NANDA - Approved Nursing Diagnoses

Activity intolerance
Activity intolerance, high risk for
Adjustment, impaired
Airway clearance, ineffective
Anxiety
Aspiration, high risk for
Body image disturbance
Body temperature, altered, high risk for
Breastfeeding, effective
Breastfeeding, ineffective
Breathing pattern, ineffective
Cardiac output, decreased
Communication, impaired verbal
Constipation
Constipation, colonic
Constipation, perceived
Coping, defensive
Coping, family: potential for growth
Coping, ineffective family: compromised
Coping, ineffective family: disabling
Coping, ineffective individual
Decisional conflict (specify)
Denial, ineffective
Diarrhea
Disuse syndrome, high risk for
Diversional activity deficit
Dysreflexia
Family processes, altered
Fatigue
Fear
Fluid volume deficit (1)
Fluid volume deficit (2)
Fluid volume deficit, high risk for
Fluid volume excess
Gas exchange, impaired
Grieving, anticipatory
Grieving, dysfunctional
Growth and development, altered
Health maintenance, altered
Health seeking behaviors (specify)
Home maintenance management, impaired
Hopelessness
Hyperthermia
Hypothermia
Incontinence, bowel
Incontinence, functional
Incontinence, reflex
Incontinence, stress
Incontinence, total
Incontinence, urge
Infection, high risk for
Injury, high risk for
Knowledge deficit (specify)

Mobility, impaired physical
Noncompliance (specify)
Nutrition, altered: less than body requirements
Nutrition, altered: more than body requirements
Nutrition, altered: high risk for more than body requirements
Oral mucous membrane, altered
Pain
Pain, chronic
Parental role conflict
Parenting, altered
Parenting, altered, high risk for
Personal identity disturbance
Poisoning, high risk for
Post-trauma response
Powerlessness
Protection, altered
Rape-trauma syndrome
Rape-trauma syndrome: compound reaction
Rape-trauma syndrome: silent reaction
Role performance, altered
Self-care deficit, bathing/hygiene
Self-care deficit, dressing/grooming
Self-care deficit, feeding
Self-care deficit, toileting
Self-esteem, disturbance
Self-esteem, chronic low
Self-esteem, situational low
Sensory, perceptual alterations (specify) (visual, auditory, kinesthetic, gustatory, tactile, olfactory)
Sexual dysfunction
Sexuality patterns, altered
Skin integrity, impaired
Skin integrity, impaired, high risk for
Sleep pattern disturbance
Social interaction, impaired
Social isolation
Spiritual distress (distress of the human spirit)
Suffocation, high risk for
Swallowing, impaired
Thermoregulation, ineffective
Thought processes, altered
Tissue integrity, impaired
Tissue perfusion, altered (specify type) (renal, cerebral, cardiopulmonary, gastrointestinal, peripheral)
Trauma, high risk for
Unilateral neglect
Urinary elimination, altered patterns
Urinary retention
Violence, high risk for: self-directed or directed at others

From the Proceedings of the Ninth National Conference of the North American Nursing Diagnosis Association, March 1990.

Total

Patient Care

**Foundations and Practice of
Adult Health Nursing**

Total

Patient Care

Foundations and Practice of Adult Health Nursing

Gail Harkness Hood, RN, DrPH, FAAN
Chair, Health Promotion Unit and
Associate Professor
University of Connecticut
School of Nursing
Storrs, Connecticut

Judith R. Dincher, RN, BSN, MSEd
Associate Professor, Department of Nursing,
Director, Nursing Program
William Rainey Harper College, Palatine, Illinois

EIGHTH EDITION
with 208 illustrations

Mosby
Year Book

St. Louis   Baltimore   Boston   Chicago   London   Philadelphia   Sydney   Toronto

Editor: Linda Duncan
Developmental Editor: Kathy Sartori
Editorial Project Manager: Jolynn Gower
Production Assistant: Pete Hausler
Book Design: Julie Taugner
Chapter Opener Art: Karen Merrill

EIGHTH EDITION

A NOTE TO THE READER
The authors and publisher have made every attempt to check
dosages and nursing content for accuracy. Because the science of
pharmacology is continually advancing, our knowledge base
continues to expand. Therefore, we recommend that the reader
always check product information for changes in dosage or
administration before administering any medication. This is
particularly important with new or rarely used drugs.

Printed in the United States of America.

Mosby-Year Book, Inc.
11830 Westline Industrial Drive
St. Louis, MO 63146

Library of Congress Cataloging-in-Publication Data
Hood, Gail Harkness.
    Total patient care :   foundations and practice of adult
    health nursing.—8th ed. / Gail Harkness Hood, Judith R.
    Dincher.
        p.   cm.
    Includes bibliographical references and index.
    ISBN 0-8016-2407-X
    1. Nursing. I. Dincher, Judith R., 1937-   . II. Title.
    [DNLM: 1. Nursing Care.   WY 100 H776t]
    RT41.H65   1991
    610.73—dc20
    DNLM/DLC
    for Library of Congress   91-15498
                                                   CIP

    93 94 95 96 GW/VH/VH 9 8 7 6 5 4 3 2

Contributors

Marion Allen, PhD
Associate Professor
School of Nursing
University of Alberta
Edmonton, Alberta

Sandra Blake, RN, MS, CIC
Nurse Epidemiologist
University of Iowa Hospital and Clinics
Iowa City, Iowa

Margaret F. Burbach, RN, CS, EdD
Professor, Nursing
William Rainey Harper College
Palatine, Illinois

Helen M. Burton, RN, BS, CDE
Nurse Manager
Diabetes Treatment Unit
New England Deaconess Hospital
Boston, Massachusetts

Marian Frerichs, RN, EdD
Professor, Medical Surgical Nursing
Northern Illinois University
DeKalb, Illinois

Peggy A. Gallagher, RN, MSN
Adjunct Faculty, Nursing
William Rainey Harper College
Palatine, Illinois

Joan Marie Hau, RN, MSN
Associate Professor
School of Nursing
St. Xavier College
Chicago, Illinois

Marcia Hill, RN, MSN
Manager, Dermatologic Therapeutics
Methodist Hospital
Clinical Assistant Professor
Baylor College of Houston
Houston, Texas

Gail Ingersoll, RN, EdD, FAAN
Assistant Professor
Chair, Division of Health Restoration
School of Nursing
University of Rochester
Rochester, New York

Suzanne L. Ivey, RN, BSN, MS
Assistant Professor, Nursing
Eastern Michigan University
Ypsilanti, Michigan

Elizabeth Laliberte, RN, MS
Assistant Professor
School of Nursing
University of Connecticut
Storrs, Connecticut

Joanne Leski, RN, MSN
Assistant Professor
William Rainey Harper College
Palatine, Illinois

Mary Lou McNiff, RN, MSN
Administrator
Brockton Visiting Nurse Association
Brockton, Massachusetts

Mary Lou Mulvihill, PhD
Professor Emeritus Biology
William Rainey Harper College
Palatine, Illinois

Anne Napier, RN, CS, EdD
Clinical Nurse Specialist Psychotherapist,
    Consultant
Boulder, Colorado

Darlene O'Callaghan, RN, MSN, MSEd
Associate Professor
School of Nursing
St. Xavier College
Chicago, Illinois

Marion A. Phipps, RN, MS, CRRN
Rehabilitation Nurse Specialist
Beth Israel Hospital
Boston, Massachusetts

Cleo J. Richard, MSN, RN
Nephrology Nurse Consultant
Escondido, California

Judy Bunnell Sellers, RN, DNSc
Associate Hospital Director
University of Connecticut Health Center
Uncas on Thames Hospital
Norwich, Connecticut

Helen Stupak Shah, RN, DNSc
Assistant Professor
School of Nursing
University of Connecticut
Storrs, Connecticut

Jean E. Steel, RNC, PhD
Associate Professor
School of Nursing
University of Connecticut
Storrs, Connecticut

Patricia Trotta, RN, MSN, OCN
Oncology Clinical Nurse Specialist
Hartford Hospital
Hartford, Connecticut

Consultants

Deloris K. Baker, RN, BSN, MA
Chicago City-Wide College/Dawson Technical
  Institute
Chicago, Illinois

Darlene C. Chiles, RN, BSN
Ohio Hi-Point School of Practical Nursing
Bellefontaine, Ohio

Nancy Claggett, RN, BSN, MS
Tri-Rivers School of Practical Nursing
Marion, Ohio

Carol J. Copeland, RN, BS
Bessemer State Technical College
Bessemer, Alabama

Edna Dilmore, RN, BS
Bessemer State Technical College
Bessemer, Alabama

Carolyn S. Edwards, RN, BSN, EdD
Wood Co. Vocational School of Practical Nursing
Parkersburg, West Virginia

Annette Gould, RN, MS
Broome-Delaware-Tioga BOCES
Binghampton, New York

Amelia V. Jameson, RN
Tri-County Technical College
Pendleton, South Carolina

Martha Jean Jett, RN
Southern State Community College
Hillsboro, Ohio

Joan M. Kulpa, RN, MSN, EdD
Bradley University
Peoria, Illinois

Leona E. McCoy, RN, MS
Flint Hills Technical School
Emporia, Kansas

Alice R. Popelka Majkrzak, RN, BSN
Sumter County Career Center
Sumter, South Carolina

Tina Mayfield, RN
Arkansas Valley Vocational Technical School
Fort Smith, Arkansas

Jayne F. Moore, RN, PhD
Intercollegiate Center for Nursing Education
Spokane, Washington

Vivian E. Mullican, RN, CS, MN
Rappanhannock Community College
Glenns, Virginia

Marion H. Nelson, RN, BSN
Great Falls Vocational Technical Center
Great Falls, Montana

Jean M. Reid, RN, MS, BSN, EdM
Practical Nursing Program
Bartonsville, Pennsylvania

Shirley J. Ruebhausen, RN, BSN, MPA, EdS
NEKA Vocational Technical School
Atchison, Kansas

Ann Tucker, RN, BA
Wood County Vocational School of Practical
    Nursing
Parkersburg, West Virginia

Shirley B. Wentz, RN, MA
Garnet Career Center School of Practical
    Nursing
Charleston, West Virginia

Preface

The original purpose of this text was to motivate the learner to approach individual health problems, health care, and nursing with concern for the safety and welfare of those who needed professional and competent care. We have done our best to maintain this 27-year standard by building on the strengths of TOTAL PATIENT CARE—its emphasis on the nursing process, its consistent review of anatomy and physiology as a basis for understanding disease processes, and its identification of physiologic, psychologic and sociologic factors affecting health and illness.

While maintaining its straightforward approach, the new edition of this core medical-surgical textbook focuses upon adult health and has undergone a major revision process. We engaged in a chapter-by-chapter review and invited some of the most respected health-care instructors and professionals to comment on both the strengths and weaknesses of the last edition. Their suggestions gave us the focus needed to make this revision complete with the most necessary skills and information needed by students in technical nursing programs to function knowledgably at the bedside.

ORGANIZATION

The approach to content remains the same as previous editions, although much has been added, condensed or simply rearranged to improve the flow and comprehension. The book is divided into three sections. PART ONE begins with an overview of the health care delivery system, the nurse's role in that system, the nursing process, and standards of care. These topics establish a foundation for nurses to operate more effectively in varied health care settings. This section then continues by identifying the physical and emotional problems frequently encountered in persons with a medical-surgical condition. An expanded section on mental disorders is featured and highlights affective disorders, organic brain syndromes such as Alzheimers disease, and addictive disorders and depression, including a discussion on suicide.

PART TWO offers the student more physiologic and pathophysiologic information that may affect and determine illness such as chapters on fluid and electrolytes, infection processes, and pain. The remainder of this section focuses on special health considerations with a particular emphasis on the psychosocial aspects of nursing care. Geriatic content has been completely revamped and expanded to include specific disorders one might encounter in caring for an elderly person. Other chapters on home-health care, death and dying, and a new chapter on long-term care cover such timely issues as death following a traumatic injury, spiritual distress, Alzheimer's disease, cancer, and care of the patient with AIDS.

PART THREE focuses on the care of patients with specific disorders. Organized by problems affecting the body systems, these chapters present common alterations in human functioning using a consistent nursing process format. Anatomy and physiology are presented as a basis for application of the nursing process, and content on assessment and diagnostic testing have been expanded to include not only the basic skills but also information on the newest and most advanced methods of diagnosing disorders. Sections on medical and nursing interventions also reflect major revision. High-technology interventions are discussed, and principles of diet therapy and drug therapy are updated and highlighted throughout in helpful boxes and tables. Psychosocial content such as guidelines for interacting with blind people and support for families coping with the effects of Alzheimer's disease contribute to the comprehensiveness of this new edition.

NURSING CARE

For all disorders, nursing care is presented in a comprehensive and consistent format. Nursing Responsibilities for Therapeutic Techniques alerts the nurse to potential or actual adverse reactions to procedures and associated nursing care. Specific preoperative and postoperative nursing interventions accompany disorders present in each chapter. Nursing Care Guidelines have been added to highlight nursing responsibilities for major disorders. Special Nursing Care Plans presenting realistic case studies covering multiple conditions that often occur in one patient, have been developed specifically for this book. Guidelines and Care Plans contain all current nursing diagnoses approved by NANDA and provide excellent models for quality nursing practice.

LEARNING TOOLS

Learning devices to enhance student comprehension are a long-time component of this text:
- KEY TERMS appear at the beginning of each chapter and are highlighted throughout.
- OBJECTIVES identify the major points within each chapter.
- Helpful TABLES and BOXES highlight important information such as pharmacology and nutrition.
- The attractive TWO-COLOR DESIGN augments the organization of each chapter and emphasizes important content.
- A complete medical-surgical GLOSSARY can be referred to allowing students to master the language of practical or vocational nursing.

Building on this group of valuable tools, we are pleased to present some new aids:
- Detailed TABLE OF CONTENTS has been added so that specific topics can be located easily and quickly.

- PRINTED ENDPAPERS, located on the inside front and back covers, provide essential information, such as NANDA diagnoses, for student reference.

TEACHING/LEARNING PACKAGE

Along with the complete revision of the text, we offer an extensively revised student workbook and an instructor's resource manual. Each chapter of the workbook and the manual parallel the chapters. Chapter summary outlines that once appeared in the text now can be found in the manual. Instructors may use these to prepare syllabi or study guides. The manual also contains learning activities suggested to develop critical thinking skills and a new testbank written especially for the users of TOTAL PATIENT CARE. The workbook presents activities designed to increase comprehension of the subject matter.

ACKNOWLEDGMENTS

We are grateful to our students, fellow faculty members, clinical associates and the reviewers who contributed to the book, including the students at the University of Connecticut who contributed to the development of the Nursing Care Plans: Teresa Concilio, Katrina Eder, Erin Halpin, Christine Lafleur, Sarabeth Robinson, Sheila Walsh, and Laura Wanat. A special tribute belongs to our contributors, without them this revision would not be as complete and useful as we feel it is.

Most important, however, is the love, understanding, patience, and support that we have received from our families. Michael and Karen Merrill have assisted with photography, art, and editing. We also thank Tom Dincher, John, Donna, and Megan Marie Dincher, Liz, Todd, and Zachary Thomas Bjur, Julie, Bob and the "developing" Breshock, and Tom and Pam Kavanaugh.

Gail Harkness Hood
Judith R. Dincher

Contents

PART ONE
Concepts Basic to Nursing

1   Introduction to Total Patient Care, *2*
Total patient care, *4*
Health, *4*
Trends affecting health care, 4
Health care cost and reimbursement, *5*
Health care delivery, *7*
Hospitals, *7*
Extended care facilities, *8*
HMOs and PPOs, *8*
Ambulatory care and home health
agencies, *9*
Government health departments, *9*
Other health care facilities, *9*
Health care team, *10*
Nursing, *10*
Nursing education and scope of practice, *11*
Medical-surgical nursing, *12*
Standards of nursing practice, 12
Nursing process, *13*
Assessment, 13
Planning, 15
Implementation, 16
Evaluation, 16
Nursing delivery systems, *17*
Theory in practice, *17*
Human needs, *18*
Patient rights, *21*

2   Physiologic Aspects of Patient Care, *24*
Causes of disease, *26*
Microorganisms, *26*
Bacteria, 26
Viruses, 29

Fungi, 30
Protozoa, 30
Nutritional imbalance, *30*
Physical agents, *31*
Chemical agents, *32*
Cellular abnormalities, *32*
Physiologic defense mechanisms, *34*
Inflammation, 35
Infection, 36
Intervention, 38
Immunity, *39*
Humoral immunity, 40
Cellular immunity, 40
Chemotherapeutic agents, *41*
Sulfonamides, 41

3   Psychologic Aspects of Patient
Care, *46*
Needs of individuals, *48*
Personality structure, *48*
Personality development, *49*
Mental health, *50*
Effects of anxiety, *51*
Defense mechanisms, *51*
Development of emotional
problems, *53*
Emotional disorders, *53*
Anxiety disorders, *53*
Psychoses, *53*
Schizophrenia, 54
Affective disorders, 55
Dexamethasone suppression test, 56
Paranoid disorders, 56
Personality disorders, *56*
Paranoid personality, 56

Schizoid personality, 56

Obsessive-compulsive personality, 56

Antisocial personality, 56

Passive-aggressive personality, 56

Organic brain syndromes: dementia, 56

Somatic disorders, 57

Addictive disorders, 57

Depression, 58

Nursing assessment of depression, 58

The therapeutic relationship in nursing, 59

Psychopharmacology, 62

Psychologic treatment methods, 62

PART TWO
Caring for the Patient with General Manifestations of Illness

4   Fluid and Electrolyte Imbalances, *68*

The nature of body fluid, 70

Gains and losses, 70

Fluid and electrolyte exchange, 71

Fluid and electrolyte imbalances, 72

Extracellular fluid volume imbalances, 72

Extracellular fluid composition imbalances, 76

Acid-base imbalance, 87

Intravenous therapy, 91

Central venous lines, 93

Peripherally inserted central catheter (PICC), 93

Shock, 93

Psychosocial support, 96

5   Preoperative and Postoperative Care, *98*

The surgical experience, 100

Negative effects of surgery, 100

Objectives of surgical nursing, 101

Outpatient surgery, 101

Admission of the patient, 102

Informed consent, 102

Preoperative preparation, 102

Nursing assessment, 102

Planning and interventions, 103

Preoperative orders, 104

Operative day, 105

Intraoperative care, 108

Surgical asepsis, 109

Sterilization, 109

The operative team, 110

Anesthesia, 110

Intraoperative complications, 116

Postoperative assessment and interventions, 116

Recovery room care, 116

Intensive care unit, 118

Continuing postoperative care, 119

Postoperative complaints and complications, 123

Complaints, 123

Complications, 125

Discharge planning, 126

6   The Patient with Pain, *128*

The nature of pain, 130

Defining pain, 130

Function of pain, 130

Pain theories, 130

Types of pain, 132

Assessment of pain, 132

Management of pain, 135

Nursing interventions and pain medication, 135

7   Community-Acquired Infections, *142*

Characteristics of the infectious process, 144

Agent, 144

Host, 144

Environment, 145

Transmission, 145

Control of communicable disease, 145

Immunization, 145

Public education, 148

Nursing's role in prevention, 148

The patient with a bacterial disease, 148

Staphylococcal infections, 148

Streptococcal infections, 150

Pulmonary tuberculosis, 150

Lyme disease, 153

Salmonella infections, 153

Shigellosis, 154

Gas gangrene, 154

Meningococcal meningitis, 155

Legionnaires' disease, 155

The patient with a viral disease, 155

Measles, 155

Rubella, 156

Chickenpox, 156

Herpes zoster, 157

Mumps, 157

Infectious mononucleosis, 157

Influenza, 158

Hepatitis, 159

The patient with a rickettsial disease, 159

Rocky Mountain spotted fever, 159

The patient with a protozoal disease, 160

Malaria, 160

Helminthic infestations, 161

Sexually transmitted diseases, 163

Syphilis, 164

Gonorrhea, 166

Acquired immunodeficiency syndrome (AIDS), 166

Herpes simplex, 167

8 Nosocomial Infections, 170

Hospital infections, 172

Incidence of nosocomial infection, 172

High-risk patients, 173

Methods of transmission, 173

Nosocomial infections, 174

Urinary tract infections, 174

Nosocomial pneumonia, 174

Surgical wound infection, 175

Nosocomial bacteremia, 177

Other sites of nosocomial infections, 178

Prevention and control, 178

Infection control committee, 178

Infection control practitioner, 178

Surveillance, 178

Preventive policies and procedures, 180

Control policies and procedures, 182

9 The Patient with Cancer, 190

Cancer: an overview, 192

Pathophysiology, 193

Causes of cancer, 195

Prevention and control, 196

Diagnostic tests and procedures, 198

Tissue sampling, 198

Imaging techniques—direct visualization, 198

Imaging techniques—Indirect visualization, 199

Laboratory studies, 201

Treatment of cancer, 201

Surgery, 202

Radiotherapy, 202

External radiation therapy, 203

Sealed internal radiation therapy, 204

Unsealed internal radiation therapy, 207

Chemotherapy, 208

Bone marrow transplantation, 212

Biological response modifiers, 212

Unproven methods, 213

Emotional care, 213

Rehabilitation, 214

10 Death and the Dying Patient, 216

Death, 218

When does death occur? 218

Prolongation of life, 218

Living will documents, 219

Fear of dying and death, 219

Emotional stages experienced in the dying process, 222

Grief and bereavement, 223

Nursing care of the dying patient, 224

Death following traumatic injury, 225

The hospice movement, 225

Nursing interventions, 226

Following death, 227

11 The Geriatric Patient, 230

Terminology, 232

Gerontology, 232

Demographics, 232

Progress and research, 233

Factors affecting aging, 233

Cultural and ethnic factors, 233

Socioeconomic factors, 234

Retirement and aging, 234

Biopsychosocial factors, 235

Aging and intelligence, 236

Aging and memory, 236

Physiology of aging, 237

Cardiovascular system, 237

Sensory system, 239

Integumentary system, 240

Musculoskeletal system, 241

Neurological system, 242

Alzheimer's disease, 243

Digestive system, 243

Urinary system, 244

Respiratory system, 245

Reproductive system, 246

Nursing the elderly, 246
  Preventing injury, 246
  Providing comfort, 247
  Meeting nutritional needs, 248
  Maintaining personal hygiene, 248
  Recognizing sexuality, 249
  Preventing complications from drug use, 250
Care of the hospitalized elderly patient, 251
  Vital signs, 251
  Sedation, 251
  Intake and output, 251
  Ambulation and convalescence, 252
Nursing homes, 252
Alternatives to institutional care, 253
  Home care, 253
  Day hospital, 253
  Foster care, 253
  Other services, 253
  Group work with the elderly, 253

12   Rehabilitation, *256*
Rehabilitation, 258
Rehabilitation nursing, 258
  Rehabilitation in each phase of health care, 259
  Rehabilitation team, 260
  Rehabilitation programs, 262
  Rehabilitation in other settings, 263
  Emotional response to disability, 263
Nursing approaches to rehabilitation care, 264
  Rehabilitation techniques, 265
  Prevention of skin breakdown, 269
  Bladder and bowel training, 270
  Sexuality, 274
  Motivation, 274
  Teaching, 275
  Continuity, 276
Summary, 281

13   Long-Term Care, *282*
Ethical dilemmas in long-term care, 284
General assessment guidelines, 285
  Functional assessment, 285
  Mental status assessment, 286
  Depression assessment, 287
Risk and specific care issues, 287
  Falls, 287
  Urinary incontinence, 289
  Constipation, 291

  Decubitus ulcers (pressure sores), 292
  Confusion, 294

14   Home Health Care, *296*
Conceptual framework, 298
Home health care, 298
  Home health services, 299
  Supportive services in the community, 299
  The home health care team, 300
Nursing in the home setting, 301
  Case study, 302
  General vs specialty care, 302
  Reimbursement, 303
  Impact of reimbursement on delivery of services, 303
  Trends, 304
  Long-term care and home health care, 304
Summary, 304

PART THREE
Nursing the Patient with Medical-Surgical Problems

15   Problems Affecting Respiration, *308*
Structure and function of the respiratory system, 310
Altered respiratory status, 312
  Dyspnea, 312
  Hypoxia, 312
  Apnea, 312
  Cheyne-Stokes respiration, 312
  Asphyxia or suffocation, 312
  Cyanosis, 312
  Hyperventilation, 312
  Hypoventilation, 312
Nursing assessment of the patient with a respiratory problem, 313
  Inspection, 313
  Palpation, 313
  Percussion, 313
  Ausculation, 314
Nursing responsibilities for diagnostic procedures, 314
  Blood examinations, 314
  Arterial blood gas studies, 315
  Sputum examination, 315
  Pulmonary function tests, 315
  Radiographic examination, 316
  Bronchoscopy, 316
  Thoracentesis, 317

Nursing responsibilities for therapeutic techniques, *317*

Psychologic care, 317

Coughing and deep breathing, 318

Suctioning, 318

Postural drainage, 319

Percussion, 320

Throat irrigations, humidifications, and aerosol therapy, 320

Endotracheal intubation, 321

Mechanical ventilation, 321

Oxygen therapy, 322

Thoracotomy, 323

Tracheotomy, 326

The patient with diseases and disorders of the respiratory system, *328*

Noninfectious respiratory conditions, 328

Infectious respiratory conditions, 335

Intervention in upper respiratory tract infections, 336

Obstructions of the respiratory system, *341*

Deviated septum and nasal polyps, 341

Enlarged tonsils and adenoids, 342

Foreign bodies, 342

Tumors of the respiratory system, *342*

Laryngeal cancer, 342

Intervention: laryngectomy, 343

Lung cancer, 344

Chest surgery, *344*

Assessment and intervention, 344

Chest wounds, *346*

Health, social aspects, and rehabilitation, *346*

16   Problems Affecting Circulation, *350*

Cardiovascular structure and function, *352*

Cardiac anatomy, 352

Vascular system, 353

Lymphatic circulation, 353

Cardiac cycle, 353

Neurohumoral controls of the heart, 354

Nursing assessment of the patient with a cardiovascular problem, *355*

Inspection, 356

Palpation, 356

Percussion, 356

Auscultation, 357

Blood pressure, 357

Electrocardiography, *359*

Electrocardiogram interpretation, 360

Disorders of rate and rhythm of the heart, *361*

Dysrhythmia, 361

Atrium, 361

Ventricle, 363

Heart block, 365

Electronic cardiac pacemakers, 366

Coronary care unit, *366*

Laboratory examinations, 367

Central venous pressure, 368

Pulmonary artery and pulmonary artery wedge pressures, 368

Exercise tolerance test, 369

Echocardiogram, phonocardiogram, and vectorcardiogram, 370

X-ray examination and fluoroscopy, 370

Cardiac catheterization, 370

The patient with diseases and disorders of the cardiovascular system, *371*

Arteriosclerosis and antherosclerosis, 371

Hypertension and hypertensive heart disease, 371

Rheumatic fever and rheumatic heart disease, 374

Bacterial endocarditis, 375

Coronary artery and heart disease, 376

Myocardial infarction, 378

Congestive heart failure, 381

Heart disease complicated by pregnancy, 385

Diseases and disorders of the arteries, veins, and lymphatics, *385*

Aneurysm, 385

Arterial occlusive disease, 386

Raynaud's disease, 386

Buerger's disease, 387

Thrombophlebitis, 387

Varicose veins, 388

Lymphangitis, 389

The patient with operative conditions of the cardiovascular system, *389*

Cardiac surgery, 390

Percutaneous transluminal coronary angioplasty, 391

Embolectomy, 391

Cardiac rehabilitation, *392*

Basic cardiac life support, *393*

Airway obstruction, *395*

17   Problems Affecting the Blood, *402*

Function of blood, *404*

Structure of blood, *404*

Plasma, 404

Erythrocytes (red blood cells), 404

Leukocytes (white blood cells), 405

Granulocytes, 405

Agranulocytes, 405

Thrombocytes (platelets), 406

Therapeutic blood fractions, 406

Blood plasma, 406

Platelets, 406

Plasma protein fractions, 407

Cryoprecipitate, 408

Packed red blood cells, 408

Leukocytes, 408

Collection of blood, 408

Testing, 408

Autologous blood, 408

Nursing responsibilities for diagnostic tests, 409

Types of tests, 409

Nursing responsibilities for therapeutic procedures, 413

Blood transfusion therapy, 413

The patient with blood dyscasis, 415

Disorders of erythrocytes, 415

Disorders of white blood cells, 422

Hemorrhagic disorders, 425

18 Problems Affecting Nutrition and Bowel Elimination, 434

Structure and function of the gastrointestinal system, 436

Process of digestion and absorption, 436

Causes of digestive diseases and disorders, 437

Assessment, 438

Diagnostic tests for disorders of the gastrointestinal system, 438

Gastric analysis and histamine test, 438

Tubeless gastric analysis, 439

Bernstein test, 439

Endoscopy, 439

Gastrointestinal series and barium enema, 441

Stool examination, 441

Diagnostic tests for disorders of the liver and biliary system, 441

Liver function tests, 441

Liver biopsy, 442

Liver scanning, 442

Cholecystography (oral), 442

Cholangiography, 443

Computerized tomography, 443

Ultrasonography, 443

Nursing responsibilities for tests and diagnostic procedures, 443

Nursing responsibilities for therapeutic techniques, 444

Gastric lavage, 444

Gastric gavage, 444

Gastrointestinal (gastric) decompression, 444

Total parenteral nutrition, 446

Abdominal surgery, 447

Preoperative and postoperative nursing care, 447

Colostomy and ileostomy nursing care, 449

Continent or pouch ileostomy, 453

Specific diseases and disorders of the gastrointestinal system, 453

Inflammatory diseases, 453

Intestinal obstruction, 461

Tumors of the gastrointestinal system, 462

Peptic ulcer, 466

Hernia, 472

Hiatus (hiatal) hernia, 473

Hemorrhoids, 473

Functional disorders, 474

Diseases and disorders of the accessory organs of digestion, 476

Diseases and disorders of the liver, 476

Diseases and disorders of the biliary system, 484

Diseases and disorders of the pancreas, 488

Tumors of the accessory organs of digestion, 490

19 Problems Affecting the Urinary System, 494

Structure and function of the urinary system, 496

Structure, 496

Function, 497

Nursing assessment, 499

History and physical examination, 499

Diagnostic tests and nursing responsibilities, 500

Urine, 500

Creatinine tests, 502

Blood urea nitrogen, 502

Kidneys, ureters, and bladder x-rays, 502

Pyelography, 502

Bladder studies, 503

Radioisotope studies, 503

Ultrasonography, 504

Computerized tomography, 504

Magnetic resonance imaging, 504

Renal biopsy, 504

Therapeutic procedures and nursing
implications, 505

Diuretics, 505

Provision for urinary drainage, 506

Diseases and disorders of the urinary
system, 510

Noninfectious diseases, 510

Infectious diseases, 512

Obstructions of the urinary system, 513

Traumatic injuries, 514

Tumors of the urinary tract, 515

Renal failure, 515

Operative conditions of the urinary
system, 522

Cystectomy, 522

Urinary diversion: ureteral transplants, 522

Cystotomy, 524

Ureterotomy and lithotomy, 525

Nephrectomy and nephrostomy, 527

20 Problems Affecting Sexuality, *534*

Structure and function of the reproductive
systems, 536

The female reproductive system, 536

The male reproductive system, 536

The role of nurse in relation to
sexuality, 539

Nursing assessment of the patient with
problems of the reproductive system, 539

Phases of reproductive function thoughout
the life cycle, 540

Puberty, 540

Menstruation, 541

Hygiene, 542

Sexual role behavior, 542

The reproductive years, 542

Menopause (climacteric), 543

Disturbances of menstrual function, 544

Dysmenorrhea, 544

Amenorrhea, 545

Menorrhagia, 545

Metrorrhagia, 545

Toxic shock syndrome, 545

Premenstrual syndrome, 546

Nursing responsibilities for diagnostic
procedures, 546

Examination of the female patient, 546

Examination of the male patient, 551

The patient with diseases and disorders of
the reproductive system, 552

Venereal disease, 552

*Conditions affecting the female external
genitalia and vagina, 552*

Conditions affecting the cervix and uterus, 556

*Conditions affecting the ovaries and fallopian
tubes, 557*

*Surgical intervention for conditions affecting
the cervix, uterus, ovaries, and fallopian
tubes, 559*

Conditions affecting the breast, 561

Conditions of pregnancy, 569

Abortion, 569

Ectopic pregnancy, 572

Conditions affecting the male external
genitalia, 573

Congenital malformation, 573

*Conditions affecting the testes and adjacent
structures, 573*

Conditions affecting the prostate gland, 575

Conditions affecting erectile function, 579

Pelvic exenteration, 580

**21 Problems Affecting Endocrine
Function,** *586*

Endocrine glands and their function, 588

Nursing assessment of the patient with
endocrine problems, 590

Nursing responsibilities for diagnostic tests
and procedures, 590

Blood chemistry, 590

Urinalysis, 590

Basal metabolic rate, 591

Protein-bound iodine test, 591

Radioactive iodine uptake, 591

Thyroid ultrasonogram, 591

Thyroid scan, 591

Triodothyroinine (T₃) resin uptake test, 591

Nursing responsibilities for therapeutic
procedures, 592

The patient with diseases and disorders of
the endocrine system, 592

Disorders of the thyroid gland, 592

Disorders of the pancreas, 595

Disorders of the parathyroid glands, 611

*Disorders of the adrenal (suprarenal)
glands, 612*

Disorders of the pituitary gland, 614

22　**Problems Affecting Neurologic Function,** *620*

Structure and function of the nervous system, 622

Nursing responsibilities for assessment, and diagnostic tests and procedures, 623

Basic neurologic examination, 623

Examination of cerebrospinal fluid, 623

Neuroradiologic studies, 625

Electrodiagnostic studies, 626

Other tests, 626

Nursing intervention, 627

Altered states of awareness, 627

Consciousness-unconciousness, 627

Confusion-delirium, 628

Increased intracranial pressure, 629

Seizure disorders, 630

Abnormal body temperature elevation (hyperthermia, hyperpyrexia), 634

The patient with diseases and disorders of the nervous system, 634

Infectious diseases, 634

Degenerative diseases, 636

Cerebrovascular accident (CVA, stroke), 641

Cerebral artery aneurysm, 646

Head injuries, 647

Neuritis and neuralgia, 649

Bell's paralysis (Bell's palsy), 651

Spinal cord injuries, 651

Rupture of the intervertebral disk, 654

Tumors of the brain and spinal cord, 656

23　**Problems Affecting Vision and Hearing,** *664*

Structure and function of eye and ear, 666

The eye, 666

The ear, 666

Nursing assessment of the patient with eye problems, 668

Diagnostic tests and procedures, 668

Loss of sight, 671

Refractive errors of the eye, 672

Contact lenses, 674

Color blindness, 674

The patient with diseases and disorders of the eye, 675

Eye irrigations, 676

Inflammatory and infectious eye disorders, 676

Noninfective eye disorders, 681

Injuries to the eye, 690

Eye enucleation, 691

Nursing assessment of patients with ear problems, 692

Diagnostic tests and procedures, 692

Hearing impairment, 693

Hearing aids, 693

Speaking to the hearing impaired, 694

The patient with diseases and disorders of the ear, 694

External ear, 694

Middle ear, 695

Inner ear, 699

24　**Problems Affecting Skin Integrity,** *704*

Structure and function of the skin, 706

Nursing assessment of the skin, 708

Assessment and description of skin lesions, 708

Nursing responsibilities for diagnostic tests and procedures, 710

Nursing responsibilities for therapeutic procedures, 710

Therapeutic baths, 710

Wet dressings, 710

Soaks, 711

Paste boots, 711

Emotional support, 711

Decubitus (pressure) ulcers, 712

The patient with diseases and disorders of the skin, 718

Bacterial diseases, 718

Fungal infections, 719

Dermatitis, 721

Lupus erythematosus, 728

Viral infections, 730

Disorders of pigmentation, 733

Disorders of glands, 733

Pruritus (itching), 734

Tumors of the skin, 734

Disorders of the appendages, 736

Infestations, 737

Burns, 738

Determination of burn depth, 738

Determination of burn extent, 738

The acute phase, 743

Objectives of treatment, 743

Methods of wound treatment—medical management, 743

Surgical management, 744

Nursing management during the acute phase, 746

25   Problems Affecting Mobility, *752*

Structure and function of the
  musculoskeletal system, *754*

  Structure, 754

  Function, 754

Position, exercise, and body mechanics, *754*

Neurovascular integrity, *755*

  Assessment, 755

  Pain, 756

  The patient with a cast, 757

  The patient with an orthopedic device, 759

The patient with diseases and disorders of
  the musculoskeletal system, *769*

  Congenital deformities, 769

  Arthritis, 770

  Infectious diseases and disorders, 775

  Traumatic injuries, 776

  Rickets, 783

  Bone tumors, 783

  Amputation, 784

Neuromuscular conditions, *787*

  Muscular dystrophy, 787

  Cerebral palsy, 787

**26   Problems Affecting Immune
  Response,** *792*

Excessive immune responses, *794*

  Allergy, 794

  Allergic reactions from insects, 797

  Anaphylactic shock, 797

  Cytotoxic, 798

  Immune complex, 798

  Cell-mediated, 798

  Assessment of people with atopic allergies, 799

  *Nursing interventions for people with atopic
    allergies, 802*

  Drug therapy, 802

  Immunotherapy, 803

  Autoimmune disease, 804

Deficient immune responses, *804*

  Primary immunodeficiencies, 804

  Secondary immunodeficiencies, 806

Nursing care of people with
  immunodeficiencies, *807*

  Acquired immunodeficiency syndrome, 807

Precautions to prevent transmission of
  HIV, *811*

Universal precautions, 811

Appendix A, *818*

Appendix B, *826*

Appendix C, *827*

Glossary, *828*

PART ONE

Concepts Basic

to Nursing

CHAPTER 1   *Introduction to Total Patient Care*

2   *Physiologic Aspects of Patient Care*

3   *Psychologic Aspects of Patient Care*

INTRODUCTION TO
Total Patient Care

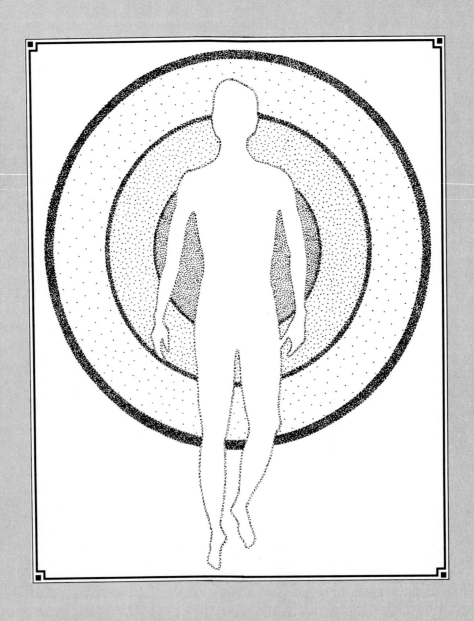

KEY WORDS

acute care
ambulatory care
analysis
assessment
case management
diagnosis related group (DRG)
documentation
evaluation
extended care facility
functional nursing
health
health maintenance organization (HMO)
holistic care
home health care
homeostasis
human needs
implementation
intermediate care facility (ICF)
long-term care
Medicaid
medical-surgical nursing
Medicare
multisystem
nursing care plan
nursing diagnosis
nursing history
nursing process
planning
preferred provider organization (PPO)
primary care
primary nursing
primary prevention
problem-oriented record (POR)
proprietary
prospective payment
retrospective payment
secondary prevention
self-actualization
skilled nursing facility (SNF)
SOAP
standards
team nursing
tertiary prevention

OBJECTIVES

1. Discuss the concept of "total patient care."

2. Define "health."

3. Discuss contemporary trends affecting health care in the United States.

4. Discuss the costs of health care and identify various reimbursement systems.

5. Identify the components of the health care delivery system in the United States.

6. Differentiate between a skilled nursing facility and an intermediate care facility.

7. Describe the services of a health maintenance organization (HMO).

8. Account for the increase in ambulatory care and home health agencies.

9. Discuss the concept of holistic care as provided by the health care team.

10. Differentiate between the levels of practice of licensed vocational/practical nurses and registered nurses with an associate degree, baccalaureate degree, or diploma.

11. Discuss the application of professional nursing standards.

12. Describe the steps in the nursing process: assessment, analysis, planning, implementation, and evaluation.

13. List techniques for effective interviewing.

14. Define the term "nursing diagnosis" and discuss the status of a universally accepted taxonomy of nursing diagnoses.

15. Discuss the role of the written care plan in providing individualized care to patients.

16. Discuss the importance of documentation.

17. Describe the "problem-oriented record" system.

18. Contrast the following organizational patterns of nursing service: functional, team, and primary nursing.

19. Discuss the value of theory in clinical application.

20. Identify the patient's rights.

TOTAL PATIENT CARE

Total patient care is a concept that provides a basis for nursing practice. The word "total" means **holistic** or "whole" and is used here to imply consideration of all human needs: physiologic, psychologic, and sociologic. The nurse is not equipped to meet all of these needs alone but plays a major role in the indentification of needs and the coordination of services and personnel in and out of the hospital. A patient is an individual who is seeking health care. Whereas the word "patient" formerly implied a passive acceptance of services, modern emphasis is on the patient as an active participant in care and a thinking consumer or client of health services. Continued use of the term "patient" is not to imply acceptance of a less active role for the health care consumer. The meaning of a word may change with time, and "patient" is used here to describe the individual who initiates, plans, and actively participates in his or her care. The word care refers to those services provided to assist the patient in maintaining or restoring optimum health. This text will focus on the care provided by the nurse to the medical and/or surgical patient who is hospitalized in an acute care or extended care facility, with a goal of cure or improvement in a specific illness or crisis.

HEALTH

The World Health Organization, an agency of the United Nations established in 1948, defines **health** as "a state of complete physical, mental, and social well-being and not merely the absence of disease." Illness is also considered to be an acute or chronic lack of adaptation to internal and environmental stressors.[12] Implied in this concept is the belief that the body is constantly at work to balance the internal environment (endocrine secretions, water, electrolytes, proteins, vitamins, minerals, oxygen) as it responds to the stressors of the external environment. When the body is able to maintain this balance, or equilibrium, this is described as the state of **homeostasis**. It is a dynamic process, requiring constant body activity in response to change.

The body must obtain the materials needed and convert or eliminate what is in excess. Illness can result from deficiency or excess. As explained by Selye,[53] the stressors may be biologic, such as hemorrhage or bacterial toxins; psychologic, such as fear and worry; or sociologic, such as financial problems or marital difficulties, but they produce a specific physiologic condition involving a syndrome of adaptation. The individual's ability to adapt to stressors will vary with time, depending on personal resources, the strength or amount of the stressor, the time at which it appears, and the gradual or sudden nature of its onset. Health is in fact a complete state of well-being, involving the whole person and environment (Figure 1-1).

Incorporating this complete state of well-being, society has begun to place greater emphasis on the values of preventive medicine, health maintenance, physical fitness, and mental vigor. Prevention of illness has been classified as primary, secondary, and tertiary. **Primary prevention** involves activities promoting general well-being, as well as specific protection for selected diseases, such as immunizations for diphtheria, measles, and tetanus. **Secondary prevention** focuses on early diagnosis and implementing measures to stop progression of disease processes or handicapping disabilities. **Tertiary prevention** deals with rehabilitation of a disabled patient to return the person to a level of maximum usefulness.[30,32]

Trends Affecting Health Care

The growing emphasis on the prevention of illness stems from the public's increasing awareness

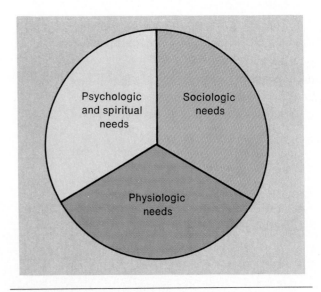

Figure 1-1

The total needs of the patient.

of health care. This awareness is but one of the trends affecting the delivery of health care in our country. Considerable changes have occurred in society and health care during the 80s and 90s. Other trends include the changing demographics in the U.S. population, advances in science and technology, and economic shifts.

The society of the United States is maturing. In 1900 the average life expectancy was 47 years, and only 4% of the population was age 65 and older. A baby born today can expect to live past 70.

The U.S. Census Bureau estimated the 1983 population to be 234 million, with 11.7% (27 million) to be age 65 and older. In 1989, they numbered 31 million, representing 12.5% of the population. By 2025, the nation's total population is projected by the Census Bureau to be 301 million, with 19.5% (58 million) to be aged 65 and older.[60] Members of the over-65 age group are heavy consumers of health care goods and services. Chronic conditions such as arthritis and hypertensive disease are present in four out of five persons age 65 and older. Although not always crippling or life threatening, these conditions may require ongoing health care and often lead to limitations in performing daily functions.

As death rates from various conditions continue to decline, the number of frail elderly (generally considered to be 85 years and older) will increase dramatically. This trend will require an expansion of long term care facilities and personnel trained in geriatric care. The increase in persons over 65 can also be attributed to the fact that "baby boomers"—the 76 million children born between 1946 and 1964 (almost one third of our total population)—are getting older. Concurrently, new technologies have extended life expectancy. Scientific technology has seen tremendous growth in the last 20 years, and these advances are reflected in modern health care.

Emerging medical technologies are permitting performance of an increasing number of outpatient diagnostic and therapeutic interventions and are drastically reducing inpatient stay requirements for some procedures. Many acute care requirements can be rendered in the home. New pharmaceuticals are developed almost weekly. Computerized information systems (telematics) aid greatly in testing, interpretation, and diagnosis and are bringing preventative health care closer to reality. Computers are also used for scheduling, billing, payroll, budgeting, surveillance, ordering, documentation, and care plans—the list is almost endless.

Technologic advances have also affected the economy of health care. Although many of these advances have reduced the cost of some services, the research and development and the initial financial outlay by the purchasing institution for such technologies is very expensive. The rising cost of health care and changes in reimbursement have greatly impacted the delivery of health care and will be discussed in the next section. One result of this impact is the increased corporatization of health care, bringing a pervasive business orientation to the industry.

The corporatization of health care refers to the development of health care multisystems that manage a large network of facilities out of a single corporate office. Such multisystems can contain costs more efficiently than single institutions. Multisystem chains can include hospitals, extended care facilities, **health maintenance organizations (HMOs)**, clinics, outpatient facilities, pharmacies, medical supply distributors, health insurance companies—almost anything and everything that has to do with health care. Multisystem chains include both national and regional systems, which are operated on a for-profit or not-for-profit basis.

The economy has also seen a steady increase in the standard of living, with a concurrent rise in the demand for health care services. Inner cities and rural communities are particularly vulnerable to limited health care services and facilities, with access to affordable and appropriate care being a significant concern to residents and providers alike.

HEALTH CARE COST AND REIMBURSEMENT

The gross national product (GNP) for health care in 1983 was 10.7% and rose to 11.5% by 1990. Currently, the United States spends more each year on health care than it does on national defense.[52] It is estimated that expenses will exceed $700 billion per year in the 1990s with continuing growth beyond. Although persons over 65 years of age represent 11% of the total population, 29% of health care expenses are made on their behalf.[4]

Health care costs have significantly escalated during the past 10 years. Federal and state agencies and private insurers have implemented various regulations to curtail the continuing spiral of costs, both through new incentive programs and changes in payment systems. Since the inception of **Medicare** and **Medicaid**, the GNP for health care has more than tripled.[52]

Medicare and Medicaid are government programs created in 1965 through an amendment to the Social Security Act. These programs are funded by taxes on the earnings of those currently employed. Medicare is a federally administered health insurance program available, regardless of income, to those over 65, to the disabled who have received Social Security benefits for more than 2 years, and to individuals with severe kidney disease. Full Medicare coverage, like most private insurance plans, requires a monthly premium and involves a deductible charge for most services that must be paid by the individual or through supplemental private insurance. In 1990 the deductible was $75 annually. The regulations for paid services constantly change and are complex in their interpretation for both provider and consumer.[62]

Medicaid is a cooperative federal and state medical assistance program for the poor. Medicaid was designed to cover areas that Medicare did not and to defray expenses for those who could not meet the cost of Medicare contributions or who had exhausted their Medicare benefits. The program is operated on a state level, although the federal government provides guidelines and a portion of the funds based on the per capita income of each state.

Currently Medicare and Medicaid cover only about 40% of health costs for the elderly and the poor.[17] Medicare provisions change often, and Medicaid programs vary from state to state. For up-to-date information in an individual state, contact the local state welfare office for Medicaid or the local social security office for Medicare.

The traditional method of reimbursement for health care services has been **retrospective**. This means that all the costs of care, eventually paid by the government, private insurance companies, and the individual were added up after they were incurred.

In 1984, **prospective** reimbursement systems were initiated in an attempt to curtail rising health care costs. The prospective reimbursement system, implemented by the Health Care Financing Agency (HCFA), required hospitals to assign **diagnosis related groups** (DRGs) to all admissions as an incentive to reduce costs. The DRG system

is currently in effect for acute care hospitals and long-term institutions and will soon cover any health care service for inpatients and outpatients. The HCFA established 470 DRG codes. These codes are based on the physician's diagnosis, the patient's age and sex, and the treatments required. The DRGs specify the number of hospital days that will be paid by Medicare. When a patient is discharged sooner than predicted for that DRG, the hospital profits. If, however, the patient requires a longer admission, the hospital pays for the excess days. The DRG codes do not consider the intensity of nursing care required by some patients. Because the intensity of nursing care varies with each patient, managing patients with high nursing care intensity has negatively affected institutional budgets. The DRG system did, however, significantly affect the length of stay for patients in the hospital (Figure 1-2).

The initial implementation of DRGs affected only the hospitalized Medicare patient. The use of DRGs by Medicare has spread to use of various prospective payment systems (PPSs) by many other government (including Medicaid) and private payers and is being extended to health care providers other than hospitals. Each type of PPS has a slightly different impact, along with advantages and disadvantages. DRGs have increased the emphasis on hospital discharge planning, as well as hospital alternatives such as skilled extended care, outpatient services, and home care. Although evidence shows that DRGs have assisted in cutting some health care costs, critics find many shortcomings in the system. The greatest concern is that DRGs put an emphasis on cost-efficiency, perhaps at the expense of quality of care.

The implications for nursing are vast. Nurses represent the major personnel expense in any hospital. The PPS provides an opportunity for nursing to demonstrate its value by clearly identifying nursing costs and relating nursing care to positive patient outcomes. Nurses are in a position to maintain quality in cost-effective care, especially if they have managerial and financial capabilities.

New methods of prepayment cannot provide all the answers to the problems of the troubled health care system. Designing systems to provide needed services to the uninsured is expected to be a major subject in state and federal legislatures. An estimated 33% of the total U.S. population has no health insurance and thus, has limited access to available services. Of those over 65 years of

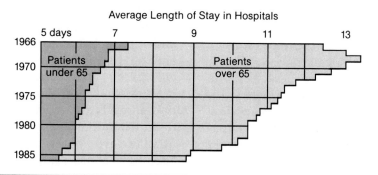

Average Length of Stay in Hospitals

Figure 1-2

Length of stay has steadily decreased with a significant drop in the early 1980s when prospective reimbursement was introduced. AHA reported an average length of stay of 7.2 days in 1987, continuing the decline. *(Courtesy of American Hospital Association)*

age, approximately 18% are not part of any health care insurance program.

People significantly handicapped by the current health care payment system include single parents, the young, the homeless, AIDS victims, and the elderly.

HEALTH CARE DELIVERY

Health care is provided in a variety of settings. These settings include hospitals, extended care facilities, HMOs, ambulatory care facilities, government and community health clinics, physicians' offices, nurses' offices, and the homes of patients. Over five million personnel are involved in health care, including over two million nurses.

The health care system is divided into three areas of care: primary (not to be confused with primary prevention), acute, and long-term care. **Primary care** is the first contact in a given episode of illness that leads to a decision of what must be done to help resolve the problem. It is provided by the individual who is responsible for the continuum of care, such as maintenance of health, evaluation, and management of symptoms, and appropriate referrals.[56] Primary care is provided by physicians and nurses. Clinical nurse specialists and nurse practitioners assume responsibility for management of acute and chronic disease as well as a variety of health promotion activities and services.

Acute care consists of "those services that treat the acute phase of illness or disability and has as its purpose the restoration of normal life processes and functions."

Long-term care consists of "those services designed to provide symptomatic treatment, maintenance and rehabilitative services for patients of all age groups in a variety of health care settings."[56] These definitions of primary, acute, and long-term care describe three areas of nursing practice, and the three levels of care in the health care system.

HOSPITALS

The *hospital* is the largest employer of nurses and other health workers. The size of the hospital may vary from under 25 to over 2000 beds. It may be governmental or nongovernmental, nonprofit or proprietary (for profit), and a general or a specialized institution, such as a children's hospital or a cancer hospital. More than a third of U.S. hospitals are either owned, leased, managed, or sponsored by a multisystem.

The hospital has numerous departments, each related in some way to the total care of patients or the operation of support services. Most hospitals have departments of dietary and food service, laundry, business and finance, physical plant (maintenance, housekeeping), nursing service, and other professional services such as radiology, pharmacy, social service, speech therapy, respiratory therapy, laboratory, medical records, and so on. Many hospitals have education departments that conduct the orientation and continuing education of the employees. These may be under a specific department, such as nursing, or may be central to the entire hospital. Another important department is that of the volunteer worker. Auxiliary members, teenage volunteers, friendly visitors, and similar volunteers provide support services, making it possible to improve care without increasing costs.

Most hospitals provide the services to both the inpatient and the outpatient. Minor surgery, diagnostics, dialysis, and physical therapy are a few of the services that may be offered on an outpatient basis. Many hospitals also offer various wellness programs to the community.

EXTENDED CARE FACILITIES

Extended care facilities, also called long-term care health centers, or nursing homes, may be part of a hospital, but most are separate institutions. Some are nonproprietary (not-for-profit), but most tend to be **proprietary.** They provide nursing care, medical supervision, and rehabilitation care, as well as furnish residential and personal services to the elderly and the disabled. Residential care means providing a pleasant, healthful place to live, a comfortable room, nutritious meals, clean laundry, the services of a barber and beautician, and the companionship of others. Personal care involves assistance with functional tasks like dressing, bathing, toileting, eating, and walking. It also includes assisting the resident in following prescribed programs of medication, diet, and exercise, as well as attending scheduled activities.

All long-term care centers do not offer the same levels of care. The Medicare and Medicaid programs have established two categories of extended care facilities according to the services they provide. A **skilled nursing facility** (SNF) is a long-term facility that has been certified in compliance with federal standards. This level of care provides 24-hour nursing services, regular medical supervision, and rehabilitation therapy. An SNF cares for the recuperating patient who no longer needs acute nursing and medical attention but still requires skilled nursing care. An **intermediate care facility** (ICF) is also certified in compliance with federal standards but provides less extensive health-related services and nursing supervision. These facilities primarily serve people who are not fully capable of living by themselves, yet are not necessarily dependent upon 24-hour nursing care.[59]

The terms "skilled nursing facility" and "intermediate care facility" describe the intensity of nursing care provided rather than the quality of care. Many extended care facilities are certified and licensed to provide both skilled nursing care and intermediate care to their residents. Medicare and other third-party payers (insurance plans) will not pay for a patient to be kept in a hospital beyond the point of need for hospital services; therefore it is more cost-effective to move a patient to an extended care facility that provides skilled nursing care. Medicare covers at least part of a "period of illness," up to 100 days of care in an SNF, but only after a stay of at least 3 days in a hospital. If care is needed beyond 100 days, the cost of care may be supplemented by Medicaid and private insurance programs. Medicaid assists with the cost of care in an SNF and an ICF. There are indications that both Medicare and Medicaid programs may institute some type of PPS for extended care facilities similar to the DRG categories currently used in hospitals. The state of New York already uses such a system for some Medicaid reimbursement for long-term care.[44] These impending changes necessitate contacting local, federal, and state offices for up-to-date information.

About 5% of persons age 65 to 85 and 20% of those over age 85 make their homes in long-term care centers. The increase in the older population and the magnitude of their health needs has resulted in a proliferation of extended care facilities.

Care is also provided in continuing care retirement communities (CCRC's). These communities provide private housing to residents with access to an adjacent SNF. Avoiding temporary or permanent moves away from one's home are viewed as a significant benefit for senior citizens. This housing trend is expected to continue.

HMOs AND PPOs

HMOs provide comprehensive health services to their members for a prepaid, fixed payment, regardless of the quantity of services provided. The distinguishing feature of HMOs is prepayment, a kind of prospective payment on an annual basis. Since the cost is fixed, the profit of the HMO will be greater if the enrollee stays well or if unnecessary diagnostic tests and treatments are avoided. Health services may be given directly or through arrangements with others and include the services of physicians, nurses, and various other health care providers.

HMOs have grown rapidly in some parts of the country, primarily in the urban areas of the

West and Midwest. More than 425 HMOs serve about 11% of the U.S. population. Most HMOs are part of a proprietary multisystem. Although the cost-effectiveness of HMOs is widely debated, HMO members do have 30% to 40% less inpatient days, and this does not appear to be at the expense of quality of care. Routine physical examinations are provided by the HMO as well as routine health maintenance programs (annual physicals, health education) and illness management.

Preferred provider organizations PPOs offer a similar delivery system to the HMO. The PPO is a group of physicians and nurses who have joined together to provide care as a group. They are not necessarily located in the same office but use each other for referrals. PPOs may or may not involve a standard fee per member annually. Provider members of the PPO furnish services on a discounted reimbursement basis in return for prompt payment and guaranteed volume. Members of a PPO are encouraged to use "preferred" providers through an incentive such as lower insurance rates.

AMBULATORY CARE AND HOME HEALTH AGENCIES

The shift in emphasis away from overnight stays in the hospital has generated a proliferation of ambulatory care and home agencies, many of them part of health **multisystems.**

Freestanding **ambulatory care** centers may be associated with a hospital or operated by a group of physicians on an extended hour basis. These centers provide immediate and convenient access to episodic care at relatively reasonable cost. There are over 3000 ambulatory care centers in the United States. Some centers are open 24 hours and have been dubbed "urgicenters."

Although most hospitals now have expanded outpatient surgery departments, freestanding outpatient surgery centers are also prevalent. These facilities also may or may not be hospital owned. The first "surgicenter" was opened in 1975 in Phoenix, Arizona, and these centers now number about 600. The relatively low complication rates associated with procedures performed at surgicenters have been attributed both to the "minor" nature of the surgeries and to "careful screening of the patients before surgery."

Home health care has long been provided by such agencies as the Visiting Nurse Association

and county health departments. The field has greatly expanded and there are now about 6000 such agencies. As the number of private (both proprietary and nonproprietary) agencies has increased, the number of government-based agencies has stayed about the same or declined. Many home health agencies are hospital or SNF based. Home health care is being offered by more hospitals than any other alternative services. Home health agencies provide services such as nursing, therapy, physical therapy, occupational therapy, social service, and home health aide/homemaker services in the client's home. The need for skilled nurses in these agencies has increased because more and more complicated and invasive procedures are being performed in the home setting. The home health nurse may enjoy a greater sense of autonomy when functioning in this more independent role.

A special type of home care, called "hospice care," is available to the dying patient who wishes to remain at home. Hospice care addresses the physical, spiritual, emotional, psychologic, financial, and legal needs of the dying patient and his or her family. This type of care is provided by an interdisciplinary team of professionals and volunteers.

GOVERNMENT HEALTH DEPARTMENTS

Departments of health are found on the federal, state, and local levels. The federal system is widespread and offers many services. The functions of state health departments are broad in scope, usually in cooperation with federal agencies and local health departments. The average health care consumer deals most often with the local health department. Local boards of health vary in the services provided. Functions usually include communicable disease control, laboratory testing, environmental sanitation services, health screening, and health education. Public health nurses may provide clinic services or care in the home or school.

OTHER HEALTH CARE FACILITIES

Health care is provided in many settings beyond the walls of the hospital or nursing home. Physicians, dentists, nurses in private practice, and incorporated group practice centers offering a va-

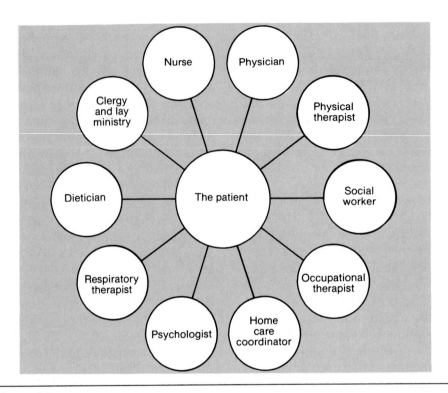

Figure 1-3
The health care team.

riety of services and expertise, play a major role in the health care system. Schools provide examinations and health teaching. Industries offer emergency services and physical examinations and are becoming more involved in programs promoting prevention and health maintenance. Community health centers are playing a major role in bringing health care closer to the people. The goal of the community health center is to provide the services needed in an atmosphere of concern and understanding tailored to meet the needs of the community it serves.

HEALTH CARE TEAM

Regardless of the setting in which care is rendered, comprehensive health care requires the efforts of a team of health professionals, paraprofessionals, and workers. In the center of the team is the patient, and it is the patient to whom the team is ultimately responsible. Often the patient lacks the ability or resources to fulfill the role of leader and coordinator of the health team. It is

the nurse, who spends the greatest amount of time with the patient, who must assist the patient and act as the patient advocate. Often, the nurse represents the patient and coordinates the efforts of the physician, physical therapist, social worker, clergy, dietitian, respiratory therapist, psychologist, home care coordinator, occupational therapist, and others. Each member of the health team is essential to the total, or "holistic," care of the patient (Figure 1-3).

NURSING

The act of nursing was once a simple function performed by the untrained. The individual who "nursed" the sick was called a "nurse." There was no formal preparation for nursing until Florence Nightingale opened her school with a prescribed curriculum of study and practical experience. As nursing evolved as a profession, nursing leaders attempted to define nursing. Florence Nightingale wrote that the goal of nursing was "to put the patient in the best condition for nature to act upon him." Virginia Henderson in 1966 wrote a classic definition of nursing—the nurse's purpose is "to assist the individual, sick or well, in the performance of those activities contributing to health or its recovery (or to peaceful death) that he would perform unaided if he had the necessary strength, will, or knowledge. And to do this in such a way as to help him gain independence as rapidly as possible."[26]

The American Nurses' Association (ANA) defines nursing as "the diagnosis and treatment of human responses to actual or potential health problems."[5] All of these definitions illustrate the consistent orientation of nurses to the provision of nursing care that promotes the well being of the people served.

Nursing has long been described as an "art and a science." Early definitions emphasized the care of the sick, whereas more recent descriptions stress the role of the nurse in prevention of disease and health maintenance as well. The necessity of viewing the patient as a whole person, including physiologic, emotional, psychologic, intellectual, social and spiritual aspects, is stressed, along with the interrelationship and interdependence of these factors as they affect health. Modern definitions include reference to the patient's family and/or significant others. The functions of the nurse are likely to be categorized according to the degree of dependence or independence of the patient. Dorothy Orem has gone beyond a definition to a theory of nursing in which she describes the "locus of decision making" and places it with the nurse, shared by the nurse and patient, or with the patient, depending on the ability of the patient to make decisions or perform activities related to health.

NURSING EDUCATION AND SCOPE OF PRACTICE

The profession's education has evolved and changed since Florence Nightingale established the first school of nursing. Today, to become a licensed vocational nurse (LVN) or a licensed practical nurse (LPN), one attends a 9- to 12-month program. To become a registered nurse (RN), one can attend a 3-year hospital diploma school, a 2-year community college associate degree program, a 4-year university baccalaureate program or a "generic masters" program. Graduates of these programs complete their education with

varying degrees of knowledge and differing skills and abilities.

The LVN/LPN is authorized to provide direct nursing care under the supervision and direction of a registered nurse, physician, dentist, or podiatrist. That supervision need not be direct and is often quite distant, with the supervisor assuming the responsibility for authorizing the LVN/LPN to function. The LVN/LPN is prepared to provide nursing care to patients with predictable nursing care problems in well-defined situations. LVN/LPN programs are offered by hospitals, community colleges, vocational centers, and some high schools. The program must be approved by the state in which it exists in order for its graduates to be eligible to take the state board examination for practical nursing. All states except California use the National Council of State Boards of Nursing Licensing Examination for Vocational/Practical Nursing. California develops and administers its own examination.

Hospital-based schools granting a diploma in nursing were the first educational programs offered in nursing. The functions and responsibilities of the graduate of a diploma school of nursing include direct patient care in hospitals, extended care facilities, and other health care agencies. The number of diploma schools has declined in recent years because of the high cost to hospitals of maintaining such programs and a trend moving nursing education into the academic setting.

The nursing graduate with an associate degree is prepared to give direct care to patients with acute or chronic well-defined health problems or to those needing information or support to maintain health—the patients usually found in hospitals, nursing homes, and other health care agencies. The practice is focused on the individual patient in consideration of that patient's relationships within a family, group, or community. The nurse with an associate degree can pursue study on the baccalaureate level. Some programs are designed to build directly on the associate degree program. Other baccalaureate programs admit associate degree graduates with advanced standing after evaluation of transfer credit in the liberal arts and sciences, and the awarding of proficiency credit earned by taking nursing examinations.

The nurse with a bachelor of science in nursing degree (BSN) is prepared to function in the acute care and extended care facility, and in the community. The additional academic background provided in the baccalaureate program prepares the graduate to assume a greater share of responsibility for health care and for directing other members of the health team. The curriculum emphasizes primary health care, preventive and rehabilitative services, health counseling, and education, and acute and long-term services. Study in such areas as nursing leadership, community health nursing, and nursing research is required of these students.

Several schools in the country have established a generic masters program. The student admitted to these programs has earned a bachelor's degree in another field related to nursing. In the 3-year course of study, the student's curriculum includes nursing knowledge and skill with a focus in an area of specialty. On graduation, the student will have earned a masters degree in nursing and is eligible for the RN examination as well. These programs attract people who may have pursued another field before choosing nursing.

Graduate education is available to candidates who have earned a bachelor's degree in nursing and meet the entrance requirements of a university graduate school. The master's degree allows a nurse to focus in an area of specialty. Most programs prepare clinical nurse specialists in a specialty area. Some prepare nurse administrators.

Although there are a variety of educational entry points in nursing, each graduate provides a unique service to patients and their families. The profession continues to differentiate the various types of practice for the future according to education and experience.[6]

MEDICAL-SURGICAL NURSING

Medical-surgical nursing is the area of nursing that deals with any illness or disease that affects the physiology of adults. The illness may have begun in childhood, during or after pregnancy, or as a result of a psychiatric problem, but once it interferes with normal physiology, the patient is said to have a medical problem and the adult is termed a "medical" patient. When the problem is treated by surgical intervention, the patient is then termed "surgical." Social and behavioral problems can affect or be affected by the patient's response and/or adjustment to physical illness and are therefore an important aspect of medical-surgical nursing. The content of medical-surgical nursing is complex and vast in scope.

The medical service usually includes those patients with serious conditions such as myocardial infarction, terminal cancer, congestive heart failure, leukemia, and AIDS. The medical patient may have entered the hospital for a series of diagnostic tests and examinations because there is some question as to what is wrong. On completion of the examinations and the establishment of a medical diagnosis, the patient may be treated and discharged or may be prepared for surgery. The patient may then be transferred to a surgical service unless medical and surgical patients are both admitted to the same units. Many patients have medical and surgical conditions at the same time. An example would be the diabetic patient who is admitted to the hospital to have the gallbladder removed.

The goal of medical-surgical nursing is to help patients help themselves. The degree of assistance required for each patient will vary with the stage of illness. It is often a temptation for nurses to "do for" patients rather than encouraging and assisting in self-care. Sometimes it is faster, at other times there is concern that the patient will not do it as well, and most often our need to help others prompts us to do what the patient should be doing independently, or with assistance. Most nurses express a desire for "helping others" as a reason for entering nursing. It is most important to remember that the best way to help a patient may be not to help at all. Promoting independence while providing support and understanding is essential to the maintenance and restoration of optimum health—that level of health that is the greatest possible for that patient.

Standards of Nursing Practice

Standards of any profession provide the public with assurances that the quality of care is maintained by its members. The ANA is responsible for establishing and maintaining the generic or general standards for nursing practice. Individual members of the nursing profession are responsible for incorporating these standards into their daily care. The generic standards provide the public with a means of determining the quality of care rendered to a patient.

The ANA and other speciality organizations have developed specific standards for many of the specialty areas of nursing practice.[3] Regardless of the specialty area, every nurse is responsible for applying the generic standards to his or her practice.

Standards of Nursing Care

Standard 1

The collection of data about the health status of the client/patient is systematic and continuous. The data are accessible, communicated, and recorded.

Standard 2

Nursing diagnoses are derived from health status data.

Standard 3

The plan of nursing care includes goals derived from the nursing diagnosis.

Standard 4

The plan of nursing care includes priorities and the prescribed nursing approaches or measures to achieve the goals derived from the nursing diagnosis.

Standard 5

Nursing actions provide for client/patient participation in health promotion, maintenance, and restoration.

Standard 6

Nursing actions assist the client/patient to maximize his or her health capabilities.

Standard 7

The client's/patient's progress or lack of progress toward goal achievement is determined by the client/patient and the nurse.

Standard 8

The client's/patient's progress or lack of progress toward goal achievement directs reassessment, reordering of priorities, new goal-setting, and revision of the plan of nursing care.

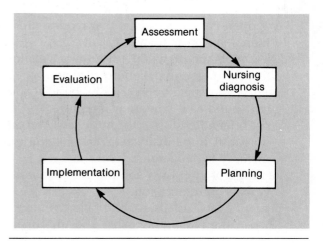

Figure 1-4
The nursing process.

NURSING PROCESS

Nursing is a dynamic interpersonal problem-solving process that facilitates the individual's potential for health. The five-step **nursing process** includes (1) assessment, (2) nursing diagnosis, (3) planning, (4) implementation, and (5) evaluation (Figure 1-4).

Assessment

Assessment requires collecting and recording data related to the patient and grouping the data into meaningful categories. It includes the physical and emotional signs and symptoms presented by the patient, as well as information obtained from other sources, such as the patient's chart, other nurses, laboratory reports, family, and visitors. A thorough nursing assessment requires systematic and careful observation of and interviews with the patient. Assessment is performed at the first encounter with the patient and recorded as a **nursing history.** It is also performed during every subsequent interaction with the patient to expand data and evaluate the response to illness or treatment.

The quality of the nursing history and subsequent patient interviews can be enhanced by the use of several effective interviewing techniques:

Approach the patient calmly and empathetically.

Explain the purpose of the questions: to provide better care by knowing more about the patient and his family.

Use terminology familiar to the patient.

Ask about the patient's immediate concerns or complaints first and save delicate, personal questions until later.

Call the patient by name.

Speak clearly, slowly, and distinctly.

Listen. Maintain the topic, but never interrupt the patient.

Ask open-ended questions that require more than a yes or no answer.

Use signals such as a nod, uh-huh, or a glance to encourage the patient to continue.

Even if your institution uses a checklist, do not sound as if you are using one.

Write brief notes during the interview. You do not want to be distracting, but relying on memory is dangerous.

Be aware of your own and the patient's non-verbal communication.

Remain open, accepting, and objective, even when the patient is hostile and uncooperative.

Use good eye contact, but never stare.

Be professional.[10,19]

Nursing diagnosis

Analysis of the data is required in the next step of the process—the development of the nursing diagnosis. A **nursing diagnosis** describes a combination of signs and symptoms that indicate an actual or potential health problem nurses are licensed to treat and capable of treating.[16] It is a concise statement that brings to mind the same behaviors in all who use it. A common characteristic of a nursing diagnosis is the determination of human function or behavior. Behavior is used here in its broadest sense, referring to an observable response. That response may be physiologic, psychologic, intellectual, emotional, or spiritual. The nursing diagnosis gives us a common language, enabling us to communicate effectively and efficiently the priority needs of the patient. It is the basis of the nursing care plan.

If a nursing diagnosis is to have universal meaning, it must be universally accepted. Nurses have been discussing the concept of the nursing diagnosis for over 30 years and it continues to evolve as the common language of nursing. The National Conference Group on the Classification of Nursing Diagnosis began meeting in 1973. Now known as the North American Nursing Diagnosis Association (NANDA), they continue to meet yearly and to develop and validate nursing diagnoses. The current list of accepted nursing diagnoses is published annually. NANDA describes the diagnosis as the problem statement, to be followed by a statement describing the etiology and signs and symptoms. This is referred to as the PES format: health problem (P), etiology (E), signs and symptoms (S). Lunney[33] has proposed a simplified system in which the diagnosis has two parts: the first part communicating behaviors that can be improved through nursing and the second part identifying factors that must be worked with to accomplish this.

Although proposed terminology differs and philosophic differences exist, there is general agreement that the nursing diagnosis must describe a behavior that is a problem to the patient and requires nursing intervention. The problem must be stated in terms that give direction to the nurse in selecting nursing interventions and identifying desired expected outcomes. For example, "ineffective airway clearance" is an accepted NANDA nursing diagnosis. It is not complete without a statement of etiology or a "related to" statement. Whether it is considered a part of, or an addition to, the nursing diagnosis, the "related to" statement is essential if the diagnosis is to be meaningful and give direction for nursing intervention. We must know "why" the airway clearance is ineffective—in other words, the etiology—to propose effective nursing interventions. The NANDA format would then follow with a description of the signs and symptoms that led to the diagnosis. Whether this grouping of significant signs and symptoms appears on the actual care plan will vary with the format adopted by a given agency. The nurse's skill and knowledge in collecting and analyzing data are essential in establishing a nursing diagnosis.

The nursing diagnosis statement can be modified to fit the individual patient. "Impaired physical mobility" is an accepted nursing diagnosis that becomes more meaningful when the impairment is further described: "Impaired physical mobility of right hand." The complete diagnostic statement would then read, "Impaired physical mobility, right hand, related to joint inflammation."

We have not yet reached the goal of a universally accepted system or taxonomy of nursing diagnoses. Proposals from any and all individuals and groups must be considered and tested. This period of development is particularly confusing to nursing students who yearn to be told precisely what is expected of them. The nursing diagnosis continues to evolve, and we will see and use diagnoses that have not been universally accepted and we will not always agree on the appropriateness. Everyone in nursing must contribute ideas and be involved in testing the work of experts in the field. A universal taxonomy will require continual change to reflect current practice.

Planning

In the **planning** stage of the nursing process, a concise written design of action is developed that is based on the nursing diagnosis. Priorities are set, appropriate nursing actions or interventions are proposed, and goals or expected outcomes are identified.

Individualized care of the total patient necessitates a written plan of care. **Nursing care plans** are intended to communicate, to prevent compli-

cations, to assure continuity of care, to identify and assure patient teaching, and to provide for discharge planning.[49] Hospitals and other health care agencies require care plans to be written for all patients.

The nursing care plan includes the nursing diagnosis or statements that identify the patient's problems and proposed nursing interventions. For each intervention there should be a statement of expected outcome criteria. The outcome criteria are the expected results of the intervention. Although the majority of the care plan focuses on inpatient nursing service, the plan should include a discharge plan (Figure 1-5).

DATE	PATIENT'S PROBLEMS	EXPECTED PATIENT OUTCOME	TARGET DATE	NURSING ORDERS
3/10	Impaired skin integrity related to 2 cm open sore on "R" ankle.	Lesion reduced in size with evidence of granulation tissue at edges.	3/17	Apply foam rubber to area surrounding lesion - change p.r.n.; foot cradle on bed to protect ankle from weight of linen.
3/10	Altered nutrition related to unregulated insulin dosage.	Weight stable. No signs of hypoglycemia. Urine negative/glucose.		Observe for signs of hypoglycemia 30" $\bar{p}$ dose of regular insulin. Urine for sugar and acetone before meals. Check FBS & 4 pm blood sugar daily & report. Weight daily. I & O.
3/10	Disturbances in self-concept related to dependence on others.	Speaks positively about personal strengths.		Anticipate needs to avoid patient having to request help. Focus on strengths and abilities to perform other hygiene needs.
3/10	Self-care deficit related to activity restriction: must use bedpan.	Stool daily or q.o.d.		Offer bedpan before am care. Provide call light and answer promptly. I & O; check stool daily.

PATIENT TEACHING PLAN	DATE INITIATED	TARGET DATE	DATE COMPLETED	OUTCOME CRITERIA FOR DISCHARGE
1500 calorie ADA diet	3/10	3/17		1. Select food items to provide 1500 calorie diet
Drawing up and administering insulin	3/11	3/18		2. Test urine for sugar and acetone
Foot and nail care	3/12	3/19		3. Draw up and administer own insulin
				4. Verbalize methods of proper foot and nail care

RELEVANT DATA—SOCIAL DATA	
Eyesight poor	
Lives alone	

| REFERRALS | ☐ SOC. SERVICE DATE | ☐ DISCH. PLANNER DATE | ☒ HOME CARE DATE 3/14 | ☒ DIETARY DATE 3/12 | OTHER DATE |

Figure 1-5

Sample nursing care plan. This sample has been typed for easier reading, but nursing care plans are handwritten and continually revised as patients' needs and conditions change.

Implementation

Implementation is the actual performance of the nursing interventions identified in the plan of care. The interventions may include direct patient care, health teaching, or other activities for the benefit of the patient or the supervision of such activities.

Important to the implementation step and the entire nursing process is documentation. Periodic patient assessment and all nursing interventions are charted in the nursing notes. These are an important part of the patient's permanent record and are considered to be legal documents. Additionally, auditing methods under DRGs, Medicare, and Medicaid can cause health care agencies, like hospitals to lose revenue through disallowance of services because of inadequate nursing documentation. Different agencies employ different methods for documentation of nursing notes. Methods may vary from a narrative type to simplified flow sheets. No matter the form, it is important that nursing documentation be complete and accurate.

One system of record keeping replaces the fragmented chart. It is termed the "problem-oriented record" and demands that all progress notes and orders be directly related to patient problems that have been identified and assigned a number. All health care workers who care for the patient use the same progress notes and order sheets; however, some institutions separate the notes according to professional discipline. Thus, there would be a separate page for nurses, physicians, and other health care workers. The **problem-oriented record** consists of four parts: *s*ubjective data, *o*bjective data, *a*ssessment, and *p*lan. This is often referred to as the **SOAP** system. The subjective data is the information the patient provides whereas the objective data is the information the nurse obtains—a conclusion or possible problem. The SOAP system is based on the nursing process and provides a mechanism for recording data.

Evaluation

The final stage of the nursing process, **evaluation,** requires a statement of expected outcome criteria or goals for each nursing intervention prescribed. The expected outcome must be stated in terms of patient behavior; that is, what the patient will be doing or what changes will be identified in the patient that will indicate successful intervention. Evaluation requires the continued assessment of

---

Example of a SOAP Note

Problem #__ Pain in abdomen
 S: "I have a dull, full pain in my stomach." Present for 2 days. Ate spicy meal 2 days ago. No bowel movements × 2 days. Remainder of systems review negative.
 O: Temp. 98.8. BP 120/80. Bowel sounds present but slow and infrequent. Stool guaiac negative.
 A: Probable constipation. R/O mass.
 P: Refer to physician
  Observe intake and output
  Record food intake

---

the patient and comparison of progress to the expected outcome. If the expected changes in the patient do not occur, alternative nursing interventions are proposed and carried out. Evaluation also implies updating the care plan and appropriate documentation.

Whereas the nursing process has been described in five stages, these stages do not occur in rigid progression. Assessment is continuous and all findings must be analyzed and may modify planning. Evaluation, although discussed last, begins with planning. If expected outcomes are not identified in the beginning, it is impossible to evaluate the effectiveness of the nursing interventions. With each change in patient behavior, the cycle begins again.

Nurses in all categories use all five steps of the nursing process. Complexity and lack of definition of patient problems demand a nurse prepared at the master's level. The associate degree nurse and diploma graduate can develop a nursing diagnosis for patients with common, well-defined health problems. They are responsible for developing a plan of care for these patients that includes proposed interventions and expected outcomes. The LVN/LPN can determine needs and provide care for patients with common, well-defined health problems as well, but in a structured setting where there is opportunity for consultation with an RN. They are able to contribute to the plan of care, perform identified nursing interventions, assess patient progress, and evaluate the effectiveness of the care of these patients.

NURSING DELIVERY SYSTEMS

In the early days of nursing, each nurse cared for one patient or "case" or a group of patients, providing all necessary services. This was known as the "case method" of patient assignment. As medicine and technology advanced, the responsibilities and duties of the nurse became more complex. As a result of the shortage of nurses during World War II, **functional nursing** was developed to use auxiliary health workers trained in a variety of skills.[46] Each person was assigned specific duties or functions that were carried out on all patients in a given unit. RNs gave medications, the LVN/ LPN gave treatments, and the aides and orderlies made beds and distributed meals. This system is still used in institutions throughout the United States.

In the early 1950s, **team nursing** was proposed to take advantage of the skills of a variety of nursing personnel while providing more comprehensive care for the patient. The RN acts as the leader of the nursing team, responsible for a predetermined group of patients. The nurse is assisted in the care of those patients by other nurses, LVNs/ LPNs, nursing assistants, and orderlies. The team leader knows and understands the condition of the patient and is able to provide for the care of each by assigning the team members according to their individual capabilities and personalities. The leader not only assigns patients but also assimilates and dispenses knowledge and is the contact with the head nurse and the physician. The team leader also has certain responsibilities for the morale of the team, for suggesting changes for team members, and for evaluation of individual work.

Essential to the team nursing concept is the team conference. It is in the conference that the team members confer on the needs of the patients and jointly establish a plan of care under the direction of the team leader.

The use of a mixture of health care personnel, coordinated by the registered nurse, is a modern version of team nursing.

Another approach to providing nursing service is termed "primary nursing." Each nurse is assigned a group of patients, preferably no more than five, and is responsible for the total care of each individual from admission to discharge. The initial assessment is performed by the primary nurse who plans the care to be given. When the primary nurse is off duty, other nurses follow the directives of the plan of care established by the primary nurse. The primary nurse involves the patient in his care, in the identification of goals, and in discharge planning. This method provides continuity of care and enables the nurse to become better acquainted with the needs of patients and families and to minister to those needs more specifically. As a result, patient centered care becomes a reality. The primary nurse accepts responsibility for the care of the patient, establishing accountability.[37,46] The primary nursing approach to patient care is not to be confused or equated with the concepts of **primary care** or **primary prevention**, both discussed earlier in this chapter.

Primary nursing in its purest form requires all care to be delivered by registered nurses. We have seen a trend to delegate less complex tasks to lesser prepared personnel with the RN maintaining responsibility for the complete care of the patient. Pairing a registered nurse with a nursing assistant or technician (partners in practice) is a modification of primary nursing.

Other nursing delivery systems have evolved from the primary nursing concept. Among these are the collaborative practice model, itself generating several variations, and the new "case management" model. Collaborative practice models encourage effective communication between the physician and primary nurse and emphasize their interdependent roles as well as the independent role functions of the professional nurse. The case management concept actually incorporates both primary and team nursing and holds the RN, as case manager, accountable for specific clinical outcomes.[67] Each agency must examine its resources, develop and state its philosophy of nursing care, and then organize its approach to nursing accordingly. Because of prospective reimbursement, a hospital's decision on which nursing delivery system to use may well rest on which approach is the most cost-effective.

THEORY IN PRACTICE

There are many theories or beliefs that explain, predict, or describe the action of the nurse. The practice of nursing draws from a wide range of theorists, both nurses and other scientists. There are an impressive and growing list of theorists who have made significant contributions to the profession and society through their study. Some of these nursing theorists include Hildegard

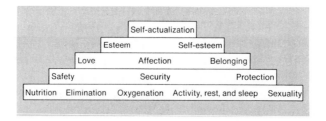

Figure 1-6

Maslow's hierarchy of human needs. *(Modified from Goble FD: The third force, New York, 1970, Grossman Publishers.)*

Peplau, Martha Rogers, Dorothea Orem, Sister Calista Roy, Imogene King, and Patricia Benner. Patricia Benner's work in caring from novice to expert has provided nurses with an understanding of their actions and given others a similar understanding of the position of the nurse in the whole of the health care team.[7,8,9]

HUMAN NEEDS

Much has been said about the identification of unmet needs and meeting the total needs of patients—physiologic, psychologic, and sociologic. One of the most extensive investigations of **human needs** was conducted by Abraham Maslow, considered a leader in the field of humanistic psychology.

Maslow identified the needs basic to all people as physiologic, safety, love and belongingness, esteem, and self-actualization. Maslow refrains from identifying the physiologic needs more specifically. The concept of homeostasis, the body's automatic efforts to maintain a constant, normal state of the bloodstream, along with recent studies of appetite, linking it in an imperfect way to an actual chemical lack in the body, has led Maslow to believe it impossible as well as useless to list fundamental physiologic needs.[39] He believes the list could become endless, depending on the degree of specificity of description. Physiologic needs are identified by Goble[23] in his study of Maslow as food, liquid, shelter, sex, sleep, and oxygen. Physiologic needs are commonly identified in nursing literature as nutrition, elimination, oxygenation, activity, rest, sleep, and sexuality.

The physiologic needs are the most important of all needs. Hypothetically, this means that an individual who is missing all needs would seek to obtain physiologic needs before any others. If all the needs are unsatisfied, the organism is then dominated by the physiologic needs. All other needs may become simply nonexistent or may be pushed into the background (Figure 1-6).

Once these physiologic needs have been satisfied, higher needs emerge and dominate the organism. When these are satisfied, again, new and higher needs emerge. Maslow refers to this organization of basic needs as a *hierarchy of relative prepotency* (superiority). Once a need is chemically gratified, it no longer dominates the organism. It now exists in a potential fashion in a sense that it may emerge again to dominate the organism if it is thwarted. A want that is satisfied is no longer a want. The organism is dominated and its behavior organized only by unsatisfied needs. If hunger is satisfied, it becomes unimportant in the current dynamics of the individual. When the human organism is dominated by a certain need, the philosophy of the future is shaped by that need. Even in the event of chronic satisfaction of basic needs, the human being is always desiring something. It rarely reaches a state of complete satisfaction except for a short time. It will always search for more at a higher level.

The needs that emerge on the next level following satisfaction of the physiologic needs are the safety needs. Maslow further describes the safety needs as security, stability, dependency, protection, freedom from fear, freedom from anxiety and chaos, and need for structure, order, law, limits, and strength in the protector.[39] The organism may equally well be wholly dominated by them. They may serve as the almost exclusive organizers of behavior, recruiting all the capacities of the organism in their service, and then the whole organism may be fairly described as a safety-seeking mechanism.[32]

In children and adults, illness is a threat to safety and a disruption of order in their lives. The disruption of regular schedule and routine that accompanies illness and hospitalization is particularly threatening to children. The child needs an organized and structured world. The child who frantically clings to his parents, as we often see in hospitals and other health care agencies, is testimony to the parent's role as protectors. The average child and, less obviously, the average adult in our society generally prefer a safe, orderly, predictable, lawful, organized world on which they can count and in which unexpected, unmanageable, chaotic, or other dangerous things do not happen. In such cases he or she has powerful parents or protectors who shield him or her from harm. The healthy and fortunate adult in our society is largely satisfied in his or her safety needs and in a real sense no longer has any safety needs as active motivators. The tendency to have some religion or world philosophy that organizes the universe and the men in it into some sort of satisfactorily coherent, meaningful whole is also in *part* motivated by safety seeking. Science and philosophy can be seen as partially motivated by safety needs. The need for safety is seen as an active and dominant mobilizer of the organism's resources only in real emergencies, for example, war, disease, crime waves, neurosis, brain injury, and breakdown of authority.

If physiologic and safety needs are fairly well gratified, the need for love, affection, and belongingness will emerge. The individual will now keenly feel the absence of friends, a sweetheart or wife, or children and hunger for a place in his group or family. Belongingness has been underrated, and it is now recognized as important to "belong" to a group, neighborhood, culture, and so on. Our society thwarts these needs, and these unmet needs are most commonly at the core in cases of maladjustment and more severe pathology.

It is Maslow's belief that love and affection, as well as their possible expression in sexuality, are generally viewed with ambivalence and are customarily hedged about with many restrictions and inhibitions. Practically all theorists of psychopathology have stressed thwarting of love needs as basic in the picture of maladjustment. Maslow places stress on the point that love is not synonymous with sex. Sex may be studied as a purely physiologic need. Ordinarily, sexual behavior is multidetermined by sexual and other

needs, chiefly love, and affection. Love needs involve both giving and receiving love.

At the next level are the esteem needs. All people in our society (with a few pathologic exceptions) have the need or desire for a stable, firmly based, usually high evaluation of themselves, for self-respect and self-esteem, and for the esteem of others. These needs may be classified into two subsidiary sets. First, these are the desires for strength, for achievement, for adequacy, for mastery and competency, for confidence in the face of the world, and for independence and freedom. Second, we have what we may call the desire for reputation or prestige (defining it as respect or esteem from other people), status, fame, glory, dominance, recognition, attention, importance, dignity, and appreciation. Satisfaction of the need for self-esteem leads to feelings of self-confidence, worth, strength, capability, and adequacy, of being useful and necessary in the world. Thwarting of these needs produces feelings of inferiority, of weakness, and of helplessness. These feelings in turn give rise to either basic discouragement or else compensatory or neurotic trends. The most stable and most healthful self-esteem is based on deserved respect from others rather than on external fame or celebrity and unwarranted adulation. Self-esteem must not be based on the opinions of others, but on real capacity, competence, and adequacy for the task.

If all the previous needs are satisfied, we may still often expect that a new discontent and restlessness will soon develop unless the individual is acting according to personal capabilities. A musician must make music, an artist must paint, and so on, if he or she is to be ultimately at peace. What a person *can* be, he or she *must* be; one must be true to one's nature. Maslow calls this need **self-actualization**. It refers to a person's desire for self-fulfillment, namely, the tendency for one to become actualized in what one potentially is—to become everything one is capable of becoming. At this level individual differences are greatest. The clear emergence of these needs usually rests on some prior satisfaction of the physiologic, safety, love, and esteem needs.

Maslow believes that there are degrees of relative satisfaction of needs. Most normal members of our society are both partially satisfied and partially unsatisfied in all their basic needs at the same time. A more realistic description of the hierarchy would be in terms of *decreasing* percent-

A Patient's Bill of Rights

The American Hospital Association presents a Patient's Bill of Rights with the expectation that observance of these rights will contribute to more effective patient care and greater satisfaction for the patient, his physician, and the hospital organization. Further, the association presents these rights in the expectation that they will be supported by the hospital on behalf of its patients, as an integral part of the healing process. It is recognized that a personal relationship between the physician and the patient is essential for the provision of proper medical care. The traditional physician-patient relationship takes on a new dimension when care is rendered within an organizational structure. Legal precedent has established that the institution itself also has a responsibility to the patient. It is in recognition of these factors that these rights are affirmed.

1. The patient has the right to considerate and respectful care.
2. The patient has the right to obtain from his physician complete current information concerning his diagnosis, treatment, and prognosis in terms the patient can be reasonably expected to understand. When it is not medically advisable to give such information to the patient, the information should be made available to an appropriate person in his behalf. He has the right to know by name the physician responsible for coordinating his care.
3. The patient has the right to receive from his physician information necessary to give informed consent prior to the start of any procedure and/or treatment. Except in emergencies, such information for informed consent should include but not necessarily be limited to the specific procedure and/or treatment, the medically significant risks involved, and the probable duration of incapacitation. Where medically significant alternatives for care or treatment exist, or when the patient requests information concerning medical alternatives, the patient has the right to such information. The patient also has the right to know the name of the person responsible for the procedures and/or treatment.
4. The patient has the right to refuse treatment to the extent permitted by law and to be informed of the medical consequences of his action.
5. The patient has the right to every consideration of his privacy concerning his own medical care program. Case discussion, consultation, examination, and treatment are confidential and should be conducted discreetly. Those not directly involved in his care must have the permission of the patient to be present.
6. The patient has the right to expect that all communications and records pertaining to his care should be treated as confidential.
7. The patient has the right to expect that within its capacity a hospital must make reasonable response to the request of a patient for services. The hospital must provide evaluation, service, and/or referral as indicated by the urgency of the case. When medically permissible a patient may be transferred to another facility only after he has received complete information and explanation concerning the needs for and alternatives to such a transfer. The institution to which the patient is to be transferred must first have accepted the patient for transfer.
8. The patient has the right to obtain information as to any relationship of his hospital to other health care and educational institutions insofar as his care is concerned. The patient has the right to obtain information as to the existence of any professional relationships among individuals by name who are treating him.
9. The patient has the right to be advised if the hospital proposes to engage in or perform human experimentation affecting his care or treatment. The patient has the right to refuse to participate in such research projects.
10. The patient has the right to expect reasonable continuity of care. He has the right to know in advance what appointment times and physicians are available and where. The patient has the right to expect that the hospital will provide a mechanism whereby he is informed by his physician or a delegate of the physician of the patient's continuing health care requirements following discharge.
11. The patient has the right to examine and receive an explanation of his bill regardless of sources of payment.
12. The patient has the right to know what hospital rules and regulations apply to his conduct as a patient.

No catalogue of rights can guarantee for the patient the kind of treatment he has a right to expect. A hospital has many functions to perform, including the prevention and treatment of disease, the education of both health professionals and patients, and the conduct of clinical research. All these activities must be conducted with an overriding concern for the patient, and, above all, the recognition of his dignity as a human being. Success in achieving this recognition assures success in the defense of the rights of the patient.

Approved by the House of Delegates of the American Hospital Association February 6, 1973.

ages of satisfaction as we move *up* in the *hierarchy of prepotency*. In other words, the higher the level of the need, the less it will be satisfied in most members of our society. It follows then that emergence of a new need does not necessarily follow *total* satisfaction of the prepotent need; rather, there is a gradual emergence by slow degrees from nothingness. As the degree of satisfaction increases, satisfaction of the next need will be increased. If only 10% of prepotent need "A" is satisfied, then need "B" may not be visible at all. As 25% of "A" becomes satisfied, 5% of "B" may emerge. If 75% of need "A" becomes satisfied, need "B" may emerge 50%, and so forth.

Maslow does not claim that these needs are to be understood as the exclusive and single determiners of certain kinds of behavior. Within the sphere of motivational determinants, any behavior tends to be determined by several or all of the basic needs simultaneously, rather than by only one of them. Eating may be partially for the sake of filling the stomach and partially for the sake of comfort and improvement of other needs.

Needs cease to play an active determining or organizing role as soon as they are gratified. This means that a basically satisfied person no longer has the needs for esteem, love, safety, and so on. The perfectly healthy, normal, fortunate person has *none of these needs*. So one who is thwarted in any of these basic needs may be envisaged simply as a sick person or at least as less than fully human. A healthy individual is primarily motivated by needs to develop and actualize fullest potentialities and capacities. If a person has any other basic needs in any *active, chronic* sense, he or she is simply an unhealthy person.

Although health evolves from gratification of basic needs, this does not produce a selfishness. It is not ego centered. On the contrary, in those who have basic needs gratified, Maslow sees compassionate and altruistic individuals. The concept of gratification postulates some positive growth tendency in the organism, which, from within, drives it to fuller development.

If one subscribes to Maslow's theory, self-actualization and health or wellness can be equated. Self-actualization is a goal and the ultimate need of all human beings and can occur when all other needs are gratified. Persons involved with promoting wellness can therefore look to Maslow's theory of human motivation based on human needs as a basis for their own theories. It treats mind and body as a whole and has as its goal optimum wellness of self-actualization, which results in the most fully developed human individual.

This examination of Maslow's theories has been limited to his hierarchy of basic needs. He has done further investigation into needs that he claims are preconditions for the basic needs, such as freedom to speak, freedom to do what one wishes so long as no harm is done to others, freedom to express oneself, freedom to investigate and seek information, freedom to defend oneself, justice, fairness, honesty, and orderliness in the group. Without these conditions the basic satisfactions are impossible or at least severely endangered. He has also studied needs that he claims go beyond the basic needs, namely, the need to know and understand and the aesthetic needs. These, too, have implications for nursing and for the education of nurses.

PATIENT RIGHTS

Emphasis on the patient as an active participant in personal health care has prompted public statements of patient rights by a variety of groups and individuals. Although not universally adopted by health care agencies, pressure is mounting for agencies to adopt standards and respect patients' rights. The House of Delegates of the American Hospital Association adopted a "Patient's Bill of Rights" during its convention in 1973, with the expectation that observance of those rights will contribute to more effective patient care and greater satisfaction for the patient, his physician, and the hospital organization.[1]

REFERENCES AND ADDITIONAL READINGS

1. American Hospital Association: Patient's bill of rights, Chicago, 1973, The Association.
2. American Hospital Association: Cost and compassion: recommendations for avoiding a crisis in care for the medically indigent, Chicago, 1986, The Association.
3. American Nurses Association: Standards of nursing practice, Kansas City, 1973, The Association.
4. American Nurses Association: Environmental assessment: factors affecting long-range planning for nursing and health care, Kansas City, 1985, The Association.
5. American Nurses Association: Nursing: a social policy statement, Kansas City, 1980, The Association.
6. American Nurses Association: Scope of nursing practice, Kansas City, 1987, The Association.
7. Benner P: From novice to expert, Menlo Park, Calif, 1984, Addison-Wesley Publishing Co Inc.
8. Benner P and Tanner C: Clinical judgment: how expert nurses use intuition, Am J Nurs 87:23-31, 1987.
9. Benner P and Wrubel J: The primacy of caring, Menlo Park, Calif, 1989, Addison-Wesley Publishing Co Inc.
10. Bernstein L and Bernstein RS: Interviewing: a guide for health professionals, New York, 1980, Appleton-Century Crofts.
11. Betz M: Primary nursing: two faces with little acquaintance, Nurs Health Care 3(10):543-546, 1982.
12. Beyers M and Dudas S: The clinical practice of medical-surgical nursing, Boston, 1977, Little, Brown & Co Inc.
13. Butler RN and Lewis MI: Aging and mental health: positive psychosocial approaches, ed 3, St Louis, 1982, The CV Mosby Co.
14. Butts PA, Berger BA, and Brooten DA: Tracking down the right degree, Nurs Health Care 7(2):90-95, 1986.
15. Discursive dictionary of health care, Washington DC, 1976, US Government Printing Office.
16. Dossey B and Guzzetta CE: Nursing diagnosis, Nursing 11(6):34-38, 1981.
17. Ebersole P and Hess P: Toward healthy aging: human needs and nursing response, ed 2, St Louis, 1985, The CV Mosby Co.
18. Easterbrook G: The revolution in medicine, Newsweek, 40-74, Jan. 26, 1987.
19. Edmunds L: Computer-assisted nursing care, Am J Nurs 82(7):1076-1079, 1982.
20. Fadden TC and Seiser GK: Nursing diagnosis: a matter of form, Am J Nurs 84(4):470-472, 1984.
21. Gebbie KM, editor: Classification of nursing diagnosis: summary of the Second National Conference, St Louis, 1976, Clearinghouse National Group for Classification of Nursing Diagnosis.
22. Gebbie KM and Lavin MA, editors: Classification of nursing diagnoses, Proceedings of the First National Conference, St Louis, Oct. 1-5, 1973, St Louis, 1975, The CV Mosby Co.
23. Goble FG: The third force, New York, 1970, Grossman Publishers.
24. Goldwater M: From a legislator: views on third-party reimbursement for nurses, Am J Nurs 82(3):411-414, 1982.
25. Gordon M, Sweeney MA, and McKeehan K: Nursing diagnosis: looking at its use in the clinical area, Am J Nurs 80(4):672-674, 1980.
26. Henderson V: The nature of nursing, New York, 1966, Macmillan Publishing.
27. Ismeurt R and others: Concepts fundamental to nursing, Springhouse, Pa, 1990, Springhouse Corp.
28. Kelley L: The nursing experience: trends, challenges, and transitions, New York, 1987, Macmillian Publishing Co.
29. Kerr AH: How the write stuff can go wrong, Nursing 17(1):48-50, 1987.
30. Leahy M, Cobb MM, and Jones MC: Community health nursing, ed 3, New York, 1977, McGraw-Hill Inc.
31. Lindeman C and McAthie M: Nursing trends and issues. Springhouse, Pa, 1990, Springhouse Corp.
32. Leavell HR and Clark RG: Preventative medicine for the doctor in his community: an epidemiologic approach, ed 3, New York, 1965, McGraw-Hill Inc.
33. Lunney M: Nursing diagnosis: refining the system, Am J Nurs 82(3):456-459, 1982.
34. Lynaugh J and Fagin C: Nursing comes of age, Image J Nurs Sch, 20(4):184-89, 1988.
35. Lysought JP: An abstract for action, New York, 1970, McGraw-Hill Inc.
36. Mackay C and Ault L: A systematic approach to individualizing nursing care, J Nurs Adm 7(1):39-48, 1977.
37. Marram GD, Bevis EO, and Schlegel MW: Primary nursing, a model for individualized care, ed 2, St Louis, 1978, The CV Mosby Co.
38. Marriner A: The nursing process, ed 3, St Louis, 1983, The CV Mosby Co.
39. Maslow AH: Motivation and personality, ed 2, New York, 1970, Harper & Row, Publishers Inc.
40. McClosky JC: Nurses' orders: the next professional breakthrough, RN 43(2):99-113, 1980.
41. McClosky JC: POR vs nursing care plan, Nurs Outlook 23:492-495, August 1975.
42. Milo N: Telematics in the future of health care delivery: implications for nursing, J Prof Nurs 2(11):39-50, 1986.
43. Minyard K, Wall J, and Turner R: RNs may cost less than you think, J Nurs Adm 16(5):28-34, 1986.
44. Mitty E: Prospective payment and long-term care: linking payments to resource use, Nurs Health Care 8(1):15-21, 1987.
45. National Commission on Nursing: Executive Summary of Final Report, 1988, The Commission.
46. Nenner VC, Eckhoff CM, and Curtis EM: Primary nursing, Superv, Nurs 8:14-16, 1977.
47. Newman MA: Nursing diagnosis: looking at the whole, Am J Nurs 84(12):1496-1499, 1984.
48. Niland MV and Bentz PM: A problem-oriented approach to planning nursing care, Nurs Clin North Am 9:238, 1974.
49. Pope S: The "problem" of nursing care plans, Superv Nurs 8:25-27, January 1977.
50. Porter LS: Is nursing ready for the year 2000, Nurs Forum 12(2):53-57, 1985.
51. Price MR: Nursing diagnosis: making a concept come alive, Am J Nurs 80(4):668-671, 1980.
52. A profile of older Americans, Washington, DC, American Association of Retired Persons, 1990.
53. Rich PL: Make the most of your charting time, Nursing 13(3):34-39, 1983.
54. Selye H: Stress without distress, Philadelphia, 1974, JB Lippincott Co.
55. Smith CE: DRGs: making them work for you, Nursing 15(1):34-41, 1985.
56. Spradley BW: Contemporary community nursing, Boston, 1975, Little, Brown & Co.
57. Steel JE (ed): Issues in collaborative practice, Orlando, Fla, 1986, Grune & Stratton Inc.

58. Ten trends to watch, Nurs Health Care 7(1):17-19, 1986.

59. US Department of Health, Education, and Welfare, Public Health Service, Office of Nursing Home Affairs: How to select a nursing home, Washington, DC, 1976, US Government Printing Office.

60. US Bureau of the Census, Projections of the population of the United States: 1977 to 2050, Pub No 704, Washington, DC, 1977.

61. US Department of Health and Human Services, Division of Nursing: Report to the President and the Congress on the status of health personnel in the United States, vol 1, Part C: Nursing personnel, Washington, DC, 1984.

62. US Department of Health and Human Services: The Medicare handbook, Baltimore, 1990.

63. Waters V: Restricting the RN license to BSN graduates could cloud nursing's future, Nurs Health Care 7(3):142-146, 1986.

64. Weeks LC and Darrah P: The documentation dilemma: a practical solution, J Nurs Adm 15(11):22-27, 1985.

65. Yorker B: Nurses accused of murder, Am J Nurs 88(10):1327-1332, 1988.

66. Zander K: Second generation primary nursing: a new agenda, J Nurs Adm 15(3):18-22, 1985.

Physiologic Aspects
of Patient Care

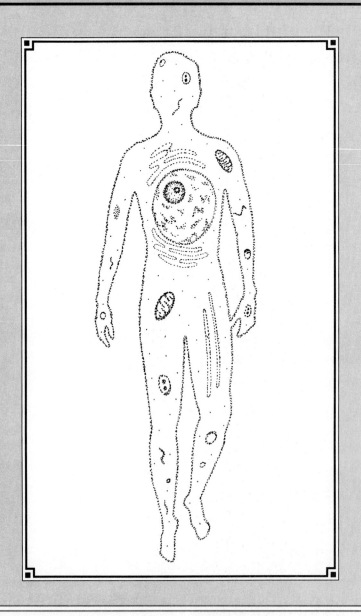

KEY WORDS

adaptation
aerobic
anaerobic
antibody
antigen
antitoxin
bactericidal
bacteriostatic
capsule
cellular immunity
chemotherapy
cilia
endogenous
endotoxin
exogenous
exotoxin
exudate
flagella
gangrene
gram negative
gram positive
host
humoral immunity
hyperthermia
hypothermia
immunity
immunization
immunoglobulins
leukocytosis
macrophage
normal flora
nosocomial
phagocytosis
septicemia
toxemia
virology
virulence

OBJECTIVES

1. Identify the major causes of illness and disease.

2. List the characteristics of the four types of microbes.

3. Describe the major physiologic defense mechanisms of the body.

4. Explain the process of inflammation and its varying manifestations throughout the body.

5. Define nursing intervention for the patient with an inflammatory condition.

6. Explain the function of the immune system in combating and preventing disease.

CAUSES OF DISEASE

Disease is any condition in which either the physiologic or psychologic functions of the body deviate significantly from what is regarded as normal. Often health and disease are viewed as a spectrum, with excellent health on one end of the scale and disease with permanent disability or death on the other end (Figure 2-1). In health, a person is successful in adapting to environmental stresses, but in illness the capacity to adapt has been limited in some way. Homeostasis is the term applied to the maintenance of a balance of physiologic processes within the body, and **adaptation** is the maintenance of a balance in interactions with the environment.[1]

Most diseases are characterized by specific signs and symptoms related to a specific disease. These signals result from pathologic processes that have interfered with normal body functioning. Since in a state of health the body functions as a whole, with each part interdependent, the malfunctioning or abnormal condition of any part of the body may affect the entire body. Often more than one specific disease, each resulting from different causes, may be present in the same person at the same time.

There are many classifications of causes of disease. Among the most common are (1) microorganisms, (2) nutritional imbalance, (3) physical agents, (4) chemical agents, and (5) cellular abnormalities.

MICROORGANISMS

Microbiology is the study of microorganisms or microbes. These are living, minute organisms, usually having a one-cell structure. Many microbes live normally within the body without causing disease or illness. They are referred to as **normal flora**. The gastrointestinal tract, the upper respiratory system, the genitourinary tract, and the skin are examples of sites where normal flora can be found. Some microbes, however, can become pathogenic, or disease producing, and invade the body, multiply, and cause disease. When this occurs, the person has an infection. Infections interfere with the normal physiologic functioning of the body causing inflammation and possibly purulent discharge. Specific symptoms depend on the site of the infection. For example, an abscess in the brain tissue will result in neurologic symptoms, whereas pneumonia will result in respiratory distress. Microbes are classified as *bacteria*, *viruses*, *fungi*, and *protozoa*.

Bacteria

The study of bacteria has shown that they have many different characteristics. In addition to the three basic shapes—round, oblong, and spiral—there are many variations of these shapes. Some may be elongated or have pointed ends, or they may be flattened on one side. Some are shaped like a comma, and others may appear square. Spirilla may be tightly coiled like a corkscrew. During cell division some remain together to form pairs, whereas others may form long chains. All of these modifications are important in identifying specific kinds of bacteria.

Bacteria may also have different chemical compositions, require different nutrients, and form different waste products. **Aerobic** bacteria grow only in the presence of oxygen, whereas **anaerobic** bacteria grow only in the absence of oxygen. Some bacteria are capable of movement.

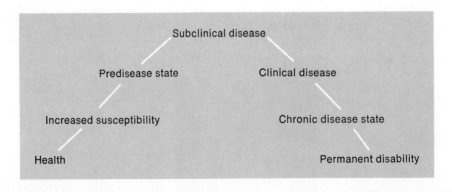

Figure 2-1
Health-illness spectrum.

Their motility is possible because of fine, hairlike projections—**flagella**—that arise from the bacterial cell (Figure 2-2). These projections cause a wavelike motion that moves the cell. A bacterium may have only one flagellum attached to one end of the cell, or there may be many flagella surrounding the cell. Locomotion of the spirochete is achieved by a wiggling motion involving the entire cell body.

Some bacteria form a specialized structure called a *spore* (Figure 2-2). Spore formation appears to occur when conditions are unfavorable for growth of the bacterium. The spore is a round body that is formed by the bacterium in the presence or absence of oxygen. The spore enlarges until it is as large as the bacterial cell and is surrounded by a capsule. Eventually the portion of the cell surrounding the spore disintegrates. The spore remains dormant until environmental conditions become favorable for growth. At that time the spore will germinate and begin reproducing in a normal manner. Characteristically, spores have a high degree of resistance to heat and disinfectants. They cannot by stained by the usual laboratory methods but require special staining techniques.

Some bacteria have the ability to form **capsules** about the cell wall (Figure 2-2). These mucilaginous envelopes seem to form when the bacterial environment is unfavorable; it is also believed that the formation may be defensive to protect the bacteria. The composition of the capsule varies with the species of bacteria. However, they may be composed of protein or fat substances, and some may contain nitrogen and phosphorus. As with spores, staining in the laboratory may require special procedures. When capsules are present, antibiotic therapy may be difficult because the capsule may prevent the drug from reaching the bacteria within the capsule.

Many diseases cannot be diagnosed and properly treated until the specific microorganism causing the illness has been identified. Identification of microorganisms is made by specially trained laboratory personnel. Most bacteria cannot be seen until a special staining process has been done. Staining is accomplished by the use of a dye applied to a specially prepared glass slide containing a small amount of the material to be examined. Most bacteria can be identified by this simple process; however, other bacteria require additional staining. Depending on whether a color can be removed by a solvent or is retained after the use of the solvent, the organism is iden-

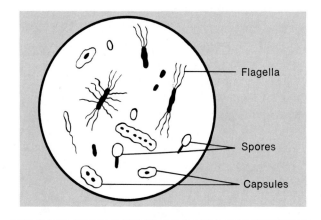

Figure 2-2
Specialized structures of bacteria: Flagella, spores, and capsules.

tified as being **gram positive** or **gram negative**. This identification is important in the treatment of the patient. This is a simple laboratory test that will assist in the selection of effective antibiotics. Different antibiotics may be required for their destruction. Some bacteria are known as acid-fast bacteria, depending on the staining process. Special staining is required for bacteria having flagella, spores, or capsules.

Body fluids and secretions suspected of containing pathogenic organisms can be collected in sterile containers and sent to the laboratory for culture and sensitivity tests. In the laboratory the collected specimens are transferred to a special culture medium that promotes growth. The culture is then studied and the pathogens are identified. Sensitivity tests are carried out to determine which antibiotics will effectively inhibit the pathogens' growth. Appropriate antibiotics are ordered on the basis of these tests.

Bacterial infections are transmitted from person to person by direct contact, by inhaling droplet nuclei, and by indirect contact with articles contaminated with the pathogen. Some are also transmitted through the ingestion of contaminated food and drink. Further information on transmission of infectious disease may be found in Chapter 7.

Bacteria have been divided into three major groups: (1) cocci, (2) bacilli, and (3) spirilla (Figure 2-3). In addition, the rickettsiae are now classified as bacteria.

Streptococci, staphylococci, and diplococci

The streptococcus bacterium is responsible for more diseases than is any other organism. Some

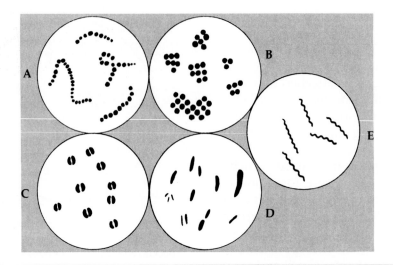

Figure 2-3

Common disease-producing bacteria. **A,** Streptococci. **B,** Staphylococci. **C,** Diplococci. **D,** Bacilli. **E,** Spirilla.

strains produce serious or even fatal diseases, other strains produce disease only under special conditions, and other strains are nonpathogenic. Disease-producing strains include beta-hemolytic streptococci, and the viridans group, also called alpha-hemolytic streptococci.

The beta-hemolytic group of streptococci is responsible for about 90% of streptococcal infections. Some of the diseases caused by this group are extremely serious and may be fatal. They include osteomyelitis, septicemia, scarlet fever, rheumatic fever, and pneumonia, as well as relatively common diseases like tonsillitis and impetigo. The organisms may also invade surgical wounds or malignant lesions. Wound infection may occur as the result of improper handwashing before changing dressings. The organisms live in the upper respiratory tract and may be spread from one person to another by direct or indirect contact.

Viridans streptococci may cause subacute bacterial endocarditis, in which the valves of the heart may be affected. Viridans streptococci may also be found in the nose and throat of well persons.

There are two primary species of staphylococcus bacteria: *Staphylococcus aureus* and *Staphylococcus epidermidis*. *Staphylococcus aureus* belongs to the pyogenic (pus-producing) group. Staphylococci may be found on the skin at all times and cause boils (furuncles), abscesses, and carbuncles. Sometimes they get into the bloodstream and cause serious complications (see Chapter 8).

Staphylococcus epidermidis is a nonpathogenic species of the staphylococcus organism that inhabits the human skin. Although this species may cause minor infections, the incidence of such infections is low.

There are several kinds of diplococcus bacteria. One type is the cause of pneumonia and was previously called the *pneumococcus*; it is now called *Streptococcus pneumoniae*. One characteristic of this organism is that it is encased in a capsule, or gelatinous envelope. Two other forms of diplococci cause gonorrhea (gonococcus) and meningitis (meningococcus).

Bacilli

The name *bacilli* means "little rod" (Figure 2-3); however, its rodlike shape is extremely variable. Certain forms of the bacillus produce spores. These forms are present in the intestinal tract of humans and animals and are discharged onto the soil. These spore-forming bacilli produce tetanus, gas **gangrene,** and anthrax (see Chapter 7). Numerous other diseases are caused by these organisms, including tuberculosis, diphtheria, pertussis, typhoid fever, and bacillary dysentery.

Spirilla

Spirilla organisms are spiral shaped like a corkscrew. Some forms of spirilla are rigid, whereas others are flexible (spirochetes). One form, which resembles a comma, is the cause of Asiatic cholera. Most of the diseases caused by the spirilla bacteria are uncommon. The spirochetes that cause syphilis are spiral shaped, but they have been separated and classified in a different order of bacteria. Lyme disease is also caused by a spirochete.

Rickettsiae

Rickettsiae are microorganisms combining characteristics of bacteria and viruses. They are parasites that flourish only within living susceptible cells. The cells provide a suitable environment and the nutrients needed for growth. The most serious diseases caused by rickettsiae are typhus fever and Rocky Mountain spotted fever. Typhus fever is spread from person to person through bites from infected body lice or fleas that have been infected from rats. Epidemic typhus is an acute, severe disease associated with overcrowding, famine, and filth. It has caused devastating epidemics resulting in the deaths of millions of people over the past centuries. Although it is rare, cases can be found in the southern United States bordering Mexico.

Rocky Mountain spotted fever has been found in almost every area of the United States, and its prevalence seems to be increasing. It is transmitted to humans through the bite of an infected tick. Several varieties of ticks carry the disease. The ticks live on many different kinds of animals found in rural and wooded areas. They may also live on common house pets such as cats and dogs. Persons working in areas where ticks are known to be abundant are more likely to become infected. The tick attaches itself to the skin, and the longer it remains attached to the skin the more likely the person is to become infected. In removing the tick from the skin, great care should be taken not to crush or squeeze it.

Symptoms of Rocky Mountain spotted fever and typhus fever are similar; in both diseases patients are usually extremely ill (see Chapter 7).

Viruses

Viruses are the smallest known agents that cause disease. They are not complete cells, but consist of a protein coat around a nucleic acid core and depend on the metabolic processes of the cell they enter. Before 1900 scientists discovered that certain agents, unlike bacteria, would pass through a laboratory filter. In addition, they were unable to observe these tiny bodies with the ordinary microscope. In 1898 Martinus W. Beijerinck called these small bodies viruses, and they became known as filterable viruses.

Major Groups of Viruses and Related Diseases

Papovavirus—papilloma (wart)
Adenovirus—bronchitis, pneumonitis, pharyngitis
Herpesvirus—herpes simplex (cold sore), herpes zoster (shingles)
Poxvirus—rubella, rabies, smallpox
Picornavirus—poliomyelitis, common cold
Reovirus—believed to cause acute respiratory tract diseases

For years scientists knew little about viruses, even though they were able to observe their effect on humans and animals. In 1941 the electron microscope became available, and a whole new era in the study of human disease was opened. With this advancement the science of **virology** was born. In addition to the electron microscope, the use of certain dyes that become luminous when exposed to ultraviolet light (fluorescent microscopy), tissue culture methods, ultracentrifuge, cytochemistry, and the development of other technical laboratory aids have resulted in rapid advances in the study of viruses.

The virus may gain entrance to the body through the respiratory tract, the gastrointestinal tract, or the broken skin resulting from an animal bite, or it may be injected by a mosquito or hypodermic needle. Viruses are selective in the type of body cells they attack, but once they have found cells showing affinity, they enter the cell and reproduce rapidly. As they multiply, they interrupt the cell activities and use the cell material to produce new virus material.

Viral infections are usually self-limiting. They run a given course, and recovery occurs. One exception is rabies, which is almost always fatal. Other viral diseases may be fatal if complications occur or if they attack extremely weak, elderly, or debilitated persons. The common cold is caused by a virus, and the aching feeling, fever, and chilly sensations may be relieved with rest and certain medicines. No medicine will cure the common cold, but discomfort can be relieved. In nearly all viral diseases, antibiotics and sulfonamide agents do not alter the course of the disease.

Viruses are classified in various ways. They can be classified according to the human diseases they cause or by the characteristics of a specific group. In the latter classification system, each subgroup may have many types or strains.

Fungi

The fungal (mycotic) infections are among the most common diseases found in humans. Fungi belong to the plant kingdom, and although many of them are harmless, some are responsible for infections. Types of fungi that are familiar to everyone include the fuzzy, black, green, or white growth on stale bread, rotten fruit, or damp clothing. Fungi are among the most plentiful forms of life. Mycotic infections are diseases caused by yeasts and molds. They may be superficial, involving the skin and mucous membranes. The most frequently involved areas include the external layers of the skin, hair, and nails. These infections are called *dermatomycosis* (ringworm). The most frequent site in children is the scalp. The condition is considered infectious, and the child may not be permitted to attend school until the infection has been cured. Other sites include men's beards (barber's itch) and the feet (athlete's foot). The infection may also occur on other parts of the body, frequently about the nails. Domestic pets may also have ringworm infection and are frequently the source of infection for humans.

Fungi also invade the deeper tissues of the body. Most of these infections produce no symptoms; however, some become serious and may be fatal. Those most common in the United States are coccidioidomycosis (valley fever) and histoplasmosis.

Coccidioidomycosis was discovered in southern California, although the disease is found in other areas of the Southwest where the climate is hot and dry. The disease affects the lungs and is believed to be contracted by inhaling the spores present in the soil, which are blown about by the wind.

Histoplasmosis also affects the lungs. This disease is widespread throughout the world; in some areas 80% of the population may be infected. The disease occurs as the result of inhaling spores present in the soil, and there is also a possibility that ingestion of the spores may cause the disease. Histoplasmosis has often been associated with various kinds of birds; however, it is now believed that the only relationship is that bird droppings enrich the soil, providing fertile media in which the fungi may proliferate.

Candida albicans may cause superficial or **systemic** infections. This fungus is a normal inhabitant of the gastrointestinal tract, the mouth, and the vagina. An infection develops when something, such as a change in pH, interferes with the balance of the normal flora, allowing the organism to grow. This change in balance can occur as a result of antibiotic therapy.

Protozoa

The protozoa are single-celled animals existing everywhere in nature in some form. Some of the parasitic forms of protozoa are found in the intestinal tract, genitourinary tract, and circulatory system of humans and animals. The disease-producing protozoa are responsible for malaria, amebic dysentery, and African sleeping sickness. Another form of protozoa causes vaginal trichomoniasis in women, often as a complication of pregnancy. It may also live in the male urethra and may be acquired or transmitted through coitus. Of the diseases caused by protozoa, the two of importance in the United States are malaria and amebic dysentery. The latter is more prevalent where sanitation is poor and personal hygiene neglected. The source of infection can be the excreta of convalescent patients or carriers, and the disease is transmitted by food handlers, contaminated food, or contaminated water supplies. The common housefly may be an intermediary vector by transmitting the organism to food.

The malaria protozoan is transmitted to humans through the bite of the female *Anopheles* mosquito. Malaria is a worldwide health problem and is one of the most serious handicaps to the development of many countries (see Chapter 7).

NUTRITIONAL IMBALANCE

Nutritional imbalance may be caused by (1) an insufficient diet or excessive diet intake, (2) an unbalanced diet, (3) an increased use of a specific nutrient, and (4) a failure of the body to use nutrients. Both nutritional excesses and deficiencies lead to an inadequate supply of nutrients to the cell. The general classes of nutrients needed by the body to carry out vital functions are water, carbohydrates, proteins, lipids, vitamins, and minerals. The individual's diet needs to include these essential nutrients for the body to be maintained, to grow to repair, and to reproduce. The necessary amount of each nutrient varies from person to person and is influenced by such factors as age and amount of activity.

Nutrition imbalance lowers the body's resistance to infection. The very young, adolescents, pregnant women, the disabled, and the poor are especially vulnerable to malnutrition. There has never been greater emphasis on diet than at the present time.

For years it has been known that a deficiency of certain vitamins can cause scurvy, beriberi, and pellagra. Lack of adequate iron in the diet can lead to anemia. Minerals serve many functions in the body. Those present in large amounts in the body are called macrominerals (see Table 2-1). Twenty-two minerals are known to be essential. Those present in small amounts are called trace minerals. These are arsenic, chromium, cobalt, copper, fluoride, iodine, iron, manganese, molybdenum, nickel, selenium, silicon, tin, vanadium, and zinc.[5]

Obesity is a major health concern in affluent countries. Defined as an excessive amount of body fat, obesity is caused when the calories consumed exceed the calories used in the production of energy. Two types of obesity have been described: upper-body (android or male) and lower-body (gynoid or female). Upper-body obesity is characterized by larger fat cells and is more prevalent among men. The lower-body type is more common among women. It is characterized by increased numbers of fat cells, especially in the gluteal-femoral region of the body. Obesity and diets high in saturated fats have been identified as risk factors in coronary artery disease. Obesity is also responsible for social isolation, glucose intolerance, hypertension, cholelithiasis, and menstrual irregularity.

Present research is concerned not only with the kinds of food necessary for health, but also how the body metabolizes and uses the nutrients. The diet may be entirely adequate from a nutritional standpoint, but because of the malfunctioning of an organ or body part, the nutritional content of the food is not properly used and the person becomes ill. For example, in diabetics the body cannot use carbohydrates despite an adequate intake.

In some countries the lack of food is so serious that people are predisposed to developing various diseases or dying from starvation. Protein-calorie malnutrition (marasmus, kwashiorkor) is of particular concern for the children in developing countries. The United States has made millions of dollars worth of surplus food and grains available to many of these countries to help combat malnutrition. However, the problem of hunger and malnutrition is still of concern in some areas of the United States. Programs such as food stamps

Table 2-1

Macrominerals	
Mineral	**Physiologic functions**
Calcium	Structural and maintenance role in bones and teeth
Chloride	Regulates stomach pH; major anion of extracellular fluid
Magnesium	Important intracellular cation; acts as activator for many enzymes
Phosphorus	Helps in bone formation and maintenance; important in energy metabolism of adenosine triphosphate (ATP)
Potassium	Major intracellular cation; necessary for transmission of nerve impulses, acid-base balance, and formation of protein and glycogen
Sodium	Major cation of extracellular fluid; regulates body fluid osmolarity and volume

for low-income families have been created to increase the purchasing power of those who qualify.

PHYSICAL AGENTS

Physical agents that result in injury to the body include trauma, changes in external temperature, electric current, exposure to radiation, and changes in atmospheric pressure. Injuries from trauma can result in closed or open wounds, fractured bones, injured organs, and disruption of blood flow. Exposure to high environmental temperatures can result in heat exhaustion or heatstroke. Severe environmental heat can cause life-threatening problems if they are not quickly recognized and treated appropriately. Overexposure to the sun's rays may result in severe burns. Fever is an example of the production of internal heat. A fever is a body temperature above 100° F (38° C) when the body is at rest. Heat can also be used therapeutically in medicine; for example, cautery is used to treat wounds, stop bleeding, and even cut tissue during surgery.

Exposure to extremes of cold may cause frostbite or actual freezing of body parts and possible death. Normally the body temperature never varies more than 1° from normal. The lethal limits for total body temperature range approximately from 71.6° to 107.6° F (22° to 42° C). In general, cold (**hypothermia**) is tolerated better than heat (**hyperthermia**). Controlled hypothermia is used in medicine for anesthesia for minor pain, and freezing techniques can be used for surgical purposes (*cryosurgery*) as in extracorporal bypass during cardiac surgery. General hypothermia may be used during surgery to decrease the activity of the body tissues. This results in a reduced need for oxygen and nourishment circulated by the blood.

Electric current may cause slight tingling, such as may be experienced in the home as a result of faulty wiring, or it may result in severe shock, burns, or death when a person is exposed to high voltage. Severe and harmful radiation injury may occur from exposure to atomic radiation, and unless proper precautions are taken, injury may result when x-ray or radium therapy is used.

Deviation from normal atmospheric pressure to increased or decreased pressure may cause illness or death. Persons traveling by air may experience extreme pain in the ears because of the rapid changes in atmospheric pressure. A condition known as the *bends*, in which severe abdominal and leg pain is suffered by divers or persons working below the land surface, is caused by the rapid decrease in pressure as the person rises to the surface.

CHEMICAL AGENTS

Studies indicate that poisoning by various chemicals constitutes a major health problem. Substances known to be toxic in large doses, such as medicines, may be taken accidentally or intentionally. There are many new drugs on the market for which no satisfactory antidote may be available. Overdoses of some drugs cause respiratory and cardiovascular depression.

Of great interest and concern in contemporary society is the prevalence of chemical dependency. Abused addictive and recreational substances have long-term consequences ranging from cardiac and liver disease to low birth weight and addicted newborns. Programs are available to assist people with chemical dependence to gain access to treatment plans. These programs are often located in hospitals and community agencies. Peer assistance programs are also available for health professionals to obtain treatment for their own chemical dependence. Some chemical agents are inhaled in the form of gas, such as carbon monoxide; others, such as lye, may be ingested. Some commonly available chemical agents that have been shown to cause harm include alcohol, caffeine, and tobacco. Cigarette smoking has been closely linked with coronary artery disease and an increased incidence of lung cancer. Of concern now is the risk to nonsmokers who breathe the second hand smoke. Various industrial processes use chemicals that are injurious if inhaled or if the chemicals come into contact with the skin.

There is increasing concern that our environment is becoming contamined by insecticides and herbicides used in agriculture, lead from combustion of gasoline in automobiles, and industrial wastes. In certain high-risk occupations such as mining exposure to gases or dust may cause acute or chronic illness. Hospitals, clinics, and other institutions have established poison control centers where information concerning a drug is available, usually on a 24-hour basis. Special educational displays, posters, and printed material have been placed in public buildings to inform the public about the harmful effects from poisons. The United States government has curtailed the use of once common food additives and some drugs because of the possible harmful effects resulting from their use. State and local governments are becoming increasingly aware of the necessity for more public information and legislation for the control of hazardous drugs, chemicals, insecticides, and sprays.

CELLULAR ABNORMALITIES

Cells are the smallest living structures that are capable of maintaining life functions and reproducing themselves. Cells of varying structure and function compose tissues, and tissues form organs, each of which contribute to the integrated holistic function of our bodies. In all pathologic conditions the cells that comprise tissues, organs, and other structures will be affected.

Although there is a significant variation in types of cells, there are structures that are common to all. A typical animal cell structure is found in Figure 2-4. The *cell membrane* forms the outer boundary, maintaining cell structure and determining which substances may move into or out of the cell. *Protoplasm* is the internal substance of the cell, composed primarily of the elements hydrogen, oxygen, carbon, and nitrogen. These are combined to form the major compounds water, carbohydrates, proteins, lipids, and nucleic acids. Protoplasm minus nuclear material is called *cytoplasm*. The specific internal structures of the cell are called *organelles* (see the box on p. 34).

The number and types of organelles will vary, depending on the type and specific function of each cell. For instance, muscle cells have numerous mitochondria to provide energy for muscle contraction. Gland cells have extensive endoplasmic reticulum and Golgi complex to provide for secretion, and white blood cells have large numbers of lysosomes that can destroy bacteria that have invaded the body.

Cells can be damaged in many ways. A lack of nutrients or oxygen may injure the cell membrane or other cell structures or cause cell death. An imbalance in the composition of the fluids surrounding cells can also create cellular damage, and drugs or toxins can alter cell membrane function (Chapter 4). Tumors are caused by cells that have been altered in some way (Chapter 9).

Defects in genes that carry traits of inheritance can result in abnormal metabolism that may or may not be compatible with life. Hereditary dis-

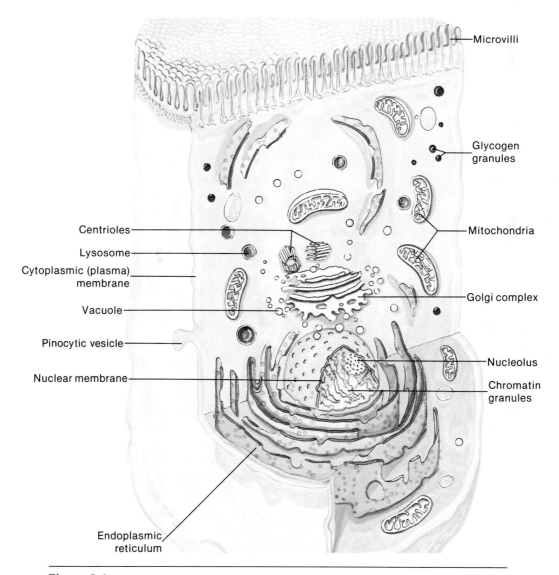

Figure 2-4

Typical animal cell. *(From Anthony CP and Thibodeau GA: Textbook of anatomy and physiology, ed 12, St Louis, 1986, The CV Mosby Co.)*

Cell Organelles

endoplasmic reticulum Network of interconnected canals winding through the cytoplasm that form proteins and serve as a means of transportation of substances throughout the cell.

golgi complex Tiny sacs believed to synthesize carbohydrate molecules that are subsequently combined with proteins; product then coated with membrane and released from the cell as a secretion.

mitochondria Delicate double-layered structure with many partitions that contain enzymes used in oxidizing glucose to form energy, which is subsequently stored as adenosine triphosphate (ATP); known as the powerhouses of the cell.

lysosomes Small sacs containing enzymes capable of digesting any cell structure.

ribosomes Small, round organelles that use genetic material to give directions for the synthesis of proteins.

centrioles Tubular cylinders that function during cell division.

nucleus Largest cell structure that stores, transmits, and transcribes genetic information[1].

---

orders such as phenylketonuria, hemophilia, and some neuromuscular disorders are examples. Traits for these conditions are carried in genes and passed from parents to offspring. Congenital defects also may be caused by environmental agents such as maternal disease and drugs. Many are believed to occur during the first few weeks of embryonic life, even before the mother realizes she is pregnant. For example, if a mother has German measles during the first trimester of pregnancy, there is a possibility that the baby will have a congenital defect. There is increasing evidence that other infectious diseases, including mumps, infectious hepatitis, and influenza, may play some part in spontaneous abortion, premature birth, stillbirth, and birth defects.

Congenital birth defects may affect any organ or system of the body, and frequently several defects involving different organs or systems may occur in the same child. In recent years certain drugs have been shown to cause alterations in fetal development. The excessive use of caffeine during pregnancy has been associated with increased fetal loss. Alcohol intake and smoking also adversely affect fetal development.[6]

PHYSIOLOGIC DEFENSE MECHANISMS

Nature has provided the body with various physiologic defense mechanisms that limit microorganisms and other substances in their ability to invade the body and cause disease. The first line of defense is the unbroken skin and the mucous membranes, which serve as mechanical barriers against invaders. Perspiration, the excretion of the sudoriferous (sweat) glands, has an average acid content on the skin of 5.65%, which is lethal to many bacteria. Lysozyme, an antibacterial enzyme present on the skin, dissolves some bacteria. This enzyme is also present in saliva and in tears.

The mucous membranes lining the respiratory tract, gastrointestinal tract, and urinary tract secrete substances that are **bacteriostatic**. The lacrimal fluid (tears) has the ability to destroy some microorganisms, and the secretions continuously bathe and wash foreign materials, including pathogens, from the eye. The high acid content of the stomach acts as a formidable barrier for pathogens that are swallowed. Any pathogens entering the intestines may be destroyed by certain enzymes secreted by the cells along the intestinal route. Vaginal secretions are normally acid, and pathogens entering the vagina are usually destroyed. Frequent vaginal irrigations will reduce the pH (acid) concentration of the vagina and thereby reduce the effectiveness of the natural barrier.

The nasal cavities, trachea, and bronchi contain fine hairlike projections called **cilia,** which are in constant wavelike motion. The cilia sweep pathogens toward the pharynx, where they may be swallowed or expectorated. If swallowed, they are destroyed by the stomach acids. The fine hairs about the external nares help prevent pathogens from entering, and if they do enter, they are trapped by cavities. The mouth has a high concentration of microorganisms. Many are swallowed and destroyed. Pathogens in the mouth usually do no harm as long as the mucous membrane remains intact. Involuntary acts also assist the body to rid itself of pathogens. Through these acts or reflexes, such as sneezing and coughing, pathogens may be eliminated from the respiratory tract. Vomiting and diarrhea eliminate bacteria and their toxins from the gastrointestinal system.

There are cells that constantly combat infectious agents and other substances entering the body. Cells that line many of the vascular and lymph channels are capable of phagocytizing bacteria, viruses, and other foreign material. Lymph nodes are located intermittently along the course of the lymphatic vessels, which drain the excess interstitial fluid that surrounds the cells of the body. These lymph nodes contain many cells that phagocytize foreign materials and thus prevent their general dissemination throughout the body. The spleen filters blood, and along with removing old red blood cells from the circulation, abnormal platelets, blood parasites, bacteria, and other substances are also removed. The Kupffer cells of the liver remove large numbers of bacteria that succeed in entering the body through the gastrointestinal tract. The bone marrow has the ability to remove fine particles from the bloodstream such as protein toxins. Phagocytic cells in the tissues throughout the body also protect various organs from invading organisms or foreign material.[3]

The white blood cells **(leukocytes)** also combat invasion. The *polymorphonuclear leukocytes,* or granulocytes, comprise the majority of these cells. There are three types of polymorphonuclear leukocytes—the *neutrophils,* the *basophils,* and the *eosinophils.* The primary function of the neutrophils is **phagocytosis,** the ingestion and digestion of debris and foreign material throughout the body. They are the first cells to arrive at the scene when an inflammatory reaction is stimulated. The ba-

sophils do not phagocytize but contain powerful chemicals such as histamine that can be released locally and assist in the inflammatory process. The eosinophils appear to play a role in allergy and foreign protein reactions. The *mononuclear leukocytes,* or monocytes, become large phagocytic cells when stimulated and also play an important role in inflammation. The *lymphocytes* are the cells primarily concerned with the development of immunity.[3]

Inflammation

One of the most important defense mechanisms is the inflammatory response. Inflammation occurs when any agent, such as a chemical substance, foreign body, severe blow, or bacteria, injures the tissue. The inflammatory process is characterized by five classic signs: redness (rubor), heat (calor), pain (dolor), swelling (tumor), and limitation of movement. When tissue is traumatized, a defensive process begins in which the body tries to localize or eliminate the injurious agent, to neutralize or destroy its poisons, and finally to repair the injured tissue (Figure 2-5). The inflammatory process begins with an increased flow of blood to the area. The tiny capillary blood vessels become dilated, allowing a

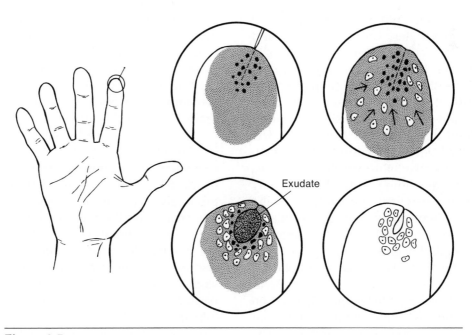

Figure 2-5

Inflammatory process. **A,** Pathogenic bacteria are introduced into tissue through portals of entry such as a pinprick. **B,** Blood supply to area begins to increase. **C,** Leukocytes begin to move out of blood capillaries. **D,** Phagocytes begin to engulf and digest bacteria; dead phagocytes, cells, and tissue fluid escape as exudate. **E,** When phagocytosis is complete, wound begins to heal.

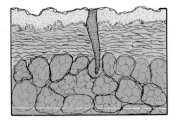 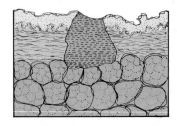 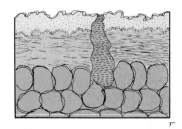

Figure 2-6
Types of wound healing: primary, secondary, tertiary.

larger amount of blood to pass through them. This is primarily caused by the release of histamine from injured cells. The leukocytes have the power to move about, and they begin to migrate out of the capillaries to the area where the pathogen has invaded the tissue. The first cells to arrive at the scene are the neutrophils, which begin to engulf and ingest any bacteria or foreign material. After several hours the monocytes follow and are transformed into large phagocytic cells called **macrophages**. It is believed that monocytes are stimulated by substances draining from the site. If the injurious agent is not removed from the site within 24 to 48 hours, lymphocytes will begin to predominate at the site and the immune process will be stimulated.

During the inflammatory process some phagocytes are killed and some tissue is destroyed. The phagocytes, destroyed cells, and some tissue fluid accumulate at the site. This is called the **exudate**. If the area has been invaded by microbes, or pathogens, an infection can occur and purulent drainage may be present. The characteristic heat and redness at the site are caused by the increased flow of blood to the area. The swelling results from the accumulation of exudate, and stimulation of the nerves in the area causes the pain. Depending on the location, any effort to move the part may be painful, causing the individual to limit movement. When phagocytosis is complete, the inflammatory condition subsides and healing begins (Figure 2-5).

Healing is the process of replacement of dead or damaged cells. Two overlapping stages occur in the process of healing. One is the regeneration of cells that were lost with identical or similar tissue. The other is formation of scar tissue. The ability of the body to regenerate new tissue depends upon the ability of the cells to multiply and form units that can function physiologically like the original cell. Damaged brain, myocardium,

and nerve tissue cannot regenerate. Scar tissue is formed by the proliferation of fibroblasts that secrete collagen precursors. This preliminary stage is called granulation tissue. Collagen is a fibrous protein present in the connective tissues of the body. Layers of collagen are deposited at the site of injury and form a dense area of scar tissue.

Wounds are repaired with a similar process. The three types of healing in wounds have been labeled as primary, secondary, and tertiary intention (Figure 2-6). Healing by primary intention means that a wound heals with its edges in close approximation and with a minimum of granulation tissue. Surgical wounds heal this way. A secondary intention healing occurs when a greater amount of tissue is damaged, and necrotic debris or inflammatory exudate is formed. These wounds take longer to heal and produce more scar tissue. Tertiary intention is sometimes called delayed primary closure. A wound that is surgically closed several days after the injury heals by tertiary intention. An example would be a heavily contaminated wound left open intentionally to drain and then closed.

Infection

Pathogenic organisms may enter the body by way of the respiratory system, digestive system, reproductive system, urinary system, and skin. They may leave the body through discharges from the nose and throat, vomitus, feces, urine, draining wounds, or drainage tubes. Pathogens may also exist via the urethral meatus in men or the vaginal canal in women. In addition, certain pathogenic organisms, such as in malaria and hepatitis B, may be transferred from a donor's blood to that of a recipient through a blood transfusion. Of great concern now is acquired immune deficiency syndrome (AIDS) (see Chapter 7). Placental transfer of microorganisms to the fetus from the mother may occur, such as in syphilis. Individuals may enter a health care facility free of infection but may develop an infection during their stay. This is referred to as a **nosocomial infection**. An example of a nosocomial infection is oxacillin-resistant staphylococcal infection (see Chapter 8).

Endogenous infection may occur when microorganisms already present in the body produce disease because of compromised defense mechanisms. An example is monilial infections in patients with diabetes.

Exogenous infection results when pathogenic microorganisms gain entrance to the body from the outside. An example is hepatitis B.

Another way in which bacteria may harm the body is by the production of powerful poisons, or toxins. These toxins are classified as **endotoxins** or **exotoxins**. Endotoxins are present in the cells of the bacteria and cause damage to the body only when the cells disintegrate. Most endotoxins are contained in organisms that cause enteric diseases such as typhoid fever and bacillary dysentery. Exotoxins are produced by bacteria and released outside the cell and are the most poisonous substances known to injure humans. Examples of diseases in which exotoxins are produced are diphtheria, tetanus, and botulism.

Some bacteria are powerful enough to resist the leukocytes and will destroy many of them, or the bacteria may produce powerful toxins that kill the leukocytes. If this occurs, the bacteria will cause disease, and either the bacteria or their toxins may be carried by the bloodstream and the lymphatic vessels to various parts of the body. The time factor is extremely important in an infection, since the longer the bacteria have to multiply, the more severe the infection will be. The physician may order bacteriostatic drugs for the patient to prevent rapid multiplication of bacteria.

Infection is classified in a number of different ways, according to the location, extent, and severity (see box to the right).

When pathogenic microorganisms invade the body and cause inflammation or infection, they may give rise to certain symptoms or conditions. Some of the conditions with which the nurse should be familiar are in the box on p. 38.

Five factors influence the ability of invading pathogens to survive and cause disease, that is, pathogenicity:

1. Whether the pathogens gain entrance by their characteristic route

2. Whether they have an affinity for only certain types of tissue
3. The degree of virulence
4. The number of pathogens that enter the body at a given time
5. The degree and character of resistance offered the invading pathogens by the host

Most bacteria enter the body by a specific route, and unless they are successful in gaining entrance by their characteristic route, they may not cause disease. For example, bacteria whose characteristic route is the respiratory system may be rendered harmless if they are swallowed. Some pathogens have a particular affinity for certain types of tissue. Once they gain entrance to the body, they go directly to that tissue, leaving other tissues unaffected. The virus causing poliomyelitis attacks only nerve tissue; other pathogens attack only the respiratory system.

Pathogens vary in their power to invade the body and produce toxins. This factor is called **virulence**. Pathogens may be highly virulent, possessing great power of invasion, with the ability to produce deadly exotoxins. Others may be of low virulence and, although able to invade the body, are too weak to produce disease.

Infection Classification

primary infection An acute infection that appears, runs its course, and resolves in a short period of time.

chronic infection The initial stages of the infection are the same as primary infections but the symptoms persist and run a prolonged course.

secondary infection Usually a complication of the primary infection. Bacteria causing a secondary infection may not always be the same as those causing the primary infection.

local infection An infection confined to a single area.

generalized infection An infection that spreads and involves the entire body.

focal infection An infection in which bacteria spread from the original site of the infection to other parts of the body.

latent infection A condition in which bacteria are still present in the body but are not active and do not cause any symptoms.

specific infection An infection caused by one kind of microorganism.

mixed infection An infection caused by more than one kind of microorganism.

Manifestations of Infection

abscess A collection of pus in a cavity or a walled-off area surrounded by inflamed tissue.

bacteremia The presence of bacteria in the bloodstream.

carbuncle An area of inflammation in the skin and deeper tissues terminating with pus formation. Sometimes constitutional symptoms accompany its presence.

cellulitis An inflammatory process that is poorly defined and diffuse, usually involving the skin and subcutaneous tissue.

exudate Accumulation of fluid within a cavity or area of inflammation that may contain cells, protein, and solid material.

furuncle A boil or an inflamed pus-filled swelling on the skin.

gangrene Death of tissue because of poor arterial or venous circulation.

granulation Budding projections formed on the surface of a wound bringing a rich blood supply to tissue.

necrosis The death of tissue or small groups of cells.

purulent discharge A discharge containing pus.

pyemia Pus in the bloodstream, causing multiple abscesses in various parts of the body.

sanguineous discharge A discharge containing blood.

septicemia The presence of pathogens or theri toxins in the bloodstream.

serous discharge A clear, watery, thin discharge.

The occurrence of disease may depend on the number of pathogens that enter the body at a given time. If a large number of pathogens enter the body, disease is more likely to occur than if only a few invade the **host**. However, the presence of a few highly virulent pathogens may result in disease, whereas a large number of pathogens of low virulence may be destroyed without causing disease. A final factor is the degree and character of resistance offered invading pathogens by the host.

Intervention

An inflammation may occur without infection (such as sunburn), but an infection is usually accompanied by inflammation. Intervention depends on the kind of injury, the extent of involvement, and the effectiveness of the defense mechanisms of the body. An infection may be local, as in the case of a boil, it may involve an entire body system such as the respiratory system, or if there is a bloodstream infection, it may affect the entire body.

Local inflammatory conditions may be painful and may cause the patient considerable discomfort. The goals of patient care are directed toward relieving the discomfort and terminating the inflammatory condition before it can affect other parts of the body. To achieve these goals, it is necessary to monitor the injured or inflamed site, carry out interventions that will aid in the healing process and ensure adequate blood flow, and provide for adequate rest and nutrients. Treatment includes rest, elevation of the part affected, application of heat or cold, use of analgesics, and occasionally incision and drainage. When infection is present, antibiotic therapy is required. Elevating the affected part above the level of the heart relieves pain and throbbing, thus increasing patient comfort.

Heat and cold are applied to the body to aid in the healing process. Heat and cold cause different physiologic responses. The initial response to local heat application is vasodilation of skin blood vessels, causing increased blood flow to the area. Increased blood flow helps reduce pain and swelling. There is increased movement of nutrients, white blood cells, and antibiotics to the site. The application of cold reduces blood flow to the site of injury. This prevents additional swelling and decreases inflammation and pain.

Whether dry or moist heat or cold are used will depend on the type of wound or injury, the location of the body part, and the presence of drainage or inflammation. Compresses and packs can be hot or cold. A compress is a moist gauze dressing that is applied to a specific area. If the skin is broken, sterile technique is used. For a moist heat compress the gauze is soaked in a solution that is 40.5° to 46° C (105° to 110° F). For a cold moist compress the temperature is 15° C (59° F). Moist heat may also be applied with soaks or baths. A sitz bath, for example, is taken to immerse the pelvic area in warm water. Soaks aid in the debridement of cleaning of wounds and are useful for the application of medicated solutions.

Dry heat can be applied with a hot water bottle, an aquathermia pack, a heating pad, or a heat lamp. Aquathermia packs contain distilled water that circulates through tubes. The desired temperature is preset and is regulated by a temperature control unit. A hot water bottle is rarely used now with hospitalized patients because they can injure the skin. Patients who use them at home should be instructed to fill them with warm tap water, 40.5° C (105° to 110° F) to prevent burns. Heat lamps can be used on small areas to increase circulation and promote healing. The nurse should be careful when applying any form of heat because of the danger of burning the patient and should assess the area frequently.

Moist cold is applied in the form of cold compresses, usually for short intervals at specified periods. Dry cold is provided by an ice bag or ice collar. An uncovered ice bag should never be applied directly to the skin and should not be used to cover wet dressings because of danger of injury to the tissues.

When local inflammation does not respond to treatment, a surgical incision may be required to provide for escape of the accumulated exudate.

Patients with generalized infections may be very ill. The temperature may be extremely high, with a corresponding increase in the pulse and respiratory rates. The white-blood cell count is increased **(leukocytosis),** and chills may occur, as well as loss of appetite, sweating, and delirium. The patient is usually confined to bed.

Acetaminophen (Tylenol) or acetylsalicylic acid (aspirin) may be given to lower the temperature. Less frequently used today, a tepid or cool sponge bath using water or a mixture of water and alcohol may also be used to decrease the patient's temperature, remove waste products from the skin, and provide comfort. Special mouth care should be given several times a day or as indicated. An emollient jelly may be used to lubricate the lips and nose to prevent dryness and crust formation. Accurate measurement of fluid intake and fluid loss from all sources is an important nursing intervention. Adequate fluid intake should be encouraged, since the patient is losing greater amounts of fluid through the skin and respiratory system.

It is important that the patient continue to produce large amounts of urine to aid in the elimination of toxins. Oral fluids should be high in nutrients, calories, and electrolytes. If sufficient fluids are not ingested, the physician may order fluids to be administered intravenously. Periodic weighing of the patient will provide information about loss of weight and body fluids. During the febrile period the diet should be liquid, followed by soft, easily digested foods and a gradual return to a general diet.

Providing back rubs, a quiet well-ventilated room, and freedom from annoying disturbances will add to the patient's comfort. The nurse

should be careful to see that young children, the elderly, and delirious patients are protected from injury. Since most patients generally feel ill, the number of visitors should be kept to a minimum.

Most patients with superficial or generalized infections will have some type of precautions taken with body secretions (see Chapter 8). The nurse should be careful to maintain medical asepsis, with special attention to handwashing (Chapter 8).

IMMUNITY

Immunology includes those mechanisms by which the body's cellular and chemical systems recognize and react to foreign substances. This is a dynamic process constantly occurring throughout life to counteract the effects of foreign materials, bacteria, viruses, foods, and chemicals that are constantly entering the body. A person with an immune system that is functioning normally is referred to as immunocompetent.

Immunity can be natural or acquired (see Chapter 7). *Natural immunity* is present at birth and depends on species, race, and the heritage of an individual. For example, humans do not suffer from foot and mouth disease found in cattle.

Acquired immunity is gained actively or passively by the individual. To develop *active immunity* a person must contract the disease or be infected with an attenuated form of the disease-producing organism. This process does not provide immediate protection against the organism since the body requires time to develop a sufficient response.

Passive immunity is gained from another source. A newborn acquires passive immunity from the mother through the placenta before birth and from breast milk afterward. Others gain passive immunity by receiving disease-specific antiserum or pooled gamma globulin containing antibodies to a number of diseases. This is a temporary type of immunity used to protect the individual from disease immediately after exposure.

Any invading agent that can elicit an immune response is called an antigen. These are usually large proteins or large polysaccharides, and many bacteria contain these substances. Some substances have a low molecular weight and cannot elicit a response by themselves. They have antigenic sites and combine with carrier substances to stimulate an immune response. If these sub-

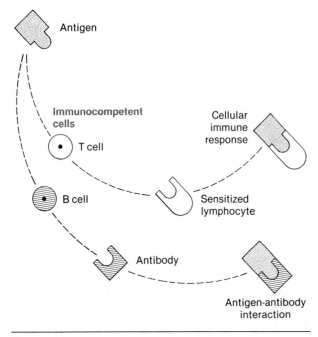

Figure 2-7

Humoral (B-cell) and cellular (T-cell) immune process.

Table 2-2

Classes of Immunoglobulins	
Name	**Characteristics**
IgG	Present in serum and amniotic fluid; activates complement; protects newborns
IgA	Present in serum, tears, saliva, GI tract, secretions, colostrum; protects mucous membranes
IgM	Present in serum; activates complement; forms antibodies for ABO blood antigens
IgD	Present in serum and umbilical cord; action unknown
IgE	Present in serum and tissues; functions in allergic and hypersensitivity reactions

stances react with another material, they can stimulate an immune response. They are called haptens. Some examples of haptens are some drugs, chemicals in dust, and breakdown products from animal dander.

The immune system is composed of specialized cells, central lymphoid tissue (the bone marrow and thymus), and peripheral lymphoid tissue (the lymph nodes, tonsils, spleen, and intestinal lymphoid tissue, e.g., Peyer's patches and the appendix). The cells responsible for the development of immunity include lymphocytes and macrophages. The lymphocytes are divided into two categories: the B lymphocytes, which are responsible for antibody formation or **humoral immunity,** and the T lymphocytes, which are responsible for cellular, or cell-mediated immunity. These lymphocytes originate in hematopoietic tissue as stem cells and migrate to lymphoid tissue for maturation and expression of their immune functions (Figure 2-7).

Humoral Immunity

Humoral immunity results when an invading agent stimulates B lymphocytes that are lying dormant in the lymph nodes to produce **antibodies.** Antibodies are proteins that are developed to react with a specific **antigen.** When the B lymphocytes are stimulated by an invading agent to produce

antibodies, they are also stimulated to produce new lymphocytes that will continue to manufacture antibodies in the future. Therefore, immunity to the agent may continue over long periods. The antibodies are called **immunoglobulins** (Ig) and can react only with the antigen that first stimulated the B cell. There are five classes of immunoglobulins, each of which has its own specific characteristics and functions—IgA, IgG, IgD, IgM, and IgE. The IgE antibody is called the reaginic antibody and is primarily responsible for allergic reactions[3] (Table 2-2).

The antigen-antibody reaction destroys or inactivates the invading agent through several processes. It can neutralize an antigen and decrease its toxic qualities, cause the agent to become insoluble in a solution or precipitate, cause agglutination or clumping of antigens, lyse cell membranes, or render the antigen susceptible to phagocytosis. Some antigen-antibody reactions have the ability to stimulate the activity of a system of nine different enzymes that are normally inactive in plasma and body fluids. This enzyme system is called the complement system and, when stimulated, assists in the process of destruction or inactivation of the invading agent.[3]

Cellular Immunity

The immune response referred to as cell-mediated or cellular is based on the function of T-lymphocytes. There are three major groups of T cells: *helper, suppressor,* and *killer* cells. The helper T cells enhance the function of the B cells. The suppressor cells inhibit the activities of other lymphocytes and provide feedback to the system. The killer cells destroy targeted enemy cells by directly binding to their surface.

Cellular immunity results when T cells are activated by an antigen. Whole cells become sensitized in a process similar to that which stimulates the B cells to form antibodies. Once sensitized, these T cells are released into the blood and body tissues, where they remain indefinitely. The cellular type of immunity is stimulated by fungi, viruses, parasites, and some bacteria that live inside other cells. Tuberculosis is a disease that stimulates cellular immunity. It is believed that there is an interaction between humoral immune processes and cellular immune processes that is thought to use the helper T cells as a switch between the two processes.

There is no absolute immunity to any specific disease to which humans are susceptible. The degree of resistance to a certain disease or agent may vary from person to person and may vary within the same person at different times.

CHEMOTHERAPEUTIC AGENTS

Chemotherapy refers to the treatment of disease with chemical drugs. In treating infections, some chemotherapeutic drugs are **bacteriostatic** and arrest the multiplication of pathogenic bacteria, whereas others are **bactericidal** in action and kill bacteria. Other drugs suppress the inflammatory response when pathogens are not involved.

Sulfonamides

The sulfonamide drugs were the first chemotherapeutic agents to be discovered and came into use after 1935. Since that time, thousands of sulfonamides have been developed, but only a few are in use today. They were originally used in the treatment of both gram-negative and gram-positive infections. Their usefulness has decreased because of the development of resistant bacteria.[4] Many other antimicrobial agents have now either replaced or are used in combination with sulfonamides. The sulfonamides are primarily bacteriostatic and act by interfering with the metabolism of the invading microorganism, preventing further growth.

Some sulfonamide drugs are especially effective in the treatment of uncomplicated infections of the urinary tract and as a preventative against infection when long-term therapy is required. Sulfonamides are also common in the treatments of ulcerative colitis, chancroid, and burns.[6] The formation of crystals in the urine and hematuria were once significant problems but are uncommon with the newer more soluble sulfonamides.[4] However, patients should still be encouraged to drink large amounts of fluids. Fluid intake should be encouraged to provide from 1200 to 2000 ml of urinary output in 24 hours.

Persons receiving sulfonamides should be observed for side effects, the most common being anorexia, nausea, and vomiting. These drugs can also cause a decrease in circulating red blood cells, white blood cells, and platelets, which can lead to the development of *purpura*, or bleeding into the skin. Any rash should be carefully observed. Signs of sensitivity such as sneezing or itching of the skin should be noted. Sulfonamides should not be given with antacids, since absorption of the drug will be lessened (Table 2-3).

Table 2-3

Partial List of Sulfonamide Agents			
Generic name	Trade name	Route of administration	Use
Sulfacetamide	Sulamyd	Topical	Ophthalmic infections
Sulfadiazine	Pyrimal	Oral, parenteral	Systemic infections; meningitis
Sulfamethoxazole	Gantanol Azo Gantanol	Oral	Systemic and urinary tract infections
Sulfisoxazole	Gantrisin Azo Gantrisin	Oral, topical, parenteral	Urinary tract infections
Sulfamethoxypyridazine	Kynex Midicel	Oral	Special indications Chronic urinary tract infections
Phthalylsulfathiazole	Sulfathalidine	Oral	Bowel-sterilizing agent
Mafenide	Sulfamylon	Topical	Burns
Silver sulfadiazine	Silvadene	Topical	Burns

Antibiotics

The development of antibiotic drugs began in 1928, when Alexander Fleming, a British bacteriologist, discovered a substance that he called *penicillin.* His findings were not immediately accepted, and it was not until about 1941 that the United States began intensive work in the development of penicillin. In the early days only penicillin and streptomycin were available, but today there are a large number of antibiotic agents. Some antibiotic drugs are effective against only gram-positive or gram-negative bacteria, whereas others are called broad-spectrum antibiotics because they are effective against both gram-positive and gram-negative bacteria.

The penicillins are the most effective and widely used antibiotics. The penicillins and their semisynthetic derivatives prevent the development of the cell wall in bacteria and therefore are bactericidal. Penicillins are used to treat a variety of illnesses, including pneumococcal pneumonia, streptococcal infections, meningococcal meningitis, gonorrhea, syphilis, and *Salmonella* infections. However, some organisms, such as *Staphylococcus aureus* and *Escherichia coli,* are capable of producing penicillinases, enzymes that destroy certain penicillins. Many new penicillins have been developed that are effective against these penicillinase producing bacteria and against other virulent organisms. The penicillins are inexpensive and have a low incidence of toxicity.

Penicillin is available in different forms and under a variety of trade names. It is administered through intramuscular injection, intravenously, or orally. Under usual conditions penicillin is nontoxic; however, in some patients allergic reactions may occur. These reactions vary from mild skin rashes to fatal anaphylactic shock. The nurse administering penicillin in any form should first be sure that the patient has had no previous reaction to it and, second, should observe the patient carefully for several hours after administration of the drug. Reactions do not always develop immediately, and fatal reactions have occurred several hours after the drug has been given.

No penicillin preparation should be administered to anyone with a previous history of an allergic reaction to the drug. Oral preparations should not be taken before or after eating for at least 1 hour, since they are poorly absorbed if acid is present in the stomach. Also, acidic fruit juices should not be used to administer the drugs.

The cephalosporin antimicrobial agents were first developed and used in the early 1960s. Cephalosporins are similar to penicillin in structure and share many physical characteristics. They are expensive, semisynthetic, broad-spectrum antibiotics. By inhibiting microbes' cell wall synthesis, they are bactericidal in action. Cephalosporins are classified into groups reflecting their introduction and use. These groups are called generations. The difference between each generation stems from their effectiveness against gram-positive and gram-negative organisms. Cephalosporins should be avoided in patients who have severe or immediate reactions to penicillins. Caution is recommended for use with patients who have preexisting renal conditions.

Tetracyclines, introduced in 1948, were the first broad-spectrum antibiotics. They block the formation of proteins in microorganisms and are **bacteristatic.** Their use has increased as resistant organisms have declined. Gastrointestinal disturbances can occur with tetracyclines, but generally the drugs are nontoxic. Allergic reactions are rare. The tetracyclines should not be administered with milk products, antacids, or iron preparations, since the combination will disturb absorption of the drug. Tetracyclines are used in the treatment of adolescent acne, chlamydial, and other uncommon infections. They are the treatment of choice in rickettsial infections. They are not used in children and pregnant women, since tetracylines bind to newly formed bones and teeth.

The group of antibiotics known as the *aminoglycosides* were in use as early as 1944 with streptomycin but were further developed after 1952. Aminoglycosides also interfere with protein synthesis in invading microbes. They are bactericidal and have a widespread clinical use. Toxic effects increase with increased dosage of the drug. The eighth cranial nerve can be affected, resulting in symptoms of hearing loss, dizziness, ringing in the ears, and imbalance. Kidney nephrons can be affected, and intake and output should be monitored.

The *macrolides* (erythromycins) are **bacteristatic,** inhibiting protein synthesis. They are effective against gram-positive cocci and can be used as a penicillin substitute in persons allergic to penicillin. Gastrointestinal disturbances may occur; allergic reactions may also occur but are not common.

Since a specific antibiotic may be ineffective against a particular organisms, sensitivity tests should be done before any antibiotic is administered. By identifying the microorganisms causing the illness, the physician can prescribe the most suitable antibiotic to cure the disease (Table 2-4).

Corticosteroids

The corticosteroids are used when inflammation is caused by some agent other than pathogens. They are hormones produced by the adrenal cortex and include cortisone and hydrocortisone, commonly referred to as adrenal steroids. One adrenal gland is located above each kidney and is composed of two parts. The inner part is the medulla, and its primary secretion is epinephrine. The outer part is the cortex, which produces several substances, some of which are necessary for life. It also produces cortisone and hydrocortisone. When the adrenal glands are surgically removed because of disease or when they fail to function, hydrocortisone is administered to replace the normal secretion.

The first corticosteroids were prepared as glandular extracts about 1928. Today the corticosteroids commercially available are of the same chemical composition but are made synthetically and have a higher potency. Chemical modification of the natural steroids has produced other more selective synthetic steroids. They are used for replacement therapy and to suppress the inflammatory and immune response.

The beneficial effects of corticosteroid therapy are the relief of inflammation, reduction of fever, and production of a feeling of well-being. The latter is probably a result of the relief of symptoms. For example, when cortisone is administered for an inflammatory condition, the classic signs of inflammation may be absent. Patients receiving cortisone feel encouraged because of the absence of symptoms; however, cortisone used therapeutically does not cure disease or alter its course, and it does not reverse any preexisting damage, such as crippling in arthritis. When used systemically the corticosteroids are powerful and dangerous drugs and have the potential for causing serious side effects that can affect every system of the body. Most physicians prescribe these drugs extremely cautiously because of the toxic effects. Abrupt withdrawal is avoided by gradually decreasing the dose to avoid potentially life-threatening adrenal insufficiency. Corticosteroids may be administered orally, intravenously, or intramuscularly, applied topically or as an ophthalmic preparation, or injected directly into an inflamed joint or lesion.

Patients receiving any of the corticosteroid preparations must be carefully observed for undesirable or toxic effects. Clear instructions regarding the drug must be given when patients are transferred to other health care facilities or discharged home (Table 2-5).

Other drugs used to relieve inflammatory conditions are the nonsteroidal antiinflammatory agents and aspirin. Aspirin, for example, is used to decrease the joint inflammation associated with arthritis. Nonsteroidal antiinflammatory drugs and aspirin have a basic effect on the biochemistry of inflammation.

Table 2-4

Partial List of Antibiotic Drugs

Generic name	Trade name	Route of administration	Average dose	Toxic and/or side effects
Natural penicillins				
Penicillin G potassium	Pentids	Oral, parenteral	Varies	Urticaria, dermatitis, erythema, gastrointestinal disturbances; anaphylactic shock possible
Procaine penicillin G	Crysticillin Duracillin	IM	300,000 units q. 12-24 h.	
Benzathine penicillin G	Bicillin	Oral IM	200,000 units 1.2 million units (single dose, absorbed slowly)	
Semisynthetic penicillins				
Penicillin V potassium	Pen-Vee-K	Oral	250 mg q. 6 h.	Urticaria, dermatitis, erythema, gastrointestinal disturbances; anaphylactic shock possible
Phenethicillin potassium	Chemipen	Oral	125-250 mg t.i.d.	

Continued on next page.

Table 2-4

Partial List of Antibiotic Drugs—cont'd

Generic name	Trade name	Route of administration	Average dose	Toxic and/or side effects
Methicillin sodium	Staphcillin Celbenin	Parenteral	6-12 g daily	
Oxacillin sodium	Prostaphlin	Oral	500 mg q. 6 h.	
Cloxacillin monohy- drate sodium	Tegopen	Oral	250-500 mg q. 6 h.	
Nafcillin sodium	Unipen	Oral	250 mg-1 g q. 6 h.	
Ampicillin	Amcill	Oral	2-4 g daily	
	Amcil-S Omnipen	Parenteral		
	Polycillin	Parenteral	1-2 g q. 6 h.	
Amoxicillin	Utimax	Oral	250 mg q. 8 h	
Ticarcillin disodium	Ticar	IM/IV	According to weight	
Dicloxacillin	Dynapen, Pathocil	Oral	According to weight	
Carbenicillin	Geopen Pyopen	IM/IV	According to weight	
Cephalosporins				
Cefotoxin	Mefoxin	Parenteral	1 g q. 6-8 h.	Reversible renal tubular ne- crosis; pain sterile abscess at injection site
Cephalothin sodium	Keflin	Parenteral, usually IV	4-12 g daily at 4- to 6-hour intervals	
Cephaloridine	Loridine	Parenteral	0.5-1 g t.i.d.	
Cephalexin	Keflex	Oral	1-4 daily in four divided doses	
Cefazolin				
Tetracycline and chloramphenicol agents				
Chlortetracycline hydrochloride	Aureomycin	Oral, topical	250 mg q. 6 h.	Gastrointestinal disturbance; kidney or liver damage with prolonged use
Oxytetracycline	Terramycin	Oral, paren- teral	250 mg q. 6 h.	
Tetracycline	Achromycin Panmycin Tetracin	Oral, paren- teral	250 mg q. 6 h.	Uticaria, anaphylactic shock. Do not take milk products/antacids with dose
Demeclocycline	Declomycin	Oral	100-300 mg q. 6 h.	
Doxycycline	Vibramycin	Oral	50-100 mg q. 12-24 h.	
Minocycline	Minocin	Oral	50-100 mg q. 12 h.	
Chloramphenicol	Chloromycentin	Oral, topi- cal, paren- teral	2-4 g daily	Bone marrow depression, gastrointestinal distur- bances
Aminoglycosides				
Streptomycin sul- fate		Parenteral	0.5-1 g 2-4 times daily	Many dose-related side ef- fects—deafness, kidney damage, neuromuscular problems
Neomycin sulfate	Myciguent Mycifradin	Oral	Varies with purpose given	
Kanamycin sulfate	Kantrex	Oral	Varies with purpose given	
Gentamicin sulfate	Garamycin	Parenteral, topical	Varies with purpose given	
Macrolides				
Erythromycin	Erythrocin Ilotycin	Oral, topi- cal, paren- teral	250-500 mg q. 6 h.	Mild urticaria, gastrointes- tinal disturbances, jaun- dice, overgrowth of bacte- ria or fungi
Erythromycin estolate	Ilosone	Oral	1-2 g daily	Liver dysfunction

Table 2-5

Partial List of Corticosteroid Preparations

Generic name	Trade name	Route of administration	Contraindications	Toxic and/or side effects
Natural steroids			1. History of tuberculosis, diabetes, hypertension	1. Headache and dizziness
Cortisone acetate	Cortogen acetate	Oral	2. Severe coronary disease	2. Hypertension
	Cortone	Parenteral, ophthalmic ointment	3. Kidney disease or failure	3. Potassium and calcium disturbances
Hydrocortisone	Cortef Cortisol Hydrocortone	Oral, IM, IV Topical	4. Skin eruptions 5. Myasthenia gravis 6. Peptic ulcer	4. Fluid and sodium retention 5. Weight gain 6. Hyperacidity and peptic ulcer
Hydrocortisone acetate	Cortef acetate Cortril acetate	Ophthalmic Intraarticular	7. Thrombophlebitis 8. Pregnancy 9. Severe emotional disturbance or psychoses	7. Masking infection 8. Weakness of involuntary muscles 9. Adrenocortical insufficiency
Hydrocortisone sodium succinate	Solu-Cortef A-hydroCort	IV	10. Osteoporosis	10. Amenorrhea
Synthetic steroids			Severe fungal infections Benefits must be weighed against potential hazards	Side effects are same as for natural steroids; toxic effects from prolonged administration of steroids:
Prednisone	Meticorten Deltasone	Oral		1. Cushing's syndrome 2. Moon face
Prednisolone	Delta-Cortef	Oral		3. Acne 4. Electrolyte imbalance
Triamcinolone	Aristocort Kenacort	Oral		5. Hyperglycemia 6. Osteoporosis 7. Spontaneous fractures
Triamcinolone acetonide	Aristocort Kenalog	Oral		8. Purpura 9. Hypertension 10. Psychic disturbances 11. Convulsions

REFERENCES AND ADDITIONAL READINGS

1. Anthony CP and Thibodeau GA: Textbook of anatomy and physiology ed 12, St Louis, 1986, Mosby-Year Book, Inc.
2. Groer ME and Shekleton ME: Basic pathophysiology: a holistic approach ed 3, St Louis, 1989, Mosby-Year Book, Inc.
3. Guyton AC: Textbook of medical physiology ed 7, Philadelphia, 1986, WB Saunders Co.
4. Hahn AB, Barkin RI and Oestreich SJK: Pharmacology in nursing ed 16, St Louis, 1986, Mosby-Year Book, Inc.
5. Muir BL: Pathophysiology: an introduction to the mechanisms of disease ed 2, New York, 1988, John Wiley & Sons Inc.
6. Pagliaro AM and Pagliaro LA: Pharmacologic aspects of nursing, St. Louis, 1986, Mosby-Year Book, Inc.
7. Phipps WJ and others: Medical-surgical nursing, ed 4, St Louis, 1990, Mosby-Year Book, Inc.
8. Porth C: Pathophysiology: concepts of altered health states ed 3, Philadelphia 1990, Lippincott.
9. Potter P and Perry A: Fundamentals of nursing, ed 2, St Louis, 1990, Mosby-Year Book Inc.
10. Smith A: Principles of microbiology, St Louis, 1985, Mosby-Year Book, Inc.
11. Thompson J and others: Mosby's Manual of clinical nursing ed 2, St Louis, 1989, Mosby-Year Book, Inc.

CHAPTER

3

Psychologic Aspects
of Patient Care

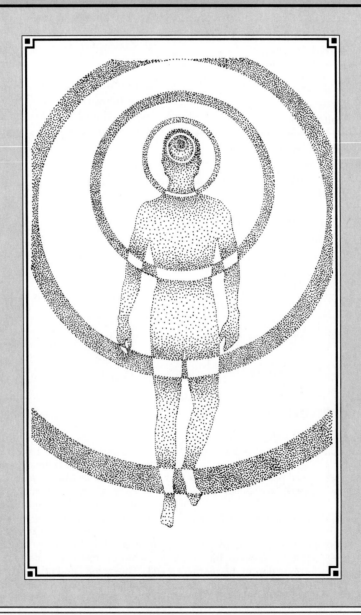

addictive disorders
adjustment disorders
affective disorders
Alzheimer's disease
anxiety
anxiety disorders
conscious
defense mechanisms
delusion
depression
dissociative disorders
ego
endogenous depression
factitious disorders
hallucination
Huntington's chorea
id
inner child
mental health
mental illness
organic psychosis
personality
personality disorder
posttraumatic stress disorder
psychophysiologic reactions
psychoses
psychosomatic disorders
regression
schizophrenia
situational depression
subconscious
superego
unconscious

1. Discuss theories of personality development and structure.

2. Explain the normal use of defense mechanisms.

3. Define and differentiate between: affective disorders, personality disorders, anxiety disorders, adjustment disorders, factitious disorders, dissociative disorders, and psychosomatic disorders.

4. Identify three types of: affective disorders, personality disorders, anxiety disorders, dissociative disorders, and psychosomatic disorders.

5. List five characteristics of schizophrenia.

6. Discuss the relationship between emotional and physical illness.

7. Describe regression and situational depression, and the potential relationship of each to the ill or hospitalized nonpsychotic patient.

8. Identify four major sources of depression, and list ten symptoms of depression.

9. List signals often given by persons thinking about suicide.

10. Identify six addictive behaviors/disorders.

11. List three common types of psychotropic drugs, and one major side effect of each.

12. Describe, discuss, and demonstrate nursing techniques that are effective therapeutic tools in the care of both psychotic and nonpsychotic patients.

The nurse may choose to practice nursing in a variety of settings. Whatever the setting, it is important for the nurse to have a knowledge and understanding of **mental health, mental illness,** and the ways in which any illness can affect the emotional well-being of a patient. Emotional reactions occur in all patients with physical illness and increase a patient's need for emotional support. Mental health and mental illness are at opposite ends of an emotional spectrum, and without emotional support, the stress of a physical illness has the potential to move a patient toward mental illness.

There is no clear-cut division between physical illness and mental illness. Physical illness affects the emotional well-being of the patient, and mental illness has an impact on the body. The mentally ill person may have physical problems, and the physically ill patient may develop emotional problems. It is never safe to assume a patient has only one or the other type of problem. Currently, a great number of the patients seeking medical care have significant emotional problems, which in turn affect their physical states. Consequently, almost all types of emotional problems can be seen in a general hospital, and many physical problems can be found in mentally ill patients. All persons have similar needs that must be met in order for them to maintain the ability to function.

NEEDS OF INDIVIDUALS

Each person is born with a definite set of basic needs. These basic needs are the same for everyone. They do not vary with age and are not changed by sex, color, race, religion, occupation, or marital status. These needs remain the same regardless of the state of the individual's emotional or physical health.

Maslow has identified a set of needs that are fundamental to all humans. The most basic of these are physiologic needs, such as food, water, warmth, and shelter. When these physiologic needs are satisfied, additional needs can emerge to be fulfilled. These higher needs include safety, love and belongingness, esteem, and self-actualization. Unmet needs have an impact on the development of the personality and can affect the way in which an individual views the world and interacts with others. Chapter 1 contains a more complete discussion of Maslow's theories of human needs.

PERSONALITY STRUCTURE

Why do people appear to be so different? One person may be angry, aggressive, and ready to fight for the slightest reason, whereas another may be passive, submissive, and always ready to give in or compromise. An individual's response to a situation is based on personality structure, which is composed of a person's genetic make-up, life experiences, knowledge, and feelings.

Sigmund Freud was notable in his time for deviating from the Viennese medical model by acknowledging the importance of emotions. He developed the concept of long-term psychotherapy called *psychoanalysis*. He referred to the awareness of the total environment as the **conscious** mind. He called the area of the mind just beneath consciousness where memories are stored the **subconscious** mind, and the reservoir of unremembered past experiences the **unconscious** mind. Because Freud was a scholar and a scientist, the goal he sought for his patients was not emotional happiness or mental health but self-knowledge and truth.

To explain the structure of **personality** and to describe and understand human behavior, Freud identified three parts of the personality: the id, the ego, and the superego.

The **id** is the part of the personality that contains impulses and drives, operating at an unconscious level of thought. Some examples of id drives include hunger, sex, and warmth. Because the id operates on the pleasure principle, it demands almost immediate satisfaction of its drives.

The **ego** is the part of the personality that deals with how the person relates to the world. It is an awareness of the conscious self, the "I." The ego has sometimes been called the executive of the personality, since it is the part in which thoughts, feelings, compromises, and solutions are formed. The ego attempts to satisfy the needs of the id, while at the same time considering the pressures from the superego.

The **superego** is that part of the personality that controls, inhibits, and regulates the impulses. It contains notions about right and wrong as taught by our parents and society. The superego operates at both the conscious and unconscious levels of thought, and aids in critical self-evaluation, self-punishment, and self-love.

Many other theories about personality structure have been developed since Freud's time. A more current theory is *Redecision Theory*, developed by Goulding and Goulding, which is based on *Transactional Analysis* and *Gestalt Therapy*.[10] This theory is often depicted by three circles representing the three parts of the personality. Each circle represents an ego state, a psychologic position an individual takes that can be observed by their behavior.

The **P**, called the *Parent ego state*, is made up of the messages received by an individual as a small child and, contains information about the world and about the child received from real parents and parenting figures. Behavior in this ego state mirrors that of parental figures.

The **A** represents the *Adult ego state*, which is the logical, thinking, data-storing part of an individual and is the place where problem-solving, negotiating, and compromising takes place. Although this part is called the Adult, it has nothing to do with age, and an individual in this ego state behaves in a nonfeeling way.

The **C** represents the *Child ego state*, which contains the instincts, intuition, spontaneity, creativity, playfulness, and feelings of the individual. This ego state is the part of an individual that thinks, feels, and behaves as the individual did in the past, particularly when he or she was a child.

In some ways, the personality structure of Redecision Theory is similar to Freud's theories. However, Redecision Theory may be more useful than Freudian theory when applied to the emotional and nursing care needs of patients.

PERSONALITY DEVELOPMENT

Regardless of the theory used to describe personality, all the parts of the personality must achieve a balance in order for a person to function effectively and survive within a society. What follows is a discussion of personality structure as described by Freud, Erikson, and the Gouldings. However, many theorists have attempted to explain how the personality develops.

Freud described three principal stages that occur in the development of the individual: the *infantile stage*, which is divided into three substages—the *oral*, the *anal*, and the *phallic;* the *latent stage;* and the *genital stage*. Each of these stages contains its own centers of importance and at each

stage the individual has needs that must be met in order for the next stage to be entered successfully.

Personality development as conceived by Erik Erikson does not stress the psychosexual aspect of all the stages of development. Instead he proposes that during the various stages of development there is a developmental task to be accomplished and that each developmental task not only contributes to some vital attribute of personality but also lays the groundwork for the next task. Erikson's first stages of emotional development are similar to those of Freud. In addition, Erikson has described a sense of autonomy as the main emotional task of the early preschool years, a sense of initiative as the main task for later preschool and early school years, and a sense of industry as the main task in the later childhood years. The developmental tasks associated with Erikson's eight stages are outlined in Table 3-1.

Goulding and Goulding describe personality development as beginning in infancy.[10] As the Child ego state of an individual grows and develops, it incorporates all the experiences an individual has had. Sometimes feelings from childhood experiences may reappear at a later time. A woman may be behaving in a perfectly appropriate way until she sees a dog, and then she may scream, cry, and cower in terror the way she did when chased by a dog as a child. Young children are very spontaneous, curious, and playful. If a child is criticized or punished for behaving in a childlike way, he or she may become unquestioningly compliant or very rebellious and may demonstrate these behaviors even in adulthood. A patient may exhibit such behavior when requested to do something by a nurse or physician. Language that is childlike is an indication that the person is in his or her Child ego state.

As the Parent ego state develops, it includes copied behavior and feelings, parental beliefs, and rules for living: the so-called "shoulds" and "should nots." This Parent ego state can both nurture and criticize the self and can nurture or criticize others. A patient who believes he "should" be a "good patient" may not ask for pain medication when he needs it and may criticize himself for needing medication at all. A nurse may be appropriately self-nurturing by refusing a third overtime shift in one week, yet simultaneously feel "selfish" in needing some time for personal matters. "You should/should not" or "Why didn't

Table 3-1

Erikson's Stages of Personality Development

Stage	Developmental task
Infancy	*Basic trust:* If the child is accepted, wanted, loved, and well cared for, he will perceive the world as friendly and supportive. If the child is not accepted, is unloved, and his needs are not met, he will become anxious and distrust the world. Basic trust is necessary to develop the capacity to love others.
Toddlerhood	*Autonomy:* As the child comes in contact with restrictions on his behavior, he must learn to adapt to the family and its rules. He becomes rebellious against his parents but desires their love and approval. A successful balance between conformity and independence will result in a child developing a sense of dignity, self-worth, and basic independence.
Preschool childhood	*Initiative:* The child's imagination expands, and he begins to explore new ideas and methods. Children unconsciously begin to imitate the characteristics of the parent of the same sex.
School-age childhood	*Industry and accomplishment:* The child learns to channel energy into constructive tasks. He competes with others at school, learns to work with peers, and develops mental and physical skills.
Adolescence	*Identity:* The physical and emotional changes that accompany adolescence bring feelings of self-doubt and confusion. The young person faces new sexual feelings, the need to choose a career, and the need to be accepted by peers. He strives for independence from family restrictions. Support during the turmoil will result in a stronger sense of identity and reinforcement of values, and the child will be ready to take his place in the adult world.
Young adulthood	*Intimacy:* Selection of a partner based on mutual trust and respect usually occurs in young adulthood. The person is mature and responsible, and to achieve this state the stages of the past must have been met satisfactorily.
Adulthood	*Generativity:* The person engages in his life work, creating a legacy that will be left for future generations.
Older adulthood	*Integrity:* Acceptance of one's place in life, continued fulfillment, a sense of accomplishment, and dignity characterize this final stage.

you . . . ?" are usually indicators that a person is in a Parent ego state.

The Adult ego state is a state of being that is observable, without feeling, where an individual stores, retrieves, and acts upon data. It is the ego state in which one has the ability in words to test out data, to determine what is reality in terms of one's own experience and that of others, and to test and prove or disprove information. A nurse doing a patient assessment, using the nursing process, or drawing up a medication would be in the Adult ego state.

MENTAL HEALTH

There is no easy formula for judging normality. What is considered "normal" can and does vary from culture to culture, country to country, and even town to town. From any point of view, the concept of normality/abnormality is a relative one.

A variety of writers have attempted to define what they consider mental health. Glasser states that a normal human being is one who is able to function effectively, obtain some degree of happiness, and achieve something of benefit to himself within the rules of the society in which he lives.[9] Morgan and Johnston define mental health as the ability to adjust to new situations, react to personal problems without marked distress, and productively contribute to society. An individual's degree of mental health may fluctuate from day to day and from situation to situation, yet maintain an overall consistency. Maslow listed the following criteria for normal personality.[12]

Maslow's Criteria for Normal Personality

1. Adequate feelings of security
2. Reasonable degree of self-evaluation
3. Realistic life goals
4. Effective contact with reality
5. Integration and consistency of personality
6. Ability to learn from experience
7. Adequate spontaneity
8. Appropriate emotionality
9. Ability to satisfy the requirements of the group, coupled with some degree of emancipation from the group
10. Adequate but unexaggerated body desires, with the ability to gratify them in an approved fashion

EFFECTS OF ANXIETY

Anxiety is a major motivating factor in a person's emotional life. A person will usually take the course of action that will reduce the feelings of apprehension, tension, and uneasiness that threaten the individual's sense of self or sense of being in control of life. These feelings stem from anticipated danger that may or may not be related to the reality of the situation. Some people are made anxious by love, some by hate, and some by the indifference of others.

Anxiety is first experienced in infancy when the child's needs are not always met and continues to occur throughout the life cycle. Throughout the course of life an individual faces many conflicts that lead to anxiety. This anxiety can be experienced in various degrees, from mild anxiety to a stage of panic.

The sudden onset of an illness, a serious accident, or the death of a loved one may create anxiety, causing sleeplessness and other symptoms. An event that changes the family lifestyle or status in the community may cause a level of anxiety that makes a person feel helpless. The person who is in an acute state of panic and threatens to harm self or others may require the nurse to stay nearby until the panic is resolved.

Not all anxiety is harmful, nor is it to be avoided at all costs. Mild anxiety can actually increase one's alertness and improve performance. In moderate anxiety one's ability to understand is decreased and learning at this time is difficult. The stage of panic results in complete incapacitation. Anxiety also has many physiologic effects on the body, which prepare the body for the "fight or flight response."

Anxiety may be recognized through many physical symptoms and communicative manifestations. A person may experience increased perspiration, restlessness, fatigue, palpitations, increased respiration and pulse rates, loss of appetite, inability to sleep, tremors, frequent urination, a "lump in the throat," vomiting, diarrhea, and a change in abdominal sensations frequently described as "butterflies in my stomach." Communication is also affected by anxiety. The anxious person may have a change in voice tone, going to a higher pitch, and may speak faster. The anxious person may be preoccupied with personal thoughts and either avoid certain topics or continually return to discussing a particular subject. Expressed in the terminology of Redecision Theory, the anxious person can be said to be in a Child ego state.

DEFENSE MECHANISMS

Because anxiety plays an essential role in influencing the personality and behavior, it is helpful to explore the varying mechanisms that people use to lower anxiety levels. **Defense mechanism** is the term used to describe the varying attempts of the unconscious mind to protect the personality by controlling anxiety and reducing emotional pressures. Defense mechanisms are used by all people to reduce anxiety and consequently affect the behavioral responses of the individual. The use of defense mechanisms is not intrinsically unhealthy. Illness, hospitalization, and incapacitation are anxiety-producing experiences, therefore an understanding of defense mechanisms is essential for those caring for the ill.

Our daily frustrations and conflicts can usually be resolved by using conscious coping mechanisms. More complex frustrations and conflicts are dealt with through unconscious defense mechanisms. All persons use defense mechanisms, and their use is not pathologic unless the individual's sense of reality is distorted. All defense mechanisms are automatic; their use is not

Table 3-2

Defense Mechanisms

Defense mechanism	Definition	Example
Compensation	The individual attempts to make up for real or imagined feelings of inadequacy.	The girl who has been made to feel unattractive works very hard to excel in school or other areas.
Conversion	Emotional conflicts that cannot be dealt with mentally are expressed through physical means.	A soldier on the front lines of battle is very fearful, but the thought of being a coward is unacceptable. Unable to resolve this conflict through thought processes, he becomes paralyzed, thus escaping the combat situation. He truly is unable to walk.
Denial	A person avoids painful or anxiety-producing reality by unconsciously denying that it exists.	A person denies unpleasant traits such as dishonesty or stubborness or refuses to believe that a loved one has died or has a terminal illness.
Displacement	Pent-up emotions are redirected toward objects or people other than the primary source of the emotion	A nursing student is chastised by the instructor. Upon returning home, the student may kick the cat, slam the door, and argue with family.
Identification	A person unconsciously enhances self-esteem by patterning himself after another person.	A hospitalized teenager so admires one of the nurses that she decides to choose nursing as a career.
Projection	A person protects himself from being aware of his own undesirable traits or feelings by attributing them to others.	The nurse believes that a particular patient does not like him or her, when in reality on an unconscious level he or she does not like the patient. The psychotic patient may state "he hates me" (I hate him) or "he thinks I am ugly" (I think I am ugly).
Rationalization	A person justifies inconsistent or undesirable behavior by giving acceptable explanations for them. (This has been called self-deception.)	A physician forgets to reorder medication for the patient and then criticizes the nurse for not giving a reminder.
Reaction-formation	A person directly reverses true feelings that are unacceptable in exactly the opposite direction.	An overprotective and hovering mother actually resents and feels hostility toward her child.
Regression	A person returns to an earlier, less mature level of adaptation, often resulting from lack of satisfaction or a threat to security; this behavior is seen in most hospitalized patients to some extent.	The 4-year-old boy suddenly starts to wet his pants and asks for a bottle after the arrival of a new baby at home. In some psychotic patients there can be a return to infantile behavior.
Repression	A person completely excludes from the consciousness impulses, experiences, and feelings that are psychologically disturbing because they arouse feelings of guilt or anxiety; conflicts that remain repressed usually seek expression, as in one's dreams.	A daughter has very intense feelings of hatred for her father and wishes he would die. This thought is very unacceptable to the daughter and she excludes it from her conscious thought, yet she frequently has dreams of funerals and cemeteries.
Sublimation	Unconscious or unacceptable desires are channeled into activities that are socially acceptable; these desires are often sexual in nature.	A person may channel sexual drives into creating artwork or composing music.
Undoing	A person symbolically acts out in reverse something already done or thought that is unacceptable; the person attempts to erase the act or the guilt.	After slapping her child's hand, the mother keeps kissing the child's fingers.

consciously planned by the individual. Their purpose is the reduction of emotional pressures to keep us from being anxious. Some of the more common defense mechanisms are illustrated in Table 3-2.

DEVELOPMENT OF EMOTIONAL PROBLEMS

Defense mechanisms are a person's unconscious attempts to adjust to or cope with difficult or anxiety-provoking situations. If these defenses are not successful in solving problems or reducing anxiety, then the person may develop emotional disorders. It is important to remember that some forms of mental illness and some emotional disorders are genetic. Some are linked to chemical imbalances in the body, some can result from medications and/or substance abuse, and some are the result of failed defense mechanisms and ineffective coping skills. When defense mechanisms fail, the resulting emotional problems are an exaggerated expression of normal behavior and are attempts to manage a difficult situation.

EMOTIONAL DISORDERS

Emotional disorders are difficult to define—they range from mild to severe, and definitions may vary according to the experiences of the person who is doing the defining and the cultural attributes and context of the patient in question. A person who is uncomfortable with the powerful expression of feelings may see a very angry person as being emotionally disturbed. Italians, who are thought to be very emotionally expressive, may see a reserved New Englander as being depressed. A nursing home patient who says, "I have stars on my ceiling, and a monkey who eats orchids in my greenhouse," may be thought of by the nurse as being senile or psychotic, unless the nurse takes the time to discover the patient was recalling her childhood when she did indeed have a ceiling with stars in her bedroom and an orchid-eating monkey in the greenhouse.

A person who is emotionally distressed is less able to act and behave in a useful and productive way.

A person may be well oriented to persons, places, and things but may not know the reasons underlying a particular behavior and so cannot modify behavior merely by willing change.

The primary sign of many emotional disorders is excessive anxiety. This anxiety can be expressed in a variety of ways. The nurse must remember that a person with emotional distress will develop certain symptoms in an attempt to control or reduce anxiety.

There are many ways to treat a person with an emotional disorder. Various forms of psychotherapy, which may be crisis-oriented, short-term, brief, or long-term, may be used. An individual may see a psychotherapist alone, as part of a couple, as part of a family, or may participate in group psychotherapy. Medication may be used alone or in conjunction with psychotherapy, and behavior modification may be incorporated into the therapy. The purpose of any psychotherapeutic treatment is to alleviate or lessen the symptoms and help the person to resume purposeful and appropriate functioning.

ANXIETY DISORDERS

Anxiety disorders are characterized by an anxious worrying that can result in a state of panic. Physical symptoms such as palpitations, shortness of breath, heavy perspiration, inability to concentrate, and sleeplessness, may be experienced, accompanied by unfocused feelings of dread. Anxiety disorders include panic disorders, phobic disorders, obsessive-compulsive disorders, conversion disorders, and posttraumatic stress disorders (Table 3-3).

PSYCHOSES

It has been said that the neurotic person builds castles, whereas the psychotic person lives in them. **Psychoses** are a group of major emotional disorders characterized by derangement of the personality and loss of the ability to function realistically in the world.

Psychoses resulting from or associated with organic brain syndromes are mental disorders caused by brain damage. These psychoses include those associated with chronic brain syndromes, alcoholic psychoses, psychoses associated with intracranial infection, and those associated with a variety of other physical conditions. Psychosis can

Table 3-3

Anxiety Disorders		
Disorder	**Description**	**Examples**
Panic disorder	General symptoms of anxiety	A person driving a car suddenly feels terrified and may have to stop driving.
Phobic disorder	Enormous fear of an object or situation, even though the person recognizes that it cannot really do him any harm.	Fear of open spaces (agoraphobia), fear of closed spaces (claustrophobia) and fear of heights (acrophobia).
Obsessive—compulsive disorder	Obsessive—repetitive thoughts. Compulsive—repetitive acts that a person is unable to stop doing.	A person constantly thinks about a love object, constantly driving by the love object's house and making him/her the total focus of all thoughts and activities.
Conversion disorder	Conversion type—blindness, deafness, paralysis Dissociative type—splits off the memory of the trauma and develops amnesia or multiple personalities.	A person sees a shooting and suddenly goes blind A person is a victim of incest and remembers nothing of the incident.
Post-traumatic stress disorder	Numbness and decreased responses following trauma; flashbacks. Acute—within six months of event; delayed—more than six months after the event. If symptoms last more than six months, they are considered chronic.	Associated with traumatic events such as being raped, earthquakes, being held hostage, or war.

also result from the stress of being in an intensive care unit. Treatment will vary according to the underlying physical situation.

Psychoses that are not directly related to physical processes are termed *functional* psychoses. These can be divided into three categories—schizophrenia, affective disorders, and paranoid disorders.

Schizophrenia

Schizophrenia is the most widespread form of psychosis and includes a large group of disorders in which there are disturbances in thinking, mood, and behavior. Although there are 10 major subdivisions of schizophrenia with unique characteristics, there are several overall characteristics possessed by all subgroups. These characteristics are listed in Table 3-4.[15]

The secondary symptoms of schizophrenia are those characterizing the 10 major subdivisions of the disorder. These symptoms are the person's desperate last attempt to reduce enormous anxiety. Discussion will be limited to the following types of schizophrenia: disorganized, catatonic, and paranoid.

Disorganized schizophrenia

Disorganized schizophrenia often begins in adolescence. Patients begin to demonstrate inappropriate emotions. They often withdraw from social contact and smile and giggle in a silly manner. There is severe regression until the behavior becomes very childlike.

Catatonic schizophrenia

The catatonic type of schizophrenia has two forms. In one phase the patient is completely inactive, mute, and appears to be in a stupor. The second phase is characterized by an agitated state. Behavior is often impulsive and sometimes destructive.

Paranoid schizophrenia

In addition to the other basic characteristics of schizophrenia, the paranoid schizophrenic is suspicious, aggressive, and has delusions of persecution. This person may hear voices, sometimes commanding action, or believe that the police are following his movements. These patients can be very convincing, and often they demonstrate manipulative behavior.

Table 3-4

Characteristics of Schizophrenia

Characteristic	Description	Example
Thought and behavioral disturbance	The individual exhibits confused thought processes that are easily sidetracked or fragmented. Speech lacks unity and clearness, and behavior may be odd, sudden, and unreasonable.	Instead of thinking, "I'm cold. The window is open and a breeze is blowing on me. I'll close the window," the schizophrenic person may think, "I'm hungry. Why is she staring at me? I see a red balloon."
Lack of affect	The individual does not display emotions, or emotions are shown inappropriately. He fails to react to others in a meaningful way.	When informed of the death of a loved one, the patient may laugh.
Withdrawal	The individual becomes secluded from the rest of the world, exhibiting decreased interest and initiative. He may have feelings of hopelessness, fear, and despair, although remaining acutely aware of his surroundings.	The person may sit for hours staring into space without speaking to anyone.
Autism	The person is detached both from reality and from the world.	The individual is extremely withdrawn and involved with his or her own inner thoughts. He or she ignores all that is occurring in the immediate area and fails to relate to others.
Regression	The individual retreats to past levels of behavior.	The person's behavior becomes more infantile.
Delusions	Persons with delusional thoughts have false beliefs based on misconceptions.	A patient may refuse all food, fearing that it may be poisoned.
Hallucinations	The person has sensory perceptions that cannot be explained by external stimuli. Any sense may be involved.	A person may hear voices or exhibit unusual behavior, such as talking to himself, listening, or unusual movements.

Affective Disorders

This category includes a group of emotional illnesses characterized by a disorder of mood. There is either extreme depression or elation. Following are types of **affective disorders**.

Major depression

A major depression occurs in people who have no previous history of depression, often happening in middle age. It is also called *involutional melancholia* and is often associated with menopause or with changes in a person's life situations. It is characterized by worrying, agitation, guilt, and feelings of hopelessness.

Bipolar disorder

Bipolar disorder, also called manic-depressive illness, is usually characterized by wide mood swings that alternate between elation and depression. In the manic phase the patient may make grandiose schemes and may go for days without sleeping or eating. The specific treatment of choice is lithium.

Postpartum depression

This can occur in the first 6 months of the postpartum period. It is characterized by weeping and lethargy, and feelings of being overwhelmed, incompetent, and helpless. Endocrine and hormonal changes, role changes, stress, or a combination of these have been proposed as causative factors.

Cyclothymic disorder

This is characterized by mood swings between elation and depression that are not as severe as those of manic-depressive illness.

Dexamethasone Suppression Test

The dexamethasone suppression test (DST) is commonly used to assess a depression that is treatable with medication. The DST is a standardized marker of depression and aids in quantifying the severity, predicting the outcome, and monitoring the treatment of depression. In normal individuals the administration of dexamethasone suppresses the secretion of cortisol. Depressed individuals are resistant to this suppression and instead hypersecrete cortisol.

The procedure consists of giving the patient 1 mg of dexamethasonse orally at 11:30 PM. The next day blood tests are taken at 4 PM and 11 PM. If either test shows a dexamethasone cortisol level over 56 µg/dL, the test is considered abnormal. The depressed patient is then treated with antidepressant medication.

Nurses need to ask the patients about their use of medications, alcohol, and steroid creams when a dexamethasone suppression test (DST) is going to be performed. Medications such as hypnotics, antianxiety drugs, anticonvulsants, and beta-blockers can alter the test results.

Paranoid Disorders

In paranoia the patient has no **hallucinations,** only fixed **delusions** of grandeur or persecution, which often center around religion. Other than the occurrence of these delusions, the personality is well balanced. There is some question as to whether paranoia is a separate category of disorders or is really a branch of schizophrenia.

PERSONALITY DISORDERS

Personality disturbances fall somewhere in the middle area of emotional disorders. The behavior of people classified as having **personality disorders** demonstrates that they have serious inner problems, yet they are in contact with reality, and most are able to adapt socially. They do not demonstrate the anxiety that is characteristic of other types of emotional problems. There is a variety of identified personality disorders. The more common forms include the paranoid personality, schizoid personality, obsessive-compulsive personality, antisocial personality, and passive-aggressive personality.

Paranoid Personality

Persons with a paranoid personality tend to be overly sensitive, suspicious, rigid, jealous, and envious. They sometimes demonstrate an exaggerated sense of their own importance and tend to blame others.

Schizoid Personality

Persons with a schizoid personality demonstrate emotional detachment, shyness, fearfulness, an inability to socialize well with others, and a tendency to daydream and withdraw.

Obsessive-Compulsive Personality

Persons classified as obsessive-compulsive are rigid, neat, inhibited, conforming, and overly conscientious. They may feel the need to perform some repetitive act in order to reduce anxiety.

Antisocial Personality

People considered to have an antisocial personality (sociopathic personality) are unable to form any meaningful attachments to other persons, groups, or society. They are selfish, irresponsible, impulsive, and unable to learn from punishment or past events. They have no sense of guilt at having done harm or damage. Many prisoners are identified as having this personality type.

Passive-Aggressive Personality

The person with a passive-aggressive personality has considerable difficulty fulfilling dependent needs and responding to authority. Behavior includes pouting, stubbornness, failure to keep appointments, procrastination, intentional inefficiency, and tardiness. The person may evoke feelings of anger in family members, friends, and co-workers.

ORGANIC BRAIN SYNDROMES: DEMENTIA

Some forms of mental illness are caused by organic brain changes. These changes can be caused by decreased blood supply to brain tissue, traumatic destruction of brain cells by either trauma or disease, or the diminishing or destruction of brain tissue caused by the aging process. Senility, or senile dementia, the pronounced loss of mental, physical, or emotional control in the elderly, was once thought to be a normal result of aging.

It is now known to have a variety of organic causes, including degeneration of the neurons of the cerebral cortex. **Huntington's chorea** is a genetically transmitted disease; all persons who have the gene develop psychosis around midlife and frequently require institutionalization. **Alzheimer's disease,** a more recently discovered chronic brain disorder, can manifest itself as early as the mid-forties in an individual. It involves a progressive destruction of nervous system tissue and brain cells; upon microscopic examination, the cells have a twisted shape. Its symptoms include involuntary muscle movements, slurring of speech, memory lapses and loss, and the gradual diminishing of thought processes and intellectual capabilities. It is sometimes possible to slow the symptoms of organic brain syndromes, but they are irreversible, and patients with these disorders progressively deteriorate.

SOMATIC DISORDERS

In the psychoses and personality disorders, the individual's anxiety is expressed through behavior. In somatic reactions an individual's emotional conflict appears to be a major factor leading to the development of pathologic changes in a previously healthy organ of the body. An example of the interaction between chronic anxiety and physical disease can be seen in a patient who develops essential hypertension as an adult. This person may have been raised in an environment that suppressed expression of anger, and may have lived for years with repressed hostility and underlying anxiety. This state can produce a slight but continual stimulation of the sympathetic nervous system, resulting in a degree of arteriolar constriction in the kidneys, skin, and most visceral organs. A decreased blood supply to the kidney can result in the development of hypertension. Other psychosomatic conditions include asthma, peptic ulcer, ulcerative colitis, hives, and migraine headaches. The specific causes of these disorders are unknown.

There is not enough knowledge yet available to prove conclusively that the causes of these diseases originate in the mind. The National Foundation of Ileitis and Colitis believes that these two diseases have been incorrectly labeled as being psychosomatic. The foundation is involved in research to determine the cause or causes of these

diseases. Whatever the cause of illness, it is the nurse's role to be supportive and caring. Those caring for patients with **psychosomatic disorders** may become impatient with or intolerant of the patient who is thought to be "doing it to himself." An unsupportive, unsympathetic attitude may be conveyed to the patient who is truly suffering.

ADDICTIVE DISORDERS

Any person who depends on drugs or alcohol, gambles excessively, works too hard, manifests anorexic, bulimic, or other addictive behaviors in an attempt to alter his feelings may be considered to have an **addictive disorder.** It is believed that those who use addictive behaviors are attempting to manage their feelings in ways that allow them to function and control their lives.

There is a wide variety of theories that attempts to explain why a person develops an addictive disorder. Some persons believe that an addiction develops as an escape from reality, whereas others state that these disorders are expressions of rage against parents, or attempts to commit suicide slowly. Some other theories suggest that addictive behavior is an attempt to combat feelings of helplessness and hopelessness and to feel more in control.

Learning theorists believe that substance abuse and addictive behaviors are learned behaviors. Because these behaviors briefly alter feelings, the individual learns to turn to this escape as a means of continuing to relieve painful feelings.

Abuse of or addiction to drugs and alcohol may be an individual's attempt to self-medicate. There have been numerous instances of persons who have stopped drinking or using drugs developing fullblown psychoses that had previously been controlled through the abuse of alcohol or drugs. It is therefore very important to assess the usual alcohol or drug use of a patient at the time of admission to an inpatient facility, since withdrawal can trigger delerium tremens (DTs), seizures, or psychotic reactions, and many medications interact adversely with alcohol. It is also important to know that there is a high incidence of alcoholism among the elderly.

Recent research indicates that a genetic factor is responsible for the development of alcoholism in more than 75% of alcoholics.

In caring for the person with an addictive disorder, it is important for nurses to be aware of their own personal attitudes toward these conditions. These patients, as well a those who attempt suicide, often arouse very judgmental reactions and great hostility in those who care for them.

DEPRESSION

The mental illnesses and personality disorders that have depression as a symptom have been covered in previous sections of this chapter. However, because of the high incidence of depression in the general population (estimated to occur in 1 of every 12 people) is can be assumed that there would also be a high incidence of **depression** among patients requiring nursing care. Thus, depression warrants a separate discussion. The types of depression include grief, **situational/reactive depression, endogenous depression** (without an identified precipitating event), chronic depression, and manic-depressive illness.

There are many signs and symptoms of depression, some of which can actually mask depression; all these should be considered when evaluating a patient for depression. These signs and symptoms include:

Mood: sad, unhappy, blue, crying, within the "normal" range

Thoughts: pessimistic, guilt-ridden, low self-esteem, loss of interest and motivation, decrease in efficiency and concentration, inability to make decisions and choices

Behavior and appearance: neglectful of personal appearance, angry/hostile, demanding, always smiling, seemingly the "good patient" (always compliant), perfectionistic, obsessive, anxious, hyperenergetic, withdrawn, dependent, indecisive, retardation of psychomotor capacities (slowing of speech and actions), agitated, apathetic

Somatic or physical symptoms: loss or increase of appetite, loss or increase in weight, constipation, insomnia, fatigue or sleeping too much, chronic pain (especially backache, headache, and abdominal pains), menstrual changes, loss of interest in sex or sexual complaints/dysfunction, palpitations, hyperventilation, difficulty swallowing, rashes, asthma, colitis, hypertension

There are many feelings that underlie or contribute to depression, chiefly feelings of helplessness, hopelessness, and worthlessness. Other feelings that may cause depression are anger, despair, guilt, resentment, hostility, dependency, negativity, inferiority, poor self-image, low self-esteem, feelings of inadequacy, and loss.

Loss can be defined in many ways and can include the loss of a significant other, a body part, a bodily function or of its mobility, a dependent state (also called *success depression*), a symbolic object, self-esteem, or self-image.

Although feelings are a significant factor in causing depression, depression can also be a part of a symptom complex of certain diseases. These diseases include thyroid disease, Addison's disease, Cushing's syndrome, systemic lupus, uremia, hypoglycemia, gall bladder disease, stroke, cardiac disease, and Alzheimer's disease.

Certain medications can also induce depression: reserpine, propranolol and other beta-blockers, methyldopa, diazepam, clonidine, corticosteroids, and oral contraceptives can all cause drug-induced depression.

Nursing Assessment of Depression

A nursing assessment and interview is useful not only in assisting with the development of any nursing care plan, but also in helping the patient feel understood and cared for. In assessing patients for depression, it is important to differentiate between the kinds and severity of depression and to recognize the components of each.

Grief: involves a real loss; is weeks to years in duration; the patient feels that everything has ended, but knows better; reaction is proportionate to loss; no loss of self-esteem.

Reactive depression: related to loss in current life situation (either real or imagined); comes and goes; can become chronic; patient manifests impaired functioning, has distorted perceptions, and may be suicidal; patient's reactions are disproportionate to loss; patient suffers loss of self-esteem.

Endogenous depression: stems from internal dynamics; other symptoms same as for reactive depression.

Psychotic depression: not necessarily a loss involved; the patient has distorted thought processes, severely impaired functioning, suffers gross distortion of perceptions (hallucinations, delusions or both); reacts disproportionately, is suicidal, and suffers loss of self-esteem.

A tool useful for evaluating whether a patient is depressed is the phrase: IN SAD CAGES.

Assessing Depression

(IN) Interest—Have interests changed recently regarding work, family, hobbies, friends? If so, how have they changed?

(S) Sleep
(A) Appetite
(D) Depressed Mood

(C) Concentration
(A) Activity
(G) Guilt
(E) Energy
(S) Suicide

Whenever a nurse is assessing depression in a patient or suspects that a patient is depressed, it is extremely important to determine whether the patient is suicidal. It is always appropriate to ask the patient very directly if he or she is suicidal or has ever thought about hurting or killing himself or herself. Asking patients directly if they are suicidal does not increase the risk of suicide; often patients will feel relieved at having an opportunity to talk about how terrible they feel. Questions that the nurse might ask when assessing a patient's risk for suicide are:

Do you feel that life is worth living?

Have you thought of hurting yourself or of committing suicide?

What do you think you might do?

Do you have the means to kill yourself?

Have you ever tried to harm yourself before? How far did you go?

On a scale of 1 to 10, how suicidal are you?

How do you see yourself in the future?

Has any member of your family committed suicide?

Suicide is the ultimate expression of anger, hostility, hopelessness, and helplessness. It is often the patient's statement of belief that "You have failed me." There are many factors that contribute to or increase the sense of hopelessness and helplessness and the risk of suicide in a patient. Any of the following increase the suicidal potential of a patient:

Previous suicide attempt

Direct or disguised suicide threat (giving away belongings or stating, "My family won't have to worry about me much longer.")

Chronic illness

Isolation

Bereavement/loss

Financial stress

Severe depression or psychosis

Alcoholism/drug abuse

Chronic use of hypnotics/sedatives

Family history of suicide

Suicide of a close friend

Over the age of 60, or between the ages of 11 and 25; there is a very high incidence of suicide among adolescents, the elderly, and the ill elderly.

Whatever the setting, it is important for the nurse to avoid trying to cheer up a depressed patient, or to make such statements as, "Things aren't that bad." The nurse should also avoid actions and attitudes that convey rejection, which can cause the patient to feel irritable and impatient, and to feel a further lowering of self-esteem. Helpful actions on the part of the nurse include encouraging the patient to express anger and hostility, acknowledging the patient's statements about feeling depressed, sad, or worthless, and being nurturing, accepting, and respectful to the patient. How would the nurse want to be treated, if the roles were reversed?

THE THERAPEUTIC RELATIONSHIP IN NURSING

The psychologist Carl Rogers is often credited with refining the use of a therapeutic relationship in the treatment of the emotionally ill. In a psychotherapeutic relationship therapists use interpersonal relationships with patients as therapeutic tools. They direct their own behavior in such a way as to be effective in the treatment of the patient. The patient's behavior is analyzed as an expression of individual needs.

Similarly, nurses need to establish therapeutic relationships with their nonpsychiatric patients. Whatever the setting, the nurse needs to use self as a therapeutic tool for patients and to develop a relationship that helps healing.

Nurses can develop meaningful and helpful relationships with their patients. They have frequent opportunities to interact with their patients, observe their behavior, and react in a manner that will have beneficial effects on the patients. Rogers has presented a variety of behaviors necessary for one to have a helping relationship. These behaviors include being genuine, offering warm acceptance of the person, and seeing the world as the patient sees it.[18]

In working effectively with the psychologic needs of patients, it is helpful to keep in mind that the patient is attempting to communicate to the nurse verbally as well as through his behavior. The nurse also is communicating with the patient in the same way. The cornerstone in any relationship, whether with family, friends, or patients, is communication. Communication implies a meaningful exchange between people, in both a verbal and a nonverbal manner.

Verbal communication involves an exchange of words on a variety of levels. Each day we may greet a neighbor by saying, "Hi, how are you?" The neighbor may reply, "Fine, thank you, how are you?" This exchange is not meaningful communication. Neither person is really interested in how the other is feeling. Often a nurse cheerfully enters the patient's room with a bright "Good morning. Isn't it a beautiful day?" without observing that the patient is lying in bed quietly crying. The nurse is not in tune with the patient's nonverbal communication (crying).

The first element in successful communication involves not talking, but *listening*. Often one is so involved with one's own thoughts or beliefs that the other person is not really heard. When a patient makes an attempt to talk with the nurse, the nurse should really try to listen to what the patient is attempting to say.

The second element in successful communication involves *supporting* what the patient is saying by not challenging or disagreeing with it.

When the patient states, "I am really afraid to have surgery tomorrow. I wonder if my doctor knows what to do?" It would be easy to reply, "There is no reason to be afraid. The doctor knows what to do." This type of reply indicates that the patient is not being heard and that his feelings are not supported. Instead the nurse may reply, "I can understand that the thought of surgery is scary. Let's talk about what worries you most." Here the nurse is supporting what the patient is saying and offering the patient the opportunity to discuss and perhaps resolve some of his fears.

A third element to be used in effective communication is *empathy*. Empathy involves a sincere attempt by the nurse to understand situations as the patient perceives them. For instance, it is easy for the nurse to become annoyed with the patient who refuses to learn to care for his colostomy. However, while talking with the patient, the nurse may learn that the patient's mother died shortly after having a colostomy.

It will not always be possible to determine why patients perceive things as they do. Situations have a variety of meanings for people, and nurses should be tuned in to what each patient is expressing.

A fourth element in successful communication involves the use of *therapeutic responses*. Therapeutic responses are ways of communicating that encourage further discussion and indicate that the nurse is listening to what the patient is saying. Table 3-5 gives examples of therapeutic versus nontherapeutic responses.

It is very important that the nurse respond to the patient's feelings, not to just his words. It is also very important that the nurse ask questions,

Table 3-5

Therapeutic and Nontherapeutic Responses

Therapeutic	Nontherapeutic
Giving broad leads—"What would you like to talk about today?"	*Turning off conversation*—"Let's not talk about your husband."
Sitting quietly, not talking—This behavior on the part of the nurse demonstrates support and interest to the patient.	*Oververbalizing*—"So then I told my boyfriend, listen here . . . "
Reflecting back to the patient what is being expressed—"It must be very lonely without your husband."	*Using cliches*—"Keep your chin up. Things will look better in the morning."
Enabling evaluation—"How do you feel about having surgery on your leg?"	*Belittling feelings expressed*—"That's not true. There is no need to feel that way, don't worry about it."

and not make assumptions about meaning. Fear and anxiety interfere with understanding, so it is important for the nurse to realize that when a patient does not follow instructions, it is not an attempt to "get the nurse," but usually means that the patient had difficulty understanding what it was that the nurse wanted. Most patients want to please, so that nurse's communications need to be clear and easy to understand.

When examining the communications between the nurses or other health care personnel and patients from the viewpoint of Redecision Theory, it becomes apparent that exchanges between people originate from one of the ego states in each person. Exchanges that originate from the Critical Parent of the Parent ego state and the Rebellious Child of the Child ego state do not generally make for effective communication.

The following is an example of a conversation between a nurse in the Critical Parent ego state and a patient in the Rebellious Child ego state.

Nurse (in Critical Parent ego state): "Mr. Donaldson, it is 5:30 AM and time for your bath. You didn't take one yesterday, and there is no reason for a man your age to have such disgusting hygiene."
Patient (in Rebellious Child ego state): "I don't take baths in the morning when I'm at home, and you can't make me take one in the morning when I'm here."

Depending on the situation, nurse/patient or nurse/nurse communications that originate from either the Nurturing Parent ego state or from the Adult ego state are most productive.

An example of communication between a nurse who is in a Nurturing Parent ego state and a patient who is in an Adapted Child ego state follows.

Nurse (in Nurturing Parent ego state): "I understand you had a pretty uncomfortable night, Ms. Alonzo. Do you need something for the pain?"
Patient (in adapted Child ego state): "Yes, I had a terrible night. I'm so tired and can't get comfortable. I just had something for pain."
Nurse (in NP): "Would you like a complete bath today, or would you rather just do a bit of washing up?"
Patient (in Spontaneous Child): "I'm too tired to take a full bath today, but I'm so hot and sticky."
Nurse (in NP): "How about my helping you with a full bath? When would be the best time for you?"
Patient (in Adapted Child): "Your help would be wonderful, but I don't want to trouble you. After my pain medication takes effect would be a good time."

The following is an example of communication with both the nurse and the patient in Adult ego states.

Nurse (in Adult ego state): "Tell me about your usual daily routine, Mr. Goldstein. What time do you usually get up? When and what do you eat? Do you take a bath or a shower, and when and how often do you do so? How do you spend your time, and what time do you usually go to bed—things like that."
Patient (in Adult ego state): "Well, I usually get up around 7 AM and have coffee while I read the paper. After a good lunch—fish, vegetable, bread, fruit, and dessert—I usually take a nap for about an hour. When I get up, I often take a shower, but not every day, because my skin is so dry. Then I go across the street and visit my friend. I come home and have some soup, or a sandwich and fruit while I watch the news. I read or watch TV until about 10 PM, then I have a cup of tea and go to bed. I always shower on Friday afternoon to get ready for synagogue and then do not wash again until after sundown on Saturday. That's part of my religion, you know. Thank you for asking how I do things when I'm at home. It's very hard being sick and being away from my routines."

Nonverbal communication is also extremely important. Nonverbal implies a form of communication that does not use words. It is our "body language." Every move of the body, every gesture may convey one's true feelings.

The incontinent patient in a nursing home who is having the bed changed for the third time in one evening may become only too aware of how loudly nonverbal communication speaks. The patient says to the nurse who is changing the bed, "I'm so sorry, my dear, I hope you don't mind." The nurse may reply "Oh, that's all right," while pulling and tugging at the sheets with an uncharacteristic roughness. The patient has "heard" the anger, although not a word of anger was said.

It is helpful for nurses to try to observe nonverbal communication carefully. Is the husband really "listening" to his wife when he is seated 2 feet from the television with his eyes glued to the screen? His body language is saying he is not. What is the mother conveying to her child when the child wraps his arms around her and she stiffens and draws away, but says, "I love you"?

The use of communication, both verbal and nonverbal, is as important a part of nursing as is performing techniques properly. Those first entering the nursing field are often unsure of themselves when conversing with patients. Often they fear saying the wrong thing. However, patients can sense whether nurses are sincere in their attempts to communicate. That attempt alone will be appreciated. Successful communication is worthwhile. It will take practice and effort but the

Figure 3-1
Participation in group sessions may help patients to express feelings. *(Courtesy Alexian Brothers Medical Center, Elk Grove Village, Ill.)*

end results of successful communication may be more important than any medication offered to the patient.

There are several general principles that should be kept in mind when attempting to develop therapeutic relationships with patients. Most important is the acceptance of the individual as he is. Patients should not be judged. Relationships are effective only if the individual perceives that the other party is interested in him as a human being worthy of dignity and respect.

Explanations of routines, procedures, and events should be given according to the patient's level of understanding. Patients should be told that their feelings can be expressed and that they will be heard. Often, having patients participate in group sessions is of therapeutic value (Figure 3-1). Mentally ill patients are usually anxious and should be treated with understanding and consistency. They should be offered reassurance for improvement in behavior, but false beliefs should not be supported. Any restrictions on behavior should be consistently enforced. By adhering to these principles, a stable, supportive atmosphere conducive to mental health can be created.

PSYCHOPHARMACOLOGY

The use of medication to treat mental illness has revolutionized the field of psychiatry. Before the 1950s, when the major tranquilizers were discovered, patients often spent their entire lives in various institutions. The medication in itself does not necessarily cure the patient but often lessens symptoms sufficiently to allow the patient to participate more easily in other forms of treatment and to function more effectively in the community. The patient may then be counseled in various community-based mental health centers rather than in an institutionalized setting.

Drugs that affect behavior are called *psychotropic* drugs. The two major drug groups in this category are the *tranquilizers* and the *antidepressants*. Tranquilizers affect the behavioral and the emotional tone of feeling (affect) of the individual. Antidepressants have a stimulating and energy-producing action that is particularly helpful in the treatment of depressive states.[11] A summary of selected psychotropic drugs is found in Table 3-6.

PSYCHOLOGIC TREATMENT METHODS

There are many kinds of psychologic illnesses. Some, such as manic-depressive illness, are treated by medication alone. It is very important that manic-depressive patients continue taking their medication, even if they feel well. It is easy for such patients to believe that they no longer need medication, to stop taking it, and to become psychotic again. Other methods of treatment include individual psychotherapy, couple or relationship psychotherapy, family psychotherapy,

Table 3-6

Selected Psychotropic Drugs

Category	Action	Side effects
Major tranquilizers *Phenothiazines* Prochlorperazine (Compazine) Triflupromazine hydrochloride (Vesprin) Thioridazine hydrochloride (Mellaril) Fluphenazine dihydrochloride (Prolixin, Permitil) Trifluoperazine (Stelazine) Chlorpromazine hydrochloride (Thorazine	Lessen psychotic process; called tranquilizers but do not tranquilize—they normalize; may reduce hallucinations; may help withdrawn persons become more active; may help calm wildly excited persons	May cause fatigue, orthostatic hypotension, depression, extrapyramidal side effects, dry mouth, agranulocytosis, sensitivity to light, menstrual irregularities; some may cause sexual dysfunction
Butyrophenones Haloperidol (Haldol)	Used especially for severe schizophrenic psychosis	
Rauwolfia alkaloids Reserpine (Serpasil)		
Lithium carbonate (Lithane, Eskalith, Lithonate)	Appears to have preventive action, particularly in bipolar disorder; first used to treat manic phase only, now used for both manic and depressive phases to stabilize behavior; some recent use with major depression (non-bipolar) Takes 1-3 weeks to become effective	Drowsiness, polyuria, polydipsia, nausea, loose stools; lithium intoxication as evidenced by ataxia, giddiness, tinnitus, tremor, vertigo, slurred speech, confusion, seizures; may advance to coma, arrhythmia, circulatory collapse Blood levels of this medication must be carefully monitored
Minor tranquilizers *Benzodiazepines* Alprazolam (Xanax) Lorazepam (Ativan) Chlordiazepoxide hydrochloride (Librium) Diazepam (Valium)	Help lessen mild anxiety states; useful in neuroses	Sedation, blurred vision, constipation, physical dependence, liver complications, decreased sexual desire May potentiate other CNS depressants and meperidine (Demerol); possible addictive effects Valium is addictive
Diphenylmethanes Hydroxyzine hydrochloride (Atarax) Hydroxyzine pamoate (Vistaril)		
Propanedols Meprobamate (Miltown, Equanil)		
Barbiturates Phenobarbital (Luminal)		
Antidepressants *Tricyclics* Amitriptyline hydrochloride (Elavil) Desipramine hydrochloride (Pertofrane, Norpramin) Imipramine hydrochloride (Tofranil) Nortriptyline hydrochloride (Aventyl)	To alleviate severe, chronic depression	Drowsiness, fatigue, dry mouth, constipation, tachycardia, orthostatic hypotension, impotence, headaches, tremors, delayed ejaculation

Continued.

Table 3-6

Selected Psychotropic Drugs—cont'd		
Category	**Action**	**Side effects**
Bicyclic Fluoxetine hydrochloride (Prozac)	To alleviate severe, chronic depression	Drowsiness, fatigue, dry mouth, constipation, tachycardia, orthostatic hypotension, impotence, headaches, tremors, delayed ejaculation
Monoamine oxidase inhibitors (MAO inhibitors) Isocarboxazid (Marplan) Phenelzine dihydrogen sulfate (Nardil)	Increase sympathetic tone of hypothalamus; increase alert behavior and appetite; take 1-2 weeks to be effective	Hypertensive crisis, especially after ingesting foods containing tyramine or tyrosine: cheese, bananas, avocados, beer, Chianti wine, excessive caffeine, chocolate, yogurt, chicken liver, yeast products, pickled herring, pickles, sauerkraut, raisins, and others; also medication containing vasopressors

and group psychotherapy. Group therapy is the treatment of choice for substance abusers, victims of family violence, adult children of alcoholics, persons with AIDS, and persons suffering from other terminal, life-threatening, or chronic illnesses.

Therapeutic approaches may entail crisis intervention, which helps an individual or family manage a current situation in which previously used coping mechanisms have failed; short-term psychotherapy, in which a person undergoes 8 to 10 weeks of psychotherapy to resolve an ongoing problem; or long-term psychotherapy, whose goal is to treat a long-standing personality disorder.

Once a very common treatment, electroconvulsive (shock) therapy is now administered very rarely and only to severely depressed patients. The shock wave causes grand mal seizures.

The goal of all treatment is to help people relieve their symptoms and to learn new behaviors and different ways of relating to others. Some forms of psychotherapy can also help people to understand themselves better.

REFERENCES AND ADDITIONAL READINGS

1. Acee AM and Smith D: Crack, Am J Nurs 87:614-617, 1987.
2. Adams F: Drug dependency in hospital patients, Am J Nurs 88:477-481, 1988.
3. Bennett G, Uourakis C, and Woolf D: Substance abuse: pharmacologic, developmental and clinical perspectives, New York, 1983, John Wiley & Sons Inc.
4. Berne E: Transactional analysis in psychotherapy, New York, 1961, Grove Press Inc.
5. Carroll BJ and others: A specific laboratory test for the diagnosis of melancholia: standardization, validation and clinical utility, Arch Gen Psychiatry 81(38):15-22, 1981.
6. Castner E: Dealing with the difficult patient, J Pract Nurs 32(5):30, 1982.
7. Cohn L: The hospitalized alcoholic: the hidden diagnosis, Am J Nurs 82:1861-1879, 1982.
8. DeGennaro MS and others: Psychotropic drug therapy, Am J Nurs 81(7):1303-1334, 1981.
9. Glasser W: Mental health or illness, psychiatry for practical action, New York, 1970, Harper & Row, Publishers Inc.
10. Goulding, MM and Goulding RL: Changing lives through redecision therapy, New York, 1979, Brunner/Mazel Inc.
11. Hahn AB, Barkin RL, and Oestreich SJK: Pharmacology in nursing, ed 16, St Louis, 1986, Mosby—Yearbook Inc.
12. Maslow AH and Mittelman B: Principles of abnormal psychology, New York, 1951, Harper & Row, Publishers Inc.
13. Minion B: Truly caring for the patient who is an alcoholic, Nurs 85(15):55-56, 1985.
14. Mittleman HS, Mittleman RE, and Elser B: Cocaine, Am J Nurs 84:1092-1095, 1984.
15. Morgan AJ and Johnston MK: Mental health and mental

illness, ed 2, Philadelphia, 1976, JB Lippincott Co.

16. Pasquali EA and others: Mental health nursing: a holistic approach, St Louis, 1985, The CV Mosby Co.

17. Powell AH and Minick MP: Alcohol withdrawal syndrome, Am J Nurs 88 3:312-315, 1988.

18. Rogers C: On becoming a person—a therapist's view of psychotherapy, Boston, 1961, Houghton Mifflin Co.

19. Schuckit MA: Drug and alcohol abuse: a clinical guide to diagnosis and treatment, ed 3, New York, 1989, Plenum Publishing Corp.

20. Taylor CM: Mereness' essentials of psychiatric nursing, ed 12, St Louis, 1986, The CV Mosby Co.

21. Vandergaer F: Cocaine: the deadliest addiction, Nurs 89 19:72-73, 1989.

PART TWO

Caring for the Patient

with General

Manifestations

of Illness

CHAPTER 4   *Fluid and Electrolyte Imbalances*

5   *Preoperative and Postoperative Care*

6   *The Patient with Pain*

7   *Community-Acquired Infections*

8   *Nosocomial Infections*

9   *The Patient with Cancer*

10   *Death and the Dying Patient*

11   *The Geriatric Patient*

12   *Rehabilitation*

13   *Long-Term Care*

14   *Home Health Care*

Fluid and Electrolyte Imbalances

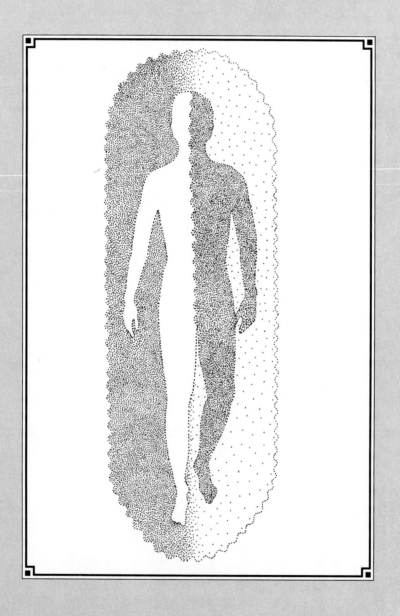

KEY WORDS

acidosis
alkalosis
anion
cardiogenic shock
cation
diffusion
disseminated intravascular coagulation
electrolyte
filtration
hypercalcemia
hyperchloremia
hypochloremia
hyperkalemia
hypernatremia
hypertonic (hyperosmolar)
hypervolemia
hypocalcemia
hypokalemia
hyponatremia
hypotonic (hypoosmolar)
hypovolemia
ionize
isotonic (isosmolar)
neurogenic shock
normovolemic shock
osmolarity
osmosis
vasogenic shock

OBJECTIVES

1. Define the components of body fluid.
2. Differentiate between intracellular and extracellular fluid.
3. Identify the major ways fluids are gained and lost from the body.
4. Explain the processes involved in fluid and electrolyte exchange throughout the body.
5. Identify the symptoms of the primary fluid and electrolyte imbalances.
6. Discuss the causes of acid base imbalance and describe the symptoms of acidosis and alkalosis.
7. Interpret blood gas values to determine types of acid base imbalance and the manifestations of each.
8. State the primary nursing responsibilities in maintaining intravenous therapy.
9. Differentiate between the major types of shock according to cause.
10. Identify goals of drug therapy in the major types of shock.
11. Outline the nursing management of the patient in shock.

THE NATURE OF BODY FLUID

Body fluids are essential to every one of the billions of cells that make up our bodies. Our body cells have been compared to the first cells that developed millions of years ago in ancient seas. Ancient cells used the ocean as a source for all their nutrients and as a means for carrying away discharged wastes. The cells in our bodies also receive nutrients and discharge wastes into the environment, but the fluid is trapped beneath our skin and volume and chemical composition are regulated precisely by intricate and complicated homeostatic mechanisms. It is believed that our body fluids today resemble ancient seas; oceans today have become more concentrated from dissolved substances from land.

Water is the *solvent* of the body, the liquid in which other substances such as electrolytes are dissolved. Although our bodies appear solid, approximately two thirds is liquid. About 75% of an infant's body weight is water, whereas average adult men have about 60% and women about 50% water in their bodies. The percentage of body weight that is water decreases with age. Obese individuals have a smaller percentage of body weight in water because fat contains little water. Therefore, the obese and the aged are at greater risk in situations involving fluid loss because they have reduced fluid reserves. Infants and very young children are at great risk because they have a higher ratio of body surface to body weight, immature kidneys that are less able to reabsorb water when necessary, and a higher percentage of fluid in the interstitial space where it is more readily lost from the body. Three fourths of the total amount of body fluid is located within the body cells as *intracellular fluid*. The remainder of the fluid is located outside the body cells as *extracellular fluid*. Approximately one fourth of the extracellular fluid is plasma or *intravascular fluid*, and three fourths is *interstitial fluid*. Intravascular fluid is in the circulating blood. Interstitial fluid is composed of the fluid in the spaces between cells, lymph, and fluids located in special areas of the body. Intraocular fluid, cerebrospinal fluid, gastrointestinal tract fluids, and fluids within body organs are considered interstitial fluid. It is the extracellular fluid that maintains the proper environment for cellular life. It supplies food, oxygen, water, vitamins, and electrolytes and carries away wastes. To maintain health, the extracellular fluid must be constantly monitored and controlled by sensitive homeostatic mechanisms for appropriate volume and chemical composition.

Substances that are dissolved in body fluids are called *solutes*. The solutes are electrolytes and nonelectrolytes. *Electrolytes* separate into particles that develop an electric charge when placed in water. For instance, salt (NaCl), when placed in water, will break up or **ionize** into sodium (Na^+) and chloride (Cl^-). **Cations** are positively charged ions, and **anions** are negatively charged ions. The principal ions in the body are listed in Table 4-1. Oppositely charged ions attract each other, and like charges repel each other. All of the electrolytes are found inside and outside the cell. However, extracellular fluid contains large amounts of sodium, chloride, and bicarbonate ions. Intracellular fluid contains large amounts of potassium, sulfate, phosphate, and protein ions. Normally the total number of positive and negative charges are equal on both sides of the cell membrane. It is helpful to know what electrolytes are found in body fluids in order to anticipate and prevent their depletion. For example, gastric secretions have a high concentration of hydrogen ions, and pancreatic secretions contain high bicarbonate concentrations. Sodium is abundant in gastric and pancreatic secretions and bile. Nonelectrolytes are compounds that do not separate into charged particles when dissolved in water. Glucose is a nonelectrolyte.

Gains and Losses

Fluid and solutes, including electrolytes are gained primarily through intake of food and water. A small amount of water is also gained as a by-product of the metabolism of carbohydrates, fats, and proteins to produce energy for body functions. Normally fluid gains approximately equal fluid losses. For example, the daily urinary output is about equal to the daily fluid intake, and the amount of water derived from solid foods plus metabolic processes approximates water lost via the lungs, stool, and skin (insensible loss). Patients can gain water and solutes from the use of nasogastric tubes, rectal tubes, and intravenous therapy. In renal failure, fluid gain is not compensated for by fluid loss.

Fluid and electrolyte deficits are common because of the many abnormal states that contribute to fluid loss. Water and electrolyte loss occurs normally through the processes of respiration, urination, perspiration, lacrimation (crying), and

Table 4-1

Normal Electrolyte Content of Body Fluids

Electrolytes (anions and cations)	Extracellular*		Intracellular (mEq/L)
	Intravascular (mEq/L)	Interstitial (mEq/L)	
Sodium (Na$^+$)	135-145	146	15-20
Potassium (K$^+$)	3.5-5.0	5	150-155
Calcium (Ca^{++})	4.5-5.5	3	1-2
Magnesium (Mg^{++})	1.5-2.5	1	27-29
Chloride (Cl$^-$)	96-106	114	1-4
Bicarbonate (HCO$_3^-$)	22-26	30	10-12
Protein (Prot$^-$)	16	1	63
Phosphate (HPO$_4^=$)	1.7-4.6	2	100-104
Sulfate (SO$_4^=$)	1	1	20
Organic acids	5	8	0

*Note that the electrolyte level of the intravascular and interstitial (extracellular) fluids is approximately the same and that sodium and chloride contents are markedly higher in these fluids, whereas potassium, phosphate, and protein contents are markedly higher in intracellular fluid.

Modified from Phipps WJ, Long BC, and Woods NF: Medical-surgical nursing, St Louis, 1987, The CV Mosby Co.

defecation. Abnormal conditions that result in loss of fluid and electrolytes include burns, wound drainage, hemorrhage, vomiting, and diarrhea. Therefore in illness, gains and losses are not always equal. Abnormal losses will accumulate as the days pass and may cause serious illness.

FLUID AND ELECTROLYTE EXCHANGE

Fluids and electrolytes move throughout the body by passive and active transport systems. Passive transport of fluid and electrolytes occurs through the processes of **diffusion** or concentration differences, **filtration** or pressure differences, and **osmosis,** which is diffusion of water molecules.

Diffusion is based on the principle that molecules and ions will flow from an area of higher concentration through a semi-permeable membrane, to an area of lower concentration or from where there is more of the substance to where there is less. Diffusion of a solute in one direction and of water in the opposite direction results in an equilibrated state. Diffusion, as it relates to body functions, occurs in such fluids as the interstitial fluid or blood plasma.

Filtration is the movement of fluid and electrolytes by the pressure or force that is exerted as a result of the weight of the solution. Movement occurs from an area of higher pressure to an area of lower pressure.

Osmosis is the diffusion of water through a semipermeable membrane—a membrane such as a cell membrane that allows only particles of a certain size to pass through. When solutions of different concentrations exist, one on each side of the semipermeable membrane, water will pass through the semipermeable membrane from the weaker solution to the more concentrated solution in an attempt to equalize the strength of the solutions on each side of the membrane. Healthy cell membranes preserve a relatively low intracellular sodium concentration in comparison to the interstitial fluid. However, the intracellular potassium level is higher than interstitial potassium levels. Figure 4-1 illustrates the process of osmosis where water molecules move toward the higher concentration of solute particles.

Osmosis through semipermeable membrane.

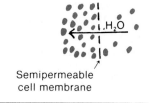

Semipermeable
cell membrane

Figure 4-1

Osmosis through semipermeable membrane.

Diffusion, filtration, and osmosis are passive transport systems. Water and electrolytes continually move between the intravascular fluid, interstitial fluid, and intracellular fluid by all of these processes. Any change in the composition of one fluid is quickly reflected in changes in the others.

Some substances can also be moved through semipermeable membranes through an active transport system. In this process, energy is needed to move molecules, or ions, from an area of low concentration to an area of high concentration. The majority of sodium in body fluids remains outside the cells, and the majority of potassium remains inside the cells as a result of this process.

Fluid and electrolyte balance is also maintained by three hormones: the *antidiuretic hormone (ADH), aldosterone,* and *parathormone.* ADH acts on the renal tubules to retain water and decrease urinary output. ADH is produced in the hypothalamus, is stored and released from the posterior pituitary gland. Aldosterone is secreted by the adrenal cortex. Aldosterone increases sodium and water reabsorption, while increasing potassium excretion in the renal tubules. The reabsorption of water and sodium results in increased circulatory volume. Parathormone is produced by the parathyroid glands. It promotes the absorption of calcium from the intestine, the release of calcium from the bones (bone resorption) and the excretion of phosphate ions by the kidneys.

The composition of the fluids in our bodies is considered to be **isotonic** or **isosmolar.** Fluids that are increased in strength (high concentration) are considered to be hypertonic or hyperosmolar, and fluids that are decreased in strength (low concentration) are **hypotonic** or **hypoosmolar.** Body fluids and fluids used in intravenous therapy are categorized according to the strength of their composition, or tonicity (osmolarity; Table 4-2). Isotonic solutions have the same tonicity as plasma. No osmosis will occur between two isotonic solutions when the two solutions are separated by a membrane, such as a cell membrane. Hypertonic solutions are stronger than isotonic solutions because they have more solutes per unit volume dissolved in them. Hypotonic solutions, on the other hand, are weaker than either isotonic or hypertonic solutions. For example, 0.45% sodium chloride (0.45% NaCl) is hypotonic to the same amount of 0.9% sodium chloride (0.9% NaCl) because it contains one half the amount of sodium chloride dissolved within it.

The differences in strengths of solutions cause movement of substances throughout the body. For example, if a hypertonic fluid is introduced into the intravascular fluid, such as can occur with some intravenous solutions, its increased concentration will quickly be equalized by diffusion into the interstitial space or cells. If the particles in the hypertonic solution cannot pass through semipermeable membranes, water will enter the vascular system by osmosis. These processes occur constantly to maintain the correct volume and concentration of body fluids.

FLUID AND ELECTROLYTE IMBALANCES

Fluid and electrolyte imbalances occur when the homeostatic mechanisms that normally control volume and concentration are ineffective. Disturbances can be primary, when the cause is directly related to the amount of fluid or electrolyte. For instance, a large amount of salt intake over a short time can result in sodium excess. Disturbances can also be of a secondary nature, when other pathologic processes in the body contribute to fluid and electrolyte imbalances. Body fluid disturbances accompany many illnesses. Every patient is a potential victim.

To provide a basis for the understanding of these processes, the most important and most common imbalances will be presented separately. It must be remembered, however, that because of the intricate and interacting nature of the mechanisms that control the body fluid composition, usually several types of imbalances occur at one time. Also, since intracellular fluid is inaccessible for analysis, fluid and electrolyte imbalances are determined by examination of the extracellular fluid. The effects of a change in one fluid compartment are rapidly transmitted to the others; therefore the extracellular fluid accurately reflects the state of all fluids throughout the body.

Extracellular Fluid Volume Imbalances

Volume disturbances of the extracellular fluid—the plasma and interstitial fluid—can be classified as a volume deficit or as a volume excess.

Extracellular fluid deficit

Isotonic extracellular fluid deficit, or **hypovolemia,** occurs when both water and electrolytes either have been lost from the body or trapped in an area of the body in such a way as to be unavailable to the circulation, which is also known

Table 4-2

Fluids Used in Intravenous Therapy			
Fluid	Hypertonic solutions	Isotonic solutions	Hypotonic solutions
Dextrose in water	10% dextrose in water 20% dextrose in water 50% dextrose in water	5% dextrose in water	
Dextrose in saline	5% dextrose and 0.45% sodium chloride 5% dextrose and 0.9% sodium chloride 10% dextrose and 0.9% sodium chloride	5% dextrose and 0.2% sodium chloride	
Saline	3% sodium chloride	0.9% sodium chloride	0.45% sodium chloride
Multiple electrolytes	5% dextrose in lactated Ringer's solution 10% dextrose in lactated Ringer's solution	Ringer's solution Lactated Ringer's solution	
Plasma substitutes		10% dextran 40 in 5% dextrose 10% dextran 40 in 0.9% sodium chloride	
Alcohol	5% alcohol in 5% dextrose		
Amino acids	8% amino acids		
Fat emulsions		Intralipid or Liposyn 10%	

as *third spacing.* Fluid accumulation at the site of burns or massive soft tissue injury, the collection of fluid in the peritoneal cavity (ascites) and shifts of fluid from the intravascular to the interstitial and intra-cellular spaces after abdominal and chest surgery are examples of third spacing.

Hypovolemia occurs with any abrupt decrease in fluid intake, acute loss of secretions or excretions, or a sudden shift of fluid to the interstitial space. Often it results from a combination of these forces. The most common cause of extracellular fluid deficit is loss of fluids through the gastrointestinal tract by vomiting and diarrhea. Other examples of conditions leading to hypovolemia include intestinal obstruction, peritonitis, fistulous drainage, and acute pancreatitis.

No specific laboratory tests indicate that a fluid deficit is occurring; however, the patient's signs and symptoms plus results from other more nonspecific laboratory tests can indicate that the condition is developing. The extracellular fluid deficit can result in an acute weight loss, often in excess of 5% of body weight, decreased body temperature, low blood pressure, increased respiratory rate, delayed vein filling, anorexia, nausea, vomiting, and shock. *Oliguria,* a urinary output below 20 ml in 1 hour or 480 ml in 24 hours, can occur in severe cases. Treatment involves cor-

recting the cause of the deficit and replacing the fluid with oral or parenteral solutions that have a normal balance of water and electrolytes. Nursing intervention for the patient with an isotonic extracellular fluid deficit is presented in Table 4-3.

Hypertonic fluid deficit

When body water loss exceeds electrolyte loss, the remaining fluid is **hypertonic.** Water moves out of the cell to dilute the extracellular fluid and dehydration results. The thirst response is triggered by the hypertonic extracellular fluid. The skin is flushed, the skin and mucous membranes are dry, skin turgor is poor, producing a "tenting" effect when grasped between two fingers, and body temperature increases (Table 4-3). This is also known as *dehydration.*

In either type of extracellular fluid deficit, the components of the blood are more concentrated from the fluid loss, therefore the hematocrit and hemoglobin values and red blood cell count are elevated.

Extracellular fluid excess

When there is an excess of water and electrolytes in the extracellular fluid, a state of **hypervolemia** exists. This commonly occurs when the kidneys

Table 4-3

Extracellular Fluid Deficit

Signs and symptoms	Nursing interventions	Expected outcomes
Isotonic deficit: hypovolemia	Monitor administration of oral and IV fluids	Correction of fluid deficit
Decreased temperature	Monitor vital signs	Increased hydration
Low blood pressure	Observe for signs of shock	Shock prevented
Tachycardia	Record body weight daily	Progressive weight loss prevented
Weak pulse	Observe skin turgor	Skin elastic
Increased respiration	Maintain accurate intake and output records	Renal function maintained—output 30 cc/hr
Delayed vein filling		
Cold extremities	Observe for oliguria	
Weakness	Monitor and communicate laboratory results	Therapy modified accordingly
Weight loss		
Nausea and vomiting	Observe fluid accumulation in "third spaces"	Fluid remobilized
Anorexia		
Decreased urinary output		
Shock		
Increased hematocrit and hemoglobin values and red blood cell count		
Hypertonic deficit: dehydration		
Thirst		
Skin flushed		
Dry skin		
Skin turgor—nonelastic (tenting)		
Increased body temperature		
Increased hematocrit and hemoglobin values and red blood cell count		

are not functioning properly or intravenous solutions are administered too rapidly. Congestive heart failure and malnutrition can also result in retention of water and electrolytes.

There are no specific tests that indicate excess of extracellular fluid; however, the hematocrit and hemoglobin values and red blood cell count may be decreased as a result of the dilution effect of the excess fluid. Patients will most commonly display symptoms of pitting edema, dyspnea, hoarseness, a bounding pulse, acute weight gain, puffy eyelids, and engorgement of peripheral veins. All symptoms are caused by the accumulation of excess fluids throughout the body. The treatment for isotonic extracellular fluid excess involves correction of the underlying cause, withholding fluids, restricting sodium intake, and administration of diuretics. Nursing intervention is presented in Table 4-4.

Water intoxication. An excess of body water that occurs without excess electrolyte levels is called water intoxication. The extracellular fluid will be hypotonic and water will move into the cells, causing the cells to swell. This results in behavior changes, confusion, incoordination, a sudden weight gain, warm moist skin, lethargy, and convulsions.

Pathophysiology of fluid shifts. *Edema* is the accumulation of fluid in the interstitial spaces. Cells are normally held closely together to facilitate the exchange of gases, nutrients, and waste products between the cells and capillaries. Excess fluid is normally removed by direct return to the capillaries or through the lymph system to maintain a negative interstitial fluid pressure. If excess fluid is not removed, a positive pressure develops, pushing the cells apart.

The pathophysiology of edema can be explained by reviewing normal capillary dynamics. Fluid leaves the capillary to nourish the cell, because fluid pressure is greater in the capillary than it is in the interstitial space. The pressure is also greater on the arterial side of the capillary. Proteins act as colloids, which means they are too

Table 4-4

Extracellular Fluid Excess: Hypervolemia (Isotonic Fluid Excess)

Signs and symptoms	Nursing interventions	Expected outcomes
Acute weight gain	Record body weight daily Maintain accurate intake and out-put records	Fluid accumulation prevented—normal weight maintained
Decreased hemoglobin and hematocrit values, and red blood cell count	Monitor and communicate labora-tory results	
Skin warm, moist Pitting edema Puffy eyelids	Observe and document skin integ-rity	
Bounding pulse Engorged peripheral veins	Monitor vital signs	Vital signs within normal limits
Dyspnea Hoarseness	Observe for pulmonary edema Restrict fluids and sodium as or-dered	Adequate oxygenation
Moist rales in lungs Cyanosis Cardiac enlargement	Administer medications as ordered	

large to pass through the semipermeable membrane of the capillary. Proteins remain in the plasma and the protein within the capillary is greater than the protein in the interstitial fluid. This creates a colloidal osmostic pressure that causes reabsorption of fluid from the interstitial space, thus returning the fluid to the capillary. The lower fluid pressure on the venous end of the capillary also facilitates fluid return to the intravascular space. Pressures that move fluid out of the capillary are greatest at the arteriole end, whereas pressures that promote fluid movement back into the capillary are greatest at the venule end. This concept is known as *Starling's law* (Figure 4-2). Edema can therefore be caused by an increase in capillary fluid pressure, a decrease in colloidal osmotic pressure in the capillary, or an increase in interstitial colloidal osmotic pressure.

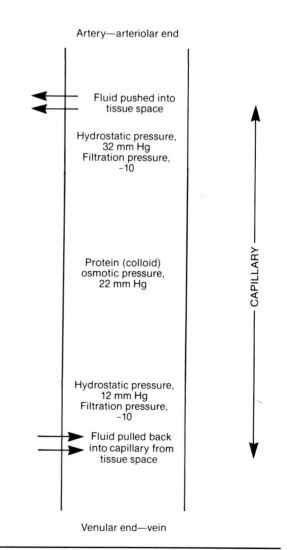

Figure 4-2

Control of fluid movement from intravascular to interstitial space and return to intravascular space. HP, hydrostatic pressure: pressure of blood against blood vessel walls. COP, colloid osmotic pressure: osmotic pressure exerted by plasma proteins, mainly albumin. FP, filtration pressure: equals HP minus COP; FP may be positive or negative.

Artery—arteriolar end

Fluid pushed into tissue space

Hydrostatic pressure, 32 mm Hg
Filtration pressure, −10

Protein (colloid) osmotic pressure, 22 mm Hg

Hydrostatic pressure, 12 mm Hg
Filtration pressure, −10

Fluid pulled back into capillary from tissue space

CAPILLARY

Venular end—vein

Fluid that shifts in this manner and is unavailable to the circulation is an example of third spacing. It can occur after burns and traumatic injury to tissue and can also be seen after abdominal and thoracic surgery. Tissue injury results in increased capillary membrane permeability, allowing fluid and albumin to leave the capillary and enter the interstitial space. This reduces plasma colloid osmotic pressure and increases colloid osmotic pressure in the interstitial space, pulling greater amounts of fluid into the interstitial space and depleting circulating volume. The patient will require fluid replacement and may need albumin to restore plasma colloid osmotic pressure. In the burned patient a normal reabsorption will take place in 48 to 72 hours. The capillaries begin to heal and plasma proteins are replaced or reabsorbed through the lymphatic system. This will cause fluid to be drawn back into the plasma and hypervolemia could result if the return is too rapid. Diuretics will be administered if fluid volume becomes excessive.[27]

Extracellular Fluid Composition Imbalances

Each of the electrolytes in the body fluid has special functions, and illness will result if the normal composition of the extracellular fluid is altered. There are two basic ways by which changes in concentration of electrolytes can be produced: (1) by altering the total quantity of the electrolyte in the body, and (2) by altering the total quantity of the water in the extracellular fluid in which the electrolyte is dissolved. For example, an excess of sodium can be caused by an increased intake of sodium, decreased output of sodium, decreased intake of water, or increased output of water. Most often a combination of these factors produces the imbalance. This principle applies to all of the extracellular electrolytes.

Sodium

Sodium is the chief cation of the extracellular fluid, accounting for 90% of all the extracellular positive ions. It is largely responsible for maintaining the proper relationships of body fluids by regulating fluid balance and osmotic pressure. It plays a vital role in numerous chemical reactions, stimulates nerve and muscle activity, assists in maintaining acid-base balance, and is necessary for kidney tubule function. A normal serum sodium level of 135 to 145 mEq/L and intracellular sodium concentrations of 10 mEq/L are necessary to balance body fluids. With an excess of sodium outside the cell or too little inside, water will leave the cell, causing it to shrink. If intracellular sodium increases or the amount outside the cell decreases (hyponatremia), water will move into the cell, causing it to swell. Both shrinking and swelling will disturb normal cellular activity in the central nervous system. The major role of sodium in neuromuscular transmission is demonstrated by the changes in muscle tone seen as early signs of abnormalities.

Sodium levels are controlled by the hormone aldosterone, which is secreted by the adrenal cortex when sodium levels are low. Aldosterone stimulates the renal tubules to reabsorb more of the sodium, which would otherwise pass out of the body in urine. Once the normal levels of sodium are reached, the secretion of aldosterone decreases. In this way the concentration of sodium is maintained within narrow limits.

Sodium deficit. When a sodium deficit occurs and the serum sodium concentration falls below normal levels, the condition is called **hyponatremia.** It is usually caused by excessive perspiration associated with the drinking of plain water, losses from the gastrointestinal tract because of (or related to) vomiting, diarrhea, or nasogastric suction, or administration of a potent diuretic. Too much salt is lost or the intake of water is excessive.

Sodium deficit can also be caused by adrenal insufficiency. The adrenals secrete aldosterone, which triggers retention of sodium by the kidneys when sodium levels fall. Without sufficient aldosterone, the patient fails to retain sodium. Dilutional hyponatremia can occur with fluid overload caused by congestive heart failure and cirrhosis of the liver or by the administration of excessive hypotonic intravenous solutions.

In a sodium deficit there are too few particles in relation to the amount of water present. The extracellular fluid is therefore hypoosmolar or hypotonic. The water moves into the interstitial spaces and the cells by osmosis in an attempt to create equilibrium. As a result the cells become swollen and cause neuromuscular irritability, producing symptoms of anorexia, restlessness, twitching, muscle cramps, weakness, irritability, mental disturbances, confusion, disorientation, convulsions, and coma. Treatment usually includes the administration of normal saline or, in severe deficit, 3% or 5% hypertonic saline solution if the kidneys are healthy. Hypertonic solutions must be administered slowly to prevent pulmonary edema. The nurse's responsibility in the management of the patient with a sodium deficit is summarized in Table 4-5.

Table 4-5

Sodium Deficit: Hyponatremia		
Signs and symptoms	**Nursing interventions**	**Expected outcomes**
Plasma sodium less than 130 mEq/L	Encourage diet high in sodium if ordered	Serum sodium level increased and within normal limits
Anorexia	Weigh daily	Early symptoms observed
Weakness	Monitor neurologic status	More severe symptoms prevented
Restlessness	Monitor vital signs	Renal compensation for low se-
Headache	Monitor administration of IV fluids	rum sodium level determined
Irritability	Monitor serum electrolyte levels as ordered every 2 to 4 hours	Volume overload prevented
Twitching	Maintain accurate intake and output records	Patient safety maintained
Muscle cramps	Observe for a change in status	Airway maintained
Abdominal cramps	Pad side rails of bed	
Confusion	Place head in lateral position if seizure occurs	
Disorientation		
Convulsions		
Coma		

If sodium is lost in equal proportions with water, the extracellular fluid remains isotonic but its volume is decreased. Serum sodium levels will be normal and the patient's symptoms will be those related to circulatory collapse caused by decreased extracellular fluid volume. Isotonic fluids are administered to replace fluid and electrolytes. When hyponatremia is caused by retention of water, treatment involves fluid restriction rather than sodium administration.

Sodium excess. Hypernatremia results when there is an excess of sodium in the serum. It can occur in any condition in which fluids that contain little sodium are lost, such as the losses accompanying profuse watery diarrhea. When the water in the plasma is decreased, the electrolyte readings will increase even though the total amount of the electrolyte in the body has not changed. Because sodium is the most abundant electrolyte, it will show the earliest changes.

When a large amount of salt is ingested over a short time, acute sodium excess can occur. Following the laws of osmosis, water from the cells will flow into a more concentrated extracellular fluid. This will help dilute the extracellular fluid but will leave the cells in need of water. Symptoms will be those of dehydration: dry mucous membranes, dry tongue, fever, thirst, flushed appearance, weakness, and irritability. Shallow rapid breathing, fluttering eyelids, and muscle spasm leading to stupor, seizures, and coma can follow. Laboratory data will indicate increased levels of plasma sodium and chloride and the specific grav-

ity of urine will be elevated. Hypernatremia occurs in victims of salt-water drowning, renal disease, and hyperaldosteronism, which results in reabsorption of too much sodium by the kidney. Normal sodium levels are restored by infusing hypotonic saline solutions, administration of furosemide (Lasix) or hydrochlorothiazide (Hydrodiuril) to promote sodium excretion, and by dietary restriction of sodium. Nursing intervention is outlined in Table 4-6.

When sodium is gained over a longer period of time, water is also retained. Sodium and water increase together in similar proportions so serum sodium levels will be within normal limits. Because the extracellular fluid remains isotonic, the cells of the body do not swell or shrink and there are no symptoms of cerebral irritability or depression. The result of this isotonic imbalance is increased volume of extracellular fluid, causing edema and circulatory overload.

Potassium

Potassium (K+) is the major intracellular cation. It is responsible for intracellular fluid balance, a regular heart rhythm, conduction of neuromuscular impulses, conversion of glucose to energy in the cell, protein synthesis, and regulation of acid-base balance. Potassium affects acid-base balance because it acts as part of the body's buffer system. If the body becomes acidotic, hydrogen ions move into the cell to reduce their number in the extracellular fluid. As hydrogen enters the cell, potassium exits in exchange for hydrogen

Table 4-6

Sodium Excess: Hypernatremia		
Signs and symptoms	Nursing interventions	Expected outcomes
Plasma sodium more than 150 mEq/L	Encourage low-sodium diet if ordered	Serum sodium levels decreased
Dry and sticky mucous membranes		
Dry tongue		
Fever	Monitor vital signs	Normal temperature maintained
Flushed appearance		
Thirst	Maintain accurate intake and output records	Deficit of water corrected
Elevated temperature	Weigh daily	
Oliguria	Monitor administration of IV fluids	Rapid correction avoided
Weakness	Observe for fluid volume changes	Efficacy of treatment determined
Irritability		
Disorientation		
Shallow, rapid breathing		
Fluttering eyelids		
Muscular spasm	Administer muscle relaxants and/or diuretics as ordered	Muscular spasms controlled
Seizures	Observe seizure precautions	
Stupor	Maintain life support systems during	
Coma	therapy	

ions, raising the serum level of potassium. This elevated serum potassium level is called a false positive because actual levels of potassium in the body have not changed. However, a serum potassium level above 5.5 mEq/L can cause toxic effects, regardless of the cause. In alkalosis the plasma is low in hydrogen ions so hydrogen leaves the cell and enters the plasma to compensate. Potassium then leaves the plasma and enters the cell and hypokalemia results. In these cases, the potassium imbalance is treated by correcting the acid or base imbalance.

Plasma potassium falls about 0.6 mEq/L for each 0.1 unit rise in blood pH. A level below 3 mEq/L is toxic. Plasma potassium increases about 0.6 mEq/L for each 0.1 unit fall in blood pH. A level above 5.5 mEq/L is toxic. The normal potassium range is 3.5 to 5.0 mEq/L.

Large amounts of potassium are found in secretions and excretions of the body, such as sweat, saliva, gastric juice, and the stool. There is no effective mechanism for conserving potassium as there is for sodium, and the body will continue to excrete potassium when the levels are already low.

Potassium deficit. Probably the most common cause of potassium deficit, or **hypokalemia,** in the United States is the use of diuretics without potassium supplementation. Loop and thiazide diuretics cause an increase in the excretion of potassium. Loop diuretics act by inhibiting the active reabsorption of chloride ions in the ascending limb of Henle's loop. Because chloride draws sodium with it, the reabsorption of sodium is also prevented. Thus, sodium chloride is retained in the tubule and excreted in urine, carrying water with it. Thiazide diuretics block sodium and chloride reabsorption in the distal convoluted tubule, resulting in increased excretion of sodium, chloride, and water. With both loop and thiazide diuretics, the high concentration of sodium in the distal convoluted tubule causes increased exchange of sodium and potassium, which in turn causes additional potassium to be pulled in and excreted.

Some diuretics are potassium sparing because they act in ways that do not cause potassium excretion. An example is spironolactone (Aldactone), which inhibits the action of aldosterone in the distal tubule. Aldosterone normally causes more sodium to be reabsorbed in the distal tubule. When its action is inhibited by aldactone, less sodium is reabsorbed and it is then excreted.

Other factors that contribute to potassium loss are insufficient potassium intake, gastrointestinal losses, inefficient gastrointestinal absorption, and

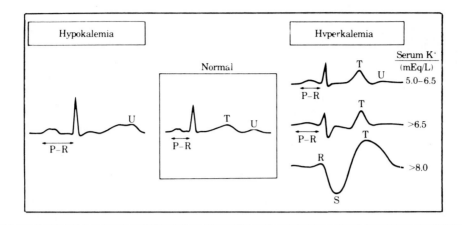

Figure 4-3

Altered cardiac conduction in hypokalemia and hyperkalemia. **A,** Normal electrocardiogram in adult. **B,** In hypokalemia T wave is flattened and U wave is prominent. **C,** In hyperkalemia, electrocardiogram changes do not always correspond to the serum potassium values given, but progression from minor to severe changes correlates to some degree with potassium level. With potassium concentration less than 6.5 mEq/L, early electrocardiogram abnormality is peaking or teneting of
T waves. The next change, shown with potassium concentration greater than 6.5, includes flattening of P wave, prolongation of P-R interval, and widening of QRS complex, with development of deep S wave. With severe hyperkalemia (8 mEq/ L), ventricular fibrillation or cardiac arrest is imminent. *(From Schrier R: Manual of nephrology, ed 2, Boston, 1985, Little, Brown & Co Inc.)*

abnormal losses of secretions and excretions from the body.

Many of the signs and symptoms of potassium deficit result from effects on the nervous and muscular systems. Skeletal muscle weakness and fatigue are common early complaints. The decreasing tone of the smooth muscle of the gastrointestinal tract can produce symptoms of anorexia, vomiting, distention, and possible paralytic ileus. Decreasing blood pressure, weak pulse, faint heart sounds, and paralysis of the respiratory muscles are later signs. Cardiac arrhythmias are common, and the electrocardiogram may show the T wave flattened and the presence of a U wave (Figure 4-3). Ventricular tachycardia and cardiac arrest may occur when the levels are very low. Hypokalemia causes the renal tubules to have a reduced ability to concentrate waste, resulting in an increased fluid loss in urinary output. Laboratory data show low potassium levels in plasma.

Oral administration of a solution of potassium salts or parenteral infusion of potassium chloride is used to treat potassium deficit. The potassium deficit should not be corrected rapidly, however, because of potassium's effect on the cardiac mus-cle. Too rapid a correction can also cause tetany. A diet high in potassium may be prescribed, for prevention or a mild deficit, including foods such as meat, fish, cereals, broccoli, and asparagus (see box page 80). The primary objective is to identify and treat the underlying pathologic process. Nursing responsibilities are outlined in Table 4-7.

Potassium excess. Hyperkalemia occurs most often when the kidneys are unable to excrete potassium adequately (renal failure). It can also occur soon after massive injury, such as burns and crushing injuries. Cellular destruction releases large amounts of intracellular potassium into the extracellular fluid. Severe infections and chemotherapy with cytotoxic drugs can also cause cellular destruction. The necrotic cells then release their intracellular potassium into the interstitial fluid. Administration of blood that is near its expiration date may also cause an excess of potassium resulting from the breakdown of old red blood cells. Acidosis will cause potassium to leave the cell and enter the extracellular fluid in exchange for hydrogen ions, resulting in an elevated serum potassium. Adrenal insufficiency and administration of intravenous potassium solutions too rapidly may result in potassium excess as well.

Table 4-7

Potassium Deficit: Hypokalemia

Signs and symptoms	Nursing interventions	Expected outcomes
Plasma potassium less than 3.5 mEq/L	Note serum potassium results Encourage diet high in potassium if indicated Monitor administration of replacement solutions	Potassium level will slowly return to normal
Muscular weakness Fatigue		

Electrocardiographic changes
    T wave flattened
    U wave present
	Monitor electrocardiogram results	Changes in heart rhythm secondary to decreased potassium detected at onset; cardiac arrest prevented

Anorexia Vomiting Distention Paralytic ileus	Monitor bowel sounds and palpate and measure abdomen for distension Maintain accurate intake and output records Observe for metabolic alkalosis (secondary to loss of acidic vomitus)	Absence of tingling and twitching; pH normal Bowel sounds present, all quadrants
Decreasing blood pressure Weak pulse Faint heart sounds Respiratory muscle paralysis	Monitor vital signs	Shock and respiratory arrest prevented

---

Sources of Potassium in Milligrams

Butternut squash, 1 cup baked, 1200
Lima beans, dry, 1 cup cooked, 1200
Spinach, 1 cup cooked, 1160
Black beans, 1 cup cooked, 1000
Soybeans, 1 cup cooked, 970
Pinto beans, 1 cup cooked, 940
Navy beans, 1 cup cooked, 790
Acorn squash, ¼ baked, 750
Green lima beans, 1 cup cooked, 720
Papaya, medium, 710
Cantaloupe, ½ medium, 680
Avocado, ½ medium, 650
Raisins, ½ cup, 650
Kidney beans, 1 cup cooked, 630
Chard, 1 cup cooked, 600

Prune juice, 1 cup, 600
Parsnips, 1 cup cooked, 590
Split peas, 1 cup cooked, 590
Blackstrap molasses, 1 tablespoon, 580
Dates, 10 medium, 520
Potato, 1 medium, cooked, 500
Orange juice, 1 cup, 500
Skim milk powder, ¼ cup, 490
Beet greens, 1 cup, 480
Banana, medium, 440
Low-fat milk, 1 cup, 430
Kohlrabi, 1 cup cooked, 430
Peas, fresh, 1 cup, 420
Brussels sprouts, 1 cup cooked, 420
Nectarine, medium, 410

Many of the early symptoms of potassium excess are nonspecific. Usually the electrocardiogram changes occur early, but the patient often is not monitored for these changes. Because potassium plays a major role in neuromuscular activity, muscle weakness is an early sign. Skeletal muscles will be weak and the patient may complain of muscle twitching. Facial and respiratory muscles may become involved and paresthesias of the face and tongue may develop. Gastrointestinal symptoms of nausea, diarrhea, and intestinal colic are also related to disturbed neuromuscular activity.

Flaccid paralysis may develop. The effect of a high potassium level on cardiac muscles is the most serious and can result in a dilated, flaccid heart. Bradycardia and dysrhythmias may lead to cardiac arrest. The conduction system of the heart is disturbed and ectopic beats are seen on the electrocardiogram. The electrocardiogram reveals tall peaked T waves, a shortened Q-T interval, and widening of the QRS complex (Figure 4-3). Laboratory data indicate levels of potassium in the plasma exceeding 5.5 mEq/L.

The treatment of potassium excess will vary according to the type and severity of the underlying problem. In mild cases potassium intake is avoided and any intravenous solutions should omit potassium. An ion-exchange resin, sodium polystyrene sulfonate (Kayexalate) can be used orally, rectally, or by nasogastric tube in the treatment of hyperkalemia. It will bind with potassium in the gastrointestinal tract, and then be eliminated. When given rectally, it is administered as a retention enema and retained for 30 to 60 minutes. A potassium-wasting diuretic such as furosemide (Lasix) will also bring down potassium levels.

If the condition is acute, 10 to 20 U of regular insulin is administered along with intravenous hypertonic dextrose solution (25% to 50%). As the dextrose accompanied by insulin enters the cell, potassium is carried along, thus lowering levels in the extracellular fluid. The effects are temporary, but it provides time so that the other measures can restore balance. Sodium bicarbonate may also be added to alkalinize the plasma. This causes hydrogen to enter the plasma from the cells in an attempt to restore acidity and potassium to leave the plasma and enter the cell in exchange for hydrogen, thus lowering serum potassium. Sodium bicarbonate also provides sodium, which antagonizes the effects of potassium on the myocardium. This effect too is only temporary.

Peritoneal dialysis and hemodialysis can also be used in emergencies. Because potassium has a depressant effect on cardiac muscle, in emergencies intravenous administration of calcium may be ordered to stimulate heart contraction by antagonizing the effects of excess potassium on heart muscle. However, calcium solutions for treatment of potassium excess should be used cautiously for the patient who is receiving digitalis preparations. Digitalis toxicity, which can cause severe visual, gastrointestinal, neuropsychologic, and cardiac disturbances, can result because calcium sensi-

tizes the heart to digitalis. Nursing interventions specific to the hyperkalemic patient are outlined in Table 4-8.

Calcium

Calcium is absorbed through the small intestine. Vitamin D is essential for the absorption of calcium. The majority of calcium in the body is stored in the teeth and bones. It is absorbed by the bones from the extracellular fluid (bone formation). It also flows from the bone back to the extracellular fluid (bone resorption) to be excreted. Although the normal levels of serum calcium are low it is an important ion for the transmission of nerve impulses. Intracellular calcium is essential for the contraction of muscle tissue; extracellular calcium is necessary for the blood clotting process and tooth and bone formation. It is needed for the absorption and utilization of vitamin B_{12} and is essential for maintaining a normal heart rhythm. Extracellular calcium stabilizes the cell membrane and blocks sodium transport into the cell, thus decreasing the excitability of the cell. A decreased serum calcium level will cause increased nerve and muscle cell excitability. Many enzyme systems are activated by calcium. Calcium levels are regulated by the parathyroid hormone. When serum calcium levels drop, the parathyroid gland increases secretion of the parathyroid hormone, which draws calcium from the bones to the circulating serum.

Laboratory tests can measure ionized serum calcium or total serum calcium. It is more difficult to measure ionized calcium so the routine test will measure total calcium. Total calcium is measured in milligrams and the normal level is 8.6 to 10.6 mg/dl. Ionized calcium is measured in milliequivalents and normal range is 4.5 to 5.5 mEq/L. Total calcium will include the calcium bound to albumin and other proteins, which is about 44% of the circulating calcium in the body. The remainder is ionized and that is the portion that is biologically active and can cause problems by being too high or too low. The amount of bound calcium decreases when serum albumin drops, causing a decrease in total serum calcium. Therefore a normal serum calcium level accompanied by low serum albumin is actually indicative of hypercalcemia because the ionized calcium now represents a higher percentage of the serum calcium. Conversely, a high albumin level causes bound calcium to increase, therefore a normal total calcium level accompanied by hyperalbuminemia actually indi-

Table 4-8

Potassium Excess: Hyperkalemia		
Signs and symptoms	**Nursing interventions**	**Expected outcomes**
Plasma potassium greater than 5.0 mEq/L	Note serum potassium results; encourage diet low in potassium if taking food	Potassium level slowly returned to normal
Electrocardiographic changes: tall, peaked T waves, shortened Q-T interval, widened QRS complex; bradycardia, arrhythmias leading to cardiac arrest	Monitor electrocardiographic results; monitor vital signs. Administer calcium solutions to neutralize potassium. Use with caution if patient is receiving digitalis preparations.	Abnormal electrical conductions detected and treated at onset. Normal sinus rhythm resumed.
Apathy, confusion	Could indicate severe imbalance; report	Oriented, alert
Abdominal and general cramps, muscle twitching and weakness	Maintain quiet environment	Muscle activity normotonic
Hyperactive deep-tendon reflexes	Monitor deep tendon reflexes	Muscle activity normotonic
Nausea, diarrhea, intestinal colic	Check bowel sounds; observe level of hydration	Bowel sounds present, all quadrants; no report of nausea or diarrhea; well hydrated
Paresthesias of the face, tongue, and extremities	Observe and report	No report of numbness
Ascending flaccid paralysis in severe cases; could result in respiratory arrest	Check respirations q 15 min to q 1 hr	Respiration 14 per minute or above

---

Formula to Correct Calcium Readings Distorted by Abnormal Albumin Levels

Hypoalbuminemia
1. Subtract patient's serum albumin from the normal level (4.0 mg/dl)
2. Multiply that remainder by a correction factor of 0.8
3. Add that product to the total calcium level found in the lab results

Example:
1.   4.0 mg/dl (normal serum albumin)
   −1.7 mg/dl (patient's albumin level)
   2.3 mg/dl (remainder)
2.   2.3 mg/dl (remainder)
   ×0.8 (correction factor)
   1.84 mg/dl (product)
3.   1.84
   +10.1 mg/dl (patient's serum calcium level)
   11.94 mg/dl adjusted total calcium level, which indicates hypercalcemia

Hyperalbuminemia
1. Subtract normal albumin (4.0 mg/dl) from the patient's albumin level
2. Multiply the remainder by a correction factor of 0.8
3. Subtract that product from the total calcium level found in the lab results

Example:
1.   6.4 mg/dl (patient's albumin)
   −4.0 mg/dl (normal albumin)
   2.4 mg/dl (remainder)
2.   2.4 mg/dl (remainder)
   ×0.8 (correction factor)
   1.92 mg/dl (product)
3.   8.6 mg/dl (patient's serum calcium level)
   −1.92
   6.68 mg/dl adjusted total calcium level, which indicates hypocalcemia

cates an ionized calcium deficit or **hypocalcemia.** The box on p. 82 shows the formula used to "correct" total calcium readings in the presence of hypoalbuminemia or hyperalbuminemia.[25]

Calcium deficit. Hypocalcemia, or calcium, deficit is often associated with excessive gastrointestinal losses. Because calcium levels in the serum are regulated by the parathyroid glands, hypoactive or absent glands can also result in a calcium deficit. The parathyroid glands can be removed inadvertently when a thyroidectomy is performed, or edema can temporarily restrict the flow of the parathyroid hormone, and calcium deficit may be a complication. Pancreatic diseases, massive subcutaneous infections, and peritonitis may result in extraction of calcium from the extracellular fluids, resulting in calcium deficit.

The signs and symptoms of calcium deficit result from neuromuscular irritability. Tingling of the extremities, muscle cramps, tetany, and convulsions can occur. Because peripheral nerves are affected first, carpopedal spasm is one of the first signs of tetany. This involves a sharp flexion of the wrist and ankle joints. Early signs of tetany are evident if carpal spasm occurs when the brachial artery is occluded by constriction, as occurs when a blood pressure cuff is applied to the upper arm and inflated. This is called **Trousseau's sign.** Also, patients can be checked for Chvostek's sign (Figure 4-4). If the face is tapped over the facial nerve in front of the temple and the face twitches, the results are positive, indicating a deficit of calcium. Electrocardiogram changes and x-ray films of bones are helpful in establishing a diagnosis, and changes in the blood clotting process can be observed. Laboratory data indicate low calcium levels in the urine and plasma.

In a mild deficit, dietary calcium is increased and oral calcium lactate is given. Administration of vitamin D will help absorb calcium from the gastrointestinal tract. To correct serious calcium deficiencies, calcium solutions are administered intravenously. Nursing intervention for a calcium deficit is outlined in Table 4-9.

Calcium excess. Hypercalcemia is a state of excess calcium in the serum. It most often occurs as a result of a tumor of the parathyroid glands; however, it is also associated with excessive administration of vitamin D, multiple fractures, multiple myeloma, and prolonged immobilization. Renal diseases may prevent calcium excretion and result in abnormally high levels in the body fluids.

Calcium excess produces depression of neuromuscular activity. Signs and symptoms include lethargy, decreased muscle tone, and deep bone pain. The high levels of calcium may cause the formation of kidney stones, which cause flank pain. Large staghorn calculi may form, which fill the pelvis of the kidney. Nausea, vomiting, anorexia, and constipation may occur, and as the

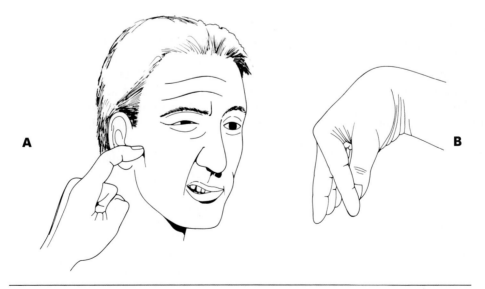

Figure 4-4

A, Chvostek's sign—a contraction of the facial muscle elicited in response to a light tap over the facial nerve in front of the ear. **B,** Trousseau's sign—a carpal spasm (hyperflexion at the wrist) induced by inflating a blood pressure cuff above the systolic pressure.

Table 4-9

Calcium Deficit: Hypocalcemia		
Signs and symptoms	Nursing interventions	Expected outcomes
Serum calcium level less than 8 mg/dl	Encourage increased dietary intake of calcium	Mild calcium deficit corrected through dietary measures
	Monitor administration of IV solutions containing calcium; monitor serum calcium	Bradycardia, which is caused by giving too much IV calcium, is prevented
Tingling of extremities; abdominal cramps; carpopedal spasm	Instruct patient regarding expected symptoms	Patient will report altered neuromuscular sensations
	Establish and maintain communication with patient, encouraging symptom report	
Positive Chvostek's sign	Check for Chvostek's sign	Absence of facial twitch
Positive Trousseau's sign	Compress brachial artery to check for sign	Absence of carpal spasm
	Monitor neurologic status	
Tetany	Observe for tetany	Normotonic
Convulsions	Maintain quiet environment, subdued lighting	Absence of seizure activity
	Establish seizure precautions	Prevention of injury
Electrocardiographic changes	Monitor vital signs	Control of arrhythmias
Delayed blood clotting	Monitor clotting times	Bleeding avoided
	Observe for hemorrhagic areas	

levels of calcium continue to rise, psychoses and coma may develop. Laboratory data will indicate high levels of calcium in the urine and plasma.

Medical treatment of hypercalcemia may include the intravenous administration of fluids and furosemide (Lasix) to dilute excess calcium and force diuresis. The underlying condition must be identified and corrected. Administration of saline and sodium sulfate or inorganic phosphate will cause diuresis and excretion of calcium through the kidneys. Steroid therapy may decrease inflammatory conditions if present and decrease the absorption of calcium. Nursing intervention for hypercalcemia is indicated in Table 4-10.

Magnesium

Magnesium is involved in the regulation of neuromuscular irritability and activates intracellular enzyme systems. Magnesium powers the sodium-potassium pump that moves potassium into cells. Without magnesium, potassium is excreted to excess. The normal serum magnesium level is 1.5 to 2.5 mEq/L. Magnesium is abundant in the foods found in a well-balanced diet. It can be lost from the gastrointestinal tract or the kidney. It plays a crucial role in maintaining normal muscle and nerve activity.

Magnesium deficit. Magnesium deficit is rarely the result of diet but does occur in cases of severe malnutrition, chronic alcoholism, prolonged diarrhea, intestinal malabsorption, and prolonged intravenous therapy lacking in magnesium. It is believed that chronic alcoholism accompanied by liver disease results in a lack of digestive enzymes that reduce magnesium absorption and cause a deficit. Hypoparathyroidism, prolonged diuretic therapy as with congestive heart failure, and the diuresing phase of renal failure can also produce a magnesium deficit. Patients with gastrointestinal cancer receiving chemotherapy are also at increased risk. The cancer interferes with absorption and the patient is frequently anorexic, which further reduces magnesium intake. Increased muscular and nervous system irritability result from magnesium deficit, producing symptoms similar to those of calcium deficit: muscle twitching, jerking, tetany, and convulsions. Cardiac arrhythmias occur in severe cases. Serum calcium and magnesium levels will provide an accurate diagnosis (Table 4-11).

The patient with a magnesium deficit will have discomfort from neuromuscular excitability. Move the patient and handle extremities gently. Keep the room quiet and lighting subdued. Use

Table 4-10

Calcium Excess: Hypercalcemia

Signs and symptoms	Nursing interventions	Expected outcomes
Serum calcium greater than 11 mg/dl	Eliminate calcium from diet Use caution if patient taking digitalis	Calcium level within normal limits Myocardial response to digitalis monitored, arrhythmias prevented
Lethargy Decreased muscle tone	Monitor neurologic status Encourage patient to communicate these symptoms	Able to perform activities of daily living
Deep bone pain Flank pain Kidney stones (renal calculi)	Observe for passage of calculi Strain urine	Stones sent to lab if passed
Hypertension Nausea	Monitor vital signs	Blood pressure within normal limits
Thirst Vomiting	Provide fluids in small, frequent amounts	Hydrated and able to take diet
Anorexia	Provide small, frequent meals	Optimum nutritional status maintained
Constipation	Encourage mobility as patient condition permits	Constipation decreased
Psychoses	Reorient patient to reality	Patient will feel more secure, less fearful
Coma, cardiac arrest	Support life systems	System integrity maintained through hypercalcemic period
	Support family members	Family members able to voice their concerns

Table 4-11

Magnesium Deficit: Hypomagnesemia

Signs and symptoms	Nursing interventions	Expected outcomes
Serum mg 1.0 mEq/L or less	Monitor serum Mg levels daily or after every 16 mEq supplement of Mg is administered Bed cradle for linens; quiet room; subdued lighting	Serum Mg between 1.0 and 3.0 mEq/L
Esophogeal and laryngeal spasm	Soft diet if PO food allowed	Swallows without choking or aspirating food
Muscle twitching: jerking, tetany	Check deep-tendon reflexes	Normotonic muscle activity
Convulsions	Administer magnesium as ordered Monitor urine output and vital signs	Urine output greater than 30 ml/hr or MD notified; Respiratory rate greater than 12 or MD notified; BP within normal limits

a linen cradle to reduce the weight of bed linens that could provoke spasms. If a diet is allowed, give soft foods to prevent choking and aspiration from laryngeal or esophageal spasms.

Treatment of a mild deficit requires increased intake of magnesium-rich foods: meat, fish, dairy products, whole grains, and green leafy vegetables. Diet can be supplemented with magnesium-based antacids such as Mylanta, Gelusil, Maalox, or Milk of Magnesia. A more severe deficit requires intravenous or intramuscular administration of magnesium sulfate. Oral replacement can be used to prevent a deficit in the predisposed individual.

The patient receiving magnesium sulfate intravenously or intramuscularly must be observed closely to avoid excess. Renal function must be observed and the physician notified if output falls below 30 ml per hour. Without adequate renal function, an excess can develop easily because magnesium is excreted by the kidneys. Vital signs and deep tendon reflexes must be checked hourly. A decrease in blood pressure or weak or absent deep tendon reflexes indicate toxicity. In addition, symptoms of flushing, generalized warmth, thirst, sweating, anxiety followed by lethargy, and decreased motor function should be reported immediately and the drug discontinued. Toxicity can produce coma. In the event that toxicity develops, calcium gluconate should be administered. It antagonizes the action of magnesium and reverses the symptoms of toxicity. If calcium gluconate is administered via the same intravenous line used for the magnesium, it must be flushed thoroughly before the calcium gluconate is added because the calcium will precipitate with the sulfates of the magnesium preparation and stop the infusion.

Magnesium excess. Magnesium excess is less common. It is found in patients with renal insufficiency who are unable to excrete magnesium adequately and in severely dehydrated patients, who develop oliguria and magnesium retention. Patients with renal failure must avoid antacids containing magnesium, such as Gelusil. Magnesium excess produces a reduction in neuromuscular irritability. Symptoms include a generalized sense of warmth, decreased deep tendon reflexes leading to flaccid paralysis, low blood pressure, depressed respirations, and drowsiness and lethargy leading to coma (Table 4-12). The electrocardiogram will reveal arrhythmias and cardiac arrest may result. Treatment must be aimed at correcting the underlying cause. Dialysis may be necessary to eliminate the excess and prevent life-threatening symptoms.

Chloride

Chloride deficit. Chloride (Cl) is the major extracellular anion. It is a component of hydrochloric acid in the stomach and plays a role in the transport of carbon dioxide by red blood cells. Chloride is excreted by the kidney and is affected by aldosterone secretion. When aldosterone is released to cause sodium reabsorption, chloride is also reabsorbed. Chloride is secreted into the gastrointestinal tract, and **hypochloremia** can occur with loss of gastrointestinal secretions as seen in vomiting, diarrhea, and nasogastric suctioning. Plasma chloride levels change with and resemble sodium levels. Chloride is lost along with sodium in the patient receiving diuretic therapy, but urinary loss of chloride may be greater than loss of sodium. Gastric fluids contain a higher proportion of chloride, so loss of gastrointestinal fluids causes

Table 4-12

Magnesium Excess: Hypermagnesemia		
Signs and symptoms	Nursing interventions	Expected outcomes
Serum Mg 3.0 mEq/L or more	Monitor serum Mg levels Prepare patient for dialysis if ordered.	Serum Mg between 1.0-3.0 mEq/L
Generalized sense of warmth	Observe and report	No report of sense of warmth
Decreased deep-tendon reflexes	Observe deep-tendon reflexes q 1 hour or as ordered.	Normotensive
Flaccid paralysis can develop	Check movement of extremities	Movement of extremities is retained
Low blood pressure	Check BP q 1 hr or as ordered	BP within normal limits
Depressed respirations	Monitor respirations; report drop to less than 14/minute.	Respirations 14/min or above
Drowsiness and lethargy	Monitor level of consciousness q 1 hour or as ordered.	Alert, oriented
Coma		
Arrhythmias and cardiac arrest	Monitor cardiac rhythm	Normal sinus rhythm

more chloride than sodium loss. When chloride is depleted and unavailable for reabsorption with sodium, the bicarbonate ion is reabsorbed to maintain the cation-anion balance. The increase in bicarbonate may cause metabolic alkalosis. The normal chloride level is 96 to 106 mEq/L. Hypochloremia occurs at less than 95 mEq/L. The symptoms of hypochloremia are the same as those of hyponatremia and metabolic alkalosis.

Chloride excess. Hyperchloremia will occur along with hypernatremia because chloride ions move with sodium ions. An example is seen in a severely burned patient when fluid is remobilized from the edematous burned areas to the vascular compartments, usually a few days after the burn is sustained.

Hyperchloremia can also result from hyperaldosteronism or renal failure. Sodium polystyrene (Kayexalate), the drug used to treat hyperkalemia, and excessive aspirin ingestion can cause chloride excess. Excess chloride interferes with bicarbonate reabsorption and results in metabolic acidosis. The symptoms are those of acidosis: lethargy, confusion, weakness, and stupor. The patient's breathing will become deep and labored as the lungs attempt to correct the problem by reducing carbonic acid by blowing off carbon dioxide. Intravenous sodium bicarbonate will be administered to return the pH to normal; the kidneys will retain the bicarbonate and eliminate chloride. A change to slow, shallow breathing indicates the patient has too much bicarbonate and is trying to conserve carbon dixoide to restore normal acidity. Frequent assessment is necessary.

Phosphates

Phosphate levels vary inversely with calcium levels. In other words, a high calcium level usually means a low phosphate level and vice versa. The parathyroid hormone that promotes calcium uptake inhibits absorption of phosphate. Both electrolytes will be deficient when the imbalance is caused by malnutrition or malabsorption.

Hypophosphatemia results from inadequate intake, poor absorption, such as in shortening of the gastrointestinal tract, loss caused by thiazide diuretics, hyperparathyroidism, and lead poisoning. Alkalosis reduces serum phosphate levels. Hypophosphatemia is treated with supplements of oral sodium and potassium phosphates (Neutra Phos). Severe cases require the intravenous administration of sodium phosphate or potassium phosphate.

Hyperphosphatemia occurs most frequently in patients with renal failure. They will also have hypocalcemia and those symptoms will be the most obvious. Patients with renal failure often take aluminum hydroxide or aluminum carbonate to bind phosphate in the gastrointestinal tract and prevent its absorption into the bloodstream.

Acid-Base Imbalance

The normal composition of body fluids depends not only on the volume of fluid and concentration of various electrolytes, but also on the concentration of the acids and bases, or alkalies, in the body. *Acids* are substances that can release hydrogen ions, and *bases* are substances that can accept hydrogen ions. It is the concentration of hydrogen ions (H^+) that determines whether a solution is acidic, basic, or neutral. The pH scale measures the amount of acidity or alkalinity of fluids. On a scale of 1 to 14, a pH of 7 is neutral. Anything below 7 is considered acidic, and anything above 7 is considered alkaline. The normal pH of extracellular fluid ranges from 7.35 to 7.45 and therefore is slightly alkaline. The normal range that will support life is from 6.8 to 7.8.[19]

The body controls pH with chemical buffers, the lungs, the cells, and the kidneys. Chemical buffers react with acids and bases to minimize changes in the pH. The primary chemical buffers are base bicarbonate (HCO_3)[7] and carbonic acid (H_2CO_3). Normally there is a ratio of 20 parts of base bicarbonate to 1 part of carbonic acid. When this ratio is upset, the body fluids will be either in a state of **acidosis** or **alkalosis.** The lungs help maintain acid-base balance by controlling the amount of carbon dioxide that is released into the air during the respiration process. Carbonic acid in the extracellular fluid breaks down into carbon dioxide and water. When respiration is suppressed, carbonic acid will build up in the body fluids because less carbon dioxide is excreted. When respirations are stimulated, the levels of carbonic acid within the body will fall. Cells serve as buffers by altering their metabolic processes either to absorb or to release hydrogen ions into the surrounding extracellular fluid. The kidneys selectively excrete or reabsorb bicarbonate as needed by the body.

There are two general types of disturbances in the body that will result in an upset of the ratio between the base bicarbonate and carbonic acid. Body metabolic processes will add or subtract bicarbonate to the extracellular fluids, and the respiratory process will add or subtract carbonic acid to the extracellular fluids. Metabolic processes can also result in production of acid. Therefore, a state of acidosis can be caused by lowering the amount of base bicarbonate or by increasing the amount of carbonic acid or metabolic acids. A state of alkalosis can be caused by increasing the amount of base bicarbonate or decreasing the amount of carbonic acid. Each of these conditions will alter the ratio of base bicarbonate to carbonic acid. Acid-base imbalances can take one or a combination of these forms, each of which alters the ratio of base bicarbonate to carbonic acid.

Metabolic acidosis

Metabolic acidosis can result either from the accumulation of too many acid by-products of metabolism or from the loss of bicarbonate. Abnormal metabolic processes such as diabetes, renal insufficiency or failure, and shock produce metabolic acidosis by the accumulation of acids within the body. Anaerobic metabolism produces lactic acidosis and fasting or starvation can produce ketosis. Bicarbonate is lost in excess in renal insufficiency, severe diarrhea, via ileostomies, ureterosigmoidostomy, intestinal or biliary fistulas, intestinal suction, and as a result of increased chloride levels.

The laboratory test used to differentiate between these two types of metabolic acidosis is the **anion gap** (or **R factor**). The anion gap is the difference between the concentration of the cations, sodium and potassium, and the sum of the chloride and bicarbonate anions. This difference reflects the concentration of anions in the extracellular fluid. When metabolic acidosis is caused by a loss of bicarbonate, the anion gap will be normal at 13 mgEq/L or below. When the cause is an excess of metabolic acids the gap will be increased above 13 mEq/L. Thus acidosis resulting from bicarbonate loss is called *normal anion gap acidosis;* acidosis resulting from excess metabolic acid is called *high anion gap acidosis.*

Signs of metabolic acidosis include hyperventilation, weakness, disorientation, diarrhea, and drowsiness leading to stupor and coma. Any state of acidosis depresses the central nervous system. The lungs attempt to compensate for the state of acidosis by increasing the rate and depth of respirations, which will reduce the amount of carbonic acid in the system. This type of breathing is known as **Kussmaul respiration.** The serum pH

level will be below 7.35, the pH of the urine will be lower than normal, and the serum bicarbonate level will be decreased or normal, depending on the cause. Serum potassium levels will be elevated when acidosis occurs.

Appropriate therapy for metabolic acidosis is treatment of the underlying cause. Bicarbonate can be given intravenously to counteract the excessive acids in the blood. Often sodium lactate is given because the liver will metabolize sodium lactate into bicarbonate. In renal failure, dialysis may be the treatment of choice. Nursing intervention is outlined in Table 4-13.

Metabolic alkalosis

Metabolic alkalosis can result either from the loss of acid from the body or from the accumulation of bases in the blood. Loss of acid can occur with excessive vomiting or gastric suction, which removes the upper gastrointestinal secretions that are high in hydrochloric acid. Administration of potent diuretics can cause loss of hydrogen and chloride ions and result in a relative increase of bicarbonate in the blood. Ingestion of an excessive amount of sodium bicarbonate or antacids will cause accumulation of base in the extracellular fluid.

The major signs and symptoms of metabolic alkalosis include nausea, vomiting, and diarrhea. Muscles have increased tone, and symptoms similar to tetany may appear. Often patients are confused and irritable, and convulsions can occur. The lungs attempt to compensate by decreasing the rate and depth of respiration to conserve carbonic acid. Plasma levels of bicarbonate are increased, the serum pH is increased, and the pH of urine is increased. Plasma potassium levels are lowered in alkalosis.

The underlying cause of metabolic alkalosis must be determined and treated. Excessive losses should be replaced, and acidifying solutions can be given orally or intravenously. The specific treatment will depend on the cause. Nursing intervention is outlined in Table 4-14.

Respiratory alkalosis

Respiratory alkalosis is caused primarily by hyperventilation, which can result from anxiety states, fever, and lack of oxygen. Some drugs can stimulate the respiratory center to cause hyperventilation. Common symptoms include headache, dizziness, paresthesias, tingling of the fin-

Table 4-13

Metabolic Acidosis: Base Bicarbonate Deficit or Metabolic Acid Excess

Signs and symptoms	Nursing interventions	Expected outcomes
Serum pH less than 7.35 Low urine pH	Monitor laboratory values	Patient's response monitored
Decreased serum bicarbonate	Keep bicarbonate readily available	pH within normal limits
Increased serum potassium	Monitor laboratory results	Serum potassium within normal limits
Blood carbon dioxide decreased	Monitor heart rhythm	
Diarrhea	Maintain accurate intake and output records	IV fluids administered at prescribed rate
		Extracellular fluid volume deficit avoided
Increased rate and depth of respirations	Monitor vital signs	Respiratory compensation for metabolic imbalances observed
Weakness, drowsiness	Monitor neurologic status and level of consciousness	Alert and oriented
Disorientation	Observe for change in status	Safety maintained
Shock	Observe for symptoms of shock	Shock prevented
Stupor	Administer medications as ordered to correct metabolic acidosis	Patient more alert
Coma	Maintain life support systems	Integrity of body systems maintained

Table 4-14

Metabolic Alkalosis: Base Bicarbonate Excess

Signs and symptoms	Nursing interventions	Expected outcomes
Serum pH greater than 7.45 Increased urine pH	Monitor laboratory values	Patient's response monitored
Increased serum bicarbonate		Abnormal laboratory results communicated
Decreased serum potassium (less than 4 mEq/L)	Observe for signs of hypokalemia	Serum potassium within normal limits
Blood carbon dioxide tension increased		
Nausea	Monitor administration of IV fluids	Fluid balance maintained
Vomiting	Maintain accurate intake and output records	
Diarrhea		
Decreased rate and depth of respirations	Monitor vital signs	Respiratory compensation for metabolic imbalance observed
Confusion	Monitor neurologic status	
	Orient patient to reality	Patient more assured, less fearful
	Observe change in level of consciousness	
Irritability	Maintain quiet environment	Decreased need for psychotropic agents
Increased muscular tone	Muscle relaxants as ordered	Decreased oxygen need; conservation of patient's energy
Tetany	Observe for tetany	Tetany avoided
Convulsions	Establish seizure precautions	Injury prevented

Table 4-15

Respiratory Alkalosis: Carbonic Acid Deficit		
Signs and symptoms	**Nursing interventions**	**Expected outcomes**
Elevated blood pH	Monitor laboratory values	Patient's response monitored
Decreased serum carbon dioxide	Observe patient for signs and symptoms of primary disease process that could contribute to respiratory alkalosis	Treatment of primary disease with correction of carbonic acid deficit
Increased urine pH		
Plasma bicarbonate normal or slightly decreased		
Serum potassium lowered		
Headache	Administer pain medication as ordered	Headache controlled
Dizziness	Reassure patient	Hyperventilation decreased
	Educate patient concerning breathing techniques	Oxygenation improved
Paresthesias	Monitor sensorium	Alert/oriented
Tetany	Observe for signs of tetany	Tetany avoided

gertips and around the mouth, and tetany and are related to increased neuromuscular irritability. The pH of the blood will be above normal, the blood gas carbon dioxide level will be low, and the pH of the urine will be increased. The bicarbonate level of the plasma may be normal or slightly lowered. Serum potassium levels are usually lowered in alkalosis. Treatment consists of sedation, emotional support, and use of a bag to rebreathe exhaled carbon dixode. Nursing intervention is outlined in Table 4-15.

Respiratory acidosis

Respiratory acidosis is caused by any condition that interferes with the normal release of carbon dioxide from the lungs. Emphysema, bronchitis, pneumonia, and asthma are conditions that interfere with the normal transport of gases across the pulmonary membrane. In addition, sedatives, narcotics, (morphine), or brain trauma may affect the respiratory center in the medulla to depress respirations.

Patients will become weak, restless, and disoriented. The pulse rate will increase, and arrhythmias may occur. Cyanosis is usually a late sign. The plasma pH will be low, and the blood gas carbon dioxide level will be elevated. The bicarbonate level will be normal or elevated in an attempt to compensate. Serum potassium is usually elevated during acidotic states.

Severe respiratory acidosis can be an emergency. Treatment measures should first involve improvement of ventilation, and mechanical ventilation may be necessary. Nursing intervention is presented in Table 4-16.

Interpretation of blood gas values. When evaluating laboratory reports of blood gas values, first determine the pH level as normal, acidosis (below 7.35), or alkalosis (above 7.45). Next evaluate the bicarbonate and carbonic acid levels. Normal bicarbonate is 22 to 26 mEq/L. Carbonic acid is measured by the $Paco_2$ and its normal range is 35 to 45. A change in bicarbonate level indicates metabolic imbalance, and a change in carbonic acid level is respiratory in origin. For example, if the pH indicates acidosis and the bicarbonate level is low while the carbonic acid or $Paco_2$ level is normal, the patient has a base bicarbonate deficit or metabolic acidosis. If the pH is acid and both bicarbonate and carbonic acid are normal, the cause is excess metabolic acid and is called metabolic acidosis. If the pH level is acid and the carbonic acid level is high while the bicarbonate is normal, the patient has a carbonic acid excess, or respiratory acidosis. With an alkaline pH level, a high bicarbonate level indicates metabolic alkalosis, whereas a low carbonic acid level indicates respiratory alkalosis.

Compensation. The "normal" value in each of these situations gradually becomes abnormal in an attempt to compensate by balancing carbonic acid and base bicarbonate levels. This will cause the pH to move toward normal. Because balance is being attempted but has not yet been achieved

Table 4-16

Respiratory Acidosis: Carbonic Acid Excess		
Signs and symptoms	Nursing interventions	Expected outcomes
Decreased blood pH	Monitor laboratory values	Arterial blood gases within normal limits
Increased serum carbon dioxide	Maintain patent airway	
Plasma bicarbonate normal or increased	Suction as necessary	
Serum potassium increased	Monitor administration of IV fluids	Serum potassium decreased via the dilutional effect of IV fluids
Weakness	Assist with transfer	Prevention of injury
Restlessness	Provide oxygen as ordered	Oxygen level increased
Disorientation	Provide emotional support	Patient verbalizes increased awareness of environment
	Monitor neurologic status	
	Reorientation	
Increased pulse	Monitor vital signs	Arrhythmias avoided
Arrhythmias	Administer medications as ordered	
Cyanosis	Perform chest percussion and postural drainage as ordered	Transport of gases across the pulmonary membrane facilitated
	Place patient in semi-Fowler's position if indicated	

(pH is still abnormal) this state is termed *partially compensated*. Once the pH has returned to normal, even though the bicarbonate and carbonic acid levels may be abnormal, the state is called *compensated* because the bicarbonate and carbonic acid have achieved a proper balance. With continued treatment, these levels will be returned to normal while a normal pH is maintained.

INTRAVENOUS THERAPY

Intravenous therapy is a primary therapeutic technique used to treat patients with fluid and electrolyte imbalances. In general three types of solutions are commonly used. *Hydrating* solutions are administered when the patient is dehydrated, and kidney function is stimulated as a result. These solutions usually contain carbohydrates in water or saline. The carbohydrate is metabolized, and the water is free to be absorbed by cells or eliminated; 5% dextrose in water is an example of a hydrating solution. *Balanced* or *maintenance* solutions provide water, electrolytes, and carbohydrates and are effective for patients who must be maintained on intravenous solutions for a period of time. These solutions are similar to normal

blood plasma. *Replacement* solutions are used primarily to replenish losses from the gastrointestinal tract occurring from vomiting, suction, fistulas, ostomies, and diarrhea. These solutions do not hydrate the patient. Lactated Ringer's solution is an example.

Fluids are introduced into veins through plastic or metal needles or through plastic catheters inserted either through metal needles or by means of a *cutdown*. The latter is a minor surgical procedure in which a small incision is made into the vein. Catheters are then anchored to the skin with a small piece of gauze under the hub of the needle and taped (Figure 4-5). A bottle or plastic bag filled with the appropriate solution and an intravenous infusion set are prepared before the procedure is started and are connected to the needle or catheter and then firmly taped in place. The fluid is started after the catheter is in place in the vein, and a proper flow rate is established.[8]

The nurse observes and monitors the patient's IV fluids. The prescribed flow rate must be regulated. The IV site is watched for *infiltration*, which is caused by displacement of the IV needle from the vein into the surrounding tissue. Infiltration is characterized by swelling of the affected tissue. The patient may experience a burning sen-

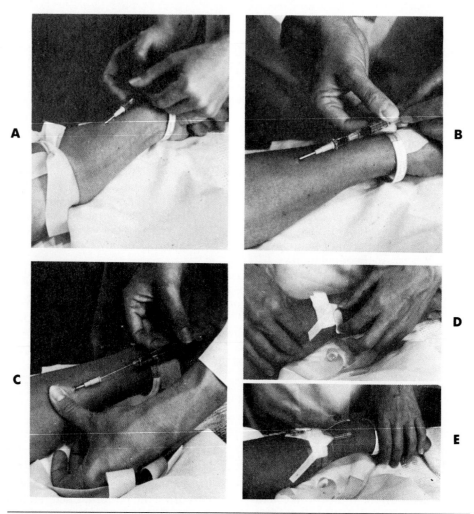

Figure 4-5
Insertion of IV catheter. **A,** Advance catheter and needle into vein as one unit. **B,** Observe for blood return in plastic hub of needle. **C,** Place fingertip over catheterized vein while gently pulling needle out of catheter. **D,** Secure hub of needle to skin by crisscrossing tape over needle hub. **E,** Loop IV tubing and secure it with tape to prevent pull on needle site. *(From Smith S and Duell D: Nursing skills and evaluation, Nursing Board Review, 481, 1986.)*

sation at the needle site. On palpation, the infiltrated site is very firm or hard to the touch and is cool and pale. Redness and warmth may also be present to varying degrees if an inflammatory process has begun. To confirm infiltration, the IV solution bottle is lowered below the patient. Blood should flow back into the IV tubing; it if does not, infiltration has occurred. Once this has taken place, the IV line must be restarted in another area.

Thrombophlebitis is a more common complication in which the vein becomes inflamed and a clot forms. Redness and edema occur at the injection site, and the patient will complain of pain along the vein. When this occurs, the IV infusion should be discontinued and warm, moist compresses applied to reduce pain and stimulate healing.

Systemic complications may occur from intravenous infusions. Nurses should be continuously alert for symptoms of circulatory overload, which are respiratory distress and increased venous pressure. Shortness of breath, increased respirations, coughing, increased blood pressure, bounding pulse, and distended veins can also be signs of circulatory overload. If infusion continues, pulmonary edema can result.

Air embolism occasionally occurs when substantial amounts of air enter the blood through an improperly running infusion. The apparatus should be checked frequently, and the infusion should be stopped or the solution changed before the bottle and tubing are empty. This will prevent air from entering the vein. Sudden vascular collapse can occur from air embolism, with the patient showing signs of shock and loss of consciousness. Other abnormal reactions that could occur include nausea, vomiting, increased pulse rate, and chills. If these symptoms appear, the infusion is stopped and the physician called. Other signs and symptoms may occur that are related to the patient's primary condition.

Central Venous Lines

Fluids can also be infused through central venous lines. A catheter is inserted into the right atrium of the heart, usually through the subclavian vein. The catheter is inserted in the operating room by the doctor. These catheters can remain in place for long periods, reducing need for frequent venipuncture. These catheters can have more than one lumen, allowing infusion of multiple solutions and/or medications. The site must be cleansed and dressed regularly and observed for signs of infection.

Peripherally Inserted Central Catheter (PICC)

Central lines can also be introduced in a peripheral brachial vein and inserted into the right atrium. These can be inserted by the registered nurse but correct placement must be verified by x-ray before the line is used.

Shock

The basic abnormality that occurs when a state of shock develops is a disproportion between the tissue needs and their supply of adequately oxygenated blood. Contributing to this is a disproportion between the volume of blood and the vascular space in which it is circulating. Lack of oxygen results, which leads to altered chemical activity within all the cells of the body. Normal metabolic processes that produce the energy needed for work within the cell are interrupted. Lactic acid is produced, which diffuses out of the cells into the extracellular fluid, causing a state of acidosis.

Types of shock

Hypovolemic shock. Shock can be classified in several ways. Hypovolemic shock results when there is a loss of fluid available to the circulation. It is caused most often by hemorrhage but can also result from loss of other body fluids, such as in dehydration caused by diabetic ketoacidosis, protracted vomiting, or diarrhea. Burns and other trauma can trap fluid at the site of the injury and decrease the volume of the bloodstream. Tissue injury occurring during trauma or surgery can increase the permeability of capillary membranes, allowing albumin to leave the circulating blood. This will disturb plasma colloid osmotic pressure and allow fluid to shift from the circulation to the tissues (Figure 4-2). Hypovolemia will result and shock is a potential danger.

Hypovolemic shock is an extension of fluid volume deficit. Loss of plasma results in hemoconcentration. Loss of fluid volume results in less venous blood returning to the right side of the heart, therefore less blood is pumped out of the heart into the vascular system. Insufficient oxygen is provided to the body cells, and abnormal metabolic processes result, leading to metabolic acidosis.

Cardiogenic shock. Shock that results from causes other than fluid loss from the circulation is termed **normovolemic shock.** Cardiogenic shock results from failure of the heart to pump adequate amounts of blood into the systemic circulation to fully perfuse and therefore oxygenate the body tissues. Cardiogenic shock is easiest to treat in its early stages but is not easily identified. The seriousness of precipitating factors tend to shadow the impending shock. Precipitating factors include arrhythmias, myocardial infarction, or congestive heart failure. Decreased blood pressure, a decreased level of alertness, and decreased renal function are all present in cardiogenic shock and reflective of the failure of the heart as a pump.

Neurogenic shock and **vasogenic shock** both occur from vasodilation, an increase in size of the vascular bed with a normal blood volume. Blood pressure decreases and therefore venous blood returned to the heart is decreased, which contributes to decreased cardiac output. In both types of shock, venous pooling results. Tissue hypoxia and cell death occur.

Although vasodilation occurs in neurogenic as well as vasogenic shock, the causative factors in each differ. The cause of *neurogenic* shock is nerve stimulation or nerve block, such as those arising from deep general anesthesia, spinal anesthesia, postural hypotension, drug reactions, brain damage, or insulin shock. *Vasogenic* shock occurs as a result of factors that directly affect the blood vessels. Vasodilation in vasogenic shock is followed by a decrease in venous return, cardiac output, blood pressure, and volume of blood to the tissues. Cellular anoxia and destruction result. Anaphylactic shock and septic shock are examples of vasogenic shock.

Anaphylactic shock results from an abnormal antigen-antibody response. The IgE antibody produced causes the release of histamine from mast cells and basophils (Chapter 26, Table 26-1). The release of histamine results in arterial and venous dilation and increased capillary permeability. Vasodilation and decreased cardiac output cause a decrease in systolic and diastolic blood pressure. Plasma leaks through the vascular bed into the interstitial space leading to circulatory collapse. Histamine contracts the smooth muscle of the bronchi, causing bronchospasm, asthma, and panting. The bronchioles constrict and contribute to hypoxemia. The patient will initially complain of dizziness, drowsiness, and itching of the eyes and ears. Confusion, diaphoresis, edema of the hands, lips, eyelids and tongue, and laryngospasm will appear quickly. The reaction rapidly progresses to complete respiratory obstruction and distress and circulatory collapse.

Treatment requires immediate elimination of the antigen, such as removing a bee stinger or stopping an infusion that caused the reaction. The patient should be placed in a supine position to increase blood flow to the brain. An open airway must be maintained and oxygen given at 5 to 10 L/min. Intravenous fluids should be started and the patient placed on a cardiac monitor. Epinephrine is given to block the release of histamine, counteract bronchospasm, and prevent circulatory collapse. Antihistamines, corticosteroids, and aminophylline are given to supplement the effects of epinephrine. On recovery from the acute episode, the patient must be fully informed of the allergy to avoid future exposure. See Table 26-2 for an outline of nursing care for the patient in anaphylactic shock.

Septic shock is caused by the metabolic end-products of bacteria. During the early phase of septic shock, the vessels are dilated and the patient may have a fever. There is still adequate blood flow to the brain, as indicated by the pa-

tient's alertness. Urinary output, reflective of renal perfusion, is adequate. The pulse may be moderately elevated, but the increase in heart rate does not support an adequate cardiac output, and systolic blood pressure slowly falls. Hyperventilation results in metabolic alkalosis.

The late phase of shock is marked by decreased mentation, which may lead to confusion and stupor. The sluggish blood is prone to clot, especially within the smaller vessels, a condition known as **disseminated intravascular coagulation.** The clotted vessels are unable to deliver oxygen and nutrients to the affected tissues. The widespread clotting depletes blood clotting factors and the patient will begin to hemorrhage. Metabolic acidosis results from cellular hypoxia and the inability of the clotted vessels to carry away cellular waste products from the affected areas. Arterial and venous constriction contribute to cold, pale, and clammy skin with a below-normal body temperature. Constriction of the renal arteries leads to decreased perfusion of the kidneys, with little urine being produced. Indeed, acute or chronic renal failure is the second most common cause of death in septic shock.

Body response to shock

Although the etiology of various forms of shock differ, many of the compensatory mechanisms that counteract the effects of shock are the same. Loss of fluid volume or a disproportion between fluid volume and the size of the vascular space will cause the blood pressure regulatory mechanisms to react.

Decreasing blood pressure will excite the vasoconstrictor center of the brain (medulla oblongata), and epinephrine and norepinephrine will be released from the adrenal medulla. The effect will be vasoconstriction of the peripheral blood vessels and an increased heart rate and strength of the contraction. These mechanisms may be successful in elevating the blood pressure and increasing the cardiac output in mild shock. The kidneys secrete the hormone renin when the blood pressure falls. Renin produces angiotensin, a powerful vasoconstrictor for peripheral arterioles.[11] To return the blood volume to normal the body releases aldosterone from the adrenal cortex, which will cause sodium reabsorption and water retention by the kidney tubules. This will increase extracellular fluid and blood volume and decrease urinary output.

Assessment of shock

The signs and symptoms of shock are similar, regardless of the etiology. The basic property of shock is decreased blood flow and therefore decreased delivery of oxygen, nutrients, hormones, and electrolytes to the cells, with a concomitant decreased removal of metabolic wastes. Signs of shock are a direct result of the body's attempt to counteract the effects of decreasing cardiac output.

Subtle early signs of shock include an increased pulse rate, increased respirations, a mild drop in blood pressure, oliguria, and restlessness. Weakness, lethargy, pallor, cool moist skin, rapid shallow respirations, decreasing body temperature, rapid thready pulse, and progressively decreasing blood pressure with a narrowing pulse pressure occur later. Pulse pressure is the difference between the systolic and diastolic blood pressures. A normal pulse pressure is 40 mm Hg. For example, a blood pressure of 128/88 would produce a pulse pressure of 40. The pulse pressure narrows in early shock because of a decreased systolic blood pressure.

Intervention for shock

Prevention of shock is the best possible treatment. Shock must be anticipated as a possible complication in any condition in which there is significant blood loss or when surgery has been performed. Early signs of shock should be observed and treatment instituted before the condition becomes life threatening.

The primary objective in treatment is to restore adequate tissue perfusion of oxygenated blood. The blood volume must be restored and hemorrhage controlled. Intravenous fluids such as lactated Ringer's solution or 5% dextrose in normal saline are given to restore fluid volume.

Blood, plasma, and plasma substitutes may also be given. A central venous catheter is inserted. Frequent monitoring of central venous pressure is done to prevent the danger of overhydrating the patient. Overloading the patient's circulatory system can lead to pulmonary edema, which will further impede the amount of oxygenation and carbon dioxide removal that can occur in the lungs. Patients receiving high-humidity oxygen can absorb some of the humidity through their lungs. Daily chest x-ray films are beneficial in monitoring the development of pulmonary edema. Diuretics, such as furosemide, may be useful in preventing fluid accumulation in the pulmonary bed. Arterial blood-gas determinations indicate the patient's oxygen and carbon dioxide levels, as well as acid-base balance.

Various types of drug therapy will be ordered according to the cause of shock. Vasoactive drugs, which affect vascular tone, can be categorized into various groups according to the following actions: constriction/dilation of arterioles, constriction/dilation of veins, or increasing myocardial contractility. Drugs that are vasoactive include norepinephrine, nitroprusside, and dopamine. For example, a patient in cardiogenic shock might be given norepinephrine, which would cause the cardiac muscles to contract with greater force, a condition that is also called a *positive inotropic effect.* The result would be an increase in cardiac output. Management is actually more complex than this. For example, an increase in cardiac contractility will also increase myocardial oxygen demand. Obviously the patient's condition must be closely monitored.

Noninotropic drugs such as nitroprusside that equally dilate arterioles and veins decrease cardiac oxygen demand and increase perfusion of peripheral vessels. However, perfusion of the vital organs will be decreased. Other drugs used in shock include antiarrhythmics (lidocaine, procainamide), antibiotics (tobramycin, gentamicin), and diuretics (ethacrynic acid).

Patients should be kept flat, and those who do not have head injuries may have their lower extremities slightly elevated. Trendelenburg's position is avoided because it pushes the abdominal organs up against the chest by gravity, thus interfering with diaphragmatic excursions and cardiac contractions. Position changes should be made slowly and gently. Observations should be made systematically and recorded in written form. Pertinent observations include blood pressure, pulse, respirations, skin color, temperature, intravenous and oral fluid intake, urinary and other forms of fluid loss, a running balance of intake and output, and level of consciousness.

Care should be taken to avoid factors that increase the severity of shock. External heat should not be applied to the patient in shock unless the patient is shivering. Shivering increases metabolic need for oxygen and causes vasodilation so the patient should be covered just enough to stop the shivering. Application of external heat would also cause peripheral vasodilation, thus supplying the peripheral tissues with blood at the expense of the vital organs and contributing to the progression of shock. Pain medications should be administered carefully to avoid extreme vasoconstriction, which can result from increased stimulation of the sympathetic nervous system.

PSYCHOSOCIAL SUPPORT

Biologic alterations in the patient with fluid and electrolyte imbalances or one who is in a state of shock have been considered in this chapter. However, the individual leads a biopsychosocial existence. Biologic alterations are likely to affect both psychologic and social spheres.

Many of the states that have been considered affect mentation to various degrees. Progressive lethargy and weakness or intermittent confusion may frighten one patient, cause another to withdraw, and inspire anger and hostility in yet another. Various family members will also have diverse responses. Responding to patients and their families in a calm, reassuring manner is often all that is needed to decrease fears, encourage communication, and lessen anger.

Patients and family members will have many questions, both verbalized and nonverbalized: Why does he twitch so uncontrollably? He was normally so active, why is he so sleepy all the time? Why doesn't my wife recognize me? Why are all those needles in her arm? What is that machine for? Factual information, communicated in words that are understood by the patient or family member is often the only answer required. However, sometimes it is not information that is sought, but someone to listen in an attentive manner. Emotional support is not necessarily exclusively verbal—it can be a gentle touch on the shoulder or the eye contact that you maintain when someone trusts you enough to ask you a question or to confide to you their anxieties.

As a member of the health care team, the nurse knows each team member's talents well enough to consult with them at appropriate times. When a family member wants to know a patient's prognosis, the physician is often the most appropriate team member to consult and refer to the family member. When a patient has financial concerns, the nurse draws from the expertise of the social worker.

The nurse, aware that the patient's psychosocial health can influence biologic health and affect response to medical and nursing therapy, incorporates this aspect of the patient's health into the plan of care.

REFERENCES AND ADDITIONAL READINGS

1. Barta MA: Correcting electrolyte imbalances, RN 50(2):30-34,1987.
2. Bear PG and Myers JL: Principles and practice of adult health nursing, St Louis, 1990, Mosby-Year Book Inc.
3. Calloway C: When the problem involves magnesium, calcium or phosphate, RN 50(5):30-36, 1987.
4. Cohen S and Wells S: Nursing care of patients in shock: pharmacotherapy, Am J Nurs 82(6):943-964, 1982.
5. Cohen S, Miller M, and Sherman R: Metabolic acid-base disorders: Physiological abnormalities and nursing actions, Am J Nurs 78(1):87-108, 1982.
6. Coleman EA: When the kidneys fail, RN 49(7):29-38, 1986.
7. Cooke SS: Major thermal injury: the first 48 hours, Crit Care Nurs 6(1):55-63, 1986.
8. Dison N: Clinical nursing techniques, ed 4, St Louis, 1979, The CV Mosby Co.
9. Gever LN: Treat shock with dopamine, Nurs 86 16(3):93, 1986.
10. Greenberg MD: Shock: its pathophysiology and treatment, Emergency 18(6):52-54, 1986.
11. Guyton AC: Textbook of medical physiology, ed 7, Philadelphia, 1986, WB Saunders Co.
12. Irwin M: Encourage oral intake: yes, but how? Am J Nurs 87(1):100-104, 1987.
13. Iveson-Iveson J: Fluid balance, Nurs Mirror 154(24):38, 1982.
14. Keithley J and Fraulini K: What's behind that I.V. line? Nurs 82 12(3):33-42, 1982.
15. Lamb C: Why is the serum sodium low? . . . Inappropriate secretion of antidiuretic hormone, Patient Care 20(7):94-98, 1986.
16. McAdams RC and McClure K: Hypovolemia: when to suspect it, RN 49(12):34-42, 1986.
17. McAdams RC and McClure K: Hypovolemia: how to stop it, RN 49(12):38-42, 1986.
18. Meador B: Cardiogenic shock: help break the vicious circle, RN 45(4):38-42, 1982.
19. Metheny N and Snively WD: Nurses' handbook of fluid balance, ed 4, Philadelphia, 1983, JB Lippincott Co.
20. Petlin A and Carolan J: Halt hypovolemic shock, RN 45(5):36-42, 1982.

21. Romanski SO: Interpreting ABG's in four easy steps, Nurs 86 16(9):58-64, 1986.
22. Sumner SM: Action stat! Septic shock, Nurs 87 17(2):33, 1987.
23. Taylor DL: Respiratory acidosis: pathophysiology, signs, and symptoms, Nurs 90 20(9):52-53, 1990.
24. Toto KH: When the patient has hyperkalemia, RN 50(4):34-37, 1987.
25. Walpert N: An orderly look at calcium metabolism disorders, Nurs 90 20(7), 60-64, 1990.
26. Wright T and Murray M: Potassium problems: which patient's in danger? RN 45(6)57-61, 1982.
27. Young ME and Flynn KT: Third spacing: when the body conceals fluid loss, RN 51(8):46-47, 1988.

CHAPTER

5

Preoperative and Postoperative Care

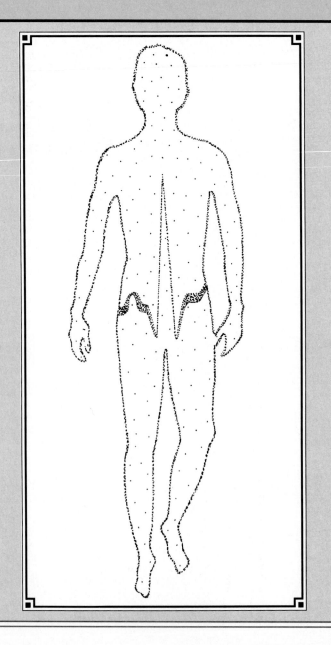

KEY WORDS

airway
ambulation
anesthesia
asepsis
atelectasis
autoclave
body image
dehiscence
embolism
evisceration
hemorrhage
hypothermia
pain relief
recovery room
sterilization
surgical procedure
thrombosis
wound healing
wound infection

OBJECTIVES

1. Identify four reasons for undergoing surgery.
2. Discuss four negative effects of surgery on the individual.
3. Describe the criteria for, and advantages of, outpatient surgery.
4. State the major goal of preoperative preparation.
5. Describe general preoperative preparation of the surgical patient.
6. Explain surgical asepsis.
7. Describe the roles of the intraoperative team.
8. List the common types of anesthesia and their uses.
9. Discuss nursing responsibilities in patient care immediately after surgery.
10. Identify nursing measures that can be used to decrease postoperative discomfort.
11. Explain nursing responsibilities in dealing with the major complications of surgical intervention.
12. Discuss discharge planning for the surgical patient.

THE SURGICAL EXPERIENCE

Modern surgery has alleviated many diseases that have crippled or killed people in past generations. Surgery is a planned alteration of physiologic processes within the body in an attempt to arrest or eliminate disease or illness. The meaning of surgery varies with each individual; however, it is generally a frightening experience to even the best prepared person. Surgery results in an invasion of one's most intimate privacy; thus confidence in the physician, the nurse, and other health care workers is an important aspect of helping the patient to cope during this time of need.

Surgical procedures may be classified in several ways. A surgical procedure may be done as an emergency or may be scheduled in advance. It may be necessary to save a life or it may be an optional (elective) procedure intended to improve health. Elective surgery can be scheduled in advance and allows the individual to prepare for the event physically and psychologically.

Knowing the purpose and anticipated outcomes of various surgical procedures can help the nurse to educate and support the patient more effectively.

Negative Effects of Surgery

Stress, increased susceptibility to infection, potential body image changes, and disruption of life-style are four negative effects of surgery that nurses should be aware of.

Stress

The stress response describes a complex physiologic and psychologic reaction to any external or internal threat to the body's equilibrium. This response can result in profound neurochemical changes in the body that initially aid the body in coping with the invasive reality of surgery. If the stress response is too severe or prolonged, however, the body's defenses become depleted. Organ failure, infection, and life-threatening electrolyte imbalance can occur. The nurse can minimize the potential for these negative effects of stress by identifying factors other than the surgical experience that may be contributing to the patient's concern. Careful preoperative preparation and teaching by the nurse will greatly lessen the patient's anxiety. During the preoperative period the physician will also carefully evaluate any other physical conditions that may increase the risk related to surgery. Some of these include electrolyte

---

Reasons for Performing Surgery

1. **Diagnostic** or **exploratory** surgery, which is performed to determine the cause and/or extent of a disease process
2. **Curative** surgery, such as an appendectomy, which attempts to remove diseased organs or tissues
3. **Palliative** surgery, which lessens the symptoms of a disease without curing it, such as a local sympathectomy for pain control
4. **Restorative** or **cosmetic** surgery, such as repair of a fracture or skin grafting for burns, which attempts to restore or improve function or appearance

---

imbalance, diabetes, liver disease, anemia, lung and heart disorders, malnutrition, obesity, and emotional instability.

Increased susceptibility to infection

Intact skin is the body's first line of defense against bacterial invasion. When the skin is surgically incised, the risk of local infection greatly increases. In addition, one of the effects of severe or prolonged stress is the suppression of the body's immune response. This combination makes infection a real possibility for every surgical patient. Antibiotic therapy may be prescribed prophylactically, but meticulous surgical and postsurgical aseptic techniques are the keys to preventing infection.

Potential body image changes

Body image, or one's subjective feelings about one's appearance, are formed in early life. A surgical procedure may significantly alter this self-perception. Operations that cause a visible change in an individual, such as amputation of a body part, involve not only a physical but also a psychologic loss. Removal of organs that have emotional and social importance, such as the uterus or testicles, may also affect a patient profoundly, despite the fact that there is no visible evidence of change. The nurse can help the patient who is undergoing surgery that may affect body image by encouraging the patient to express his concerns. A number of community support groups exist, such as ostomy clubs and branches of Reach to Recovery for women who have had mastectomies.

Table 5-1

Criteria for Outpatient Surgery	
The patient	**The procedure**
Accepts the idea of outpatient surgery	Is elective and one that does not produce severe alterations in physiologic status
Can follow postoperative discharge instructions	
Has a home environment and support system that will foster early postoperative recovery at home	Does not require acute or intensive postoperative care such as transfusions or intensive monitoring
Has no other medical conditions that pose a serious risk for home recovery	Generally causes only minimal pain that can be managed by oral analgesics

Disruption of lifestyle

Every person who undergoes a major surgical procedure will have at least a temporary change in lifestyle. If rehabilitation will be prolonged, or normal function has been permanently altered, a person's career, job security, and social activities may be jeopardized. The nurse can often help the patient to identify these potential changes and assist in the development of coping strategies through referral to appropriate agencies and resources.

Objectives of Surgical Nursing

The objective of surgical nursing is to prepare the patient mentally and physically for surgery and to assist in full recovery in the shortest time possible with the least discomfort. The nursing care of surgical patients is a step-by-step process, beginning before the patient is admitted to the hospital and terminating when recovery is complete and the patient returns to a normal routine. The nurse who is assigned the care of surgical patients needs to have a broad understanding of individual reactions to the surgical procedure. Every surgical patient experiences fear and anxiety, so the nurse must be able to recognize the verbal and nonverbal expressions of these emotions and respond in a helping manner. Open communication must be maintained between the nurse and patient, the nurse and family, the patient and surgeon, and the family and surgeon. The nurse can assist the patient and family by reporting appropriate concerns and questions to the surgeon as they arise. The nurse must possess a wide range of technical skills, as well as a keen sense of critical observation. The line between safety and danger in the care of many surgical patients, especially older patients, may be a narrow one. The alert nurse must recognize early signs of impending compli-cations and report them so that preventive measures may be taken.

Outpatient Surgery

In past decades a patient needing elective surgery that could not be done in the doctor's office was admitted to the hospital one or several days before the surgery for preoperative testing and preparation. Many of these surgical procedures are now performed with the patient being admitted, treated, and discharged on the same day. These *outpatient (same-day)* surgeries have the following advantages:

1. Reduced stress because the patient is not hospitalized.
2. Lower costs, which not only benefit the individual but are also passed on to the health care industry.

However, not all surgeries can be done on an outpatient basis. The criteria for determining whether a procedure can be done on an outpatient basis are summarized in Table 5-1.

Although surgical procedures done in the outpatient setting may not be as extensive or critical as those that take place in the traditional surgical setting, the role and responsibilities of the nurse remain challenging. The nurse still needs to *assess* and *teach* the patient, and to plan for the patient's *discharge*. All of this must be accomplished in a short span of time. Ideally, patient assessment and teaching can take place several days before the procedure when the patient comes to the hospital or free-standing surgical clinic for preoperative diagnostic testing. Use of the telephone interview and written assessment and discharge planning forms also help to make the outpatient surgical experience safe and satisfactory for the patient.

ADMISSION OF THE PATIENT

Surgical patients admitted to the hospital in emergency situations may be suffering from traumatic injuries received in an accident or from a condition requiring immediate surgery, such as acute appendicitis; in these instances, patients may be taken to the operating room with limited preparation. In the absence of an emergency, patients are admitted the day before or the morning of surgery according to prearranged plans made by the surgeon. Often much of the testing necessary for surgery is completed before admission to the hospital. If diagnostic studies or specialized care is required, the patient may be admitted several days before surgery.

The nurse should be ready to receive the patient at the time of admission, and a friendly, interested, and unhurried attitude will help to make the patient feel secure. The physical condition of the patient should be assessed and a complete orientation to the unit given. The nurse should be alert to any fears or apprehensions expressed by the patient and transmit such information to the surgeon. The patient and family should be encouraged to communicate freely with the physician.

A complete history, including previous illnesses, accidents, or surgeries, and a history of the present illness, its symptoms, duration, and related information are secured from the patient. In the cases of children and older persons, members of the patient's family may be helpful in supplying information. The physician, assisted by the nurse, will examine the patient. (Refer to a textbook on basic nursing for the procedure.) Often a number of laboratory examinations may be completed before admission, including urinalysis, a complete blood cell count, and determination of hemoglobin value, bleeding time, clotting time, and hematocrit level. In some cases a blood glucose test or electrocardiogram may be ordered. Many hospitals automatically require a chest x-ray examination of each patient admitted.

The physician will evaluate the patient's nutritional status for dehydration and malnutrition. When severe vomiting and diarrhea have occurred, there may be an electrolyte imbalance and a protein and vitamin deficiency that will result in decreased resistance to infection and delayed wound healing. The patient may be given total parenteral nutrition, also called hyperalimentation, for several days before surgery to improve nutritional status and to prevent these complications from occurring. (See Chapter 18 for an additional discussion of hyperalimentation.)

If hemorrhage or slow bleeding has occurred, there may be a decrease in hemoglobin value and red blood cells. It may be necessary to transfuse the patient with whole blood or packed cells or to administer electrolytes and vitamins intravenously before surgery.

INFORMED CONSENT

A written statement giving consent to have the operative procedure performed is required before surgery. This statement, witnessed by an authorized person, protects the patient from unsanctioned surgery and protects the surgical team from claims that unauthorized surgery was performed. It implies informed consent, which means that the physician has provided the patient with an explanation of the surgical procedure, the possible consequences of the surgery, and what can be expected during the postoperative period.

Patients sign their own operative permits if they are of legal age and mentally capable. A responsible family member may sign the permit if the patient is a minor or if the patient is unconscious or judged to be incapable of understanding his actions. Refusal to have the operation is the patient's privilege. The operative permit, when signed, becomes a part of the patient's chart.

PREOPERATIVE PREPARATION

The preparation and care of the patient before surgery has one major goal—to promote the best possible physical and psychologic state of the patient before surgical therapy. To achieve this goal, the patient's individual needs must be ascertained and his strengths and limitations evaluated. A plan of care can then be developed to assist the patient in adjusting physically and emotionally to the surgical experience.

Nursing Assessment

Before any surgery the patient must be assessed by the nurse for the following:
1. Knowledge and understanding of the surgical procedure and the recovery phase
2. Physiologic status
3. Psychologic status

Preoperative patient teaching

One of the nurse's most important responsibilities during the preoperative period is to teach the patient about the upcoming surgery and postoperative strategies that will speed recovery. The nurse must first find out what the patient already knows, what explanations the physician has already given, and how much the patient needs and wants to know. Excessive and detailed descriptions of the surgical experience may actually increase preoperative anxiety.

Physiologic status

The patient's physiologic status is explored both by the physician and nurse in separate admission histories and examinations. Often the nurse can elicit information that the patient may have neglected to mention to the physician, which will be of great importance for a successful surgery.

Psychologic status

An evaluation of the patient's psychologic status and readiness for surgery is also essential. If the patient is extremely anxious, perhaps even convinced that surgery will be fatal, the surgeon should be informed. If further explanation by the surgeon does not alleviate excessive anxiety, surgery is often postponed or canceled. The nurse should assess the following:

1. The level of anxiety and specific concerns about surgery
2. Coping patterns of the patient
3. Support systems, which may include family, friends, and religious beliefs and practices
4. Factors that may increase stress levels, such as marital or family discord and financial problems.

Planning and Interventions
Preoperative instruction

Preoperative instruction can help to relieve some of the patient's anxiety. Nursing personnel must know what information has been given to the patient regarding his surgery. Often, questioning the patient about what he has been told will enable the nurse to clarify and reinforce his knowledge. The patient's anxieties, needs, and resources should be taken into consideration, since they will vary considerably from patient to patient. The amount of information given to the patient should depend on the ability to comprehend and the anticipated emotional reaction. It is not

---

Patient History

Information collected for the patient history should include:

1. Past surgical experiences, problems, or complications.
2. Other illnesses or chronic conditions that the patient has that increase surgical risk, such as diabetes, liver disease, obesity, and cardiorespiratory deficiencies.
3. The potential for activity postoperatively.
4. Medications the patient may be taking that could affect recovery, as well as allergies or intolerance to medications.
5. Habits such as smoking, excessive use of alcohol, or a sedentary lifestyle that could impede recovery.

---

appropriate for the nurse to discuss the diagnosis and prognosis of the patient. These matters should be referred to the physician.

The nurse should be able to explain the purposes of, and preparation for, diagnostic tests, meaning of x-ray procedures, laboratory tests, medications, and nursing procedures. Often the operative procedure and postoperative expectations can be discussed with the patient. Preoperative instruction should be spaced so that the patient has time to assimilate the information and ask questions. Various studies dealing with preoperative instruction have indicated that the well-prepared patient recuperates more rapidly, needs medication less frequently, and develops fewer complications after surgery. In addition, the time of hospitalization is often shortened.[1]

Specific patient instruction is often given concerning deep breathing and coughing, turning and moving, medications, and special equipment that may be used postoperatively. Patients should be taught how to take a deep breath slowly and exhale slowly in a sitting position. This provides good ventilation of the lungs and oxygenation of the blood. After practicing this several times, the patient should take a short breath and cough deeply. Coughing helps remove secretions from the lungs. The patient can be taught to splint an abdominal or thoracic incision by interlacing the fingers and placing the palms over the incision site, or a towel or small pillow can be used. This lessens the muscular strain around the incision when the patient coughs.

Specific positions to be assumed postoperatively should be explained to the patient. Position should be changed frequently after surgery to improve circulation, increase respiratory function, and prevent venous stasis. Leg exercises may be taught if it is anticipated that the patient will not be ambulatory within a day after surgery. These exercises include extension and flexion of the knee and hip joints and rotation of the foot in a circular manner. Other exercises may be recommended according to the patient's specific surgical procedure.

Reassurance that medications will be available postoperatively to control discomfort will help to lower the patient's anxiety. Any special equipment such as drainage tubes and equipment, intravenous therapy, or assisted breathing apparatus should be explained to the patient before surgery. Knowledge of this special equipment will help decrease postoperative anxiety. Many patients are placed in intensive care units after extensive surgical procedures. Electronic monitoring equipment may be frightening to the patient and family if they are not given a simple explanation of how it is used to contribute to patient care. The patient's family often believes that the patient is in a critical condition when placed in the intensive care unit. They should be given the same information the patient is given. Explanation concerning the patient's care can often be given during visiting hours when the family is present.

Psychologic preparation

Preparation for surgery should begin as soon as the patient is told that an operation is necessary. The anticipation of any surgical procedure will result in an emotional reaction. Much can be done to alleviate fears before admission as well as during hospitalization. The patient's reaction will depend on many factors, including personality structure and the pattern of reaction to stressful events in the past.

A surgical operation is a stressful situation in which the patient may believe there is danger of acute pain, serious damage to the body, disability, and death. In addition, there is a fear of the unknown; this can be complicated by fear of anesthesia or fear of separation from activities, family, and friends. The average patient also worries about financial problems, family responsibilities, and employment status. Anxiety will usually increase as the time for surgery draws near.

The nurse can assist the patient, family, and surgical personnel by listening and helping him to verbalize his fears. Often the patient only wants the opportunity to express his fears to a caring, understanding, and accepting person. Members of the patient's family are often not able to listen or empathize with the patient because of their own feelings and stress.

Patients are more willing to express their feelings if they have established a good relationship with a member of the nursing team. Therefore, nurses should try to establish an atmosphere of acceptance and understanding. No attempt should be made to minimize the patient's fears by dismissing these fears as "normal." Thorough discussion of the patient's concerns, with appropriate explanations or referral to the physician, should be carried out by the nurse. Denial may be one of the major defense mechanisms that the patient uses to deal with stress. With this in mind, the nurse should not attempt to give detailed descriptions or instructions to the patient who is unwilling to hear them. Nurses can help dispel any misconceptions and let the patient know that they or the physician are available to discuss concerns. Occasionally, it is helpful to have the patient talk with other people who have had similar surgery. The patient's family should be included in any discussions or explanations whenever possible. They should be encouraged to understand the anxiety the patient faces and to visit often.

Preoperative Orders

The evening before surgery the physician will write the preoperative orders for the patient. Hospitals and physicians will vary in the kind of preoperative preparation desired; however, certain routine procedures are fairly common.

Diet

It is essential that the patient be optimally nourished before surgery. Usually nothing by mouth (NPO) is allowed from midnight until surgery the next morning. (If the planned surgery is not scheduled until late in the day or will be done under local anesthesia, however, the patient may be allowed to eat during the immediate preoperative period.) Withholding food and fluids minimizes the chances of vomiting and aspirating vomitus into the lungs during or immediately after the surgery. Instructions concerning the elimination of food and fluid should be given to the patient before surgery. Accidentally ingesting food or water will usually delay surgery, increasing the hospital stay and expense. The nurse is responsible for removing water from the patient's room and for communicating the patient's NPO status to everyone involved in care.

Elimination

For some types of surgery the physician may request that the patient be catheterized and that a catheter be left in place to keep the bladder empty. A distended bladder can complicate operative procedures on the lower abdomen and increase the chances of bladder trauma during surgery. If the patient is not catheterized, the patient should void before surgery.

Most surgical patients are given an enema preoperatively; however, the procedure is not uniform. The enema may consist of soapsuds, saline, or tap water. There is increasing use of commercially prepared enemas, which are more comfortable for the patient. The reasons for administering a preoperative enema are found in the box below.

Bisacodyl (Dulcolax) suppositories may be ordered instead of enemas. When bowel surgery is to be performed, "enemas until clear" may be ordered, that is, enemas must be given until no fecal matter returns with the solution. The nurse should be sure that all enema solution is returned, and failure to achieve results should be reported to the physician. If an enema is ordered preoperatively, the return of bowel elimination may not occur for several days after surgery; the normal pattern of elimination will take longer to return.

Skin preparation

Formerly it was customary for the nurse to shave the patient on the night before surgery. Recent research shows that this practice is 10 times more likely to cause wound infection than shaving the incisional area just before surgery.

Hair is removed from the area with a sharp, disposable razor. Strokes should be with the grain of the hair shaft to avoid nicking or scraping the skin (Figure 5-1) because such cuts may become sites of infection. If the skin is injured, the surgeon may refuse to perform the surgery. Caution must be used in shaving around moles or warts, and any skin eruption must be reported. In shaving areas such as the axilla and pubic area, the nurse may clip the long hair first to make shaving easier. Care should be taken not to expose or embarrass the patient, who should be left dry and comfortable after the procedure. Scrubbing the operative site the night or morning before surgery with an antiseptic such as povidone-iodine has also been found to decrease wound infections.

Sedation

A sedative is usually ordered by the physician to be given at bedtime the evening before surgery to ensure that the patient gets adequate sleep and rest. After administration of the sedative, the patient should be instructed to remain in bed, since dizziness or confusion may be experienced. In the case of elderly persons, side rails should be used and patients should be observed at frequent intervals. The call light should always be placed within easy reach, and the patient should be taught how to use it properly.

Operative Day
Visitors

On the operative day it is best that visiting be limited to avoid unnecessary stimulation; the patient should be allowed to rest and should be kept as quiet as possible. Close family members should be advised to arrive at least 1 hour before the scheduled time of surgery. Time should be allowed for personal hygiene such as bathing, oral care, and shaving.

Assessment

The vital signs—temperature, pulse, respiration, and blood pressure are checked and recorded. Any elevation of temperature must be reported immediately. All pins and combs are removed from the hair.

The nurse should check the chart carefully to be sure that all data such as laboratory reports of blood and urine have been recorded and that a signed operative permit is attached to the chart.

Reasons for Administering a Preoperative Enema

1. To remove feces from the intestine before surgery on the gastrointestinal tract
2. To relieve the patient of postoperative pain that might be caused by straining to have a bowel movement after abdominal surgery
3. To avoid an impaction postoperatively
4. To avoid exertion or the tendency to strain after certain kinds of surgery, such as eye surgery

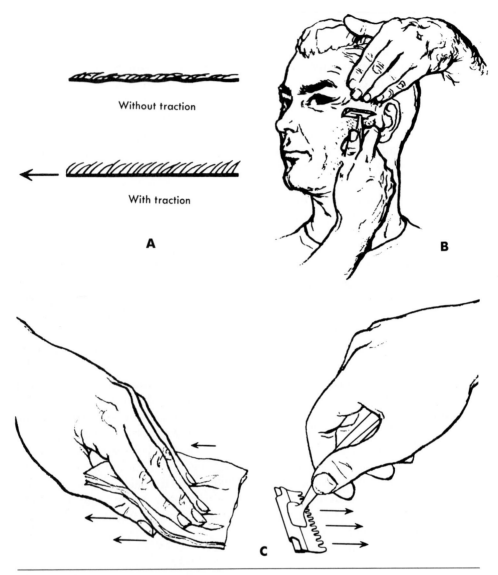

Figure 5-1

Skin shaving. **A,** Skin traction is provided with free hand in direct opposition to slant of hair to tighten and smooth skin and raise hairs in more upright position. **B,** Hair and horny layer of skin are shaved off. **C,** Traction is applied with sponge, and hoe-type razor head is held against skin and stroked with the grain of the hairshaft as shown in B. *(From Pate MO: The preparation manual, Long Island City, NY, Edward Weck and Co Inc.)*

Operative permits should be signed before administration of medications. All preoperative medications and procedures should be accurately charted before the patient goes to the operating room, and a new physician's order sheet should be attached to the record. Charge vouchers and special forms should be included.

Prostheses

Just before transportation to surgery, dentures and removable bridges should be removed and placed in a container marked with the patient's name, then put in a safe place to avoid loss or damage. Contact lenses and any prostheses should be removed and stored.

Makeup

Procedures vary among anesthesiologists, but frequently the anesthetist prefers that all makeup be removed before the patient goes to surgery. Any reduction of oxygen to the tissues may be observed in the lips, face, and nail beds, or it may be detected by the color of the blood at the operative site. Some anesthesiologists believe that removal of nail polish is unnecessary because the hands are covered with sterile drapes and are not accessible, and others have suggested that colored nail polish be removed from one or two fingers.

Valuables

Valuables such as money and jewelry should be listed in the patient's presence, sealed in an envelope, and locked up or given to a responsible member of the family. The nurse should be familiar with the policy of the hospital concerning the care of valuables and should use every precaution to protect the patient's personal property. Often considerable sentiment is attached to the wedding ring, and the patient may be allowed to wear it; however, it should be anchored securely with tape to avoid loss.

Preoperative orders

The patient is given a hospital gown that ties in the back, and all personal articles of clothing are removed. The patient's hair may be covered with a surgical cap. Depending on the type of surgery, and the patient's age and condition, the physician may order a retention catheter inserted into the urinary bladder preoperatively. The physician may also order intravenous fluids or insertion of a gastric tube preoperatively. The surgeon may request that midthigh or knee-high elastic stockings be applied or that the patient's legs be wrapped with elastic bandages to help prevent thrombophlebitis. If elastic stockings are ordered, the nurse should follow the manufacturer's directions for measuring and applying them; if elastic bandages are ordered, 4-, 5-, or 6-inch bandages should be used to wrap the patient's legs from the metatarsals to midthigh, and the bandages should be fastened securely.

Preoperative medications, which are ordered by the anesthesiologist, are usually administered parenterally. The purpose of preoperative medications is to reduce the patient's anxiety about anesthesia and to provide for a smoother induction. Some medications will also reduce secretions.

Some of the preoperative medications commonly prescribed are classified and described in Table 5-2. Preoperative medications are ordered individually for each patient, and consideration is given to the patient's age, his general condition, the presence of other diseases that require med-

---

NURSING CARE GUIDELINES
Preoperative Preparation

Nursing Diagnoses
- Anxiety related to unknown outcomes and unknown environment
- Provide restful environment
- Potential sleep disturbance related to anxiety and unfamiliar surroundings
- High risk for injury while premedicated
- Knowledge deficit, postoperative exercise and activity

Nursing interventions
General
- Explain operative process
- Provide opportunity for verbalization of fears
- Demonstrate and practice deep breathing and coughing
- Explain postoperative positioning
- Explain special procedures and equipment; demonstrate when possible
- Demonstrate and encourage pertinent exercises
- Explain dietary restrictions, for example, nothing by mouth after midnight
- Prepare skin as ordered
- Explain and administer medications
- Provide for spiritual needs

Immediate
- Check that identification band is in place
- Remove and store hairpins, dentures, jewelry, contact lenses, and prostheses
- Store valuables
- Give patient a hospital gown
- Check skin preparation
- Have patient void; chart time and amount
- Administer and chart medications
- Instruct the patient to remain in bed and put the bedrails up
- Complete chart:
  Operative permit signed
  Laboratory data complete
  Order sheets, progress rates, history, and so on included
  Charge vouchers and forms included
  Special procedures completed and charted

Expected Outcomes
- Best physical and psychologic
- Adjustment to the surgical experience
- No postoperative complications

Table 5-2

Preoperative Medications		
Classification	Action	Nursing considerations
Sedatives		
Secobarbital Sodium (Seconal) Pentobarbital Sodium (Nembutal) Promethazine (Phenergan)	Relieve anxiety; has relaxing effect	May cause confusion, hypotension, and dizziness; potentiate narcotics
Tranquilizers		
Diazepam (Valium) Midazolam HCI (Versed)	Relieve anxiety	May cause confusion, hypotension, and dizziness; potentiate narcotics
Narcotics		
Meperidine HCI (Demerol) Morphine sulfate	Sedation and pain relief	May cause nausea, respiratory and circulatory depression
Anticholinergics		
Atropine sulfate Glycopyrrolate (Robinul)	Control secretions; maintain clear airway	Causes dry mouth, tachycardia
H$_2$ receptor antagonists		
Cimetidine (Tagamet) Ranitidine (Zantac) Famotidine (Pepcid)	Decrease gastric secretions and acidity	Occasional mild dizziness

ications, and the anesthetizing agent to be administered.

The medication is ordered to be administered on call or at a specific hour, and it is important that the nurse give the medication on time so that its maximum effect is reached during induction of anesthesia. If for any reason the medication is not administered as directed, the anesthesiologist should be notified so that the necessary adjustments may be made. The hospital may require that identification be attached to the patient's wrist, including such information as the patient's name, room number, medication given, hour administered, and signature of the nurse.

Just before being medicated, the patient should be requested to void and the amount and time should be noted; the inability to void should be reported to the physician. Vital signs should be taken and recorded. Advise the patient to stay in bed after the medication has been given and put the bedrails up.

Transport

The patient may be transferred to the operating room in his own bed or by stretcher. He should be moved carefully and with as little confusion as possible. The patient should be protected from drafts and exposure by applying cotton blankets and should be made comfortable with a small pillow. The nurse or transport personnel should accompany the patient and remain until relieved by a member of the operating room staff. The patient's record is given to the operating room nurse, who is also advised verbally of the patient's name and any significant problem existing at the moment.

INTRAOPERATIVE CARE

Aseptic surgery had its beginning about 1867 with the work of Joseph Lister, an English surgeon. At that time wound infection complicated most surgeries, and puerperal infection was common in obstetric wards. After observing the process of wound infection, Lister concluded that it was caused by microbes. It was not until 1878 that Robert Koch demonstrated that the organisms so well described by Louis Pasteur actually were present in infectious lesions. However, based on this belief, Lister began using a solution of carbolic acid in the operating room, as well as saturating dressings over wounds. These measures resulted in a remarkable decrease in the incidence of wound infection.

Although modern science has progressed far since Lister, the basic definition of **surgical asepsis** remains unchanged. It is a condition in which there is complete absence of germs. Asepsis is absolute; there is no compromise or modification. Many situations are encountered on the clinical unit that require aseptic techniques, such as catheterization or changing surgical dressings. The slightest error may mean prolonged illness or hospitalization for the patient. The nurse should know the methods used to achieve asepsis and the variables that determine the effectiveness or ineffectiveness of the method employed.

Surgical Asepsis

Surgical asepsis prevents organisms from entering the body. Surgical aseptic techniques are employed whenever the skin or mucous membranes are perforated or incised. Any object that comes in contact with a wound must be absolutely free of pathogenic organisms to prevent all contaminants from entering the area of operation or any wound. Procedures in operating rooms are carried out under strict surgical asepsis; this involves preparation of the patient's skin and sterilization of all instruments, linens, dressings, or other materials coming in contact with the wound. It includes special attire for the surgeon and assistants, properly cleaning and disinfecting all inanimate objects in the room, and maintaining proper temperature and humidity. It may include sterilization of the air. It is also called sterile technique and aseptic technique.

Sterilization

Sterilization is a process by which all forms of living microorganisms are completely destroyed, including spores and viruses. The method of sterilization is determined by the supplies and equipment that are to be used. In surgical asepsis all supplies and equipment are sterilized before use and are handled only with sterile equipment. Two factors are important in determining the type of sterilization to be used:

1. The type of microorganism; some pathogens are easily destroyed by ordinary methods of disinfection, whereas others are extremely resistant.

2. The degree of contamination; the greater the amount of contamination, the longer it will take to ensure complete destruction of pathogenic organisms.

Heat is one of the most effective and convenient methods of destroying microorganisms. Boiling is a form of moist heat and is one of the oldest methods of sterilization. It is commonly used in the home and under most conditions is satisfactory. Equipment to be sterilized by boiling must be completely immersed in the water, and timing begins when the water begins to boil. Most vegetative forms of bacteria will be killed if boiled for 10 to 20 minutes.

Steam under pressure is the most dependable method of sterilizing, since it will rapidly destroy all forms of microorganisms. This method of sterilizing is called **autoclaving.** Steam enters the autoclave under pressure, which increases the temperature of the steam. During the sterilizing process the temperature is maintained at about 250° F (121° C) and at 15 to 17 pounds of pressure for a specified time. At the completion of the process the pressure is reduced to zero and the load is allowed to dry.

Dry heat sterilization uses circulating hot air provided by an electric oven sterilizer. It may be compared to an ordinary baking oven. It will penetrate many different materials, such as oils and closed containers that are not affected by steam. The kind of materials, the way they are prepared, and the loading of the oven will determine the length of time necessary for sterilization to be accomplished. In general, the time required for hot air sterilization will vary between 1 and 6 hours and in some cases may be longer.

Ethylene oxide is a chemical found in both liquid and vapor form. If the liquid form comes into contact with the skin, it causes blisters; inhaling the gas causes nausea, vomiting, dizziness, and irritation of the mucous membranes. Research has demonstrated that exposure to ethylene oxide gas will kill all forms of vegetative bacteria, including spore-forming types, and viruses. During the past decade its use has increased in sterilizing equipment that cannot be subjected to other methods of sterilizing, for example, medical and surgical equipment such as instruments with lenses (cytoscope, cystoscope, and bronchoscope) and plastic equipment such as infant incubators and the artificial kidney machine. It is also useful for sterilizing polyethylene tubing and some rubber goods.

The use of ethylene oxide gas requires special types of sterilizers. The process by which sterilization is accomplished is complex and involves several factors, including temperature, time, concentration of the gas, moisture, and proper packaging of materials. The actual sterilizing time varies from 1 to 4 hours; however, before the supplies or equipment can be used, all the residual gas must be allowed to dissipate. It is for this reason that materials exposed to ethylene oxide are not used for 24 to 36 hours.

The sterilization of materials usually occurs in the central service department of the hospital. In addition to being responsible for the mechanics of sterilization, this department provides supplies of uniform quality and contributes to reducing costs by the efficient use of expensive equipment.

The Operative Team

Those giving care to the patient during the intraoperative period are generally prepared to be sterile or nonsterile members of the surgical team. Sterile members of the team include the surgeon, who may be assisted by another physician, and the scrub nurse or technician. Unsterile personnel include the anesthesiologist (physician) or anesthetist (nurse), the circulating nurse, and various technicians. To best serve the needs of the patient at a critical time, team members must work efficiently as a unit.

The scrub nurse

As the sterile nursing member of the operative team, the primary role of the scrub nurse is to anticipate the needs of the surgeon and assist at the operative site. This nurse prepares the instruments and materials to be used by the surgeon (Figure 5-2) and may assist with the surgical procedure if no other medical personnel assume this role. The scrub nurse or technician must have a thorough knowledge of aseptic technique (Figure 5-3), as well as the ability and stamina to work efficiently under pressure. Manual dexterity and good organizational skills are also important.

The circulating nurse

The circulating nurse has the major role in managing the operating room. This nonsterile team member must have an overall picture of the needs of the patient, as well as those of the other members of the team. This individual must be a registered nurse. Some of the duties of the circulating nurse are as follows:

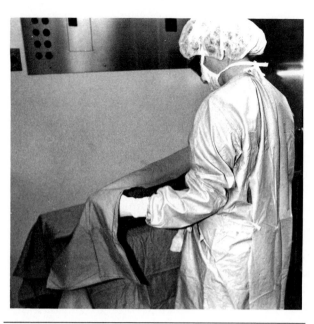

Figure 5-2
Scrub nurse protects gloves with cuff of drape when opening inner wrapper of pack, which will serve as sterile table cover. (*From Meeker MH and Rothrock JC: Alexander's care of the patient in surgery, ed 9, St Louis, 1991, Mosby-Year Book Inc.*)

1. Maintain a safe environment for the patient. This may take the form of observing breaks in sterile technique, providing for safe use of complex equipment, and keeping the operating room free from hazards.
2. Anticipate the need for, and obtain supplies and equipment for the sterile team.
3. Communicate information about the patient's status to other members of the health team and the patient's significant others.

Anesthesia

Most patients have some fear of anesthesia, such as going to sleep and not waking up, or some fear of the unknown. Some patients may fear waking up and experiencing pain during surgery, acting bizarrely when anesthetized, or experiencing uncomfortable after-effects such as nausea and vomiting.

Most fears can be allayed if the patient is well informed about the anesthetic chosen and the effects it will produce. The kind of anesthetic is selected for the individual patient, considering the patient's physical condition, age, preference, and the type, site, and length of the operation to be

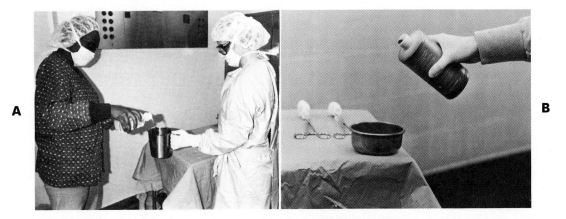

Figure 5-3
A, When pouring solution into receptacle held by scrub nurse, circulating nurse maintains safe margin of space to avoid contamination of sterile surfaces. **B,** Care must be used when pouring solution into receptacle on sterile field to avoid splashing fluids onto sterile field. Placement of receptacle near edge of table permits circulating nurse to pour solution without reaching over any portion of sterile field. *(From Meeker MH and Rothrock JC: Alexander's care of the patient in surgery, ed 9, St Louis, 1991, Mosby-Year Book Inc.)*

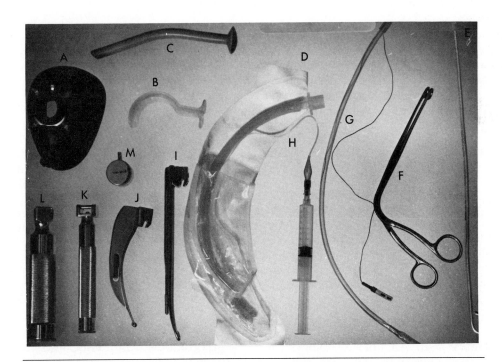

Figure 5-4
Commonly used anesthesia equipment. **A,** Mask. **B,** Oral airway. **C,** Nasal airway. **D,** Tongue blade. **E,** Stylet for endotracheal tube. **F,** Magill forceps. **G,** Esophageal stethoscope with temperature monitor. **H,** Endotracheal tube. **I,** Miller blade. **J,** Macintosh blade. **K,** Pediatric laryngoscope handle. **L,** Laryngoscope handle. **M,** Precordial stethoscope. *(From Meeker MH and Rothrock JC: Alexander's care of the patient in surgery, ed 9, St Louis, 1991, Mosby-Year Book Inc.)*

Table 5-3

Selected General Anesthetics

Drug	Characteristics	Nursing considerations
Inhalant agents		
Isoflurane (Forane)	Volatile liquid: provides good muscle relaxation; rapid induction and recovery; potentiates muscle relaxants significantly.	Depresses respirations; monitor rate and quality of respirations closely.
Halothane (Fluothane)	Volatile liquid: rapid induction but poor degree of muscle relaxation. Evidence suggests liver damage may be side effect. Shivering commonly occurs as patient awakens.	Anesthesiologist should be informed if patient has any history of liver disease, alcoholism, or gallbladder disease. Keep patient warm postoperatively. Monitor closely for cardiac arrhythmias.
Enflurane (Ethrane)	Volatile liquid: slow acting but fairly good muscle relaxation and analgesia can be achieved. Can cause fatal arrhythmias, particularly in presence of epinephrine-like drugs.	Monitor vital signs closely and provide for safety during what is often a prolonged (45-minute) wake-up period.
Nitrous oxide	Gas: very popular, weak agent that is used in combination with oxygen and other anesthetic agents. Nonexplosive; may create hypoxia.	Monitor for hypoxia and be prepared to administer oxygen.
Intravenous agents		
Short-acting barbiturates: methohexital (Brevital), thiamylal (Surital), thiopental (Pentothal) sodium	Thiopental sodium is most popular of this group. Given at onset of surgery to provide rapid and smooth induction. May cause laryngospasm, respiratory depression, and sudden hypotension.	Assess respiratory status closely postoperatively.
Narcotic and nonnarcotic analgesics: morphine, meperidine, droperidol (Innover), fentanyl	Used with other anesthetic agents to provide effective analgesia during surgery. Major side effect is respiratory depression.	Monitor respirations closely. Keep naloxone (Narcan) on hand to keep reverse narcotic effect. Use narcotics sparingly or in decreased doses during the first 12 postoperative hours.
Ketamine (Ketalar, Ketaject)	Dissociative agent used for short procedures. Provides analgesia and loss of memory of procedure without putting patient to sleep. Often used in pediatric surgery.	Protect patient from additional stimuli (noises, touching) during wake-up period. In adults, may cause confusion and excitement for 24 hours after surgery. Assess for hypertension and respiratory depression.

performed (Figure 5-4). An anesthesiologist, a physician who specializes in the selection and administration of anesthesia, chooses the anesthetic agents following a preoperative visit. During the visit the anesthesiologist assesses the patient's physical and emotional state, discusses individual preferences, explains the procedure of administering anesthesia, answers questions, and in general promotes confidence and helps to relieve anxiety.

Anesthesia is effected by the anesthesiologist or an anesthetist. A nurse anesthetist is a professional nurse who has received postgraduate training in the administration of anesthetics and who functions under the supervision of an anesthesiologist.

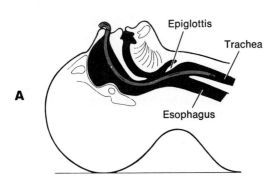
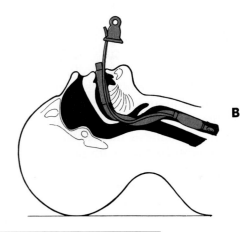

Figure 5-5

A, Intranasal intubation. Note adapter at proximal end of tube that can be used to attach anesthetic equipment. **B,** Oral intubation. Note inflated cuff.

Patients will be under close surveillance at all times during the operation and during the immediate postoperative period.

Some hospitals have anesthetizing rooms in which the patient is anesthetized; when the surgeon is ready, the patient is wheeled into the operating room. It should be remembered that the patient is sedated and in a strange and sometimes frightening environment. There should be no bright lights or unnecessary noise and talking.

The kind of anesthetic administered may affect the postoperative condition and return to consciousness. An understanding of anesthetizing agents will help the nurse assess the patient's condition and anticipate postoperative needs.

Types

Anesthesia is classified as *general* or *regional*. When the surgeon wishes all sensations in the entire body to be suspended temporarily, the patient is given a general anesthetic. When only a part of the body is involved, the patient may be given a regional anesthetic. General anesthetics include drugs that are administered by inhalation or by injection into the bloodstream (Table 5-3).

Inhalation anesthesia. Drugs used in inhalation anesthesia may be in the form of liquids that vaporize, with the patient inhaling the vapor; examples include Forane and halothane. Inhalation drugs are also in the form of gases such as nitrous oxide. Several examples of inhalants are described in Table 5-3.

Inhalation anesthetics render the patient un-

conscious, therefore pain is eliminated. They also provide muscle relaxation and alleviate anxiety because the patient is asleep. All drugs used to achieve inhalation anesthesia are administered in combination with oxygen or air by a mask or through a tube that is inserted into the trachea or bronchi.

Endotracheal intubation ensures that the airway will remain open and that the lungs can be aerated even when the chest wall is entered. The endotracheal tube is held in place by a balloon that is inflated after it is inserted (Figure 5-5). The presence of the balloon and the pressure it exerts on the walls of the trachea will cause some irritation of the mucosa; occasionally, postoperative edema in the area can cause respiratory difficulty. Therefore, the patient must be watched carefully for symptoms of respiratory obstruction when endotracheal tubes have been used.

Intravenous drugs. Some drugs given intravenously are administered in combination with inhalation anesthesia. These anesthetics reduce the amount of the inhalation anesthetics required. The drugs used are short-acting barbiturates that produce unconsciousness in 30 seconds. The most common drugs in use are thiopental (Pentothal) sodium and thiamylal (Surital). When large amounts have been given, the patient will not return to consciousness quickly. The patient must be watched carefully for laryngeal spasm (which may be indicated by retraction of the soft tissues about the neck muscles), severe cyanosis, and restlessness.

Other intravenous agents are commonly used to maintain anesthesia throughout the surgical procedure. These include narcotics such as morphine, meperidine (Demerol), and fentanyl (Sublimaze). These are often used in conjunction with nitrous oxide and referred to as nitrous-narcotic anesthesia. Ketamine (Ketalar) results in a dissociative anesthesia that leaves the patient awake in a trance-like state with no pain or memory of the surgery.

Muscle relaxants. Curare and succinylcholine (Anectine) are powerful muscle-relaxants that may be administered to increase relaxation of abdominal muscles during surgery or to facilitate endotracheal intubation. Pancuronium (Pavulon) is a synthetic neuromuscular blocking agent used primarily to produce skeletal muscle relaxation during surgery after general anesthesia has been induced. It is compatible with all the general anesthetics currently in use.[5] Both drugs may cause respiratory difficulty, and the patient should be watched extremely carefully.

Regional anesthetics. Regional anesthetics are local anesthetics used to inhibit nerve impulses to various parts of the body. A local anesthetic drug is injected in and around nerves, resulting in anesthesia of the area supplied by the particular nerves.

Several different drugs may be used including procaine (Novocain), tetracaine (Pontocaine), and lidocaine (Xylocaine; Table 5-4). Regional anesthesia may be divided into the categories of spinal, epidural, nerve block, infiltration, and local.

Spinal anesthesia. A solution of a local anesthetic drug may be injected into the subarachnoid space, which contains cerebrospinal fluid. The drug anesthetizes nerves as they leave the spinal cord. The method of injection is the same as that for any spinal puncture (Figure 5-6).

This type of anesthesia is used for surgery involving the abdomen, perineum, and lower extremities. Use of this method on the upper part of the body would paralyze the respiratory muscles and the diaphragm.

Under spinal anesthesia, the patient may remain awake; therefore it is necessary to avoid any careless conversation that may be misinterpreted by the patient. During the operation the patient may be aware of pressure or pulling sensations but no pain. After spinal anesthesia the patient generally is kept flat in bed for several hours. Vital signs, especially blood pressure, should be watched because hypotension may occur. Sensations to the anesthetized part do not return immediately, and careful positioning of the patient is important to prevent later discomfort. The patient may have severe headache, which is thought to be caused by spinal fluid leaking from the puncture site. The headache often lasts for several days, but analgesics plus an increased oral intake will help alleviate the discomfort. Measures taken by the anesthesiologist to reduce the incidence of headache include the use of fine-gauge needles and the placement of a "blood patch" at the insertion site to prevent the leakage of spinal fluid.

Epidural anesthesia. This form of anesthesia

Table 5-4

Selected Regional Anesthetics		
Drug	**Characteristics**	**Nursing considerations**
Procaine (Novocain)	Used for infiltration, spinal, nerve block; widely used in dentistry. Available with or without epinephrine.	Observe for allergic reaction. If combined with epinephrine for use on injured fingers or toes, may cause poor local circulation.
Benzocaine (Solarcaine)	Use topically and available commercially	Avoid use near eyes. May cause skin irritation.
Lidocaine (Xylocaine) hydrochloride	Used topically and for infiltration nerve block, such as epidural, caudal, and spinal. Rapid action and long duration. Also used to treat cardiac arrhythmias. Comes with and without epinephrine.	Monitor for changes in vital signs, excitability.
Tetracaine (Pontocaine)	Used topically and for infiltration nerve block, such as spinal and caudal. More potent and has more toxicity and longer duration than other agents.	Protect patient from injury, burns during period when no sensation is present.

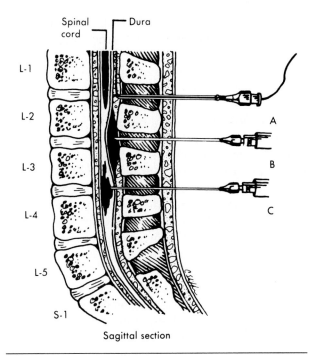

Spinal cord — Dura

L-1
L-2
L-3
L-4
L-5
S-1

A
B
C

Sagittal section

Figure 5-6

Location of needle point and injected anesthetic relative to dura. **A,** Epidural catheter. **B,** Single injection epidural. **C,** Spinal anesthesia. (Interspaces most commonly used are L4-5, L3-4, and L2-3.) *(From Meeker MH and Rothrock JC: Alexander's care of the patient in surgery, ed 9, St Louis, 1991, Mosby-Year Book Inc.)*

involves the injection of a local agent into the extradural space outside the spinal canal. Examples of epidural anesthesia are the sacral and caudal blocks, which are used to anesthetize the perineum during deliveries.

Peripheral nerve block. This type of anesthesia is used to provide anesthesia or freedom from pain in body structures innervated by selected nerve systems. Examples include the brachial, femoral, and sciatic nerves.

Infiltration anesthesia. Infiltration anesthesia is achieved by injection of a local anesthetic drug directly into the tissues. This type of anesthesia precedes minor operations in which tissue is incised. Local anesthesia should be used whenever possible; however, it should not be used if patients are extremely apprehensive.

Because all drugs used for local anesthesia are potentially toxic, the patient should be carefully observed for signs of itching of the skin, twitching, convulsions, cyanosis, nausea, and vomiting. Blood pressure, pulse, and respiration should also be carefully checked. The patient is conscious but may be drowsy if a sedative has been administered before the surgical procedure.

Topical anesthesia. Drops, sprays, lotions, and ointments are types of topical anesthetics. They are applied directly to the skin or mucosa for temporary anesthesia before simple procedure or for pain relief. Many of these products are sold over the counter in pharmacies.

Alternative forms of anesthesia

Hypothermia. **Hypothermia** is a means of decreasing oxygen consumption during anesthesia and surgery by slowly lowering the body temperature to between 82° and 86° F (28° and 30° C). As the amount of oxygen needed by the tissues decreases, less blood is required to meet tissue needs. The circulation can then be briefly compromised or interrupted to facilitate surgery performed in vital areas, such as in cardiac and neurosurgical operations.

Hypothermia is induced by covering the patient with a blanket containing coils through which a mixture of ice water and alcohol circulates. For some major cardiac and neurologic procedures, blood may be cooled outside the body and reinfused into the patient. Dangers exist in lowering the temperature and also in rewarming the body after surgery. Continuous care and observation are necessary. During rewarming, the patient must be closely watched for cardiac arrhythmias, respiratory depression, unstable temperatures, and skin irritations. Careful monitoring of intake and output vital signs is essential.

Local hypothermia refers to lowering the temperature of a part of the body, such as a leg. This procedure is primarily used to anesthetize the limb before amputation, avoiding the necessity for general anesthesia. The extremity is packed in ice for approximately 2 to 3 hours, or the blanket device can be used. It is useful for patients who are poor surgical risks but requires constant observation of the patient and close coordination in the operating room.

Acupuncture. Acupuncture is an ancient Oriental method of achieving anesthesia in which fine metal needles are inserted beneath the skin at particular body points to provide anesthesia. There is no clear explanation as to why it is effective, but the technique has been successfully used, particularly for minor procedures.

Hypnosis. The power of the mind over the body forms the basis for this anesthetic practice. Pain is controlled by the power of suggestion. Such methods as hypnosis and acupuncture do have the advantage of having none of the side effects that chemical anesthetics may cause; however, they are not widely used or well regarded by the medical establishment in this country.

Intraoperative Complications
Malignant hyperthermia

Malignant hyperthermia is a rapid rise in body temperature that can be triggered by the anesthetic agents or muscle relaxants used during surgery. Its exact pathophysiology is not known, but it is related to a defect in cellular metabolism resulting in hypercalcemia. Early warning signs of this potentially fatal complication are tachycardia, muscle rigidity, and a rapid rise in temperature (as much as 1° C every 5 minutes). Treatment consists of cardiopulmonary support during which efforts are made to stabilize vital signs, cool the patient with ice, and reduce muscle spasms with dantrolene (Dantrium). Because this condition is hereditary, the nurse preparing the patient for surgery should ask if there has been any family history of this condition or of sudden death during surgery. Patients known to have experienced this complication should be advised to wear a Medic Alert bracelet identifying this problem.

POSTOPERATIVE ASSESSMENT AND INTERVENTIONS

Recovery Room Care

Patients recovering from anesthesia must be watched constantly until they have recovered from anesthesia and their vital signs are stable. Most hospitals maintain facilities for the immediate postoperative care of the patient, and the patient is transferred from the operating room to the recovery unit on a specially designed bed or stretcher. The recovery room is generally located near the operating room and is equipped with the necessary supplies, drugs, and equipment for care in any emergency that might arise. The recovery room is considered a part of the surgical suite and is under the supervision of the anesthesiologist.

The anesthesiologist accompanies the patient from the operating room to the recovery room and advises the nurses of the patient's condition and any special problems that require care or attention. The anesthesiologist will make sure that the patient's airway is clear and that vital signs are satisfactory. Before leaving the patient, the anesthesiologist will inform the recovery room nurse of the patient's condition, and the postoperative vital signs should be taken. The patient should be protected by side rails on the bed, which may be padded to prevent injury to a particularly restless patient. The patient should be moved as carefully as possible. Anesthetics are stored in the body during surgery, and until they are eliminated, every movement of the patient, such as from operating table to stretcher or bed, riding in elevators or wheeling around corners in corridors, may cause serious changes in the vital signs. Regardless of the type of surgery the patient has undergone, immediate postoperative care should include the maintenance of privacy and warmth, mouth care, back care, position changes, proper body alignment, and appropriate wound care.

Airway

The immediate responsibility of the nurse is to make certain that the **airway** is clear and that it remains clear. The patient should be turned and placed in Sims' position with the head flat to allow for drainage of blood or mucus from the mouth. When it is not possible to turn the patient, the head should be turned to the side. If increased secretions obstruct the respiratory passages, they are aspirated with a catheter attached to suction. If the suction is on, the catheter must be pinched while it is being inserted to prevent damage to the mucous membrane. If secretions have been removed but evidence of respiratory difficulty is still present, the nurse's thumbs and fingers should be placed at the angle of the jaw on both sides and the jaw should be pushed forward (Figure 5-7). The tongue may be grasped with a piece of gauze and pulled forward. If these measures do not relieve the difficulty, the anesthesiologist should be called. Often the anesthesiologist leaves an airway in place until the patient shows signs of regaining consciousness (Figure 5-8).

Breathing

The patient's respiratory rate should be checked at frequent intervals; shallow, quiet, and slow respirations may be an early sign of respiratory difficulty. The movement of air in and out of the lungs can be felt by holding the hand near the patient's mouth. Respiratory rates of 30 or above or below 16 should alert the nurse to difficulty. Signs and symptoms of anoxia that should be observed are included in the box on p. 117.

Many anesthetics and anesthetic adjuncts depress the respiratory mechanism. Narcotic anesthetics, sedatives, and neuromuscular blockers all have a negative effect on respiratory activity. The recovery room nurse must be aware of the types

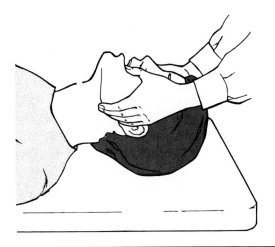

Figure 5-7

Method of pushing jaw forward to relieve respiratory difficulty.

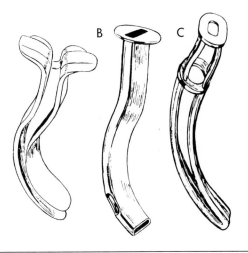

Figure 5-8

Artificial airways. **A,** Plastic. **B,** Rubber. **C,** Metal.

of agents used during the surgery and the time of their administration.

The patient who has had a neuromuscular block (curare, succinylcholine) is often requested to lift the head or in some other way demonstrate the return of muscle control before the airway is removed.

Patients whose respirations are below 12 per minute as a result of narcotic anesthesia may be medicated with a narcotic antagonist such as naloxone hydrochloride (Narcan) or levallorphan tartrate (Lorfan). These drugs, given parenterally, work rapidly to reverse narcotic-induced respiratory depression.

Signs and Symptoms of Anoxia

Slow, sighing respirations
Rapid, shallow breathing
Noisy respirations
Dyspnea
Rapid, thready pulse
Apprehension
Restlessness
Pallor
Cyanosis

Circulation

Blood pressure and pulse should be taken as ordered or as the patient's condition indicates. The patient's preoperative blood pressure should be known for comparisons. A falling systolic pressure or cardiac arrhythmias should be reported immediately. A critical systolic pressure must be determined for each patient individually based on preoperative readings. A drop in blood pressure may occur after the administration of certain types of anesthetics, muscle-relaxing drugs, or some tranquilizing drugs. It may also occur as the result of moving the patient or of unrelieved pain. The pulse should be checked for rate, rhythm, and volume. A drop in blood pressure and a weak, rapid, thready pulse with cool, moist skin may indicate severe bleeding or shock, and the physician should be notified immediately. Treatment is based on the cause, and the physician will order the appropriate procedures.

Dressings

The nurse must check dressings and bed linens beneath the patient frequently for evidence of drainage or bleeding. If bright red blood appears, the dressing should be observed again within a short period. The surgeon should be notified if there is any increase in bleeding. Dressings should also be checked for constriction.

Drainage

All drainage tubes are connected to the appropriate type of drainage. They should be properly connected and patent. Gastric tubes are connected to suction; urinary drainage tubes are connected to the proper drainage container (Figure 5-9).

Intravenous therapy

It is the nurse's responsibility to carefully observe the patient who is receiving intravenous fluids.

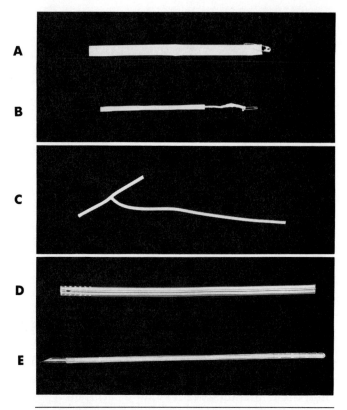

Figure 5-9

Commonly used surgical drains. **A,** Penrose drain. **B,** Cigarette drain. **C,** T-tube. **D,** Abramson all-purpose drain with three lumens. **E,** Saratoga sump drain. *(From Phipps, WJ and others: Medical-surgical nursing: concepts and clinical practice, ed 4, St Louis, 1991, Mosby-Year Book Inc.)*

The rate of flow is ordered, and the number of drops per minute must be regulated. The injection site should be watched for swelling, which indicates that the cannula has slipped out of the vein and fluid is entering the soft tissues. When the nurse aspirates the line with a syringe, blood should appear in the tubing. If blood does not appear, the intravenous fluid has infiltrated. The patient's complaint of burning pain at the site is often the first sign of inflammation or infiltration. When these symptoms occur the intravenous infusion should be removed and restarted in another area. Nurses should be continuously alert for possible complications such as respiratory difficulty, circulatory overload, and thrombophlebitis. Further information concerning fluid and electrolyte imbalance can be found in Chapter 4.

Physician's orders

The nurse should check the physician's orders for any procedures or medications, such as admin-istration of intravenous fluids or blood, and carry out all orders.

Relief of pain

As the patient begins to awaken, he may complain of pain. Patients who are extremely apprehensive before surgery may show evidence of pain early in the postoperative period. Before giving pain-relieving drugs, the nurse should consider the length of time since the preoperative sedatives were administered, the type and action of the anesthetizing agent used, the status of vital signs, the age of the patient, and the preoperative emotional state. Whenever any question arises concerning the administration of a narcotic, the physician should be consulted. The patient should be closely monitored for signs of respiratory depression and hypotension.

Voiding

The patient should be encouraged to void while still in the recovery room. With the return to full consciousness and the awareness of pain, the patient becomes tense and voiding may become difficult. The nurse should encourage the patient to void before painful stimuli cause tension or after the pain has been relieved by analgesics. If the patient has an indwelling catheter, the nurse should position the collection unit for optimum drainage. An accurate record of urinary output should be maintained.

Transfer to patient's room or special unit

The length of time the patient remains in the recovery room will be determined by his immediate postoperative condition. When the vital signs are stabilized and consciousness has been regained, the patient may be transferred from the recovery room. The patient is considered conscious by demonstrating orientation to person, place, and time. At the time of transfer the nurse from the recovery room gives a report about the condition of the patient, including any problems that occurred during this immediate postoperative period. If the patient needs continuing close monitoring, transfer to a special unit may be necessary.

Intensive Care Unit

The evolution of the intensive care unit (ICU) began early in the 1960s. Nearly all units were in large metropolitan hospitals. Now even small rural hospitals have a few beds set aside for the care of critically ill patients. The nurse-to-patient ratio is low, and the nurses have extensive training to provide expert nursing care and to meet any emergency that might arise. Today the number of beds has increased, and the numbers and kinds of patients admitted to the ICU have also increased. A patient is admitted to the ICU because of the need for intensive nursing and medical care, which it is assumed cannot be given in the regular clinical units. A large number of diseases and disorders are a potential threat to the life of the individual. When vital processes are compromised, intensive nursing and medical care may maintain those processes until the inner resources of the human body can effectively take control.

The increasing number of patients whose lives may be saved cannot always be cared for adequately in a single unit. Separate intensive care units for specific kinds of patients, such as burn units, shock units, coronary care units, respiratory care units, neurosurgical units, neonatal and pediatric care units, and renal care units, exist in most large hospitals. Nurses assigned to these units have participated in special courses and are considered experts in intensive care nursing.

Nursing personnel in the ICU include the head nurse, who is responsible for the nursing care given to all patients. The head nurse organizes and plans the work, assigns duties, and supervises all personnel in the unit. Nurses, technicians, and respiratory therapists participate in patient care in the ICU. The ICU is frequently the scene of crisis situations, and personnel must be able to use good judgment and make accurate decisions quickly in any emergency. Emergencies must be anticipated and appropriate measures initiated even before the physician arrives. Many ICUs have special protocols, or standing orders, that allow the nurse to administer oxygen, medications, and intravenous fluids to save the life of the patient. Special equipment such as monitors, respirators, and defibrillators are always available. The respiratory therapist has become increasingly important in helping to maintain inhalation equipment and its proper functioning and in the proper administration of various types of respiratory therapy by continuously monitoring ventilators and supervising the administration of oxygen or aerosol therapy.

Visitors are strictly limited in the ICU. Usually only close members of the family are permitted to visit for short periods. Extraneous diversion such as flowers, radios, televisions, and telephones are often prohibited. When the condition improves so that intensive care is no longer needed, the patient is transferred to a room in a clinical unit.

Continuing Postoperative Care

The continued postoperative care of the patient is directed toward the prevention of complications, rehabilitation, and a return to normal living. A member of the family should be permitted to see the patient and in some instances may be allowed to remain with the patient.

Comfort and safety measures

Postoperative patients should be protected by side rails on the bed. A pillow may be placed under the patient's head, and the head of the bed may be slightly raised. Because the patient is sensitive to temperature changes, care should be taken to avoid chilling by exposure to drafts; electric fans or air conditioners should not blow directly onto the patient. The patient may feel cool to the touch and may complain of being cold. This is because of air-conditioned operating and recovery rooms, as well as a normal circulatory response to stress. The patient may be covered with a blanket until the skin is warm and dry, after which the blanket should be removed to prevent overheating. The patient who becomes too warm will become restless, and excessive perspiration will result in the loss of body fluids and important electrolytes.

Oral and back care should be given and the face and hands washed. The patient is turned onto the side in Sims' position, with a pillow placed to the back and between the legs to give support. If intake of water is not permitted, the lips should be moistened with cool water at intervals. The room should be well ventilated and free from unnecessary noise.

The patient should be turned regularly every 2 hours from side to side unless the type of surgery performed limits positioning. Turning is essential to prevent respiratory complications and thrombus formation.

Coughing and deep breathing

The purposes of having the patient breathe deeply and cough are to remove mucus and other secretions that accumulate in the respiratory passages during anesthesia and to facilitate expansion of the lungs. Research suggests that forceful expulsive coughing may compromise respiratory recovery by collapsing the alveoli. Coughing exercises therefore are generally done only for patients with secretions and mucus present in the bronchial passageways. When the patient has been taught these exercises preoperatively, and understands their importance, procedures are accomplished more readily and thoroughly.

Many hospitals use techniques such as encouraging the patient to yawn, use of the incentive spirometer, and specific respiratory therapies such as intermittent positive pressure breathing. All of these techniques stimulate deep breathing. If coughing is indicated, it is encouraged after deep breathing, it should be deep and should result in expectorating the mass of mucus from the respiratory passages. Better results may be obtained if the patient is placed in a sitting position and the nurse assists by splinting the incision with a folded towel or pillow to relieve the strain. Pain medication administered approximately 1 hour before coughing and deep breathing will benefit the patient who is experiencing discomfort. If the patient is unable to cough up mucus and secretions accumulated in the respiratory passages, they should be removed by suctioning. Patients who have surgery of the brain, the spinal cord, or the eyes should not be permitted to cough, since this will increase intracranial pressure.

Lung sounds should be evaluated regularly (i.e., at least once each shift) to assess the lungs for secretions or diminished breath sounds.

Voiding

The postoperative patient should void within 8 to 10 hours after surgery. The combination of anesthesia, surgery, pain, and apprehension can result in the patient's inability to urinate. A distended bladder can be palpated by examining for fullness above the symphysis pubis. Often the patient is uncomfortable and may void only in small, frequent amounts.

If the patient's condition permits, the bathroom may be used with the assistance of the nurse. Providing adequate hydration through intravenous fluids or taking increased fluids by mouth when permitted will facilitate voiding. Running water while the patient is attempting to void, placing the patient's hands in warm water, or pouring warm water over the genital area may help. The patient should be catheterized as a last resort and only when the bladder is distended and palpable above the pubis and the patient complains of distress.

If the patient has an indwelling urinary catheter, the nurse should monitor the output every 2 hours for the first 24 hours. Care should be taken to position the collecting unit below the patient to facilitate gravity drainage. Routine catheter care should be followed to minimize the possibility of bladder infection. Records should be maintained of all output (see Chapter 19).

Bowel function

After surgery of the gastrointestinal tract, peristalsis is temporarily absent and usually does not return for approximately 48 hours. The patient's expulsion of flatus or spontaneous movement of the bowels indicates that normal peristalsis has returned. Bowel sounds should be checked once each shift in all four quadrants of the abdomen with a stethoscope, and the nurse should question the patient concerning the passing of gas. Cathartics are not usually administered to surgical patients, and they are not encouraged to have bowel evacuation for several days after surgery. Patients who are accustomed to having a daily bowel movement often become worried.

Diet

Most surgical patients are not given food until peristalsis returns, because it may result in nausea, vomiting, and gas formation. They may be allowed sips of cool water (ice chips moisten the mucous membrane and may help to prevent nausea), and they are usually given intravenous fluids. Before administering oral fluids after surgery, the nurse should check the physician's orders and check the patient's ability to swallow. Initially fluids should be given slowly, a few sips at a time. Patients having surgery other than on the gastrointestinal tract may be allowed a soft or regular diet soon after surgery; however, most patients do not feel like eating and may need encouragement. Liquids such as fruit juices, tea, and water are generally desired by the patient and are better tolerated than are solids.

Tubes

When the patient has a retention catheter in the urinary bladder or a nasogastric tube such as a Levin or Salem Sump tube, the nurse must check it frequently to be sure it is draining properly. Irrigations or special procedures that may have been ordered by the physician should be carried out regularly. All drainage should be measured, observed, described, and recorded on the patient's chart.

Dressings

Dressings are observed at intervals for bleeding or drainage. If drainage soaks through the dressing, it may be reinforced with additional dressings until an order has been secured for changing. All wound dressing must be carried out under strict surgical asepsis to promote wound healing. Most hospitals have routine procedures for dressing wounds that have been approved by the surgical staff. These procedures, including types of dressings and equipment used, will vary among hospitals and surgeons. Some types of dressings, such as those used for severe burns or plastic surgery, may be changed only by the surgeon, and the patient may be given a light anesthetic for the procedure. Abdominal binders may be worn to support the incision while the patient is up. By the time the patient leaves the hospital, no dressing may be required.

Various types of drains may be buried under the surgical dressing. The Penrose drain is a soft rubber tube of varying widths that is used in any situation in which leakage of fluids is anticipated. It is often used when abscessed cavities must be drained. It functions through capillary action, drawing fluid away from the organ in which it is placed, along its surfaces, and out of the body through an opening near the surgical incision. Drain sites must be carefully observed and the characteristics and amount of any discharge should be noted. Surgical nurses may be requested to advance drains a certain amount at intervals. This repositioning helps keep the drain functioning properly. Dressings covering drains may require frequent changing and are often held in place with Montgomery straps (Figure 5-10) to avoid the repeated use of tape on the skin.

Because moist dressings provide an ideal medium for bacteria, many surgeons use a closed drainage system in which the drainage tube has its own collecting reservoir. Systems such as the Hemo-Drain and Jackson-Pratt wound suction apparatus provide low suction through compression of an attached reservoir or can be attached to continuous or intermittent suction machines (Figure 5-11).

Exercises

Unless contraindicated, exercises should be started as soon after surgery as possible or by the end of the first postoperative day. This is especially important if early ambulation is to be delayed. Exercises stimulate circulation, prevent venous stasis, prevent contractures and loss of function, and facilitate recovery. The patient should be encouraged to exercise the fingers, hands, arms, feet, and legs. Leg exercises are particularly important to prevent thrombus formation. Legs should be alternately flexed and extended by bending the knees and straightening the legs while the patient is lying in bed. Frequently reminding the patient to perform these exercises will encourage active participation in his recovery.

Pillows should not be placed under the patient's knees, and the knee gatch of the bed should

Figure 5-10
Montgomery straps may be used when frequent dressing changes are anticipated.
(From Meeker MH and Rothrock JC: Alexander's care of the patient in surgery, ed 9, St Louis, 1991, Mosby-Year Book Inc.)

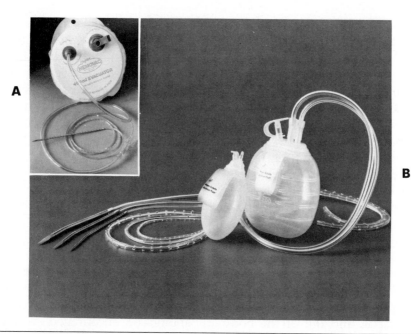

Figure 5-11
Closed wound drainage systems. **A,** Portable self-contained. **B,** Jackson-Pratt 100 ml
and 400 ml reservoirs with round silicone drains and attached trocars. (**A,** *From Perry,
AG and Potter PA: Clinical nursing skills and techniques, ed 2, St Louis, 1990, Mosby–Year
Book Inc.* **B,** *Courtesy American V Mueller, American Hospital Supply Corp, Chicago, Ill.
From Gruendemann, BJ and Meeker MH: Alexander's care of the patient in surgery, ed 9, St
Louis, 1991, Mosby-Year Book Inc.)*

not be elevated. The practice of letting the patient
sit on the side of the bed or be up in a chair with
the legs dependent for extended periods of time
is discouraged. All of these cause pressure on the
veins and engorgement of blood in the lower
limbs and contribute to clot formation.

Wound healing

Wounds generally heal by primary or secondary
intention. Surgical wounds that are sutured
closely at the time of surgery heal by primary intention and generally leave a minimum of scarring. If a wound is large, with edges that cannot
be approximated, it must be allowed to heal by
secondary intention—or the filling in of the area
from the bottom with scar tissue. Open wounds
are far more susceptible to infection. Generally the
nurse is involved in frequent dressing changes
that may include packing of these wounds with
antiseptic gauze or the application of moist dressings. Montgomery straps may be used to avoid
tape injuries to the skin when dressings must be
changed frequently.

Ambulation

Early **ambulation** facilitates the normal functioning of all body organs and systems, thereby reducing the danger of postoperative complications.
Erect posture and activity encourage deep breathing and help prevent lung congestion. Walking
stimulates the venous circulation, helping to prevent thrombosis. Problems such as urinary retention and constipation occur less often in patients
who ambulate early in the postoperative period.

After most major surgery, patients are allowed
out of bed on the first postoperative day. Patients
who have recently had anesthesia should be subjected only to slow, gradual changes out of bed.
If at any time faintness or nausea is experienced,
they should return to the last previous comfortable position and remain for a few minutes before
trying to rise again. Getting out of bed and walking soon after a surgical experience will cause apprehension and fear of pain. The benefits of early
ambulation should be well explained, before surgery if possible, to obtain the best results. The
type of surgery and the condition of the patient

will determine when ambulation may be started and the extent of walking permitted. Ambulation means walking, not sitting in a chair; however, it should be a gradual process and should not tire the patient. Some elderly persons may need to be elevated to a sitting position in bed before they are allowed out of bed. When allowed out of bed, they should be assisted by the nurse, and only a few steps may be sufficient at first. Ambulation permits the patient to be independent and self-sufficient and to carry out most self-care activities. It decreases feelings of helplessness, shortens the hospital stay, and enables the patient to regain strength more readily. Postoperative care is summarized in the boxed material to the right.

POSTOPERATIVE COMPLAINTS AND COMPLICATIONS

Complaints
Pain

Pain is a subjective symptom indicating physical or emotional distress, which varies widely among individuals and cultures. The nurse should remember that pain is always real to the person experiencing it and that efforts should be made toward its relief.

The patient may verbally complain of discomfort, or the pain may be manifested in other ways. Facial expressions are an excellent indication of pain, for example, clenched teeth, wrinkled forehead, widely open or tightly shut eyes, and grimacing. Often a patient will groan, cry, gasp, or cry out. Body movements can also indicate the presence of pain, for example, muscle tension, immobilization of a part or of the whole body, kicking, tossing and turning, and rubbing. Observation of these symptoms can help the nurse and physician to assess the level of pain and provide adequate relief. Often patients are unaware that they are permitted to have a pain medication or are reluctant to ask for one.

The patient's first complaints of pain occur early in the postoperative period and are usually the result of the traumatic effects of surgery. One of the primary responsibilities of the nurse is to evaluate the patient's need for pain medication. When a patient complains of pain, the nurse should note the location of the pain, ask whether it is constant or intermittent, and ask whether it is a sharp, dull, or burning sensation. This infor-

---

NURSING CARE GUIDELINES
Postoperative Care

Nursing diagnoses
- Potential fluid deficit/excess related to fluid loss, fluid shift (third spacing), and fluid therapy
- Pain related to tissue trauma, pressure, or spasms
- Potential infection related to broken skin and traumatized tissue
- High risk for injury, electrolyte loss, shock, falling related to surgical intervention
- Immobility related to activity restrictions
- Potential urinary retention related to surgical intervention, anesthesia
- Knowledge deficit related to postoperative instructions
- Potential impaired gas exchange related to anesthesia and reduced lung expansion

Nursing interventions
Immediate
- Maintain patent airway
- Observe for signs of anoxia
- Suction secretions from respiratory passageways as necessary
- Check vital signs frequently
- Check dressings frequently
- Observe for early signs of shock
- Maintain proper drainage and/or suction
- Provide for pain relief
- Regulate and observe infusion of intravenous fluids
- Monitor temperature
- Evaluate status of orientation

Continuing
- Provide for comfort
- Monitor vital signs as necessary
- Encourage deep breathing and coughing
- Encourage voiding
- Check for flatus or bowel sounds
- Turn and position frequently
- Maintain patency of drainage tubes
- Measure and record intake and output
- Care for wound using aseptic technique
- Observe for bleeding and drainage
- Evaluate need for pain medication
- Encourage exercises and ambulation
- Observe for postoperative complications

Expected outcomes
- Physical and psychologic needs met
- Rehabilitation and return to normal living
- No complications

mation should be recorded on the patient's chart and communicated to the charge nurse and physician. The early administration of a pain-relieving drug such as morphine, meperidine (Demerol), or anileridine (Leritine) will often provide relief for several hours and permit restful, quiet sleep. Pain resulting from the surgical procedure should diminish after the first 24 to 48 hours, after which new orders are often written for pain management. Pain may be the result of other causes, such as abdominal distention, urinary retention, and casts that are too tight and are pressing on a nerve. Headache sometimes results from spinal anesthesia, and patients having abdominal surgery will experience pain when coughing deeply. The apprehensive and nervous patient may complain of more pain than the calm, passive individual. Elderly patients may tolerate more pain than do younger persons, and obese persons often need larger amounts of drugs to relieve pain.

Whatever the cause of pain, the nurse should make every effort to relieve it and to make the patient comfortable. Changing the patient's position, washing the face and hands, rubbing the back with alcohol, applying a cold cloth to the forehead, or just sitting with the patient may provide relief and decrease the need for drugs. Drugs such as morphine depress respiration and should not be given when respiration is compromised, when the blood pressure is below what has been established as normal for the patient, or when blood pressure is unstable, since it may contribute to shock. Narcotics should be given 1 hour before postoperative activities such as ambulation. Nursing care should then be given when the patient is receiving the most benefit from the medication. The patient should be told that the medication is for pain. The psychologic effect of knowing that something is being done relieves anxiety and tension, which contributes to the effectiveness of the drug. When a narcotic has been given to an elderly person the nurse must be particularly observant of the patient, since the drug may cause restlessness or disorientation.

Pain medication is now frequently administered intravenously with a PCA pump. Morphine or meperidine cartridges are attached to intravenous fluid tubing in a mechanical pump. The patient controls the flow of the medication by pushing a button. The patient is instructed to push the button if any discomfort is present. An overdose is prevented by setting the control on the machine to allow infusion at a predetermined interval. The amount of drug administered is also controlled by settings on the machine. This method gives the patient the ability to control pain and prevent its occurrence. When using a PCA pump, less medication is required than in the traditional method of allowing pain to return before medication is given.

Nausea and vomiting

Postoperative nausea and vomiting may be the result of any one of several causes, including the anesthetic, sensitivity to drugs, surgical manipulation, or serious postoperative complications. Patients who have experienced considerable preoperative vomiting and who fear vomiting postoperatively may be more inclined to do so. Often a nasogastric tube attached to suction siphonage is left in place for 24 to 48 hours to keep the stomach empty and to reduce the incidence of nausea and vomiting. Nausea and vomiting resulting from anesthesia should not last longer than 8 hours. When vomiting appears to be the result of drugs, the physician will usually change the medication order. Most postoperative vomiting is mild and self-limiting, requiring little treatment; however, several drugs belonging to the group known as phenothiazines may have an antiemetic effect for some patients and are often ordered by the physician. Some of these include prochlorperazine (Compazine), thiethylperazine (Torecan), promazine (Sparine), and promethazine (Phenergan). H_2 receptor antagonists such as cimetidine (Tagamet) and ranitidine (Zantac) also reduce postoperative nausea and gastrointestinal distress. If the patient is permitted to have fluids by mouth, sips of hot tea with lemon, ginger ale, or cola drinks may be given to relieve nausea. Persistent vomiting may be serious because it results in loss of body fluids and electrolytes.

Retention of urine

An overdistended bladder may cause the patient considerable discomfort and actual pain. Patients having surgery of the rectum, pelvis, or lower abdomen commonly have difficulty voiding. When the nurse has exhausted all measures designed to help the patient void, catheterization under strict surgical asepsis is indicated. Because continued inability to void will result in loss of bladder tone, the physician may order a retention catheter inserted until the patient's condition improves (see Chapter 19).

Abdominal distention

Abdominal distention occurs when gas accumulates in the stomach and intestines. It occurs to some extent in most surgical patients, giving rise to "gas pains." Because of the temporary loss of peristalsis, gas is not moved through the intestinal tract, accumulating in the greatest amount in the large intestine. The cause for the accumulation of gas in the intestinal tract is not clearly understood. Severe abdominal distention may interfere with respiratory function. Measures to provide relief include the use of a well-lubricated rectal tube, which should be inserted just past the internal sphincter. The tube should not be left in longer than 30 minutes, because spasms of the sphincter may occur; however, it may be used every 3 to 4 hours if it provides relief. The surgeon may order a Levin or Salem tube inserted through the nose into the stomach and attached to suction to prevent the stomach from becoming dilated with gas and to prevent paralysis of the intestines (paralytic ileus). Drugs that stimulate peristalsis, for example, neostigmine (Prostigmin) or metoclopramide (Reglan), are sometimes ordered. Early ambulation can prevent or reduce the amount of distention.

Complications

The incidence of postoperative complications has been reduced through more careful preoperative preparation for surgery, improved surgical procedures, and improved postoperative care. However, several postoperative complications continue to occur and probably always will to some extent. The most common symptoms associated with postoperative complications is fever. Although the average postoperative patient will have a slight temperature elevation for the first day or two after surgery, temperatures persistently remaining above 100° F (38° C) indicate possible problems. The most serious complications are hemorrhage, surgical shock, respiratory disorders, thrombosis, embolism, wound infection, dehiscence, and evisceration.

Hemorrhage and shock

Blood loss may occur during the surgical procedure in the operating room or after the surgery has been completed and the patient has been returned to his room. The surgeon will evaluate the amount of blood loss during surgery and, if the loss has been great enough, will order the patient transfused with whole blood. **Secondary hemorrhage** may result from an untied blood vessel or the slipping of a ligature. It may involve a capillary, vein, or artery and may be external or internal (into a body cavity or organ). All hemorrhage creates an emergency situation, requiring that immediate steps be taken to control bleeding and restore blood volume.

The nurse should be conscientious about inspecting the dressing for evidence of bleeding from the wound. A small amount of oozing may be controlled by placing a sterile dressing over the site and applying a pressure bandage. If an extremity is involved, the part may be elevated. When bleeding is internal, the patient will be returned to the operating room so that the wound can be opened. The nurse should be alert to the symptoms that may indicate internal bleeding. Early detection is important to prevent damage to the cells and vital organs, and in some cases even death.

Symptoms of hemorrhage are essentially those of hypovolemic shock. Early signs include restlessness, apprehension, an increasing pulse rate, and oliguria. Later the skin becomes pale, moist, and cool, the respiratory rate increases, the pulse rate increases, the temperature becomes subnormal, and the blood pressure falls. The patient will complain of thirst and gasp for air as bleeding continues. In addition to blood on dressings, external evidence of hemorrhage may be observed, such as blood in vomitus, in urine, or from the lungs (hemoptysis). Patients receiving anticoagulant drugs should always be watched for bleeding into the skin or from a body orifice. If a patient shows signs of hemorrhage, the nurse should remain calm and reassure the patient while carrying out emergency measures until the surgeon arrives. Specific nursing measures are outlined in Chapter 4.

Other causes of postoperative shock are sepsis, cardiac failure, drug reactions (including anesthetic drugs), transfusion reactions, pulmonary embolism, and adrenal failure. Each cause results in a pathologic process that ultimately produces cardiovascular collapse and poor oxygenation of all body tissues. The symptoms of each type of shock are essentially the same as those given for hypovolemic shock. Treatment depends on the cause; however, oxygen and intravenous solutions are administered. The patient is kept flat and warm, and vital signs are checked at frequent intervals and recorded. Further information on shock can be found in Chapter 4.

Respiratory disorders

Many respiratory complications can be prevented through careful postoperative care. Those patients who have respiratory disease preoperatively are most likely to develop complications after surgery. The nurse should observe the patient preoperatively for coryza, coughing, or sneezing and report such symptoms to the physician. The most frequent complications are bronchopneumonia, hypostatic pneumonia, bronchitis, pleurisy, and **atelectasis** (see Chaper 15). Maintaining a clear airway, instructing the patient to breathe deeply and cough, regular turning, placing the patient in Fowler's position, and encouraging early ambulation are nursing interventions designed to prevent respiratory complications.

Thrombosis and embolism

Several factors contribute to the formation of a blood clot or **thrombus** in the vein. The complication is most common in middle-aged persons who are required to maintain a schedule of bed rest. Other predisposing factors include tight abdominal binders, injury or pressure to veins occurring in the operating room at the time of surgery, decreased respiration and blood pressure, or any condition that results in the decreased flow of blood through the veins. **Embolism** occurs when a blood clot breaks away from a vessel and enters the circulation. Emboli originating from thrombi in veins will usually follow the normal circulatory pathways until the next capillary system is reached, that of the lungs. Pulmonary embolism is a serious complication of surgery and is described more fully in Chapter 15. Postoperative exercises, early ambulation, and frequent change of position are nursing interventions that aid in preventing these complications.

Wound infection

Surgical **wound infections** usually are manifest by the fifth postoperative day. The organism most often involved is *Staphylococcus aureus*, although *Escherichia coli*, *Proteus vulgaris*, *Aerobacter aerogenes*, and *Pseudomonas aeruginosa* are also involved. A postoperative wound infection is classified as a hospital-acquired or nosocomial infection (see Chapter 8). Factors such as pre-existing illness, obesity, advanced age, complicated surgery, and forms of therapy such as radiation and chemotherapy predispose the patient to postoperative infections. Poor surgical technique and failure to use an aseptic technique during wound care can also result in infection. Infected wounds are cleaned and irrigated by the physician, and often a drain is placed in the incision. The drainage is cultured, and appropriate antibiotic drugs are administered. Clean incised wounds should heal without infection if they are uncontaminated.

Dehiscence and evisceration

Dehiscence and **evisceration** may result from infection, abdominal distention, coughing, and poor nutrition. They occur more often in the chronically ill and the obese patient, usually on the sixth to seventh postoperative day. Both are caused by the sloughing out of sutures or staples before healing takes place. In dehiscence some or all of the sutures may give way, causing the edges of the skin to separate. When evisceration occurs, the incision suddenly opens up and the intestines are released to the outside (Figure 5-12). The patient may state that he felt as if something gave way, and inspection of the dressing reveals a clear, pink drainage. Any pink drainage from the wound of a postoperative patient should be investigated immediately. The wound should be covered with a sterile dressing or a sterile towel and held loosely in place with a binder. The surgeon should be notified immediately. The nurse should remain calm and reassure the patient. The patient should be placed in a low Fowler's position, and food or fluids should be withheld until the patient is seen by the physician. Generally the patient is returned to surgery and the wound is resutured.

DISCHARGE PLANNING

Careful planning for the transition from the postoperative unit to the home setting or extended-care facility is essential for optimum recovery. This planning is done by the patient, family, nurse, and other appropriate members of the health care team. Postoperative hospital stays have decreased in length dramatically in the past decade, which has increased the need for teaching the patient and family numerous procedures and therapies that were once only carried out in the hospital setting. Nowhere is the need more evident than in the outpatient surgery setting. It is not unusual for postoperative patients to be discharged with sutures and surgical drains still in place, dressings, and even ongoing intravenous infusions.

The nurse should consult with the physician

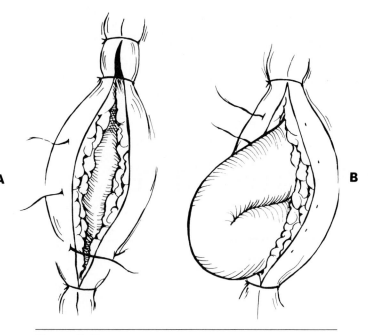

A

B

Figure 5-12

A, Wound dehiscence. **B,** Evisceration. *(From Meeker MH and Rothrock JC: Alexander's care of the patient in surgery, ed 9, St Louis, 1991, Mosby-Year Book Inc.)*

Discharge Criteria or Outcomes for the Postsurgical Patient

1. The incision is clean and dry and healing is in progress.
2. The vital signs are within preoperative normal levels and the patient is afebrile.
3. The patient has only mild to moderate pain, which is managed by oral analgesics.
4. The patient is able to carry out activities of daily living without a significant increase in pain or fatigue.
5. The patient verbalizes knowledge of signs and symptoms of postoperative complications.
6. Elimination patterns have been reestablished.
7. The patient can describe any dietary or activity changes necessitated by surgery.
8. The patient demonstrates an ability to care for the incision, take medication, or do any procedures needed for continuing convalescence (or a family member demonstrates this ability).
9. The patient can describe the schedule of follow-up care with the physician.
10. The patient verbalizes knowledge of community resources and support groups that may be useful in promoting recovery.

---

in determining what care the patient and family can provide at home, as well as what community resources and home nursing care agencies may be necessary. If dressing changes or other procedures will be done at home, the nurse should not only teach the patient and family how to do these, but should provide a 2-day supply of equipment, written instructions, and the location in the community where additional supplies can be obtained. Patients being discharged should also know the time of their appointment for follow-up care with the physician. If the patient is being discharged to an extended care facility, a written summary of the medical regimen and nursing care plan should be completed by the physician and nurse and should accompany the patient.

Discharge criteria or outcomes for the postsurgical patient are included in the box above.

REFERENCES AND ADDITIONAL READINGS

1. Brunner LS and Suddarth DS: Textbook of medical-surgical nursing, ed 5, Philadelphia, 1985, JB Lippincott Co.
2. Burrell LO and Burrell ZL: Critical care, ed 4, St Louis, 1983, The CV Mosby Co.
3. Cope AL: Pain: its psychological aspects, J Pract Nurs 27(1):30-31, 1977.
4. Croushore TM: Postoperative assessment: the key to avoiding the most common nursing mistakes, Nurs 79 9(4):46-51, 1979.
5. Hahn AB, Barkin RL, and Oestreich SJK: Pharmacology in nursing, ed 15, St Louis, 1983, The CV Mosby Co.
6. LeMaitre GD and Finnegan JA: The patient in surgery: a guide for nurses, ed 4, Philadelphia, 1980, WB Saunders Co.
7. Long BC and Phipps WJ: Essentials of medical-surgical nursing, St Louis, 1985, The CV Mosby Co.
8. Neuberger GB: Wound care: what's clear, what's not, Nurs 87 17(2):160-163, 1987.
9. Rayder M and others: Problem: a new nurse asks why preoperative teaching isn't done . . . three answers from experience, Am J Nurs 79:1992-1995, 1979.
10. Schumann D: Symposium on wound healing. Preoperative measures to promote wound healing, Nurs Clin North Am 14:683-699, 1979.
11. Schumann D: How to help wound healing in your abdominal surgery patient, Nurs 80 10(4):39, 1980.
12. Sorenson KC and Luckman J: Medical-surgical nursing: a psychophysiologic approach, Philadelphia, 1987, WB Saunders Co.

The Patient with Pain

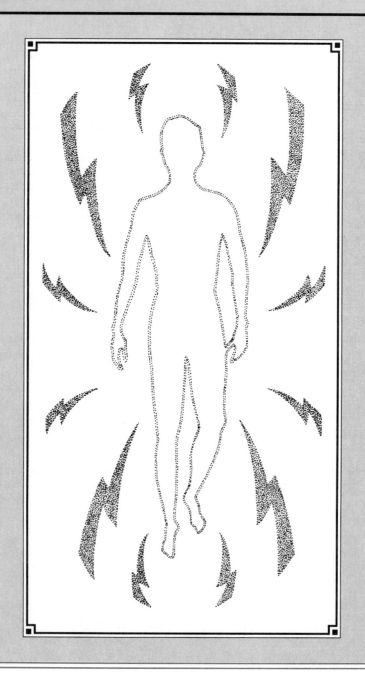

KEY WORDS

acute pain
addiction
chronic acute pain
chronic benign pain
chronic cancer pain
distraction techniques
endorphins
epidural analgesia
gate control theory
intrathecal analgesia
neurotransmitters
pain
patient-controlled analgesia
physical dependence
placebo
referred pain
relaxation techniques
tolerance
transcutaneous electrical neural stimulation
  (TENS)
venous access devices
visual analog scale

OBJECTIVES

1. Discuss the role of the nurse in pain management.

2. Define pain.

3. Identify applications of the gate control theory to pain management.

4. Identify the components of a pain assessment.

5. Describe medications appropriate for mild, moderate, and severe pain.

6. Discuss the nurse's role in administering pain medications.

7. Describe nonpharmacologic measures appropriate for the nurse to use in pain relief

The alleviation of pain is one of the most frequent problems faced by nurses giving care to patients. Nurses have a well-established central role in the successful management of pain. Regardless of the clinical setting in which the nurse practices, whether in a hospital, a long-term care facility, a physician's office, or the patient's home, the nurse will have numerous opportunities to work with patients who are anticipating or experiencing pain. The nurse's role includes assessing the individual with pain, administering therapeutic modalities, and monitoring the effectiveness of the interventions.[19] The nurse can be the key link in facilitating communication between the individual with pain and the family and other members of the health care team.

Pain is frequently the symptom that brings the patient to the physician. The physician assumes the primary responsibility for diagnosing the cause of the pain and for treating the disease process or pathology causing the symptom. It is the nurse, however, who has the most direct contact with the patient during the long hours that he experiences pain and is therefore in a position to make a major contribution to any program of pain relief. Nurses are held accountable for the management of the pain program for patients under their care.

THE NATURE OF PAIN

The nature of pain has been of considerable interest throughout history. Pain is a nebulous sensation. Scientists cannot directly measure its intensity nor see it in action. Patients often have difficulty in describing their pain and sometimes even have trouble in fixing its location. To primitive humans and to some individuals even today, pain was intimately involved with religion. It was viewed as a curse, the result or payment for doing evil. Pain was sometimes deliberately inflicted in an attempt to appease the gods and redeem the soul.

In more recent years scientists have come to realize that pain is both a physical and a psychologic phenomenon. **Pain** can be viewed as having two components: (1) the sensation or *perception* of pain, which involves the nerve pathways and the brain; and (2) the *reaction* to pain, which takes into account the emotional side of pain. The reaction to pain is a complex response, involving the highest cognitive (thinking) mechanisms. Research has shown that the capacity for perceiving pain

is essentially the same in all people under normal circumstances. The reaction to pain, however, varies widely from one person to another and even in the same individual under different circumstances.

Defining Pain

Pain is an intensely personal, complex biochemical event. It is a symptom that arises in response to a noxious stimulus or tissue injury; occasionally, pain may persist after the tissue damage has healed or may be felt in the absence of obvious tissue damage.[16] Much of the difficulty in precisely defining pain occurs because it is a very personal, subjective experience that can only be interpreted in terms of its meaning to the person feeling it. To the patient, pain is simply "what hurts." Nurses can experience their own pain but can only make judgments about the pain of others.

McCaffery's definition of pain best meets the needs of nurses in caring for patients in pain: "Pain is whatever the experiencing person says it is, existing wherever he says it exists."[10] Using this definition, the nurse accepts that the patient is having pain; the patient does not have to prove that pain exists.

Function of Pain

Pain can serve as a protective mechanism for the body, signaling that tissues are damaged or threatened with damage. It is frequently the first symptom that tells the individual something is wrong with the body and urges that person to seek medical assistance. Pain can also protect the body from further injury; for example, the pain caused by contact with a hot object causes the person to withdraw from the object. Sometimes, however, the protective function of pain becomes lost or obscured, such as the pain of long-term arthritis or chronic back pain. No longer is the pain a useful mechanism warning of danger. In such individuals the reaction to pain and methods of adapting to living with pain become of great significance to the health care team.

Individuals who cannot feel and respond to pain, either because of a loss of sensation (such as spinal cord injury) or because of the absence of pain receptors (genetic deficiency), are very susceptible to injury; the nurse must be extremely vigilant when providing care to these patients.

Pain Theories

Science does not yet have a satisfactory explanation for pain transmission and pain relief; therefore, it must resort to theory—the best guess available on the basis of current evidence. In 1965 Melzack and Wall proposed the **gate control theory** that has generated much research and has provided a partial explanation of how pain is transmitted and perceived (Figure 6-1).[18] According to this theory, pain sensations travel along small-diameter C-δ (C delta) fibers and go through a "gate" located in the spinal cord and from there on to the brain. These pain sensations can be blocked at this gate by stimulating the large-diameter A-δ (A delta) fibers, which carry generalized sensations. The gate can also be closed by brain activity. Psychologic factors, the memory of previous pain experience, and many physical or mental activities can also influence the perception of pain.

Examples of the application of this theory would include the use of transcutaneous electrical neural stimulation, rubbing (massage, backrubs),

the use of counterirritants, such as Ben Gay and Deep Heat ointments, or the use of heat or cold. In each instance the fast-moving impulses coming from the peripheral nerve receptors reach the "gate" first and close it to the impulses coming along the slower pain fibers. The brain receives and interprets the general sensation message and does not receive the pain message.

Current research on pain focuses on the neurochemical nature of pain. It is now known that the body is capable of secreting narcotic-like substances called **endorphins.** These substances lock into narcotic receptors on nerve endings in the brain and spinal cord and thus block the transmission of pain sensations. Differences in the amount of endorphins present in different individuals may help explain differences in pain perception. Research has shown that such things as prolonged pain or constant stress can decrease the amount of endorphins; brief pain or brief stress

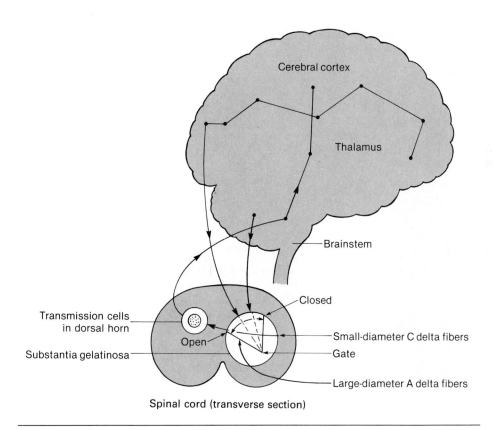

Spinal cord (transverse section)

Figure 6-1

Gate control theory. Pain sensations, traveling along small-diameter C delta fibers, go through "gate" (located in the substantia gelatinosa), through transmission cells, and on to brain. These sensations can be blocked at gate by stimulation of large-diameter A delta fibers, which carry general sensations. Gate can also be closed by brain activity.

will increase the amount. It is interesting to note that intense physical exercise such as jogging can temporarily increase an individual's endorphin level.

Much is now known about the pain experience, but even more is yet to be discovered. For the person in pain, the answers cannot come quickly enough.

Types of Pain

Pain is often classified into three major categories based on etiology.[19] **Acute pain** occurs after injury or surgery and usually subsides within a predictable time span. Observable responses to acute pain are found in Figure 6-2. **Chronic acute pain** occurs almost daily over a long period. Examples of this include cancer or burn pain. This pain may last for many months before being cured or controlled and may end only with the death of the patient. **Chronic benign pain** is persistent or recurs over a period of months or years. Examples of this type of pain include backache, headache, and arthritis.

Another method of classifying pain is by the location or source of the pain. Superficial pain occurs when the skin or surface structures are affected by a painful stimulus. The pain localizes to the site of the stimulation and is usually described as having a prickling or burning quality. Deep pain arises from deeper structures such as the muscles and visceral tissue; it may be localized to the site of the stimulus or more likely will be poorly localized with a dull and aching quality. Deep pain is often felt at a site distant from the area of stimulation, an occurrence known as **referred pain** (Figure 6-3). Referred pain is projected from various internal organs of the body to the body surface; for example, cardiac pain that arises in the heart but is projected to the jaw, left arm, and epigastric region.

Assessment of Pain

A detailed and accurate description of the patient's pain is essential for the accurate diagnosis and treatment of the underlying cause. Because pain is subjective, the patient should be encouraged to describe in detail the nature, intensity, and location of pain (see box). A helpful pain assessment tool is found in Figure 6-4. The nurse will find it helpful to follow a specific pattern, such

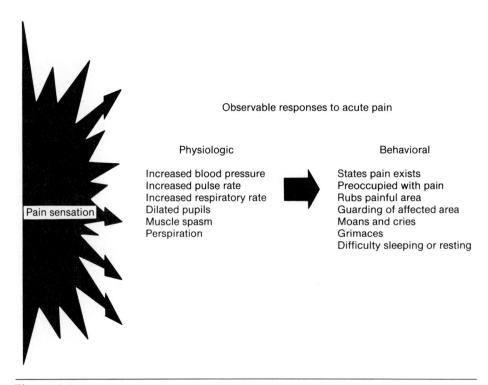

Figure 6-2

Observable responses to acute pain. *(Modified from McCaffery M and Beebe A: Pain: clinical manual of nursing care, St Louis, 1989, The CV Mosby Co.)*

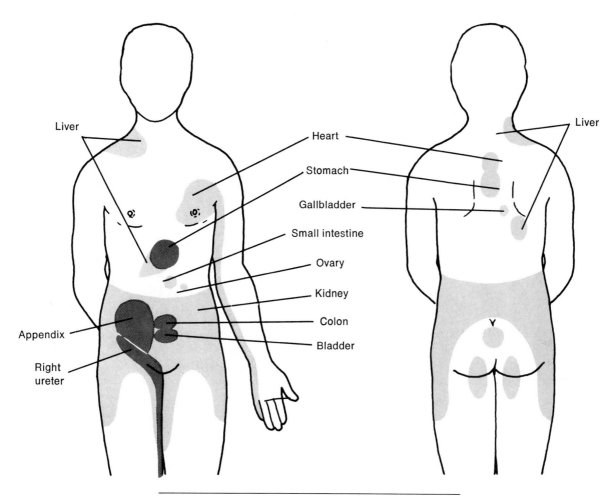

Figure 6-3
Areas of referred pain.

as the following, for assessing each painful episode.[15]

Quantifying the degree of pain before and after medications or other interventions is a useful way to monitor the effectiveness of the therapy. Two methods that are widely used are questionnaires and rating scales. The McGill-Melzack Pain Questionnaire measures both sensory and affective dimensions of pain.[17] Rating scales can be used in any patient care setting with a minimum of time or cost. The patient is asked to rate his pain on a scale of 1 to 10 (or 1 to 100), either verbally or on a visual analog scale (Figure 6-5).[9] It is important to remember that all pain measurements are subjective. A single measure is not significant in itself; what is important is the change over time.

The **visual analog scale** is a 10 cm line representing a continuum from no pain to the worst imaginable pain. The patient makes a pencil mark at the point on the line that describes the intensity of his pain at that time.

A problem that nurses frequently face in the assessment of pain is the wide variation of how pain is experienced and reported by patients. The nurse may use the term "pain" to mean one thing, and the patient may interpret it to mean something quite different. A patient may respond "No" to a question about pain and yet be in need of assistance. It is frequently helpful to use a variety of terms, such as ache, pressure, hurt, and discomfort, to determine just what the patient is experiencing. Also, it is important to use the phrase "patient reports" pain rather than "patient complains of" pain. The negative connotation of the word "complain" may influence the patient or others in their relationship to him.

The young child and the elderly patient pre-

INITIAL PAIN ASSESSMENT TOOL   Date_____

Patient's Name_____Age_____Room_____

Diagnosis_____Physician_____

                                              Nurse_____

I. LOCATION: Patient or nurse mark drawing.

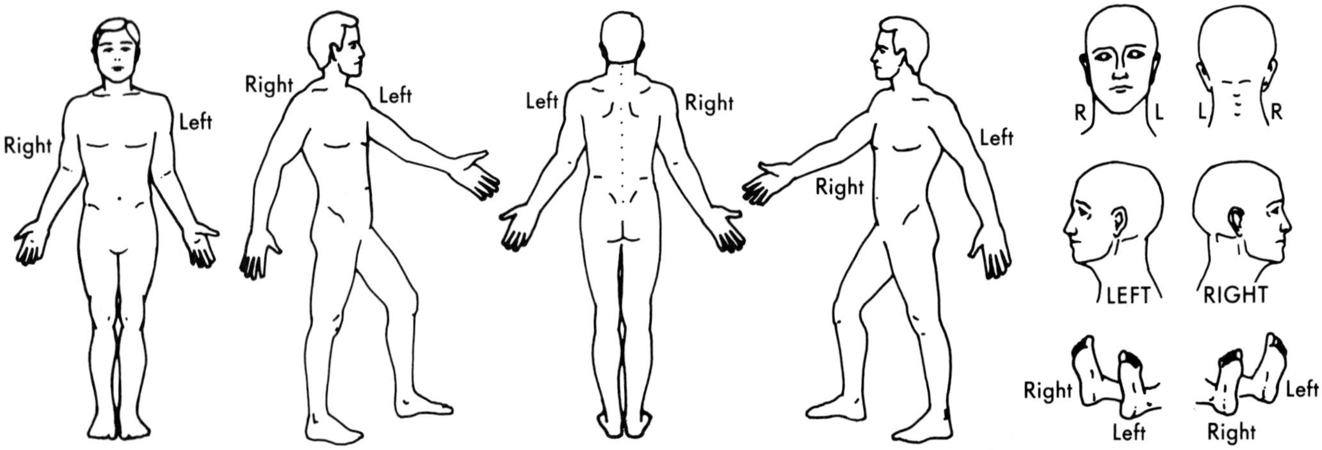

II. INTENSITY: Patient rates the pain. Scale used _____

    Present:_____
    Worst pain gets:_____
    Best pain gets:_____
    Acceptable level of pain:_____

III. QUALITY: (Use patient's own words, e.g. prick, ache, burn, throb, pull, sharp)_____
    _____

IV. ONSET, DURATION VARIATIONS, RHYTHMS:_____

V. MANNER OF EXPRESSING PAIN:_____
    _____
    _____

VI. WHAT RELIEVES THE PAIN?_____
    _____
    _____

VII. WHAT CAUSES OR INCREASES THE PAIN?_____
    _____
    _____

VIII. EFFECTS OF PAIN: (Note decreased function, decreased quality of life.)
    Accompanying symptoms (e.g. nausea)_____
    Sleep_____
    Appetite_____
    Physical activity_____
    Relationship with others (e.g. irritability)_____
    Emotions (e.g. anger, suicidal, crying)_____
    Concentration_____
    Other_____

IX. OTHER COMMENTS:_____
    _____

X. PLAN:_____
    _____

Figure 6-4

Initial pain assessment tool. *(From McCaffery M and Beebe A: Pain: clinical manual of nursing care, St Louis, 1989, The CV Mosby Co.)*

Assessment of Pain

1. History of pain—prior occurrences, factors that precipitated the pain, activities that increased or decreased the pain, methods used to relieve the pain, usual time of occurrence of pain episodes
2. Physiologic characteristics—increase in pulse and respiratory rates, increase in diastolic and systolic blood pressure, pallor, dilated pupils, diaphoresis, nausea; because of the body's ability to adapt to abnormal situations, these physiologic signs may be absent or decreased in prolonged acute pain or chronic pain
3. Verbal statements—description of the quality or character of the pain (aching, burning, prickling), severity of pain using a scale (mild, moderate, severe), location of pain (precisely located or diffuse), frequency and duration of pain, meaning of pain to the individual
4. Facial expressions—clenched teeth, tightly shut lips, tightening of jaw muscles, strained look, and so forth
5. Body movements—lying quietly or rigidly, restless or purposeless movements, protective or guarding movements toward a specific area, rubbing movements

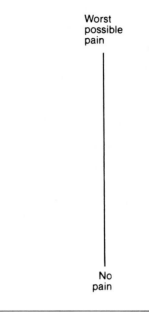

Figure 6-5
Visual analog scale (VAS). (Not drawn to scale).

sent special problems with pain.[14,16] The nurse needs to be especially alert to nonverbal cues; the child often cannot describe the pain, and the elderly patient often is reluctant to "complain" or is fearful of being over medicated. In either case, the nurse needs to play an active role to prevent undue suffering resulting from undertreatment of pain.

MANAGEMENT OF PAIN

When a specific underlying cause of the pain can be identified, medical management is directed toward eliminating the problem that caused the pain. For example, the pain of appendicitis or cholecystitis can be eliminated through surgical removal of the involved organ, and the pain associated with infection can be relieved with antibiotics. When an underlying cause cannot be identified or eliminated, a patient may be referred to a "pain clinic," where a multidisciplinary approach will be used to diagnose and treat the pain.

In such a clinic the major focus is to help patients learn a variety of methods that allow them to control their pain and manage it on a daily basis.

Nursing Interventions and Pain Medication

The administration of a drug should not be the only or even the first action considered by the nurse when responding to a patient's report of pain. Many times offering reassurance or employing general comfort measures will greatly reduce the need for pain medication.

Various medications (see Table 6-1) are used to alleviate pain by interacting with some aspect of the pain experience.[7,11,12,14] Aspirin and other nonsteroidal antiinflammatory drugs are frequently used for mild to moderate pain.[22] These drugs block the production of prostaglandins near the injury that activate nerve endings, which send pain signals to the brain. Tricyclic antidepressant drugs (e.g., amitriptyline, doxepin, imipramine) may be used to elevate mood and also to raise the levels of **neurotransmitters** that stimulate the body's production of endorphins.

For moderate to severe pain, opiate drugs are likely to be used. Morphine molecules fit into receptor sites on certain cells in the brain and central nervous system and block pain messages from being received. Frequently combinations of drugs are used (e.g., aspirin and codeine), thus attacking the pain problem from several approaches.

Table 6-1

Drugs for Pain

Drug (generic and trade name)	Preparations (route of administration and dosage)	Action	Nursing considerations
Mild to moderate pain			
Acetaminophen (Datril, Tylenol)	325-650 mg PO every 3-4 hours prn (maximum of 4000 mg daily)	Mild analgesic; antipyretic (reduces fever)	Can mask a fever/infection; overdose or chronic use can cause liver damage; monitor liver function tests
Acetylsalicylic acid (aspirin)	325-650 mg PO every 3-4 hours prn	Mild analgesic; antipyretic; anti-inflammatory	Increases prothrombin time and can cause gastric bleeding; give with full glass of water or milk to minimize adverse GI reactions.
Codeine	30-60 mg PO every 3-4 hours 15-60 mg SC or IM every 3-4 hours	Mild to moderate analgesic narcotic	Most frequently used in combination with aspirin or acetaminophen; high doses (e.g., 60 mg) may cause restlessness and excitement; watch for constipation and urinary retention
Ibuprofen (Advil, Motrin, Nuprin)	200-400 mg PO every 4-6 hours	Antiinflammatory with analgesic effects	Individual responses vary greatly and drug interactions may occur; dosages may need to be adjusted
Moderate to severe pain			
Hydromorphone hydrochloride (Dilaudid)	1-2 mg SC, IM or IV every 4-6 hours 2-12 mg PO every 4-6 hours 3 mg rectal suppository every 6-8 hours	Very potent synthetic narcotic analgesic (8 to 10 times stronger than morphine); used for severe pain	Use smallest dose possible (See morphine sulfate for nursing care concerns)
Levorphanol tartrate (Levo-Dromoran)	2-3 mg PO or SC every 4-6 hours	Very potent synthetic narcotic analgesic (4 to 5 times stronger than morphine); used for severe pain	Strong sedative and respiratory depressant; slow onset of peak effect (60-90 minutes) but prolonged duration (6-8 hours)
Meperidine hydrochloride (Demerol)	50-150 mg IM or PO every 3-4 hours	Synthetic narcotic most commonly used for postoperative pain	Less spasmodic and constipating than most narcotics; rapid onset and short duration of effect (2-4 hours); significantly less effective orally; prolonged use can cause central nervous system symptoms (e.g., dizziness, seizures)
Methadone hydrochloride (Dolophine)	2.5-10 mg IM, SC or PO every 3-4 hours	Synthetic narcotic used for severe pain	Administration may be painful; longer-acting and less sedating than morphine

Table 6-1

Drugs for Pain—Cont'd

Drug (generic and trade name)	Preparations (route of administration and dosage)	Action	Nursing considerations
Morphine sulfate	5-20 mg SC or IM every 4 hours 10-30 mg PO every 4-6 hours 4-10 mg injected very slowly	Potent analgesic; considered best first choice for relief of severe pain.	Standard narcotic to which all other narcotics are compared. Affects smooth muscle of GI and GU tracts, causing contraction of bladder and ureters; decreases intestinal peristalsis; watch for urinary retention, constipation, and respiratory depression
Pentazocine (Talwin)	30 mg IM or IV every 3-4 hours 50 mg PO every 3-4 hours (maximum dose of 600 mg/day)	Analgesic for moderate pain (one third as potent as morphine); often used as a preoperative medication or to supplement anesthesia	Can antagonize effects of morphine and other narcotics and may elicit withdrawal symptoms in patients who have been taking other narcotics regularly

Traditionally, most analgesic drugs were administered on an "as needed," or prn, basis; current thinking is to suppress the pain "around the clock" (ATC). By giving medications according to a time schedule, a patient's body maintains a sufficient level of drug to keep the pain at bay and to prevent anxiety from building and the memory of suffering from becoming established.

It is critical that the nurse be aware of the significant variations in drugs, in peak effects, in duration of effects, and in side effects. Also, the nurse must be alert to the differences that result from oral versus parenteral administration of a medication. The peak effect of most parenteral narcotics is 1 hour, whereas the peak effect of most oral forms of the same drug comes two or more hours later. In most instances oral analgesics have a longer duration of effect than parenteral drugs. A careful assessment of these factors must be made and incorporated into the plan of care for any patient receiving medications.

Patients should be given analgesics for pain before the pain becomes severe. If the patient has to wait too long for relief, discomfort and anxiety increase and significantly more medication is needed to adequately control the pain. Ideally, the patient should not need to ask for analgesics for pain relief; the observant nurse will assess the patient's need and work according to the principle of prevention rather than treating already existing pain.

Addiction

Pain medications should not be withheld from patients because of fear of tolerance or dependence. **Addiction (psychologic dependence)** must be distinguished from physical dependence or drug tolerance.[7,14,20,24] With drug **tolerance,** increasingly larger doses are needed to provide the same effect as was produced by the original dose. The first sign of tolerance is that the duration of the drug's effect is shortened; next, other side effects, such as constipation and euphoria, disappear. Tolerance can be handled by increasing the dose of the drug, or occasionally, by switching to another medication with an equivalent analgesic effect.

If a patient receives narcotics on a continuous basis for several weeks, it is assumed that physical dependence will occur.[24] **Physical dependence** is an altered state produced by the repeated administration of a drug; when the drug is stopped, withdrawal symptoms occur. In the clinical setting pain seldom stops abruptly. Patients who become physically dependent can be weaned off the drug by gradually diminishing doses as the pain subsides.

Addiction is a behavioral pattern rooted in a psychologic desire for the euphoric effects of narcotics and is characterized by an overwhelming involvement with getting and using the drug. Most patients do not request analgesics unless they have pain. In fact, it is far more frequent that patients with pain refuse analgesics unnecessarily because of fear of addiction. Most experts agree that psychologic dependence (addiction) is rare when narcotics are administered to patients with pain during short hospital stays.

Placebos

A **placebo** is an inactive substance or procedure that is used with a patient under the guise of an effective treatment.[14,22] Placebos can only be used when prescribed by a physician. Their most frequent use is as a control measure in research. Their use is documented on the patient's chart just as any other drug or therapy.

Approximately one third of the population reacts to placebos; that is, they will experience effects when given a placebo. Research has shown that the effects of placebos are physical as well as psychologic. The exact mechanism by which placebos work is not known, but research suggests that placebos stimulate the brain to produce endorphins and other chemicals, thus calling on "the doctor within." To a large extent, the ability of a placebo to cause effects is a measure of the faith or confidence the patient has in his physician or nurse. Administering placebos sometimes creates an ethical dilemma for the nurse. If a placebo is being given for an inappropriate purpose (e.g., to "prove" that the pain is not "real"), the nurse has the right to refuse to give it. In such a situation, the nurse should discuss the problem with the nursing supervisor so that the action will have administrative support and the patient will receive attention for his pain.[14]

Patient-controlled analgesia

Patient-controlled analgesia is a method of delivering pain-killing drugs.[14] A variety of mechanical pumps are now used to allow patients to administer analgesic medications to themselves to control pain. The pumps are calibrated to provide specific amounts of drugs at time intervals determined by the physician. They are equipped with safety features that prevent overdosing. Research has shown that patient-controlled analgesia can often provide better pain relief than periodic injections because patients can receive relief at the first sign of pain. Studies also show that patients like the idea of controlling their own pain; anxiety and tension are decreased and ultimately less narcotic is used. As the cost of these devices decreases, it is likely that use of this method of analgesic delivery will increase greatly.

Spinal analgesia

Narcotics are sometimes administered via catheters into the epidural or subarachnoid space in the spinal cord.[21] Analgesia is the result of the drug's direct effect on receptors within the spinal cord instead of within the brain. Fewer side effects (e.g., sedation, disorientation) are seen by this route than with the systemic administration of narcotics.

The spinal route can be used for both acute and chronic pain. The most common uses are for postoperative pain (e.g., cesarean section, orthopedic surgery) and for **chronic cancer pain** that is poorly controlled by systemic medications.

The spinal route for the administration of drugs for pain control is new and many aspects of its use are not yet fully known. Nurses must have specific, additional inservice education on this method before being assigned to care for patients on **epidural** or **intrathecal analgesia**.

Venous access devices

Autoinfusers, drug pumps, and right atrial catheters allow consistent access and regulated flow for continuous intravenous morphine or other drugs. The continuous infusion maintains constant blood levels of the drug and provides better pain control with smaller amounts of the drug than when given by injection or orally. These devices have been proven safe and effective in both the hospital and the home environment.[7]

Transcutaneous electrical neural stimulation

Transcutaneous electrical neural stimulation (TENS) is most commonly used for pain that is fairly well localized.[4,14] TENS modulates pain by stimulating peripheral nerves with electrical current applied to the skin via electrodes connected to a small battery-operated pulse generator (Figure 6-6). This stimulation enhances the production of endorphins, thereby mobilizing the body's own pain defenses. This method may be used alone or in conjunction with other modalities.

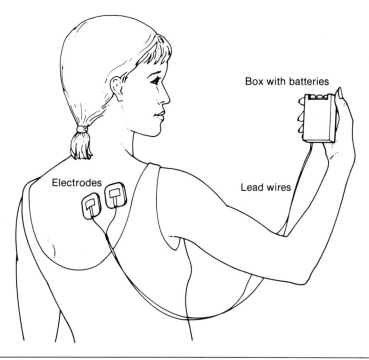

Figure 6-6
Three major components of a TENS unit with two electrodes placed on the upper back of the patient to relieve shoulder pain. *(From McCaffery M and Beebe A: Pain: clinical manual of nursing care, St Louis, 1989, The CV Mosby Co.)*

TENS may be used in the control of acute pain, especially pain from injuries such as sprains and lacerations, and postoperative pain. The use of TENS for the postoperative patient frequently decreases (although not completely) the need for narcotic analgesics, thus decreasing unwanted side effects such as respiratory depression, nausea, and vomiting, and slow bowel functioning.

In most clinical settings the physician or physical therapist introduces the patient to TENS. The treatment is usually administered by nurses who have had special education in the use of TENS. The patient is encouraged to handle the equipment and experiment with the settings to determine the best location for the electrodes and the most comfortable frequency and duration of current for his pain. Before the electrodes are attached to the skin, the nurse should wash the area with soap and water to reduce resistance, then rinse and dry. The nurse applies enough electrode gel to ensure adequate conduction but not so much that the gel oozes from under the electrode, tapes the electrodes in place, turns the stimulator on, and slowly advances the output control until stimulation is felt. Most patients describe the stim-

ulation as a buzzing or tingling sensation. The nurse assists the patient in adjusting the controls to provide the most comfortable sensation that gives the maximum pain relief.

TENS does not work the same for everyone. Some patients experience great relief immediately; for others, relief comes only after repeated applications. Some patients find that the analgesia may last for hours or even days after the current is turned off; others experience relief only for a limited time. Nurses can provide support and encouragement to their patients while they experiment with this device. Most patients obtain considerable relief from TENS.

Noninvasive interventions

A number of physical or mental activities can be used to help the patient focus his attention on sensations other than pain.[13,14,26] **Distraction** is a very useful technique if the patient is experiencing mild to moderate pain. In the presence of severe pain, distraction tends to increase anxiety and tension and thus increase pain. Examples of distraction include talking on the telephone, watching television, working on hobbies or crafts, and performing rhythmic breathing techniques. It is critical to remember that distraction does not make the pain go away; it only makes it more bearable.

Any procedure that helps the patient relax can help relieve emotional and muscle tension and lessen pain. A wide variety of **relaxation techniques** are available, such as progressive relaxation exercises, meditation, biofeedback, and self-hypnosis. The Lamaze method of childbirth is an example of a procedure that uses both distraction and relaxation procedures. Most relaxation techniques require time and effort to master but are very useful, especially for the patient with chronic pain.

Many patients have worked out their own methods for coping with pain; the nurse should ask the patient to describe procedures that have helped in the past and to support and encourage the patient as he attempts to use them again in his present pain situation. As with the use of analgesics, it is important to begin pain control methods before pain becomes severe.

The boxed material at the end of the chapter summarizes nursing interventions for the patient with pain.

Neurosurgical procedures

A number of neurosurgical techniques for blocking pain transmission have been tried.[23] Peripheral nerve blocks using local anesthetics such as lidocaine can provide temporary relief of pain in some acute painful situations such as neuralgias, thrombophlebitis, or musculoskeletal conditions. For longer term effects (up to 6 months) absolute alcohol or phenol may be used. These substances are used infrequently because of their toxic effects—they may produce necrosis and sloughing of superficial tissue.

When pain becomes severe and cannot be controlled by other means, surgical interruption of the pain pathways may be necessary. A peripheral *neurectomy* may be performed if the pain is localized to a specific area such as an arm or leg. When pain is more diffuse (e.g., cancer pain), the pain pathways in the spinal cord may be interrupted. This procedure is known as a *chordotomy* and can be done at various levels, depending on the location of the pain. Other procedures that may be performed include *rhizotomy*—cutting pain pathways in the brainstem—and destruction of small, specific sites in the brain by means of radiation or a heating current applied by a probe. The nurse must be aware that when these procedures are

performed, the body is no longer protected from injury because of the loss of sensation in that area affected by the surgery. These patients are therefore particularly susceptible to pressure sores.

> ### NURSING CARE GUIDELINES
> ### *Patient in Pain*
>
> **Nursing diagnoses**
> - Altered comfort: acute pain, chronic pain
>
> **Nursing interventions**
> - Assure the patient that you know the pain is real and that you will help him deal with it
> - Provide general comfort measures—turning, repositioning, back rubs, and changing damp dressings
> - Provide support for painful areas when moving patient, such as placing a pillow to the abdominal incision area
> - Teach the patient about anticipated pain—when to expect pain, the quality of the pain, and pain relief measures available
> - Individualize pain control measures considering a variety of approaches
> - Use pain control measures before pain becomes severe—get ahead of the pain. Include measures the patient believes will help
> - Provide distraction—meaningful and interesting sensory stimulation such as radio, television, hobbies, and conversation
> - Provide cutaneous stimulation to block pain transmission—gentle massage, pressure, application of menthol rubbing agents to skin or around painful area, application of heat or cold as indicated, and transcutaneous electrical neural stimulation (TENS)
> - Promote relaxation—instruct the patient to breathe deeply and "let go" on expiration; assist him to relax his body while contracting one muscle group (e.g., arm, leg)
> - Assist patient to use guided imagery—to imagine a pleasant event as a substitute for the pain experience
>
> **Expected outcomes**
> - Comfort improvement
> - Use of measures for relief of discomfort
> - Understanding of the rationale for therapy
> - Demonstration of increased tolerance for pain by returning to work, using analgesics less, or increasing daily activities

REFERENCES AND ADDITIONAL READINGS

1. Barbour LA, McGuire DB, and Kirchoff KT: Nonanalgesic methods of pain control used by cancer patients, Oncol Nurs Forum 13(6): 56-60, 1986.
2. Booker J: Pain: it's all in your patient's head (or is it?), Nurs 82 12:47-51, 1982.
3. Cummings D: Stopping chronic pain before it starts, Nurs 81 11(1):60-62, 1981.
4. Davis AJ: Teaching your patients to use electricity to ward off pain, RN 39:43-45, 1978.
5. Davitz LJ and others: Suffering as viewed in six different cultures, Am J Nurs 76:1296-1297, 1976.
6. DiBlasi M and Washburn CJ: Using analgesics effectively, Am J Nurs 79:74-76, 1979.
7. Foley KM: The practical use of narcotic analgesics, Med Clin North Am 66:1091, 1982.
8. Hauck S: Pain problem for the person with cancer, Cancer Nurs 9(2):66-76, 1986.
9. Jacox A: Pain: a source book for nurses and other health professionals, Boston, 1977, Little, Brown & Co.
10. McCaffery M: Nursing management of the patient with pain, ed 2, Philadelphia, 1979, JB Lippincott Co.
11. McCaffery M: How to relieve your patient's pain fast and effectively—with oral analgesics, Nurs 80 10(11):58-63, 1980.
12. McCaffery M: Patients shouldn't have to suffer: how to relieve pain with injectable narcotics, Nurs 80 10(10): 34-39, 1980.
13. McCaffery M: Relieving pain with noninvasive techniques, Nurs 80 10(12):55-57, 1980.
14. McCaffery M and Beebe A: Pain: clinical manual for nursing practice, St Louis, 1989, The CV Mosby Co.
15. McGuire LA: A short, simple tool for assessing your patient's pain, Nursing 11(3):48-49, 1981.
16. Meinhart NT and McCaffery M: Pain: a nursing approach to assessment and analysis, Norwalk, Conn, 1983, Appleton-Century-Crofts.
17. Meissner J: McGill-Melzack pain questionnaire, Nurs 80 1:50-51, 1980.
18. Melzack R and Wall P: Pain mechanisms: a new theory, Science 150:971-978, 1965.
19. National Institutes of Health Consensus Development Conference Statement: The integrated approach to the mangement of pain, U.S. Department of Health and Human Services, Public Health Service Pub No 1986-491-292:41148, Bethesda, Md, 1986, National Institutes of Health.
20. Newman RG: The need to redefine "addiction," N Engl J Med 308:1096-1098, 1983.
21. Paice JA: Intrathecal morphine infusion for intractable cancer pain: a new use for implanted pumps, Oncol Nurs Forum 13(3):41-47, 1986.
22. Perry S and Heidrich G: Placebo response: myth and matter, Am J Nurs 81:720-725, 1981.
23. Portenoy RK and others: Maximizing control of cancer pain, Patient Care 20:24-45, 1986.
24. Porter J and Hick H: Addiction rare in patients treated with narcotics, N Engl J Med 302:124, 1980.
25. Stewart E: To lessen pain: relaxation and rhythmic breathing, Am J Nurs 76:958-959, 1976.
26. West BA: Understanding endorphins: our natural pain relief system, Nurs 81 11:50-53, 1981.
27. Wilson RW and Elmassian BJ: Endorphins, Am J Nurs 81:722-725, 1981.

Community-Acquired Infections

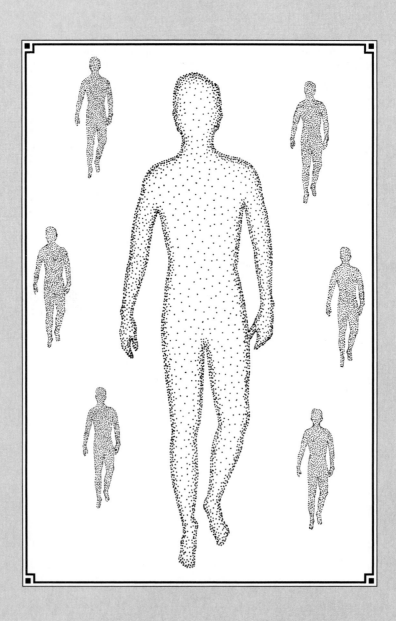

KEY WORDS

active immunity
antitoxin
carrier
epidemiology
fomite
host
immunoglobulins (Ig)
incubation period
infectious disease
Koplik's spots
natural immunity
passive immunity
pathogen
strawberry tongue
syndrome
vector

OBJECTIVES

1. Discuss the interrelationships between the agent, host, and environment in the development of infectious disease.

2. Describe the major means of transmission of communicable diseases.

3. Explain the role of immunization in prevention of communicable diseases.

4. Differentiate between the common infectious diseases in the community setting according to agent, host, and environmental characteristics.

5. Define the nurse's role in treatment, prevention, and control of communicable disease.

One of the greatest accomplishments of the twentieth century has been the control of communicable diseases in humans. There are remarkable contrasts when we examine health trends during the past 90 years. Those born at the beginning of our century had an average life expectancy of 47.5 years. In 1900 tuberculosis accounted for 25% of all deaths. Seventy-five percent of major illnesses resulted from acute infectious diseases. These took a particularly devastating toll on infants.

Public health measures, such as clean drinking water, effective waste control, availability of a variety of foods, better methods of food handling, and public enlightenment have been largely responsible for the remarkable decrease in these illness burdens. Medical advances have produced immunizing agents, such as serums and vaccines, that aid human immune processes in preventing disease or in modifying its severity. Antibiotics have reduced the impact of many diseases and enhanced recovery with minimal complications. The result, over what is a relatively short period of time, has been a decline in disease-related deaths, particularly infant deaths, and an increase in life span.

Life expectancy is more than 75 years now and our population is not only increasing, but growing older. Illnesses have changed. With the exception of acquired immunodeficiency syndrome (AIDS), chronic noninfectious diseases have replaced infectious diseases as the leading causes of morbidity and mortality in the United States. Atherosclerosis, the underlying disease process in heart attacks and strokes, and conditions such as cancer, diabetes, emphysema, and arthritis now comprise the majority of the health burden of the United States. These illnesses last a long time, demand more monitoring and care, and have contributed, in part, to the increase in medical costs during the latter part of the century.

Despite the remarkable success in reducing the impact of infectious diseases upon society, an ongoing program of infectious disease prevention and control must be maintained. Infectious processes continue to account for a major proportion of acute illnesses. Pneumonia remains among the ten highest causes of death, and lost schooldays and workdays per year from infectious diseases are significant. The AIDS epidemic is also testimony to need for ongoing surveillance, prevention, and control.

CHARACTERISTICS OF THE INFECTIOUS PROCESS

A communicable disease is an **infectious disease** where the causative organism is transmitted, from where it lives and multiplies, to another person or place. It can be transmitted directly from one person to another, or indirectly through a carrier or vector. The development of the infection depends on the interaction of the causative **agent,** the **host,** and the *environment* (Figure 7-1). The interaction between the agent, the host, and the environment must be correct for an infectious disease to develop. For instance, organisms such as tetanus spores cannot grow and multiply in oxygen-rich environments. Others, such as the tubercle bacillus, thrive in persons who are malnourished, fatigued, and exposed to poor sanitary conditions.

Agent

The infectious agent is usually a microorganism called a **pathogen,** although parasites such as helminths (small wormlike animals) and insects such as lice can cause communicable disease. Infectious agents are classified as bacteria, viruses, rickettsiae, protozoa, and helminths (see Chapter 2). All infectious agents have intrinsic properties that are unique to the microorganism or parasite. These characteristics include size, chemical character, requirements for growth, antigenic properties, ability to produce toxin, ability to become resistant to chemicals, and others. Some organisms require moist, warm, dark breeding grounds, and others can survive in dry, warm, or cold settings until the proper conditions exist for them to grow and multiply. The virulence of the organism can vary, particularly in those organisms that are subject to change, such as the influenza viruses. For some organisms, existence in a dormant state is possible. Knowledge of these intrinsic properties is essential to the prevention and control of infectious agents.

Host

Presence of an infectious agent does not always produce disease. A susceptible host must be present. Many underlying host factors determine whether the person will develop the infection. Factors that contribute to susceptibility include the person's general health, immune status, and age, and the amount or dose of the infectious agent and the duration of exposure.

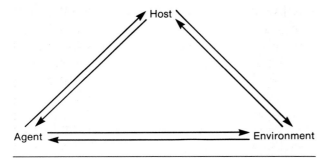

Figure 7-1

The interaction between the agent, host, and environment must be correct for an infectious disease to develop.

Infectious processes can produce a wide variety of clinical effects in the host, ranging from inapparent (subclinical) infection to mild, moderate, or severe clinical illness or death. Inapparent infection can occur when the infectious agent invades the host and begins to grow and multiply but does not produce symptoms of illness. The host's immune system is able to combat the infection without visible effects. Such a person may become a **carrier** capable of infecting others without having evidence of the disease. This characteristic of early infection with the human immunodeficiency virus (HIV), the causative agent in AIDS, has produced great problems for prevention and control of its spread. Depending on the agent characteristics, people with active infections are communicable for varying lengths of time, but an average is from 3 to 7 days.

Environment

The interaction between the agent and host occurs in the environment. Environmental conditions can alter the infectivity, pathogenicity, virulence, and immunogenic properties of the agent.[28] Conditions such as heat, moisture, light, and oxygen concentration can be factors in the development of infectious diseases. Modification of the environment is one way that the agent-host-environment interaction may be changed to prevent or control the communicable disease. For example, the boiling of contaminated objects has long been used to destroy organisms and prevent their spread.

Pathogens are transmitted to the susceptible host by an infected person or animal (carriers), or through an intermediate **vector,** often an arthropod such as a mosquito. The vector transmits the pathogen through innoculation (bite) or by contamination of the environment through food or water. Lyme disease is an example of an epidemic illness in the United States that is transmitted by a small tick vector.

Transmission

Transmission of infectious diseases through **direct contact** involves close association with a carrier in an infectious state. An outbreak of impetigo in a preschool environment is an example of direct transmission of the *Staphylococcus* organism from person-to-person. Transmission through **indirect contact** occurs when objects, **fomites,** become contaminated and harbor infectious organisms. For example, lice can be transmitted from one child to another through a contaminated teddy bear. Organisms on objects can be transferred through hand-to-mouth contact to the susceptible person. Organisms can also be transmitted through **vehicles** such as water, milk, food, contaminated intravenous fluids, prepackaged supplies, and blood products. Respiratory infections often are transmitted by contaminated droplets suspended in air by coughing, sneezing or talking. Some organisms remain viable in dust for very long periods of time, causing outbreaks of infections months or years later.

CONTROL OF COMMUNICABLE DISEASE

Prevention and control of communicable disease depends on interference with the normal pattern of transmission of the organism. This may be done by altering characteristics of the agent, the host, or the environment. One of the most common methods of breaking the chain of infectious events is to enhance the immunity of the host. Other methods involve alteration or destruction of the agent, or interruption of the life cycle of the organism through environmental changes.

Immunization

Immunization increases the body's immune defenses against the infectious agent without actually producing the disease. **Natural immunity** results from the passage of a mother's antibodies across the placental barrier into the circulation of the fetus. The mother's antibodies protect the newborn infant from specific infectious organisms. Natural immunity is transitory, protecting the newborn infant for the first 3 to 6 months of life, when mortality is the greatest.

Active immunity

Active immunity results from the stimulation of the body's immune system to produce either *antibodies* or specialized cells that have the ability to destroy or neutralize foreign microorganisms. It occurs after an infectious agent is introduced into the body, producing either an illness or an inapparent illness, or through immunization. Immunity is the most durable if the person acquires the infectious disease. However, severe or fatal complications can result from some infections. It is also possible for a recovered person to become a carrier—harboring microorganisms and transmitting them to others unknowingly.

Following exposure, part of the microorganism acts as an *antigen*, a substance that is usually composed of large protein or polysaccharide molecules and is capable of inducing a specific immune response (see Chapter 2). The body responds with the production of antibodies **(immunoglobulins)**. These are protein molecules that are specific to the antigen, and can interact with the antigen to interfere with the infectious process.

Artificially acquired active immunity results from the injection into the body of a vaccine or serum that contains antigen of the microorganism. These immunizations are given before the person has been exposed to the illness, if possible. Boosters are given periodically to maintain immunity since the immune response from a vaccine or serum is not as strong as that resulting from an acute illness. Active immunity is acquired by the administration of a vaccine or toxoid. Vaccines that contain live organisms are called live attenuated vaccines. The organisms have been weakened so that they do not cause disease. Noninfective vaccines contain organisms that have been killed by heat or chemicals. Toxoids contain the toxin that is produced by the organism, but the toxin has been rendered harmless.

Most children receive immunizations early in life, since young children can suffer severe complications from many infectious diseases. These immunizations prevent diphtheria, pertussis, tetanus, polio, measles, mumps, and rubella and *Haemophilus influenza type B*. Recently, the U.S. federal government has recommended the addition of a sixth universal immunization against

Hepatitis B. It is recommended for children who are 18 to 24 months of age and who are in groups thought to be at increased risk of disease, such as those who attend day care centers. Studies have shown that this vaccine does not stimulate a good immune response in younger children. The best response occurs in children 24 months and older. The vaccine is not recommended for children under 18 months of age.

A schedule of childhood immunizations can be found in Table 7-1. Vaccines are available either singly or in combinations other than those indicated, such as measles-rubella (MR).

Measles is a serious contagious disease. It occurs frequently in the United States as a result of low immunization levels of the population. Every child and young adult should receive protection from this disease, since complications can result in encephalitis, mental retardation, pneumonia, and death. Side effects of the vaccine occur infrequently, but a mild temperature elevation or skin rash may appear.

The measles vaccine is a live virus vaccine that has been attenuated or reduced in virulence. It is believed that one dose is sufficient to produce long-lasting immunity.

Measles vaccine should not be administered to children who are sensitive to eggs. Contrain-

Table 7-1

Childhood Immunization Schedule*	
Vaccine	**Age**
Hib—*Haemophilus influenzae* type B vaccines (PRP-HbOC/PRPOM)	2 months
DTP vaccine—diphtheria-pertussis-tetanus	2 months 4 months 6 months
DTP booster	15 months
Td vaccine—tetanus-diphtheria	6 years (school entry) 14 years Every 10 years thereafter
OPV—oral polio vaccine	2 months 4 months
OPV booster	15 months 4-6 years (school entry)
MMR vaccine—combined measles-mumps-rubella	15 months

*(American Academy of Pediatrics: Haemophilus influenzae Type B conjugate vaccines: recommendation for the immunization of infants and children at 2 months of age and older, and updates, AAP News, pp 16-17, March 1991)

dications for administration of measles virus vaccine include leukemia or other malignant disorders. Children whose resistance is low because of receiving steroid therapy, radiation, alkylating drugs, and antimetabolites should not be given the measles vaccine. Administration of the vaccine during pregnancy should be avoided.

Administration of live mumps virus vaccine provides an active immunity against mumps. The vaccine is prepared in chick embryo cell culture and therefore should not be given to persons sensitive to the proteins of eggs. Contraindications for its use are the same as for measles vaccine. Mumps can be a serious disease resulting in deafness and encephalitis.

Live rubella virus vaccine provides active immunity against rubella (German measles). The vaccine should not be given to pregnant women because of the possibility of producing the disease in the unborn child. Rubella has caused defects of the heart, brain, eye, and ears in children whose mothers have had rubella during the first trimester of pregnancy. Rubella vaccine is given to all children to prevent spread of the disease to pregnant women and their unborn children. The Centers for Disease Control in Atlanta recommends that educational and training institutions seek proof of rubella immunity from all women students and employees. The vaccine may be given to women of childbearing age only if pregnancy will be avoided for at least 2 months. It should not be given during febrile illnesses but should be postponed until recovery occurs. Other

---

Contraindications for Immunizations

Hypersensitivity to egg protein, animal tissues, or antibiotic used in vaccine preparation
Altered immune states
    Lymphoma
    Leukemia
    Generalized malignancy
    Dysgammaglobulinemia
Immunosuppressive therapy
    Steroids
    Antimetabolites
    Alkylating agents
    Radiation
Pregnancy in some instances, especially measles
Febrile illness—immunization should be delayed
    until recovery

---

contraindications are the same as for measles and mumps. The label on the bottle should be read before administering the vaccine to determine the kind of cells from which the vaccine has been prepared. This is important in preventing hypersensitivity reactions. A summary of the contraindications for immunization is found in the box below left.

Disposable syringes and needles should be used, or the jet and hypospray may be used, in administering vaccines. The latter is most often used in mass immunization programs. If the preparation being used contains alum or aluminum hydroxide, it should be given intramuscularly. In children under 3 years of age it should be placed in the anterolateral aspect of the upper thigh, and in children over 3 years of age it may be given in the deltoid muscle. Fluid toxoid or vaccines in a saline suspension may be given subcutaneously.

The liquid oral poliovirus vaccine may be administered to infants by placing it on the tongue with a dropper. In older children it may be placed on a lump of sugar before ingestion.

Passive immunity

Passive immunity is acquired by injecting a serum that contains antibodies to the infectious organism into the susceptible host. Since the person receives antibodies that have been formed elsewhere, there is no direct stimulation of his own immune system. The immunity that is acquired is temporary, rarely lasting longer than 3 weeks. It is useful in emergency situations and in the treatment of specific diseases. Administration of immunoglobulin (gamma globulin) to prevent infectious hepatitis in exposed people is an example.

Antitoxins are serums containing antibodies that react against the toxin that is produced by the particular microorganism infecting the body. Thus the administration of an antitoxin is for the purpose of neutralizing the poisons produced by pathogens and does not have any effect on the organism itself. Chemotherapeutic drugs may be given to the individual to destroy the organism. Examples of antitoxin serums include diphtheria antitoxin, tetanus antitoxin, and antisnake (antivenom) serum. Serums are sometimes derived from sources other than animals.

Immunoglobulin (Ig, or gamma globulin) is a fraction of the plasma of human blood containing antibodies against certain diseases. It is occasionally used in treating or modifying measles in a nonimmune person. It may also be used to prevent infectious hepatitis in exposed persons. Other diseases for which it has been used include rubella, mumps, and poliomyelitis. Immunoglobulin is prepared in a sterile solution for subcutaneous or intramuscular injection; it is never given intravenously. Emphasis should be placed on active immunization to prevent those diseases for which vaccines are available.

Public Education

The present generation of people have less concern about communicable childhood diseases. The incidence of these diseases has decreased to such an extent that fear of them or their consequences no longer exists. While this has contributed significantly to the increased quality of life, problems still exist. Immunization rates throughout the United States have gradually declined, especially among some religious groups. As a result we have seen a rise in the incidence of some diseases such as measles.

Many states have attempted to remedy this situation by passing laws requiring immunizations for children before attending school. However, these laws do not reach all segments of the population. Preschool children and aged people are not included. Some local health departments operate well-child clinics for the purpose of monitoring immunization status and general wellness. The United States has launched a nationwide campaign to increase the levels of immunity throughout the country. In some community areas immunization levels in the population had fallen to 50% or less. There is a continual need for study and development of programs that will reach all members of the population.

There also is a need for public education programs regarding positive health practices that are important in the prevention of disease. Sociologic factors may have a profound effect on the incidence of certain infectious diseases. In areas that have a low socioeconomic status, inadequate housing, poor sanitary facilities, inadequate refuse collection, and possibly even contaminated water supplies, reservoirs of infection may exist.

Poor nutritional standards also decrease resistance to disease and provide the opportunity for pathogens to invade the human body. The social picture is often one of apathy and lack of motivation, coupled with lack of transportation accessibility, and availability of medical and clinical services. This contributes to the failure to secure immunization of young children, and pro-

duces conditions for a potential epidemic of infectious disease. Also, the high mobility of some segments of the population means that a person exposed to an infectious disease, or who is a possible source of disease, may be miles away from the point of contact within a few hours. Therefore the worldwide spread of infectious diseases is more of a problem now than ever before.

Nursing's Role In Prevention

Nurses play an important part in prevention of infectious disease. Every nurse must be informed of the recommended immunizations and encourage all people to maintain correct immunization records and have boosters when necessary. Every nurse should engage in public information or educational programs and counsel individuals in their health practices whenever possible. Nurses can observe human behavior as it relates to health and illness and can offer solutions to problems related to disease prevention. Often it is the overlooked common, everyday event that is the ultimate answer to the problem. It is the task of each individual nurse to keep informed as to changes in health practices and disseminate this information to the public.

THE PATIENT WITH A BACTERIAL DISEASE

Due to improved public health standards and the widespread use of immunizations, many infectious diseases have a less significant impact on our population now than at the beginning of the century. Four common infectious diseases that are caused by bacterial organisms are diphtheria, pertussis, tetanus, and typhoid fever. Other infectious diseases are prevalent among certain groups in specific geographical locations, or on a seasonal or cyclic basis. New illnesses occasionally appear and can become widespread in a relatively short period of time. The Lyme disease epidemic is an example.

Staphylococcal Infections

Staphylococcal organisms are normal inhabitants of the upper respiratory tract, skin, and gastrointestinal tract of many people. It is estimated that between 20% and 40% of all persons are asymptomatic carriers of *Staphylococcus aureus*, providing a source of infection for themselves and for others when host resistance is lowered. Transmission usually occurs through direct contact with purulent discharge from an infected person. Transmission through fomites or airborne particles is rare. The **incubation period** is 4 to 10 days. The organism is communicable as long as purulent lesions continue to drain or the carrier state persists. Staphylococcal infections occur worldwide; however, they are more prevalent in overcrowded areas where personal hygiene is poor. There are no specific preventive measures other than cleanliness and adherence to strict aseptic technique where appropriate.

In the community, *S. aureus* infections are usually manifest as skin lesions such as impetigo, boils, carbuncles, abscesses, wound infections, and conjunctivitis. Some toxin-producing strains can cause a distinctive scaulded skin **syndrome.** Infection around the nose and mouth can spread backward into the cranial vault where there are no mechanical barriers to halt its spread. For this reason, infected pimples or acne must not be squeezed or traumatized. Systemic disease is rare, usually occurring in those who are immunosuppressed or suffering from a debilitating illness. However, septicemia, pneumonitis, lung and brain abscesses, pneumonia, endocarditis, osteomyelitis, and other complications can occur. Staphylococcal pneumonia frequently complicates influenza.

Prevention is best accomplished through education in personal hygiene, especially in handwashing. Prompt treatment with topical antibiotics, or systemic antibiotics if the infection has disseminated, will reduce transmission. Outbreaks in schools, camps, and other population groups are reportable to public health authorities.

Toxic shock syndrome

During 1980 and 1981 an epidemic of toxic shock syndrome (TSS) occurred that was associated with toxin-producing strains of *S. aureus.* It is a severe illness characterized by sudden onset of high fever, vomiting, profuse diarrhea, and myalgia, and can lead to hypotension, shock, and death. A deep red "sunburn" rash develops within a few hours, followed by desquamation of the skin about 10 days after onset, especially on the palms of the hands and soles of the feet. Approximately 95% of the reported cases in women occurred during the menstrual period and most were associated with the use of vaginal tampons. In cases of TSS not associated with menstruation, including cases in men, *S. aureus* has been isolated from

focal lesions of skin, bone, lung, and stool. Aggressive fluid and electrolyte and antistaphylococcal antibiotic therapy is required.[3]

Nurses in community and school settings should communicate information regarding the risk of TSS. Menstrual TSS can be prevented by avoidance of vaginal tampons. However, intermittent use of tampons, frequent changing of tampons, and avoidance of products that have the potential to irritate mucous membranes reduces the risk of TSS.

Staphylococcal food poisoning

The *S. aureus* toxin is also one of the principal causes of food poisoning in the United States. The foods commonly involved are those touched by the food-handler without subsequent cooking, or those that are improperly heated. Foods such as pastries, custards, salad dressings, and sliced meats can be contaminated by purulent discharges. If the food then stands at room temperature for several hours before eating, an environment that is favorable to reproduction of the organism and subsequent toxin production is created. Acute gastroenteritis occurs approximately 1 to 6 hours after ingestion of the food. Severe nausea, cramps, vomiting, and diarrhea can occur and last for several hours. Duration of illness is 1 or 2 days; hospitalization may be required. Deaths are rare.

Often the food is consumed by large groups of people, causing an outbreak that is reportable to public health authorities. Individual cases are rarely identified. An **epidemiologic** investigation can determine the population at risk, the place and time of exposure, and ultimately the food item responsible for the attack. The implicated food will have the highest attack rates. Most of the ill will have eaten the food, and most of the well will have not eaten the food.

Prevention includes reduction of food-handling time with no more than 4 to 5 hours at room temperature, refrigeration of perishable food at 40° F (4.4° C) or lower, and maintenance of hot foods above 140° F (60° C). Nurses should promote these practices as an everyday concern in all households. Also, persons with boils, abscesses, and other purulent lesions of the hands and face should be excluded from handling food. All food-handlers should be educated in performing proper hygiene techniques. These include handwashing, cleaning of fingernails, keeping the food preparation area clean, and using proper temperature control, thus reducing the danger of infections.

Streptococcal Infections

Streptococci, like staphylococci, are found almost everywhere in the environment. These infections probably cause more illness than any other group of organisms. They can attack any part of the body and cause both primary and secondary disease. Many distinct strains exist, although not all are pathogenic. Streptococci are normal inhabitants of the respiratory tract in humans. Group A beta-hemolytic *Streptococcus pyogenes* produces the most significant variety of diseases in man. Streptococcal sore throat and skin infections are the most common; cellulitis, mastoiditis, otitis media, pneumonia, wound infections, septicemia, scarlet fever, and other diseases can occur.

Streptococcal sore throat is prevalent in temperate and semitropical regions. In the United States, epidemics in New England and in the Great Lakes region are frequent. Transmission results from direct contact with another infected person or object. Organisms usually enter the body through the respiratory tract or through a wound. Nasal carriers are often transmitters of the organism. Outbreaks of streptococcal sore throat may follow ingestion of contaminated foods, particularly milk and milk products. Following a short incubation period of 1 to 3 days, the organism becomes established in the lymphoid tissues causing a local cellulitis. The infectious process can easily spread since toxins released by the organism prevent the normal inflammatory process from walling off the lesion.

Infected persons exhibit fever, sore throat, exudative tonsillitis or pharyngitis, and tender anterior cervical lymph nodes. Petechiae may be present in a diffusely red throat. Symptoms can be minimal, however. Repeated attacks of streptococcal sore throat or other illnesses due to different types of streptococci are also relatively common. With antibiotic therapy, transmission is generally limited to 24 to 48 hours. Untreated cases can transmit the organisms for an indefinite period of time. Complications such as scarlet fever, rheumatic fever, or acute glomerulonephritis may appear in 1 to 5 weeks following infection, but this is rare when adequate treatment is begun at an early stage.

Scarlet fever includes all of the symptoms that occur with a streptococcal sore throat, although it may be associated with infections at other sites.

It has an abrupt onset with chills, vomiting, headache and high temperature. In approximately 24 hours a fine, erythematous rash occurs that blanches on pressure and feels like sandpaper. It occurs most often on the neck, chest, axillary folds, elbow, groin, and the surface of the inner thighs. Usually the rash does not affect the face. The tongue has a furred appearance that gradually disappears and becomes characteristically red **(strawberry tongue).** The incidence and severity of scarlet fever has decreased in recent years, although the mortality rate in some parts of the world has been as high as 3%.[3]

One of the most important factors in control of these infections is the identification and treatment of streptococcal infections before serious complications result. The treatment of choice is penicillin therapy for at least 10 days. Treatment initiated within the first 24 to 48 hours will decrease severity, reduce complications, and prevent the development of most cases of acute rheumatic fever. Infected people should be observed carefully for complications that may appear throughout the course of the illness. Preventive measures nurses should convey include education of the public regarding the transmission of the organism, and the relationship of streptococcal infections to scarlet fever, acute rheumatic fever, and other complications.

Pulmonary Tuberculosis

Tuberculosis is one of the oldest known diseases. It is one of the most devastating worldwide diseases of all time, attacking any organ or tissue and resulting in years of chronic invalidism or death. In 1882, Robert Koch discovered *Mycobacterium tuberculosis* as the causative organism and modern treatment became possible. Significant advances have been made in the treatment, prevention, and control of the disease, resulting in downward trends in morbidity and mortality in many countries. In 1987 the incidence rate in the United States was 9.3 new cases per 100,000 population. The incidence has risen slightly in recent years, primarily as a complication of the immunosuppression accompanying persons infected with the HIV virus. Tuberculosis case rates are highest among the elderly. Morbidity and mortality increase with age, are higher in males than females, and are higher in nonwhites than whites.[12] Tuberculosis is also more frequent among people of a lower socioeconomic status, where factors such as overcrowding increase the risk of infection.

Transmission

Transmission of the *Mycobacterium tuberculosis* organism occurs when a susceptible person inhales an airborne droplet nuclei from the sputum of an infected person. When a person with active tuberculosis coughs, sneezes, or expectorates, the infectious organisms are carried into the air as droplets, or droplet nuclei. However, prolonged contact is usually necessary for infection to occur and transmission through indirect contact is rare.

The incubation period for a primary tuberculosis lesion is approximately 4 to 12 weeks. Persons who have the microorganisms in their system will react positively to a tuberculin skin test (10 mm or greater), although the disease may not be present. People can transmit the organism to others as long as the organism is being discharged from the body. Progressive development of the disease is greatest within 1 to 2 years of infection, although it may remain as a latent infection throughout a lifetime. Pulmonary tuberculosis is most common, although dissemination of the organism through lymphatic drainage and the circulation can result in involvement of many parts of the body.

Assessment

Primary pulmonary infections usually go unnoticed by the individual. As a result of the stimulation of the body's immune system, lesions containing the tubercle bacillus often become walled off and calcified, isolating the organism and preventing spread of the disease. However, the organisms may remain viable, and if the person's resistance falls at a later time, an active case of tuberculosis may develop.

Symptoms are often the result of toxic manifestations produced by the infection. Mild fever, fatigue, and gradual weight loss can occur early, while cough, chest pain, dyspnea, and hemoptysis become prominent only when the disease has progressed. Profuse sweating may occur at night. The spitting of blood (hemoptysis) may occur when cavitation extends into a blood vessel. There can be a wide variety of symptoms with tuberculosis, and there is no specific pattern in which they occur.

Case finding

When tuberculosis is suspected, there must be a complete history and physical examination, including routine laboratory examinations. A history of exposure is of special significance. Diag-

nosis of active tuberculosis is made by finding the tubercle bacillus in smears of sputum. Frequent sputum examinations are required to isolate the tubercle bacillus, and failure to find it does not always rule out the diagnosis of tuberculosis. Under some conditions it may not be possible to secure sputum for examination; a gastric lavage is then done, and the gastric contents are examined. A bronchoscopic examination is often done to secure secretions from the bronchial tree or directly from portions of the lung. X-ray films visualize calcified nodules in the lung and can be used to follow the progression of the disease following diagnosis.

The tuberculin test is a diagnostic aid that indicates the presence of infection but does not necessarily indicate the presence of the disease. The tuberculin test is presently used as a screening method to detect persons with infection and to rule out persons who do not have tuberculosis.

The Mantoux test is the skin test of choice for identifying infected persons. It involves inoculation of tubercle bacillus extract (tuberculin) intradermally on the inner surface of the forearm. Purified protein derivative (PPD) is usually used. The reaction is an example of delayed (cellular) hypersensitivity reaction. The test is read between 48 and 72 hours after administration. If the site of induration is 0 to 4 mm, the test is considered to be negative; if the induration is 5 to 9 mm, it is doubtful; and if it is 10 mm or more, it is positive. The amount of induration or hardness is important, not the amount of redness present. A positive reaction indicates that a patient has had contact with the tubercle bacillus, but active tuberculosis may not be present. In general, the more intense the reaction to the test, the greater the likelihood of an active case of tuberculosis being present. Positive reactions may be suppressed in patients who are acutely ill with tuberculosis, receiving corticosteroid drugs, or infected with certain other infectious diseases, such as measles.

Other skin tests are available for screening large groups of people but not for diagnosis. These include the tine test and the Mono-vacc. These tests pierce the skin at several points at the same time. The reaction is considered negative if the areas of induration are less than 2 mm. If there is a meeting of the reactions of two or more puncture sites, the reaction is considered positive. Positive reactions should be tested further for presence of the disease.

Ideally, everyone should have an annual examination for tuberculosis. Periodic testing should be routine for all medical and nursing personnel. X-ray examination should be restricted to positive reactors. The greatest emphasis in screening should be on high-risk groups such as contacts of active tuberculosis cases, patients in general hospitals and mental institutions, immigrants from areas in which tuberculosis is common, and populations of lower socioeconomic status. All active cases must be reported to local health departments so that contacts may be examined and monitored.

Drug therapy

Following diagnosis, the stage of the patient's disease is evaluated, and an individual schedule of treatment is planned. Effective chemotherapy reverses the infectiousness of tuberculosis within 2 weeks of initiation, and prevents progression of the illness. A combination of agents is used to affect the organism in different stages of growth. Primary drugs include isoniazid (INH), rifampin, streptomycin, pyrazinamide (PZA), and ethambutol hydrochloride in varying combinations. The standard treatment is INH plus rifampin for 9 months.[38] Secondary drugs are available for cases resistant to the primary drugs. Any treatment considers the stage of the disease, its activity, and the patient's resistance to the drug.

Patients must be monitored for the onset of toxic symptoms that would necessitate a change or discontinuance of the drug. Numbness, tingling, and weakness of the extremities are toxic signs that may be observed when isoniazid is being given. Streptomycin may cause deafness, dizziness, unsteadiness of gait, ringing in the ears, or severe headache. Toxic symptoms are more likely to occur in older persons or in those who have been taking the drug for several years. Since patients with tuberculosis often receive chemotherapeutic drugs over a prolonged time, regular laboratory examinations are important. These examinations may include urinalysis, blood urea nitrogen test, liver function tests, and serum glutamic oxaloacetic transaminase (SGOT) test. In addition, visual acuity and hearing tests should be done at intervals if indicated. Depending on the extent of the disease and patient response, drug therapy is usually given for 9 to 12 months.

Nursing intervention

Tuberculosis is not a highly infectious disease, and prompt specific chemotherapy limits the release of tubercle bacilli into the air within a few days after therapy has been initiated. The patient needs instruction on the proper handling of sputum to prevent organisms from becoming airborne. When the patient coughs or sneezes, moist droplets are carried into the air. Some droplets will fall into the immediate environment, whereas others will remain suspended in the air as droplet nuclei. Good ventilation will carry droplet nuclei on air currents where they may be killed by sunlight or ultraviolet light. When the patient is taught to cover his nose and mouth when coughing or sneezing, the dissemination of moist droplets into the environment is reduced or eliminated. When the patient understands the importance of this procedure, cooperation can usually be expected. Tissues used to cover coughs or to collect sputum may be placed in public sewer systems or into a paper bag and burned.

Nurses should emphasize the importance of continuing to take the prescribed medications. One of the main factors in the continued transmission of tuberculosis is lack of adequate patient education and follow-up to ensure that therapy is completed. Patients should understand the nature and extent of the illness and recognize that medication must be continued as prescribed. Failure to take the medication on a regular basis will impede the healing process and contribute to the possible development of resistant strains of the organism.

Prevention and control

In addition to drug therapy, a variety of other prevention and control measures are recommended that interfere with transmission patterns in other ways. A vaccine known as BCG (bacille Calmette Guérin) is available; however, the amount of protection that it produces against tuberculosis is variable. In the United States, where the risk of infection is low, immunization is not generally indicated. It may be used for medical personnel who risk exposure to undiagnosed cases, contacts of active tuberculosis cases, and newborns whose mothers have active tuberculosis.[1] If used, it is given only to persons who have a negative tuberculin test. Improving social conditions and educating the public about prevention of the spread of tuberculosis organisms can help to control the transmission of the organisms. Tuberculin testing in high-risk groups, increased availability and accessibility of medical diagnosis and treatment, and nursing case management are important methods for casefinding and control of spread. The use of chemotherapeutic drugs is now recommended for known contacts exposed to tuberculosis, who tested positive but do not have the disease.

Tuberculosis has occurred among persons infected with the HIV virus.[8] The HIV infection causes immunosuppression, which allows latent tuberculosis infection to progress to a clinically apparent disease. *Mycobacterium tuberculosis* infection, in the presence of laboratory evidence for HIV infection and involving at least one site outside the lung, is now diagnostic of AIDS.[19] Clearly, prevention and control efforts will need to focus on those with or at risk for HIV infection.

In 1989, the U.S. Department of Health and Human Services released a strategic plan for the elimination of tuberculosis in the United States by the year 2010. The report also established an interim target case rate of 3.5 per 100,000 by the year 2000. The three-step plan includes: (1) more effective use of existing prevention and control measures, especially for high-risk populations; (2) development and evaluation of new technologies for diagnosis, treatment, and prevention; and (3) rapid assessment and transfer of newly developed technologies into health care practices.[7] An effective tuberculosis elimination effort such as this requires good epidemiologic surveillance data that targets the affected populations and geographic areas.

Lyme Disease

Lyme disease was first identified by a Yale rheumatologist in 1975 when he analysed an unusual cluster of arthritis cases that occurred in Lyme, Connecticut. Since then cases have spread rapidly in the Northeast, the Midwest, and the California coast, reaching epidemic proportions. Cases have been diagnosed in almost every state and in many other countries throughout the world. Cases have been recorded in Europe for several decades, leading epidemiologists to suspect that the organism was introduced in this country through migratory birds. The true incidence is unknown, since health care workers are not required to report the disease to public health authorities.

The organism *Borrelia burgdorferi* is the causative agent. The bacterial spirocete is transmitted to humans through the bite of a small tick vector the size of a poppy seed. Studies of the life cycle of the tick indicate that it commonly feeds upon an infected white-footed mouse in its larval stage, medium-size mammals including people in its nymph stage, and white-tailed deer as adults.[39]

The tick deposits the organism in the capillary system as it feeds on the host's blood, often from 12 to 24 hours. The incubation period is from 3 to 21 days after tick exposure. The human immune system responds weakly to the infection, and antibodies do not appear in any quantity until 4 to 6 weeks have passed. Because of this, laboratory tests are not helpful in early stages, and may produce false negative results.

Like other spirocete infections such as syphilis, symptoms of Lyme disease resemble many other diseases. The majority of people may first realize they were bitten when a characteristic rash at the site of the bite appears. It is an expanding red circle, often with a small welt in the center. Flulike symptoms such as fever, headache, fatigue, and stiff neck are common, along with swelling of the knee joints. If Lyme disease is not treated promptly, generalized arthritis, severe fatigue, arrhythmias, and symptoms of central nervous system involvement such as numbness, facial paralysis, visual disturbance, and seizures may occur. Permanent structural damage to joints may develop. Early treatment with antibiotics will usually prevent complications. Advanced cases may require prolonged intravenous or intramuscular antibiotics. Ceftriazone (Rocephin) penetrates the blood-brain barrier and is used in people with central nervous system involvement.

Various measures have been used to interfere with the transmission of Lyme disease. However, the most effective measures so far are to prevent the bite of the tick. People are advised to (1) check their bodies for "moving freckles" when in an area known to be tick-infested; (2) tuck pants into long socks and wear a long-sleeved shirt in tick-infested areas; (3) wear light colors and tightly woven fabrics; (4) spray insect repellent containing the ingredient DEET on your skin; (5) avoid tall grass and low brush; (6) keep pets free of ticks; (7) remove ticks with tweezers. Large-scale spraying has been ineffective in reducing the tick population, and efforts to treat infestations in mice by cotton-soaked insecticides are expensive and practical only in small areas.[39]

Salmonella Infections

Salmonellosis is an acute gastroenteritis caused by certain species of the genus *Salmonella*. It is usually classified with food poisoning because food is the most common vehicle of infection. The proportion of cases that are recognized and reported are probably very small. Outbreaks that are reported usually involve hospitals, schools, restaurants, and nursing homes. Infections usually occur as a result of food contaminated at its source, cross-contaminated during processing, or contaminated at some point by an undetected carrier.[1] Most chicken should be considered contaminated and should be handled and cooked accordingly. The organism is also found in cracked eggs, meat and meat products, and other types of poultry. Infection is prevented by thorough cooking of all foodstuffs derived from animal sources and by education of all food handlers.

The incubation period is from 6 to 72 hours, usually from 12 to 36 hours. It is followed by a sudden onset of frequent, bulky stools and then watery diarrhea. Abdominal pain, nausea and vomiting, headache, and fever may occur. Anorexia and loose stools may persist for several days. The organism may localize in any part of the body, causing a variety of complications. Generally, deaths are uncommon and occur only in the very young and elderly.

Treatment is supportive. The infection is usually self-limiting, and antibiotic treatment may prolong the carrier state. Antibiotics are indicated when complications occur, however. The primary objective in care is to maintain hydration; fluid and electrolyte losses may need to be replaced intravenously.

Shigellosis

Shigellosis (bacillary dysentery) is an acute inflammatory diarrheal disease of the colon caused by the *Shigella* bacillus bacterium. The inflammatory condition, which may also involve portions of the ileum, results in severe ulceration and, if sufficiently intense, may destroy the mucous membrane of the colon, although perforation may not occur. The disease is spread by the fecal-oral route, often through contaminated water, food, or feces. The organism has been isolated from milk products and shrimp. It usually occurs in crowded areas where sanitary conditions are poor.

The incubation period is usually between 1 and 7 days, with an abrupt onset. The primary symptom is severe diarrhea with abdominal cramping. The diarrhea results in loss of fluids and electrolytes, and the patient becomes severely dehydrated. The stools contain blood, pus, and mucus. The temperature may range from low-grade elevation to 102° to 104° F (39° to 40° C) in the afternoon. Urination may be painful, and the patient has a constant desire to defecate.

Intervention

A problem in the treatment of bacillary dysentery has been the resistance of the organisms to various antimicrobial drugs. At present, tetracycline, ampicillin, and trimethoprim-sulfamethoxazole are considered to be effective. Intravenous fluids and electrolytes are given to combat dehydration. The patient should be isolated with enteric precautions taken. A low-residue diet is offered, and the use of milk and cream should be avoided. The disease is considered to be self-limiting, and mortality is low when treatment is secured.

Gas Gangrene

Gas gangrene is a serious infection caused by a gas bacillus of the *Clostridium* genus, which is a spore-forming type of organism that produces a gas and a toxin. The specific organism is anaerobic, lives in the intestinal tract, and may find its way into a wound through soiled clothing. The gas bacillus, like the tetanus bacillus, has the power to live in the absence of air. Thus it may infect penetrating wounds such as gunshot wounds, compound fractures, or lacerated wounds.

The onset is usually sudden and may occur 1 to 4 days after injury. Severe pain and edema develop, and although there may be little fever, the pulse rate may be rapid, weak, and thready. The respiratory rate is increased, and the blood pressure may fall. There may be a peculiar odor from the wound, which often is the first indication of the infection. The slightest unusual odor should be reported immediately to the physician. As the infection extends into the surrounding muscles, skin color change and gas bubbles may be seen at the site of the wound or may be expressed from the muscles. Unless it is treated promptly, the disease is fatal.

Intervention

The most important aspect of treatment is the excision of all infected tissue. Gas gangrene antitoxin is given, and antibiotic therapy is started. Supportive treatment may include blood transfusion and intravenous fluids. When an extremity is involved, amputation may be necessary to save a patient's life. The patient must be isolated, and rigid medical asepsis must be carried out. The nurse must remember that spore-forming bacteria are not destroyed by ordinary disinfecting methods and that contaminated equipment and linens must be autoclaved. Gas gangrene is dangerous and may spread to other patients unless precautions are taken.

Meningococcal Meningitis

Meningococcal meningitis is an acute bacterial infection of the membranes that cover the brain and spinal cord. The causative organism is *Neisseria meningitidis.* It occurs worldwide, most commonly in the winter and in the spring. Children and young adults are usually the victims, although outbreaks have occurred in adults living under crowded conditions. The disease is not a significant health problem in the United States, although a vaccine is available that can be used under special circumstances. Generally, it is recommended for military personnel in the United States and for civilians who travel to areas of the world where meningococcic infection is epidemic. Circumstances may also arise where it is indicated for special groups that have been exposed. The treatment of choice is penicillin (see Chapter 22).

Legionnaires' Disease

Legionnaires' disease is primarily a respiratory infection caused by bacterium recently named *Legionella pneumophila.* It is not considered a significant health problem in the United States, although occasional outbreaks occur. It is believed to be transmitted by airborne droplets from contaminated water sources. The sources of several outbreaks have involved various types of air conditioning systems, although the organism has been isolated from a creek near a contaminated water-cooling system. Although it is believed that the organism is free living in soil, this has not been proved. Symptoms of infection include fever, malaise, nonproductive cough, and respiratory difficulty. Some patients have complained of chest pain, abdominal pain, and other gastrointestinal symptoms. Complications have included renal damage and encephalitis. The organism is sensitive to erythromycin.

THE PATIENT WITH A VIRAL DISEASE

Measles

Measles (rubeola) is a highly infectious and often severe viral disease occurring in young children. Although measles is preventable through active immunization, the disease still occurs in a significant number of people (1.5 cases or less per 100,000 people).[12] Before a measles vaccine was

available, more than 400,000 cases were reported annually in the United States. Since the introduction of the vaccine in 1963, the number of cases per year has decreased by more than 90%. However, the incidence of measles has increased somewhat in all age groups with the highest incidence rate in preschoolers who were never vaccinated. Measles control in the future depends on the success of continuing programs to immunize all susceptible persons who can tolerate the vaccine.

The onset of measles is usually sudden after an incubation period of 7 to 14 days. It occurs most often in the late winter or early spring. In the beginning the disease is often mistaken for a severe cold. Coryza, lacrimation of the eyes, which are red and sensitive to light, sneezing, and a bronchial cough appear. The child may have fever, with temperatures ranging from 103° to 105° F (39.5° to 40.5° C), and often appears severely ill. During this period examination of the throat may reveal small white spots with a reddened base, which are called **Koplik's spots.** In approximately 4 days a macular type of rash begins to appear about the face and gradually extends over the entire body. The rash gradually coalesces to form a slightly elevated eruption that reaches its height in approximately 48 hours, after which it begins to fade. After disappearance of the rash a fine desquamation of the skin occurs.

With the development of the rash the acute symptoms begin to subside, and if complications do not develop, recovery may be expected in 10 to 14 days. Measles is often complicated by bronchopneumonia, otitis media, and encephalitis. Encephalitis accompanies rubeola in about one of each 1000 children affected and may cause brain damage and mental retardation.

Intervention

There is no specific treatment for measles. The child with measles should be isolated from other children, and care should be taken in the disposal of nose and throat secretions. The patient is usually more comfortable in a darkened room because of the sensitivity to light. Sponge baths may be given to reduce fever, and fluids should be encouraged. Bed rest is indicated, and exposure to drafts or respiratory infections should be avoided. The nurse should be alert to complaints of earache or enlargement of the cervical lymph nodes, and if they should occur, the physician should be notified. During the febrile period the diet should be liquid or soft. Cough medicines have little effect on the cough, and antibiotic therapy does not alter the course of the disease.

Prophylaxis

For children who have not had measles, active immunization should be given at 15 months of age. Maternal measles antibody in the serum of the child under age 1 year limits the effectiveness of the measles vaccine in producing an active immunity. If an unvaccinated child has been exposed to measles, immunization given with 72 hours may provide protection.

The measles vaccine produces a mild or subclinical, noncommunicable infection in 95% of susceptible children (see page 146). It is recommended that persons who were immunized with live measles vaccine before 12 months of age and those who received an inactivated vaccine that was available between 1963 and 1967 should be reimmunized.

Rubella

Rubella (German measles) is sometimes called *3-day measles* because of the short duration of the disease. The symptoms may be similar to those of rubeola but are usually much milder, and Koplik's spots are absent. Some cases may be so mild that the rash is the first and only significant indication of the disease. The lymph nodes behind the ears are almost always enlarged.

The incubation period of the disease is from 12 to 23 days. Isolation and careful handling and disposal of respiratory secretions are important during the course of the disease.

Pregnancy

The occurrence of rubella during pregnancy has been found to present a major hazard to early fetal development. The rubella virus infects the placenta and spreads to the fetal circulation. The time of gestation and the length of time that the virus survives and continues to grow in fetal tissue will determine the effects on the fetus. The greatest incidence of defects takes place between the second and the sixth week of gestation. After 8 weeks, heart defects, cataracts, and glaucoma decrease, but brain and ear defects may continue to occur into the second trimester of pregnancy. Fetal defects do not develop during late pregnancy. Since 75% of rubella cases occur in school-age children, they represent the reservoir of infection for exposure of pregnant women and women of childbearing age.

Prophylaxis

In 1969 the U.S. government licensed live rubella virus vaccine for general distribution. Children in kindergarten and early grades may be the source of community epidemics and should be high on the priority list to be immunized. A single dose of rubella vaccine produces protective antibodies in approximately 95% of susceptible persons. It is often combined with measles or measles-mumps vaccines and given at 15 months of age (see page 146).

The vaccine should not be given to pregnant women or to women who may become pregnant within 3 months of receiving the vaccine. Persons with febrile illness should not be immunized until they have recovered from their illness. The vaccine has not been reported to be associated with allergic reactions; however, some vaccines do contain trace amounts of antibiotics. Therefore label information on the vaccine bottle should be reviewed carefully before administering the vaccine to patients with allergy to antibiotics.

The immunization of male adolescents and adults is useful in preventing and controlling epidemics. Since rubella vaccine is in general use, several factors are important: (1) surveillance of epidemics, (2) accurate diagnosis and reporting of cases, and (3) reporting of all birth defects related to rubella.

Chickenpox

Chickenpox is the second most frequently reported communicable disease (following gonorrhea) in the United States. The herpes varicella-zoster (V-Z) virus is the causative agent, transmitted by direct contact with skin lesions or by airborne transmission of respiratory tract secretions. The incubation period is 2 to 3 weeks and the period of communicability is usually 1 to 2 days before onset of the characteristic rash.

There is a sudden onset of slight fever with a maculopapular rash. The rash is superficial, first appearing on the chest, abdomen and back, gradually extending to other parts of the body. The lesions appear in crops, and small reddened spots are often observed in the throat before the rash appears on the skin. The rash goes through a series of stages, beginning with a macule, then progressing to a papule, vesicle, and crust. Headache, loss of appetite, and malaise are also common symptoms. Scratching of the lesions may lead to secondary infections, and scar formations may result. The disease is self-limiting and there is no specific treatment. Isolation is generally considered unnecessary, but items contaminated with nose and throat discharges should be carefully discarded.

Although chickenpox is usually a relatively benign disease, infection in a child who has leukemia may result in a widely disseminated infection. More children are surviving with leukemia because of the use of chemotherapeutic drugs; however, infection with chickenpox may be fatal. Live attenuated varicella vaccines have been developed and administered safely to children with leukemia.

Herpes Zoster

Herpes zoster (shingles) is a local manifestation of recurrent infection occurring with the chickenpox virus, usually in an older adult. Vesicles erupt on the skin in crops or in irregular patterns along a sensory nerve. Eruptions commonly appear along the chest wall, and occasionally the ophthalmic branch of the trigeminal nerve may be involved. Severe pain and paresthesias can occur over the infected nerve. The pain is controlled with analgesics, and topical steroid applications may promote healing.

Mumps

Mumps (parotitis) is an infectious disease caused by a specific virus that primarily affects children. However, susceptible adults may contract the disease. It has continued to decrease in incidence since the vaccine was licensed in December 1967. There are now approximately 1.5 cases per 100,000 people per year.[12] Mumps is characterized by inflammation and swelling of the parotid glands on one or both sides, and the salivary glands may be affected; however, 40% of the cases of mumps are believed to be subclinical. The incubation period is 14 to 21 days but may extend beyond 21 days. The disease is transmitted through droplet infection from the upper respiratory tract.

Symptoms depend on the severity of the attack, which may include slight to moderate elevation of temperature, with general malaise and pain on moving the jaw or opening the mouth. A characteristic condition associated with mumps is an acute sensitivity to acid substances.

Occasionally, other glands in the body may become involved, the most common being the testes in the male past puberty. Encephalitis, aseptic meningitis, and unilateral nerve deafness are the most serious complications. The question of mumps occurring during early pregnancy as a possible cause of fetal malformations has come under investigation.

Intervention

The patient should be isolated until all symptoms of the infection have subsided. Warm or cold packs may be applied to swollen, tender salivary glands. If orchitis develops, bed rest, narcotic analgesics, support of the inflamed testis with a bridge, and ice packs may make the patient feel more comfortable. The diet should be liquid or soft, and any food or drink with a tart or acid taste should be avoided. If it remains uncomplicated, the disease may run a course of approximately 7 to 10 days.

Prophylaxis

Although available singly, mumps vaccine is usually combined with measles-rubella vaccine and administered at age 15 months. Administration of the vaccine within 1 to 2 days after exposure offers some protection to the susceptible person.

Infectious Mononucleosis

Infectious mononucleosis is an acute infection caused by the Epstein-Barr (EB) virus, which is closely related to the herpes viruses. Infection with the virus is worldwide, but infectious mononucleosis occurs primarily in developed countries where contact with the virus is delayed from early childhood until age 15 to 25 years. Infection with the virus at an early age results in a subclinical infection that usually goes unnoticed. A syndrome resembling infectious mononucleosis may be caused by herpesvirus type 6 or the cytomegalovirus (another member of the herpesvirus group of organisms).[3]

The disease seems to have a low degree of communicability. It often occurs among groups of young people living together, as in college dormitories. The disease has been referred to as the "kissing disease" because transmission appears to be by the oral route and the exchange of saliva. The name *mononucleosis* was derived from the atypical lymphocytes among the white blood cells (see Chapter 17).

The disease is characterized by sore throat, fever, enlarged lymph nodes, headache, and vomiting, and in persons with severe cases the spleen may be enlarged or jaundice may occur. The incubation period is believed to be 4 to 14 days but may be as long as 6 weeks.

There is no specific treatment for the disease, which is self-limiting. During the acute phase the patient should be confined to bed. Mild analgesics such as aspirin may be given to relieve the discomfort from the sore throat and enlarged glands. Antibiotics have no effect on the course or the outcome of the disease. In severe cases, steroid therapy may be recommended. Although serious complications, including neurologic problems, are possible, their occurrence is rare. Chronic fatigue syndrome may be an outcome of the infection.

Influenza

Influenza is an acute viral disease of the respiratory tract. Epidemics and pandemics of influenza have been known since the sixteenth century. The worst pandemic of modern times occurred in 1918 and 1919 when it was estimated that 20 million people died, over half of these in the United States. Several serious epidemics have occurred since then. The disease occurs in cycles, but sporadic illness occurs during nonepidemic years. Each year, most states report cases of influenza to the Centers for Disease Control, although only epidemics are required to be reported. Attack rates during epidemics have been estimated from less than 15% of the population to 25% in large communities. True incidence data is difficult to obtain.

Three types of influenza virus have been identified: A, B, and C. Types A and B have long been associated with epidemics; type C has appeared only sporadically and in localized outbreaks. Strains of influenza A are described by geographic origin, strain number, year of isolation, and by an index that identifies the antigenic characteristics of the strain. Hemagglutinin (H) and neuraminidase (N) are surface antigens of the virus that stimulate antibody production. Each strain has specific configurations. For instance, the viral strain that caused the Hong Kong influenza epidemic in 1968 is described as A/Hong Kong/1/68 (H3N2).

The mode of transmission is by direct contact through droplet infection, often airborne in crowded, enclosed areas. The incubation period is short, usually from 24 to 72 hours, and the period of communicability is limited to 3 days from the onset of clinical symptoms. The typical onset is sudden with chills, a temperature of 102° F or above, aching of the head, back and extremities, sore throat, cough, sneezing, and weakness. In uncomplicated cases the acute period usually lasts from 3 to 5 days. Some cases begin with gastrointestinal symptoms, bronchopneumonia, or sinusitis. Influenza is especially hazardous for the elderly, and mortality from influenza-related pneumonia rises. Generally the treatment is symptomatic; antibiotics may be given if a secondary infection such as a bacterial pneumonia occurs (see Chapter 15).

Susceptibility to the influenza viruses is universal. Infection produces immunity to the specific infecting virus, and infections with related viruses broadens immunity. However, type A influenza viruses undergo "antigenic shifts" where distinctive new hemagglutinin or neuraminidase surface antigens are formed. These result from changes in the genetic material of the virus. These new variants of influenza create new epidemics when enough of the population is susceptible.

Vaccines have been created to immunize people at high risk, including health care workers. Since the antigenic characteristics of the current strains provide the basis for selecting the virus strains included in each year's vaccine, the vaccines may not be effective if new strains appear. Because the proportion of elderly people in the United States is increasing, and chronic diseases are more prevalent, an increased emphasis on control measures is necessary for the future. It is recommended that the following groups be targeted for vaccination programs (in order of priority):

1. Children and adults with chronic disorders of the cardiovascular or pulmonary systems
2. Residents of chronic care facilities
3. Healthy individuals 65 years or older
4. Children and adults with chronic metabolic diseases, renal dysfunction, anemia, or immunosuppression
5. Children and teenagers who are receiving long-term aspirin therapy because they are at risk of Reye's syndrome following influenza infection
6. Physicians, nurses, and other personnel having extensive contact with high-risk patients since they may transmit the virus causing nosocomial infections in patients
7. Providers of care to high-risk people in the home[10]

Local health planning and education in schools and institutions, along with surveillance of the extent and progress of outbreaks, are other means of prevention and control.

Hepatitis

Viral hepatitis is an infectious disease that attacks the liver, causing a diffuse inflammatory reaction. Several distinct infections actually occur, differing in etiologic and pathologic characteristics. Their prevention and control measures also vary (see Chapter 18).

Hepatitis A incidence was 10.4 cases per 100,000 people in 1987.[12] The virus is transmitted from person to person by the fecal-oral route, and contaminated food is a common vehicle. The incubation period is from 15 to 50 days, averaging 28 to 30 days. The virus is excreted in the feces long before clinical symptoms appear, although the carrier is thought to be most infectious just before onset of symptoms. Since the disease has a low incidence in infants and preschool children, mild, inapparent, and asymptomatic infections are probably common.

The onset of viral hepatitis is abrupt with fever, malaise, nausea, and abdominal discomfort, followed by jaundice within a few days. The illness varies from mild symptoms to a severely disabling disease lasting several months. Severity increases with age, although complete recovery is normal. Presently, no vaccine for active immunization is available. Immunoglobulin (IG) may be given to exposed persons or to those who anticipate travel to highly endemic areas as a prophylactic measure. All feces, blood, and body fluids from the infected individual should be treated as potentially infectious. Prevention and control measures used focus upon education of the public toward good sanitation, personal hygiene, and handwashing.

Hepatitis B (HBV) has a similar incidence rate to Hepatitis A: 10.7 cases per 100,000 people in 1987.[12] The infection occurs worldwide with little seasonal variation. The virus is composed of a core surrounded by an outer coat containing the surface antigen. Transmission occurs when blood, serum, or plasma from an infected person is introduced parenterally, often through venipuncture equipment or needle sticks. The infection can also be transmitted through contamination of open wounds or through exposure of mucous membranes to infected body fluids. Fecal-oral transmission has not been demonstrated. The average incubation period is from 60 to 90 days. Blood is infective weeks before the onset of symptoms, through the clinical course of the illness, and during the chronic carrier state that may last for years. Surface antigen can be detected in the serum several weeks before onset of symptoms and into the carrier state.

The onset is usually insidious with vague abdominal discomfort, anorexia, malaise, nausea and vomiting, and joint pain. Fever may be mild or absent. Jaundice is common, accompanied by dark urine, clay-colored stools, and pruritus. The illness ranges from inapparent infection to acute hepatic necrosis that may be fatal. Treatment is symptomatic only, planned to strengthen the patient's resistance to infection. The patient's contacts and those who are accidentally exposed can be immunized with an inactive viral antigen (HB). Preventive measures include strict discipline in blood banks, use of blood and blood products only when essential, and sterilization of all reusable equipment.

Non-A, non-B hepatitis resembles hepatitis B clinically and epidemiologically. It is usually less severe in the acute stage, but asymptomatic or symptomatic chronicity is common. The incubation period is from 2 weeks to 6 months. Treatment, control, and prevention measures are similar to HBV.[3]

THE PATIENT WITH A RICKETTSIAL DISEASE

The rickettsia are microorganisms now classified as bacteria. They are intracellular parasites that attack the reticuloendothelial system of humans. (see Chapter 2). The diseases resulting from rickettsial infections are not transmitted from person to person, but through the bite of a tick or body louse. The most common disease in the United States is Rocky Mountain spotted fever caused by *Rickettsia rickettsii*.

Rocky Mountain Spotted Fever

The incidence of Rocky Mountain spotted fever is greater along the eastern seaboard and in the southeastern states than in the Rocky Mountain area. There are three types of ticks that may be responsible for the disease: the American dog tick, the Rocky Mountain wood tick, and the Lone Star tick. The disease is seasonal, being more common from April to August, and in some areas presents an occupational hazard. When occupations take persons into areas heavily infested with ticks, the risk is greater. The disease is frequently contracted by persons vacationing or picnicking in areas in which ticks exist. If the disease is untreated, the fatality rate is high. The incubation period is 3 to 14 days.

Assessment

The disease may be mild, with the person remaining ambulatory, or it may be severe, with death occurring within a few days after its onset. Early symptoms may be loss of appetite, malaise, irritability, and vague aches and pains. The disease may have an abrupt onset, beginning with a chill, severe headache, an elevation of temperature to 104° F (40° C) or more, and severe aching. There may be an unproductive cough, nosebleed, and abdominal pain with nausea and vomiting. The face is flushed, there is profuse sweating, the mouth is dry, and the tongue is coated. In persons with severe cases there may be rigidity of the neck, mental confusion, delirium, incontinence, constipation, and severe prostration; convulsions and coma may occur. On the third or fourth day a rash appears, beginning on the wrists and ankles but gradually spreading over the body, and it may include the scalp and the mucous membranes of the mouth and throat. The rash is petechial in type and tends to fade on pressure; it is rose colored in the beginning but darkens as the disease continues. The acute illness may last for 2 or 3 weeks, with the temperature remaining high for as long as 10 days. The pulse rate is usually slow in relation to the amount of fever present, but in persons with severe cases it may become weak and rapid.

Intervention

The treatment of Rocky Mountain spotted fever is with chloramphenicol (Chloromycetin) or tetracycline, and treatment should be administered early in the disease, preferably with the beginning of the skin rash. The use of antibiotic therapy may bring about remarkable improvement in the symptoms and will reduce the febrile period. Other treatment consists of administering intravenous fluids if sufficient fluid is not taken orally. Blood transfusions may sometimes be indicated.

Care is the same as that for any patient with febrile disease. The patient is on a regimen of bed rest, and measures to control the temperature, such as giving sponge baths and administering antipyretic drugs, are instituted. Special mouth care and eye irrigations may be necessary. The diet should be high in protein with extra between-meal feedings that are also high in protein.

Prophylaxis

No vaccine is currently licensed in the United States. Preventative measures are similar to Lyme disease. Persons who work in tick-infested areas and persons who go camping or picnicking in areas in which they may be exposed to ticks should use tick repellents, avoid sleeping on the ground, wear long pants tucked into socks, and inspect clothing and skin carefully. Areas such as the hairline and under the arms should be given special attention. In removing ticks it is important to avoid crushing them or leaving the head embedded in the skin. The greatest danger of infection occurs after the tick has fed for 6 to 8 hours.

THE PATIENT WITH A PROTOZOAL DISEASE

There are approximately 30 known protozoal diseases. Most of these diseases have a low incidence rate in the United States, but are prevalent in other parts of the world. Most cases occur in travelers who have been to countries where the infections are endemic. Examples include amebiasis and giardiasis, which affect the intestine; toxoplasmosis and malarias, which are systemic diseases; and trichomoniasis, which affects the genitourinary tract and is considered a sexually transmitted disease. Trichomoniasis is widespread throughout the world. Malaria is a serious, worldwide disease, reportable to the Centers for Disease Control.

Malaria

Malaria is transmitted from person to person by a mosquito known as the *Anopheles quadrimaculatus*. Control of the disease in the United States has been brought about primarily by destruction of mosquito breeding places and adequate treatment of persons with malaria. Most cases that have occurred in the United States have been in persons returning from travel to areas of the world where the disease still exists.

There are four species of the parasite that cause malaria in humans; the most serious is known as *Plasmodium falciparum*. The parasite is injected into the body by the female mosquito seeking a blood meal before ovulation. The parasites invade the liver, where they grow and multiply. After 12 to 14 days (the incubation period), they enter the bloodstream and invade red blood cells. The symptoms that result are caused by the continual lysis of red blood cells.

Assessment

Symptoms begin with headache and a gradually increasing fever. The typical malaria pattern soon develops: there is a severe chill, followed by a high fever, with temperatures ranging from 103° to 105° F (39.5° to 40.5° C), and then a rapid fall in temperature followed by profuse sweating. This sequence may repeat itself every 48 hours, and between the episodes the patient may be reasonably well. However, over time without adequate treatment, there is a gradually developing anemia with enlargement of the spleen.

Intervention

Oral administration of chloroquine (Aralen) is the treatment of choice for most cases of malaria. However, in areas were *Plasmodium falciparum* has become resistant to chloroquine, quinine sulfate is given, along with tetracycline.[3] Travelers to Asia, Africa, or South America, where the chloroquine-resistant organisms are present, are advised to take mefloquine for prophylaxis. This drug is contraindicated for pregnant women; other drug therapy will be recommended. Administration of the drug should begin 2 weeks before departure and continue for 6 weeks after leaving the malarious area.

Helminthic Infestations

Metazoa are parasites that belong to the animal kingdom. When they invade the human body, this is referred to as a *helminth infection*. The Metazoa are divided into two groups: (1) Platyhelminthes, which includes tapeworms, and (2) Nematoda, or roundworms. This second group of Metazoa includes *Ascarisiasis* parasites, hookworms, pinworms, and *Trichinella* parasites (Figure 7-2).

Parasites often ingest nutrients in the gastrointestinal tract of the infected person, causing a state of malnutrition even though the person is eating a balanced diet. Some parasites feed on the host's blood, causing severe anemia. Irritation and damage to tissue can occur, and if the parasites grow or increase in numbers, blood vessels, ducts, and even the gastrointestinal tract can be blocked. Pinworms are sometimes found in the appendix when acute appendicitis has necessitated its removal. Some parasites produce toxins that injure tissue or cause severe allergic tissue reactions.

Platyhelminthes (flatworms)

Tapeworms (Cestoda). Tapeworms are flatworms and nearly all flatworms are segmented. At one end there is a head and a neck called the *scolex*; in relation to the size of the worm the head is tiny. The scolex contains a mechanism enabling the worm to attach itself to the mucous membrane of the intestinal tract (Figure 7-2). Three forms of the worm are known to infect humans in the United States: (1) dwarf tapeworm, (2) beef tapeworm, and (3) fish tapeworm.

The dwarf tapeworm is the smallest of the tapeworms. It is most prevalent in areas where the sanitation is extremely poor. Infection occurs as the result of ingestion of the eggs of the worm, which hatch in the human intestinal tract. The cycle begins when the worms produce eggs that are discharged in the feces. Improper handwashing after using the toilet is the medium by which the eggs are conveyed to the mouth and thus to the intestinal tract.

The beef tapeworm reaches the human intestinal tract through the ingestion of insufficiently cooked or raw beef containing the larvae of the worm. The cycle begins when the larvae produce worms. The eggs produced by the worms are present in human feces and are deposited onto the soil where cattle graze. A cow ingests the eggs, which hatch in the small intestine. The larvae (an intermediate stage in the development of the worm) lodge in the animal's tissues. A person who eats raw or undercooked beef containing the larvae may become infected. The beef tapeworm is known to grow to a length of 25 feet, and as long as the head remains attached to the mucous membrane of the intestinal wall it will continue to grow and produce eggs. The beef tapeworm is the one most commonly found in the United States.

The fish tapeworm, like the beef tapeworm, requires an intermediary host, and human infection occurs in a similar way. Human feces containing the eggs are deposited into fresh water where the eggs mature into tiny embryos. The embryos are usually eaten by small shellfish, which are ultimately eaten by larger fish. The embryo then matures in the tissues of the fish. In areas where fish is eaten raw or is insufficiently cooked, infection may occur. The fish tapeworm

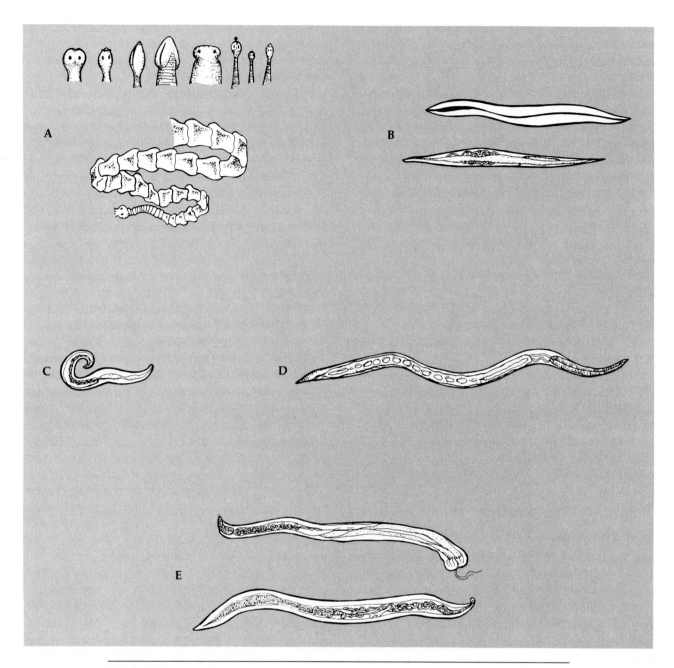

Figure 7-2
Metazoa. **A,** Tapeworm; heads and body. **B,** Pinworm. **C,** Trichina. **D,** Ascaris.
E, Hookworm.

may grow to 30 feet in length and may live for many years in the human intestine. Fish tapeworm infection is believed to be more prevalent than previously thought. Infection is known to result in severe anemia, and it is reported that the worm absorbs large amounts of vitamin B_{12} from the intestinal tract.

Praziquantel (Biltricide) or niclosamide (niclocide) is the drug of choice for both beef and fish tapeworm infestations.[3]

Nematoda (roundworms)

Ascariasis. *Ascariasis* is a genus of large roundworm resembling the common earthworm (fishworm). It varies in length from 4 to 12 inches, and the female worm may produce as many as 27 million eggs. When human feces are deposited on the ground, they become mixed with the soil, where the eggs may live for indefinite periods. Infection results from ingestion of the eggs containing the larvae, which reach the small intestine where the worms mature. Infection with *Ascariasis* may be serious and cause complications such as intestinal obstruction, perforation of ulcers, appendicitis, and similar conditions.

Administration of mebendazole (Vermox), pyrantel pamoate (Antiminth) or piperazine salts provide effective treatment.

Hookworms

There are two species of hookworm, and both may cause human infection. One species is most common in the southern United States; the other species is most prevalent in Europe and Asia. As with many other kinds of worms, the source of infection is soil that has been contaminated with human feces containing the eggs. The larva of the hookworm will penetrate the unbroken skin of the feet and legs and enter the body by way of the hair follicles and sweat glands. It penetrates lymph and blood vessels and may reach the lungs, where it is often coughed up and expectorated. If swallowed, the larva will reach the small intestine, where the worms mature. The worm attaches itself to the intestinal mucosa by a pinching kind of hook. A mature worm will produce from 5000 to 10,000 eggs daily. The hookworm is reported to ingest as much as 50 ml of the host's blood daily, which results in a severe iron-deficiency anemia. It also damages and ingests bits of tissue from the intestinal mucosa and frequently causes allergic reactions.

Mebendazole (Vermox), albendazole (Zentel), and pyrantel pamoate (Antiminth) are effective in treating the infestation. Examination of stool specimens should be repeated after 2 weeks.

Pinworms (threadworms, seatworms)

Pinworms are found worldwide, and they represent the most common helminth infection in the United States. Prevalence is highest in school-age children and lowest in adults. Often entire families are infected at the same time. The pinworm is a tiny worm, and infection is self-induced by the anal-oral route. The ingested eggs pass into the stomach, and the worm matures in the large intestine. When the mature worm is ready to lay its eggs, it crawls to the outside and deposits its eggs in folds about the rectum and anus, after which it dies. The life cycle is approximately 4 to 6 weeks. Severe itching occurs about the area, and through scratching the hands become infected with the eggs, which are then carried to the mouth, and the entire cycle begins again. Reinfection may cause the number of worms present in the gastrointestinal tract to increase over several months.

Several drugs are effective in eliminating the infestation, among them pyrantel pamoate (Antiminth), mebendazole (Vermox), albendazole (Zentel), and pyrvinium pamoate (Povanyl). Treatment is repeated after 2 weeks. Taking daily showers, frequently changing underclothes and bedsheets, washing hands frequently, discouraging nailbiting, and providing education in personal hygiene help prevent outbreaks.

Trichinellosis (trichinosis)

Trichina is a parasitic organism of the genus *Trichinella* responsible for trichinosis. The primary source of trichinosis is insufficiently cooked pork and pork products that are infected with the worm. The larva that is present in the meat passes into the intestinal tract, and the worm matures in the intestine, where it becomes embedded in the mucosa. The larva is then released and eventually reaches the bloodstream. After entering the general circulation, the larva is carried to skeletal muscle tissue and becomes encased in a cyst. There are several stages of the infection during the development of the worm and its passage through the body. During the various stages of the infection symptoms may be acute, with fever, increased leukocyte count, allergic manifestations, and psychologic symptoms. After encasement the primary symptom is rheumatic-like pain. The disease is serious in that 5% to 10% of persons infected will die.

Thiabendazole has been effective in treatment of the infestation when given during the very early, intestinal stage of the disease. Mebendazole (Vermox) is used in the muscular stage of the disease. Corticosteroids are indicated only in severe cases.

SEXUALLY TRANSMITTED DISEASES

Five diseases have been traditionally classified as sexually transmitted diseases (STDs) reportable to public health authorities: syphilis, gonorrhea, chancroid, lymphogranuloma venereum, and granuloma inguinale. Acquired immune deficiency syndrome (AIDS) has recently been added to the list. The incidence rates of chancroid, lymphogranuloma venereum, and granuloma inguinale are only 2 cases per 100,000 people or less. Syphilis and gonorrhea are still significant health problems, and AIDS is the epidemic of the twentieth century.

There are other conditions that are often sexually transmitted, such as trichomoniasis, venereal warts, herpes simplex type 2, and some chlamydial infections, but reporting of these conditions is not required. The most common conditions are discussed below. Table 7-2 outlines the characteristics of venereal diseases.

Syphilis

Syphilis is a widespread communicable disease. Nearly 65,000 cases were reported in 1987, resulting in a case rate of 35.8 per 100,000 people.[12] It primarily involves people between 15 and 30 years of age. Social factors are significantly related to the disease. It is more common in urban settings and among male homosexuals in some areas. It also is more common in males than females.

Table 7-2

Characteristics of Sexually Transmitted Diseases

Disease (pathogen)	Transmission/incubation	Symptoms	Prevention and control
Condyloma acuminata, genital warts (human papilloma virus)	Direct contact 2-3 months average	Fleshy, cauliflower-like growths around genitalia	10%-25% podophyllin in tincture of benzoin; intralesional recombinant interferon alpha-2b (Intron A); sexual contacts should be examined and treated, if indicated
Chancroid (*Haemophilus ducreyi*)	Direct contact 3-5 days, up to 14 days	Painful ulcers at site, painful regional lymph nodes	Ceftriaxone or erythromycin; report to health authorities; prophylactic treatment of contacts
Lymphogranuloma venereum (*Chlamydia trachomatis*)	Direct contact, usually sexual intercourse	Small, painless papule or nodule often unnoticed; suppuration of regional lymph nodes and invasion of adjacent tissues; fever, chills, headache, joint pain	Tetracycline; treatment of recent contacts; report to health authorities
Other chlamydial infections (*Chlamydia trachomatis*)	Direct contact through sexual intercourse	Males; urethritis Females; mucopurulent cervicitis Itching, burning on urination	Tetracycline or doxycycline; prophylactic treatment of sexual partners; reportable in some states
Granuloma inguinale (*Calymmatobacterium granulomatis* presumed agent)	Direct contact through sexual activity	Small, beefy-red nodule, slowly spreads; often painless; can spread to other parts of the skin, mucous membranes	Tetracycline, co-trimoxazole, or chloramphenicol for 3 weeks; report to health authorities; examine sexual contacts
Trichomoniasis (*Trichomonas vaginalis*)	Direct contact with vaginal and uretheral discharges or contaminated articles	Petechial lesions; profuse, thin, foamy, yellow discharge with foul odor; sometimes asymptomatic vaginitis, and/or urethritis	Metronidazole (Flagyl); sexual partners should be treated concurrently

Syphilis is contracted almost exclusively through direct sexual contact with exudates from a person infected with the bacterial spirocete *Treponema pallidum*. Susceptibility is universal. Saliva, semen, blood, and vaginal discharges may carry the organism. Fetal infection may occur through transfer of the organism through the placenta. The incubation period is from 10 days to 10 weeks, usually 3 weeks. Four stages of development have been identified: the primary, secondary, latent, and late stages. The period of communicability of untreated patients is variable and indefinite.

Primary syphilis

The primary lesion appears as a painless papule occurring on the male prepuce or female vulva, vagina, or cervix. It may become an indurated chancre. The serologic blood test is usually negative at this time. During the primary stage the disease is highly infectious. The primary lesion disappears in 3 to 4 weeks with or without treatment, and no topical application will hasten its healing. Positive identification of the specific spirochete may be made at this time by a dark-field examination (a special attachment on the microscope). When adequate treatment is given early during the primary stage, the serologic test may remain negative. Without treatment the disease progresses to the secondary stage. The secondary stage usually begins 2 to 8 weeks after the appearance of the chancre.

Secondary syphilis

As a result of the invading organisms, several symptoms develop, including a rash. The rash may be a slight erythema or may be extensive, with macular, papular, or pustular lesions. The rash may involve the entire body, especially the palms and soles, locations that strongly suggest the diagnosis. Lesions called *mucous patches* appear about the mouth and lips, and the throat may be sore. A papular type of lesion (condyloma latum) appears about the genitals. All moist lesions are infectious, and positive dark-field examination may often be secured from these secondary lesions. Other symptoms include alopecia, pain in the bones, gastric disturbances, inflammation of the eyes, loss of appetite, and malaise. Without treatment the symptoms of secondary syphilis may disappear slowly and recur at intervals for as long as 2 years, and the disease is considered highly infectious during this stage.

Latent syphilis

The latent stage is generally considered to cover 4 years or more from time of onset of the disease. During this period there is no clinical evidence of the disease after disappearance of secondary lesions, except for the reactive serologic test. However, it is during this time that the organism is attacking the vital structures and causing an inflammatory condition. The body's defenses may be sufficient to overcome the destructiveness of the organism; however, there is no way to determine which individuals may ultimately suffer severe disability. The serologic test remains reactive, and the disease is potentially infectious through sexual contact. Latency sometimes continues throughout life and spontaneous recovery may occur.

Late syphilis

The late stage occurs 5 to 20 years after initial infection. Disabling lesions occur in the cardiovascular system and central nervous system. This stage is often referred to as neurosyphilis, cardiovascular syphilis, or gummatous syphilis. These late manifestations impair health, limit occupational efficiency, and shorten life.

Congenital syphilis

Mothers with untreated syphilis often have a history of repeated abortions. If the pregnancy is completed, the fetus may be stillborn, or if the infant survives, it may have syphilis. An infant with congenital syphilis may have a rash on the face, palms of the hands, soles of the feet, and buttocks, with the latter often taken for diaper rash. There may be mucous patches in the mouth and a nasal stuffiness and rhinitis (snuffles), and the bones and abdominal organs are often involved. The syphilitic lesions of the infant are infectious, just as are those of the adult. The child who survives may develop complications at any time before 16 years of age. These complications include changes in the bones, deformed permanent teeth, interstitial keratitis, and eighth nerve deafness. The central nervous system may be involved, and mental retardation may occur in a small number of children.

Intervention

The present treatment of syphilis is administration of long-acting penicillin G. At the present time there is no evidence that the syphilitic organism is becoming resistant to penicillin; however, caution must be exercised because more individuals are becoming sensitive to penicillin. The same care should be exercised as when administering penicillin to a patient for any condition. Treatment may extend over a period of several days or may be given in one initial dose. Patients who are sensitive to penicillin may be treated with tetracycline or erythromycin.

The fundamental approach to controlling syphilis is to interview patients in order to identify contacts. All identified contacts of confirmed cases of syphilis should receive preventive penicillin therapy and be educated about the disease. The privacy of the individual must be protected. Preventive measures assumed by nurses include health and sex education, discouragement of sexual promiscuity, and encouragement of syphilis serology during prenatal examinations. Control of prostitution and assuring availability and accessibility of care are broader goals for health care personnel.

Gonorrhea

Gonorrhea remains an epidemic in the United States. It is an infection of the genitourinary tract with the organism *Neisseria gonorrhoeae* (gonococcus bacterium). Gonorrhea is the infectious disease reported the most frequently, having a case rate of 323 per 100,000 people. It is very common in the United States among sexually promiscuous male homosexuals. With the introduction of resistant strains of the organism, the incidence has increased worldwide.[12]

Transmission of the organism occurs through direct contact with exudates from the mucous membranes of infected people. The incubation period is 2 to 7 days. Without treatment the infection may be self-limiting or result in a chronic carrier state. In females, urethritis or cervicitis initially occurs. It is often mild and may go unnoticed. Chronic endocervical infection is frequent, and the uterus may be invaded as the infection progresses. Because of the sometimes mild nature of the disease in women, many cases go untreated and spread the infection to others. The period of communicability may extend for months if untreated. A disseminated gonococcal infection develops in approximately 5% of those infected, causing arthritis, fever, and skin lesions.[3]

The characteristic symptoms begin with burning, urgent, and painful urination. There may be redness and edema of the urinary meatus. After the initial symptoms a purulent urethral discharge occurs in the male, and a discharge may be expressed from the vaginal glands, ducts, and the urethra in the female. In the absence of treatment or with inadequate treatment the disease may become chronic and lead to complications. Epididymitis and prostatitis may occur in the male, and salpingitis and pelvic inflammatory disease (PID) may occur in the female. An acute inflammatory condition in the fallopian tube may result in atresia and sterility.

Intervention

The treatment for gonorrhea consists of administering penicillin G, 4.8 million units at one visit. Ampicillin or tetracycline can also be used. However, certain strains of the gonococcus are becoming resistant to penicillin. For persons who are sensitive to penicillin, other antibiotics may be administered. Minocycline (Minocin), a semisynthetic derivative of tetracycline, has been used as an alternative agent to treat gonorrhea. Interview of patients and tracing of contacts are fundamental elements of a control program. Preventive measures are the same as for syphilis.

Acquired Immunodeficiency Syndrome (AIDS)

AIDS is a syndrome of clinical events resulting from an acquired deficiency of the immune system. It was first recognized as a disease entity in 1981 when the description first appeared in the Centers for Disease Control publication *Morbidity and Mortality Weekly Report*. It is the most severe disease state of a continuum of illnesses that are related to infection by the human immunodeficiency virus (HIV). It has grown in proportion so rapidly that it has been labeled a worldwide plague.

At the end of 1988, 82,764 cases of AIDS in the United States and its territories had been reported to the Centers for Disease Control. Of these cases, over half have died. The annual incidence rates vary according to geographic areas, from 0.6 cases per 100,000 persons in North Dakota to 81.2 cases per 100,000 persons in Washington, D.C. It is estimated that up to 420,000 men and 60,000 women in the United States will be diagnosed with AIDS by 1993.[6] Homosexual or bisexual men account for the majority of all reported cases of AIDS in the United States. Persons using intravenous drugs are second in frequency, followed by heterosexual partners of persons at risk.

Transmission

HIV has three main modes of transmission: (1) sexual contact with an infected person; (2) exposure to infected blood or blood products, often through needle-sharing among IV-drug users; and (3) transmission from an infected woman to her fetus or infant.[8] The retrovirus has the characteristics of a "slow" virus in that its incubation period is months or years, the resulting disease is relentless, progressive, and often fatal, and the virus is recoverable through all stages of illness. It is estimated that 1 million to 1.5 million Americans are infected with HIV.[6] Although these people may be asymptomatic, they can transmit the virus to others.

Pathophysiology

When HIV enters the body it begins to attack a specialized group of white blood cells called T-4 lymphocytes (helper cells) that form an essential part of the cell-mediated immune system (see Chapter 26). Over time, the alterations in these cells decrease the individual's ability to fight off certain opportunistic infections and malignancies. There is a wellness to illness continuum. Initial infection with HIV may produce an acute transitory viral syndrome. At the resolution of the acute infection, HIV antibodies may be detected (seropositive). The period of asymptomatic infection may last for months or years.

Clinical manifestations may begin with symptoms of AIDS-related complex (ARC). ARCs are diagnosed when a person who has been infected by HIV has at least two well-developed symptoms of immunodeficiency with at least two laboratory abnormalities. Symptoms such as fever, night sweats, fatigue, lymphadenopathy, and weight loss are common. ARCs may be a precursor to AIDS or remain in a mild form. It is not known whether ARCs reflect a chronic disease state or are due to immune abnormalities. AIDS is the life-threatening complication of HIV infection. The case definition for AIDS depends on the status of laboratory evidence of HIV infection and incorporates the presence of "indicator" diseases such as Kaposi's sarcoma or *Pneumocystis carinii* pneumonia.[11] Specific care for the patient with AIDS is found in Chapter 26.

Prevention and control

Currently there is no cure or preventive vaccine for AIDS. Azidothymidine (AZT) and ribavirin are two common antiviral agents used to interfere with HIV replication. A variety of drugs are used to treat opportunistic infections. Blood and body fluid precautions are essential for those caring for HIV infected people. Preventive measures are focused on safe sexual practices and use of clean drug paraphernalia. Use of condoms and limiting the number of sexual partners will decrease the risk of HIV transmission. Public health measures such as blood product screening, perinatal counseling, and contact tracing can reduce the risk of exposure and transmission. Many agencies, among them the National Gay Task Force, are actively engaged in educating the public.

Herpes Simplex

There are four major types of herpes viruses. The herpes simplex virus (HSV) types 1 and 2 cause both genital and oral infections. Other viruses included in this family are the Epstein-Barr virus, which causes mononucleosis; the varicella-zoster virus, which causes chickenpox and shingles; and the cytomegalovirus (CMV), which can result in severe congenital abnormalities. The majority of oral HSV infections are caused by type 1, and most genital lesions are caused by type 2. However, either strain can be found in the oral and genital areas, as well as in other parts of the body as lesions on the skin. Recurring cold sores around the external surface of the mouth are considered oral herpes. HSV-1 and HSV-2 infections can be distinguished only by tissue culture.

Most people have been exposed to HSV-1 and/or HSV-2 infections. Random sampling of various populations for the presence of antibodies to the virus have estimated that 40% to 100% of the general population have been exposed at some time to the viruses.[1]

Pathophysiology

HSV infections are believed to be transmitted by skin-to-skin contact with an infected lesion. The virus enters the body through a break in the skin or mucous membranes, and transmission is not necessarily sexual in nature. Incubation is from 2 to 12 days. It enters the nervous system at the site of infection, resides in that area permanently, and can remain dormant indefinitely. An outbreak of active infection can be triggered by such things as local trauma, sunlight, emotional stress, and the presence of other debilitating diseases. Asymptomatic transmission can also occur, posing extensive problems for prevention and control of the infection.

The initial or primary infection is usually the most severe and lasts from 7 to 21 days. An initial infection in the mouth causes severe stomatitis, but the lesions will not recur. A fluid-filled vesicle forms first, followed by shallow ulcerations. When this occurs in the genital area, itching, burning, tingling, and sometimes severe pain may be present. Edema, swollen lymph glands, and a thin, white discharge may occur. The number of lesions may vary considerably. Moist lesions heal more slowly than dry lesions. Outbreaks may recur, although they become progressively more mild and less frequent, and lesions last from 4 to 10 days.

Prevention and control

There is no cure for oral or genital herpes. Topical 5-iodo-2' deoxyozidine (Idoxuridine) may modify acute symptoms. Acyclovir (Zovirax), used orally, intravenously, or topically, may reduce shedding of virus, diminish pain, and accelerate healing time. Keeping lesions dry and clean is essential. A vaccine for HSV is under study, but it will have little effect for those who have already been infected. Prevention of herpes focuses on avoidance of contact with open lesions. Health care personnel should wear gloves when in contact with mucous membranes that may be infected with herpes simplex virus. Using a condom during sexual activity may decrease the risk of infection.

HSV infections during pregnancy have devastating effects on the fetus, particularly if it is an initial infection. The infection in the infant can be systemic and result in death. A cesarean section may be performed to prevent infection in the newborn when the mother has an active infection.

Also, HSV-2 infections have been related to cervical cancer.

The emotional problems associated with a herpes infection can be severe. When a mother unknowingly infects her infant or a person passes on the infection to a sexual partner, guilt and despair can result. The social stigma of venereal disease may be very destructive. Empathy and acceptance are imperative.

• • •

The sexually transmitted diseases have frequently been termed "social diseases" because of the factors in society that have contributed to their existence, including poverty, poor housing, low income, ignorance, and in more recent times the high mobility of people, increased consumption of alcohol, ease of treatment, and a change in value systems. All these factors have contributed to the increase in the incidence of sexually transmitted diseases.

Prevention and control continues to be a major health focus. Preventive measures include educational programs, especially in schools, on general health, sex education, and preparation for marriage. Most states require premarital and prenatal examinations, including blood serology. Discouragement of sexual promiscuity along with teaching methods of personal prophylaxis will help protect members of the community. Facilities for early diagnosis and treatment should be available in all communities. Control measures include mandatory reporting of all cases to local health departments so that all contacts can be investigated. Interviewing of patients and tracing contacts are fundamental in control of transmission.

REFERENCES AND ADDITIONAL READINGS

1. Baum SG and Phillips CF: Just who is at risk for mumps? Patient Care 23(4):48-56, 1989.
2. Beck M et al: A mean strain of strep, Newsweek 116(4):57, 1990.
3. Beneson AS: Control of communicable diseases in man, ed 15, Washington, DC, 1990, American Public Health Association.
4. Boley T et al: Herpes zoster: etiology, clinical course, and suggested management, J Am Acad Nurse Pract 2(2):64-68, 1990.
5. Breslin E: Genital herpes simplex, Nurs Clin North Am 23(4):907-915, 1988.
6. Centers for Disease Control: HIV prevalence estimates and AIDS case projections for the United States: report based upon a workshop, MMWR 39(No. RR-16):1-31, 1990.
7. Centers for Disease Control: A strategic plan for the elimination of tuberculosis in the United States. 38(Suppl S-3):1-25, 1989.
8. Centers for Disease Control: AIDS and human immunodeficiency virus infection in the United States: 1988 update, 38(Suppl S-4), 1989.
9. Centers for Disease Control: General recommendations on immunization, 38(13):205-214, 1989.
10. Centers for Disease Control: Prevention and control of influenza, MMWR 36(24):373-380, 385, 1987.
11. Centers for Disease Control: Revision of the CDC surveillance case definition for acquired immunodeficiency syndrome, 36(Suppl 1S):3S-9S, 1987.
12. Centers for Disease Control: Summary of notifiable diseases, United States, 1987, 36(54), 1988.
13. Cohn JA: Virology, immunology, and natural history of

HIV infection, J Nurs Midwifery 34(4):242-250, 1989.

14. Cuzzell JZ: Clues: pain, burning, and itching, Am J Nurs 90(7):15-16, 1990.

15. Dawkins BJ: Genital herpes simplex infections, Prim Care 17(1):95-113, 1990.

16. Enterline JA et al: Condylomata acuminata (venereal warts), Nurse Pract 14(4):8, 10, 12, 1989.

17. Ferrar A: Germs that kill healthy people, Ladies Home Journal 107(9):147-148, 1990.

18. Fogel C: Gonorrhea: not a new problem but a serious one, Nurs Clin North Am 23(4):885-897, 1988.

19. Gee G and Moran TA: AIDS: concepts in nursing practice, Baltimore, 1988, Williams & Wilkins.

20. Gingrich MM: Should you take zidovudine after a needle stick? Nurs 90 20(9):18, 1990.

21. Glittenberg JE: Problems of global control of tuberculosis, J Prof Nurs 6(2):73, 129, 1990.

22. Graham JM et al: Chlamydial infections, Prim Care 17(1):85-93, 1990.

23. Gurevich I: Counseling the patient with herpes, RN 53(2):22-28, 1990.

24. Holman S: Epidemiology and transmission of HIV infection in women, Nurs Midwifery 34(5):233-239, 1989.

25. Lutz R: Stopping the spread of sexually transmitted diseases, Nurs 86 16:47-50, 1986.

26. Madsen LA: Tuberculosis today, RN 44-50, 1990.

27. Mandell GL, Douglas GR and Bennett JE: Principles and practice of infectious diseases, ed 3, New York, 1990, John Wiley & Sons Inc.

28. Mausner JS and Kramer JS: Epidemiology: an introductory text, ed 2, Philadelphia, 1985, WB Saunders Co.

29. McElhose P: The "other" STDs: as dangerous as ever RN 51(6):52-59, 1988.

30. Melvin SY: Syphilis: resurgence of an old disease, Prim Care 17(1):47-57, 1990.

31. Moy JG: The patient with gonococcal infection, Prim Care 17(1), 59-53, 1990.

32. Nettina SL: Syphilis: a new look at an old killer, Am J Nurs 90(4):68-70, 1990.

33. Nettina SL et al: Diagnosis and management of sexually transmitted genital lesions, Nurse Pract 15(1):20, 1990.

34. Noble RC: Sequelae of sexually transmitted diseases, Prim Care, 17(1):173-181, 1990.

35. Pritchard VG et al: Streptococcal outbreak, J Gerontol Nurs 14(2):19-23, 1988.

36. Rapini RP: Venereal warts, Prim Care 17(1):127-144, 1990.

37. Shoop NM: Prepare for the 1990s: update: tuberculosis, hepatitis, and acquired immunodeficiency dyndrome, Gastroenterol Nurs 12(3):200-203, 1990.

38. Stumacher RJ: Clinical infectious diseases, Philadelphia, 1987, WB Saunders Co.

39. Tiny tick, big worry, Newsweek, 113:65-70, 1989.

40. Unsuspected chlamydia, Emerg Med, 21(16):93-94, 1989.

41. Whelan, M: Nursing management of the patient with Chlamydia trachomatis infection, Nurs Clin North Am 23(4):877-883, 1988.

Nosocomial Infections

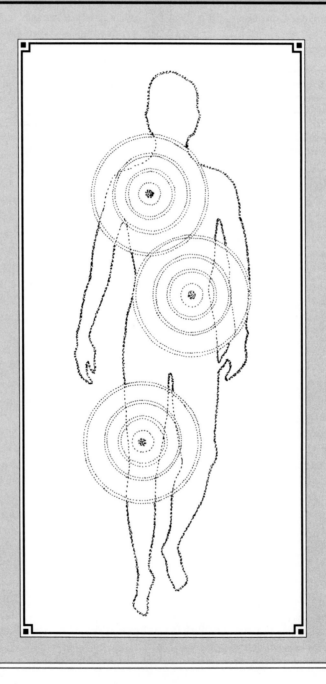

OBJECTIVES

1. Differentiate between nosocomial and community-acquired infections.

2. Name the most common sites, hospital services, and types of organizations associated with hospital-acquired infections.

3. Explain factors that put a patient at high risk for infection.

4. Identify measures to prevent and control urinary tract infections, surgical wound infections, pneumonia, and bacteremia.

5. Specify the standards required for infection control in hospitals.

6. Define antiseptics and disinfectants.

7. Identify effective surveillance methods for hospital-associated infections.

8. Contrast the differences between category-specific isolation, disease-specific isolation, universal precautions, and body substance isolation.

9. Discuss the emotional responses patients with nosocomial infections may experience.

HOSPITAL INFECTIONS

Infections have always been associated with hospitalization. In fact, infection following surgery was once so common that the drainage from a wound was referred to as "laudable pus." Fortunately, today's hospitals reflect the impact of increased knowledge of disease causation, pathogenesis, environmental control, and patient response in the diagnosis and treatment of infections.

Nosocomial infection has been defined as a clinically active infection occurring in a hospitalized patient that was not present or incubating at the time of admission. Residual infections that were acquired during previous admissions and infections acquired in the hospital but that appear after discharge are also classified as nosocomial. The term "nosocomial" is derived from the Greek words *nosos*, illness or disease, and *komeo*, to take care of. One of the first private hospitals in ancient Greece was called a nosocomium.

In contrast to nosocomial infection, a *community-acquired* infection is found in patients who enter the hospital with a known or incubating infection. In this case the symptoms of infection may be present or may appear during hospitalization. Any infection, whether hospital-acquired or community-acquired, may be serious if it spreads to other susceptible persons.

Not only does the patient bring fixed patterns of behavior with him to the hospital, but he also brings microorganisms in his nose, throat, and intestinal tract and on his skin. Although some of these microorganisms are harmless and some may be beneficial, others have the potential for precipitating hospital infection if circumstances are favorable. Any patient or hospital employee may either be a source or recipient of a nosocomial infection.

The hospital is an environment contaminated by patients, visitors, and hospital personnel. People admitted to hospitals are exposed to an increased variety and increased concentration of microbial agents. Often they are exposed to new organisms that are peculiar to the hospital environment and that have developed increased virulence and resistance to drugs. Illness decreases the body's resistance and therefore increases the patient's susceptibility to infection.

Also, diagnostic and treatment methods may weaken or bypass normal defensive barriers, placing some patients at a **high risk** for nosocomial infections. During use, medical-surgical supplies and equipment may become contaminated. Ventilators, respiratory therapy equipment, pressure monitoring devices, intravenous catheters, and urinary catheters are all examples of equipment that bypass normal body defenses and become a source of infection. Even prepackaged sterile supplies designed to protect the patient can become contaminated and serve as a source of nosocomial infection.

Incidence of Nosocomial Infection

The Centers for Disease Control initiated the National Nosocomial Infections Study (NNIS) in 1969 to gather ongoing data from a variety of hospitals in the United States. Their statistics indicate that there are approximately 3.4 nosocomial infections per 100 discharged patients, or an infection rate of 3.4%, when all infections from all types of hospitals are considered. Infection rates appear to be associated with the type of facility and service that is offered. Large teaching hospitals have the highest reported incidence of nosocomial infection; small nonteaching hospitals have the lowest. It has been suggested that this latter finding is partly a result of severity of illness and increased length of hospitalization often found in larger hospitals.[9]

The Study of the Efficacy of Nosocomial Infection Control (SENIC) represents a large-scale study conducted by the Centers for Disease Control during 1975 and 1976. In this study a statistical sample of all U.S. hospitals were used. The national nosocomial infection rate was determined to be 5.7 nosocomial infections per 100 admissions.[16]

Other nosocomial rates reported range from 3% to 15% of all patients admitted to hospitals. However, the 6% rate established by the SENIC study is the generally quoted rate. It is estimated that more than 8 million extra hospital days are required every year to care for patients with nosocomial infections. The estimated annual cost of this care is about $4 billion nationwide. It is also estimated that 20,000 deaths per year are directly attributable, and another 60,000 attributable in part, to nosocomial infections. These figures indicate that nosocomial infections are a leading cause of death in the United States.[15] Infection control programs can be a real cost benefit to the hospital if the program results in decreased morbidity and mortality incurred because of nosocomial infections.

The 1984 NNIS data show that the urinary tract is the most common site infected in hospitalized patients, followed by lower respiratory tract and surgical wound infections. Infections of these three sites account for almost three fourths of all nosocomial infections. The hospital services with the highest rates include surgical, medical, and gynecologic units, followed by obstetric and newborn nursery units. ***Escherichia coli, Pseudomonas aeruginosa,*** *enterococcus faecalis*, and ***Staphylococcus aureus*** are the most frequently reported **pathogens.**

High-Risk Patients

Nosocomial infections can be classified as either exogenous or endogenous. **Exogenous** infections are acquired from sources outside the patient or from the environment. **Endogenous** infections result when circumstances permit the potentially virulent organisms that normally reside within the host to multiply, causing a pathologic condition within the patient. When endogenous infections occur, the host's normal defense mechanisms are deficient or compromised. A person with deficient defense mechanisms is called a *compromised host.*

There are many underlying host factors that determine whether a person will or will not develop an infection. Age and underlying disease are two of the most important determinants. Newborn infants, especially those of low birth weight, have immature immune systems and therefore have fewer physical resources to combat infectious microorganisms. The elderly have less efficient immune systems and thus have a decreased resistance to infection. Chronic disease, such as renal failure, diabetes, or cancer, and burns, malnutrition, or a state of shock can all predispose to infection. Treatment measures that invade body cavities bypass natural defense mechanisms, creating a direct route for microorganisms to gain entrance to body organs and cause infection. Urinary catheterization, intravenous infusions, peritoneal dialysis, and surgical incisions of the skin are examples. Ionizing radiation and immunosuppressive drug therapy can depress the immune response, placing the patient at high risk for infection. The extensive use of antibiotics may also be responsible for decreasing host resistance and the development of more virulent and resistant strains of organisms.

METHODS OF TRANSMISSION

Microorganisms are transmitted by various routes, and the same microorganism may be transmitted by more than one route. For example,

varicella-zoster virus (chickenpox) can spread either by the airborne route or by direct contact. There are four main routes by which organisms are transmitted to a susceptible host. These routes are contact, airborne, vehicle, and vectorborne transmission.

Contact transmission is the most common method by which microorganisms are transmitted from one person to another. Contact transmission can be divided into three subgroups: direct contact, indirect contact, and droplet contact. *Direct contact* involves person-to-person spread and occurs when there is physical contact between the source and the susceptible person. Contact occurs constantly during daily patient care, with hands having the most contact with the patient. Therefore, thorough handwashing is the best means of preventing transmission by direct contact. *Indirect contact* involves personal contact of the susceptible host with a contaminated intermediate object. For instance, an inadequately disinfected endoscope can indirectly transfer organisms. *Droplet contact* occurs when an infectious agent briefly passes through the air. The infected sources and the susceptible host are usually within a few feet of each other. This is considered "contact" transmission rather than airborne, since droplets usually travel no more than 3 feet. Organisms are usually dispersed when an infected person coughs, sneezes, or talks.

Airborne transmission occurs when infectious agents remain suspended in the air for long periods of time. Organisms carried in this manner can be widely dispersed by air currents before being inhaled by or deposited on the susceptible host. Tuberculosis is a disease transmitted by this route. Good ventilation systems help to prevent the transmission of infectious agents by the airborne route.

Vehicle transmission occurs when contaminated items such as blood, blood products, food, water, or drugs serve as the vector of transmission to multiple persons. Examples of this type of transmission are the spread of salmonellosis from contaminated dairy products or the contraction of acquired immunodeficiency syndrome (AIDS) from infected blood.

Vectorborne transmission occurs when insects or other animals serve as intermediate hosts for an infectious agent. For example, malaria is transmitted by mosquitos and Rocky Mountain spotted fever is transmitted by ticks. Vectors have not played a significant role in the transmission of nosocomial infection in the United States.

NOSOCOMIAL INFECTIONS

Urinary Tract Infections

Urinary tract infections (UTIs) are the most common site of nosocomial infections occurring in hospitalized patients. About 80% of the nosocomial UTIs are associated with the use of genital urinary manipulations.[23] Catheter-associated urinary tract infections are caused by a variety of pathogens including *Escherichia coli*, **Klebsiella,** *Proteus, Enterococcus, Pseudomonas, Enterobacter, Serratia,* and *Candida.* Many of these microorganisms are part of the patient's endogenous bowel flora, but they can also be acquired by cross contamination from other patients, hospital personnel, contaminated solutions, or nonsterile equipment.

Host factors that appear to increase a person's susceptibility to catheter-associated UTIs include debilitation, chronic disease, and the presence of pathogenic bacteria in the periurethral area. Women and the elderly have higher contraction rates of such infections. Whereas most UTIs are of low morbidity and mortality, infections can occasionally lead to such complications as prostatitis, epididymitis, cystitis, pyelonephritis, and **bacteremia.**

Infecting microorganisms gain access by several routes. Microorganisms that inhabit the meatus or distal urethra can be introduced directly into the bladder when the catheter is inserted. Also, infecting microorganisms can migrate to the bladder along the outside of the catheter and the periurethral mucous sheath or along the internal lumin of the catheter after the collection bag or catheter drainage tube junction has been contaminated.

Nursing measures that can prevent or control urinary catheter-associated infections relate to optimal catheter care for patients who require drainage systems. The most direct method to prevent catheter-associated bacteriurea is to avoid catheterization. Urinary catheters should be inserted only when necessary and should be left in place only as long as necessary. Indications for the use of an indwelling catheter include relief of urinary obstruction, neurogenic bladder, aid in surgery, and as a means of accurate measurement of output. Routine use of indwelling catheters for incontinence is not appropriate unless there is concern about massive skin breakdown.

Once a urethral catheter is in place, urinary tract infection is best avoided by maintaining a closed system and by minimizing the duration of catheterization. Urine specimens should be obtained without opening the catheter collection tube junction. Special ports in the system allow for aseptic collection of urinary specimens. These ports should be cleansed with a disinfectant before aspiration of the urine with a sterile needle and syringe.

Urinary flow should be unobstructed. The catheter and collecting tubing should be kept from kinking and the collecting bag should be emptied regularly using a separate collecting container for each patient. Nosocomial transmission has occurred between patients when contaminated urine collecting devices have been used from one patient to another.[24] Routine changing of indwelling catheters does not reduce the risk of urinary tract infection.

Handwashing is extremely important and should be done immediately before and after any manipulation of the catheter. It is imperative that hands be washed between handling catheters of different patients.

Nosocomial Pneumonia

Nosocomial pneumonia is the second most common nosocomial infection. It accounts for 15% of nosocomial infections in U.S. hospitals. Nosocomial pneumonia is associated with mortalities ranging from 20% to 50% and is the most common fatal nosocomial infection.[23]

A majority of these pneumonias occur in intensive care unit settings or post-surgical recovery rooms. The NNIS consistently reports that more than 60% of nosocomial pneumonias are caused by aerobic gram-negative bacilla. *Pseudomonas aeruginosa* alone accounts for 16.9% of nosocomial pneumonias. *Klebsiella, Enterobacter* species, *Escherichia coli, Serratia marcescens,* and *Proteus* are other gram-negative bacteria that may cause nosocomial pneumonia. *Staphylococcus aureus,* a gram-positive organism, is the second most common **etiologic** agent causing hospital-acquired pneumonia. It accounts for 12.9% of the cases.[9] Less common etiologic agents causing hospital-acquired pneumonia include anaerobic mouth flora, **Streptococcus** *pneumoniae, Branhamella catarrhalis,* Influenza A virus, *Haemophilus influenzae, Legionella* species, and *Aspergillus.*[7]

Nosocomial lower respiratory viral infections can occur and are often reflective of the occurrence of a virus in the community. During community outbreaks, viruses are introduced into the hospital by patients, employees, and visitors. These viral infections may be particularly severe in high-risk, debilitated patients. Respiratory syncytial virus (RSV), parainfluenza virus, and influenza are responsible for a large proportion of viral nosocomial pneumonia cases.

It is also now evident that *Legionella pneumophila* accounts for a small number of cases of nosocomial pneumonia. Because of the special testing techniques required to diagnose *Legionella*, the true frequency of this pathogen is unknown. Some hospitals have experienced clusters of nosocomial *Legionella* pneumonia. These are usually related to environmental factors such as contamination of potable water or air conditioning systems.

A number of factors predispose patients for hospital-acquired pneumonia. Intubation of the respiratory tract is associated with a high frequency of nosocomial pneumonia. The use of endotracheal tubes bypasses the protective defense mechanisms of the upper respiratory tract.

In addition, hospitalized patients often have impaired host defenses because of clinical conditions such as chronic obstructive lung disease, cystic fibrosis, leukemia, central nervous system depression (coma), and electrolyte imbalance. These patients can become colonized with potential pathogens from their own endogenous flora or from exogenous sources such as hands of hospital personnel and contaminated respiratory therapy equipment. It is believed that a colonized patient becomes infected through aspiration of upper respiratory tract secretions.

Diagnosis of a nosocomial pneumonia may be difficult. A positive culture of respiratory tract secretions does not distinguish between **colonization** and infection of the lower respiratory tract. Therefore, the clinician must rely on a change in clinical symptoms such as altered mental status, change in fever, change in chest x-ray, cough, sputum production, and elevated leucocyte count to make a diagnosis. However, these clinical conditions may be present without the occurrence of pneumonia.

Prevention of nosocomial respiratory tract infections is based on reducing the acquisition of potential bacterial pathogens in the upper airways and thereby decreasing the risk for aspiration of these organisms. Handwashing is essential in the prevention of all nosocomial infections. Hands should be washed after contact with respiratory secretions whether gloves are worn or not. Hands must be washed before and after contact with a patient who is intubated or who has had a recent tracheostomy.

General nursing techniques such as keeping the airway open and having the patient turn, cough, and deep breathe, plus early ambulation after surgery, are important in preventing postoperative pneumonia. Before surgery patients should receive instruction regarding measures that will reduce the risk of nosocomial pneumonia. During this teaching patients should demonstrate and practice adequate coughing and deep breathing. It is important to control the pain in a postoperative patient so that pain will not interfere with coughing and deep breathing.

Close adherence to the guidelines for use of respiratory therapy equipment will also decrease the incidence of nosocomial pneumonia. Only sterile fluids should be nebulized or used in a humidifier. Nebulizers (including medication nebulizers) and their reservoirs and cascade humidifiers should be changed or replaced with sterilized or disinfected ones every 24 hours. Warm humidifiers that create droplets to humidify should not be used.

Patients with tracheostomy should have their tracheostomy suctioned using sterile techniques. The risk of cross-contamination and excessive trauma increases with frequent suctioning. Therefore, suctioning should be done only using a "no touch" technique and gloves on both hands. A sterile catheter should be used for each series of suctioning. If flushing of the catheter is necessary because of tenacious mucous, sterile fluid should be used to remove secretions from the catheter. Fluid used for one series of suctioning should be discarded.

Patients with potentially transmissible respiratory infections should be isolated from other patients according to the hospital isolation guidelines. To prevent nosocomial acquisition of viral infections from employees, health care workers with acute respiratory infections should not be assigned to the direct care of high risk patients. In addition, all health care workers assigned to care for high risk patients should receive an influenza vaccine annually to decrease the risk of transmission to patients.

Surgical Wound Infection

Surgical wound infections are the third most frequent nosocomial infection in most hospitals.

They are divided into categories of incisional or deep infections. Incisional infections account for 60% to 80% of surgical wound infections. The remainder are classified as deep infections.

A wound is considered infected if purulent material drains from it, even without a positive wound culture. Wounds are classified according to the likelihood and degree of wound contamination at the time of the operation. A widely accepted classification scheme outlined by the American College of Surgeons, predicts the relative probability that a wound will become infected. Clean wounds have a 1% to 5% risk of infection; clean contaminated, a 3% to 11% risk of infection; contaminated, a 10% to 17% risk of infection; dirty, over a 27% risk of infection.[8]

Another index developed to predict the likelihood of surgical wound infection is a multivariate index developed and tested during the SENIC study. This index includes four risk factors which are: having an abdominal operation; having an operation that lasts longer than 2 hours; having a contaminated, dirty, or infected operation by the traditional classification system; and having three or more discharge diagnoses.[14]

Age is one host factor that may influence the risk of infection. Persons over age 65 have twice the chance of contracting nosocomial surgical wound infections as younger persons. Obesity, severe malnutrition, infection at other sites, and extended preoperative stays in the hospital are other host factors associated with an increased risk of infection.

Gram-negative aerobic bacteria make up approximately 40% of the pathogens isolated from surgical wounds. However, *Staphylococcus aureus* remains the most frequently isolated species from surgical wounds. Microorganisms that infect surgical wounds can be acquired from the patient, the hospital environment, or hospital personnel. However, the patient's own flora is responsible for most infections. Sources of infection include the gastrointestinal tract, respiratory tract, genital tract, urinary tract and the skin and anterior nares. Most infections, whether acquired from the environment or the patient's own flora, appear to be acquired in the operating room. Few infections are acquired after the operation if the wounds are closed primarily. Open wounds and the presence of drains increases the risk of infection in the postoperative period.

Measures to prevent surgical wound infection actually begin before the operation. An important preoperative measure is to treat any active infection before surgery. Shortening the preoperative hospital stay of the patient also reduces risk of infection.

Historically, hair adjacent to or in the area of the proposed surgery has been removed to prevent hair from contaminating the wound during the operation. However, several recent studies suggest that shaving with a razor can injure the skin and increase the risk of infection. Therefore, clipping hair, using a depilatory, or not shaving at all, have been suggested in place of shaving.[12]

Before surgery, skin at the operative site should be thoroughly cleansed with an antiseptic solution to remove all superficial skin flora, soil, and debris. The surgical team must also scrub their hands to minimize the normal flora on their skin. The surgical scrub is designed to kill and remove as many bacteria as possible, including resident bacteria. Once hands are scrubbed, members of the surgical team wear sterile gloves that act as an additional barrier to prevent the transfer of microorganisms to the surgical wound.

To reduce airborne contamination, ventilation systems that produce 20 changes of highly filtered air per hour are installed in modern operating rooms. Some operating rooms, especially those used for orthopedic surgeries involving joint replacements, have installed laminar flow ventilation units.

Operative technique is the most important measures to prevent wound infection. Perforation of the bowel during surgery prolongs the operation and increases the risk of postoperative infection.

One highly recommended preventive measure, resulting from the findings of the SENIC study, is to report surgical wound infection rates to individual surgeons. This reporting may decrease surgical wound infection rates by 20%.[14]

The postoperative period usually does not contribute greatly to the risk of surgical wound infections. However, wounds can become contaminated and infected if they are not handled with aseptic technique. Aseptic technique is especially important if the wound is not completely closed. Wounds should be kept covered with a sterile dressing until they are sealed, usually around 24 hours after the operation. Nursing personnel can reduce the risk of surgical wound infection by washing hands and using a "no touch" technique for surgical wound dressing changes.

Another approach to preventing surgical

wound infection is the use of prophylactic antimicrobial therapy. Prophylactic antibiotics are recommended for operations associated with a high risk of infection or for operations considered severe or life threatening. Antibiotics used for prophylaxis should be started shortly before the operation and promptly discontinued after the operation.

If the wound becomes infected, patients should be placed on either drainage and secretion precautions or contact isolation.

Nosocomial Bacteremia

Nosocomial bacteremia is defined as the isolation of an organism from a properly obtained blood culture specimen in a patient with clinical signs of sepsis who is admitted with neither signs nor symptoms of infection nor a positive blood culture. Nosocomial bacteremia can be divided into two categories. Primary bacteremia occurs without any recognizable focus of infection with the same organism at another site. These infections are considered to be related to intravenous (IV) fluid therapy when an intravenous line is present. Secondary bacteremia results from an infection at another site.

The focus in this section will be on primary nosocomial bacteremia associated with intravascular devices. Secondary bacteremia is reduced by giving attention to prevention and control of infections at other body sites.

Intravascular related infections consist of those related to microbial contamination of the cannula, the cannula wound, or the infusate. Most of these infections are cannula related.

Factors that influence a patient's risk of acquiring cannula related infection include the patient's susceptibility, the type of cannula used, the method of insertion, duration of cannulation, and the purpose of the cannula. Plastic cannulas have been associated with a higher risk of infection than steel cannulas. Peripheral catheters that remain in place longer than 72 hours are associated with a marked increase in the rate of infection. Central cannulas, which are used for monitoring central venous pressure, are also associated with high rates of infection.

Staphylococci are the most frequently encountered pathogens in catheter related infections. *Staphylococcus aureus* is a frequent cause of device-associated infection. However, the coagulase-negative *Staphylococci* have become more common causes of these infections in the past few years.

Staphylococci account for $\frac{1}{2}$ to $\frac{2}{3}$ of the bacteremia associated with these devices. Gram-negative bacteria and candida are also important pathogens in the etiology of bacteremia.[6]

Infections related to microbial contamination of infusate occur far less frequently than cannula related infections. Contamination can occur during the manufacturing process or hospital preparation. Infections caused by contaminating infusate usually result from gram-negative bacilli.

Nursing interventions are important in preventing vascular related infections. As with other nosocomial infections, handwashing is of major importance. Hands should always be washed before inserting an IV cannula and before performing any manipulation of the cannula or line.

In adults the upper extremity should be used in preference to lower extremity sites for IV cannulation. The IV site should be scrubbed with an antiseptic before venipuncture. The cannula should be secured to stabilize it at the insertion site. A sterile dressing should be applied over the insertion site. The date of the insertion should be recorded in a place where it can be easily found. Many institutions record the date of insertion in both the medical record and on the dressing or tape at the IV site.

Patients with IV devices should be evaluated at least daily for evidence of cannula related complications. This can be accomplished by palpating the insertion site through the dressing or by visual examination through a transparent polyurethane dressing. Pain or tenderness warrants removal of the dressing and inspection of the site. Peripheral cannulas should be replaced every 48 to 72 hours. If a peripheral IV must remain in place longer than 72 hours the site should be inspected and dressed frequently. This frequent changing of central catheters is currently a controversial issue. In addition, any cannula inserted without proper asepsis, such as in an emergency setting, should be replaced at the earliest opportunity. If purulent thrombophlebitis, cellulitis, or IV related bacteremia is diagnosed or strongly suspected, the entire IV system should be changed.

Intravenous administration tubing is routinely changed every 72 hours. Tubing used for hyperalimentation sets should be routinely changed every 24 to 48 hours. Tubing should be changed immediately after the administration of blood, blood products, or liquid emulsions. Once started, all parenteral fluids should be completely used or discarded in 24 hours.

The nurse caring for a patient with an intravascular device must always remember to follow strict aseptic technique in the care of these patients. Although nosocomial bacteremia occurs infrequently, it can be life threatening.

Other Sites of Nosocomial Infections

While the four previously discussed sites of infection account for the majority of nosocomial infections, about 10% to 15% fall into the category of "other nosocomial infections." These infections include skin and subcutaneous infections, central nervous system infections, gastroenteritis, and endometritis. In preventing these infections, the nurse must always remember routes of transmission, the practice of good handwashing, the use of adequate aseptic technique in all procedures, and the importance of general skin care for all hospitalized patients.

PREVENTION AND CONTROL

The first recommendations regarding hospital acquired infections were developed by the American Hospital Association and published in 1958.[20] Since that time, the Joint Commission on Accreditation of Healthcare Organizations (JCAHO), the Centers for Disease Control (CDC) of the United States Department of Health and Human Services, and various state licensing laws have established standards for infection control in hospitals. The general recommendations made by these organizations include (1) the establishment of an active hospital-wide infection control program, (2) the establishment of a multidisciplinary committee that will be responsible for monitoring the infection control program, (3) the development of specific written infection control policies and procedures for all services in the hospital, and (4) the development of a practical system for reporting and evaluating infections among patients and personnel.

Infection Control Committee

The primary function of the infection control committee is to determine and provide for meaningful implementation of hospital policy relating to the investigation, control, and prevention of infections within hospitals. Standards of care must be developed that reduce the risk of hospital-associated infections among both patients and personnel. It is the committee's responsibility to establish mechanisms for effective nosocomial infection surveillance, institute control measures such as isolation requirements and aseptic procedures, review bacteriologic services, monitor antibiotic therapy, undertake educational programs, and establish techniques for discovering infections that are not manifest until after discharge of the patient.[6]

The composition of infection control committees will vary with individual hospitals. However, membership should include the hospital epidemiologist, physician representatives of the major clinical departments, the infection control practitioner, an administration representative, the pathologist, nursing service representatives, and representatives from other departments of the hospital as appropriate for the individual facility. Often a representative from the local health department is invited to become a member.

Infection Control Practitioner

The infection control practitioner is the member of the infection control team who is primarily responsible for the development, coordination, and supervision of the entire infection control program within the hospital. Most hospitals are employing registered nurses with a bachelor of science degree in nursing as infection control practitioners.

One function of the infection control practitioner is to collect, analyze, and report data regarding nosocomial infections. This activity is called surveillance. Other functions of the infection control practitioner include monitoring patient care activities, developing and updating specific prevention and control policies, participating in education programs, conducting special studies, and collaborating with all disciplines and departments in the facility. Probably the most important attribute of the effective infection control practitioner is an understanding of human nature and the ability to develop effective interpersonal relationships. The Association for Practitioners in Infection Control (APIC) and the CDC have recommended that there be one infection control practitioner for every 250 beds in an acute care facility and one for every 500 beds in a long-term health care facility.

Surveillance

The purpose of a **surveillance** program is to detect, record, and report hospital-associated infections in a systemic fashion so that effective and practical control measures can be instituted. In the past, surveillance centered on reports from the bacteriology laboratory and observations made by nursing personnel or house staff whose time was devoted primarily to the care of patients. As a result, underreporting of nosocomial infection was a serious problem. At present there is no single surveillance system that will provide complete information on the occurrence of hospital-associated infections; therefore, a combination of techniques appropriate for the individual institution are used.

Laboratory reports remain an important source of information. Urine, chemistry, and culture reports along with postmortem reports are checked. Criteria for nosocomial infections at various body sites must be established. A chart review is done to determine if a nosocomial infection is present.

X-ray report summaries, especially those involving the respiratory and gastrointestinal tracts, may provide evidence of infection. If the surveillance system includes identification of all community-acquired infections for control purposes, patients admitted with known infections or suggestive symptoms should be investigated. Temperature records are examined, and patients with one or more oral temperature recordings of 100° F (37.8° C) within the preceding 24-hour period should be reviewed for evidence of nosocomial infection. Also, charts of all patients receiving antibiotics may be reviewed to determine the reason for administration.

Daily rounds on patient units can be a means of gathering much of the data. Information is often offered by the nursing staff, physicians, and others that can provide clues to possible nosocomial infections or identify possible sources of infection. One method that may be used is the observation of individual patient nursing care plans for clues that are thought to indicate that the patient is at high risk for developing a nosocomial infection. Patients who have one of the risk factors are noted and their charts reviewed. Some factors that increase the patient's risk for infection are found in the boxed material to the right.

Two areas that are often neglected when surveying for nosocomial infections are those that appear in hospital personnel and discharged patients. Physicians should be encouraged to notify the infection control practitioner when infections develop after discharge from the hospital. Also, employees with potentially communicable dis-

---

Factors Increasing Risk of Infection

Diseases or disorders
Burns
Circulatory impairment
Cirrhosis
Extensive dermatitis
Hepatitis
Immune deficiencies
Malignancies
Malnutrition
Open wounds
Renal failure
Shock
Trauma

Therapeutic techniques
Bladder catheterization
Central nervous system shunts
Decubiti care
Hyperalimentation
Immunosuppressive therapy
Radiation therapy
Respiratory therapy
Surgery
Tracheostomy

---

eases, such as upper respiratory tract illness, skin infections, and enteric diseases, should not be allowed to handle food, equipment, or other objects that come in direct contact with patients, nor should they be allowed to participate in patient care. A special program for monitoring personnel should be implemented, since the etiologic agents of most acute communicable diseases are frequently harbored by clinically normal persons. Employees developing hospital-associated infections should also be monitored. Often the diagnosis of nosocomial infection in employees is overlooked.

Knowledge of the usual prevalence, or **endemic,** rate of infection in a hospital allows the infection control practitioner to identify areas that require investigation, institute more specific control measures, or detect epidemics if they occur. Information such as this can also be used for staff education and in the evaluation of new control measures.

Not all hospital-associated infections can be prevented. The patient's underlying disease condition or methods of therapy increase his vulnerability to both exogenous and endogenous microorganisms. Hospitals with well-developed surveillance systems have demonstrated that after an initial reduction of nosocomial infection rates, presumably as a result of the impact of surveillance activities, a relatively stable endemic level of infection remains.

Preventive Policies and Procedures

The best basic measures to prevent and control infectious diseases are the use of general sanitary practices and aseptic techniques. *Prevention* refers to the elimination of the occurrence of an infectious process, whereas **control** pertains to restricting the spread of infectious processes. The single most important technique in both prevention and control is proper handwashing.

Handwashing

Every person has a relatively stable resident bacteria population on the skin. New bacteria may be added and, unless removed, may become part of the resident population and be spread to other persons. Nurses are constantly coming into contact with contaminated equipment and material. In providing nursing care, they are frequently moving from patient to patient and may unconsciously transfer pathogenic organisms from one patient to another and even endanger their own health. The safest way for nurses to protect themselves and their patients is by thorough and careful handwashing.

Ideal facilities for proper handwashing include a sink with knee or foot controls, hot and cold running water, soap, and paper towels. Antiseptics should be used in handwashing when the nurse is involved with an invasive procedure. Handwashing should be done before moving from patient to patient. The combination of soap, running water, friction, and time is the essential factor in good handwashing procedures. Hands should then be thoroughly rinsed, keeping them in a downward position to prevent water from running up the arms, draining back again, and contaminating the hands. Nails and areas between the fingers should receive special attention. Hands should be thoroughly dried. Times when handwashing should be performed are included in the box to the right. Failure of hospital personnel to wash hands in these situations is a frequent cause of hospital-acquired infection.

Antisepsis and disinfection

The use of disinfectants in cleaning equipment and other surfaces is an important part of the pre-

vention of infectious disease. An *antiseptic* is a chemical agent that inhibits the growth of microorganisms but does not always kill them. Chemicals that are applied to living tissue, such as the skin, are often referred to as antiseptics.

A **disinfectant** is an agent that will destroy microorganisms. A **germicide** or a **bactericide** is synonymous with a disinfectant. However, the term "disinfectant" usually refers to a chemical that is used on inanimate objects. An example would be the use of glutaraldehyde in disinfecting surgical instruments. Although disinfectants are able to destroy pathogenic microorganisms, they are not able to destroy their **spores,** which are the reproductive elements of the cell. Some chemicals can be used as an antiseptic or a disinfectant, depending on the strength of the solution.

When using any antiseptic or disinfectant, several factors must be considered. These include the strength of the solution, the time allowed for disinfection, the temperature of the solution, the character of the material to be disinfected, and the proper disinfectant to be used. The greater the strength of the solution, the greater the germicidal power of the disinfectant. Microorganisms respond differently to disinfectants, depending on their strain and stage of development. Weak solutions having antiseptic value may be completely ineffective for disinfecting highly contaminated instruments.

Most disinfectants do not act quickly. Usually, the greater the strength of the solution, the shorter the time required to kill the microorganism. Disinfecting time is shortened when the material is clean or free from blood, feces, and pus. For example, wiping the mucus from a thermom-

---

When to Wash Hands

- Before and after the workday
- After the direct care of any patient
- After handling any equipment
- Before performing invasive procedures, whether or not sterile gloves are worn
- Before and after contact with any wound
- Before contact with patients at high risk for infection
- After contact with a source likely to be contaminated with virulent microorgansims, such as secretions or excretions
- Between contacts with different patients in special care units

eter before placing it in a disinfecting solution will shorten the time necessary to destroy any microorganism. An ideal disinfectant would kill bacteria, fungi, animal parasites, and viruses in 10 minutes, even in the presence of organic material. However, no disinfectant has been found suitable for all purposes.

Chlorine compounds

Chlorine is a poisonous gas, and its inhalation for even a short time may cause damage to the respiratory tract. Almost no chlorine occurs free in nature; it is prepared by chemical methods. Chlorine dissolves in water and is used extensively for purification of drinking water and in disinfection of water in swimming pools. Chlorine also combines with other elements to form compounds. For example, sodium hypochlorite (household bleach) is frequently used for disinfecting renal dialysis equipment because of its activity against the hepatitis virus. It is widely used for disinfection of toilets and other bathroom fixtures, as a bleach for laundry, and as a sanitizer for dishwashing.

Phenol compounds

Carbolic acid was the first germicide used. It is irritating and toxic to the skin, and its use has been declining because less toxic germicides have become available. By irritating sensory nerve endings in the skin, it acts as a local anesthetic and therefore is used in lotions such as calamine lotion to relieve pruritis. A mixture of phenols (creosol), generally in a 5% solution, is used to disinfect feces. A solution of creosol (Lysol) in a 1% to 2% solution is often used to disinfect sinks and toilets.

Hexachlorophene is a chlorinated diphenol that has been incorporated into soaps, lotions, ointments, shampoos, and oils to reduce the pathogenic bacteria on the skin. Optimum antibacterial effects have resulted with continued use of the product. It has been used in surgical scrubs and in the preoperative preparation of the skin. Use of hexachlorophene on infants should be limited because it can be absorbed into the body and cause neurologic side effects. The compound should be thoroughly rinsed from any skin surface after application. Alcohol and other solvents should not be used when hexachlorophene is used.

Ammonium compounds ("quats") are used as environmental disinfectants. Quaternary ammonium compounds do not kill spores, viruses, or tubercle bacilli. Another limitation is that soap inactivates their germicidal activity. These compounds are not to be used as skin antiseptics. They are often ineffective against gram-negative bacteria and have been associated with outbreaks caused by this group of bacteria.

Alcohol

Alcohol is available in several preparations, primarily as an antiseptic. Ethyl alcohol is used in a 50% to 70% concentration. Isopropyl alcohol has greater antiseptic values than ethyl alcohol. It may be used in full strength concentrations of 99% or as isopropyl rubbing alcohol, which is 70% concentration in a water solution. Isopropyl rubbing alcohol is generally used in the hospital for giving alcohol rubs and sponges and may be used as a skin antiseptic before parenteral injections and venipunctures. Alcohol evaporates, and unless care is taken, its germicidal qualities will become ineffective. Alcohol will not kill spores, and its use in disinfecting instruments is limited because it corrodes.

Iodine

Iodine has been in use for many years as an antiseptic and disinfectant. It has been used in preparation of the skin for surgery. Although it is one of the most effective chemical disinfectants, it has certain disadvantages. It may burn the skin and cause tissue damage, it corrodes instruments, and it stains. Iodine is prepared in an aqueous solution and in an alcohol solution. A 2% solution of tincture of iodine contains 2% iodine, 2.4% potassium iodide, and 46% ethyl alcohol. If tincture of iodine is used in the home, it should be in a dark bottle, kept tightly closed, labeled *poison*, and placed out of reach of children.

Iodophors are available both as disinfectants and as antiseptics. They combine iodine with another agent such as a detergent, and in combination the iodine is gradually released. Iodophors are free from the objectionable properties of iodine and are safe to use as antiseptics on the skin and mucous membranes. These agents have a persistent effect if they are not rinsed off. Iodophors are marketed under a number of trade names.

Aldehydes

Glutaraldehyde is the most common aldehyde used for disinfection of hospital equipment. This agent is active in the presence of organic matter and is active against bacteria, fungi, viruses, and spores. Solutions are unstable and have an effective life of 2 weeks to 30 days. Also, glutaraldehydes may cause chemical burns on human skin and mucous membranes. Therefore thorough rinsing is necessary after disinfection. Glutaraldehydes are used for disinfection of respiratory therapy equipment, anesthesia equipment, lensed instruments, and items that cannot be steamed or gas sterilized.

Others

Other disinfectants include *silver nitrate* and *boric acid*. Silver nitrate in a 1% solution has been used to treat the eyes of most newborn babies to prevent ophthalmia neonatorum caused by the *Neisseria* organism. However, the tetracyclines are now used to treat this condition, because they produce less eye irritation and are also effective against *Chlamydia* infections.

Hydrogen peroxide solution consists of hydrogen peroxide and water and is used to clean wounds and to treat Vincent's infection (trench mouth). It is generally used in a 3% to 6% solution, and its germ-killing capability is a result of its oxygen-releasing ability. The solution should be kept in a tightly closed bottle in a cool, dark place because it decomposes rapidly. It should not be used in any closed body cavity where oxygen cannot escape.

The appearance of new chemical disinfectants and the wide divergence in practice between hospitals make it increasingly important for the nurse to be familiar with a disinfectant and its use.

Personnel and equipment

Hospital policies should be established that help prevent the transmission of infectious organisms. Personnel in charge of direct patient care should be free of infection and responsible for practicing sanitary measures. All hospital personnel should maintain their immunization levels, treat all illness promptly, and refrain from patient care when they are ill. The employee health service should be used whenever necessary.

All patients should be assessed for infection when admitted, and attempts should be made to assure that visitors are free of infection or disease. The hospital environment should be kept as free of pathogenic microorganisms as possible. All patient areas should be cleaned daily, and provisions should be made for adequate ventilation. Equipment and supplies should be sterilized or disinfected, and aseptic technique must be maintained where it is indicated.

High-risk areas

The nursery, delivery room, operating room, recovery room, intensive care unit, and other specialized units such as the hemodialysis unit are considered high-risk areas. Patients in these areas are usually considered compromised hosts and are therefore highly susceptible to infection or disease.

Patients who are identified as being at high risk for infection should have protective measures implemented as part of their care. Attempts should be made to decrease patient contact with infectious agents. Catheters and tubes that bypass normal defense mechanisms should be used judiciously. Special instructions should be given to the patient and family regarding health maintenance and avoidance of contact with other infected persons. Thorough handwashing must be practiced between all patient contacts.

Control Policies and Procedures
Isolation

The nursing care of the patient with infectious disease involves the two basic principles of medical asepsis: (1) to confine all pathogens to a given area, preventing their spread from an infected patient to others; and (2) to protect susceptible people from pathogens present in the environment or carried by other persons. Isolation is a means of interrupting the transmission of infectious organisms, since sources of infections and susceptible hosts are more difficult to control. The procedure establishes a barrier around the patient in an attempt to prevent the spread of infection either to or from the patient. Nurses assigned to the care of a patient in isolation should have a basic knowledge of the infectivity of the disease and its mode of transmission, as well as an understanding of the high risk factors involved with susceptible patients.

The *CDC Guideline for Isolation Precautions in Hospitals* published in 1983 recommends one of two different systems for isolation precautions: category specific or disease specific. Each hospital's infection control committee should determine which system will best meet the needs of their hospital.

Category-specific isolation precautions

Seven isolation categories have been defined. They are derived by grouping diseases for which similar isolation precautions are indicated. A category ending with the term *isolation* requires a private room. A category ending with the term *pre-*

cautions indicates a private room is not necessary.

Strict isolation prevents transmission of highly contagious or virulent infections that may spread by both air and contact routes. A common disease requiring strict isolation is chickenpox.

Contact isolation prevents transmission of highly transmissible or epidemiologically important infections that do not warrant strict isolation. Multiple-resistant bacterial infections or colonizations, pediculosis, pneumonia caused by *Staphylococcus aureus* or group A *Streptococcus*, scabies, and major skin, wound, or burn infections are examples of diseases or conditions requiring contact isolation.

Respiratory isolation prevents transmission of infectious diseases primarily over short distances through the air (droplet transmission). Measles, *Haemophilus influenzae* meningitis, meningococcal meningitis or pneumonia, and mumps are some of the diseases requiring respiratory isolation. Tuberculosis isolation (AFB, or acid-fast bacilli isolation) is the category for patients with pulmonary tuberculosis (TB) who have a positive sputum smear or a chest x-ray film that suggests active tuberculosis. Laryngeal TB is also included in this category. In general, infants and young children with pulmonary TB do not require isolation because they rarely cough and their bronchial secretions contain few AFB. This category is referred to as AFB, rather than tuberculosis, to protect the patient's privacy.

Enteric precautions prevent infections that are transmitted by direct or indirect contact with feces. Transmission usually requires ingestion of the infective agent. Amebic dysentery, hepatitis A, and gastroenteritis caused by *Campylobacter* species, *Cryptosporidium* species, *Salmonella* species, and *Shigella* species are examples of diseases requiring enteric precautions.

Drainage/secretion precautions prevents spread of infections that are transmitted by direct or indirect contact with purulent material or drainage from an infected body site. Minor skin, wound, or burn infections; minor **abscesses;** and conjunctivitis are included in this category.

Blood/body fluid precautions prevent infections transmitted by direct or indirect contact with infective blood or body fluids. Diseases included in this category are Creutzfeldt-Jakob disease, hepatitis B, malaria, and HIV infection.

Instruction cards have been designed to give concise information about category-specific isolation precautions. Samples of these cards are shown below and on pp. 184-187. The appropriate card should be posted where it is visible to all personnel providing care to the patient.

Disease-specific isolation precautions

This type of precaution is an alternative to the category system of isolation. With this system each infectious disease is considered individually. Most common infectious agents and diseases are

---

Strict Isolation

Visitors—report to nurses' station before entering room

1. Masks are indicated for all persons entering room.
2. Gowns are indicated for all persons entering room.
3. Gloves are indicated for all persons entering room.
4. HANDS MUST BE WASHED AFTER TOUCHING THE PATIENT OR POTENTIALLY CONTAMINATED ARTICLES AND BEFORE TAKING CARE OF ANOTHER PATIENT.
5. Articles contaminated with infective material should be discarded or bagged and labeled before being sent for decontamination and reprocessing.

Diseases requiring strict isolation*

Diphtheria, pharyngeal
Lassa fever and other viral hemorrhagic fevers, such as Marburg virus disease†
Plague, pneumonic
Smallpox†
Varicella (chickenpox)
Zoster, localized in immunocompromised patient, or disseminated

From: CDC Guidelines, Infection Control 4: No 4, 284-290, 1983.
*A private room is indicated for strict isolation; in general, however, patients infected with the same organism may share a room. See *Guideline for Isolation Precautions in Hospitals* for details and for how long to apply precautions.
†A private room with special ventilation is indicated.

Respiratory Isolation

Visitors—report to nurses' station before entering room

1. Masks are indicated for those who come close to patient.
2. Gowns are not indicated.
3. Gloves are not indicated.
4. HANDS MUST BE WASHED AFTER TOUCHING THE PATIENT OR POTENTIALLY CONTAMINATED ARTICLES AND BEFORE TAKING CARE OF ANOTHER PATIENT.
5. Articles contaminated with infective material should be discarded or bagged and labeled before being sent for decontamination and reprocessing.

Diseases requiring respiratory isolation*

Epiglottitis, *Haemophilus influenzae*
Erythema infectiosum
Measels
Meningitis
   Bacterial, etiology unknown
   Haemophilus influenzae, known or suspected
   Meningococcal, known or suspected
Meningococcal pneumonia
Meningococcemia
Mumps
Pertussis (whooping cough)
Pneumonia, *Haemophilus influenzae*, in children (any age)

From: CDC Guidelines, Infection Control 4: No 4, 284-290, 1983.

*A private room is indicated for respiratory isolation; in general, however, patients infected with the same organism may share a room. See *Guideline for Isolation Precautions in Hospitals* for details and for how long to apply precautions.

---

listed in the *CDC Guideline for Isolation Precautions in Hospitals,* as are specifications for the required precautions (private room, mask, gown, and gloves). An instruction card is prepared and displayed near the patient.

Gowns should be worn whenever clothing might be soiled by infective materials. Gowns should be worn once, changed whenever wet, and discarded aseptically. Masks help prevent the spread of microorganisms that are transmitted through the air. They should cover the nose and mouth, be used only once, and be changed periodically. Handwashing before and after each contact with the patient is the single most important way of preventing transmission of infection. Gloves should be used when handling infected materials; they should be used once and discarded.

If contaminated, equipment taken into the room should be sterilized or disinfected. Linens should be bagged in leak-proof bags as should other contaminated objects that are taken from the room. It is essential that these bags be labeled so they can be dealt with appropriately.

Many hospitals modify these guidelines to meet their specific requirements. Sometimes precautions may be required although the patient does not fully meet the criteria for any type of isolation. For example, patients with urinary tract infections who are catheterized can serve as res-

ervoirs of infection for other catheterized patients in the same room. Practices must be occasionally modified for an infected patient needing constant care or emergency therapy. Isolation procedures should be revised as each patient's disease resolves or progresses. When the patient poses no risk to others, isolation should be terminated.

Universal precautions

In August of 1987 the CDC published a new set of recommendations for the prevention of HIV transmission in health care settings. The recommendations are referred to as Universal Blood and Body Fluid Precautions or Universal Precautions. Because it is impossible to recognize or be aware of all patients infected with bloodborne pathogens at the time care is given, Universal Precautions need to be implemented for all patients undergoing medical care.

Universal Precaution recommendations include the following;

1. All health care workers should routinely use appropriate barrier precautions to prevent skin and mucous membrane exposure when contact with blood or other body fluids of any patient is anticipated. Gloves should be worn for touching blood and body fluids, mucous membranes, or nonintact skin of all patients; for handling items or surfaces soiled with blood or body

---

Contact Isolation

Visitors—report to nurses' station before entering room

1. Masks are indicated for those who come close to patient.
2. Gowns are indicated if soiling is likely.
3. Gloves are indicated for touching infective material.
4. HANDS MUST BE WASHED AFTER TOUCHING THE PATIENT OR POTENTIALLY CONTAMINATED ARTICLES AND BEFORE TAKING CARE OF ANOTHER PATIENT.
5. Articles contaminated with infective material should be discarded or bagged and labeled before being sent for decontamination and reprocessing.

Diseases or conditions requiring contact isolation*

Acute respiratory tract infections in infants and young children, including croup, colds, bronchitis, and bronchiolitis caused by respiratory syncytial virus, adenovirus, coronavirus, influenza viruses, parainfluenza viruses, and rhinovirus

Conjunctivits, gonococcal, in newborns

Diphtheria, cutaneous

Endometritis, group A *Streptococcus*

Furunculosis, staphylococcal, in newborns

Herpes simplex, disseminated, severe primary or neonatal

Impetigo

Influenza, in infants and young children

Multiple-resistant bacteria, infection or colonization (any site) with any of the following:

1. Gram-negative bacilli resistant to all aminoglycosides that are tested. (In general, such organisms should be resistant to gentamicin, tobramycin, and amikacin for these special precautions to be indicated.)
2. *Staphylococcus aureus* resistant to methicillin (or nafcillin or oxacillin if they are used instead of methicillin for testing)
3. *Pneumococcus* resistant to penicillin
4. *Haemophilus influenzae* resistant to ampicillin (betalactamase positive) and chloramphenicol
5. Other resistant bacteria may be included in this isolation category if they are judged by the infection control team to be of special clinical and epidemiologic significance.

Pediculosis

Pharyngitis, infectious, in infants and young children

Pneumonia, viral, in infants and young children

Pneumonia, *Staphylococcus aureus* or group A *Streptococcus*

Rabies

Rubella, congential and other

Scabies

Scalded skin syndrome (Ritter's disease)

Skin, wound, or burn infection, major (draining and not covered by a dressing or dressing does not adequately contain the purulent material), including those infected with *Staphylococcus aureus* or group A *Streptococcus*

Vaccinia (generalized and progressive eczema vaccinatum)

From: CDC Guidelines, Infection Control 4: No 4, 284-290, 1983.

*A private room is indicated for contact isolation; in general, however, patients infected with the same organism may share a room. During outbreaks, infants and young children with the same respiratory clinical syndrome may share a room. See *Guideline for Isolation Precautions in Hospitals* for details and for how long to apply precautions.

---

fluids; and for performing venipuncture and other vascular access procedures. Gloves should be changed after contact with each patient. Masks and protective eyewear or face shields should be worn during procedures that are likely to generate droplets of blood or other body fluids to prevent exposure of mucous membranes of the mouth, nose, and eyes. Gowns or aprons should be worn during procedures that are likely to generate splashes of blood or other body fluids.

2. Hands and other skin surfaces should be washed immediately and thoroughly if contaminated with blood or other body fluids. Hands should be washed immediately after gloves are removed.
3. All health care workers should take precautions to prevent injuries caused by needles, scalpels, and other sharp instruments; during disposal of used needles; and when handling sharp instruments after procedures. To prevent needlestick injuries, needles should not be recapped,

AFB (Tuberculosis) Isolation

Visitors—report to nurses' station before entering room

1. Masks are indicated only when patient is coughing and does not reliably cover mouth.
2. Gowns are indicated only if needed to prevent gross contamination of clothing.
3. Gloves are not indicated.
4. HANDS MUST BE WASHED AFTER TOUCHING THE PATIENT OR POTENTIALLY CONTAMINATED ARTICLES AND BEFORE TAKING CARE OF ANOTHER PATIENT.
5. Articles should be discarded, cleaned, or sent for decontamination and reprocessing.

Diseases requiring AFB isolation*

This islolation category is for patients with current pulmonary TB who have a positive sputum smear or a chest x-ray appearance that strongly suggests current (active) TB. Laryngeal TB is also included in this category. In general, infants and young children with pulmonary TB do not require isolation precautions because they rarely cough and their bronchial secretions contain few AFB compared with adults with pulmonary TB. To protect the patient's privacy, this instruction card is labeled AFB (acid-fast bacilli) isolation rather than tuberculosis isolation.

From: CDC Guidelines, Infection Control 4: No 4, 284-290, 1983.

*A private room with special ventilation is indicated for AFB isolation. In general, patients infected with the same organism may share a room. See Guideline for Isolation Precautions in Hospitals for details and for how long to apply precautions.

Enteric Precautions

Visitors—report to nurses' station before entering room

1. Masks are not indicated.
2. Gowns are indicated if soiling is likely.
3. Gloves are indicated for touching infective material.
4. HANDS MUST BE WASHED AFTER TOUCHING THE PATIENT OR POTENTIALLY CONTAMINATED ARTICLES AND BEFORE TAKING CARE OF ANOTHER PATIENT.
5. Articles contaminated with infective material should be discarded or bagged and labeled before being sent for decontamination and reprocessing.

Diseases requiring enteric precautions*

Amebic dysentery
Cholera
Coxsackievirus disease
Diarrhea, acute illness with suspected infectious etiology
Echovirus disease
Encephalitis (unless known not to be caused by enteroviruses)
Enterocolitis caused by *Clostridium difficile or Staphylococcus aureus*
Enteroviral infection
Gastroenteritis caused by
   Campylobacter species
   Cryptosporidium species
   Dientamoeba fragilis
   Escherichia coli (enterotoxic, enteropathogenic, or enteroinvasive)
   Giardia lamblia
   Salmonella species
   Shigella species
   Vibrio parahaemolyticus
   Viruses—including Norwalk agent and rotavirus
   Yersinia enterocolitica
   Unknown etiology but presumed to be an infectious agent
Hand, foot, and mouth disease
Hepatitis, viral, type A
Herpangina
Meningitis, viral (unless known not to be caused by enteroviruses)
Necrotizing enterocolitis
Pleurodynia
Poliomyelitis
Typhoid fever (*Salmonella typhi*)
Viral pericarditis, myocarditis, or meningitis (unless known not to be caused by enterovirsuses)

From: CDC Guidelines, Infection Control 4: No 4, 284-290, 1983.

*A private room is indicated for Enteric Precautions if patient hygiene is poor. A patient with poor hygiene does not wash hands after touching infective material, contaminates the environment with infective material, or shares contaminated articles with other patients. In general, patients infected with the same organism may share a room. See Guideline for Isolation Precautions in Hospitals for details and for how long to apply precautions.

Drainage/Secretion Precautions

Visitors—report to nurses' station before entering room

1. Masks are not indicated.
2. Gowns are indicated if soiling is likely.
3. Gloves are indicated for touching infective material.
4. HANDS MUST BE WASHED AFTER TOUCHING THE PATIENT OR POTENTIALLY CONTAMINATED ARTICLES AND BEFORE TAKING CARE OF ANOTHER PATIENT.
5. Articles contaminated with infective material should be discarded or bagged and labeled before being sent for decontamination and reprocessing.

Disease requiring drainage/secretion precautions*

Infectious diseases included in this category are those that result in production of infective purulent material, drainage, or secretions, unless the disease is included in another isolation category that requires more rigorous precautions. (If you have questions about a specific disease, see the listing of infectious diseases in Guideline for Isolation Precautions in Hospitals, Table A, Disease-Specific Isolation Precautions.)

The following infections are examples of those included in this category provided they are not (a) caused by multiply-resistant microorganisms, (b) major (draining and not covered by a dressing or dressing does not adequately contain the drainage) skin, wound, or burn infections, including those caused by *Staphylococcus aureus* or group A *Streptococcus*, or (c) gonococcal eye infections in newborns. See Contact Isolation if the infection is one of these 3.

Abscess, minor or limited
Burn infection, minor or limited
Conjunctivitus
Decubitus ulcer, infected, minor or limited
Skin infection, minor or limited
Wound infection, minor or limited

From: CDC Guidelines, Infection Control 4: No 4, 284-290, 1983.
*A private room is usually not indicated for Drainage/Secretion Precautions. See Guidelines for Isolation Precautions in Hospitals for details and for how long to apply precautions.

Blood/Body Fluid Precautions

1. Masks are not indicated.
2. Gowns are indicated if soiling with blood or body fluids is likely.
3. Gloves are indicated for touching blood or body fluids.
4. HANDS SHOULD BE WASHED IMMEDIATELY IF THEY ARE POTENTIALLY CONTAMINATED WITH BLOOD OR BODY FLUIDS AND BEFORE TAKING CARE OF ANOTHER PATIENT.
5. Articles contaminated with blood or body fluids should be discarded or bagged and labeled before being sent for decontamination and reprocessing.
6. Care should be taken to avoid needle-stick injuries. Used needles should not be recapped or bent; they should be placed in a prominently labeled, puncture-resistant container designated specifically for such disposal.
7. Blood spills should be cleaned up promptly with a solution of 5.25% sodium hypochlorite diluted 1:10 with water.

Diseases requiring blood/body fluid precautions*

Acquired immunodeficiency syndrome (AIDS)
Arthropodborne viral fevers (for example, dengue, yellow fever, and Colorado tick fever)
Babesiosis
Creutzfeldt-Jakob disease
Hepatitis B (including HBsAg antigen carrier)
Hepatitis, non-A, non-B
Leptospirosis
Malaria
Rat-bite fever
Relapsing fever
Syphilis, primary and secondary with skin and mucous membrane lesions

From: CDC Guidelines, Infection Control 4: No 4, 284-290, 1983.
*A private room is indicated for Blood/Body Fluid Precautions if patient hygiene is poor. A patient with poor hygiene does not wash hands after touching infective material, contaminates the environment with infective material, or shares contaminated articles with other patients. In general, patients infected with the same organism may share a room. See Guidelines for Isolation Precautions in Hospitals for details and for how long to apply precautions.

purposely bent or broken by hand, removed from disposable syringes, or otherwise manipulated by hand. After they are used, disposable syringes and needles, scalpel blades, and other sharp items should be placed in puncture-resistant containers for disposal. The puncture-resistant containers should be located as close as practical to the use area. Large-bore reusable needles should be placed in a puncture-resistant container for transport to the processing area.

4. Although saliva has not been implicated in HIV transmission, the potential exists. This has not been scientifically documented, however. Mouthpieces, resuscitation bags, or other ventilation devices should be available for use in areas where the need for resuscitation is predictable. This minimizes the need for emergency mouth-to-mouth resuscitation.

5. Health care workers who have exudative lesions or weeping dermatitis should refrain from all direct patient care and from handling patient-care equipment until the condition resolves.

6. Pregnant health care workers are not known to be at greater risk of contracting HIV infection than health care workers who are not pregnant. However, if a health care worker develops an HIV infection during pregnancy, the infant is at risk of an HIV infection resulting from perinatal transmission. Because of this risk, pregnant health care workers should be especially familiar with, and strictly adhere to, precautions to minimize the risk of HIV transmission.[10]

Implementation of Universal Precautions makes the use of blood and body fluids unnecessary. Whether or not to use the blood and body fluid precaution card to identify patients known to be infected is currently controversial.

Health care employers are now being regulated by the Occupational Health and Safety Administration (OSHA) and are being charged with providing a safe working environment for all health care workers. Under the proposed OSHA standards, hospitals will be obligated to provide the necessary protective equipment and education to ensure appropriate implementation of Universal Precautions.

Body substance isolation

A system of isolation proposed by Lynch and others departs from the standard CDC isolation systems.[22] This system is referred to as body substance isolation (BSI) and is used for all patients. Gloves are worn for any anticipated contact with blood or body fluids. Gloves are changed between all patients. Handwashing after patient contact is indicated. Gowns, aprons, masks, or goggles are worn when blood or body fluids are likely to contact the clothing, skin, or face. Private rooms may be necessary for those patients with diseases transmitted through the air or for patients who soil the environment with body substances.

Under this system of isolation a body substance isolation card is placed in all patient rooms. A separate "stop sign alert" card with instructions is placed outside of the rooms of patients with airborne infections. Masks are worn for these particular patients. Other forms of isolation are not used under this system.

No standard system of isolation is appropriate for all hospitals. Each hospital must evaluate its own patient population and the attitudes of its employees. Many hospitals are now using a combination of the category specific isolation system and Universal Precautions. All of these systems of isolation need analysis to determine which best meets the objective of diminishing the transmission of infection.[23]

Emotional support

Hospital-acquired infections cannot help but evoke feelings of anxiety, frustration, and hostility in the patient and family. Through no fault of his or her own, the patient has acquired an infection that may mean additional hospital days, increased hospital costs, time away from work, or disruption of home life. Isolation procedures are time consuming and costly and may discourage personnel from giving the best possible care to the patient. The solitude that usually accompanies isolation deprives the patient of normal social relationships, and emotional reactions are likely to occur.

A wide range of emotional reactions can be seen in isolation patients. They may exhibit overt abusive or aggressive behavior or show signs of withdrawal and depression. The excessive demands made by some patients can be extremely frustrating to nursing personnel. Family members may fear the possibility of developing the infection themselves and avoid contact with the patient. The procedures of gowning, masking, and frequent handwashing may convey feelings of rejection.

Every patient in isolation should have a basic understanding of what to expect. A thorough explanation of the ways in which the infection is transmitted and the procedures of isolation that tend to interrupt transmission should be given to both the patient and family. When they realize the significance of isolation and their roles in preventing further transmission, cooperation and acceptance can be achieved. Much can be done to relieve the patient's anxiety by maintaining a friendly, understanding, sympathetic, and reassuring manner.

REFERENCES AND ADDITIONAL READINGS

1. American College of Surgeons: Manual on control of infection in surgical patients, ed 2, Philadelphia, 1984, JB Lippincott Co.
2. Barlett P and others: Toxic shock syndrome associated with surgical wound infections, JAMA 247:1446-1450, 1982.
3. Barrett-Connon E and others: Epidemiology for the infection control nurse, St Louis, 1978, The CV Mosby Co.
4. Bennet JV and Brachman S: Hospital infections, Boston, 1986, Little, Brown & Co Inc.
5. Castle M: Hospital infection control: principles and practice, New York, 1987, John Wiley & Sons Inc.
6. Centers for Disease Control: Guidelines for the prevention of nosocomial infections, Atlanta, 1982, US Department of Health and Human Services.
7. Centers for Disease Control: Guidelines for prevention of nosocomial pneumonia, Atlanta, 1982 US Department of Health and Human Services.
8. Centers for Disease Control: Guidelines for the prevention of surgical wound infections, Atlanta, 1985 US Department of Health and Human Services.
9. Centers for Disease Control: National nosocomial infections study report, annual summary-1984, Atlanta, 1986, US Department of Health and Human Services.
10. Centers for Disease Control: Recommendations for prevention of HIV transmission in health-care settings, MMWR 36(25 suppl), 1987.
11. Centers for Disease Control: Update: universal precautions for prevention of transmission of human immunodeficiency virus, Hepatitis B virus, and other bloodborne pathogens in health-care settings. MMWR 37:377-387, 1988.
12. Cruse PJE and Foord R: The epidemiology of wound infection, A ten year prospective study of 62,939 wounds, Surg Clin North Am 60:27-40, 1980.
13. Garner JS and Simmons BP: CDC guideline for isolation precautions in hospitals, Atlanta, 1983, US Department of Health and Human Services.
14. Haley RW: Managing hospital infection control for cost effectiveness, Chicago, 1986, American Hospital Publishing Inc.
15. Haley RW and others: Identifying patients at high risk of surgical wound infection: a simple multivariate index of patient susceptibility and wound contamination, Am J Epidemiol 121:206-15, 1985.
16. Haley RW and others: The nationwide nosocomial infection rate, Am J Epidemiol 121:159-167, 1985.
17. Hargiss CO: Infection control: putting principles into practice, Am J Nurs 81:2165-2186, 1981.
18. Hargiss CO and Larson E: Guidelines for prevention of hospital-acquired infections, Am J Nurs 81:2175-2183, 1981.
19. Harris AA, Levin S, and Trenholme G: Selected aspects of nosocomial infections in the 1980s, Am J Med 77:3-10, 1984.
20. Infection control in the hospital, ed 4, Chicago, 1979, American Hospital Association.
21. Kreiswirth BN and others: Nosocomial transmission of a strain of *Staphylococcus aureus* causing toxic shock syndrome, Ann Intern Med 105:704, 1986.
22. Lynch P and others: Rethinking the role of isolation practices in the prevention of nosocomial infections. Ann Intern Med, 107:243-6, 1987.
23. Mandell G, Douglas G, and Bennett J: Principles and practices of infectious diseases, ed 3, New York, 1990, Churchill Livingstone Inc.
24. Rutela WA and others: *Serratia marcescens* nosocomial infections of the urinary tract associated with urine measuring containers and urinometers, Am J Med, 70:659-63, 1981.
25. Stamm WE: Nosocomial infections: etiologic changes, therapeutic challenges, Hosp Pract 16:75-88, 1981.

The Patient with Cancer

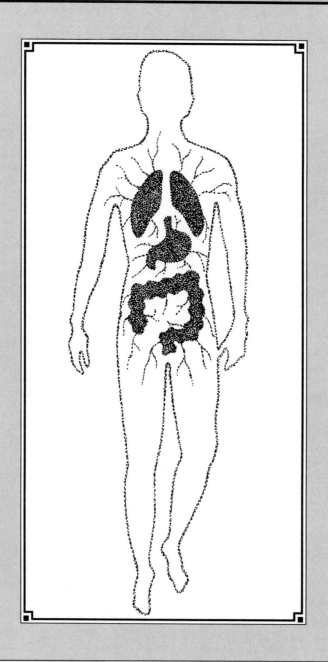

KEY WORDS

benign
bone marrow transplantation
carcinogens
carcinoma
chemotherapy
computerized tomography
desquamation
ionizing radiation
leukopenia
magnetic resonance imaging
malignant
mammography
metastasis
myelosuppression
neoplasm
oncogenes
oncology
palliative
proctosigmoidoscopy
radiation therapy
radioisotope
sarcoma
thrombocytopenia

OBJECTIVES

1. Appreciate cancer as a health care problem.
2. Describe the predominant characteristics of cancer.
3. Identify the major causes of cancer.
4. List recommended methods of prevention and early detection.
5. Describe the common methods of diagnosis and treatment of cancer.
6. Discuss nursing care of the patient receiving radiation therapy.
7. Discuss nursing care of the patient receiving chemotherapy.
8. Discuss the emotional impact of cancer on the patient and family.

CANCER: AN OVERVIEW

Cancer is characterized by abnormal and unrestricted cell division and by the spread of these cells into healthy tissues of the body. Without appropriate medical intervention this dissemination of cancer cells can become widespread, leading to tissue destruction, which may ultimately cause the death of the individual. Cancer is one of the oldest diseases known to humans; its cause has been a puzzle for centuries and remains so.

The annual number of deaths from cancer in the United States is exceeded only by those resulting from heart disease. In 1990 it was estimated that approximately 510,000 Americans would die of cancer that year.[2] According to present trends, one out of four persons and three out of four families will be affected by cancer at some time. Cancer attacks rich and poor, young and old, with equally devastating effects. The largest number of malignant tumors occurs in four areas of the body: the lungs, the colon-rectum, the breasts, and the prostate, in order of cancer incidence.

Cancer of the lung is the leading cause of cancer deaths in both men and women. Recently the incidence of lung cancer has been decreasing in men, but it continues to increase in women. Since 1987, more women have died each year from lung cancer than from breast cancer. In 1990 it was estimated that 142,000 people in the United States would die from lung cancer—92,000 men and 50,000 women. The survival rate for cancer of the lung is extremely low, with only about 13% of the victims living as long as 5 years after the disease was diagnosed. These statistics are unfortunate because the disease is largely preventable. At least 83% of the cases of lung cancer are directly related to cigarette smoking.[2]

Cancer of the colon and rectum kills approximately 60,900 persons each year, according to 1990 estimates, and ranks second as a cause of cancer deaths.[2] There has been a small increase in survival rates during the past two decades. Approximately two out of three patients might be saved by early diagnosis and prompt treatment—the keys to survival. Early diagnosis by a digital rectal examination and a stool blood (guaiac) slide test can help save more lives from colon-rectum cancer than from any other tests. The stool blood test consists of taking two separate stool samples on each of 3 consecutive days and examining them for the presence of blood. It is now recommended that all persons 40 years of age and over have a digital rectal examination annually; an annual stool blood slide test should be added at age 50, and a proctosigmoidoscopy examination should be given every 3 to 5 years.

Cancer of the breast is the most common cancer among women over the age of 40. In 1990 it was expected that 150,000 new cases of breast cancer would be diagnosed and that 44,000 women would die from the disease. When cancer of the breast is diagnosed early at a localized stage, 90% of those affected will survive 5 years or longer; when diagnosis and treatment are delayed, with consequent regional spread, the 5-year survival drops to 68%; when women have distant metastases, the survival rate is 18%.[2] Despite new methods of detection and treatment, the death rate from cancer of the breast has not been substantially reduced. If present trends continue, one of every 10 women in the United States will develop breast cancer.[2] This fact has effectively been brought to the attention of the American public by the mastectomies performed on several prominent women. As a result of better public awareness, more women now perform breast self-examination (BSE), have screening mammograms, and seek medical attention early.

The most frequent sites of malignant neoplasms are found in Figure 9-1.

The United States Congress appropriates millions of dollars to the National Cancer Institute for research and training. Each year, in addition to the work done by the National Cancer Institute, Congress provides grants and contracts to other organizations whose research activities may be applied to prevention, detection, diagnosis, and treatment of malignant disease.

The National Cancer Act of 1971 provided funds for the establishment of cancer research centers throughout the nation. These centers are carefully reviewed by the National Cancer Advisory Board and receive funding from the National Cancer Institute, the American Cancer Society, and many other sources. The American Cancer Society is one of the oldest and largest voluntary health agencies in the United States; it is dedicated to eliminating cancer through research, education, patient service, and rehabilitation. In 1990 the American Cancer Society spent an estimated 90 million dollars in funding research grants and fellowships.[2]

The ultimate objective of all cancer research is the control of cancer in humans. Progress toward

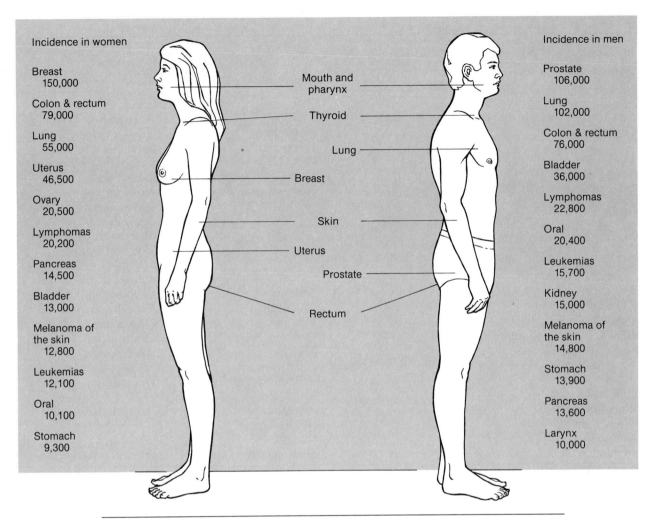

Incidence in women

Breast
150,000

Colon & rectum
79,000

Lung
55,000

Uterus
46,500

Ovary
20,500

Lymphomas
20,200

Pancreas
14,500

Bladder
13,000

Melanoma of
the skin
12,800

Leukemias
12,100

Oral
10,100

Stomach
9,300

Mouth and
pharynx

Thyroid

Lung

Breast

Skin

Uterus

Prostate

Rectum

Incidence in men

Prostate
106,000

Lung
102,000

Colon & rectum
76,000

Bladder
36,000

Lymphomas
22,800

Oral
20,400

Leukemias
15,700

Kidney
15,000

Melanoma of
the skin
14,800

Stomach
13,900

Pancreas
13,600

Larynx
10,000

Figure 9-1

Most frequent sites of malignant neoplasms. *(Redrawn from 1990 Cancer Facts and Figures, Atlanta, 1990, American Cancer Society, Inc.)*

realizing this objective is measured by: (1) increased knowledge about malignant disease, (2) identification and control of factors related to cause and prevention, and (3) improvement in detection, diagnosis, and treatment.

Pathophysiology

The basic structural unit of all forms of animal and plant life is the cell. Each organ of the body is composed of many different types of cells joined together to perform specific functions. It is the coordination of all cellular activities that allows the body to function as a whole organism. All cells have the genetic capability of dividing and multiplying, and they normally do so in response to a specific need of the body. However, a normal cell can undergo changes that will transform it into a cancer cell. Cancer cells are able to divide and multiply, but not in a normal manner. Instead of limiting their growth to meet the specific needs of the body, cancer cells continue to reproduce in a disorderly and unrestricted manner.

New growths of abnormal tissue, whether benign or malignant, are referred to as **neoplasms,** or tumors. **Benign** tumors do not tend to progress, whereas **malignant** tumors tend to become progressively worse, often resulting in the death of the individual. Although benign tumors are usually harmless, occasionally they will involve vital organs, such as the brain, with fatal results. Normally, they do not spread and are easily removed. The word ending *-oma* means tumor, and

Table 9-1

Classification of Neoplasms		
Origin	**Benign**	**Malignant**
Epithelial tissue		Carcinoma
Squamous cells (skin and mucous membrane)	Papilloma	Squamous cell carcinoma
Gland cells	Adenoma	Adenocarcinoma
	Polyp	Basal cell carcinoma
Pigmented cells	Nevus	Malignant melanoma
Endothelial tissue		Endothelioma
Blood vessels	Hemangioma	Angiosarcoma
Lymphoid tissue		Lymphosarcoma
		Leukemia
		Malignant lymphoma
		Hodgkin's disease
Plasma cells		Multiple myeloma
Connective tissue		Sarcoma
Fibrous tissue	Fibroma	Fibrosarcoma
Cartilage	Chondroma	Chondrosarcoma
Adipose tissue	Lipoma	Liposarcoma
Bone	Osteoma	Osteosarcoma
Muscle tissue	Myoma	Myosarcoma
Smooth muscle	Leiomyoma	Leiomyosarcoma
Striated muscle	Rhabdomyoma	Rhabdomyosarcoma
Nerve tissue		
Nerve fibers	Neuroma	Neurogenic sarcoma
	Neurofibroma	
Glia cells	Glioma	Glioblastoma
Meninges	Meningioma	Malignant meningioma

Table 9-2

General Characteristics of Neoplasms	
Benign tumor	**Malignant tumor**
1. Slow, steady growth	1. Rate of growth varies, usually rapid
2. Remains localized	2. Metastasizes
3. Usually contained within a capsule	3. Rarely contained within a capsule
4. Smooth, well defined, movable when palpated	4. Irregular, more immobile when palpated
5. Resembles parent tissue	5. Little resemblance to parent tissue
6. Crowds normal tissue	6. Invades normal tissue
7. Rarely recurs after removal	7. May recur after removal
8. Rarely fatal	8. Fatal without treatment

the site of the tumor is indicated by the stem. Tumors are usually named according to the type of tissue from which they arise (Table 9-1).

Malignant tumors differ from benign tumors in several important aspects (Table 9-2). They are capable of continued growth that will compress, invade, and destroy normal tissue. Malignant cells break away from their original sites and are transported by the blood or lymph to new sites where they begin to grow. This is called **metastasis.** During this process of spread, malignant cells are temporarily stopped by the lymph nodes, but they may grow and multiply there. The body's immune system is constantly attempting to rid the body of these metastasizing cells and is generally successful, with only a fraction of 1% surviving.

However, this percentage is sufficient to establish tumors in other portions of the body. Cancer spreads by the following:

1. Direct extension into adjacent tissue
2. Permeation along lymphatic vessels
3. Embolism through lymphatic or blood vessels
4. Diffusion or seeding within a body cavity

The reason why a single body cell suddenly fails to divide and multiply in a normal manner is not known, but tumors are found in all kinds of tissue and in all parts of the body. **Carcinoma,** a malignant tumor, is the most common form of cancer. Carcinomas arise from epithelial cells. These cells form coverings such as the skin, and they line cavities such as the mouth, stomach, and lungs. Other kinds of epithelial cells are found in glandular organs such as the breast. Another form of cancer is the **sarcoma,** which occurs less frequently than do carcinomas. Sarcomas arise from connective tissue such as bone, muscle, and cartilage. The carcinomas and the sarcomas are called solid tumors. Cancer can also develop in the blood-forming and lymphoid organs. *Leukemia* is an abnormal, uncontrolled multiplication of white blood cells. *Lymphoma* arises in the lymph system, especially the lymph nodes and spleen, and is characterized by overproduction of lymphocytes. There are two main forms of lymphoma: Hodgkin's disease and non-Hodgkin's lymphoma. *Multiple myeloma* is caused by an overproduction of plasma cells in the blood and bone marrow.

CAUSES OF CANCER

Although the specific cause of cancer is unknown, many theories have been developed. Agents that can cause malignant changes in healthy cells after prolonged exposure are referred to as carcinogenic agents, or **carcinogens.** These include viruses, chemical agents, physical agents, hormones, and diet. Hereditary factors are also important.

Viruses are thought to cause some forms of human cancers, but it has been difficult to isolate specific human cancer-causing viruses. One virus has been shown to cause a rare adult leukemia, and other viruses have been linked with increased risk of certain cancers. Cancer-causing viruses are able to enter and alter the genetic material that controls cell growth.

Chemical agents include a wide variety of substances often found in increased amounts in certain occupations and in polluted environments. Some of the most common chemical carcinogens include hydrocarbons, such as in cigarette smoke, air pollutants, tar, soot, aniline dyes, benzene, asbestos, vinyl chloride, cobalt, chromium, nickel, and arsenic compounds. The relationship between cigarette smoke and lung cancer has been well established, and there is increased evidence that secondary smoke is a hazard. Snuff, a form of smokeless tobacco, has been implicated as a cause of mouth cancer. This is of concern because of the increased use of "dipping snuff" in young males.[2]

Physical agents include ultraviolet radiation from sunlight and ionizing radiation from natural gamma rays, x-rays, and radioactive isotopes. Skin cancer is found more often in persons exposed to prolonged periods of sunlight, and it is more common in fair-skinned persons. The greater pigmentation of dark skin appears to protect against the effects of ultraviolet rays. Persons acutely or frequently exposed to ionizing radiation have an increased incidence of cancers, especially leukemia. This is seen in the survivors of the atom bomb, in persons cured of an earlier cancer by the use of radiation therapy, and in radiation workers before strict exposure precautions were enforced. Physical trauma from chronic irritation of parts of the body can be a contributing cause of cancer. Bladder stones, chronic infections, and parasitic infestations can produce a chronic inflammatory condition that will predispose a person to cancer.

Hormones have been implicated in the development of some forms of cancer. Prolonged estrogen therapy has been linked to an increased incidence of endometrial cancer. Use of diethylstilbestrol (DES) during pregnancy has been related to development of vaginal carcinoma in female children. In prostate cancer and in some breast cancers, tumor growth can be slowed by treatments that stop the natural production of sex hormones.

Dietary factors have been linked to the development of certain cancers. It is thought that some diets may increase the risk of cancer, and other diets may offer some protection from cancer. High fat diets have been associated with increased risk of colon, breast, prostate, and endometrial cancer, while fiber is thought to have a protective role against colon cancer. Various vitamins, particularly vitamins A and C, may decrease the risk of cancer.[2,3] Some food additives have been suspected to be carcinogenic, and excessive alcohol use has been linked to increased risk of cancer of the mouth, larynx, and esophagus.

Human cancer is thought to be caused by a combination of many factors, both environmental and genetic. Recent research suggests that certain genes in each cell control cell growth. Some of these genes, called **oncogenes,** can somehow be activated to produce a protein that causes the cell to begin growing in an abnormal or malignant fashion.[9] What "switches on" the oncogenes is not yet known, but many of the carcinogens discussed above are being studied. Some scientists believe that we form cancer cells in our bodies throughout life, and that our immune system is constantly detecting and eliminating the abnormal cells. This concept has stimulated research involving the immune system of the body. Some immunologists suggest that cancer may be caused by a failure of this system and that strengthening the body's natural immune defenses may help to destroy malignant tissue.

PREVENTION AND CONTROL

Cancer usually begins as an alteration in one microscopic cell of the body. At this time the individual is asymptomatic and considered to be an active, healthy person. As the cancer cell begins to divide without restraint, symptoms will eventually occur. The first symptoms are insidious and not readily apparent to the victim. A small, painless lump, a vague change in bowel habits, or a chronic cough may be the only prodromal sign of a devastating illness, and often these poorly defined symptoms are not considered valid reasons for seeking medical attention. If left untreated, cancer cells will continue to invade adjacent healthy tissue and eventually will spread to other parts of the body, where new cancer growths will be established. Because of this characteristic pattern of development, cancer is difficult to detect in its earliest stages. If the disease is not readily diagnosed, the chances for cure are greatly reduced, since spread of the disease has already occurred. Early diagnosis and prompt treatment could save more than 50% of all cancer patients; currently the survival rate is four in ten patients.

It is clear that cancer must be prevented or controlled at an early stage. Future efforts must be concentrated on promoting research, controlling environmental carcinogens, and educating

---

Five Protective Steps Against Cancer
1. Eat more vegetables from the cabbage family.
2. Add more high-fiber foods to your diet.
3. Choose foods high in vitamin A.
4. Choose foods high in vitamin C.
5. Reduce weight.

Five Risk Factors of Cancer
1. High fat diet
2. Salt-cured, smoked, nitrite-cured foods
3. Cigarette smoking
4. Excessive alcohol
5. Exposure to the sun

---

the public and health professionals about methods of prevention and early detection. Nurses can play a particularly important role by promoting primary and secondary prevention.

Primary prevention refers to the steps that can be taken to avoid factors that might lead to the development of cancer. The American Cancer Society recommends 10 steps to a healthier life and reduced cancer risk.[3]

Other risk factors include excessive x-rays, estrogens, and exposure to harmful chemicals and fibers like asbestos.

Secondary prevention refers to steps taken to diagnose cancer as soon as possible after it has developed and while it is still potentially curable. Early detection of cancer in people without symptoms is a major goal of all cancer organizations. The American Cancer Society and other agencies recommend certain guidelines for cancer-related checkups (Table 9-3). Simple steps to early diagnosis include monthly breast self-examination (BSE), testicular self-examination, mammograms, Pap smears, stool bloods, and proctosigmoidoscopy. All nurses should urge their patients to practice these preventive health behaviors and teach them the seven warning signs of cancer (see box at right).

Public awareness and concern about prevention and early detection of cancer is growing. All commercial advertising of cigarettes on radio and television has been banned, and airlines no longer

Table 9-3

American Cancer Society Guidelines for Cancer-Related Checkups in People Without Symptoms, According to Age[2]		
Site	**Increasing age** ⟶	
Breast	Women age 20 and over should perform BSE monthly. Women 20 to 40 years of age should have a physical breast examination every 3 years.	All women should have a baseline mammogram at age 40. Women 40 to 49 should have a mammogram and breast examination every 1 to 2 years.	Women age 50 and over should have a mammogram and breast examination every year.
Lung	Primary prevention: help smokers stop smoking and keep non-smokers from starting.		
Colon-rectum		Men and women over age 40 should have a digital-rectal examination every year.	Men and women over 50 should have a stool-blood test every year and a proctosigmoidoscopy every 3 to 5 years.
Cervix/ uterus	Women age 18 and over, and sexually active younger ones, should have an annual Pap test and pelvic examination. After 3 or more consecutive normal annual examinations, a Pap test may be done less frequently at physician discretion.		Endometrial tissue sample at menopause for high risk women
Skin	Primary prevention: avoid exposure to sunlight, use sunscreens, and protect children from traumatic sunburns.		
Basic	"Cancer-related health checkup" every 3 years for those 20 to 40 years of age	"Cancer-related health checkup" every year for all persons age 40 and over	

Seven Warning Signals of Cancer

1. **C**hange in bowel or bladder habits
2. **A** sore that does not heal
3. **U**nusual bleeding or discharge
4. **T**hickening or lump in breast or elsewhere
5. **I**ndigestion or difficulty swallowing
6. **O**bvious change in wart or mole
7. **N**agging cough or hoarseness

If a warning signal occurs, see a doctor.

---

allow smoking on flights. Educational programs in schools and spot filmstrips on television are designed to acquaint the public about the hazards of smoking and to encourage persons who smoke to discontinue the habit. Quit-smoking classes and support groups are now widely available and often are provided by companies for their employees. Public education programs have also alerted more women to the benefits of BSE, mammograms, and Pap smears. Colorectal screening programs are often run by community agencies.

The National Cancer Institute and the American Cancer Society spend a large amount of money on public and professional education. The National Cancer Institute sponsors a toll-free information line, accessible in all parts of the country by dialing 1-800-4-CANCER. Trained counselors provide the most up-to-date answers about cancer prevention, detection, and treatment. The American Cancer Society has units in all states and provides free information to the public about cancer, as well as services to people with cancer.

DIAGNOSTIC TESTS AND PROCEDURES

Before a physician or pathologist can make a diagnosis of cancer, the patient must be carefully examined, a tissue sample must be obtained, and the primary location and anatomic spread (stage) of the cancer must be established.

Tissue Sampling

A definite diagnosis of cancer can only be made when a pathologist sees malignant cells in a tissue specimen viewed under a microscope. There are a number of techniques for making a tissue diagnosis.

Exfoliative cytology

Exfoliative cytology or Papanicolaou (Pap) smear test is used as a means of studying cells the body has shed during the normal sequence of growth and replacement of body tissues. If cancer is present, cancer cells are also shed. By studying these cells under the microscope, malignant conditions can be diagnosed before symptoms are noticed by the patient. The test was originally developed to diagnose early cancer of the cervix and can now be used effectively to study cells shed from the stomach, esophagus, lung, colon, bladder, and discharge from the breasts. If cancer cells are found, a biopsy is always done.

Secretions from the cervix are secured during a pelvic examination. It is a simple, painless procedure that should be performed yearly in women age 18 and over.

The specimens are sent to a laboratory, and results are sent to the physician and often to the patient. The appearance of the cells under the microscope is graded into five classes:

Class I	Normal
Class II	Abnormal; may indicate infection
Class III	Suspiciously malignant
Class IV	Probably malignant
Class V	Malignant

The nurse should understand that the Pap test is primarily a screening test, and that further examination may be necessary to confirm a diagnosis. The nurse can assist the patient by telling her how to prepare for the examination. The Pap smear is not done during a menstrual period; a douche should not be taken for several hours before the test; the physician may want the patient to avoid coitus and a tub bath for 24 hours before reporting for the test. This simple test has resulted in a decrease in the death rate from cervical cancer.

Biopsy

A biopsy is the surgical removal of a piece of tissue for microscopic examination. There are several biopsy techniques. A needle biopsy can be done of tumors close to the skin, visible on x-rays or scans, or seen during endoscopic procedures. Fine needle biopsies are easy to do but yield only a few cells. Larger bore needles give bigger tissue samples, and an incisional biopsy involves taking a small sample out of the tissue mass. An excisional biopsy involves removing all of the known tumor.

Various biopsy procedures may be used, and they may be performed in the physician's office, in the clinic, or in the hospital. If the biopsy is taken from an external lesion, preparation will include the use of an antiseptic and injection of a local anesthetic, such as 2% procaine solution. Using a special biopsy instrument, the physician removes a small amount of tissue for examination, after which a sterile dressing is applied. Although the biopsy is a simple procedure, it may not seem simple to a frightened, nervous patient. The frozen-section biopsy enables a tissue specimen to be quickly examined during an operation to immediately determine whether the tissue is benign or malignant. The specimen is quickly frozen, cut, and immediately stained. Although this technique is not satisfactory for a detailed study of the cells, possible malignancies can be promptly identified. Permanent sections of the tissue are prepared so that special stains can be used to help the pathologist make a definite diagnosis. Patients should be told that these biopsies usually take several days to process and that diagnosis may be delayed until then.

Imaging Techniques—Direct Visualization

The primary location and anatomic spread of a cancer can be determined by a number of imaging

Much of this material has been taken from the class text. (handwritten)

techniques using direct or indirect visualization. Direct visualization techniques involve introducing fiber-optic endoscopy tubes into hollow organs and viewing internal surfaces. Fiber-optic tubes contain lighting, magnifying devices, and attachments that allow brushings or biopsies to be performed.

Bronchoscopy

Bronchoscopy allows examination of the trachea and bronchii of the lungs using a local or general anesthesia. The bronchoscope is inserted through the nose and advanced into the upper airway. Biopsies or brushings of suspicious areas can be done through the tube. The patient's throat must be numbed during this procedure to prevent discomfort and gagging. After the procedure, the patient should be warned not to eat or drink until the gag reflex returns. The nurse should be alert if the patient shows signs of bleeding or has trouble breathing after the procedure.

Esophagoscopy and gastroscopy

Esophagoscopy and gastroscopy allow visualization of the esophagus and stomach by the use of a flexible tube inserted through the patient's mouth. Biopsies or washings can be taken during the procedure. The patient should be instructed not to eat or drink after midnight before the procedure. The patient will be given medication before the gastroscopy to make him or her relaxed and sleepy. It is important that someone accompany the patient to drive him or her home after the procedure.

Proctosigmoidoscopy

Proctosigmoidoscopy is the examination of the anus, rectum, and sigmoid colon by use of a rigid tube up to 10 inches long. Tumors, polyps, or ulcerations may be studied by examination and biopsy. In preparing the patient for the proctosigmoidoscopy, it is extremely important that all fecal matter be removed before the examination; this is usually accomplished by cleansing enemas. Laxatives and cathartics are seldom given before the procedure, but the nurse should be familiar with the exact preparation desired by the physician. The patient is placed in the knee-chest position and draped to expose only the anal area. In some situations, however, it may be desirable to place the patient in a side-lying position. The patient should be given information about the examination and should know what to expect. He or she should know that there may be some discomfort, but that the procedure is usually not painful. Since the examination is often fatiguing, especially for the elderly person, the nurse should arrange for the patient to rest after the procedure and should provide some light nourishment.

Colonoscopy

Colonoscopy allows the examination of the entire colon by means of a long flexible tube. Preparation of the bowel is more extensive than for a sigmoidoscopy. The patient must be on a liquid diet and use laxatives and enemas before the examination.

Imaging Techniques—Indirect Visualization

Indirect visualization techniques include radiographic tests such as chest x-rays, mammograms, gastrointestinal series, barium enemas, CAT scans, and **radioisotope** studies and nonradiographic tests such as ultrasounds and magnetic resonance imaging.

Radiographic studies can be done with or without contrast. Noncontrast x-ray studies include chest x-rays, mammograms, and abdomen and bone films. Contrast x-ray studies use materials such as air, iodine containing dyes, or barium to outline an organ. Examples of contrast x-rays include lymphangiograms, myelograms, and barium studies of the gastrointestinal tract.

X-rays are electromagnetic waves similar to light and heat waves and are produced in a vacuum tube. They have the ability to penetrate most substances and alter a photographic plate, producing an image of those substances through which the rays pass. The image reflects the varying densities of the tissues, such as bone, soft tissue, fat, and air. In this way, body cavities, organs, and bones can be visualized, thereby assisting the physician in diagnosis and treatment. Fluoroscopy is an x-ray technique by which the radiologist is able to visualize internal structures while they are functioning. For example, fluoroscopy of the chest enables the radiologist to view the expansion and contraction of the lungs.

Nurses may be requested to assist while diagnostic x-ray films are being made. Precautions must be taken to avoid exposure to radiation. If the nurse remains in the room with the patient, a lead apron and possibly gloves should be worn.

The following are some of the most commonly ordered indirect imaging studies for cancer diagnosis and staging.

Mammography

Mammography is a safe, simple, nontraumatic technique for detecting the presence of breast tumors. Using a low-energy beam, films of the soft breast tissue are taken without the use of a radiopaque medium. In many instances it is possible to differentiate between a benign and malignant tumor. The x-ray procedure is recommended for women who have signs and symptoms of breast disease, a familial history of breast cancer, a previous breast biopsy or breast surgery, or large, pendulous breasts that make palpation difficult. Yearly mammography is now recommended as a screening test for all women age 50 and over. A baseline mammography should be done at age 40, then one every 1 to 2 years until age 49. Mammography is combined with breast self examination (BSE) and physical examination of the breast by a health care provider to detect early breast cancer. The technique of BSE is shown on page 550.

Barium enema

When the physician wishes to visualize the colon above the sigmoid, a careful preparation of the patient is required. Procedures vary; however, all fecal matter must be removed from the colon. This is extremely important because any residue left in the colon may interfere with a correct diagnosis. Usually the patient takes nothing by mouth after midnight, and laxatives, rectal suppositories, and enemas are given as ordered. Often enemas are given until the solution returns free of fecal material. A poorly prepared patient may delay the examination, resulting in inconvenience to the x-ray department and additional expense to the patient.

The patient reports to the x-ray department at the scheduled hour, and is given an enema of barium, a radiopaque substance, which he or she is asked to retain. The radiologist observes the filling of the colon, using the fluoroscope, after which x-ray films are taken. The patient is then allowed to evacuate the barium. Sometimes the radiologist has the patient return after evacuation of the barium. The colon is distended with air, and additional x-ray films are taken. The patient may feel exhausted after the examination, and a period of rest is desirable. Because barium retained in the bowel becomes difficult to expel, a warm oil retention enema or a laxative such as magnesium citrate may be ordered following the examination.

Gastrointestinal series

The gastrointestinal (GI) series is an x-ray examination of the upper gastrointestinal tract using a radiopaque contrast medium. It is used to determine pathology of the stomach and duodenum.

The patient should be told not to eat or drink for at least 6 to 8 hours before the examination. Food in the stomach will result in misleading x-ray films. The patient reports to the x-ray department at the scheduled hour, and is given a mixture of barium to drink. The fluoroscope is used to observe the barium as it passes through the esophagus into the stomach. X-ray films are then taken at specific intervals over several hours to study the movement of the barium from the stomach into the small intestine. The patient should not be given any food until the x-ray department notifies the nurse that they are finished with the tests. Many patients find the examination fatiguing, especially elderly persons. The patient is usually hungry and should be served a warm, appetizing meal, made comfortable, and allowed to rest undisturbed. A cathartic may be included in the barium mixture or ordered following the examination to hasten the elimination of the barium from the intestines.

Computerized tomography

Computerized tomography (CT), also known as computerized axial tomography (CAT scan), is a computer-aided x-ray examination that has proved to be a major breakthrough in diagnostic technique. Conventional x-ray films can only differentiate between bone, soft tissue, fat, and air with any precision. The CT is 100 times more sensitive to differences in tissue densities, and individual organs and structures within organs can be visualized. A narrow x-ray beam is rotated around the patient, and multiple exposures are made. Sensitive detectors record the results, which are then processed by a computer. An image of the body section exposed to the x-ray beam, a tomogram, is then constructed. Each image represents a horizontal cross-section or "slice" of the body. This diagnostic device can be used to detect tumors and other pathologic conditions without performing special procedures that are often painful, complicated, invasive, or risky.[8]

Since the x-rays are focused on a few thin layers of the patient's body, patients receive no more radiation than with a conventional x-ray examination. The patient will lie on an adjustable hydraulic couch and the scanner will rotate around the chosen site. As the scanner rotates it will make a clicking noise, which can frighten the unsuspecting patient. Patients must hold completely still because motion will disturb the image. Often snug-fitting restraints will be used as appropriate. The procedure is safe, painless, and usually requires no specific preparation or follow-up. Sometimes a contrast medium is given to highlight certain parts of the body. If the contrast is given intravenously, the patient should be warned that it may produce a warm sensation. If the patient is allergic to iodine or contrast medium, the x-ray personnel should be alerted. If oral or intravenous contrast medium is to be used, the patient is usually told not to eat or drink for several hours before the test. Check with the radiology department for instructions specific for each test.

Radioisotope studies

Radioisotopes are elements that emit rays of energy. They occur naturally as radium or uranium, or can be artificially produced from other elements. The most widely used radioisotopes in medicine are altered forms of iodine, phosphorus, cobalt, iron, and gold. The patient needs no specific preparation other than explanation of the procedure. At a specified time the patient will be given an intravenous injection of an isotope, which has a tendency to accumulate in the organ to be studied. In the radioisotope laboratory, a sensing device charts or maps the areas of the organ that have picked up the radioactive material. Variations from normal are seen as lighter or darker areas and indicate abnormality of the organ, often a malignancy. For example, radioactive iodine is readily assimilated by the thyroid gland, and pathogenesis can be detected during a thyroid scan. It is now possible to scan most major organs, such as the brain, kidneys, liver, pericardium, and bone. Such minute amounts of radioactive material are used, and it is eliminated so quickly, that the patient is not considered radioactive.

Magnetic resonance imaging

Magnetic resonance imaging (MRI) is relatively new. It uses a magnetic field and radiofrequency sound waves to produce excellent images of the soft tissues, veins and arteries, and the brain and spinal cord. The procedure is not invasive and poses no risk of radiation exposure. However, it is costly ($700 and up) and may be lengthy, taking up to 1½ hours. The patient must lie still for pe-

riods of up to 20 minutes, must remove all metal objects, and lie on a narrow stretcher that is rolled into a shallow tunnel. Despite efforts to prevent claustrophobia with mirrors, a call button, and a voice-activated intercom, the procedure is frightening to many people. Patient teaching by the nurse is essential to help decrease anxiety. Guided imagery and rhythmic breathing may be useful for distraction and for giving the patient control.[11]

Ultrasound

Ultrasound uses high-frequency sound waves instead of x-rays to show the structure and function of internal organs. A sound wave transducer (transmitter and receiver) is moved over the skin. The sound waves pass through the skin and, as they strike various organs, they send echoes back to the transducer. Each tissue produces a distinctive echo that can be identified by the transducer. The sound waves are changed into electrical energy that forms an image on a screen. With the advent of CAT scans and MRIs, ultrasound has been used less. However, it is still a good diagnostic test for some cancers and is often used to complement x-ray tests. The advantages of ultrasound are that there is no radiation exposure, no discomfort, and no injections. Most of the time no special preparation is needed. The patient will be asked to fast for several hours before a gastrointestinal ultrasound and to drink fluids and keep the bladder full for pelvic exams.

Laboratory Studies

Analysis of chemicals in the blood may be useful in diagnosing the type and extent of the cancer. Some cancers produce substances called tumor markers. For example, carcinoembryonic antigen (CEA) is commonly found in metastatic colon cancer. Elevated acid phosphatase levels may be found in persons with prostate cancer. These tests are not very useful in screening for cancer, however, because the acid phosphatase levels are also elevated in many benign conditions. However, they are used to evaluate response to treatment.

TREATMENT OF CANCER

Cancer may be treated in four ways: surgery, radiotherapy, chemotherapy, and biotherapy. Early diagnosis and treatment may result in cure, whereas delayed diagnosis and treatment may result in treatment that is palliative only, with death the inevitable outcome. For many, cancer becomes a chronic illness, and nursing care focuses on rehabilitation and efforts to optimize the quality of life.

Surgery

Surgery is often the primary treatment for cancer and may be performed for various purposes. It may be preventive, diagnostic, curative, or **palliative** and may range from the removal of a small tumor to extensive surgical excision. The surgical removal of a potentially dangerous mole or polyp may be considered preventive surgery. Sometimes cancer of an internal organ is suspected, but diagnosis cannot be made without a surgical biopsy. In many instances the removal of a malignant tumor before metastasis occurs results in a permanent cure. For example, in cancer of the cervix the surgeon removes the entire uterus, the cervix being its distal end. When metastasis becomes widespread, surgery may be only palliative, such as relieving an intestinal obstruction or controlling pain. Some surgery is extensive, with removal of the regional lymphatics and adjacent tissue. When surgery is performed early before metastasis occurs, it offers the patient the best chance for cure.

Research is underway to find ways to increase chances of cure by surgery. The effects of chemotherapy and/or radiation treatment administered before, during, or after surgery are being investigated. This is called "adjuvant therapy." Some inoperable tumors have been reduced in size by drugs or radiation so that surgery can be performed. A course of chemotherapy and/or radiation therapy given after all visible tumor has been removed may reduce the risk of recurrence in some cancers. Adjuvant chemotherapy is commonly used for the treatment of early stage breast cancer after surgery and/or radiation.

Newer surgical techniques and tools have been developed. Cryosurgery is being used to treat some cancer of the skin, mouth, and other superficial lesions. This technique destroys tumors by freezing them with liquid nitrogen. Laser surgery, which uses intense light beams, can vaporize some cancerous lesions like those on the larynx.

Palliative surgery treats the complications of cancer when total removal or destruction of cancer cells is impossible. This method contributes to the patient's comfort and may prolong life. An example of palliative surgery is the creation of a colostomy to bypass a cancerous lesion in the bowel. Reconstructive or plastic surgery may be used to correct defects caused by the original surgical intervention. Many women are now choosing to have breast reconstruction after a modified radical mastectomy for breast cancer.

The preoperative and postoperative nursing care of patients having surgical procedures involving cancer is essentially the same for any other kind of surgery and will be reviewed in the appropriate sections. However, psychosocial needs are often more intense, since the potential or actual diagnosis of cancer exists.

Radiotherapy

Radiotherapy, or **radiation therapy,** refers to the use of ionizing radiation to treat tumors. Radiation is ionizing when it can break atoms of a substance into smaller parts that carry a positive or negative charge. Most radiation we are familiar with, such as heat and light, is not ionizing. X-rays, gamma rays, and radioactive particles (alpha and beta particles, neutrons, protons) are types of ionizing radiation. When **ionizing radiation** passes through living tissue it damages DNA molecules and leads to disruption of cell function and division. The principle in using various forms of radiation to treat cancer is to give doses large enough to destroy cancer cells without causing irreparable damage to normal tissue surrounding the tumor. Although both normal and malignant cells can be destroyed, most malignant cells are more susceptible to ionizing rays than are normal cells. Radiation therapy may be used to obtain a cure, alone or in combination with surgery and/or chemotherapy, or for palliation of symptoms when cure is impossible.

Ionizing radiation is considered hazardous material because acute and chronic exposure causes cellular changes that can lead to gene mutation, birth defects, and carcinogenesis. Wherever radiation is being used, whether for diagnostic or treatment purposes, precautions must be taken to minimize patient and personnel exposure. Persons who work in radiation areas are carefully monitored to ensure that they do not receive more than the maximum permissible dose each year (5 rem). Nurses are most at risk for exposure to radiation when caring for patients receiving internal radiation therapy. Safety precautions are discussed in that section. The symbol for a radiation area is shown in Figure 9-2.

Two general types of radiation therapy tech-

Caution

Radiation

Figure 9-2
Radiation symbol.

niques are currently used: external beam radiation (teletherapy) and internal radiation therapy (brachytherapy). External beam therapy is given from outside the body using various radiation generating machines. Internal radiation therapy places a radiation source close to the tumor. Sealed sources can be placed into the tumor-containing tissue or into a cavity close to the tumor. Unsealed internal radiation uses solutions of radioisotopes that emit ionizing radiation.

External Radiation Therapy

External radiation is most often delivered to the patient by machines that generate x-rays or contain radioisotopes, like cobalt-60, that emit gamma rays. Most machines used today generate supervoltage radiation that can be accurately directed to deep tumors while sparing the skin from damage. Radiation is generally given in small doses over a period of time, usually 5 days per week for 4 to 8 weeks. Palliative radiation takes less time. This method of delivering radiation, called *fractionation*, may increase cancer cell destruction while minimizing damage to normal tissues.

Nursing intervention

External radiation therapy may be given on an outpatient or an inpatient basis. Most patients know that they are receiving radiation therapy for cancer, and preparation of the patient and the family is very important. The course of therapy that has been prescribed for the patient is usually explained by the physician. Nurses can often clar-

ify uncertainties, answer questions, and explain the radiation procedure more fully. Patient teaching of self-care measures while receiving external radiation therapy is essential, especially if the patient receives therapy as an outpatient. New patients are usually extremely apprehensive and need much reassurance and support. The term "radiation therapy" often incites fear in both the patient and family and often is viewed as the last resort when all else has failed.

The purpose and procedure must be discussed, along with the patient's perception of radiation therapy. It should be stressed that the patient will not become radioactive. Every patient should understand that the treatment is administered while lying on a table in a room alone. Often the machine will rotate around the patient, making a clicking sound. The patient will be able to communicate with technicians outside the room and will be observed continually. During the treatment, which may take 1 to 3 minutes, the patient must remain as still as possible. Shielding will be provided for sites not to be treated. It is helpful if the patient can be oriented to the surroundings and the machine before the first treatment.

X-ray therapy is more effective when the patient's nutritional status is good; a high-calorie, high-protein diet is generally recommended. The nurse should see that the bowels are evacuated and the bladder is emptied before the patient reports for the treatment. This is particularly important if the patient is receiving therapy to the back, abdomen, or pelvis. The patient should have had adequate sleep and rest. Any ointment or dressings should be removed and the skin thoroughly cleansed before the patient reports to the x-ray department. Indelible ink or tattoo marks are used to outline the area that will receive radiation. This is called *simulation*. These markings are used to position the machine before each treatment. The patient should be instructed not to remove markings while undergoing treatment. The nurse should see that the patient reports to the x-ray department promptly at the scheduled hour. Elderly, debilitated, and seriously ill patients should be accompanied and should not be left alone.

Patients receiving external radiation therapy may experience nausea, vomiting, and diarrhea. This is most common when radiation is given to or near the gastrointestinal tract. Several small feedings per day may be tolerated better than regular meals. If vomiting is severe, food intake may be reduced to liquids only, and then increased to 3000 ml per day to compensate for fluid loss. Several drugs, including dimenhydrinate (Dramamine), prochlorperazine (Compazine), and perphenazine (Trilafon) have been helpful in controlling nausea and vomiting; if diarrhea occurs, it can usually be controlled with paregoric or diphenoxylate (Lomotil). Fatigue and weakness are common. Rest periods should be provided after therapy and encouraged throughout therapy.

The patient should know that there may be some reddening of the skin, which may turn dark in color, become dry, itch, and slough (**dry desquamation**). The nurse should avoid referring to the reddening as a burn. Ointments, deodorants, powders, and other products should not be used unless approved by the radiation department. Whether the patient may shower or bathe depends on the policies of the radiation department. Bathing of the area outlined for therapy is usually avoided, but if it is permitted, only mild soap such as Dove or Basis should be used, and scrubbing of the area should be avoided. If radiation is being applied to the trunk, no constricting clothing should be worn. The patient should avoid exposure to the sun and extremes of hot and cold, such as the use of hot-water bottles, ice caps, electric pads, and sunlamps.[16,20]

Steam baths, whirlpools, and saunas should be avoided. If the skin is not broken, cornstarch may be lightly applied over the radiated areas to control itching. If the skin blisters, cracks, or "weeps," a process called wet desquamation, the cornstarch should be discontinued. Great care should be taken to avoid infection, and the radiologist should be consulted for further treatment.

The cumulative effects from radiation may involve damage to the bone marrow where blood cells are formed. White blood cells are highly sensitive to radiation and may be destroyed. The resulting leukopenia produces an increased susceptibility to infection. Low platelet levels produce **thrombocytopenia,** and an increased tendency to hemorrhage may result. This complication necessitates that the patient be protected from injury. Anemia may also occur from depression of red blood cell formation. Complete blood counts are generally done on a weekly basis.

Additional symptoms may occur, depending on the site being treated. Radiation to the scalp may cause alopecia, or loss of hair. Cystitis may occur with radiation to the pelvis, and pneumo-

nitis may occur with radiation to the chest wall. Radiation to the mouth, throat, and neck often results in mouth soreness and ulceration (stomatitis). Patients should be encouraged to report any symptoms that may occur so that appropriate comfort measures can be started. Symptoms gradually get worse during the treatment course and usually resolve within a few weeks after treatment ends. A summary of nursing interventions is given in the boxed material to the right.

Although great care is taken during treatment planning to minimize radiation effects on normal tissues, damage can occur. Radiation effects can be divided into acute (during treatment to 6 months after) and chronic (variable onset after 6 months).[16] Many of the acute changes were discussed above. They involve mostly tissues that contain many dividing cells like the skin, mucous membranes, hair follicles, and bone marrow. Acute reactions are often reversible. Chronic changes involve tissues with cells that divide more slowly like muscles and the vascular system. These changes are rarely reversible. Chronic effects include tissue fibrosis, tissue necrosis, fistula formation, and cataracts. See Table 9-4 for a summary of the acute and chronic side effects of external radiation therapy.

Sealed Internal Radiation Therapy

Internal radiation therapy involves the temporary implantation of sealed applicators containing a radioactive substance into various organs of the body. Applicators may be inserted into the patient's mouth, tongue, neck, vagina, cervix, or other body cavity. Radium is a radioactive element that has been used in this way to treat cancerous lesions for some time. The supply of radium is limited and costly. However, it remains almost unchanged over many years and therefore can be used over and over. As radium slowly disintegrates it gives off a radioactive gas called radon. Although radium is kept in a sealed container, a tiny pinhole can result in leakage of the gas and consequent exposure of other patients and personnel. For this reason cesium-137, a radioactive isotope, is now being used instead of radium in hospitals. Other radioisotopes commonly used are iodine-125 and gold-198.

The radioactive isotope is prepared in a number of ways, such as in needles, tubes, capsules, and wires. External molds, created specifically for each patient, can be applied to the skin and mucous membrane. The specific form used is deter-

Table 9-4

Side Effects of External Radiation Therapy	
Time of occurrence	**Side effect**

Acute (during treatment and up to 6 months following treatment; usually reversible)	Skin reactions
	  Erythema
	  Dry desquamation
	  Wet desquamation
	Nausea and vomiting
	Diarrhea
	Fatigue
	Bone marrow suppression
	Stomatitis
	Cystitis
	Pneumonitis

Chronic (after 6 months of radiation therapy; often permanent)	Fibrosis (lung, bladder, heart) Fistulas Necrosis (bone, nerve) Paresthesia Cataracts Cancer

---

NURSING CARE GUIDELINES
External Radiation Therapy

Nursing diagnoses

- Anxiety related to the procedures and effects of radiation
- Potential altered health maintenance related to lack of knowledge of radiation therapy
- Potential altered nutrition caused by effects of radiation therapy

Nursing interventions

- Purpose and procedure should be explained by physician and reinforced by nurse
- Encourage high-calorie, high-protein diet
- Encourage high fluid intake
- Skin markings are not to be removed
- Observe for radiation reactions
  Nausea
  Vomiting
  Diarrhea
  Skin reddening
  Skin breakdown
  Fatigue
  Weakness
  Anorexia
  Leukopenia
  Thrombocytopenia
  Anemia
  Specific symptoms according to radiation site
- Give reassurance and support

Expected outcomes

- Understanding of the purposes of the therapy and procedures used
- Less anxiety related to fear of the unknown or misconceptions
- Understanding of the importance and rationale of maintaining a high-calorie, high-protein diet and high-fluid intake during therapy
- Skin markings present
- Caring for skin, taking measures to prevent skin breakdown and infection
- Observation of signs and symptoms of radiation reactions
- Adjustment of activities to compensate for fatigue

---

mined by the area to which radiation is to be applied; for example, needles may be used to treat cancer of the mouth, whereas tubes or capsules are generally used for internal radiation of the uterus. Whatever isotope is used, the radiologist determines the exact length of time that it should remain in place, and it must be removed at exactly the specified time. It is removed by the physician using long-handled forceps, washed, and placed in a lead-lined container.

Nursing intervention

The patient who is to have an implanted radiation source is prepared in the same way that most surgical patients are prepared. For a cervical implantation, a cleansing enema is given the night before treatment; a douche may also be given. A bedtime sedative is administered to ensure sleep and rest, and the patient is allowed nothing by mouth after midnight.

During surgery the physician will position the applicator and either insert the radioactive substance at that time or wait until the patient has returned to the hospital bed. The former is known as "preloading" and the latter as "afterloading." Afterloading is often preferred, because fewer hospital personnel are exposed to the radiation.

The psychologic preparation of the patient receiving an implantation is important. Patient care during the treatment is minimal, and the patient is usually in isolation. The nurse can offer reassurance to the patient and help relieve the patient's anxiety by making frequent stops at the patient's door. Upon return to the unit, the patient is placed in a single room, and a sign is placed on the bed and door indicating that the patient is receiving radiotherapy. The patient should be instructed to lie quietly to avoid any displacement of the radioactive source. The vital signs are checked at frequent intervals until they are stable, and the temperature, pulse, and respiration are checked every 4 hours unless the nurse is directed otherwise. The patient should maintain a high-fluid intake. Talking should be discouraged when implants are placed in the mouth.

When applicators are placed in the cervix, the patient is positioned with head and chest fairly low. The patient should be turned frequently and encouraged to breathe deeply. The legs should be held close together and straight, and the patient should be carefully rolled to the side when turning. No perineal care is given while the applicator is in place in the cervix. Usually the treatment will only last for 1 or 2 days.

The patient may have a Foley catheter inserted into the bladder to prevent distention, and it should be checked at intervals to ascertain that it is draining properly. Patients should be watched for any bleeding and leaking of urine around a Foley catheter, and the radiologist should be notified if such complications occur. Patients are usually given a low-residue diet and diphenoxylate to prevent bowel movements that might dislodge the implant. However, if needed, the patient should use the bedpan for bowel evacuation and should be instructed not to strain. The contents of the bedpan should be inspected carefully before the nurse disposes of them. All emesis, clothing, and bed linens are inspected before they are removed from the unit. Dark threads are attached to the applicator and brought to the outside, where they are fastened to the skin. The patient should be cautioned to avoid any pulling on the threads, and they should be counted every 4 hours and recorded on the patient's chart. Long forceps and a lead carrier are kept in the patient's room in case the applicator is accidentally displaced. Dislodged applicators should never be picked up with the hands. The forceps and carrier can also be used for removal of the implant, although this is often done in the radiology department. If any radioactive source becomes dislodged, the radiologist should be notified immediately.

The patient should be observed for symptoms of a radiation reaction. Nausea, vomiting, malaise, and anorexia may indicate that alteration of the treatment is necessary. An elevated temper-

ature may indicate an infection. The physician must be notified of any unusual symptoms that may occur. A summary of nursing intervention is found in the boxed material below.

The radiologist calculates the dose of radioactive source necessary to destroy cancer cells, and the exact hour that the radioactive source is to be removed is noted on the patient's chart; it may also be noted on a tag placed on the patient's

---

NURSING CARE GUIDELINES
Sealed Internal Radiation Therapy

Nursing diagnoses
- Anxiety related to the procedures and effects of radiation
- Potential altered health maintenance related to lack of knowledge of radiation therapy
- Potential altered nutrition resulting from effects of radiation therapy

Nursing interventions
- Purpose and procedure should be explained by physician and reinforced by nurse
- Follow precautions as ordered
- Attach radiation symbol to door of room
- Instruct patient to lie quietly
- Check vital signs frequently
- Encourage high fluid intake
- Check position of applicator every 4 hours
- Observe for symptoms of radiation reaction
- Observe for specific symptoms according to radiation site
- Maintain measures for self-protection
- Time—limit amount of time spent in the room; organize well
- Distance—approach patient only when necessary; communicate from doorway
- Shielding—use shielding if available
- Never touch a radiation source with bare hands; if the applicator becomes dislodged, pick it up with long forceps, place it in a carrier, and notify the radiologist immediately
- Provide opportunities to communicate using the principles of time, distance, and shielding

Expected outcomes
- Understanding of the purposes of the therapy
- Less anxiety related to fear of unknown or misconceptions
- No motion while the radioactive applicator is in place

wrist. The radiologist should be notified at least 30 minutes before the hour of removal, and a tray with the necessary equipment should be at the patient's bedside. After removal of the radioactive source, the patient should be given a warm cleansing bath and made comfortable on a freshly made bed. On discharge of the patient, the equipment and utensils in the room are not radioactive and require only routine cleaning.

It is important to realize that there is nothing explosive about the radioactive material used. The patient does not become radioactive when the sealed applicator is removed from the body and no radiation remains. Body excretions are not radioactive unless part of the source has become dislodged and is present in the excretion. Nurses cannot become radioactive by caring for a patient with sealed internal radiation therapy, and they cannot expose others to radiation. However, nurses and other hospital personnel are exposed to some radiation when caring for these patients. Appropriate precautions should be taken by all those who come in contact with the patient. Visitors should be instructed to limit the length of their visits, and stay at least 6 feet from the patient. Pregnant women and children should not be allowed to visit the patient.

Self-protection

There are three main factors that determine the amount of radiation the nurse will receive while caring for the patient. First, the amount of *time* spent with the patient should be the absolute minimum required for whatever care is necessary. However, nursing care should be planned so that good care is provided without the nurse presenting a hurried appearance. Second, the nurse should understand that as the *distance* from the source of radiation (the patient) is increased, there is a significant decrease in the amount of radiation exposure. When caring for a patient with a cesium source in the pelvis, the nurse should plan care so that no more than 30 minutes a day is spent at a distance of no less than 3 feet from the source. At a distance of 6 feet, a safe time would be 2 hours a day. This general guideline also applies to visitors.

Speaking to the patient frequently from the doorway provides reassurance to the patient and allows the patient the opportunity to communicate without exposing personnel to undue radiation. A bedside telephone will help the patient keep in touch with family. When a radioisotope has been placed in the pelvic area, a drawsheet placed on the operating room table under the patient may be used to lift her from the table onto the stretcher and from the stretcher onto the bed, thus avoiding close contact. Walking at the head rather than at the side of the stretcher while transferring the patient also reduces exposure. Third, *shielding* must be considered for self-protection. Various materials, such as a lead sheet or shield, can be placed between the nurse and the patient to absorb the radiation.

All personnel who spend considerable time in radiation areas should wear badges with small dental film inside. This film is developed at intervals and observed for fogging that might indicate overexposure. It is important to understand that these badges are to measure an individual nurse's exposure to radiation. Nurses should not use another person's badge or lend their badge to others. Radiation safety officers are employed by most hospitals that are providing radiation therapy. The officer monitors patient safety and calculates safe working times and distances for each isotope and dose.

Unsealed Internal Radiation Therapy

Unsealed internal radiation therapy involves the administration of radioisotopes orally or by injection. Depending on the radioisotope used and its pattern of distribution in the body, the radioactivity may be localized or widely spread throughout the body.

Nursing intervention

Radioactive iodine (^{131}I) is commonly used for the treatment of thyroid diseases. Like many other isotopes, radioactive iodine circulates in the blood stream and is eliminated from the body by the kidneys. When large doses are given for treatment, special care must be taken in the handling and disposal of the patient's body fluids (blood, urine, feces and vomitus). Sheets and dressings should be handled with gloves and stored until they may be disposed of safely. Usually the radioactivity decreases to one half in 8 days, and approximately 50% is excreted in 1 day. Precautions are rarely necessary after a week has passed. Isotopes of phosphorus, cobalt, and gold are also used for therapeutic purposes. Each has specific characteristics and will necessitate varying protective measures.

It is important to note that the patient receiving therapeutic doses of a radioisotope does become a source of radioactivity as long as the radioisotope remains within the body and continues to emit radiation. Nursing personnel must know which radioisotope was used, how long it will continue to emit radiation, how and when it was administered, and how it is distributed and excreted by the body. The radiation safety principles of time, distance, and shielding must be used, and patients should be placed in isolation. The boxed

material below left summarizes the nursing interventions for a patient receiving unsealed radiation therapy with radioactive iodine; the nursing actions for this radioisotope are similar to those used with other radioisotopes.

Chemotherapy

Cancer is a disease involving cellular metabolism. Much of the present cancer research is directed toward finding chemicals that will control the growth and multiplication of malignant cells. **Chemotherapy** now plays a major role in the early curative treatment of cancer patients as well as providing palliative measures for the patient who has widespread metastasis. New drugs are continually being developed, and several may be combined to provide the most satisfactory results. Drugs may also be used in combination with surgery and/or radiotherapy.

Chemotherapeutic drugs disrupt the internal metabolism of cells so that they are either prevented from multiplying or directly killed. The drugs are usually classified according to their mechanism of action. *Alkylating agents* react with nuclear material of cells to impair cell division and growth. *Antimetabolites* block the formation of normal nuclear material. *Antibiotics* used in cancer therapy are highly toxic drugs; they are not used to treat infections. Some appear to destroy nuclear material, although their mechanisms of action vary. *Plant alkaloids* disrupt cell division; the action of *hormones* is unknown. Steroid therapy is sometimes used as cancer therapy, principally to alter certain hormones. A summary of the common chemotherapeutic drugs is found in Table 9-5.

Although chemotherapeutic drugs are effective in preventing the multiplication of cancer cells or destroying them, normal tissue is affected as well. Tissues that multiply rapidly are affected the most, such as cells in the gastrointestinal tract, hair follicles, and bone marrow. As a result, side effects can be expected from the administration of these drugs. The severity of the side effects is usually related to the strength of the dose given, and reducing the dose or discontinuing the drug will minimize the symptoms.[5,18]

Nursing intervention

Chemotherapy is the most dreaded form of cancer treatment. It is not uncommon for patients to refuse treatment because they fear side effects such as vomiting and hair loss. Nurses play an important role in helping patients find ways of coping

---

NURSING CARE GUIDELINES
Unsealed Internal Radiation Therapy

Nursing diagnoses
- Anxiety related to the procedure and effects of radiation
- Potential altered health maintenace related to lack of knowledge of radiation therapy
- Potential altered nutrition resulting from effects of radiation therapy

Nursing interventions
- Purpose and procedure should be explained by the physician and reinforced by the nurse
- Follow precautions as ordered
- Attach radiation symbol to door of room when patient is receiving therapeutic doses of radioisotopes
- Check patient's room for:
  - Solid waste container
  - Solid linen container
  - Other containers as directed by hospital radiation safety officer
- Instruct patient to remain in the room
- Instruct patient on use of the bathroom and waste containers
- Check that all meals are served on disposable items
- Maintain visitor restrictions—no one under age 18, no pregnant women
- Maintain measures for self-protection—use principles of time, distance, and shielding
- Wear gloves when handling any body fluids

Expected outcomes
- Understanding of the purposes of the therapy and procedures used
- Less anxiety related to fear of the unknown or misconceptions
- Isolation and use of containers for urine, feces, and vomitus
- Participation in maintaining nutrition and fluid intake

with the physical and emotional reactions to chemotherapy.[18]

Common gastrointestinal symptoms include nausea and vomiting, anorexia, diarrhea or constipation, and possibly distortion of taste. Nausea and vomiting most often occur within a few hours after administration of the drug, although they may not occur at all in some patients. The drug therapy should be thoroughly explained to the patient. Some hospitals give patients an information sheet explaining their drug regimen. The patient should realize that medications will be ordered to prevent the symptoms, and that these should be taken regularly before and after treatment. Small, frequent feedings are suggested, and patients are encouraged to increase their fluid intake.

Soreness and ulceration of the mouth may occur. Good oral hygiene, including frequent rinsing of the mouth, is encouraged, and antibacterial mouthwashes may be ordered. Dry, cracked lips may be soothed with petroleum jelly. Patient information sheets may be useful (box on p. 210). Alopecia, or loss of hair, may be a significant psychologic event. Wigs, scarves, and cosmetics can effectively conceal the hair loss.

The patient should be encouraged to purchase a wig before the hair is lost, usually a few weeks after chemotherapy is first given. Reassure the patient that hair will grow again once the treat-

Table 9-5

Selected Cancer Chemotherapeutic Drugs

Class	Drug	Type of malignancy
Alkylating agents	Busulphan (Myleran)	Chronic myelocytic leukemia
	Carboplatin (Paraplatin)	Ovarian
	Carmustine (BCNU)	Brain
	Chlorambucil (Leukeran)	Chronic lymphocytic leukemia
	Cisplatin (Platinol)	Testicular, ovarian, lung
	Cyclophosphamide (Cytoxan)	Lymphoma, breast, ovarian
	Dacarbazine (DTIC)	Melanoma
	Ifosfamide (Ifex)	Lymphoma
	Lomustine (CCNU)	Brain, lymphoma
	Mechlorethamine (Nitrogen mustard)	Hodgkin's disease
	Melphalen (Alkeran)	Multiple myeloma
	Thiotepa	Bladder
Antimetabolites	Cytarabine (Cytosar, Ara-C)	Leukemia
	5-Fluorouracil (5-FU)	Colon, breast
	Mercaptopurine (6-MP)	Leukemia
	Methotrexate (MTX)	Leukemia, lymphoma, breast
Antibiotics	Bleomycin (Blenoxane)	Testicular
	Dactinomycin (Actinomycin-D)	Wilm's tumor
	Daunorubicin (Cerubidine)	Acute leukemia
	Doxorubicin (Adriamycin)	Acute leukemia, sarcoma, breast
	Mithramycin (Mithracin)	Hypercalcemia of cancer
	Mitomycin C (Mutamycin)	Stomach, pancreas
	Mitoxantrone (Novantrone)	Leukemia, lymphoma
Plant alkaloids	Vinblastine (Velban)	Lymphoma
	Vincristine (Oncovin)	Acute leukemia
	Ectoposide (VP-16-213, VePesid)	Lung, testicular
Hormones	Androgens (Testosterone)	Breast
	Corticosteroids (e.g. Prednisone)	Leukemia, lymphoma
	Estrogens (e.g. DES)	Prostate
	Progesterone (e.g. Megace)	Breast
	Antiestrogens (e.g. Tamoxifen)	Breast
	Antiandrogens (e.g. Eulexin)	Prostate
Enzymes	L-Asparaginase	Acute lymphocytic leukemia

Education for Chemotherapy Patient—Mouth and Throat Problems

The linings of the mouth and throat are among the most sensitive areas of the body. Cancer patients—especially those receiving chemotherapy or radiation treatments—often complain of soreness in these areas. These problems seem directly related to the treatment. Recent surgery in the head and neck area also may result in difficulty in chewing and swallowing. Remember that part of the healing process in this area of the body depends on your eating well and drinking fluids.

- If you have mouth or throat problems, be sure to see your dentist.
- If you have sores under your dentures, do not wear them when you do not need them for eating. Check with your dentist.
- If your mouth is dry, ask your physician whether the medicines you are taking are causing the dryness.
- If your gums, tongue, and throat become dry or sore, follow the treatment prescribed by your physician or nurse after you have discussed the problem with them.

Do you have trouble chewing and/or swallowing because of soreness or dryness?
- Try a softer diet. Use your favorite foods but make changes that will soften them.
- Use a blender. If you like vegetable soup, for example, heat it before blending it. Food tastes better if it is cooked before it is blended. It is easier to blend warm food.
- Cut meats up in small pieces and add gravy to them. This also helps when you blend them.
- Use butter, gravies, or cream sauces on meats and vegetables.
- Choose soft foods as mashed potatoes, yogurt, scrambled or poached eggs, egg custards, ricotta cheese, milk shakes, puddings, gelatins, creamy cereals, and macaroni and cheese.
- Make stews, casseroles, and simmered foods, adding more liquids to make them softer.

From U.S. Department of Health and Human Services: Eating hints, Bethesda, Md, 1980, National Cancer Institute.

---

ment is discontinued. Not all chemotherapy drugs cause hair loss, so first check which drugs the patient will be receiving.

New nursing research has shown that "icing" the scalp before chemotherapy reduces loss of hair. There are several commercial caps available that "ice" the scalp and are used to reduce hair loss in chemotherapy. This procedure may be uncomfortable to the patient. Also, the treatment cannot be used for patients with tumors that can metastasize to the skin, because the ice cap will prevent the chemotherapy from reaching this area and create a sanctuary for the cancer cells. Another approach to reducing hair loss is to apply a tourniquet below the hairline of the scalp before intravenous chemotherapy, and leave it on the scalp 10 to 15 minutes after injection.

Suppression of the bone marrow **(myelosuppression)** produces the most serious side effects. The bone marrow is continually producing the three major types of blood cells: white blood cells, platelets, and red blood cells. Chemotherapy will temporarily stop the division of blood cells in the marrow. This leads to a drop in the number of circulating blood cells (nadir counts) 1 to 2 weeks after chemotherapy is given. Complete blood counts should be checked weekly or more often if indicated. **Leukopenia,** the reduction in number of white blood cells, can increase the risk of infection. To reduce this risk, patients undergoing chemotherapy should be instructed to:

1. Inform the physician or nurse about any signs of infection—cough, increased temperature, change in discharge from orifices, skin breakdown.
2. Maintain good hygiene techniques—clean nails and hair; wash hands before meals.
3. Maintain good perineal care, including washing genitalia after urination or bowel movements.
4. Avoid individuals with colds and flu, and avoid crowds during the flu season.

Antibiotics are given at the first sign of infection. Patients with very low white blood cell counts may be hospitalized and placed on "reverse isolation" with good handwashing precautions. Strict reverse isolation using laminar air flow rooms, or plastic bubbles, is only used in bone marrow transplant units for patients with extreme bone marrow suppression.

Thrombocytopenia, a low platelet count, increases the chance of hemorrhage. If the platelet count is low, or the patient exhibits signs or symptoms of bleeding, platelet transfusions are indicated. Anemia may require transfusion of packed red blood cells. Other side effects can occur that are specific to the type of drug given. For instance, cardiac toxicity and altered functioning of the reproductive system can occur with some types of antibiotic or hormone therapy.

Other organs that can be damaged by some chemotherapeutic drugs include kidneys, lungs, liver, and peripheral nerves. It is important to look up the expected side effects of the drugs the patient is receiving.[18]

See Table 9-6 for a summary of the general side effects of chemotherapy and suggested nursing actions.

Drug therapy is usually given intermittently to minimize side effects, and a variety of routes are used. Drugs may be administered orally; however, the intravenous route is more common.

When chemotherapeutic drugs are administered intravenously, the drug flows through the entire circulatory system; this is a relatively short and painless procedure.

Some drugs are vesicants and will cause tissue damage if they leak outside the vein. Intravenous sites must be observed carefully, and integrity of the patient's veins must be preserved. Venous punctures should be done only when absolutely necessary. Blood for testing can be obtained by fingerstick.

A new technique for delivering chemotherapy is by use of ambulatory infusion pumps. These portable, battery-operated syringe pumps are designed to deliver continuous drug therapy. The pump is small and light enough to attach to the patient's belt and enables the patient to receive continuous chemotherapy while engaged in daily activities in the community.

The technique of isolation-perfusion has been

Table 9-6

Side Effects of Chemotherapy and Suggested Nursing Actions

Side effect	Intervention
Gastrointestinal	
Nausea	Provide frequent small meals; have patient eat when least nauseated
Vomiting	Suggest effervescent fluids such as soft drinks, which may relieve nausea
Anorexia	Teach patient the need for increased protein, carbohydrates, and vitamins
	Teach patient to have frequent nutritious snacks
Diarrhea	Inform physician if diarrhea is continual
	Instruct patient about importance of maintaining high fluid intake during episodes of diarrhea
Skin—stomatitis (breakdown of the mucous membranes of the mouth)	Teach patient to avoid smoking, alcohol, and irritating food
	Teach patient to brush teeth with soft toothbrush and rinse after brushing with baking soda and water at least twice a day
	Encourage patient to report changes in skin of mouth (bleeding, ulcerations, severe stomatitis)
	Recommend high-protein liquids/blenderized food until mouth sores heal
	Recommend cold food such as frozen fruit sticks or frozen ice cream sticks to ease pain of stomatitis
Alopecia (loss of hair)	Encourage patient to use wigs, scarves, and hats
	Provide opportunities to talk about change in patient's body image
Bone marrow suppression	Obtain complete blood counts as ordered
Leukopenia (reduced WBCs)	Teach patient to report early symptoms of infection, such as fever, cough, sore throat, and urinary frequency
	Instruct patient in good hygiene practices, including perineal care
	Teach patient to avoid crowds during flu season
Thrombocytopenia (reduced platelets)	Teach patient to report early signs of bleeding, such as easy bruising, blood in urine or stool
	Teach patient to avoid physical trauma
Anemia (reduced RBCs and hematocrit)	Teach patient to report symptoms of anemia, such as fatigue, shortness of breath, and dizziness
	Encourage patient to set priorities for activities and to pace daily routine

in use for some time. The tumor area is isolated from the general circulation, and an extracorporeal circulation to the isolated tumor area is established. This method necessitates passing the returning venous blood through an oxygenator and then returning it to the artery.[4] In intraarterial chemotherapy the drug is placed in an artery supplying the tumor area and given under pressure. The tumor receives the full strength of the drug, and the drug is thus weakened before it reaches the general circulation. Not every tumor can be treated by perfusion. Intracavitary therapy involves the instillation of a drug into a body cavity, such as the pleural cavity. The method of administration depends on the type of drug, the location of the tumor, and the condition of the patient.

Since chemotherapy drugs alter the genes of the cell, it is important for the nurse to prevent self-exposure when caring for the patient receiving chemotherapy. Latex gloves should be worn when handling any chemotherapy tubing, waste, and patient excreta for 48 hours after drug administration, since some of the drugs are excreted in the urine and stool.[7,15]

Bone Marrow Transplantation

In the 1980s, **bone marrow transplantation** became an important means of treating leukemia. Transplantation is currently being used in over 15 different diseases including leukemias, lymphomas, multiple myeloma, and various solid tumors.[12]

A bone marrow transplant allows very large doses of drugs to be given to kill all the cancer cells, then restores the patient's bone marrow so that life threatening bleeding or infection is avoided. In leukemia, high doses of chemotherapy and radiation are given to eradicate all leukemic cells from the patient's body as well as to suppress the patient's immunity to donor marrow. The patient's bone marrow is then replaced by bone marrow from a compatible donor or from the patient. There are three basic types of bone marrow transplantation: *autologous*—patient is his or her own donor; *allogeneic*—person with compatible tissue is donor (usually a sibling); *syngeneic*—identical twin is donor.

The donor marrow is obtained from the hip bone using a special syringe and needle. As the procedure can be painful, it is usually done under general anesthesia. The donor may be stiff for a few weeks. The donated bone marrow is infused into the patient's blood stream and travels to the bone where it begins to produce a new population of blood cells. If the marrow successfully grows, (engrafts) and no leukemic cells recur, the patient may be potentially cured of the leukemia.

For several weeks after the transplant, while the new marrow is developing, the patient will be kept in the hospital in a bone marrow transplant unit. During this time he or she will be very susceptible to infections and may bleed easily. Blood products, antibiotics, and antifungal medications can be used to support the patient. Germ-free precautions will be strictly enforced. The patient will be in the hospital for 1 to 2 months, and then followed very closely as an outpatient. The immune system takes up to 9 months to recover.

A complication of allogeneic, but not autologous or syngeneic, transplants is graft versus host disease. This results when the donor T-lymphocytes recognize the patient's cells as foreign and attack them. Symptoms, which can range from minor to severe, include skin rash and peeling, nausea, vomiting, diarrhea, liver dysfunction, photophobia, eye dryness, and burning.

As this major procedure becomes increasingly available in different parts of the country, nurses will be caring for more pretransplant and posttransplant patients. The nurse needs to be prepared to assist the patient and family in coping with both the physical and emotional reactions that result from such an intensive treatment.

Biological Response Modifiers

Although advances in the use of combinations of surgery, radiation therapy, and chemotherapy have resulted in increased survival for cancer patients, effective treatment is still not available for many types of cancer. In recent years, cancer treatment research has focused on the use of **biological response modifiers (BRMs),** which include immunotherapy and biological therapy.

BRMs are agents that make the cancer patient's biological response to the tumor cells more effective. As well as strengthening the patient's immunologic response, some BRMs have direct antitumor activity, and some have other biologic effects that help fight cancer. Research on BRMs is a rapidly expanding field thanks to technologic advances in gene cloning and hybridoma technology. Gene cloning allows production of large quantities of purified human BRMs, and hybridomas can produce monoclonal antibodies against specific tumors.

Earlier attempts at immunotherapy used non-

BRMs Currently Tested Against Cancers

Interferons are naturally produced in response to viral infections. They have many biological actions including antitumor effects. Alpha, beta, and gamma are the three types of interferons.

Interleukin-2 (IL-2) is naturally produced by T-lymphocytes and stimulates the growth of cells called lymphokine-activated killer (LAK) cells that can kill tumor cells.

Tumor necrosis factor (TNF) is a substance produced by certain white blood cells that can directly kill tumor cells causing necrosis but does not harm normal cells.

Monoclonal antibodies are antibodies produced by a single clone of B-lymphocytes directed against an antigen on a tumor cell. They have been called "magic bullets."

Colony stimulating factor (CSF) is another substance produced by certain white blood cells that increases the growth of other white blood cells in the bone marrow. Use of the BRM might allow use of higher doses of chemotherapy drugs by preventing life threatening leukopenia.

Differentiating agents are agents that cause cancerous or precancerous cells to mature into normal cells. These include growth factors and some hormones.

specific stimulation of the immune system with bacteria (BCG or *C. parvum*) or viruses, or active specific immunization with tumor cells. There were some tumor responses reported with these methods, but interest has now shifted to the newer BRMs.

Nursing interventions

BRM therapy results in many of the same side effects as chemotherapy, but there are some unique nursing care problems associated with use of biologic agents. Because many BRMs stimulate the immune system to function more efficiently, patients receiving this therapy will have symptoms similar to those suffered during a bacterial or viral infection. These flulike symptoms include chills, fever, headache, malaise, and fatigue. Comfort measures include body temperature stabilization with use of acetaminophen (Tylenol), appropriate clothing, cooling blankets, and tepid baths. Attention should be paid to proper intake

of fluids and nutrition, and the patient should be allowed plenty of rest. Gastrointestinal effects of nausea, vomiting, anorexia, and altered taste should be dealt with in similar ways to those recommended for chemotherapy patients. BRMs may also cause skin rashes and itchiness, subtle mental status changes, and cardiac and blood circulation dysfunction. Nurses must be alert for any of these physiologic changes in patients receiving BRMs.[10,17]

Immunotherapy has not achieved the success in treating cancer that was once expected. However, research on BRMs is progressing rapidly. Most biologic agents are still investigational but some, like interferon, are being released for more general use. Nurses will become increasingly involved with caring for patients receiving BRMs and will need to be prepared to help manage the side effects.

Unproven Methods

Beyond the above treatment options, there are other methods used. These methods do not withstand scientific trials and have been referred to as quackery. In the last 20 years Laetrile has received extensive publicity as a treatment that might cure cancer. Laetrile was studied by the National Cancer Institute for several years and was found to be a toxic drug that was *not* effective as a cancer treatment. To date, the best hope of cure for cancer lies with the standard treatments—surgery, radiation, chemotherapy, and biotherapy.

EMOTIONAL CARE

One of the most important aspects of care of the patient with cancer is psychologic support. Many times this is more important than the physical care of the patient. Anxiety and depression are common emotional reactions to cancer. Many patients suffer from feelings of guilt and see their illness as a punishment for their own past. Overt anger is also a common behavior pattern in cancer patients and usually is accompanied by acute anxiety. Although they may not be verbalized, these feelings are close to the surface, and hope is the one indispensable aspect of treatment that must permeate all persons involved in the patient's care.

Public education has gone far in making people more conscious of the seriousness of cancer, and although many patients may know consciously or unconsciously that the diagnosis is cancer, they still hope that a cure may be found in time for them. In the past many physicians believed that patients should not be told that they had cancer. Education has resulted in a greatly enlightened public. The modern communication media have been used to present fictional drama concerning cancer. These factors have helped bring about changes in the knowledge and understanding of cancer.

It is believed that a majority of patients suspect or know that they have cancer without being told. The nurse should be aware of statements made by the patient indicating that he is looking for some confirmation of his belief. The patient may say, "I'm sure that I have cancer" or "Did the doctor tell you that I have cancer?" Answers to such statements and questions may not be easy to give. The patient must be allowed to fully express concerns and be given the opportunity to ask questions. It is essential that nursing personnel be aware of the patient's understanding. However, the individual's knowledge or understanding does not eradicate the emotional impact when the cancer diagnosis is given. Cancer is a threat to survival, and most persons want to look forward to life, not death.

When caring for the cancer patient, the nurse must objectively examine personal attitudes and beliefs. The nurse's own feelings about cancer can be projected to the patient and family, both verbally and nonverbally. It is important that the nurse support the therapy being offered to the patient and reassure the patient and family. It is best to stress the progress and events of the day rather than refer to the future optimistically. The nurse must realize that cancer can be cured and that patients can live with cancer under control for many years.

The ability to communicate with the cancer patient does not always involve the spoken word. A soothing back rub, change of position, or refreshing drink may be more meaningful to the patient than any verbal conversation. Members of the patient's family often need emotional support as well as the patient. Giving emotional support to the family may mean providing a blanket or a pillow at night, or giving them a report of the patient's condition during surgery. Collaborative practice between the nurse and physician can be effective in joint understanding of the patient's fears and special problems. The patient with cancer, perhaps more than patients with other conditions, appreciates visits from the hospital chaplain or a minister. The nurse can be helpful in arranging for such visits. When everything has been done for the patient that is humanly possible, and the physician has terminated therapeutic measures, the nurse should continue to provide physical comfort and emotional support to the patient and family.

REHABILITATION

Rehabilitation of the patient with cancer is an obligation of those responsible for his care. The patient is confronted with unique problems that are seldom experienced by patients with other diseases. Often adjustments in body image and self-concept must be made. The patient may have a permanent colostomy, a permanent tracheostomy, loss of voice, or a ureterostomy. The thought of facing life with the loss of these normal functions may be overwhelming to the patient. If mutilating surgery is to be performed, the patient should know before the surgery what to expect and should be assured that care will be provided as well as information regarding self-care.

Patients who are to have laryngectomies should be visited by the speech therapist, who can explain how they will be taught to speak again. In preparation for eventual hospital discharge and after surgery, patients should be permitted to assist with procedures. These procedures may include management of the tracheostomy, suctioning, colostomy irrigations, oral irrigations, or gastrostomy feedings. Patients who have had mastectomies should be taught arm exercises. All patients should be encouraged to return to their normal activities as soon as possible.

If patients are in a terminal phase of illness, they should remain ambulatory and perform daily activities of self-care as long as possible. Many will be able to do so until the last stages of their terminal illness. Although the prognosis may be poor, with only a few months remaining, many patients return to their normal work for weeks or months. Most cancer patients today remain at home and often are employed. Hospitalizations are intermittent and only when necessary. Nursing care can be given in the home by a community health nurse, and hospice programs are available in many communities, often as part of the nursing agency (see Chapter 14 for more detail). While the patient is still hospitalized, the home care nurse may visit the patient to jointly plan for the care that will be needed at discharge.

Often, patients are helped and encouraged when given an opportunity to meet and talk with a person who has had similar surgery. These self-help groups may be very effective for the patient and family. Some of the groups involved in the rehabilitation of patient's with cancer are:

1. *Reach to Recovery.* The American Cancer Society, Inc., (ACS) sponsors this organization. On receiving a physician's referral, a trained ACS volunteer who has had breast cancer surgery will visit a woman who has just had this surgery. The volunteer teaches the woman exercises to help her recover and offers practical advice on adjusting to a mastectomy.

2. *International Association of Laryngectomees.* Also sponsored by the ACS, this organization assists persons with recent laryngectomies to make early adjustments to loss of voice and overcome psychosocial problems. Local clubs may be called "Lost Chord" or "New Voice."

3. *I Can Cope* and *Living with Cancer.* These are educational programs designed to inform cancer patients and their families about this disease. Programs include classes on what cancer is, how to live within its limits, and what resources are available to patients and families.

4. *Make Today Count.* This is a mutual support group for persons with life-threatening illnesses. The purpose is to allow these people to discuss their personal concerns so that they may deal with them in a positive way.

5. *United Ostomy Association.* Local chapters are composed primarily of persons with ostomies, with the purpose of providing mutual aid, moral support, and education to those who have had a colostomy, ileostomy, or urostomy.

REFERENCES AND ADDITIONAL READINGS

1. Abernathy E: Biotherapy: an introductory overview, Oncology Nursing Forum, 14 (6 suppl:13-15, 1987.
2. American Cancer Society, Inc: 1990 cancer facts and figures, Atlanta, Ga, 1990. American Cancer Society, Inc.
3. American Cancer Society, Inc: Taking control: ten steps to a healthier life and reduced cancer risk, Atlanta, 1987, No 201915, American Cancer Society, Inc.
4. Bouchard-Kurtz R and Speese-Owens N: Nursing care of the cancer patient, ed 4, St Louis, 1981, The CV Mosby Co.
5. Brager BL and Yasko J: Care of the client receiving chemotherapy, Reston Va, 1984, Reston Publishing Co, Inc.
6. Brunner LS and Suddarth DS: Textbook of medical-surgical nursing, ed 6, Philadelphia, 1988, JB Lippincott Co.
7. Cloak MM and others: Occupational exposure of nursing personnel to antineoplastic agents, Oncol Nurs Forum 12 (5):33-41, 1985.
8. Haughey CW: CT scans, Nurs 81 11(12):72-77, 1981.
9. Holleb AI: The American Cancer Society cancer book, Garden City, NY, 1986, Doubleday and Co, Inc.
10. Irwin MM: Patients receiving biological response modifiers: overview of nursing care, Oncol Nurs Forum 14(6 suppl):32-37, 1987.
11. Kyba FN, Ogburn-Russell L, and Rutledge JN: Magnetic resonance imaging, Nurs 87 17(1):44-48, 1987.
12. Public Education Information Department: Bone marrow transplantation: questions and answers, New York, 1987, Leukemia Society of America.
13. McNally JC, Stair JC, and Somerville ET, (eds): Guidelines for cancer nursing practice, Orlando, Fla, 1985, Grune & Stratton, Inc.
14. Morra M and Potts E: Choices: realistic alternatives in cancer treatment, rev ed, New York, 1987, Avon Books.
15. Occupational Safety and Health Administration: Work practice guidelines for personnel dealing with cytotoxic (antineoplastic) drugs, Washington, DC, 1986, OSHA-US Department of Labor.
16. Strohl RA: The nursing role in radiation oncology: symptom management of acute and chronic reactions, Oncol Nurs Forum 15(4):429-34, 1988.
17. Suppers VT and McClamrock EA: Biologicals in cancer treatment: future effects on nursing practice, Oncol Nurs Forum 12(3):27-32, 1985.
18. Walters P: Chemo: a nurse's guide to action, administration, and side effects, RN 53(2):52-66, 1990.
19. Wood HA: Radiation therapy implants. In Johnson BL and Gross J (eds): Handbook of oncology nursing, New York, 1985, John Wiley & Sons, Inc.
20. Yasko JM: Care of the client receiving external radiation therapy, Reston, Va, 1982, Reston Publishing Co, Inc.

Death and the Dying Patient

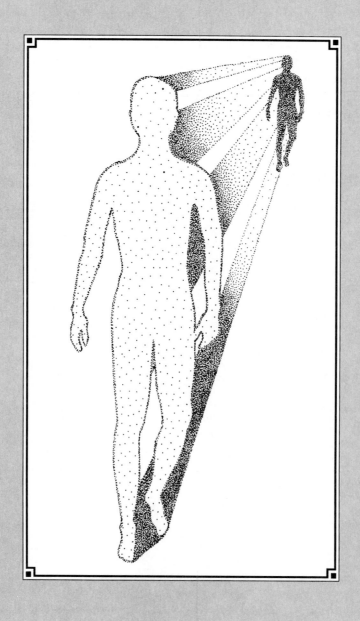

KEY WORDS

acceptance
anger
anticipatory grief
bargaining
bereavement
denial
depression
grief
hospice
living will
respite
thanatology
unfinished business

OBJECTIVES

1. Discuss the changing attitude of society toward death.

2. Define the term "thanatology."

3. Discuss the "living will" and explain how this document contributes to "death with dignity."

4. Discuss fears experienced by the dying patient.

5. Identify the behaviors characteristic of each stage of dying: denial, anger, bargaining, depression, and acceptance.

6. Discuss the phase of grief and bereavement.

7. Identify physical, emotional, and spiritual needs common to the dying patient.

8. Identify expected behavior in the dying patient and suggest nursing interventions that will provide needed support.

DEATH

Until recent years Americans have had the reputation of being a death-denying society. Ministers, nurses, and physicians have experienced long-standing frustrations in attempting to provide support for dying patients and their families.

In the 1960s and 1970s death, dying, grief, and bereavement became the focus of new study and research by various disciplines. Elisabeth Kübler-Ross, through her writings concerning her work with dying patients, peaked the interest of the general public. **Thanatology,** the scientific study of death, found its way into the course offerings of many universities across the United States. Death has become a popular topic of books, articles, film, and video presentations. The hospice movement, discussed in this chapter, had its roots in England and has rapidly developed in the United States as a support system for the dying and their families.

For the nurse, death and dying can be an everyday reality of practice and must be addressed. As Kübler-Ross states, death is the "final" stage of growth and as such should be faced and experienced fully. The nurse has a unique opportunity and a major responsibility to help the patient and his family through the experience of dying and death.[8]

It is necessary to understand how the physiologic and psychologic factors surrounding death affect the individual. Many of the physiologic processes are well known, and the nurse or physician can predict death with reasonable accuracy. However, the psychologic and spiritual impact of impending death on the patient is less understood.

As each patient moves toward his or her own death, each views the experience and accepts death in his or her own way. There is no specific pattern applicable to all persons. Through the study of death and dying, nurses and other members of the health care team will grow in their ability to understand the terminally ill person and provide support for the family and significant others.

When Does Death Occur?

The question of when death occurs is highly controversial. A diagnosis of death is usually made when there is an absence of heartbeat and cessation of respiration. These signs as the only criteria for determining death were questioned when the first transplantation of a human heart was accomplished in 1967. Physicians who were interested in organ transplants believed that a new definition should be found. The principal reason for this is that the organ from a donor must be removed as quickly as possible after death. A question that has not been resolved concerns whether a person is actually dead even though the heart may still be beating.

In an effort to answer the question, "When is death?" physicians employ the electroencephalograph to measure brain activity. They believe that the absence of brain activity, even though the heart is still beating, indicates that death has taken place. Based on this assumption, several definitions have been proposed.

In 1968 Healey and Harvey[14] defined death as "the irreversible cessation of (1) total cerebral function, (2) spontaneous function of the respiratory system, and (3) the circulatory system." Christiaan Barnard believed that a person may be considered dead when (1) the heart shows no electrical activity for 5 minutes, (2) there is no spontaneous respiration, and (3) there is the absence of reflexes.[14] Most physicians accept a definition based on the absence of brain waves.

The use of the electroencephalograph in determining when a person is dead is now commonly used when a patient is being kept alive by extraordinary means and the decision must be made to continue or discontinue life support. In most situations physicians determine death by the more traditional method: absence of heartbeat and cessation of respiratory function. This determination has been a medical responsibility until recently and continues to be so within institutional settings. However, a law passed in 1982 in New Jersey permits registered nurses working with dying patients in home settings to pronounce death when a physician is not available.[13]

Prolongation of Life

New technologies and drugs have made it possible to prolong the lives of some terminally ill patients. Dying patients, when transferred from home to hospital, find themselves surrounded by technologically advanced equipment but often in a lonely, sterile atmosphere without friends or family to support them.

The use of life support measures is a common subject of television programs and magazine articles as well as health care ethics committees. The question is posed: If death is inevitable, should not care be directed toward making the patient as comfortable as possible rather than prolonging life? This problem is dealt with daily in hospitals and nursing homes. The practice of using **extraordinary means** to prolong the life of a terminally ill patient becomes a tangled web of ethical, religious, legal, and moral questions to which there are no decisive answers.

Living Will Documents

Concern for Dying, an educational council in New York, provides national leadership in addressing issues involving the rights of the dying patient. The council has prepared a living will document that enables individuals to state in advance their wishes regarding the use of life-sustaining procedures in the event of terminal illness (Figures 10-1 and 10-2). One of the main goals of Concern for Dying, a nonprofit organization, is the nationwide support for living will legislation. To date 42 states and the District of Columbia have enacted living will legislation that offers guidelines for health care professionals involved in making decisions about life and death. Questions regarding the legality of such documents center around the timing of when the will is drawn up and the mental status of the patient at that time. Living will legislation, although still controversial, is one of the first steps in an attempt to regulate and standardize the criteria on which life-and-death decisions are made for the terminally ill.[10]

The Patient Self-Determination Act became effective in December of 1991. It requires hospitals, nursing homes, hospices, home health care agencies, and provider agencies to advise patients upon admission of their right to accept or refuse medical treatment and their right to execute an advance directive. The advance directive can be in the form of a living will or a durable power of attorney that designates an individual to make decisions about treatment should the patient be unable to make those decisions. It will not be easy for most people to deal with this question and it is hoped that public education will prepare individuals for this event. It is necessary that patients discuss their wishes regarding treatment with the individual given durable power of attorney. The durable power of attorney would cover all health care choices and not be limited to questions related to terminal illness, as is the living will.

In situations lacking previous direction, it becomes the responsibility of the physician to determine what measures are taken. The wishes of the patient and family are sought when possible. The nurse's assessment of the patient and communication with the family contribute to the decision-making process. The nurse is not responsible for these decisions but should encourage communication between all parties so that they are agreeable to the plan of treatment. Timing is important here, as physicians may be willing to withhold treatment but reluctant to withdraw a treatment once started.[16]

The decision to use any measure should be guided by what will contribute to the patient's comfort, safety, and well being. If the use of oxygen relieves labored respiration, it should not be considered a heroic measure. However, administering a new antibiotic drug that can in no way alter the outcome would be considered questionable.

Fear of Dying and Death

A difference exists between the fear of dying and the fear of death. Fear of dying is usually present when the health of the individual is so compromised that there is a distinct possibility that the person may die. This fear may lead the person to seek and/or accept extraordinary measures to prolong life and prevent death.

When all measures used to preserve life have failed and death is imminent, the person may fear death. This fear focuses on the physical cessation of vital functions and what will happen when mortal life ceases. The fear of death may also be related to psychological and spiritual factors, frequently overlooked, which are often of primary importance to the dying patient. The boxed material on p. 222 lists some common fears of dying patients.

Although research into fear of dying is limited, there is some evidence that not all persons fear dying. Kastenbaum and Aisenberg[5] report that fear and anxiety may be experienced by the dying patient, but depression is far more common. The patient with severe, painful physical symptoms may experience anxiety, whereas the patient who is aware of the terminal condition may experience a greater degree of depression.

There are many variables related to the fear of dying, including age, culture, social status, educational and occupational background, serious chronic disease, and the mental health status of the individual. The aged person who has undergone biologic changes characteristic of his or her age group appears to show less fear of dying than a younger person.

Death means the end of everything that an individual has held dear and enjoyed throughout life. Although one mourns his or her loss, fears are primarily related to the unknown. What hap-

To My Family, My Physician, My Lawyer
And All Others Whom It May Concern

Death is as much a reality as birth, growth, and aging—it is the one certainty of life. In anticipation of decisions that may have to be made about my own dying and as an expression of my right to refuse treatment, I, _____, being of sound mind, make this statement of my wishes and instructions concerning treatment. (print name)

By means of this document, which I intend to be legally binding, I direct my physician and other care providers, my family, and any surrogate designated by me or appointed by a court, to carry out my wishes. If I become unable, by reason of physical or mental incapacity, to make decisions about my medical care, let this document provide the guidance and authority needed to make any and all such decisions.

If I am permanently unconscious or there is no reasonable expectation of my recovery from a seriously incapacitating or lethal illness or condition, I do not wish to be kept alive by artificial means. I request that I be given all care necessary to keep me comfortable and free of pain, even if pain-relieving medications may hasten my death, and I direct that no life-sustaining treatment be provided except as I or my surrogate specifically authorize.

This request may appear to place a heavy responsibility upon you, but by making this decision according to my strong convictions, I intend to ease that burden. I am acting after careful consideration and with understanding of the consequences of your carrying out my wishes. *List optional specific provisions in the space below. (See other side.)*

------ **Durable Power of Attorney for Health Care Decisions** (Cross out if you do not wish to use this section) ------

To effect my wishes, I designate _____, residing at _____

_____, (phone #) _____, (or if he or she shall

for any reason fail to act, _____, residing at _____

_____, (phone #) _____) as my health care surrogate—that is, my attorney-in-fact regarding any and all health care decisions to be made for me, including the decision to refuse life-sustaining treatment—if I am unable to make such decisions myself. This power shall remain effective during and not be affected by my subsequent illness, disability or incapacity. My surrogate shall have authority to interpret my Living Will, and shall make decisions about my health care as specified in my instructions or, when my wishes are not clear, as the surrogate believes to be in my best interests. I release and agree to hold harmless my health care surrogate from any and all claims whatsoever arising from decisions made in good faith in the exercise of this power.

I sign this document knowingly, voluntarily, and after careful deliberation, this _____ day of _____, 19____.

_____
(signature)
Address _____

_____

I do hereby certify that the within document was executed and acknowledged before me by the principal this _____ day of _____, 19____.

_____
Notary Public

Witness _____

Printed Name _____

Address _____

_____

Witness _____

Printed Name _____

Address _____

_____

Copies of this document have been given to:

This Living Will expresses my personal treatment preferences. The fact that I may have also executed a declaration in the form recommended by state law should not be construed to limit or contradict this Living Will, which is an expression of my common-law and constitutional rights.

(Optional) my Living Will is registered with Concern for Dying (Registry No. _____)

Distributed by Concern for Dying, 250 West 57th Street, New York, NY 10107 (212) 246-6962

Figure 10-1

A Living Will. *(Reprinted with permission from Concern For Dying, 250 West 57th Street, New York, NY 10107.)*

How to Use Your Living Will

The Living Will should clearly state your preferences about life-sustaining treatment. You may wish to add specific statements to the Living Will in the space provided for that purpose. Such statements might concern:

- Cardiopulmonary resuscitation
- Artificial or invasive measures for providing nutrition and hydration
- Kidney dialysis
- Mechanical or artificial respiration
- Blood transfusion
- Surgery (such as amputation)
- Antibiotics

You may also wish to indicate any preferences you may have about such matters as dying at home.

The Durable Power of Attorney for Health Care

This optional feature permits you to name a surrogate decision maker (also known as a proxy, health agent or attorney-in-fact), someone to make health care decisions on your behalf if you lose that ability. As this person should act according to your preferences and in your best interests, you should select this person with care and make certain that he or she knows what your wishes are and about your Living Will.

You should not name someone who is a witness to your Living Will. You may want to name an alternate agent in case the first person you select is unable or unwilling to serve. If you do name a surrogate decision maker, the form must be notarized. (It is a good idea to notarize the document in any case.)

Important Points to Remember

- Sign and date your Living Will.
- Your two witnesses should not be blood relatives, your spouse, potential beneficiaries of your estate or your health care proxy.
- Discuss your Living Will with your doctors; and give them copies of your Living Will for inclusion in your medical file, so they will know whom to contact in the event something happens to you.
- Make photo copies of your Living Will and give them to anyone who may be making decisions for you if you are unable to make them yourself.
- Place the original in a safe, accessible place, so that it can be located if needed—not in a safe deposit box.
- Look over your Living Will periodically (at least every five years), initial and redate it so that it will be clear that your wishes have not changed.

The Living Will Registry

In 1983, Concern for Dying instituted the Living Will Registry, a computerized file system where you may keep an up-to-date copy of your Living Will in our New York office.

What are the benefits of joining the Living Will Registry?

- Concern's staff will ensure that your form is filled out correctly, assign you a Registry number and maintain a copy of your Living Will.
- Concern's staff will be able to refer to *your* personal document, explain procedures and options, and provide you with the latest case law or state legislation should you, your proxy or anyone else acting on your behalf need counselling or legal guidance in implementing your Living Will.
- You will receive a permanent, credit card size plastic mini-will with your Registry number imprinted on it. The mini-will, which contains your address, Concern's address and a short version of the Living Will, indicates that you have already filled out a full-sized witnessed Living Will document.

How do you join the Living Will Registry?

- Review your Living Will, making sure it is up to date and contains any specific provisions that you want added.
- Mail a photo copy of your original, signed and witnessed document along with a check for $25.00 to: Living Will Registry, Concern for Dying, 250 West 57th Street, Room 831, New York, New York 10107.
- The one-time Registry enrollment fee will cover the costs of processing and maintaining your Living Will and of issuing your new plastic mini-will.
- If you live in a state with Living Will legislation, send copies of any required state documents as well.
- If you have any address changes or wish to add or delete special provisions that you have included in your Living Will, please write to the Registry so that we can keep your file up to date.

Revised March 1989

A LIVING WILL

And Appointment of a Surrogate Decision Maker

Prepared by
CONCERN FOR DYING
An Educational Council

Figure 10-2

A Living Will. *(Reprinted with permission from Concern For Dying, 250 West 57th Street, New York, NY 10107.)*

Common Fears of Dying Patients
1. Unrelenting pain
2. Changes in body image
3. Loss of control of bodily functions
4. Lack of truth-telling regarding physical condition
5. Loss of decision-making control in planning care and quality of life issues
6. Loss of privacy
7. Nonresolution of unfinished business
8. Abandonment by family or significant others
9. Dying alone

pens after death? Is there an afterlife? Is death a painful experience? What will happen to the body after death? The individual who has well-developed spiritual or religious beliefs may have fewer fears about death.

Patients may also have concerns about the losses and grief family members will experience at the time of their death. Family discussions regarding the future helps to allay these concerns. As death approaches and the sensorium changes, fears tend to subside and the patients often appear composed. Kübler-Ross found that when there is opportunity for communication, counseling, and resolution of problems, death can be more easily accepted.[7]

Emotional Stages Experienced in the Dying Process

Observation of terminally ill patients indicates that patients experience stages of well-defined emotional feelings when moving through the dying process.[8] The sequence in which these emotions are experienced is varied. Not all patients experience each of these emotional stages, nor do they exhibit the behavior characteristics of each stage. Family and friends of the patient also experience these emotional stages, and frequently the stage they are experiencing is not synchronized with the stage being experienced by the patient. These stages are identified as denial, anger, bargaining, depression, and acceptance.[7]

Denial

When patients are unable to face the diagnosis of terminal illness, they often deny its existence. In essence they are saying, "No, not me." **Denial** is

a defense mechanism to protect individuals from thoughts they are unable to accept at that time.

Anger

Patients are not ready to accept that their illness is terminal. They become angry and displace that anger on those around them. Patients in this stage may be rude to their family, demanding of the nurse, and hostile to the physician. The patient experiencing anger asks, "Why should it be me?"

Bargaining

Anger may subside and patients begin to think about how they can buy additional time. "Yes me, but . . . ." Their first approach may be to God, negotiating for an extension of time to achieve a long-sought goal in exchange for leading a better life.

Depression

Depression is marked by feelings of loss and despair. "What is the use?" The ravages of disease and illness begin to take their toll; as the patient becomes weaker, illness cannot be denied any longer. The patient becomes sad, may show less interest in visits from family and friends, may withdraw, and become uncommunicative.

Acceptance

The final stage is one of **acceptance.** "I am ready." This stage may be one of active acceptance or a passive state in which the patient is too weak and tired to fight to maintain life any longer. The struggle is over and the patient longs for quiet and rest before a final journey.[7]

All of these five stages may not be observed. Every patient will not pass sequentially from the stage of denial through acceptance in exact order. Patients will often move back and forth entering the next stage and regressing back to a previous stage. The patient's family may experience the same stages, but not necessarily in the same order or at the same time. The patient may still be in the stage of anger while the family has progressed to bargaining. This may cause problems in communication, making it more difficult for them to be supportive of one another. Both will need the assistance of the nurse to work with them through their individual stages. The longer the period of dying, the more likely the patient and the family are to move back and forth from one stage to another.

Even if and when the patient reaches the stage

of acceptance, hope continues. Throughout terminal illness the patient never loses hope that some new drug, treatment, or medical discovery will alter the outcome of the illness. Hope enables the patient to live as fully as possible despite weakness and vulnerability.

GRIEF AND BEREAVEMENT

Grief is a normal emotional reaction to loss. Grief may be in response to the loss of material possessions, of self-identity, or of some body function or part. Separation from loved ones as in war or incarceration may cause one to grieve. Death of a close relative or friend may cause an intense emotional response.

The dying patient may grieve over the loss of independence, the impending loss of life, the meaningful experiences of the past, and the separation from loved ones. When the patient dies, attention is then focused on the significance of the death to family and friends.

Following the death, a period of **bereavement** is experienced by the family and friends of the deceased. More distant members of the family group may also mourn the loss of the relative. Nurses who have had a long association in the area of terminally ill patients may grieve their death. Studies of bereavement indicate that a wide range of behavioral patterns may accompany grief. Some individuals are able to accept the situation and appear to have the emotional stability to adjust to the loss, whereas others may develop psychosomatic complaints. In some instances physical illness may develop after the loss of a close friend or relative. If grieving is not experienced at the time of death, it may be experienced later, at the time of another loss.

Loss of a loved one rates high on the stress scale. Those experiencing the loss are vulnerable to illness. Support from friends and community is an important ingredient in working through the grieving process. Recently developed sources of help available in many communities today are bereavement support groups, often a part of hospital, church, or hospice programs.

According to the United States census, the number of widows far exceeds the number of widowers. Women who lose their husbands are especially vulnerable to bereavement because of its consequences. An elderly woman who loses her husband may not experience the same problems associated with bereavement as a younger widow. Age, stage of development, and life experience are the related factors. To maintain self-respect and self-identity is of paramount importance for the younger widow. The death of a mate can mean deprivation through loss of income, lowering the standard of living to which she is accustomed. Not only is she deprived of her husband's companionship, but she may be left with the responsibility of raising a family alone. If she is not already working, it may become necessary to seek employment to support herself and the children. According to Parkes,[12] when there is loss, there is also deprivation. The individual is most acutely aware of loss at the time of death and may not think about deprivation until some time later. However, deprivation invariably follows loss.

Parkes has indicated that grieving is a psychologic process with three distinct phases. After the death of an individual the survivor may be numb with grief, protesting the reality of the event. The survivor may experience physical changes such as loss of appetite, nausea, inability to sleep, weakness, and restlessness. A feeling of nonreality may exist, and the individual may be preoccupied with thoughts of the deceased. It is during this time that the survivor is surrounded by friends and sympathizers.

After the funeral rites have taken place the support systems often diminish. The individual is alone, and the second phase of grieving begins. This phase is characterized by despair. It is common to experience depression, a decrease in energy level, and a sense of being slowed down in thought process and actions. The final stage, before recovery, is characterized by detachment. Feelings of apathy, loss of interest, and absence of spontaneity may be present. The length of these stages varies, eventually culminating in some subtle "breakthrough" behaviors, such as reaching out to a new activity, interest, or person, accompanied by a fleeting sense of beginning to be able to enjoy some aspects of life once again.

Many variables affect the grieving process, and there is no clear-cut pattern that can be applied to every individual. The stages of grief are said to be similar to the stages of dying. Grief is a response to loss. Therefore it is logical that the bereaved, like the dying person, will move along a similar but individual path. For some persons the period of grief may be only a few weeks, whereas for others it may last more than a year. The process may vary if the death is sudden and

---

Characteristic Experiences of the Grieving Process
1. Feelings of nonreality
2. Despair
3. Detachment
4. Breakthrough behaviors
5. Recovery

unexpected, or if it occurs after a prolonged terminal illness. If the family or loved ones have participated in the care and support of the patient, a part of the grief work will take place before the death. This phenomenon is referred to as **anticipatory grief** and is thought to assist the individual in moving at a faster pace through the grieving process.

NURSING CARE OF THE DYING PATIENT

The nurse's responsibility in caring for dying patients includes caring for their families and friends as well as for themselves. Several studies indicate that nurses sometimes avoid dying patients. It has been proposed that the reason is that caring for the dying patient stimulates nurses to think about their own deaths.

Schoenberg[16] believes that there are three factors relevant to the nursing care of the dying patient. First, the educational system fails to teach the student nurse how to care for the dying patient. Second, the system of medical practice in the hospital is one of noninvolvement, thus discouraging the nurse from providing more than the basic elements of care. Third, the nurse does not receive the emotional support necessary to work through personal feelings and develop a philosophy about the care of the dying patient. Recently, efforts have been made to incorporate content on working with the dying patient into the curricula of both nursing and medical schools.

In working with the terminally ill, the nurse grows along with the patient and family. The nurse moves through the same stages of grieving as the family and patient. To fulfill the emotionally demanding role of providing support to the patient, the nurse must be able to receive support from some other source. Individual sessions with more experienced nursing personnel, as well as group sessions with pastoral care staff, social workers, and psychologists are used as methods of providing support to the nurse. An expansion of this type of support system is desirable to help nurses grow through these experiences and to prevent staff burnout.

The nursing care of the terminally ill patient deals with the physical, psychosocial, and spiritual health of the patient. Terminal illness does not mean that the patient is facing immediate death. Many illnesses from which the patient is not expected to recover are marked by long remissions that are punctuated by exacerbations at infrequent intervals. Such is the case with cancer and AIDS.

During the patient's admission to the hospital the nurse should come to know the patient, learning about the social and cultural background, religious or spiritual orientation, and personal problems that are of particular concern. The nurse should assess how the patient is dealing with the illness and identify the emotional stages the patient and family are experiencing in the dying process. In addition, the nurse can assist the patient in identifying the **unfinished business** of life—those matters the patient wishes to address before death.

Many patients are aware of their prognosis, whereas others may not be. Some patients, suspecting they have a terminal illness, will seek confirmation from the nurse. The nurse should be aware of this possibility and be prepared to handle it sensitively. It is especially important that the nurse know what the physician has told the patient and the family. Many experts in the field of death and dying believe that the patient always knows the truth whether or not the family or physician has shared the prognosis. In this case the nurse can be of greatest help to the patient by facilitating and encouraging open expressions of feelings and concerns. By conveying this information to the physician and the family, the nurse can assist all parties involved to face the subject of death openly.

If staffing patterns permit, the same nurse should be assigned to care for the patient on each admission. When this is possible, the patient develops a feeling of trust, security, and confidence. When the patient is admitted for the last time, the personal relationship that has been established may help to bridge the gap between living and dying.

Death Following Traumatic Injury

Supporting patients and families in the intensive care unit following sudden and unanticipated traumatic injury provides a special challenge to the nurse when death is imminent. In today's technologically advanced environment it is possible to lose sight of the patient as a person and to disregard what the patient considers to be in his or her best interests. High priority should be placed on comfort and communication in regard to both patient and family. These are crucial elements in ensuring a dignified death for the terminally ill patient. Often the nurse's role is one of asking questions to help the patient, family, and physician steer the situation toward responsible and appropriate treatment.[16]

When death is inevitable, the patient and family have few choices. In many situations organ and tissue donations are choices that can be offered to the patient and family. Giordano states that offering this option to a grieving family can be a final act of care in assisting them through their grief. The nurse must be well informed about the policies and procedures of the hospital and unit and be able to provide this information to the family. The nurse may also help in determining which family member to approach when a potential donor is identified. This individual should be the family member who has demonstrated emotional strength and clear thinking throughout the ordeal. The consent of the next of kin will also be required. Organs presently used for transplant include the kidney, heart, liver, pancreas, heart, and lung. Tissue identified are the eyes, skin, bone, heart valves, and others.[3]

The Hospice Movement

The special needs of the dying patient and his family are addressed by the **hospice** concept. The term "hospice," in its original use, meant a resting place for travelers on a difficult journey. The hospice concept had its beginnings in England and has rapidly spread throughout the United States in the last decade.

There are three basic types of hospices: home-based, which provides a support system to enable a patient to die at home; free standing, which is available as a haven for the terminally ill to come to die; and defined areas or teams, which exist in the general hospital setting. The hospice concept requires the cooperation of various disciplines, including nurses, physicians, pharmacists, social workers, dieticians, clergy, and volunteers. All work together to address the terminally ill patient's physical, emotional, and spiritual needs (Figure 10-3).

Figure 10-3
Hospice team. *(Courtesy of Hospice of the North Shore, Evanston, Ill.)*

The following goals are basic to hospice care:
1. Maintaining the patient in as symptom-free a state as possible. In some cases this means addressing the problem of pain control. The nurse, physician, and pharmacist work together to keep the patient as nearly free of pain as possible and at a level of alertness that will enable interaction with family and friends.
2. Supporting the patient to continue to define quality of life, maintain control, and make decisions about care.
3. Encouraging patients to live fully, supporting them in their efforts to communicate with family and friends in tying up the unfinished business of life. The nurse, social worker, and clergy often work together to attain this goal.
4. Being available to the family, providing them with individualized and appropriate support. Volunteers are important members of the hospice team in providing **respite** care for family members, as well as assistance in household chores and running errands.

If nurses are in tune with the needs of dying patients, many of these goals can be accomplished in either the home or hospital setting.

As previously stated, a patient faces death in an individual way. In most instances the patient does not want to feel abandoned and desires the presence of a close friend or relative. Frequent visits to the patient's room by the nurse, a gently placed hand on the patient's shoulder, and a kindly spoken word convey to the patient that he or she is not alone. Small objects belonging to the patient, such as family pictures, should be placed within easy viewing distance. The creative use of light, flowers, and music can provide a comforting atmosphere. The patient should be placed in an area where he or she can hear people moving about and thus not feel alone.

Nursing Interventions
Physical care

The physical care of the patient must continue to the end. The patient may be unable to take care of personal hygiene needs. Bathing, including perineal, oral, and skin care, and a regular schedule for turning the patient are essential. Oral care must not be neglected. Many terminally ill patients breathe through their mouths, which causes mucous membranes to become dry and sore. Poor oral condition will interfere with speech and swallowing. When dentures cannot be worn, drooling will occur. Pathogenic organisms and oral secretions may cause stomatitis and maceration of tissues around the mouth. These conditions may cause the patient actual pain.[16] Oral care should be given at regular intervals and be sufficient to keep the tissues clean and free from odor.

Terminal illness is often accompanied by pain. Ongoing assessment of pain is important. The patient's need for frequent pain medication administered intramuscularly for greater effectiveness is often the only reason the patient remains in the hospital, rather than going home to die. Pain and the effects of the pain medication affect the patient's appetite, leading to poor nutritional status and further debilitation. The sensory effects of the pain medication can make it impossible for the patient to think clearly and to deal effectively with loved ones. Recent developments in pain control include new methods of using morphine. An increase in the use of oral morphine is noted. Higher concentrated solutions of morphine are available for oral use, as well as sustained-release morphine tablets. The use of a stool softener is an important adjunct to pain control medication to prevent the additional discomfort of constipation.

Effective pain control is possible if medications are given around the clock, with the dosage adjusted according to the patient's individual and changing needs. This method of medication administration is more successful in controlling pain breakthrough and erasing pain memory. It replaces the demand or prn method.

Emotional support

As noted previously, patients who have a terminal illness experience a variety of emotional responses. It is important that the patient express these feelings. The nurse can best facilitate expression of feelings by being an attentive listener. The patient may be demanding and angry, tearful, or withdrawn. The nurse's continued presence and support during these times conveys feelings of care and concern, lessening the patient's fear of abandonment. Attentive listening will enable the nurse to identify the patient's specific concerns or unfinished business. If the nurse is not able to assist the patient in problem solving, referral may be made to a social worker, a minister, or a psychiatrist, as appropriate to the situation.

Reminiscence therapy and relaxation techniques may also be effective in providing emotional support to the patient. In addition, the use of humor has been recognized as playing an important part in interacting with the terminally ill. Humor is thought to provide a sense of power and self-worth when emotional pain is overwhelming.[4] Herth states that humor is closely related to self-concept and provides a sense of perspective, hope, and joy. This serves to empower the individual, resulting in a sense of control over life. Shared humor also serves as a connecting mechanism diminishing the feelings of isolation associated with dying.

Spiritual support

Preparation for providing support to patients in spiritual matters begins with nurses assessing their feelings regarding their own deaths and dying experiences. Identifying personal spiritual beliefs is a process that continues throughout a nurse's career and lifetime, enabling continued growth in the nurse's supporting skills.

If the nurse can suspend judgment and tendencies to interpret and analyze, an atmosphere of openness can be created for discussing the patient's spiritual concerns. It is within this climate that patients may feel comfortable sharing their spiritual philosophy or religious beliefs. Listening and affirming the patient's beliefs and assisting the patient to participate in familiar religious rituals are essential. When requested to do so, the nurse may pray with or read to the patient from the patient's personal religious text. Regardless of the nurse's beliefs, support should be provided to the patient within the patient's own spiritual or religious framework. With the patient's permission, referral can be made to the patient's minister or the hospital pastoral care staff.

Support of the family

Being attentive to the needs of the patient's family is an extension of caring for the dying patient. Emotional support at this time includes providing time for the family to spend with the patient with as few interruptions as possible. A quiet and private place where the family can be together is also important. Family members should be given the opportunity to express their feelings as death approaches.

When the patient dies, the family should have the opportunity to view and spend time with the deceased family member. After removal of the body, the nurse should assist the family in gathering the patient's belongings. A dignified man-

ner in handling the body and the patient's belongings may convey to the family the nurse's respect for the deceased and concern for their feelings. The box below provides additional guidelines for the care of the dying patient and his family.

Following Death

Each hospital, county, and state has its own policies and procedures regarding death, in addition to the legal requirements for autopsy, signing death certificates, and interstate transport of bodies. Nurses should become familiar with the policies and procedures of the hospital, county, and state in which they practice.

Guidelines for the Care of the Dying Patient and his Family

1. Decisions concerning the use of extraordinary means to prolong life are the responsibility of the patient, the family, and the physician. Input from other members of the health care team may often be helpful.
2. Encouraging the patient to be a decision maker concerning his or her care and treatment for as long as the condition permits is basic to maintaining dignity and feelings of self-worth.
3. It is the responsibility of the nurse to see that physical care and emotional and spiritual support are available to the dying patient. The nurse plays an important part in this care and should involve others of the health care team as is appropriate.
4. The patient may identify one or two members of the family or the hospital staff with whom he or she feels comfortable discussing innermost feelings. Choices of these individuals should be respected.
5. The nurse should assess how the patient's family members and friends are dealing with the impending loss of their loved one and should encourage them to express their feelings and direct them toward additional support from the health care team as is necessary.
6. Various cultures and religions have ritualistic practices that help a bereaved individual to move through the grief process. These should be encouraged and respected.
7. The expression of feelings of guilt by the bereaved in regard to past life experiences with the deceased is a common occurrence.
8. Family and friends should be made aware of local bereavement support groups.

Case Study

Mr. Brian D. is a 32-year-old homosexual diagnosed with AIDS. He has been hospitalized for 7 days because of recurring high fever, cachexia, and a persistent, debilitating cough. For several days Mr. D. has refused inhalation therapy and other treatments. He has requested to have the blinds drawn in his room during the day shift and has spent the last 2 days lying with his eyes closed facing the wall when awake. Today he refused both his breakfast and lunch trays. In replying to the nurse's statement of concerns he stated, "I feel sad and empty. How can God let this happen to me?" He asks the nurses to tell his family and partner, Bruce, that he prefers not to see them during visiting hours.

Nursing diagnosis: spiritual distress[10]
Related data:

1. Withdrawn, lying with eyes closed facing wall
2. Flat affect
3. Does not comply with treatment regimen
4. Lack of appetite
5. States "I feel sad and empty. How can God let this happen to me?"
6. Refuses visitors

Expected outcomes

1. The patient will express anger and other feelings.
2. The patient will increase his or her level of acceptance of self, God, and others.
3. The patient will experience an increased sense of meaning in living with an illness.
4. The patient will maintain communication with and accept support from partner and family.
5. The patient will develop an increased sense of hope and inner peace.

Nursing interventions

1. Take time to sit with the patient and listen in a nonjudgmental manner.
2. Nonjudgmental listening—encourage the patient to reminisce about past experiences and their significance to his or her life. Help the patient focus on successes and the value of positive experiences.
3. Assist the patient to place the illness experience into the context of the total life experience. Pray with patient as patient desires.
4. Discuss the patient's significant relationships with family and partner and ways to maintain and strengthen them. Discuss grace in relation to accepting help from others. Provide for privacy needs during visiting hours. Be available to family with ideas on how to best support the patient.
5. Assist the patient in relaxation techniques. Suggest use of music therapy, meditation, and prayer. Offer referral to pastoral care per patient's wishes.

Adapted from Standard care plans, spiritual distress and hope, McFarland G and McFarland E: Nursing diagnosis and intervention, St Louis, 1989, The CV Mosby Co.

REFERENCES AND ADDITIONAL READINGS

1. Anderson G and others: Living wills: do nurses and physicians have them? Am J Nurs 86:271-275, 1986.
2. Amanta M: Hospice in the United States: multiple models and varied programs. Nurs Clin North Am 20(1):269-279, 1985.
3. Giordano M: Organ and tissue donation: a nurses's final act of care, J Adv Med Surg Nurs 2(1):59-63, 1989.
4. Herth K: Contributions of humor as perceived by the terminally ill, Am J Hospice Care 7(1):36-40, 1990.
5. Kastenbaum R and Aisenberg RB: The psychology of death, New York, 1972, Springer Publishing Co, Inc.
6. Kovalev M and Vermel I: The legal definition of death, World Health 9:1143, 1982.
7. Kübler-Ross E: On death and dying, New York, 1969, The Macmillan Co.
8. Kübler-Ross E: Death: the final stage of growth, Englewood Cliffs, NJ, 1975, Prentice-Hall, Inc.
9. The living will—where it stands, Geriatric nursing 6(1):18-20, 1985.
10. McFarland G and McFarlane E: Nursing diagnosis and intervention, St Louis, 1989, The CV Mosby Co.
11. Miller J: Inspiring hope, Am J Nurs 85:22-25, 1985.
12. Parkes CM: Bereavement, New York, 1972, International Universities Press, Inc.
13. Reinhard S and Aughenbaugh DA: Policy for pronouncement of death, Nurs & Health Care 6:489-491, 1985.
14. The right to die with dignity, New York, 1971, Euthanasia Educational Fund, Inc.
15. Schoenberg B and others: Psychosocial aspects on terminal care, New York, 1972, Columbia University Press.
16. Wilson V and Jacobson E: How can we dignify death in the ICU? Am J Nurs 90(5):38-42, 1990.

CHAPTER

11

The Geriatric Patient

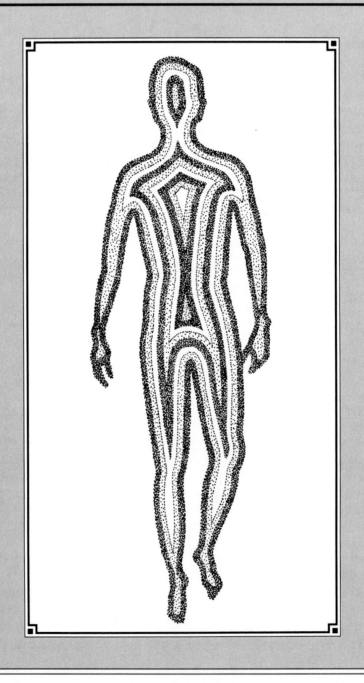

KEY WORDS

Alzheimer's disease
biopsychosocial
delirium
dementia
diagnosis-related groups
geriatrics
gerontology
home care
life span
Medicare
nursing home
reality orientation
reminiscing
remotivation
retirement
senescence
sexuality

OBJECTIVES

1. Differentiate between "geriatrics" and "gerontology."
2. Discuss the effects of the increasing number of persons over 65 years of age on the health care system in the United States.
3. Discuss socioeconomic and cultural factors that affect persons over age 65.
4. Identify biologic, psychologic, and social changes related to aging.
5. Identify the typical adjustments required of the aging person.
6. Discuss the factors involved in maintaining mental health for the person over age 65.
7. Discuss current theories of the causes of aging.
8. Discuss the effects of aging on intelligence and memory.
9. Identify the physiologic changes that occur with aging.
10. Identify assessment techniques used to evaluate the physiologic changes of aging.
11. Identify nursing interventions related to physiologic changes that occur with aging.
12. Discuss nursing measures to prevent injury and promote comfort for the aged person.
13. Describe the modifications in diet required by those over age 65.
14. Identify factors that contribute to sexual satisfaction in the elderly person.
15. Discuss the effects of age-related pathophysiologic changes on drug action and toxicity.
16. Discuss the reaction of the elderly to central nervous system depressants and stimulants.
17. Explain the need for reducing dosages of most drugs prescribed for the elderly.
18. Identify alternatives to institutional care of the aged person.

TERMINOLOGY

Some of the terms associated with the care of the aging patient include geriatrics, gerontology, and senescence.

The term **geriatrics** is defined by Webster's as the branch of medicine that deals with the diseases and problems of old age and aging people.[29] It is derived from the Greek word, geras, meaning old age.

GERONTOLOGY

Gerontology is the scientific study of the process of aging and its phenomena (facts and events).[29] The science of gerontology is interdisciplinary and includes the social, biologic, and psychologic aspects of aging, and iatros, meaning physician.

Senescence represents the last stage in the life cycle. It is preceded by the process of growth and development during which the individual attains maturity; then a gradual decline begins. Senescence is not a pathologic condition but a normal biologic process (see Figure 11-1).

DEMOGRAPHICS

It has been stated that the elderly comprise the fastest growing minority group in the United States. In 1900 only 4% of the population was 65 years of age or older. In 1989, there were an estimated 31 million people, or 12.5% of the population, who were 65 years of age or over. It has been predicted that by the year 2030, 50 million people will be age 65 or over and will make up 17% of the total population.

As the number and proportion of older adults increases, the proportion of working adults (ages 18 to 64) decreases. This means that there are fewer persons contributing to the national economy and fewer family members to provide support for the elderly, both financially and in times of crises. Thus the government may have to assume a greater role in providing these services to the older population.[11]

Since the turn of this century, life expectancy has greatly increased, from an average of 47.3 years in 1900 to 75 years for the person born in 1984. In general, women live longer than men.

Geographically, there has been a gradual shifting in locale of the elderly. During the decade of the 1960s alone, 500,000 elderly persons left the northern states while the southern states gained 450,000. The area with the largest number of elderly people is the South (8.5 million) followed by the North Central with 6.5 million, the Northeast with 6 million, and the West with 4 million.[11]

What do these statistics mean to the nurse and the nursing profession? There are significant changes in the increasing number of elderly persons needing the expertise of nurses prepared in geriatric care. It can be predicted with reasonable accuracy that this trend will continue for many decades. The increase in life expectancy means that people are healthier as they move into their later years. They will need information and guidance regarding health promotion and maintenance to keep them in a healthy state. Longer life

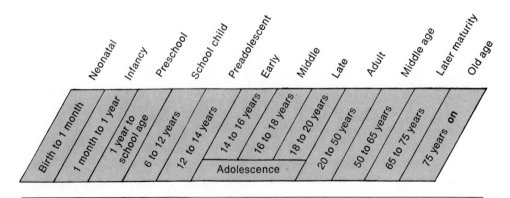

Figure 11-1

Life span is continuous but has been divided into stages, each presenting different needs. Geriatric patient is near end of continuum and has his own special needs.

expectancy means that many more people will move into the "old-old" population.[3] This group will create the most intensive demand for health care services, especially long-term care services. Nurses have long been the caretakers of the elderly, and nurses should avail themselves of every opportunity to increase their understanding and skill in meeting the nursing needs of this population (Table 11-1).

PROGRESS AND RESEARCH

It may be said that since 1961, when the first White House Conference on Aging was held, there has been a new awakening to the needs of the elderly. Although many recommendations were formulated and submitted to this conference, one of the most important was the eventual enactment of legislation establishing **Medicare** and the Older Americans Act.

Benefits under Medicare became available July 1, 1966. Some changes have been made in the original act; however, millions of older Americans have received and are continuing to receive hospital and medical care under its provisions. The Older Americans Act became law in 1965. Since then, numerous changes and amendments have been made, and some parts have been completely rewritten. Certain parts of the act are administered by the federal government through the Department of Health and Human Services, whereas other parts are implemented by state and local agencies. The act covers a wide range of services to the elderly.

Special emphasis has been placed on meeting nutritional needs of elderly persons. Numerous programs are funded under various parts of the Older Americans Act. Among these programs are homemaker services, home health aides, foster grandparents program, employment referrals, housing, health screening, research and demonstration programs, and training programs in the field of aging.

The Social Security Act as revised in 1965 and its subsequent amendments provide monthly benefits for elderly persons. Periodic increases in benefits have been granted to cover increased living costs. Along with the Social Security benefit, the ceiling on earned income has been raised without loss of the monthly benefit. This makes it possible for elderly persons to continue part-time work. Many universities and medical centers have opened research centers to study the biologic and psychologic factors related to aging to also improve the aged person's quality of life.

Although tremendous strides have been made to provide a better life for millions of elderly Americans in the United States, not all are receiving these benefits. Many communities have active ongoing programs, whereas other communities lag far behind with little interest in improving the life of the elderly.

Table 11-1

Nine Most Common Causes of Death Among Persons 75 Years and Older By Frequency of Occurrence per 100,000 Population of That Age Group		
	Men	**Women**
Heart disease	3498	2245
Malignancies	1840	948
Cerebrovascular accident (CVA)	661	572
Chronic obstructive pulmonary disease (COPD)	505	164
Pneumonia and flu	338	184
Accidents	149	83
Diabetes	129	128
Suicide	53	7
Liver disease	43	25

From U.S. Bureau of the Census: 1988. Statistical abstract of the United States, 108th ed., US Government Printing Office, Washington, DC. (In Ebersole P and Hess P: Toward healthy aging, ed 3, 1990, The CV Mosby Co.)

FACTORS AFFECTING AGING

Cultural and Ethnic Factors

Many variations exist in the cultural patterns of different groups of people, as well as within families at different periods. In early Oriental cultures the older members of society were revered and called the "wise ones." In primitive cultures the elderly persons were the source for information and knowledge. They always knew where to find food and water, and they traveled with the tribe. When they became too feeble to travel and could not be cared for, they accepted death. In the early culture of the United States the older citizens were also important. They were consulted about the political and educational affairs of the community. They were respected because of the knowledge that they had acquired during their lives. Present-day American culture is youth oriented, and the elderly occupy a lower position and endure lower prestige. They may look back with feelings of nostalgia to a time when there was solidarity of the family unit, and youth showed respect and devotion to the aged members of the family. The social system imposes retirement and forces the individual to find new roles at a time when it is more difficult to make decisions than it was at an earlier age. Limited financial resources affect most elderly as inflation reduces the buying power of a fixed income from pensions or Social Security payments.

Socioeconomic Factors

Housing is a pressing problem. The elderly wish to remain in their own homes, in familiar surroundings. In the earlier agricultural society this was inevitable because many generations shared the same homestead. When grandparents became less capable of taking care of themselves, the children were there to care for them. In today's society, we find each nuclear family—mother, father, and children—in a separate home. When the children grow up, they in turn establish their own home, leaving mother and father in an "empty nest." As mother and father grow old and infirm and become unable to maintain a household or care for themselves, they may be forced to leave their home. Whether they move in with one of their children or enter a home for the aged, an adjustment is necessary and often difficult. Often, abrupt changes are made without consideration of individual differences and needs. Lifetime patterns are not easily changed and must be evaluated in terms of what they mean to the individual.

Mrs. Smith, an 83-year-old widow, lived in two small basement rooms of a house in a textile mill village. The public health nurse was appalled at the lack of sanitation and sought ways to place Mrs. Smith in a clean, comfortable room. When Mrs. Smith was approached with the suggestion, her reply was, "All I want is to be left alone with my things."

Under the Federal Housing Act, funds have been made available for construction of housing units for the aged. "High rise" apartment complexes for the elderly are found in many urban areas. Many of these provide no other services for the elderly; although they may solve the problem of housing, they may create numerous other problems for the residents.

Many elderly are forced to leave their homes because of urban renewal and readjust their life-long patterns of living.

Mrs. Clay had lived for 46 years in the home that had been her parents'. However, when urban renewal came, Mrs. Clay had to move. In reference to her new home Mrs. Clay said, "I like it quite well, but it's very inconvenient. You see, I was right there in town. Out here I have to call a taxi every time, and I don't always have the money."

Not all elderly are confronted with this problem. Those with adequate financial resources are able to maintain their desired life-style, but the majority of the elderly need assistance through community services. The elderly of tomorrow need to plan today.

Retirement and Aging

During the early history of the United States when the economy was rural and agricultural, there was little concern about **retirement.** Individuals worked well into their later years, and even when they were advanced in years, chores kept the elders occupied and provided an opportunity for them to make a contribution to society. Today's society remains essentially work oriented, but the twentieth century finds the older worker pressured into retirement to provide jobs for the young.

Retirement is now mandatory for many people at age 70. Although retirement is thought of as a positive reward for labor, a special time free from worry, many persons facing retirement have difficulty coping with this abrupt change in life-style. The increased number of women in today's labor force makes retirement a concern for men and women alike.

In retirement, sustained activity is no longer required. The absence of social roles for the elderly makes a work substitute difficult to find. Enforced inactivity over an extended period can be harmful to the health of the retired person. Add to this the effect of bereavement for a spouse, friends, and even children, and there may be a tendency for the individual to give up and withdraw.

The basic needs of the retired older worker are to feel financially secure, to be useful, to form new associations and interact with people, to maintain a sense of dignity and self-respect, and to feel needed and wanted in society. The fulfillment of these needs begins in the middle years of life by careful planning for the future and requires that society provide roles for its older members.

Biopsychosocial Factors
Causes of Aging

The biologic process of aging causes physiologic changes in the total human organism. Changes usually develop slowly, and many persons consider themselves to be in good health. Although these changes vary among individuals, most elderly persons complain of physical symptoms that should be given medical attention. While proclaiming good health, the individual may have poor nutrition, need dental care or dentures, need glasses, may be constipated, need a hearing aid, or be dehydrated. In addition, many elderly persons have pathologic conditions that require hospital, medical, and nursing care. Frequently, the stressful situations related to psychosocial problems affect the physical condition of the individual.

Scientists continue to investigate the cause of aging, not only to extend life, but to achieve a life free of degenerative disease. Some believe that the aging process is programmed by genes, whereas others theorize that it is related to a chemical block of thyroxine. The most recent evidence relates the aging process to the immune system. It has been found that a type of white blood cell, the T cell, provides resistance to cancer cells, viruses, bacteria, and fungi, but loses its effectiveness with age and therefore the host loses immunity to disease. It is believed that these cells decrease because the thymus gland shrinks with age, and it is the thymus gland that secretes chemicals stimulating the bone marrow cells to produce T cells.

Experiments have been conducted in which T cells removed from animals were frozen for as long as 15 years and then reinjected. The T cells maintained their youthful immune powers while frozen and were perfectly normal when thawed. When the frozen cells were reintroduced into the aging host, the immune system returned to the potency found in young adulthood. Scientists believe that this dwindling immunity is responsible for the degenerative diseases of aging such as cancer, arthritis, diabetes, and kidney disease, as well as an increase in susceptibility to infection. The prospect of controlling the degeneration that ac-

companies old age is, indeed, an extremely exciting one.

Mental Health

It is generally believed that individuals who were well adjusted and able to meet problems and make adaptations during their younger years are better prepared to face problems with advancing years. Erikson identified this stage of life as that of ego integrity versus despair. Erikson defines integrity as "the acceptance of one's own and only life cycle and of the people who have become significant to it as something that had to be and that, by necessity, permitted no substitutions."[10] Achieving integrity means that the individual accepts past events, experiences, and lifestyle, including the mistakes one has made along the way. The person who does not achieve ego integrity feels despair or disgust about the course of one's life, and may blame circumstances on someone or something else. He or she experiences regret that it is too late to start over or change that life.

The older person may be confronted with fears of illness, physical suffering, helplessness, and death. Chronic disease or illness results in low morale, but when meaningful friendships exist, even when health is poor, the individual is less likely to suffer from low morale. At these times a mental health clinic can provide emotional support and give the individual a feeling of friendship, warmth, and a sense of personal worth.

Many elderly persons depend on others for part or all of their care. Dependency results in loss of dignity, diminished self-esteem, and lowered morale. When disease and illness are superimposed on normal aging changes, adaptation is difficult for the individual.

The dependency that elderly persons experience may give rise to feelings of resentment toward family, friends, or those trying to help. They may become demanding, tend to magnify normal aches and pains, and complain of loss of sleep and of various digestive disturbances. However, vague symptoms can be indicative of underlying pathologic conditions. It must be remembered that older persons have many adjustments to make at a period of their lives when they tolerate stress situations poorly. Following are some adjustments that the older person may have to make:

1. Death of a spouse, friends
2. Retirement and reduced income

3. Identification with an older age group
4. Adjustment to depleted physical energy and a gradually changing body.

Most elderly persons become aware of the shortness of time. They become concerned about changes in their bodies and their loss of strength or the presence of disease. The grief after the loss of a spouse or close friend may cause the person to question continued existence. The individual may progress to a state of depression and prefer self-destruction to continuation of life. With the increased incidence of geriatric suicide, the nurse caring for elderly patients should be alert to warning signs. The person who expresses a desire to die or makes threats of suicide should not be taken lightly. It is during such periods of loneliness and depression that the individual needs emotional support. Some communities have volunteers who make regular visits or frequent telephone calls to elderly persons. An 85-year-old woman who has lost all of her family lives alone in her home. She often says, "I wish the Lord would take me. No one calls me, and I just sit here alone for days."

Many of the concepts held concerning psychosocial factors in old age have never been proved and are now being questioned. It is only recently that research, although limited, has enabled society to learn some of the factors that affect the social life and attitudes of elderly persons.

It has been stated that chronologic age may be unrelated to old age. Elderly people are individuals and must be treated as such. It has been suggested that older persons represent a "subculture." Society has fostered such a culture through community programs that tend to segregate older persons, such as senior citizen centers, golden age groups, and adult day-care centers. These programs take older persons out of the mainstream of society and provide little opportunity for interaction with younger persons.

There is a wide range of activities designed to keep older persons in the mainstream of life and in contact with society. Some of these activities operate under the Older Americans Act and others through local community programs. The success of a mental health program for the elderly depends on a social consciousness within the community that is oriented toward mental health. The nurse can be an innovator of new ideas and can be a source of inspiration, not only to individuals but also the community in the development of an ongoing mental health program for its elderly population.

Maintaining mental health does not mean doing *for* the older person; it means doing *with* the older person. A large number of elderly citizens want something to do and want to feel that they are useful. Many are ambulatory and able to remain in their own homes, where they are happier. For some this is not possible. Older persons face many social and economic problems in later life. In many instances these problems can have a profound impact on their lives. A community counseling service should be available where the person may have privacy, quiet, and an unhurried atmosphere to talk over problems. Groups of elderly persons in the community can be formed to develop social contacts. With the help of a group leader, the members of the group assist each other in devising methods to handle problems faced in the community.

Aging and Intelligence

It is a myth that intelligence decreases with age. Although the elderly will achieve lower scores on intelligence tests, this is usually because of slower reaction time and more time needed to complete the examination rather than a deficit in the ability to think. The elderly replace speed with accuracy, and research shows that they often do better than younger persons when the time limit is removed. Leading an active life, including the mastery of new knowledge and skills, is considered essential to maintaining intelligence in the elderly.

Aging and Memory

It is common in our society to place the blame on advancing age when one experiences any lapse in memory. Scientific tests have shown that depression, not aging, is more often the cause of memory lapse.[30]

The elderly are sometimes described as rigid in their approach to problem solving. The tendency to persist in a particular approach to a problem despite additional information suggesting a change is believed not to be associated with the age of this individual but with the level of education achieved. It is also demonstrated that the greater the number of years that has elapsed since the individual was involved in formal schooling, the more likely it is that the individual will solve problems by the application of relevant items in his stored experience. Analyzing a problem and employing a new solution depend on recent exposure to this type of thinking, which is commonly found in the educational setting. All of these facts point to the importance of continued lifelong learning in the maintenance of mental functioning.

PHYSIOLOGY OF AGING

When a person has reached maturity, a gradual aging of all body tissues and organs begins. Loss of cells and loss of physiologic reserves make up the dominant processes of aging. By the time a person has reached 70 years of age, the aging process may be well advanced. The rate and extent of aging varies among individuals, and the rate at which various organs age may also vary. Although there is considerable variation among individuals and within the same person, the years of physiologic change are often long and protracted. Table 11-2 shows various physiologic changes in elderly persons.

Cardiovascular System

The heart size usually remains the same, but it may decrease in size as a result of decreased physical demands and activity. The heart rate becomes slower and cardiac output is reduced; as a result, there is less blood carrying oxygen and nutrients to all the organs and tissues in the body. This in turn affects the function of these organs. In the presence of stress, physical or psychologic, reduced cardiac output means there is less oxygen to meet the increased need caused by the stress. The heart needs more rest between beats; therefore tachycardia easily results in heart failure. Arteriosclerotic changes are common in the elderly, but it is not clear whether these changes are natural to the aging process or if they are simply a common pathologic process seen in the aged population. Nonetheless, these changes make the blood vessels less elastic and more resistant to blood flow, resulting in elevated blood pressure. Exercise can increase cardiac output, and daily exercise such as walking is excellent for the elderly.

Assessment

Assessment of the cardiovascular system should begin with noting the rate, rhythm, and character of the pulse for 1 full minute in a resting state. Pulses are checked bilaterally for symmetry because older people have arterial insufficiency. Blood pressure is taken first with the person lying down and then standing. Orthostatic hypoten-sion is common in the elderly. The medications the person is taking should be assessed for their effects on blood pressure. The presence or absence of pedal edema is evaluated when palpating pedal pulses. The temperature of the hands and feet is noted. Cool, dry extremities reflect a decrease in peripheral circulation. Family history of heart disease should be questioned. The individual's lifestyle including smoking, diet and obesity, exercise, and stress should be assessed.

Common pathologic conditions

Cardiovascular problems are among the most common diseases of the elderly. Controversy exists however, about whether these problems are the result of the aging process or the result of longstanding lifestyle. Some recent studies support the theory of lifestyle as the cause of many cardiovascular pathologic conditions. The effects of the aging process do, however, contribute to the progress of pathologic conditions.

Hypertension. Hypertension is very common among the elderly population. Hypertension is defined as blood pressure that is consistently above what is considered normal. A person is considered hypertensive with a systolic blood pressure greater than 160 mm Hg and/or a diastolic pressure greater than 90 mm Hg. The diastolic reading is more important than the systolic pressure. See Chapter 16 for a complete discussion of the pathophysiology, assessment, and intervention of hypertension.

Arteriosclerosis and atherosclerosis. The changes that occur in the heart and vascular system begin early in life and progress over the years. Atherosclerosis is a form of arteriosclerosis, a condition in which the blood vessels lose their elasticity, or "hardening of the arteries." Atherosclerosis results from fatty deposits (plaque) that form in the intima of the blood vessels. These changes make it increasingly difficult for blood to flow through the vascular system. The flow of blood to the kidneys, brain, and lower extremities is often affected. The condition may become severe enough to cause serious disease of the heart, such as coronary artery disease, myocardial infarction, and congestive heart failure. There is a direct link between atherosclerosis and arterial occlusive disease. See Chapter 16 for coverage of these conditions.

Cerebrovascular accident (CVA). Cerebrovascular accident (CVA or stroke) is one of the leading causes of death in the elderly and is the

Table 11-2

Physiologic Changes in the Elderly

Body system	Physiologic changes*	Results*
Cardiovascular	↓ Heart size ↓ Cardiac output ↓ Heart rate ↑ Atherosclerosis	↓ Oxygenation ↑ Chance of heart failure ↑ Blood pressure
Sensory	↓ Accomodation ↓ Diameter of pupil ↑ Opacity of lens	↓ Light to retina ↓ Night vision ↑ Sensitivity to glare ↓ Peripheral vision ↓ Color vision
	↓ Functioning of middle and inner ear	↓ High-frequency sounds ↓ Balance
Integumentary	↓ Sebaceous secretions ↓ Subcutaneous fat ↓ Thickness of epidermis	↑ Dry skin ↑ Wrinkling ↑ Susceptibility to heat and cold ↑ Thickness of nails ↓ Hair color and distribution
Musculoskeletal	↓ Bone calcium ↓ Water of intervertebral disks ↓ Blood supply ↓ Elastic tissue ↓ Muscle mass	↑ Curvature of spine—osteoporosis ↓ Height ↓ Mobility ↑ Risk of falls and fractures
Nervous	↓ Brain cells ↓ Nerve fibers ↓ Touch receptors	↓ Reflexes ↓ Memory ↓ Pain recognition
Digestive	↓ Gastric secretions ↓ Peristalsis ↓ Sensory receptors ↓ Number of teeth	↑ Constipation ↓ Appetite ↓ Ability to taste ↓ Ability to chew ↓ Nutritional status
Urinary	↓ Blood supply ↓ Nephrons ↓ Muscle tone ↑ Size of prostate	↑ Urine concentration ↓ Bladder capacity ↑ Residual urine ↑ Chance of infection ↓ Urinary stream
Respiratory	↓ Elasticity ↑ Thickness of capillaries ↓ Number of capillaries	↓ Gas exchange ↑ Shortness of breath ↑ Risk of disease
Reproductive	↓ Estrogens ↓ Seminal fluid	↓ Epithelial cells of vulva ↑ Chance of vaginitis ↓ Breast mass ↓ Ovary size ↓ Uterus size ↓ Vaginal secretions

* ↑ , Increased; ↓ , Decreased.

result of an interruption of circulation in the brain. Hypertension is a major factor in the occurrence of a stroke. See Chapter 16 for pathophysiology and intervention of CVA.

Nursing interventions

The most important nursing intervention relating to the cardiovascular system is the strategy to prevent cardiovascular disease. Promoting a healthy lifestyle in all individuals will decrease the incidence of cardiovascular pathologic conditions in the elderly. The importance of a good diet cannot be overemphasized. The nurse should encourage and assist the elderly in decreasing their intake of salt, saturated fats, and alcohol, and increasing their intake of grains, fresh fruits, and vegetables. A regular program of exercise tailored to the individual is very important. Smokers should be encouraged to quit. Nursing interventions for individuals with cardiovascular problems include monitoring and evaluating the effects of the medical therapies. The nurse will need to teach the patient about the medications prescribed by the doctor, their side effects, and the importance of continuing the medication.

Sensory System

The status of the individual's sensory system affects the way in which the individual reacts to the environment and the people in it. Deficits in hearing or vision have the effect of isolating an individual from what is going on around him or her.

Vision

With aging there is a gradual decrease in visual accommodation. This means that the elderly require more time to focus when looking from one site to the other. Night vision is reduced, and more time is needed for the eyes to adjust to the dark. Increased lens opacity causes light to scatter and makes the elderly person more sensitive to glare. These changes cause many older people to discontinue driving at night. Senile miosis, a condition that decreases the size of the pupils, results in a decreased amount of light reaching the retina. Therefore the elderly need more light to work, read, and walk safely. Peripheral vision, the ability to distinguish objects at the edges of the visual field, is reduced. Sometimes the elderly do not communicate with people sitting beside them simply because they do not see them. The lens yellows with age, causing the elderly difficulty in discriminating colors. Blues and greens tend to fade and are easily confused. Reds, oranges, and yellows can be seen best.

Assessment. The patient should be asked about visual problems such as double vision, blurring, tunnel vision, or any other visual disturbance. Headaches or pain in or around the eye should be noted. Vision can be assessed by using an eye chart or by determining if the person can recognize the number of fingers held up by the examiner at 2 and 10 feet away. Newspaper headlines can also be used to check vision. Peripheral vision can be determined by wiggling the fingers while slowly bringing them toward the patient's center of vision. Color discrimination can be checked by using a color chart, colored paper, or colors in the environment.

Common pathologic conditions. The most common visual problems of the elderly are cataracts, glaucoma, senile macular degeneration, and diabetic retinopathy. These problems are covered in Chapter 23.

Nursing interventions. Nurses should be aware of visual changes with aging in order to assist elderly clients in adapting to these changes. When moving back and forth between brightly lit and darker areas, such as coming indoors on a sunny day or coming out of a darkened theatre into the daylight, elderly individuals should pause to allow the eyes to accommodate to the change. Sunglasses help to reduce glare in bright daylight. The elderly who drive at night can be advised to use lighted and divided highways to reduce the glare from oncoming cars. Indoors, lamps and windows should be shaded to allow adequate light but reduce glare. Supplemental light should be provided for tasks such as reading or sewing. Adequate lighting of stairs is essential. Stair edges should be marked with contrasting color. Night-lights will aid the elderly when they need to arise during the night. Older patients who have decreased peripheral vision should be approached from the front, and objects should be placed directly in front of them. With the decrease in color discrimination, tactful guidance may be necessary to assist the elderly in selecting matching clothes and in advising older women on the application of cosmetics.

Hearing

Hearing impairment is common and is first demonstrated by an inability to hear the higher frequencies. This affects the individual's ability to discriminate words, and there will be certain words that the individual will not be able to hear or will confuse with other words. Background words are not heard fully; this results in reduced sensory stimulation and may lead to withdrawal and social isolation. Changes in the middle and inner ear may result in some loss of balance. Ear wax becomes drier and may accumulate in the ear.

Assessment. Hearing should be assessed by an examiner standing behind the individual, first covering one ear and then the other. The examiner, speaking in a normal voice, should ask the person to respond to questions or repeat a series of words. Both ears should be checked.

Nursing interventions. When caring for the elderly, the nurse should stand directly in front of and face the individual, speak clearly, and at a moderate rate. It is important not to overarticulate, shout, or mumble. Shouting may not help the person hear better; it may make it more difficult. Hearing aids can help with some types of hearing loss; however, some individuals may refuse to wear a hearing aid.

Taste and smell

It has been generally thought that the senses of taste and smell decrease with age. The little research that has been done in this area has not supported this theory. However, factors such as smoking or medication do affect taste and smell.

Touch

As with the other senses, it is generally thought that the sense of touch decreases with age. There is some evidence that a person's ability to detect temperature extremes or pain is affected as one ages, but more and better research is needed in this area. Individuals with an impaired sense of touch may be unable to determine whether a surface (such as a coffee pot) or water is hot enough to cause injury. A decreased sense of pain may result in the person's not realizing the extent of an injury such as a broken hip following a fall. The nurse can assess the individual's sensitivity to temperature using containers of hot and cold water, and to pain using the sharp and dull ends of a safety pin. Those whose sense of touch is diminished can be counseled to be extra vigilant to prevent injury.

Integumentary System

The signs of aging are perhaps most visible in the skin and hair. The epidermis and dermis become thinner, although there may be some thickening in areas exposed to sunlight. Decreased vascularity in the dermis leads to increased fragility of the skin. This results in easier bruising and increased susceptibility to skin problems such as decubiti. There is less secretion of the sebaceous glands causing the skin to become dry. Wrinkling of the skin is caused by loss of subcutaneous fat and a decrease in water content of the skin. The nails become hard and brittle, leading to cracking and splitting. Hair becomes lighter and thinner. About half of the population over age 50 has at least 50% gray body hair. The elderly are more susceptible to heat and cold; heat applications must be at a reduced temperature to avoid burns. Since reduced activity results in reduced heat production, elderly persons will often feel cold when others are comfortable.

Assessment

Examination of the skin should be done by exposing all areas under good lighting. Pressure areas need to be checked for signs of redness or open lesions. Skin folds should be parted to check for irritation or signs of infection. Note the moisture of the skin and the size and location of any skin lesions. The elderly bruise easily and may have reddened areas called senile purpura.

Common pathologic conditions

The most common skin disorders among the elderly are skin cancers, keratoses, pigmentary disturbances, psoriasis, dermatitis, and urticaria.[25] The immobile elderly are more prone to develop decubitus ulcers. See Chapter 24 for discussion of these conditions.

Dryness and itching (pruritus) are very common among the elderly. In most cases, dry skin is the cause of pruritus. However, other systemic problems should be ruled out in the case of severe pruritus. Conditions that may aggravate dry skin and itching include dry heat and air conditioning, daily hot baths or showers, and use of harsh or deodorant soaps.

Nursing interventions

The goal of nursing should be to maintain the integrity of the skin. Because the skin of the older person is more fragile, it should be given more gentle care. The use of very hot water, harsh or deodorant soaps, and rubbing alcohol should be avoided. A complete bath 2 or 3 times a week is sufficient supplemented with partial baths. When bathing the elderly, use gentle and superfatted soaps, and pat the skin dry rather than rubbing. Use of creams and lotions while the skin is still slightly damp is recommended. Do not use bath oil in the water because this makes the bathtub slippery and increases the likelihood of falling. Use cornstarch in skin folds rather than talcum powder. Talcum tends to cake and irritate when it becomes moist. Skin should be examined frequently for early signs of irritation or pathologic conditions. Proper humidity in the heated or air-conditioned environment should be maintained. Nutrition greatly influences skin condition, and older people should be taught the importance of a sound and healthy diet.

Musculoskeletal System

Aging of the musculoskeletal system affects bones, joints, muscles, and muscle attachments. There is a decrease in bone mass and a thinning of the intervertebral discs of the spinal column that results in a shortening of the trunk. This, along with a general flexion of the joints, results in a decrease in height, forward projection of the head and neck, and kyphosis. Loss of bone mass and postural changes increase the risk of fractures and falling. Fear of falling frequently leads to decreased mobilization which then decreases bone mass. There is a decrease in muscle fiber as muscle regeneration slows. Muscles atrophy and are replaced by fibrous tissue. These changes result in decreased muscle strength. Subcutaneous tissue is redistributed, with a decrease in the face and extremities and an increase around the abdomen and hips. Changes occur in the cartilage of the joints, especially the weight-bearing joints such as knees and hips, causing stiffness. These changes can be aggravated by joint stress, obesity and decrease in ambulation. While a decrease in muscle strength and increased joint stiffness cannot be halted, they can be significantly slowed with exercise.

Assessment

Assessment of the musculoskeletal system is done by first noting the curvature of the spine. Ask the individual to bend forward, sideways, and slightly backward to check the range of motion of the spine. Then ask the person to sit. This routine will assess the spinal muscles and hip muscles. Assess the upper extremities, symmetrically checking each joint in active and passive range of motion. Palpate the joints, noting deformities, tenderness, or areas of warmth. To check the

lower extremities, observe the individual's gait. Examine the joints as with the upper extremities, but note carefully the internal and external rotation of the hips.

Common pathologic conditions

The most common problems affecting the musculoskeletal system in the elderly include arthritis, osteoarthritis, gout, and fractures. See Chapter 25 for more information about these pathologic conditions.

Osteoporosis. Osteoporosis is a condition characterized by decreased bone density accompanied by increased porosity and brittleness of the bone. The bones become very fragile and fracture easily, often following only minimal trauma. The sites most affected are the vertebra, the hip, and the wrist. The kyphosis or "dowager's hump" seen in many older women is caused by collapse fractures of the thoracic vertebra. Osteoporosis results from the aging of the bone remodeling process. Before the approximate age of 45, bone formation or absorption is greater than bone loss or resorption. After age 45 the process reverses, and more bone is resorbed resulting in bone loss. Risk factors that appear to increase the occurrence of osteoporosis include cigarette smoking, high caffeine intake, excessive alcohol intake, a high protein diet, a history of low dietary calcium, low Vitamin D, a slender body build with little body fat, and a sedentary lifestyle. Bone loss increases significantly following menopause in women, putting them at greater risk. Treatment of osteoporosis is aimed at prevention. There is no way to replace bone already lost, but there are ways of slowing its progress. Ideally, prevention begins in the early years of life. Building up of the bones throughout childhood and early adulthood with adequate calcium intake provides for greater bone mass. When bone loss begins later in life, there is a greater percentage of bone mass left. Later prevention of osteoporosis includes exercise, calcium, and estrogen. Weight-bearing exercise such as walking, jogging, bicycling, and dancing stimulate bone formation and retard bone mass reduction.[13] Older adults should increase their intake of dietary calcium to the equivalent of 3 or 4 glasses of skim milk per day. Alternate sources of calcium include cheese, yogurt, canned salmon (with the bones), and calcium supplements. Estrogen replacement therapy after menopause is recommended for those at high risk of osteoporosis.

Nursing interventions

A person's sense of self is directly affected by his or her ability to be independently mobile. Likewise, a healthy mental attitude will stimulate the individual to take measures to maintain motor function. Nurses can assist the older adult to assume a positive mental attitude and outlook on life. Exercise is extremely important in maintaining motor function. Every older adult will benefit from exercise; however, it must be appropriate to the capabilities of the individual. Walking, swimming, dancing, jogging, stretching, and aerobics are all beneficial in maintaining muscle strength and joint movement. Pain management for the elderly with muscle and joint pain is essential in maintaining mobility.[25] Good nutrition is important to supply the energy, vitamins, and minerals needed to maintain a healthy state. Safety is of primary concern in preserving motor function. The nurse should assess the person's environment and recommend measures such as the use of grab bars, appropriate lighting, and the use of canes or walkers when appropriate. Area rugs and other obstructions that could cause falls and injuries should be removed.

Neurological System

Changes occurring in the nervous system of the aging adult include a decrease in the number of functioning neurons. This is a gradual change, becoming more pronounced over age 70. The loss of neurons means the loss of neuronal interconnections resulting in slower conduction of nerve impulses. For this reason, it is more difficult for the elderly to maintain body homeostasis. Recovery from stress is slower and incomplete. The elderly are at risk for hypothermia and hyperthermia that may become life threatening. Reaction time is also decreased among the elderly. Reflexes are diminished and motor activity is slower. Tremors are common, especially in the head, face, and hands. The sense of pain is also diminished, and the elderly may be free of pain in such acute disorders as myocardial infarction or pneumonia. Older adults take longer to fall asleep, have shorter periods of deep sleep, and awaken more frequently during the night.[25]

Assessment

Assessment of the nervous system is a complex process, but several simple techniques can provide valuable information. Careful observation of the person's gait will reveal the ability to coordi-nate muscle movements. The reflexes may be slowed, but should be equal bilaterally. Sometimes severe arthritis can depress the knee-jerk reflex. Sensory testing can be done by using a cotton wisp for light touch and a safety pin for deep touch. Touch the skin at different places bilaterally, from head to toe, while the person's eyes are closed. The person is asked to say when the wisp is felt. Deep touch is assessed in the same way, using an open safety pin, first the point, and then the head. The person is asked to identify "sharp" and "dull."

Common pathologic conditions

The most common pathologic conditions of the neurological system among older adults are grouped under the term organic brain syndrome. Two subcategories of organic brain syndrome are delirium and dementia. **Delirium** (acute confusional states) is usually a temporary, reversible condition frequently associated with physical or mental illness in older adults.[25] **Dementia** (chronic brain syndrome) is a progressive decline in an individual's intellectual function. Parkinson's disease is also classified under organic brain syndrome; however, the decline in intellectual function is often absent in Parkinson's. See Chapter 22 for a discussion of Parkinson's disease.

Delirium. Delirium is associated with metabolic changes and disruptions. It can be caused by cardiovascular changes such as cerebral vascular accident, decreased blood supply, congestive heart failure or infection and by metabolic disturbances such as hypokalemia or hyperkalemia, hypoglycemia or hyperglycemia, acidosis, or alkalosis. Psychologic disturbances such as depression, grief, fatigue, or severe emotional stress, and environmental factors such as sensory deprivation or sensory overload can also be responsible for a state of delirium. Symptoms include sudden onset of confusion, disorientation, hallucinations, and incoherent speech, anger, apathy, or changes in psychomotor activity. The delirium state is usually temporary and can be reversed by identifying and correcting the underlying condition that is causing it.

Dementia. Dementia is a group of pathologic conditions characterized by a gradual decline in intellectual function with symptoms such as loss of memory for recent and remote events, impaired ability to problem solve or to make judgements, and personality changes. The most common of the dementias is Alzheimer's disease.

Alzheimer's Disease

Alzheimer's disease is a chronic, degenerative, and irreversible disease. It is more common in women. No genetic links have been found; however, it does have familial tendencies. The disease results in characteristic changes in the brain that can only be identified on autopsy: cerebral atrophy, senile plaques, and neurofibrillary tangles. The cause of Alzheimer's disease remains unknown. There is a great deal of research being conducted to isolate a cause, and there are many theories including environmental factors, such as aluminum, head trauma, and infection, as well as immunologic and genetic factors.[2] While aluminum is found in the damaged cells, some believe it only enters the cell as a result of the damage, rather than being the cause. There is no cure, and death usually occurs in an average of 5 to 8 years, although some Alzheimer's victims have been known to live for 15 to 20 years after contracting the disease.

Alzheimer's is classified into three stages. The *first stage*, the forgetful or mild stage, is characterized by short-term memory loss, mild disorientation for time and date, difficulty in completing mathematical calculations, and subtle behavioral changes such as a decreased interest in work, family, or recreation.[25] The *second stage* is the confused stage, and symptoms include extreme confusion, suspiciousness and paranoia, and difficulty with daily living activities such as driving, money management, and home maintenance. Patients are easily lost even in familiar places and will wander off, especially at night. They have difficulty functioning in environments other than home. During this stage patients neglect personal hygiene and withdraw from social groups. Individuals may become extremely depressed if they are aware of what is happening.[14,25] The *third stage* is the dementia or terminal stage in which people have flat affect and no longer ambulate. They do not recognize family or friends, are unable to communicate, and have no interaction with the environment. They become malnourished, emaciated, and are incontinent.[14,25]

Assessment

There are no definitive tests to confirm a diagnosis of Alzheimer's disease. Only by examination of the brain on autopsy can the diagnosis be confirmed. Diagnosis is made on the basis of cognitive and behavioral symptoms and by ruling out other physiologic and psychologic disorders.

Since the goal of nursing care will be to keep the individual functioning at his or her highest possible level, the nurse will need to assess the patient's abilities on an ongoing basis. Those areas that should be assessed include level of consciousness, reality orientation, memory, ability to reason, ability to carry out activities of daily living, interaction with others, and response to environmental stimuli.[29]

Nursing interventions

To date there is no cure for Alzheimer's disease. Medications may be used to decrease agitation or depression, but the use of drugs is controversial. The focus of nursing care for Alzheimer's patients is to maintain the highest possible level of functioning for each person. Most Alzheimer patients are cared for at home during the early stages of the disease and institutionalized for the terminal period. As the disease progresses, care becomes more and more difficult for family members. They need reassurance and assistance in developing and maintaining an everchanging plan of care. Community resources for families of Alzheimer patients are frequently lacking, but the nurse can assist by working through the political and social systems to provide this desperately needed support. Care of the Alzheimer patient, at home or in an institution, should include establishing effective verbal and nonverbal communication, providing a safe and structured environment, maintaining normal daily living patterns, maintaining mobility and exercise as much as possible, providing cognitive stimulation in the environment, maintaining optimal nutritional status, and maintaining bowel and bladder continence as long as possible.[25]

Digestive System

Most of the problems associated with the gastrointestinal system of the elderly are the result of pathologic conditions and not part of the normal aging process. The loss of teeth commonly attributed to aging is preventable with good dental hygiene earlier in life. There is a slight decrease in gastric secretion and a slowing of peristalsis in the bowel. This may lead to various complaints, one of the most frequent being constipation and its complications, colon flatus, and fecal impaction. Pathologic conditions in the older adult are the same as those seen in all adults. Chapter 18 discusses problems associated with the gastrointestinal system.

Constipation

Constipation is a common complaint among the elderly. It is most important to determine the person's definition of constipation. Many people subscribe to the theory that daily bowel movements are necessary and that less frequent movements indicate constipation. They spend a great deal of time and money attempting to induce daily movements. Many become laxative dependent. The nurse can help to reeducate these elderly people about good bowel hygiene (see below). Laxatives should be taken only under the direction of a physician.

Assessment

Assessment of the elderly digestive tract includes a good oral examination. The condition of the mucous membrane should be noted. Examine the teeth for the presence or absence of caries and good hygiene. If dentures are in place, have the individual remove them to inspect the gums. A stethoscope can be set lightly on the abdomen to listen for bowel sounds. It may take 1 to 5 minutes to hear sounds in any one area. Increased sounds can mean a hyperactive intestine as in diarrhea, and decreased sounds can be a sign of a paralytic ileus or obstruction. A rectal examination will provide information about anal sphincter tone. Fecal impaction may be present if large amounts of hard stool are in the rectum. The stool should be tested for signs of occult blood.

Nursing interventions

Nursing interventions for the GI system will focus on providing for and maintaining a healthy state of functioning in the patient. Good mouth care and attention to dental problems are essential. Teaching about and providing a healthy diet are important. It is not easy for older adults to change lifelong eating habits, so this may present a challenge to the nurse. Healthy bowel habits are necessary to prevent constipation. This would include: a sufficient intake of high fiber foods and raw fruits and vegetables, 6 to 8 glasses of water daily, a regular program of exercise, and a regular, unhurried time for bowel movements. The use of laxatives and enemas should be discouraged unless prescribed by a physician. Institutionalized elderly will need more assistance in assuming the above habits for healthy bowel management. The use of laxatives, cathartics, and enemas should not be routine in institutions that care for the elderly.

Factors Affecting Dietary Patterns of the Elderly
1. Reduced income
2. Inadequacy of cooking facilities
3. Loneliness and having to eat alone
4. Physical inability to prepare food
5. Loss of teeth or poorly fitting dentures
6. Lack of transportation or delivery service

Urinary System

With aging there is a decrease in the number of nephrons in the kidneys and a decrease in the blood supply that adversely affect the functioning of the urinary system. The kidneys become less efficient in concentrating or diluting urine. The renal threshold for glucose is elevated, and individuals tested for high blood glucose will not show elevated levels in the urine. Excretion of drugs is altered, and the elderly must be closely observed for signs of drug toxicity. The smooth muscle and elastic tissue of the bladder is replaced with fibrous connective tissue. This results in decreased bladder capacity and increased frequency of urination. The elderly also experience more nocturia. There is a decrease in the force of the stream, and some may experience stress incontinence. For these reasons many elderly may limit their appearance in public or long trips. Some decrease their fluid intake to avoid embarrassment. Bladder outlet changes may cause obstruction in the male and incontinence in the female.[25]

Assessment

Assessment of the urinary system is done indirectly by asking the elderly about their urinary habits. The kidneys themselves are rarely palpated. If there is a severe kidney infection, the individual can have flank tenderness. The amount, color, and odor of urine is one way to assess the urinary system. The external meatus of both men and women should be inspected and kept clean to prevent infections. If the urinary bladder is overfilled with urine, it can be palpated above the pubic bone.

Common pathologic conditions

Decrease in the function of the urinary system causes certain pathologic conditions to be regularly seen among the elderly. The diminished efficiency of the kidneys may result in acute and chronic renal failure (see Chapter 19). Bladder problems such as urinary retention, urinary tract infections, and cancer of the bladder appear (see Chapter 19). Urinary incontinence is especially troublesome in women, while benign prostatic hypertrophy and prostate cancer affect men (see Chapter 20).

Nursing interventions

The elderly may feel uncomfortable talking about a genitourinary problem and may live with the problem rather than facing the embarrassment of mentioning it. The understanding nurse will appreciate these feelings and will provide a private, gentle, and sensitive environment to assist the individual. Nursing interventions should be focused on maintaining normal functioning of the urinary system. Mobility and activity promote normal functioning, so the nurse should encourage the elderly to remain as active as possible. Older adults should be aware of their patterns of elimination and should plan their schedules accordingly, if possible. Medications that affect elimination, such as diuretics, should be taken in the morning so that they do not interfere with sleep. When away from home the elderly should locate the washroom in any public place before it is needed. Clothing can be modified to permit ease and speed in its removal. The environment should also be modified according to individual needs, such as providing unobstructed pathways to the bathroom, using night lights, and having hand rails alongside the toilet to assist in getting up and down. Maintaining adequate fluid intake is essential for bladder functioning, and good personal hygiene is important to decrease the incidence of infection and to control odor. Exercises can be taught to decrease incontinence (Kegel exercises). These exercises involve tightening of the muscles of the pelvic floor in a regular, scheduled pattern. To make the person aware of the appropriate muscles, instruct them to do the following:

1. Stand or sit with the muscles of the legs, abdomen, and buttocks relaxed.
2. Imagine trying to keep from having a bowel movement by tightening the muscles around the anus.
3. When urinating, attempt to stop the flow midstream, hold it, then restart it.

These exercises should be done on a regular basis several times every day.[6]

Respiratory System

The function of the pulmonary system decreases with age, and the loss reduces the reserve necessary during stress. These losses are not great enough, however, to interfere with ordinary activity.[25] Skeletal changes reduce the flexibility of the rib cage, and it tends to remain expanded. The respiratory muscles weaken, resulting in reduced ability of the thoracic cavity to enlarge with inspiration and to recoil with expiration. Smoking, immobility, and obesity can further compromise lung function. Because the lungs are less elastic, more air remains in the lungs, and less air is exchanged. Thickened and decreased capillaries reduce the exchange of oxygen and carbon dioxide in the lungs. The elderly become short of breath more readily and have greater difficulty recovering from respiratory diseases.

Assessment

Assess the respiratory system by first looking at the shape of the chest. Note the condition of the skin and whether the accessory muscles are used for breathing. Breathing should be unstrained and symmetrical. Auscultation of the lungs is done posteriorly first and then anteriorly, going side to side, top to bottom. The individual is asked to take a deep breath through the mouth while the stethoscope is placed on the chest. Observe the person carefully for signs of hyperventilation while conducting the examination. Breath sounds may be distant, but should be clear. Soft or loud crackles or wheezes are considered abnormal sounds.

Common pathologic conditions

The most common respiratory diseases among the elderly include chronic obstructive pulmonary disease (COPD), emphysema, chronic bronchitis, asthma, tuberculosis, and lung cancer. These are not problems brought on by aging of the lungs but are the result of lifestyle, including smoking and air pollutants. Pneumonia is also common in older adults. Several factors contribute to the increased incidence of pneumonia among the elderly: weakened immune system, immobility, chronic illness, and debility. Institutionalized elderly are more vulnerable. These respiratory diseases are discussed in Chapter 15.

Nursing interventions

As with other systems, mobility and exercise play an important role in maintaining a healthy respiratory system. Exercise will help to reduce the effects of aging on the lungs and will increase the muscle tone of the chest and the individual's ability to fight off infection. The elderly who smoke should be encouraged and assisted in quitting. For those older adults who have lung problems, the nurse can assist in adapting the environment to reduce irritants. This might mean the use of filters, humidifiers or dehumidifiers, and air conditioning. Older persons at risk for lung diseases should have flu vaccines when advised. Colds and other respiratory infections should be attended to promptly.[25]

Reproductive System

After menopause women experience a decrease in estrogens, tissue changes in the vulva and vagina, a thinning of the epithelial cells, and the loss of normal vaginal acidity. The elderly woman is more susceptible to vaginitis because of these changes. The breasts, uterus, and ovaries begin to atrophy. Men will experience a reduction in seminal fluid. The prostate may enlarge and the testes may become smaller and less firm.

Assessment

Assessment of the breast tissue in elderly women is important because cancer is a concern. The breasts are inspected for symmetry, nipple discharge, or dimpled skin. Circular palpation is done from the axilla, gradually working toward the nipple. The nipple is squeezed to check for discharge. A pelvic examination for the elderly woman can be helpful in determining pelvic muscle tone and a possible cystocele, rectocele, or uterine prolapse. These are all factors that can contribute to incontinence. Some of these conditions can be noted with careful external inspection. A pelvic examination should be conducted by a physician or nurse practitioner.

The elderly man is examined externally for signs of phimosis (tight foreskin), testicular swelling, hydrocele, or herniations. A physician or nurse practitioner should evaluate the status of the prostate gland by rectal examination.

Common pathologic conditions

Problems of the reproductive system in elderly females include relaxation of the pelvic musculature (cystocele, rectocele and uterine prolapse) and cancer of the reproductive organs. Breast cancer is the most common form. In elderly males benign prostatic hypertrophy and cancer of the

prostate are often seen. These conditions are discussed in Chapter 20.

Nursing interventions

The focus of nursing interventions should be education. Many elderly will feel embarrassed to discuss problems related to their reproductive organs. The nurse will need to be sensitive to their embarrassment and provide an environment in which they can more easily discuss this subject. Adult women should be taught breast self-examination and encouraged to practice it monthly. Annual mammograms are recommended for women over 50. Regular physical examinations are recommended for both sexes, including Pap smears for women and digital rectal exams for men.

NURSING THE ELDERLY

The process of aging does not necessarily mean a process of decline. Although the elderly are more susceptible to illness, aging does not mean sickness. Physical changes do occur, but physical debility is not a normal part of the aging process. Nursing care of the aging individual requires respecting each as a unique and valued person. This includes the manner of addressing the person. Every adult person should be asked how he or she would like to be called. Use of an elderly person's first name by a much younger person is considered by many as a breach of etiquette. To address an older adult as "Grandma" or "Gramps" or "dear" is inappropriate and degrading. The care of the elderly includes procedures designed to protect the person from injury, provide comfort, meet nutritional needs, maintain personal hygiene, and provide care during illness and convalesence. The nurse should also recognize the elderly's sexuality and their changing susceptibility to drugs.

Preventing Injury

Injuries resulting from accidents are a major and largely preventable cause of death and illness in the elderly. A great many of the accidental deaths are the result of complications following falls.

Since most falls occur in the home, precaution should be taken to protect elderly persons. Scatter rugs should not be used unless they are secured by rubber mats beneath them. Toys left on the floor and furniture moved to unfamiliar places may be responsible for a fall. Rubber mats should be placed in bathtubs and support should be provided to assist persons stepping from the tub (Figure 11-2).

Night-lights and lights in bathrooms and on stairs should be left on at night, and increased illumination should be provided in the evening. Elderly persons are susceptible to accidents on streets and highways at dusk or in the evening; to avoid such accidents, an elderly person should be accompanied, should carry a flashlight, and should have reflectorized material attached to clothing.

Providing Comfort

Elderly persons may be burned more easily than younger persons because their pain receptors do not respond as readily. For this reason, heating pads or hot-water bottles should not be used. Elderly persons often need extra clothing or wraps. The feet may be cold because of circulatory changes. Shawls or sweaters, warm socks, or extra blankets may be used. The patient should not be positioned directly in front of or in a draft caused by a fan, air conditioner, or open window.

Short rest periods of 15 or 20 minutes after meals will be of greater value than long naps that

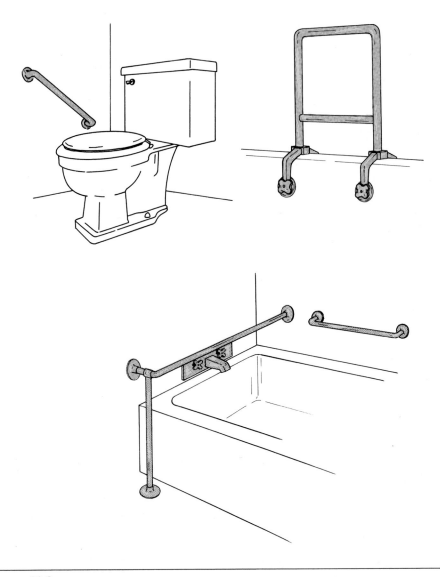

Figure 11-2
Hand bars placed on bathtubs and beside toilets provide support for patient and prevent falls from loss of balance.

may interfere with sleep at night. Older people frequently complain of sleepless nights and on such occasions may get up and walk about the house. Many times they try to follow the same pattern of sleep as they did when younger, when more sleep was required. Providing evening entertainment such as television or games will occupy the elderly person until a later hour and postpone sleep, providing for a sound sleep and a more refreshed feeling on waking.

Meeting Nutritional Needs

As a group, elderly people appear to be highly susceptible to malnutrition. In senescence the metabolic processes decrease from 10% to 30%, physical activity decreases, and the individual needs fewer calories. However, if appetite fails, the individual will become malnourished. Some elderly persons are obese and continue to follow dietary patterns of overeating, particularly of rich foods. They, too, may be undernourished, not in calories but in dietary essentials.

The diet should include all of the nutritional requirements, that is, carbohydrates, fats, proteins, vitamins, minerals, and water. Because of reduced physical activity and a decline in metabolic activity, elderly persons need fewer calories than when they were younger. Caloric needs must be evaluated individually. Men may require more calories than women, and some persons are more active than others and expend more energy, which requires more calories. It has been suggested that there should be a reduction in calories of 7% to 8% every 10 years after a person has reached 25 years of age.

The diet should include four basic food groups:
1. Meat, fish, poultry, and eggs
2. Milk
3. Fruits and vegetable
4. Breads and cereals

The basic food groups apply to all persons regardless of age, with the calories adjusted through smaller or larger servings. There is some evidence that proper use of food in the body depends on all nutrients being present at approximately the same time. Although the "basic four" diet provides a simple, systematic guide to food selection, it does not regulate intake of salt, cholesterol, and saturated fat. Additional information must be provided to guide the elderly in selecting a diet that is well balanced and at the same time is low in salt, cholesterol, and saturated fat.[8]

The frequency and the amount of food served is also important, and it is recommended that the daily food requirement be divided into six small meals. Vitamin and mineral supplements should be used only on the advice of the physician. Whenever possible, the individual should eat with the family, and food should be prepared the way the person likes it and served attractively. The elderly should be allowed to participate in food selection and preparation if they are able; guidance in including all essential foods in the diet should be provided as necessary.

Maintaining Personal Hygiene

Daily baths result in excessive dryness and scaling of the skin, often accompanied by itching. Inadequate rinsing may cause a dermatitis, producing a great deal of discomfort from burning and itching of the affected parts. Complete baths should be reduced to two or three a week with careful rinsing and drying. However, attention should be given to the perineal area on a daily basis. Bath oils may be added to the water, but extra caution must be taken to prevent falls, since these oils make the tub more slippery. Showers, taken with a hand-held shower head in a stall that has a seat or is large enough for a bath chair, provide for thorough rinsing, and are less difficult to maneuver in and out of than bathtubs. An elderly person should not be alone in a locked bathroom. To assure privacy, a sign on the door or hanging from the doorknob can tell others that it is "occupied." Because of diminished activity of oil glands, the hair should be shampooed less frequently. Shampoos containing alcohol should be avoided because of their drying effect.

Cold weather and dry furnace heat can aggravate the problem of dry skin. Older people who spend the winter in cold climates should take extra precautions to prevent skin problems. Wearing soft clothing and using skin lotions can help prevent dryness.

Care of the feet is also important. Warm soaks with thorough drying, particularly between the toes, followed by massage with baby oil or lanolin will prevent excessive drying. A member of the family or the nurse should trim the nails. If financial resources permit, the individual may be taken to a podiatrist for foot care. Visits may be scheduled at 4- to 6-week intervals. Corns, calluses, and infections require special care.

Many elderly people will have partial or full dentures. Some will have teeth missing. The loss of teeth and presence of dental caries or poorly fitting dentures affect the person's general health by interfering with dietary needs. Normal shrinking of the gums exposes the soft parts of the tooth structure, which are more sensitive to injury. Improperly fitting dentures may cause the gums to become sore. Regular gum massage will stimulate circulation and help to keep gums healthy. For those who have their own teeth, regular visits to the dentist are necessary. Teeth should be brushed after meals with a mild dentifrice and a soft-bristle brush, and dentures should be brushed after each meal.

Sluggishness of the bowel may accompany aging; it is primarily the result of inactivity and faulty diet. When it occurs, it is not unusual for the person to resort to the use of some form of laxative that was seen advertised or that a well-meaning friend or neighbor has suggested. Laxatives, as with any other medication, should be prescribed by the physician. However, regularity of bowel habits should be encouraged, and when possible, diet should include some soft bulk to facilitate bowel evacuation. Simple measures such as prune juice at night or a glass of warm water with a little lemon juice before breakfast may be all that is required.

Decreased muscle tone and reduced capacity of the bladder may cause urinary incontinence. This may result in embarrassment for the individual. A medical examination should be done to rule out infection or other pathologic condition. Clothing should be changed as often as necessary to prevent odor and skin excoriation. If there is no pathologic condition, incontinence can be prevented by planning frequent use of the bathroom, commode, or bedpan during the day and limiting fluids after the evening meal.

The individual should be encouraged to maintain good personal hygiene and personal appearance with reference to hair and clothing. For many elderly persons some member of the family will have to help with or supervise daily care. The same principles of personal hygiene apply to the individual who may be hospitalized or in a nursing home.

Recognizing Sexuality

Society has held the stereotyped belief that sexual desires and activity begin to diminish in the mid-forties until they cease completely some time in the later years and that this is appropriate. The elderly who are sexually active are considered perverse or at best lying about their activities. Open expressions of **sexuality** between elderly partners are often met with the disapproval of grown children because they believe that sex is not appropriate for this age group. The work of Kinsey and Masters and Johnson and recent studies conducted at Duke University are proving quite the opposite.

Whereas Kinsey's work did not deal with a very large sample of elderly persons, it did show us that most men over age 60 were capable of sexual intercourse[18] and that sexual activity in females varied more with marital status than it did with age.[19] Masters and Johnson devoted a great deal of their study to the sexual responses of aged persons. They found that, physically, men over age 60 were slower to respond sexually, and the physiologic response of women was diminished somewhat, but that both are capable of orgasm, especially those who are frequently exposed to effective stimulation.[23,24] Studies continue to add to the evidence that sex continues to play an important role in the lives of many elderly persons. These studies, along with the work of Masters and Johnson, lead us to some overall conclusions that are quite different from the stereotype held by society, namely that there is no specific age when sexual activity will and should cease. Frequency of sexual activity is related to the availability of a socially sanctioned partner rather than age. An individual who has frequent sexual experiences earlier in life will continue to have more frequent sexual experiences later in life than the person who is less active in early years. Good physical health affects sexual functioning and will affect the quality and quantity of sexual activity in the elderly.

These current findings should be considered by the nurse working with the elderly. Nurses must become comfortable with the idea that the elderly have or desire to have an active sex life. The elderly do receive pleasure from sex, and sexual problems may in turn trouble older persons. The nurse must educate others in this area and try to remove prejudices. The nurse must consider each elderly person as an individual in the area of sexuality, as well as in other human needs. The elderly person's sexual needs will be affected by his or her present and previous lifestyle rather than by some concrete standard of performance. Most importantly, the nurse must realize that the elderly need touch and affection as much or even more than they need specific sexual expression.

Preventing Complications from Drug Use

Twenty-five percent of all medications are taken by the 10% of the population who are over age 65. For this reason and because of the physiologic effects of aging on drug action, drug use in the elderly must be carefully examined.

It is said that 85% of all prescriptions written by a physician are based on what the patient says. When it is considered that the average patient wants nothing more while visiting the physician than to get out and avoids telling the physician anything that will make him look "sick," one realizes that most physicians are prescribing drugs on inadequate information. With these facts in mind it is important that patients, particularly the high–drug use group called the elderly, know about their drugs, understand their actions, and keep their physicians informed. It is equally important for the nurse to be aware of age-related factors that affect drug action and increase toxicity in this age group.

The age-related factors that account for changes in drug action and increased toxicity are numerous. Gastric emptying time is slowed in the older person, and the motility of the gastrointestinal tract is slower. Intestinal blood flow is reduced; absorption by the cells is also reduced. For these reasons, drugs taken orally and absorbed in the gastrointestinal tract are absorbed more slowly than they would be in a younger person. Metabolism slows with age and any drug that affects or is affected by metabolism will be needed in lower doses. For example, dosage of antibiotics should be reduced because an elderly person retains antibiotics in the body longer than a younger person. The absorption and distribution of a drug changes with age. Passage across the blood-brain barrier, however, is always good, which means that the drug will manage to get to the brain even though it may not be supplied as well to other parts of the body. This accounts for confusion frequently being an early sign of drug toxicity in the elderly. Excretion is another factor affecting drug action. The nephrons in the kidney are reduced 50% to 60% with aging, and liver function decreases, both of which slow the rate at which drugs are excreted from the body. Cumulative actions can be a problem if doses are not reduced to account for the aging process.

When evaluating drug dosages ordered for the elderly, one must remember that recommended drug dosages are tested on 25-year-old, healthy men of approximately 150 pounds. One commonly used drug, diazepam (Valium), has a recommended adult dosage of 15 to 50 mg per day, usually given in three or four doses. In the elderly it is found that 5 to 15 mg of diazepam per day is the maximum that should be given and that 2 mg per dose or 6 mg per day is probably the most beneficial. Diazepam is commonly ordered for the elderly, but at 5 or 10 mg three times a day. Like diazepam, all tranquilizers and antidepressants should be administered in reduced dosages. Dosages ordered for elderly patients, as well as the symptoms they are exhibiting, should be examined. If they are showing confusion, it could be related to these drugs being excreted slowly by the body and crossing the blood-brain barrier in toxic levels. Confusion may be one of the earliest signs of toxicity. When older persons act confused, they are frequently labeled senile; medications should be checked to see if, in fact, the confusion may be drug induced.

Sedatives and other nervous system depressants have an intensified effect on the elderly; therefore, only small doses of the drugs should be given. Elderly persons may exhibit bizarre behavior when given a sedative or hypnotic. Confusion, disorientation, irritability, and incontinence commonly occur.

Barbiturates include in their action an ability to slow the heartbeat. For this reason it is best to avoid the use of barbiturates for the elderly, and some authorities believe that they should not be used at all. If an elderly patient is taking a barbiturate, signs of reduced heart action should be watched for; extreme care should be exercised if that patient has a heart problem. Be sure to report these symptoms to the physician immediately so that the medication order might be reconsidered.

Drug idiosyncrasies are common in the elderly. In drug idiosyncrasies the action obtained from the drug is just the opposite of the intended desired action. For example, if a sleeping pill is given and the individual has an idiosyncrasy to

---

Care of the Elderly

Nursing goals
Protect from injury
Provide comfort
Meet nutritional needs
Maintain personal hygiene
Recognize sexuality
Prevent complications from drug therapy

that particular drug, sleeplessness will result rather than sleep.

Drug interactions are a problem not only for the elderly but for all individuals taking drugs. Drugs interact with foods and with other drugs in ways that may affect the action of the drug. The dangers of giving aspirin with anticoagulants and causing an increase in bleeding are well known. Antacids are not to be given with an antibiotic because they tie up the antibiotic and reduce its effectiveness. There are literally hundreds and hundreds of possible drug interactions, and the nurse should consult drug references to identify the possible interactions for each drug the patient is taking.

It is important that all drugs taken by the elderly be identified, including those prescribed by *each* physician as well as over-the-counter drugs that the elderly may not even consider as drugs or medications. A very careful history must be taken in order to identify every drug that the elderly person is taking to avoid interactions and possible toxic effects.

The route and method of administration must be clearly understood by elderly persons as well as by younger persons taking medications. If the drug is to be taken under the tongue or taken without chewing, it is important that the person understands those directions to achieve therapeutic effect.

An elderly person with organic brain syndrome may resist taking medications. Some will very aggressively refuse. It is necessary to observe the patient swallow the drug and to be sure that the patient has not hidden the drug under the tongue, in the buccal cavity, in the hand or bed linen, or in any other number of places. Stay with the patient while he or she takes the drug, being sure that it is gone from the mouth. It may even be necessary to check the mouth after the person has supposedly taken the drug to be sure that it has been swallowed and that he or she does not aspirate.

The boxed material at left summarizes major nursing goals in the care of the elderly.

CARE OF THE HOSPITALIZED ELDERLY PATIENT

Nursing elderly patients with acute medical or surgical conditions is different in many respects from nursing younger persons. The normal aging changes that have occurred produce physiologic and psychologic patterns that would not be observed in younger persons. Nursing care will probably require more time because the elderly person is slower to move and act. More assistance may be required in performing activities of daily living. A gentle touch is also important, since the older person is susceptible to injury to skin, bones, and connective tissue. The assistance of other nursing personnel may be necessary to aid in turning, lifting, and ambulating the older patients and to prevent injury.

Vital Signs

Blood pressure is influenced by age, but the range of systolic pressure may be rather wide; however, the diastolic range is less wide. Any significant change in blood pressure should always be reported. The blood pressure of elderly persons may be affected by chronic disease or the stress of illness. In the elderly person a small change may be more important than it would be in a younger person. In an older person the pulse rate may be less significant than the volume and rhythm. The rate must be considered together with other symptoms and the patient's condition. It is not uncommon for the pulse in an elderly person to be intermittent, and patients who are receiving digitalis often exhibit changes in the normal rate and rhythm of the pulse. Most people over 70 years of age have premature beats, which occur sooner than expected in the rhythmic pattern. The nurse should develop a sensitivity to what is felt and be able to report it accurately.

Sedation

Elderly patients often do not tolerate sedative drugs as well as do younger patients; after surgery smaller amounts of narcotics are generally required. Changing the patient's position, giving a warm drink, or sitting with an anxious patient will often be of greater value than administering a drug. When a hypnotic is administered to an elderly person at bedtime, it is important for the nurse to check on the patient frequently. Often the patient may become confused, try to get out of bed, and fall, causing serious injury. When administering any medication to elderly persons, it is well not to use the term "drugs," since many of them associate drugs with addiction.

Intake and Output

Total fluid intake, including that contained in foods, should be sufficient to produce 1500 ml of urine in 24 hours. Since many older persons are dehydrated, fluids will often be retained until a physiologic balance has been established. A severely dehydrated patient may retain and absorb solution administered as an enema. Persuading an individual to take oral fluids is often a frustrating experience, and small amounts at frequent intervals will often be better accepted than a large amount at one time. When fluids are restricted because of a cardiac or other condition, the nurse should understand the amount permitted and calculate it carefully. In some conditions and postoperatively, the physician may order the administration of solutions intravenously. An important factor in the administration of intravenous fluids to elderly persons is the rate of flow. Severe cardiac disturbance may result if fluids are administered too rapidly. Unless ordered otherwise by the physician, 1000 ml of fluid should not be administered in less than 4 hours. Frequently, elderly persons do not tolerate blood transfusions well. The blood should be administered slowly, and the patient should be carefully observed during the procedure.

Careful records of intake and output should be maintained and accurate measurements made.

Ambulation and Convalescence

Recovery from acute illness is often accompanied by chronic disease, which may affect the rate of recovery. Older people require longer periods for recovery than do younger persons, and their progress is slower. The elderly should be out of bed as much as their condition permits to prevent complications. The process of ambulation should be slow and progressive, beginning by elevating the patient in bed. The next step is to have the patient sit on the side of the bed, and then sit up in a chair for 15 to 20 minutes beside the bed, taking a few steps, gradually lengthening the time up and the extent of walking. The patient should be observed for color, respiration, and pulse rate, and if faintness or dizziness occurs, the patient should be returned to bed. An elderly person out of bed for the first time should not be left alone.

The older patient recovering from surgery or serious illness may become anxious and frustrated because of the slow rate of recovery and long convalescence. The nurse should recognize that these emotions can affect the patient's desire to participate in care and continue with prescribed activities; a caring attitude, encouragement, and support are important aspect of care.

When caring for elderly patients in the hospital or in the home, the nurse should speak clearly and distinctly and be sure that the patient understands. This is especially important when giving medications or treatments, since the patient may respond to a name that is not his own.

When working with elderly patients in the hospital or in the home, the nurse should not expect to make requests and secure a quick response. The patient may respond with "all right" or "in a minute." Directions should be given slowly, making certain that the patient understands. The patient may indicate that he understands, but action may be slow. The older person should not be hurried, since this may create confusion and render the patient unable to respond appropriately.

The boxed material below summarizes nursing care of the hospitalized elderly patient.

NURSING HOMES

Only 5% of the elderly population live in institutions, but of these, most are in **nursing homes.** Many of those residing in nursing homes could be cared for in their own homes. There is a move to provide additional services to families to make home care feasible, but nursing homes remain an important provider of health care. Nursing homes may provide sheltered care for the ambulatory patient, intermediate care, or skilled care for the patient requiring extensive nursing services. A home may provide only one or all three of these levels of care, and the home is chosen according to the nursing needs of the prospective resident.

Nursing homes approved for Medicare require that the personnel maintain nursing care plans for each patient. Plans should be based on the immediate and long-term needs of the patient.

Care of the Hospitalized Elderly Patient

Nursing interventions
Recognize changes in vital signs.
Monitor sedation closely.
Maintain adequate fluid intake and output.
Assist with ambulation and convalescence.
Prevent injury and complications.

As in the general hospital, they should reflect the thinking of the entire nursing staff.

The average nursing home resident differs little from most other persons of the same chronologic age. In addition to the normal degenerative changes, many have chronic diseases and may be malnourished and debilitated. The nursing care must be individualized according to the individual's particular needs. Some patients will be ambulatory and be able to provide much of their own care; others will need assistance with personal hygiene, and some must have total care. The patient's psychologic needs should be met, reassuring personal worth and seeking to maintain a sense of dignity and self-respect.

ALTERNATIVES TO INSTITUTIONAL CARE

Home Care

If the patient is to be cared for in his or her own home, the family and the community must provide the necessary services. Most elderly persons prefer to remain in their own homes and are happier when they can do so. Each person must be carefully evaluated medically and socially for home care. When the person's potential for self-care has been determined, an individualized program is planned. Many of the services under the Older Americans Act such as meals, transportation to physicians or clinics, home health aides, and homemaker service, as well as visits by the public health nurse or visiting nurse may be needed. "**Home care** can preserve the elderly person's independence, dignity, and identity—precious human qualities that are often lost when the elderly person is placed in an institution"* (see Chapter 14).

With the introduction of the prospective payment system and **diagnosis-related groups,** the incentive to provide alternatives to hospitalization is greater. Home care programs and preventive programs are expanding in an effort to keep elderly individuals from being hospitalized. Health maintenance organizations have become more involved in providing Medicare benefits to the el-

derly. This involvement has created greater use of alternate care services such as home care, day care, and preventive programs.

Day Hospital

Experimental programs for daytime care of the aged are being tried in both the United States and Canada. The objective is to prevent or delay admission to an institution and to promote independence. Individuals must be ambulatory; however, the patient may be permitted to use a walker or a cane. Emergency care is available if needed. A kitchen may be available for retraining and motivation. Transportation is provided, and a noon meal is provided in a cafeteria. Each person is encouraged to participate in group activities and in various crafts. A team approach is used with a physician, nurse, dietitian, psychiatrist, and occupational therapist. Patients are evaluated as to progress and may become sufficiently independent to maintain themselves at home. Thus some leave the program, and others are admitted.

Foster Home

The care of the elderly in a foster home has had limited success. The concept that an elderly person will be a happier person in a home environment and be able to share in family relationships has been difficult to implement in many communities. Disadvantages have centered around the lack of medical care and the foster home being operated for profit.

Other Services

The extended care facility provides short-term, intermediate, and convalescent care. It may be a part of a general hospital or be operated as an independent institution. Its function is to provide care after an acute illness until the person is able to return home.

A variety of community outpatient services is available in many communities. These include mental health clinics, physical therapy, dental clinics, speech clinics, and numerous social services.

Group Work with the Elderly

Working with the aged in groups can be very effective in meeting psychosocial needs. Group work of this nature is not to be confused with group psychotherapy, which deals with people who have psychiatric problems. Group work has been employed to treat and prevent psychosocial

---

*From Connecticut testing home care plan for the aged, Aging 223:8, May 1973.

problems in the elderly as well as to maintain mental health. Groups have been conducted for reality orientation, remotivation, reminiscing, and health teaching. In some instances the family is also involved with the group.

Reality orientation groups are used with regressed aged persons, especially those with chronic brain syndrome. A small group of four or five persons meets daily with their leader, who emphasizes time, day, month, weather conditions, and the like, which are then posted on a board for all to see throughout the day. Remotivation groups are the next step in progression after reality orientation. The leader must have specialized training to conduct these groups.

Reminiscing groups have been pioneered by Ebersole, a psychiatric nurse.[8] Reminiscing is an adaptive response to aging and can be used effectively to preserve and rebuild self-concept and maintain social integrity. It will help elderly persons to remember who they are and thus stimulate self-esteem.

Nurses should be encouraged to investigate possibilities of working with groups, seek whatever training is required, and implement or assist in group work with the elderly when opportunities arise. Group work requires the support and cooperation of everyone in the agency if it is to be successful.

REFERENCES AND ADDITIONAL READINGS

1. Boyer G and Boyer J: Sexuality and aging, Nurs Clin North Am 17:421-427, 1982.

2. Burns EM and Buchwalter KC: Pathophysiology and etiology of Alzheimer's disease, Nurs Clin North Am 23(1), 11-29, 1988.

3. Burnside IM: Nursing and the aged: a self-care approach, ed 3, New York, 1988, McGraw-Hill Book Co.

4. Burnside IM: Working with the elderly: group process and the techniques, ed 3, N Scituate, Mass, 1984, Duxbury Press.

5. Butler RN, and Lewis M: Aging and mental health, ed 3, St Louis, 1982, The CV Mosby Co.

6. Carnevali DL and Patrick M: Nursing management for the elderly, ed 2, New York, 1986, JB Lippincott Co.

7. Compion M and Maletta G: Behavior; a symptom of cognitive and functional disorders. In Gordon G and Stryer R, (eds): Creative long-term care, administration, Springfield, Ill, 1983, Charles C Thomas, Publisher.

8. Ebersole P and Hess P: Toward healthy aging; human needs and nursing response, ed 3, St Louis, 1990, The CV Mosby Co.

9. Enloe C: Managing daily living with diminishing resources and losses. In Cornwall D and Patrick M, Nursing management for the elderly, ed 2, Philadelphia, 1986, JB Lippincott Co.

10. Erikson EH: Identity and the life cycle: psychological issues, New York, 1950, International Universities Press.

11. Esberger KK and Hughes ST Jr: Nursing care of the aged, Norwalk, Conn, 1989, Appleton & Lange.

12. Eustis NN, Greenberg J, and Patten S: Long-term care for older persons: a policy perspective, Monterey, 1984, Brooks/Cole Publishing Co.

13. Goodman CE, Osteoporosis and physical activity. AAOHN 35:539-542, 1987.

14. Hall GR: Care of the patient with Alzheimer's disease living at home, Nurs Clin North Am 23(1): 31-46, 1988.

15. Hewner SJ: Bringing home the health care, J Gerontol Nurs 12(2): 29-30, 32-35, 1986.

16. Kane RL, Ouslander JG, and Abrass IB: Essentials of clinical geriatrics, New York, 1984, McGraw-Hill, Inc.

17. Keough J. In Huey, FL: What teaching nursing homes are teaching us, Am J Nurs 85:678-683.

18. Kinsey AC and others: Sexual behavior in the human male, Philadelphia, 1948, WB Saunders Co.

19. Kinsey AC and others: Sexual behavior in the human female, Philadelphia, 1953, WB Saunders Co.

20. Kirkpatrick M: A self care model for osteoporosis, AAOHN 35:531-535, 1987.

21. Langland R: Effects of touch on communication with elderly confused clients, J Gerontol Nurs 8: 152-155, 1982.

22. Madson S: How to reduce the risk of postmenopausal osteoporosis, J Gerontol Nurs 15(9): 20-24, 1989.

23. Masters WH and Johnson VE: Human sexual response, Boston, 1966, Little, Brown & Co, Inc.

24. Masters WH and Johnson VE: Human sexual inadequacy, Boston, 1970, Little Brown & Co, Inc.

25. Matteson MA and McConnell ES: Gerontological nursing: concepts and practice, Philadelphia, 1988, WB Saunders Company.

26. Parsons CL: Group reminiscence therapy and levels of depression in the elderly, Nurse Pract 11: 68-76, 1986.

27. Profile of older Americans: 1990, Program resources department, AARP and AoA, Washington, DC, 1990, US Department of Health and Human Services.

28. Tagg PI: Neighborhood resources for the elderly, Home Health Care Nurse 4(2): 24-29, 1986.

29. Webster's medical desk dictionary, Springfield, Mass, 1986, Merriam-Webster, Inc.

30. White JE: Osteoporosis: strategies for prevention, Nurse Pract 11(9): 36-51, 1986.

31. Yurick AG and others: The aged person and the nursing process, ed 3, Norwalk, Conn, 1989, Appleton & Lange.

12

Rehabilitation

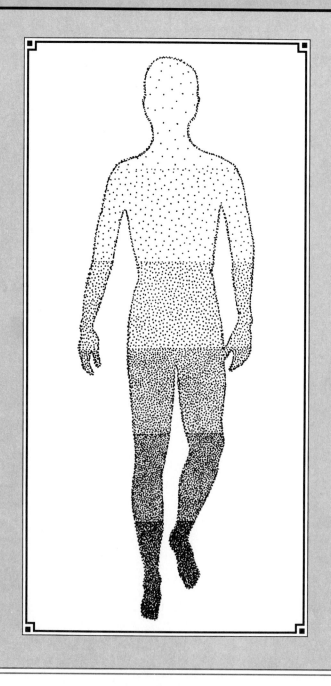

KEY WORDS

activities of daily living (ADL)
adaptation
amputee
body image
braces
continuity
contractures
motivation
prosthesis
prosthetist
rehabilitation
therapist

OBJECTIVES

1. Identify the goals of rehabilitation.

2. Discuss the concept of a rehabilitation team, its members, and their roles.

3. Identify types of facilities and agencies that provide rehabilitation services.

4. Discuss the rehabilitative aspects of each phase of patient care: primary, secondary, and tertiary.

5. Identify the normal emotional responses to disability and discuss related nursing interventions.

6. Identify nursing activities that prevent deformity and preserve function.

7. Discuss methods of bladder and bowel training and regulation.

8. Discuss the role of the rehabilitation nurse as a motivator and teacher.

9. Discuss the care of prostheses and braces and the care of the skin beneath them.

10. Describe the physical preparation of the patient for crutch walking.

11. Discuss important points related to the safe teaching of crutch walking.

12. Give examples of self-help devices for the handicapped.

REHABILITATION

The concept of **rehabilitation** is broad and far reaching and is a fundamental process in providing total patient care. Many definitions and interpretations of this process exist, but they all share a common meaning. Basically, rehabilitation is the process of assisting individuals who have been ill or who have become disabled in recovering to their highest possible level of independence and well-being. The need for rehabilitation occurs when a person's previous way of life is changed by illness or injury. Depending on the type of disability, the physical, mental, vocational, social, and economic aspects of a person's life may be altered. Some disabling events may be minor and the need for rehabilitation limited. Others may require extensive rehabilitation that involves many facets of a person's life.

Most authorities believe that a very important concept of rehabilitation is that individuals be restored to their full ability of which they are capable in all areas—physical, emotional, social, educational, and vocational. The rehabilitation process helps patients to live the most productive lives possible. Instead of the classic emphasis on disease, diagnosis, and therapeutic procedure, rehabilitation stresses restoration of normal function, prevention of complications, education of patient and family, adaptation, and retraining. **Adaptation** is the process of adjusting to life changes that occur with disability. The patient must participate in the adaptation process, or rehabilitation will be incomplete or unsuccessful.

The following situation exemplifies rehabilitation. Forty years ago Mr. J., who is without legs, would have looked forward to spending the rest of his life in a wheelchair, dependent on public support and charity. Restoration of physical function, however, has restored his independence, self-sufficiency, and self-image.

Mr. J., 35 years of age, is married and the father of five children. One day while at work he was driving his pickup truck along a rain-slicked expressway when, without warning, a large truck suddenly crossed the highway and crashed into his vehicle. Mr. J. was rushed by ambulance to the hospital, where his condition was considered serious. Both legs were so badly injured that above-knee amputation was necessary. Today Mr. J. has been fitted with artificial legs and is learning how to walk with them. He is being trained for a new kind of work. He is enthusiastic and anxious to progress with ambulation. He is optimistic and ready to proceed with his training and is looking forward to complete independence and being able to care for his family.

REHABILITATION NURSING

Rehabilitation may be viewed as an underlying theme of all nursing care. Regardless of the care setting, acute care hospital, long-term care facility, rehabilitation facility, or the community, nurses use patient-care practices and techniques that aim at restoration of function and prevention of complications. These approaches form some of the basic tenets of nursing practice. For example, the nurse caring for the bed-bound patient uses methods to position the patient and provide movement and exercise to prevent skin breakdown and respiratory complications. As the patient improves, the nurse uses a range of techniques: methods to improve mobility through transfer training, strengthening exercises, and ambulation; emphasis on improved ability of the patient to participate in **activities of daily living (ADLs)** such as bathing, grooming, dressing, and feeding; and, if needed, methods to assess and correct incontinence.

Although principles of rehabilitation are integral to all nursing practice, rehabilitation nursing is viewed as a specialty practice area within nursing. In 1988, the Association of Rehabilitation Nurses in cooperation with the American Nurses Association defined rehabilitation nursing and stated its goals as follows:

Rehabilitation nursing is a specialty practice area within the scope of professional nursing practice. Rehabilitation nursing is the diagnosis and treatment of human responses of individuals and groups to actual or potential health problems stemming from altered functional ability and altered life-style.

The goal of rehabilitation nursing is to assist the individual with disability and chronic illness in the restoration and maintenance of maximal health. The rehabilitation nurse should be skilled at treating alterations in functional ability and life-style resulting from physical disability and chronic illness.*

---

*American Nurses Association and Association of Rehabilitation Nurses: Rehabilitation nursing, Kansas City, MO, 1988. American Nurses Association.

Rehabilitation nurses care for patients with a wide range of disabling conditions, such as stroke, spinal cord injury, brain injury, amputation, cancer, congenital deficits, and problems of addiction. In addition to providing nursing care that is based on the rehabilitation philosophy of maximizing function and preventing complications, rehabilitation nurses understand the impact of these conditions on the patient. For instance, in caring for the person with a brain injury, the nurse must have the ability to assess behavioral and communication problems occurring secondarily to the injury. In caring for the person with a spinal cord injury, the nurse must understand the need for specialized approaches to bowel and bladder care.

In this chapter some of the basic techniques of rehabilitation nursing will be described. For a more detailed description of rehabilitation nursing care of patients with specific disabilities, a rehabilitation nursing textbook should be consulted (See boxed material below).[2,10]

Rehabilitation in Each Phase of Health Care

Health care may be divided into three phases or stages: *primary health care* refers to preventive efforts, *secondary health care* deals with the period of acute illness, and *tertiary health care* involves recovery and rehabilitation from illness or accident. Rehabilitation philosophy and practices are part of all aspects of health care and are integral to each phase of nursing care.

Primary health care

In this phase of health care, emphasis is placed on *prevention* of disease and accidents. One aspect is the protection of all susceptible individuals against those diseases for which positive immunizing agents are available. The crippling conditions of poliomyelitis have been nearly eliminated by the administration of the polio vaccine. Another aspect involves early assessment and edu-

cation about chronic disease to decrease long-term disability. Hypertension, when detected early, can be managed through a variety of approaches including dietary management, smoking cessation, exercise, and, when needed, medications. If carefully managed, the long-term risks associated with hypertension—heart disease, renal disease, and stroke—can be reduced. Also, methods to promote safety in the work place, enhanced driving safety through reduced speed and use of seat belts, and reduction of pollutants in the environment are examples of preventive health practices.

Nurses working in primary care and in all other health care settings have the opportunity to educate individuals and groups in many preventive health practices. These include the importance of regular medical and dental evaluation, well-balanced nutrition, exercise, smoking cessation, approaches to management of chronic disease, and appropriate use of medications. These practices focus on keeping the individual at a maximum level of health and well-being.

Secondary health care

Rehabilitation nursing concepts are essential aspects in caring for acutely ill patients. During the hospital stay the nurse must recognize the potential impact of illness and disability on the individual's physical function and emotional state. With ongoing nursing assessment, the extent of patients' *functional limitation* (ability to care for themselves, mobility, continence) can be determined and support provided to the patients and their families. Even at the earliest stages of illness and disability, realistic short-term and long-term goals should be established with patients that reflect their potential for participation in rehabilitation programs. The nurse uses these goals in planning daily care.

Planning with the physician and other members of the health care team, the nurse helps the patient to participate in a program of increased activity. The nurse needs to continually assess the effects of this increased activity on the patient. For the elderly, fatigue may have a greater impact on recovery and increased activity than for younger patients. As a result, activity tolerance must be carefully assessed in an acutely ill older person. Measuring vital signs, observing respiratory and color changes during activity, and determining endurance for participation in sitting, transferring, and walking are a few of these assessment parameters.

Focus of Rehabilitation
Physical
Emotional
Social
Educational
Vocational

Of great importance during this time is the prevention of *secondary complications* such as pressure sores or contracture formations that may occur because of the patient's immobility and altered physical and medical status. Keeping the patient as mobile and well-nourished as possible is the goal. Maintaining body alignment, controlling joint range of motion, and preventing excessive pressure against the patient's skin will help reduce the incidence of secondary problems.

Tertiary health care

The period of recovery is one of convalescence, which is a gradual process that may extend over a considerable period and be punctuated with one or more relapses. As soon as the acute phase of illness has passed, a careful evaluation of the disability should be made, and a program of therapy should be planned for the individual patient. If the nurse's concept of rehabilitation includes all patients, irrespective of disability, the nurse will guide many individuals with nondisabling illnesses in self-help activities and an early return to normal living. There is no time in the course of any illness when rehabilitation begins or ends. It should run concurrently with the illness, whether the illness is acute or chronic, temporary or permanent, disabling or nondisabling. Many more patients are being rehabilitated and returned to useful and productive lives than in the past. Research has contributed to rehabilitation through the development of new and improved prostheses, techniques, and methods. When rehabilitation procedures are begun early, hope is given to the individual, mental depression and discouragement may be decreased, and the disabling conditions resulting from prolonged bed rest may be prevented.

Rehabilitation of the aged and chronically ill may be a long process. The short-term and long-term goals have to be adjusted to fit the individual's potential. It may take longer for an older person to attain certain skills; again, fatigue, decreased endurance, and stamina may be more of a factor for an older person than for a younger one. Dependency and low self-esteem may cause the aged person to reject participation in rehabilitation.[4] However, exercise and increased activity may have a powerful impact on the level of health and well-being of the elderly.[13] For a person with chronic illness, full participation in the level of activity that a rehabilitation program requires may be diminished by the isolation the illness has im-

posed, fear of failure, and hopelessness. It may not be possible to restore all patients to the level of independence they desire. For some patients, severe disability may limit the potential for total independence and care options. The continued guidance and support of the intradisciplinary team is needed when the severity of disability is recognized by the patient and family. The services of the entire team are needed to identify approaches in finding a supportive environment for the patient in the community or in a long-term care setting.

Rehabilitation Team

Any comprehensive program in rehabilitation requires a group of experts in various areas of restorative care, since no single profession can provide all the necessary services for a complete rehabilitation program. This group, or intradisciplinary team, meets regularly to establish patient goals, evaluate progress, and revise the treatment plan (Figure 12-1).

Patient

The most important member of the rehabilitation team is the patient. Success in a rehabilitation program can only occur if the patient has an understanding of his or her disability, is involved in setting goals, and participates in the plan of care. Because of the stress of adapting to all the life changes imposed by the disability, the patient may have lost motivation for this level of participation. Involvement of family and a significant other is often pivotal in helping the patient find such motivation. Family and friends can often provide the impetus for participation that the patient is unable to find on his or her own. Meetings with the patient, family, and members of the team provide the information necessary for a more successful outcome. Such meetings should occur during the early part of the program to aid the patient in adjustment, then on a regularly scheduled basis in preparation for discharge.

Nurse

The role of the nurse in a rehabilitation setting is a diverse one. Nurses function as care givers, teachers, coordinators, evaluators, and resources for patients and family members. The nursing staff frequently spends the most time with the patient, being present 24 hours a day. This affords the opportunity for nurses to observe, assess, teach, reinforce, and evaluate the effects of the

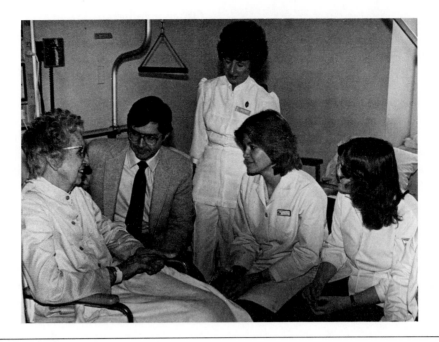

Figure 12-1
Multidisciplinary rehabilitation team meets regularly to discuss patient progress, goals, and approaches. *(Courtesy Copley Memorial Hospital, Aurora, Il.)*

total rehabilitation program. Nurses use assessment criteria to determine the patient's level of disability, stage of adaptation and adjustment, and learning needs. Nursing care is based on these findings. In some settings, the nurse coordinates the intradisciplinary team meetings. The nurse, as well as other members of the team, contributes pertinent information that provides a clear picture of the patient's progress over time. Nurses and other team members' documentation on patient progress may be an important aspect of rehabilitation.

Physician

The physician member of the team may be a psychiatrist, trained as a medical specialist in physical rehabilitation. However, in some settings, the physician on the team may be a member of another medical specialty such as neurology, orthopedics, oncology, cardiology, and pediatrics. Physicians trained in these areas, who choose to practice in a rehabilitation setting, often have a special interest in this phase of care. The physician assesses the medical status of the patient and prescribes various evaluative procedures, medications, consultations, and therapies as needed, and provides important information about the pa-

tient's status to other members of the team, the patient, and the family.

Physical therapist

The physical **therapist** deals with exercise, muscle strengthening, and problems of mobility. After initial assessment of muscle strength and joint range of motion, the therapist implements exercises and therapeutic techniques ordered by the physician. Ongoing assessment and evaluation are reported to the team, together with specific approaches that work well for the particular patient. The physical therapist also implements prescriptions for splints, braces, prostheses, and wheelchairs, and is a good resource for the nurse when problems arise with this equipment.

Occupational therapist

The occupational therapist (OT) evaluates the impact of the disability on the patient's physical and cognitive ability in a variety of domains. An occupational therapist assesses (1) the patient's ability to perform in a variety of activities of daily living such as bathing, dressing and eating, (2) the patient's cognitive ability to perceive and understand the environment in order to function in a safe and meaningful way, and (3) movement problems. With the nurse, physician, and speech therapist, the OT may assist with evaluation and treatment of chewing and swallowing problems. An occupational therapist's treatment approach may include exercise regimens, modalities such as heat, cold, or vibration, and craft activities to strengthen the patient's muscles and improve coordination and balance. Methods to improve concentration ability and the prescription of assistance devices such as splints, adapted eating utensils, and dressing aids may also be included.

Vocational therapist

The vocational therapy department uses counselors to assess the patient's job skills, educational needs, interests, and motivation. Therapists also arrange for job retraining when necessary and direct disabled persons to appropriate vocations.

Psychologist

Emotional problems are bound to occur in a crisis situation such as sudden disability. Disruptions of lifestyle, family structure, and body image result in profound psychologic problems. The psychologist uses testing and interviewing to identify problems and works with the patient and family to develop coping mechanisms and methods of adjusting to the disability. Advising other team members on how to deal with patients undergoing emotional distress is an important role of the psychologist.

Social worker

The problems of housing, finances, transportation, and family relationships are addressed by the social worker. This team member is the link between the institution and the community, assisting the patient and family to solve the problems of transition.

Recreational therapist

Recreation and play are as important to total patient care as physical and emotional support. The recreational therapist assesses interests and provides for involvement in games, sports, hobbies, music, and other forms of diversion. Structured programs within the institution are implemented to meet patient needs, and trips to the "outside world" to movies, bowling lanes, plays, and other activities assist the individual to apply some of the adaptation skills learned in the rehabilitation process.

Other members

Often the rehabilitation team will include a speech therapist, dietitian, orthopedist, dentist, teacher, and members of other professions, depending on the type of disability.

Rehabilitation Programs

Personal disability resulting from World War II placed emphasis on the need to establish programs and centers for rehabilitation treatment. Over the past 40 years there has been a rapid growth in such rehabilitation programs. Today there are over 7000 rehabilitation facilities in the United States. These facilities provide a wide range of services to disabled individuals. Rehabilitation programs are based in a variety of settings, within acute care hospitals, free standing facilities, long-term care facilities, and in the community. Centers are operated by for-profit and not-for-profit organizations, state vocational agencies, insurance companies, private agencies, and a variety of community agencies.

In 1954 the Vocational Rehabilitation Act was passed by the U.S. Congress. This law provided funds to state agencies for improvement and expansion of rehabilitation services. The primary objective of the Social and Rehabilitation Service (formerly called the Vocational Rehabilitation Department) is the education and training of persons for employment. Many handicaps can be corrected, rendering the individual employable and economically independent and self-sufficient. A 50-year-old woman who was a widow was employed to care for an elderly patient in the home. She was unable to continue because of severe varicose veins. Through vocational rehabilitation she received medical care and hospitalization for vein stripping, thereby enabling her to continue with employment.

The original Vocational Rehabilitation Act was updated in 1973 and amended in 1978 to include a comprehensive definition of independent living.[12] The amendment mandated that any institution receiving federal funds must make its facilities open and accessible to the handicapped. This includes not only government buildings, but national parks and recreation areas as well.

The services under the Social and Rehabilitation Service have been greatly expanded to cover many more types of disabilities. The developmental disabilities' program now extends services to persons afflicted by mental retardation, cerebral palsy, convulsive disorders, and other neurologic disorders. A primary problem has been the shortage of trained personnel. In an effort to overcome this problem, the Social and Rehabilitation Service has provided grants to universities and certain institutions to train individuals in vocational rehabilitation. Medicare, administered by the Social Security Administration, now includes rehabilitative services for both hospitalized patients and those recuperating elsewhere. The Veterans Administration provides rehabilitation services for veterans.

Some public school systems operate special classes for children with cardiac disease and those in need of sight saving. There are schools for children who are blind and deaf, have cerebral palsy, or are mentally retarded. The National Foundation for Asthmatic Children operates a school in Tucson, Arizona. Through the expanding medium of educational television, many handicapped individuals are being served. There is also growing concern about the problems of chronic alcoholism and drug addiction. Centers, public and private, are being opened in many large cities to treat and rehabilitate these persons.

Federal and state governments are developing programs for research in mental retardation. It is not only important to learn more about the causes of mental retardation, but also to learn how many of the mentally retarded can be rehabilitated to lead normal, productive lives in the community. Physical and mental retardation is not the only area in which rehabilitative services are needed. Society has become aware of other kinds of sickness. Millions of persons are in need of rehabilitative services, such as the economically depressed, the elderly, migrant workers, juvenile offenders, children and young people who are addicted to drugs, and alcoholics. Some rehabilitative efforts are being made in these areas, but much remains to be done.

Rehabilitation in Other Settings

Outside of established rehabilitation centers, the team usually consists of physician, nurse, patient, and family. The nurse who has a basic understanding of rehabilitation and whose philosophy includes the whole patient is a key person in rehabilitation. In the acute care setting, where the rehabilitation process must begin, it is often the responsibility of the nurse to plan and coordinate the patient's rehabilitation program, recognizing the impact of acute illness and disability on function, and initiating early interventions. When caring for patients in extended care facilities, the nurse works with the patient performing those activities or exercises prescribed by the physical therapy department. The patient being cared for at home may benefit from the services of a physical therapist, speech therapist, or occupational therapist, provided either through private agencies or public health departments. Whereas the patient may participate in rehabilitation therapy sessions daily in a rehabilitation center, visits are usually less frequent in other settings. It is the nurse's responsibility to supervise and conduct ongoing therapy as prescribed by each therapist, and to report the patient's progress.

Emotional Response to Disability

Disability is a general term that refers to the limiting effects of an acute or chronic condition on an individual over time. A disabling event often creates a period of crisis for the patient. With loss of body function, loss of ability to work, or loss of ability to function independently, feelings of self-worth may be changed for a limited period or for a long time. The individual's **body image** may undergo significant changes. The person may gradually realize that he or she is different, and that life will probably be changed forever. The individual may wonder how family, friends, and colleagues will accept him or her. Fear, worry, anxiety, and apprehension are increased; the person may enter a period of shock and dismay. Discouragement and depression are common during this early time.

Many factors can influence a person's ability to cope with a disabling event. Some of these factors include age, type and severity of disability, and the meaning of the loss to the person. The age at onset of disability and the needs at certain periods of life may have an impact on how well the person copes. As an example, a person born with a physical handicap may adjust to the limitations in life but experience difficulty at certain times. Adolescence may be such a time; the adolescent goal of independence from family may be difficult because of the physical care needs. The disabled adolescent may refuse to participate in long-established care routines as a form of seeking independence. Another example of the impact of age on the reaction to disability may be seen in the elderly disabled person. He or she may experience difficulty in accepting the rationale for participation in the difficult work of recovery, feeling that he or she is just "too old" for such an effort.

The person who becomes disabled from a traumatic event may experience an acute emotional reaction to the loss and changes that occur. The reaction may be severe enough to limit the person's participation in rehabilitation. Individuals with *chronic progressive disease* may adapt to the gradual changes in function but experience emotional distress if acute medical problems require hospitalization, or when care supports cannot meet their needs. When the person with chronic progressive disease reaches a point in the course of their disease when independent living is no longer possible, the need for placement in an extended-care facility may create great distress.

The meaning of the loss of function that has resulted will vary with every person. Loss of an arm may affect a professional pianist or carpenter more severely than a school teacher or chemist. Much depends on how the loss affects the patient's everyday life. Personality problems that develop after a disability may occur as a result of the patient's personality characteristics before the injury. A person who can easily be made to feel inadequate before the injury will have more emotional stress after the injury. Initial nursing assessment of the patient and family is important. A psychosocial history obtained on admission will help the nurse plan therapeutic interventions geared to the specific patient and family.

The initial reaction to a physical injury is *shock*. The patient experiences disbelief, anxiety, and fear, which are considered part of the mourning process. *Loss* of anything that is meaningful to the patient will produce a period of grief. The patient may be unable to look at the change, attempting to deny its existence. Gradually the patient will begin to talk about the change, and often nurses are the first to be questioned about the disability. The patient may ask to see the disabled part and may seem both fascinated and revolted. During this stage of adjustment, depression and anger may be present. Eventually the patient may realize that life cannot be as it was before and will begin to examine the values placed on conventional "normality." He or she may realize that the disability need not alter his or her entire life, and may begin to react more openly with others. Time is essential for this process of adaptation and adjustment.

Similar reactions occur with patients facing surgery or progressively deteriorating diseases. However, the surgical patient usually has time to begin adapting before surgery. Patients with chronic illnesses have time to adjust to each stage of the illness.

The patient's family

A family's response to a patient's illness and loss of function is based on many factors. The relationships of the individuals involved, methods of family coping, role of the patient in the family, and economic issues may all have an impact on this response. During the acute phase of the condition the family will suffer from anxiety, apprehension, and fear. The family should be given emotional support, comfort, and all the information possible during this critical period. If the patient is the breadwinner, the spouse may be distressed about how medical and hospital bills will be paid or how to provide for the family. A serious disability may mean social isolation for the family, as well as for the patient. To set an individual apart from other individuals means loneliness and depression. As soon as the prognosis can be made, long-term goals should be established for the patient. The family should be given information about sources of help in rehabilitation and economic assistance. A social worker may help the family with plans, but if a social worker is unavailable, nurses should be familiar with community agencies and with the sources of help for a family in trouble. Specific support groups are available for families of disabled persons. For example, the National Head Injury Foundation* provides information, education, resources, and peer support for patients and their families.

NURSING APPROACHES TO REHABILITATION CARE

The nurse, as a member of the rehabilitation team, must assume a share of responsibility for guiding the patient toward health and independence. Many nurses will be working with the physician without the services of other persons who contribute to a comprehensive rehabilitation program. Therefore it is increasingly important for

---

*National Head Injury Foundation, 33 Turnpike Road, Southboro, MA 01772

the nurse to be familiar with the local and state agencies that can provide services to the patient. Each patient must be accepted as an individual, and each will have his or her own special problems. The nurse should understand that the patient may go through several stages characterized by varying emotional reactions before being able to adapt and adjust to the illness or disability. The nurse should not attempt to change the patient's life patterns but, through listening and understanding, provide support while the patient moves toward adaptation and a new way of living.

In caring for patients, particularly those who are immobile, the nurse needs to use rehabilitation techniques to promote maximum functioning and to prevent secondary complications. These techniques include (1) range of joint motion, (2) positioning and transferring of the patient in bed and in a chair, (3) encouraging patient participation in self-care, and (4) prevention of skin breakdown. Depending on the needs of the patient, the nurse may have to develop a program of bladder and bowel care. The nurse may be asked questions by the patient about sexuality and sexual function in disability. Teaching the patient the implications of his diagnosis, reinforcing aspects of self-care, and providing for continuity of care are underlying themes of nursing care of the disabled.

Rehabilitation Techniques
Range of joint motion

Each joint of the human body has a potential range of motion that is normal for that joint. In order for movement to be maintained, the limbs of the body must be moved to stretch the muscles, ligaments, and tendons that surround and support each joint. This stretching occurs with normal daily activity. However, when illness or injury limits normal movement there is a potential to lose movement in joints. Without the stretching associated with normal movement, the muscles, tendons, and ligaments surrounding joints can become shortened, limiting the amount of possible movement. When this occurs a **contracture,** or fixed movement, of the joint may develop. In the person with loss of muscle strength, the development of a contracture can occur within a relatively short period of time. A contracture can limit function in a joint and cause secondary complications. For example, a foot contracted in a position of foot drop may not be able to support the foot and leg for walking, or a stroke patient with

an elbow severely contracted in the flexed position may develop skin breakdown because of pressure and maceration of the skin.

When a patient is immobilized either because of illness or injury, nurses need to provide the movement necessary to keep joints as mobile as possible. This type of movement regimen, *range of joint movement* (ROM), needs to be provided several times a day to each joint to prevent stiffness and contracture formation. Joints that should be exercised include the neck, shoulders, elbows, wrists and fingers, hips, knees, ankles, and toes. For many patients, the exercises will be passive, and the nurse will exercise the joints without assistance from the patient. Passive exercise accomplishes several things for the patient: (1) it helps to keep joints mobile, (2) it promotes venous return and lymphatic flow and (3) it helps prevent excess demineralization in the bone that is exacerbated by inactivity. If the patient is able to move he or she can perform active range of motion by taking the limbs through all the potential degrees of movement.

The normal range of motion for some of the joints is described in Figure 12-2. Normal range of motion for joints include:

Neck. The neck is able to rotate from side to side, flex toward the chest and extend toward the back, and extend away from the flex toward the shoulders on each side.

Shoulders. The shoulders are able to rotate (with arms moving in a circular motion), flex forward, extend backwards, move away from the body (abduction), and move toward the body (adduction).

Elbows. The elbows are able to flex toward the upper arm and extend away from the upper arm.

Hips. The hips are able to rotate in a circular motion, flex toward the body, extend and hyperextend away from the body, and move toward the body (adduction) and away from the body (abduction).

Knees. The knees are able to bend (flex) and to straighten (extend).

When providing exercises for range of joint motion, the nurse should never push or stretch the joint beyond the point of stiffness, pain, or discomfort. A physical therapist and occupational therapist can assist with care of tight and painful joints. When providing such exercises, the nurse should support the limb and the joints involved. As an example, if a nurse is flexing a patient's hip,

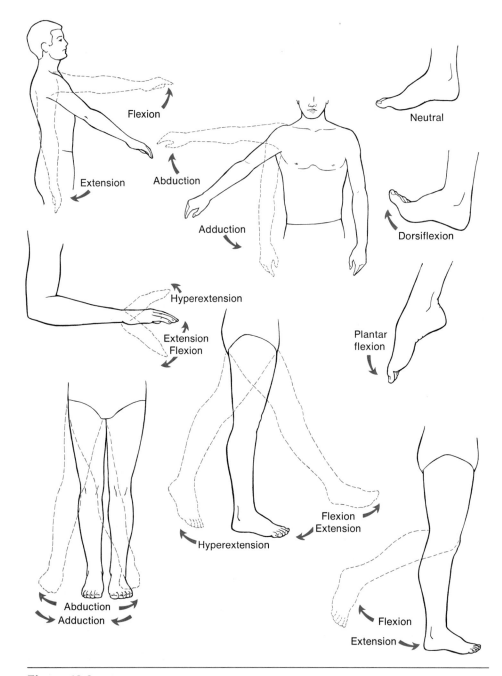

Figure 12-2
Range of motion. Methods of exercising joints to prevent contractures and to stimulate circulation.

the patient's leg should be cradled in the nurse's arm at the knee. The nurse gently holds the hip down with the other hand to prevent lifting up of the hip. When providing this exercise the nurse should stand as close as possible to the patient with the height of the bed adjusted to prevent back, shoulder, and arm strain. Use of the principles of body mechanics is important while lifting

or moving the patient during range of motion exercises (see boxed material on p. 267).

If the patient has weakness or paralysis in one limb or on one side of the body, the patient can be taught self-range of motion exercises. The nurse or therapist can instruct the patient to cradle and lift the weaker limb with the strong limb. A stroke patient can use the strong arm to lift and

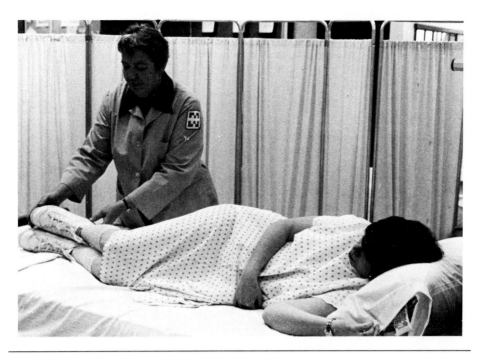

Figure 12-3
High-topped canvas shoes maintain foot alignment regardless of patient's position in bed. Shoes are worn with socks for 3 hours, removed for 1 hour, and reapplied. *(Courtesy William Rainey Harper College, Palatine, Il.)*

Guidelines for Providing Range of Joint Motion

Never push or stretch the joint beyond the point of pain.
Provide support to the limb and joints involved.
Stand as close to the patient as possible.
Teach the patient and family how to perform range of motion exercises.

---

exercise the weak arm and can use the strong foot and leg by pushing it under the weak leg and lifting.

In acute care hospitals, nursing homes, rehabilitation hospitals, and adult day care programs in the community, nurses and therapists organize patients to participate in group exercise programs. Some of these programs incorporate self-range of motion and active range of motion as part of the program. These programs have been found to have additional benefits such as increased activity tolerance and socialization.[12]

Positioning
In addition to exercises, good body alignment in either a sitting or lying position is important in preventing deformities and skin breakdown. When the patient is in a lying or supine position, legs and feet should be kept in line with the torso of the body, and an adjustable footboard that extends above the toes should be used to help prevent foot-drop and keep covers off the feet. Heels should be kept free from pressure, with toes pointing toward the ceiling. High-topped tennis shoes with socks, or foot splints, can be used intermittently (3 hours on, 1 hour off) to prevent foot-drop (Figure 12-3). Unlike a footboard, these shoes and splints maintain proper alignment when the patient is positioned on either side.

When the patient is flat in bed, excessive hip flexion and outward rotation of the hips and legs should be avoided because of the potential for development of contractures or skin breakdown.

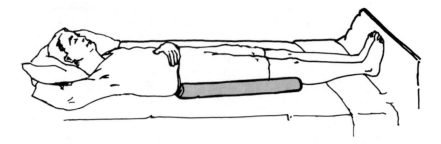

Figure 12-4
Trochanter roll is placed against patient's body between hip and knee to prevent external rotation of hip and excessive pressure against hip and side of ankle.

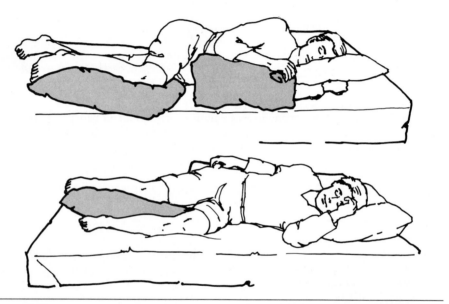

Figure 12-5
In side-lying position, arm and leg should be supported with pillows. The patient's trunk and limbs can be positioned toward front of body or toward back.

A firm bed mattress will reduce hip flexion. However, patients who use a soft bed surface or who have had an above-the-knee amputation are at risk to develop a hip flexion contracture that can severely limit ambulation and mobility. To prevent outward rotation of the hip and leg, place a rolled towel or trochanter roll along the side of the body between the hip and knee (Figure 12-4). Arms and hands should be positioned to provide support and comfort. Hand rolls can be used to maintain a functional position and prevent wrist-drop if paralysis is present. In a side-lying position, proper alignment should be maintained. The patient's top leg may be flexed, brought forward, and supported by pillows, and the arm should be supported in a flexed position (Figure 12-5). Patients need to be turned regularly every 1 to 2 hours and should be encouraged to turn themselves even more often if possible. Variations in positioning will depend on the patients' condition and diagnosis. A sagging bed makes it difficult to maintain good body alignment, and a board placed between the springs and mattress will help provide firmness.

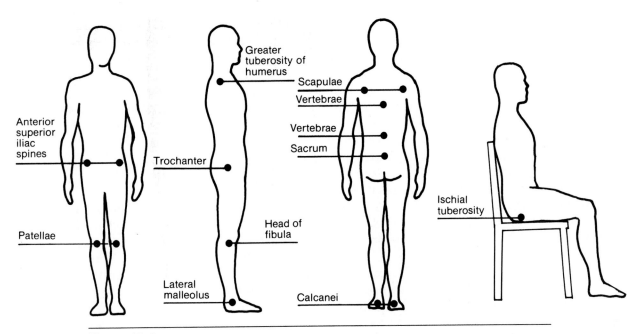

Figure 12-6
Bony prominences of the body.

Patient participation

The nurse can promote activity and exercise by encouraging the patient to participate in his or her own care. For the patient who has been acutely ill, this activity may be of a limited nature. Turning independently in bed and balancing oneself while sitting on the side of the bed may increase strength, endurance, and balance. Brushing one's own hair or teeth may promote upper extremity strength and trunk balance. Gradually the patient should engage in increased activity. The nurse and the physical therapist need to work together to reinforce patient independence in transfers in and out of bed, standing, and walking. As the patient increases in activity level, strength and endurance will increase.

Prevention of Skin Breakdown

Prevention of skin breakdown is an important aspect of care of the immobile or disabled person. Skin breakdown, or pressure sore formation, occurs when there is excessive pressure over the bony prominences of the body when the patient is lying or sitting (Figure 12-6). The common names for this problem, bedsore or decubitus ulcer, are inaccurate terms because the real culprit is pressure, not the bed or lying down (the term *decubitus* comes from the Latin word meaning

lying down). Pressure decreases or totally prevents the flow of blood to tissue over the bony prominences thus depriving the tissue of needed oxygen. This hypoxic tissue cannot survive, and a wound forms. The size and depth of the wound depends on the intensity of pressure and the length of time the pressure is unrelieved.

Other factors play an important role in this development; they include the nutritional status of the patient, mobility, sensory ability, medical status, continence, and circulatory status. Changes in the skin also occur with aging. The skin has less elasticity, is drier, and has less subcutaneous tissue, factors that make the older patient more susceptible to skin breakdown. On admission, the nurse needs to identify the patient at risk for the development of a pressure sore.

Pressure relief must be instituted in all patients at risk. In addition to turning the patient at 1- to 2-hour intervals, pressure-reducing devices such as air or water mattresses should be used. Cleansing of the skin and close attention to the condition of the skin are necessary. If the skin is too dry, lubricating creams and ointments should be applied. If the skin is too moist, a light application of a drying powder may be beneficial.

Consultation with a nutritionist is important for the patient who is not taking in an adequate diet or fluids. This is particularly true when laboratory values indicate that the person has low levels of protein, which is essential for healing and maintaining skin integrity. Vitamin and mineral levels are also important. A bladder and bowel program should be planned for the incontinent person to prevent skin maceration.

The patient who sits in a wheelchair or other type of chair should be protected from pressure on the sitting surfaces of the body through the use of a wheelchair cushion. A bed pillow does not provide adequate pressure relief. A 4-inch foam cushion may be fine for most patients, whereas a more detailed type of cushion may be required by other patients.

The treatment of a pressure sore is based on the size and depth of the wound. Many hospitals have developed protocols for the selection of cleaning agents and dressings for the wounds, based on size and depth.[14] Some pressure sores extend down to bone and can place the patient at risk of death because of infection. In all types of pressure sores methods to prevent infection are important aspects of care.

Pressure sores are for the most part a preventable problem. If there is no pressure, an ulcer does not form. However, scrupulous attention must be paid to the patient at risk because the ulcer could develop within a few hours if pressure is unrelieved.

Patients should be out of bed as much as possible, depending on their condition; this is especially true of older patients. Moving from bed to chair provides activity for muscles that otherwise receive little exercise. It also provides for better ventilation of the lungs by helping to prevent the accumulation of fluid at the base of the lung.

Patient transfers

The patient's level of independence in transferability should be assessed by the physical therapist and nurse. As a patient's strength and endurance increase, the ability to lift himself or herself out of bed into a chair or commode increases. Patients with severe disabilities may be totally dependent in this area or in need of moderate to minimum assistance. Safety is of prime importance when transferring a patient. The prevention of injury to the patient and the nurse must be considered before the patient is moved. Carefully planning the transfer and describing each step to the patient and other care providers will help to decrease the possibility of injury. The transfer of some patients may require the use of equipment such as hydraulic lifts or transfer boards or belts. All staff using this equipment must be thoroughly familiar with the techniques involved. The longer the handicapped person remains in bed, the more his or her self-confidence declines and the more he or she dreads the responsibilities of becoming a self-reliant individual.

Bladder and Bowel Training
Bladder training

Urinary incontinence is a major health care problem. The impact of this problem is felt not only in financial terms, which are great, but also in the disruption of the incontinent person's social and personal life. In the elderly, urinary incontinence is one of the three major causes of nursing home placement. Urinary incontinence can also lead to secondary problems such as skin breakdown or falls from slipping in urine.

Care of the incontinent patient involves assessment of the underlying cause of the incontinence and development of approaches to improve the patient's condition. The nurse must work closely with the patient and family, the physician, and other health care team members to find methods to improve the patient's incontinence or, if needed, to determine alternative interventions that are safe and convenient for the patient. Of particular importance in caring for the elderly incontinent patient is recognizing that urinary incontinence is not normal in old age but an abnormal development that often has multiple identifiable causes.

There are a variety of ways to describe urinary incontinence. One of the most useful approaches is to categorize incontinence as either a temporary condition that can be corrected or as an established or fixed condition that cannot be corrected.[15] Nursing assessment and interventions are important aspects of the care of patients with either type of urinary incontinence.

Temporary incontinence has been described as an uncontrolled leakage of urine that may be reversible once the underlying causes are corrected.[15] Recognized causes of temporary incontinence include confusion, infection, medication side effects, immobility that may limit the patient's access to toilet facilities, constipation, and inadequate fluid intake. Additionally, elderly women may develop urinary incontinence because of cellular changes that occur in the lower urinary tract following menopause. This condition, *atrophic urethritis*, may be corrected with medication. Often patients will have a combination of factors that lead to temporary urinary incontinence. For example, elderly patients admitted to the acute care hospital for pneumonia or a hip fracture may develop fever, decreased fluid intake, confusion, immobility, and constipation. Urinary incontinence may be an outcome of these multiple factors. Once the medical problem is corrected, the incontinence usually improves.

Fixed urinary incontinence is not reversible; however, like temporary incontinence it may have multiple causes. Also, there are several different types of fixed incontinence. Generally, pathologic changes within the urinary tract and its supporting structures or within the nervous system pathways that integrate bladder function lead to this problem. The care of patients with fixed incontinence requires medical assessment to identify the cause and to define the specific type. The physician and nurse work closely with the patient and family to plan the best method to manage the incontinence. Some neurologic disorders, such as multiple sclerosis or spinal cord injury, leave the patient with fixed urinary incontinence. The medical evaluation may include specific procedures to describe the type of fixed urinary incontinence. Based on these findings, management of the incontinence may involve specific bladder programs, such as a bathroom scheduling regimen or a program of intermittent catheterization, as well as medications and some form of urine-collecting device.

Nursing assessment of the patient with either type of incontinence involves obtaining a patient history and performing a physical assessment. Interviewing the patient and family about the incontinence may provide important and helpful information. The nurse might ask specific questions of the patient and family, such as the following:

What problems are you having with urination?

Can you feel when your bladder is full?

How long can you wait to get to the bathroom after you feel the need to empty your bladder?

Do you need to get out of bed at night to urinate?

Do you have any dribbling or urine when you laugh, cough, or sneeze?

Do you have pain or burning with urination?

Have you noticed a change in the color or odor of your urine?

The nurse may need to assess the patient's mental status, since confusion can lead to incontinence. A limited mental status evaluation includes the patient's orientation to person, place, and time, as well as long- and short-term memory. If possible, the nurse should assess the patient's ability to get in and out of bed and in and out of the toilet facility, as well as the ability to manage clothing and toilet tissue. For the bedbound patient the nurse may assess the patient's ability to manipulate a urinal or bedpan. A 48-hour record of the patient's fluid intake and urinary output is helpful in determining fluid balance. A 48-hour history of urinary incontinence is best recorded by the use of an incontinence chart indicating the patient's condition, wet or dry, at 2-hour intervals (Figure 12-7). Keeping this chart may help to detect a possible pattern or urinary incontinence. The physician and nurse should work together in assessing the patient's physical status to determine bladder fullness or distention and to determine if the bowel is impacted with stool. The physician may decide to perform a neurologic examination, including an evaluation of reflex activity needed for normal bladder function. The patient's medical record should be reviewed to identify important factors that could be relevant to bladder problems, such as a medical diagnosis, medications, laboratory values, or previous surgeries.

Once this information is collected and documented, the nurse and other members of the health team should plan specific interventions. All reversible causes of incontinence need to be identified. Once such factors as confusion, fever, constipation, dehydration, immobility, and decreased fluid intake are corrected, incontinence may diminish. If incontinence persists or is unrelated to these factors, the assessment should continue and a bladder program should be developed.

A bladder program (or "bladder/training program" as it is sometimes called) may not correct the underlying cause of the incontinence, but it may correct the incontinence or decrease the episodes of incontinence. Bladder training is based on clear patterns of communication between staff and patients to regulate fluid intake and develop a pattern or schedule of urinary elimination. The patient's past voiding history, fluid intake record, and incontinence chart are reviewed to establish this schedule. If no pattern of incontinence can be identified from the incontinence chart, the nurse should establish a bladder program sched-

INCONTINENCE RECORD

Patient's name _____

Room number _____

Date:		Date:		Date:	
Time	Wet or dry	Time	Wet or dry	Time	Wet or dry
8 am		8 am		8 am	
10 am		10 am		10 am	
12 N		12 N		12 N	
2 pm		2 pm		2 pm	
4 pm		4 pm		4 pm	
6 pm		6 pm		6 pm	
8 pm		8 pm		8 pm	
10 pm		10 pm		10 pm	
12 MN		12 MN		12 MN	
2 am		2 am		2 am	
4 am		4 am		4 am	
6 am		6 am		6 am	

Figure 12-7

Example of 48-hour incontinence record.

ule. The patient's schedule and expected outcome should be clearly documented and understood by all staff, as well as the patient and family. The patient's response to the bladder program must be documented and communicated to all involved.

An example of a bladder program developed for a patient who is consistently incontinent after meals may include the following:

Fluid intake 2000-3000 ml/day: 200 ml every 2 hours beginning at 6 AM and ending at 8 PM. Fluids are restricted at night. A variety of fluids preferred by the patient should be offered.

Voiding routine On arising, ½ hour after each meal, ½ hour before going to bed. If the patient is incontinent between voiding times, the times and surrounding events should be noted.

For the patient who has no clear pattern of incontinence, a bladder program might include a similar fluid regimen but a voiding routine of every 2-hour toileting. When the patient attempts to void, he should have privacy and be placed in a comfortable position.

Success in bladder training depends on patient cooperation. Behavior modification techniques have been used successfully in motivating patients to cooperate with a bladder retraining program. Behavior modification is a therapeutic program that involves rewards or positive reinforcers for desired behavior. The likes and dislikes of each patient will vary. An action or reward that is positive for one patient may be negative for another. The desired behavior, in this case, continence, is more likely to be repeated if the patient experiences some reward for that behavior. The reward may be material or it may be in the form of praise, but it must be seen as a reward by that individual patient if it is to be effective. The patient is checked every 2 hours; if dry, a reward is given. If incontinent, no reward is given. Appropriate use of the toilet or commode is also rewarded. The short-term goal of staying dry or using the commode appropriately will lead to the long-term goal of independent use of facilities and continence. The entire staff must fully understand the program and its methods and implement it appropriately.

An indwelling catheter should be avoided as a method to treat incontinence because the patient with an indwelling catheter has a high probability of developing a urinary tract infection. Some estimates indicate that 70% of patients develop a urinary tract infection within 72 hours of catheter insertion. However, an indwelling catheter is necessary for many individuals, such as those with an acute illness, those with surgery, or when the patient cannot urinate. Bladder training of the patient with an indwelling catheter is controversial. If the patient has a urinary tract infection, the physician may decide to treat the infection with medication. Another approach used is to simply remove the catheter as the source of infection rather than treating the patient with medication. There is some disagreement also regarding the benefit gained by clamping and unclamping the indwelling catheter before removal. Whereas some authorities believe that it is necessary to clamp the catheter periodically to increase bladder capacity and sensation, others believe that the bladder can hold as much urine as is necessary and that the catheter should be removed abruptly. Whether the catheter is clamped or removed abruptly, the patient's attention should be directed to the sensation aroused by the expansion of the bladder as it fills and the contraction of the bladder as it empties.

Bladder training may help patients with either temporary or fixed incontinence. However, other approaches may be necessary because of the extent and type of bladder dysfunction. If the patient has no sensation of bladder fullness and no ability to empty the bladder, a program of intermittent catheterization may be initiated. The scheduling of this program is based on fluid intake and volume of catheterized urine. Initially the patient is catheterized every 4 hours, and then this schedule is decreased to every 6 to 8 hours while the patient is awake. Depending on the type of bladder dysfunction, this program may eventually allow for reflex bladder—emptying without catheterization. For some patients, intermittent catheterization becomes the only method of urinary elimination, and the patient may be taught self-catheterization. A clean rather than sterile technique may be used by the patient doing self-catheterization in the home. This technique allows the patient to reuse catheters after washing them

with soap and water. Sterile techniques should be used for self-catheterization in the hospital.

Some individuals may need to use an indwelling catheter on a long-term basis. Urinary tract infection is a constant threat with long-term catheterization; these individuals should be followed up by a physician if discharged home with the catheter. Adequate fluid intake, care of the catheter and collecting bags, and attention to skin care must become part of the daily routine.

Urine-collecting devices are another method of managing incontinence. A condom-collecting system may be beneficial to some men. The condom should be changed daily, with close attention given to skin care and cleaning. Several urine-collecting devices are available for women. These products fit over the perineum and are connected to a drainage bag. Proper fit is a problem for many women; if the fit is not tight, urine will leak. Close attention to skin care is also essential in use of these devices.

Diapering may be the method chosen by some individuals to manage their urinary incontinence, particularly if soiling of clothing or falling in urine is a problem. However, all other treatment interventions should be evaluated before adopting this method. Preventing skin problems because of wet diapers becomes an important aspect of care. Many diapering products are available and should be selected based on the individual's specific needs. Diapers must be changed when wet in the bedbound patient because of the high potential for skin breakdown. Some disposable diapers are made to keep the layer next to the skin dry while absorbing the urine in other layers.

Bowel training

Bowel retraining is similar to bladder retraining in that a pattern or routine must first be established and the patient rewarded for compliance. Bowel function is aided by the addition of high-residue foods to the diet. Whole-grain breads, bran cereal, prune juice, and fresh fruits have been found to be very effective in stimulating bowel function. Adequate fluid supply is also essential to normal bowel function. Medication may be prescribed to soften the stool and/or increase peristalsis. Harsh laxatives and enemas should not be used to regulate bowel function. Dietary restrictions and other physician orders should be considered, and the physician should be consulted when planning a retraining program for the incontinent patient.

The squatting position on the toilet or bedside commode is most effective for evacuation. The abdominal muscles contract when the thighs are flexed against the abdomen and increase inter-abdominal pressure, which aids in expelling feces. If the toilet seat is too high to allow this position, a footstool or sturdy box should be placed under the patient's feet. The patient who cannot assume this squatting position will have more difficulty in establishing regular bowel patterns. Exercises that strengthen the abdominal muscles will aid evacuation, and the contraction and relaxation of perineal muscles will assist in the control of bowel evacuation. A regular time for evacuation should be established. The gastrocolic reflex reaches its maximum effect 30 minutes after eating. If agreeable with the patient and his family, the evacuation time is scheduled 30 minutes after breakfast. The patient is assisted to the commode or toilet and allowed to stay there for 10 or 15 minutes. The patient is also instructed to use abdominal and perineal exercises to assist the movement of feces but not to strain to produce a bowel movement. Privacy must be provided, and the patient should feel relaxed. Roughage and fluid should be increased or decreased in the diet as necessary to maintain normal bowel function.

If the patient does not have full control of voluntary muscles, this routine may not be practical or possible. A study of new bowel regimen showed success with a nonresidue diet and weekly suppositories. Seriously disabled, incontinent men in a Veterans Administration hospital treated with this routine had predictable weekly defecations and maintained a satisfactory physical condition. When a patient begins a schedule such as this, fecal impaction can become a problem but can usually be corrected by adjusting fluid intake. In some cases pharmacologic agents or enemas may be necessary. A 3- or 4-day trial of any pharmacologic agent is necessary to determine its effect on the patient. Administration of 500 ml of fluid into the intestinal tract will usually result in complete evacuation. A routine can be established that prevents accidental elimination. It is important to remember that enemas are to be used only when the patient's physical condition makes normal elimination impossible.

Sexuality

When considering the total patient and his family, the area of sexuality must be addressed. To discuss this with patients, nurses must be in touch with their own feelings about sexuality and be knowledgeable about the effects of disability on sexual function. The patient may be hesitant to ask questions or bring up the subject of sex, but if the nurse lets it be known that it is an appropriate topic, the patient may initiate discussion. Experts in this field (often handicapped persons themselves) are available for referral, and literature is available in nursing journals, from rehabilitation hospitals, and state rehabilitation departments.

If the nurse feels unqualified or uncomfortable with the topic of sexuality, he or she should let the patient know that it is an appropriate topic to raise but that another team member could better address these concerns. In a rehabilitation setting, there is often a team member who is an expert in the area of sexuality and sexual counseling who can assist the patient or help others on the team counsel the patient. In other types of settings the sexual concerns of patients are not always discussed. Across the country, there are currently many training programs to help health professionals become more knowledgeable in this important area of health.

Motivation

Motivation is an important aspect of rehabilitation. In order for disabled persons to gain some level of independence, they must possess the desire to participate in the difficult work of recovery. Motivation is the force, the desire, and the drive necessary for this participation. This work is not only physically demanding, but it is also emotionally and spiritually stressful. Nursing staff are with the patient 24 hours each day, and therapy treatments are often long. During the length of hospitalization that some disabilities require, the nurses, therapists, patients, and family members often develop strong relationships that are a vital part of rehabilitation. Nurses and therapists can use their relationships with patients to help patients create a desire for self-sufficiency and independence. Emphasizing capabilities and improvements can be of great value at a time when patients are discouraged.

Nurses must realize that patients may experience periods of regression as they move toward independence. When patients are unsuccessful in efforts at learning new skills or tasks, they may feel "what's the use," and frustration and depression may result. It is then that the nurse needs to gently stress what has been accomplished, no matter how small, and encourage the patient to talk about frustrations and fears. The nurse needs to acknowledge the fact that rehabilitation is hard work and express an understanding of this to the patient.

The nurse will encounter patients who may have received maximum benefit from rehabilitation, but in whom only partial recovery has been achieved. An understanding approach to these patients is extremely important, since they may be resentful and have periods of depression. The patient must be told that these feelings are normal and understandable. Conveying acceptance, along with a positive attitude stressing what the patient can do, may help to eliminate the feeling of rejection and antagonism.

The nurse must be constantly alert to the emotional stress and pain of the patient and encourage the expression of feelings. Stress may become so great that the patient is unable to find the energy to participate in the work of rehabilitation. In this case the entire intradisciplinary team must be involved in the discussion of assisting the patient through this period. Psychiatric counseling is often beneficial to the patient to identify ways of coping and adapting. Group counseling, comprised of patients with similar disabilities, and group leaders (psychiatric therapists, social workers, nurses, or occupational or physical therapists) can be most helpful. Some patients may need the assistance of psychotropic medications to deal with the depression and hopelessness they feel as a result of their illnesses and disabilities.

The patient who has sustained brain damage resulting from the disability may be unable to communicate feelings to staff and family, and the level of frustration may be great. The nurse needs to work closely with the speech and language therapist to assess this patient's level of comprehension and communication. A plan of intervention and communication will be devised based on this assessment.

Teaching

The nurse assumes a major role in teaching the patient. For a patient participating in a rehabilitation program this teaching might include:

   Reinforcement of skills taught in therapy sessions such as self-care activities, transfers, and crutch walking
   A description of the illness or disability and a description of the expected course of the disease process

   Health practices that the patient needs to incorporate into daily living to stay healthy
   Those symptoms that indicate a health problem has developed and medical care is needed
   A method to find health care when needed
   A description of the rationale for medications and potential side effects of medications
   Approaches to locating home supports when needed

The nurse must assess the learning needs and learning abilities of the patient before establishing a teaching plan. An important question to ask is, "What does the patient and family need to know to have an easier transition at time of discharge?" In teaching a patient an activity or providing some important information, the environment should be as conducive to learning as possible. Providing teaching during a nonstressful time of day, in a quiet place, and without any sense of haste is important. This is especially true for the elderly who do not have difficulty learning new material in general, but have difficulty learning new skills in a limited period of time.[6] Finding a quiet environment in a busy hospital setting may be difficult, but with planning, not impossible. Some patients will tire easily and will need frequent rest periods.

Along with teaching, the nurse should provide some educational materials to patients and family members. The stress of learning new information may decrease retention. Having reference materials available to reinforce new information may help the patient and family with understanding and application of new ideas. Not all educational materials contain correct information or are appropriate to the needs of all patients. In some hospitals or agencies, nurses participate in patient-education committees. One task of this type committee is often the review of patient educational materials for acceptability, readability, and accuracy.

A basic principle of teaching-learning is progressing from the simple to the complex. Simple activities should be taught first and each mastered before a new one is begun. The patient may become discouraged and need much encouragement; even the slightest progress should be noted. The patient must be treated as an adult and never belittled or demeaned if unable to master a new skill or retain new information. Patience may have to be learned by those who become frustrated and overwhelmed by the amount of detail needed to

---

```
┌─────────────────────────────────────────────┐
│              Patient Teaching               │
│                                             │
```

Assess the learning needs and learning ability of patient and family members.

Provide an environment conducive to learning.

Review educational materials before giving them to patient and family.

Progress from the simple to the complex.

Treat the patient and family as adults.

Provide time for practice, discussion, and feedback.

Evaluate the need for a group teaching program.

Evaluate the impact of teaching.

---

complete some skills. Some persons may never develop this degree of patience, and participation in rehabilitation remains a difficult task.

Providing a patient the opportunity to practice a task or discuss information is another important aspect of teaching. To teach the patient, the nurse must avoid helping him or her. After giving instruction, demonstration, and the opportunity for return demonstration and practice, the nurse must let the patient do the work or task alone. Nurses working in rehabilitation have to learn "to hold their hands behind their backs," and let the patients do for themselves, even if that doing involves a great deal of struggle.

Another approach to teaching new skills or new information is the use of group teaching sessions for both patients and families. Bringing together patients with like disabilities provides the opportunity for the nurse to reach a larger audience and for patients to share their insights, questions, and frustrations with each other. Within these group situations, patients often develop close relationships with each other and can learn new ways of coping. Laughter, one of the most important coping skills, often becomes an important part of these group activities. Group teaching programs for families can also provide information, support, and coping strategies (see boxed material above).

Continuity

There must be **continuity** between the care the patient receives in the hospital and the care given in the home, as well as continuity in the care given by all members of the rehabilitation team. The patient must be taught one way to perform an

activity and practice on a single method. If the patient is taught different ways, he or she will become confused, frustrated, and discouraged. The nurse can assist each therapist who is working with the patient by observing and reporting progress or lack of progress. The nurse will be able to report to the therapist any significant problems that arise in connection with the activities being practiced by the patient. If the patient is to leave the ward for therapy, it is important that the nurse see that the appointment is kept promptly and that the patient is in a presentable condition. As progress is made, the patient may be held responsible for preparation and for keeping appointments with little or no help from the nurse.

Prostheses

A **prosthesis** is an artificial substitute for some part of the body. The most common types of prostheses are artificial legs, arms, eyes, and breasts. Prostheses for amputees must be fitted for the individual patient, and they are adapted to the weight and size of the patient. They are made of various types of materials; however, those made of plastic material are light in weight, easy to keep clean, and do not absorb body odors. Prostheses for legs are held in place by pelvic belts, waistbands, or suction cups. Temporary prostheses for above- and below-the knee amputations can be fitted immediately following surgery, although this is not always done. These prostheses are made of casting materials contoured to the amputation stump and provide a rigid dressing that controls bleeding and swelling postoperatively. A temporary peg, or pylon, and foot are attached to the cast, which allows the patient to dangle and stand with aid within a few days after surgery. There are many advantages to this procedure. The patient is more active, muscle activity and circulation are stimulated, and the process of physical rehabilitation begins immediately. An upright position soon after surgery encourages the patient and helps in adjusting to an altered body image. Some authorities also believe that phantom pain (sensation arising from the area of the amputated leg) is decreased with the use of a temporary prosthesis.

The **amputee** is confronted not only with a physical problem, but also with social, vocational, and psychologic problems which require the services of the entire rehabilitation team and a skilled **prosthetist**.

When healing is underway, the stump must be molded to a conical shape to fit into the prosthesis. Compression bandages are generally used for this purpose. However, elastic stump-shrinking socks are also used and often are more desirable, since the art of wrapping the stump is difficult to achieve. Careful washing of the stump is important, and bandages should be removed and rewrapped several times a day. There is a greater variety of prostheses available for the patient with lower extremity amputation than for the patient with upper extremity amputation.

It is more difficult to develop an upper extremity prosthesis that is both cosmetically acceptable and functional. The hook-type is most frequently used, and cosmetic hands are available to fit over the hook on some models. This prosthesis is very difficult to master. The new myoelectric prosthesis is more acceptable cosmetically and has capabilities not previously available. It is capable of gross hand motion, index finger–thumb opposition, grasp, and wrist pronation and supination. It does not, however, provide fine movements of the fingers and hand. It is most effective when the lost extremity is on the nondominant side. The right-handed person who loses his left arm will not require as much fine movement in the prosthesis. When the prosthesis arrives and the patient begins to wear it, the patient and the family should be instructed in care of the stump and the appliance. Not all patients are suitable candidates for an artificial extremity, and numerous factors, with careful examination of the individual patient, have to be considered.

In teaching a patient to care for a prosthesis, the following areas should be addressed. Cleanliness is important to prevent skin problems; the socket of the prosthesis should be washed, rinsed, and dried daily. Lint and dirt should be removed and joints lightly oiled once a week. Joints should be inspected for loose or worn parts and replacements made promptly by a prosthetist. Any problems or changes in the fit (as occur normally when the stump shrinks) should be reported as well.

The skin beneath the prosthesis is prone to irritation and breakdown if not carefully cared for and inspected. Daily hygiene is essential; soap and water followed by a thorough rinsing is adequate. The patient should avoid creams or preparations containing alcohol. When a stump sock is used, it must fit well and be free of wrinkles and mended areas. The sock is also washed daily in cool water and mild soap. A lower extremity stump will shrink over time, requiring adjustments to be made in the socket of the prosthesis. The patient should be warned against padding the stump or socket with cotton or washcloths, since the uneven pressure distribution that results will cause pressure areas on the skin and possible infection. A change in stump size requires a visit to the prosthetist to adjust the prosthesis.

An artificial eye is made of glass or plastic and is painted by a skilled artist to match the patient's other eye. Eyes made of glass are heavier than those made of plastic and are easily broken if dropped. Those made of plastic, although lighter, are less durable and may be scratched unless care is taken. The prosthesis may be used as soon as the socket is healed, which may be from 3 to 6 weeks after surgery.

When the eye is removed for cleaning, it can be washed with soap and water and stored in a clean piece of gauze or a labeled envelope. It will need to be moistened before it is reinserted; sterile saline is generally used for this. The patient will have to be taught how to remove and insert the prosthesis; he or she may be nervous at first but will soon master the technique and develop skill and confidence. When a patient with an eye prosthesis is admitted to the hospital, the nurse should realize that the patient has a special method of caring for the eye and should supply whatever equipment needed and not try to change the person's methods.

Researchers at the University of Utah have developed an artificial eye that receives images and sends signals to the brain so that the individual can actually see. The equipment used is being miniaturized to make the eye practical. This prosthesis will bring sight to the blind rather than fill a cosmetic need.

Braces

The overall purpose of using **braces** is to improve patient mobility. Specifically, they may be used to support the body weight, to limit involuntary movement of the body, and to prevent and correct deformities. Braces may be of the short-leg or long-leg type and may have attachments, depending on the purpose for which they are used. Braces usually consist of a steel frame with joints, hinges, and straps; belts are used to secure them in place. Braces are generally attached to the heel of the shoe. An inside lining protects the body from friction.

Proper care of the brace should be taught and

emphasized to the patient. All locks should be opened weekly and lint and dirt removed. A drop of machine oil should be placed in each joint and the excess wiped away, since any oil left on leather will cause deterioration. The leather parts may be washed with warm water and saddle soap, then dried and polished. The brace should be checked at intervals to be sure it is keeping the part in good position. Shoes should be kept in good repair and should have rubber heels. Knees pads are part of the brace and should be worn with it. The skin should be inspected daily for discoloration, bruises, abrasions, or evidence of friction. Children who wear braces during their growth periods should have them checked at intervals by the physician, and any change indicated should be made properly. A brace that is too small for a growing child may do more harm than good.

Braces may be used to support the torso and should be applied with the patient lying down with the body in good alignment. A cotton shirt worn beneath the brace helps to absorb perspiration and body odors and contributes to comfort.

Preparing the patient for braces is no less important than preparing him for any other artificial aid. The patient needs to be prepared physically through range of motion and other exercise and by proper position in bed. To be prepared psychologically, the patient should understand why the braces are necessary, how they will help, and how to care for them. Unless the patient is prepared for the aid, he or she may resent it and develop negative attitudes, in which case its value may be minimized. Young persons may be concerned with the cosmetic effect and must be given the chance to express their feelings.

Crutches

Crutches are assistive walking devices (Figure 12-8). They may be used temporarily or permanently, but in either case the nurse has an important function in helping to prepare the patient for crutch walking. As soon as the physician determines that the patient has improved sufficiently, exercises should be started to strengthen the muscle groups involved in the use of crutches. These include the muscles of the neck, arms, shoulders, chest, and back. Various types of exercises may be started while the patient is in bed, using such equipment as a trapeze placed over-

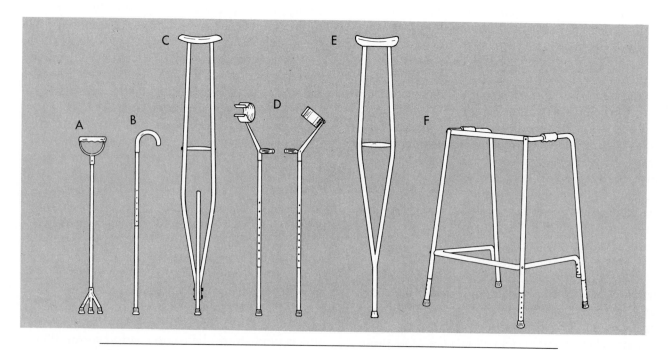

Figure 12-8

Types of crutches and canes. **A,** Quadripod cane. **B,** Adjustable aluminum cane. **C,** Adjustable aluminum crutch. **D,** Adjustable aluminum Canadian crutch. **E,** Nonadjustable wooden crutch available in various lengths. **F,** Walker.

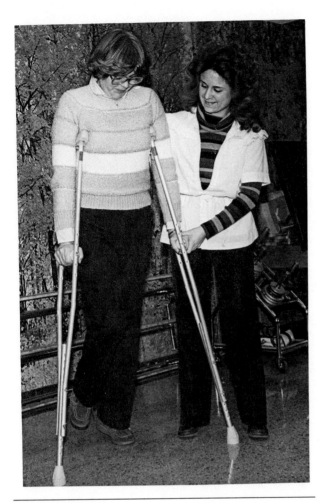

Figure 12-9

In assessing patient using crutches, nurse observes fit, posture, and gait. *(Courtesy Copley Memorial Hospital, Aurora, Il.)*

Important Points to be Considered in Crutch Walking

1. The patient should be measured for crutches so that they will be the right length. Crutches should be adjustable and have heavy rubber tips.
2. Padding of the axillary bar is generally discouraged, since it encourages the patient to place weight or lean on it. By doing so, the patient may develop a paralysis of the radial nerve (crutch paralysis). Crutches that are too long or too short may also cause crutch paralysis. Crutch length should be adjustable so that the patient bears *no* weight in the axilla.
3. The patient should be taught from the beginning to maintain good posture. The head should be held high and straight, with the pelvis over the feet (Figure 12-9).
4. Crutch walking must be taught, and several short lessons a day will be of more value to the patient than a long one resulting in fatigue.
5. When ambulation is begun, it is desirable to have an attendant in front of the patient and one behind him; however, they should not touch the patient.
6. Whether the patient is able to bear weight or shift weight will depend on the disability and the physician's order. Some patients, especially elderly ones, may learn to use a walker before using crutches.

---

head or a rope fastened to a pulley at the foot of the bed. The patient can be taught how to do pushups by placing his palms flat on the bed, or sawed-off crutches can be used in the bed. During the patient's confinement to bed, the legs should be put through the full range of motion several times a day. Before standing, the patient should be taught and should be able to move from the bed to the chair. Standing and balance are important prerequisites to ambulation. Many older people have a poor sense of balance and coordination. They may be fearful and find it difficult to strengthen muscles before walking; therefore the nurse will need to have a great deal of patience in working with them. Ideally, parallel bars should be used in helping the patient stand and achieve balance; however, two beds placed end to end will achieve the same results. The physical therapist usually assists the patient with standing and balance during initial attempts to walk with crutches. In many places it will be the responsibility of the physician and the nurse.

Gait

There are several types of gait, and the type used will depend on the disability. The most common types of gait include four-point gait, two-point gait, and swing-to or swing-through gait (Figure 12-10). In four-point gait the patient bears weight on both legs, one at each step so there are always three points of contact with the floor. This type of gait requires constant shifting. In two-point gait there are two points of contact with the floor. This method is similar to the four-point gait but faster. In swing-to gait the patient places the crutches ahead, then lifts his or her weight on the crutches and swings the body to the crutches. Swing-

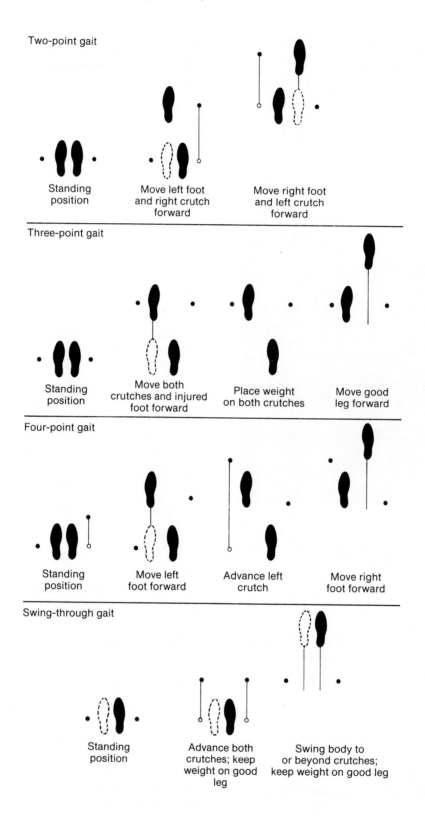

Figure 12-10

Crutch walking. **A,** Two-point gait. **B,** Three-point gait. **C,** Four-point gait. **D,** Swing-through gait.

through gait is similar except that the patient lifts his or her weight and swings beyond the crutches. In three-point gait, weight is placed on the crutches and unaffected leg. It may be used when partial weight bearing is permitted.

A patient who has been taught to use crutches should have mastered sufficient daily care activities to be independent when leaving the hospital, and should also have been taught how to get up and down steps and into and out of cars.

Self-help devices

If the patient is to learn to perform daily care activities successfully, many modifications and adaptations will be needed. A wide variety of devices are available to help the handicapped person. Others may be developed simply by the skill of an ingenious nurse or a member of the family.

SUMMARY

Rehabilitation is a tremendous challenge to all nurses. The saving of lives and the increase in the life span can have little meaning to disabled and handicapped patients unless they can believe that they are respected members of the society in which they live. With knowledge, skill, understanding, patience, and perseverance, the nurse can assist patients in the realization of independent living.

Tools and Procedures to Assist the Handicapped Person

1. Sponge instead of washcloth for bathing
2. Sponge attached to a long handle with a pocket for soap
3. Loose clothing with large armholes
4. Front closing for clothing with grippers rather than buttons
5. Neckties already tied
6. Elastic shoelaces and long-handled shoehorns
7. Suction cups or sponge rubber mats for dishes
8. Runways and ramps constructed for wheelchairs use
9. Hand rails
10. Wheelchair or ordinary chair with seat cut to fit over toilet
11. Lavatories, sinks, appliances, and electric outlets placed at a height easily reached by the patient
12. Special eating utensils, such as silverware with padded or curved handles, glass holders, and place guards
13. Food arranged clockwise on the plate and tray for the blind patient

---

REFERENCES AND ADDITIONAL READINGS

1. Banja JD: Rehabilitation and empowerment, Arch Phys Med Rehabil 71(8):614-615, 1990.
2. Dittmar S, (ed): Rehabilitation nursing, St Louis, 1989, The CV Mosby Co.
3. Glennon TP and Smith BS: Questions asked by patients and their support groups during family conferences on inpatient rehabilitation units, Arch Phys Med Rehabil, 71(8):699-702, 1990.
4. Hesse K and Campion E: Motivating the geriatric patient for rehabilitation, J Am Geriatr Soc 31(10):586-589, 1983.
5. Jette A, (ed): Functional disability and rehabilitation of the aged, Top Geriatr Rehabil 1(3):1-9, 1986.
6. Katzman R and Terry R: The neurology of aging, Philidalphia, 1983, FA Davis Co.
7. Kowalsky E: Grief: a lost life style, Am J Nurs, 78(3):418-420, 1978.
8. Learman LA and others: Pygmalion in the nursing home. The effect of caregiver expectations on patient outcome, J Am Geriatr Soc 38(7):797-803, 1990.
9. Lewis C: Improving mobility in older patients, Rockville, Md, 1989, Aspen Publications.
10. Martin N, Holt N, and Hicks D: Comprehensive rehabilitation nursing, New York, 1981, McGraw-Hill Book Co.
11. Mumma C (ed): Rehabilitation nursing: concepts and practice, ed 2, Evanston, Ill, 1987, Rehabilitation Nursing Foundation.
12. Paillard M and Nowak K: Use of exercise to help older adults. J Gerontol Nurs 11(7):36-39, 1985.
13. Payton O and Poland J: Aging process: implications for clinical practice, Phys Ther 63(1):41-47, 1983.
14. Phipps M and Bauman B: Staging care for pressure sores, Am J Nurs 84(8):999-1003, 1984.
15. Resnick N: Urinary incontinence in the elderly, Med Grand Rounds 3:281-290, 1984.
16. Schmitt N: Patients perception of laughter in a rehabilitation hospital, Rehabil Nurs 15(3):143-147, 1990.
17. Smith E (ed): Exercise and aging, Top Geriatr Rehabil 1(1):1-88, 1985.
18. Straus A and others: Chronic illness and the quality of life, ed 2, St Louis, 1984, The CV Mosby Co.
19. Sudarsky L: Geriatrics: gait disorders in the elderly, New Engl J Med 322(20):1441-1446, 1990.
20. Werner-Beland J: Grief responses to long-term illness and disability, Reston, Va, 1980, Reston Publishing Co, Inc.

Long-Term Care

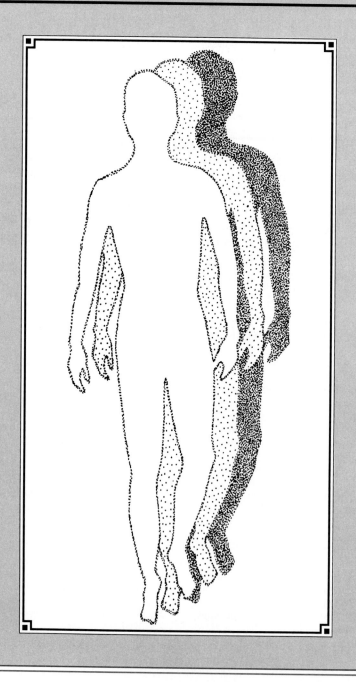

OBJECTIVES

1. Explain the relationship of a nursing home to long-term care.

2. Explain how the concepts of autonomy, independence, and maintenance or promotion of function guide care of the nursing home resident.

3. Define medical ethics.

4. Explain differences between life sustaining measures and "do not resuscitate" orders.

5. Discuss 12 general areas important for a nursing assessment of the older person.

6. Discuss risk factors and preventive measures for falls among the elderly nursing home resident.

7. Discuss problems associated with use of restraints and identify alternatives.

8. Discuss assessment and interventions for the older nursing home resident with urinary incontinence.

9. Discuss assessment of the older nursing home resident with constipation.

10. Explain risk factors for preventive measures, and interventions for skin breakdown among elderly nursing home residents.

11. Differentiate between delirium, depression, and dementia.

12. Discuss possible interventions for the confused nursing home resident.

At one time, the words long-term care or nursing home might have conjured up images of very old confused people living out their last days in sadness and neglect. Today **long-term care** means an extension of the health care system to care for people in all stages of chronic illness and people at all levels of ability. In the near future, more people age 65 and over will need a variety of long-term care maintenance and new models of health care are being developed to accommodate this expected increase.

The nursing home is only one of many types of long-term care available to the patient today. It represents a new home for the person who enters. The older person who moves into a nursing home generally cannot live independently. This does not mean that the person is dependent; rather the person has a different functional level than other older people living independently in the community.

The typical nursing home resident is at least 84, female, widowed, has limited finances, and has little support from family. In addition, the resident will have age-related physiologic changes and multiple chronic diseases requiring a wide variety of medications. The older person in a nursing home requires very complex health care to meet all his or her needs.

Caring for the resident of a nursing home is one of the most rewarding and challenging areas of nursing practice. The nurse in long-term care has the opportunity to be creative and independent, acting as a case manager and promoting interdisciplinary care.

There are three related concepts that guide care of the resident: autonomy, promotion of **independence,** and maintenance or improvement of function. **Autonomy** can be defined simply as self-governance or not being controlled by outside forces or individuals. An autonomous person makes decisions about care, chooses activities and organizes care according to his or her preference, and generally takes charge of any situations that arise. Although complete autonomy is not always possible, each nursing plan of care must be established with the input of the resident and the family as appropriate. It is important for the nurse to remember that the 84-year-old person is a special type of survivor that is usually quite capable of decision-making if given the chance. If the nurse promotes autonomy and independence, then maintenance of or improvement of function are likely to follow.

ETHICAL DILEMMAS IN LONG-TERM CARE

When promoting autonomy, issues of an ethical nature are bound to arise. Ethics is a philosophic discipline and medical ethics is a new field within ethics. Medical ethics explores grounds for deciding moral actions. Medical ethics asks questions such as, "What is informed consent?", "When is a person considered informed?", "What is quality of life?", and "When is it morally right to make decisions for someone else?"

There are, of course, no absolute answers to these and other ethical questions. The purpose of asking questions and raising issues is to clarify thoughts and values, specify the dilemma, and identify information needed to make decisions. An **ethical dilemma** occurs when there are conflicting values and answers to questions.

Ethical dilemmas typically arise when deciding end-of-life issues. Nurses need to know if there has been any discussion with the resident and/or the family about life-sustaining measures. Often little or no information is available. Many times the do not resuscitate (DNR) order has been written, but there is no mention of other life-sustaining measures. Cardiopulmonary resuscitation is only one of many life-sustaining measures. Others include artificial feedings (gastric and nasogastric feedings), ventilators, antibiotics, and even transfer to an acute care hospital for an acute illness.

Discussions about options for life-sustaining measures and their impact on quality of life should be discussed with each older person, family members, and the surrogate decision-maker well before acute episodes require immediate emergency decisions. Each long-term care facility needs specific policies and procedures relating to all aspects of life-sustaining measures.

While end-of-life **decision-making** is of major importance, it is not the only decison-making needed in long-term care. Although independence and decision-making abilities in the older patient are valued by health care professionals, the older patient is frequently excluded from decisions about treatments and care. It is often assumed that the older person is cognitively impaired or should be spared difficult decisions. Involvement in discussions about goals and interventions promotes feelings of self-determination. The older person values independence as does the health care professional.

GENERAL ASSESSMENT GUIDELINES

The nursing assessment is crucial for identification of barriers to autonomy, independence, and functional abilities. The combination of changes in physiology, multiple chronic illnesses, multiple medications, and years of life experience makes assessment difficult. Signs and symptoms of acute illness are often vague or seem unrelated to a particular illness. Because of this, the initial nursing assessment must be complete so that even subtle changes will be recognized.

Each nursing home will have different assessment instruments. However, all nursing assessments should include health practices, activity, exercise, elimination patterns, coping styles, nutrition, sleep patterns, sexuality, support systems including family and friends, cognition/perception, spirituality, and self-concept.

When gathering data on the older person, the nurse must remember that the person admitted to the nursing home has had an average of 84 years of experience. It is important to find out what the person was like as a youth, young adult, adult, and older person. Questions about childhood activities, family relationships, household responsibilities, education, leisure activities, activities with family and friends, occupation, and roles and relationships all add to the understanding of the person today. Previous behavior patterns, learning styles, interaction styles, and coping styles will continue in some form. Using this information, nursing interventions can be creative and individualized to maintain resident autonomy as much as possible.

In addition to a general assessment, specific assessment data must be gathered on each nursing home resident regarding functional status, mental status, and depression.

Functional Assessment

A **functional assessment** identifies the person's level of independence focusing on abilities rather than disabilities. Each person's ability to perform activities of daily living are often assessed using a numerical scale.

Most facilities use standardized forms. Both physical activities of daily living (ADL) and instrumental activities of daily living (IADL) need to be assessed. Physical ADLs are bathing, dressing, eating, ambulating, managing a wheelchair, and using the toilet. IADLs involve balancing a checkbook, housekeeping, going to the store, doing laundry, answering the telephone, and managing medications. Many times ADLs are assessed, but assumptions are made that the person is able to perform the IADLs.

Assessment of both ADLs and IADLs allows the health care worker to design a plan of care that considers the resident's abilities to function independently. The functional assessment provides a baseline from which goals and interventions are developed. The resident should be involved in planning care by using the functional assessment to discuss the resident's goals. Each step can be discussed and mutually agreed on in the development of the plan.

The nurse may identify other members of the health care team that can assist the resident in reaching goals. The resident and health care team may then establish a contract that clearly outlines the strategies to be used in achieving the resident's goals. For instance, a person may need to improve muscle strength. The nurse or physical therapist may design an individualized exercise program that the resident will perform independently on a routine basis. In this way, both play a role in improving functional status.

IADLs provide insights into abilities. The resident can be encouraged to continue activities according to abilities, goals, and within the constraints of the facility. It may be possible for the resident to be responsible for taking medications either by coming to the nursing station for them or by keeping them in the room. Nursing interventions may also include allowing the person to make financial decisions, do laundry, make their own bed, or clean their room. There are a number of creative approaches to the care of the older person that can be developed using the functional assessment as the base.

The functional assessment also serves as a means of evaluation. Through periodical assessments, it can be demonstrated to the resident that abilities have improved or remained at the same level. When assessing functional status, each function may be evaluated numerically using a scale such as that illustrated in the box on p. 286. As abilities change, the numbers change. The choice of a functional assessment instrument depends upon the intended use in the facility.

Many functional assessments for the elderly do not indicate the small changes that may be very important to the older person. For instance, to be able to stand, the person must first be able to move to the edge of the chair or bed, push up with the

---

Functional Assessment

0 = Independent
1 = Independent with assistive device
2 = Needs assistance/supervision
3 = Requires device and assistance of another
    person
4 = Dependent

---

arms, and push with the legs. Each step can be used to evaluate progress toward goals.

Useful functional assessments that could be incorporated into a nursing assessment are the Katz Index of ADL,[8] the Barthel Index,[12] the PULSES Profile,[14] the Rapid Disability Scale,[10] and the Scale for Instrumental Activities of Daily Living.[9]

Mental Status Assessment

Every person entering a nursing home needs a mental status assessment. A mental status assessment examines cognitive functions such as the ability to think and make decisions. In addition to an admission assessment, it is important to ascertain previous **mental status** and mental status after 3 months of institutionalization. Many times the older nursing home resident was first admitted to an acute care hospital, treated for an acute illness, and then transferred to the long-term care facility.

Before the acute episode, the person may have had no problems with mental status. The acute episode and change in environment may cause changes in mental status that have not resolved on admission to the nursing home. Knowledge of past function helps identify recent changes and give direction for care. Often when the person adjusts to the new environment, intact mental status will return. Mental status assessment is also performed any time the nurse feels that there has been a change in cognitive function.

There are three purposes of the exam. The first is to give baseline information about the cognitive state so that change can be identified. The second purpose is to screen for problems or potential problems. Third, the mental status exam helps identify areas of strength and weakness, and areas in need of additional evaluation.

There are multiple mental status questionnaires that are useful in long-term care. Because altered mental status can involve many parts of

the central nervous system, the mental status exam uses a variety of questions aimed at identifying specific areas of dysfunction. Thus, assessment of mental status is more than examination of orientation.

The Folstein Mini-Mental State Exam[6] is one of the most widely used assessment instruments. It is easy to use and assesses orientation, short-term memory, ability to attend to tasks (attention), calculation, recall (memory), and language. Each area provides neurologic information and may assist in identification of the area of the brain affected and extent of the problem.

Types of information asked include the following:

Orientation: What is the day, month, year and season? Where are you?

Short-term memory: The nurse would name three unrelated objects such as apple, pen, chair and ask the person to repeat them.

Attention/calculation: The person is asked to count backwards by 7 or, if unable to count, to spell "world" backwards.

Recall: After completing the attention task, the person is asked to name the three objects named in the question before (apple, pen, chair).

Language: The person is asked to name two objects that the nurse points to such as a watch and pencil; to repeat a sentence after the nurse; to follow a three stage command; to read a sentence and follow the directions given in the sentence "Close your eyes"; write a sentence of their choosing; and copy a complex figure.

Another popular mental status test is the Short Portable Mental Status Questionnaire[16]. This 10-item scale assesses orientation, remote memory, and calculation.

Types of questions asked include the following:

Orientation: What is the date, day of week, name of facility, telephone number.

Memory: What is your age, birth date, the president now and one before, mother's maiden name.

Calculation: Count backward by 3 starting at 100.

At first, the nurse may be uncomfortable using the mental status assessment. There are various ways to put yourself and the resident at ease. Test it out on other professionals in the facility to gain comfort and confidence and identify problem areas. When administering it to the resident, explain that sometimes as a person gets older, they have trouble with memory or doing certain things and that the information will help the staff provide the best possible care. This approach will give the person permission to miss answers and talk about problems with memory. Also, it will let the person know that it is part of a normal procedure and that they are helping the nurse by answering the questions.

Depression Assessment

Because **depression** affects many older people but is often not diagnosed or treated, all nursing assessments should include a measure of depression. The Geriatric Depression Scale[26] is frequently used as an initial assessment and as part of a periodic assessment of the older person. The 30-item scale is useful for screening and identifying a treatable condition.

The questions can be either read to or by the person. Responses are either "yes" or "no" and examine life satisfaction, interest in activities and life, thoughts about the future, mood, memory, concentration, and decision-making. The scale is easy to use and assists the nurse in identifying areas of concern to the person.

RISK AND SPECIFIC CARE ISSUES

Falls

Falls and the associated morbidity and mortality represent a major problem for the elderly. Sequelae include fractures, decreased mobility, loss of confidence, psychologic distress, and imposed isolation due to fear of falling. Resulting disability leads to loss of function and independence. Autonomy is threatened.

Risk factors for falls include altered gait and balance. The gait of the elderly person at risk for falls may be slow, with short irregular shuffling steps. The change in gait produces a less secure base of support and an inability to recover from a change in balance.

Gait and balance

Balance is a function of vision, proprioception, stabilizing muscles, and vibratory senses. Problems may be caused by vestibular (inner ear) alterations resulting in vertigo and dizziness. Proprioception involves knowing where extremities are in space. Changes in proprioception produce errors in placing the foot.

Muscle strength

Muscle strength may also contribute to putting the person at risk. It was once thought that muscle weakness and atrophy were "normal" consequences of aging. Researchers in the area of biology of aging find, however, that the person who has a regular exercise program does not lose strength and endurance. In addition, older people who have not exercised, but who begin a regular exercise program, have increased strength and endurance.

Aging muscle without exercise loses lean mass, strength, and endurance, particularly in the essential weight bearing muscles of the legs. Immobility produces progressive loss of muscle tone and weakness and may be associated with psychogenic vertigo and dizziness. Immobility also contributes to loss of calcium from the long bones resulting in an increased risk of fractures.

Balance, gait, and muscle strength are probably the most important risk factors for falls. However, there are numerous contributory factors that must be assessed.

Sensory change

Sensory change in vision and hearing contribute to altered depth perception. Visual acuity decreases and the ability to distinguish blues and greens diminishes. Glare, especially highly waxed floors, disturbs depth perception and may actually "blind" the person so that perception of surroundings is difficult, if not impossible. Glaucoma alters peripheral vision.

Medications

Medications produce a variety of risk factors including orthostatic hypotension, dizziness, and confusion. Each medication must be evaluated by the pharmacist for interaction with other drugs being taken and interaction with the physiologic state of the resident.

Incontinence

Incontinence is another major risk factor. The older person may be attempting to get to the bathroom in a hurry and fall, or may dribble urine and slip and fall. Assessment and treatment of urinary incontinence may correct problem with falling.

Age/gender, history of falls and confusion

Age and gender are associated with falls. The older the person, the more at risk. Women are more likely to fall than men. Previous history of falls represents yet another important risk factor.

Assessment must include information on falling at home or within the nursing home. Residents who fall tend to fall again. Confusion also places the person at risk for falls and tends to be in combination with all the risk factors.

The risk of falling is complex and requires careful evaluation. Table 13-1 lists risk factors that should be part of the nursing assessment and used to explore additional assessment and/or plan interventions.

Interventions

Examination of the list of risk factors associated with falls helps identify possible interventions. Change in environment, stressful life events, or change in medications all place the person at risk. Additional orientation to the new facility and extra supervision and observation, particularly at night, will decrease the risk. Evaluation of mental status and depression helps to identify the extent of the problem. Taking time to listen to concerns and offer support assist the person in gaining an understanding of events. Autonomy and independence should be encouraged.

Medications are the culprit in many problems of old age. The pharmacist should evaluate medication interactions. The blood pressure should be taken when the person is reclining and again upon standing to identify orthostatic hypotension. Periods of dizziness, confusion, or change in mental status should be observed and related to routine medications or medications taken as needed.

The resident should be referred to physical and occupational therapy for a thorough evalua-

tion of function, with an emphasis on potential for falls. The treatment plan should address individual risk factors for falls. Group and individual exercises should be encouraged. Even the person in a wheelchair can benefit from regular exercise. Make sure lighting is adequate and glare kept at a minimum. Bright colors for bed spreads and walls help perceptual problems.

Records of incontinence and bladder and bowel patterns help identify when the person should be taken to the bathroom. A common time for falls is at night when the person is trying to climb over the side rails of the bed to get to the bathroom. If used at all, half side rails are best. These assist the person in moving in bed and provide a means of stabilization when sitting up on the edge of the bed.

One of the most common, but incorrect, methods of preventing falls is to apply physical restraints. Interestingly, a high percentage of falls occur when restraints are in place and side rails up.[24] Of all possible interventions, this is the most harmful to the person's sense of autonomy, independence, function, and self-esteem. Restraints often increase agitation, and may contribute to incontinence, skin breakdown, confusion, and depression. Several states have laws against using restraints that are all-encompassing. Physical restraints (vest, wrist and ankle restraints), psychologic restraints (medications), and restricting activity by not having needed devices (such as a walker or cane) within reach are all illegal.

The controversy over restraints remains. Concerns of nurses and long-term care management center on the potential increase in injuries from

Table 13-1

Assessment—at Risk for Injury—Falls					
Risk factor	Yes	No	Risk factor	Yes	No
Admission (within 2 weeks)			Incontinent (urine)		
Transfer to unit or room change			Hearing deficit		
Medication change (within 30 days)			Visual deficit		
Cardiac medications			Confusion		
Antihypertensives			Head injury		
Diuretics			CVA		
Tranquilizers			Amputee		
Sleeping medications			Diabetic		
Pain medication			Metastatic disease		
More than 5 medications			Degenerative neuromuscular disease		
			Previous falls		

falls, and the related liability. While the move to restraint-free environments is relatively new in the United States, it is not new in England and other European countries. In England and the United States, the number of falls and injury from falls has not been found to increase when restraints are removed.[5]

Identification of alternatives to restraints occurs after exploring the need for restraints. If the reason is the potential for falls, an evaluation of the risk factors and measures to correct risk factors provides the nurse with alternatives. Exercise programs, activity programs, lower bed height, and locating the person close to the nurses station are possible interventions to permit removal of restraints.

Urinary Incontinence

Urinary incontinence, the involuntary loss of urine, presents a problem to at least 10 million noninstitutionalized American adults and accounts for approximately 10 billion dollars spent on products to manage the problem. Urinary incontinence causes significant disability and dependency and is a leading cause of institutionalization.

It is often assumed that urinary incontinence (UI) is a consequence of aging, that there is no corrective treatment, and therefore, one must learn to live with it. Urinary incontinence, however, is a symptom rather than a disease and is not a normal part of the aging process. Unfortunately, the evaluation and treatment of UI is often neglected by health care professionals. When treated appropriately, mobility, function, and independence show significant improvement.

In long-term care, 50% or more of the residents probably will have urinary problems. UI is complex, with multiple causative factors. There are three main types of UI: stress incontinence, urge incontinence, and overflow incontinence. Although there are three distinct types, older people often have two or three types at the same time. The nurse plays a vital role in treatment of UI through a complete assessment that includes a mental status examination, functional assessment, documentation of the pattern of incontinence, and assessment aimed at identification of the type of incontinence.

Stress incontinence

Stress incontinence, the involuntary leakage of small amounts of urine, usually in response to increased intraabdominal pressure, accounts for about 35% of incontinence in older people. The person will complain of losing small amounts of urine, usually during the day, when coughing, laughing, sneezing, bending, or changing position. Stress incontinence occurs primarily in women who have had three or more pregnancies. Additional assessment may reveal the presence of a cystocele, rectocele, uterine prolapse, or urethral prolapse, atrophic vaginitis due to lack of estrogen, obesity, or use of certain antihypertensive medications.

Urge incontinence

Urge incontinence (UI) is the involuntary loss of large amounts of urine associated with a strong desire to void. It probably accounts for 60% to 70% of UI in older people. The person complains of losing large amounts of urine day or night, having a strong desire to void but being unable to hold urination until reaching the bathroom. The person will experience leaking urine 3 to 5 seconds after coughing, rather than with coughing, as in stress incontinence. Additional assessment may reveal moderate to high caffeine intake (coffee, tea, cola), atrophic vaginitis, diabetes, infection, degenerative neurologic conditions such as a CVA or Parkinson's disease, alcoholism, and use of certain medications such as sedatives and diuretics.

Overflow incontinence

Overflow incontinence, the involuntary dribbling of urine due to an obstruction of the bladder outlet, probably accounts for 10% to 15% of the UI in older people. The person complains of dribbling during the day without warning. When voiding, there is a hesitancy and interruption in the stream of urine and the feeling of incomplete emptying of the bladder. If catheterized, there would be over 100 ml of residual urine present in the bladder. Additional assessment may reveal a fecal impaction, enlarged prostate, diabetes, a spinal cord injury or disc disease, or use of certain drugs such as alcohol, antihistamines, decongestants, phenothiazines, and muscle relaxants.

The person with UI requires a thorough evaluation by the health care team. In addition to the causes identified for each type of incontinence, there are multiple environmental contributory factors to assess. Immobility or being unable to get to the bathroom, commode, or bedpan, unfamiliar surroundings, inadequate lighting, dehydration causing concentration of urine, and irritation of the bladder wall are all correctable factors that need to be considered in assessment of UI.

Voiding record

There are a variety of methods to record voiding patterns.[7] The purpose of the record is to identify the pattern of incontinence in terms of frequency, amount, and conditions surrounding the incontinent episode. It can be kept by the resident, family, and/or nursing staff. The record requires cooperation by everyone as it encompasses at least one 24-hour period. The resident is observed on an hourly basis to determine whether the person was incontinent, dry, or voided normally. The amount of urine should be documented. If the person was incontinent, the following should be noted on the record: the approximate amount of urine, awareness of the urge to eliminate, associated conditions (coughing, sneezing, impaction or urge to defecate, walking or changing position), and the availability of appropriate facilities. In addition, an accurate record of the amount, type, and time of fluid intake is kept. Analysis of this record will help determine the person's normal patterns of elimination and assist in development of nursing interventions.

When assessing elimination patterns of older people the nurse should ask questions that help identify the type of incontinence. Questions such as "Do you ever lose urine when you don't want to?", "Do you lose urine when you sneeze, laugh, or cough?", "Do you have trouble getting to the bathroom on time?", "Do you wear something to keep you dry during the day and/or night?" will elicit a great deal of important information.

Urinary incontinence is complex. A thorough assessment will help identify the type of UI enabling the health care team to determine appropriate interventions.

Intervention

Interventions depend upon the type of incontinence and, whenever possible, removing the cause. The goal of all treatment is to promote independence and improve function.

For stress incontinence, Kegel exercises aim at strengthening the pelvic floor and can be taught by the nurse. The person is taught to find the pelvic floor muscle by trying to stop a stream of urine. The muscle that is pulled is the muscle to be exercised. The person is instructed to tighten the muscle, hold it for a count of 10 and relax it for a count of 10. This is repeated 10 to 15 times in the morning, afternoon, and evening. The exercise can be done at any time, in any place. When teaching the exercises, the nurse needs to emphasize the importance of relaxation as well as

tightening. Also, be sure the person is not using the abdomen, legs (or crossing legs), or buttocks or holding the breath while exercising. Developing a schedule that can be posted for the person to see and mark off when completing the exercise places responsibility on the person as well as serving as a reminder.

Additional interventions for stress incontinence include oral or topical estrogen for atrophic vaginitis, development of a weight loss program, use of loose garments, evaluation of medications, (particularly antihypertensive medications) possible use of anticholinergic medications, surgery, and habit training.

The purpose of habit training is to avoid large amounts of urine in the bladder. It begins by examining the voiding record to identify normal frequency patterns. A regular, rigid voiding schedule is established. The person is taken to the bathroom every 2 hours whether or not there is a desire to void and regardless of incontinence.

There are multiple interventions for *urge incontinence* that can be initiated by the nurse in cooperation with the health care team. First, make sure the environment facilitates normal voiding. Make sure the bathroom, commode, bedpan, or urinal is accessible and assistive devices needed for independence are close at hand. Remove obstacles and make sure lighting is adequate. It may be necessary to have the resident's eyes examined and vision corrected or mobility improved with the input of physical therapy. Occupational therapy may help design easy-to-open clothing.

Bladder training and habit training are also useful. The goal of bladder training is to increase the interval between voiding to 4 hours. The person is taught to inhibit the urge to void and increase bladder capacity, thus increasing the interval between voiding. Relaxation exercises often help the person overcome the urge. The nurse works with the resident encouraging slow, deep breathing until the urge disappears. The resident is encouraged to wait 5 minutes and then void. If an accident occurs before the 5 minutes, shorten the waiting time to 3 minutes. When it becomes easy to wait 3 minutes, increase the time to 4 or 5 minutes. Gradually increase the waiting time. To have a successful bladder training program, the person must maintain adequate intake usually between 2000 ml to 2500 ml per day. Natural diuretics such as coffee, tea, cocoa, cola, and grapefruit juice should be avoided. Additional interventions include evaluation of medications that could cause incontinence.

Often *overflow incontinence* is neurogenic in etiology. The resident and family can be taught measures to assist in voiding. Sitting on the toilet or commode places the person in the correct position. Deep breathing, blowing through a straw leaning forward, and the Crede maneuver (manual pressure on the bladder) may initiate voiding. Each of the techniques may be successful at different times. Because it does not work once does not mean that it will not work at another time. Successful management depends on patience and a willingness to try various methods.

Another treatment of choice for overflow incontinence is intermittent catheterization. Treatment of incontinence in many health care settings involves placement of an indwelling catheter which in turn places the person at risk for infection, decreases independence and mobility, increases the risk of trauma, and increases the need for medical supervision. Sterile intermittent catheterization by the nurse or clean technique taught to a cognitively intact person, simulates normal voiding patterns and decreases the risk of infection. In addition, intermittent catheterization promotes independence and functional abilities.

The first intervention for incontinence associated with outlet obstruction is to relieve the obstruction. This may be by removal of the fecal impaction or surgery for an enlarged prostate. Next, evaluate medications, identifying those that tighten sphincters or contribute to urinary retention.

Care of the person with urinary incontinence represents a challenge to the nurse and requires thorough assessment and creative problem solving with the resident, the family, and the health care team.

Constipation

As with all problems encountered in the long-term care setting, constipation has multiple causative factors. The elderly use more over-the-counter preparations to promote bowel elimination than any other age group. Persistent use of laxatives tends to inhibit normal patterns thereby creating an impression of constipation that stimulates perpetual use of laxatives. Also, in a misguided attempt to prevent incontinence, the older person may decrease fluid intake thereby increasing the tendency toward constipation. Diets lacking in roughage and fruit, medications, inhibitory practices (ignoring the bowel reflex as well as use of laxatives), and lack of exercise all contribute to the problem of constipation. Added to this list are

cultural beliefs about the importance of regular, often translated as daily, bowel movements.

Assessment

An accurate assessment is essential for planning appropriate interventions. Assessment should include the following:

Time: What are the usual days and the time of day of bowel movements?

Frequency: Are bowel movements daily, three times a week, twice a week, or weekly?

Consistency: Is the stool formed, hard, soft, or loose?

Fluid intake: List the amount of daily fluid intake, and the type of fluid.

Nutrition: A 24-hour recall is helpful for a variety of assessment areas including elimination. Ask specific questions regarding foods and amounts consumed at meals, for snacks, and at bedtime. Note amounts of cereals, fresh fruit, vegetables, breads.

Stimulants: Identify what the person uses to stimulate a bowel movement. This includes coffee, prunes, bran, and other natural laxatives, plus medications, enemas, suppositories, and digital stimulation.

Habits associated with elimination: What is the usual place for elimination? Are activities such as reading or smoking done during bowel evacuation?

Medications: Certain medications cause constipation such as anticholinergic drugs, aluminum or calcium antacids, and high doses of aspirin.

Exercise: List the amount and type of exercise.

Physical assessment: A rectal examination to check for impaction, bowel sounds, and skin turgor (dehydration), and a palpation of the abdomen for masses should be performed. Chronic medical conditions should be noted.

Intervention

If constipation and impaction are present, the cleansing of the bowel must take place before a bowel program can be successful. Laxatives and enemas should be used as needed to clean the bowel. Then, the assessment data can be used to identify normal patterns and begin a re-education of the bowel. When developing a bowel program, it is usually easier to re-establish old patterns than to develop new ones. If the person usually had a bowel movement at bedtime, retraining should begin at this time using the natural cues found effective by the person. Nutritional stimulants such as bran may be added to the morning or afternoon foods, prunes or other dried fruits may be served, and fresh fruit or bran cereal can be suggested as a snack.

If no bowel movement occurs within the first 48 hours, a gentle stimulant such as a glycerine suppository at the time the person normally has a bowel movement may be needed. Whenever using artificial bowel stimulants, start with the most natural and work up to the more irritating.

Encourage the person to respond to the urge to evacuate the bowel. Make sure the environment is conducive by providing privacy and ensuring that the bathroom, commode, or bedpan is accessible. No bowel program will work immediately. Each intervention should be given approximately 2 weeks to be effective. The person will usually respond to encouragement and support. Punishing words or actions will place an unnecessary barrier to success. For most people, it is unnatural to be dependent on others for toileting. Whenever possible, the nurse should facilitate independence.

Decubitus Ulcers (Pressure Sores)

As a person ages, changes take place in the skin that contribute to the potential for skin breakdown. With aging, there is a decrease in vascularity, subcutaneous fat, elasticity, hair folicles, and temperature and touch receptors. The result is skin that is fragile, easily injured and difficult to heal.

Additional risk factors include immobility, diabetes, incontinence, poor nutrition, inadequate fluid intake, and edema. Assessment must include all factors plus an accurate description of the altered skin. Pressure sores, also called decubitus ulcers, are the most common form of alteration in skin integrity caused by continued unrelieved pressure. They develop over bony prominences where the pressure causes occlusion of capillaries and local inflammation from inadequate nutrient exchange.[18]

Pressure sores should be assessed and described using a standard classification system. Identification of stages helps determine interventions (Figure 13-1).

It is extremely useful to photograph pressure sores, with the inclusion of a tape measure in the photograph to indicate the size. The photograph serves as both a means to assess the extent of the problem and evaluate effectiveness of treatment. Before photographing the pressure sore, permission from the patient or family must be obtained. The picture with the date and location of the wound along with the treatment plan are then placed in the record. Pictures should be taken weekly until the lesion is healed.

Intervention

One of the key factors to healing pressure sores is a consistent approach by all who care for the person. The proposed treatment must be given time to work. All long-term care facilities need to develop a skin protocol that fits their facility and residents. The protocol outlines assessment, identification of the person at risk, preventive measures and, when pressure sores develop, a protocol for intervention. The treatment protocol requires collaboration with the physician but the nurse plays a primary role in care of pressure sores.

Initial interventions aim at identification of the person at risk and prevention. Once pressure sores begin to develop, interventions are designed according to the extent of the lesions and center around relief of pressure. Basic nursing interventions include turning every 2 hours, use of special mattresses such as a waterbed mattress, a circulating air mattress, or an egg crate mattress, special cushions for the wheelchair, range of motion exercises, ambulation, and special skin care.

In addition, residents and families can be taught the prevention of pressure sores and encouraged to take part in the treatment plan. Residents who are in chairs for extended periods of time should be taught to change position frequently by pushing up on the arms of their chairs to relieve pressure. Isometric flexion exercises of the buttocks can also be performed to increase circulation and relieve pressure. Residents may need to be reminded to follow their treatment plan.

There are numerous products on the market for management of pressure sores. Treatment must begin as soon as redness develops. Once the skin breaks, dressings that provide a moist environment have been found the most successful.[1,17] Dressings such as Duoderm and Opsite are useful for Stage 2 and some Stage 3 pressure sores. Deeper wounds, and wounds with a great deal of drainage, require dressings such as Sorbsan, and karaya powder that absorb the exudate without drying the wound.

When necrotic tissue is present, the pressure sore must be debrided. Noninvasive wet-to-dry dressings are often the treatment of choice. It

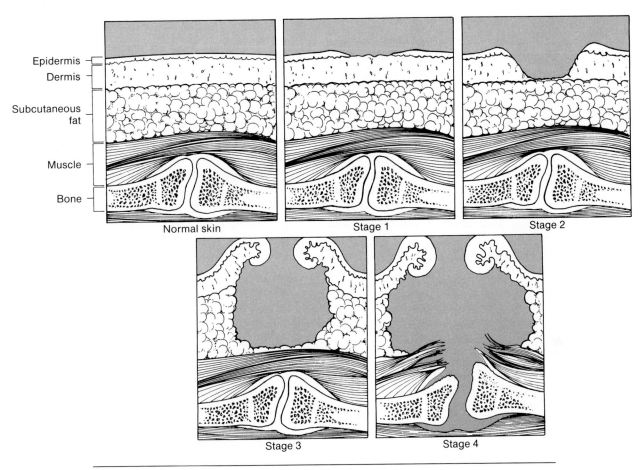

Epidermis
Dermis
Subcutaneous fat
Muscle
Bone

Normal skin   Stage 1   Stage 2

Stage 3   Stage 4

Figure 13-1
Normal skin and pressure sore formation.

The appearance of pink granulation tissue heralds the end of the debridement process.

In addition to the physician, other members of the health care team need to be involved in the treatment plan. An in-depth nutritional assessment and treatment plan needs to be instituted. If a pressure sore is draining, the person is losing albumin, a necessary factor in healing. Nutritional interventions include an increase in protein, either at meal time or by the use of supplements. Periodic albumin levels are needed to monitor the nutritional sufficiency. Physical and occupational therapy may be helpful in development of an activity plan. Provision of special cushions for the wheelchair or the provision of assistive devices will help the person move independently.

Pressure sores severely limit independence and threaten functional ability. Prevention and treatment decisions often rest on the nurse. Resident, family, and staff teaching are important aspects of practice in addition to coordination of care with the interdisciplinary team.

Pressure Sore Stages

Stage 1: Inflammatory response (redness, swelling and heat), with or without a break in the skin.
Stage 2: Shallow ulcer with distinct edges and drainage, surrounded by an area of redness, heat, and swelling. The dermis is involved.
Stage 3: Irregular ulceration involving subcutaneous fat, drainage may be copious.
Stage 4: Deep ulceration that extends into the muscle tissue with visualization of ligaments and bone. The wound and drainage from the wound are foul smelling, and the borders are thick and pigmented.

---

must be remembered, however, that this debridement process takes time to be effective. Other measures include use of a scalpel and scissors to remove necrotic tissue followed by enzyme creams such as Elase to continue debridement.

Confusion

Confusion in the elderly is poorly understood and evaluated. Unfortunately, confusion is often considered a consequence of aging by both the older person and the health care professional. Confusion is a symptom rather than a disease and may actually be the presenting symptom for any number of underlying conditions. The primary cause of confusion among the elderly is medication. When assessing the medications the person takes, have the family bring in all medications they can find at home. This should include prescription medications, over-the-counter medications, and medications taken by other members of the household. Often older people trade medications or take medications prescribed for a condition long since resolved.

Other causes of confusion include infections (such as a respiratory or urinary track infection), metabolic problems (diabetes, thyroid conditions), nutrition, sensory disturbances, tumors, anemia, atherosclerosis, alcohol abuse, trauma, and environmental factors. Confusion is not a simple phenomenon. The person with confusion often requires an extensive evaluation to determine the cause.

There are three "D's" associated with confusion in the elderly: delirium, depression, and dementia. Although discussed separately, the older person frequently has two and often three of the conditions at the same time.

Delirium

Delirium is a common nonspecific presentation of illness in the elderly and is often the first sign of underlying disease. It is a symptom in need of evaluation. Delirium and acute confusional state may be used interchangeably to describe the same syndrome. Delirium replaces terminology once used including acute organic brain syndrome, acute dementia, and toxic confusional state. Delirium is a global cognitive impairment of memory and organization of thought. Onset is sudden, characterized by uncooperative behavior, drowsiness and/or hyperactivity, mood swings, inappropriate language, delusions, hallucinations, and confused visual-spacial relationships. Symptoms are more severe at night. The mental status examination will show an inability to attend to tasks and an altered level of consciousness.

Depression

Another common cause of confusion is **depression.** Again, confusion may be the presenting symptom. Depression often goes unrecognized and untreated in the older population, yet the elderly are at the highest risk for successful suicides. It is likely that between 30% and 50% of the residents in long-term care have some type of depression. In addition to confusion, the depressed older person will have a variety of somatic complaints and are frequently labeled hypochondriacs.

Conditions often associated with depression include thyroid and adrenal abnormalities, Parkinson's disease, CVA, medications, and other psychiatric syndromes. The mental status examination will reveal only mild, if any, impairment. Interviews with the person will be difficult with many "I don't know" answers. The score on the Geriatric Depression Scale will indicate a depression with a score of over 11.

Dementia

Dementia, once called organic brain syndrome, is a term used to describe a global cognitive dysfunction with impairment in short- and long-term memory, orientation, abstract thinking, judgment, and personality changes. Disturbances in cortical function creating aphasia (language disorders), apraxia (inability to carry out motor function), and agnosia (failure to recognize objects and people that are familiar) are also included. The mental status examination will show a global cognitive impairment but depending on the stage of the illness, the person may be able to attend to tasks and perform calculations.

There are many different types of dementia however, the most common is dementia of the Alzheimer's type (DAT). Unlike delirium, the onset of DAT is slow and insidious, the disease progressive and irreversible. The disease process continues for many years and places considerable burden on the family. Families will report that the person is not quite the same but may have trouble describing the problem. Getting lost while walking or driving or leaving burners on the stove are frequently the behaviors that force the family to take the person to the physician.

When assessing the person with dementia, the nurse will note many "near miss" answers to questions and an attempt on the part of the person to conceal problems. The person may also be unsociable, uncooperative, and hostile as well as confused and disoriented. Because confusion is one of the presenting symptoms, and there is no differential diagnosis for dementia, there needs to be a complete evaluation that includes laboratory tests, x-rays, CT scans, magnetic resonance imagery, psychiatric and neurologic testing.

Intervention

Caring for the person with alteration in thought processes is difficult. The person with delirium needs a consistent, quiet, and calm approach to care. The environment should be organized to avoid extremes and excessive sensory input. Have the room quiet with familiar people to provide care, avoid changing personnel and routines, and decrease lighting at night. Orientation to person, time, and place may be helpful. Once the underlying condition is corrected, the delirium will clear. Mental status will become normal providing there is no other cognitive problem.

Depression should be treated with both medications and therapy. There may be a resistance to therapy from the health care workers and the older person. Beneath the resistance is the belief that therapy for the older person is not cost effective and of little use. The older person, however, will benefit and regain independence and function as well as have improved mental status. Reminiscence, life review, and support groups are useful and beneficial interventions that can be initiated by the nurse.

The nursing home resident with dementia needs structure and consistency. Routines are helpful. Because wandering may be a problem, warning devices that let the nurse know that the person is out of bed or opening a door should be used. They allow the person freedom of movement, independence, and functioning ability while maintaining a safe environment. The person can also be seated close to the nursing station for closer observation.

Of primary importance when caring for the person with dementia is care of the family. Placement of the loved one in a long-term care facility was probably a difficult decision. Watching the slow deterioration and not being recognized are difficult adjustments for any family member. Reassuring the family, offering support, and providing information are helpful in their anticipatory grieving process.

REFERENCES AND ADDITIONAL READINGS

1. Alvarez OM, Martz PM, and Eaglstein WH: The effect of occlusive dressings on re-epithelialization and collagen synthesis, J Surg Res 35:142-148, 1983.
2. Bates B: Guide to physical examination, ed 3, Philadelphia, 1983, JB Lippincott Co.
3. Berecek KH: Etiology of decubitus ulcers: treatment of decubitus ulcers, Nurs Clin North Am 10:157-210, 1975.
4. Burnside I: Nursing and the aged, ed 3, New York, 1988, McGraw-Hill Inc.
5. Evans LK and Strumpf NE: Patterns of restraint: a cross cultural view, Gerontologist 12:272, 1987.
6. Folstein MF, Folstein SE, and McHugh PR: Mini-mental state: a practical method of grading the cognitive state of patients for the clinician, J Psychiatr Res 12:189-198, 1975.
7. Greengold BA and Ouslander JG: Bladder retraining, J Gerontol Nurs, 12:31-35, 1986.
8. Katz S and others: Studies of illness in the aged. The index of ADL: a standardized measure of biological and psychosocial function, JAMA 185:94-98, 1963.
9. Lawton HP and Brody EM: Assessment of older people: self-maintaining and instrumental activities of daily living, Gerontologist 9:179, 1969.
10. Linn MW and Linn BSW: The rapid disability rating scale-2, J Am Geriatr Soc 30:378-382, 1982.
11. Mace N and Rabins P: The 36-hour day, New York, 1981, Warner Books Inc. 1981.
12. Mahoney F and Barthel D: Functional evaluation: the barthel index, Maryland State Med J 61-65, 1965.
13. Matteson MA and McConnell A: Gerontological nursing: concepts and practice, New York, 1988, WB Saunders Co.
14. Moskowitz E and McCann C: Classification of disability in the chronically ill and aging, J Chronic Dis 5:342-346, 1957.
15. Neugarten B: Middle age and aging, Chicago, 1968, University of Chicago Press.
16. Pfeiffer E: A short portable mental status questionnaire of the assessment of organic brain deficit in elderly patients, J Am Geriatr Soc 23:433-441, 1975.
17. Pollock SV: Wound healing: a review, J Dermatol Surg Oncol 5:389-993, 1979.
18. Reuter JB and Cooney TG: The pressure sore: pathophysiology and principles of management, Ann Intern Med 94:661-666, 1981.
19. Rodriquez E, editor: Restraints, focus on geriatric care and rehabilitation 4:1-8, 1990.
20. Strumpf NE and Evans L: Physical restraints of hospitalized elderly: perceptions of patients and nurses, Nurs Res 37:132, 1988.
21. Wells T, editor: The rehabilitation management of urinary incontinence, Top Geriatr Rehab 3:1-77, 1988.
22. Wieman HM and Obear ME: Falls and restraints in a skilled nursing facility, J Am Geriatr Soc 34:907, 1986.
23. Williams TF, editor: Rehabilitation in the aging, New York 1984. Raven Press.
24. Yesavage JA and others: Development and validation of a geriatric depression screening scale: a preliminary report, J Psychiatr Res 17:37-49, 1983.

Home Health Care

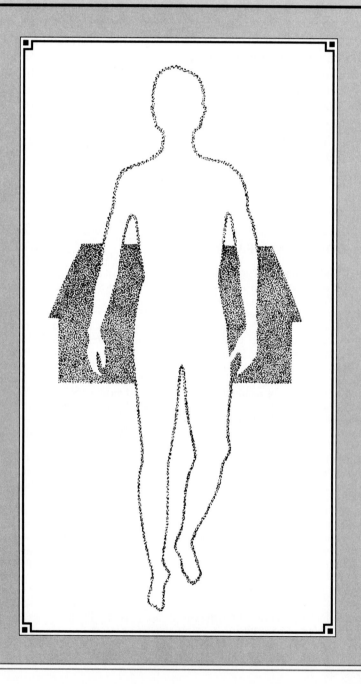

KEY WORDS

control
diagnosis-related groups (DRGs)
environment
family
populations
reimbursement
socioeconomic
team

OBJECTIVES

1. Identify the concept of "home health care."
2. Describe the historical development of home health care.
3. Identify the types of home health agencies.
4. Identify the services provided by home health agencies.
5. Discuss the concept of the team in home health care.
6. Discuss the role of the nurse in the home setting and the activities provided.
7. Identify the sources of reimbursement for home health services.
8. Identify trends and future directions in home health care.
9. Discuss the relationship of long-term care to home health care.
10. Give examples of the rewards and opportunities in home health care.

CONCEPTUAL FRAMEWORK

Home health care is provided in the home to maintain or restore a person's health and well-being. The concept of home health care has grown out of a rich tradition in the history of nursing. It has evolved in response to the needs of patients and families in community settings. Since the early part of the century when nurses began to work in the urban slums of the nation, home health services have been a dynamic and energetic force in health care.

"Community health nursing practice promotes and preserves the health of populations by integrating the skills and knowledge relevant to both nursing and public health. The practice is comprehensive and general, and is not limited to a particular age or diagnostic group; it is continual and is not limited to episodic care."[1]

HOME HEALTH CARE

Home health care in the United States, as we know it today, had its origins in the late nineteenth century. The movement began as "visiting" or "district" nursing. In many communities, interested and benevolent citizens formed associations, raised funds, and hired nurses to visit the "sick and poor" in their homes. These developments occurred when urban areas in America were undergoing expansion. Immigration was at its peak and thousands of foreign-born people thronged the cities. Epidemics of influenza, cholera, and other highly contagious diseases were rampant. Physicians were in short supply, and it was the nurse who stepped in to help the family care for their sick. The development of district nursing was a response to the needs of this population.

In many cities the first of these organizations were the visiting nurse associations and district nurse associations. These were formed as charitable entities to provide nursing services to those who could not afford to pay for nursing care. Early organizations developed in such cities as Buffalo, New York, Boston, and Philadelphia (Figure 14-1). The focus of the service was not only to provide nursing care as needed but to also teach family members concepts of good hygiene and cleanliness. These concepts of teaching and prevention continue to be a part of home health care today.

Figure 14-1

Two visiting nurses in Boston's North End, 1909. *(Courtesy Boston Visiting Nurse Association, Boston; Nursing Archives, Mugar Memorial Library, Boston University.)*

Because care occurs in the home setting, the **family** is the unit of service and plays a major role in the delivery of service. Because service takes place in the community setting, the **socioeconomic,** cultural, political, and **environmental** characteristics of the community influence the practice of home health care.

As the needs of the population grew, the visiting nurse associations began to respond to those needs, and many municipalities and government agencies began to assume responsibility for community health services. Their role emphasized controlling outbreaks of communicable diseases.

However, as the health problems of the nation changed from tuberculosis to heart disease, cancer, and stroke, so did the programs of those official agencies who provided public health nursing.[4]

Over time, visiting nursing has evolved into public health nursing into community health nursing into home care nursing. The National Association for Home Care estimates that today there are 3000 home health agencies nationwide.[8] The following types of organizations deliver home health services:

Voluntary agency—A nonprofit organization with a volunteer board of directors (e.g., visiting nurse associations [VNAs]).

Official agency—A tax-supported unit of a governmental or municipal organization (e.g., a health department of a town or city).

Proprietary agency—A for-profit organization delivering home health services (e.g., investor-owned national chains such as Medical Personnel Pool, Upjohn, Inc.).

Hospital-based agency—A unit or a department of a hospital that delivers services to persons leaving the hospital who still need nursing care in their own homes.

Home Health Services

Most home health agencies offer a range of services.

Skilled nursing

Skilled nursing care involves assessment of client needs, establishment of the plan of care, and carrying out the plan of care. Some examples of skilled nursing provided in the home setting include monitoring and evaluation of medication regimens, dressing care, catheter care, injections, and other therapeutic treatments (Figure 14-2).

Home health aide

Services rendered by the home health aide include personal care, assistance with activities of daily living, meal preparation, and incidental housekeeping activities.

Rehabilitation services

Physical therapy, occupational therapy, and speech therapy are forms of rehabilitation. These services are provided by a registered therapist and include the evaluation and assessment of the patient's status, development of a rehabilitation program, and implementation of this treatment plan.

Rehabilitation can include range-of-motion exercises, strengthening exercises, and assistance with ambulation and mobility. Patients who benefit from rehabilitation services are those who have had cerebrovascular accidents, those with neurologic injuries and disease, and those with orthopedic conditions such as fractures. The goal is to restore function, to develop maximum independence, and to provide ways in which patients may cope with a long-term disability.

Medical social work

Social work services include counseling, support for patients and their families, coping with the problems of illness and disease, and assistance in learning to use community resources. Patients may also be advised about and provided assistance with financial problems, such as budgeting and how to apply for financial aid.

Specialty care

Home health services now encompass many areas that were traditionally provided in the hospital setting. These include administration of medications through heparin locks, parenteral and enteral therapy, ostomy care, and respiratory therapy. In addition, it is possible to have a full array of laboratory services available for patients at home, including electrocardiographic monitoring, pneumograms, and x-ray films.

Other services

Home health services available to special populations include pediatric care, hospice care, psychiatric care, and gerontologic community health nursing services.

Supplies and equipment

The home health agency can supply directly or make arrangements for such items as dressings, catheters, walkers, wheelchairs, and hospital beds. The ability to provide this service allows patients to be cared for in their homes in an environment that mimics the hospital setting.

Supportive Services in the Community

Other supportive services in the community augment professional services and family support and enable patients to remain at home. The following services may be provided directly by the home health care agency or arranged for by the nurse in the organization[8]:

Day care—Offers supervised activities and

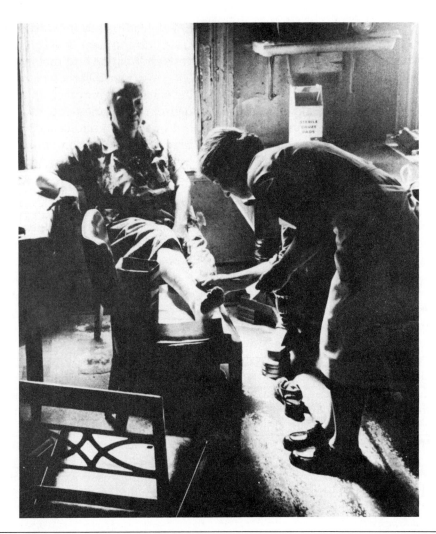

Figure 14-2
A visiting nurse provides care to a patient with leg ulcers, 1962. *(Courtesy Boston Visiting Nurse Association, Boston; Nursing Archives, Mugar Memorial Library, Boston University.)*

meals at a specific site, such as a senior center or long-term care facility (e.g., a chronic disease/rehabilitation hospital, extended care facility).

Telephone reassurance—Provides contact by phone and offers support for those who are homebound and alone.

Friendly visitors—Volunteers visit those who are unable to get out of their homes themselves. These workers provide socialization and companionship.

Meals on Wheels—A service provided to the geriatric population either in their homes or in a group residential setting. The purpose of Meals on Wheels is to relieve family members of the burden of meal preparation

and to provide older people with a well-balanced diet.

Homemakers—Homemakers assist persons with meal preparation, housekeeping, laundry, or food shopping.

Personal Emergency Response Systems—A system available to persons living alone at home. Electronic devices are connected by telephone to a central location that alerts relatives and emergency services in the event of a fall or accident.

The Home Health Care Team

The team concept is essential for deliverying services to persons in their own home. In addition to the registered nurse (RN), who serves as the

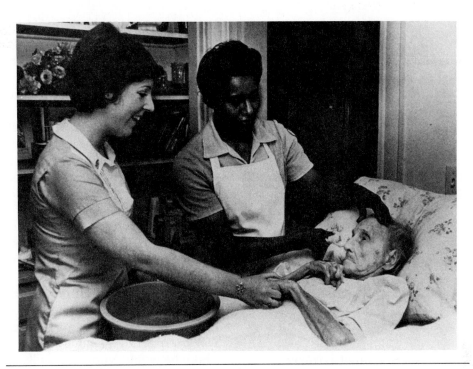

Figure 14-3
A visiting nurse instructs the home health aide in bedside care, 1970s. *(Courtesy Boston Visiting Nurse Association, Boston; Nursing Archives, Mugar Memorial Library, Boston University.)*

coordinator and case manager, other nursing roles contribute to the care of patients at home including the licensed practical nurse (LPN) and the *home health aide.* Both of these workers assist in the care of patients in the home setting and function in collaboration with the RN. The RN supervises the home health aide in carrying out the plan of care (Figure 14-3). The *physician* is also a member of the team and authorizes the medical orders in the care plan. The *social worker,* acting on the physician's medical orders, provides support and counseling and focuses on assisting the patient and family or significant other in coping with the socioeconomic consequences of the disease, illness, or disability. Others brought into the home as needed include the *physical therapist, occupational therapist,* and *speech pathologist.* A *nutritionist* may help patients remain at home by providing nutrition counseling and teaching about special and therapeutic diets.

NURSING IN THE HOME SETTING

Nursing is the core service in the delivery of home health care. The nurse, working within the framework of a team that includes the patient, family, physician, and others, is the case manager. He or she is responsible for assessing the patient, developing the care plan, implementing the care plan, and evaluating this plan and its outcome. Using the nursing process, the goal of the nurse is to treat the symptoms of illness and disease, minimize disability, and promote health within the context of home and community.

The nurse in the home setting not only collaborates with the team but arranges for other programs and services to be made available to the patient and family at home. The nurse may use other community resources to allow the patient to remain at home. Meals on Wheels is an example of a community program by which a hot meal is delivered each day to those who are unable to prepare their own food. For those who cannot carry out simple homemaking and housekeeping chores, a homemaker may be provided to dust, shop, make beds, and do laundry.

A major responsibility of the nurse is to link patients and their families to available community resources, such as welfare programs, counseling resources, and rehabilitation services in the community.

Case Study

Mr. S. is a 48-year-old married man who is a self-employed carpenter. He has two children, a 15-year-old boy in high school and a 12-year-old girl in junior high. Up until he was seen in the emergency room of the local hospital, he had been very healthy and had not seen a physician for many years.

Mr. S. was seen in the emergency room after experiencing an acute onset of chest pain while scraping paint from a house. Tests and a physical examination confirmed an acute evolving myocardial infarction. During his hospital stay, the diagnosis was an anterior wall myocardial infarction with continuing hypertension. While he was in the hospital, Mr. S. appeared to be ambivalent about the instructions he received concerning his condition, diet, medications, and activity restrictions. He also verbalized anxiety regarding his finances. His blood pressure was still unstable, and he was receiving antihypertensive agents.

Because Mr. S. would be discharged from the hospital shortly to conform to his insurance guidelines, he was referred to the local home health agency for follow-up teaching and monitoring of his compliance with his medical regimen.

A nurse from the local visiting nurse and home health agency visited Mr. S. at his house the day after his discharge from the local hospital. She explained to him and his wife that the physician had requested visits to review his medications, which now included warfarin (Coumadin) and methyldopa (Aldomet), and to assist in his recovery at home. During the visit the patient expressed concern regarding finances; although ambulatory, he was still unable to return to his previous level of activity as a carpenter. Through the interview it became apparent that the patient was denying the extent of his illness.

After a physical assessment of the patient, which included a cardiac evaluation, a blood pressure reading, and measurement of pulse rate, the patient appeared to be asymptomatic. However, the patient did not seem to understand the continuing need to take his medications when he did not have any symptoms or feel sick. In developing the plan of care, the nurse established a teaching plan that included his wife. Arrangements were made for him to be seen by the social worker who could assist in getting the family the necessary financial help they required. The nurse worked with the social worker to focus on the patient's adjustment to illness, including his denial of the illness. A diet with "no added salt" had been prescribed and his wife's need for assistance in developing a diet plan that included foods low in salt was identified.

The nurse told the family she would return the next day to visit Mr. S. again. She continued the visits each day for a week, offering support, encouragement, teaching, and reviewing the patient's physical status. Through the help of the social worker, the family received financial aid. This reduced the patient's anxiety level, making him more amenable to learning about his disease, its signs and symptoms, and the limitations imposed by the diagnosis. He also began to understand the importance of taking his medications. The nurse continued to see Mr. S. each week, reviewing his dietary intake with his wife and providing overall monitoring of his status. Through counseling with the social worker, Mr. S. was preparing to enter a job training program, where he would learn new skills and become employed in a less strenuous job. The nurse was in contact verbally and in writing with the patient's physician throughout his home care program. She provided feedback and information on his status, which was reviewed with the physician. When Mr. S. and his wife were independent in all aspects of his care, the nurse informed the physician of her intent to discharge him from service.

General vs Specialty Care

The nurse practicing in the home setting historically has been viewed as a generalist, providing care to patients and families of all age groups and with all health problems, diseases, and disabilities. The nurse cares for patients with cardiac problems, diabetes, cancer, and pulmonary disease, among others. In caring for patients, the nurse integrates principles of teaching and learning in the plan of care. The focus is teaching the patient and family the necessary care and techniques to allow the patient to remain at home.

Increasingly, as the technology of health care changes, many specialized services have been developed and have been provided by home health agencies. Specially prepared nurses offer services directly to the patients and offer consultation to others providing services. Some specialty areas now available include pediatric care, ostomy care, oncology, psychiatric–mental health services, hospice care, and geriatric care.

Also, as the technology traditionally available only in the institutional setting becomes more readily adaptable to the home setting, nurses have responded to these changes. Nurses are providing home care to patients who require infusion therapy, parenteral and enteral nutrition, and oxygen and respiratory therapy (Figure 14-4).

Reimbursement

Home health services are reimbursed through a variety of third-party payers. Major support comes from Medicare and in most states Medicaid. Private insurance coverage for home health services is currently limited but growing as insurance companies compare the higher cost of hospital care to home care. A growing market in health maintenance organizations (HMOs) has led to the provision of home health services to the subscribers of those types of insurance plans. HMOs view home health services as one way to substitute for the more expensive types of care.

Voluntary agencies typically charge for services on a "sliding-scale" basis. Many of these agencies also receive funds from the United Way to help support those patients who cannot afford the full cost of home health care. Patients may also pay on a private basis for these services.

Impact of Reimbursement on Delivery of Services

The most significant impact on the development and growth of home health care came over 20 years ago with the initiation of Title XVIII (Medicare) and Title XIX (Medicaid) of the Social Security Act.

Under the Medicare legislation (Title XVIII), the Home Health Benefit was created and home health services developed for older Americans. What had been known as community health nursing gradually began to evolve into home health care. Increasingly, the traditional visiting nurse association has become known as the certified home health agency. The titles and names of many organizations were amended to reflect these changes (e.g., Visiting Nurse and Home Health Agency). Under the regulations of the Medicare program, agencies must provide skilled nursing and one other service, such as physical therapy, occupational therapy, or speech therapy. Many agencies provide these services plus other programs such as the home health aide. Agencies must meet federally defined standards known as the "Conditions of Participation" to be eligible for reimbursement of their services.

When Medicare legislation passed in 1966,

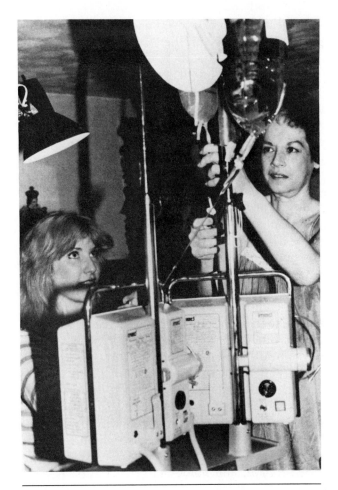

Figure 14-4

A patient learns to care for an infusion pump with the assistance of the nurse from the home health agency, 1980s. *(Courtesy Boston Visiting Nurse Association, Boston; Nursing Archives, Mugar Memorial Library, Boston University.)*

states were also eligible to receive federal funds for health services to those entitled because of income levels. This program, known as Medicaid (Title XIX), also provided support for home health services in most states. These two pieces of legislation had sweeping effects on the delivery of home health services in the United States and led to the growth and proliferation of many kinds and types of home health services. What had once been a socially benevolent service provided through district nursing in the framework of public health and community nursing was now a distinct component of the health care system that had come of age.

To be eligible for reimbursement under Title XVIII and Title XIX for home health services, agencies must be surveyed each year to evaluate their compliance with the "Conditions of Participation." This evaluation is usually carried out by the health department in each state. Over the years this process has mandated that home health agencies develop practices, programs, and procedures that meet certain standards. The standards are related to the administrative, program, and quality assurance structure of the home health agency. These governmental mandates have affected the delivery of services and have required agencies to develop comprehensive programs and more sophisticated administrative systems. The mandates have not only lead to a more consumer-oriented philosophy but also have driven up the costs of services remarkably. What had been provided free or for a minimum charge in the early days of visiting nursing is currently more expensive. Compared to the costs of hospital care or other types of institutional care, however, home health care is much less expensive and frequently more humane and desirable.

The Older Americans Act of 1972 made possible the payment of a broad range of supportive and social services that allow elderly persons to remain at home. These federally supported programs include homemaker services, home health aide services, and home-delivered meals.

Trends

Recent changes in the methods by which the federal government and other payers reimburse hospitals for services has had an impact on home health services. More patients who a short time ago would have been cared for in the acute care setting of the hospital are being cared for at home. This is because of the DRG system **(diagnosis related groups),** which has given hospitals an incentive to discharge patients earlier from the hospital than ever before. These patients are more acutely ill, have more intense needs for services, and require more care than ever before. This trend is a throwback to the tradition of caring for the sick at home. Long before hospitals and other health care institutions came into being, ill persons were cared for in their homes by family members or neighbors.

The method of prospective payment based on the DRG system reimburses at a fixed rate hospitals who care for Medicare beneficiaries. Hospitals are reimbursed according to the patient's diagnosis, and a specified number of hospital days is allowed for each diagnosis.

Increasingly, products are being developed that allow patients to remain at home safely. These products include portable respirators, cardiac monitors, and pumps for administering nutrients, antibiotics, and pain medications. In addition, the home setting can be adapted easily to meet the needs of patients. Psychologically, patients do well and can recover faster, because they can sleep in their own beds, eat the food they like, and maintain control over their own lives.

Long-Term Care and Home Health Care

As the elderly population continues to increase through the year 2000, the need for services for this group will grow proportionately—including the needs for supportive, maintenance, and chronic care. Nursing is the pivotal profession in the delivery of long-term care, and there is increasing support to have long-term care delivered in the home and community setting.

Currently the largest single age group served by home health agencies consists of those persons over 65 years of age. The Medicare program does not pay for custodial care or long-term care of elderly persons in the home, however. Coverage is available only for acute episodes of illness evidenced by documented skilled care. The Medicare term *skilled nursing* described the administration of tasks such as catheterization, injection, and dressings. The needs of those who require long-term care, the disabled elders, for the most part do not fall within this narrow designation.

Elderly persons are in need of supportive and custodial services. These services allow them to remain in the community and include assistance with ADL such as bathing, routine monitoring of medications, and teaching and reinforcement of health practices, diet, exercise, and hygiene. Currently these services are not reimbursed. For those who are eligible because of income levels, Medicaid pays for the cost of these services in many states. But for many Americans, there are significant gaps in coverage for long-term care.[6]

The United States must grapple shortly with these issues to ensure that its citizens are not caught in a "no-care zone." It must also formulate policies for the future to ensure that the growing long-term care needs of the elderly population will be met and financed appropriately.

SUMMARY

Home health care is a challenging and rewarding opportunity to serve people and is one of the fastest growing areas of health care delivery. Practitioners draw on a variety of resources to coordinate a total program of services for patients to allow them to remain at home.

Elderly patients are the heaviest users of home health services. They also benefit from such supportive services as those provided by homemakers, companions, and Meals on Wheels. With future trends anticipating extraordinary growth in the elderly population, there is certain to be a subsequent surge in providers of home health care. Home health care has been identified by the American Nurses' Association as the future of nursing.

Home health care also affords many special opportunities and rewards for the clinician who must use his or her ingenuity and creativity to deliver care in a variety of environments. LPNs are finding opportunities in the home health care setting as well. Working with other members of the team in carrying out the plan of care can provide rewards and challenges. These include an opportunity to learn and understand about the aspects of care that are unique to the home and community setting. The psychosocial impact of illness and disability on the patient and family are more readily apparent in the home setting than in the institution. These factors affect the services provided and cannot be separated from the medical and health needs of the patient. Because care is provided in the home, the patient maintains control and mastery over his environment. Indeed, the home health nurse is viewed as a guest and helper in the home setting.

REFERENCES AND ADDITIONAL READINGS

1. Council of Community Health Nurses: Standards of community health nursing practice, Kansas City, Mo, 1986, American Nurses' Association.
2. Freeman RB: Public health nursing practice, Philadelphia, 1963, WB Saunders Co.
3. Gardner M: Public health nursing, New York, 1937, The Macmillan Publishing Co, Inc.
4. Health Advocacy Services Program Department: A handbook about care in the home, Washington, DC, 1985, American Association of Retired Persons.
5. Janczak DF: Changes in rural public health nursing program: a community profile, Home Health Care Nurse, 1985.
6. Jarvis LL: Community health nursing: keeping the public health, Philadelphia, 1981, FA Davis Co.
7. Leader S: Home health benefits under Medicare, Washington, DC, 1986, American Association of Retired Persons.
8. McNiff ML: HMOs and home care: a VNA's experience, Caring 5:30-33, 1986.
9. McNiff ML: Impact of managed care systems on home health agencies, Home Health Care Nurse 6:3, 1988.
10. National Association for Home Care: Homecare, Washington, DC, 1985, The Association.
11. Pavasaris BA: A classification tool in home health care, Home Health Care Nurse 7:1, 1989.
12. Spiegal AD: Home health care, Owings Mills, Md, 1983, National Health Publishing.
13. Wolf RS and others: A model for the integration of community based health and social services, Home Health Serv Q 6:4, 1985/1986.

PART THREE

Nursing the Patient

with Medical-

Surgical Problems

CHAPTER 15 *Problems Affecting Respiration*

16 *Problems Affecting Circulation*

17 *Problems Affecting the Blood*

18 *Problems Affecting Nutrition and Bowel Elimination*

19 *Problems Affecting the Urinary System*

20 *Problems Affecting Sexuality*

21 *Problems Affecting Endocrine Function*

22 *Problems Affecting Neurologic Function*

23 *Problems Affecting Vision and Hearing*

24 *Problems Affecting Skin Integrity*

25 *Problems Affecting Mobility*

26 *Problems Affecting Immune Response*

Problems Affecting Respiration

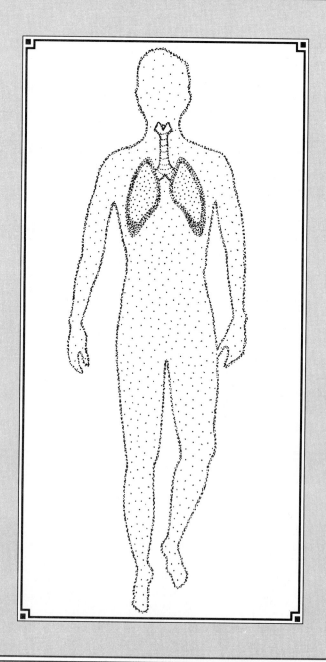

OBJECTIVES

1. Describe the normal passage of oxygen and carbon dioxide through the respiratory system.

2. Identify signs and symptoms that indicate a patient is experiencing hypoxia, carbon dioxide retention, or both.

3. Explain to patients the purpose of the respiratory diagnostic test.

4. List at least three nursing observations that relate to the care of a patient with closed chest drainage.

5. Identify at least four nursing interventions that assist patients in reducing retained secretions in the tracheobronchial tree.

6. Describe nursing responsibilities involved when caring for a patient receiving oxygen therapy.

7. Compare nursing assessment and intervention indicated for a patient with chronic obstructive pulmonary disease (COPD) with the assessment and intervention indicated for a patient with pneumonia.

8. Identify three actions the nurse can teach patients to decrease the spread of respiratory tract infections.

9. Compare the nursing assessment and intervention indicated for a patient with a laryngectomy with the assessment and intervention indicated for a patient with a temporary tracheostomy.

STRUCTURE AND FUNCTION OF THE RESPIRATORY SYSTEM

The respiratory system is a continuous series of passages—beginning with the nasal cavities and terminating with the tiny alveoli in the lungs—that make exchange of gases between the blood and the air possible. The upper respiratory system includes the nasal cavities, pharynx, larynx, and trachea (Figure 15-1). The nose transports, warms, and humidifies air going to and from the lungs. It filters air by bouncing molecules back and forth along its convoluted pathways, where impurities are trapped by nasal hair and moist mucous membranes. Both air and food pass through the pharynx; air then enters the larynx through the opened epiglottis, a "trapdoor" that shuts on swallowing. The larynx contains the vocal cords and is located at the upper end of the trachea. The trachea, a 4- to 5-inch-long and 1-inch-wide tube composed of smooth muscle supported by regularly spaced rings of cartilage, maintains an open passageway for airflow. At its lower end (the carina), the trachea divides, forming the right and left main bronchi. Mucous membrane lines the entire upper respiratory tract, and many of its cells contain fine hairlike projections called *cilia*. Mucus and impurities continually sweep toward the pharynx, where they are expectorated or swallowed.

The right and left bronchi, their subdivisions, and the lungs comprise the lower respiratory system (Figure 15-1). The bronchi, similar in structure to the trachea, are lined with ciliated mucosa, and each enters a lung, where it divides and branches, forming bronchioles. This structure resembles an inverted tree. Further branching produces microscopic alveolar ducts, which end in alveolar sacs called *alveoli*. Inside each lung 300 million alveoli are interlaced in a network of capillaries. Here, oxygen is transferred to the blood and carbon dioxide is removed from the blood to be eliminated from the body. Some of the cells in the alveoli secrete a liquid called *surfactant* that serves to increase lung compliance (ease of inflation) and to keep alveoli evenly inflated and dry.[10]

The left lung is divided into two lobes, whereas the right lung has three lobes. The uppermost part of the lung is called the *apex* and the lower part is the *base*. The lungs are separated by a space called the *mediastinum*.

The lower part of the system and part of the trachea are enclosed in a bony framework known as the *thoracic cage*. The thoracic cage is separated from the abdominal cavity by the diaphragm, which contracts to create a partial vacuum during inspiration and relaxes during expiration, permitting abdominal organs to push upward and help force air from the lungs. The thoracic cavity is lined with a serous membrane, the *parietal pleura*, and each lung is enclosed in a saclike structure of serous membrane, the *visceral pleura*. Pleural cells secrete a clear, sticky fluid that allows the membranes to glide over one another with little friction. This pleural space can become inflamed and fill with air or fluid, causing a disruption in the negative pressure of the pleural cavity. This loss of normal negative pressure causes the lung to contract and eventually collapse.

Respiration is controlled primarily by the respiratory center in the medulla oblongata of the brain. The phrenic, glossopharyngeal, and vagus nerves innervate the diaphragm, larynx, tracheobronchial tree, and lungs and transmit impulses to and from the respiratory center. In addition, chemoreceptor bodies located in the medulla oblongata and in the aortic and carotid arteries influence respiration as a result of their sensitivity to changes in concentrations of carbon dioxide, oxygen, and hydrogen ions in the cerebrospinal fluid and arterial blood.[10]

The function of the respiratory system is the exchange of gases, which is accomplished through the process of respiration. Respiration is both external and internal. External respiration (**ventilation**) consists of the movement of oxygen into the lungs (inhalation) and the removal of carbon dioxide out of the lungs (exhalation). During the inhalation phase, oxygen from inspired air passes through the permeable membranes of the alveoli and capillaries, reaching the blood. Oxygen then combines with hemoglobin in the red blood cells and is transported by the circulatory system to the body cells. Internal respiration is the process by which oxygen is transferred from blood to body cells and carbon dioxide is passed from body cells to blood to be eliminated from the body. Normally, respiration is a regular rhythmic process that is involuntary in most instances. Any condition interfering with this normal function is serious; if all oxygen is cut off, death will ensue in 4 to 6 minutes. The cells of the brain cannot be deprived of oxygen for more than 3 minutes without causing irreversible brain damage. Therefore restoration of respiratory function takes precedence over correction of any other condition.

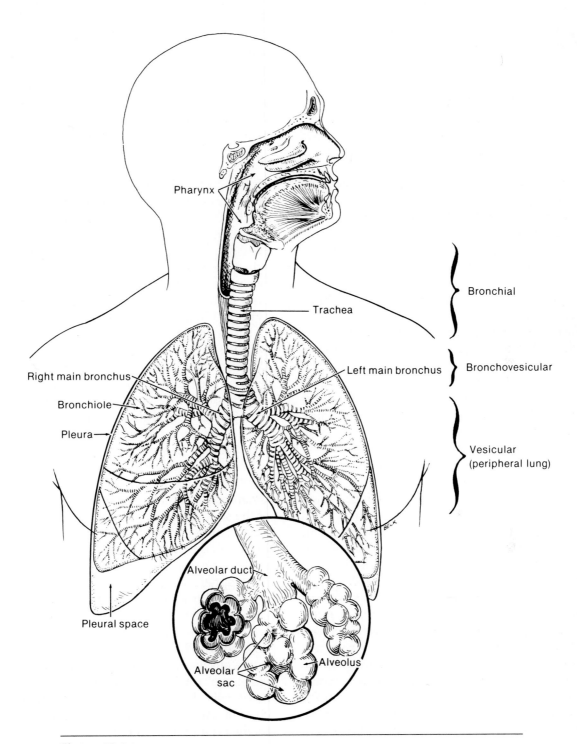

Figure 15-1

Pharynx, trachea, lungs, and location of breath sounds. (*Modified from Anthony CP: Textbook of anatomy and physiology, ed 11, St Louis, 1983, The CV Mosby Co.*)

ALTERED RESPIRATORY STATUS

Because nurses care for patients with a variety of respiratory difficulties, familiarity with the most common deviations from normal respiration and their significance is essential.

Dyspnea

When breathing becomes difficult and labored and requires considerable exertion, patients are said to be dyspneic. **Dyspnea** is a subjective symptom of respiratory difficulty. It may result from pain, pulmonary disease, anemia, heart failure, obstruction, or emotional factors. Characteristics of the condition include pallor, restlessness and anxiety, increased pulse and respiratory rates, or rattling sounds in the respiratory passages. When patients are unable to breathe except in a sitting position, they are said to be **orthopneic**. Dyspnea is one of the most frightening symptoms for patients and their families. Patients often feel their lives are threatened, and as they become more anxious, their dyspnea may increase. The nurse caring for the dyspneic patient should be calm, reassuring, and confident, and should attempt to determine the underlying cause of the problem.

Hypoxia

Hypoxia is an insufficient supply of oxygen available to the body tissues. Its causes are many and varied. Decreased oxygen in the environment, pulmonary diseases, inadequate transport of oxygen by the red blood cells or circulatory system, or tissue edema can result in decreased oxygen supply to cells of the body. Hypoxia is a symptom of an underlying disease or disorder, and treatment is directed toward relieving the cause. The condition may be acute if the supply of oxygen is reduced quickly, as in airway obstruction or blockage by respiratory secretions, or it may be chronic. The signs and symptoms of hypoxia vary with the extent of the lack of oxygen and the underlying cause. Generally, early signs of hypoxia are changes in behavior, decreased judgment, drowsiness, lassitude, and headache. Occasionally, patients will become restless and excited. As the condition progresses, shortness of breath, rapid pulse, blood pressure changes, nausea, delirium, convulsions, and coma can occur. **Cyanosis** is a late sign of hypoxia and usually is not evident until the hypoxia is well advanced. **Hypercapnia** (hypercarbia) is an abnormally high level of carbon dioxide in the body.

Apnea

Apnea is cessation of breathing. An increased respiratory rate may lead to increased oxygen in the blood and decreased carbon dioxide. Periods of apnea are a mechanism to compensate for this condition. Periods of apnea may be associated with Cheyne-Stokes respiration.

Cheyne-Stokes Respiration

In the critically ill patient, Cheyne-Stokes respiration may be a sign of approaching death. Respirations follow an irregular rhythmic pattern, beginning with slow, shallow respirations that increase in depth and rapidity to a maximum point, which is followed by a gradual decrease. A period of apnea lasting from 10 to 60 seconds follows, after which the respiratory pattern is repeated (Figure 15-2).

Asphyxia or Suffocation

When carbon dioxide increases in the tissues and oxygen is deficient, the patient may die from **asphyxia** or suffocation. The condition may result from anything that cuts off the supply of oxygen, such as drowning, interference by foreign bodies, or inhalation of smoke.

Cyanosis

Cyanosis is characterized by a bluish discoloration of the skin and mucous membrane. It results from a deficiency of oxygen in the blood and an increase in carbon dioxide. Cyanosis may occur suddenly, or it may develop gradually. It usually is present in dyspneic conditions and is associated with many cardiovascular disorders. The nurse should always report any evidence of cyanosis.

Hyperventilation

In the absence of disease, normal respiration provides the amount of oxygen necessary for the body cells. In hyperventilation, inhalation is increased. As a result, carbon dioxide decreases in the blood and oxygen enters the alveoli in excess of the physiologic needs of the body. If continued, it may lead to changes in the circulation and upset the otherwise normal ventilatory process.

Hypoventilation

Hypoventilation is the opposite of hyperventilation and occurs when the amount of carbon dioxide retained is above normal limits and the amount of oxygen entering the alveoli is below that necessary to meet the body's needs.

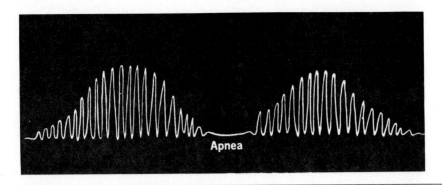

Figure 15-2
Cheyne-Stokes respiration. Note rhythmic pattern that repeats itself after period of apnea.

NURSING ASSESSMENT OF THE PATIENT WITH A RESPIRATORY PROBLEM

Nursing assessment of the patient with a problem affecting respiration begins with a detailed health history. The nurse should question the patient about specific areas, including dyspnea, chest pain, cough, sputum production, hemoptysis, cyanosis, abnormal respiratory patterns or sounds, exercise tolerance, allergies, recent respiratory tract infections or exposure to others with respiratory tract infections, medications, smoking habits, occupational respiratory hazards, and family health history. Following the history, the nurse performs a systematic physical assessment of the patient.

Inspection

The first step in respiratory tract assessment is *inspection*. Both the anterior and posterior chest are observed for lesions, scars, skin color, and any deformities. Deformities that might be evident are pigeon chest, barrel chest, funnel chest, and kyphosis and scoliosis. The patient's posture also should be noted. The rate, depth, type, and quality of respirations are assessed. The nurse should consider the following questions during the examination: Is the breathing regular or irregular? Are the respirations deep or shallow? Do both sides of the chest expand equally? Is the patient experiencing intercostal retractions? Is the breathing pattern abdominal, thoracic, or paradoxic? Cyanosis is identified by careful examination of the nail beds, lips, and mucous membranes of the oral cavity.

Palpation

The second step is *palpation*. The patient should be in a sitting position, although a supine position is acceptable if the patient is unable to sit up. The nurse places warmed hands side by side with the thumbs close together and the fingers spread out over the anterior chest wall. The patient takes several deep breaths, and the respiratory movements of both sides of the chest are compared. The nurse's thumbs should move apart at the same time and be equally distant. The patterns of expansion and contraction are noted, as are equal or unequal expansion, depression of the chest wall during inspiration, degree of expansion, and diaphragmatic excursion. The nurse palpates the chest for any painful areas, swelling, masses, or crepitation. The trachea is palpated for position; it should be vertical and stretch downward on inspiration. The nurse repeats the procedure on the posterior chest wall.

Vibrations produced by the normal spoken voice, vocal fremitus, also may be palpated. The nurse places the hand palm down on the chest wall and has the patient repeat the phrase "ninety-nine" or "blue moon," then compares the transmission of the vibrations on both sides of the chest. An increase in fremitus will occur with secretions or consolidation in the lung, as in pneumonia or atelectasis. Bronchial obstruction or the presence of air or fluid in the pleural space will cause a decrease in or absence of fremitus.

Percussion

The third step in the respiratory assessment is *percussion*. Tapping the surface of the chest wall with the fingers produces sounds that may indi-

...nsity in the lungs. *Resonance* is ...it is hollow, low pitched, non-... where the chest is thinnest. ...normally over the scapulae and ...houlder muscles and over solid organs such as the heart and liver. An area of consolidation, which can occur in pneumonia, will produce a dull sound. A *tympanic* sound may be heard over an area where air is trapped, as in the hyperinflated lung of an emphysemic patient. The tympanic sound will be louder, longer, higher pitched, and drumlike.

Auscultation

The final step in the assessment procedure is *auscultation*. The patient is instructed to maintain a sitting position and to breathe through the mouth. The surroundings should be calm and quiet with a comfortable room temperature. The diaphragm of the stethoscope is placed firmly against the chest wall to decrease the sounds produced by skin or hair rubbing against it. A systematic approach is used, starting at the right scapular area and comparing the sounds heard there with the sounds heard in the left scapular area. The nurse continues down both sides of the posterior chest to the base of the lungs. The procedure is repeated on the anterior chest, also comparing both sides. The nurse should listen through several respiratory cycles over each area.[14]

Breath sounds reveal important data about the patient's condition. The nurse must learn to listen and distinguish between the three normal types of breath sounds. *Vesicular breath sounds* are heard over most of the normal lung. They are soft, low-pitched, breezy sounds heard longer during inspiration because they reflect the passage of air into the alveoli. *Bronchial breath sounds* normally are heard over the trachea. If heard elsewhere, they are abnormal and indicate areas of consolidation. Bronchial sounds are loud, high pitched, and hollow with an expiratory phase greater than the inspiratory phase. *Bronchovesicular breath sounds* are heard over the mainstem bronchi anteriorly on either side of the sternum in the first and second intercostal spaces and posteriorly between the scapulae (Figure 15-1). If heard elsewhere, they are abnormal. Bronchovesicular sounds are a mixture of vesicular and bronchial sounds and are softer and slightly lower pitched than bronchial sounds. Their inspiratory and expiratory phases are near equal. The breath sounds should be evaluated for quality, pitch, intensity, location, and duration.

Abnormal breath sounds called *adventitious sounds* may be superimposed over normal breath sounds. They are the result of inflammation of the pleurae, air passing through narrowed airways, or moisture. Adventitious sounds are crackles, rhonchi, wheezes, and pleural friction rubs. Crackles (rales) are caused by the passage of air through moisture or secretions in the alveoli and small airways and are described as fine, medium, or coarse.[3] They resemble the crackling sound of a cellophane wrapper being gently crinkled. They also can be simulated by rubbing pieces of hair together between the fingers close to the ear. They usually are heard only on inspiration. *Rhonchi and wheezes* are caused by air passing through the larger airways that have been narrowed by accumulation of fluids and secretions, by mucosal edema, or by smooth muscle spasms. Rhonchi usually are heard more on expiration and are described as musical, bubbling, or snoring sounds. Wheezes may be expiratory or inspiratory or both. *Pleural friction rubs* are caused by the inflamed pleural linings rubbing together. They produce a grating, squeaking sound, such as that produced by two pieces of leather rubbing together. Absence of normal breath sounds in their proper locations should also be considered abnormal. Any abnormal breath sounds heard during assessment should be described precisely according to type, location, intensity, duration, and associated symptoms. These should be recorded accurately and changes reported promptly to the physician.

NURSING RESPONSIBILITIES FOR DIAGNOSTIC PROCEDURES

Blood Examinations

Routine blood examinations usually are ordered for patients with respiratory disease and include a red blood cell count, white blood cell count, and hemoglobin determination. Abnormal increases in the number of white blood cells may indicate mobilization of the body's defenses against a respiratory tract infection, whereas significant decreases in red blood cells and hemoglobin decrease the oxygen-carrying capacity of the blood. Depending on the specific diagnosis of respiratory disease, the physician may order additional blood studies.

Arterial Blood Gas Studies

Studies of the partial pressure or tension of carbon dioxide ($Paco_2$) and oxygen (Pao_2), measurement of the oxygen and carbon dioxide carried in the blood, and determination of blood pH are necessary in the diagnosis and treatment of patients with acute and chronic lung diseases. These studies determine how well the lungs are ventilating, how well the blood is being oxygenated, and the amount of acid in the blood, respectively. Arterial blood gases are the most accurate means of assessing a patient's respiratory function. The partial pressure of oxygen (Pao_2) and oxygen saturation (Sao_2) represent the amount of oxygen present in arterial blood. Sao_2 indicates the percentage of hemoglobin bound with oxygen. Pao_2 indicates the pressure at which the oxygen is bound to the hemoglobin. The nurse should assess both values, because a patient may have a Pao_2 within normal limits but a low Sao_2, indicating that the hemoglobin is not carrying an adequate amount of oxygen to the cells. The partial pressure of carbon dioxide indicates the adequacy of alveolar ventilation. Any change in the Pco_2 up or down by 10 mm Hg causes a shift in blood pH by 0.08 units in the opposite direction, leading to an acid-base imbalance. An increase in Pco_2 indicates hypoventilation and will affect the blood pH, with respiratory acidosis resulting. A decrease in Pco_2 indicates hyperventilation, resulting in respiratory alkalosis. (See Table 15-1 for a description of normal arterial blood gas values.)

Sputum Examination

The examination of sputum is done by persons trained in laboratory methods, but the collection of the specimen is usually a nursing responsibility. Sputum consists of material coughed up from the lungs and may contain pathogenic and nonpathogenic organisms. If sputum is to be used for diagnosis, it must be collected in the correct manner. Specimens should be collected early in the morning when sputum production usually is greatest. Before collection, patients should rinse their mouths with clear water, after which they should be encouraged to cough deeply and expectorate into a sterile container.

If an adequate specimen is not obtained, sputum may be obtained by cough induction using

Table 15-1

Normal Blood Gas Values of Arterial Blood*	
Pco_2—partial pressure of carbon dioxide	34-45 mm Hg
Po_2—partial pressure of oxygen	80-100 mm Hg
O_2 saturation—percentage of hemoglobin carrying oxygen	97%-100%
pH—acidity or alkalinity of blood sample	7.35-7.45
Base excess—alkaline substances in blood sample	$-2 = +2$

*Arterial blood is obtained through puncture of an artery, such as the femoral or radial, with a small needle or from a catheter previously placed into the artery. After the sample is drawn, it must be placed on ice and sent immediately to the laboratory for analysis.

aerosolized mist inhalations or nasotracheal suctioning. The physician also may obtain a transtracheal aspirate with a needle puncture through the cricothyroid membrane. If the patient is intubated, tracheal aspiration is accomplished by attaching a mucus trap to the suction source during routine suctioning of sputum. The specimen should be properly labeled and sent immediately to the laboratory. Sputum collected more than 24 hours before laboratory examination may have no diagnostic value.

The general appearance of sputum depends on the kind of substances and pathogenic organisms it contains. It is usually described as purulent, mucopurulent, bloody, serous, or frothy. Normally sputum is odorless, but in suppurative conditions of the lungs, such as lung abscess, it may have a foul odor. Sputum examination using the Papanicolaou smear technique may be useful in detecting the presence of cancer cells. The amount, odor and appearance of all sputum should be recorded on the patient's record.

Pulmonary Function Tests

Pulmonary function tests evaluate lung function and may indicate the existence of some impairment or the necessity for additional investigation. They also are helpful for monitoring the patient's respiratory status and evaluating the effectiveness of therapy. These tests measure the volume of air the patient inhales and exhales. Lung volumes and capacities are obtained from these measurements.

The most common pulmonary function test is performed by spirometry. Several measurements of lung volumes and capacities are obtained, including total lung capacity, vital capacity, inspiratory capacity, residual capacity, tidal volume, expiratory reserve colume, forced expiratory volumes in 1 and 3 seconds, and maximum voluntary ventilation. These measurements reveal whether the patient has an obstructive or restrictive disease process and can monitor improvement or deterioration in lung function when measured over time.

Normal lung volumes and capacities are obtained in the pulmonary laboratory using a **spirometer**, which consists of an air-filled drum inverted over water. As the patient breathes in and out through a connecting mouthpiece and tube, the drum rises and falls and a graphic record (spirogram) is produced. Small portable mechanical instruments often are used at the bedside in clinical practice. A record of total lung capacity is obtained by asking the patient to take a breath and expand the lungs to the greatest extent possible. The patient then exhales forcefully, expelling all the air possible and producing a measure of vital capacity. The largest volume of air inspired after a normal inspiration is a measure of inspiratory capacity, whereas residual capacity is tested by the amount of air retained in the lungs after a maximum expiration. In chronic obstructive pulmonary disease the volume of gas expired usually is decreased. Other tests include gas dilution, plethysmography, and diffusing capacity. The nurse should relieve any apprehension patients may have by explaining the purpose of these procedures and that they will be asked to breathe deeply several times into a small tube. Patient cooperation is important for accurate results.[5]

Radiographic Examination

X-ray examination of the chest is one of the most common of all radiographic procedures. It is ordered by the physician to detect disease of the chest or to monitor change over time. Many hospitals require routine chest x-ray films of all patients admitted. When chest x-ray films have been ordered, the nurse should see that the patient wears a hospital gown tied in the back. Pins must not be used, and bras with metal hooks and any other article of clothing containing metal must be removed, because the presence of metal will produce a shadow over the film. When chest x-ray films are taken in the outpatient clinic, the patient is instructed to strip to the waist and put on a gown tied in the back. Patients are transported to the x-ray department by stretcher or wheelchair and should be accompanied by an attendant. If the patient is too ill to be taken to the x-ray department, a portable x-ray machine may be taken to the patient's bedside; the preparation of the patient, however, is the same.

Fluoroscopic x-ray examination is a screening procedure to detect any pathologic condition of the chest during breathing or swallowing. It also is performed to follow the course of barium while it is moving through the esophagus into the stomach. Patients should be told they will be in darkness for a short period of time but that there will be no discomfort involved. The preparation of the patient for fluoroscopic examination is the same as that for x-ray examinations of the chest.

Computed tomography (CT) is a method in which the lungs are scanned in successive cross-sections by a narrow x-ray beam. The results are subsequently analyzed by computer to identify small nodules, tumors, or other abnormalities that may not be visible on conventional x-ray films.

Pulmonary angiography, a test in which radiopaque dye is injected into the pulmonary circulation, followed by a series of x-ray films, and ventilation/perfusion lung scans are radiologic tests performed to detect pulmonary emboli.

Bronchoscopy

In the past, visualization of the trachea and bronchi was limited by the large, rigid, metal bronchoscope used. With the advent of smaller, flexible, fiberoptic bronchoscopes, a more accurate picture of the airway is able to be transmitted. The fiberoptic bronchoscope also allows easier passage through the nasal or oral route. The bronchoscope is passed through the mouth into the trachea and major bronchi after a topical anesthetic has been administered. The room is darkened, and visualization of the bronchial tree is possible when light is reflected through the instrument. The examination is used to permit the physician to remove foreign bodies that have lodged in the bronchi, to suction secretions for laboratory examination, to observe the respiratory passageways for disease, and to obtain biopsy specimens.

The emotional preparation for bronchoscopy is important. The procedure results in a certain amount of discomfort, and the apprehensive, fearful patient may cooperate poorly. Explaining to patients what to expect and teaching them how to breathe during the procedure and how to relax will provide a greater feeling of security and help relieve their anxiety.

Before a bronchoscopy, no food or fluid by mouth is allowed after midnight. Postural drainage may be ordered in the morning to remove any secretions that may have drained into the trachea or bronchi during the night. Special mouth care should be given after postural drainage, and dentures and bridges should be removed. A sedative usually is ordered for the patient. If the procedure is done in the operating room, usual preoperative nursing measures will be required.

When patients return to their room, they should be positioned according to the physician's instructions. No food or fluids should be given until normal reflexes have returned. Patients should be watched carefully for respiratory difficulty, because edema of the larynx may occur. If a biopsy has been done, sputum may be tinged with blood for several days; the nurse should be alert for any unusual bleeding, however, and the physician should be notified immediately if this occurs. If throat soreness and discomfort are prolonged, a mild analgesic such as aspirin may be ordered. Persistent throat soreness and hoarse voice should be evaluated, because injury to the trachea or larynx during the procedure can occur.

Thoracentesis

Fluid from the pleural cavity may be removed for diagnosis or for treatment. Fluid in the pleural cavity often is detected on x-ray examination; in some cases, however, dyspnea may be present because of compression of the lung on the affected side. If the lung is compressed, diminished expansion of the chest on the affected side will be observed. Fluid in the pleural cavity may follow pneumonia, **pleurisy,** and tuberculosis. It also may occur in patients with cancer, heart disease, and kidney disease. When accumulation of fluid results from kidney disease or heart disease, both sides usually are affected, whereas only one side is involved in other disorders. When it occurs as a result of pneumonia, pus formation may occur (*empyema*).

When thoracentesis is to be done, the patient should be informed about the procedure. The nurse should remember that what seems like a simple procedure may be frightening to the patient and that every means should be used to relieve the patient's anxiety. The procedure usually is carried out in the patient's room; the patient is in a sitting position with head and arms resting on a pillow placed on the overbed table. Using aseptic technique, the skin is cleansed generally in the area of the eighth or ninth rib interspace, after which a local anesthetic is injected into the tissues. The patient must be cautioned not to move while the needle is being inserted to avoid damage to the lung or pleura. The primary function of the nurse is to observe the patient and assist during the procedure. The pulse and respiration should be checked several times, and the patient should be observed for diaphoresis or any change in skin color. Fluid withdrawn from the chest is observed for color, consistency, and amount. A description of each is recorded in the medical record. The specimen is sent to the laboratory for analysis.

NURSING RESPONSIBILITIES FOR THERAPEUTIC TECHNIQUES

Any condition resulting in respiratory difficulty produces anxiety and apprehension for the patient and must be viewed as potentially serious. Respiratory embarrassment often results from oxgyen deficiency, which may have several causes. The nurse should be familiar with the underlying condition responsible for the oxygen deficit. To meet the patient's oxygen needs, the nurse must be able to recognize the signs of oxygen deficiency. Symptoms will depend on the degree of deficiency; however, not all patients exhibit the same effects. Symptoms include restlessness, excitement, confusion, increases in respiratory and pulse rates, headache, sighing and yawning, nausea and vomiting, and anorexia. Blood pressure may be normal or elevated, but as air hunger increases, the blood pressure falls, cyanosis appears, and twitching of muscles may occur.

Psychologic Care

Inability to secure sufficient air is a frightening experience, particularly for children, and parents who may be anxious and apprehensive may pass their anxiety on to the child. When a patient's life is threatened, the nurse also may be anxious, but if anxiety in the patient or family is to be relieved, the nurse must remain calm. Although the psychologic care of each patient depends on the patient's own needs and the particular situation, the nurse maintains a calm approach to the problem,

has basic knowledge and ability to plan or organize patient care, and performs technical skills
competently, setting the stage for patient confidence and relief of anxiety. Explanations in simple
terms will help to relieve patient anxiety.

Coughing and Deep Breathing

Coughing, suctioning, postural drainage, and
percussion are used to remove secretions and to
provide adequate ventilation in the lungs by maintaining a clear airway. Increased secretions and
sputum from the respiratory tract may cause mucous plugs to form, obstructing the passages and
preventing free exchange of gases. Depending on
the disease present and the condition of the patient, procedures must be instituted to remove
secretions. For some patients, their own deep productive coughing may be sufficient. For others,
the nurse may be responsible for clearing the airway. Patients with **hemoptysis** (expectoration of
pure blood) should not be encouraged to cough.
When possible, the patient should be placed in a
sitting position; if coughing is painful, the nurse
should assist the patient by splinting the chest.
Sputum should be collected in tissues and placed
in paper bags at the bedside or kept in a sterile
container to assess 24-hour sputum production.
The patient should be taught to take a deep
breath, hold it a second, and cough on expiration.
Tissues should be folded and placed in the cupped
hand. Nurses who handle sputum should wash
their hands thoroughly after each encounter or
follow universal precautions (Chapter 8). Persistent shallow coughing is of no value and only tires
the patient.

Many cough medicines are available on the
market. Some may be purchased over the counter
in drugstores, whereas others require a physician's prescription. Cough medicines may be narcotic or nonnarcotic antitussives and are classified
as demulcents, expectorants, or sedatives. The
kind of cough remedy prescribed depends on the
condition for which it is needed and the result
desired. Demulcents are protective and may be
expected to relieve irritation of the throat by providing a soothing effect and protecting the mucous membrane from air. Demulcents often are
found in gargles, lozenges, and syrups that contain various flavoring agents such as wild cherry.
Some lozenges contain an analgesic that adds little, if anything, to its effectiveness. Expectorants
act to increase or modify mucous secretions in the
respiratory tract, making mucus less thick and
more easily expectorated. The expectorant drug

used is glyceryol guaiacolate (Robitussin TG), and
iodide preparations. Sedative agents reduce
coughing by depressing the cough reflex. They
may contain a narcotic or barbiturate, which also
depresses the respiratory center. Their use usually
is limited to disorders involving extremely painful
coughing. If an allergic factor is involved, an antihistaminic agent may be ordered. Often in an
acute infection, nasal congestion contributes to
the patient's discomfort. Phenylephrine (Neo-
Synephrine), ephedrine sulfate, or any of the numerous sprays and drops available may be ordered by the physician.[6]

Suctioning

When the patient is unable to cough, secretions
may be removed by suctioning. When the patient
is in respiratory distress because the airway is obstructed, the nurse may observe the following
signs: gurgling, increased pulse and respiratory
rates, a harsh respiratory sound, restlessness,
anxiety, pallor with cyanosis about the mouth, or
generalized cyanosis. If the distress is caused by
mucus obstructing the airway, the patient should
be suctioned immediately, carefully, and thoroughly to relieve the symptoms and restore a patent airway.

The procedure used to suction a patient involves attaching a whistle-tip catheter to tubing
connected to a continuous suction device. The
whistle-tip catheter provides the nurse fingertip
control over suctioning. During suctioning, sterile
gloves are worn and sterile catheters used to prevent contamination of the respiratory tract. When
aspirating secretions, the nurse should maintain
strict aseptic technique to prevent serious complications. Separate catheters must be used for
nasal secretions and for tracheobronchial secretions. The nurse should use caution to avoid injuring the mucous membranes. If the patient is
conscious, the procedure should be explained
fully before beginning. When the patient has an
oral airway tube or a tracheal tube, the suction
catheter is inserted through the tube.

The patient should be hyperventilated and hy-
peroxygenated before and after suctioning, because both air and secretions are removed during
suctioning. Several methods may be used to oxygenate patients: (1) if they are able, instruct patients to deep breathe for 1 minute; (2) have patients used a face mask and rebreathing bags with
oxygen attached; (3) if patients are on mechanical
ventilation, increase the oxygen to 100% for 1 minute and manually depress the sigh cycle button

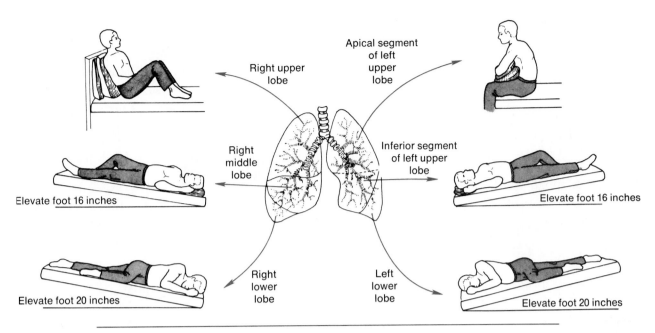

Figure 15-3
Postural drainage positions for draining various portions of lung.

two or three times; or (4) manually ventilate patients with an Ambu bag adapted to deliver 100% oxygen. Suction should not be applied until after the catheter has been inserted and is being withdrawn. The whistle-tip catheter is rotated while it is being withdrawn, and suction should be intermittent by removing and replacing the finger to the tube valve during a withdrawal of the catheter. If possible, patients should be placed in Fowler's position before beginning the procedure. Each suction should not exceed 10 seconds, and an interval of 3 minutes should elapse before repeating the procedure. During this time, oxygen is administered and the patient is reconnected to the mechanical ventilator. When suctioning through an airway or endotracheal or tracheostomy tube, the catheter should be inserted until resistance is felt (the carina).

During suctioning the tip may come in contact with the carina, causing stimulation of the patient's cough reflex. Although this assists the patient in expectorating secretions, the coughing could be violent enough to expel the tracheostomy or endotracheal tube and it is very uncomfortable for the patient. The nurse should ensure that the tube is secured before suctioning. The patient should be informed that suctioning may cause coughing, and the suction catheter tip should be withdrawn from the carina to reduce further

cough stimulation. Careful washing of the hands should precede and follow suctioning patients.[4-6]

Postural Drainage

Postural drainage is used to drain excessive secretions (including pus from lung abscess) from the lungs. Drainage is facilitated by placing the patient in a position that allows gravity to aid in the procedure. The position of the patient should be determined by the area of the lung to be drained. The upper lobes of the lung can best be drained in the sitting position, the lower lobes in a lying position (Figure 15-3). Positions vary, however, according to the patient's condition, strength, and respiratory function. Gravity drainage of the lungs can be accomplished in several ways. In most cases younger patients tolerate lowering of the head better than elderly or debilitated patients. If possible, the mouth should be approximately 20 inches lower than the base of the lungs. Special beds and tables are available; however, the patient's own bed may be used. During the procedure patients should be encouraged to cough deeply, and after returning to bed they may be expected to cough and expectorate large amounts of sputum. One highly satisfactory method uses the Gatch bed, in which the knee section is elevated as high as possible and the patient lies over the bend. A board is placed across

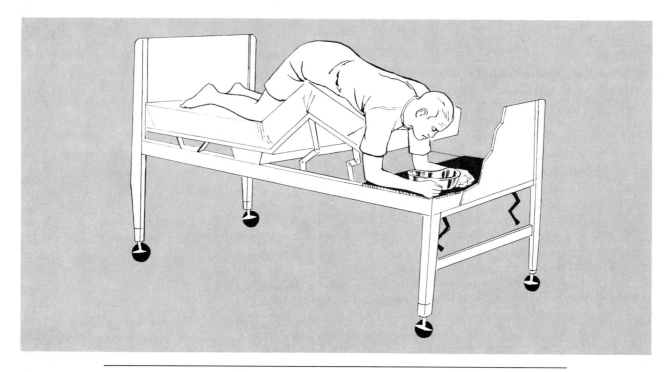

Figure 15-4
Postural drainage using Gatch bed.

the bed frame and protected with towels, thus providing a place for a receptacle for sputum and a place to rest the hands (Figure 15-4). The procedure is more effective when patients have been taught and practice breathing with their diaphragms.

Elderly patients with hypertrophic arthritis may be unable to bend the body over the bed for postural drainage, but fairly satisfactory results may be obtained by elevating the foot of the bed. Postural drainage often is fatiguing for debilitated patients. They may be able to remain in the position for only a few minutes. However, with each effort they experience less discomfort. The procedure should be supervised by the nurse and is best carried out midway between meals to prevent nausea and vomiting. The patient's teeth should be brushed after the procedure, and an antiseptic mouthwash may be used if desired. The patient should be protected from chilling during the procedure and should be allowed to rest after returning to bed.

If the physician orders the drainage measured, it should be collected in a receptacle suitable for measuring. The color, amount, and consistency should be recorded on the patient's chart.

Percussion

Percussion is a techique of rhythmically clapping and vibrating the chest wall over the involved area to help loosen mucus plugs and move them into the bronchi, where they may be drained out or expectorated. It is performed with a cupped hand, often in conjunction with postural drainage and is not painful. Clapping and vibrating are not employed when a danger of hemorrhage is present or if the patient complains of pain. The procedure should be performed by a nurse or therapist trained in the technique.

Throat Irrigations, Humidifications, and Aerosol Therapy

Persons suffering from nasopharyngeal and bronchial infections often secure relief with warm throat irrigations. A physiologic saline solution at a temperature of 120° F (49° C) usually is employed, and irrigations may be used several times a day. The application of heat to the irritated membranes promotes drainage of secretions, stimulates circulation, and relieves pain, swelling, and muscle spasm. The nurse may assist the patient with the procedure, or the patient may be taught to carry out the procedure under supervision.

Normally, as the patient inspires room air it is heated and humidified in the upper airway. When the upper airway is bypassed or when added water vapor is desired to improve patient comfort to maximize secretion mobility, or to deliver inhaled medications, humidifiers or nebulizers are used. Humidifiers add water vapor to inhaled air. They are used primarily to moisten dry mucous membranes when the patient receives oxygen therapy. Cool humidifiers provide additional water vapor in the inspired air and usually are adequate if the patient is breathing through the upper airway. If the upper airway is bypassed with a tracheostomy, the water vapor must be heated to provide sufficient humidification to prevent drying of mucous membranes and retention of thick secretions.

Nebulizers add water or medication particles to inhaled air by breaking it up into small particles, producing a mist therapy. The smaller the particle size, the deeper into the lung it can be inhaled. Nebulizers are effective in administering highly humidified air or oxygen to patients with respiratory problems. The administration of bronchodilators and mucolytic agents by nebulization is a common part of the therapeutic regimen. The medication is inhaled as a fine mist of droplets suspended in air. A hand-held nebulizer can be used, or the medication can be administered with oxygen under pressure. When oxygen is forced through the nebulizer containing the medication, it carries fine particles of the medication deep into the respiratory tract. Breathing slowly and deeply, the patient holds his breath for 3 or 4 seconds after an inspiration, and exhales through pursed lips. The procedure is repeated until all the medication has been inhaled as ordered. The teeth should be brushed and the mouth rinsed after the procedure to prevent soreness. Nearly all forms of respiratory therapy given will include some form of humidity or aerosol.[15]

Endotracheal Intubation

In endotracheal intubation, a tube is passed through the nose or mouth into the patient's trachea. Like a tracheostomy tube (Figure 15-5), it has an inflatable cuff that must be inflated and managed in the same manner. The endotracheal tube often is placed during an emergency to facilitate the patient's breathing and the patient then receives mechanical ventilation. If continued ventilatory support is required for more than 3 to 4 weeks, a **tracheotomy** usually is performed.

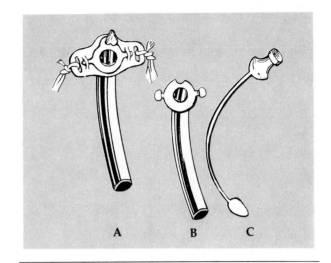

Figure 15-5
Tracheostomy tube. **A**, Outer cannula. **B**, Inner cannula. **C**, Obturator.

Mechanical Ventilation

Pulmonary **ventilation** is the process of taking oxygen into the lungs and releasing carbon dioxide in the exhaled gas. Under certain conditions the patient is unable to maintain optimum levels of arterial oxygen, carbon dioxide, or both. When this occurs, the patient's survival depends on mechanical ventilation.

Several conditions exist for which the patient may need ventilatory assistance. Among these disorders are drug overdose, chronic obstructive pulmonary disease (COPD), respiratory failure, certain neuromuscular disorders, cardiac arrest, and pulmonary edema caused by ventricular failure.

When mechanical ventilation is used, the patient usually must be intubated with an artificial airway and connected to an artificial respirator. The natural airway is bypassed, requiring some form of humidity to prevent drying of mucous membranes and thickening of respiratory secretions. Patients receiving mechanical ventilation therapy require close and careful monitoring. The nurse must be familiar with the respirator and its connecting tubing. Ventilator settings are ordered by the physician and should include tidal volume, respiratory rate, frequency of sighs, and percentage of oxygen. Most ventilators have several modes or types of ventilatory support to choose from. Each requires a different contribution or effort by the patient to support breathing. These modes include control, assist/control, intermittent mandatory ventilation (IMV), and continuous positive airway pressure (CPAP). The mode should be ordered according to the severity and type of breathing problem. Positive end expiratory pressure (PEEP) often is used with patients receiving mechanical ventilation to improve the oxygen transfer across the lung. The nurse should continuously monitor patients' exhaled tidal volume, respiratory rate, inspired oxygen level, and peak pressure (pressure required to deliver the tidal volume into the patients lungs) while they are receiving mechanical ventilation. The heart and rhythm, blood pressure level, and skin color should be observed carefully. Blood gas studies are obtained frequently to evaluate and optimize ventilatory support. Often an arterial catheter is placed to avoid frequent arterial punctures.

The nursing care of patients receiving ventilation therapy includes monitoring, positioning to provide optimum ventilation, turning the patient every hour, and carrying out passive range-of-motion exercises. All fluid intake and output should be recorded. Suctioning of secretions and airway maintenance must be assessed at least every 2 hours. Adequate nutrition and fluid balance should be maintained. If bronchodilating drugs are administered, the patient should be observed for side effects. The nurse should provide emotional support and explain procedures and equipment if the patient is conscious. These patients often are anxious and require sedation. Before administering sedatives or narcotics, the blood pressure, pulse, and ventilator parameters should be checked.[3]

Oxygen Therapy

The administration of oxygen is supportive treatment for patients in whom **oxygenation** is deficient. The many devices available for oxygen therapy are divided into two groups, low-flow and high-flow systems. Low-flow systems contribute partially to the inspired gas the patient breathes (i.e., part of each breath contains room air). Low-flow systems do not provide a constant or known concentration of inspired oxygen. As the patient's breathing patterns change, the amount of oxygen inspired also changes. Examples of low-flow systems include the nasal cannula, face mask, and nonrebreathing mask with reservoir bag. High-flow systems provide the total amount of inspired gas. A specific percentage of oxygen is delivered independent of the patient's breathing pattern. Examples of high-flow systems include Venturi masks and aerosol masks connected to a nebulizer.

The decision to administer oxygen, the amount to deliver, and the method to be used depend on the purpose for which it is administered.[3] The effectiveness of oxygen in the treatment of the patient depends on the pathologic process present. The physician will indicate the method by which oxygen is to be given and the number of liters per minute. The nurse responsible for carrying out the order should act promptly and should remember that, although oxygen may be beneficial, it also may be dangerous. Therefore, when the patient is receiving oxygen, careful patient observation should occur.

Many patients and their families believe that oxygen is administered as a last resort. Although most patients receiving oxygen are seriously ill, the nurse should make every effort to reassure the patient and relieve the anxiety of the family. If patients are conscious or semiconscious, the nurse should explain all procedures, assuring them they will breathe better and be more comfortable. If patients are sick enough to receive oxygen, the method of administration should be such that they receive its maximum benefit. To achieve this, the nurse should be familiar with the equipment and ensure that it is in working order.

Oxygen by nasal cannula

The oxygen cannula is made of plastic and consists of two prongs, which are placed in the nostrils, and either a strap about the head or a plastic bow similar to the bow on glasses, which fits over the ears. The flow meter should be set at the number of liters ordered by the physician; the oxygen should be allowed to flow through the cannula before its insertion, because the patient may receive a blast of oxygen meant to flush the system. Oxygen concentrations from 24% to 40% may be delivered. At a flow rate of 6 L per minute the nasal cannula will deliver a concentration of 40% oxygen. This is the maximum rate a cannula should deliver. The nasal cannula works on the same principle as the Venturi mask, except that the work of mixing oxygen and air is done in the nasopharynx and oropharynx. Therefore whether a patient breathes through the nose or mouth does not matter because oxygen and atmospheric air are mixed before they enter the trachea and lungs. Proper placement of the prongs is important to avoid a direct stream of oxygen against the nasal mucosa. Even with correct positioning of the prongs, a greater degree of nasal drying occurs with this method. The nasal cannula is useful when an extremely low concentration of oxygen is needed.

Oxygen by mask

A simple oxygen mask will provide concentrations of oxygen from 40% to 60%, depending on the patient's ventilatory pattern. As the patient inspires, room air is drawn in through the holes in the mask and around the edges, mixing with the oxygen. Normally, flow rates of 5 to 8 L per minute are ordered. These masks are comfortable and are used when higher concentrations of oxygen are desired than can be delivered by nasal cannula.

Venturi masks, aerosol masks, and nonrebreathing masks are other types of masks that may be ordered for the patient. Venturi masks are high-flow systems that can deliver oxygen concentrations from 24% to 40%. Aerosol masks are used with nebulizers and can be adjusted to deliver oxygen concentrations from 22% to 100%. Nonrebreathing masks can be high- or low-flow systems, depending on the oxygen flow rates and how well the mask fits. With nonrebreathing masks the exhaled air escapes and a valve prevents it from being rebreathed. A reservoir bag from which the patient can obtain more oxygen during inspiration also is attached. Oxygen concentrations from 60% to 100% may be delivered.

All patients do not tolerate oxygen by mask equally well. The head strap should be adjusted to the position most comfortable for the patient. The patient who is apprehensive or who has acute dyspnea may have a feeling of suffocation. Depending on the patient's condition, the mask should be removed and the face bathed and dried every 2 hours. The mask must be removed and replaced with a nasal cannula during meals. The minimum flow for any type of mask should be 5 L per minute. Because moisture tends to collect in the mask, it should be regularly wiped dry.

Oxygen precautions

Regardless of what method of oxygen administration is used, certain precautions must be adhered to when a patient is receiving oxygen. "No smoking" signs should be conspicuously displayed, and the patient and his visitors must understand that smoking is not permitted because oxygen supports combustion. Electric appliances such as heating pads, razors, blankets, or call sig-nals should not be used. When oxygen tanks are being used, they should be secured in such a way that they will not be tipped over. They should not be placed near lamps, radiators, or other heating devices.

Hyperbaric oxygen

The use of hyperbaric oxygen in the treatment of disease is still in the experimental stage. Not all authorities agree on its value; however, most agree that it may serve as an adjunct to other therapy. Approximately 50 different conditions reportedly are being treated with hyperbaric oxygen, including cancer, in which it has been used as an adjunct to radiation therapy.[1] Researchers also have determined that there is a danger of severe side effects from hyperbaric oxygen. Hyperbaric oxygenation is achieved by exposing the patient to pressure greater than normal atmospheric pressure. As a result, the amount of oxygen dissolved in the plasma is increased, causing an increase in oxygen levels in the tissues of the body. Therapy is carried out in either small or large steel chambers that the patient may enter alone or with staff members, and all personnel involved are subjected to rigid physical examination and training.

Thoracotomy

A **thoracotomy** is a surgical opening into the thoracic cavity to remove blood, pus, or air or to expedite reexpansion of a lung after accidental injury or surgery. A thoracotomy may be done to explore the thoracic cavity for evidence of disease, including cancer. If indicated, a biopsy may be done.

Patients having any type of open chest surgery are given endotracheal anesthesia. Anesthesia given in this way makes it possible to keep the unoperated on lung expanded and functioning during surgery. Normally, the pleural space contains a negative or subatmospheric, pressure. The pressure within the lungs is normally that of atmospheric pressure. Inspiration causes the negative pressure in the pleural space to become even greater and creates a type of vacuum that "pulls" air into the lungs, expanding them. However, when the pleura is entered through surgery or trauma to the chest wall, atmospheric pressure enters the pleural space and the lung collapses. The negative pressure that kept the lungs expanded no longer exists. Therefore after chest surgery, the patient will usually have one or more drainage tubes placed in the pleural cavity. The tubes permit the escape of air so that the lung will expand and allow for drainage of fluid from the pleural space. Often one tube will be placed in the upper chest to remove air, and another tube will be placed in a lower position to remove fluids. The chest catheters are then attached to a closed drainage system.

Two basic types of closed chest drainage are used: gravity (water seal) and suction drainage. Gravity drainage is accomplished by attaching the tubing leading from the chest to a long glass-connecting tube that is inserted into a sterile drainage bottle containing sterile water. The glass-connecting tube is inserted below the water level, providing a seal to prevent air from backing up into the pleural cavity. If the system is working correctly, the water in the long glass-connecting tube will rise during inspiration and drop during expiration as air and fluid pass out into the water (Figure 15-6). The water level should be marked so that an accurate measurement of drainage may be made. The bottle is placed on the floor or below the level of the bed, and under no circumstances should it be lifted up because this will allow fluid to drain back into the chest cavity. If the bottle is placed on the floor, it should be secured with adhesive tape or placed in a metal holder to prevent knocking it over. The entire system must be kept upright. Occasionally, two bottles may be used for gravity drainage, one accepting the drainage and the other supplying the water seal. This setup has two advantages. First, it allows the nurse to make a more accurate observation of the volume and type of drainage. Second, it prevents an increase in the fluid level of the water-sealed bottle, which would create resistance to the flow of air and fluid from the pleural space. The drainage bottle is placed between the patient and the water-sealed bottle.

The application of suction may be necessary to reexpand the lung. Suction can be applied through the use of a suction outlet. A three-bottle system is illustrated in Figure 15-7. The suction reaching the patient's chest is controlled by the depth to which the tube is submerged in the suction control bottle. The physician will order the amount of sterile water and the positioning of the tube in the suction control bottle. The submerged tube in the suction control bottle should bubble continuously but gently as air is drawn in to reduce suction from the source. If this does not occur, the nurse should check for an air leak into

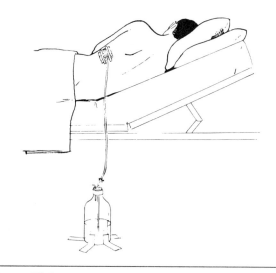

Figure 15-6
Thoracotomy tube is connected to sterile closed drainage. Note bottle is fastened to floor.

the pleural space or into the drainage setup or for mechanical problems with the suction machine. If the bubbling is too vigorous, the suction machine should be inspected because it may be turned up higher than necessary.

In most hospitals, disposable drainage systems based on the principles of the three-bottle suction are used. These systems also consist of a suction control chamber, a water-sealed chamber, and drainage chamber (Figure 15-7). Evacuation of air and fluid are possible, and certain newer versions allow for reinfusion of the patient's own blood loss if the amounts are significant. The physician orders the amount of pressure to be exerted through the chest tube. The nurse monitors the water levels within the drainage system to ensure that evaporation has not resulted in less pressure being delivered than ordered. The nurse also monitors the water-sealed chamber for evidence of an air leak, which is observed as bubbling in the water. The extent of bubbling can range from intermittent to continuous with respirations. Careful documentation of the frequency and extent of an air leak should be noted in the medical record, and the nurse should compare findings to previous descriptions.

A patient may experience an air leak from the lungs from various causes. As the patient inhales, air is taken into the lungs, and small amounts of air may be released from a leak that escapes into the pleural cavity. If no escape route exists for the air, the patient may develop a tension pneumo-

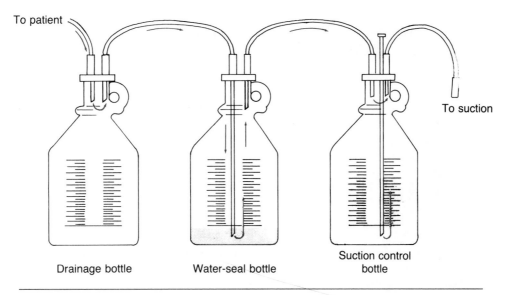

To patient

To suction

Drainage bottle   Water-seal bottle   Suction control
bottle

Figure 15-7
Three-bottle water-seal chest drainage.

thorax that could be life-threatening. For this reason, the practice of clamping chest tubes is discouraged. If a water-sealed bottle breaks and the patient is known to have an air leak, the tubing is left open while a new setup is prepared. An open pneumothorax will occur, but this is less serious than a tension pneumothorax. While the new setup is arranged, a temporary water seal can be made with a bottle of sterile saline or a clean cup of tap water. If an air leak has not occurred, the patient is told to cough or exhale hard to push out any air in the pleural space and the tube is double-clamped close to the chest. The nurse should leave the clamps on for only 1 to 2 minutes while preparing the new setup and should observe for signs of a possible tension pneumothorax.[3]

The only other reasons to clamp the chest tube are to locate the source of leaks in the system and to replace drainage bottles. If continuous bubbling is noted in the water-sealed bottle, the nurse starts clamping close to the chest and works down to the drainage unit. When the tube is clamped between the air leak and the water-sealed bottle, the bubbling will stop. If the cause is a loose connection, it is reconnected; if the drainage unit is cracked, it is replaced. If the air leak is into the patient's pleural space, the physician should be notified immediately. The nurse must remember to assess the reasons why the patient has a chest tube; if a new air leak develops, it must be investigated immediately.

The nurse should be familiar with the purpose for which the drainage is being used and the kind of drainage to expect. If the drainage contains excessive amounts of blood, the physician should be notified. Blood clots may form in the tubing, causing an obstruction. To prevent this from happening, the physician may order the tubing to be milked. This should be done carefully to avoid generation of significant amounts of pressure in the chest. Frequent checking is necessary to ascertain that the system remains airtight, that it is working correctly, and that the tubing does not become kinked when the patient is lying on his or her side. If a small pillow, folded towel, or rubber ring is placed under the chest when the patient is in a side-lying position, it will help to prevent obstruction of the tube.

Several alternate chest drainage units that duplicate or modify the one-, two-, and three-bottle systems currently are used in hospitals. The Pleur-evac is a sterile, plastic, disposable unit that provides water-sealed drainage using the principles incorporated in the three-bottle drainage system (Figure 15-8). It can be hung from the bed or contained in a disposable floor stand. The Argyle Double Seal unit is also based on the three-bottle system but has a fourth chamber as well. This fourth chamber is an additional water seal that is vented to the atmosphere to relieve a possible pressure buildup within the system. It looks similar to the Pleur-evac but reads from left to right.

The Heimlich chest drainage valve does not

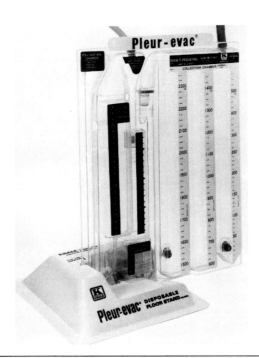

Figure 15-8
Adult-pediatric nonmetered Pleur-evac. *(Courtesy Dekna-tel, Inc, Queens Village, NY.)*

use a water-sealed unit. It is a sterile, disposable flutter valve that is attached between the chest drainage catheter and a drainage collection bag. The flutter valve allows fluid and air to pass through it but prevents any reflux of fluids and air. It has the advantage of allowing the patient more mobility because it works in any position.

Tracheotomy

Tracheotomy is any endotracheal intubation in which an incision is made into the trachea through the skin and tissues of the neck to create an artificial airway. Some confusion has arisen concerning the term **tracheostomy**, which is used by some physicians and nurses. The surgical procedure performed by the physician in creating the airway is a *tracheotomy*, after which a *tracheostomy* tube of the proper size is inserted. Some commercial distributors label tubing as tracheostomy tubes, indicating equipment and not procedure. When a tracheotomy results in a permanent airway, as in a **laryngectomy**, a *tracheal stoma*, or *tracheostoma*, results, and the term used is *tracheostomy*. This interpretation is consistent with the medical definition—to provide with an opening or mouth.

A tracheotomy may be an elective procedure, or it may be performed in an emergency. If at all possible, it should be done in the operating room under strict aseptic technique. Indications for a tracheotomy may include any condition in which respiration is compromised, such as blockage of the upper respiratory tract, respiratory failure, the need for long-term assisted mechanical ventilation, the possibility of aspiration in the comatose patient, or a need for effective removal of excessive secretions. After the surgical procedure, a tracheostomy tube is inserted into the opening and securely tied about the patient's neck with cotton tape. A sterile gauze dressing (unfilled) covers the surgical wound around the tube (Figure 15-9). The tracheostomy tube may consist of two or three pieces: the outer cannula, inner cannula, and obturator (Figure 15-5) or simply a single cannula and an obturator. In double-cannula tubes, the obturator is used to guide the outer cannula through the surgical opening into the trachea, after which it is removed and the inner cannula inserted into the outer cannula and locked in place. Single-cannula tubes usually are used because newer materials and adequate humidification eliminate the need for a removable inner cannula.

Cuffed tracheostomy tubes are most commonly used. These tubes are made of plastic material and have a cuff surrounding the middle portion of the tube that can be inflated with air (Figure 15-10). The cuff prevents air from leaking around the sides of the tube and holds the tube in place. The use of these tubes provides a leak-proof system that is a definite advantage with mechanical ventilation. Although the newer low-pressure, high-volume cuffs minimize irritation to the tracheal mucosa, the intercuff pressure should be measured at least every 8 hours. The pressure should be kept at 18 to 21 mm Hg to allow for adequate capillary blood flow. If increased intracuff pressures are required, the physician should be notified and the tube changed to a larger size.[8]

The nurse should remember that patients with cuffed tracheostomy tubes in place will not be able to speak because air does not pass directly through the larynx. These patients should be assured that they will be able to speak normally again when the cuffed tracheostomy tube is removed.

A primary nursing responsibility is the maintenance of a patent airway. A patient who has a newly formed tracheostomy will need frequent

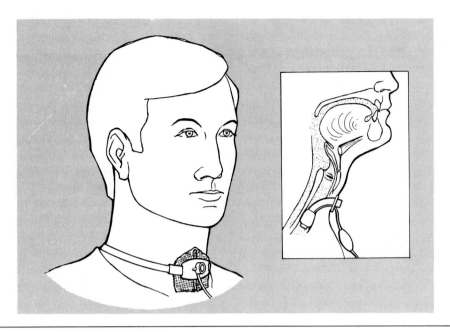

Figure 15-9
Cuffed tracheostomy tube is in place and tied around patient's neck. Wound is protected with sterile dressing.

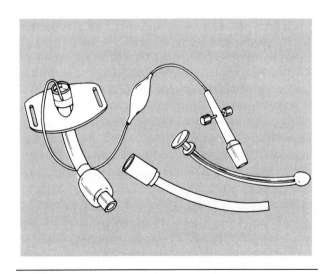

Figure 15-10
Cuffed tracheostomy tube.

suctioning. If a form of mechanical ventilation is not used, a nebulizer may be used to keep secretions moist. A mid-Fowler's position provides comfort and facilitates breathing. Provisions must be made for the patient to communicate because he or she will be unable to speak. Patients are usually apprehensive and fear choking. The nurse must observe the patient for complications, which may include apnea, cyanosis, shortness of breath, bleeding from the wound, and hypotension. Blood pressure measurements should be taken before the surgical procedure and at intervals thereafter. An extra sterile tracheostomy set of the same size, a pair of scissors, and a tracheotomy dilator should be kept at the patient's bedside for emergency use in case the tube becomes displaced. Any patient undergoing a tracheotomy should not be left alone for the first 24 hours after insertion of the tube.

If discharged with a tracheostomy tube, the patient must be taught how to care for the tube. Suction equipment should be available at home. Persons who have a permanent tracheostomy must be instructed not to swim and to use caution when bathing so that water is not aspirated. Any scarfs or collars worn about the tracheostomy opening should be made of porous materials.

Whatever the purpose of a tracheotomy, whether it is temporary or permanent, the nurse should remember that the life of the patient depends on nursing skill in keeping the airway clear because it is the only means by which the patient can breathe.

THE PATIENT WITH DISEASES AND DISORDERS OF THE RESPIRATORY SYSTEM

Diseases of the respiratory system may result from many different causes, including infection, benign or malignant tumors, physical or chemical agents, allergy, senescence, and emotional factors. Specific symptoms vary with the particular disease; however, characteristics of many diseases are coughing with or without sputum, hemoptysis, dyspnea, cyanosis, and pain. Chest pain usually is related to breathing difficulties because the pleura, lungs, and bronchi do not have nerves that transmit pain impulses. Respiratory diseases can be classified in many ways, but generally they fall into two groups: those that are not infectious and those that are infectious and that are caused by specific disease organisms.

Noninfectious Respiratory Conditions
Epistaxis

Nosebleed rarely is fatal or even serious, but it may cause the patient considerable anxiety. A number of causes of **epistaxis** exist. The nasal cavities are supplied by a fine network of blood capillaries, and anything causing congestion of the nasal membrane may rupture a small capillary and result in bleeding. The condition may occur in persons with hypertension, cardiovascular disease, blood dyscrasias, and some communicable diseases. Epistaxis also may be caused by injury to the nose, picking, or forceful blowing.

Assessment. The cause should be determined by careful examination and assessment. Data to be obtained include history, frequency and duration of bleeding episodes, any precipitating factors, signs of upper respiratory tract infections or allergic conditions, present medications that might influence clotting, and measures used to try to stop the bleeding. The patient should also be observed for site, color, and amount of bleeding; signs of respiratory difficulty; and signs of progressing hemorrhage. The physician will order laboratory tests to determine the extent and possible cause of the bleeding.

Intervention. Nursing procedures include placing the patient in Fowler's position with the head forward. The patient should be encouraged to let the blood drain from the nose, breathe through the mouth, and avoid swallowing the blood, because this may cause nausea and vomiting. The nostrils should be compressed tightly below the bone and held for 10 minutes or longer. This procedure will control most cases of epistaxis. Other procedures include holding ice in the mouth, placing iced compresses over the nose, holding an ice collar to the throat, and spraying the nostrils with phenylephrine (Neo-Synephrine). If bleeding cannot be controlled, the physician should be called, and packing the nose may be necessary. Hemostatic agents such as Gelfoam, packing saturated with 1:1000 solution of epinephrine, petroleum gauze, and oxidized cellulose (Oxycel) often are used. In rare cases, cauterizing the bleeding vessel may be necessary.

Cystic fibrosis

Cystic fibrosis, mucoviscidosis, is a genetic disease affecting 1 of every 1600 to 2000 live births of white infants. Although it is a disorder of the exogine glands, one principle characteristic is the production of large amounts of tenacious sputum. When this sputum collects in the tracheobronchial tree, obstruction, infection, atelectasis, and air trapping can occur. Cough, increased respiratory rate, and dyspnea also may be evident. Treatment is aimed at decreasing symptoms and preventing infection. Parents are taught a regime of chest percussion and vibration, postural drainage, and administration of bronchodilators and antibiotics when indicated.[16]

Chronic obstructive pulmonary disease (COPD) or chronic airflow limitation (CAL)

Diseases that interfere with ventilation cause psychologic, physical, and social problems for the individual. Fear, tension, frustration, and panic accompany these diseases. One of the most important aspects of medical and nursing care is the relief of anxiety. Inadequate ventilation causes a disturbance in the homeostasis of the body. Electrolyte balance is affected, changes occur in the extracellular fluid, and serious cardiac complications may occur. The constant shortness of breath, fatigue, and limitation of activity may cause retirement from employment, limitation of social activities, and feelings of social isolation and depression. COPDs include **emphysema**, chronic **bronchitis**, and **asthma**, each of which may result in varying degrees of incapacitation for the individual (see the boxed material).

Pulmonary emphysema

Pulmonary emphysema affects persons of all social and economic levels. An estimated 10 million persons in the United States have emphysema and one of every four wage earners past 45 years of age is disabled because of the disease. The disease is more common in men than in women, and reports indicate that most men past 70 years of age have destructive emphysema. The cause of emphysema is unknown; however, chronic bronchitis and asthma frequently are associated with emphysema. Research has indicated that cigarette smoking is the most important agent in the development of pulmonary emphysema. Air pollution, changes in temperature, and humidity appear to have an adverse effect on the disease.

Pathophysiology. In pulmonary emphysema the alveolar walls and capillaries are destroyed, decreasing the area available for the exchange of gases between the bloodstream and the air. Chronic irritation to the bronchi, bronchioles, and alveoli causes inflammation, with swelling and secretions. The lumen of the bronchioles narrows, especially during expiration, and air becomes trapped in the alveoli. The alveoli become distended, and then they rupture or become scarred and thickened with a loss of elasticity. Infections hasten the process. Expiration of air depends on the elasticity of the lungs, but because of lost elasticity and obstructed bronchioles, all of the inspired air cannot be forced out of the lungs. Increased pressure in the alveoli causes them to collapse. Distended air sacs (blebs) occurring on the surface of the lung may rupture and allow air to enter the pleural cavity, causing spontaneous pneumothorax. The pathologic changes cause a decrease in vital capacity and an increase in the residual volume of air retained in the lungs. Oxygenation of the arterial blood is decreased, and carbon dioxide tension of the arterial blood is increased. The retention of carbon dioxide in the blood may result in respiratory acidosis or carbon dioxide narcosis, stupor, and coma.

Assessment. Emphysema has an insidious onset, with dyspnea being the predominant symptom. As the disease progresses, the dyspnea is not only experienced on exertion but also at rest. Other manifestations of the disease include hypoxia, coughing with copious amounts of mucopurulent sputum, a barrel-shaped chest, use of accessory muscles of respiration, wheezing, grunting on expiration, peripheral cyanosis and digital clubbing, chronic respiratory acidosis, chronic weight loss, anorexia, and malaise. Any emotional upset, exertion, or excitement increases the dyspnea and respiratory stress.

NURSING CARE GUIDELINES
Chronic Obstructive Pulmonary Disease

Nursing diagnoses
- Anxiety related to respiratory difficulty
- Possible alteration in self-concept related to functional limitations
- Ineffective airway clearance
- Ineffective breathing patterns
- Respiratory dysfunction
- Potential ineffective coping patterns due to effects of illness on lifestyle
- Potential alteration in nutrition
- High risk for infection

Nursing interventions
- Prevent acquisition of respiratory tract infections
- Encourage patient to secure influenza vaccine in early autumn
- Encourage patient to discontinue cigarette smoking
- Direct patient to avoid drafts and sudden temperature changes
- Teach patient pulmonary hygiene to expectorate secretions: postural drainage, coughing, use of expectorants, bronchodilators, high humidity
- Teach breathing exercises, "pursed-lip" breathing
- Administer oxygen only if ordered and in low concentrations (flow rate, 1 to 2 L per minute)
- Observe for complications: cor pulmonale, congestive heart failure
- Encourage daily exercise program to recondition and strengthen muscles
- Encourage nourishing diet, several small meals a day
- Encourage fluid intake
- Encourage self-care activities within limits of patient's ability

Expected outcomes
- Understanding of methods to prevent respiratory tract infections
- Understanding of methods to maintain optimum health
- Performance of daily breathing exercises and pulmonary hygiene
- Not smoking
- Understanding of signs and symptoms of potential complications

Intervention. The most important factor in the treatment of patients with emphysema is prevention. The patient should be protected from respiratory tract infections, the occurrence of which intensify breathing problems. Many physicians believe that an antibiotic should be administered to emphysema patients during the fall and winter months. Laboratory examination of sputum should be performed to determine the specific bacteria present. Tetracycline or another broad-spectrum drug usually is given. The patient should be encouraged to secure an influenza vaccine early in the autumn. Because cigarette smoking is hazardous, every effort should be made to persuade the patient to discontinue the habit. The patient should avoid drafts and changes of temperature. Windows should be kept closed, and air conditioning is desirable. The patient should have a sleeping room and bath on the first floor if possible. Treatment is palliative and is directed toward making breathing as easy as possible. Some patients do better in moderate climates with minimum temperature changes.

Coughing is the emphysema patient's first defense. Deep breathing, incentive spirometry, and aerosolized bronchodilators aid in loosening secretions and optimizing ventilation. Low, small, grunting coughs after deep breaths while the abdominal muscles are supported, usually produce the best results. The patient may be taught to inhale by using the stomach muscles and exhale by blowing gently through pursed lips. Chest physical therapy such as percussion, vibration, and postural drainage often is effective in removing secretions from affected lungs.

Bronchodilators may be helpful for patients with bronchial obstructions. Medications used include aminophylline preparations, which are administered in rectal suppositories. Isoproterenol hydrochloride (Isuprel), isoetharine (Bronkosol), or metaproterenol (Alupent) used in a nebulizer help many patients. For patients in whom the bronchodilating drugs become ineffective, steroids may be added. Usually 5 to 10 mg of prednisone given orally once a day is ordered. If steroid therapy is continued, the patient must have an increased intake of potassium and be monitored for adverse side effects.

Because of the constant high level of carbon dioxide in the blood and tissues of the emphysema patient, the body comes to rely on low levels of oxygen as the main stimulus for respiration. Administering high concentrations of oxygen to such a patient may depress his or her respirations.

If ordered, oxygen should not be administered with a flow rate greater than 2 to 3 L per minute. It should be started slowly and the patient observed for restlessness, apprehension, flushed skin, shallow respirations, and stupor. The patient also should be observed for signs of right ventricular failure (cor pulmonale). Because the capillaries in the lungs have been destroyed by the disease process, the heart has to work harder to pump blood through the diseased lungs. Edema of the feet and legs and distended neck veins may indicate the onset of right ventricular failure. Gastric ulcers also tend to occur in patients with emphysema, although the specific cause is unknown.

Physical therapy should be part of every patient's therapy program. Its purpose is to recondition and strengthen muscles that have become soft and flabby and have lost their tone because of inactivity. Patients should be encouraged to follow a graded program of daily exercise. They usually breathe most easily when sitting up and may feel less well in the morning because secretions have collected in the lungs and bronchi during the night. A hot drink may help loosen tenacious sputum so that it may be coughed up. By the end of the day patients may feel completely exhausted. They should be encouraged to care for themselves within the limits of their ability. The diet should be nourishing, eliminating gas-forming foods. The appetite may be poor, and several small, attractive meals a day may be better than large meals. The taking of fluids should be encouraged to avoid the tendency toward dehydration. The nose and mouth should be kept clean, and all nursing care should be adapted to the needs of the individual patient. These needs will change as the disease progresses, and the physician, nurse, patient, and family must work together to plan a way of life for the patient.

Chronic bronchitis

Chronic bronchitis often occurs with pulmonary emphysema. In pulmonary emphysema defining the pathologic changes in the lungs is possible. In chronic bronchitis, the changes are functional and cannot be observed on x-ray examination. However, physiologic findings in obstructive chronic bronchitis are similar to pulmonary emphysema. The incidence of chronic bronchitis is greater among persons who smoke cigarettes, and cigarette smoking is considered to be the primary etiologic factor. Other inhalants may be contributing factors. For instance, severe air pollution has been found to aggravate the disorder and cause respiratory failure.

Pathophysiology. In chronic bronchitis, an abnormal increase in the mucus-secreting cells of the bronchial epithelium and the mucus-secreting cells of the trachea occurs. The goblet cells (so called because of their shape) of the surface epithelium are increased. The bronchi become thickened, and fibrosis of the bronchioles with infiltration by inflammatory cells may occur. Chronic infection of the mucous membrane usually is present, and the sputum may contain a variety of pathogenic microorganisms. The normal function of the cilia is impaired, so they are unable to move secretions upward where they may be coughed up. Because of this, mucous secretions may form plugs in small bronchi, where they become media for infection.

Assessment. The most common physiologic response in chronic bronchitis is a persistent cough with large amounts of sticky but fairly thin liquid mucus. In the presence of shortness of breath, the vital capacity is reduced, and dyspnea, cyanosis, and wheezing occur. Severely debilitated patients may be unable to cough and clear the respiratory passages, and respiratory function is compromised.

Intervention. The treatment consists primarily of the patient adopting a healthy lifestyle. Patients should secure adequate sleep and rest, eat a well-balanced diet, and should participate in some form of recreational activity. They should be cautioned to avoid exposure to respiratory tract infections, dust, and other irritants. Work that requires the individual to be outside during cold or wet weather should be avoided. If change of employment is necessary, the patient may be referred to the Social and Rehabilitation Service.

The most effective single factor in treatment is to require that the patient stop smoking. Most methods of treatment, including bronchodilators, nebulized agents, or oral medications, have been shown to have limited effect on chronic bronchitis. However, some patients may think that they do provide some relief. Although antibiotics often are administered to prevent infection, the time to begin such therapy is debatable. When chronic bronchitis with obstruction of the airways has existed over a long period, the patient may develop respiratory failure and right ventricular failure.

The nursing care of the hospitalized patient with chronic bronchitis is essentially the same as that for emphysema.

Asthma

Asthma can be classified as *extrinsic asthma*, meaning that it is caused by substances outside the body. These substances are antigens to which the individual is hypersensitive. About half of all persons with asthma fall into this category. When determining any extrinsic factor is impossible, the disease is considered to be *intrinsic asthma*, or asthma resulting from internal causes. Most frequently, intrinsic asthma is caused by chronic recurrent respiratory tract infection. Attacks may be precipitated by emotional stress, irritating fumes, changes in temperature and humidity, and increased physical activity. No cure for asthma is available. About one in four persons who develop the disease in childhood will have a spontaneous recovery, and about an equal number will become progressively worse. Few adults with asthma have spontaneous recoveries, and become progressively worse, with attacks lasting longer, becoming more frequent, and gradually becoming chronic.

Pathophysiology. In acute attacks of asthma, the lumina of the small bronchi become narrow and edematous. Spasm of the bronchial muscles occurs. The mucous-secreting glands of the bronchi secrete a thick, tenacious mucus, which obstructs the narrowed passages of the bronchi. Inspiration and expiration become difficult, and in an effort to get more air, the patient uses the auxiliary muscles of respiration. More air is forced into the lungs than can be expelled, causing the lungs to increase in size. The vital capacity is decreased, whereas an increase in the residual volume of air occurs. Because of inadequate ventilation, cyanosis occurs. The heart is not affected, and the respiratory rate remains about normal. After the acute attack subsides, the narrow lumen widens and the patient is able to cough and produce large amounts of thick, stringy sputum. Although the lungs return to their normal size after an attack, continued episodes will lead to permanent impairment and emphysema.

Assessment. The characteristic physiologic symptoms of asthma are shortness of breath accompanied by wheezing and coughing. Severity of symptoms indicates severity of attack. Pronounced wheezing progressing to absent breath sounds with a normal or rising Pa_{CO_2} are an ominous sign, indicating the need for immediate intervention. In asthma, as in chronic bronchitis and emphysema, the process of exhaling is more difficult than inhaling. Patients can reduce dyspnea markedly by sitting up with their head tilted forward during exhalation. After the normal exhalation the patient should gradually contract the abdominal muscles until no more air can be expelled from the lungs and then inhale. This procedure will reduce the effort required for exhaling. As a result of the ventilation difficulty, the patient may become cyanotic, and in prolonged attacks asphyxiation and death may occur if the patient is not treated with appropriate interventions, including mechanical ventilation. The patient generally perspires freely, the pulse may be weak, nausea and diarrhea may occur in children, and the patient may complain of pain in the chest caused by the respiratory effort. Children are more likely to have an elevation of temperature, which often is caused by some infection. The cough of persons with asthma usually is tight and dry in the beginning, but as the attack continues, the thin, mucous secretion becomes copious, thick, and stringy and is expectorated with difficulty.

Intervention. Treatment and care of asthma is directed toward three factors: (1) relief of the immediate attack, (2) control of causal factors, and (3) general care of the patient.

When parents of asthmatic children anticipate an approaching attack, medication that provides bronchodilation should be given early. Adequate hydration should be provided by offering the child small drinks at frequent intervals. If the attack progresses, 0.1 to 0.2 ml of a 1:1000 solution of epinephrine may be given subcutaneously. Adults with an attack of asthma may be given 0.3 to 0.5 ml of a 1:1000 solution of epinephrine subcutaneously.

Other drugs used in the treatment of an attack of asthma include terbutaline and aminophylline parenterally, combined with an aerosolized medication such as isoproterenol (Isuprel), isoetharine (Bronkosol), or metaproterenol (Alupent). These medications in various forms may be continued as part of the patient's long-term therapeutic regimen along with corticosteroids and cromolym sodium to prevent recurrent attacks.[13,15]

During an acute attack of asthma the patient should be placed in a sitting position and made as comfortable as possible. The overbed table may be prepared as for the patient with a cardiac problem (Chapter 16) and placed in front of the patient. Because the patient perspires profusely, clothing and bed linens should be changed frequently to keep him or her dry and prevent chilling. Humidification of inspired air helps loosen secretions so that they may be expectorated more easily. Dietary orders should be carried out, and the patient should be encouraged to take adequate amounts of fluids. If the fluid intake is inadequate, intravenous fluids may be ordered. Most attacks subside in 30 to 60 minutes, although they may continue for days or weeks. The patient who has frequent attacks of asthma may eventually become resistant to all forms of treatment and may develop what is called *status asthmaticus*, in which acute symptoms continue and a prolonged attack can cause exhaustion and require mechanical ventilation. Severe attacks of asthma are frightening to all concerned, and the patient and family needs reassurance and support.

The control of asthma depends on finding the cause and eliminating it. If the disease is caused by extrinsic factors (allergy), identification of the offending allergen may be made through skin tests, and the patient can be desensitized. If intrinsic factors are suspected, a thorough physical examination should be made to determine a source of infection, specific organisms, or other physical factors.

Patients with asthma should be advised against smoking, and should avoid exposure to cold, wet weather. A program of personal hygiene, with sleep, rest, and breathing exercises, should be instituted.

Pulmonary embolism and infarction

Pulmonary embolism occurs when a blood clot or other foreign matter becomes lodged in a branch of the pulmonary artery or arteriole. Pulmonary infarction is the death of a portion of lung tissue resulting from an insufficient blood supply, and it often occurs as a result of pulmonary embolism. Clots usually arise as the result of poor venous circulation or thrombosis. They break away from the vein in which they are formed and are carried by the venous blood through the right side of the heart and into the capillary system of the lungs, where they become lodged. Pulmonary embolism may occur as a postoperative or postpartum complication or from prolonged bed rest. The seriousness of the condition depends on the size of the blood vessel affected. If a large vessel is occluded, death may occur instantly.

Assessment. The symptoms vary with the severity of the condition, but the most common sign is sudden chest pain. Productive cough with blood-tinged sputum, rapid shallow respiration, fever, increased pulse rate, and (in severe cases) cyanosis and shock may be present. The nurse may be the first person to observe the signs and should be alerted when the patient complains of severe pain in the chest.

Intervention. Treatment includes absolute bed rest for 2 days and the administration of anticoagulant drugs such as heparin sodium, usually given intravenously for its immediate effect, and bishydroxycoumarin (Dicumarol), which is administered orally. New fibrinolytic drugs that dissolve large embolisms, such as urokinase or streptokinase, are currently used in some centers. The nurse must remember that, when the patient is receiving anticoagulant therapy, coagulation studies must be performed daily with careful monitoring for bleeding. Breathing will be assisted by placing the patient in a high Fowler's position; nursing care is similar to that for a patient with a myocardial infarction (p. 380). The major factor in pulmonary embolism is prevention, and the nurse shares much of the responsibility. To prevent pulmonary embolism, many surgeons require patients undergoing major surgery to wear elastic stockings while in bed. Some physicians order a minidose of heparin (5000 U sq. b.i.d) for patients needing long-term bed rest. Early mobility is encouraged to prevent venous stasis.[18]

Acute pulmonary edema

Acute pulmonary edema is a medical emergency occurring in patients with heart disease. Although the symptoms are primarily in the lungs, the basic cause is failure of the left side of the heart to adequately pump blood through the body. As a result, excessive amounts of blood collect in the left side of the heart, the pulmonary veins, and eventually the pulmonary capillary system. The increased pressure in the capillaries causes the serous portion of the blood to be pushed through the capillaries into the alveoli. As the alveoli become filled with fluid, the patient begins to suffocate in his own secretions, showing symptoms of severe dyspnea, cyanosis, wheezing, moist respirations, and a rapid and weak pulse rate. Assessment and nursing intervention are covered in Chapter 16.

Atelectasis

The conditions of **atelectasis** and pneumothorax (see next section) result in collapse of the lung but under different circumstances and for different reasons (Figure 15-11). Atelectasis is a common postoperative complication that can occur when the patient breathes rapidly and shallowly to prevent pain from the surgical site. It also occurs in association with bedridden patients, smokers, obese patients, premature infants, and patients with respiratory tract infections or chronic obstructive lung disease.

Pathophysiology. Atelectasis occurs from the blockage of air to a portion of the lung. It may result from pressure against the lung caused by air or fluid in the pleural cavity, tumors, an enlarged heart, or any abdominal condition that pushes the diaphragm upward. It also may result from an obstruction within one of the bronchi. A foreign body or a thick plug of mucus may completely occlude a bronchus, shutting off all air to a portion of the lung. As the air in the isolated part of the lung is absorbed by the capillaries and new air no longer enters, the part involved collapses. No separation of the visceral and parietal pleural occurs, however, and no air enters the pleural space. Treatment is removal of the obstruction by whatever means are necessary.

Assessment. The severity of the symptoms depends on the degree of alveolar tissue involved, the rate at which the obstruction develops, and the presence of a secondary infection. Patients who develop atelectasis usually have dyspnea, anxiety, cyanosis, tachypnea, tachycardia, decreased blood pressure, elevated temperature, and pain on the affected side. Rales and decreased

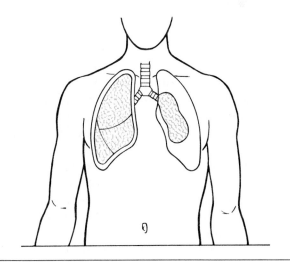

Figure 15-11

Pneumothorax, atelectasis, and pneumoperitoneum all result in collapse of lung. Example of pneumothorax showing air-filled pleural space. Atelectasis and pneumoperitoneum may lead to pneumothorax if hole is present in lung or diaphragm.

breath sounds may be auscultated in the affected areas.

Intervention. The key to treatment of atelectasis is prevention. Postoperative and other high-risk patients should be taught how to cough and breathe deeply. Mobility should be encouraged, and bedridden patients should be turned and repositioned every 1 to 2 hours. Incentive spirometers may be used to promote deep inspiration and to improve ventilation and bronchial drainage. Chest percussion and postural drainage will assist in expectoration of bronchial secretions. Suctioning, oxygen, and administration of aerosols and humidity also are used.

Pneumothorax

Pneumothorax is a condition in which air fills the pleural space between the lung and the chest wall, and the lung consequently collapses (Figure 15-11). A common cause is the rupture of a bleb on the surface of the lung, which is a complication of emphysema. However, pneumothorax may occur during severe episodes of coughing in a patient with chronic respiratory disease. Chest injuries or wounds in which the membrane covering the lungs is torn allow air to escape into the pleural space. Spontaneous pneumothorax may occur without any known cause. Tension pneumothorax develops when air enters the pleural space through a tear or hole in the lung tissue or through a sucking chest wound and cannot escape. This causes positive pressure to build rapidly, leading to collapse of the lung and a potential mediastinal shift.

Assessment. A sharp, sudden pain in the chest may occur, followed by dyspnea, diaphoresis, weak and rapid pulse rates, falling blood pressure, lack of chest movement, and decreased breath sounds on the affected side; apprehension and shock sometimes follow. If the condition is not severe, the air may absorb or may be aspirated with a needle. A closed thoracotomy may be required for some patients.

Intervention. The care of the patient depends to a large extent on the condition resulting in the collapse. Pain must be relieved and the patient made as comfortable as possible. The patient with spontaneous pneumothorax may be placed in a high Fowler's position and encouraged to breathe normally. The pulse and respiratory rates should be checked at frequent intervals and all exertion reduced to a minimum. X-ray films usually are taken to determine the amount of air in the chest cavity. Oxygen may be given and preparation made for a thoracentesis. A continuous flow of air into the pleural cavity may require closed chest drainage.

Adult respiratory distress syndrome (ARDS)

Adult respiratory distress syndrome—also referred to as shock lung, wet lung, stiff lung, oxygen toxicity, and congestive lung syndrome—is a combination of symptoms resulting from direct or indirect injury to the lung. Some of the many factors that contribute to the development of ARDS are viral and bacterial pneumonia, chest trauma, head injury, surgery, any form of shock, oxygen toxicity, smoke inhalation, aspiration of toxic irritants, near drowning, drug overdose, fat or air emboli, sepsis, disseminated intravascular coagulation, massive blood transfusions, renal failure, pancreatitis, and radiation injury to the lung.

Pathophysiology. An alteration in the alveolar capillary membrane occurs, and the increased capillary permeability causes fluids to leak into the interstitial spaces, small airways, and eventually the alveoli. The lungs become edematous and hypoxia occurs. The fluid affects the activity of surfactant (the lipoprotein that helps to maintain the elasticity of the alveolar tissue), and the alveoli collapse. This leads to shunting of blood through the fluid-filled or collapsed alveoli, which interferes with oxygen transport. Plasma and red blood cells escape from the damaged capillaries, causing hemorrhage.

Assessment. Symptoms may occur within hours of the lung injury or may not appear for several days. Initially, the patient experiences rapid, shallow breathing and dyspnea. The dyspnea and tachypnea rapidly become more severe, with hypoxia, intercostal retractions, cyanosis, crackles and rhonchi, and tachycardia appearing. The hypoxia and cyanosis respond poorly to oxygen therapy. As the ventilation-perfusion imbalance worsens, the hypoxia becomes overwhelming, resulting in hypotension and signs and symptoms of respiratory and metabolic acidosis.

Intervention. Treatment is aimed at maintaining adequate alveolar ventilation and tissue oxygenation and at correcting the underlying cause. High concentrations of oxygen are administered through a tightly fitting mask, which allows for the use of continuous positive air pressure. Frequently, the patient requires intubation with mechanical ventilatory support and positive end-expiratory pressure (PEEP). Positive end-expiratory pressure improves ventilation and perfusion by stretching the stiff lung tissue and keeping the alveoli from collapsing. In some cases, high-frequency jet ventilation may be required. This method of ventilator therapy allows for delivery of high levels of PEEP without raising peak mean-airway pressure to the extent required by conventional ventilators. It ventilates the patient with small tidal volumes and high-respiratory rates.[12] Nursing care consists of continued support of the patient's respiratory function and the detection and prevention of complications. Frequent assessments should be made of vital signs, breath sounds, intake and output, arterial blood gases, and serum electrolytes. Airway patency should be maintained by suctioning using a sterile technique; ventilator settings are checked frequently. The patient's position should be changed frequently and passive range of motion performed. The environment must be quiet and relaxed and adequate rest periods planned. The nurse will be working closely with the physician and respiratory therapist; any respiratory changes should be reported immediately to the physician.

Infectious Respiratory Conditions

A large number of diseases of the respiratory tract are infectious. Most of these diseases, bacterial or viral in nature, find their way into the respiratory tract when an individual breathes in air saturated with the disease organism. Many infections follow a pattern, beginning with what appears to be a common cold but gradually involving all parts of the respiratory tract. A large number of infections of the lower respiratory tract have their beginnings with upper respiratory infections.

Invasion of the upper respiratory system by pathogenic microorganisms, usually viral, causes inflammation and edema of the mucous membranes. The mucus-secreting glands become hyperactive, producing large amounts of serous to mucopurulent exudate. The cervical lymph nodes enlarge and are tender. Air passages become occluded, causing impaired pulmonary ventilation. Respiratory rates increase in an effort to get more air to the lungs, and the heart works harder to supply the body's tissues with oxygen. The body mobilizes its forces to combat the invading pathogen, and leukocytosis occurs. The inflammatory condition of the mucous membranes causes the throat to become red, sore, and dry; the voice

becomes hoarse; and a dry painful cough develops. The pathogen may invade the contiguous mucous membranes of the sinuses and the ears.

Acute coryza (common cold)

Acute coryza may be caused by one or several viruses. The causative virus is believed to be present constantly in the upper respiratory tract. A person's susceptibility to the virus increases periodically from a wide variety of factors. Symptoms usually appear within 24 to 48 hours after exposure and may be transmitted to others several hours afterward. Symptoms include a chilly sensation and sneezing. The nasal membranes feel hot, dry, and congested. A slight throat irritation may occur, followed by a thin, serous nasal discharge. Nasal congestion causes pressure, which results in headache and tenderness of cervical lymph nodes. If the infection remains uncomplicated, it generally subsides in approximately 1 week. If nasal discharge becomes purulent, it is an indication that the infection is complicated by bacterial invasion.

Acute pharyngitis

Bacteria or viruses from acute coryza may extend to the pharynx, or pharyngitis may occur without prior evidence of a cold. The throat becomes inflamed and red, the tonsils and cervical lymph nodes become tender, and a sensation of rawness and a dry cough may occur. Chronic pharyngitis may result from chronic infection of the sinuses or nasal mucosa and may not produce any significant symptoms. Acute pharyngitis usually responds to symptomatic treatment, with recovery occurring in about a week. If the condition is caused by one of several bacteria, such as the hemolytic streptococcus, *Staphylococcus aureus*, or *Haemophilus influenzae*, symptoms may be more serious and complications may ocur.

Acute laryngitis

Acute laryngitis generally is secondary to other upper respiratory tract infections. The mucous membrane lining the larynx becomes inflamed, and the vocal cords become swollen. The disease is characterized by hoarseness or loss of voice and cough. Acute laryngitis may occur in children, especially at night (croup), and results in an alarming dyspnea that usually is not serious. The child should not be left alone. Often the attack can be relieved by warm or cool moist inhalations or, for very young children, a croup tent. Although rare, a tracheotomy may be required in some cases. If it remains uncomplicated, acute laryngitis usually clears in a few days.

Tonsillitis

Acute follicular tonsillitis is an inflammation of the tonsils, often caused by streptococcus or staphylococcus bacteria. The throat is sore and painful, swallowing is difficult, and generalized aching of muscles, with chills and an elevation of temperature occur. If tonsillitis is caused by the hemolytic streptococcus, the symptoms may be more severe, with nausea and vomiting and an increase in the leukocyte count developing. The primary concern is the prevention of complications such as rheumatic fever and nephritis. Repeated attacks of tonsillitis may require surgical removal of the tonsils, a **tonsillectomy**.

Sinusitis

Sinusitis may be acute or chronic. It usually occurs as the result of other upper respiratory tract infections, and because mucous membranes of the nasal cavities are continuous with the sinuses, infection may be spread easily to the sinuses. Inflammation of the sinuses may occur from obstructions such as nasal polyps or from a deviated septum that blocks the drainage from the sinuses. It also may be a complication of influenza or pneumonia. If an acute sinusitis is left untreated, it may become chronic or may lead to more serious conditions such as meningitis, brain abscess, osteomyelitis, and septicemia. The primary symptom of sinusitis is pain, and its location is related to the sinus involved. When the maxillary sinus is affected, the pain occurs over the cheeks and may radiate downward to the teeth. A frontal sinus infection causes pain in and above the eyes. The bone over the affected sinus usually is sensitive to slight pressure, and puffiness over the area may be observed. Depending on the extent of the infection and the particular microorganism involved, the patient may have an elevation of temperature, nausea, and loss of appetite. When a continuous postnasal dripping into the back of the throat occurs, coughing and soreness of the throat may result. Acute sinusitis causes discomfort and frequently results in loss in working time and other activities of daily living.

Intervention in Upper Respiratory Tract Infections

The treatment of upper respiratory tract infections is directed toward relief from the discomfort of symptoms and prevention of complications. Bedrest is desirable during the acute stage of the infection, and precautionary measures should be taken to prevent the spread of the infection to others. Nasal sprays, moist inhalations, hot saline gargles, throat irrigations, and aspirin provide symptomatic relief. Drugs should not be taken without a physician's order. At present, antibiotics are not considered to be effective in respiratory tract infections of viral origin. Fluid intake should be increased, and if the temperature is elevated more than 1° F, medical attention should be sought. When pharyngitis or laryngitis accompanies acute coryza, relief may be obtained by steam inhalations or with an ice collar for the throat. If coughing is disturbing, an analgesic cough mixture or a mild sedative for rest at night may be ordered. When severe pharyngitis is present, the nurse should be alert to the possibility of dangerous complications. Temperature and pulse and respiration rates should be checked every 4 hours unless otherwise ordered. The diet should be liquid or soft, with fluids forced. A daily bowel evacuation, using enemas or mild laxatives if necessary, should occur. If the infection is caused by bacteria such as streptococci, the patient should be observed for skin rash, which might indicate scarlet fever. Blood cultures, a white blood cell count, and urinalysis may be ordered. In bacterial infections, an elevation of the white blood cell count may be seen. When the larynx is involved, talking should be avoided or reduced. Antibiotic drugs may be ordered when the infection is caused by bacteria. Most patients with respiratory tract infections are more comfortable when placed in a low (15 degrees) Fowler's position, which provides for better drainage of secretions. A cool (68° to 70° F [20° to 21° C]), well-ventilated room with high humidity that is free from drafts provides a greater degree of comfort than an overheated room.

Influenza

People often associate certain respiratory symptoms with influenza, and frequently say, "I have the flu." In reality, most of these persons have one of the respiratory tract infections just reviewed. Epidemics and pandemics of influenza have been known since the sixteenth century. The worst pandemic of modern times occurred in 1918 and 1919, when an estimated 20 million people died, over half of these in the United States. During this epidemic, the disease was first named *influenza*. In 1957 and 1958, a serious epidemic of influenza (Asian influenza) developed, with more than 7000 deaths occurring in the United States. The disease occurs in cycles, but variations of specific strains are believed to cause sporadic illness during nonepidemic years.

The disease is caused by a virus that has been identified and classified as type A, B, or C. Type D is now known as parainfluenza 1, and strains of A are known as A prime, or A_1 and A_2. In 1968, 1969, and 1974, various parts of the world, including the United States, experienced a fairly mild form of influenza caused by a new strain of the A_2 virus, which was called A_2 *Hong Kong–like virus.*

Assessment. The first symptoms of influenza occur with unbelievable rapidity, and the typical picture is one of chills, an elevated temperature of 102° to 104° F (39° to 40° C); severe aching of the back, head, and extremities; sore throat; cough; considerable prostration; sneezing; coated tongue; and weakness. If the infection is uncomplicated, the acute period usually lasts from 3 to 5 days. Some cases do not follow the typical pattern but begin with gastrointestinal symptoms, bronchopneumonia, pleurisy, or sinusitis. Influenza is especially hazardous for elderly persons, and the mortality from influenza-pneumonia generally rise sharply during an influenza epidemic.

Intervention. The patient should remain on a regimen of bed rest during the acute phase and should resume activities gradually after the temperature is normal. The patient should avoid overheated or cold rooms and should be protected against chilling. Analgesic and antipyretic drugs may be administered to relieve discomfort and reduce fever, and sedative cough mixtures may be given to relieve throat irritation. Fluid intake should be more than 3000 to 5000 ml per day. Humidity provided by steam inhalations helps to keep nasal passages clear and soothes inflamed membranes. The patient with influenza is uncomfortable and feels very ill; however, influenza alone usually is not serious. The danger with this condition lies in complications caused by streptococcus or staphylococcus bacteria. Bronchopneumonia is the most frequent complication, and very young, elderly, or debilitated persons are more likely to develop it.

Persons with uncomplicated influenza should remain at home. If admitted to the hospital, the patient runs the risk of acquiring a bacterial infection that could cause serious complications. Viral infections are self-limiting, and there is no known drug that will cure them.

At present, immunization for influenza is not recommended for healthy adults and children. Although its effectiveness may be limited, it is advised for persons of all ages who have debilitating diseases such as rheumatic heart disease, cardiovascular disorders, chronic bronchopulmonary disease, and diabetes. The vaccine also is advised for all health care workers. The individual should be given one dose of the vaccine according to the manufacturer's directions. Local or mild systemic reactions occur in about half the recipients of the vaccine. The vaccine should not be given to anyone who is hypersensitive to eggs because an allergic reaction might occur.

Acute bronchitis

Bronchitis is caused by inflammation of the bronchial tree and the trachea. As a rule, it is secondary to infection in the upper respiratory tract, but it also may result from bronchial irritation caused by exposure to chemical agents or as a complication of communicable diseases such as measles. Acute bronchitis usually begins with hoarseness and cough, slight elevation in temperature, muscular aching, and headache. The cough may be dry and painful, but it gradually becomes productive. Bedrest is indicated as long as the temperature is elevated. Treatments should be directed toward preventing the extension of the infection. Either plain or medicated steam inhalations soothe irritated respiratory passages. Aerosol therapy may be given, and antibiotics may be ordered. Sedative or expectorant drugs may be ordered for the cough. If no complications occur, recovery may be expected in a week to ten days.

Pneumonia

Pneumonia is a disease of the lungs caused by bacteria or any of several viral agents. It may occur in comatose or oversedated patients and in those whose pulmonary ventilation is inadequate. It may result from aspiration of infected secretions from the upper respiratory or gastrointestinal tracts, may complicate certain viral diseases such as measles or influenza, and may cause complications, including empyema, septicemia, meningitis, and endocarditis. Most pneumonia is caused by *Streptococcus pneumoniae* (pneumococcus).

Pathophysiology. Infected secretions from the upper respiratory tract drain into the alveoli, where the normal defense mechanisms such as ciliary action and coughing are unable to remove them. An inflammatory process begins, and in-

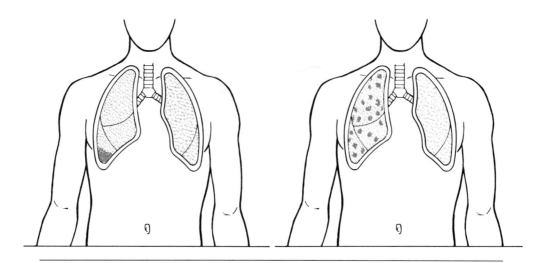

Figure 15-12

A, Bacterial pneumonia may affect one or more lobes of lung. **B**, Viral pneumonia appears as patchy distribution throughout lung.

creased amounts of fluid are released in the area. The serous fluid moves easily into additional alveoli and bronchioles. As the process continues, less surface area is available for the absorption of oxygen and the release of carbon dioxide. Leukocytes and a few erythrocytes begin to accumulate in the affected alveoli, and the number increases until they eventually completely fill each alveolus, resulting in consolidation (Figure 15-12, *A*). Phagocytosis begins in the consolidated alveolus, and the area is finally cleared. In the beginning, only one lobe of the lung may be involved, but the infected fluid may spread to the bronchial tree of another lobe, setting up another infection process.

Assessment. Symptoms may vary with the individual; however, the onset of bacterial pneumonia usually is sudden and accompanied by a severe chill and chest pain. These symptoms are followed by an elevation of temperature, which may be as high as 105° F (40.5° C), with an increase in pulse and respiratory rates. The patient develops a cough, which may be painful and constant. At first the sputum may be clear or tinged with blood, but within 48 hours it develops a characteristic rusty appearance. The sputum is thick and tenacious and may be expectorated with difficulty; suction should be available if needed to help clear the airway. Leukocytosis is present, with the number of white blood cells ranging from 20,000 to 30,000. The skin is hot and moist, the lips dry, and the tongue parched. Occasionally nausea,

vomiting, diarrhea, and jaundice appear. Fever blisters (herpes simplex) may appear on the lips and nose, and sores may cover the tongue. Restlessness and delirium may accompany pneumonia and may forebode a crucial situation.

Legionnaires' disease is an acute bacterial bronchopneumonia caused by a gram-negative bacillus. It derived its name from the 1976 American Legion convention in Philadelphia, where it affected 180 people and caused 29 deaths. The bacteria is airborne and has an affinity for stagnant water such as that found in air-conditioning and cooling systems. Thus it tends to affect people who work together in one building or who come together in large groups, such as at conventions. It tends to occur epidemically, particularly during the summer, with a severity ranging from a mild pneumonitis to a multilobar pneumonia with a 10% to 15% mortality. The symptoms are similar to bacterial pneumonia, except that the cough may be unproductive at first and signs of gastrointestinal upset are more likely to be present.

Pneumonia caused by a virus usually appears as a patchy infection throughout the lung (Figure 15-12, *B*). The onset is slower and is characterized by chilly sensations or chills, fever, profuse sweating, aching, and a painful cough. The sputum is mucopurulent and may contain blood. The white blood cell count is normal. The temperature elevation generally runs an irregular course, varying widely even during the day, and may continue for as long as 3 weeks. Viral pneumonia rarely is fatal, and although the patient is extremely uncomfortable, the seriousness is less than that of bacterial pneumonia. However, these patients may require a longer period of convalescence.

Intervention. Nursing care of patients with pneumonia is a major factor in the progress and prognosis of the illness. Pneumonia is debilitating and exhausting. Treatment and care are directed toward keeping the patient as comfortable as possible, planning care to avoid any unnecessary expenditure of energy, and using antibiotic and sulfonamide agents to assist the body's defenses to overcome the infection. The type of antibiotic drug used will depend on the particular organism present and whether the organism remains sensitive to the drug. Sputum for diagnosis should be secured before treatment with the antibiotic is started. Meperidine (Demerol) often is used to relieve pain. Cough analgesics and increased humidity tend to relieve coughing. If the patient is cyanotic or dyspneic, oxygen may be ordered.

The patient's room should be well ventilated, with the temperature from 68° to 70° F (20° to 21° C), and free from drafts. A restful, quiet environment should be provided. The patient should be positioned to allow for the greatest comfort and may be placed in a high, 90-degree Fowler's position or on the affected side. The position should be changed frequently. The nursing care plan should be made to provide nursing care with periods of uninterrupted rest. Visiting should be limited sharply during the acute phase of the disease. Temperature, pulse, and respiratory rates are checked every 4 hours, and blood pressure readings should be taken at least once a day. The diet usually consists of liquids, and the total fluid intake should be increased from 3000 to 4000 ml per day. The patient may have to be encouraged to take food or fluids. If pneumonia occurs in a patient with cardiac disease, the nurse should determine if fluids and sodium are to be restricted. Intake and output records should be maintained. Intravenous fluids designed to maintain electrolyte balance may be ordered. Special mouth care will have to be given several times each day. A lubricant should be applied to the lips and to soften any crusts on the nares. Fever blisters should be kept dry.

Abdominal distention frequently accompanies pneumonia. Measures to relieve distress include the insertion of a rectal tube for no longer than 20 minutes or a small saline solution enema. Neostigmine bromide (Prostigmin) may be or-

dered if other measures fail. With decreased peristalsis, a gastric tube may be inserted and attached to suction siphonage. The nurse should be alert to a fall in temperature with a weak rapid pulse, a drop in blood pressure, increased cyanosis, and dyspnea. Bed rails always should be available, and if restlessness and delirium occur, the patient must be watched carefully and not left alone. Although the use of antibiotics has decreased the death rate from bacterial pneumonia, some patients succumb to the disease. Expert nursing care is essential.

Patients with pneumonia that is caused by the staphylococcus bacteria should be isolated, and careful medical asepsis should be carried out. Patients with pneumonia that is caused by other pathogens do not need to be isolated, but the nurse should be careful about handwashing and proper handling of the disposal of sputum (see the box on p. 340).

Tuberculosis

Pulmonary tuberculosis is caused by an acid-fast bacterium, the tubercle bacillus (*Mycobacterium tuberculosis*). When the bacillus enters the lung, the body responds by surrounding the bacteria with monocytes, which fuse together forming large giant cells. Fibrous tissue grows around the area and the central portion of this growth of cells becomes necrotic. The entire inflammatory process is called granulomatous inflammation. If the number of organisms entering the lung is small and the body's resistance is high, healing occurs by scarring. If a large number of organisms are inhaled into the lung, the inflammation overwhelms the body's defenses and a more extensive destruction of lung tissue occurs. This destruction results in lung cavities.[2]

Tuberculosis can be a primary or secondary disorder. Secondary tuberculosis usually occurs late in life or when individuals are immunocompromised. Detection of tuberculosis is through acid-fast stained sputum specimen and chest x-ray examinations. Treatment usually requires more than one drug; often triple therapy in the form of streptomycin, isoniazid (INH), and rifampin is prescribed[17] (see Chapter 7). Patients with infectious tuberculosis must be kept from interacting with others who have not developed immunity to the disease and should receive adequate rest to recover from the illness. Nursing interventions for patients with pneumonia should be initiated.

NURSING CARE GUIDELINES
Pneumonia

Nursing diagnoses
- Anxiety related to respiratory difficulty
- Ineffective airway clearance
- Respiratory dysfunction
- Potential alteration in nutrition
- Potential fluid volume imbalance

Nursing interventions
- Check vital signs every 4 hours
- Observe for respiratory distress
- Administer antibiotics as ordered
- Administer pain medication as needed
- Administer oxygen as needed
- Provide well-ventilated room, free from drafts
- Position patient in Fowler's position or lying on affected side; change position frequently
- Monitor intake and output and intravenous infusions as ordered
- Encourage high fluid intake
- Provide oral and nasal hygiene
- Provide rectal tube or enema or nasogastric tube to relieve abdominal distention
- Teach proper disposal of sputum
- Isolate patient if staphylococcal pneumonia present
- Follow careful medical asepsis techniques

Expected outcomes
- Avoidance of respiratory complications
- Understanding of proper disposal of sputum
- Maintaining an adequate nutritional and hydration state
- Understanding of the type of pneumonia
- Understanding of methods to prevent respiratory tract infections and maintain optimum health
- Understanding of the use, time, dosage, and side effects of prescribed medications

---

Acquired immunodeficiency syndrome (AIDS)

Patients with acquired immunodeficiency syndrome (AIDS) are at great risk for pulmonary infection, particularly pneumonia caused by *Pneumocystis carinii*. Patients with AIDS also are at risk for development of tuberculosis and Legionnaire's Disease.[2]

The onset of the infection may be rapid or may occur over several weeks, with individuals reporting gradual weakness and increased shortness of breath. The usual symptoms include fever, malaise, dyspnea, and dry cough. Chills, chest pain, and sputum production also may occur in some patients. Respiratory failure may develop and despite intensive mechanical ventilation and other interventions, death is common.[9]

Pleurisy and empyema

Pleurisy results from inflammation of any part of the pleura. Several forms of the disease exist, which are referred to as dry pleurisy, wet pleurisy, or pleurisy with effusion, and empyema, which is characterized by pus formation. Although the disease may occur spontaneously, it is more likely to be a complication of pneumonia or tuberculosis. The disease has been less common since the development of antibiotic therapy.

Assessment. The first symptom may be a severe knifelike pain on inspiration, which may be referred to the shoulder or to the abdomen on the affected side. A cough, dyspnea, and vomiting may occur, and the patient may hold the abdomen with a boardlike rigidity.

Pleurisy with effusion is less dramatic than dry pleurisy, and the first symptom may be dyspnea, occurring when the accumulation of fluid in the pleural cavity has become large enough to compress the lung. The acuteness of the dyspnea depends on the size of the effusion; other symptoms are related to the cause and may include an elevation of temperature. If the fluid becomes purulent and empyema develops, the temperature may reach 105° F (40.5° C), with chills, profuse perspiration, and prostration.

Intervention. The treatment of pleurisy depends on the type and stage of the disease and is directed toward removing the underlying cause through the administration of the appropriate antibiotic to combat the infection. If fluid is present in the pleural cavity, a thoracentesis may be performed and the fluid aspirated, followed by the instillation of penicillin. If the pleural fluid has become purulent and empyema has developed, adequate drainage and specific antibiotics must be provided. With antibiotic therapy, the need for an open thoracotomy almost has been eliminated. Patients with pleurisy usually are apprehensive and worried, and the nurse needs to be sympathetic and understanding. Practicing good bedside nursing and providing as much comfort as possible in a quiet environment will do much to hasten recovery. Patients will be more comfortable if they lie on the affected side and turn toward the affected side when coughing. Pain should be relieved, and generally the use of aspirin is sufficient. If dyspnea is severe, oxygen may be administered. Because pleurisy often follows a debilitating disease, an adequate diet is important. The diet should be high in protein, calories, vitamins, and minerals; supplemental feedings may be helpful.

Bronchiectasis

Bronchiectasis is characterized by a permanent dilation of one or more of the bronchi from repeated infections. A single lobe of one lung or one or more lobes in both lungs may be affected. The left lung tends to be involved more often than the right lung, although in approximately 50% of patients, both lungs are involved. The cause of the disease is unknown, and although some cases are believed to be congenital, most appear to result from chronic bronchitis and severe attacks of infectious respiratory diseases. It is primarily a disease of the young, often affecting persons 20 years of age or younger.

Assessment. In the early stages, no symptoms may be present, but as the disease progresses, the most characteristic symptom is a productive cough. The cough is worse in the morning and any change in position may produce paroxysms of coughing. The cough produces large amounts of purulent sputum, which may be tinged with blood. Hemoptysis occurs in a large number of cases, although it usually is not serious. As the disease gradually worsens, fever, chills, fatigue, loss of weight, clubbing of the fingers, and loss of appetite may occur. The diagnosis is made by x-ray examination (bronchography), and bronchoscopy. The only cure is surgical removal of the affected area (lobectomy). However, each patient must be carefully evaluated in relation to pulmonary function and prognosis because all patients are not suitable candidates for such surgery.

Intervention. Palliative treatment consists of measures to improve the general health, such as adequate diet, rest, and prevention of respiratory tract infections. Cigarette smoking, alcohol, and excessive exercise should be avoided. Irritants from air pollution may contribute to recurrent episodes of acute respiratory tract infection. Sputum cultures often indicate the presence of specific microorganisms, and antibiotic therapy for the particular pathogen is administered. Postural drainage should be part of the patient's daily routine, and moist inhalations may make thin, tenacious sputum easier to raise. Many patients are treated on an outpatient basis, but in severe exacerbation the patient is admitted to the hospital. The nurse

should encourage and reassure the patient and assist with postural drainage or other chest therapy. Mouth care must be given several times a day, and the use of an antiseptic mouthwash before meals may be desirable. The patient should be constantly on the alert for obstruction of the airway by large plugs of mucus.

OBSTRUCTIONS OF THE RESPIRATORY SYSTEM

Obstructions of the respiratory system may result from any of the following: a deviated septum, nasal polyps, enlarged tonsils and adenoids, aspiration of foreign bodies, dry secretions, and laryngeal tumors.

Deviated Septum and Nasal Polyps

The nasal septum divides the two nasal cavities. Most people have some irregularity of the septum, but unless it is great enough to obstruct breathing, they are unaware of the condition. In addition, during childhood, injuries to the nose including fractures can be received. If not cared for, these injuries may result in a bending of the septum to one side or the other, and if the deviation is severe, it causes a partial blocking of the respiratory passageway on one side. When obstruction occurs, surgical correction is necessary.

A polyp is a small tumor attached to the mucous membrane of the nose. It may have been caused by prolonged inflammation of the sinuses, and because it obstructs free drainage of secretions, the inflammatory condition may be aggravated. Surgical removal may be necessary to relieve the inflammatory condition.

Respiratory obstruction from a deviated septum or nasal polyps may be corrected by a surgical procedure called *submucous resection*. The procedure is performed while the patient is under local anesthesia, after administration of preoperative sedation. After the procedure, the nose is packed for approximately 12 hours. If tampons are used, the strings should be fastened to the cheek with a bit of adhesive tape, and the patient should be instructed not to blow his or her nose. The patient is placed in a Fowler's position, and analgesics are administered to relieve pain. Because the patient will be breathing through the mouth, he or she may be given chipped ice to help keep the mouth moist. Cold cream may be applied to the lips, and iced compresses may be applied over the nose. The patient should be observed for hemorrhage, indicated by expectoration of bright red blood, frequent swallowing, or increased flow of bright red blood through the packing. After removal of the packing, the patient is allowed a diet as desired and bathroom privileges. The patient should be told to expect a loss of the senses of smell for about 1 week.

Enlarged Tonsils and Adenoids

The pharyngeal tonsils (adenoids) are a mass of lymphoid tissue located at the back of the nose in the upper pharynx. The palatine tonsils, also composed of lymphoid tissue, are located on each side of the soft palate in the throat. These tissues are normally larger in childhood, and under normal conditions, removal is not considered necessary unless they become infected with bacteria and do not respond to conservative treatment. If they become extremely large and obstruct breathing through the nose, the child may have to breathe through the mouth to get enough air. The tonsils also may obstruct the eustachian tube opening into the back of the throat and may cause some loss of hearing. Removing these lymphoid structures surgically may be necessary to restore normal breathing and hearing.

Intervention

Tonsillectomy for an adult may be performed while the patient is under local anesthesia. On return from surgery patient is place in the Fowler's position. When a general anesthetic has been given, the patient should be placed on his or her side or abdomen with a pillow under the abdomen and the head hyperextended. Vital signs should be checked as for any postoperative patient. An ice collar is applied to the throat for relief of discomfort. The patient should be instructed not to cough or clear the throat, and talking should be discouraged for several hours. Postoperative hemorrhage should always be watched for, and care is directed toward its prevention. The patient should not be allowed to gargle the throat before healing begins because this may dislodge a clot and produce bleeding. If nausea is not present and if no bleeding develops, water or chipped ice may be given. If temperature elevation occurs, the surgeon should be notified. A trace of blood is to be anticipated, but any unusual amount of bright red blood should be reported immediately. Because children may hemorrhage and swallow blood, the nurse should watch the pulse rates and blood pressures of children who have had tonsillectomies. Suction equipment and packing should be available for emergencies.

Foreign Bodies

Children are likely to put small objects into their nose, such as beans, peanuts, and corn, which are sometimes aspirated into the lungs. If the object is visible, it can be removed with a pair of tweezers. If the object has lodged in the back of the nose or pharynx, the child should be kept quiet and taken to a physician.

Emergency treatment is necessary if foreign materials become lodged in the throat or trachea. If the object cannot be dislodged by the finger, the nurse should stand behind the choking individual, hold the individual below the rib cage, and quickly squeeze (similar to a bear hug). This will force out residual air and the foreign object from the respiratory tract. This is called the Heimlich maneuver (see Chapter 16). The Heimlich maneuver also may be used in children, or the child may be picked up by the heels and shaken. This will often cause the child to cough out the object.

Aspirated foreign bodies are more likely to enter the right main bronchus, which is larger and in a more vertical position. If the object is small, coughing will occur and slight dyspnea will develop. Often the aspiration of a foreign body will create an acute emergency, making prompt removal with a laryngoscope or bronchoscope necessary, and occasionally a tracheotomy may be required to prevent death. The nurse needs to approach the situation with calmness and efficiency in carrying out emergency orders. When foreign bodies are removed from the bronchus or lung, the child may be hospitalized, and the child's vital signs must be watched. The throat may be sore, and steam inhalations may be ordered with sedative or analgesic drugs to relieve discomfort. The child is positioned on the side without a pillow.

TUMORS OF THE RESPIRATORY SYSTEM

Benign or malignant tumors may occur in any part of the respiratory system. Malignant tumors of the upper respiratory system are less common than are tumors in other parts of the body.

Laryngeal Cancer

Cancer of the larynx accounts for a small percentage of neoplasms. As with malignant tumors in other parts of the body, the cause of carcinoma of the larynx is unknown, although persons with laryngeal cancer frequently are heavy smokers. When the condition is diagnosed, early cure is possible. The disease is most common in men after 45 years of age.

Assessment. The first symptom of laryngeal cancer that may be observed is hoarseness of the voice, which becomes progressively worse without treatment. If this symptom is neglected, metastasis to other structures will occur, and pain on swallowing or pain in the vicinity of the "Adam's apple" will radiate to the ear. Ultimately, the airway will become obstructed and dyspnea will occur. Carcinoma of the larynx is diagnosed by history and visual examination of the larynx with a laryngoscope. A biopsy is done for laboratory confirmation of the clinical findings. Depending on the location of the tumor and the extent of involvement, a partial or a total laryngectomy is performed.

Intervention: Laryngectomy

Speech is the means by which a person maintains personal and social relationships. Its loss is a threat to the individual's feelings of security, adequacy, and acceptance. One of the most important decisions of a patient's life is made when he or she consents to a total **laryngectomy**. When a total laryngectomy is performed, the larynx, the vocal cords, the thyroid cartilage, and the epiglottis are removed surgically. The trachea is sutured to the anterior surface of the neck as a permanent tracheostomy. Because the patient no longer breathes through the nose, he or she has little sense of smell. The patient must be prepared emotionally for the loss of normal speech and the change in normal breathing. After surgery, the patient should be given an explanation of the operation. This may be done by discussing the way in which normal speech is produced and how the operation will affect the production of normal speech. In addition, the patient should be given some information about speech therapy and should be told that he or she will be taught to speak again.

After surgery the patient may be placed in the intensive care unit because continuous nursing care should be provided for the first 48 hours or longer if necessary. If the patient is admitted directly to his or her room, it should be prepared to receive the patient after surgery. Heated nebulizers are used to humidify the air. Equipment for caring for and cleaning a tracheostomy tube should be available, as well as suction, tissues, and a pencil and paper or slate. Some surgeons do not insert a tracheostomy tube because the method of suturing keeps the wound open. If a

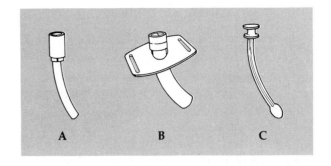

Figure 15-13
Laryngectomy tube. **A,** Inner cannula. **B,** Outer cannula. **C,** Obturator.

tube is inserted, it is a laryngeal (laryngectomy) tube (Figure 15-13), which is slightly larger in diameter and shorter than the ordinary tracheostomy. If a tube is inserted, an extra sterile set the same size as the one inserted should be available at the bedside for emergency use if the first tube comes out.

The most important function of the nurse is to keep the airway clear. The nurse must be available to wipe or suction secretions when the patient coughs to prevent aspiration. In the beginning, suctioning may be necessary as often as every 5 minutes. The suction catheter should not be inserted more than the length of the tube, and if secretions cannot be removed, the physician should be notified. Efforts should be made to prevent wound infection by maintaining aseptic technique. Oxygen may be administered for 1 or 2 days.

The character of respirations must be observed for any increase in rate, wheezing, or crowing sounds, indicating airway obstruction. Secretions may be tinged with blood for the first 1 or 2 days, but any continued blood may be from internal hemorrhage and should be reported. Meticulous mouth care with an antiseptic mouthwash should be given frequently. If intravenous fluids are given, they should not be placed in the arm that the patient uses for writing, if possible. The patient may not be allowed anything by mouth for a week. Feedings are given by means of a gastric tube passed through the patient's nose. When the patient is allowed food by mouth, it should be soft until healing is complete. Some surgeons do not order tube feedings but allow patients to eat soft food and drink liquids if they feel well enough. A patient with a laryngectomy usually is most comfortable in a 45-degree Fowler's position, which makes breathing easier. The lips should be kept moist with cold cream, and crusts should not be allowed to form about the nares.

As patients improve they should be taught how to care for their own tracheostomy, and if they are unable to do so, some member of the family should be taught. When a tube is used, it may be left in place for appoximately 6 weeks. As soon as the neck wounds have healed, the therapist may begin speech training. Esophageal speech has proved to be the most successful means of communication after a laryngectomy. This is taught at special speech clinics in larger cities. If esophageal speech cannot be learned, a vibrator or an electronic artificial larynx can be used. Much assistance can be obtained from local chapters of the American Cancer Society, Inc., including information on a Lost Cord Club or a New Voice Club. Most patients with total laryngectomies are able to return to normal roles in life. However, they should be advised against occupational hazards such as dust and fumes and should seek to protect themselves against respiratory tract infections.

Lung Cancer

The incidence of malignant tumors (carcinoma) of the lung has been increasing. It is more common in men than in women, although the incidence in women is steadily climbing. Tumors may result from metastasis from somewhere else in the body or may appear as primary tumors. Depending on the location and size of the tumor, the patient may or may not experience symptoms. A cough and dyspnea usually are the only signs, and the tumors may have been present for some time before detected. Immediate treatment is essential, and surgical removal of the cancerous part usually is indicated. The removal of one or more lobes of the affected lung or the entire lung depends on the location and extent of tumor growth. X-ray therapy and chemotherapy also are used.

CHEST SURGERY

Surgery of the chest is performed to cure or to relieve disease conditions such as bronchiectasis, lung abscess, lung cancer, cysts, and benign tumors. Open heart surgery also involves opening the chest. The kind of operative procedure used depends on the purpose for which it is to be done. An exploratory thoracotomy is done to confirm a diagnosis of lung or chest disease. Often a biopsy is done and the chest is closed, with the possibility

of future operations to treat the disease process. In some conditions only a small portion of lung tissue may be removed; this procedure is called segmental resection of the lung. Removal of an entire lobe of one lung is a **lobectomy**, whereas removal of an entire lung is a **pneumonectomy** (Figure 15-14). The latter is done most frequently for treatment of bronchogenic carcinoma. Many patients will be cared for in intensive care units or in cardiopulmonary units immediately following surgery.

Assessment and Intervention

Patients being considered for a lobectomy or pneumonectomy are screened carefully by the surgeon, because not all patients are eligible for this kind of surgery. Many patients will be seen in the surgeon's office, and tests and examinations will be performed on an outpatient basis. Some patients will be admitted to the hospital for their preoperative preparation, which is both psychologic and physical. Patients may have been chronically ill for a long time, affecting their physical conditions. Emotional reactions to the proposed surgery may be affected by poor physical status. While efforts are being directed toward improving the physical condition, efforts should be made to remove the patient's fears through reassurance. The nurse should encourage the patient to communicate feelings and should report any special problems to the physician. During this period efforts are made toward correcting any condition that might affect the outcome of surgery.

Preoperative preparation

The patient should know that several examinations and tests will be performed. A bronchoscopic examination, electrocardiogram, x-ray examination of the chest, and sputum examination may be performed. Tests of pulmonary function and a number of blood tests may be done. Most patients receive blood transfusions before surgery, and antibiotic drugs are administered. Drugs by nebulization also may be ordered. Mouth hygiene is extremely important, and the nurse should ascertain that the teeth are brushed after each meal, in the morning, and at bedtime. Postural drainage is done several times daily, first when the patient is awakened in the morning and last at bedtime. The patient should be encouraged to cough deeply and to expectorate as much mucus as possible during postural drainage. The diet should be nourishing, and the patient should be weighed daily. Unless contraindicated, the pa-

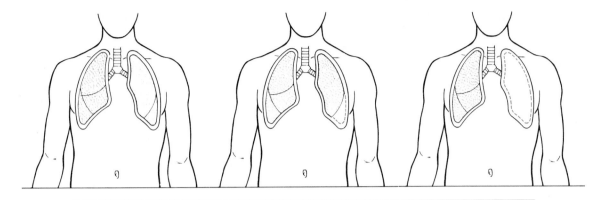

Figure 15-14

Lobectomy and pneumonectomy. **A**, Normal lung. **B**, Lobectomy with lower lobe of left lung removed. **C**, Pneumonectomy with entire left lung removed.

tient should be ambulatory during the preoperative preparation to maintain muscle tone. An explanation concerning the nursing procedures to be carried out after surgery should be given to the patient. The patient should be told that he or she will be admitted to the intensive care unit for 1 to 2 days postoperatively, that there may be pain because the nerves between the ribs have been cut, that blood and other fluids will be received, that oxygen will be administered, and that vital signs will be checked frequently for several hours. If a chest catheter will be used after surgery, the patient should be told that it will drain the fluid and air that normally accumulate after chest surgery. The patient should be taught incentive spirometry with coughing and deep breathing techniques and how to do arm and shoulder exercises.

Postoperative preparation

The intensive care unit is prepared for the patient's return from surgery and equipped for any emergency that might arise. Oxygen, ventilators, monitors, infusion pumps, a thoracentesis tray, a tracheotomy tray and tubes, chest drainage tubes, and closed drainage systems are needed. A wall suction source with catheters for oral and nasal suctioning also may be required.

After surgery, the blood pressure, pulse, and respiration rates are checked every 15 minutes for 3 hours, and then every 30 minutes until ordered otherwise by the surgeon. Oxygen is administered by a mechanical ventilator, nasal cannula, or mask for as long as necessary. When the patient returns to his or her room, blood may be administered intravenously, to be followed by intravenous fluids. Because a reduction in lung capacity requires a period of physiologic adjustment, fluids

should not be allowed to drip at a rate faster than 50 or 60 drops per minute, unless ordered by the surgeon. This procedure will avoid overloading the circulation and precipitating pulmonary edema and is especially important in older patients. Fluids by mouth are allowed early in the postoperative period. If the patient has a chest tube in place, the nurse must be familiar with the operation of the closed chest drainage system.

When the patient is conscious and the vital signs have stabilized, the head of the bed may be elevated to an angle of approximately 30 to 45 degrees. Orders concerning the positioning of the patient should be received. The patient with a pneumonectomy usually is turned every hour from the back to the affected side and should never be completely turned to the unoperated side. This allows the fluid left in the space to consolidate and prevents the remaining lung and the heart from shifting toward the operative side (mediastinal shift). The patient with a lobectomy may be turned to either side, and the patient with a segmental resection usually is not turned onto the affected side unless this position is ordered by the surgeon.

Medication for pain will be needed for several days and must be planned for the individual patient. Coughing and incentive spirometry will be painful, and better cooperation will be secured from the patient if pain-relieving medication is administered before he or she is instructed to cough. Coughing must be deep enough to bring up secretions, and the nurse should splint the chest when the patient coughs. Both the anterior and the posterior side of the chest must be splinted. The nurse's forearms or palms of the hands or a towel placed around the chest and held tightly may be employed. If the mucus is thick and the patient has difficulty bringing it up, steam inhalations or aerosol therapy may be ordered. If efforts to cough and bring up mucus fail, the surgeon should be notified.

Exercises are begun early in the postoperative period to facilitate lung ventilation and to maintain normal muscle tension in the shoulder and the trunk. At first the exercises are performed passively by the nurse, but as soon as the patient is ambulatory or able to sit on the side of the bed and stand, they are performed actively by the patient. The physical therapist will assist with exercises, but in the absence of the physical therapist, the nurse must be able to teach and to help the patient with exercises.

The nurse must be constantly on the alert for signs indicating serious complications. Cyanosis, dyspnea, and acute chest pain may foretell atelectasis and should be reported immediately. The nurse must check the apex beat of the heart and note its location; any change should be reported. Pallor, an increase in the pulse rate, and any significant drop in blood pressure may indicate internal hemorrhage. Dressings should be checked frequently for the presence of bright red blood, which may indicate external hemorrhage.

Early ambulation of the patient with a lobectomy may begin the first or second postoperative day. The patient is allowed first to sit on the side of the bed or to stand beside the bed. Patients undergoing a pneumonectomy may not be allowed out of bed until later. Ambulation depends on the individual patient and progress made.

CHEST WOUNDS

Injuries to the chest are serious surgical emergencies and may involve the thoracic cage, pleura, lungs, heart, diaphragm, and abdominal organs. The care of the patient will be determined by the extent of the injury. Patients with chest wounds are often apprehensive, and the nurse should explain procedures done to or with the patient. Patients with fractured ribs usually have considerable pain, and the administration of a sedative before turning or moving the patient is advisable. Multiple adjacent rib fractures can result in a free-floating segment of the rib cage (flail chest). When this occurs, the free segment loses continuity with the rest of the chest wall and moves paradoxically. On inspiration, when the rest of the rib cage is moving outward, the flail segment sinks inward.

On expiration, when the rib cage is moving inward, the flail segment bulges outward. Because pressure within the chest is decreased as a result of this paradoxical movement, movement of air is decreased. Previously, all patients with flail chest were treated with mechanical ventilation. Now, mechanical ventilation is avoided unless absolutely necessary. Patients are given analgesics to help decrease pain and to facilitate deep breathing and coughing. The patient should be encouraged to cough and breathe deeply and should be ambulatory as soon as his or her condition permits.

Penetrating wounds may be caused by any foreign object. Knife and bullet wounds may penetrate the lungs, resulting in an air leak. When this occurs, the air may compress the lung, causing pneumothorax, or bleeding into the pleural cavity may occur, causing the lung to collapse. Both are serious because they may lead to cardiac or respiratory arrest unless immediate emergency treatment is given. The patient should be observed for dyspnea, and the blood pressure, pulse, and respiratory rates should be checked at frequent intervals. Oxygen may be administered, and a thoracentesis may be done with a catheter inserted and connected to closed drainage to remove air and blood. If the injury is such that surgical repair is necessary, a thoracotomy is performed at a later time. An antibiotic and tetanus toxoid injection generally is administered. In cases in which respiration is severely compromised, a tracheotomy may be required to provide for adequate ventilation.

HEALTH, SOCIAL ASPECTS, AND REHABILITATION

Through public health education and the use of chemotherapeutic agents, the incidence of many infectious respiratory diseases has been reduced and serious complications avoided. However, the increasing number of patients with AIDS needing preventive and acute care for respiratory problems and the potential for respiratory complications in patients with trauma or prolonged illness make respiratory assessment and intervention important in the care of these individuals. When caring for patients with infection, nurses should realize the importance of self-protection and protecting other patients and workers. Nurses should use every opportunity to emphasize to patients with respiratory disease the importance of avoiding acute infections. In addition, nurses who have acute respiratory tract infections should isolate themselves from individuals at risk.

Many patients are handicapped socially, vocationally, and emotionally because of respiratory diseases. When severe dyspnea is present, it interferes with work capacity, and the individual may be unemployable. Persons with copious bronchial secretions and sputum may become self-conscious, and they may be isolated socially because others may fear they have a communicable disease. The individual then may withdraw from society, sometimes becoming preoccupied with personal health problems. Prolonged unemployment and chronic illness bring financial worries to the patient and family. Providing emotional support and encouragement and assisting with identification of community supports will help patients adjust to their illnesses.

Persons with certain types of respiratory conditions, such as the patient with a laryngectomy, lobectomy, or pneumonectomy, may need special rehabilitation services. Speech training may be needed to enable the individual to assume a normal position in society. Rehabilitation of this type may include reeducation and training for occupations requiring less expenditure of energy for persons with reduced vital capacity. The necessity to provide leisure-time activities and recreational pursuits for persons who will not be able to work is another aspect of rehabilitation. The nurse should be familiar with the community agencies offering services that assist individuals in returning to independent, productive lives.

NURSING CARE PLAN
Patient with Pneumonia

The patient is a 61-year-old male who comes to the emergency department with a complaint of shortness of breath, chills, fatigue, and "feeling terrible." He states that he has not been well for 1 week with loss of appetite, muscle aches, and feeling "very drawn."

Denies COPD, cardiac disease, hypertension, and diabetes mellitus.
Has a history of smoking one pack per day (PPD) of cigarettes since the age of 13 (48-year smoking history).
Denies alcohol abuse.
Has good health behaviors as evidenced by yearly physicals.
Involved in physical sports until 4 years ago; now his activity level is sedentary.

Married 40 years, supportive caring wife.
Three adult daughters, all with young children, live locally and visit often.
Full-time truck driver now (retired as a limosine driver).
Practicing Catholic religion.
Active social life, with many friends.
Owns own home.
Insured through private medical insurance.
Hobbies: gardening and fixing cars.

Alert and oriented × 3 (time, place, and person).
Febrile to 101-103.
Respiratory: Bilateral scattered rales throughout entire lung fields. Respirations 24 to 26, regular but labored. Some use of accessory muscles. Painful cough with small amount of sputum (thick, tenacious, yellowish mucoid). Oxygen at 3 L.
Abdominal: Soft nontender, nondistended abdomen with bowel sounds heard in all four quadrants. Bowel movement on day of admission.
Skin: Clean and intact. No broken skin areas, no pressure sores, and no rashes.
Cardiovascular: Pulse 86 to 90, regular. PMI heard at apex. No murmurs, nor jugular distension. Brachial, radial, femoral, popiteal and pedal pulses heard bilaterally.

WBC 18,000. Hgb 12.2. Hct 39. Electrolytes WNL.
PPD planted right forearm.
Sputum sent for culture and acid fast bacillus (AFB).
Urinalysis WNL.
Chest x-ray consistent with pneumonia bil lower lobes.

IV—D5 1/2 N/S at 100 ml per hour
Ancef 1 g in 50 ml D5W over 20 minutes every 6 hours.
Tylenol 1 to 2 tabs prn for discomfort

Continued on next page.

NURSING DIAGNOSIS

Ineffective airway clearance related to secretions as evidenced by abnormal
breath sounds (rales) and labored breathing.

Expected patient outcomes	Nursing interventions	Evaluation for expected outcomes
The patient will breathe effectively and his airway will remain patent as evidenced by normal breath sounds, normal respiratory rate, rhythm, and depth. His fluid intake will be 2000 to 3000 ml per 24 hours.	Monitor position for maximal aeration of lungs (90-degree Fowler's). Encourage frequent position changes every 2 hours when awake. Monitor vital signs every 4 hours, more frequently if abnormal. Ascultate lungs every shift. Compare findings and document. Teach effective coughing and deep breathing exercises. Demonstrate effective splinting when coughing or straining. Liquid diet only. Force fluids every 2 hours when awake. Patient likes fruit juices and ginger ale without ice. Explain rationale for increased liquids. Mouth care to combat dryness of oxygen and secretions. Monitor IV site for patency and infiltration. Regulate IV to 100 ml per hour. Encourage sputum expectoration. Provide tissues and paper bag for hygenic disposal.	Patient's airway will remain clear and allow for adequate ventilation. He will demostrate an effective cough, and change his position frequently. Vital signs will return to normal. Respiratory assessment will have absence of rales, rhonchi, wheezes, or stridor. Intake will be approximately 1000 ml per shift, (combined po and IV).

NURSING DIAGNOSIS

Anxiety related to respiratory difficulties.

Expected patient outcomes	Nursing interventions	Evaluation for expected outcomes
Will experience decreased anxiety, and be able to discuss feelings related to health status and shortness of breath.	Teach relaxation techniques. Use a caring approach; provide time to actively listen. Encourage participation in care as tolerated. Discuss his physical feelings and relate these to his compromised lung status. Assist him to compare and contrast behaviors of progress.	The patient will show decreased anxiety through facial expressions and body language. He will begin to participate in his own care. He will discuss his fears and feelings and identify behaviors of progress.

NURSING DIAGNOSIS

Activity intolerance related to imbalance between oxygen supply and demand,
as evidenced by shortness of breath (SOB) and increased respiratory rate with activity.

Expected patient outcomes	Nursing interventions	Evaluation for expected outcomes
The patient will identify controllable factors that cause fatigue and will demonstrate skill in conserving energy. He will receive adequate rest while in the hospital.	Provide environment conducive to rest. Turn down lights when resting. Monitor for noise level. Keep room temperature at 68° to 70° F. Limit visitors to short visits. Explain rationale.	The patient will list factors that cause fatigue and show increasing tolerance with activity level after periods of rest.

Expected patient outcomes	Nursing interventions	Evaluation for expected outcomes
	Plan nursing care to include uninterrupted rest periods. Encourage patient to help plan activity progression. Accompany patient if short of breath to bathroom while fatigued. Monitor physiologic responses to increased activity (vital signs).	He will become proficient in conserving energy while performing activities of daily living (ADLs) and have vital signs that remain within normal parameters.

NURSING DIAGNOSIS

Knowledge deficit related to course of illness and health risk
behaviors (smoking) as evidenced by verbal questioning.

Expected patient outcomes	Nursing interventions	Evaluation for expected outcomes
The patient will acquire knowledge related to illness, hospitalization, and postdischarge behaviors and potential risk behaviors.	Explain the rationale for rest, increased fluids, and activity monitoring. Discuss behaviors that suggest need for modification of ADL's. Initiate discussion on smoking. Ask if patient motivated to stop smoking. Discuss any previous attempts to quit and identify the rationale for previous failures. Cite statistics related to risks of smoking, including cardiovascular and pulmonary problems. Recommend self-help groups for support.	The patient will: State factors that contributed to his illness. Identify behaviors of progress and discuss the rationale for rest, increased fluids, and ADL monitoring. Participate in the decision with his physician of returning to work. Identify the risks involved in smoking, and cite his motivational level to quit. Plan to attend a self-help smoking cessation group.

REFERENCES AND ADDITIONAL READINGS

1. Bolton ME: Hyperbaric oxygen therapy, Am J Nurs 81:1199–1201, 1981.
2. Crowley LV: Introduction to human disease, ed 2, Boston, 1988, Jones & Bartlett.
3. Dossey BM, Guzzetta CE, and Kenner CV: Essentials of critical care nursing: body–mind–spirit, Philadelphia, 1990, JB Lippincott Co.
4. Fuchs P: Streamlining your suctioning techniques. I. Nasotracheal suctioning, Nurs 84 14(5):55, 1984.
5. Fuchs P: Streamlining your suctioning techniques. II. Endotracheal suctioning, Nurs 84 14(7):46, 1984.
6. Fuchs P: Streamlining your suctioning techniques. III. Tracheostomy suctioning, Nurs 84 14(7):39, 1984.
7. Malasanos L, Barkauskas V, and Stoltenberg-Allen K: Health assessment, ed 4, St Louis, 1990, The CV Mosby Co.
8. Mapp CS: Trach care: are you aware of all the dangers? Nurs 88 18(7):34–43, 1988.
9. Meredith T and Acierno LJ: Pulmonary complications of acquired immunodeficiency syndrome, Heart Lung 17:173–178, 1988.
10. Porth CM: Pathophysiology: concepts of altered health states, ed 3, Philadelphia, 1990, JB Lippincott Co.
11. Purtilo DT and Purtilo RB: A survey of human diseases, ed 2, Boston, 1989, Little, Brown & Company.
12. Smith S: High-frequency jet ventilation in the treatment of idiopathic pulmonary fibrosis complicating ARDS: a nursing challenge, Crit Care Nurs Q 11(3):29–35, 1988.
13. Sodbinow E: AANA Journal course: advanced scientific concepts—update for nurse anesthetists, pulmonary pharmacology: bronchodilators. AANA J 56:542–551, 1988.
14. Stevens SS and Becker KL: How to perform picture-perfect respiratory assessment, Nurs 88 18(1):57–63, 1988.
15. Thompson JM and others: Clinical nursing, St Louis, 1986, The CV Mosby Co.
16. Wells PW and Meghdadpour S: Research yields new clues to cystic fibrosis, MCN 13:187–190, 1988.
17. West JB: Respiratory physiology: the essentials, ed 4, Baltimore, 1990, Williams & Wilkins.
18. Zschoche DA, ed: Mosby's comprehensive review of critical care, St Louis, 1986, The CV Mosby Co.

CHAPTER

16

PROBLEMS AFFECTING
Circulation

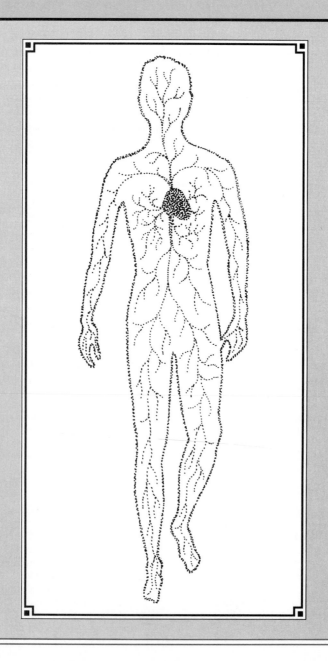

aneurysm
angina pectoris
angioplasty
arteriosclerosis
ascites
atherosclerosis
atrial fibrillation
bacterial endocarditis
cardiac output
cardiogenic shock
central venous pressure
cholesterol
defibrillation
depolarization
diuretic
dysrhythmia
electrocardiogram
embolectomy
hypertension
ischemic heart disease
isoenzyme
lumen
lymphangitis
myocardial infarction
occlusion
oscilloscope
pacemaker
plaques
pulmonary edema
Purkinje's fibers
risk factor
sinoatrial node
sinus bradycardia
sinus tachycardia
stenosis
thrombophlebitis
varicosities
ventricular fibrillation
ventricular tachycardia

1. Describe the normal flow of blood through the heart and circulatory system, and trace the normal electric conduction through the heart.

2. Identify common cardiac dysrhythmias and their effect on cardiac output.

3. List at least three precautions the nurse should teach to patients with permanent pacemakers.

4. Demonstrate the preparation of patients for cardiac diagnostic tests and identify nursing interventions after tests.

5. Compare nursing assessment and interventions indicated for a patient with acute pulmonary edema with those indicated for a patient with congestive heart failure.

6. Compare the nursing assessment and interventions indicated for a patient with angina pectoris with those indicated for a patient convalescing from a myocardial infarction.

7. Describe those items that should be included in a patient education program on hypertension.

8. Identify nursing assessment and interventions related to the postoperative care of a patient with a vein ligation and stripping.

9. Describe nursing responsibilities related to the preoperative and postoperative phases for a patient undergoing cardiac surgery.

10. Demonstrate skills to appropriately assess a patient with a cardiovascular problem.

11. List steps of basic cardiac life support.

12. Describe the sequence of events to care for a patient with an obstructed airway.

CARDIOVASCULAR STRUCTURE AND FUNCTION

Cardiac Anatomy

The heart, a hollow muscular organ, pumps blood throughout the cardiovascular system. It is located behind the sternum, within the mediastinum between the lungs and above the diaphragm. The base of the heart is located just below the second rib. The lower part of the heart, the apex, is pointed downward and to the left. The heart is protected anteriorly by the rib cage and sternum and posteriorly by the rib cage and vertebral column.

Heart chambers

The heart is made up of four chambers (Figure 16-1). The upper chambers are the *right* and *left atrium*. The lower chambers, the *right* and *left ventricles*, are thick muscle-walled chambers. The right and left side of the heart are separated by a *septum*.

The right atrium receives venous blood from all body tissues except the lung. The right ventricle pumps venous blood through the pulmonary artery to the lungs, where carbon dioxide is exchanged for oxygen. Oxygenated blood from the lungs is received in the left atrium. The left ventricle pumps blood through the aorta to all parts of the body.

Heart muscle

There are three distinct layers of heart muscle. The outer layer, the *epicardium*, is a thin transparent layer and frequently is infiltrated with fat. The *myocardium*, the middle layer, consists of striated cardiac muscle fibers that permit the heart to contract. The inner layer of heart muscle, the *endocardium*, is a thin layer of endothelial tissue that lines the inner heart cavity and covers the valves of the heart and the chordae tendineae, which are tendons that hold the cardiac valves open. The endocardium is continuous with the inner lining of the vessels. Inflammation of the endocardium is called *endocarditis* and may be caused by a microorganism. These microorganisms include bacteria, fungi, rickettsiae, and rarely viruses and parasites.

The heart is surrounded by a membranous sac called the *pericardium*. The pericardium consists of an external fibrous layer and an internal serous layer that adheres to the heart and the epicardium. Pericardial fluid is found between the two pericardial layers. This serous fluid lubricates the two layers with each heartbeat. Inflammation of the pericardium is called *pericarditis*. A frequent

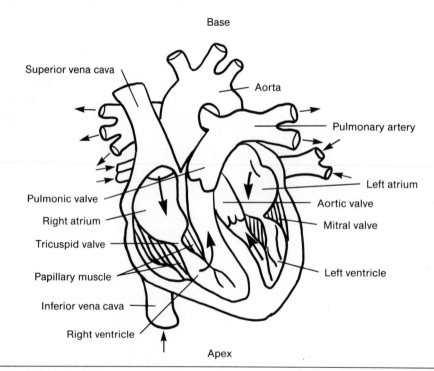

Figure 16-1
Blood flow through heart.

cause is open heart surgery. Other causes are uremia, myocardial infarction, viral or bacterial infections, tumors, anticoagulants, or trauma.[10]

Heart valves

The forward flow of blood through the heart is controlled by a series of one-way valves that prevent backflow within the heart. Heart valves are nonmuscular tissue. The *tricuspid valve* between the right atrium and ventricle and the *mitral valve* between the left atrium and ventricle are often called atrioventricular valves because they direct the blood flow between the atria and ventricles. The valve between the right ventricle and pulmonary artery is the pulmonic valve, and the aortic valve is between the left ventricle and aorta. These valves are called *semilunar valves.*

The heart, like other organ systems, has its own blood supply. The coronary arteries are the first branches from the aorta. They surround the heart and provide blood to all portions of the myocardium and the heart's electrical conduction system. Coronary veins return deoxygenated blood to the right atrium.

Vascular System

Blood vessels

Blood vessels are a network of arteries, arterioles, capillaries, venules, and veins that circulate blood to and from the heart. This network is divided into the *systemic circulation* and the *pulmonary circulation.* The circulatory system transports nutrients and oxygen to body cells and carries waste products to organs of the body to be eliminated. All systemic arteries branch from the aorta. Blood in veins of the systemic circulation flows into the *superior* or *inferior vena cava,* which then flows into the right atrium.

Pulmonary circulation carries blood from the right ventricle to the lungs and back to the left atrium. The right and left pulmonary arteries arise from the right ventricle and immediately subdivide into a series of short branches, ending in capillaries that encircle the lung air sacs (alveoli), pick up oxygen, and release the waste product carbon dioxide. The capillaries gradually come together to form pulmonary veins that carry oxygenated blood from the lungs to the left atrium.

Blood and blood components

Blood volume makes up about 8% of a person's total body weight. This percentage varies according to weight, sex, age, altitude, environmental temperature, nutrition, and pregnancy.[10] During a normal pregnancy the blood volume changes to approximately 50% over nonpregnant levels.[4,7] About 40% of the blood is composed of circulating cells, and the other 60% is plasma.[22] Red blood cells transport hemoglobin, which has the unique property of binding and releasing oxygen. The percentage of red blood cells is measured as a hematocrit value. White blood cells make up about 1% of the circulating blood volume and are the body's first enzymes and chemicals needed for the inflammation process and coagulation of blood. Plasma, which is similar to tissue (interstitial) fluid but contains 7% proteins, contributes to cardiovascular function by maintaining blood volume, blood viscosity, and osmotic pressure.

Lymphatic Circulation

Lymphatic fluid is excess tissue (interstitial) fluid that has accumulated around body cells. Lymphatic drainage maintains equilibrium of the fluid surrounding body cells. Lymphatic vessels begin as tiny lymphatic capillaries similar to blood capillaries. These unite and form large vessels that empty into veins. Lymph moves as a result of skeletal muscle contraction, negative intrathoracic pressure, and the suction effect of blood flow in the veins. Distributed along the lymphatic vessel system are small round bodies, lymph nodes, that serve as filters to remove proteins. Lymph node function is related to the immune system (see Chapter 2). The lymphatic fluid flow depends on venous pressure and the condition of venous vessels. Venous vessel obstruction or elevated venous pressure can affect interstitial fluid volume and the dynamics of capillary exchange.

Cardiac Cycle

Blood circulating throughout the cardiovascular system is regulated by the cardiac cycle, which coordinates activities of the heart. The cardiac cycle consists of two phases, *systole (contraction)* and *diastole (relaxation).* The cardiac cycle is less than 0.8 seconds long and includes systole, when atrial and ventricular muscular contractions are propelling blood forward, and diastole, when the heart muscle relaxes and is refilled with blood.

Heart sounds

S_1, S_2, S_3, and S_4 are the four heart sounds produced by contraction and relaxation of the heart muscle and closure of the heart valves. S_1 and S_2 are normally heard. S_3 and S_4 are considered ab-

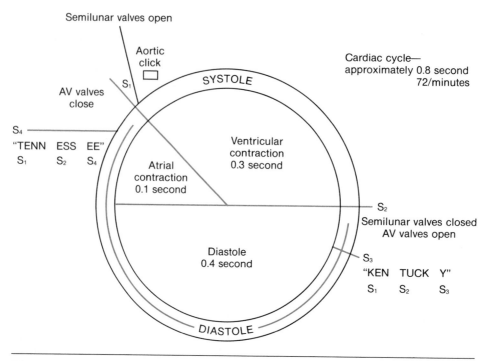

Figure 16-2
Heart sounds and cardiac cycle.

normal heart sounds unless proven otherwise.

The first heart sound, S_1, corresponds to the onset of ventricular contraction and is associated with closure of the mitral and the tricuspid valves. The second heart sound, S_2, (Figure 16-2) occurs at the end of ventricular contraction and coincides with the onset of ventricular diastole. S_3, if present, occurs early in diastole, just after the S_2.

The S_3 sound results from vibrations produced by rapid ventricular filling, which is transmitted by the ventricular muscle. A third heart sound is not an unusual finding in children and young adults, but suggests altered cardiac function such as chronic heart failure in adults.

The fourth heart sound, S_4, occurs during ventricular diastole after atrial contraction and immediately before S_1. The S_4 sound results because the ventricle is dilated but resistant to filling. This is common in patients with **hypertension.**

Normal electrical cardiac conduction

The heart has its own electric conduction system that initiates the cardiac cycle and maintains the regularity of the cycle (Figure 16-3). The conduction system is composed of the *sinus node, atrioventricular (AV) junctional tissue, the bundle of His,* and the *His-Purkinje system.* The sinus node, located near the junction of the superior vena cava and right atrium, initiates the electrical impulse. The impulse spreads over both atria, resulting in contraction. Simultaneously the impulse activates the AV node. The AV node is situated in the right atrium, near the coronary sinus and above the tricuspid valve. The cells organize in a parallel manner before entering into the bundle of His. The AV node delays the electrical impulse transmission from the atria to the ventricles to permit maximum filling of the right and left ventricles before the electrical impulse reaches them. After passing through the AV node the electrical impulse stimulates the bundle of His, which divides into the right and left bundle branches. It then subdivides further into the **Purkinje's fibers,** causing the ventricles to contract. The electrical conduction system is extremely complex and is located under the endocardial surface of the heart. That is why the conduction system is highly susceptible to disease and lack of blood supply.

Neurohumoral Controls of the Heart

Many physiologic entities can control the heart. Some of these controls are the *sympathetic* (stim-

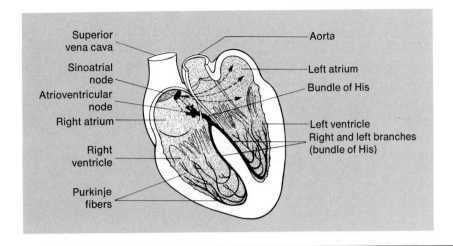

Figure 16-3
Conduction system of heart.

ulating) and *parasympathetic* (inhibitory) *nervous systems.*

Alpha-, beta₁-, and beta₂-adrenergic receptors

Stimulation of alpha-receptors raises blood pressure by constricting peripheral vascular arterioles; stimulation of beta₁-receptors affects the conduction system; stimulation of beta₂-receptors causes peripheral vasodilation and relaxation of constricted bronchial muscles.

Baroreceptors

Baroreceptors are located in the carotid sinus and affect heart rate by monitoring blood pressure.

Chemoreceptors

Chemoreceptors respond to oxygen deficiencies or increased carbon dioxide levels.

Temperature

An increase in body temperature stimulates the AV node to discharge impulses faster. Conversely, a lowered body temperature decreases the heart rate.

Electrolytes and hormones

Epinephrine stimulates the sympathetic nervous system, causing the heart rate to increase. Excess potassium within the heart muscle causes the heart to become dilated and flaccid, decreasing the heart rate. Also, excess potassium can impede conduction of electrical impulses from the atria to the ventricles. Low-potassium levels may increase the automaticity of the heart muscle, and ectopic beats may occur.

NURSING ASSESSMENT OF THE PATIENT WITH A CARDIOVASCULAR PROBLEM

Nursing assessment begins with a comprehensive history of the patient's problem. The review of seven dimensions of a patient problem assures that no detail of the problem is overlooked. The seven dimensions include the following: body location, quality, quantity, chronology, setting, aggravating/alleviating factors, and associated symptoms.

When assessing the cardiovascular system it is also important to identify risk factors that, if present, indicate an increased chance of developing a cardiovascular problem. **Risk factors** are conditions that have been identified through research as contributing to cardiovascular problems (Table 16-1).

After obtaining the patient's cardiovascular history, the nurse conducts a systematic physical examination. The objective of this physical examination is to gain information about the muscular movement of the patient's heart. The four techniques of physical assessment are *inspection*, *palpation*, *percussion*, and *auscultation*. The physical assessment is performed with the patient in the following positions: sitting, supine, and lying on the left side.

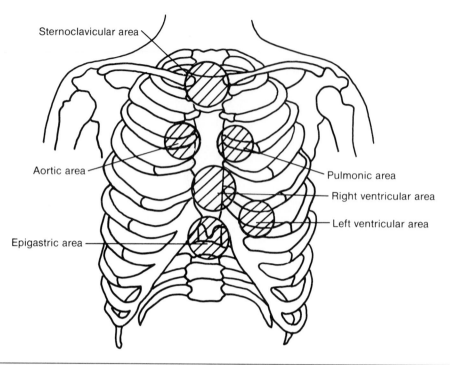

Sternoclavicular area

Aortic area

Epigastric area

Pulmonic area

Right ventricular area

Left ventricular area

Figure 16-4

Areas of inspection and palpation for cardiac assessment.

Table 16-1

Cardiac Risk Factors	
Unavoidable	**Avoidable**
Increasing age	Hyperlipidemia
Gender (men >	Hypertension
women)	Obesity
Family history of heart	Cigarette smoking
disease	Physical inactivity
Glucose intolerance	Stress
	Use of oral contraceptives
	in women

Inspection

Inspection includes visual assessment of the shape of the patient's chest and assessment of the pericardium for pulsations (Figure 16-4).

Normally, no pulsation will be visible unless the patient is very thin, in which case a slight pulsation may be detected. The location of an abnormal pulsation requires further assessment.

Palpation

Palpation is used to detect pulsation or vibration (thrills) that may not have been identified with inspection or to further assess pulsations identified during inspection. The same areas of the pericardium are assessed (Figure 16-4). The best palpation technique to detect vibrations is to use the palmar bases of the fingers of the right hand to locate a vibration and then to use the pads of the middle and index fingers to make finer assessments. Detection of vibrations suggests the presence of a pathologic condition and requires further assessment. Special attention should be given to locating the point of maximum impulse (PMI). This is the most lateral pulsation of the left ventricle detected over the apex of the heart. Normally the apical impulse is located 3 to 3.5 inches (approximately 7.5 to 9 cm) from the midsternal line. A displaced apical impulse or one that has abnormal vibration indicates cardiovascular disease. An abnormal vibration is classified as a *lift* if it can be seen at more than .08 inch (2 cm) to the left of the chest wall; a *heave* is an impulse whose force pushes out against the palpating hand.

Percussion

Percussion is an assessment technique that produces sound by tapping a body part, thus indicating the size, density, and location of an underlying structure. Percussion may be used to

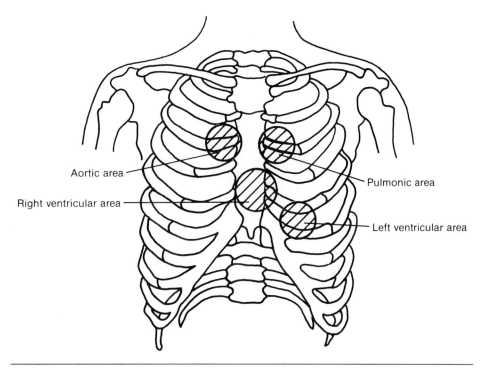

Figure 16-5
Areas of cardiac auscultation.

identify cardiac borders; however, x-ray examination and fluoroscopy are more accurate diagnostic measures. Normally there are midsternal shifts to the left in pregnant women and patients with liver cirrhosis.

Auscultation

Auscultation is the perception and interpretation of sound through a stethoscope (Figure 16-5). It is the most difficult technique because the ear must be trained to identify normal sounds and recognize specific characteristics of abnormal sounds. Variations in sounds are described by the sound, location, time, intensity, and pitch. Specific heart sounds include the vibrations produced from all cardiac events and are influenced by the viscosity and velocity of blood, elasticity of the heart valves, and distention of the cardiac chambers. Normally the heart has two distinct sounds, S_1 and S_2. Additional sounds, S_3 and S_4, may be present, as may heart murmurs (Table 16-2).

The nurse listens systematically in all areas of the heart, first with the diaphragm and then with the bell of the stethoscope. The diaphragm picks up high-pitched sounds and the bell low-pitched sounds. It is vital for the nurse to have confidence in hearing S_1 and S_2 before expecting to identify

S_3, S_4, or murmurs. Table 16-2 outlines the characteristics of the four heart sounds.

Murmurs are vascular sounds that produce vibrations within the heart or great blood vessels (i.e., aorta, pulmonary vein) and are most commonly associated with **stenosis** or regurgitation. Murmurs may be considered a normal finding if no other signs or symptoms of cardiovascular disease are found.

The heart sounds that may be heard are an ejection click (the opening of pulmonic and aortic valves), an opening snap (opening of the mitral and tricuspid valves), or the splitting of either S_1 or S_2 (single sound perceived as two sounds). Splitting may be physiologic (occurring with respirations) or pathologic (related to a cardiovascular problem).

Blood Pressure

Assessment of the cardiovascular system also includes measurement of blood pressure. Systolic blood pressure, the top reading of the blood pressure measurement, measures stroke volume and pressure exerted against the interior walls of the aorta, whereas diastolic blood pressure, the bottom number of the blood pressure measurement indicates the resistance of the blood vessels. To

Table 16-2

Characteristics of the Four Heart Sounds				
	S₁	S₂	S₃	S₄
Sound	Lubb	Dubb	Ken–tuck—y S₁, S₂, S₃	Tenn–ess–ee S₁, S₂, S₄
Location	Mitral tricus- pid valve	Aortic-pulmonic area	Apex	Medial to apex
Time	Systolic; longer than S₂	Diastolic; shorter than S₁	Early diastole	Late diastole, pre- systole
Intensity	Louder at apex	Louder at base	Dull	Higher than S₃
Pitch	Low	Higher than S₁	Low pitch	Duller than crisp S₁
Clinical inter- pretation	Normal	Normal	Normal in children or after exercise, may be sign of conges- tive heart failure or mitral regurgitation	Normally not heard; associated with hypertension, aor- tic or pulmonic stenosis

Korotkoff Sounds	
Phase	Description
1	Beginning of faint sound (systolic blood pressure)
2	Swishing sound
3	Loud, crisp sound
4	Cessation of sound (diastolic blood pressure)

Table 16-3

Arterial Pulse Assessment		
	Normal	Clinical alteration
Rate	60-100	<60, good physical condition, or myocardial damage >100, response to exercise, anxiety, smoking, myocardial infarction
Rhythm	Regular	Irregular, cardiac disease
Quality	Strong	Weakened, congestive heart failure, aortic stenosis, shock sounding, fever, anemia, hy- perthyroidism, atherosclerosis Bruit—abnormal swishing sound of blood flowing through partially occluded vessel

ensure an accurate reading, the blood pressure cuff must fit adequately around the patient's arm. Because blood pressure sounds are low pitched they are best heard with the bell of the stetho- scope. The audible vibrations within an artery are called *Korotkoff sounds* and are divided into four phases. Blood pressure readings vary with age, with lower limits of 90/60 mm Hg and upper limits of 140/90 mm Hg in adults. Systolic pressure may vary 5 to 10 mm Hg in both arms.

A blood pressure measurement is usually taken with the patient sitting. Often it is important to measure the patient's blood pressure while lying or standing. Normally the blood pressure measurement should remain the same in any po- sition. A decrease in systolic measurement of more than 10 mm Hg or a decrease in diastolic measurement of more than 5 mm Hg suggests postural hypotension, possibly caused by anti- hypertensive medication, prolonged bed rest, or low-fluid volume.

Arterial pulses

The carotid, radial, brachial, femoral, popliteal, dorsalis pedis, and posterior tibial are the blood vessels most commonly assessed (Table 16-3). It is important to compare vessels on both the right and left sides. Extremities that are cool and pale suggest arterial vessel involvement, whereas warm, cyanotic extremities indicate venous prob- lems.

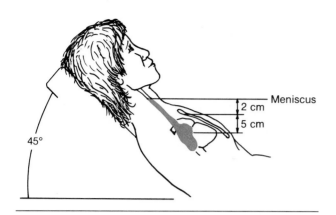

Figure 16-6
Jugular venous pressure.

Venous measurement

Inspection of the jugular venous pulse is a good indicator of hemodynamics of the right side of the heart. Jugular pulsations reflect atrial contractions (Figure 16-6). The internal jugular veins give a more accurate pressure measurement than the external jugular veins, which are more visible. Normally the jugular venous pressure is found 3 cm above the sternal angle with the bed at a 45-degree angle. A change in the jugular venous pressure is most significant when compared with previous jugular venous pressure readings. Increased readings suggest hypervolemia and decreased readings suggest hypovolemia. To measure the jugular venous pressure, raise the head of the bed to a 45-degree angle and observe pulsations of the internal jugular vein. If internal jugular vein pulsations cannot be visualized and the patient's clinical condition does not contraindicate, ask the patient to hold his breath and bear down. If pulsations still cannot be visualized, lower the head of the bed until pulsations are visualized. Hold a pencil on a horizontal plane next to the neck of the patient where the jugular pulsations are. Place a ruler on the sternal angle (the angle of Louis, a bony ridge between the manubrium and the sternum at the level of the second intercostal space) and extend the ruler vertically. Measure in centimeters the point where the horizontal pencil crosses the ruler.

Lymph node

Lymph node evaluation is part of the cardiovascular assessment. Normally lymph nodes should not be felt on palpation.

Edema

Edema is the accumulation of excess interstitial fluid. It is most commonly found in the lower extremities and the sacral area if the patient is supine. Edema is not a normal finding and is suggestive of chronic heart failure. It may also be a sign of venous disease, arterial occlusion, or lymphatic obstruction. Edema of one extremity suggests a local cause, whereas bilateral edema indicates a systemic cause. Edema may be described as pitting if indentation of the edematous area persists after finger pressure is withdrawn. Pitting edema is described by the measurement of the depth of the indentation in millimeters or centimeters.

ELECTROCARDIOGRAPHY

Heart muscle contraction results from an electrochemical process when electrically charged particles on the outer and inner surface of the cell membrane move in and out of the cell. The electrical events of the heart are polarization, or resting stage; **depolarization** during heart muscle contraction; and repolarization as the heart muscle relaxes.[49] The electrical events can be visualized with electrocardiograph machines. These machines measure the electrical current generated by the heart muscle contraction and display a continuous picture of the electrical current on an oscilloscope. An **electrocardiogram** (ECG) is the written output of an electrocardiograph machine and appears on graph paper. Time intervals are measured horizontally and amplitude or force is measured vertically.

To obtain an ECG, positive and negative electrodes are placed on specific areas of the chest wall and limbs, with the heart between two electrodes. This procedure provides different views (leads) of the heart's electrical activity. The direction (deflection) of the waveforms on the graph paper depend on whether the electrical wave is moving toward the positive electrode or the negative electrode or in a line between the two electrodes.

Heart monitoring is useful for identification of normal and *abnormal heart rhythms* (**dysrhythmias**). Detection of dysrhythmias permits immediate pharmacologic or mechanical (**defibrillation**/cardioversion) intervention. This intervention can prevent the occurrence of more serious problems.

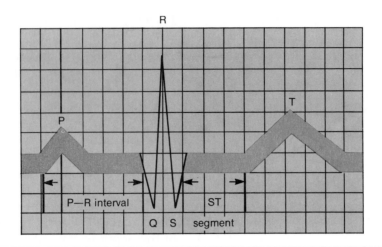

Figure 16-7
ECG of one heartbeat.

Electrocardiogram Interpretation

Each heart muscle contraction should produce a P, Q, R, S, and T wave on the ECG graph paper (Figure 16-7). The first positive deflection occurring above the baseline is the P wave, which represents the **sinoatrial (SA) node** firing and the passing of electrical current through the atria. The QRS complex, or waves, are a series of negative positive-negative deflections that demonstrate the wave of electrical current passing through the bundle of His, the bundle branches, and Purkinje's fibers. It shows that the ventricles have contracted. The positive deflection after the QRS complex in the T wave represents the repolarization, or resting period, of the heart. During this period, the heart will not accept an impulse from the SA node, thus allowing the electrical charges to realign on either side of the cell membrane.

The spaces between the waves are called segments. The PR interval is the space between the P and QRS complex. This represents electricity passing through the AV node. Between the QRS complex and the T wave lies the ST segment, which represents the completion of the ventricle contraction and the repolarization period.

Every ECG should be interpreted by following five basic steps (see box). Following these steps will foster a systematic approach to ECG interpretation and reduce confusion.

Rate

The ventricular rate is usually considered the heart rate. It can be felt in the radial pulse and is

---

Five Steps To ECG Interpretation

1. Determine rate, the number of counted heart beats per minute
2. Determine rhythm, the regularity with which the heart beats
3. Determine the presence or absence of P waves
4. Determine the length of the PR interval
5. Determine the configuration of the QRS complex

---

the counted beats per minute. When reviewing an ECG the ventricular rate is determined by counting the number of R waves in a 6-second strip. (If the rhythm is irregular, an exact rate cannot be determined.) The atrial rate can be calculated by counting the P waves in a 6-second strip.

Rhythm

The rhythm reveals whether the patient's heart is beating regularly or irregularly. The atrial and ventricular rhythm should be identified. The atrial rhythm is determined by measuring the distance between two consecutive P waves. Calipers for marking the point on paper at each consecutive P wave will accomplish this measurement. Then line up the two dot points with the next two P waves (moving left to right). If the distance is equal between all the P waves, the rhythm is regular; if it is unequal, the rhythm is irregular. The ventricular rhythm is determined using the same method, only measuring the R-wave intervals.

P wave

The presence of a P wave indicates that the SA node originated the impulse and is a result of atrial depolarization.

PR interval

The PR interval measures the AV conduction time. It is measured from the onset of the P wave to the beginning of the QRS complex. The normal PR interval is 0.12 to 0.2 seconds. A shorter PR interval means the impulse originated in an area other than the SA node. A longer PR interval signifies a delay in the impulse as it passes through the AV node.

Configuration and location

Evaluation of the configuration and location of the P, Q, R, S, and T waves on a rhythm strip reveals information about the location and extent of myocardial damage. Each wave should be evaluated systematically. All P waves should be similar in shape and size. A difference indicates irritation in the atrial tissue or damage near the SA node. All P waves should point in the same direction. The direction should be appropriate for the lead being recorded. P waves should precede QRS complexes. Next, review the QRS complexes for shape, size, direction, and location in relation to the T wave. QRS complexes close to the T wave mean the ventricles are contracting prematurely. The T wave represents ventricular relaxation. The closer the QRS is to the T wave, the greater the risk is of serious ventricular dysrhythmia.

The ST segment can be slightly elevated above the baseline but should not be depressed. It then curves very slightly into the start of the T wave. An abnormality of the ST segment is an early sign of myocardial infarction.

T waves should also be observed for size and shape and should point in the same direction as the QRS complex. T waves should follow the QRS. Elevated or "tented" T waves can be a sign of elevated potassium levels.

DISORDERS OF RATE AND RHYTHM OF THE HEART

The pulse is one of the most sensitive indices for assessing heart function. Nurses should develop a keen sensitivity to what they feel when obtaining a peripheral pulse. When the heart is functioning normally, the pulse is felt as smooth, regular, equally spaced beats of equal strength and volume, which occur from 60 to 100 times per minute. Under certain conditions, changes occur in the pulse rate, its rhythm, and volume. Some of these conditions are called *cardiac dysrhythmias.*

Dysrhythmia
Cardiac dysrhythmias

Cardiac dysrhythmias occur in well persons and those with cardiovascular disease. Any deviation from normal sinus rhythm is defined as a dysrhythmia. **Dysrhythmias** may result from an abnormal rate, a site of impulse formation in other than the SA node, or from abnormal conduction within the system. Dysrhythmias are categorized by site of origin, either sinus, atrial, nodal (junctional), or ventricular. The nurse may be the first person to detect changes in the patient's pulse.

Sinus dysrhythmia

The SA node originates sinus dysrhythmia, but the discharge varies. The heart rate increases and decreases as the SA node fires prematurely or late (Figure 16-8). Normally, the SA node is at a rate of 60-100 times per minute. If the rate falls below 60 per minute, the process is termed **sinus bradycardia.** If, however, the rate is greater than 100 times per minute, it is termed **sinus tachycardia.**

Atrium
Premature atrial contraction

Normally the SA node originates the impulse to begin the cardiac cycle. Sometimes, however, an impulse will arise from another area of the atrium; such an impulse is called a premature atrial contraction (PAC). The impulse usually occurs earlier than expected and is represented by a P wave that has a different configuration than P waves representing impulses that begin in the SA node. The QRS complex is usually normal but may have a different configuration. A short pause is usually present between the T wave and the next P wave (Figure 16-9).

PACs are a common dysrhythmia and are found in patients with rheumatic heart disease, hyperthyroidism, or even people without heart disease. In many patients no treatment is indicated. Patients with symptoms may receive a mild sedative. If underlying heart disease is thought to be the cause of the PACs, drugs such a quinidine,

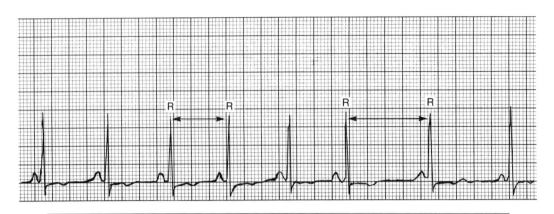

Figure 16-8
Sinus dysrhythmia.

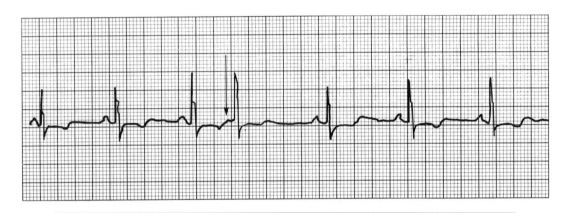

Figure 16-9
Premature atrial contraction (PAC).

digitalis, disopyramide, or propranolol may be prescribed.

Atrial flutter

Atrial flutter is an atrial rhythm occurring at a rate of 250 to 350 beats per minute (Figure 16-10). The impulse does not originate from the SA node. The ventricular rate is less than the atrial, usually about one half the atrial rate. The regular, rapid atrial rate results in a "saw-tooth" flutter wave on an ECG tracing. QRS complexes do not follow each flutter because the ventricles cannot respond as rapidly as the atria. The QRS complex will appear normal unless an aberrant conduction is present. Such cardiovascular problems as coronary artery disease, rheumatic heart disease, or cor pulmonale are usually present in patients with atrial flutter. The ectopic focus becomes the pacemaker that originates all impulses. The impulse is normally conducted through the AV node into the ventricles. The ventricles initially respond to every second or third atrial beat unless the rhythm persists.

Cardiac output will remain within the normal limits as long as the ventricular rate is within the normal limits and no treatment is needed. Treatment is indicated when the ventricular rate is so rapid that the ventricles cannot fill. The goal of treatment is to slow the ventricular rate or change the rhythm to a sinus node–initiated impulse. Digitalis is the first drug of choice.

Atrial fibrillation

Atrial fibrillation is an atrial rhythm with a rapid atrial rate of 400 to 600 per minute and a ventricular rate of 140 to 170 per minute because the AV node cannot conduct every atrial impulse (Figure 16-11). P waves are absent and the ECG tracing

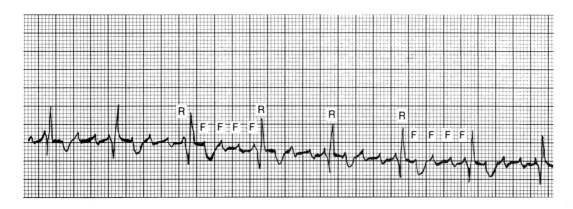

Figure 16-10
Atrial flutter. **R,** R wave. **F,** flutter wave.

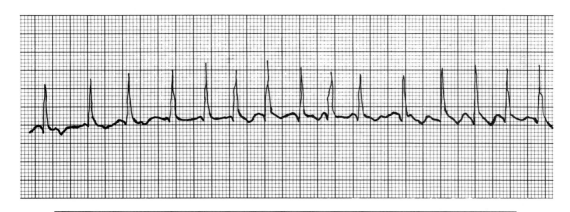

Figure 16-11
Rapid atrial fibrillation.

has classic fibrillation waves. QRS complexes are normal or reflect aberrant conduction. In healthy young people, atrial fibrillation may be a transient dysrhythmia. Continuous atrial fibrillation is associated with heart disease. PACs usually precede atrial fibrillation. Cardiac output decreases and there is a risk of peripheral atrial emboli. The radial pulse is slower than the apical pulse because some systolic contractions are weaker and cannot be palpated in the arteries.

Treatment depends on cardiac output. If cardiac output remains adequate, digitalis is used to increase AV node blocking and to allow more time for the ventricles to fill. Quinidine may help in maintaining a sinus rhythm. The patient's pulse should be checked for a slow rate before giving digitalis or quinidine. If it is slow, the drug should be withheld and the physician notified. Signs and symptoms of digitalis toxicity are increased pulse rate, nausea, dizziness, and visual disturbances.

If cardiac output falls, cardioversion is the treatment of choice to return the heart rate and rhythm to normal. Cardioversion is a procedure that gives the heart external electrical stimulation. The external electrical stimulation will interrupt the irregular conduction pattern of the heart and return it to normal sinus rhythm. The patient's heart rhythm is monitored and the electric shock is delivered during ventricular contraction. Delivery of electric shock at any other time could cause severe, life-threatening dysrhythmia. Cardioversion is performed by a physician with a patient's written consent. The nurse monitors the patient's heart rate, rhythm, blood pressure, and respirations throughout the procedure.

Ventricle
Premature ventricular contractions

Premature ventricular contractions (PVCs) are ventricular contractions that do not originate from

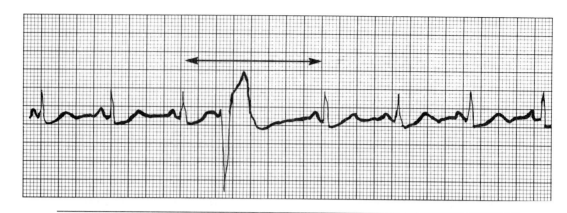

Figure 16-12
Isolated premature ventricular contraction (PVC).

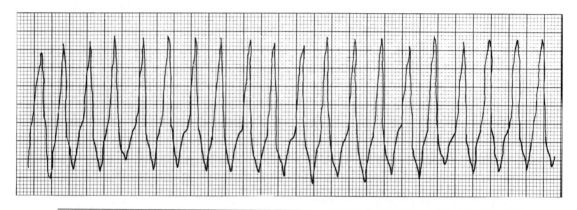

Figure 16-13
Ventricular tachycardia (rapid).

the AV node (Figure 16-12). Ventricular contraction results from a site in the Purkinje's fibers and occurs earlier than a sinus beat. A P wave does not precede the QRS complex. Instead, an inverted P wave may follow the PVC. The QRS complex is widened, notched, and may be of greater amplitude. The T-wave deflection is in the opposite direction of the QRS complex. A "compensatory" pause usually follows the PVC as the heart waits for the next SA node impulse.

PVCs are the most common dysrhythmias. They may occur in people with or without heart disease. PVCs may be expected in patients after a myocardial infarction or cardiac surgery or in patients with myocardial irritability.

Rare PVCs are not treated. Multiple PVCs, two or three consecutive PVCs, or those close to the T wave of the previous beat are treated with antiarrhythmic drugs such as lidocaine, procain-

amide, quinidine, and propranolol. If the cause of PVCs is hypokalemia, potassium chloride replacements are given; if the cause is digitalis toxicity, the digitalis is discontinued.

Ventricular tachycardia

Ventricular tachycardia is a serious dysrhythmia that results from a series of rapid, regular impulses originating in a ventricular ectopic focus (Figure 16-13). Ventricular contraction does not follow atrial contraction. The ventricular rate ranges from 100 to 220 beats per minute. P waves are rarely seen. The QRS complex is widened and notched with greater amplitude. The T wave may be buried in the QRS. If it is visible, it will deflect in the opposite direction of the QRS. **Ventricular tachycardia** is a complication of digitalis toxicity or myocardial infarction. Ventricular tachycardia must be terminated promptly. Treatment consists of drug

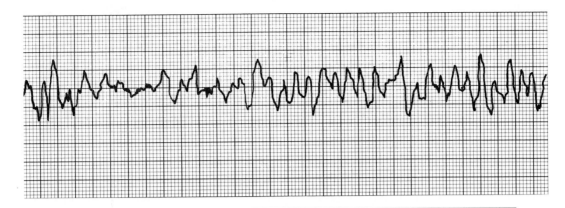

Figure 16-14
Ventricular fibrillation.

therapy such as lidocaine, procainamide, or bretylium. If digitalis toxicity is the cause, the digitalis should be discontinued and potassium given. Electrical countershock is usually effective.

Ventricular fibrillation

Ventricular fibrillation is rapid, irregular "twitching" of the ventricles, demonstrated by a wavering baseline and bizarre waveform (Figure 16-14). Ventricular fibrillation may result from myocardiac infarction, digitalis and quinidine toxicity, or a PVC occurring at the apex of the preceding T wave (R on T phenomenon). During ventricular fibrillation, the ventricles cannot deliver blood to the body. If untreated, death will ensue. Immediate treatment is defibrillation with direct-current countershock. Often ventricular fibrillation can be overtaken by aggressive treatment of PVCs that are encroaching on the T wave or occurring in multiples.

Heart Block

Heart block results from a disturbance in the conduction system, specifically at the AV junction. Heart block is categorized as first-degree, second-degree, or third-degree blocks.

First-degree AV block is identified by a PR interval greater than 0.2 second. The impulse originates in the SA node and travels normally through the atria. The conduction is delayed at the AV junction but passes through, and the ventricles respond normally. First-degree block may result from digitalis, quinidine, or procainamide therapy. Usually no treatment is necessary.

Mobitz type I Wenckebach block results from the same conduction defect as first-degree block. However, with each beat the conduction delay through the AV junction increases progressively, until the sinus impulse is completely blocked and no QRS complex occurs. This dysrhythmia is commonly seen in patients with inferior myocardial infarction and digitalis toxicity. The only treatment is discontinuance of the digitalis.

Mobitz type II is demonstrated by conduction of some sinus impulses through the AV junction with a prolonged P-R interval; however, other sinus impulses are blocked completely. The ventricular rate is a fraction of the atrial rate. This is a more serious dysrhythmia, is usually seen in acute anterior myocardial infarction, and indicates damage to the ventricular septum. Treatment may include isoproterenol and epinephrine infusion or transvenous pacing.

Third-degree block occurs when none of the sinus impulses are conducted through the AV junction. The atrial rate is usually regular and of normal rate but faster than the ventricular rate. The ventricular rate is usually 30 to 45 beats per minute. The PR interval is variable. If the QRS complex is normal, it will be widened only if the ventricular impulse originates below the bundle of His. Complete heart block may be due to digitalis toxicity, age, myocarditis, acute myocardial infarction, or cardiac surgery. Isoproterenol is used to treat third-degree block and temporary or permanent cardiac pacing.

Bundle-branch block is a conduction delay through the right or left bundle. The P-R interval is normal, and the QRS complex is prolonged by at least 0.12 second and may be notched and widened. Myocardial infarction, hypertension, and cardiomyopathy are common causes of bundle-branch block. It can also be drug induced by procainamide or quinidine or caused by hyperkalemia. Treatment is focused on the underlying problem.

Electronic Cardiac Pacemakers

Electronic cardiac pacing is indicated for any condition in which the SA node of the heart fails to initiate or conduct the impulse at the rate needed to obtain good cardiac output. Pacemakers may be internal or external and may provide a fixed rate (asynchronous) or demand (synchronous) pacing of the ventricles.

The **pacemaker** is an electrically operated mechanical device that enables the ventricle to contract normally. It may also be used in an emergency or for a temporary period, or it can be implanted permanently in the patient's chest. Several approaches are possible in initiating the use of the pacemaker. If it is to be temporary, a catheter may be inserted through a vein, often the jugular or subclavian vein, and it is attached to an external pacemaker. Patients with an occasional blockage of the electric impulses in the heart, such as after heart surgery or a myocardial infarction, may need this type of pacemaker. Usually it is inserted in the operating room or in a special laboratory, such as the cardiac catheterization laboratory, and the catheter is passed directly into the right ventricle using fluoroscopy.

Permanent pacemakers are necessary if the patient has irreversible cardiac damage to the conductive nerve pathways of the heart. A permanent pacemaker is also inserted through a vein, but the battery box is permanently implanted within the subcutaneous tissue of the patient's chest or abdomen. Occasionally, the patient's chest is opened and the electrodes are sutured into the ventricle. Internal pacemakers may be powered by a mercury battery, which lasts 1½ to 2 years, by lithium, which lasts 7 to 10 years, or by nuclear energy, which lasts 10 to 20 years.

Assessment and intervention

The nursing care of the patient is determined by the procedure used. In any case the patient will have a wound that must be protected from infection. If a catheter is inserted into a vein, care must be taken to prevent its displacement. When a temporary pacemaker is in use, all electric equipment in the room must be grounded, and only one machine may be connected to any electric outlet. Any exposed electrodes should be insulated. The nurse should remember that the implanted pacemaker is a foreign object, and the patient should be observed for any elevation of temperature that might indicate trouble. The nurse should also be certain that an infusion set and a defibrillator are at the bedside for emergency use. Patients with implanted pacemakers often are apprehensive and fearful. The primary responsibilities of nurses include assisting the patient in accepting the instrument and relieving fear and apprehension. Every patient must be taught the importance of daily counting his pulse for a full 60 seconds while at rest. Those with fixed rate pacemakers should report any change of more than 5 beats per minute to the physician. Patients should know the rate at which the pacemaker is set. They should be taught the meaning and symptoms of battery failure (see box below).

All patients with pacemakers should carry identification/alert cards with information about the manufacturer and the type, model, and milliamperage at which their pacers are set. Newer models of pacemakers generally have metal shielding to protect them from external interference. Most electrical devices can be used safely. Microwave ovens now have special shields and will usually not affect the pacemaker. Arc-welding equipment and power transmitters should be avoided. Patients should be taught to use caution near the antitheft devices in some stores. Airport metal detectors may be triggered, so the patient may need to provide a pacemaker identification card.

CORONARY CARE UNIT

The coronary care unit (CCU) or the cardiopulmonary unit is a specially designed unit of the hospital. The unit is equipped with all supplies and equipment, including emergency drugs, to meet the needs of each patient admitted to the

---

Symptoms of Battery Failure
Dizziness
Light headedness
Syncope
Chest pain
Shortness of breath
Peripheral edema
Palpitations
Confusion

unit. It provides for continuous monitoring of the cardiac function.

The overall objective of the CCU is to save lives. During the early development of these units, emphasis was placed on the prompt treatment of patients with cardiac arrest. With increased knowledge and understanding about coronary artery disease, the emphasis is now placed on preventing cardiac arrest. If not identified, treated, and controlled, minor disorders of rhythm and dysrhythmias may lead to serious dysrhythmias, heart failure, and death. It cannot be expected that all patients admitted to the unit will survive; however, the mortality has been significantly reduced.

Large medical centers have specially designed separate CCUs; however, some community hospitals care for coronary disease patients in intensive care units (ICUs) along with other seriously ill patients. There are definite disadvantages to this system, especially when the ICU is a ward type of arrangement. However, the environmental location of the patient is not always what is most important—the quality of nursing care often is. Nurses are the key to the success of the CCU. They will usually be the first to offer basic life support and to start treatment of life-threatening dysrhythmias. Nurses are with the patient 24 hours a day and are in a position to assess and detect the first sign of trouble. Their immediate assessment of the problem and appropriate emergency action may be lifesaving. The CCU, with its effective monitoring system and trained personnel, has effectively reduced in-hospital death from heart attacks.

Patients in a CCU may experience extreme emotional and physical stress. They are anxious about loss of function, helplessness, finances, family, and the possibility of death. The CCU environment is foreign and frightening. Coronary care nurses must have technical proficiency and sensitivity to care for CCU patients and families in crisis. Much can be done to reassure patient and families by supplying information that will relieve anxiety, by listening carefully to the patient, and by treating the patient as an adult. The caring and empathy on which nursing was founded is demonstrated during the patient's most serious crisis.

Nurses in the CCU are often responsible for keen assessment of the patient's physiologic changes and for taking ECGs, observing and recording cardiac monitor readings, maintaining oxygen therapy, and observing and regulating in-travenous fluids. They should also be prepared to provide basic cardiac life support, defibrillation, and intravenous infusions.

Laboratory Examinations

It is usually important to conduct several laboratory studies in order to establish an accurate diagnosis or to follow the course of the cardiovascular disease.

Complete blood count

The routine laboratory examination comprises a count of red and white blood cells, an estimate of hemoglobin, and a differential count, which includes many different cells that are usually few in number. An increase in the number of white blood cells indicates that an inflammatory condition or tissue destruction is present. Determination of red blood cell count and hemoglobin level helps physicians to determine how well the blood is being oxygenated.

Sedimentation rate

The sedimentation rate is used to determine the extent of inflammation and infection that is present in the patient. The sedimentation rate is usually increased in rheumatic fever and in myocardial infarction. It is useful both in diagnosing rheumatic fever and in following the course of the disease.

Blood cultures

When **bacterial endocarditis** is suspected, the diagnosis may be established by finding the causative organism in the blood. Often several blood cultures may be necessary before a positive diagnosis can be made.

Serum enzyme tests

Enzymes are proteins that are present in all body cells. Certain enzymes are specific to particular tissues and are present in high concentrations in these tissues, such as the heart, liver, and kidneys. When damage occurs to these tissues, significant amounts of the enzymes are released into the bloodstream.

Cardiac **isoenzymes** are specific to heart muscle tissue and are useful in diagnosing acute myocardial infarction. One isoenzyme is lactic dehydrogenase (LDH), numbered 1 to 5. Within 48 hours following a myocardial ischemic attack, 80% of patients will have an increased LDH. Another isoenzyme contributing to the diagnosis of myocardial infarction is the CPK (creatine phosphokinase). There are three classes of enzymes, CPK-MM, CPK-BB, and CPK-MB. The CPK-MB is specific to myocardial tissue and increases within 4 to 8 hours after the onset of chest pain and peaks at 24 hours. Blood samples are drawn and analyzed every 3 to 6 hours after the onset of symptoms so that the pattern of isoenzyme can be established.

Blood chemistries

The mechanisms controlling metabolic balance are frequently disturbed during serious illness. Serum electrolytes are important to determine the status of sodium, potassium, chloride, carbon dioxide, bilirubin, calcium, creatinine, glucose, magnesium, phosphorus, alkaline, phosphatase, urea nitrogen, and uric acid levels in CCU patients.

Cholesterol

Cholesterol is one of the lipid, or fat-like, substances in blood. Increased levels of lipids (hyperlipidemia) have been found to be a risk factor for coronary artery disease. It is thought the lipids accumulate within the inner lining of blood vessels, decreasing the blood vessel diameter. This is called **atherosclerosis.** The narrowed blood vessels decrease the circulation efficiency of the blood laden with oxygen and nutrients. If the heart muscle does not receive enough oxygen, a person experiences chest pain, which is a symptom of impending myocardial muscle damage. Studies

---

Foods High in Saturated Fat and Cholesterol

Whole milk
Dairy cream and substitutes made from tropical
  oils
Cheese
Butter
Red meat heavily marbled or fatty:
  Prime cuts
  Sausage
  Bacon
  Ribs
  Ground meat with high-fat percentages
  Cold cuts
Lard
Meat fat
Poultry skin
Coconut or palm oil
Hydrogenated vegetable shortening

---

show that blood cholesterol levels can be lowered by decreasing the dietary intake of foods high in saturated fat and cholesterol (see box).

Blood gases

Arterial blood gases help to determine the status of the patient's oxygenation and acid-base balance.

Coagulation studies

Because many of the patients in CCUs have had a thrombolic insult, the use of anticoagulation therapies is not unusual. Coagulation studies include platelet counts, prothrombin time counts, partial thromboplastin time (PPT) and activated partial thromboplastin time (APTT) counts, activated clotting time counts, fibrinogen level studies, thrombin time counts, and recalcification time counts.

Central Venous Pressure

Central venous pressure (CVP) provides information about circulating blood volume. It is a direct reflection of right atrial pressure (RAP) and an indirect reflection of the preload of the right ventricle. *Preload* refers to the amount of stretch in the ventricular muscle just before contraction.

This measurement gives some indication of the ability of the heart to pump blood. A physician introduces a catheter into a peripheral or central vein and then into the vena cava or right atrium. The catheter is secured and attached to an intravenous solution with a manometer attached (Figure 16-15). Placement is verified by a chest x-ray examination. A sterile, occlusive dressing covers the site. The tubing and dressing should be changed according to hospital policy, at which time the site should be observed for any sign of redness, swelling, and drainage. These signs or any complaints of pain from the patient should be documented and reported to the physician.

The pressure is measured in centimeters of water. The normal range of CVP measurement is 4 to 10 cm. An increase in CVP indicates decreased contractility of the myocardium, vasoconstriction, or increased circulating blood volume. Conversely, a decreased CVP reading indicates increased myocardial contractility, vasodilation, or hypovolemia.

Pulmonary Artery and Pulmonary Artery Wedge Pressures

Because the CVP does not provide an accurate reading of pressure in the left side of the heart,

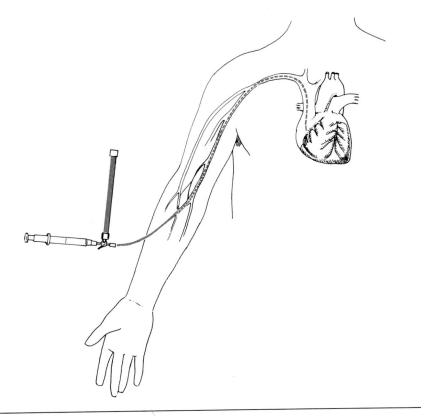

Figure 16-15
Central venous pressure.

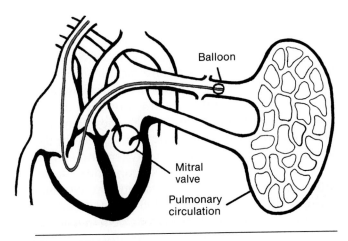

Figure 16-16
Pulmonary artery catheter in wedge position during diastole.

patients who are critically ill often receive pulmonary artery (PA) catheters. During diastole, an open column of blood extends from the pulmonary artery through the lungs and into the heart to the open mitral valve. This permits measurement of left ventricular preload.

The physician inserts the PA catheter into a central vein (subclavian or jugular). It is also possible to use the femoral or brachial veins. The multilumen catheter is advanced into the right

ventricle and from it into the pulmonary artery (Figure 16-16). The catheter is attached to a pressure transducer and intravenous solution. Placement is verified by a chest x-ray examination. Measurement is done with an electronic monitor. The PA catheter has a distal balloon that, upon inflation, can provide the pulmonary artery wedge pressure indicating function of the left side of the heart. In addition to providing these measurements, an additional **lumen** within the catheter terminates in a thermister (a device for measuring very small changes in temperature) port and permits measurement of cardiac output. Complications associated with placement of a PA catheter include infection, pulmonary artery rupture, pulmonary thromboembolism, catheter kinking, arrhythmias, and air embolism.

Exercise Tolerance Test

An exercise tolerance test (ETT) is valuable in diagnosing ischemic heart disease. The patient's ECG is continually monitored while he or she is subjected to a gradually increasing level of exercise on a motorized treadmill or bicycle. A depression in the ST segment of the ECG indicates lack of oxygen to the heart muscle. The ETT is also used to diagnose dysrhythmias and to evaluate the patient's cardiac tolerance of exercise. The patient needs to understand what the test includes because his cooperation is necessary. He should also know that if he experiences any pain, dyspnea, or extreme fatigue, the test will be stopped. The patient is advised to avoid smoking, to have nothing by mouth except water for several hours before the test, and to wear clothing suitable for exercise. Medications that affect the heart may be withheld.

Echocardiogram, Phonocardiogram, and Vectorcardiogram

The echocardiogram, phonocardiogram, and vectorcardiogram are noninvasive tests that pose no risk or discomfort to the patient. Before testing, the patient should be informed that the procedures are painless and that he or she must lie quietly for approximately 30 minutes.

The echocardiogram uses high-frequency ultrasonic waves bounced off the heart to locate and record the motion of cardiac structures. The data are transmitted through an **oscilloscope** and recorded on photographic paper or film. An echocardiogram is useful in determining the function of the left ventricle and cardiac valves, especially the mitral valve. It also indicates the presence of cardiac tumors, pericardial effusion, and congenital heart defects.

The phonocardiogram expands the limits of heart sounds that may be heard with a stethoscope. Microphones are placed on the surface of the body, and a graphic recording is made of sounds that originate in the heart and the great vessels. An ECG is taken at the same time.

The vectorcardiogram is a three-dimensional graphic picture of the heart's electric conduction performance. The vectorcardiogram depicts the same information as the twelve-lead ECG but in a different form. The patient preparation is the same as for an ECG.

X-ray Examination and Fluoroscopy
X-ray films

The use of x-ray examination is one of the most valuable tools for appraisal of the size and shape of the heart. The heart is opaque to x-rays, but contour may be readily outlined, and the thoracic aorta may be seen. Fluoroscopic examination allows visualization of the heart in motion. The outline of the heart may be traced on the fluoroscope screen and copied on paper for further study, a procedure called *orthodiagraphy*. The lungs may be evaluated at the same time because congestion of

the lungs occurs early in heart failure and may be the first sign of heart failure.

Angiography

Examination of the chambers of the heart, valves, and blood vessels is made by injecting a contrast medium into a vein or artery. X-ray films called *angiograms* are then taken. Selective angiography uses a smaller amount of the contrast medium and injects it in or near the area to be studied. This method has proved more satisfactory than injecting the contrast medium into the vein. Selective angiography makes it possible to study any part of the vascular system. Patients undergoing this procedure should be questioned carefully concerning allergies because some persons are sensitive to the dye. Preceding the examination food is usually withheld from the patient to avoid nausea and vomiting, and a mild sedative may be given. These patients are usually fearful and apprehensive and need a great deal of education and reassurance. After the procedure the patient should be monitored for bleeding from the site of the injection, and blood pressure readings monitored.

Cardiac Catheterization

Cardiac catheterization requires a staff of well-trained physicians and nurses and is usually done only in medical centers where facilities exist for open heart surgery. The purposes of cardiac catheterization are to measure the pressure in the heart chambers and pulmonary arteries, to obtain blood samples from the heart and vessels for determination of the amount of oxygen and carbon dioxide present, and to detect congenital or acquired defects. The catheterization may be done on either the right side or the left side of the heart. A cutdown is usually made over a vein in the arm or leg, and a small catheter is introduced into the vein. It is slowly passed through the vein to the heart with the aid of the fluoroscope, and x-ray films are taken along the route. The examination permits a more precise diagnosis. The left side of the heart may be catheterized in a similar way by inserting a catheter into the femoral artery and passing it up the aorta and into the heart. If atrial stenosis is present, a needle can be passed into the heart by means of a special bronchoscope, or the heart may be entered directly through the chest wall.

Before catheterization, the procedure is explained to the patient and a signed consent is

Postcatheterization Nursing Intervention

1. Direct the patient to remain in bed for 3 to 6 hours.
2. Monitor vital signs every 30 minutes for 2 hours, then every hour for 4 hours or until stable.
3. Check insertion site for bleeding, hematoma, and swelling. Place a sandbag over the insertion site for 4 to 6 hours.
4. Check pulses and signs of circulatory compromise in the limb of insertion.
5. Encourage the patient not to flex or hyperextend the leg in which the catheter was inserted for 12 hours.

obtained. Nursing care of the patient after catheterization includes surveillance of vital signs and insertion site, and assisting the patient to resume precatheterization status (see box).

THE PATIENT WITH DISEASES AND DISORDERS OF THE CARDIOVASCULAR SYSTEM

The leading cause of death in the United States is cardiovascular disease. Since the initiation of a massive campaign to educate people about risk factors in 1968, mortality has been steadily declining.[41] In the last decade this decrease has been 30%. Annually, approximately 1.2 million Americans suffer a myocardial infarction.[41] Reducing morbidity and mortality from heart disease is a primary concern of health care providers. The nurse needs to be aware of the risk factors and should encourage patients to modify habits that predispose them to heart disease.

Arteriosclerosis and Atherosclerosis

Arteriosclerosis is a process of degeneration and decreased elasticity of the artery walls caused by chronic inflammation and scarring. This degenerative process weakens the vessel walls, predisposing them to hemorrhage, thrombosis, and hypertension. It is also related to the aging process. **Atherosclerosis** is a type of arteriosclerosis that affects the large arteries, such as the aorta, its major branches, the coronary arteries, and the large arteries of the brain. It is very serious because it is the underlying cause of most heart and brain infarcts.

Pathophysiology

The disease is characterized by deposits of fat (usually cholesterol) within the inner lining of the arteries. This deposit initiates a low-grade inflammatory reaction and healing process, which eventually results in hard, irregular, multicolored **plaques,** which fibrose and calcify within the inner lining of the arteries (Figure 16-17). This process weakens and narrows the walls of the major arteries, and partial or complete obstruction can occur. Whenever obstruction occurs, the tissue beyond the obstruction is deprived of its blood supply, and death of the tissue may result. The deprivation of blood to the heart is referred to as **ischemic heart disease,** and the pathologic condition involves the coronary arteries.

Intervention

There is no effective treatment or cure for arteriosclerosis and atherosclerosis. The process probably begins early in life and develops gradually over the years. Surgical procedures have been developed that will remove plaques from certain areas and increase the circulation beyond. Earlier in this chapter several factors that increase the risk of heart disease are reviewed. To decrease the risk of ischemic heart disease, the individual must establish good health habits during the early years of life. It is believed that the process can be slowed by modifications in daily living. A reduction of dietary cholesterol will usually cause a decrease of the serum cholesterol. Most cholesterol in the diet comes from animal fats. Foods that should be eliminated from the diet include whole milk, butter, eggs, organ meats, and other animal fats (see box on p. 368). The use of polyunsaturated oils, skim milk, and low-fat cheese and the addition of complex carbohydrates should be considered. The nurse should encourage young persons to establish good dietary patterns and not to smoke or to stop smoking.

Hypertension and Hypertensive Heart Disease

Hypertension refers to an elevation of blood pressure, that is, a blood pressure higher than would normally be expected for the individual's age, weight, and sex. Secondary hypertension affects 5% to 10% of people with the disease and can be attributed to a specific cause. When the pathologic

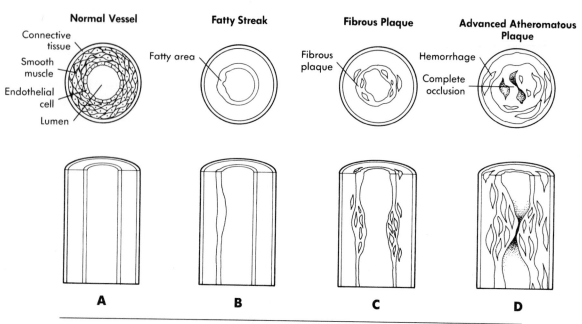

Figure 16-17

The progression of atherosclerosis shown in both the longitudinal and the cross-sectional views. **A,** Normal vessel. **B,** First stage, fatty streaks. **C,** Second stage, fibrous plaque development. **D,** Third stage, advanced (complicated) lesions. *(From Thelan LA, Davie JK, and Urden LD: Textbook of critical care nursing, diagnosis and management, ed 1, St Louis, 1990, The CV Mosby Co.)*

condition is treated, the blood pressure returns to normal. When an abnormally high blood pressure occurs without any known cause, it is called essential or primary hypertension, which is the type affecting 80% to 90% of hypertensive individuals.

A common feature of hypertension is elevation of both blood pressure parameters: systolic and diastolic. In some patients the systolic blood pressure is elevated without diastolic blood pressure elevation. This is often seen in elderly patients and patients with hyperthyroidism or aortic insufficiency. When the diastolic pressure is elevated without the increase in systolic pressure, it indicates a rise in peripheral vascular resistance. This is commonly seen in young people.[10]

The course of this disease is insidious. Some people who are hypertensive remain untreated for years. If the disease is left untreated, severe organ damage can occur, resulting in myocardial infarction, cerebral vascular accidents, heart failure, renal failure, and sometimes death.

Three major systems of control that have an interdependent effect on blood pressure are (1) sodium and extracellular fluid volume, (2) the sympathetic nervous system, and (3) the renin-angiotensin system.

Lifestyle Treatment of Hypertension
Weight control
Dietary sodium restriction (for "salt-sensitive" patients)
Alcohol restriction
Caffeine restriction
Exercise (avoid isometric; encourage aerobic)
Smoking cessation

Sodium

Normally when a person consumes salt a series of physiologic responses are triggered that result in the excretion of salt. However, a person with hypertension has an altered response to sodium excretion and requires higher filtration pressures in the kidneys to remove the sodium.

Sympathetic nervous system

Increased levels of plasma norepinephrine have been found in some hypertensive individuals, which suggest higher levels of sympathetic activity, especially in people with borderline hypertension, high cardiac output, and a rapid heart

---

> ### Sodium Restricted Diets
>
> Mild restriction: 2 to 3 g
> - Salt *lightly* in cooking
> - No added salt
> - Restrict consumption of pickles, olives, bacon, ham, chips, and heavily salted processed foods
>
> Moderate restriction: 1 g
> - No salt in cooking
> - No added salt
> - Salt-free substitutions for canned or packaged foods
> - Meat and milk in moderate portions
>
> Strict restriction: 0.5 g
> - Meat, milk, and eggs in small portions

rate. As a person ages, the number of beta-receptor cells decreases, contributing to the higher norepinephrine levels.

Renin-angiotensin system

Renin is a hormone that limits the formation of the potent vasopressor angiotensin II. Angiotensin II raises blood pressure directly through vasoconstriction and increased sympathetic nervous system activity, and indirectly through increased aldosterone, increased antidiuretic hormone, and increased thirst.

Whatever the cause, pathologic changes in the arterioles leads to constriction and increased peripheral resistance. As the disease progresses, the deterioration in the blood vessels affects vital organs such as the retina, brain, kidney, and heart.

The blood pressure of some patients is higher during office visits than at home. In addition, the technique for obtaining a blood pressure reading affects the reading, such as the correct blood pressure cuff size for the patient's arm. Blood pressure should be measured in both arms while the patient is supine, sitting, and standing. The patient's arm should be at the level of the heart and be supported. The patient should not wear constrictive clothing.

A thorough personal and social history should be obtained, including the patient's life stressors and dietary and exercise habits. The patient's knowledge of hypertension and willingness to comply with the medication regimen should be evaluated. The impact of seasonal variations, such as constriction of blood vessels from cold weather, may increase the blood pressure reading.

When symptoms occur, the first sign may be headache, followed by fatigue, dyspnea on exertion, deteriorating vision, and kidney disorders. As blood flows from arteries into capillaries and veins and meets resistance, blood from the heart is pumped at an increased pressure to compensate for this resistance and to maintain the circulatory flow. Gradually, the walls of the left ventricle and the arteries become thickened. The left ventricle is enlarged because it works harder and harder to force the blood out into the body. Eventually the heart cannot function efficiently, and congestive heart failure ensues.

Assessment

Hypertension has been termed the "silent killer," because individuals often remain asymptomatic until signs of vital organ damage begin to appear. The patient may complain of headache, fatigue, dyspnea on exertion, blurred vision or dizziness, and faintness. The only true indices of hypertension involve the blood pressure. One blood pressure reading is not diagnostic; several should be made at weekly intervals for the outpatient and hourly or daily for the hospitalized patient.

Intervention

There is no agreement on the best treatment method for essential hypertension. Most agree, however, that several factors need to be considered, such as age, sex, family history, living habits, and whether vascular changes have occurred. The height of the diastolic blood pressure is more important than the height of the systolic pressure. The goal of treatment is to maintain the patient's blood pressure as close to an individual normal as possible. Risks of cardiovascular complications drop when the diastolic readings are maintained below 90 mm Hg.[26]

It is most important to set realistic treatment goals for the patient's blood pressure, weight, and diet. Lifestyle and habits are difficult to change (see box on p. 372). Sodium restricted diets are often recommended (see box above left). The mean arterial pressure (MAP) is used for establishing blood pressure goals. The ideal MAP is equal to or less than 100. It is calculated using the following formula:

MAP = diastolic blood pressure
+
one third of the pulse pressure
(systolic blood pressure minus the diastolic blood pressure)

When choosing antihypertensive therapy, many things must be considered. The stepped-care approach is one form of treatment.

Generally it is best to use a low dose of medication whenever possible. This will reduce drug side effects, increase tolerance, and improve compliance. The less frequently the medication must be taken, the better the rate of compliance. Consider the physiologic changes in elderly patients, as well as characteristics such as race and sex. Studies show young people with more norepinephrine do well with beta-blockers. Blacks do well with diuretics. Converting enzyme inhibitors are effective in people with renal vascular hypertension and patients who do not tolerate diuretics. If blood pressure control is not satisfactory, the drug should be reevaluated and factors such as compliance and duration of drug action should be taken into account. Another goal of treatment is to preserve the quality of the patient's life. Offering the patient several treatment options increases the person's participation through the opportunity to make choices.

Rheumatic Fever and Rheumatic Heart Disease

Rheumatic fever is primarily a disease of children and young persons, occurring between 5 and 15 years of age. Rheumatic fever usually begins with hemolytic streptococcus sore throat, which develops rapidly. The throat appears very red, and swallowing is difficult. The glands under the jaw are enlarged and tender, and the temperature may be elevated as high as 104° F (40° C). Throat cultures may be taken and the causative organism isolated. In 2 to 3 weeks after recovery from the throat infection, indications of rheumatic fever appear. It is not the streptococcus organism that is thought to be the causative agent, but rather the toxins released by the organism. The body forms antibodies against these toxins that can react with many tissues of the body, producing a wide variety of symptoms. Rheumatic fever, however, is a preventable disease. Through the use of antibiotic therapy for patients with streptococcal infections, almost all primary attacks of rheumatic fever could be eliminated. Once it has occurred, however, the patient is susceptible to future attacks.

Assessment

Rheumatic fever has no specific set of symptoms because the signs vary with the age of the indi-

---

Stepped-Care Treatment of Hypertension

1. Nonpharmacologic approaches.
2. Partial dose:
   Diuretic—Chlorothiazide (Diuril), hydrothiazide (Hydrodiuril), chlorthalidone (Hygroton)
   Beta-blocker—propranolol hydrochloride (Inderal), atenolol (Tenormin), metoprolol bitartrate (Lopressor)
   calcium antagonist—nifedipine (Adalat, Procardia)
   angiotensin-coverting enzyme (ACE)—captopril (Capoten), enalapril (Vasotel)
3. If blood pressure remains high, doses are adjusted. Substitution is made to an ACE inhibitor or calcium antagonist.
4. If blood pressure remains high, a vasodilator—minoxidil (Loniten)—is added. The substitution outlined in step 2 may be reserved for this step.
5. If blood pressure remains high, a third or fourth drug may be added.

---

vidual. A diagnosis is established through careful laboratory examinations and observation of the patient. The leukocyte count and the sedimentation rate usually increase. Fever may occur, including a pulse rate consistent with the fever. Any increase in the pulse rate should be viewed as serious because it may be the first indication of heart damage. Some degree of anemia may be present because of dietary deficiencies. The younger the child, the less likely it is that the joints will be involved. When the joints are involved, they are swollen and tender, and a characteristic of the disease is that the joint pain moves from joint to joint. Nodules may appear on the joints and subcutaneously, developing in crops. As one crop disappears, another appears. Some patients develop inflammation of the heart (carditis). This may be followed by a systolic murmur that is heard at the apex of the heart, and endocarditis is always a possibility. Rheumatic fever may be recurring, and each new attack further damages the heart. The formation of scar tissue in the heart may cause the valves to leak, resulting in insufficiency, or a narrowing of the valve may occur, resulting in stenosis. The mitral and aortic valves are most often affected, but the other valves may be involved. Extensive damage to the heart muscle at the time of a severe attack of rheumatic fever may result in heart failure and death. However, the disease is likely to become chronic, resulting in death years later. Some individuals recover with no heart damage, but careful medical supervision over a long period is necessary to eliminate the possibility of heart involvement.

Intervention

Emphasis is placed on prevention through extensive and immediate treatment of patients who have throat infections and are taking antibiotic drugs to eradicate the hemolytic streptococcus bacteria. Antibiotic therapy may continue at regular intervals for as long as 5 years after an attack of rheumatic fever.

Complications

Mitral and aortic stenosis. Mitral stenosis and aortic stenosis are the most serious complications of repeated attacks of rheumatic fever. Although mitral insufficiency, mitral valve prolapse, and aortic insufficiency also can occur. Valves may become thickened and fused together, causing heart failure. Symptoms include dyspnea on exertion and **pulmonary edema,** a direct result of failure of the left side of the heart.

Treatment varies with the severity of the condition. Conservative treatment involves limitation of activity, reduction of sodium intake, and administration of digitalis and diuretics. If the patient becomes increasingly incapacitated when undergoing this therapy, surgery may be necessary. Mitral stenosis can be treated surgically by performing a mitral commissurotomy, replacing the mitral valve. The surgeon makes an incision into the left atrium and inserts the finger, a knife, or a dilator through the valve and breaks apart the stenosed tissue. Aortic stenosis is treated by replacing the aortic valve with open heart surgery using a heart-lung machine.

Bacterial Endocarditis

The endocardium is the serous membrane that lines the inside of the heart and covers the flaps of the valves. Bacterial endocarditis is an inflammation of this lining caused by bacteria, and it may be acute or subacute.

Subacute bacterial endocarditis

Subacute bacterial endocarditis may occur in persons who have had rheumatic fever with damaged heart valves or in persons with congenital defects of the valves. It is believed to result from hospital-acquired infection after various types of surgery, including open heart surgery. It may also occur after dental extraction or tonsillectomy. Usually the causative organism belong to the *Streptococcus viridans* group of organisms.

The organism is present in the bloodstream and directly invades the heart. The valves are usually involved and become inflamed and covered with bacterial growth. The healing process may result in scarring, which will gradually reduce the effectiveness of the heart.

Assessment

The classic presentation of the patient with endocarditis includes fever, anemia, and a heart murmur. The onset is generally insidious over a period of several weeks, and the symptoms, which may be numerous, gradually become more serious. There may be weight loss, cough, headache, and joint pains. Tachycardia is common. One of the most characteristic symptoms is the appearance of petechiae, small hemorrhages from capillaries. These frequently occur in the conjunctiva, mouth, and legs. Small nodes, called Osler's nodes, occur on the tips of the fingers and toes, and clubbing of the fingers is common. The tendency for hemorrhage gives rise to menstrual disorders, and hematuria may occur. Emboli from the vegetative lesions on the heart valves may be carried to the lungs, spleen, or kidneys. Confirmed diagnosis is usually made on finding the organism in blood cultures.

Intervention

Long-term parenteral administration of antibiotics effective against the causative organism is the medical plan of therapy. Patients may be hospitalized for about 2 to 3 weeks, and bedrest is indicated. Penicillin against sensitive streptococci is the drug of choice. If allergy is present, alternative therapy is a first generation chephalosporin or vancomycin. The duration of antibiotic therapy is long because the microorganisms are protected by the dense platelet-fibrin vegetation that surrounds them. A diet high in calories is often indicated, so the patient may need creative nursing encouragement to overcome loss of appetite. Observation of the patient for petechiae, location of pain, vomiting, speech difficulty, paralysis, visual disturbances, hematuria, and changes in vital signs is important for the nurse.

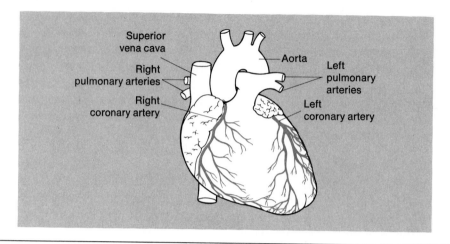

Figure 16-18

Coronary arteries arise from aorta just above heart, one on left side and one on right side.

Coronary Artery and Heart Disease

The two coronary arteries, right and left, arise from the aorta just above the aortic semilunar valves, at the point where the ascending aorta begins. They are the first blood vessels to branch off from the aorta. Each coronary artery fans out over the heart muscle (myocardium) and subdivides into smaller branches that supply the myocardium with oxygen and nutrients (Figure 16-18).

Pathophysiology

The primary cause of coronary artery disease is atherosclerosis. The major factor in coronary artery disease is the gradual buildup of cholesterol, other fatty substances, macrophages, and various cellular debris within the inner lining of the arteries. The walls of the vessels become inflamed, and calcification of the debris takes place, forming **plaques** that obstruct the flow of blood. The process is insidious and develops over years with few or no symptoms. Symptoms occur when obstruction of one of the coronary arteries or its branches is severe enough to deprive the heart of its oxygen supply. When the oxygen supply is cut off from any part of the heart muscle, the affected tissue will die. Angina pectoris and myocardial infarction are the most common diseases that result from coronary obstruction.

Angina pectoris (anginal syndrome)

The cause of **angina pectoris** is arterial spasm resulting in a decreased blood flow through the coronary arteries, which causes less oxygen to reach the myocardium. The disease is usually the result of atherosclerosis; however, conditions such as hypertension, diabetes mellitus, syphilis, or rheumatic heart disease can predispose a patient to the disorder.

Assessment

The characteristic symptom of angina pectoris is a sudden, agonizing pain in the substernal region of the chest; the pain may be sufficiently severe to completely immobilize the person. The pain may radiate to the left shoulder and down the inner side of the arm into one or more of the fingers or to the jaw (Figure 16-19). The pain is inconsistent, and frequently the patient is unable to describe it because of its many variations. At times it may appear only as a digestive upset. During an acute episode the face of the patient may have an ashen appearance and the patient may be covered with cold, clammy perspiration and may be unable to speak. The pulse rate may remain normal, the pulse volume does not change, and the blood pressure shows little or no change. The patient may be extremely apprehensive, and the great physical and mental pain may trigger thoughts of death.

Any one of several factors may precipitate an attack of angina, including exposure to cold, emotional upsets, an unusually heavy meal, particularly at night, or any activity that will increase the work of the heart or cause a decreased supply of blood to the heart muscle.

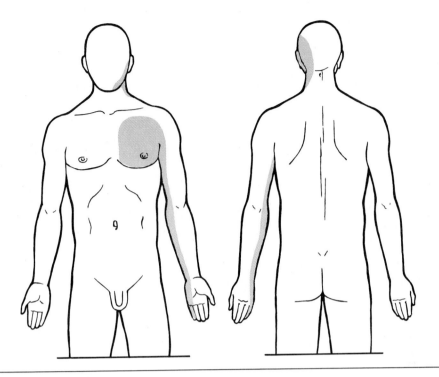

Figure 16-19
Area to which pain radiates in angina pectoris.

Intervention

The treatment of angina pectoris requires the treatment of the individual as a whole rather than treatment of the disease only. The patient needs to understand the nature of the pain and the causative factors. The nurse can assist the patient in regulating a daily plan of living to reduce or eliminate the attacks of pain. The patient should be protected from the cold by wearing warm clothing in cold weather. The use of tea, coffee, and tobacco should be discouraged, and meals should be regular and of moderate proportion. If the patient is overweight, plans should be made for a gradual reduction to a nearly normal range for age and height. Rest and relaxation are essential elements of treatment. Adjustments should be made when necessary to relieve the individual of tension and emotional strain. Treatment of angina is directed toward relieving the attack and decreasing the frequency and severity of attacks. The sublingual administration of nitroglycerin, 0.32 to 0.65 mg, or isosorbide dinitrate (Isordil), 5 to 10 mg, to relieve the immediate attack may be ordered (Table 16-4). These medications dilate the arteriole system and increase the blood flow to the heart muscle. All nitrate preparations may cause flushing of the skin and an increase in pulse and respirations, and a headache may occur. Patients with angina pectoris should always carry a nitrite preparation with them and may use it freely. Propranolol (Inderal) is also often used on a daily schedule with a nitrate preparation to reduce cardiac muscle work and oxygen need. These medications are given on a schedule established to cause maximum vasodilation at the times when the patient is most active. Therefore the patient must be educated as to the specific times to take the medications, as well as the actions, uses, and side effects of the drugs.[17]

A major aspect of nursing care is to relieve the patient's anxiety. This is particularly important if attacks occur at night. The nurse must rely on the patient for information concerning the quality, intensity, and duration of pain. Medication should be given promptly. The patient may be raised to a sitting position and made comfortable. The patient needs support and reassurance, and these can best be provided if the nurse is calm, has a well-modulated voice, is firm, yet provides care with gentleness, understanding, sympathy, and efficiency. The nurse must be able to differentiate between dyspnea as a subjective complaint and dyspnea resulting from congestive failure, when the respiration is wheezy and the patient is cyanotic.[11]

Table 16-4

Common Drugs Used in Patients with Cardiac Disorders

Drug	Preparations	Action	Nursing considerations
Nitroglycerine (Nitrostat)	0.15-0.6 mg SL	Relaxes coronary vessels	Monitor blood pressure and pulse rate; patient should sit or lie down
Nitroglycerine (Nitro-Bid)	10-200 μg/min (IV) ½-2 inches ung (15 mg/inch) 1 disk (topical)		CCU/ICU patients; check local reaction
			Apply to skin that is free of hair; rotate sites
Propanolol (Inderal)	10-40 mg po q 6 hr	Decreases preload and afterload	Note signs of heart failure
Nifedipine (Procardia)	10 mg po tid	Calcium channel	Give ac and hs blocker
Digoxin (Lanoxin)	0.125-0.5 mg po qd (maintenance)	Increases force of contractions	Check apical pulse 1 minute; hold if <60
Quinidine gluconate (Quinaglute)	200-400 mg po q 4-6 hours	Antiarrhythmic	

Myocardial Infarction

Myocardial infarction (MI) occurs when one of the coronary arteries or its branches (Figure 16-17) suddenly becomes **occluded.** The cause may be a coronary thrombosis, in which a blood clot forms and interrupts the blood supply. Blockage from other causes, such as vasoconstriction of the arteries or sudden atherosclerotic changes, is referred to as a coronary occlusion. The part of the heart supplied by the vessel is deprived of its blood supply and as a result dies. The area becomes soft and necrotic (infarct); it is gradually replaced by fibrous tissue; and collateral circulation is established.

Men in middle life who generally consider themselves to be in robust health are often the persons who have MIs. They usually have some degree of atherosclerosis and may or may not have hypertension. In some cases the condition may develop slowly, and often the individual has what he believes to be mild indigestion. The diagnosis may be difficult to establish at this stage.

Assessment

The typical symptoms of acute MI include a severe pain in the area of the lower sternum and upper abdomen, which may continue to increase in severity and radiate to the shoulders and down the arms or to the jaw. The left shoulder and the left arm are more frequently affected. The pulse becomes rapid, weak, and irregular. Vomiting may occur, and the patient is covered with cold, clammy perspiration. The blood pressure may fall, and all the signs of **cardiogenic shock** are present. Most patients are acutely aware of their condition and are extremely apprehensive. In a few hours the temperature rises, but the elevation does not exceed 101° F (38.3° C). Both the leukocyte count and the sedimentation rate are increased. An electrocardiogram is obtained on the patient's admission to the hospital and will be repeated at intervals to monitor the patient's progress. An x-ray examination of the chest is also done.

Three laboratory tests have proved to be beneficial in assessing the damage that occurs to the heart. The death of cardiac muscle results in the release of intracellular enzymes into the bloodstream. These enzymes are also located in tissue other than heart muscle; however, their presence indicates that damage of tissue has occurred (p. 367). This, plus ECG changes and the presence of typical symptoms, leads to a firm diagnosis. The serum glutamic-oxaloacetic transaminase (SGOT) level may rise as early as 4 to 6 hours after the infarct. It peaks in 1 or 2 days and returns to normal in about 4 days. The LDH level becomes elevated within a day after cardiac damage, peaks in 3 days, and returns to normal within 1 or 2 weeks. The CPK-MB level is often elevated within

3 to 5 hours after the initial symptoms, peaks in about 24 to 36 hours, and returns to normal in 3 days if no further damage has occurred.[1]

Intervention

Most patients with MIs are taken to the CCU or ICU. The goal of intensive therapy is to stabilize and prevent further increase of the infarct size or complications. The relief of pain is of primary importance, and morphine or meperidine (Demerol) is usually administered intravenously. Oxygen is administered by nasal cannula or mask. Intravenous infusions are started immediately (usually in the emergency room). Cardiovascular shock and consequent collapse of the vessels are a constant threat, and a vein should be kept open for the administration of emergency drugs.

Vasopressor drugs may be ordered and infused slowly. The drip rate is regulated by the blood pressure, which is taken with the pulse at frequent intervals (e.g., every 5 to 15 minutes). The nurse caring for a patient receiving vasopressor medications should remember that they are dangerous drugs, and extreme caution must be used while they are being administered. The patient's temperature is taken every 4 to 6 hours. While the use of anticoagulant therapy in the management of patients with MIs is controversial, an anticoagulant drug such as heparin sodium is usually given to prevent venous thrombosis or pulmonary embolism. Patients who are at high risk for systemic embolism because of atrial fibrillation or congestive heart failure may receive a full dose of anticoagulation with heparin. Similar indications exist for the use of oral anticoagulant therapy. The prothrombin time (PT) is closely monitored while the patient receives anticoagulant therapy. The optimal range of PT for a patient is one and one-half to two and one-half times the control time.[48] The patient should be observed for signs of bleeding while receiving anticoagulant therapy. Bleeding may occur from the gums or from sites of injections. All emesis, urine, and stools should be tested for occult blood. Any sudden signs of dyspnea and changes in rate, rhythm, or volume of the pulse should be reported at once.

Thrombolytic therapy as an attempt to recannulize the obstructed coronary arteries by dissolving the clot has become routine for patients who are treated within a short time (ideally, less than 6 hours) of the infarct. Currently there are three agents capable of dissolving the thrombus; urokinase (Abokinase, Breokinase), streptokinase (Kalikinase), and tissue-type plasminogen activator (t-PA).[47] Additional criteria may apply before a patient is selected for this relatively new therapy. Limits have been given for age, ECG findings, duration of chest pain, and predisposition to hemorrhage in the research trials of these drugs.[45]

The patient with MI must be assured of maximum rest from the moment of the attack. Procedures should be planned to allow long periods of undisturbed rest. During the acute phase only close members of the patient's family are permitted to visit so that they do not interfere with rest. Complete bedrest is the usual way of providing maximum rest; however, studies indicate that the work demanded of the heart may be lessened if the patient is in an upright position. Therefore some physicians will permit the patient to sit in an armchair for short periods several times a day. Most patients have bedside commode privileges. The patient should be assessed closely for any cardiovascular changes. Gradually the patient's activity is increased, using ECG readings and serum cardiac isoenzyme levels as a guide.

The diet prescribed depends on the patient's condition and may be liquid, soft, or regular. Foods known to be gas producing should be avoided. Bowel elimination may be regulated by mild laxatives and stool softeners. The patient should not strain.

Currently, early mobilization of MI patients is routine in most settings. The need for limited movement and exercise was recognized as early as the eighteenth century. However, in the 1950s and 1960s, it was common practice to keep patients on strict, hospitalized bedrest for 6 weeks. In the late 1960s the use of early mobilization of acute MI patients began to show positive results.[20] Currently, cardiac rehabilitation programs are located in most large hospitals. Patients are permitted limited, planned progression in activity as soon as they are stabilized in CCUs. (For further discussion, refer to the section on Cardiac Rehabilitation.)

As the heart heals, collateral circulation develops and the necrotic tissue in the myocardium heals with fibrotic scar formation. The first 2 weeks after an MI are considered the most dangerous, and the patient's condition must be watched closely for 4 weeks. Healing usually occurs in 6 weeks, although convalescence generally takes 2 to 3 months. Gradually, the patient will be able to return to a normal or nearly normal life.

The management and care of the patient with MI must be individualized, depending on the severity of the attack, complications, and progress. Cardiac monitoring equipment has made it possible to detect cardiac disturbances that otherwise would have been missed. Nurses should realize that machines can contribute much to the care of the patient but may also increase the patient's fear, anxiety, and apprehension unless he or she understands their contribution to care. Above all, it should be remembered that machines cannot provide emotional support or intelligent, empathetic understanding essential to the patient's progress (see box at right).

Complications

Cardiogenic shock, pulmonary edema, dysrhythmias, and congestive heart failure can occur as complications of a MI.

Cardiogenic shock. Cardiogenic shock occurs when the heart fails to pump an adequate amount of blood to the vital organs. Whenever a portion of the heart muscle dies, that area can no longer contract and do its share of the work required to pump the blood through the circulatory system. Therefore the cardiac output will decrease and less blood will be available to supply oxygen and nutrients to the body tissues.

Symptoms of the resulting cardiogenic shock include cold, clammy, and moist skin, pallor, apathy, decreasing blood pressure, a weak, thready, irregular, and rapid pulse, shallow and rapid respirations, and, as the condition progresses, cyanosis of the lips and nail beds and dilated pupils. (See Chapter 4.)

Acute pulmonary edema. Acute pulmonary **edema,** or left-sided heart failure, is always a medical emergency. Although it is caused by cardiac failure, it is the pulmonary system that is affected. Because the left side of the heart cannot adequately pump blood to the body, excessive amounts of blood collect in the left side of the heart, the pulmonary veins, and pulmonary capillaries. The increased pressure in the capillaries causes the serous portion of the blood to be pushed through the capillaries into the alveoli. Fluid rapidly reaches the bronchioles, and the patient begins to suffocate in his own secretions. This acute condition is ever present in patients with chronic heart disease but can follow cerebrovascular accidents, head trauma, rapid administration of intravenous fluids, and poisoning from barbiturates and narcotics.

NURSING CARE GUIDELINES
Myocardial Infarction

Nursing diagnoses
- Alteration in cardiac output related to decreased cardiac perfusion
- Alteration in tissue perfusion related to interruption of arterial blood flow
- Alteration in comfort (chest pain) associated with poor cardiac perfusion
- Self-care deficit related to weakness
- Anxiety associated with inability to control illness
- Impaired physical mobility associated with discomfort and activity intolerance
- Potential alteration in fluid volume related to cardiac failure
- Potential ineffective breathing patterns related to discomfort and pulmonary vascular congestion
- Potential ineffective individual coping related to effect of illness on life-style
- Potential impaired gas exchange related to pulmonary vascular congestion
- Potential fear of death

Nursing interventions
- Check vital signs frequently
- Maintain complete bedrest, transfer to chair as ordered, increase activity gradually
- Observe for signs and symptoms of cardiogenic shock, pulmonary edema, cardiac dysrhythmias, and congestive heart failure
- Allow for long periods of undisturbed rest
- Restrict visitors and space visits so they do not interfere with rest periods
- Administer pain medication as needed
- Administer oxygen as needed
- Regulate bowel elimination with laxatives and diet; do not permit straining at defecation
- Alleviate anxiety or apprehension
- Restrict sodium and cholesterol intake; provide well-balanced diet

Expected outcomes
- Vital signs within normal limits
- Free of cardiorespiratory complications
- Purposes of sodium- and cholesterol-restricted diets stated
- Purposes of prescribed medications described
- Myocardial infarctions defined and risk factors identified
- An exercise rehabilitation plan and any activity limitations described
- Adjustments to health problem and any changes necessary in lifestyle being made

Assessment. The patient with pulmonary edema becomes cyanotic and dyspneic. The pulse is weak, rapid, and respirations become wheezy and sound moist with gurgling. The patient is unable to breathe unless sitting up and may develop a productive cough with frothy, pink-tinged sputum. The patient may be restless, apprehensive, and covered with cold, clammy perspiration.

Intervention. Objectives of care for the patient in acute pulmonary edema are to achieve physical and mental rest, relieve hypoxia, decrease the venous return to the heart, and improve the function of the heart. The nurse should remain with the patient. The patient should be placed in a high Fowler's position, or be allowed to remain in any position of comfort. Physical and mental relaxation is most important. Morphine sulfate may be given to relieve anxiety and apprehension and helps to achieve muscular relaxation. Because morphine is a respiratory depressant, the patient must be carefully observed; morphine is generally not given to patients with obstructive pulmonary disease. Oxygen is administered using a nonrebreathing mask or nasal cannula.

Rotating tourniquets may be ordered to reduce the venous pressure and the venous return of blood to the right side of the heart. This allows more blood to be pooled temporarily in the extremities and slows its return to the heart. The physician orders the procedure and specifies the interval for rotation and the time that the procedure is to be continued. It then becomes the responsibility of the nurse to understand the technique of compression and release of the tourniquets and to recognize any complications should they occur.

When rotating tourniquets are ordered, either of the following methods may be used: (1) four blood pressure cuffs (if available) or (2) the commercial automatic rotating tourniquet machine that is supplied with four pneumatic cuffs. The tourniquets are placed on the distal third of the arm between the elbow and the shoulder and on the distal third of the thigh between the knee and the hip. One extremity is always left free. The tourniquet is secured and must not be tight enough to obliterate the arterial pulse. Moving clockwise or counterclockwise, one tourniquet is removed at the prescribed interval, usually 15 minutes. The fourth tourniquet is applied first, and then one is removed so that tourniquets are on three extremities at one time. The procedure continues for the time specified by the physician.

When the tourniquets are discontinued, they are removed one at a time, observing the same order and interval until all have been removed (Figure 16-20). The nurse should maintain a time schedule at the bedside so that the procedure may be carried out in the proper order.

If the patient is conscious, the procedure and its purpose should be explained to him. The blood pressure should be taken before beginning the procedure and at intervals during the procedure. The pulse should be taken after the application of each tourniquet. The tourniquet must be tight enough to occlude the venous flow but must not occlude the arterial flow. If the arterial flow is occluded, it may cause pulmonary embolism or phlebothrombosis. Special attention must be paid to color and warmth of the skin, and peripheral pulses should be monitored. When the procedure has been completed, the nurse should complete the patient's record with the following information: (1) the time the procedure was begun and ended, (2) the interval of rotation, (3) blood pressure and pulse readings, (4) any medications given, (5) urinary output, and (6) the patient's response to the procedure.

During the procedure the nurse should observe the patient for hypotension, quality of peripheral pulses, and any decreased urinary output. If they should occur, it should be reported immediately.

Congestive Heart Failure

Congestive heart failure occurs when the **cardiac output** (the volume of blood ejected by the heart each minute) can no longer meet the needs of the body tissues. It may be the result of bacterial endocarditis, damage from rheumatic fever, syphilitic heart disease, arteriosclerosis, hypertension, or myocardial infarction. It may also occur from other disorders, including chronic obstructive pulmonary disease and blood transfusions. It may affect the right or the left side of the heart, but ultimately both sides are affected.

Pathophysiology

When the heart fails to pump sufficient blood to meet the needs of the body, all body organs and tissues are affected. The pulmonary vascular system becomes congested because it is no longer emptied sufficiently by the left atrium and ventricle. As the pressure in the heart chambers increases, the blood begins to back up in the atria and the large veins. Blood returning to the heart cannot be pumped rapidly enough into the con-

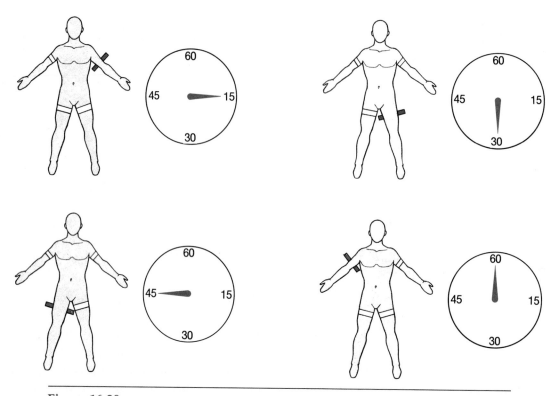

Figure 16-20

Procedure for rotating tourniquets to reduce pulmonary edema. Note that tourniquets are rotated clockwise each 15 minutes and that one extremity remains free.

gested pulmonary vessels, and the venous system becomes engorged. As the pressure in the venous system rises, other organs of the body become congested. The decreased cardiac output causes a diminished flow of blood to the kidneys and reduces the glomerular filtration rate. With reduced renal blood flow, sodium and water are retained in the body and contribute to generalized edema. Because of increased venous pressure and stasis, fluid is pushed out of the capillaries and venules. The liver and other organs become congested, and fluid escapes into the abdominal cavity, termed **ascites**.

Assessment

The early symptoms of congestive heart failure are (1) shortness of breath, usually apparent on exertion such as climbing stairs or walking rapidly, (2) a slight cough, more of a hacking type, (3) a tendency to become easily fatigued, (4) slight abdominal discomfort, and (5) swelling of the feet and ankles. The edema of the feet and ankles subsides at night when the person is in a supine po-

sition. As the disease becomes advanced, the dyspnea may be of a panting type and may be so severe that the person must remain in an upright position (orthopnea). The cough is dry, and hemoptysis may occur. The edema may extend to the face, neck, sacrum, and extremities and is a pitting type (dependent edema). There may be cyanosis, enlargement and tenderness of the liver, and decreased urinary output. Abnormalities of the pulse may be found, and the patient may or may not complain of pain in the chest and abdomen. When there is left ventricular failure, acute pulmonary edema may occur. Dyspnea is increased, cyanosis occurs, and a productive cough is present. This is always a serious emergency, and immediate treatment is necessary. When right ventricular failure occurs there may be excessive weight gain. As the venous pressure increases, the patient complains of more pain in the upper abdomen. The patient is weak and experiences loss of appetite, excessive perspiration, and nocturnal diuresis. Pitting edema, particularly in the lower extremities, occurs, which is related to the abnormal weight gain. The central venous pressure is elevated but will gradually decrease with effective treatment.

Intervention

In the treatment of congestive heart failure the three primary objectives are to reduce oxygen requirements, decrease the edema, and increase the cardiac output. To accomplish these objectives, three approaches are usually taken: rest to reduce the oxygen requirements; medications to reduce the edema, with digitalis to improve the cardiac output; and proper diet to reduce sodium intake and increase potassium.

Rest

The patient with congestive heart failure must be treated on an individual basis, and many patients with mild or moderate failure can avoid serious complications such as venous stasis or pulmonary embolism if they are out of bed and leading a relatively normal life. Because of this, many physicians do not confine such persons to long periods of bedrest. If the condition is severe, bedrest is usually necessary, and the length of rest is determined for the individual patient. The hospital environment should be quiet and restful. The nurse needs to be aware that emotional exertion, like physical exertion, increases the metabolic activity and increases oxygen needs. The patient may fear immediate danger and prolonged helplessness. The nurse should be alert to signs that indicate anxiety, frustration, and fear. The patient may express these feelings verbally or may show them by uncooperativeness and hostility. The patient may feel safe only when someone is nearby, and arrangements may have to be made for a member of the family to stay near the patient. Reassuring the patient mayoften be accomplished best by a calm, cheerful attitude and efficient, confident administration of care (see the boxed material at right).

Drugs

The goal of drug therapy is to reduce cardiac work load and increase cardiac output and cardiac reserve. **Diuretics** are drugs administered for the purpose of removing the excess water that has been retained by the body. In the presence of the diuretic, urinary output is increased, edema and ascites are relieved, and breathing is made easier. All diuretics produce similar effects—excretion of

---

NURSING CARE GUIDELINES
Congestive Heart Failure

Nursing diagnoses

- Alteration in cardiac output related to cardiac failure
- Ineffective breathing patterns related to pulmonary vascular congestion
- Impaired gas exchange related to pulmonary vascular congestion
- Alteration in tissue perfusion related to interruption of arterial and venous blood flow
- Impaired physical mobility related to weakness
- Anxiety associated with inability to control illness and ineffective breathing patterns
- Self-care deficit related to weakness
- Alteration in fluid volume related to decreased renal blood flow
- Potential fear of death associated with severity of illness
- Potential ineffective individual coping mechanisms caused by effect of illness on life-style
- Potential alteration in thought processes related to poor tissue perfusion

Nursing interventions

- Position patient in Fowler's position with back, arms, and legs supported for optimum respiratory ventilation
- Observe for signs of fluid excess—pitting edema, dyspnea, cough, pulmonary edema, distended neck veins, tachycardia
- Check vital signs frequently
- Observe for signs of disorientation or mental confusion
- Observe for signs of hypokalemia
- Administer digitalis preparation as ordered and observe for signs of toxicity
- Administer diuretics as ordered
- Administer oxygen as needed
- Turn every 2 hours
- Provide quiet, restful environment
- Allow for periods of rest after activity
- Restrict sodium intake as ordered
- Weigh daily

Expected outcomes

- Optimum respiratory ventilation achieved
- Vital signs within normal limits
- No or minimum signs of fluid excess exhibited
- Proper rest and sleep achieved
- Purposes of sodium-restricted diet and prescribed medications stated

sodium chloride and water. Because potassium is also lost, the patient must have his or her potassium level checked daily and supplemented as necessary. Food rich in potassium are shown in the box. When severe ascites is present, the patient may require an abdominal paracentesis, or if fluid has accumulated in the chest cavity, a thoracentesis may be done.

The physician usually orders an inotropic agent, usually digitalis in some form, to slow the heart rate and increase the force of the beat, thereby improving cardiac output. The maximum effect can be obtained by giving several large doses. This treatment is called *digitalization*. During this time the patient must be carefully monitored for toxic symptoms such as nausea, vomiting, irregular pulse, diarrhea, anorexia, and visual disturbances. If any of these symptoms occur, the drug should be withheld and the physician notified. As soon as the maximum effect has been obtained, the patient is given a maintenance dose. The nurse should remember to count the pulse before administering digitalis. If the rate is below 60 or over 100 beats per minute, the drug is withheld and the physician is notified.

A mild sedative may be needed for sleep and rest at night. Meperidine (Demerol) or morphine sulfate may be ordered to relieve pain; however, nursing measures such as changing the patient's position and keeping the patient informed of his progress may relieve the need for sedation. A mild laxative or stool softener is given to avoid straining while defecating. When dyspnea or cyanosis is present, oxygen may be administered.

Diet

Patients with congestive heart failure, as well as patients with other heart diseases, are prescribed a sodium-restricted diet. The body requires a certain amount of sodium, and any excess is excreted by the kidneys. In patients with congestive heart failure in which water is retained in the tissues, sodium is retained as well. Sodium contributes to water retention, but when sodium is absent, water is excreted. The sodium-restricted diet is often misunderstood and interpreted by the patient to mean no consumption of salt. The selection of foods that are low in natural sodium is most important. Foods high in potassium should be encouraged to compensate for potential potassium loss.

Meals for patients should be small to keep the diaphragm low, providing for expansion of the

---

Foods Rich in Potassium	
Almonds	Lima beans
Apricots	Molasses
Bananas	Mushrooms
Beet greens	Oats
Bran flakes	Parsnips
Broccoli	Peanuts
Brussel sprouts	Poultry
Buttermilk	Potatoes
Citrus fruits and juices	Seafood
Dates	Swiss chard
Fish	Walnuts
Garlic	Yeast

---

lungs. The patient's fluid intake and output must be monitored carefully.

Other interventions

The patient should be placed in a position that affords the greatest amount of comfort and rest. Most patients are comfortable in a high Fowler's position with the back, arms, and knees supported with pillows. A small pillow may be placed at the back of the head and one in the small of the back. This position allows for maximum lung expansion for best ventilation and slows the venous blood return to the heart.

A patient on complete bedrest is predisposed to venous stasis. If the patient is unable to move his legs, the nurse should provide passive exercise every 1 or 2 hours, flexing the extremities. Often therapeutic elastic stockings are applied to promote venous return. Complete bed baths may be too fatiguing for the patient, and partial baths, with special care of the skin and all bony prominences, may be adequate. Because of poor circulation, the patient is susceptible to decubitus ulcers, and frequent inspection and massage are required for their prevention. Accurate intake and output records are necessary. The patient should be weighed daily. Loss of fluid will cause a marked decrease in weight. The patient should be assisted on and off the bedpan. An orthopedic pan may facilitate the procedure with less strain on the patient. Some patients may be permitted to use a bedside commode.

The patient should be observed for any change in the rate, rhythm, or volume of the pulse, skin color, dyspnea, increase or decrease of edema, and any evidence of mental confusion of psychoses. During the acute stage of the illness, visitors should be limited to immediate members of the family, who should not tire the patient with lengthy conversations or disturbing affairs. As the patient improves, the activity level is gradually increased.

Heart Disease Complicated by Pregnancy

It is estimated that 2% to 4% of pregnant women have heart disease, which is a cause of maternal mortality and may contribute to premature and perinatal deaths. The largest number of cases of heart disease in pregnant women result from rheumatic fever, with a small number from congenital defects and about the same number from hypertensive heart disease. Frequently, the woman may be unaware that she has heart disease until she visits an obstetrician for antepartum care. Treatment is designed to prevent congestive heart failure. The obstetrician may consult a cardiologist to assist with the management of the patient.

Assessment

The medical history generally includes history of rheumatic fever, chorea, congenital heart disease, and heart murmur. A careful evaluation of the cardiac problem is made, and the patient's activity is planned according to the cardiac findings. Activities requiring the greatest amount of energy output should be reduced or eliminated. The patient is advised to get adequate rest at night and have several rest periods during the day. She is cautioned against exposure to respiratory tract infections such as colds and sore throats. Beginning at the third trimester of pregnancy, the greatest burden is placed on the heart. At this time the patient should be carefully observed for increased dyspnea, cough, hemoptysis, peripheral edema, anemia, or increased pulse rate. The patient may be hospitalized, have fluids restricted, undergo digitalization, and be placed on a sodium-restricted diet.

Intervention

Most patients will be seen in the physician's office or in a clinic during their antepartum period. The nurse in the physician's office or clinic may be the first person to see the patient. The nurse should observe the patient carefully on each visit and report any noticeable symptoms to the physician. The nurse should be familiar with the physician's orders for the patient and be able to help the patient understand them. The patient will usually be required to visit the physician every 2 weeks. The nurse may assist in encouraging the patient and in helping to prevent and relieve anxiety.

The patient's respiratory and cardiac status are monitored carefully during labor. Dyspnea may be relieved by placing the patient in a semirecumbent position. The pulse and respiratory rates should be taken frequently. Emergency equipment and supplies should be available for any emergency. During the postpartum period the patient should not become fatigued. Rest periods and moderation in activities should be continued following discharge.

DISEASES AND DISORDERS OF THE ARTERIES, VEINS, AND LYMPHATICS

Aneurysm

When the wall of an artery becomes weakened from disease or from injury, it may become distended at the weakened place. The distended part is called an **aneurysm.** The most frequent causes are arteriosclerosis and syphilis. Almost all aneurysms involve the aorta, with most of them occurring in the arch of the aorta. However, they may occur in arteries located elsewhere in the body. A fusiform aneurysm affects the entire circumference of the artery, similar to a partially blown-up, long balloon (Figure 16-21). A saccular aneurysm involves only a portion of the artery wall and forms an outpouching on the side of an otherwise normal artery (Figure 16-22). The distended part fills with blood and gradually becomes larger and larger, until it may appear as a pulsating tumor.

Assessment

The symptoms are related to the structures, bones, or nerves that are compressed by the aneurysm. Most aneurysms are below the diaphragm in the abdominal aorta. A frequent presenting symptom is back pain. Aneurysms are diagnosed through imaging techniques, such as x-ray, CT, or ultrasound examinations.

Intervention

Treatment consists of decreased physical activity to reduce the work of the heart and to decrease the arterial pressure. Many aneurysms are cor-

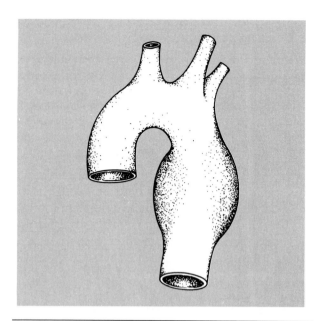

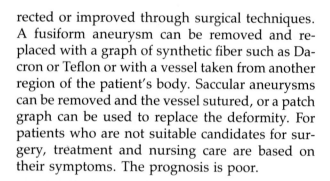

Figure 16-21
Fusiform aneurysm.

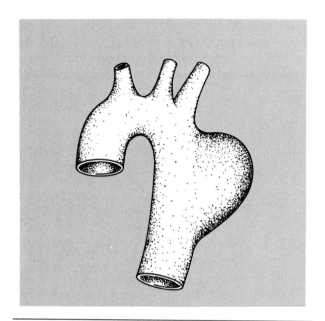

Figure 16-22
Saccular aneurysm.

rected or improved through surgical techniques. A fusiform aneurysm can be removed and replaced with a graph of synthetic fiber such as Dacron or Teflon or with a vessel taken from another region of the patient's body. Saccular aneurysms can be removed and the vessel sutured, or a patch graph can be used to replace the deformity. For patients who are not suitable candidates for surgery, treatment and nursing care are based on their symptoms. The prognosis is poor.

Arterial Occlusive Disease

Arterial occlusive disease has been directly linked to atherosclerosis. The buildup of plaques in the intimal layer of the arteries leads to narrowing and obstructions, which decrease the blood flow in the main arteries. Smoking, high-cholesterol diets, obesity, a family history, hypertension, and diabetes may all be considered predisposing factors. The disease is more common in men than women. Any of the major arteries may be affected, with the prognosis dependent on the location and severity of the occlusion.

Assessment

A health history should include information on risk factors and health habits. Signs indicating diminished blood flow and oxygenation to the affected tissues include diminished or absent peripheral pulses, pallor, coldness of extremities, tingling or numbness, and muscle cramping at rest or after exercise. Diagnostic tests such as arteriography and oscillometry are done to determine the location of the occlusion and the extent of the decreased blood flow.

Intervention

Treatment is aimed at improving circulation and preventing ischemia and depends on the location, cause, and size of the obstruction. General care measures include encouraging the patient to follow a moderate exercise program that includes walking. Chilling and cold environments should be avoided. Meticulous foot care should be performed daily. Any position that cause legs to be crossed or hips and knees flexed for long periods should be discouraged. The wearing of restrictive clothing such as garters or tight shoes should be avoided. Medical treatment may include the use of vasodilators or anticoagulants. Surgery may be necessary to restore circulation and may include bypass grafts, endarterectomy, patch-grafting, or a sympathectomy.

Raynaud's Disease

Raynaud's disease is a chronic condition primarily affecting women. Attacks are often triggered by cold or emotional stress. Vasospasm of the arteries of the hands or feet leads to blanching of the fingers or toes. This is accompanied by a sensation of coldness and numbness followed by throbbing pain, tingling, and swelling.[15] The patient should be reassured that the disease is unlikely to lead to serious disability; the symptoms will be more a matter of inconvenience. The patient should keep the extremities warm and avoid contact with cold objects. Stressful situations that precipitate the attacks should be identified and coped with accordingly. Care should be taken to prevent injury or infection to the affected extremities. Smoking should be discouraged. Vasodilators are not usually prescribed unless the symptoms are severe. A sympathectomy may be helpful for patients who have not obtained relief by any other method.

Buerger's Disease

Buerger's disease (thromboangiitis obliterans) is an acute inflammation of the arteries and veins of the lower extremities that leads to the development of lesions that eventually cause thrombus formation. This results in decreased blood flow to the legs and feet. Leg ulcers and gangrene are frequent complications. The incidence is highest among young men who are heavy smokers. Intermittent claudication—muscle cramping occurring after exercise but relieved by rest—is a common symptom. Other symptoms include coldness, numbness, and tingling in the lower extremities; absent or diminished peripheral pulses; and redness or cyanosis. Smoking is known to have a negative influence on the course of the disease, so the patient should be advised to stop. Skin and foot care to prevent infections is vital. Exposure to cold and trauma should be avoided. Vasodilators may be used, and a sympathectomy may be performed.

Thrombophlebitis

Simple phlebitis is the inflammation of the wall of a vein, whereas **thrombophlebitis** is inflammation with the presence of a blood clot in the vein. Many factors predispose a person to this condition, including age, occupation, obesity, prolonged abdominal or pelvic surgery, injury to the extremities, dehydration, and any condition that restricts the individual to bedrest over an extended time. Thrombophlebitis may occur easily in older persons with sclerotic changes in the veins that cause the blood to flow slowly.

The nurse can contribute much toward the prevention of thrombophlebitis by carrying out several nursing procedures. Active exercise while the patient is in bed, including dorsiflexion (bending backward) and plantarflexion (bending forward) of the toes, should be done several times each hour or for 3 minutes each hour while the patient is awake. This simple exercise will do more to stimulate circulation than will massage or telling the patient to move his legs. Fluid intake should be encouraged to prevent dehydration, and accurate intake and output records should be maintained.

Elevating the knees by changing the position of the Gatch bed and placing pillows under the knees should be avoided, since these procedures will compress the undersurface of the knee, causing a pooling of blood and increased pressure in the veins of the calf of the leg. The same situation occurs when the patient is sitting in a chair, which permits the calf of the leg and the knee to be compressed. Placing the patient's feet on a stool will avoid pressure on veins under the knee. Tight abdominal binders and dressing and the use of drugs that depress respiration should be avoided after surgery.

Assessment

The veins of the lower extremities are usually affected. The patient may complain of pain or cramps in the calf of the leg, and these pains may follow the course of the vein. Tenderness and abnormal distension of the vein may be noted. There is usually an increase in temperature, and the sedimentation rate is also elevated. The most serious complication of thrombophlebitis is pulmonary embolism with a possible pulmonary infarction.

Intervention

Treatment of the patient with thrombophlebitis depends on whether superficial veins or deep vessels are involved and on the extent of involvement. If the phlebitis involves only the superficial veins, anticoagulant therapy may not be ordered. Bedrest with continuous hot, moist packs is generally ordered, and as soon as the acute condition has subsided, the patient may be allowed out of bed with an elastic stocking on the extremity. If the phlebitis involves the deep veins, anticoagulant therapy with heparin is usually ordered. A phlebogram will determine the exact site and extent of the involvement. A surgical procedure known as thrombectomy (removal of a thrombus from the vein) may be done. Hot compresses using Turkish towels soaked in warm water (with excess water removed) are then wrapped loosely about the extremity and covered with plastic. An Aquamatic K pad may also be used. Elastic stockings should be put on before the patient gets out of bed and removed several times during the day and the leg inspected. Elastic stockings should not be rolled at the top.

Varicose Veins

Varicose veins develop when blood flow in the legs becomes permanently sluggish and the veins permanently dilate. Other forms of venous **varicosities** are hemorrhoids and varicocele. Several factors contribute to the cause of varicose veins. The underlying cause may be a congenital weakness in the walls of the vein, an abnormal placement of the valves in the vein, or a defect of the valves. The immediate causes include severe physical strain such as that produced by long standing and lifting heavy objects. Pressure on pelvic veins from the enlarging uterus during pregnancy, pelvic tumors that may press on the veins, obesity, and wearing tight round garters also contribute to the development of varicose veins.

Assessment

About 50% of all women and 25% of men 40 years of age or older have varicose veins. They develop insidiously, beginning in young adults and gradually increasing in severity with increasing age. At first there may be no symptoms, but eventually the patient may complain of pain in the feet and ankles, with a tired, heavy feeling in the legs. Swelling may occur in the feet, which usually subsides during the night and reappears as soon as the patient is up on his feet again. Pigmented areas may appear on the skin above the ankles with eczema-like lesions; these lesions ultimately may break down, and ulcers may occur. The rupture of the varicose vein through an ulcer may cause considerable blood loss.

Intervention

The treatment of patients with varicose veins include bedrest and elevation of the extremity, the use of an elastic stocking or an elastic bandage, or the surgical removal of the vein (vein stripping). Sometimes when small veins are involved, the physician may inject a solution into the vein that will cause it to sclerose without providing a permanent cure.

Vein ligation and stripping

Ligation and stripping is one of the most common types of surgery performed on the veins. Before surgery the physician will determine whether the deep veins of the extremity are open. Not all patients with varicose veins will need to have them surgically removed, but when edema and pigmentation (which may lead to ulceration) occur, surgery is usually advised. Sometimes veins are so distended that they become unsightly, and surgery may be done for cosmetic reasons.

The physician usually visits the patient on the evening before surgery and marks the route of the veins that are to be removed. The long saphenous vein, which branches from the groin and extends to the ankle, is often the one removed. One or both extremities may be involved. The entire leg and pubis are shaved, with special care given to the groin, which will be the site of ligation. Other preparation is the same as that for other surgical patients. Although the surgical procedure may be performed while the patient is under local anesthesia, it is long and painful, and the patient is usually given a general anesthetic.

Postoperative intervention

When the patient returns from surgery, the extremity will be wrapped with elastic bandages. Small, sterile dressings will cover the areas in which veins were ligated. These dressings should be checked frequently for evidence of bleeding. Bandages should be removed only on the physician's order. The knee section of the Gatch bed should not be raised, but the foot of the bed may be elevated about 8 inches to facilitate the return of venous blood. The foot and toes should be observed for skin color and edema, and the patient should be encouraged to move them as soon as possible. The patient may have some pain for 2 or 3 days, and meperidine may be ordered for relief. Most patients are ambulatory the first day after surgery or as soon as they have recovered from anesthesia. Patients should not sit or stand but should walk. Patients are usually discharged after 2 or 3 days, and an elastic stocking is worn for several weeks. Patients should be advised against the use of depilatory cream on the legs, especially where the skin may be thin. They should avoid scratching and bruising the legs. They should not sit with the legs crossed and are advised to avoid the use of panty girdles that may compress veins in the groin and thighs.

Lymphangitis

Lymphangitis is an acute inflammation of the lymph vessels caused by the invasion of bacteria such as the streptococcus organism. It is characterized by red streaks that follow the course of the vessel involved. The patient may experience an elevated temperature and chills. In some patients the lymph nodes along the course of the vessel may be swollen and tender. Usually, however, the inflammatory condition terminates at the first lymph node. The condition may be serious if the causative organism reaches the bloodstream because septicemia may occur.

Intervention

Treatment of lymphangitis is based on controlling the underlying cause. Warm, moist dressing may be ordered for application over the affected vessels, and scrupulous skin care and immediate attention to all abrasions should be given. The affected part is elevated, and sulfonamide or antibiotic therapy is ordered. The condition generally responds quickly to therapy. In some cases, abscess formation may occur, and incision and drainage may be necessary.

THE PATIENT WITH OPERATIVE CONDITIONS OF THE CARDIOVASCULAR SYSTEM

Surgery of the cardiovascular system is one of the most significant accomplishments of medical science in this century. Currently it saves lives and provides lifetimes of health free from crippling cardiac conditions.

Heart surgery requires a vast array of equipment and a staff of highly trained, efficient professionals. In no other aspect of medical-surgical care is the team concept of greater importance than in operative procedures involving the heart. Judgment, technical competency, and skill in observation are demanded of the nurse, and an ability to understand the feeling and emotional response of the patient is of equal importance. Whether the patient is an adult or a child, the nurse's responsibility begins in the physician's office and continues long after the surgery has been completed and convalescence and rehabilitation have returned the patient to his optimum condition.

Because almost all cardiac surgery is performed in large medical centers, patients may be away from their families and friends. They will be in an unfamiliar environment and may be fearful of what is happening to them. The warm, friendly attitude of the nurse contributes greatly to the patient's feeling of security and may lead him to verbalize fears, anxiety, and problems.

Cardiovascular surgery may be performed to correct congenital or acquired conditions. It may be performed inside the heart (open heart surgery), or it may be done to relieve or correct some condition outside the heart (closed heart surgery). It may involve the valves of the heart, the heart muscle or its covering, or the great blood vessels of the body. Surgery is also used to treat coronary artery disease. The coronary artery bypass is one of the most frequently performed heart operations in the United States. To create the bypass, the surgeon removes a vein from the patient's leg and sutures one end to a new opening in the aorta near the junction of the coronary arteries. The other end is connected to the coronary artery beyond the diseased area. This procedure bypasses the obstruction to blood flow and increases the oxygen supply to the heart muscle immediately. The operation does not "cure" the process of atherosclerosis, the primary cause of coronary artery disease. The patient must maintain a low-fat, low-cholesterol diet and follow recommendations designed to prevent the progression of the atherosclerosis, or the bypass arteries may also become occluded.

Open heart surgery can be performed only with the use of a heart-lung machine. Although there are many models, all machines provide gas exchange (oxygen and carbon dioxide), which normally occurs in the lungs, and then pump oxygenated blood to the body tissues, duplicating the action of the heart. This process is called a cardiopulmonary bypass. In addition, the patient's body temperature is lowered during surgery to slow metabolic processes.

Cardiac surgery may be performed on very young infants, middle-aged persons, and selected older persons. Not all persons needing surgery are suitable candidates for cardiac surgery, and not all those having surgery will be completely cured. Sometimes damage already done cannot be corrected, but further damage can be prevented. The physician may recommend surgery to the patient, but the final decision is always the patient's. In the case of a young child the parent must make the decision, which is not always easy because there is some risk involved and sometimes, even when the child may be helped, there is no possibility of complete cure.

Cardiac Surgery
Preoperative care

The patient is admitted to the hospital a day before surgery and is usually very apprehensive. Before surgery, the patient receives detailed examinations, including laboratory studies and special tests and examinations outlined earlier in this chapter. The physician will plan for a conference with the patient and family to give them information about the surgery. The nurse should participate in the conference to reinforce information at a later time.

Before surgery, the patient's weight and vital signs are recorded to establish a normal baseline. The patient continues with a sodium-restricted diet and current medication regimen. Unless contraindicated, the patient should be up and walking around to maintain strength and muscle tone. If the patient is a child, the nurse may use the opportunity to learn the child's interests, habits, likes, and dislikes to establish a friendly mutual acceptance. This will be extremely important in the postoperative care of a child. The room should be attractive and cheerful, and the child should be provided with his favorite toys.

The surgeon and nurse will review with the patient details of the postoperative care. The patient should be taught how to breathe deeply and cough and may practice this procedure under supervision because it will be essential after surgery. The patient should be informed that chest tubes, nasogastric tubes, an endotracheal tube, a urinary catheter, and intravenous lines may be used, that vital signs will be monitored frequently, and that pain medication will be available.

The physical preparation is similar to that for most surgical patients. The skin preparation usually covers a wide area from chin to ankles. A sedative for sleep and rest is recommended the evening before with fluids restricted after midnight. Although the fear is not always verbalized, the patient may expect to die, and may have made necessary material preparation. On the day of surgery members of the family and a religious counselor should be permitted to visit the patient.

Postoperative care

The first 48 hours after heart surgery are the most critical for the patient. The patient is transferred to an ICU for close assessment and sophisticated hemodynamic monitoring.

Vital signs

The apical-radial pulse, blood pressure, and respiration are checked and recorded every 15 minutes until the patient is stable and then are checked hourly. The rhythm, rate, and strength of the pulse should be observed, and the nurse should constantly observe for dysrhythmias. The pressures inside the heart are also monitored. The physician should indicate the lowest level of systolic pressure that the patient can tolerate without harmful effects. If the surgery has involved coronary arteries, systolic pressure must be watched more closely. Any elevation of temperature of more than 102° F (39° C) should be reported, because temperature elevation increases the work of the heart.

Respiratory assistance

For the first few hours after surgery, the patient is given assisted ventilation and oxygen. This procedure decreases the possibility of hypoxia and resulting dysrhythmias. Oxygen administration may continue for several days.

Chest catheters may be used to provide closed drainage for both the right and left pleural cavities or for one side only. They are attached to a water-sealed drainage system and must be kept free of clots and kinks (Chapter 15). Drainage should be observed for excessive amounts of blood. The amount of drainage in 24 hours will depend on the type of surgery and may vary from 400 to 1200 ml in some patients. Absence of drainage must be promptly reported because fluid may be accumulating in the chest cavity, resulting in serious cardiac complication. When turning the patient, the nurse should provide for adequate slack in the tubing to prevent disconnection or displacement of the chest catheters.

The patient is encouraged to cough and breathe deeply every 2 hours. Some patients may be placed in a semi-Fowler's position and turned from side to side every 2 hours; others may be turned to one side only; and patients undergoing some types of surgery must remain flat and may not be turned.

One of the purposes of deep breathing and coughing is to bring up secretions and maintain a clear airway. The nurse may assist the patient by supporting the chest and upper abdomen with a pillow. Deep coughing is often a problem because the patient fears pain, so coughing and deep breathing are most effective about 30 minutes after receiving pain medication.

Other interventions

A nasogastric tube is inserted and connected to suction to keep the stomach empty. The patient is usually maintained on a regimen of intravenous fluids for 1 or 2 days. Blood samples are taken daily for several days to monitor serum electrolyte values.

Activity is increased as the patient's recovery permits. Patients usually sit in a chair 24 hours after surgery and ambulate short distances 24 to 48 hours after surgery. The patient then begins a prescribed exercise program. Patients report most pain during the first 48 hours because of rib retraction during surgery. Meperidine or morphine sulfate is usually ordered.

Most patients are allowed fluids by mouth as soon as nausea and vomiting have ceased; however, intravenous infusions are maintained for a few days. Occasionally, fluid intake is restricted, and an accurate measurement must be maintained. A sodium-restricted diet is usually given to the patient as tolerated.

Prevention of complications

Antibiotics are routinely given to all patients to prevent infection. An x-ray examination of the chest and ECG are usually done within the first 24 hours of surgery. Dressings should be checked frequently for evidence of any unusual bleeding. Any numbness, tingling, pain, or loss of motion, in the extremities should be reported. Assessments for shock, hemorrhage, pneumothorax, pulmonary edema, and congestive heart failure are made at regular intervals. Disorientation is common after heart surgery but should always be noted and reported. The patient may have profuse sweating. The bed should be kept dry.

Ambulation

The type of surgery and the condition and progress of the patient will determine the return of ambulation activity. The process should be a gradual one, and initially walking may consist of only a few steps. Most patients are discharged 7 days after surgery.

The surgical removal of a patient's diseased heart and its replacement with a normal heart (heart transplant) has been accomplished in some large medical centers.

A summary of nursing care is found in the box on p. 392.

Percutaneous Transluminal Coronary Angioplasty

Percutaneous transluminal coronary angioplasty (PTCA) offers patients with symptomatic coronary artery disease another treatment option in addition to coronary artery bypass grafting (CABG). PTCA provides favorable results in terms of risks, success rate, cost, and physical capacity following the procedure. However, restenosis (recurrence of stenosis) data differ greatly between these two options. The rate of restenosis within 6 months following PTCA is 30%. With CABG, the recurrence rate is 81% to 96% for saphenous and internal mammary artery grafts, respectively.[25]

The **angioplasty** procedure involves dilating the stenosed coronary arteries with a double-lumen balloon catheter.[30] The procedure is performed with local anesthesia in the cardiac catheterization laboratory. The coronary artery is usually accessed using the femoral percutaneous approach; however, the brachial percutaneous approach or a cutdown can also be used.

Nursing care patients undergoing angioplasty is similar to a patient undergoing surgery. The patient and the family need to be knowledgeable about the angioplasty procedure to reduce anxiety and establish trust and cooperation. During the procedure the nurse instructs the patient to report feelings of chest pain. The nurse will also continuously monitor the patient's blood pressure, heart rate, and rhythm.

Immediately after the angioplasty procedure the patient is transferred to the CCU or the unit that ensures close hemodynamic monitoring. Specifically, the patient is monitored for excessive bleeding at the catheter insertion site, chest pain, or dysrhythmias, which could indicate that the newly dilated artery is closing.

Patient education after the procedure should focus on modifying risk factors by changing nutritional and dietary patterns. The patient's length of stay is usually 3 days or less, so patient education must be concise.

Embolectomy

The surgical removal of an embolus from an artery (or infrequently a vein) is called an **embolectomy.** Throughout this text, stress is placed on the prevention of venous stasis and clot formation. Ar-

---

NURSING CARE GUIDELINES
Cardiac Surgery

Nursing diagnoses

- Ineffective breathing patterns related to discomfort and musculoskeletal impairement associated with chest surgery
- Alteration in comfort associated with surgical intervention
- Anxiety related to inability to control illness
- Impaired physical mobility associated with discomfort and activity intolerance
- Self-care deficit related to discomfort and activity intolerance
- Fear of death
- Potential alteration in cardiac output associated with decreased cardiac function
- Potential alteration in tissue perfusion related to interruption of arterial blood flow
- Potential impaired gas exchange associated with possible decrease in cardiac function
- Potential alteration in fluid volume related to altered cardiac function

Nursing interventions
Preoperative phase

- Explain laboratory tests to patient
- Monitor apical-radial pulses and blood pressure
- Weigh daily
- Continue sodium-restricted diet, diuretics, and digitalis preparations as prescribed
- Provide activity as tolerated
- Teach deep-breathing and coughing exercises
- Explain postoperative care and equipment to patient
- Provide emotional support, anticipating needs
- Observe for signs and symptoms of cardiorespiratory complications

Immediate postoperative phase

- Check vital signs every 15 minutes until stable and then hourly for 24 hours
- Observe for cardiac dysrhythmias

- Monitor pressures within heart
- Report any temperature elevation above 102° F (39° C)
- Administer oxygen and assisted ventilation as ordered
- Assist patient to cough and breathe deeply every hour
- Maintain patency of closed chest drainage; observe for excessive drainage
- Administer intravenous infusions as ordered
- Maintain patency of nasogastric tube; give good oral and nasal hygiene
- Observe for signs of electrolyte imbalance and fluid retention
- Encourage progressive activity as tolerated and ordered
- Maintain patency of indwelling urethral catheter
- Measure and record hourly urine output: report if less than 30 ml per hour
- Check and record specific gravity of urine every hour
- Administer pain medication as needed
- Observe for complications—shock, hemorrhage, pneumothorax, pulmonary edema, cyanosis, congestive heart failure
- Check dressings frequently for amount and type of drainage
- Observe for disorientation or psychosis
- Provide frequent rest periods

Expected outcomes

- Vital signs within normal ranges
- Deep breathe and cough exercise performed every hour
- Normal fluid and electrolyte balance achieved
- Relief from pain obtained
- Proper rest and sleep obtained
- Postoperative or cardiorespiratory complications absent

---

terial occlusion usually occurs as a result of decreased blood flow in narrowed vessels. This can be due to hypovolemia, decreased cardiac output, or atherosclerotic diseased vessels. An embolus may lodge in an artery and completely shut off blood flow to the part supplied by that artery. Symptoms are pain, changes in sensation, and discoloration of the affected body part. Often, emergency surgery is required to correct the problem.[11] When an embolectomy has been performed, the extremity must be protected from in-

jury. No external heat or cold should be applied. Anticoagulant drugs are administered to prevent clot formation, and antibiotics are given to prevent infection. Vital signs are observed, as in all surgical procedures.

CARDIAC REHABILITATION

Cardiac rehabilitation is designed to maintain or restore the cardiac patient to his or her optimum

---

Cardiac Rehabilitation Goals

Prevent or delay complications
Improve participation in activities of daily living
Resume work
Attain a positive psychologic adjustment
Reduce cardiovascular risk factors

Four Phases of Cardiac Rehabilitation

Phase I *In-patient (CCU):* ambulation and range of motion achieved (when patient is considered stable)
Phase II *Remainder of hospitalization:* gradual increase in exercise with stair climbing
Phase III *Convalescence at home:* expanded moderate-intensity exercises
Phase IV *Long-term (lifelong) conditioning:* exercise, prescribed by exercise specialist nurse in conjunction with cardiologist

level of physiologic, psychologic, educational, and social function. It includes educational and exercise programs, counseling, and social networking for patients with myocardial infarctions, chronic angina, and cardiomyopathy and for those who have undergone cardiac surgery. The goals of cardiac rehabilitation are described (see box). Cardiac rehabilitation generally includes four phases (see box).

Patients report that while hospitalized their greatest source of information and care was the nurse. Patients and their families should have all available information about their physical condition, treatment plan, and the hospital environment.

The population of the United States is increasing, and every year more people are reaching the age when heart disease most often manifests itself and takes it greatest toll. Diseases of the heart and blood vessels cost the country approximately $20 billion annually, with atherosclerotic coronary artery disease accounting for the majority of the money spent. The intangible results are deprivation of the family, physical and mental suffering, and loss to society when the individual is unable to function as a social being. However, research has provided guidelines for the prevention of some kinds of heart disease, and through adequate medical care and evaluation, followed by sound programs of rehabilitation, many heart patients can become contributing members of society.

BASIC CARDIAC LIFE SUPPORT

Two organizations are primarily responsible for basic cardiac life-support standards in the United States, the American Heart Association and the American Red Cross. These standards are taught by certified instructors across the nation to health-care providers and the general public. Once lost, cardiac function must be restored as quickly as possible to avoid cerebral damage. All nurses should be prepared in *cardiopulmonary resuscitation* (CPR).

Before starting basic life support, it must first be determined that the patient is unresponsive. This is accomplished by gently tapping the person's shoulder and asking "Are you OK?" If the person does not respond, call for help. *Do not leave the person.* Next, assess the person for the presence or absence of respirations by turning the patient on their back (Figure 16-23).

Open the person's airway. Without muscle tone, the tongue and epiglottis will obstruct the pharynx and larynx. The head tilt–chin lift technique is an effective method for opening the airway. To accomplish the head tilt, place one hand on the person's forehead and use the palm of your hand to apply firm, backward pressure to tilt the head back. Place the fingers of the other hand under the lower jaw near the chin, and lift to bring the chin forward. The jaw is supported and helps to tilt the head back (Figure 16-24). This procedure should not be attempted on persons with suspected cervical or head injuries.

Determine breathlessness by placing your ear over the person's mouth and nose while maintaining an open airway. Observe the person's chest to see if it rises and falls, listen for air rushing during exhalation, and feel for airflow (Figure 16-25).

Begin rescue breathing by sealing the mouth and nose. Deliver two breaths of 1 to 1½ seconds each. Observe chest rise and fall (a sign of adequate ventilation) and then listen and feel for movement of air. If the patient is unable to ventilate, reposition the head and repeat rescue breathing. If the person cannot be ventilated after repositioning the head, begin the procedure for airway obstruction.

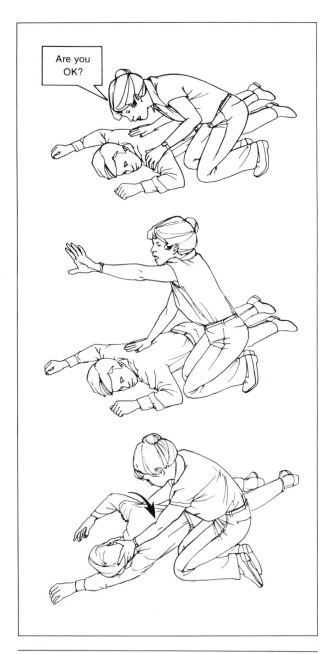

Figure 16-23

Initial steps in cardiopulmonary resuscitation. *Top,* Determining unresponsiveness. *Center,* calling for help. *Bottom,* correct positioning. *(From Standards and guidelines for cardiopulmonary resuscitation and emergency cardiac care, part 2, 255:2915-2932.)*

Figure 16-24

Head tilt/chin lift method of opening airway. *(From Standards and guidelines for cardiopulmonary resuscitation and emergency cardiac care, part 2, 255:2915-2932.)*

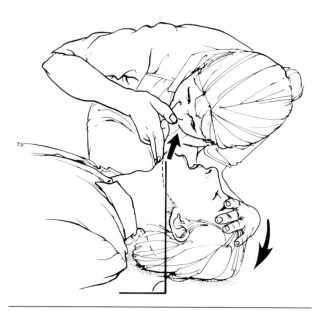

Figure 16-25

Determination of breathlessness. *(From Standards and guidelines for cardiopulmonary resuscitation and emergency cardiac care, part 2, 255:2915-2932.)*

Assess for circulation. Palpate the carotid artery (5 to 10 seconds) because it is the strongest palpable pulse. If the pulse is absent, begin external cardiac compressions. It is important to take time to adequately check for a pulse, because external cardiac compressions are dangerous to a beating heart.

Kneel by the person's shoulders, placing the palm of your hand on the sternum and two fingers above the xiphoid process (Figure 16-26). Place your second hand on top of the first. Compress the sternum 1½ to 2 inches for adults and ½ to 1½ inches for a child. Compressions should be equal. Hands remain on the sternum during up-

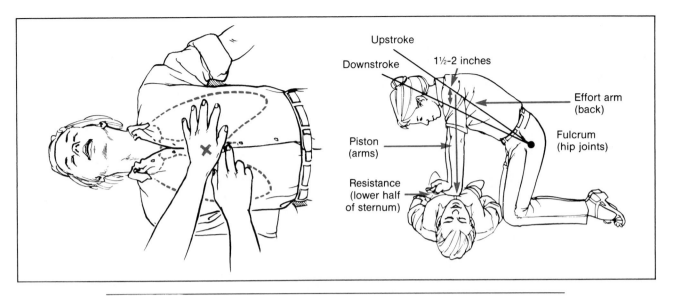

Figure 16-26
External chest compression. *(From Standards and guidelines for cardiopulmonary resuscitation and emergency cardiac care, part 2, 255:2915-2932.)*

stroke, when the chest should relax completely. The compression rate should be 15 to 18 to maintain a rate of 80 to 100 beats per minute for adults and children, 100 beats per minute for infants. Go back to the head of the patient, position the head, and administer two breaths. Complete four cycles of 15 to 18 compressions and two ventilations before rechecking for a carotid pulse. If the pulse returns, stop cardiac compressions. Once spontaneous respirations begin, mouth-to-mouth resuscitation can be stopped.

AIRWAY OBSTRUCTION

An airway may be partially or completely obstructed. If the airway is partially obstructed, the person will exchange air. If air exchange is good, the person can cough forcefully, dislodging the obstruction. Sometimes the air exchange is good initially but becomes poor. If the air exchange is poor, the person's cough will be ineffective. There will be a high-pitched noise with inhalations and even cyanosis. With complete airway obstruction the person cannot speak, breathe, or cough and may clutch the neck (Figure 16-27). This is the universal choking sign.

Ask the person to speak. If the person cannot, attempt to clear the person's airway. Stand behind the person, wrapping your arms around the victim's waist (Figure 16-28). Make a fist with one

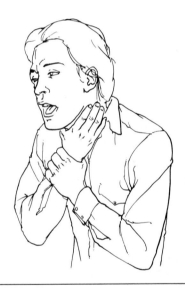

Figure 16-27
Universal distress signal for choking. *(From Standards and guidelines for cardiopulmonary resuscitation and emergency cardiac care, part 2, 255:2915-2932.)*

hand and place the thumb side against the person's abdomen, in the midline, slightly above the naval and well below the tip of the xiphoid process. Grasp your fist with the other hand. Press the person's abdomen with quick upward thrusts. This process is frequently called the *Heimlich maneuver,* named for Dr. Harry J. Heimlich who developed it. Each thrust should be distinct and

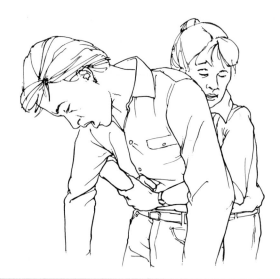

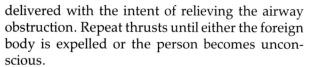

Figure 16-28

Heimlich maneuver. Conscious victim with foreign-body airway obstruction. *(From Standards and guidelines for cardiopulmonary resuscitation and emergency cardiac care, part 2, 255:2915-2932.)*

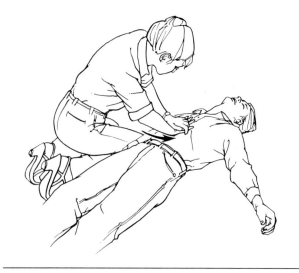

Figure 16-29

Heimlich maneuver. Unconscious victim with foreign-body airway obstruction. *(From Standards and guidelines for cardiopulmonary resuscitation and emergency cardiac care, part 2, 255:2915-2932.)*

delivered with the intent of relieving the airway obstruction. Repeat thrusts until either the foreign body is expelled or the person becomes unconscious.

If the person lapses into unconsciousness, position the person on his or her back, open the mouth by grasping both the tongue and lower jaw between the thumb and fingers, lifting the mandible. (This is the tongue-jaw lift.) Using your finger, sweep your finger deeply into the mouth to remove any foreign material. Attempt to ventilate the person by using the tongue-jaw lift to open the mouth. If the airway is still obstructed, straddle the person's thighs, place the heel of one hand against the person's abdomen, midline above the naval and well below the xiphoid (Figure 16-29). Place your second hand directly on top of your first hand. Press into the abdomen with quick, upward thrusts, six to ten times. Check the person's mouth again for foreign material by sweeping a finger deeply into the mouth. Reposition the head and attempt to ventilate. If the airway is still obstructed, straddle the persons' thighs again and repeat the process until the airway is clear. If the person does not breathe spontaneously after a foreign body is removed, ventilate the person and check for a pulse; if no pulse is present, begin cardiac compressions.

The abdominal thrust should not be practiced on an individual who is not experiencing airway obstruction. Nurses should seek complete train-

ing in first aid for obstruction of the airway with a foreign body through the American Red Cross or the American Heart Association. Thousands of lives could be saved each year if more people were trained in these rescue maneuvers.

If the airway is obstructed by secretions, it must be cleared by suction or by gravity drainage. The patient with multiple injuries must not be turned on the side to drain secretions because there is always the possibility of spinal cord injury. If a vertebral fracture is suspected, the patient's neck should *not* be hyperextended to open the airway. The nurse places one hand on each side of the patient's head, holding it in a fixed, neutral position. The mandible is pushed forward with the index fingers without tilting the head backward. Two fingers then can be inserted into the patient's mouth to remove foreign bodies or secretions if suction equipment is not available.

If the patient is breathing, respirations should be assessed. The force of expiration, the presence of noise or retractions, and the patient's skin color will warn of inadequate oxygenation. It is also important to note whether or not the chest wall is intact and that chest movements are symmetric. The patient with a flail chest moves the chest in a direction opposite to the rest of the thorax during respirations. The patient will be cyanotic, respirations will be noisy, and the patient will have a deathlike pallor. Another life-threatening condition is tension pneumothorax. The pleural space of the affected side becomes filled with air, causing lung collapse. Decreased breath sounds are heard on the affected side, and the trachea shifts to the unaffected side. The neck veins become distended, and there are changes in the level of consciousness. A fracture of the larynx will obstruct the airway completely. A laryngeal fracture should be suspected if there are bruises on the neck or if subcutaneous emphysema is observed in the neck area. Air is forced into the subcutaneous tissues when the larynx is damaged. The patient may also exhibit hoarseness, cough, and hemoptysis. These conditions usually require a tracheostomy to maintain a patent airway.

NURSING CARE PLAN
Patient with Congestive Heart Failure and Oliguria

The patient is a 68-year-old woman with morbid obesity who was admitted directly from her Physician's Office to the Emergency Department with a medical diagnosis of oliguria and congestive heart failure. She has been on continuous oxygen at home due to chronic hypoxia, sleep apnea, and now with increasing dyspnea. She has noticed increasing generalized edema, and currently has a dry hacking cough that interferes with sleep. She complains of mild abdominal pain unrelated to eating or stooling.

She was cardioverted in the emergency department for atrial fibrillation. An echocardiogram done at that time visualized a mural thrombi, and she was given anticoagulants. Lasix and Metalazone were administered to increase urinary output. Calan (Verapamil) was given to dilate the coronary arteries and decrease oxygen demand. Procan was given as an antiarrythmiac. She was admitted to the coronary care unit for 5 days and then transferred onto a medical unit.

Past medical history

Hospitalized as a child for a fractured femur from a bicycle accident.

Pregnancies complicated by excess weight, preeclampsia and gestational diabetes.

C-sectioned × 3 with viable infants. All infants weighed over 10 lbs.

Abdominal hysterectomy 12 years ago due to excessive bleeding and fibroid tumors. Uterus removed along with both ovaries and tubes.

Maintained on estrogen therapy until age 60.

States she has always been "heavy."

Diabetes mellitus type II, (non-insulin dependent), (NIDDM), × 25 years.

Hypertension for 20 years. Has been on various antihypertensive meds with moderately good response. Quality compliance to drug therapy.

COPD- chronic hypoxia and difficulty with activities of daily living (ADLs). Uses oxygen at home via nasal cannula.

Biventricular congestive heart failure for past 2 years.

Sleep apnea, prefers to sleep in recliner.

Chronic renal failure. Requires diuretics daily.

Atrial fibrillation in past. Responded to meds. Cardioversion in the emergency department—first time needed.

Psychosocial data

Married. Supportive husband with three adult children. (Two live out of state). Six grandchildren. One granddaughter in college lives in the home. Gives some assistance to her grandmother.

Jewish religion. Husband cantor in Temple.

Retired from lighting supply company as cashier, (sedentary activity).

Has private health insurance plus Medicare.

Own home, one level, few stairs. Wheelchair ramp being built onto side of house.

Has never smoked. Denies overuse of alcohol and/or drugs.

No known food allergies. Allergic to sulfa drugs, ? allergy to some tapes.

Assessment data

Oriented × 3 (time, place, and person).

Vital signs: T 97 rectally, P 62, R 20. B.P. 162/78.

Weight on admission: 362 (bed scale).

Current weight: 351 lbs (6 days later).

Height: 5 ft 1 in

Skin: Multiple open weepy blisters on left thigh and right arm. Both draining clear fluid. Many open areas on back of thighs and buttocks. Evidence of irritation from scratching.

Blister on right great toe, covered with a bandage.

Respiratory: Decreased breath sounds in lower lobes bilaterally.

Bibasilar crackles (rales) heard.

Upper lobes clear to ascultation.

Cardiovascular: Apical pulse = 68. Heard at apex. Regualr rhythm > Neck veins distended.

Abdominal: Pendulous abdomen with many fatty indentations.

Difficult to hear bowel sounds due to the depth of adipose tissue.

Continued on next page.

Abd. girth 64 to 68 inches. Abd. nontender, soft on palpation.

Midline scars from previous surgeries.

Musculoskeletal: Grossly edematous extremities. 3+ pitting edema.

Negative pedal, posterior tibial, popiteal pulses. Positive femoral pulses felt bilaterally.

Urinary: Foley catheter draining cloudy urine. Specific Gravity = 1.024

Lab data

Hgb 9.1 Hct 29 Blood sugar = 212
BUN 63 (normal 5-20)
Creatinine clearance 3.7 (normal = 0.8-1.4 mg/dl)
K 5.2 Na 136
Oxygen sats at 94-97 on oxygen at 2 L. Drops to 78-80 when off the oxygen.

Medications

40 units NPH insulin daily in morning
4 units regular insulin/coverage if blood sugar over 160.
Prednisone 15 mg po daily
Calan SR 240 mg po daily
Procan SR 500 mg po TID
Digitalis 0.125 mg po BID
Metalazone 5 mg po daily
Colace 100 mg po BID
Ducolax 10 mg × 1 prn constipation (rectally).
Diet: 1800-calorie ADA diet, with 800 ml fluid restriction.

NURSING DIAGNOSIS

Alteration in cardiac output related to cardiac failure, as evidenced by increasing shortness of breath, and inability to perform ADLs.

Expected patient outcomes	Nursing interventions	Evaluation for expected outcomes
Patient demonstrates no signs of hyperkalemia on ECG. Patient maintains intake of no more than 800 ml, and output no less than 25 ml per hour. Urine specific gravity remains between 1.010 and 1.020. Hct stays above 30. BUN, creatinine, sodium, and potassium stay within acceptable levels. Patient's skin shows signs of healing and remains infection free. Patient assists with some ADLs without undue fatigue. Patient remains on bed rest to conserve energy while dyspnea remains. Patient participates in passive exercises every 1 to 2 hours when awake. Patient demonstrates her skill in selecting permitted foods such as those low in sodium. Patient describes signs and symptoms that require reporting to her physician. Upon discharge, patient cites foods that are rich in potassium.	Monitor BP, pulse, cardiac rhythm, temperature, and breath sounds every 4 hours. Record and report changes from baseline. Take temperature rectally if dyspnea present. Carefully monitor I & O, and specific gravity every 4 hours. Monitor BUN, creatinine, electrolytes, Hgb and Hct. Discuss patient's food preferences, and plan according to dietary restrictions. Assist her with meal planning. Provide mouth care every 4 hours. Keep her mucous membranes moist with a water-soluble lubricant. Keep on oxygen at 2 L via nasal cannula. Explain the rationale for not increasing the oxygen above 2 L at home. Support patient with positive feedback about adherences to restrictions. Give skin care every 4 hours. Examine skin daily for signs of breakdown/infection. Change patient's position at least every 2 hours. Elevate edematous extremities. Maintain on bedrest while dyspnea present.	Patient will experience decreased shortness of breath. Patient will gradually show improvement in her ability to perform ADLs. Patient's BP will remain within the normal range. Signs of hyperkalemia, (peaked or elevated T waves, prolonged P-R intervals, widened QRS complexes or depressed ST segments) do not appear on ECG. Patient's I & O remain within established limits. Patient's skin remains free of infection, and shows signs of healing with no new blister apparent. Patient's Hct remains above 30. Patient identifies the signs and symptoms to report to her physician.

Expected patient outcomes	Nursing interventions	Evaluation for expected outcomes
	Teach patient to conserve energy. Increase her level of activity as tolerated. Ambulate with assistance until patient's strength improves. Apply antiembolism stockings to increase venous return. Remove for 1 hour every 8 hours. Teach patient foods that are rich in potassium (bananas, all citrus fruits and juices, broccoli, bran flakes, raw carrots, prunes).	

NURSING DIAGNOSIS

Fluid volume excess related to congestive heart failure.

Expect patient outcomes	Nursing interventions	Evaluation for expected outcomes
Patient's body weight will decrease by 2 to 3 lbs daily. Patient's hemodynamic status will be restored to a normal range. Patient's electrolyte levels, BUN, and creatinine will come to as near a normal range as possible. Patient's pulmonary status will be restored to an acceptable range. Patient will report less dyspnea and experience more comfort. Patient and her family will demonstrate an adequate knowledge base regarding fluid volume excess related to congestive heart failure.	Weigh daily before breakfast. Check for signs of further dependent edema, such as sacral edema, increasing pitting edema, and increased ascites. Monitor fluid restriction of 800 ml. Help patient to make a schedule for timed amounts. Provide sour hard candy to decrease thirst and improve taste. Explain the reasons for fluid and dietary restrictions. Assess skin turgor for signs of dehydration. Measure abdominal girth daily. Compare to previous measurements. Provide sodium restricted diet. Teach foods low in sodium. Administer diuretics as ordered. Monitor for increased output as response. Assess for peripheral edema. Measure girths to check for decreases. Explain the cause for fluid volume excess. Provide information regarding congestive heart failure, the relationship of diet, medications, activity and follow-up care. Ask patient to repeat back teachings. Check for any misinformation.	Patient will show a gradual decrease in weight and overall girth. Urine specific gravity will decrease as urine output increases. Electrolyte levels, BUN, and creatinine will return to as near a normal range as possible. Patient plans a 24 hour intake schedule. Patient shows increasing comfort and less shortness of breath. Patient states the rationales for restricted fluids, medications, and the need for compliance to orders. Complications of excess fluid do not remain.

NURSING DIAGNOSIS

Self-care deficit related to shortness of breath, morbid obesity, and fatigue as evidenced by her inability to carry out aspects of self-care such as bathing and personal hygiene.

Continued on next page.

Expected patient outcomes	Nursing interventions	Evaluation for expected outcomes
Patient's self-care needs are met. Patient demostrates the use of assistive devices. Patient discusses her feelings related to body image. Patient grows in her ability to perform some parts of the tasks of bathing and personal hygiene.	Identify patient's optimum time to attempt self-care (morning after a period of rest after breakfast). Provide privacy. Encourage a discussion of feelings related to body size and overall edema. Provide dignity to nursing care by showing feelings of acceptance. Place all articles of self-care within her reach. Praise patient for any attempts of self-care. Allow ample time to perform tasks. Rewarm the bath water if cold. Monitor for fatigue. Encourage her to plan rest periods before moving on to new tasks. Assist her when necessary. Check her color and overall adaptations. Provide constructive feedback.	Patient grows in her ability to perform some self-care needs. Patient discusses and shows signs of acceptance of her body image. Patient grows in her ability to accept constructive feedback, and plans ways to incorporate new learnings upon discharge.

NURSING DIAGNOSIS

Alteration in elimination related to immobility and diet as evidenced
by hard formed stool and painful defecation.

Expected patient outcomes	Nursing interventions	Evluation for expected outcomes
Patient displays normal bowel sounds. Patient will have a bowel movement every 2 to 3 days without undue strain. Patient states an understanding of factors contributing to constipation, such as diet, immobility and fluid intake.	Assess bowel sounds and bowel habits daily. Consult with dietician for use of prune juice as a fruit exchange. Administer Colace or Dulcolax as needed. Encourage as much movement as possible when awake. Progressive ambulation is best once dyspnea decreases. Discuss foods that are high in bulk and roughage Provide commode at bedside. Maintain privacy. Allow time for evacuation. Keep toilet articles within reach. Instruct patient to avoid straining if possible. Tell patient that abdominal massage may relieve discomfort and promote defecation.	Patient has less pain on defecation. Patient's bowel pattern returns to a more normal pattern for her. Patient identifies the relationship between inactivity, diet, and bowel habits. Patient uses the dietician as a resource person to discuss food exchanges and foods high in fiber and bulk.

REFERENCES AND ADDITIONAL READINGS

1. Appleton D and LaQuaglia JD: Vascular disease and post-operative nursing management, Crit Care Nurse 5(5):34–42, 1985.

2. Barden C and others: Balloon aortic valvuloplasty: nursing care implications, Crit Care Nurs 10(6):22–30, 1990.

3. Bates B: The heart, pressures, and pulses. In Bates B, ed: A guide to the physical examination, ed 4, Philadelphia, 1987, JB Lippincott Co.

4. Boley T, Curtis J, and Schmaltz R: Last hope for a failing heart, Am J Nurs 90(5):672–677, 1989.

5. Brewer C and Markis J: Streptokinase and tissue plasminogen activator in acute myocardial infarction, Heart Lung 15(6):552–568, 1986.

6. Brewer-Senerchia C: Thrombolytic therapy: a review of the literature on streptokinase and tissue plasminogen activator with implications for practice, Crit Care Nurs Clin North Am 1(2):359–372, 1989.

7. Briody M: The role of the nurse in modification of cardiac risk factors, Nurs Clin North Am 19:387–395, 1984.

8. Brown KR and Jacobson S: Mastering dysrhythmias: a problem solving guide, Philadelphia, 1988, FA Davis Co.

9. Budny J and Anderson-Drevs K: IV inotropic agents: dopamine, dobutamine, and amrinone. Crit Care Nurse 10(2):54–62, 1990.

10. Bullock BL and Rosendahl PP: Pathophysiology. Glenview, IL, 1988, Scott, Foresman & Co.

11. Burden L and Rodger J: Assessing chest pain and intervening efficiently, Nurs Life 6(2):33–40, 1986.

12. Carcio H: Assessment of the heart and peripheral vascular system. In Carcio H, ed: Manual of health assessment, Boston, 1985, Little Brown & Co, Inc.

13. Carnesas A: Anticoagulation and cardiovascular disease: determining therapeutic options, Hosp Formul 20:1238–1244, 1985.

14. Conover MB: Understanding electrocardiography, ed 4, St Louis, 1984, The CV Mosby Co.

15. Delp H and Newton R: Effects of brief cold exposure on finger dexterity and sensibility in subjects with Raynaud's phenomenon, Phys Ther 66:503–507, 1986.

16. Dougherty CM: The nursing diagnosis of decreased cardiac output, Nurs Clin North Am 20:787–799, 1985.

17. Eberts MA: Advances in the pharmacologic management of angina pectoris, J Cardiovasc Nurs 1(1):15–29, 1986.

18. Gardner PE: Cardiac output: theory, technique and troubleshooting, Crit Care Nurs Clin North Am 1(3):577–589, 1989.

19. Glick MS: Caring touch and anxiety in myocardial infarction patients in the intermediate cardiac care unit, Int Care Nurs 2(2):61–66, 1986.

20. Greenland P and Briody M: Rehabilitation of the MI survivor, Postgrad Med Cardiac Rehab 75(1):79–94, 1984.

21. Guzetta CE and Dossey BM: Cardiovascular nursing, St Louis, 1984, The CV Mosby Co.

22. Guyton AC: Textbook of medical physiology, ed 8, Philadelphia, 1990, WB Saunders Co.

23. Hall LT: Cardiovascular lasers: a look into the future, Am J Nurs 90(7):27–30, 1990.

24. Huang SH and others: Cardiac rehabilitation of the myocardial infarction patient. In Huang SH and others, eds: Coronary Care Nursing, Philadelphia, 1989, WB Saunders Co, pp 423–434.

25. Hudak CM, Gallo BM, and Benz JJ: Critical care nursing, Philadelphia, 1990, JB Lippincott Co.

26. Kaplan N: Clinical hypertension, ed 4, Baltimore, 1986, Williams & Wilkins.

27. Kelleher RM: Cardiac drugs: new inotropes, Crit Care Nurs Clin North Am 1(2):359–372, 1989.

28. Kennedy GT: Captopril in the treatment of chronic CHF, Crit Care Nurse 10(2):39–46, 1990.

29. Linden B: Unit-based phase 1 cardiac rehabilitation program for patients with myocardial infarction, Focus Crit Care 17(1):15–19, 1990.

30. Loan T: Nursing interaction with patients undergoing coronary angioplasty, Heart Lung 5:368–374, 1986.

31. McCrum AE and Tyndall A: Nursing care of patients with implantable defibrillators, Crit Care Nurse 9(5):48–71, 1989.

32. Miracle JK: Anatomy of a murmur, Nurs 86 16(7):26–32, 1986.

33. Moynihan M: Assessing the educational needs of post-myocardial infarction patients, Nurs Clin North Am 19:441–447, 1984.

34. Nissen G: Streptokinase therapy in acute myocardial infarction, Heart Lung 13:223–230, 1984.

35. Ohler L, Fleagle DJ, and Lee BI: Aortic valvuloplasty: medical and critical care nursing perspectives, Focus Crit Care 16(4):275–287, 1989.

36. Perloff D: Hypertension in women. In Douglas PS and Brest AN, eds: Heart disease in women, Philadelphia, 1989, FA Davis Co, pp 207–242.

37. Riegel B: The role of nursing in limiting myocardial infarct size, Heart Lung 14:247–255, 1985.

38. Runions J: A program for psychological and social enhancement during rehabilitation after myocardial infarction, Heart Lung 14:117–125, 1985.

39. Ryan AM: Stopping CHF while there's still time, I, RN 49(8): 28–33, 1986.

40. Searle L: RN master care plan: the patient in congestive heart failure, RN 49(8):34–35, 1986.

41. Shoemaker WC and others: Textbook of critical care, ed 2, Philadelphia, 1989, WB Saunders Co.

42. Smith ND and Abram J: Valvular heart disease of rheumatic origin, Hosp Med 20(10):77–89, 1984.

43. Standards and guidelines for cardiopulmonary resuscitation (CPR) and emergency cardiac care (ECC), JAMA 255:2905–2984, 1986.

44. Stanley M: Helping an elderly patient live with CHF, II, RN 49(9):35–37, 1986.

45. Thelan LA, Davie JK, and Urden LD: Textbook of critical care nursing: diagnosis and management, St Louis, 1990, The CV Mosby Co.

46. Thompson JM and others: Mosby's manual of clinical nursing, St Louis, 1989, The CV Mosby Co.

47. Underhill SL and others: Cardiac nursing, ed 2, Philadelphia, 1989, JB Lippincott Co.

48. Underhill SL and others: Cardiovascular medications for cardiac nursing, Philadelphia, 1990, JB Lippincott Co.

49. Van Meter M and LaVine PG: Reading EKGs correctly, Horsham, PA, 1981, Intermed Comm, Inc.

50. Vitello-Cicciu JM: Therapeutic advances in cardiovascular disease, Crit Care Nurs Clin North Am 1(2):307–436, 1989.

51. Warbinek E and Wyneso MA: Designing nursing care for patient with peripheral arterial occlusive disease: update, I, Cardiovasc Nurs 22(1):1–5, 1986.

52. Williams SR: Nutrition and diet therapy, St Louis, 1989, The CV Mosby Co.

53. Yacone L: Acute MI: the first crucial hours, I, RN 49(1):20–25, 1986.

PROBLEMS AFFECTING
The Blood

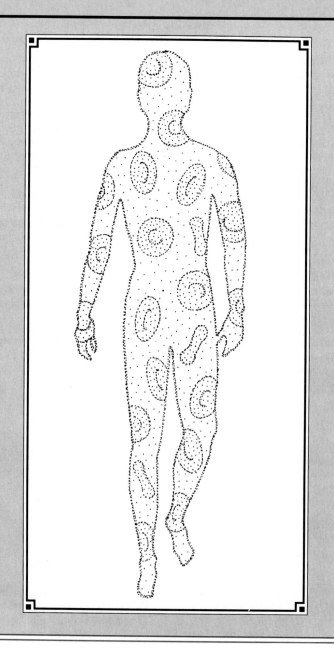

KEY WORDS

anemia
blood dyscrasias
cryoprecipitate
ecchymoses
erythrocytes
erythropoiesis
erythropoietin
granulocytes
hemoglobin electrophoresis
hemophilia
Hodgkin's disease
homeostasis
immunoglobulins (Ig)
leukapheresis
leukemia
leukocytes
leukocytosis
leukopenia
lymphocytes
molecules
monocyte
osmotic pressure
petechia
phlebotomy
pica
plasma pheresis
polycythemia
purpura
sickle cell anemia
splenomegaly
thrombocytes
viscosity

OBJECTIVES

1. Discuss the importance of the blood components as a measure of health and illness.

2. Describe the common diagnostic tests for blood disorders.

3. Differentiate between iron-deficiency, pernicious, sickle cell, and plastic anemias according to their pathophysiologic features and nursing assessment and intervention.

4. Discuss the significance of leukocytosis and leukopenia as indicators of illness.

5. Define the major aspects of nursing intervention for the patient with leukemia and anemia.

6. Discuss the cause, manifestations, and nursing intervention in caring for patients with hemorrhagic disorders.

FUNCTION OF BLOOD

The blood is the transportation system of the body. Through its vast network of vessels it carries oxygen to the cells and returns carbon dioxide to the lungs to be eliminated. It transports food to nourish the cells so that they may carry on their normal functions and carries away waste products of cell metabolism. Water, electrolytes, hormones, and enzymes, all of which have important functions in helping to keep the body in a state of equilibrium (**homeostasis**), are transported by the blood. Heat is carried by the blood, thereby regulating body temperature. Immune cells and antibodies that help to prevent disease are also important parts of the blood. Through a complex system, the blood provides clotting and prevents serious loss of fluids in case of injury. It also prevents clot formation in blood vessels, which would seriously interfere with oxygen reaching the cells of the body. Any disease or condition that affects the blood or its transport system may pose a serious threat to the individual.

STRUCTURE OF BLOOD

The blood is slightly sticky and has a characteristic odor and a faint salty taste. It is bright red in the arteries because it is carrying oxygen; it is dark red in the veins because the cells have taken up the oxygen and the blood is carrying carbon dioxide to be eliminated by the respiratory system. The blood is composed of two parts: the liquid part called *plasma*, which constitutes slightly more than half of the total volume, and the formed elements, or cells. The cells have been divided into several groups: (1) **erythrocytes,** or red blood cells; (2) **leukocytes,** or white blood cells; and (3) **thrombocytes,** or platelets.

Blood volume remains fairly constant in one person, but there are variations among individuals. Factors such as age, sex, size of the body frame, and the amount of adipose tissue may affect the volume of circulating blood.

Plasma

Plasma contains no cells and is estimated to be about 90% water. It is a clear, straw-colored fluid with a large number of substances dissolved in it. Among the most important of these substances are the *plasma proteins*, which include *serum albumin, serum globulin, and fibrinogen* (see Figure 17-

1). The proteins have some individual functions, but all of them are important in nutrition and regulation of blood volume through osmotic pressure. Serum albumin, in particular, influences blood volume because it comprises more than half of the total proteins. Serum globulins are divided into alpha, beta, and gamma globulins. The gamma globulins are significant in the immune response because they are the body's antibodies. Fibrinogen contributes to blood coagulation through its role in the formation of fibrin. Other substances dissolved in plasma include the following: urea, uric acid, glucose, respiratory gases, hormones, and electrolytes. Minute amounts of other substances essential to meet the body's needs are also found in plasma. Plasma can be separated from the formed elements, and because it contains the proteins that assist in the clotting of blood, it may be administered for several bleeding disorders.

Erythrocytes (Red Blood Cells)
Formation

Erythrocytes are formed in the red bone marrow, which develops in the pelvis, vertebrae, ribs, skull, and proximal ends of the femur and humerus.[19] Before birth the production is carried on by the liver and the spleen. The production of erythrocytes, **erythropoiesis,** is a continuous process, and in the absence of disease, the number remains relatively constant.

Number

The number of erythrocytes in men (4.5 to 6 million/mm³ blood) is usually slightly higher than the number of erythrocytes in women (4.3 to 5.5 million/mm³ blood). In the newborn infant the number may be increased (5 to 7 million/mm³ blood), but it gradually decreases to adult levels by 15 years of age. Every minute of every day, healthy adults produce 150 million red blood cells, replacing those that have been destroyed.[19] Recent discovery of substances called hematopoietic growth factors has contributed to an understanding of erythrocyte homeostasis. **Erythropoietin** is one of the growth factors that stimulates marrow production of red blood cells. It is thought that the kidney produces erythropoietin in response to low-tissue–oxygen levels. In addition to the growth factors, effective erythropoiesis requires healthy bone marrow with normal stem cell populations and adequate supplies of folic acid, vitamin B_{12}, and iron.

Hemoglobin

The main ingredient of the erythrocyte is hemoglobin. Within each red blood cell there are millions of molecules of hemoglobin. The amount of hemoglobin in the red blood cell depends on adequate iron storage, which is essential for the synthesis of hemoglobin and for the oxygen-carrying ability of the hemoglobin **molecule.** Hemoglobin carries oxygen to the cells of the body, thus the amount of oxygen available to the cells depends on the amount of hemoglobin in the blood. Hemoglobin is measured in grams per deciliter of blood, whereas red blood cells are measured in millions per cubic millimeter of blood.

Blood loss

Loss of blood through hemorrhage causes a decrease in circulating fluid, the number of red blood cells, hemoglobin, and, in turn, the amount of iron. Because the oxygen-carrying power of the blood has been decreased, the heart has to work harder to supply the cells with oxygen. Thus a person suffering from loss of blood may be expected to have an increased pulse rate. There will also be an increase in respirations as the body attempts to provide more oxygen for circulation.

Chronic blood loss also causes **anemia,** although the blood volume in the vascular system is stabilized more readily. Certain diseases of the blood and blood-forming organs may affect the production of erythrocytes so that the number is decreased or their structure is immature. In some genetic diseases, the erythrocytes may have an abnormal shape. In contrast to the disease states mentioned that cause anemia, some disorders cause an overproduction of erythrocytes. Having too many red blood cells in the circulation is undesirable and may at times be life-threatening.

Leukocytes (White Blood Cells)
Formation

Leukocytes, in a manner similar to erythrocytes and thrombocytes, arise from stem cells in bone marrow. Disorders of white blood cells can result from overproduction, underproduction, or abnormal maturation of any one or all leukocyte cell lines.

Number

Leukocytes, or white blood cells, are not as numerous as the erythrocytes, or red blood cells. The number of white blood cells in 1 mm³ of blood varies between 5000 and 10,000. The number is essentially the same for men and women. When there is an increase of more than 10,000 white blood cells, it may indicate the presence of some pathologic condition. Such an increase is called **leukocytosis.** Under some conditions, there may be a decrease in the number of leukocytes, which is called **leukopenia.** *Granulocytopenia* is a term that is used interchangeably with leukopenia but refers specifically to a low number of circulating granulocytes or neutrophils.

Classification

Leukocytes are classified as granular or nongranular, depending on the color of their cytoplasm and the shape of their nuclei. Granular leukocytes are called **granulocytes,** and approximately 50% to 75% of leukocytes are granulocytes. About 50% of the mature granulocytes released from the bone marrow into the circulation adhere to the walls of small blood vessels.[19] The remainder pass from the circulation into the tissues to perform their specific functions. The nongranular leukocytes, or *agranulocytes,* comprise less than one third of the cells and include the **lymphocytes** and **monocytes.** The granulocytes are divided into three types: *neutrophils, basophils, and eosinophils.*

Granulocytes

The primary function of the *neutrophils* is *phagocytosis,* the ingestion and digestion of debris and foreign material throughout the body. They are the first cells to arrive at the scene when an inflammatory reaction is stimulated. Neutrophils are attracted to the foreign substance in response to chemotactic stimuli that are released from inflamed tissue and involve the complement system and lymphocytes. Neutrophils are also referred to as myelocytes, "polys," and granulocytes.

The *basophils* do not phagocytize material but contain powerful chemicals such as histamine that can be released locally. They are important during the inflammatory process in modulating the formation of clots and their growth. The specific function of these cells in the body is not completely understood.

The *eosinophils* appear to play a role in allergy or foreign protein reactions and are elevated in number in patients with allergies or parasitic infestations.

Agranulocytes

The *monocytes* become larger phagocytic cells when stimulated and also play an important role in the inflammatory process. *Lymphocytes* are the primary cells concerned with the development of immunity. Although they arise from stem cells in the bone marrow, maturation occurs in the lymphatic or reticuloendothelial systems.

The leukocytes have many functions in the body, and their ability to move about helps to protect the body from infection and to repair damaged tissue (Figure 2-5). A count of white blood cells is often an important aid to the physician in establishing a diagnosis; for example, in suspected acute appendicitis an increase in the number of white blood cells together with clinical symptoms may indicate to the physician the need for an appendectomy.[3]

Differential count

A differential count is a measure of the total number of white blood cells and the percentages of each of the five classes. For many patients, one drop of blood obtained from a fingertip is sufficient for this test. After the specimen is placed on a slide, it is examined under a microscope and each type of leukocyte is identified and counted. Each type of cell is reported as a percentage of all classes of white blood cells. In various diseases certain kinds of cells may be increased; for example, in some bacterial infections, the number of lymphocytes may increase.

Thrombocytes (Platelets)
Formation

Thrombocytes, or platelets, are tiny fragile elements in the blood. They are formed in red bone marrow and are thought to be minute fragments of larger cells called *megakaryocytes*.

Number

The exact number of platelets is unknown, but various estimates have placed the number from 150,000 to 500,000/mm³ of blood. In certain hemorrhagic disorders, a decrease in the number of platelets may cause serious bleeding, whereas in other diseases there may be an abnormally high number of platelets, called *thrombocytosis*.

Function

The primary function of platelets is to control bleeding. When an injury to a blood vessel occurs, the platelets concentrate at the site of the injury and control bleeding by forming thrombotic plugs and by releasing a substance, factor III, which is necessary for coagulation and the formation of

Average Normal Blood Values	
Erythrocytes	
Men	4.5-6.0 million/mm³ blood
Women	4.3-5.5 million/mm³ blood
Newborns	5.0-7.0 million/mm³ blood
Leukocytes	
Men	5000-10,000/mm³ blood
Women	5000-10,000/mm³ blood
Newborns	15,000-45,000/mm³ blood
Platelets	150,000-400,000/mm³ blood
Hemoglobin	
Men	14-18 g/dl blood
Women	12-16 g/dl blood
Newborns	15-20 g/dl blood

fibrin. They continue their activity in helping to shrink the clots and bring together the margins of the damaged vessel.

THERAPEUTIC BLOOD FRACTIONS

Blood may be broken down into its component parts so that patients with certain conditions may be given specific blood fractions to meet their individual needs (Figure 17-1).

Blood Plasma

Plasma may be separated from whole blood that has been stored, or it may be separated from fresh blood taken from a donor and immediately frozen. The primary use of plasma is for conditions in which clotting of the blood is defective. When fresh blood plasma is used, it contains all of the factors essential for clotting, including the antihemophilic factor.

Platelets

Platelets may be separated from whole blood and administered to patients with severe hematologic disorders, open heart surgery, and postoperative bleeding. The demand for platelets has increased, and it is now believed that patients with active bleeding from any site, internal or external, whose platelet count is below 20,000/mm³ of blood should receive platelets. The administration of platelets has been a lifesaving measure for many

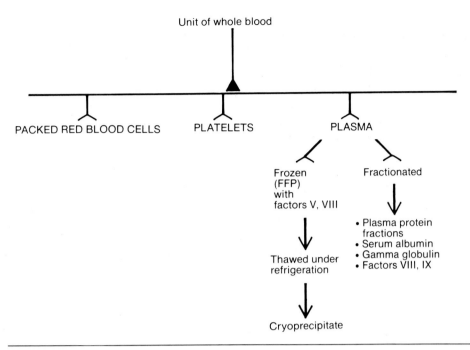

Figure 17-1
Reduction of unit of whole blood into fractions.

patients receiving chemotherapy for malignant disorders.

Platelets are administered most often in the form of a concentrate that has been separated from one or more units of whole blood. The advantage of the platelet concentrate is that it may be infused in only 50 ml of fluid. When long-term administration is required, it avoids overloading the circulatory system.

Pheresis

In **plasma pheresis,** pheresed platelets that are matched with human lymphocyte antigen (HLA) are preferred over pooled or random donor platelets for patients who are at risk for developing antibodies to donor platelet antigens. The life span and functional capacities of platelets are diminished when these antibodies develop. This also interferes with successful bone marrow transplantation. With the exception of hemolytic reactions, the patient receiving platelets may have reactions similar to those from whole blood transfusions. Therefore close observation of the patient is essential.

Plasma Protein Fractions

Plasma proteins may also be given as individual blood components.

Gamma globulin

The primary use of gamma globulin is in the prevention or modification of infectious disease. Immune human gamma globulins are fractions of blood obtained from persons with circulating antibodies against a specific disease. Such persons may have antibodies as a result of having had the disease or having been immunized against it. When administered to nonimmune persons, immune human gamma globulin prevents disease or complications of diseases such as tetanus, mumps, pertussis, or rubella.

Serum albumin

Purified human serum albumin may be administered to assist in maintaining **osmotic pressure** of the plasma. It is useful in any condition in which the albumin:globulin ratio has been lowered. It may be administered to burn patients, for hypovolemic shock, and in liver disease.

Fibrinogen

Fibrinogen is an essential factor for the clotting of blood. A deficiency may be a congenital disorder or an acquired condition resulting from massive hemorrhage, prolonged active bleeding, or other hematologic conditions dependent on the clotting mechanism.

Cryoprecipitate

Cryoprecipitate, prepared by the thawing of fresh frozen plasma, contains an average of 150 mg of fibrinogen and is used to restore the plasma level to normal ranges.[2] Cryoprecipitate also contains factor VIII (the antihemophilic factor) factor XIII, and von Willebrand's factor. A deficiency in any one of these coagulation factors can result in severe bleeding. Cryoprecipitate may be used to correct the deficit; however, the specific factor concentrate that is deficient is usually preferred.[2]

Packed Red Blood Cells

Packed red blood cells are red blood cells without the plasma. By centrifuging whole blood, the cells and the plasma are separated. In conditions in which the blood volume is normal but the number of red blood cells and hemoglobin is decreased, packed red blood cells may be given. Because packed red blood cells are placed in only a small amount of fluid, the danger of overloading the circulatory system is avoided. The removal of plasma containing white blood cells and antibodies reduces the risk of allergic reaction. To provide safer transfusions to recipients, whole blood is rarely administered except when specifically indicated, as in massive hemorrhage or total blood transfusions to newborns.

Leukocytes

Leukocytes may be obtained through a special process called **leukapheresis** (or granulocytapheresis). Because leukocytes cannot be obtained in sufficient amounts from a single unit of blood, it is necessary to obtain them from a single compatible donor by removing the leukocytes and replacing the blood. The procedure yields leukocytes that are predominantly granulocytes. Recipients of this component are those with life-threatening, low white blood cell counts who have infections that are unresponsive to antibiotic therapy, and those with leukemia, immunosuppressive disorders, and those undergoing extensive field radiation therapy or intensive chemotherapy. Granulocytes have a short survival time and must be infused as soon as possible after collection, in less than 24 hours. The infusion must be given slowly and the recipient should be observed closely for negative reactions. The long-term therapeutic benefit of granulocytes transfusion is still questionable and continues to be evaluated.

COLLECTION OF BLOOD

The collection and storage of blood began during World War II. Because of the progress of medical science, the need for whole blood, plasma, and blood fractions has become essential in the practice of modern medicine. Along with the increased demand, improved methods of collection, storage, and distribution have taken place. At present there are three main collection systems: the American Red Cross, hospitals, and commercial centers. The American Red Cross maintains regional centers for the collection of blood and mobile units that may be taken to communities, industrial plants, or college campuses. The arrival of the mobile unit is usually the culmination of drives for donors sponsored by local citizens. Most hospitals collect blood to meet their individual needs. Frequently, donors are members of the patient's family, friends of the patient, or other persons interested in the patient. In an emergency, when large amounts of blood may be needed, the hospital may call on citizens of the community or the American Red Cross to help meet its needs. In most instances donors to hospitals and the American Red Cross do not receive payment for their blood. Commercial centers that offer a small fee to donors have come under attack and are being scrutinized and frequently banned by state governments.

Testing

Although all prospective donors are examined and interviewed, donors may be unwilling or unable to provide an accurate history about exposure to and incidence of blood-transmitted diseases, including acquired immune deficiency syndrome (AIDS), hepatitis, syphilis, malaria, cytomegalovirus (CMV), or Epstein-Barr virus. Therefore the Federal Drug Administration (FDA) requires the testing of all donated blood for antibody to immunodeficiency virus type 1 (HIV-1), hepatitis B surface antigen (HBsAG), and human T-cell lymphotropic virus (HTLV-I) and for syphilis. Such donor screening and testing, however, does not totally eliminate the risk of transmitting disease by transfusion.[1]

Autologous Blood

In many areas blood-collection agencies can store autologous (one's own) blood for use in elective surgery. Recent technologic developments also allow the reinfusion of a patient's blood shed during surgical procedures. These developments contribute to the safer use of blood products but have limited application in high-blood–use groups.

NURSING RESPONSIBILITIES FOR DIAGNOSTIC TESTS

A large number of tests performed on the blood are done for diagnostic purposes, but some are useful in guiding the physician in the course and treatment of disease. Some tests are performed on capillary blood and require only a few drops, which is usually secured by pricking the finger or the earlobe. Blood for other tests requiring a larger amount of blood is secured from a vein with a needle and syringe. Some of the more common tests are reviewed here, and others are found in different sections of this book, according to their relation to specific diseases. Table 17-1 lists normal hematologic values for various diagnostic tests.

Types of Tests
Complete blood count
The complete blood count (CBC) is the most common of all tests made on the blood. It consists of a count of the erythrocytes and leukocytes, measurement of hemoglobin, and hematocrit and a differential count of the leukocytes. A platelet count is often included. The physician orders the examination, which is made by persons trained in laboratory methods. However, it is often the responsibility of the nurse to execute the proper forms and notify the laboratory of the physician's request. Many hospitals require that routine blood counts be completed for all patients on admission, and some hospitals route the patient from the admission office to the laboratory for the examination before the patient is admitted to the clinical unit. Elevated red blood cell counts may indicate polycythemia or dehydration; lowered counts may suggest anemia. Elevated white blood cell counts may result from infection or leukemia, whereas decreased counts may suggest bone marrow depression from various causes (Figure 17-2).

Hemoglobin
Hemoglobin (Hgb) is the oxygen-carrying pigment of the red blood cells that gives blood its red color. Its primary function is to transport oxygen from the lungs to the tissues of the body. Hemoglobin determinations measure the total amount of hemoglobin in the peripheral blood and are important in diagnosing different types of anemias.

Hemoglobin electrophoresis
Hemoglobin electrophoresis is used to identify various abnormal hemoglobins in the blood. The most common abnormal hemoglobin causes sickle cell anemia.

Hematocrit
The test for hematocrit measures the relative volume of cells and plasma in the blood. In anemia after hemorrhage and in extracellular fluid excess the hematocrit value is lowered, and in dehydration it is increased. A microhematocrit test may be done using capillary blood secured by pricking the finger.

Coagulation tests
Tests for coagulation measure the ability of the blood to clot, which may be affected by many factors. Tests most frequently used to measure the clotting ability of blood are the prothrombin time, partial thromboplastin time, coagulation time, and bleeding time.[18]

Bleeding time. Bleeding time is one of the four primary screening tests for coagulation disorders. A small stab wound is made in either the earlobe or forearm; the bleeding time is recorded; and a measurement is made of the rate at which a platelet clot is formed. The bleeding time test is significant in detecting vascular abnormalities and of moderate value in detecting platelet abnormalities or deficiencies. Currently, its principle use is in the diagnosis of von Willebrand's disease, a hereditary defective molecule of factor VIII and a type of pseudohemophilia.[8]

Prothrombin time. Prothrombin is converted to thrombin in the clotting process. When prothrombin time is increased, it indicates a longer time for clotting to occur. When greatly increased, the prothrombin time warns of a person at risk for bleeding or hemorrhage. The time may increase in the presence of some diseases or when the patient is receiving coumarin therapy. The test should be done frequently on all patients receiving coumarin therapy. A decreased prothrombin time may indicate intravascular clotting and suggest a patient at risk for thrombus formation.

Partial thromboplastin time. A more sensitive test than the prothrombin time is the partial thromboplastin time (PTT). The PTT, as it is com-

Table 17-1

Normal Values for Complete Blood Count Tests

Test	Normal ranges	
White blood cells (leukocytes)	5000-10,000 mm³	
Differential white blood cell count	Absolute values (mm³)	Relative values (% of total white blood cells)
Granulocytes		
Neutrophils	3000-7000	60%-70%
Eosinophils	50-400	1%-4%
Basophils	25-100	0.5%-1%
Agranulocytes		
Lymphocytes	1000-4000	20%-40%
Monocytes	100-600	2%-6%
Red blood cell count		
Men	4.5-5.4 million	
Women	3.6-5 million	
Red blood cell indices		
Mean corpuscular volume	84-99 µ³/red blood cell	
Mean corpuscular hemoglobin	26-32 µ³/red blood cell	
Mean corpuscular hemoglobin concentration	30%-36%	
Hematocrit values		
Men	40%-50%	
Women	37%-47%	
Hemoglobin values		
Men	14-16.5 g/dl	
Women	12-15 g/dl	
Platelet count	150,000-400,000 mm₃	
Normal values for coagulation tests		
Bleeding time		
Earlobe method	1-6 min	
Forearm method	1-9 min	
Prothrombin time	11-16 sec	
Partial thromboplastin time	30-45 sec	
Fibrinogen level	160-415 mg/dl	
Lee-White clotting time	5-10 min	

monly called, is affected by reduction of even one of the clotting factors. Heparin dosage is frequently regulated by monitoring the PTT to assist in maintaining specific levels of therapy. When the PTT is greatly increased, the possibility of bleeding is also increased. Patients should be assessed for any sign of bleeding, such as ecchymoses, bleeding from gums or any body surface, tarry stools, or bloody urine. A low PTT may indicate a patient at risk for clot formation.

Sedimentation rate

The test for sedimentation rate measures the time required for the red blood cells to settle to the bottom of a test tube, usually based on a duration of 1 hour. The test is most often used to observe

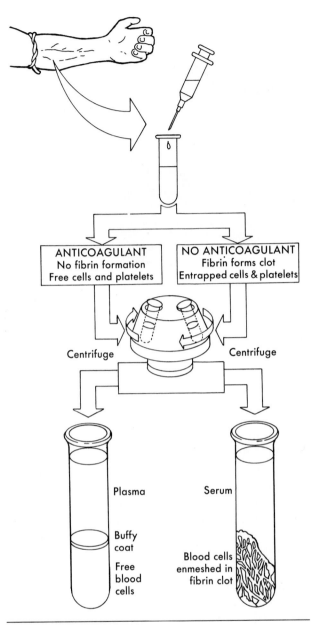

Figure 17-2

Liquid and cellular blood components. When blood is drawn and mixed immediately with an anticoagulant, fibrin formation is prevented. Most cellular studies are done with anticoagulated blood. Centrifugation provides an upper liquid layer of plasma and a lower layer of free cells and platelets. A buffy coat, composed mainly of white blood cells, may appear between the plasma and red cell layers. Serum results if the blood is allowed to coagulate; fibrinogen is converted to a fibrin clot in which platelets and cells adhere. *(From Powers: Diagnostic hematology, ed 1, St Louis, 1989, The CV Mosby Co.)*

the course of some diseases such as rheumatic fever and rheumatoid arthritis.

Blood gas analysis

A blood gas analysis is used to measure the oxygen and carbon dioxide content of the blood and to determine the functional ability of the lungs to maintain adequate gas levels in the blood. Blood is secured from the radial or femoral artery. The test is used primarily in respiratory diseases and disorders and guides the physician in the administration of oxygen and/or medications (Chapter 15).

Schilling test

Intrinsic factor secreted by the gastric mucosa is necessary for the absorption of vitamin B_{12}. The Schilling test is used to diagnose pernicious anemia, in which the intrinsic factor is deficient, resulting in a reduction of vitamin B_{12} absorption. Normally a person ingests and absorbs more vitamin B_{12} than needed, with the excess excreted in the urine. However, when vitamin B_{12} cannot be absorbed, it passes on through the gastrointestinal system without appearing in the urine. To perform the Schilling test, an injection of vitamin B_{12} is given to meet body needs, with subsequent administration of oral radioactive vitamin B_{12}. If absorption is unimpeded, the excess vitamin B_{12} should be found in the urine. All urine is collected for 24 hours and the amount of radioactive vitamin B_{12} measured. Little or no radioactive vitamin B_{12} in the urine indicates an absorption problem. The next step is to determine whether the malabsorption results from intrinsic factor deficiency or some other cause such as intestinal disease. The Schilling test is repeated, and oral intrinsic factor is added. If the radioactive vitamin B_{12} in the urine now rises, it is clear that a intrinsic factor deficiency is the problem, establishing a diagnosis of pernicious anemia. If radioactive vitamin B_{12} remains low, other malabsorption causes are implicated.

Bone marrow aspiration

Aspiration of bone marrow is done to obtain a specimen of cells for biopsy. Examination of the cells indicates their reproductive ability and is useful in the diagnosis of certain blood dyscrasias. A local anesthetic is injected into the area surrounding the biopsy site. The most common site in adults and children over 18 months of age is the posterior iliac crest (Figure 17-3). The nurse's role

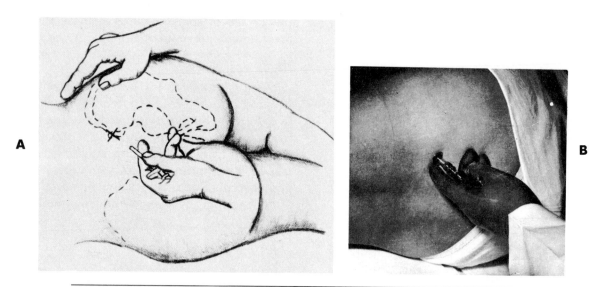

Figure 17-3

Bone marrow aspiration; posterior iliac crest. **A,** Drawing of anatomical site. **B,** Photograph of aspiration technique. *(A from Miale, JB: Laboratory medicine hematology, ed 6, St Louis, 1982, The CV Mosby Co. B from Bauer, JD: Clinical laboratory methods, ed 9, St Louis, 1982, The CV Mosby Co.)*

is to reinforce the explanation of the procedure with the patient and to assist with positioning. Guided imagery techniques can be used to elicit patient cooperation and to minimize the pain associated with the procedure. Because of the risk of bleeding, pressure should be applied to the site for a full 5 minutes and the patient closely observed.[16] If the patient has a problem with prolonged bleeding, the puncture site should be assessed frequently for oozing or frank bleeding and pressure applied if this occurs (Figure 17-4).

Blood chemistry

The chemical analysis of blood involves a large number of tests, some of which are carried out on whole blood, a few on plasma, and others on blood serum. Many of these tests are related to the diagnosis of specific diseases and are discussed elsewhere. However, blood for chemical analysis is usually collected early in the morning while the patient is in a fasting state. The patient may not be allowed anything by mouth after midnight, and breakfast may be withheld.

Blood typing and cross-matching

In administering blood, it is important for the blood of the donor and the blood of the recipient to be compatible. If it is not, the patient may suffer a severe or fatal reaction. There are many different systems for matching blood, and more than 100 different blood factors are known. However, the most familiar system classifies blood types as A, B, AB, and O (Table 17-2). It is always best to transfuse the patient with blood of his own type when possible; however, if the same type cannot be secured or if there is a delay in typing and cross-matching, the O type may be used in an emergency, but the patient must be watched carefully for indications of a reaction. Usually 500 ml of whole blood administered to a patient will elevate the number of red blood cells and the amount of hemoglobin by 15% in 24 hours. Plasma may be administered to people of all blood types, but because reactions may occur from plasma, the same precautions should be taken as for administering whole blood.

Rh factor

In addition to the kinds of protein substances found in the four types of blood, some persons have an extra protein substance called the *Rh factor*. Approximately 85% of all persons have this protein and are said to be *Rh positive;* the remaining 15% are said to be *Rh negative*. It is just as important to determine the Rh factor in cross-matching blood for transfusion as it is to determine the blood type. If an Rh-negative person is transfused with Rh-positive blood, he may develop antibodies against the Rh-positive factor. If given further transfusions with Rh-positive blood,

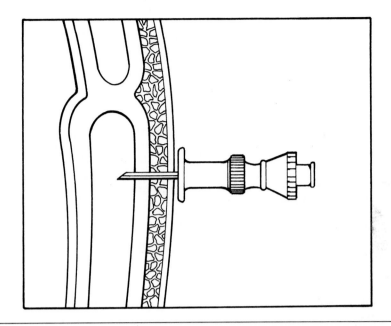

Figure 17-4

Bone marrow aspiration: penetration into marrow cavity. *(From Powers, LW: Diagnostic hematology, ed 1, St Louis, 1989, The CV Mosby Co.)*

Table 17-2

ABO Blood Types	
Recipient's blood type	Compatible donor type
A	A, O
B	B, O
AB	A, B, AB, O
O	O

he may develop severe reactions. An Rh-positive fetus in utero may precipitate the formation of antibodies in an Rh-negative mother. If any of these antibodies reaches the fetal circulation, it may cause the infant to be stillborn or may result in the disease called *erythroblastosis fetalis.*

NURSING RESPONSIBILITY FOR THERAPEUTIC PROCEDURES

Blood Transfusion Therapy

There are three primary reasons for administering blood: (1) to replace or maintain blood volume, (2) to preserve the oxygen-carrying function of the blood, and (3) to increase or maintain the coagulation abilities of the blood. A transfusion introduces whole blood, or any of its components, from a donor into the bloodstream of the recipient. Before administration, the compatibility of the blood that is to be given must be checked with that of the patient. Incompatibility can result in severe hemolytic reactions that may be fatal to the patient.

Procedures

When the physician writes an order for blood transfusion, the request is sent to the laboratory, along with a sample of the patient's blood, so that typing and cross-matching can be done and the number of pints or units to be administered prepared. The nurse should assemble the necessary equipment and record the patient's vital signs. The registered nurse is responsible for the administration and handling of blood once it arrives on the unit. Most institutions require that two registered nurses check the blood before administration. The blood should be checked for expiration date, and the label indicating the patient's name, room number, and identification number should be compared to the patient's identification band. The patient's blood group and Rh status should be compared with the donor's blood group and Rh status. If any discrepancy is found, the blood is not given. Blood brought to the unit should be used immediately or returned to the

Table 17-3

Blood Transfusion Reactions		
Type of reaction	Cause	Symptoms
Allergic reaction	Hypersensitivity to antibodies in donor's blood	Urticaria, pruritus, fever, anaphylactic shock
Hemolytic reaction	Incompatibility	Nausea, vomiting, pain in lower back, hypotension, increase in pulse rate, decrease in urinary output, hematuria
Pyogenic febrile reaction (most common)	Antibodies to donor platelets or leukocytes, or contamination of blood	Fever, chills, nausea, headache, flushing, tachycardia, palpitations

blood bank. It is administered through an infusion set with a filter in the drip chamber that will remove any precipitates or clots that may form. The infusion line is primed and rinsed with saline because other solutions can cause hemolysis of the cells. The blood filter should not be used for more than 4 hours and a unit of blood should not be transfused for over 4 hours.

After the transfusion has begun, the nurse should carefully observe the patient while the first 50 ml is infused. Symptoms of severe reaction are usually seen during the first 50 ml or less of blood infusion. Start the infusion slowly, 5 ml per minute or less for the first 15 minutes. Vital signs should be taken before and 15 minutes after the transfusion is started and frequently during the transfusion. The patient should be observed for symptoms of potential complications.

Transfusion reactions

Transfusion reactions from contaminated blood, presence of antibodies to donor cells and allergic reactions can occur after only a small amount of blood has been given. If symptoms of a reaction occur (Table 17-3), the transfusion should be discontinued, the intravenous tubing changed, and the vein kept open with a slow saline solution drip. The blood should not be destroyed but should be saved for examination in an effort to determine the cause of reaction.

Circulation overload

Circulation overload is a complication that can result from too rapid fluid infusion. Cough, increasing pulse rate, dyspnea, and edema are symptoms of this complication. Packed cells rather than whole blood are indicated for patients who are susceptible to circulatory overload. This includes people with cardiac and renal impairment and the elderly.

Air embolism

Air embolism is a rare but often fatal complication from a blood transfusion and is caused by air being allowed to enter the circulation. This is most likely to occur when blood is being given under pressure.

Interventions

Policies and procedures related to transfusion of blood or its components vary in each institution, but the care of the patient should always include measures to prevent transfusion reactions through proper identification of blood donor and recipient compatibility, and careful handling of the blood product to prevent contamination and hemolysis. The specific action the nurse takes varies with the type of reaction that is suspected. In general, vital signs should be monitored throughout the transfusion and the patient assessed for signs and symptoms that indicate a reaction. When a hemolytic reaction is suspected, the nurse monitors the patient for shock, taking frequent blood pressure and pulse measurements, recording accurate intake and output, and obtaining a first-voided urine specimen. If the patient complains of itching and wheezes within the first few minutes of the transfusion, an allergic reaction should be suspected. Chills and fever occurring about 1 hour after the start of a transfusion indicates a pyogenic reaction. If the physician determines that these symptoms are not due to a hemolytic reaction or to contaminated blood, the patient may be treated with antipyretics and steroids to alleviate the symptoms, and the transfusion is then continued. Symptoms that indicate an air embolus include chest pain, acute shortness of breath, and shock. The patient should be turned immediately onto the left side and the head lowered. This is a rare complication but requires immediate action if it occurs.

THE PATIENT WITH BLOOD DYSCRASIAS

Blood dyscrasias refer to diseases or disorders of the blood and blood-forming organs. These include a wide range of conditions with varying prognoses. Life-style may predispose persons to certain disorders, whereas heredity may account for others. Often the cause is unknown. Similarly, treatment may cause a dramatic response or simply be palliative. Some diseases may be controlled, but a lifetime of compliance to treatment is required.

The following is a partial classification of diseases and disorders of the blood and the blood-forming organs. These include red blood cell, white blood cell, and hemorrhagic disorders.

Disorders of Erythrocytes
Anemia

Anemia is not a disease but a condition resulting from one or a combination of causes. It is defined as a lower than normal number of red blood cells and quantity of hemoglobin. The major manifestations of anemia, including pallor, decreased activity tolerance, and orthostatic hypotension, result from the body's attempts to provide adequate levels of oxygen to the brain and other vital organs. Vasoconstriction of skin, kidney, and peripheral blood vessels is the mechanism that is responsible for the symptoms of anemia. It accompanies several diseases, and its development may be so insidious that an individual is unaware of the condition until symptoms appear. It may develop slowly when there is a slow bleeding from the intestinal tract, or it may develop quickly if there is a massive hemorrhage. Anemia is usually present in diseases in which there is destruction of red blood cells or when there is immature development of the red blood cells. Any condition that causes a decrease in red blood cells, in hemoglobin, and in iron will cause varying degrees of anemia.

Assessment of the patient with anemia. The nurse should examine the patient's skin for the texture and level of hydration and for the presence of any ulcerated areas. Assess the eyes for pallor of the conjunctiva or a yellowish tinge to the sclera and for brightness or luster. The oral cavity is assessed for color and the tongue for any evidence of sores or swelling. The patient should be asked about the presence of such symptoms as headaches, ringing in the ears, dizziness with position changes, difficulty concentrating, or difficulty

---

Blood Dyscrasias

Red blood cell disorders
  Anemia
    Hemorrhagic
    Iron-deficiency or nutritional
    Pernicious
    Sickle cell
    Aplastic

  Polycythemia

White blood cell disorders
  Leukocytosis
  Leukopenia
  Infectious mononucleosis
  Hodgkin's disease
  Leukemia

Hemorrhagic disorders
  Hemophilia
  Purpura
  Splenomegaly

---

swallowing. Other areas included in the assessment are the diet history and a past or present history of blood loss from the rectum, hemorrhoids, urine, vomitus, and prolonged or frequent menstrual bleeding. The nurse should inquire about a history of gastric ulcer, gastric or colon surgery, anemia, or a family history of anemia or blood disease.

Hemorrhagic anemia. Anemia resulting from loss of blood may be acute or chronic. Acute anemia or *hypovolemic shock* occurs when there has been a sudden loss of a large amount of blood. This may be caused by traumatic injury, *hemoptysis*, hemorrhage at childbirth, ulcerative lesions, and disorders of coagulation. Anemia may result from lesser degrees of hemorrhage or slow bleeding such as that from a bleeding gastric ulcer or bleeding hemorrhoids.

Pathophysiology. The loss of blood decreases the amount of circulating fluid and hemoglobin and the amount of oxygen carried to the tissues of the body, which must have oxygen to survive. Blood loss may be classified as severe, moderate, or mild. The degree and rapidity with which the blood loss occurs is related to the severity and number of symptoms observed in the patient.

Severe blood loss may be caused by trauma if large blood vessels are ruptured or severed. Massive uterine hemorrhage may accompany childbirth, or it may result from cancer. A ruptured tubal pregnancy may release large amounts of blood into the peritoneal cavity. Severe blood loss can also occur when the number of platelets in the blood is low or when the coagulation process is abnormal.

Less severe blood loss occurs in many conditions, including prolonged or frequent menstrual periods, a bleeding gastric ulcer, or bleeding hemorrhoids.

Assessment. When blood loss is severe, the patient may experience hematogenic or hypovolemic shock. Prostration, thirst, a rapid pulse rate, pallor, hypotension, clammy skin, or mental confusion because of decreased oxygen supply to the brain can occur. When anemia is caused by slow bleeding, the symptoms are less dramatic. Fatigue is a primary symptom. The volume and rate of the pulse is normal. On exertion the blood pressure may drop and tachycardia may occur. There is a tendency toward fainting and dizziness because of orthostatic hypotension. If bleeding continues for a prolonged period, pallor will develop and shortness of breath on exertion, headache, drowsiness, and menstrual disturbances may occur.

Intervention. In a case of massive hemorrhage, measures are taken to control the bleeding, treat for shock, and replace the volume of circulating fluid (see Chapter 4). Patients should be observed for evidence of further bleeding. They should lie flat and be kept warm, and vital signs should be taken at frequent intervals. Care should be taken to prevent injury to a restless or confused patient.

The immediate concern in chronic bleeding is to locate and remove the cause. This requires a carefully taken history and physical examination. Laboratory examination and x-ray studies may be required. Depending on the degree of anemia, blood transfusions may be given and iron therapy instituted.

The patient may or may not be given iron preparations. If liquid preparations are administered, they should be given through a straw or drinking tube and the teeth and mouth cleansed after each administration to avoid staining the teeth. If there is any disorder of the intestinal tract that makes the oral administration of iron undesirable, it may be given intramuscularly in the form of iron dextran (Imferon). It is given in the gluteal muscle in 1- to 5-ml injections daily or less frequently and may be continued until the hemoglobin returns to normal. Deep injection using the Z-tract method is necessary to avoid leakage into subcutaneous tissue which causes staining of skin.

An oral dose of iron should be given with orange or another citrus juice because an acid condition enhances absorption. Conversely, milk, milk products, and antacids inhibit absorption. Ideally, iron should be administered 1 hour before meals. However, if gastric irritation occurs, iron may be given with meals, taking care to avoid milk products at that time. Patients should be told that they will have dark stools during the time they are receiving oral iron preparations.

Iron-deficiency (hypochromic) anemia. Anemia caused by iron deficiency is the most common type of anemia. It is estimated that 90% of the iron-deficiency anemia in adults is found in women. It is the most common cause of anemia in infancy and childhood. The iron stored by the fetus in utero is depleted during the first 6 months after birth. Iron deficiency after 6 months is usually a result of inadequate iron in the diet. Average normal daily iron requirements are found in Table 17-4.

About two thirds of all iron in the body is in the hemoglobin of the blood (Figure 17-5). For the most part this iron is used over and over, with essentially no excretion, and small reserves are available if needed. Reserves are stored in the bone marrow, spleen, liver, and muscle; in men-

Table 17-4

Average Normal Daily Iron Requirements	
Sex and age-group	**Amount**
Men and postmenopausal women	10 mg
Women during childbearing period	18 mg
During pregnancy	15-35 mg
Infants	1.5 mg/kg of body weight (about 5-15 mg)
Children	10-18 mg
Adolescent boys	10-15 mg
Adolescent girls	10-25 mg

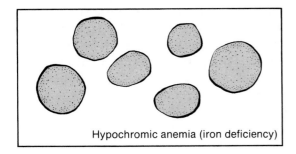

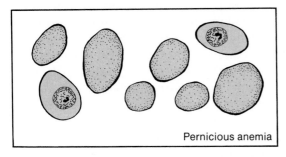

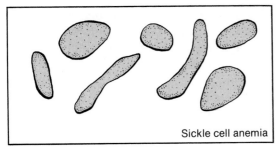

Figure 17-5

Red cells in three types of anemia. *(From Brooks SM and Paynton-Brooks, N: The human body, structure and function in health and disease, ed 2, St Louis, 1980, The CV Mosby Co.)*

Table 17-5

Commonly Used Iron Preparations	
Preparation	**Average daily dose***
Oral administration	
Ferrous sulfate (Feosol) (most common and least expensive)	300 mg
Ferrous gluconate (Fergon)	900 mg
Ferrous fumurate (Ircon)	600-800 mg
Ferrocholinate (Chel-Iron, Ferrolip)	1-2 g
Intramuscular injection	
Iron dextran complex	50-250 mg
Iron sorbitex (Jectofer)	2-4 ml
Intravenous injection	
Dextrifferon (Astrafer)	1.5 ml in 5% solution

*Based on extent of the anemic disorder.

struating women almost all of the body's iron is stored in the red blood cells. Sources for storage include iron recycled from the destruction of old blood cells and dietary intake. Because iron is not lost through normal excretion, anemia caused by loss of iron has to result from some other cause. In the adult, diet is a factor only if iron is being lost because of some other cause. These causes include excessive menstrual bleeding, repeated pregnancies with blood loss and transfer of iron to the fetus in utero, and blood loss from the gastrointestinal tract, as might occur from carcinoma. In some cases, the body fails to assimilate and utilize the iron.

Pathophysiology. Loss of blood is the most common cause of iron deficiency anemia, which is characterized by a decrease in hemoglobin in the red blood cells. Although the red blood cell count may be within a normal range, the cells are small, microcytic, and poorly shaped and therefore are unable to carry their normal amount of hemoglobin. The body gradually exhausts its supply of stored iron, and the blood develops an abnormally low-color index (hypochromia). Iron is an essential constituent of enzymes within the cells, and without it, the metabolism of the cell is affected and eventually the entire body suffers.

Assessment. Iron-deficiency anemia develops gradually, and the individual may consult a physician because of fatigue and weakness. Sometimes during the early stages, the anemia may be found on a routine physical examination. Symptoms include **pica,** pallor, dyspnea, palpitation, and loss of appetite. The nails become brittle and poorly shaped, the tongue is sore, and in some instances there may be difficulty in swallowing. The hemoglobin level will be found to be as low as 10 mg/dl of blood, and if the condition is severe it may be lower. The most reliable test for the diagnosis of iron-deficiency anemia is a bone marrow biopsy.

Intervention. In the absence of observed bleeding, a thorough examination should be made to locate any internal source of bleeding. Treatment for iron-deficiency anemia is the administration of iron and the identification and treatment of the cause. Commonly used iron preparations are found in Table 17-5. Iron is absorbed much more slowly when administered orally than it is when injected, and administration may have to be continued for several months. For varying reasons some patients cannot be given iron orally and receive it intramuscularly. When iron is injected, the results are faster and the duration of therapy is shortened; however, it does carry some risk; fatal reactions have been reported but are rare.

Most patients with iron-deficiency anemia are cared for in the physician's office or the outpatient clinic. Patient education regarding iron therapy and proper diet is vital. Foods high in iron should be identified: liver, egg yolks, lean meat, red kidney beans, dried raisins and apricots, yellow vegetables such as carrots and turnips, spinach, and wholewheat bread.[16] Teenagers in particular need help with diet modification. Patients should be evaluated for compliance with iron-replacement regimens because of the drug's tendency to cause gastrointestinal problems. If the patient is experiencing side effects that prevent compliance, there are actions that can be taken to minimize the discomfort. When the problem is constipation, reducing the daily dose is helpful; for gastric distress the patient can be instructed to take the drug with meals. Another reason for noncompliance may be the cost of the drug. Consult the pharmacist for a less expensive preparation, or contact a social worker who may be able to identify sources of financial assistance. Usually 300 mg of ferrous sulfate taken three times a day for 4 months is sufficient to correct the deficiency once the underlying cause has been treated.[19]

Pernicious anemia (vitamin B_{12} deficiency anemia). Until 1928 pernicious anemia was considered incurable, and the patient was subject to remissions, relapses, and ultimately death. Although the disease remains incurable, modern treatment has made it possible for the patient to have a normal life span. Patients with pernicious anemia who die usually do so from some other cause. The disease primarily affects middle-aged and older persons. Individuals who have had a total or partial gastrectomy will inevitably develop the disease because the gastric fundus (the source of the intrinsic factor) has been removed. Persons who are strict vegetarians and persons with a history of surgery or disease of the ileum are at risk for vitamin B_{12} deficiency anemia. Pernicious anemia is not the same as iron-deficiency anemia; however, it is believed that iron-deficiency anemia of long duration may predispose an individual to pernicious anemia.

Pathophysiology. An intrinsic factor secreted by the fundus of the stomach is necessary for the absorption of vitamin B_{12} by the intestinal mucosa. Persons having pernicious anemia lack the intrinsic factor and thus develop vitamin B_{12} deficiency. Vitamin B_{12} is a necessary element in the production of erythrocytes and in nervous system function. The red blood cells in the bone marrow fail to mature, and their rate of destruction exceeds their rate of production. The erythrocytes that do reach the bloodstream may be few in number and abnormally large, or megaloblastic. The red blood cell count may be low and the hemoglobin will be decreased. The skin may appear a pale lemon-yellow color (mild jaundice) because of the excessive death rate of the red blood cells, which causes the bile pigments to be increased in the blood serum. There is little or no secretion of hydrochloric acid in the stomach.

Assessment. The onset of pernicious anemia is usually insidious, with symptoms of a slowly developing anemia. Pallor develops gradually with a yellowish tint to the skin. There may be palpitation, nausea, vomiting, flatulence, indigestion, constipation, and often diarrhea. There is soreness and burning of the tongue, which appears smooth and red with infection about the teeth and gums. Fever, weakness, anorexia, and difficulty in swallowing may also occur. Neurologic symptoms may develop, including tingling of the hands and feet and loss of sense of body position. Cerebral symptoms include loss of memory, mental confusion, and depression. Personality changes and behavior problems can occur.

Severe neurologic impairments can result from inappropriate treatment and inadequate diagnostic evaluation of vitamin B_{12} anemia. These impairments include partial or total paralysis, which results from destruction of the nerve fibers of the spinal cord. Peripheral nerve damage causes the paraesthesia and lack of position sense seen in this disorder.

Intervention. Once the diagnosis has been established, the treatment consists of injections of hydroxocobalamin (vitamin B_{12}). If the anemia is severe, the patient may be transfused with packed red blood cells. The patient may also require treatment for coexisting conditions such as cardiovascular disorders. Injections of vitamin B_{12} must be continued throughout the person's lifetime. Treatment is individualized, but one injection every 2 months may keep the patient free of symptoms.

The nursing care of the patient depends to some extent on the stage the disease had reached when it was discovered. While confined to the hospital, vital signs should be checked daily and recorded. An increase in pulse and respiration is to be expected from the body's adjustment to transfer oxygen to the cells, especially with exertion, but any great change should be reported immediately. Special mouth care should be performed by the patient several times a day, using a cleansing solution that is nonirritating to the mucous membrane of the mouth.

Meals should be carefully planned to provide a diet high in protein, vitamins, and minerals. It is better to use complete proteins of a high order, such as meat, milk, eggs, and shellfish. Because the patient may have a poor appetite, considerable encouragement to eat may be needed. The attractive preparation and serving of food will often stimulate the patient's appetite. Unusually hot, acid, salty, and spicy foods should be avoided because of the soreness of the mouth. Constipation may be treated with mild laxatives prescribed by the physician.

Patients with pernicious anemia are especially sensitive to cold, and extra lightweight warm blankets may be needed. Cotton flannel night-clothing, a warm bed jacket, and bed socks will make the patient more comfortable. Hot-water bottles and electric heating pads should be avoided because of the danger of burning the patient.

Nursing care of the patient with a vitamin B_{12} deficiency anemia also includes evaluation of patient problems such as self-care deficits, fatigue, weakness, activity intolerance, and potential for injury. The goals of care are to conserve energy and prevent injury. Energy can be conserved by assisting the patient with physical care and balancing activities with rest periods. Passive exercises will maintain bone and muscle mass depleted during prolonged inactivity. As soon as they can be tolerated, active exercises like progressive ambulation should be instituted. Loss of independence and altered self-image are common problems and need to be considered in the plan of care. Maintenance of skin integrity is managed by frequent skin inspections, position changes, and the use of protective devices. Intensive and comprehensive rehabilitation programs are appropriate for individuals with severe neurologic deficits and can be instituted when the anemia is corrected.

Most patients with pernicious anemia are older than 40 years of age, and lifetime patterns have been established. Learning that they have an incurable disease may cause considerable emotional shock for some patients. The patient may reject the diagnosis and lose valuable time needed for therapy. The nurse may help the patient by stressing how regular treatment will help the patient feel well, be well, and live a happy normal life. Persons who are economically depressed may need assistance from a community social agency and Medicaid, and elderly persons may be provided for through the Medicare program.

Sickle cell anemia. Sickle cell anemia is found almost exclusively in blacks, and its distribution is worldwide. The disease is a genetic hemolytic blood disorder affecting both men and women. Approximately one of every 10 black Americans carries the gene for the abnormal sickle hemoglobin and therefore has the sickle cell trait. The disease is diagnosed most frequently in children, often in infancy, and the mortality is high. Half of these patients live beyond 20 years of age, although survival rates are increasing with improved care.

Screening clinics have been established in many areas of the United States to identify persons with the trait. Although there is no preventative treatment or cure for the disease, counseling helps the person to avoid the factors that may predispose him or her to a serious exacerbation. Also, couples who either have the trait or have sickle cell disease should be advised of the risks involved so they can make informed decisions about becoming parents. The risk of having a child with sickle cell anemia depends on the genetic characteristics of the prospective parents.

Pathophysiology. Sickle cell anemia is caused by an abnormal hemoglobin molecule (hemoglobin S). When the molecule is present in the red blood cell, it causes the cell to acquire a sickle or crescent shape when the oxygen supply is decreased. The sickle-shaped cell cannot move normally through the blood vessels and tends to block or clog small vessels. As tissue hypoxia worsens and as more oxygen is given up to the tissues, further sickling occurs, blood **viscosity** increases, hemolysis increases, and more clots form in the microcirculation; a sickle cell crisis ensues.

Assessment. The life of the sickled cell is short, and the production of new cells is not fast enough to keep oxygen supplied to the tissues of the body. The person may experience attacks of severe pain in various organs and in the bones. There may be fever, anemia, and thrombi in the lungs and spleen, and the spleen may be enlarged. Leg ulcers may occur. Because of red blood cell destruction, jaundice is frequently seen. Children develop abnormal growth patterns, and infections account for the high mortality in the very young. These persons are especially susceptible to osteomyelitis as a result of salmonella infections and to pneumonia caused by the pneumococcus bacteria. The rate of maternal complications in pregnancy, such as hemorrhage and eclamptic conditions, is reported to be high.

Intervention. Treatment is preventive and supportive. Children should be immunized against preventable diseases. Any activity that causes stress or requires strenuous exercise and would limit oxygen supply should be avoided. Good health habits, including rest, proper diet, avoiding respiratory tract infections, and regular medical supervision should be encouraged. If an acute exacerbation (crisis) occurs, the patient is admitted to the hospital and placed on a regimen of bedrest. The patient may experience fever; severe pain in the chest, joints, and abdomen; edema; and leukocytosis. Routine administration of analgesics is indicated for pain during a crisis as is assistance with activities of daily living and frequent rest periods. Because dehydration contributes to sickling, administration of fluids by mouth or intravenously is very important. Local applications of heat may be used to relieve pain, but cold applications should not be used because they promote sickling. Bacterial infection is a serious complication of sickle cell anemia, and immunizations to prevent pneumococcal pneumonia in these patients is recommended.

Death from sickle cell anemia usually results from long-term effects of repeated tissue damage in major organs such as the heart, kidneys, and liver. The parents of a patient with sickle cell anemia and the patient need a great deal of encouragement and emotional support during the long course of chronic illness. Repeated hospitalizations that begin in early childhood frequently cause ineffective family and patient coping. The loss of independence can lead to depression and to noncompliance with crisis prevention approaches. The adolescent is particularly vulnerable to ineffective coping because many activities such as vigorous athletics need to be avoided, as do situations where exposure to infection is a risk. It is very difficult to achieve the developmental

tasks of childhood and adolescence while having to cope with a chronic and life-threatening illness. Early referral to resources such as the Sickle Cell Foundation can provide the patient and family with support. The nurse needs to maintain a sensitive awareness of the needs of each age group afflicted with sickle cell anemia. A common need is the presence of a trusting relationship with health care providers. An area of potential conflict in this relationship is that of pain management. In a sickle cell crisis, pain is severe. However, it is often ineffectively managed because of caregiver attitudes and lack of knowledge. When the patient seeks pain relief but cannot obtain it because of these problems, trust is threatened and the patient experiences alienation from the staff. If the patient uses strategies that exacerbate the alienation, a vicious cycle begins and the patient suffers needlessly. The nurse is in the best position to prevent this escalation of events through early recognition and confrontation.

Aplastic anemia. Aplastic anemia results from bone marrow failure that is congenital or acquired; in approximately 50% of cases the cause is unknown.[16] It may be induced by radiation, chemicals, or drug therapy, especially with antineoplastic drugs and chloramphenicol. This is a severe, life-threatening anemia with a poor prognosis, requiring careful medical management and excellent nursing care.

Pathophysiology. In aplastic anemia insufficient red blood cells are produced as a result of an interference with the stem cells in the bone marrow. In rare instances only the red blood cells are affected, but usually there is depression of all the cells originating in the bone marrow. This depression of red blood cells (erythrocytes), white blood cells (leukocytes), and platelets (thrombocytes), is referred to as *pancytopenia.*

Assessment. The reduction of erythrocytes produces classic signs and symptoms of anemia: pallor, weakness, dyspnea, and hypoxia. The patient may be tired, lethargic, or confused because of the lack of oxygen to the brain. Infection poses a very real threat because of decreased white blood cells (leukopenia). Thrombocytopenia (reduced thrombocytes or platelets) increases the risk of bleeding. Even an intramuscular injection may produce a site for fatal bleeding. About 50% of persons with aplastic anemia die, most from infection or bleeding.[16]

Intervention. The cause of aplastic anemia must be identified promptly and removed or discontinued. Bone marrow suppression is expected with certain antineoplastic drugs or radiation therapy, and therefore frequent monitoring of laboratory values should be done to maintain control. The margin for therapeutic treatment in such cases is exceedingly narrow. Supportive treatment includes transfusions of packed red blood cells and platelets as indicated.

Blood transfusions are avoided to prevent iron overloading and the development of antibodies to tissue antigens. Platelet transfusions that are HLA (human lymphocyte antigen) matched are used to treat serious bleeding in the thrombocytopenic patient. Cautious use of blood transfusion is necessary to minimize the risk of rejection for the bone marrow transplant candidate. Antibiotics are not given prophylactically but may be lifesaving when given for a specific infection.[6]

A splenectomy may be required in patients with hypersplenism when it is responsible for destruction of normal platelets or for marrow suppression of platelet production. Steroids and androgens are sometimes used in an attempt to stimulate the bone marrow. Antithymocyte globulin has recently become an important therapy for patients who are not candidates for bone marrow transplantation.

Bone marrow transplantation is the treatment of choice in patients under the age of 50 who have a compatible donor. Lectin separation of donor T lymphocytes offers hope for patients without a suitable donor. Bone marrow transplantation involves several processes: immunosuppression of the recipient with total lymph node irradiation and high-dose cyclophosphamide, followed by aspiration of donor marrow from the anterior and posterior iliac crests. Approximately 100 aspirates are taken. The bone marrow is then infused intravenously into the recipient and migrates to the bone marrow cavities. Establishment of the graft (engraftment), if it takes place, occurs in 10 to 30 days. During that period the patient is at enormous risk for severe and irreversible bleeding and infection.

The patient receives immunosuppressive therapy for about 6 months to prevent rejection and graft-vs-host disease. In 30% to 70% of patients graft-vs-host disease occurs with varying degrees of severity. The long-term physical problems include skin changes that cause contractures and muscular wasting, fluid and electrolyte abnormalities caused by chronic diarrhea, fatigue, and jaundice and pruritus caused by inflammation of the liver. Patients and families are confronted with numerous stressors: prolonged hospitalization and isolation from friends and support systems, an altered patient self-concept as a result of physical changes and inability to carry out role responsibilities, and the need to learn complex care regimens after discharge from the hospital.

Patients with aplastic anemia are highly susceptible to infection, and thus nursing care should be directed toward prevention. Strict aseptic technique must be adhered to for dressing changes and administration of intravenous fluids or medications. Meticulous care to prevent impaired skin and mucous membrane integrity includes avoiding intramuscular injections and the administration of rectal medications or the use of rectal thermometers. When bedrest is prescribed, the patient should be assisted to changed position frequently to prevent the development of decubitus ulcers caused by tissue hypoxia. Protective devices such as egg-crate or water mattresses are indicated.

Bowel movements must be kept soft and regular to prevent irritation to the mucous membrane, which could act as a site for infection. Rest periods and assistance will help alleviate the shortness of breath and conserve energy. Thrombocytopenia should alert the nurse to observe carefully for any signs of bleeding and prevent even the slightest trauma. The patient's urine and stool should be monitored for occult or gross bleeding. Assessment of the oral cavity includes noting the presence of bleeding gums (epistaxis) or bleeding from denuded mucosal areas. Medications should be given orally whenever possible. Although the prognosis is poor, careful medical and nursing management improves the chance of survival.

Polycythemia

Polycythemia is a chronic disease that occurs most frequently in middle-aged men of Jewish ancestry.

Pathophysiology. The disease is caused by a proliferation of erythrocytes in the bone marrow. The red blood cell count may range from 7000 to 10 million/mm³ of blood. The disease occurs in two forms: primary and secondary. The cause of primary polycythemia is unknown. In the absence of cardiorespiratory disease the oxygen content of the blood is normal, but the rate of flow is decreased and the **viscosity** is increased. The decreased rate of flow and increased viscosity may lead to thrombosis in small blood vessels. The leukocyte count is increased in true or primary polycythemia and may reach 25,000 to 50,000/mm³. Increased numbers of platelets predispose the patient to intravascular thrombosis. The spleen and liver are enlarged, and bleeding in the form of ecchymosis occurs in mucous membranes and skin. The secondary form of the disease accompanies several other chronic disorders, including cardiac and pulmonary disease. This form has been associated with benign and malignant tumors, particularly malignant tumors of the kidney. In the absence of infection the leukocyte count is near normal. The causative factor in secondary polycythemia is decreased oxygen in the blood.

Assessment. Symptoms are caused by the effects of the massive numbers of red blood cells, which result in hyperviscosity of the blood and hypervolemia. The patient appears plethoric with an appearance of fullness and may complain of headache, fatigue, night sweats, pruritus, paraesthesia, and dyspnea. The spleen and liver will be enlarged and bruises may be seen on the skin and mucous membranes. These persons appear to be predisposed to gout and peptic ulcers.

Intervention. The objective of treatment of polycythemia is to suppress the bone marrow, reduce the blood cell mass, maintain the hematocrit value at or below 50%, and reduce the leukocyte and platelet count. **Phlebotomy** and the removal of up to 500 ml of blood at intervals may accomplish the objectives for some patients. Chemotherapeutic drugs may also be used, including melphalan (Alkeran), chlorambucil (Leukeran), and busulfan (Myleran). Radioactive phosphorus (³²P) may be administered intravenously. Combinations of phlebotomy with chemotherapy and/or radioactive phosphorus are used to provide sustained control of this disease.

The survival time is long, and patients will be required to continue receiving medication. Persons who survive 10 years or longer frequently develop leukemia. The role of the nurse is supportive and directed at minimizing the symptoms. The patient should be encouraged to maintain good health habits and regular medical supervision.

Disorders of White Blood Cells
Leukocytosis

Leukocytosis is an increase in the number of white blood cells. It is both a protective and a destructive

mechanism. In many diseases that are potentially dangerous, leukocytes are increased and play an important role in helping the body to overcome an infection. In some forms of leukemia large numbers of immature leukocytes are produced, causing changes in the spleen, liver, and lymph nodes. Although the number of leukocytes is increased, the cells are immature and do not afford protection against infection.

Leukopenia

Leukopenia is a condition in which the number of leukocytes is greatly reduced. When the granulocytes are reduced, serious bacterial infection may occur. There are numerous conditions causing leukopenia, including chemical agents known to be toxic to the body. Among these are the antineoplastic drugs. Whenever leukopenia occurs, the patient should be protected from infection. The protective mechanism afforded by the leukocytes has decreased, and the patient's life could be in danger if infection should develop.

Infectious mononucleosis

Infectious mononucleosis is an acute infectious disease involving the white blood cells. The number of leukocytes may be increased from 10,000 to 25,000/mm³. The lymphocytes are also increased, some of which will be immature, although most will be mature. The clinical manifestations of the disease involve the lymphoid tissues of the body, particularly the lymph nodes and the spleen (see Chapter 7). The *Paul-Bunnell* (heterophil antibody) *test* is used to determine the presence or absence of antibodies to the Epstein-Barr virus, which causes infectious mononucleosis.

Hodgkin's disease

Hodgkin's disease is classified as a malignant lymphoma and involves the lymph nodes and lymphatic tissues. The disease occurs more frequently in men than in women, and in those 15 to 34 and over 50 years of age. In the past Hodgkin's disease was always fatal, but now many persons can be cured. Early diagnosis in stage I and treatment with radiation can offer a 90% to 100% cure.

Pathophysiology. The cause of Hodgkin's disease is unknown, although environmental, genetic, infectious, and immunologic causes have been studied.

Assessment. The first sign of the disease in two thirds of cases is an asymptomatic enlarge-

---

NURSING CARE GUIDELINES
Anemias

Nursing diagnoses

- Altered nutrition: less than body requirements related to anorexia
- Activity intolerance related to an imbalance between oxygen supply and demand
- Ineffective breathing pattern related to fatigue
- Fear related to prescribed treatment plan
- Altered family processes related to hospitalization
- Potential complication: hemorrhage secondary to thrombocytopenia
- Potential injury related to weakness
- Knowledge deficit related to prescribed diet and medication therapy
- Pain related to decreased oral mucous membrane integrity
- High risk for impaired skin integrity related to immobility

Nursing interventions

- Encourage small frequent meals
- Provide pleasant dining environment
- Give frequent rest periods
- Increase activity as tolerated
- Elevate head of bed as tolerated
- Prevent unnecessary exertion
- Provide positive reinforcement
- Provide an atmosphere of acceptance
- Promote an open and trusting relationship with the family
- Encourage family to visit patient whenever possible

- Monitor for signs of active bleeding
- Avoid aspirin and aspirin-containing products
- Encourage patient to request assistance with activities
- Keep environment free of clutter
- Assess and document patient's level of understanding of iron-replacement therapy
- Provide educational literature on foods high in iron
- Provide frequent oral hygiene
- Provide cool, bland foods
- Keep skin clean and dry
- Encourage frequent turning and movement

Expected outcomes

- Tolerates prescribed diet
- Participates in required activity
- Demonstrates effective breathing pattern
- Verbalizes sources of fear
- Family members participate in patient's care
- Complete blood count is within normal range for patient
- Vital signs are within normal limits for patient
- Verbalizes need for assistance
- Verbalizes an understanding of iron-replacement therapy
- Describes foods high in iron
- Mucous membranes remain intact
- Verbalizes pain relief
- Skin remains intact

---

ment of a lymph node in the neck. As the disease progresses, the deep lymph nodes in the mediastinum and the retroperitoneal cavity with the adjacent tissues are involved.

When systemic symptoms such as loss of 10% of body weight, fever, and night sweats are present, the prognosis is less favorable regardless of the stage of disease at diagnosis; this is denoted as "B" in the staging system, for example, stage IIB Hodgkin's disease. The spleen and liver become enlarged, and in about one fifth of cases the bone marrow is affected. Symptoms are associated with the extent of lymph node and organ involvement. Mediastinal lymph node involvement can compress the trachea and underlying lung tissue, causing dyspnea and difficulty in swallowing. Retroperitoneal involvement is associated with edema of the lower extremities and

back pain. Jaundice and fatigue are symptoms of liver involvement. The diagnosis is usually established by biopsy of a lymph node and identification of large atypical cells called Reed-Sternberg cells.

Intervention. Hodgkin's disease is classified into stages according to pathologic findings and the probable prognosis. From stage I each subsequent stage represents increased activity and progression of the disease. Depending on the stages, treatment may be curative or only palliative. In the stages I and II, treatment consists of radiotherapy of the involved lymph nodes and the contiguous tissues with a view toward cure. In later stages a combination of radiotherapy and chemotherapy is used. When the disease becomes widespread, radiotherapy has little benefit and chemotherapeutic drugs and steroids are administered in cycles. Although cure may not be achieved in the late stage of the disease, remission extending over several years may occur.[6]

Nursing management of the patient with Hodgkin's disease includes intervention to reduce the effects of problems such as dyspnea, pain, fatigue, pruritus, and impaired skin and mucous membrane integrity. The patient is especially susceptible to infection and should be protected against respiratory tract infections and skin infections, which may result from scratching. Treatment of Hodgkin's disease contributes to the severity of the patient's problems.

Leukemias

Leukemia is a neoplastic disorder resulting in widespread proliferation of white blood cells and their precursors throughout the body. It is a disease of the bone marrow, which is where leukocytes are formed. Specific causes of leukemia are unknown, but ionizing radiation, viruses, and genetic abnormalities have been linked with the disease.

Leukemia may be acute or chronic and is also classified according to the type of cells involved, such as the granulocytes, monocytes, and lymphocytes.

Acute lymphoblastic leukemia is the form most common in children, but chronic forms may also occur. Chronic leukemia is more common in persons older than 45 years of age, but acute leukemia may occur in adult persons of any age. Approximately 50% to 60% of all leukemia in the United States is classified as acute leukemia.

Acute leukemia. The acute leukemias are divided into lymphocytic leukemia (ALL), which originates from lymphocytes, and myelocytic leukemia (AML), which originates from granulocytes. Acute lymphocytic leukemia (ALL) occurs primarily in children, and acute myelogenous leukemia (AML) occurs primarily in adults. In children the disease usually affects those 2 to 4 years of age, with most deaths occurring in children under 2 years of age. Regardless of the type of the cells involved, whether in children or adults, the characteristics and progress of the disease are similar.

Pathophysiology. Abnormal growth of immature cells or *blasts* will occur. AML is diagnosed when bone marrow aspiration and biopsy show an overgrowth of very immature cells of the myeloblast. ALL is characterized by cells that are precursors of lymphocytes call lymphoblasts.[4]

Early in the course of acute lymphoblastic leukemia, lymphatic tissues are involved, including lymph nodes and the spleen. The enlarged lymph nodes may be the first signs of the disease in some persons. In all forms of acute leukemia, the leukemic cells multiply in the bone marrow. Their proliferation causes a decrease in the production of red blood cells and shortens their life. The platelets are also reduced. With the reduction of erythrocytes, anemia may develop, and the decreased platelets interfere with the blood-clotting mechanism, which results in bleeding. During the course of the disease almost all organs of the body become involved. With treatment, remissions may occur during which blood cell production may return to nearly normal.

Assessment. The onset of the disease often begins with a slight cold or tonsillitis. The temperature may range from low grade to high. The child may complain of headache and abdominal pain; in the very young child, pain may be evidenced by crying, restlessness, and reluctance to move or be moved. In the adult the onset of the disease may be traced to a cold from which recovery was slow. This is followed by prostration, weakness, anemia, and anorexia. If the anemia is severe, there may be pallor. Ulcerations may occur about the mouth, skin, and rectum. Bleeding varies from ecchymosis and petechiae to purpura, which may become necrotic and ulcerative. Bone pain results from the rapid proliferation of cells in the marrow. Symptoms will vary widely as various organs or parts of the body are involved.

Intervention. Tremendous progress in the treatment of leukemia has been made during the last decade using a complex combination of drug and radiation therapy (Chapter 9). The survival of children with acute lymphoblastic leukemia has increased from an average of 3 months before modern therapy to the point where the majority of those treated have no evidence of the disease after 5 years. Acute nonlymphocytic (myelocytic) leukemia has shown less response to treatment. Only 50% of these patients respond to treatment.

Bone marrow transplantation may be selected as the treatment of choice in patients with suitable donors if the initial remission of the acute leukemia has been induced. Before transplantation, the patient's bone marrow cells and leukemic cells must be killed by massive chemotherapy and total body irradiation. The patient may succumb to infection, hemorrhage, or graft-vs-host disease.

Many of the symptoms concurrent with leukemia are the result of treatment rather than the disease. Side effects of the chemotherapeutic drugs and reactions to radiation therapy should be noted (Chapter 9). If the person receives blood transfusions, packed red blood cells, or platelets, he must be observed for transfusion reaction. When numerous transfusions are given, the danger of reaction is increased. Hematomas or hemorrhage may occur from any trauma to the skin. Infections and hemorrhage account for many complications of leukemia, and the nurse must be constantly alert to protect the patient from infection and to report immediately any severe bleeding or indication of infection. Specific nursing responsibilities are summarized in the box on p. 426.

The child with acute leukemia may come into the hospital several times during the course of the disease. Examinations and treatment may be painful experiences for him, and he may be fearful. The nurse should do everything possible to relieve the anxiety of both the child and the parents. Parents need tender, loving care at this time as much as, and perhaps more than, the child.

Chronic leukemia. Chronic leukemia is confined almost entirely to adults and develops slowly. The chronic leukemias are divided into lymphocytic (CLL) and myelogenous (CML) leukemia. The individual may be completely asymptomatic when the disorder is discovered on a routine physical examination.

Pathophysiology. In chronic myelogenous leukemia the spleen becomes enlarged to the extent that the patient can palpate it and becomes aware of a heavy feeling in the upper left abdomen. Chronic lymphocytic leukemia may progress slowly, or it may progress rapidly to a fatal termination. The leukocyte count is increased, and lymph nodes throughout the body are enlarged but are not painful. Chronic myelocytic leukemia is characterized by the presence of a chromosomal marker, the Philadelphia chromosome, and by a progressive fibrosing of the bone marrow.[19]

Assessment. All forms of chronic leukemia are characterized by similar symptoms, including weakness, fever, bone pain, loss of appetite, loss of weight, anemia, enlargement of body organs, and hemorrhage.

Intervention. The desired objectives of treatment in chronic leukemia partially depend on the kind of cells that are involved. In chronic myelogenous leukemia, the purpose of treatment is to bring about a reduction in the number of leukocytes, thrombocytes, and spleen size. When the white blood cell count is kept at or near normal, other symptoms are modified. In chronic lymphocytic leukemia, the primary consideration is directed toward relief of the conditions that arise from the increased production of lymphocytes, such as the enlarged and painful lymph nodes and spleen, anemia, and decrease in the number of platelets. Drugs commonly used in chronic leukemia include chlorambucil (Leukeran), hydroxyurea, corticosteroids, and cyclophosphamide (Cytoxan). Irradiation of lymph nodes is often used, and blood transfusions may be given if the anemia is severe. Although drugs are not curative, they help to prolong life expectancy for patients with chronic leukemia. The median survival for patients with chronic myelogenous leukemia is 3½ to 4 years, whereas that for patients with chronic lymphocytic leukemia is 6 years.[4] The nursing care during severe relapses is the same as that for patients with acute leukemia. When the patient is ambulatory in the hospital or in the home, regular daily rest periods should be oberved to minimize fatigue and weakness.

Hemorrhagic Disorders
Hemophilia

Hemophilia is a general term that is applied to a group of diseases that have certain things in common. They are all hereditary bleeding diseases that have a prolonged bleeding time. They all exhibit a deficiency in one or more of the factors essential for coagulation of the blood.

Pathophysiology. The most common form of the disease is *classic hemophilia A*. This form appears only in males and is transmitted by the female. *Christmas disease* (hemophilia B) occurs in the same manner as hemophilia A, but is due to a deficiency of factor IX. A third form of the disease is *von Willebrand's disease* (hemophilia C, vascular hemophilia), which occurs in both men and women.

Assessment. Severe bleeding may occur in any part of the body. Repeated hemorrhages into joints (hemarthrosis) such as ankles, knees, and elbows may damage them to the extent that mobility is difficult. Hemorrhage into muscles may lead to contractures. Bleeding occurs into soft tissues and throughout the gastrointestinal tract, and minor injuries such as cuts, lacerations, or bruises may lead to fatal bleeding. There may be hematomas and hematuria, and anemia is often present.

NURSING CARE GUIDELINES
Leukemia

Nursing diagnoses
- High risk for infection related to neutropenia
- Potential complication: hemorrhage secondary to thrombocytopenia
- High risk for injury related to decreased strength and endurance
- Activity intolerance related to weakness and fatigue

Assessment
- Monitor temperature
- Check pulse rate, respiratory rate, blood pressure, temperature
- Assess mental status for restlessness, confusion
- Inspect oral cavity for ulceration, white or gray patches
- Assess skin for broken areas, signs of inflammation, tenderness, drainage
- Inspect perirectal area for inflammation, tenderness
- Auscultate lungs for sounds of congestion
- Monitor white blood cell counts
- Inspect skin for petechiae, purpura
- Check urine, stool, emesis, sputum for frank or occult blood
- Assess mental status for changes
- Inspect eyes, nose, ears, gums for evidence of bleeding
- Inspect IV sites, bone marrow biopsy sites, perirectal area for signs of bleeding
- Monitor platelet count
- Assess mental status for signs of agitation, restlessness, confusion
- Note pulse changes with patient activity
- Assess patient for orthostatic hypotension
- Check patient for dizziness with position changes
- Monitor hematocrit, hemoglobin levels
- Assess pulse changes with each activity
- Evaluate patient ability to perform self-care without shortness of breath

Nursing interventions
- Report temperature elevation, vital sign changes, abnormal findings
- Wash hands frequently and before and after patient contact
- Avoid IM injection, Foley catheters, rectal thermometers, suppositories
- Reduce number of visitors
- Prevent patient contact with persons who have respiratory tract infections, flu
- Sponge patient with tepid water for elevated temperature
- Administer antibiotics as ordered
- Assist patient with frequent position changes while in bed; provide skin care
- Use protective devices such as egg-crate mattress to prevent skin breakdown
- Encourage deep breathing and coughing; administer gentle chest physical therapy
- Provide frequent oral hygiene
- Report any bleeding or abnormal findings
- Apply pressure to venipuncture, bone marrow biopsy sites for 5 minutes
- Provide patient with soft toothbrush; instruct patient to use electric razor when shaving and shoes or slippers when ambulating
- Keep side rails up while patient is in bed
- Instruct patient to change position slowly and wait for assistance with ambulation
- Avoid heat to painful areas; use cold or gentle massage
- Provide reality orientation frequently
- Conserve patient energy
- Assist patient with self-care activities
- Space tests, activities; provide frequent rest periods
- Teach energy conservation techniques
- Instruct patient to report activities that increase fatigue

Expected outcomes
- Describes signs and symptoms of infection and preventative measures
- Maintains adequate nutrition
- Free from bleeding
Hemoglobin, hematocrit, and platelet count are within normal range for patient
- Avoids physical trauma
- Verbalizes a need for assistance
- Spaces activities throughout the day
- Demonstrates progression with activity and endurance
- Strives toward independence

Intervention. Treatment is first preventative. The individual with hemophilia in any form must be guarded against injuries. Contact sports are contraindicated. Parents should receive instruction concerning activities for young children and should know when an injury is serious enough to call the physician. Genetic counseling should be available to the family. If there has been a severe hemorrhage, fresh whole blood may be given. At the present time cryoprecipitate or commercial concentrates of factor VIII are the treatment of choice for persons with hemophilia A. In hemophilia B, concentrates containing the deficient factor IX may be administered. In hemophilia C, cryoprecipitate is given. Mild to moderate hemophilia A and von Willebrand's type I may be treated with a synthetic analog of vasopressin. This has been shown to increase factor VIII levels and can reduce the risk of AIDS and hepatitis transmitted by blood transfusions. Nurses monitor the patient for side effects of the drug, which include fluid retention, tachycardia, hyponatremia, and hypokalemia. The blood pressure and pulse rate are measured frequently during the infusion and fluids are usually restricted. Patients experiencing pain from joint or muscle complications may need analgesics to relieve pain. Analgesics containing aspirin or narcotics are usually avoided.

When injections are unavoidable, the nurse should use a small needle and apply firm pressure to the injection site for some time after the injection. The patient should be helped to remain quiet by the use of a recommended sedation, if necessary. The diet should be high in iron, vitamin C, and protein, with high-protein drinks between meals. The application of cold compresses and pressure sometimes lessens the amount of bleeding into the tissues. Persons with hemophilia should inform physicians and dentists of this condition. Identification should be worn or carried, indicating that the person has hemophilia and the type.

Some psychosocial concerns are common to the hemophiliac and family and need to be addressed. In hemophilia A and B, the gene is transmitted by the mother, who may experience guilt feelings and compensate by overprotecting the child. As in sickle cell anemia or in any chronic condition that requires extra attention for the affected child, sibling rivalry and jealousy may be exaggerated. The hemophilic child learns early that trauma is associated with bleeding and may use defense mechanisms like denial to cope. In adolescence and young adulthood this can be manifested in risk-taking behavior. Other adaptations include stress-related spontaneous bleeding and passive reliance on others, neither of which are effective coping responses. The nurse can assist the patient and family by recognizing these responses and confronting them. Referral to the National Hemophilia Foundation may be helpful.

Vascular purpuras

Assessment. Purpura is a condition in which there are small, spontaneous hemorrhages into the skin or mucous membrane. Tiny hemorrhages appearing as pinpoint purplish spots are called **petechiae;** larger hemorrhages are called **ecchymoses.**

Pathophysiology. Purpura may be divided into two categories: those associated with the destruction of platelets and those caused by failure of the bone marrow to produce platelets. *Idiopathic,* or *autoimmune thrombocytopenic purpura* (ITP) is caused by the destruction of the platelets in the blood. The destruction results in a greatly reduced number of platelets and leads to bleeding. The disorder occurs in an acute form in children and may progress to a chronic disorder. It also occurs as a chronic disorder most commonly in young adult females. Destruction of the platelets is caused by an antiplatelet factor in the plasma. In the chronic form it may occur as a complication of a primary disease or after the ingestion of certain drugs. In some forms the platelets are deposited in large numbers in the spleen, causing splenomegaly. The second form of the disease, *thrombocytopenic purpura,* is caused by a failure in the production of platelets, which may be the result of damage to the bone marrow. Drugs and chemicals or conditions that require massive blood transfusions may result in purpura.

Intervention. Treatment and care depend on discovering and eliminating the cause. If purpura is caused by the destruction of platelets, both the acute and the chronic stages of the disorder are treated with steroids. In some situations removal of the spleen may be indicated. If purpura is caused by a drug, withdrawing the drug will usually correct the condition.

Splenomegaly

The spleen is located in the upper part of the abdominal cavity under the lower part of the rib cage. It has four major functions: removal of microorganisms from the blood, formation of red blood cells under abnormal conditions, removal of old red blood cells and platelets from the circulation, and storage of blood. In blood dyscrasias, in which blood cell production in the marrow is compromised, the spleen may assume the function of producing all the blood cells. Not all of the functions of the spleen are understood. Enlargement of the spleen occurs in several diseases and is called **splenomegaly.**

Pathophysiology. Chronic congestive splenomegaly is frequently associated with certain blood dyscrasias in which removal of the spleen, *splenectomy*, may be indicated. Various disorders affecting the spleen may also require its removal. Injury to the organ, especially a crushing type, is always a surgical emergency. Splenectomy is done only as a reluctant, final intervention in children.

Postoperative nursing intervention. The nursing care of the patient after a splenectomy is essentially the same as that for other patients after abdominal surgery (Chapter 5). Because the spleen has a rich blood supply and the patient may have a blood dyscrasia, it is important that the patient be carefully observed for postoperative hemorrhage. The patient should be carefully monitored for the development of a subphrenic abscess in the dead space created by removal of the spleen.

NURSING CARE PLAN
Patient with Aplastic Anemia

The patient is a 40-year-old male on the medical unit with a diagnosis of aplastic anemia. He presented himself to his private physician 2 weeks earlier with complaints of fatigue, epistaxis, easy bruising, and hematuria. Since admission, he has undergone multiple diagnostic studies, and is currently being prepared for transfer to an oncology regional center as a potential candidate for a bone marrow transplant. Various members of his extended family are being considered as potential donors, but no one has been identified as a tissue match as yet.

He states that he lost 20 lbs prior to admission, but has regained 5 lbs since admission. Second hospital day—he received 10 units of cryoprecipitate. Third hospital day—he received 1 unit of fresh frozen plasma. Fourth hospital day—he received 2 units of packed red blood cells. (PRBC). Implantation of a porta-cath in the right subclavian region was performed under local anesthesia.

He has no known food or drug allergies. Aspirin and nonsteroidal antiinflammatory drugs (NSAIDs) are contraindicated due to his pathologic condition.

Past medical history

No previous hospitalizations. History of occassional premature ventricular contractions (PVCs), noted on recent inoffice ECGs. He has hypertension (HTN), which is under control with the drug Tenormin, 50 mg daily.

Spontaneous passing of a kidney stone (nephrolithasis), 1 year prior to current illness.

He is a Vietnam veteran and was exposed to agent orange while on ground patrol in that country (prolonged exposure).

Some health risk behaviors: Smoked 3 to 4 packs per day times 21 years. Drinks 2 to 3 cans of beer per day times 15 years.

Health strengths: Has yearly physical exams. Eats a low fat diet, exercises at least twice per week, (plays tennis). Works out at the gym when he feels that his weight is climbing.

Family history

Father died at age 67 from myocardial infarction (MI).

Mother alive and well, age 65, only health problem is HTN, which is under control with medication.

Older brother Sam died 3 months ago from a motor vehicle accident.

Younger brother Joe, age 38. Excellent health, lives in Europe.

Two sisters, ages 33 and 34, both in good health. Supportive relationships. All said to be willing to be tested as a candidate for the bone marrow transplant.

Psychosocial data

Married for 16 years. Periods of separation times 2. States that the last visits to the marriage counselor has strengthened their communication skills and now they have a quality "understanding" relationship. One daughter Sally, age 14. She is currently being shielded from the knowledge of the gravity of her father's illness. Large extended family on wife's side.

Has worked at automotive factory for 22 years. Has HMO-oriented health insurance plan.

Religion: Protestant. Goes to church on a sporadic basis.

Hobbies: Bowling, fishing, some contact sports. Likes TV, but dislikes reading.

Assessment data

Chronically ill-appearing male. Oriented × 3 (time, place, and person).

Height 6 ft Weight 195 lbs.

Skin: Pale, with evidence of multiple bruises in various stages of healing. Bruises mostly on trunk and upper arms.

No rashes, no evidence of skin breakdown.

Anterior chest wall has 2 intact sutured incisions with no dressings. Very slight serosangineous drainage from lower incision. No redness or edema present in either incision.

Hematoma 5 by 6 cm noted to the right of incisions. (Patient keeping ice over the swelling).

Respiratory: Rate 16-20. Regular depth and rhythm. Clear to percussion and ascultation.

Abdominal: Soft, nondistended. Positive bowel sounds heard in all four quadrants.

Cardiovascular: Apical pulse of 78. Best heard over apex.

Musculoskeletal: Full range of motion all joints.

Lab data

WBC 6,000
RBC 2.69
Hgb 7.3
Hct 23.4 } All low = pancytopenia

Platelets, 114,000

Oxygen saturation level = 79-81 without additional oxygen. Improves up to 95 with 4 L oxygen continuously.

BUN, creatinine, chloride and potassium WNL.

Calcium high at 11.2 (nl = 8.5-10.4).

Sodium (Na) high at 148 (nl = 135-145).

Albumin low at 3.2 (nl = 3.3-5.0).

PT high at 14.0.

PTT high at 42.5.

Continued on next page.

Medications

Tenormin 50 mg po daily (HTN).
Allupurinol 300 mg po BID.
Aquamethyton 15 mg po BID.
Solu-Medrol 20 mg po every 6 hours.

IV 1000 ml normal saline at 100 ml per hour. May D/C if po intake adequate. Convert to a hep lock.

NURSING DIAGNOSIS

Potential for infection related to pancytopenia and surgical incision

Expected patient outcomes	Nursing interventions	Evaluation for expected outcomes
Incision site remains free of signs and symptoms of infection. Patient's vital signs and lab values remain within his normal limits. No pathogens appear in cultures. Patient shows no evidence of skin breakdown.	Monitor vital signs at least every 4 hours and report any deviations from the baseline. Minimize the risk of infection by careful handwashing. (All personnel, family, visitors, and staff need to comply). Use strict aseptic technique when inserting IV lines, changing dressings, and/or providing wound care. Have patient cough and deep breathe every 4 hours to help remove secretions and prevent pulmonary complications. Help patient turn every 2 hours. Provide skin care especially to bony prominences to prevent venous stasis and skin breakdown. Ensure adequate nutritional intake. (Needs 2000 calories range daily). Offer high protein supplemental snacks. Likes milkshakes if cold. Arrange for reverse isolation if WBC count falls low. Monitor the flow and number of visitors. Explain the rationale to patient and family. Educate patient and his family about good handwashing techniques and/or any other factors that increase infection risks.	Patient's temperature and vital signs remain within the normal range. Patient's WBC and differential count remain within a normal range. Cultures do not grow pathogens. Patient demonstrates appropriate personal/oral hygiene. Patient's incision site (port-a-cath) remains clear and pink and free of purulent drainage. Patient's IV sites do not show signs of inflammation. Patients skin does not exhibit signs of breakdown. Patient lists risk factors that contribute to infection. Patient remains free of infection.

NURSING DIAGNOSIS

Potential for injury or fatigue related to altered hemodynamics as evidenced by critically low platelet count, increased PT and PTT values, decreased Hct and Hgb, easy bruising, and excessive bleeding.

Expected patient outcomes	Nursing interventions	Evaluation for expected outcomes
Patient carries out activities of dialy living (ADLs) without excessive weakness or fatigue. No signs of active bleeding appear. Patient's clotting profile returns to as near normal as possible. Patient maintains adequate ventilation.	Monitor daily lab values and document findings. Report any abnormal values immediately to the physician. Assess for excessive bleeding, fatigue, or new bruising. Inspect skin daily during bath. Guiac all stools.	Patient's lab values will improve after the infusion of platelets and packed RBCs. Fatigue will be lessened, and patient will identify ways to conserve energy. Bruising will diminish. There will be no signs of bleeding, either overt or covert.

Expected patient outcomes	Nursing interventions	Evaluation for expected outcomes
Patient communicates understanding of precautions needed to prevent bleeding. Patient's lab values of platelets, RBCs, Hgb and Hct, PT and PTT will improve and fatigue, bruising, and excessive bleeding will diminish.	Place patient on neurovital signs. Monitor for changes in level of consciousness (LOC or any signs of confusion. Keep on oxygen at 4 L. Check oxygen saturation levels every 4 hours. Monitor for a fall of O_2 saturation level if off oxygen. Assess for hematuria, epistaxis, blood in the stool, or dyspnea. Maintain IV hydration as ordered. Monitor intake and output. Force fluids (at least 1000 ml per shift) while on the allupurinol. Maintain patient safety measures such as no aspirin or nonsteroidal antiinflammatory drugs (NSAID) products. No intramuscular injections while platelet count is so low. Hold any venipuncture sticks for 5 minutes. Assist patient in and out of bed. Monitor for safety. Monitor administration of blood and blood products. Assess baseline vital signs prior to any procedure, and during the procedure according to hospital protocol. Check lab values before and after treatments and watch for adverse reactions during the administration of any blood or blood products, (assess for rash, hives, fever or generalized urticaria). Teach patient ways to conserve energy (i.e., alternate periods of rest). Inform patient of the adverse effects of smoking and encourage him to stop.	Patient will have no untoward reaction during transfusion therapy. Patient's clotting profile will return to normal limits. Patient will improve in his ability to carry out his ADLs.

NURSING DIAGNOSIS

Potential for anxiety related to his diagnosis, as evidenced by restlessness, insomnia, aggression towards staff and family, changes in communication patterns, and verbalization of inability to cope and meet role expectations.

Expected patient outcomes	Nursing interventions	Evaluation for expected outcomes
By discharge, patient and his wife will discuss all the changes brought on by his illness. Both parents will begin to share information with 14-year-old daughter. This information will be geared to her developmental level, and will foster discussion with her (The pattern of exclusion will be stopped).	Spend 10 mintues with patient twice a shift. Convey a willingness to listen. Offer verbal reassurance such as, "I know you're frightened, I'll stay with you." Give patient concise explanation of anything about to occur.	Patient will report decreased restlessness and anxiety. He will have longer periods of uninterrupted sleep. Patient and his family will have quality discussions on the projected effects of his illness and changes that might be necessary in their lifestyle.

Continued on next page.

Expected patient outcomes	Nursing interventions	Evaluation for expected outcomes
Patient will identify his usual coping patterns and state which ones will assist him now. Patient and his family will begin to discuss treatment choices, and write down any questions that are unclear to them.	Avoid information overload, since an anxious patient cannot assimilate many details. Make no demands on patient. Identify and reduce as many environmental stressors as possible. Have patient state what kinds of activities promote feelings of comfort and encourage him to perform them. Remain with patient during severe anxiety. Include him in decisions related to care when feasible. Support the family in coping with patient's anxious behavior. Allow extra visiting periods with his family, if this seems to allay his anxiety. Teach patient relaxation techniques to be performed at least every 4 hours, such as guided imagery, progressive muscle relaxation, and meditation. Praise patient for initiating discussion with daughter. Encourage her to share feelings. Refer patient to community or professional mental health resources as needed.	Daughter will be included in the family discussions, and the exclusion behaviors will be eradicated. Patient and his wife will identify their usual patterns of coping and relate these to the perceived illness threat. They will draw strength from one another. Patient will practice relaxation techniques on an ongoing basis.

NURSING DIAGNOSIS

Knowledge deficit related to lack of information regarding treatment protocol as evidenced by questioning drugs, side effects, and infusion therapies.

Expected patient outcomes	Nursing interventions	Evaluation for expected outcomes
Patient communicates a need to know. By the time of the transfer to the oncology center, patient will state an understanding of what has been taught. Patient and his primary nurse will set realistic learning goals.	Establish an environment of mutual trust and respect to enhance learning. Ascertain what patient already knows. Clarify any misinformation. Negotiate with patient to develop goals for learning. Select teaching strategies (such as discussion of visual materials and demonstration). Answer his questions honestly. Refer him to his physician on matters related to medical protocol. Give clear explanations on the drugs that he is taking. Explain the dose, time, and need for compliance. Teach skills that he must incorporate into his daily lifestyle (i.e., dressing changes). Have patient give a return demonstration.	Patient expresses a desire for new knowledge related to his treatment protocol. He demonstrates newly learned skills and health-related behaviors. Patient develops realistic learning goals. Patient can state each drug he is taking, the correct dosage, the rationale for use, and some common side effects. Patient writes down any questions related to his medical regimen so as to further enhance his knowledge about his illness. Patient indicates an openness to discuss the potential of bone marrow transplantation and the availability of a matched donor.

Expected patient outcomes	Nursing interventions	Evaluation for expected outcomes
	Provide emotional support if patient questions the overall prognosis. Discuss bone marrow transplantation once the concept has been introduced to him. Encourage his further questions. Reinforce the prevention of infection necessity.	

REFERENCES AND ADDITIONAL READINGS

1. American Association of Blood Banks: Blood transfusions outside the hospital, Am J Nurs 89(1):486–489, 1989.
2. American Red Cross: Circular of information for the use of human blood and blood components, 1989, The American Red Cross.
3. Anthony CP and Thibodeau GA: Textbook of anatomy and physiology, ed 12, St Louis, 1987, The CV Mosby Co.
4. Beare P and Myers J: Principles and practice of adult health nursing, St Louis, 1990, The CV Mosby Co.
5. Brown S: Behind the numbers on the CBC, RN 53(2):46–51, 1990.
6. Brunner L and Suddarth D: Textbook of medical-surgical nursing, ed 6, Philadelphia, 1988, JB Lippincott Co.
7. Buchsel P and Kelleher J: Bone marrow transplantation, Nurs Clin North Am 24(4):907–949, 1989.
8. Fischbach F: A manual of laboratory diagnostic tests, ed 3, Philadelphia, 1988, JB Lippincott Co.
9. Froberg J: Part I: the anemias—causes and courses of action, RN 52(1):24–30, 1989.
10. Froberg J: Part II: the anemias—causes and courses of action, RN 52(3):52–57, 1989.
11. Froberg J: Part III: the anemias—causes and courses of action, RN 52(5):42–47, 1989.
12. Hood L: Interferon, getting in the way of viruses and tumors, Am J Nurs 87(4):459–464, 1987.
13. Kneisl C and Ames S: Essentials of adult health nursing, Menlo Park, 1988, Addison-Wesley Publishing Co.
14. Konradi D and Stockert P: A close-up look at leukemia, Nurs 89 19(6):34–41, 1989.
15. Lederer JR and others: Care planning pocket guide: a nursing diagnosis approach, ed 3, Redwood City, 1990, Addison-Wesley Nursing.
16. Luckmann J and Sorenson K: Medical surgical nursing, ed 3, Philadelphia, 1987, WB Saunders Co.
17. Perdew S: Facts about AIDS: a guide for health care providers, Philadelphia, 1990, JB Lippincott Co.
18. Phipps WJ and Long B: Medical surgical nursing: a nursing process approach, ed 2, St Louis, 1989, The CV Mosby Co.
19. Rifkind RA and others: Fundamentals of hematology, ed 3, Chicago, 1986, Year Book Medical Publishers, Inc.
20. Simonson G: Caring for patients with acute myelocytic leukemia, Am J Nurs 89(3):304–309, 1989.
21. Van Devanter N and others: Counseling HIV-antibody positive blood donors, Am J Nur 87(8):1026–1030, 1987.

PROBLEMS AFFECTING

Nutrition and Bowel Elimination

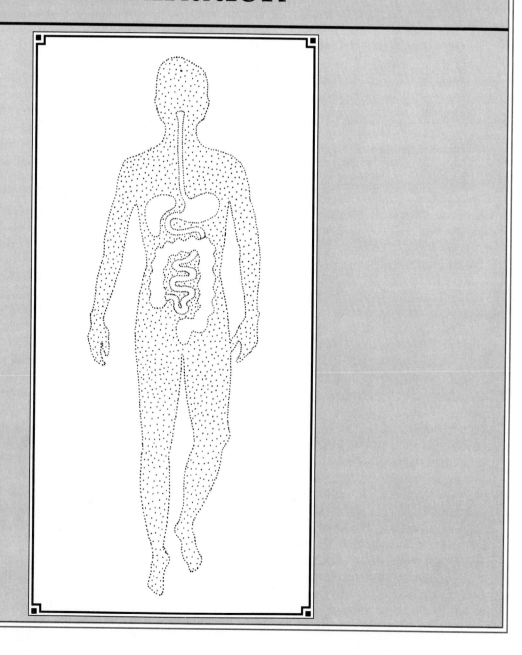

KEY WORDS

anastomosis
appendicitis
biliary system
cardiospasm
cholangiography
cholecystectomy
cholecystography
cirrhosis
colostomy
computerized tomography
dysphagia
esophagoscopy
gastrectomy
gastroscopy
hemorrhoids
hepatic coma
hepatitis
herniorrhaphy
hiatus hernia
hyperalimentation
ileostomy
ileus
intussusception
laparotomy
occult blood
pancreatitis
paralytic ileus
peptic ulcer
peristalsis
proctoscopy
pyloric spasm
sigmoidoscopy
stomas

OBJECTIVES

1. Describe the pathway of food through the gastrointestinal tract.

2. Discuss factors that may affect the process of digestion and absorption.

3. Explain the following diagnostic tests, including purpose, procedure, and preparation of the patient: gastric analysis, endoscopy, gastrointestinal series, barium enema, liver function tests, liver biopsy, cholecystography, and cholangiography.

4. Identify signs and symptoms of impending complications following surgical treatment of common gastrointestinal disorders, including peptic ulcer, appendicitis, diverticulitis, intestinal obstruction, hernia, hiatus hernia, and hemorrhoids.

5. Discuss the prevention of and interventions for peritonitis as a complication of gastric ulcer and appendicitis.

6. Discuss the care of the ostomy patient, including skin care, application of appliances, psychologic aspects, and use of irrigation equipment for colostomy patients.

7. Describe the nursing care of the patient with a gastrostomy tube, including skin care, feedings, and psychologic aspects.

8. Discuss the nursing care of the patient during gastrointestinal decompression.

9. Discuss the purpose of total parenteral nutrition and the potential side effects of too rapid administration.

10. Identify measures to prevent the transmission of infectious and serum hepatitis (hepatitis A and hepatitis B).

11. Discuss the nursing care of the patient with cirrhosis of the liver and hepatic coma.

12. Identify nursing interventions to prevent complications following cholecystectomy.

STRUCTURE AND FUNCTION OF THE GASTROINTESTINAL SYSTEM

The gastrointestinal (GI) system, or alimentary tract, is also called the digestive system because its function is the digestion and absorption of food. The system begins in the mouth and terminates at the anus. The mouth is also called the *buccal,* or oral, *cavity.* Three sets of salivary glands pour their secretions through ducts that open into the mouth. The teeth and tongue are considered accessory organs of digestion. The esophagus, which is about 10 inches long, leads from the mouth to the stomach. In its descent it passes through the thoracic cavity behind the trachea and the heart. A sphincter muscle, the cardiac sphincter, guards the opening between the esophagus and the stomach. The muscle relaxes to permit the passage of food or fluids, after which it contracts to prevent backward flow. The stomach is a pouchlike structure located in the upper part of the abdominal cavity under the liver and the diaphragm. It is divided into three parts: the fundus, the upper part nearest the esophagus; the middle section, or body; and the pylorus, which is the lower part. Located between the stomach and the small intestine is the pyloric sphincter, which relaxes to permit passage from the stomach into the small intestine and contracts to prevent the contents of the intestine from returning to the stomach. Spasms of the cardiac and the pyloric sphincter sometimes occur and are considered functional disorders.

The small intestine, which is about 20 feet long, consists of three sections but has no break in its continuity. The section nearest the stomach is the duodenum, the middle section is the jejunum, and the lower section is known as the ileum. Most of the digestion and absorption of food takes place in the small intestine.

The large intestine is only about 6 feet long but is much larger in diameter than the small intestine. It is also divided into three sections. The cecum, which begins where the large intestine joins the small intestine, is only a few inches long. The ileocecal valve guards the passageway between the ileum and the large intestine. The vermiform appendix, located at the end of the cecum, is a small, wormlike tube. The colon from the cecum ascends upward on the right side of the abdomen, then crosses over the abdomen below the stomach and continues downward on the left side. Thus the colon has been separated into the

ascending, transverse, and *descending* colon. As the colon descends, the final portion is shaped like an S and is called the *sigmoid colon.* The sigmoid then joins the rectum, which is about 7 to 8 inches long. The final inch makes up the anal canal. The opening from the anal canal to the exterior is guarded by two sets of muscles, the internal sphincter and the external sphincter. The final opening to the exterior is the anus. The alimentary tract is lined with muscles that contract involuntarily to produce the wavelike contractions called **peristalsis**.

The liver, gallbladder, and pancreas are accessory organs. They assist the process of digestion by contributing specific secretions and enzymes essential for normal digestion and use. The liver, located on the right side of the body under the diaphragm, is the largest of the organs. It has many functions and is considered one of the most vital organs of the body. The gallbladder is shaped like a pear and lies under the liver. It stores and concentrates bile and releases it into the duodenum during the process of digestion. The pancreas is a slender organ, fishlike in shape, which is located at the back of the stomach with a portion extending into a C-shaped curve of the duodenum. Located within the pancreas are the cells called *islands of Langerhans* that secrete insulin.

Because much of the care of the patient depends on the specific parts of the gastrointestinal system affected, the nurse is encouraged to review in greater detail the structure and function of the system.

PROCESS OF DIGESTION AND ABSORPTION

Digestion is the process by which food is prepared so that it may be absorbed and used by the body. Absorption is the process in which nutrients pass into the circulation so that they may be carried to the body tissues. Digestion is accomplished by two processes: (1) mechanical digestion and (2) chemical digestion.

During mechanical digestion, which begins in the mouth, food is cut and ground into small pieces *(mastication).* Its passage from the mouth to the stomach is facilitated by mucus from the salivary glands and the mucus-secreting glands along the esophagus that lubricates and aids in easy passage. Food entering the stomach from the esophagus passes through the *cardiosphincter* (valve). The muscle relaxes to allow food to enter the stomach, then contracts to prevent its backward flow. When the semiliquid contents of the stomach *(chyme)* enter the small intestine (duodenum), their passage is controlled by the *pyloric sphincter* (valve), which relaxes and contracts much the same as the cardiosphincter. Food is moved along the entire route by wavelike muscular contractions **(peristalsis)**. Mechanical digestion may be best described as a cutting, grinding, and churning process. As this action goes on, numerous enzymes are being secreted that chemically act on the various food constituents.

Chemical digestion is the action of enzymes on the proteins, carbohydrates, and fats by breaking them into simple compounds in preparation for absorption. *Ptyalin* is secreted in the mouth and acts on starches; however, this action is limited and largely destroyed by the hydrochloric acid in the stomach. Several enzymes are secreted in the stomach, including the hormone *secretin*, which stimulates the pancreas to secrete its enzymes. The breakdown of proteins begins in the stomach. Hydrochloric acid is secreted in the stomach, and the acidity must remain at about pH 2 for enzyme action. There is little action on fats in the stomach. The major part of chemical digestion occurs in the small intestine, where all of the food constituents undergo enzymatic action. An enzyme from the pancreas aids the digestion of fats. Bile produced in the liver and stored in the gallbladder is released into the duodenum and is required to dissolve fats and fat-soluble vitamins. Other vitamins, minerals, and water that are present require no enzyme action.

When chemical action is complete, through several processes, absorption begins. Carbohydrates and proteins enter the circulation through the portal system, whereas fats enter the lymph vessels and eventually reach the portal system near the thoracic duct. The large intestine (colon) has several functions before the cycle is complete. There are no enzymes in the large intestine. After the residue from the small intestine passes through the ileocecal valve and enters the colon, water and some electrolytes such as sodium and chloride are absorbed into the blood. Bacteria in the colon putrefy undigested foods, synthesize vitamin K and vitamins B_{12}, B_2, and B_1, and produce gas that assists in propelling the feces toward the anus. The urge to defecate is a reflex stimulated by distention of the rectum. Voluntary relaxation of the rectal sphincter assists defecation.

It takes 24 to 40 hours for feces to pass through the large intestine.

The liver plays an important role in metabolism of carbohydrates, fats, and proteins. The liver assists in the regulation of blood glucose by converting carbohydrates to glycogen, storing glycogen, and then converting it to glucose as needed. When glycogen stores are low, the liver deaminates (removes the ammonia) from amino acids to make glucose and glycogen or ketones for energy. It synthesizes and catabolizes fatty acids and neutral fats to form ketone bodies and active acetate (sources of cell energy). Its role in protein metabolism includes synthesis of amino acids and supply of plasma proteins for tissue repair. It synthesizes the proteins, prothrombin, and fibrinogen for blood coagulation. The liver stores vitamins, including vitamin K and the other oil-soluble vitamins, and is the primary site of vitamin B_{12} storage.

There are many factors that affect the process of digestion and absorption. Elderly persons, who have lost their teeth and have no dentures or have poorly fitting dentures will have problems with mastication. Thus the mechanical process of cutting and grinding will be compromised. The patient who must remain in a recumbent position may have difficulty in swallowing, because food does not pass down the esophagus as easily as in a sitting position. Emotions affect the secretion of enzymes or may cause severe and painful contractions of the sphincter muscles. Pathologic disease may affect any part of the system; some may be treated medically, whereas others may require surgery. The lack of specific nutrients or sufficient calories may result in malnutrition or starvation.

CAUSES OF DIGESTIVE DISEASES AND DISORDERS

Many conditions can disrupt normal functioning of the gastrointestinal system. Some diseases are pathologic conditions, such as cancer or appendicitis. Many complaints have no pathologic basis but result from some emotional problem, such as stress, and are called psychophysiologic disorders.

Other conditions may be the result of traumatic injury or congenital malformation. In some conditions the body may be unable to use certain nutrients, as in diabetes. When the islands of Langerhans in the pancreas fail to produce insulin, the body cannot use carbohydrates. Changes occur in the system that are normal results of the aging process, such as decreased mobility, which can cause constipation. Frequently, elderly persons do not understand these degenerative changes and believe they have a disease.

Despite the multiplicity of digestive disorders, relatively few symptoms are directly related to the digestive system. These symptoms are clinically defined as nausea, vomiting, constipation, diarrhea, loss of appetite, difficulty in swallowing, abdominal pain, blood in stools, and vomiting of blood (hematemesis).

Assessment

Similar symptoms may occur in several different diseases, and the nurse can assist the physician by making careful observation of the patient's complaints and reporting and recording them.

The nurse should be familiar with the correct anatomic location of abdominal pain so that it can be properly identified and its location reported (Figure 18-1). The pain should be described as throbbing, aching, stabbing, dull, intermittent, or constant. The abdomen should also be observed for distention.

Nausea and vomiting may be the result of organic disease or may occur from emotional disturbances. Nausea and vomiting frequently occur after the administration of a general anesthetic. The patient may complain of nausea but without any emesis. If vomiting occurs, the amount, character, relation to food or fluid intake, presence of bright red blood, and presence of fecal matter, which can be detected by appearance and odor, should be recorded and reported.

Stools should be observed for frequency, color, consistency, presence of mucus, bright red blood, coffee-ground appearance (indicating old blood), odor, and macroscopic parasites (worms).

Other observations that may be important to the physician include belching gas or expelling large amounts of flatus and the condition of the patient's appetite. The patient's mental state should also be observed for depression, anxiety, apprehension, restlessness, or crying episodes. Vomiting, frequent liquid stools, diaphoresis, and hemorrhage or oozing from wounds result in loss of electrolytes. Procedures such as gastric suction and repeated enemas also cause loss of electrolytes. Because a serious imbalance of electrolytes may result, it is important for the nurse to observe patients carefully for any signs and symptoms of

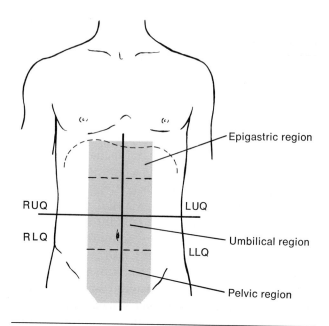

Figure 18-1

Anatomic quadrants and regions of abdomen.

electrolyte loss and to report this at once to the physician (Chapter 4). Tissue turgor should be assessed to determine the state of hydration, along with the appearance of the mucous membranes. The presence and location of edema and abdominal distension should also be noted.

DIAGNOSTIC TESTS FOR DISORDERS OF THE GASTROINTESTINAL SYSTEM

Several diagnostic tests and procedures are performed on the gastrointestinal system. Some are performed to aid the physician in establishing a diagnosis when symptoms of a disease are present. Tests may be done to rule out the existence of a specific disease, and some may be done as a preventative measure to discover a disease before symptoms occur, when treatment may be most advantageous. There may be some variation in procedures among physicians and hospitals, and the nurse should understand the physician's orders.

Gastric Analysis and Histamine Test

The test for gastric analysis is performed to examine the acidity of the stomach contents. Cells of the stomach secrete hydrochloric acid, which aids digestion. Too much acid may be present in persons with conditions such as peptic ulcer; in persons with diseases such as pernicious anemia or gastric malignancies, the acid may be absent. Although some health care professionals have questioned the accuracy of the results of gastric analysis, the test is still considered a worthwhile adjunct to other tests.[2] The patient receives nothing by mouth after supper the evening before the test, and in the morning a tube is passed through the nose into the stomach. A large syringe is attached to the tube, and the contents of the stomach are aspirated. Usually, several specimens are secured at intervals according to the physician's direction. Each specimen must be carefully labeled with the time it was taken and its numeric order. A clamp is placed on the tube between specimens and the tube taped to the patient's face. The physician may wish to stimulate the flow of gastric secretions and will order a subcutaneous injection of histamine or betazole (Histalog). This is known as the histamine test. The gastric secretions are then aspirated at 15-minute intervals for 1 hour or longer. Because some patients are sensitive to histamine and may have a reaction, a tray with a syringe containing a 1:1000 solution of epinephrine should be ready for emergency use.

The procedure should be explained to the patient, and he or she may be assured that, although it may be uncomfortable, it is not painful. An emesis basin should be given the patient because gagging may produce vomiting during the procedure. The test may be performed in the physician's office or in an outpatient clinic. The procedure may be carried out by the nurse under the physician's direction, or it may be done by a laboratory technician.

Tubeless Gastric Analysis

The tubeless method of determining the presence of hydrochloric acid in the stomach is more comfortable for the patient because it does not require the passage of a tube. The test indicates the presence or absence of free hydrochloric acid but cannot be used to determine the *amount* of free hydrochloric acid if it is present. It is useful as a screening technique for detection of gastric achlorhydria (absence of free hydrochloric acid). Preparation of the patient may be the responsibility of the technician or the nurse. All food is withheld after midnight until the test is completed. In the morning the patient voids and the specimen is discarded. The patient is then given 250 mg of caffeine sodium benzoate. After 1 hour the patient voids, and the entire specimen is saved, labeled, and sent to the laboratory. The patient is then given one packet of an exchange resin, azure A (azuresin [Diagnex Blue]) with a glass of water. If there is free hydrochloric acid in the stomach, the resin will cause the release of a substance in the stomach that will then be absorbed from the small intestine and excreted by the kidneys within 2 hours.[15] Thus 2 hours later the patient voids and the specimen is sent to the laboratory. The absence of detectable amounts of dye in the urine indicates that free hydrochloric acid probably was not secreted.

Bernstein Test

The Bernstein, or acid perfusion, test aids in differentiating esophageal pain caused by esophagitis from that caused by angina pectoris. A nasogastric tube is measured for placement in the midesophagus. It is inserted and advanced to the stomach and the contents aspirated. The tube is then withdrawn so that it is located in the midesophagus and is attached to a bottle of normal saline. A second bottle of 0.1 normal hydrochloric acid is hung next to the saline. The saline is infused at about 125 drops per minute for about 10 minutes, then the infusion is changed to the hydrochloric acid drip without the patient's knowledge. The acid drip is continued for 15 minutes or until the patient complains of burning or pain in the chest, whichever comes first. The saline and hydrochloric acid drips are repeated for two more cycles. The test is negative if no pain arises after 15 minutes of hydrochloric acid instillation. The test is ended with the instillation of saline.

Preparation for the examination requires fasting for 8 hours and withholding any drugs that may interfere with the production of acid, such as antacids and pain medications. The patient should be instructed that the nurse will be instilling medications into the nasogastric tube and will be trying to reproduce his chest pain. The test takes 30 to 60 minutes to complete.

Endoscopy

The gastrointestinal tract may be examined by endoscopy. One procedure allows direct visualization of the esophagus **(esophagoscopy),** stomach **(gastroscopy),** or duodenum *(duodenoscopy),* or all three of these organs (esophagogastroduodenoscopy, or EGD). Another permits visualization of the large intestine *(colonoscopy),* and others allow visualization of the lower gastrointestinal tract **(proctoscopy, sigmoidoscopy).** The endoscope is an instrument containing a cablelike cluster of glass fibers that transmit light and return an image to a scope at the head of the instrument (fiber-optics). Pictures can be taken of suggestive lesions by attaching a camera to the head of the scope; biopsy can be performed through the scope when desired. In addition to its use in diagnosing inflammatory, ulcerative, infectious, and neoplastic diseases of the gastrointestinal tract, it can be used for removal of a foreign body.

Esophagogastroduodenoscopy (EGD)

For a complete EGD or any portion of this examination, the patient is usually medicated before the procedure with a tranquilizer such as diazepam (Valium) or a narcotic such as meperidine hydrochloride (Demerol). Atropine may be given to reduce secretions. An intravenous line is started or a heparin lock inserted for administration of additional medication of emergency medications. The patient must fast for 6 to 12 hours before the examination. A surgical consent form must be signed before the patient is medicated; the patient should be instructed on the purpose and procedure. Vital signs should be taken before any medication is given and again before the patient is transferred to the examination room.

Before insertion of the flexible tube of the endoscope, the vital signs are taken once more, and the blood pressure cuff is left in place to monitor the patient's blood pressure during the procedure. The patient's throat is sprayed with an anesthetic, and a mouth guard is inserted to protect the teeth and keep the mouth immobile. The young child must be restrained and may require anesthesia to prevent injury. The tube is inserted through the mouth and into the esophagus with the head bent forward. The physician will instruct the patient to change the position of the head and chin as the tube is passed through the various parts of the gastrointestinal tract. Additional medication for relaxation is given intravenously if needed. Air is sometimes instilled to open the lumen of the bowel and flatten tissue folds; water can be instilled to rinse materials from the lens or from a lesion. Suction may be applied to remove fluid and secretions. The patient will experience feelings of pressure as air is inserted. The tube is withdrawn when the physician has completed visualization of the organ in question.

After the test is completed, the patient's vital signs are taken before transfer. If the patient is an outpatient, further observation is performed in the recovery area. The hospitalized patient can be returned to his or her room. Vital signs are to be taken every 15 minutes for 1 hour, every 30 minutes for the next hour, then hourly until 4 hours after the examination. If they remain stable, vital signs are then taken every 4 hours for 24 hours. Food and fluid are withheld until the gag reflex returns. The nurse should assess for the presence of the gag reflex by touching the back of the throat with a tongue blade. The patient will experience a sore throat and some belching from the instillation of air. More severe pain in the throat, neck, stomach, back, or shoulder could indicate perforation; the physician should be notified immediately and the patient's vital signs monitored. Elevation of temperature is another indication of perforation. The patient should be instructed to observe emesis and stool for blood and report it immediately.[8]

Colonoscopy

The colonoscope is inserted anally. The large intestine must be thoroughly cleansed to be clearly visible. The patient should maintain a clear liquid diet for 48 hours before the examination, should be given a laxative such as magnesium citrate or castor oil the evening before, and should be administered tap water or saline enemas until they are returned clear 3 to 4 hours before the procedure. Soapsuds enemas are not given because they irritate the mucosa and stimulate mucous secretions that may hinder the examination. A sedative may be given intramuscularly or intravenously to help the patient relax. Vital signs must be monitored as outlined for the patient undergoing an EGD. The patient is positioned on the left side, and the colonoscope is lubricated and inserted into the rectum. The patient will experience an urge to defecate. He is instructed to breathe deeply and slowly through the mouth to relax the abdominal muscles. Air may be introduced to distend the intestinal wall. Flatus will escape around the instrument when air is instilled, and the patient should be instructed not to try to control it. Suction can be used to remove blood or liquid feces. When the instrument is advanced to the descending sigmoid junction, the patient is assisted to the supine position, if necessary, to facilitate advancement of the instrument. Abdominal palpation of fluoroscopy may guide the colonoscope through the large intestine. The procedure is contraindicated in patients who are pregnant or have diseases of the bowel that would predispose them to perforation, such as ischemic bowel disease, acute diverticulitis, peritonitis, and active colitis. Following the examination, the patient's vital signs should be monitored per the routine postoperative procedure, and he or she should be observed for side effects of the sedatives and for perforation. Malaise, rectal bleeding, abdominal pain and distention, fever, and mucopurulent discharge should be reported to the physician immediately. The patient will pass large amounts of flatus and may be embarrassed unless privacy is provided. A normal diet can be resumed after recovery from sedation. Some blood may be present in the stool if a polyp is removed.[8]

Proctoscopy and sigmoidoscopy

Proctoscopy and sigmoidoscopy are examinations that enable the physician to visualize the lower portion of the gastrointestinal tract. The proctoscope is used to examine the rectum, whereas the sigmoidoscope can be inserted further to visualize the lower 10 inches of the gastrointestinal tract. The use of the flexible fiberoptic instrument allows further examination of the colon beyond the range of the rigid sigmoidoscope and is less uncomfortable for the patient.

Preparation for both procedures includes the administration of an enema before the examination. Diet and fasting orders will vary with the physician; they should be checked and followed closely.

The procedure is performed with the patient in the knee-chest or lateral position. The patient usually assumes a kneeling position on a special proctoscopy table that "breaks" in the middle so he can bend at the waist. The patient is secured to the table while it is rotated so that his head is lowered and his buttocks are elevated. This position facilitates insertion of the instrument and allows the physician to assume a comfortable position during the procedure. The patient will feel pressure during insertion and advancement of the instrument and when air is instilled to distend the bowel lining. The position and procedure may be embarrassing to him. After the examination the patient should be observed for signs of perforation as in postoperative intervention for other endoscopic procedures.

Gastrointestinal Series and Barium Enema

The purpose of the gastrointestinal series and the barium enema is to detect any abnormal condition of the tract, any tumors, or other ulcerative le-

sions. The gastrointestinal series is an examination of the upper gastrointestinal tract. As the patient drinks a radiopaque substance such as barium, the physician observes its passage through the esophagus into the stomach with the fluoroscope. X-ray films are taken over several hours. When the physician wishes to visualize the lower intestinal tract above the sigmoid, an enema containing barium is administered. The radiologist observes the filling of the colon, using the fluoroscope, after which x-ray films are taken.

Nursing intervention related to both procedures includes ensuring that the patient takes no food or fluids after midnight before the procedure, administering cleansing enemas before the colon x-ray film is taken, administering cathartics as prescribed, and monitoring the patient's bowel movements following the procedure for excretion of the barium. If the barium is not excreted properly, an impaction and intestinal obstruction could result.

Stool Examination

Stools may be examined for bacteria, parasites, blood, or chemical analysis. The process of digestion changes blood that might be coming from the stomach or the intestine so that it will not be observed in the stool on inspection. Chemical examination is then necessary to detect **occult** (hidden) **blood.** In some instances the patient may be given a meat-free diet for 3 days before the test, whereas in other situations any random stool may be sent to the laboratory. Stools may also be examined for other substances that may indicate disorders of the biliary tract, pancreas, or some problem of digestion of food.

Stool specimens may be examined for various kinds of parasitic infections. The specimen is secured and kept in various ways, depending on the type of parasite sought. Most stool specimens must be taken to the laboratory as soon as they are secured and must be kept warm.

DIAGNOSTIC TESTS FOR DISORDERS OF THE LIVER AND BILIARY SYSTEM

Liver Function Tests

The primary functions of the liver are to secrete bile, assist in the digestion of proteins and fats, assist in the regulation of blood glucose, synthesize the proteins that function in blood clotting (prothrombin and fibrinogen), and maintain water balance in the body. Therefore a number of different tests are performed to detect liver disorders and determine liver function. Most tests are made on blood serum and a few on urine and feces. Some laboratories may require tests be made while the patient is in a fasting state. Because of variations in procedure, the nurse should understand the orders. The liver function tests that may be performed include the bilirubin and galactose tolerance tests, among others.

Bilirubin test

The bilirubin test may be performed on blood, urine, or feces. Bilirubin, a pigment resulting from a breakdown of hemoglobin, is excreted with bile into the small intestine, where it is converted to urobilinogen. Some of the urobilinogen is excreted, and some is returned to the liver where it is reconverted into bilirubin. Normally, little appears in the blood, but when obstructions of the liver ducts occur, bilirubin is picked up by the blood, resulting in jaundice. Thus in jaundice there is an increase of bilirubin in the blood.

Galactose tolerance test

Galactose, a sugar, is converted to glycogen by the liver. When liver cells are damaged, this function of the liver is impaired. The test is commonly done when jaundice is present and also when diabetes is suspected. The patient is required to be in a fasting state. The patient is given galactose in water to drink, and urine specimens are collected each hour for 5 hours.

Other liver function tests

Several other tests may be performed, including the *icterus index* and *serum cholesterol* tests discussed in Chapter 16. The *serum glutamic-oxaloacetic transaminase* (SGOT), *serum glutamic-pyruvic transaminase* (SGPT), and *lactic dehydrogenase* (LDH) tests are used in several diseases, including liver disease. The *alkaline phosphatase level* is elevated in obstructive disorders of the biliary tract.[15]

Test values

Approximate normal values of liver function tests are as follows:

Bilirubin	Direct, 0.1-0.4 mg/dl serum Indirect, 0.2-0.7 mg/dl serum
Galactose tolerance	Not more than 3 g after 5 hours
SGOT	5-40 units/ml
SGPT	5-35 units/ml
Alkaline phosphatase	1.5-4 Bodansky units/dl (several methods, with some variation according to method used)

Liver Biopsy

The procedure of liver biopsy is used to assist in establishing the diagnosis in various diseases affecting the liver. Several other examinations precede the biopsy, including tests of bleeding time, prothrombin level, and venous pressure (Chapter 17). A biopsy needle is inserted through a small incision in the skin, and a small cylinder of liver tissue is removed. The patient is asked not to breathe while the needle is being inserted and to remain as quiet as possible during the test. After the procedure the patient must be carefully observed for signs of hemorrhage and should be positioned on the right side for several hours with a pillow under the costal margin. If the patient shows any signs of increased pulse rate, decreased blood pressure, pain, or obvious apprehension it should be reported to the physician immediately.

Liver Scanning

Radioactive isotopes are administered to the patient and are readily concentrated in the liver. Radiation from the isotopes is recorded by a scanning device. The procedure helps to differentiate normally functioning areas of the liver from nonfunctioning areas. The liver scan is generally one of the most reliable tests to detect liver disease; however, it may not detect very small lesions or very early liver cell disease.

Cholecystography (Oral)

Through the use of a radiopaque dye, it is possible to visualize the gallbladder and the extrahepatic biliary system with **cholecystography.** This assists the physician in detecting calculi (stones), inflammatory conditions, or tumors of the gallbladder. After a low-fat evening meal the patient is given a synthetic radiopaque drug, usually iopanoic acid (Telepaque) orally. The number of tablets ordered is based on the weight of the patient. The tablets should not be crushed and should be taken one at a time, at 5 minute intervals, with one or two sips of water. Thereafter, nothing is permitted by mouth. If the tablets are vomited, the physician should be notified. In the morning a cleansing enema may be ordered. After the x-ray films are taken, a high-fat diet may be given to stimulate the gallbladder to contract, expelling the dye into the bile ducts. X-ray films are again taken to visualize the biliary system. The nurse should be sure that the examination has been completed before permitting the patient to have food. The patient should be observed for any toxic symptoms from the radiopaque drug.

Cholangiography

In **cholangiography** a cholangiogram allows for visualization of the biliary ducts. It may be used when a patient cannot tolerate or is unable to absorb the oral agents. The contrast medium may be injected into the blood (*intravenous cholangiography*), into a T tube inserted after a cholecystectomy (*T-tube cholangiography*), or through the skin directly into the ductal system (*percutaneous cholangiography*). The patient should be informed that the procedure may involve positioning on a tilting x-ray examination table that rotates into vertical and horizontal positions and that injection of the contrast medium may cause nausea, vomiting, hypotension, flushing, and urticaria. A severe reaction may produce anaphylactic shock. Before the examination a consent form must be signed and a patient history taken to determine hypersensitivity to iodine, seafood, or contrast media used in other diagnostic tests. During the procedure someone must remain with the patient to observe his or her response, and the vital signs should be checked frequently during and after the procedure until they are stable.

Computerized Tomography

Computerized tomography (CT) involves the passage of multiple x-ray beams through the upper abdomen while detectors record the strength of the x-ray beam as it is deflected off various tissues (tissue attenuation). This information is reconstructed by a computer as a three-dimensional image on an oscilloscope screen. Because attenuation varies with tissue density, CT can distinguish various tissues; intravenous contrast media can be injected to accentuate different densities. Defects in the tissue are seen as different in density from normal tissue.

The patient is positioned supine on a radiographic table that is moved into the center of the scanner. A series of transverse x-ray films is taken and recorded on magnetic tape. This information is then fed into the computer, and selected images are photographed. If a contrast medium has been ordered, it is injected after this first series of films is completed. The patient must be observed for an allergic reaction to the contrast medium. CT is ordered for examination of the biliary tract, liver, and pancreas. It should be done before or at least 4 days after barium studies because barium will hinder visualization.

Ultrasonography

Ultrasound examination may be ordered for examination of the gallbladder and biliary system, the liver, spleen, and pancreas. High-frequency sound waves are channeled into the region to be examined, and the echoes that result are converted to electric impulses, which are displayed as a pattern of spikes or dots on an oscilloscope screen. The pattern of the dots varies with tissue density and reflects the size, shape, and position of the organ being examined. There is no exposure to radiation. The ultrasound picture resembles an x-ray picture, but closer examination will reveal the series of dots or spikes that create the image. When a good view is obtained, photographs are taken for later study.

The patient is instructed to fast for 8 to 12 hours before the examination to reduce the amount of gas in the bowel, which hinders transmission of ultrasound. When the gallbladder is to be examined, the patient is given a fat-free meal the evening before to promote accumulation of bile in the gallbladder. During the procedure the room may be darkened slightly to improve visualization on the oscilloscope. The test will take 15 to 30 minutes for each organ being examined. A water-soluble lubricant is applied to the face of the transducer, and then transverse scans are taken at frequent intervals and at angles appropriate for the organ being examined. After the procedure the patient should be cleansed of the lubricant and may resume his usual diet. No other follow-up care is necessary.

Nursing Responsibilities For Tests and Diagnostic Procedures

When the physician writes the order for examinations and tests, the forms should be properly completed and the laboratory or x-ray departments should be notified without delay. Specimens to be collected by the nurse should be secured promptly, labeled properly, and sent to the laboratory. Proper identification of the patient's room or bed when food or fluids are to be withheld is a nursing responsibility. The patient should be readied and transported to the x-ray department or laboratory at the scheduled hour. If for any reason an appointment cannot be kept at the specified time, the department should be notified as early as possible. Medications ordered before and in preparation for tests and studies should be administered promptly and recorded. Any patient receiving intravenous dye should be carefully assessed for allergies before and for reactions after the procedure.

Most patients are completely unfamiliar with the various procedures and tests and will be nervous and apprehensive. They may be anxious and worried over what the examination will reveal. The nurse should be able to explain in simple words some of the things that the patient may expect. Through careful, thorough, and accurate preparation of the patient, the nurse will be indicating an interest in his welfare and giving support and encouragement.

NURSING RESPONSIBILITIES FOR THERAPEUTIC TECHNIQUES

Gastric Lavage

Gastric lavage refers to the washing out of the stomach. The purpose may be to remove poisonous ingested substances or any other irritating substance, to relieve nausea and vomiting, or in some cases to prevent nausea and vomiting. A stomach tube and approximately 4000 ml of a solution—which may be tap water, physiologic saline, 5% solution of sodium bicarbonate, or in case of poison, the specific antidote—is used. Not more than 500 ml of solution should be instilled into the stomach at one time. It is then siphoned back and the procedure repeated. In the case of poison, the siphoned solution may have to be saved for laboratory analysis. Emotional and physical support of the patient is very important during this procedure.

Gastric Gavage

Gastric gavage is used to provide nourishment for patients who are unable to eat from loss of appetite, unconsciousness, excessive weakness or debilitation, or obstruction of the esophagus. Patients with depression psychosis, premature infants, or infants with plastic repair of the mouth may be fed in this manner. The tube is introduced through the nose into the stomach in the same manner as a Levin tube. Liquid feedings or medications are introduced through the tube and may flow by gravity or be controlled by pump. The patient should be in a semi-Fowler's to high Fowler's position during the feeding and for at least 30 minutes after it is completed. Signs of pain, gastric distention, or vomiting should be reported at once.

Gastrointestinal (Gastric) Decompression

Decompression of the gastrointestinal tract may be employed for several different reasons, such as removing air and fluids from the stomach. A nasogastric tube (Levin or Salem tube) is generally used for this purpose. The tube is lubricated with a water-soluble jelly and passed through the nostril down the esophagus to the stomach. The tube is taped to the cheek or bridge of the nose to avoid pressure against the nostril and is connected to an intermittent electric suction machine such as the thermotic drainage pump (Figure 18-2). Intermittent gastric suction (suction automatically turned on and off by the machine to provide gentler suction) is frequently used to prevent postoperative distention and to relieve postoperative vomiting. For these purposes, the tube may be inserted before the patient goes to surgery. When surgery on the stomach is performed, the surgeon may insert the tube after completing the surgery. The tube protects the suture line from pressure after surgery. The length of time that the tube remains in the stomach is determined by the physician; it may be approximately 48 hours or until peristalsis returns. The nurse's role in assessing for bowel function (bowel sounds, passing of flatus) is vital in determining this.

Intestinal decompression

Intestinal decompression may be necessary when an obstruction along the intestinal route is suspected or in the case of paralytic ileus. Several types of long tubes may be used for this purpose, including the Harris tube, Miller-Abbott tube, or Cantor tube (Figure 18-3). These tubes are long, soft rubber tubes with a balloon at or near the end and eyes through which secretions may be drained. The Miller-Abbott tube has two lumens; one opens into the balloon into which mercury is placed, the other is attached to suction. The tube is inserted through the nostril and is advanced along the intestine by peristaltic action or by the weight of the mercury. Secretions along the route are removed by gentle suction. The tube usually remains in the intestinal tract for several days, and

Figure 18-2
Gomco Thermotic Pump. *(Courtesy Allied Healthcare Products, Inc, St Louis, Mo.)*

then removed gradually.

All decompression tubes are generally attached to some type of suction apparatus, and it is important that the equipment used be in working order. The tubing for gastric suction is pinned or clipped to the patient's gown, allowing sufficient slack to permit the patient to turn without displacement of the tube. Care should be taken to prevent the tubing from becoming kinked or obstructed by the patient lying on it. Patients usually complain of considerable discomfort from the nasogastric tube. The nostrils become dry and crusted from increased mucous secretions. The throat is irritated, and the mouth and lips are dry from mouth breathing. The patient is often receiving nothing by mouth but should be allowed to rinse the mouth frequently. Equal parts of glycerine and lemon juice may be applied to the mucous membrane of the mouth with an applicator.

NURSING CARE GUIDELINES
Gastrointestinal (Gastric) Decompression

Nursing diagnoses
- Potential fluid volume deficit related to loss of gastrointestinal secretions
- Alteration in nasal and oral mucous membrane related to abstinence from oral food and fluids and presence of tube

Nursing interventions
- Maintain patency of decompression tube
- Irrigate as necessary with 30 ml normal saline (may need a physician's order)
- Tape nasogastric tube to nose or cheek; do *not* tape intestinal decompression tubes; ensure that no pressure is placed on nostril
- Administer nothing by mouth unless ordered; physician may permit sips of water or hard candy
- Cleanse nostril through which tube passes at least once every 8 hours; lubricate with water-soluble jelly
- Administer mouth care every 2 hours; rinse with mouthwash and lubricate lips and mucous membranes with lemon and glycerin swabs
- Pin nasogastric tubing to gown to prevent displacement with patient turning; loop intestinal decompression tubing on bed to prevent displacement
- Attach to low suction unless otherwise ordered
- Empty drainage bottle every 8 hours and record
- Observe and record color, appearance, odor, and presence of blood, bile, or mucus
- Notify physician if tube is not draining, despite attempts to irrigate
- Assess for signs of fluid/electrolyte deficit

Expected outcomes
- Decompression tube patent and draining
- Soft abdomen—no increase in abdominal girth
- Nares moist, free of pressure from tube
- Moist oral mucous membranes
- Fluid and electrolyte balance maintained
- Verbalized concerns about condition and frustrations related to decompression tube

---

This preparation will form a protective coating that helps to prevent drying. Cold cream or petroleum jelly may be applied to the lips. The nares about the tube should be cleansed with applicators and warm tap water or a water-soluble jelly. Some physicians may allow the patient to have occasional chipped ice, sips of water, or hard fruit

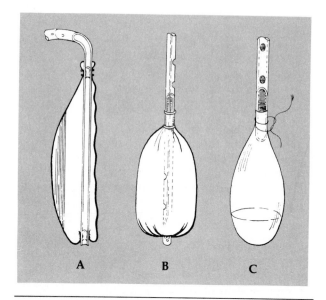

Figure 18-3

Decompression tubes. **A,** Harris tube. **B,** Miller-Abbott tube. **C,** Cantor tube.

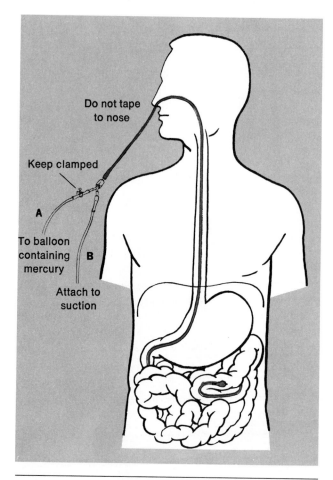

Figure 18-4

Intestinal decompression tube in place. Note that tube is not taped to nose. **A,** Arm of Y tube leading to balloon containing mercury or air must be kept clamped. **B,** Arm of Y tube is attached to rubber tubing leading to suction.

candy to relieve throat discomfort. Chewing of gum results in some swallowing of air; therefore some physicians disapprove of it.

Drainage tubes may become blocked with blood clots or mucus, which obstruct the flow. The physician often orders irrigation of the tube with sterile physiologic saline solution every 2 hours or as necessary to keep it open and draining. Not more than 30 ml of solution should be gently injected through the tube. Careful aspiration of the solution may be necessary to ensure patency of the tube, but any vigorous effort to aspirate the tube should be avoided. If the suction apparatus is working properly and the tube is open, the solution will return. Accurate records of irrigation solution used must be maintained, and the amount must be deducted from the total gastric drainage. The secretions in the drainage bottle are measured every 8 hours and recorded. The appearance, odor, and presence of blood, bile, or mucus should be noted. If the nurse observes that the tube is failing to drain despite efforts to irrigate it, this should be reported immediately to the physician.

When intestinal decompression tubes are used, they should *not* be taped to the nose because they are designed to move through the intestine by gravity and peristaltic action. Caution must be used in irrigating these tubes to ensure that the solution is injected into the opening that is attached to suction. The other opening is into the

balloon containing air or mercury and is clamped off. To avoid error, both outlets should be labeled. Measurement and observation of drainage are the same as that done with the gastric tube (Figure 18-4).

Total Parenteral Nutrition

Total parenteral nutrition (TPN) is a technique to maximally provide for the assessed nutritional needs of the patient who cannot or should not digest or absorb nutrients. The patient's nutritional deficits are carefully determined along with an appropriate formula for nutritional support. Patients selected for this procedure are generally poorly nourished as a result of surgery, trauma, or disease and are unable to adequately meet their own nutritional needs. Patients with gastrointestinal disorders frequently fall into this category because of an interruption of the normal digestion and absorption processes of the system.

Hyperalimentation involves the intravenous infusion of nutrients, which is accomplished with a concentrated solution of at least 10% dextrose in water, proteins, and electrolytes. Emulsified fats can also be infused. Because these solutions are so concentrated, a large vessel must be used so that the amount of plasma in the vessel can sufficiently dilute the solution to prevent complications. The infusion rate must be kept constant for proper dilution to occur, as well as to prevent complications that could arise from sporadic infusion of such a concentrated solution so high in glucose. Nausea and headache are often early signs of too rapid administration. Later symptoms may include severe dehydration and convulsions. The box at right summarizes nursing diagnoses and care commonly seen in the patient requiring TPN.

ABDOMINAL SURGERY

The abdomen is opened for several surgical procedures, and the incision into the abdomen is called a **laparotomy.** Surgical procedures within the abdominal cavity may include surgery of the stomach, the small intestine, the large intestine, and the accessory organs of digestion. The upper part of the uterus, fallopian tubes, and ovaries are within the abdominal cavity; therefore the abdomen may be opened for the surgical removal of any or all of the pelvic organs. Surgery may also involve certain other structures within the abdominal cavity such as lymph nodes and blood vessels, or it may provide for drainage of blood or pus. An exploratory laparotomy may be performed when it is not possible to make an accurate diagnosis before surgery. Because the nursing care of the patient may involve procedures related to the particular type of surgery, the nurse should become familiar with the following terms and their meanings:

abdominal resection Removal of portion of the bowel, with or without permanent colostomy.

appendectomy Removal of the appendix.

cholecystectomy Removal of the gallbladder.

gastrectomy Removal of all or part of the stomach.

gastrostomy A surgical opening into the stomach.

herniorrhaphy Surgical repair of the hernia.

NURSING CARE GUIDELINES
Total Parenteral Nutrition (TPN)

Nursing diagnoses
- Fluid volume deficit related to interference with usual intake patterns
- Impaired swallowing related to weakness, absent swallowing reflex, and inflammation
- Alteration in nutrition (less than body requirements) related to inability to ingest or digest food
- Alteration in oral mucous membrane related to abstinence from oral foods and fluids
- High risk for infection related to insertion site and introduction of foreign matter
- Self-care deficit related to weakness
- Disturbance in self-concept related to altered nutritional pattern

Nursing interventions
- Monitor intake and output
- Monitor patient's vital signs every 4 hours
- Measure urine, blood, or both for glucose every 6 hours
- Maintain constant intravenous flow rate
- Monitor insertion site and report any evidence of redness, swelling, oozing, or tenderness
- Change intravenous tubing at least every 24 hours
- Change intravenous dressing at least every 72 hours using sterile technique
- Weigh patient daily
- Monitor serum electrolytes

Expected outcomes
- Cessation of weight loss or gain
- Maintenance of fluid and electrolyte balance
- Normal blood glucose levels
- Absence of infection through the intravenous line or at venipuncture site

---

hysterectomy Removal of the uterus.

oophorectomy Removal of the ovaries.

salpingectomy Surgical removal of the fallopian tubes.

splenectomy Surgical removal of the spleen.

Preoperative and Postoperative Nursing Care

The preoperative nursing care of the patient who is to undergo abdominal surgery is essentially the same for all the abdominal surgical procedures just defined (Figure 18-5). The basic postoperative care is also the same with slight variations in specific nursing procedures (Chapter 5). The patient

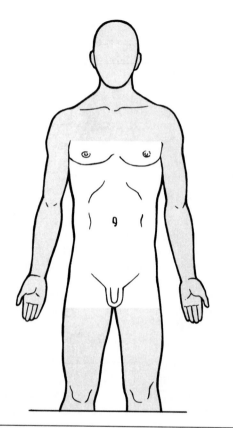

Figure 18-5

Areas of skin to be prepared for abdominal surgery.

may be admitted to the hospital the morning of or up to 3 days before surgery, depending on the preparation required. During this time the nurse should try to establish a relationship with the patient and family. The nurse must evaluate the patient's understanding of the surgery and identify areas in which further clarification is needed. The patient's feelings and fears about the surgery should be determined so that problems that may be encountered during the postoperative period can be identified. During this time, the nurse offers encouragement, relieves anxiety, and reassures the patient that efforts will be made to meet his or her individual needs.

Cleansing enemas are usually given before abdominal surgery, unless an inflammatory condition contraindicates this procedure. If the large bowel is to be entered during surgery, a series of cleansing enemas with oral antibiotics are given to "sterilize" the bowel and reduce risks of peritonitis postoperatively. Complete blood count, urinalysis, and chest x-ray examination are routine, with additional laboratory and diagnostic tests ordered by the physician as indicated. The

most important aspect of preoperative nursing care is patient teaching. The patient must know what to expect in preparation for surgery, the expected postoperative course, the method and importance of turning, coughing, and deep breathing, care of the wound and dressings, antiembolism exercises, and ambulation. The nurse must evaluate the patient's understanding of the preoperative instructions by observing behavior that indicates that the patient has in fact learned. For example, a patient who has "learned" about coughing and deep breathing would be expected to demonstrate the technique and explain the importance of performing it regularly. All preoperative teaching and evaluation of patient learning should be documented in the patient record.

Postoperatively, the nurse should observe the patient's vital signs, observe for abdominal distention, note the passing of stool or flatus, and listen for the return of bowel sounds. Peristalsis is usually interrupted after abdominal surgery, producing a period of adynamic or paralytic ileus for 12 to 36 hours. Normal intestinal function is regained soon thereafter without specific treatment unless the patient is fed before peristalsis returns. Food and fluids should be withheld until bowel sounds can be heard or until the patient has passed flatus. A nasogastric tube may be inserted to drain intestinal contents until peristalsis returns. Intravenous infusions are given to provide necessary fluids, electrolytes, and nutrients until oral feedings can be resumed. If a patient begins to vomit after surgery, oral intake should be withheld and any emesis and distention reported to the physician.

Distention can be detected by observing the abdomen and palpating it. Increasing distention can be determined by measuring the abdomen at the largest portion with a tape measure and marking the area with a pen so that a comparison of later measurements will be accurate. Measurements should be done once each shift and by the same person everyday if possible. To listen for bowel sounds, the diaphragm of the stethoscope is placed over all four quadrants and sounds are listened to for 3 to 5 minutes. Normal bowel sounds are gurgling, swishing, or tinkling noises. The absence of sound or an occasional tinkle is usually related to an **ileus** or functional obstruction. The abdomen is palpated after listening for bowel sounds because palpation can induce some reflex peristalsis, which could be mistaken for true peristalsis.

Paralytic ileus

Paralytic ileus, or the inability of the intestinal tract to move contents through it because of an absence of peristalsis, is a frequent complication after peritonitis. Bowel function is also affected by pH and electrolyte imbalance, anesthetics, pain killers and other drugs, emotions, the extent of the trauma, and the concentration of albumin in the plasma. When normal intestinal function is slowed or stopped, gas, fluid, and waste products collect in the intestines. This results in a rapid increase of pressure within the intestine, distention, and pressure on surrounding areas such as the diaphragm. Decompression is vital at this time to prevent life-threatening complications such as intestinal perforation and atelectasis.

The box on p. 445 summarizes commonly found nursing diagnoses and nursing care of the patient undergoing gastric decompression.

COLOSTOMY AND ILEOSTOMY NURSING CARE

Both colostomy and ileostomy provide an artificial opening through which fecal matter may be eliminated. A **colostomy** may be temporary or per-manent; an ileostomy is usually permanent. Although both procedures are designed for the same purpose, the nursing care and the patient's problems are different. The basic nursing care of these patients is the same as that for any patient undergoing abdominal surgery. The colostomy is usually performed on the left side of the transverse or on the descending colon (Figure 18-6), therefore fluids and electrolytes will be absorbed, leaving a solid or semisolid fecal mass. The colostomy in this location can be more easily managed than one in the ascending colon because of the firmer consistency of the stool and the absence of irritating chemicals and enzymes from the digestive juices. During the early postoperative period after a colostomy, considerable drainage may occur, which is increased after the return of peristalsis. If the colostomy is done on the ascending or transverse colon, the drainage is almost continuous and is in a semiliquid state.

A transverse colostomy is usually temporary and is performed to divert the feces from the affected portion of the bowel to allow healing. In a double-barreled colostomy the transverse colon is brought to the surface of the abdomen, and two openings (**stomas**) are present. One opening, generally the one on the patient's right, is the stoma

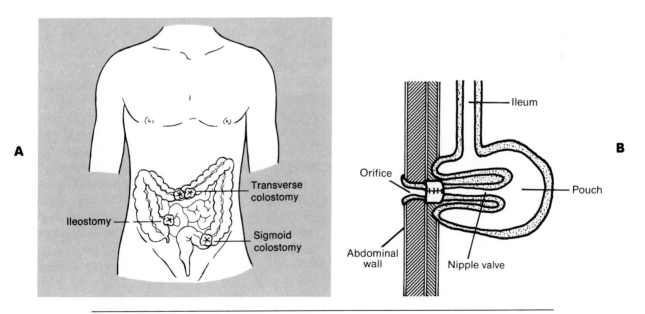

Figure 18-6

A, Colostomy opening is usually on left side of abdomen, whereas ileostomy is on right side of abdomen. If double-barrel colostomy is created, proximal and distal ends of colon are brought out onto abdomen as two separate stoma, separated by skin. **B,** Continent ileostomy (Kock's pouch). Distal ileum is fashioned into pouch that is then sutured to interior abdominal wall.

through which stool will pass. The opening on the left will lead to the resting bowel; this non-functioning stoma is called a mucous fistula. A similar and preferred procedure is the loop colostomy, in which the transverse colon is brought to the surface and a plastic rod inserted beneath the loop to prevent it from slipping back into the abdominal cavity. The bowel may not be opened to form the stomas for several days.[15] A permanent colostomy usually involves the sigmoid colon, and the proximal end is brought to the surface and sutured (Figure 18-6).

The care of the patient is directed toward preventing contamination of the surgical wound and keeping the skin in a healthy state. The stoma and mucous fistula, if present, should be pouched immediately after surgery or on the first postoperative day to protect the skin from drainage and prevent contamination of the surgical wound. Dressings are applied to drains and the incision site, and Montgomery straps should be used if drainage demands frequent changes. When applying the pouch, the skin is cleansed with plain water. If petroleum jelly–gauze was applied in the operating room, it must be removed and the skin cleansed with water and defatted for the pouch to adhere. A drainable pouch should be used so that it can be emptied without being removed. The amount, color, and character of the drainage should be measured, assessed, and recorded; the absence of drainage after the colostomy should be reported. The nurse must observe the color of the stoma and observe for prolapse, retraction, or tearing of peristomal sutures. Changes in color of the stoma could indicate ischemia and potential necrosis.[5]

If the patient has a distal transverse or descending colostomy, evacuation of the colostomy may be regulated with irrigation. The physician will order irrigations to begin in the hospital, a few days after surgery. After an average of 6 weeks of daily irrigations, the patient will become regulated enough to wear a small, closed pouch or gauze dressing; most prefer the security of the small pouch. The patient is monitored at home to assist in choosing an appropriate closed pouch. When regulated, the colostomy will not drain between irrigations. Most patients must irrigate daily, whereas some will retain stool for 2 days between irrigations. If the colostomy is located in the ascending or proximal transverse colon, the stool will be liquid to soft and irrigation will not prevent a continual drainage of stool. A drainable

collecting pouch with a skin barrier or Stomahesive must be worn at all times to collect the stool and avoid irritation of the skin from the digestive enzymes that may be present in this type of stool. The pouch should be emptied when it is one-third to one-half full and changed daily or every other day. A colostomy located in the descending or sigmoid colon will be controlled successfully with irrigation unless there are other complicating factors present.

When irrigations are used, they are usually planned to coincide with the patient's former habits of defecation and family living patterns. During irrigation, 500 to 1000 ml of fluid is used in a container placed 18 to 20 inches above the stoma; if placed higher, the fluid will travel further into the bowel than necessary and require extra time to return. A tubing with a cone on the end is inserted into the stomal opening; the cone prevents the tubing from being inserted further than ½ to 1 inch into the colostomy. A catheter without a cone should not be used because perforation of the bowel could result. The physician or experienced nurse may use a catheter to bypass an intestinal stricture or to help remove a food blockage. The water for irrigation should be at body temperature.

The odor of intestinal gas and feces can be controlled by diet and personal hygiene. Each person reacts differently to foods; therefore new foods should be added gradually to the diet to identify any that stimulate bowel activity and gas formation. Fresh vegetables and fruits, nuts, whole grains, bran, and other high-fiber foods increase stool volume and gas; however, some people find that a steady high-fiber diet eventually decreases gas and fecal odor. Yogurt and buttermilk may reduce odor, probably because of the bacteria normally present in these foods, as will green leafy vegetables containing chlorophyll. Ingestion of bismuth, charcoal, or chlorophyll tablets may be helpful, but a physician should be consulted before a patient takes any of these preparations. Emptying and cleaning or changing the drainage pouch as necessary and keeping the skin around it clean are important to prevent odor. A few drops of liquid deodorizer on a tissue or cotton ball may be placed in the pouch, as may charcoal or chlorophyll tablets. Aspirin or sodium bicarbonate (baking soda) should never be used because of the danger of irritation of the stoma, which could result in bleeding.

An **ileostomy** is an opening into the small intestine through which fecal material is eliminated (Figure 18-6). The colon and rectum no longer function, and elimination occurs through an opening in the wall of the abdomen. Generally a loop of ileum is brought to the surface in the lower right quadrant and sutured to the skin. The procedure is usually permanent, and the colon and rectal tissue are removed (total proctocolectomy).

The contents of the small intestine are liquid and contain large quantities of digestive enzymes that are irritating and will cause excoriation and ulceration of the skin. The ileostomy drains freely and almost continuously day and night so that an appliance is necessary to collect the fluid. Regular bowel movements can never be achieved through the ileostomy. A temporary disposable ileostomy bag is applied at the time of surgery to prevent fecal drainage from coming in contact with the skin and the incision. The bag prevents ulceration of the skin and interference with wound healing. The temporary bag has an adhesive back, which is applied to the skin and will stay in place until it is pulled off or removed with a solvent such as ether or benzene. The bag will need to be changed frequently, depending on the particular type of bag used. The skin must be carefully cleansed and completely dried during the change, because moisture results in failure of the appliance to adhere, allowing seepage onto the skin. The best results are obtained if the bag is changed before the patient has eaten. A skin preparation may be applied to protect the skin and may promote healing if ulceration has occurred.

The stoma continues to shrink for up to 6 months, and the patient must be refitted every 6 to 8 weeks. When the stoma ceases to shrink, the patient can be fitted for a permanent appliance. They are made of plastic material and will last for a year or two. Disposable pouches are also available but may be too expensive to use for a long period. Odor control is less of a problem with a disposable pouch (Figure 18-7). The patient should be taught how to change the appliance, how to care for it, and how to care for the skin around the stoma. Most ileostomy patients need to empty the bag four or five times a day by removing the clamp or band and allowing the contents to flow into the toilet. The bag can then be washed using a small Asepto syringe and warm, soapy water, followed by a clear warm water rinse. Skin problems should be prevented, but when they arise, the use of a Stomahesive wafer placed over medication such as mycostatin (Nys-

tatin) powder is helpful. The appliance is changed once or twice a week to avoid skin irritation from frequent changes. At each change the skin is washed, inspected for irritation, and dried thoroughly before another pouch is applied. The appliance that has been removed should be washed in cool, soapy water to eliminate odors and increase the life of the appliance. With time the consistency of the ileostomy discharge becomes less liquid and thicker and thus easier to manage.

The patient may be placed on a low-residue diet following surgery but will later be ready for a general diet. Adequate fluid intake and careful diet are necessary to prevent obstruction. Food with high-fiber content, gas-forming foods, fried and smoked foods, highly seasoned food, and skins of fruits, nuts, seeds, and popcorn may need to be avoided. A rule of thumb is to avoid foods that were not easily digested or that were found to be gas forming before the surgery. The patient must be instructed to chew all foods thoroughly and eat slowly. Obstruction is indicated by nausea, abdominal distention with low back pain, or abdominal cramps accompanied by emesis; the physician should be consulted immediately.[5] Gastrointestinal upsets are more serious for patients with an ileostomy. Fluid and electrolyte imbalances occur more readily because the fluid reabsorption function of the colon no longer exists. Symptoms of electrolyte imbalance include headache, fatigue, drowsiness, nausea, and anorexia. Some patients complain of muscle cramps, but they are more likely to complain of flaccid muscles, weakness, and fatigue resulting from a deficiency of potassium, a muscle stimulant. Potassium is normally reabsorbed into the body in the large intestine, which has been removed.[4]

The necessity for good psychologic preparation for the ostomy patient cannot be overemphasized. Usually the patient consents to the ostomy so that he or she may once again become a contributing member of society. However, the creation of a new opening for the passage of fecal matter produces much emotional trauma. Preoperative preparation should begin in the physician's office and continue throughout the hospital stay. The nurse should explain the procedure, familiarize the patient with the equipment, and allow the patient to verbalize his feelings. The use of pictures and charts to describe the anatomy of the gastrointestinal system and the surgical procedure will be helpful. The stoma should be de-

A

Figure 18-7

A, The Guardian two-piece ostomy system by Hollister provides a complete selection of skin barrier styles (cut-to-fit, presized, convex, nonconvex, floating flange, and stationary flange), pouch styles (drainable, closed, and urostomy), irrigator drains, and stoma caps. Drainable and closed pouches are available with transparent or opaque pouch film in small or full sizes. Guardian pouches securely attach to Guardian skin barriers and are used by people with colostomies, ileostomies, and urostomies. **B,** The FirstChoice one-piece drainable ostomy pouches by Hollister provide a complete selection of preattached skin barrier styles (cut-to-fit, presized, convex, and nonconvex) with either transparent or opaque pouch film. FirstChoice drainable ostomy pouches are used by people with colostomies and ileostomies. *(Courtesy of Hollister, Inc.)*

B

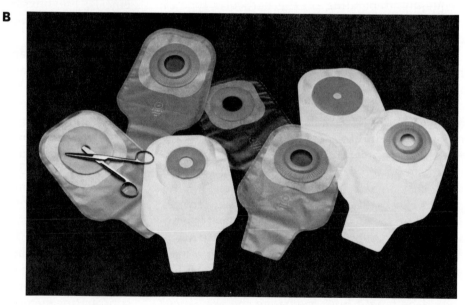

scribed as a red bowel, which may protrude and have little feeling. Preoperative visits from other persons who have ostomies are essential; volunteers from local clubs involved in the United Ostomy Association are usually available. Patients need encouragement, instruction, reassurance, and praise when learning to care for the ileostomy. Dietary restrictions must be explained to the patient and family, and the patient must re-

alize the need for continual medical supervision. Most of the patient's concerns will involve control of the odor and bowel excretions and the amount of time that must be devoted to care. Nursing personnel can assist the patient in planning schedules and referring the patient to helpful resources.

The psychologic care of the patient with a colostomy or an ileostomy is more demanding than the physical care. Few other types of surgery produce greater emotional trauma and require greater understanding by all who care for the patient. The patient with a colostomy is usually of middle age or older, whereas the patient with an ileostomy is often a young adult or in his teens with his whole life before him. The patient is often a frail, undernourished, debilitated person whose response to the shock may be so severe that he hopes to die. A colostomy may be only a palliative procedure to improve the quality of life of a patient with terminal cancer.

In the weeks, months, or years ahead the patient must develop social confidence. This can be facilitated by careful teaching of the patient concerning care and control of his ostomy to avoid unpleasant incidents. During the early postoperative period the patient will be concerned and fearful about recurrence and metastasis if the surgery was indicated by malignancy. An optimistic attitude and regular reexamination by his physician will do much to reassure the patient. If employed, the patient should return to regular employment as soon as possible. If retraining is necessary, he should contact the Office of Social and Vocational Rehabilitation. Today an ostomy is no barrier to employment and social acceptance.

CONTINENT OR POUCH ILEOSTOMY

A newer type of ostomy—the continent or pouch ileostomy (Kock's pouch)—is being done on an increasing number of patients with ulcerative colitis and multiple polyposis. It requires no appliance because the surgeon forms a reservoir using about 16 inches of the terminal ileum (Figure 18-6). The last 4 inches are used to create a nipple valve, which controls release of contents. The immediate postoperative care of the patient with a pouch ileostomy is similar to that of other ostomy patients, with the addition of maintaining patency of the pouch through a temporary drainage system. As the sutures heal, the drain is clamped for gradually increasing periods of time, allowed to drain between each period, and eventually removed. The capacity of the reservoir or pouch gradually increases with time until it is able to hold 500 to 1000 ml and requires draining only two or three times a day, using a Silastic catheter inserted into the stoma. A small, absorbent dressing is taped over the stoma, and the patient will be drainage free for another 5 or 6 hours. The drainage procedure takes no more than 5 or 10 minutes.[16] Whereas these patients must adjust to some change in body image, this is not so drastic as it would be with a conventional ileostomy. They will require support in the transition from the "sick role" to health and in adjusting to the stoma.

The boxed material on p. 454 summarizes postoperative nursing care of the patient with a colostomy or ileostomy.

SPECIFIC DISEASES AND DISORDERS OF THE GASTROINTESTINAL SYSTEM

Inflammatory Diseases
Stomatitis

Inflammation of the mouth results from several causes and may affect the entire mouth or only a small part of the mucous membrane. Among the causes of stomatitis are vitamin deficiency, infection by specific organisms such as fungi or bacteria, certain drugs, and some viral diseases. Symptoms may include a burning sensation, pain, formation of ulcers, the presence of membranes as in diphtheria, tender bleeding gums, a disagreeable odor to the breath, and sometimes fever. Treatment depends on identifying and treating the cause. Vincent's stomatitis, commonly called *trench mouth*, often occurs in epidemics and is fairly common. The condition responds readily to penicillin and good mouth hygiene.

Thrush (candidiasis) is caused by a fungal organism, *Candida albicans*. The disease appears as small white patches on the mucous membrane of the mouth and tongue. The same organism is responsible for monilial vaginitis in the adult, and newborn infants may become infected as they pass through the birth canal. The infection may be spread in the nursery by the carelessness of nursing personnel. Handwashing, care of feeding equipment, and cleanliness of the mother's nipples are important to prevent spread. There are several methods of treatment, including 1 to 4 ml of nystatin (Mycostatin) dropped into the infant's mouth several times a day. Thrush may also occur in adults who are receiving broad-spectrum antibiotics, particularly chlortetracycline or tetracycline. Treatment for the adult is the same as for the infant.

The possibility of transmission of some inflammatory diseases of the mouth has been questioned. However, when bacterial disease is known

---

NURSING CARE GUIDELINES
Colostomy and Ileostomy

Nursing diagnoses

- Potential fluid volume deficit related to reduced absorption of fluids
- Potential altered nutrition (less than body requirements) related to absorption disturbances
- Pain related to abdominal muscle manipulation
- Impaired skin integrity related to incision and stoma site
- Altered gastrointestinal tissue perfusion related to bowel diversion/reconstruction
- Potential ineffective individual coping related to change in body image
- Knowledge deficit related to care of stoma and appliance

Nursing interventions

- Administer the standard immediate postoperative care
- Administer standard care for nasogastric decompression tube
- Listen for bowel sounds once every 8 hours and note passing of flatus through ostomy
- Measure abdominal girth once every 8 hours to detect distention
- Maintain sterile, dry dressing to abdominal wound; change as necessary to keep dry; use Montgomery straps for frequent dressing changes
- Maintain seal of drainable pouch around ostomy; apply immediately after surgery
- Empty pouch when half full; check every 2 hours; flush with perineal bottle after emptying
- Minimize odor in appliance with commercial deodorizer; do not place aspirin or sodium bicarbonate in bag—may come in contact with stoma and cause irritation and excoriation
- Change pouch as often as necessary to maintain tight seal to skin, at least daily for 5 days
- Remove adhesive from skin with solvent such as ether or benzene
- Cleanse skin with water when changing appliance

(most authorities avoid the use of soap); dry thoroughly

- Apply skin preparation or Stomahesive to protect skin
- Cut or use precut openings in temporary appliance and fit closely around stoma; apply Stomahesive powder for irritated skin around stoma
- Immediately change appliance to ileostomy if it begins to leak; secretions from the small intestine contain enzymes that will quickly ulcerate the tissue
- Close bottom of appliance with clamp; save clamp when changing appliance
- Report absence of drainage from ostomy
- Never irrigate ileostomy; irrigate colostomy only if ordered by physician
- Gradually involve patient in self-care
- Facilitate expression of feelings about altered body image and provide support during the grieving process
- Maintain intravenous infusions until oral intake is adequate; gradually increase diet from clear liquids to low residue; maintain general diet with restrictions on gas-forming and hard-to-digest foods, which can be taken eventually
- Never give laxative and instruct patient to avoid laxative (even after barium studies)
- Never take rectal temperature
- Instruct patient to avoid antacids with magnesium—it is added to prevent constipation and will cause diarrhea

Expected outcomes

- Maintenance of patency of the gastrointestinal tract
- Prevention of injury to stoma
- Maintenance of skin integrity around stoma
- Control of odor and fecal leakage from stoma bag
- Adaptation of patient to new body image
- Independence and self-care by patient

---

to exist, nurses should use every precaution to protect themselves and all other patients. Nursing care should consist of cleansing the mouth and teeth of any foreign material, rinsing the mouth, and lubricating the lips. The mouth should be inspected using a flashlight and tongue blade. The frequency of oral care depends on the patient's condition, and whatever procedure is used should meet the needs of the patient and should be con-

sistent and effective. The nurse should be alert in identifying patients who are in need of special mouth care and should encourage good oral hygiene in all patients.

Gastritis

Inflammation of the stomach is the most common stomach ailment and may result from substances that produce an irritation of the membrane. It may be caused by food infection, dietary indiscretion, excessive ingestion of alcohol, or excessive use of salicylates such as aspirin. If the condition is acute, fever, epigastric pain, nausea and vomiting, headache, coating of the tongue, and loss of appetite may occur. If the condition results from ingestion of contaminated food, the intestines are usually affected, and diarrhea may occur. Food is generally withheld as long as vomiting persists, and if vomiting is severe, intravenous infusions are administered. Histamine-inhibiting drugs such as cimetidine (Tagamet) and ranitidine (Zantac) may be given. Chronic gastritis may indicate the presence of ulcers or malignancy, or it may accompany uremia and liver disease. The treatment consists of a bland diet, antacids, and avoidance of irritating foods and situations that might further the condition. The underlying cause must be treated.

Enteritis

Inflammation of the intestine accompanying gastritis is called *gastroenteritis*. Enteritis occurs in conjunction with some infectious diseases, such as typhoid fever, dysentery, tuberculosis involving the intestines, and most cases of food infection. The severity of the condition depends on the virulence of the organism causing the condition. The primary symptoms are diarrhea and abdominal cramping. When the infection is from food, the symptoms occur within a few hours after the contaminated food has been eaten. Fever may or may not occur, but dehydration and weakness are usually present. Diarrhea is present in many types of infections and may be the forerunner of serious infections, especially in children.

Treatment is based on identifying the cause by using stool examination or cultures from suspected food. Precautions should always be taken until the cause of the diarrhea has been established. Patients with infectious enteritis should be isolated and medical asepsis carried out. Bedrest is indicated, and only liquids are given by mouth. When vomiting is present, oral fluids may be withheld, and the appropriate electrolyte solutions are administered parenterally to replace those lost through diarrhea and vomiting. Antibiotic or sulfonamide drugs may be ordered by the physician in treating some types of enteritis.

Regional enteritis

Pathophysiology. Regional enteritis, or Crohn's disease, is an inflammatory process that may involve any part of the alimentary tract from the mouth to the anus but usually involves segments of the small bowel. The most common location of lesions is the terminal ileum, although the duodenum and jejunum can also be involved. Twenty percent of cases occur in the colon. This disease occurs most often in young adults, and there seems to be a higher incidence among Jewish persons. Mortality is not high, but the disease often results in disability and incapacity requiring long medical or surgical treatment.

Regional enteritis is a slowly progressive, relentless, persistent inflammation. The small bowel becomes soggy, congested, and thickened. In the later stages sections of the intestinal wall become permanently fibrosed, thickened, and the tract narrowed. The involvement of segments of the bowel creates a "skip" pattern.

It has been suggested that regional enteritis is essentially a disorder of the lymphoid tissue. This would explain the frequent involvement of the terminal ileum and anus, which both have a rich lymph supply. Stricture and the formation of abscesses or fistulas to other loops of the small bowel, colon, abdominal wall, bladder, or vagina may be present. The fistulas are probably extensions of fissures and occur in approximately one third of the patients. A partial bowel obstruction occurs frequently and may recur in the same patient; however, a complete obstruction is uncommon.

Assessment. The symptoms are mild and intermittent at first. Exacerbations often follow dietary indiscretions (milk, milk products, fatty foods), emotional upsets, or illness. Abdominal pain, cramping, tenderness, flatulence, nausea, fever, and diarrhea will occur in an acute attack. The more typical picture is the chronic type with diarrhea accompanied by mild pain. It may be aggravated by illness or emotional upsets but is usually less severe than diarrhea associated with ulcerative colitis. The stool is usually soft or semiliquid and may be quite foul smelling and fatty. Urgency to expel stools may awaken the patient at night. A large amount of flatus is also likely to be present. The passing of gross blood is rare and would indicate extensive ulceration.

Diagnosis. Diagnosis is made by a series of x-ray examinations, including an upper gastrointestinal tract series (barium swallow) and barium enema. Proctosigmoidoscopy may be beneficial to rule out other diseases such as ulcerative colitis or diverticulitis or to obtain a rectal biopsy.

Intervention. Treatment of regional enteritis is not specific or curative but is supportive, palliative, and aimed at attaining remission of the disease. Regional enteritis has a tendency to recur, and complete spontaneous resolutions are rare. Medical treatment initially attempts to reduce active inflammation and is more likely to be successful early in the course of the disease before permanent structural changes have developed. Metronidazole (Flagyl) is believed to be beneficial in Crohn's perianal disease. Loperamide hydrochloride (Immodium) is used to treat cramping. Immunosuppressive drugs, such as azothioprine (Imuran) decrease antibody-reducing cells and have been effective. Complications such as fistulas, abscesses, strictures, or hemorrhage require surgical treatment. Nursing care is centered around rest, relief of pain and diarrhea, and psychologic support. Surgical treatment is aimed at correcting complications or removal of the affected portion of the intestinal tract or both. Ileostomy may be necessary.[9]

Ulcerative colitis

Ulcerative colitis involves the colon almost exclusively and is one of the most serious diseases of the gastrointestinal tract. Although the disease has been reported since 1875, the specific cause is still unknown. There appears to be little evidence that the disease is caused by pathologic organisms. Possible causes include food allergies, emotional factors, and autoimmune reactions. Once the disease becomes established, it often becomes chronic. The disease may be acute, progressing rapidly to a fatal outcome, or it may remain low grade.

The disease may be controlled medically but is cured only by surgical intervention and removal of the diseased colon. The disease usually attacks young adults and may be found in children and adolescents; it almost always occurs before 30 years of age. The disease is important because it may result in disability and dependence of the individual. Ulcerative colitis begins in the rectum and spreads upward in the colon, eventually involving the mucous membrane and all layers of the intestinal wall.

Assessment. The symptoms begin rather insidiously, with increasing distress and frequency of stools until the individual may have as many as 20 to 30 stools a day. The presence of ulcers on the lining of the intestine results in blood loss and anemia and possibly in severe hemorrhage. The patient becomes debilitated, pale, weak, and thin, and electrolytes are constantly being depleted from the severe diarrhea. Because of the nutritional deficiency, symptoms of vitamin deficiency may occur. The diagnosis is made on the basis of the history and physical examination, including sigmoidoscopy, x-ray examination, and stool specimens.

Intervention. Treatment includes complete bedrest. Bathroom privileges may be permitted in some cases. Rest must be both physical and emotional. Some physicians believe that psychotherapy should accompany medical treatment because understanding the patient and his or her problems is a primary factor in patient response to treatment. Sedation such as phenobarbital or a tranquilizer is given after meals and at bedtime, and a hypnotic such as pentobarbital sodium (Nembutal) or chloral hydrate may be ordered for sleep at night. Several drugs are designed to control diarrhea and abdominal discomfort.

Anticholinergics may decrease muscle spasm but have little effect on diarrhea. Opiates may cause distention and megacolon. Small doses of opium tincture or diphenoxylate (Lomotil) may be useful. The drug of choice is sulfasalazine (Azulfidine). In this instance it is not used for its antibiotic effect but because it decreases diarrhea and associated symptoms. It also reduces the incidence of relapse when used on a long-term basis. Its specific action is unknown, but it is retained by the connective tissue of the intestinal mucosa and submucosa. Remission and improvement occur in 70% of the patients. A hot-water bottle or electric heating pad to the abdomen and hot sitz baths may provide some relief. Adrenocorticotropic hormone has given good results for some patients, but its effect may vary in the same patient at different times. Because of its side effects, it is seldom given unless other measures fail. The diet is high in proteins, calories, and vitamins.

Patients with ulcerative colitis should have a quiet, pleasant environment and should be protected from chilling and secondary infection. Because diarrhea constitutes one of the major problems, bathroom facilities should be readily available; a bedside commode or, if the patient is not ambulatory, a padded bedpan should be within reach of the patient. After defecation the anal area should be carefully cleansed and a soothing ointment applied. The frequency, amount, and character of stools should be observed and recorded. Care must be taken if enemas are given because perforation of the bowel may easily occur. Room deodorizers should be available to eliminate unpleasant room odors, and plans should be made for airing the room daily.

Patients with ulcerative colitis are usually debilitated and thus are predisposed to decubitus ulcers.

Preventative measures should be taken early by using any of the procedures reviewed in Chapter 24. The skin is dry, and superfatted soap should be used, followed by lanolin. Special mouth care must be given several times a day with the application of cold cream or petroleum jelly to the lips. Because the appetite is poor, the patient will need much encouragement to eat, and consideration should be given to the patient's food desires because he will often know which foods cause him the most discomfort. Food intake should be carefully noted because diet is important in treating patients with ulcerative colitis. During the acute stage of the disease the patient may be receiving intravenous infusions and blood transfusions. Perforation of intestinal ulcers may occur, resulting in hemorrhage and peritonitis. Any drop in blood pressure and increase in pulse rate or abdominal pain should be reported. The patient is usually given some mild sedative drug to relieve nervous tension and an antispasmodic drug to decrease peristalsis.

The psychologic care of the patient with ulcerative colitis requires the empathic understanding of everyone concerned with his care. The patient is often insecure, sensitive, and apprehensive. A carefully prepared nursing care plan will contribute to the continuity of care, which is important in meeting the patient's needs for a feeling of security. Because the patient's behavior may be characterized by periods of depression and changes in mood, the nurse must be prepared to accept such changes and continue to provide intelligent, personalized nursing care.

If medical management is unsuccessful, surgery is indicated to remove the diseased colon. The patient usually has an ileostomy, but ileoanal anastomosis, removal of the entire colon with anastomosis of the ileum to a small portion of remaining rectum, is sometimes performed. There is a danger of the disease remaining in the rectum and spreading to the attached ileum, causing a "backwash ileitis." Sphincter control to prevent inadvertent discharge of stool is a postoperative goal when anastomosis is performed. An advance in technique called ileoanal pull-through

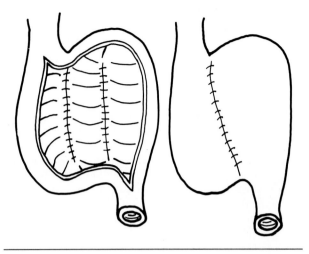

Figure 18-8
Internal pouch for ileoanal anastomosis (Soave procedure).

that creates a pouch of ileum provides greater capacity for fecal material and reduces the problem of sphincter control experienced by these patients (Figure 18-8).

The continent or pouch ileostomy (p. 449) has been successful with ulcerative colitis patients.

The box on p. 458 summarizes nurses diagnoses and care of the patient with this disease.

Appendicitis

One of the most common causes of an acute abdominal condition in children and young adults is **appendicitis.** The risk of fatal complications is increased when treatment is delayed. Factors that have helped reduce deaths from appendicitis during past years include early recognition of the disease, improvement in surgical techniques and anesthesia, the use of antibiotics, and intensive nursing care.

Pathophysiology. The vermiform appendix is a small tube in the right lower quadrant of the abdomen. The lumen of the proximal end is shared with that of the cecum, whereas the distal end is closed. The walls of the appendix contain lymphoid cells, and although the appendix has been generally considered to have no specific function, it is now believed to share with other lymphoid tissues of the body in preventing infection. The appendix fills and empties regularly in the same way as the cecum. However, the lumen is tiny and is easily obstructed. If it becomes obstructed, the blood supply is disrupted, it becomes distended, and inflammation occurs.

NURSING CARE GUIDELINES
Ulcerative Colitis

Nursing diagnoses

- Anxiety related to inability to control disease
- Alteration in bowel elimination: diarrhea related to inflammatory process
- Alteration in comfort (abdominal pain) related to gaseous distention and intestinal cramping
- Potential ineffective individual coping related to effects of disease on life-style
- Potential fluid volume deficit related to increased excretion of liquid stool
- Alteration in nutrition (less than body requirements) related to food intolerance, anorexia, increased excretion of liquid stool
- Disturbance in self-concept related to debilitating effects of disease

Nursing interventions

- Spend at least 15 minutes daily in active listening with patient
- Assess level of comfort; give analgesics or sedatives as ordered
- Weigh patient daily
- Note and chart color, consistency, and frequency of all stools
- Listen to bowel sounds every 4 hours and report absence
- Report drop in blood pressure, increase in pulse rate, or abdominal pain

- Maintain bedrest with commode or accessible bathroom
- Check vital signs every 4 hours
- Measure intake and output, including liquid stools
- Encourage diet high in protein, calories, and vitamins and low in residue
- Force fluids to 2000 ml daily—200 ml every 2 hours between 8 AM and 10 PM and 400 ml during night
- Maintain intravenous infusions if ordered
- Carefully cleanse anus after bowel movement; rinse with water rather than using harsh papers
- Apply petroleum jelly (Vaseline) or other soothing ointment to excoriated anus
- Minimize room odor with ventilation and commercial deodorizers
- Encourage self-care as physical condition permits

Expected outcomes

- Evidence of adequate hydration: skin elastic, mucous membranes moist
- Maintaining weight gain
- Verbalized satisfaction with ability to control disease
- Verbalized concerns and fears about effect on lifestyle
- Abdomen soft and full of distention and pain
- Rectal tissues intact, free of excoriation
- Patient identifies and avoids foods that increase flatus, distention, and discomfort

---

Pathogenic bacteria present in the intestinal tract, often *Escherichia coli,* begin to multiply in the appendix, and infection develops with the formation of pus. If distention and infection are severe enough, the appendix may rupture, releasing its contents into the abdomen. If this occurs, the infectious material may be walled off and the infection localized with an appendiceal abscess. If it is not localized, the infectious material spreads to the abdominal cavity and generalized peritonitis occurs.

The symptoms most characteristic of acute appendicitis are pain, fever, and nausea and vomiting. In adults the pain may be felt in the lower right quadrant of the abdomen, halfway between the umbilicus and the crest of the ileum *(McBurney's point)*. In children pain may be experienced near the umbilicus. Mild leukocytosis and loss of appetite may also be present.

Intervention. The surgical removal of the appendix (appendectomy) is often performed as an emergency operation. In most patients having any abdominal surgery, the appendix is routinely removed. When appendicitis is suspected, surgery is usually done as soon as the diagnosis has been completed to avoid rupture and complications. If the appendix has ruptured, treatment will vary among physicians. Over the decades there has never been agreement among physicians as to the best method of treatment. Some physicians prefer a conservative approach and large doses of antibiotics are administered, whereas other physicians believe that the abdomen should always be opened and the appendix removed.

In a clean appendectomy (without rupture) recovery is usually rapid, requiring 5 to 7 days. The postoperative care is directed toward preventing wound infection and pulmonary compli-

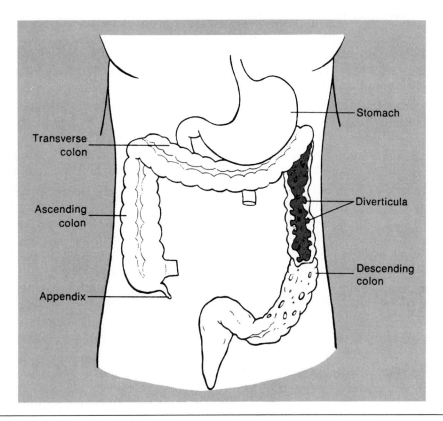

Figure 18-9
Diverticula.

cations. The patient is ambulatory on the first postoperative day. When drainage is necessary because of an abscess, dressings must be changed as necessary and disposed of carefully. Recovery is slower, and the patient must be watched for complications such as hemorrhage, intestinal obstruction, and an increased elevation of temperature and pulse rate, which may indicate the formation of a secondary abscess.

Diverticular disease: diverticulosis and diverticulitis

Diverticula are pouches of mucosa and submucosa that protrude or herniate through the circular muscles of the intestinal wall (Figure 18-9). Diverticula can occur anywhere in the large bowel but are most frequently found in the sigmoid colon.[5] They are rarely found in persons under age 40, but it is estimated that one out of every three persons over age 60 has some diverticula. The incidence in nonindustrialized countries is very low, and the condition is practically nonexistent in African populations. There is increasing evidence that a low-residue diet may cause diverticula. When diverticula are present, the individual is said to have *diverticulosis.* When one or more diverticula become inflamed, fecal matter penetrates the thin-walled diverticula, resulting in inflammation and abscess formation outside the bowel called "diverticulitis."

Pathophysiology. There is no agreement among authorities on the cause of diverticula. The role of diet in causing the disease continues to be investigated. Diverticula develop when the muscles of the colon hypertrophy or become thickened. Both the circular muscles and the longitudinal muscles and muscular fibers (teniae coli) are involved. As these muscles thicken, the colon becomes segmented by the circular fibers during peristalsis. Between these circular fibers little sacs develop. Increased pressure in the colon results in the protrusion of mucosa through the weakened muscle in the little sacs, resulting in diverticula and diverticulosis.

Once diverticula develop, there is the possibility that the protrusion will continue and perforation will occur, resulting in diverticulitis. This complication can be in the form of very small or microperforations into the fat layer around the bowel or larger macroperforations opening into the peritoneal space. Microperforations result in the formation of abscesses and localized peritonitis. Macroperforations produce severe generalized peritonitis. The body responds as it does to any inflammatory process. Complications of diverticulitis include fistulas, septicemia, obstruction, and hemorrhage.

Those who theorize that diet is the cause of the disease believe that a lack of fiber causes the muscle thickening that predisposes the individual to formation of diverticula. A lack of fiber in the diet results in less bulk in the stool. The lumen of the bowel is not forced to widen, and the pressure within that lumen is therefore increased (intracolonic pressure). The sigmoid is normally the narrowest segment of the bowel; interestingly, it is the most common site of diverticula. Fiber also affects stool transit time—the time it takes for stool to move through the bowel. Stool that moves faster will have less water absorbed and will thus be softer and easier to eliminate. Increased intracolonic pressure is believed to be the cause of the muscle hypertrophy, which leads to the formation of diverticula.

Assessment. The patient with diverticulosis may not display any problematic symptoms. Complaints of constipation and diarrhea are probably related to the cause of the disease rather than a symptom of the disease. When diverticula perforate and diverticulitis develops, the patient will complain of mild to severe pain in the lower left quadrant of the abdomen and will have fever and an elevated white blood cell count and sedimentation rate. If the condition goes untreated, septicemia and septicemic shock can develop. This patient will be hypotensive, have a rapid pulse rate, and may have some loss of consciousness. Obstruction can occur, and the patient will experience abdominal distention, nausea, and vomiting. Hemorrhage occurs in about 10% to 20% of patients and may be mild and go unnoticed for some time or be severe and result in shock.[15]

Intervention. The traditional treatment for diverticulosis is based on the belief that muscle atrophy is responsible for the disease and includes a low-residue diet, stool softeners, and bedrest. Those who agree that increased intracolonic pressure and muscle thickening are the causes employ a different treatment regimen, involving a high-fiber diet of bran, fruits, and vegetables. Diverticulitis is sometimes treated with sulfa drugs when the patient has uncomplicated signs of inflammation. Microperforation resulting in localized abscess is treated with a combination of antimicrobials effective against gram-negative, gram-positive, an anaerobic organisms. Fluids and electrolytes must be administered intravenously, and a nasogastric tube is inserted and attached to suction. Analgesics are given intramuscularly for pain. Activity is restricted by bedrest. Surgery to resect the bowel may be necessary. Macroperforation always requires surgery; a temporary or permanent colostomy or bowel resection may be performed, depending on the severity of the disease and the extent of complications.

Nursing intervention is aimed at monitoring vital signs and fluid balance, providing relief of pain, and assessing response to treatment. The patient must be observed closely for signs of septicemia and shock. The schedule for antibiotic therapy must be strictly followed. When surgery is necessary, nursing interventions follow the recommendations for the specific procedure performed.

Peritonitis

Peritonitis is an inflammation of the peritoneum and the abdominal cavity and is often a complication of a bacterial infection. Infection may develop from a perforated peptic ulcer or ruptured appendix. It may be caused by infection from the internal female organs. Although infrequent, it may occur from trauma to abdominal organs or be carried by infection in the bloodstream. The inflammatory process may be localized, with abscess formation, or it may be generalized, with bacteria spreading throughout the entire abdominal cavity. Sometimes peritonitis occurs without any known cause.

Generalized peritonitis is an extremely serious condition characterized mainly by severe abdominal pain. The patient usually lies on his back with the knees flexed to relax the abdominal muscles, and any movement is painful. Nausea and vomiting occur. Constipation or diarrhea may occur early, but as the condition progresses, peristalsis ceases and constipation occurs with no passage of flatus. The abdomen becomes distended, tense, rigid, and very tender. The pulse is weak and rapid, and blood pressure falls. Leukocytosis and marked dehydration occur; the patient may collapse and die.

Intervention. The patient is placed in a semi-Fowler's position and is given meperidine or morphine sufficient to relieve pain. A nasogastric tube is inserted and connected to suction to keep the stomach empty. Intravenous fluids are administered to prevent dehydration and to maintain electrolyte balance, and appropriate antibiotic therapy is started. Further care or indications for surgery depend on the cause of the peritonitis and the patient's condition. The patient receives nothing by mouth, and special mouth care is needed, including lubrication of the lips. All intake and output, including vomitus, must be accurately measured and recorded. The patient should be observed for pain, and the type of pain and its location should be described, recorded, and reported. The patient often realizes the seriousness of his condition, and the nurse should facilitate expression of fears and provide emotional support.

Intestinal Obstruction

An obstruction of the small or large intestine may occur when any condition exists that prevents the free passage of bowel contents through the intestine. The obstruction may be partial or complete and is always regarded as serious. The relief of intestinal obstruction is ultimately a surgical procedure; however, the cause of the obstruction, its location, and the condition of the patient will be considered by the physician.

Pathophysiology

An intestinal obstruction has many causes, some of which include a strangulated hernia, twisting of the bowel (volvulus), cancer, postoperative adhesions, paralytic ileus, and stricture. The most common causes are postoperative adhesions and hernia. Obstruction may occur in the small or the large intestine. In the large intestine it is less dramatic than when it occurs in the small intestine. When an obstruction cuts off the blood supply, as in a strangulated hernia, the part will die and gangrene will develop. Most obstructions occur in the small intestine and affect the normal homeostasis of the body. The continuous vomiting causes loss of electrolytes and loss of hydrochloric acid from the stomach, leading to alkalosis. The loss of water and sodium from the body may cause acidosis and severe dehydration.[2]

Assessment

The symptoms vary according to the location and the extent of the obstruction. When the obstruction is high in the small intestine, symptoms appear earlier and are more acute than when the large intestine is obstructed. The early symptoms are abdominal pain, vomiting, and constipation. The pain is often wavelike, and vomiting may be projectile. The gastric contents are first vomited, but as peristalsis is reversed, bile and fecal matter from above the obstruction are vomited. When the obstruction is in the colon, vomiting may not occur. The patient may eliminate blood or pus from the bowel, but no fecal matter or flatus passes. Extreme thirst occurs; the tongue and mucous membranes of the mouth and lips become parched. Abdominal distention develops and is greater when the obstruction is in the colon. Signs of shock may appear, and without treatment, the patient may die within a few hours.

Intervention

A long intestinal decompression tube, such as the Miller-Abbott, Cantor, or Ampro tube, is inserted by the physician to remove gas and fluids from the stomach and intestine and to relieve the distention. The patency of the tube should be checked frequently and maintained by irrigating the tube every 1 to 2 hours with 30 ml of normal saline. The volume, character, and consistency of the drainage should be observed and recorded. Any irrigating fluid that does not return on aspiration should be noted on the intake and output record. A long intestinal tube is intended to travel down the intestinal tract and should never be taped.[2] Intravenous fluids are administered to correct the dehydration and replace the electrolytes lost through vomiting. All vomitus should be accurately described, and any fecal matter should be saved to be examined for occult blood. Temperature, pulse, and respiration rates are taken every 4 hours, and more often if the patient exhibits signs of hypovolemic shock. The patient is placed in Fowler's position to prevent respiratory embarrassment, which might occur from the abdominal distention, to help prevent gastric regurgitation, and to encourage passage of small intestine contents into the colon. Careful records of urinary output should be maintained, and if retention occurs, the patient should be catheterized. The patient should be assisted with frequent cleansing of the mouth and changes in position. The environment should be kept well ventilated and free of odors by prompt care of vomitus and the use of a deodorizer if necessary.

Preoperative and postoperative intervention

Surgery for intestinal obstruction depends partly on the cause of the obstruction, its location, and the condition of the patient. In some cases surgery may be relatively simple, whereas in other situations the cause may complicate the surgical procedure. In obstructions resulting from a strangulated hernia, the cutting off of the blood supply may have caused the bowel to become gangrenous, and resection of the affected bowel may be necessary. Before surgery, the patient is given a small enema under low pressure. Intravenous fluids are administered to replace electrolytes lost through vomiting and to provide nourishment. After surgery, if the bowel has been resected, oral feeding is withheld to give the anastomosis time to heal. A nasogastric tube attached to suction aids in keeping the stomach empty. Accurate intake and output records must be kept. Other postoperative care is the same as that for any abdominal surgery.

Tumors of the Gastrointestinal System
Mouth cancer

Tumors of the lips, tongue, and mouth may be benign or malignant; cancer of the tongue is the most common type of tumor of the mouth. Although the cause of mouth cancer is unknown, it is believed that irritation resulting from smoking, consumption of alcohol, dental appliances, and rough, jagged teeth are predisposing factors. Malignant tumors of the mouth metastasize early to adjacent structures such as the lymph nodes in the neck and muscle tissue. Cancer of the mouth is often associated with leukoplakia, a condition characterized by the formation of white patches on the mucous membrane of the tongue or cheek. Cancer of the mouth is more common in men than in women and is responsible for 3% to 6% of deaths from cancer. When the disease is discovered early, the prognosis is good.

Intervention. Malignant lesions may involve the lips, tongue, or mucous membrane lining the mouth, and surgery or radiation or both may be used in the treatment. Any surgery of the mouth interferes with the normal functions of respiration, speech, and eating and will involve certain nursing problems. The mouth cannot be rendered completely free of pathogenic organisms but should be kept as clean as possible to prevent infection.

Preoperative care of the mouth for patients with malignant tumors requires meticulous attention. The teeth should be brushed before and after meals, and dental floss should be used to remove any particles between the teeth. Dentures and bridges should be cared for in the same manner. Warm mouthwashes or irrigations with an antiseptic solution may be ordered by the physician. If necrotic tissue is present, various preparations may be used to loosen the tissue and deodorize the mouth. A solution of 1 teaspoon of salt and 1 teaspoon of baking soda in 1 quart of warm water may be used for frequent mouthwashes. Also, 1.5% hydrogen peroxide may be used as a mouthwash with moderate pressure irrigation. Depending on the site and the extent of the lesion, eating may be difficult. The diet should contain soft food and be free of acids and citrus foods, which may cause pain; frequent small feedings may be more desirable than large meals three times a day. The emotional factors involved in this kind of surgery require that the nurse have an understanding of the patient's feelings. The patient may fear permanent disability or disfigurement and should be given as much information before surgery as is necessary to help relieve his or her anxiety. If the malignancy involves the lymph nodes in the neck, a radical neck dissection may be done in an attempt to remove all affected tissue.

After surgery, the patient's speech will be affected, and a pad and pencil should be at the bedside. The patient may have a tracheotomy or a tracheostomy, and nursing care will be the same as that outlined in Chapter 15. A nasogastric tube may be inserted through the nostril and connected to suction. The physician will order the position in which the patient should be placed. Depending on the suture line and the extent of surgery, suction of secretions and mucus may be gently done, or a wick of gauze may be placed in the mouth and allowed to drain into an emesis basin. The physician may order mouth irrigations to be performed, using a prescribed solution and sterile equipment. Intravenous infusions may be given. If a radical neck dissection has been done, blood transfusions may be needed, and a large pressure dressing may be applied to help prevent edema and splint the affected body part. Some physicians place a perforated catheter in the wound and attach it to a small portable suction apparatus (Hemovac). This removes secretions as soon as they accumulate and promotes healing. If this method is used, no gauze dressings are applied and the area may be sprayed with a plastic material. The method of feeding will depend on the site and the extent of the surgery, and nasogastric tube feedings may be necessary in the beginning. When a portion of the tongue has been removed, a thread is often passed through the remaining portion of the tongue and fastened to the outside of the cheek with adhesive tape to keep it from obstructing the airway. The patient must be watched carefully for hemorrhage and respiratory difficulty because edema may occur and obstruct the airway. A tracheostomy tray, a suction machine with a soft rubber catheter, and oxygen should always be available for emergency use.

Cancer of the mouth may be treated by external radiation or by implanting radium needles or radon seeds (Chapter 9). When radium needles are used, they are attached to threads fastened to the outside of the cheek with adhesive tape, and the patient must be cautioned against any pulling on the threads. The threads must be checked and counted several times a day and recorded on the patient's chart. A pad and pencil or slate should be provided for the patient because talking will be difficult. Mouth hygiene is important, and a spray may be ordered and used while the needles are in place. Any equipment used must be carefully inspected for radium that may have become dislodged. The physician will give directions concerning food and fluids. The patient should always be watched carefully for hemorrhage, edema, or choking.

Esophageal cancer

Cancer of the esophagus occurs mostly in men and accounts for over 6000 deaths each year in the United States. Despite all therapy the 5-year survival rate for esophageal cancer is poor—at only about 4%. In the majority of cases only palliation is possible.[14]

Dysphagia (difficulty in swallowing) with the ingestion of solid foods is the prime symptom in 90% of cases; weight loss may also occur. Pain does not occur until the disease is well advanced, and swallowing difficulty may be intermittent in the beginning so that there is usually a delay in reporting symptoms to a physician. This is unfortunate because metastasis does not occur until after extensive local infiltration. Hence, the slightest dysphagia should be investigated promptly and thoroughly with **esophagoscopy,** esophagrams, and cytologic examinations of esophageal washings. The tumor metastasizes to the lymph nodes in the neck and chest and eventually to the liver and the bones. The patient becomes thinner and more malnourished as the disease progresses. Radiation may be used for palliation when metastasis has occurred. The only hope for cure is

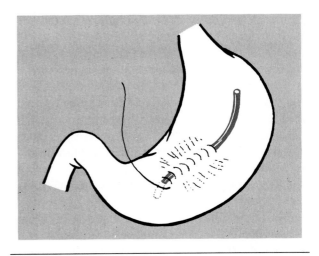

Figure 18-10

Gastrostomy tube is inserted into stomach and secured with sutures. End of tube or catheter is brought out through opening in abdomen so that feedings may be given.

early diagnosis and surgical removal of the lesion. The tumor and lymph nodes may be removed and the esophagus anastomosed to the stomach (esophagogastrostomy), or a portion of the intestine may be anastomosed between the esophagus and the stomach after the tumor is removed. If the patient is not a candidate for major surgery, or if the tumor is inoperable, a gastrostomy may be performed for feeding purposes.

Gastrostomy care

The patient with a gastrostomy has a permanent opening into the stomach through which a tube has been inserted for the purpose of feeding (Figure 18-10). The stomach is sutured to the abdominal wall to prevent stomach contents from entering the abdominal cavity, and the catheter is secured into a small incision. The nurse should understand the physician's orders concerning the tube. If the tube inserted by the physician happens to come out, the physician should be notified immediately. Some physicians use the Barnes-Redo prosthesis, which is sutured into the gastrostomy opening. The appliance has a cap that may be removed for feeding and then replaced.[15] The nursing intervention for the patient includes caring for the skin, maintaining patency of the tube, good oral care, and administering the prescribed feeding as ordered by the physician. Often there is a slight seepage of secretions about the tube, which will cause excoriation of the skin.

Careful washing with mild soap and water, thorough drying, and the application of a bland ointment will usually keep the skin in a healthy condition. If the tube becomes blocked, it may be gently irrigated with a bulb syringe and physiologic saline solution. Force should not be used, and if the tube is not easily unplugged, the physician should be notified. A second tube should be sterilized and available if a replacement is needed.

The diet is prescribed by the physician, and food should be warmed by placing it in a pan of warm water. The patient is placed in a semi-Fowler's position, and the feeding is allowed to flow by gravity. (Refer to a textbook on basic nursing.) The amount of food taken should be recorded so that the physician may determine if the amount of food that the patient is receiving provides sufficient calories. The preparation of gastrostomy feedings has been greatly simplified because of the commercial feedings that are now available. These preparations contain all of the nutritional requirements of a normal diet.

The patient with a gastrostomy has an emotional adjustment to make that may be difficult. The realization that he or she will not be able to eat normally may be traumatic, and the patient will need a great deal of support and encouragement. The nurse can help the patient by providing privacy for the feeding, by preparing an attractive tray with the feeding in an opaque container such as an attractive pitcher or teapot, and by using a colorful tray cover. The patient is often allowed to chew some food but now swallow it, which stimulates the flow of the digestive juices and aids digestion. As the patient begins to accept this method of feeding, he should be encouraged to participate in administering the feeding and caring for the skin. It is usually important for a member of the family to be taught the preparation of the diet, as well as the gastrostomy care and feeding of the patient. After the patient leaves the hospital, the home health nurse may visit the patient to supervise, instruct, and provide encouragement.

Stomach cancer

The incidence of cancer of the stomach has declined by more than 35% during the past 3 decades and continues its downward trend annually. Patients who do not produce sufficient acid in the stomach are vulnerable to stomach cancer. Diet has been implicated as a predisposing factor because low-socioeconomic groups, for whom diet is high in starch and low in fresh fruit and vegetables, have a higher incidence of this disease. The incidence is also high in parts of the world where there is heavy consumption of smoked fish and smoked meat, such as Japan, Iceland, Chile, and Hawaii.[4]

The early symptoms are so poorly defined that most individuals delay medical treatment until the malignancy is well established. Frequently, symptoms related to the metastasis rather than the cancer prompt the patient to consult the physician. Symptoms include loss of appetite, a feeling of fullness after meals, epigastric distress, nausea, vomiting, weight loss, anemia, vomiting blood that has a coffee-grounds appearance, blood in the stools that appears dark and tarry, and pain. A palpable mass may be felt through the abdominal wall, but this often indicates that the condition is inoperable. Early diagnosis is most important.

The patient is admitted to the hospital and a series of diagnostic tests are begun, including gastroscopic x-ray and fluoroscopic examination of the entire gastrointestinal tract. Gastric analysis is performed; cytologic examination using the Papanicolaou technique to determine the presence of cancer cells may be done following lavage. Emesis may be saved for examination, and stool specimens are examined for the presence of occult blood.

The only treatment is a partial or total gastrectomy. The malignant growth often causes chronic starvation, and several days of preoperative treatment may be necessary to correct anemia and malnutrition. Once the patient is nutritionally stable, the surgeon will remove all or part of the stomach, depending on the findings.

Intervention for the patient after a total gastrectomy differs from that after a subtotal gastrectomy, because the chest cavity must be entered to remove the entire stomach. There will be little nasogastric drainage because secretions are normally formed in the stomach, which has been removed. Small frequent feedings, beginning with tap water and progressing to bland foods, are given. The patient should be given easily digested foods, eat slowly, and chew his food thoroughly. In the absence of the intrinsic factor normally produced by the stomach, vitamin B_{12} cannot be absorbed and a regular injection of vitamin B_{12} is necessary to prevent pernicious anemia. The patient may undergo chemotherapy. A combination of chemotherapeutic agents has been found to be more effective than a single drug. Radiation may be used with chemotherapy but radiation alone has not proved effective against gastric cancer.

Cancer of the small intestine

Malignant lesions develop less frequently in the small intestine than in other segments of the gastrointestinal tract. Symptoms, which include intestinal obstruction, bleeding, and upper abdominal pain, do not appear early. Treatment is surgical removal. The prognosis is poor because these tumors tend to metastasize early in the liver and local lymph nodes. A considerable portion of the bowel wall becomes involved before symptoms appear, making early diagnosis almost impossible.[4]

Colorectal cancer

Cancers of the colon and rectum are the most prevalent internal cancers in the United States, occurring equally in men and women. Early detection and treatment lead to a good prognosis, but most patients are still diagnosed and operated on late in the course of the disease. Etiologic factors are not definite, but certain conditions appear to be more prone to malignant changes, including ulcerative colitis and diverticulosis. Evidence suggests that a low-fiber diet is related to colorectal cancer. Evidence also suggests that a diet rich in beef and saturated fats leads to an increased incidence of colorectal cancer. It is theorized that carcinogens are formed from degraded bile salts and that stool, which remains in the large bowel for a longer period as a result of too little fiber to stimulate its passage, may overexpose the bowel to these carcinogens. Another theory relates diverticulosis to low-fiber diets, proposing that the lack of fiber necessitates stronger muscle contractions to excrete hard stools, increasing pressure on the colon wall, which leads to outpouching, or diverticula. Thus the reduced weight of stool and the increased time it takes for stool to pass (transit time), which results from a low-fiber diet, have been related to both diverticulosis and cancer of the colon. As stated earlier, the individual with diverticulosis is already considered more prone to malignant changes.

Symptoms may partly depend on the portion involved. Rectal bleeding is still the most common symptom. Alternating constipation and diarrhea is common, along with excessive flatus, cramplike pains in the lower abdomen, and abdominal distention. Obstruction is most likely to occur if the tumor is on the right side or in the transverse colon, in which fecal contents are still fluid. The individual may complain of weakness, loss of appetite, and loss of weight, and anemia may be present. Hemorrhoids and cancer frequently coexist. Rectal bleeding can never be assumed to be the result of hemorrhoids alone, without an examination that rules out cancer. The diagnosis is made on the basis of abdominal and rectal examinations, which include a barium enema and a gastrointestinal series, proctoscopic and sigmoidoscopic examination, and examination of the stools for occult blood. Three fourths of all colon and rectum cancers can be detected with the aid of the sigmoidoscope, and it is important to include this examination in the routine physical examination for all adults over 40 years of age. Any change in normal bowel habits should be reported to the physician.

Treatment is always surgical, but preoperative radiation therapy may also be used, along with chemotherapy. The type of surgery depends on the anatomic position of the carcinoma. Whenever possible, the tumor is removed and an end-to-end **anastomosis** (bringing together the healthy sections of the colon after the tumor has been removed) is performed. If the tumor has obstructed the bowel, a temporary colostomy may be done to divert bowel contents, and resection will be done after the obstruction has been decompressed. If the tumor is in the sigmoid or rectum, an abdominoperineal resection is performed, removing the rectum and constructing a colostomy on the abdominal wall. Patients who have inoperable disease may be treated with radiation therapy or chemotherapy. A colostomy may be performed to divert the bowel contents if an inoperable tumor is causing obstruction.

Preoperative intervention. Patients who are to undergo bowel surgery may be admitted to the hospital several days before surgery to allow time for preparation. The patient is given a low-residue, high-calorie diet during this time. Sulfonamide agents and neomycin are administered orally to reduce the bacterial level in the colon. Enemas are given until the solution returns clear. The abdomen and perineal area is shaved, and a catheter is inserted for urinary drainage. An intestinal decompression tube is inserted to keep the stomach empty and prevent distention. The psychologic preparation of the patient is extremely important. If the physician anticipates that a colostomy will be necessary, the patient should be prepared for it. The patient needs to understand that he may expect to lead a normal life.[7]

Postoperative intervention. Postoperative care includes the care of all tubes, such as a Miller-Abbott tube, a nasogastric tube, a urinary drainage catheter, or drains placed in the perineal wound. The character and appearance of all drainage must be observed and recorded. Considerable drainage may occur from the perineal wound for the first 24 hours, and dressings should be changed or reinforced frequently and observed closely for hemorrhage. Antibiotics are usually administered to prevent or control infection. The patient receives nothing by mouth, but intravenous fluids are given to maintain hydration and replace electrolytes. If an abdominoperineal resection was done, the perineal wound may have been packed, and the packing is removed gradually by the physician. When all packing has been removed, irrigation of the wound may be ordered for once or twice a day. The physician should give specific directions regarding how the wound is to be irrigated and the solution to be used. Irrigation is a mechanical method of removing tissue and debris. Later the physician may order sitz baths. Routine care is given the colostomy.

These patients usually have more difficulty with ambulation as a result of the perineal wound, and the nursing procedures of encouraging deep breathing and coughing, turning the patient, and giving leg exercises are of special importance. The patient is usually very ill, and turning is difficult because of pain; therefore the nurse should assist the patient and provide support with pillows. Pain-control measures are also important.

Benign tumors

Benign tumors may occur anywhere in the gastrointestinal tract and usually take the form of polyps, which occur most frequently in the stomach and the large intestine. Symptoms may resemble those of malignant growths, but surgical procedures are less radical. The diagnosis is made by proctoscopic and x-ray examination.

Peptic Ulcer

A **peptic ulcer** is an open lesion in the lining of the part of the digestive tract exposed to stomach juices (hydrochloric acid and pepsin). It involves loss of tissue from the mucosa or submucosa, may go as deep as the muscle layer, and may penetrate

the serosa into the abdominal cavity (perforated ulcer). Peptic ulcers are most often found in the upper duodenum just below the pylorus (duodenal ulcers), are commonly found in the stomach (gastric ulcers), and may be found in the lower esophagus—in other words, all the places bathed by the gastric juices.

The exact cause of peptic ulcers is unknown, but there is evidence of hereditary predisposition. A bacteria has been identified that may cause the inflammation and that theory is being investigated. The incidence in relatives of an ulcer patient is three times higher than in persons unrelated to someone with an ulcer. Men are afflicted more often than women, and it is more common in people with type O blood. Emotional stress, hurried and irregular eating, and excessive smoking are considered predisposing factors. Ulcers seem to develop in people who are emotionally tense, but a definite link has not been established. Ulcers can be caused by pancreatic tumors, which secrete excessive amounts of the hormone gastrin (gastrinomas [Zollinger-Ellison syndrome]). For reasons that are unknown, the incidence of both gastric and duodenal ulcers has declined over the last two decades.[6] It has been estimated that about 10% of adults in the United States will have a peptic ulcer at some time in their lives.

Pathophysiology

Peptic ulcers occur when the lining of the lower esophagus, stomach, and duodenum are "digested" by the digestive juices, gastric acid, and pepsin. The lining is usually protected from its own juices by a barrier of mucus and epithelium. Erosion occurs when there is an increase in the concentration or activity of gastric acid or pepsin or when there is a decrease in the normal resistance of the protective barrier.

Gastric juices are released in three phases. The first is the cephalic, or psychic, phase, a reflex action in response to parasympathetic fibers in the vagus nerve. This reflex action takes place when food is seen, smelled, or even imagined. Second, in the gastric phase, juices are secreted in response to a hormone, gastrin, which is formed by cells in the antrum of the stomach. Gastrin is released when partly digested proteins are present. The third is the intestinal phase. When hydrochloric acid enters the duodenum, it stimulates the secretion of the hormone secretin. Secretin stimulates bicarbonate secretion from the pancreas, and these alkaline secretions enter the duodenum and neutralize the acid. Secretin also inhibits the production of gastric juices during the gastric phase.

The glands in the mucosa lining the stomach secrete the substance that provides the protective barrier. These mucous secretions are a mixture of mucopolysaccharides and mucoproteins. This mucus adsorbs pepsin and protects the stomach by allowing hydrochloric acid to pass through to the surface of the gastric mucosa very slowly. This gastric mucosal barrier prevents the mucosa from being digested by its own secretions. The ability of the mucosa to resist digestive action is also influenced by blood supply, acid-base balance, the condition of the mucosal cells, and the ability of the epithelium to regenerate.

It was once thought that people with peptic ulcers simply secreted more acid than others. This has been found to be true for those with duodenal ulcers and gastric ulcers near the duodenum, but people with gastric ulcers seem to secrete subnormal amounts of acid.[18]

In times of stress the sympathetic nervous system takes over and prepares the body for "fight or flight" by inhibiting the blood flow to the digestive organs and decreasing the production of juices. In some people chronic stress seems to enhance the action of the parasympathetic system on the abdominal organs, thus stimulating gastric juice production and the entire digestive process.[6] These persons will develop a peptic ulcer in response to chronic stress.

Severe injury or illness, burns, head injury or intracranial disease, and ingestion of alcohol or drugs that act on the gastric mucosa often result in gastric erosions called "stress ulcers." The exact mechanism is unknown, but it is thought to be caused by a decrease in blood supply, which in turn causes a decrease in energy metabolism within the gastric mucosa. The gastric mucosal barrier is then disrupted and its protective ability decreased. Gastric juices are then allowed to act on the mucosa, and multiple lesions develop very rapidly.

Assessment

Symptoms may vary with the location and severity of the ulcer. If the ulcer erodes through a blood vessel, bleeding or severe hemorrhage may result. In the case of hemorrhage, the vomited blood has a coffee-grounds appearance. If slow bleeding occurs, the blood generally passes through the intestinal tract and stools are dark and tarry in appearance.

Pain is the characteristic symptom and is described by the patient as dull, burning, gnawing, or boring; it is located in the midline of the epigastric region. With a gastric ulcer the pain occurs 60 to 90 minutes after eating; with a duodenal ulcer, 2 to 4 hours after eating. Pain of duodenal ulcer is relieved by eating or antacids, and patients usually have pain during the night that awakens them. They are usually free of pain when they wake in the morning because the flow of gastric secretions is lowest at this time. The pain is caused by the irritation of the ulcer by the gastric acid; exposed sensory nerve endings at the edges and base of the ulcer or increased motility and spasm of the muscle at the ulcer site are thought to produce the pain. Although pain is the typical symptom, many variations are found in its presence or absence, its character, and its duration. Nausea and vomiting may or may not be present and, when present, are often the result of pyloric obstruction, which may result from ulcerous inflammation or scarring. Many patients are anemic because of loss of blood but are usually well nourished because they eat to relieve the pain. The diagnosis is established through a gastrointestinal series, endoscopic examinations (p. 440), and examination of stool specimens for occult blood. The histamine test and cytologic examination of gastric washings may be done to rule out malignancy (p. 438). If the patient with a suspected gastric ulcer fails to secrete hydrochloric acid after an injection of histamine, it is likely that he has a malignancy in the stomach.

The nursing care guidelines for patients with peptic ulcers are found in the boxed material on p. 468.

Table 18-1 compares duodenal and gastric ulcers.

Intervention

The goals of therapy are to relieve pain, heal the ulcer, prevent complications, and prevent recurrence. Symptoms may be relieved before the ulcer heals, which may take 4 to 8 weeks. The patient should understand that he must continue treatment even though the symptoms disappear. Treatment will include rest, diet, medication (antacids, anticholinergics, sedatives, histamine blockers), and in some cases, surgery.

Rest

The patient must have physical rest and relief of tension. Diversional activity such as reading, watching television, or making crafts should be encouraged. Stress should be reduced for the pa-

NURSING CARE GUIDELINES
Peptic Ulcer

Nursing diagnoses

- Alteration in comfort: pain related to action of gastric secretions on inflamed mucosa
- Knowledge deficit related to medications and diet prescribed to promote healing and over-the-counter drugs that must be avoided
- Nutrition (potential for more than body requirements) related to frequent ingestion of food to prevent ulcer pain
- Sleep pattern disturbance related to pain at night
- Anxiety related to inability to manage stress
- Potential fluid volume deficit related to sudden hemorrhage at ulcer site
- High risk for injury (peritonitis) related to possible perforation

Nursing interventions

- Observe and record time and characteristics of pain
- Offer and administer analgesics as needed
- Administer antacids as ordered
- Provide quiet environment
- Plan treatments to provide rest periods
- Spend 15 minutes each shift when patient is awake, listening to patient's concerns and encouraging expression of feelings
- Provide diversional activities as needed
- Explain all procedures and anticipate needs
- Check vital signs four times a day
- Observe all stools, emesis, and sputum for blood and report findings
- Palpate abdomen to detect distention once each shift
- Observe for nausea every 4 hours when awake
- Observe skin color and temperature
- Reinforce dietary instructions and restrictions
- If patient is a smoker, facilitate efforts to avoid smoking
- Teach dangers of aspirin and over-the-counter drugs containing aspirin

Expected outcomes

- Absence of pain
- Absence of blood in stool
- Afebrile state
- Vital signs stable and within normal limits
- Verbalization of reason for medications ordered and frequency and timing of dosage
- Ability to select and eat foods for well-balanced diet that complies with physician's orders
- Verbalization of concerns and fears

tient whenever possible. Everything that is done, as well as the goals of treatment, should be carefully explained; being informed reduces the patient's anxiety. The patient must identify those factors that aggravate the condition, and a good listener is necessary for the patient to vent his feelings and examine his or her life-style. Listening alone may help, and nurses may discover problems that should be referred to the physician, social worker, or other qualified professionals.

Diet

The traditional milk and cream (sippy) diet is no longer used although patients will still ask about it. It has been found that, although milk products do buffer gastric acid, the high protein and fat in milk stimulates further acid production. Some authorities recommend a diet that eliminates only those foods that stimulate secretion, highly seasoned foods, highly fibrous foods, and those that cause pain to the patient. An even more liberal approach eliminates only those foods that cause pain. When milk is prescribed, skimmed milk is used. In the early stages of healing the patient will have to be more cautious and may be given small, frequent feedings. Foods that stimulate gastric acid secretion and motility, such as extremely hot or cold foods, coffee, alcohol, and seasonings, should be avoided at first and then used with moderation to test tolerance. Because gastric contractility is increased when the stomach is empty or overly full, small, frequent feedings are indicated.[3]

Drug therapy

Antacids are used to bring relief of symptoms, but there is no conclusive evidence that they promote healing. Antacids may be ordered every hour at first, with the frequency then gradually reduced. The antacids should be prescribed by the physician, who will select the one best for the individual patient. Some antacids such as sodium bicarbonate are absorbed systemically and may cause alkalosis. An antacid made of calcium carbonate (Dicarbosil, Tums) is not desirable because it produces rebound gastric secretion. The calcium carbonate also is absorbed into the bloodstream, producing hypercalcemia and possible renal damage with long-term treatment. Magnesium and aluminum hydroxide mixture (Maalox) may cause loose stools, whereas magnesium trisilicate and aluminum hydroxide (Gelusil) and aluminum hydroxide gel (Amphojel) may be constipating.

Table 18-1

Comparison of Duodenal and Gastric Ulcers

	Duodenal	Gastric
Incidence	Male:female ratio—4:1	Male:female ratio—2:1
Blood group	Most frequent in type O blood	Equal for all types
Acid production	Excessive	Normal
Pain	2-4 hours after eating and during night	1-1½ hours after eating
	Pain free in morning on arising	Rarely at night
	Relieved by eating	Relieved by vomiting
		Not relieved by eating
Vomiting	Rare	Common
Bleeding	Blood in stool (melena)	Hematemesis
State of hydration and nutrition	Usually well nourished from frequent ingestion of food	Poorly nourished, possible dehydration from vomiting

Some patients alternate these two drugs to prevent problems in elimination. Camalox is a mixture of the two but also contains small amounts of calcium carbonate, which stimulates acid secretion. Antacids can affect the absorption of some drugs; therefore they should be given 1 to 2 hours before or after other drugs. In the event of constipation or diarrhea, the patient should consult his physician. No cathartics should be taken unless prescribed by the physician because they increase peristaltic activity.

Anticholinergics, such as methantheline (Banthine) and propantheline (Pro-Banthine), may be prescribed with antacids because they block stimulation from the vagus nerve, which causes the secretion of hydrochloric acid. They also decrease gastric motor activity and permit antacids to remain in the stomach longer. Anticholinergics should be used with caution, however, because they can cause gastric obstruction.[3]

The introduction of cimetidine (Tagamet) in the late 1970s brought about dramatic results in treating ulcers. Cimetidine and ranitidine (Zantac) are antihistamines; they act by blocking the action of the histamine H_2 receptors, thereby inhibiting the secretion of hydrochloric acid. These drugs relieve the pain and promote healing of the ulcer. Their effectiveness in treating ulcers has greatly reduced the need for surgical intervention. Because antacids can decrease the absorption of cimetidine, they should not be given concurrently.

It is generally agreed that smoking, caffeine, and alcohol should be eliminated by the patient with an ulcer. Smoking reduces the bicarbonate content of pancreatic juice, which is the neutralizer of gastric acid in the duodenum. An extremely tense patient may be better off smoking than trying to quit, but there are few who fall into this category. Both regular coffee and decaffeinated coffee stimulate acid output. Tea, cocoa, cola, and chocolate also contain caffeine and should be avoided. Alcohol reduces the ability of the mucosa to resist the effects of gastric secretions. It should be avoided while the ulcer is healing and taken only occasionally after the ulcer has healed. An ounce of liquid antacid taken ½ hour before a drink will limit its effect on the mucosa.

Mucosal resistance is also reduced by many medications, including acetylsalicylic acid (aspirin), steroids, phenylbutazone, reserpine, indomethacin, and many over-the-counter drugs containing aspirin. Aspirin may also act as an anticoagulant and precipitate hemorrhage at the ulcer site. The patient must be alert to avoid medications that contain aspirin and should be taught to read labels thoroughly for ingredients.

Complications

The major complications occurring in peptic ulcer are hemorrhage, perforation, and obstruction. When a large hemorrhage occurs, measures are taken to control the bleeding and to restore the volume of circulating fluid. The patient is transfused with whole blood or plasma, and intravenous fluids are administered to maintain urinary output and electrolyte balance. The patient may be given tranquilizing agents or barbiturates to relieve restlessness and apprehension.

A nasogastric tube is inserted to remove acid and the protein load from the stomach, prevent nausea and vomiting, and monitor blood loss. While the tube is in place, the patient will need

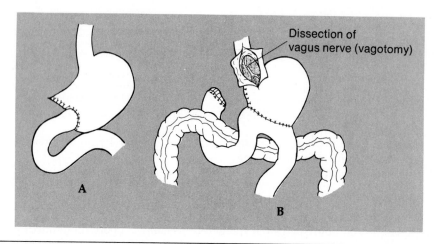

Dissection of
vagus nerve (vagotomy)

A

B

Figure 18-11

Types of gastric resections and anastomoses. **A,** Billroth I partial gastric resection with anastomosis of remaining segment of stomach to duodenum. **B,** Billroth II partial gastrectomy with anastomosis of stomach to jejunum. Duodenum has been closed. Vagotomy is often performed in conjunction with either of these procedures.

frequent mouth care and cleansing and lubrication of the nostril through which the tube is passed. The tube must be checked frequently to see that it is patent and draining. All intake and output should be recorded with a description of the color and consistency of the gastric drainage. Nothing is given by mouth to promote physiologic rest for the stomach and avoid further irritation. Fluids and electrolytes will be given per intravenous infusion. Because gastric drainage removes fluids and electrolytes from the body, the nurse must be alert for signs of fluid and electrolyte imbalance. Dry skin, oliguria (urine output of less than 30 ml per hour), and hypotension indicate a deficit in fluid volume (hypovolemia). Shallow respiration could indicate metabolic alkalosis, and muscle weakness may be a sign of potassium and sodium deficiencies.

Gastric perforation occurs when an ulcer erodes through the wall of the stomach or the duodenum and the contents from the stomach are released into the peritoneal cavity. The result may be peritonitis. Emergency surgery is required to close the perforation. The gastric contents that have escaped into the peritoneal cavity are aspirated by suction during the operation. A solution containing antibiotics may be placed in the abdominal cavity before the abdomen is closed. Surgical procedures include gastrectomy (gastric resection), vagotomy (resection of the vagus nerve to decrease stomach function), and antrectomy (removal of a large amount of the acid-secreting

mucosa of the stomach) or vagotomy and pyloroplasty (enlarging of the pyloric sphincter to allow reflux from the duodenum).[9,15]

Another complication is obstruction of the pyloric sphincter, which results from scarring and fibrosis caused by the healing or breakdown of an ulcer. The muscle becomes spastic, edematous, and stenosed, gradually obstructing the passage from the stomach to the pylorus. Surgery is usually required to relieve the condition, and vagotomy with pyloroplasty is the procedure most often employed.[6]

Gastric resection (gastrectomy)

Peptic ulcers that do not respond well to medical management, and chronic peptic ulcers may be treated surgically by performing a gastric resection, or **gastrectomy.** A total or subtotal gastrectomy may be done, and several different types of surgical procedures may be used (Figure 18-11). Usually, the ulcer and a large amount of acid-secreting mucosa of the stomach are removed (antrectomy), and the remaining portion of the stomach is anastomosed to the small intestine (gastroenterotomy). The remaining portion of the stomach may be joined to the duodenum (Billroth I) or jejunum (Billroth II). A patient whose duodenum is deformed as a result of a duodenal ulcer will require the remainder of his stomach to be joined to his jejunum, whereas a patient whose duodenum is normal may have the remainder of his stomach joined to his duodenum.

A vagotomy may be done at the same time. This procedure includes resection of the vagus nerve, and secretions of hydrochloric acid and gastric motility are lessened. The more extensive surgical procedures, such as gastrectomy, produce side effects such as the dumping syndrome. A vagotomy with a pyloroplasty or segmental resections are used because of the lower incidence of side effects and a low ulcer recurrence rate.

The patient who is about to have a gastrectomy has probably been ill for a long time and feels discouraged and worried, often fearing that the condition may be cancer. During this time an explanation of the various treatments and procedures and the reasons for them will help relieve his tension and apprehension. During the preoperative period the patient is encouraged not to smoke and is given an explanation of what to expect postoperatively.

Postoperatively the patient will have a nasogastric tube connected to suction siphonage and is given nothing by mouth for 24 to 48 hours. Drainage from the gastric tube should be watched carefully. Initially, the drainage may be bright red, but this changes to dark brown or dark red within 6 to 12 hours after surgery. Within 24 to 36 hours the drainage becomes greenish-yellow, indicating normal secretions containing bile. If large amounts of bright red blood continue, the physician should be notified.[9] Dressings have to be watched also for any evidence of bleeding, which should be reported promptly. The nurse should check the suction frequently to be sure that it is working properly because distention of the stomach will strain the suture line. Vomiting usually indicates obstruction or kinking of the drainage tube in the stomach; the surgeon should be notified immediately. The nurse should never try to reposition the tube because it may damage the suture line or the anastomosis. There may be an order to irrigate the tube with 30 ml of normal saline to keep the tube open. No irrigation should be done unless ordered.[9] Intravenous fluids are given to maintain fluid balance in the body. All intake, including fluids, output, including gastric drainage, must be measured and recorded. Mouth care and care of the nares about the tube must have frequent attention.

The tube is removed when peristalsis returns and sutures begin to heal. The nurse assists the physician in determining the return of peristalsis by listening for bowel sounds with a stethoscope and by questioning the patient about passing flatus. Oral fluids, beginning with water, may be started before the tube is removed; if so, the tube is clamped during and shortly after oral intake. Diet is gradually resumed on the physician's order, usually beginning with small, frequent feedings, increased as tolerated by the patient. Any feelings of fullness, nausea, or vomiting should be reported.

When a total gastrectomy is performed, the entire stomach is removed and the small intestine (jejunum) is anastomosed to the esophagus. Patients having this procedure must be given injections of vitamin B_{12} for most of their life. The stomach mucosa secretes the intrinsic factor that is essential for the absorption of this vitamin from the intestinal tract; without it, no vitamin B_{12} will be absorbed. In addition, the patient must eat small, frequent meals. A complication that occasionally occurs is the dumping syndrome, which includes a sensation of nausea, weakness, and faintness after meals, frequently accompanied by profuse perspiration and palpitations and a sense of fullness in the epigastric area. It is believed that these symptoms may be caused by the rapid emptying of large amounts of food and fluid through the gastroenterostomy into the jejunum, rather than passing through the entire stomach and the duodenum before entering the jejunum. The intestinal contents are more hypertonic than they would be if they had passed through the entire stomach and the duodenum, and they attempt dilution by drawing fluid from the circulating blood volume into the intestine, consequently reducing the blood volume and producing a syncope-like syndrome. This may occur after many of the surgical procedures used to treat gastric ulcer, and approximately 20% of patients experience this reaction after gastric surgery.[6]

Dumping generally subsides within 6 months to 1 year and may be avoided by eating frequent small meals, avoiding chilled foods and fluids, lying down after meals, reducing carbohydrate in the diet, and taking fluids between meals rather than with meals. The physician may prescribe sedatives and antispasmodics to delay gastric emptying.

On discharge from the hospital the patient should be given instructions concerning diet and the importance of eliminating irritants such as coffee, alcohol, tobacco, and aspirin. Foods that contain many spices are usually prohibited. The patient needs to follow a regimen that is relatively free from tension.

If the patient has a gastrostomy tube, the nurse must be careful when changing dressings to keep those around the tube separate from those around the wound. The tube must be handled carefully to avoid displacement.

Hernia

A hernia, commonly referred to as a rupture, is the projection of a loop of an organ, tissue, or structure through a congenital or acquired defect. Most hernias have their origin in the abdomen.

The most common type of hernia is the umbilical hernia, which is frequently seen in infants as the result of a congenital weakness of the abdominal wall. A femoral hernia is more common in women, and an inguinal hernia is more common in men. Another type of hernia, **hiatus** (hiatal) **hernia**, is the projection of the stomach or the intestines through the diaphragm into the thoracic cavity (see next section). If the protruding structure can be returned by manipulation to its own cavity, it is called a reducible hernia. If it cannot, it is called an irreducible or incarcerated hernia. The size of the defect through which the organ passes largely determines whether or not the hernia can be reduced.

When the blood supply to the structure within the hernia becomes occluded, the hernia is said to be strangulated and gangrene may result, requiring immediate surgery. In some cases an incarcerated hernia may be reduced by elevating the foot of the bed and administering a narcotic to the patient to relieve pain. If the patient cannot reduce the hernia or if pain continues after reduction and the incarceration has existed for 6 hours, surgery is usually recommended. The treatment of choice for all hernias is surgery; however, sometimes surgery is inadvisable because of the patient's condition or some other reason. For such persons a mechanical appliance called a *truss* may provide some relief.

Surgery

The surgical procedure for repair of a hernia is called **herniorrhaphy** (Figure 18-12). To prevent recurrence of the hernia and facilitate closure of the defect, a *hernioplasty* may be performed, using fascia, filigree wire, mesh, or a variety of plastic materials to strengthen the muscle wall.

The preoperative care for the repair of a hernia is the same as that for any uncomplicated abdominal surgery. Postoperative care includes prevention of wound infection and avoidance of any

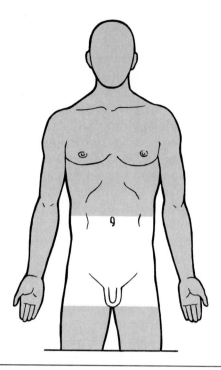

Figure 18-12

Area of skin to be prepared for herniorrhaphy.

strain on the wound for approximately 2 weeks. Early ambulation is encouraged to prevent abdominal distention. After repair of an inguinal hernia, tenderness and swelling of the scrotum may be reduced by applying ice packs. If scrotal edema does occur, the use of a suspensory may provide some relief. The urinary output should be watched because retention sometimes occurs and catheterization may be necessary. Food and fluids are usually permitted as soon as nausea ceases. If the operation is uncomplicated and progress is generally satisfactory, the patient is discharged in less than a week but is not permitted to return to work for several weeks. Children and young adults are often ambulatory on the first postoperative day, and infants and young children are often sent home the first or second day because they respond to recovery better in their home environment. If they remain in the hospital, they should be kept amused and prevented from crying, which might strain the sutures. Any evidence of abdominal distention or coughing after hernia repair should be reported to the physician immediately.[15] Some hospitals perform outpatient walk-in and walk-out surgery for simple hernia repairs and other types of uncomplicated surgery. The repair is completed in the morning, and the patient rests at home in the evening.

Hiatus (Hiatal) Hernia

The **hiatus hernia**—*hiatus* meaning, opening—is a common pathologic disorder of the upper gastrointestinal tract. It is most common in women 50 years of age or older. The disorder may be asymptomatic, or it may cause symptoms that are distressing to the patient. The diagnosis is made by esophagoscopy and barium and x-ray examination. Cytologic studies are usually made to eliminate a diagnosis of cancer.

Pathophysiology

Before entering the stomach, the esophagus passes through a small opening in the diaphragm. Under normal conditions the opening in the diaphragm encircles the esophagus securely. Thus the esophagus is held within the thoracic cavity, whereas the stomach remains in the abdominal cavity. For some reason, often congenital, the esophageal sphincter fails to remain tight, permitting the opening to become enlarged and relaxed. When this occurs, the upper portion of the stomach may protrude upward through the relaxed muscle into the thoracic cavity. Frequently this type of hernia may occur when the individual is in a prone position, and it will return to its normal position when the individual is in an upright position.

Assessment

When symptomatic, a hiatus hernia may cause the person considerable distress. The primary symptom is heartburn caused by the gastric contents of the stomach being regurgitated into the esophagus. There may be substernal pain that may radiate, simulating angina pectoris. Vomiting and abdominal distention may occur.

Intervention

Treatment includes dietary measures with small meals consisting of bland foods. Antacids may be given if symptoms are not relieved. The patient is advised not to smoke and to avoid wearing a girdle or tight-fitting belts or clothes. Sleeping with several pillows at night may provide comfort. Straining for bowel elimination, coughing, and bending are discouraged. If the condition does not respond to conservative treatment, surgery may be performed. The surgical approach may be thoracic, and the patient will have a thoracotomy and chest drainage. The surgery may be abdominal, and the nursing care is the same as that for other kinds of abdominal surgery.[9]

Hemorrhoids
Pathophysiology

Hemorrhoids (piles) are dilated veins similar to varicose veins. They may occur outside the anal sphincter as external hemorrhoids or inside the sphincter as internal hemorrhoids. The small bluish lumps characteristic of external hemorrhoids may disappear spontaneously, leaving a small skin tag. Occasionally the hemorrhoid will become thrombosed, and a blood clot will develop within the vein. In addition to hemorrhoids, anal fissures (cracks in the mucous membrane) and an anal fistula (duct extending from one tissue surface to another) may be present. Hemorrhoids result from numerous factors, including (1) prolonged constipation, (2) heavy lifting, (3) straining in an effort to defecate, and (4) pregnancy or large pelvic tumors. Certain forms of liver disease and high blood pressure may also contribute to the disorder.

Assessment

Symptoms may include an awareness of a mass in the rectum near the anus. Constipation is almost always present. Bleeding may occur and will appear as bright red blood that is not mixed with feces. The dilated veins may become thrombosed, causing severe pain. Although hemorrhoids rarely become malignant, bleeding and constipation are symptoms of cancer of the rectum. For this reason, all patients with these symptoms should have a thorough examination to rule out cancer, including a sigmoidoscopy and barium enema. Hemorrhoids do not cure themselves, and medical or surgical care is necessary.

The patient with rectal disorders has special problems in that "piles" have been a subject of jokes and laughter for decades. Individuals have been reluctant to talk about the problem and even to seek medical care. When bleeding occurs, severe anemia may result unless medical care is obtained.

Intervention

When the patient presents himself for examination, the nurse should be aware that this has been a difficult decision for him and should assure him of absolute privacy and protect his self-respect. Medical treatment of the patient with hemorrhoids consists of warm compresses to stimulate circulation and healing and analgesic ointments such as dibucaine (Nupercaine). Sitz baths help to reduce pain and edema, and bulk stool softeners such as Metamucil or Fiber-con, bran and other natural food fibers are recommended to assist in the passage of fecal material. Steroid suppositories may be given to relieve inflammation. External hemorrhoids may be excised in the physician's office. Internal hemorrhoids occasionally are treated with injection of a solution that will cause sclerosing or hardening of the dilated vein. This causes the vein to shrink and adhere to underlying muscles as it heals with fibrous tissue. Internal hemorrhoids may also be treated by ligating them with rubber bands. Tight bands are applied with a special instrument in the physician's office, causing constriction, necrosis, sloughing, and scarring.[2] Fixation to underlying muscle is also accomplished with infrared photocoagulation, in which the tissue is destroyed by creating a small burn causing inflammation and scarring cryotherapy destroys the tissues by freezing. The Nd-YAG laser is also used for fixation and excision of hemorrhoids.

Hemorrhoidectomy

Standard treatment involves surgical excision of the hemorrhoid (hemorrhoidectomy), leaving the wounds open or closed (Figure 18-13). A laxative may be given before surgery. After surgery the patient is often positioned on his stomach, but he may lie on his back with a support under the buttocks. Although this surgery is not considered a major procedure, pain may be acute, and narcotics may be given and analgesic ointments applied. Sitz baths are given to relieve pain and promote healing. If a spontaneous bowel elimination does not occur within 3 days, an oil retention enema may be given, followed by a cleansing enema. Dressings may or may not be used. Vital signs should be checked frequently for the first 24 hours to rule out internal bleeding because hemorrhage is the most serious complication. Difficulty in voiding may occur, and the patient usually is allowed out of bed to urinate. Ambulation may be allowed on the night of the surgery or the next morning. A soft diet is permitted on the evening of the surgery; a full diet is given on the first postoperative day. The patient is advised to include fiber and plenty of fluids and to exercise moderately to promote regular bowel function.

Functional Disorders

Functional disorders can occur when no pathologic disease can be demonstrated. However, most functional conditions may also occur when

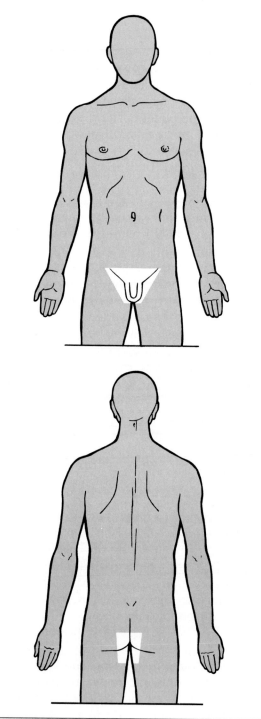

Figure 18-13
Area of skin to be prepared for hemorrhoidectomy.

there is a pathologic condition. Therefore they should not be considered lightly, and every effort should be made to determine the presence or absence of disease. These complaints can be psychosomatic, and these patients may benefit from counseling and psychotherapy.

Indigestion

Indigestion may be the result of disease somewhere in the body, but as a functional disorder, it does not have a pathologic basis. Some hypersensitive persons who are tense and anxious may become aware of normal sensations present in the stomach, usually related to the digestive process. These individuals may interpret such sensations as pain. They complain of pain in the upper abdomen, usually related to the eating of food. Such persons may describe the pain in a variety of ways and frequently attribute their discomfort to specific foods. Often these persons resort to the habitual use of sodium bicarbonate or some popularly advertised antacid, which may provide temporary relief. Treatment is based on examination to rule out the existence of disease and the encouragement of improved mental health.

Constipation

Constipation is the most common disorder of the gastrointestinal tract and is as old as the human race. Many people still believe that failure to have a daily bowel movement results in absorption of poisons, and they attribute several complaints to this "absorption of poison." There is no single cause for constipation; it may be the result of several factors, including nervous tension, faulty diet, inadequate fluid intake, lack of sufficient exercise, and inadequate toilet facilities. It must be kept in mind that constipation is a symptom of many organic diseases. During an acute illness constipation may occur because of reduced food intake and reduced intestinal motility. This type of constipation is usually relieved as soon as health returns. The patient in the hospital may repress the reflex of defecation because he does not want to ask for the bedpan or because he hates to use the bedpan. When there is delay in answering the patient's signal, the desire to defecate may also be repressed.

Constipation may occur during the latter part of pregnancy as a result of pressure on the lower bowel, or it may be a complication after delivery in the postpartum period. The patient may be able to relieve the disorder during the antepartum period by drinking more water and eating fresh fruit and vegetables and food containing roughage. Laxatives should be taken only on the physician's order.

Elderly people frequently suffer from constipation as a result of the slowing down of the digestive process and inadequate diet. Often they have a cabinet full of laxatives and fall prey to popular advertisements in an effort to have a daily bowel movement.

The treatment of constipation must be based on the type of constipation and the patient's individual needs, and the presence of possible organic disease must be ruled out. When mineral oil is administered for constipation, it should be given at bedtime to avoid interference with the absorption of the fat-soluble vitamins. Several laxatives, or stool softeners, are on the market under the trade names of Peri-Colace, Dialose, Sof-Cil, and Milkinol. Laxatives should be prescribed by the physician and should be discontinued as soon as possible.

Cardiospasm and pylorospasm

Sphincter muscles are located between the esophagus and the stomach (cardiac valve) and between the stomach and its outlet into the duodenum (pyloric valve). Normally, these muscles contract to prevent the backward flow of food material and gastric secretions and relax to allow food to enter the stomach from the esophagus and to permit the passage of food from the stomach into the duodenum. Under certain conditions these muscles fail to relax at the proper time and may contract vigorously. These severe contractions are called *spasms*. They give rise to symptoms of inability to swallow, regurgitation of food, epigastric pain, and vomiting. Spasms of the pyloric sphincter may be associated with peptic ulcer, but emotional factors are believed to be the primary cause of **cardiospasm** and **pylorospasm.** Treatment may include regulation of the diet, administration of antispasmodic and sedative drugs, and helping the individual to solve his emotional problems. If cardiospasm is severe, dilation of the constricted esophagus may be necessary.

Anal sphincter spasm

Sphincter muscles surrounding the anus and rectum relax to permit defecation. When the individual has severe hemorrhoids or fissures (cracks) in the anus or mucous membrane of the rectum, spasms of the sphincter muscles may occur. Difficult and painful defecation may then result. The treatment is correction of the cause or dilation of the sphincter muscles.

Hyperacidity

Hyperacidity, commonly called *heartburn*, may occur as the result of a pylorospasm that contributes to reverse peristalsis. The gastric juice in the stomach is forced up through the cardiac valve into the esophagus, in which it gives the characteristic burning sensation.

Psychic vomiting

Psychic vomiting occurs in persons with emotional and psychologic problems. It may occur after every meal or infrequently, particularly when the individual is faced with a tense situation. Often the amount of food vomited is small and is regurgitated rather than vomited; thus it does not interfere with the normal nutrition. However, if large quantities of food are regurgitated at frequent intervals, the individual may become malnourished. Psychic vomiting is not uncommon in children and frequently occurs after breakfast. If the child expects to face an unpleasant situation at school, it may provide a means of escape.

Air swallowing

Air swallowing is a functional condition in which the person swallows air and then belches it up with a loud noise. Persons often master the technique so well that it is impossible to detect the individual swallowing the air.

DISEASES AND DISORDERS OF THE ACCESSORY ORGANS OF DIGESTION

Diseases and Disorders of the Liver
Viral hepatitis

Viral **hepatitis** is an infectious disease that attacks the liver. It is caused by distinct but similar viruses that produce almost identical symptoms but vary in their incubation period and mode of transmission. These viruses are known as the A virus (short-incubation virus), formerly called infectious hepatitis; B virus (long-incubation virus), previously called serum hepatitis; and a third virus not yet positively identified, known as non-A, non-B. The incubation period for the A virus is 15 to 50 days, for the B virus 50 to 150 days, and for non-A, non-B the incubation time is 14 to 182 days.[2]

The source of the virus causing type A hepatitis is primarily human feces. It is spread by the oral intake of food, milk, or water contaminated with the virus. There is some evidence that the virus can also be transmitted by the parenteral introduction of the hepatitis virus through blood, blood products, or the equipment used for venipuncture or other procedures that require penetrating the skin. The virus is excreted in the feces long before clinical symptoms appear. The carrier is thought to be most infectious just before the onset of symptoms, and the victim is believed to be free of the virus within 7 to 9 days after jaundice appears.[11] It is known that an individual may have and carry the disease but not be diagnosed because it can occur in a mild form that is not severe enough to produce jaundice.[15]

The source of the virus that causes hepatitis B is the blood of persons who have the infection or who are carriers of the virus. The virus is present in semen, saliva, and blood and is transmitted by sexual contact or blood products—usually through accidental needle sticks or sharing of needles by IV drug users.[10]

The third variety of hepatitis, called non-A, non-B because it has not been positively identified, is transmitted in the blood and is the major cause of transfusion-related viral hepatitis. It is often seen in parenteral drug abusers and is common among personnel working in renal transplantation units.

Pathophysiology. A diffuse inflammatory reaction occurs, and liver cells begin to degenerate and die. As the liver cells degenerate, the normal functions of the liver slow down. Degeneration, regeneration, and inflammation may occur simultaneously and may distort the normal lobular pattern of the liver and create pressure within and about the portal vein areas. These changes may be associated with elevated serum transaminase levels, a prolonged prothrombin time, and a slightly elevated serum alkaline phosphatase level. In most instances of nonfatal viral hepatitis, regeneration begins almost with the onset of the disease. The damaged cells and their contents eventually are removed by phagocytosis and enzymatic reaction, and the level returns to normal. The outcome of viral hepatitis may be affected by such factors as the virulence of the virus, the preexisting condition of the liver, and the supportive care provided when symptoms appear.

Assessment. Symptoms may be mild or severe and include loss of appetite, fatigue, nausea and vomiting, chills, headache, and temperature that may range from 100° to 104° F (38° to 40° C). Jaundice usually appears in 4 to 7 days but may not occur before 30 days and may be absent in some patients. The temperature usually returns to normal when jaundice appears, but the an-

---

NURSING CARE GUIDELINES
Viral Hepatitis (Type A and Type B)

Nursing diagnoses

- Activity intolerance related to fatigue
- Alteration in comfort related to abdominal distention, liver tenderness, and pruritis
- Deficit in diversional activity related to prolonged bedrest and a protracted course of disease
- Alteration in nutrition (intake less than body requirements) related to anorexia, fatigue, nausea, and vomiting and altered metabolism of nutrients by liver
- Potential impairment of skin integrity related to severe pruritis
- Potential sensory deprivation related to isolation restrictions
- Disturbance in self-concept (body image) related to presence of jaundice
- Anxiety related to uncertainty of diagnosis

Nursing interventions

- Follow appropriate isolation procedures:
  Wear gown and gloves when in contact with patient or wastes
  Have patient remain in room; explain reason for isolation and the procedures to patient and family
  Use disposable dishes and utensils and double bag to discard and burn
  Double bag all linen and trash
  Keep thermometer in room and discard when patient is discharged
  Discard stool carefully in toilet unless community waste treatment system is not capable of removing this pathogen

Destroy and safely discard all needles or other materials used to puncture skin in a secure box in room
- Observe for depression resulting from elevated bilirubin; explain to patient
- Maintain bedrest, increasing ambulation as jaundice recedes
- Bathe skin, apply lotions, and administer medications as ordered to relieve itching caused by increased bilirubin; avoid soap and use warm water
- Administer oral hygiene twice daily
- Plan care to promote rest and conserve energy
- Assess food likes and dislikes; provide between meal nourishments
- Reduce light in room if patient has photophobia
- Weigh daily before breakfast
- Instruct patient on the effects and transmission of the disease
- Visit patient regularly to prevent sensory deprivation

Expected outcomes

- Afebrile
- Skin intact and free of itching
- Oral mucous membranes moist and free of lesions
- Able to select and ingest well-balanced diet
- Maintains or gains weight
- Performs activities of daily living
- Verbalizes comfort with diversional activities
- Absence of hepatitis in those in contact with patient
- Verbalizes understanding of the effects of hepatitis and the way it is spread

---

orexia and nausea persist. Children usually have a milder form of infectious hepatitis, with no jaundice and with symptoms predominantly appearing as those of an intestinal or respiratory illness. The jaundice is caused by the inability of the liver to remove satisfactorily the waste products of red blood cell destruction (bilirubin) from the bloodstream. Bilirubin is a pigment that gives bile and consequently stools their normal color. When obstruction to the elimination of bilirubin occurs, the pigment accumulates in the bloodstream and is ultimately deposited in the body tissues. It can first be detected in the whites of the eyes. The urine becomes dark as the kidney attempts to remove the excess pigment from the bloodstream.

Pruritus, abdominal pain with tenderness over the liver, and photophobia occur. The diagnosis is based on symptoms, liver function tests, and a liver biopsy, with prothrombin and clotting time tests preceding the biopsy.

Intervention. There is no specific treatment for hepatitis. Therapy is planned to strengthen the patient's resistance to the infection, and rest and a nourishing diet are primary considerations. Antibiotics may be administered to prevent secondary infection, and antihistamines may be given to relieve the itching. Fluid intake is encouraged during the acute stage, and if a sufficient amount is not taken, intravenous infusions may be given. Diet is of major importance and should provide all the necessary nutrients. Because the appetite is poor, the patient will need considerable encouragement to eat, and records of food intake should be kept. If the patient does not eat, tube feedings may be ordered.

Prevention is the most important goal in controlling hepatitis. Patients, their families, and health care providers must be knowledgable about the way in which the virus is transmitted and take the steps needed to prevent its spread.[2] All patients with hepatitis A should be advised of enteric precautions. The patient should be given a thorough explanation of the reasons for the precautions and should be instructed in the proper handling of his own secretions and body wastes and in thorough methods of handwashing. Gown and gloves should be worn when handling excreta, giving enemas, taking rectal temperatures, handling food wastes, drawing blood, disposing of urine, or carrying out any other procedure or hygiene measure that involves direct contact with the patient. The patient's urine and stool should be isolated and disposed of properly.

When the patient has hepatitis B, utmost care must be given to syringes, needles, and other instruments that are contaminated with the patient's serum. Only disposable needles and syringes should be used and health care personnel should wear gloves when performing procedures and handling equipment. A vaccine is available for hepatitis B and persons who are at high risk for developing the disease should be immunized. Health care personnel who are at high risk for contact with the disease should be vaccinated, including those in the emergency room, operating room, and intensive care units, dialysis employees, phlebotomists, and laboratory technicians.[2]

Non-A, non-B hepatitis is spread mainly through blood transfusions. Spread of this type of hepatitis is prevented by proper handling of blood products and instruments and by screening of blood before transfusion.

The patient's environment should be made as pleasant as possible. Tepid baths, rubs, and oral care are important, and a soothing lotion may provide relief from skin pruritus. The patient may be disturbed over the long illness and the resulting financial problems. The nurse should attempt to encourage the patient and help to provide diversional activities to relieve the monotony of his convalescence. With children the problems of a long convalescence may be greater, and it will require the help of everyone involved to keep them occupied and contented. Physical and emotional support are essential to recovery during this long convalescence.

A more severe course will be seen in the patient with a fulminating viral hepatitis that involves a sudden and severe degeneration and atrophy of the liver and may lead to hepatic collapse and death. Steroid therapy is instituted to attempt to reverse the process. Subacute fatal viral hepatitis causes acute massive necrosis, finally destroying enough of the liver to cause death.

Table 18-2 compares the types of viral hepatitis; the box on p. 477 summarizes nursing care of the patient with type A or B hepatitis.

Cirrhosis

Cirrhosis (scarring) of the liver is a disease in which the cells of the liver undergo degeneration and are replaced by fibrous tissue. The basic cause is not clearly understood but appears to be repeated injury to the liver cells. Although the liver cells have a great potential for regeneration, repeated scarring decreases their ability to be replaced. Cirrhosis is more common in men of middle age and later life, but it may occur in younger persons. In the United States cirrhosis as a cause of death is outranked only by heart disease, cancer, and cerebral hemorrhage in the 45- to 61-year-old age group. Several types of the disease have been identified, each with a different cause, but the final result is the same for all types. The most common form of the disease in the United States is Laennec's portal cirrhosis, which appears to be related to chronic malnutrition and alcoholism.

Pathophysiology. Cirrhosis is a disease that develops slowly and may progress gradually over a period of years. There is a slow destruction of the functional cells of the liver. As the cells degenerate, they become infiltrated with fat and the organ increases in size (fatty cirrhosis). The regenerated nodules are separated by bands of fibrous scar tissue. The process restricts the flow of blood to the organ, which contributes to its destruction. As the blood supply continues to be diminished and the scar tissue increases, the organ becomes atrophied. The damaged liver cannot metabolize protein normally; therefore protein intake may result in an elevation of blood ammonia levels.

Liver cell damage reduces the liver's ability to synthesize albumin. The progressive liver damage also obstructs the portal vein as it enters the liver. This obstruction of the circulation results in portal

Comparison of Types of Viral Hepatitis

	Type A hepatitis	Type B hepatitis	Non-A, non-B hepatitis
Other names	Infectious hepatitis, IH virus, short incubation virus	Serum hepatitis, SH virus, long-incubation virus	Hepatitis C, hepatitis D, type C hepatitis
Causative organism	Hepatitis A virus	Hepatitis B virus	Non-A, non-B virus
Mode of transmission	Fecal-oral route: oral ingestion of virus from feces, contaminated shellfish, milk, water, poor sanitation, nasopharyngeal secretions Introduction to blood via blood, blood products, contaminated venipuncture or parenteral injection needles, biting insects	Blood-borne; blood, serum, plasma, contaminated equipment used for venipuncture or parenteral injection Maternal transmission to fetus Sexual contact	Blood-borne: blood, serum, plasma, contaminated equipment used for venipuncture or parenteral injection
Incubation period	15-50 days	50-150 days	14-182 days
Immunity	Homologous	Homologous	
Severity	Most have few symptoms Not jaundiced	Severe Potential for chronic liver disease	Variable; potential for chronic liver disease
Signs and symptoms	Usually mild May not produce jaundice Headache, malaise, loss of appetite, fatigue, nausea, vomiting, chills, headache, elevated temperature Can resemble flu with respiratory and gastrointestinal symptoms	Variable; may be severe Similar to type A Jaundice usual; accompanied by dark urine and clay-colored stools and pruritus Abdominal pain, liver tenderness	Variable
Mortality	<0.5%	1%-5%	1%-3%

hypertension, or increased pressure in the veins that drain the gastrointestinal tract. This increased pressure forces fluid and albumin into the peritoneal cavity, which is called ascites. Reduced synthesis of protein and the leaking of existing protein result in hypoalbuminemia (reduced protein or albumin level in the blood), which reduces the blood's ability to regain fluids through osmosis. Protein must be present in adequate amounts to create colloidal osmotic pressure and "attract" the fluid to pass back into the blood vessels after it escapes in the capillaries. As fluid leaves the blood and the circulating volume decreases, the receptors in the brain signal the adrenal cortex to increase secretion of aldosterone to stimulate the kidneys to retain sodium and water. The normal liver inactivates the hormone aldosterone, but the damaged liver allows its effects to continue (hyperaldosteronism). Retention of fluid and sodium then results in increased pressure in the blood

vessels and lymphatic channels, adding to the problem of portal hypertension. Ascites is therefore a result of portal hypertension, hypoalbuminemia, and hyperaldosteronism.[11]

Gradually, veins in the upper part of the body become distended, including the esophageal veins, and esophageal varicosities develop that may rupture, causing severe hemorrhage. Skin lesions appear on various parts of the body (spider angiomas), which appear to be small, dilated blood vessels. Pressure on the center of the lesion causes its temporary disappearance.

Assessment. Early symptoms may include loss of appetite, nausea and vomiting, fever, and jaundice. When enough cells of the liver become involved to interfere with its function and obstruct its circulation, the gastrointestinal organs and the spleen become congested and cannot function properly. The patient loses weight and experiences diarrhea and constipation. Anemia occurs

---

NURSING CARE GUIDELINES
Cirrhosis

Nursing diagnoses

- Activity intolerance related to fatigue, anemia, weight of ascites, and peripheral edema
- Alteration in comfort related to liver inflammation and ascites
- Alteration in fluid volume (excess) related to increased intraabdominal pressure and decreased osmotic gradient
- High risk for injury related to thrombocytopenia and leukopenia and esophageal varices
- Noncompliance with diet modification and alcohol restrictions
- Alteration in nutrition (intake less than body requirements) related to anorexia, fatigue, and mouth odor
- Disturbance in self-concept (body image) related to jaundice and ascites
- Potential impairment of skin integrity related to decreased activity, ascites, and peripheral edema

Nursing interventions

- Check vital signs every 4 hours and more often if evidence of hemorrhage is present
- Observe mental status and report changes (confusion, headache)
- Assist with activities of daily living as needed to conserve energy
- Provide for adequate rest
- Give frequent, attractively served, small feedings tailored to patient's food preference and dietary restrictions
- Check tolerance for foods after each meal
- Cleanse skin, avoid soap, and apply soothing lotions to relieve pruritus
- Administer mouth care and offer mouthwash frequently

- Observe for gastrointestinal hemorrhage as evidenced by epistaxis, hematemesis, melena, anxiety, restlessness, and feeling of epigastric fullness
- Observe for edema by measuring ankles daily
- Observe for ascites by measuring abdominal girth daily
- Measure intake and output
- Weigh daily

Expected outcomes

- Select foods for a well-balanced diet that comply with any restrictions of fluid, protein, and sodium
- Explain the importance of avoiding alcohol
- Identify prescribed medications and their dosage, frequency of administration, and side effects
- State reason for avoiding over-the-counter drugs unless recommended by physician
- Identify need for rest and describe modifications of personal schedule to obtain adequate rest
- Describe methods to prevent bleeding and explain importance
- Identify situations to be avoided to prevent infection
- Demonstrate ability to monitor weight, abdominal girth, temperature, and bleeding and discuss need for daily evaluation
- Identify signs and symptoms that should be reported to physician immediately: weight gain, increased abdominal girth, elevated temperature, bleeding, bloody or tarry stools, changes in behavior or memory
- Identify date of return visit to physician or clinic

---

because of nutritional deficiency. Epistaxis, purpura, hematuria, spider hemangioma, and bleeding gums may be present. The patient becomes weak and depressed. Late symptoms include ascites, hematologic disorders, splenic enlargement, and hemorrhage from esophageal varices or other distended gastrointestinal veins. The patient may lapse into a coma, and death may occur. See above for guidelines for care of the patient with cirrhosis. A nursing care plan for a patient with cirrhosis is found on p. 490.

Intervention. Treatment varies with the symptoms and their severity, but there is no specific treatment for the disease. Diet is the one important factor; when the patient has no appetite,

it may take more than encouragement to persuade him to eat. Food should be served when the patient feels like eating.

The diet should contain enough protein for tissue repair and minimum maintenance but may need to be reduced if ammonium levels in the blood are elevated. Salt (sodium) is restricted to reduce edema and ascites, and potassium supplements may be necessary to replace potassium lost in gastric drainage and as a result of diuretic therapy. To eliminate sodium without causing potassium loss (and associated alkalosis), furosemide (Lasix) and spironolactone (Aldactone) may be given in combination. Spironolactone antagonizes aldosterone, which acts on the kidney to lose potassium while reabsorbing sodium. Chlorothiazide (Diuril) or chlorthalidone (Hygroton) are other diuretics that may be used to decrease edema and ascites. Careful records of food intake should be maintained and recorded. All fluid intake and output are measured and recorded, and the patient is weighed daily.

When ascites is present, an abdominal paracentesis may be done. (Refer to a textbook on nursing.) Also, when ascites is present, the patient may be more comfortable if he is placed in a supine position, but his position should be adjusted to afford him the greatest amount of comfort and the least respiratory embarrassment. Special attention must be given to the skin because the poor nutritional status and tissue edema may contribute to the development of decubiti (Chapter 24). Oral care should be given frequently and regularly; a mouthwash before meals may make food a little more appetizing. The patient's environment should be quiet and conducive to rest, and precautions should be taken to protect him from exposure to secondary infections.

Gastrointestinal bleeding occurs in 40% to 60% of cirrhosis patients. It may be from a lesion associated with erosive gastritis, peptic ulcer, or esophageal varices. Endoscopy must be performed to determine the cause of bleeding. Blood transfusions are given to replace blood loss and treat anemia. Hemorrhage may be treated by infusing vasopressin (Pitressin) in the area adjacent to the site of the bleeding during angiography (insertion of a catheter in the femoral artery, threaded up the aorta, past the renal arteries into the superior mesenteric artery). If the vasopressin drip does not stop or control bleeding, a Sengstaken-Blakemore tube may be inserted. This is a triple-lumen tube that has an esophageal balloon, a gastric balloon, and a gastric tube with suction openings at the tip (Figure 18-14). The tube is passed through the nose, and when it is in place, the balloons in the stomach or esophagus or both are inflated to press against the bleeding vessels and control the hemorrhage. The gastric aspiration is attached to low–Gomco-intermittent suction. When either balloon is inflated, a Levin tube is passed into the esophagus through the mouth and attached to low suction to drain the saliva that cannot drain into the stomach. The balloon must be deflated periodically to prevent necrosis. The patient is allowed nothing by mouth.

Surgical intervention. Surgery to correct complications of cirrhosis involve creating a portacaval, splenorenal, or peritoneovenous (LeVeen) shunt.

Portacaval or splenorenal shunt. The increased portal pressure found with liver disease can be reduced by surgical shunting of some of the portal blood directly into the inferior vena cava (Figure 18-15). This reduces the flow of blood through the portal system. A portacaval shunt involves the anastomosis of the portal vein to the inferior vena cava so that the liver is bypassed, whereas the splenorenal shunt requires the removal of the spleen and the splenic vein is anastomosed to the left renal vein. A more conservative procedure relieves portal pressure by adding a graft between the superior mesenteric vein and the inferior vena cava. This is elective surgery that may be only palliative in nature.

LeVeen (peritoneovenous) shunt. When diet and medication fail to control ascites, a peritoneovenous shunt, also called the LeVeen shunt,

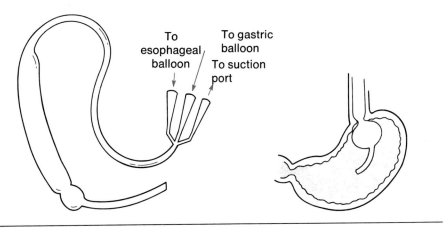

Figure 18-14
Sengstaken-Blakemore tube.

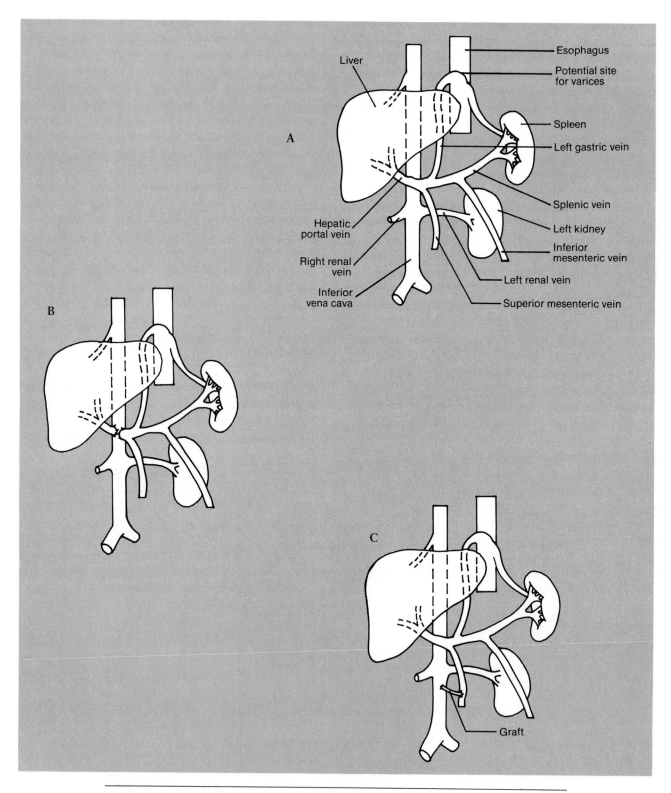

Figure 18-15

A, Normal portal circulation. **B,** End-to-side portacaval shunt. Large amount of blood is diverted from its usual route to liver and flows directly into inferior vena cava. Portal vein and vena cava are anastomosed just outside liver. Encephalopathy is a danger, since ammonia and other toxins enter systemic circulation directly instead of going to liver for detoxification. **C,** Side-to-side mesocaval shunt. In this more conservative procedure, graft is added between superior mesenteric vein and inferior vena cava to reduce blood flow to liver and reduce pressure.

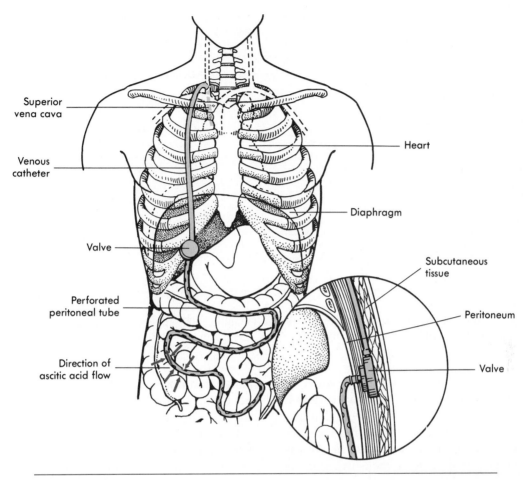

Figure 18-16

LeVeen shunt showing placement of catheter. (From Phipps, WJ, Long, BC, and Woods, NF: Medical-surgical nursing: concepts and clinical practice, ed 3, St Louis, 1987, The CV Mosby Co.)

may be performed. It is a surgical procedure in which a specially designed tube containing a one-way pressure valve is placed so that one end is in the peritoneum. The other end is threaded through the subcutaneous tissue of the chest wall and placed in the jugular vein or superior vena cava (Figure 18-16). The segment of tubing that lies in the peritoneum is perforated to allow passage of peritoneal fluid into the tubing. When the pressure valve is open, fluid enters the tubing, flows upward, and empties into the superior cava, where it is then recirculated with the blood. The valve is triggered by the patient's breathing. When the patient inhales, the diaphragm descends and causes an increase in pressure in the fluid in the peritoneum (intraperitoneal fluid pressure) and a decrease in the pressure in the superior vena cava (intrathoracic superior vena cava pressure). This change in pressure causes a pressure difference between the two locations, caus-

ing the valve to open and forcing the fluid to flow into and up the tube.

Although this procedure controls ascites, there are additional risks involved. The tube can become occluded, ascitic fluid can leak from the incision site, and the blood can become too diluted. As with any surgical procedure, there is a risk of wound infection, and the candidate for a LeVeen shunt is predisposed to infection because of general debilitation and a poor nutritional state.[11]

Hepatic coma

Hepatic coma is a degenerative condition of the brain that follows liver failure. It is thought to be the result of increasing levels of ammonia in the bloodstream, which results in hepatic encephalopathy. Symptoms progress from inappropriate behavior, confusion, flapping tremors, and twitching of the extremities to stupor and coma.[2]

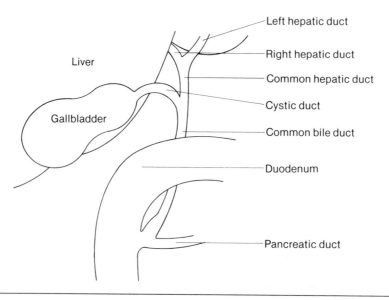

Figure 18-17

Biliary system: gallbladder and ducts. (From Bonaparte, BH, editor: Gastrointestinal care: a guide for patient education, New York, 1981, Appleton-Century-Crofts.)

Intervention. The underlying cause must be treated and the patient given supportive care that will prevent further damage to the liver. The patient should receive the supportive care necessary for any patient who has liver disease or who is unconscious. However, special measures such as central venous monitoring and tracheostomy care may be necessary. The kidney output should be watched carefully because renal failure may occur. Intravenous infusions and intermittent positive-pressure breathing therapy may be given. Drugs that are normally detoxified by the liver are avoided, but medications that stimulate the removal of ammonia from the bloodstream through the kidney may be administered, along with antibiotics to prevent infection. Hemodialysis may be used to remove the ammonia from the blood.

Diseases and Disorders of the Biliary System

The **biliary system** consists of the gallbladder and the ducts leading from the liver to the gallbladder and then to the duodenum. About 1 L of bile per day is formed in the liver and excreted into the left or right hepatic ducts, which merge to become the common hepatic duct (Figure 18-17). Bile passes through the hepatic duct to the cystic duct leading to the gallbladder, where it is stored and concentrated. When needed for digestion, bile is released from the gallbladder into the cystic duct, flows through the common bile duct, and empties into the duodenum. Bile salts are the metabolically

active components of bile. In the intestine, they act on fat to make it more soluble and to break it up into tiny particles that can pass through the intestinal wall. Cholesterol and lecithin in bile keep bile salts in suspension. Bile facilitates the absorption of fat-soluble vitamins, iron, and calcium and activates the release of pancreatic and intestinal enzymes.

Disorders of the biliary system are common in the United States and are responsible for the hospitalization of more than one-half million people per year.[11] Disorders include tumors (which are rare), infections, congenital malformations, and the two most common conditions—cholecystitis (inflammation) and cholelithiasis (stone formation).

Cholecystitis

Cholecystitis is an inflammation of the gallbladder. It is more common in women than men, and sedentary, obese persons are more likely to be affected. The incidence increases with age, becoming highest in persons in their 50s and 60s.

Pathophysiology. Cholecystitis can be caused by an obstruction, a gallstone (cholelithiasis), or a tumor. A large variety of organisms may contribute to acute gallbladder disease. Because the bile cannot leave the gallbladder, more water is absorbed, and the bile becomes more concentrated and irritates the walls of the gallbladder. A typical inflammatory response occurs, and the

---

Biliary System Terminology

chole Pertaining to bile.

cholang Pertaining to bile ducts.

cholangiography X-ray examination of bile ducts.

cholangitis Inflammation of a bile duct.

cholecyst Pertaining to the gallbladder.

cholecystectomy Removal of the gallbladder.

cholecystitis Inflammation of the gallbladder.

cholecystography X-ray examination of the gallbladder.

cholecystostomy Incision and drainage of the gallbladder.

choledocho Pertaining to the common bile duct.

choledocholithiasis Stones in the common bile duct.

choledochostomy Exploration of the common bile duct.

cholelith Gallstone.

cholelithiasis Presence of gallstones.

---

gallbladder becomes enlarged and edematous. Chronic inflammation results in thickening of the walls, which become fibrous, replacing normal muscle and mucosal tissues. This can further affect the ability of the gallbladder to empty and concentrate bile. As the tissues of the gallbladder become damaged, bacteria or other irritants can become trapped and contribute to a chronic inflammatory process. There is danger of rupture of the gallbladder and spread of infection to the hepatic duct and liver. When the disease is severe enough to interfere with the blood supply, the gallbladder wall may become gangrenous.

Assessment. The condition may be acute, with a sudden onset of nausea and vomiting and severe pain in the right upper quadrant of the abdomen, or chronic, evidenced by several milder attacks of pain and a history of fat intolerance. The attacks may be so mild the patient avoids medical attention until he develops jaundice or severe pain from obstruction in the biliary ducts. A fibrous gallbladder cannot be seen with a cholecystogram, even after a double dose of contrast medium.

Intervention. Treatment usually requires surgical removal of the gallbladder (cholecystectomy), but some physicians prefer to wait until the acute infection subsides. Others prefer to operate immediately to avoid the risk of rupture and subsequent peritonitis. If treated medically, the patient is given nothing by mouth; a nasogastric tube is passed and attached to suction if vomiting is present; intravenous glucose, electrolytes, and antibiotics are administered; and meperidine may be given for pain. When the attack subsides, a diet low in fat is resumed. Nursing intervention includes monitoring fluid balance and vital signs, observing for symptoms, and relieving pain. If surgery is planned, routine preoperative nursing care for abdominal surgery is ordered.

Cholelithiasis

Cholelithiasis is the presence of stones in the gallbladder. About 10% of the people in the United States have stones in the gallbladder, and about 6000 people die each year as a result of this disorder. Before the age of 50 years, it is more common in women; the incidence is equal in men and women after age 50 years. It is more common in diabetic persons, women who have been pregnant, and obese people.[19]

Pathophysiology. Stones are composed primarily of cholesterol, bilirubin, and calcium. They may be large, measuring inches across, or very small stones, referred to as gravel. The cause of gallstone formation is not fully understood, and there are numerous theories. Evidence suggests that gallstones form when the bile excreted by the liver is abnormally high in cholesterol and lacks the proper concentration and proportion of bile salts. Individuals with an increased cholesterol level may be predisposed to the formation of gallstones. When the balance of cholesterol, lecithin, and bile salts is disturbed, precipitation of bile salts may cause the formation of gallstones. Stasis of bile from delayed emptying may result in excess saturation of bile with cholesterol and promote the precipitation of bile salts. Infection can create an area of irritation that may become a site for stone formation. Inflammation may cause gallstones, and stones may also cause inflammation.

Assessment. Symptoms result from the inflammation in the gallbladder and the presence of stones. Pain is located under the right rib cage in the upper right quadrant of the abdomen and may radiate to the right shoulder. The gallbladder can be palpated for assessment. Decreased flow of bile produces fat intolerance and the symptoms of abdominal distention, nausea and vomiting, and flatulence. Symptoms may first appear after ingestion of a heavy meal containing fatty foods. If the disease is severe, the pain and tenderness are increased, with elevation of temperature, increased pulse and respiratory rates, and an increase in the number of leukocytes. The cholesterol level will be elevated.

Pain is more severe when the bile passages are obstructed by a stone. The pain may be referred to the back and right shoulder and may last for several hours; it is usually accompanied by nausea and vomiting and profuse perspiration. The patient may be jaundiced. The patient is usually scheduled for a cholecystography to confirm the presence of stones.

Intervention. Some mild attacks of cholelithiasis may be treated medically. Antispasmodic drugs may be given, a nasogastric tube is inserted and attached to suction, and intravenous fluids are administered. After the acute phase a low-fat, low-cholesterol diet may be ordered.

Traditionally, cholelithiasis has been treated primarily by surgical removal of the gallbladder, or cholecystectomy. While this remains the treatment of choice, other options are available for some patients. Extracorporeal shockwave lithotripsy and dissolution with bile acids are being used with increased frequency.

Extracorporeal shockwave lithotripsy

Extracorporeal shockwave lithotripsy (ESWL) is the application of shockwaves to bombard and disintegrate the gallstone. Oral dissolution therapy is prescribed for many patients after ESWL to dissolve the remaining fragments. With the use of ESWL, recovery time and patient discomfort are significantly reduced. A major drawback of ESWL is the likelihood of recurrence of the gallstones. Because the procedure is new, further studies are needed to validate this.[19]

Oral dissolution therapy

Oral bile acids, chenodeoxycholic acid and ursodeoxycholic acid (UDCA), currently are used to dissolve small cholesterol gallstones. Taken in pill form, this form of treatment is used alone or in conjunction with extracorporeal shockwave lithotripsy. It is very expensive, ranging from $1300 to $1600 per year and may need to be continued for up to 2 years. There is a high (up to 40%) incidence of recurrence of the stones over a 5-year period.[16]

Cholecystectomy

Surgical removal of the gallbladder (**cholecystectomy**) is indicated when the patient has chronic or acute cholecystitis or cholelithiasis. Careful evaluation and examination of the patient's general condition must precede the surgery. If the patient is over age 40 years, an electrocardiogram is done; if jaundice is present, tests of liver function and prothrombin time are ordered. Other preoperative testing and care is the same as that for any abdominal surgery.

In cholecystectomy an incision is made just under the ribs in the right upper quadrant of the abdomen (right subcostal incision). The gallbladder is excised from the posterior liver wall. The physician can also explore the common bile duct (choledochostomy). After common duct exploration a T tube is inserted to allow adequate bile drainage during healing of the duct. It also provides a route for postoperative cholangiography if desired (T-tube cholangiogram). The T tube is placed in the common bile duct with one arm directed toward the hepatic duct and the other toward the duodenum. A Jackson-Pratt or Penrose drain is often inserted and brought out through a stab wound to provide an escape route for drainage caused by inflammation of tissues in the operative area. The drain is removed when drainage stops.

A recent innovation in cholecystectomy involves the use of the laser and the laparoscope. Laser laparoscopic cholecystectomy can reduce a patient's hospital stay to 48 hours and recovery time to a few days. The large abdominal incision is avoided because the gallbladder is visualized through a laparoscope inserted through a small incision in the navel. The scope acts like a television camera, projecting a magnified view of the abdominal organs on a color-video screen. The laser and other instruments are introduced into the abdomen through three tiny openings. The gallbladder is grasped with a forceps; the bile is aspirated with a needle; and the organ collapses. It is detached with the laser and removed through the laparoscope. If stones are present, they are removed before the gallbladder is detached. The laser seals the operative area and adhesive strips close the tiny opening. The incision in the navel is closed with a single suture. Eliminating the large incision results in less pain, less blood loss, rapid return of bowel function, and prompt return to normal food intake. It is considered an option for patients with chronic pain but not for those with acute cholecystitis.

Postoperative intervention. Vital signs must be monitored and dressings observed frequently and carefully for drainage or hemorrhage. The

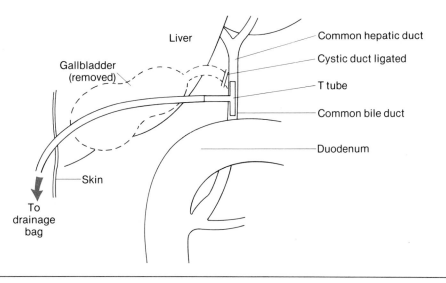

Liver

Gallbladder
(removed)

Common hepatic duct

Cystic duct ligated

T tube

Common bile duct

Duodenum

Skin

To
drainage
bag

Figure 18-18
T tube in common duct.

dressings will usually require reinforcement at the drain site. The patient is placed in the Fowler's position to facilitate drainage; he or she should be helped if necessary to turn frequently and perform leg exercises to prevent embolism. Deep breathing and coughing are important, and the patient will need considerable encouragement because of the location of the incision. He or she will tend to avoid deep breaths because expansion of the rib cage and chest wall will be painful. The nurse can assist by splinting the incision with a towel or small pillow. Respiratory therapy or the use of an inspiration spirometer are ordered to ensure adequate lung ventilation and expansion. Pain medication should be given frequently in the early postoperative period to facilitate movement and deep breathing. The patient is usually dangled the night after surgery and ambulated the first postoperative day. An abdominal binder may be ordered to provide support during ambulation.

Fluid balance is maintained with intravenous therapy; potassium is usually added to compensate for loss from surgery. A nasogastric tube is usually inserted and connected to suction to prevent nausea, vomiting, and abdominal distention. The nurse should be sure the tube is draining properly, and if it becomes obstructed, it may be irrigated with physiologic saline solution. Usually, 30 ml of solution is sufficient to determine its patency. The patient is given nothing by mouth while the nasogastric tube is in place, although sips of water or ice chips may be allowed to keep the mouth moist. The nurse should check the phy-

sician's order before giving ice or fluids to the patient, and the patient should be allowed to rinse the mouth frequently. Glycerin or petroleum jelly should be applied to the lips, and the nostril through which the tube is passed should be cleansed and lubricated.

Dressings are reinforced until the physician gives an order for them to be changed. Dressings may have to be changed frequently to keep the patient comfortable and prevent excoriation of the skin. Montgomery straps should be used to prevent skin irritation from frequent removal of adhesive tape. A small, closed drainage pouch may be applied to the drain site to collect drainage and protect the skin. The physician may have placed a hemovac drain in the surgical site.

If a T tube has been inserted in the common bile duct, the long segment of the tube is brought out to the skin through a small stab wound and sutured to the skin (Figure 18-18). The site of the T tube should be observed carefully. A large amount of bile staining the dressing could indicate leakage around the T tube and/or blockage of the tube. The T tube is attached to drainage. Bile will flow into the bag instead of down the common bile duct if the bile duct is edematous. Positioning the drainage bag at the abdominal level rather than at a lower point will create more resistance for the flow of bile into the bag.[19] Bile will only flow into the bag if the resistance in the common duct is greater. The greater the edema, the greater the resistance in the common duct. If positioned at the abdominal level, it is secured by pinning it to tape applied to the skin. Otherwise, the weight of the bag would pull on the long tube and cause tension on the insertion site in the common duct. The bag must be positioned so the tube is not kinked, otherwise bile will not be able to drain from the liver. The position of the bag and tube and the color and amount of drainage must be checked at frequent intervals during the first 24 hours and recorded. The tube must be emptied as often as necessary to keep it no more than one-half full. The T tube should drain 300 to 500 ml in the first 24 hours after surgery. This amount will decrease as edema decreases because the bile will then flow to the duodenum; it should be less than 200 ml by the fourth day. After oral intake is resumed, the physician may order the tube clamped for about 1 hour during meals to aid in the digestion of fat. The T tube is left in place for about 10 days, but some patients are discharged from the hospital with the tube. The physician will remove the tube when the common bile duct is patent for drainage of bile. The patient must be observed for jaundice, as evidenced by yellowing of the skin, sclera, and mucous membranes. Dark-colored urine and lack of color in the stool indicate an obstruction in the biliary ducts. These symptoms should be reported to the physician immediately.[15] If the patient was jaundiced before surgery, there should be a clearing of the skin, sclera, and mucous membranes, and the stool and urine should return to normal color.

Bowel sounds should be checked at least daily to determine the return of peristalsis. A clear-liquid diet is usually ordered 24 to 48 hours after surgery and increased as tolerated. Some physicians wait for the return of bowel sounds to begin the patient on a clear liquid diet, whereas others believe the clear-liquid diet will encourage the return of peristalsis, which is also facilitated by ambulation.

When a solid-food diet is started, it will usually be low in fat. Many patients who were troubled with flatulence or nausea after eating certain foods will continue to experience these problems after a cholecystectomy. The patient should be instructed to experiment with different foods, trying small amounts of those that previously caused discomfort and gradually eliminating those that continue to do so.

Throughout the postoperative period the patient must be observed for complications. Jaundice will appear if the common duct is occluded by stones or there is stricture of a duct. A decrease

in blood pressure and a rise in the pulse rate indicate hemorrhage. Dressings must be observed for hemorrhage and leakage of bile. An elevated temperature could indicate peritonitis or wound infection. Pancreatitis may occur following cholecystectomy. There is also the discouraging possibility that the symptoms experienced before surgery will return. This may be caused by another stone in the ducts, but sometimes the cause cannot be identified.

At the time of discharge, the patient should be instructed on any restriction in activity or diet. The diet is usually low in fat. The patient should be able to describe the restrictions and identify the signs of complications that should be reported to the physician.

The boxed material shown at right outlines the nursing care guidelines for the patient who has undergone conventional cholecystectomy, cholecystostomy, or choledochostomy (see following sections). This would be modified for the patient undergoing laser laparoscopic cholecystectomy.

Cholecystostomy

A cholecystostomy is an opening into the gallbladder. It is usually considered a temporary measure and may be performed if the patient cannot tolerate a cholecystectomy. An incision is made in the fundus (the top, rounded section) of the gallbladder. The gallbladder is then emptied of stones, and a tube with a large lumen is sutured into the gallbladder for drainage during the postoperative period.

Choledochostomy

A choledochostomy is the opening and exploration of the common bile duct, usually performed to remove stones. A T tube is inserted for drainage, as already described for cholecystectomy. The procedure is usually performed in conjunction with a cholecystectomy.

Diseases and Disorders of the Pancreas
Pancreatitis

Inflammation of the pancreas often occurs when chronic gallbladder disease is present. However, many persons who develop **pancreatitis** have no other illness, and the exact cause is unknown. The condition may become chronic after several acute attacks. An acute attack may develop suddenly, with intense pain in the epigastric region, vomiting, elevation of temperature, and increased leukocyte count. In patients with a severe form of

---

NURSING CARE GUIDELINES
Cholecystectomy, Cholecystostomy, or Choledochostomy—Postoperative Care

Nursing diagnoses

- Ineffective breathing pattern related to pain and splinting of high abdominal incision
- High risk for injury related to accidental obstruction of bile drainage
- Alteration in comfort (pain) related to the abdominal incision
- Potential impairment of skin integrity related to wound drainage
- Knowledge deficit related to diet modifications, activity restrictions, and signs of biliary obstruction after discharge

Nursing interventions

- Check vital signs every 15 minutes until stable, then every 4 hours
- Assist patient to cough and to take 10 deep breaths hourly; assist to splint incision while coughing
- Turn every 2 hours
- Facilitate deep breathing and activity by relieving pain with analgesics as ordered
- Ambulate as early as permissible
- In presence of T-tube
  Maintain patency of T-tube and prevent tension on tube
  Promote T-tube drainage by placing patient in low Fowler's position, progressing to semi-Fowler's position
  Observe, describe, and record amount and character of drainage at least once every 8 hours

  Empty bag when half full
  Clamp as ordered by physician after surgery
- Maintain intravenous fluid therapy as ordered
- Maintain patency of nasogastric tube if present
- Observe for nausea, vomiting, and abdominal distention
- Observe color of skin and sclera for jaundice, indicating obstruction of the bile flow
- Note color and consistency of all stools
- Reinforce primary dressing and observe drainage; after primary dressing is removed by physician, change and apply sterile dry dressing as necessary; use Montgomery straps if drainage is profuse
- Reinforce dietary instructions for fat-restricted diet

Expected outcomes

- Afebrile
- Wound approximated, no sign of inflammation
- Vital signs stable and within normal limits
- Weight stable
- Skin, sclera, and mucous membranes clear of jaundice
- Stool and urine normal in color
- Selects and tolerates low-fat diet
- Demonstrates care of T-tube if present on discharge
- Identifies activity restrictions
- Identifies date of return visit to physician

---

the disease the pancreas may be destroyed by its own enzymes, with hemorrhage into the pancreatic tissue and the abdominal cavity. Shock then occurs, and the patient often dies.

In treating patients with simple pancreatitis, food and fluids are withheld to avoid stimulating pancreatic activity, and intravenous fluids are administered. The most common complaint is constant pain radiating to the back and both sides. The pain is treated with morphine or meperidine. When the disease becomes chronic, the gland contains scar tissue that impairs its function. Mild to severe pain continues; weakness, jaundice, and diarrhea may occur; and the patient becomes weak and debilitated. Because of continued pain and the necessity for narcotic drugs, the patient may present problems of addiction. These patients need good nursing care and emotional sup-

port. The care is the same as that for other chronic diseases.

Pancreatectomy

There is no specific surgery to cure pancreatitis. An exploratory laparotomy may be done to confirm the diagnosis and treat general peritonitis or perforation of the organ. In severe cases a partial or total pancreatectomy may be performed. If it is necessary to remove the entire pancreas, the secretion of insulin will be eliminated, and it will be necessary for the patient to take insulin for the rest of his life. The preoperative preparation of the patient is the same as that for other abdominal surgery. In addition to the routine postoperative care, the patient should be observed for complications such as peritonitis, jaundice, and intestinal obstruction. The stool should be observed for a light-colored, frothy appearance and any evidence of undigested particles of fat.

Tumors of the Accessory Organs of Digestion

Malignant or benign tumors may occur in any of the accessory organs of digestion. Tumors of the pancreas are usually malignant, and in some instances surgery may be done for their removal. Most malignant lesions of the liver are the result of metastasis from primary tumors elsewhere in the body. Treatment consists of removing the diseased lobes (lobectomy). Liver transplants are performed with variable success.

Careful preoperative preparation and expert postoperative nursing care is necessary. After sur-

gery, the patient must be constantly observed for hemorrhage, which is always a possibility. All vital signs are checked at frequent intervals. The patient will have chest tubes connected to closed chest drainage and will have a nasogastric tube connected to suction siphonage. Food and fluids are withheld for several days, and mouth care is important. Ambulation is usually delayed for several days.[15] Cancer of the gallbladder and bile ducts is rare. When it occurs, it generally begins in one of the ducts and metastasizes to the liver. Patients with cancer of the accessory organs of digestion experience loss of appetite, loss of weight, general weakness, secondary anemia, and a general feeling of discomfort (Chapter 9).

NURSING CARE PLAN
Patient with Cirrhosis

The patient is a 45-year-old male who enters the emergency department of the veteran's hospital complaining of fever, burning on urination, constipation, and general malaise. He states he began feeling poorly 3 nights ago and noticed that his "eyeballs were turning yellow just like last time." He states he gave up drinking 4 years ago. He has no known food or drug allergies.

Past medical history

History of chronic alcoholism since age 30.
Appendectomy at age 15, no other surgeries.
Pneumonia at age 40. Has smoked 1 to 2 packs cigarettes per day since age 12.
Multiple VA admissions for chronic nutritional anemia related to alcoholism.
Patient—poor historian; old records not available.

Family history

Both parents deceased, causes unknown.
Has 2 siblings, sister (with whom he lives), and younger brother who lives out of state. States he has no contact with brother.
Sister works as receptionist for lawyer, and has 2 adult children living in the home.
Family relations described as "strained."

Psychosocial data

Lives with sister since second divorce 2 years ago. Previous divorce 6 years earlier. First marriage lasted 12 years. States he supports and visits 3 daughters from first marriage (ages 13, 15, and 17.) Conflicting stories of involvement with them.

Works as a carpenter at a local insurance company. States he enjoys work and rarely misses going to work. Considers himself as a "master cabinet maker" and works with woods as a hobby.
States he has few close friends.
Attends AA meetings "when he thinks of it."
Served in the Army during Vietnam as a clerk/cook.
Denies use of drugs and/or alcohol for 4 years.

Assessment data

General: thin male who appears malnourished. Color pale.
Height 5 ft 10 in, weight 140 lbs 20% ↓ Ideal body weight (IBW).
Oriented × 3 (time, place, and person).
Skin: intact, olive coloring with some scaly patches on anterior chest (2 to 3 cm). Patient states some pruritis.
Eyes: obvious yellow sclerae. EOM intact.
Respiratory: nonproductive cough, especially in the morning.
Rales heard bilateral bases. Resp. regular rate and rhythm, 22-24.
Cardiovascular: Apical rate 78. Regular. PMI at apex. No bruits, all pulses intact.
Abdominal: soft, slight distention. Bowel sounds hypoactive (14-16), heard in all four quadrants. Liver palpable at right costal margin with firm sharp edges and small nodules.
GU: complaining of burning on urination. Urine dark amber, cloudy.
Vital Signs: T 100, P 68-72, R 20. B.P. 110/64.

Lab data	*Medications*
Hgb 9.4 Hct 29 BUN 45 SGOT 96.	Folic acid 1 mg po daily.
SGPT 52 Total bilirubin 7.2.	Feosol 120 mg BID.
Alk Phosp 20 Serum amylase 24 IU/L.	Prednisone 20 mg daily.
WBC 4500 Platelets 200,000.	Multivitamin tab 1 daily.
Electrolytes WNL.	Nembutal 100 mg po hs.
Urine ph 5.1 Specific Gravity 1.028.	Ascorbic acid tab 1 daily.
4+ albumin, many RBC, casts.	Tylenol 325 to 650 mg po prn fever/discomfort.
Urine culture—*E. coli* present.	

NURSING DIAGNOSIS

Urinary elimination pattern related to infection as evidenced by cloudy urine, burning sensation and culture of *E. coli*.

Expected patient outcomes	Nursing interventions	Evaluation for expected outcomes
Patient will maintain fluid balance; intake will equal output. Patient will voice increased comfort upon urination. Complications will be avoided. Patient will discuss the need to monitor urologic state of hygiene and will demonstrate skill in managing elimination pattern.	Observe voiding patterns. Document urine color, characteristics, I & O, and patient's daily weight. Identify patient's fluid choices (ginger ale, water, and orange juice). Force fluids up to 800 to 1000 ml per shift. Instruct patient regarding need for personal cleaning of perineal area to avoid stool contamination of urethra. Provide supportive measures as indicated (Tylenol ordered). Assist with general hygiene. Encourage patient to ventilate feelings regarding discomfort.	Patient's fluid intake will equal output. Patient expresses feelings of comfort. Patient discusses need for attention to personal hygiene and will identify daily practices of self-care. Patient does not show evidence of skin breakdown, infection, or other complications. Patient maintains urinary continence.

NURSING DIAGNOSIS

Denial related to alcoholism as evidenced by statements of abstinence for 4 years.

Expected patient outcomes	Nursing interventions	Evaluation for expected outcomes
Patient describes knowledge and perception of present health problems. Patient lists daily activities and rationale for changes. Patient expresses knowledge of alcohol abuse and cites known causative factors. Patient indicates, by conversation or behavior, an increasing awareness of reality.	Provide for a specific amount of uninterrupted noncare related time daily (Primary nurse directed). Encourage patient to express feelings related to present problem, its severity, and potential impact upon life pattern. Encourage patient to cite significant losses in his relationships, and to identify any insight into his own role in these losses. Listen to patient with nonjudgmental acceptance. Correct any gross misperceptions. Discuss "enabling" behaviors and their role in fostering his alcoholism.	Patient discusses present health problems and their relationship to alcohol abuse. Patient describes ADLs and reports any stressors that contribute to the need for a drink. Patient identifies his need to maintain consistent contact with AA members and to attend meetings on a regular basis. Patient identifies an increasing awareness of reality either verbally or through behavior.

Continued on next page.

Expected patient outcomes	Nursing interventions	Evaluation for expected outcomes
	Discuss his relationship with his sister and each daughter. Encourage honesty in his descriptions. Discuss the philosophy of AA and explore his member contacts. Identify the need for regular attendance at meetings.	

NURSING DIAGNOSIS

Noncompliance with diet modification as evidenced by less than body requirements, constipation, and urinary infection.

Expected patient outcomes	Nursing interventions	Evaluation for expected outcomes
Patient will show no further evidence of weight loss, and will take in 2200 calories daily. Patient will gain approximately 2 lbs per week. Patient (and his sister) will identify special dietary needs. Patient (and his sister) will demonstrate the ability to plan nutritionally sound diet prior to discharge.	Obtain and record patient's weight daily. Determine food preferences and provide them within the limits of planned caloric needs (high carbohydrate, high calorie, and high protein). Prefers pasta, some lean meats, salads, and fruits. Dislikes many vegetables and fiber foods (states his best meal is breakfast). Give small frequent feeds. Elevate head of bed during meals. Check tolerance for foods after each meal. Refer to dietician or nutritional support team for dietary management. Monitor bowel sounds once per shift. Teach principles of basic four food groups. Involve sister in instruction. Discuss foods high in fiber. Try to identify one that patient approves. Provide oral hygiene before meals. Discuss role of alcohol as appetite suppressant, and physiologic damage of taking drink with no food in stomach. Calorie count daily.	Patient will maintain present weight of 140 lbs and show a gradual increase of 1 to 2 lbs by the end of the week. Patient will take in between 1800 to 2200 calories per day. Patient (and his sister) will discuss the basic four food groups and list sample foods in each group. They will plan a sample diet menu for 1 week postdischarge based on proper food nutrient exchanges. Patient will continue to eat quality breakfasts and will identify foods that can be eaten for snacks.

NURSING DIAGNOSIS

Social isolation related to inadequate personal resources as evidenced by statements of "few friends," history of two divorces, and estranged relationships with brother and daughters.

Expected patient outcomes	Nursing interventions	Evaluation for expected outcomes
Patient interacts with caregivers in a positive way. Patient expresses feelings related to a lack of supportive relationships. Patient expresses a desire to be involved with others. Patient uses resources available through the agency (social services, home health care, self-improvement classes, AA) to establish a realistic plan for the future. Patient states his plan to participate in social activities not involving drinking.	Assign the same caretaker to build a trusting relationship. Plan a 15-minute period every shift to sit with patient. If he does not talk, allow silence. Involve patient in planning his own care. Maintain on bed rest while acutely ill, but monitor for quality interactions. Discuss patient's living accommodations and life-style outside of hospital. Refer to social services for follow-up if necessary. Praise sister for visiting. Inquire into past friendships that hold potential for renewal.	Patient interacts in a positive manner (eye contact, pleasant voice). Patient expresses feelings toward significant persons in his life. Patient identifies need to be involved with support groups. Patient uses available resources. Patient states a plan to participate in social activities.

REFERENCES AND ADDITIONAL READINGS

1. Anthony CP and Thibodeau GA: Textbook of anatomy and physiology, ed 12, St Louis, 1987, The CV Mosby Co.
2. Beare PG and Myers JL: Principles and practice of adult health nursing, St Louis, 1990, The CV Mosby Co.
3. Beyers M and Dudas S: The clinical practice of medical-surgical nursing, ed 2, Boston, 1984, Little, Brown & Company.
4. Bouchard R and others: Nursing care of the cancer patient, ed 4, St Louis, 1981, The CV Mosby Co.
5. Broadwell DC and Jackson BS, eds: Principles of ostomy care, St Louis, 1982, The CV Mosby Co.
6. Broadwell DC and others: Continent ileostomy and ileoanal reservoir: two surgical alternatives for patients once requiring conventional ileostomies, Point View 23(3):12–15, 1986.
7. Brunner LS and Suddarth DS: Textbook of medical-surgical nursing, ed 6, 1987, JB Lippincott Co.
8. Ford RD: Diagnostic tests handbook, Springhouse, PA, 1987, Springhouse Corp.
9. Given BA and Simmons SJ: Gastroenterology in clinical nursing, ed 4, St Louis, 1984, The CV Mosby Co.
10. Haddrey WC: Viral hepatitis today, Emerg Med 21(6):124–126, 131–136, 1989.
11. Luckmann J and Sorensen KC: Medical-surgical nursing: a psychophysiologic approach, ed 3, Philadelphia, 1987, WB Saunders Co.
12. Metheny NM and Snively WD, Jr: Nurses' handbook of fluid balance, ed 4, Philadelphia, 1983, JB Lippincott Co.
13. Nortridge JA: Helpful hints for assessing the ostomate, Nurs 82 12(4):72–77, 1982.
14. Patrick M and others: Medical-surgical nursing: pathophysiological concepts, New York, 1986, JB Lippincott Co.
15. Phipps WJ, Long BC, and Woods NF: Shafer's medical-surgical nursing, ed 8, St Louis, 1986, The CV Mosby Co.
16. Rowland GA, Marks DA, and Torres WE: The new gallstone destroyers and dissolvers, Am J Nurs 89(11):1473–1476, 1989.
17. Sheridan E, Patterson H, and Gustafson E: Falconer's the drug, the nurse, the patient, ed 7, Philadelphia, 1987, WB Saunders Co.
18. Thompson J and others: Clinical nursing, St Louis, 1986, The CV Mosby Co.
19. Vergunst H and others: Extracorporeal shockwave lithotripsy of gallstones: possibilities and limitations, Ann Surg 210(5):565–575, 1989.
20. Williams SR: Nutrition and diet therapy, ed 5, St Louis, 1985, The CV Mosby Co.

CHAPTER

19

PROBLEMS AFFECTING
the Urinary System

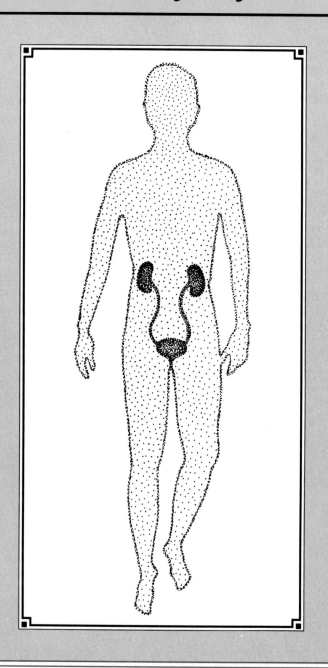

KEY WORDS

acute renal failure

anuria

blood urea nitrogen (BUN)

calculus

chronic renal failure

creatinine

cystectomy

cystitis

cystostomy

dialyzer

diuresis

diuretic

glomerulonephritis

glomerular capillaries

hematuria

hemodialysis

hydronephrosis

ileal conduit

lithiasis

micturition

nephrectomy

nephron

nephrostomy

nephrotoxic

peritoneal dialysis

polyuria

pyuria

urea

uremia

ureter

ureterotomy

urinalysis

urine osmolality

OBJECTIVES

1. Explain how the nephron forms urine.

2. Identify four hormones produced in the kidney and their functions.

3. Differentiate between routine, sterile, and clean-catch urine specimens.

4. Discuss the purpose and nursing responsibilities related to the common diagnostic tests and procedures performed on the urine, kidneys, ureters, and bladder.

5. Discuss the prevention and observation for side effects of diuretic therapy.

6. Describe the assessment of acute poststreptococcal glomerulonephritis and nursing intervention for the patient.

7. Identify methods of preventing complications and renal damage in the patient with an infection of the urinary tract.

8. Discuss nursing intervention for the patient with urinary calculi and methods of preventing their formation.

9. Compare and contrast the nursing assessment and intervention for patients with acute and chronic renal failure.

10. Explain the purpose of dialysis and differentiate between peritoneal dialysis and hemodialysis.

11. Differentiate preoperative and postoperative nursing intervention for patients with the following methods of urinary diversion: cutaneous ureterostomy and ileal conduit.

12. Identify the nursing responsibilities related to dressings, drains, and urinary drainage tubes following surgery on the urinary tract.

13. Discuss the psychosocial aspects of caring for the patient with a disorder involving the urinary system.

STRUCTURE AND FUNCTION OF THE URINARY SYSTEM

Structure
Macroscopic anatomy

The urinary system consists of two *kidneys*, two **ureters**, one urinary *bladder*, and one *urethra* (Figure 19-1). The kidneys are located in the posterior abdominal cavity, one on each side of the vertebral column and are protected and surrounded by muscles, fascia, fat, and different abdominal organs. Additionally, the posterior upper portion of each kidney is protected by ribs. A thin cellophane-like *capsule* covers each kidney and contains blood vessels, lymphatic vessels, and nerve fibers. Pain can be felt if the capsule is stretched or punctured.[18]

The **ureters** are fibromuscular, mucosa lined, narrow tubes approximately 25 to 30 mm in length that originate in the kidneys and terminate in the bladder. The urinary bladder, a muscular sac that holds approximately 300 to 500 ml of urine, is located in the pelvis between the rectum and the pubic bone. The urethra is a mucosal tube that connects the bladder to the urinary meatus. The urethra is shorter in the female, approximately 3 to 5 cm in length and longer in the male, approx-

imately 20 cm in length. Because the ureters, urinary bladder, and urethra are innervated, pain can be felt in any of these structures.[18] The kidneys produce urine that is transported unchanged via peristalsis through the ureters to the bladder, through the urethra and out the urinary meatus.

Microscopic anatomy

The structural-functional unit of the kidney is the **nephron**, and there are more than a million in each kidney. A nephron is composed of five parts: Bowman's capsule, proximal convoluted tubule, loop of Henle, distal convoluted tubule, and collecting duct (Figure 19-2). The nephron wall is one cell thick and supported by a *basement membrane* which is composed of collagen and glycoproteins.[18] The beginning of each nephron is shaped like a cup and is called *Bowman's capsule*. It surrounds a cluster of **glomerular capillaries** that are also supported by a basement membrane (Figure 19-3).

Extending from each Bowman's capsule is the *proximal convoluted tubule*. It is proximal because it is the segment nearest the tubule's origin from Bowman's capsule; it is convoluted because it is twisted. The proximal tubule narrows and becomes the descending limb of the *loop of Henle*; it later becomes the ascending limb, widens, and

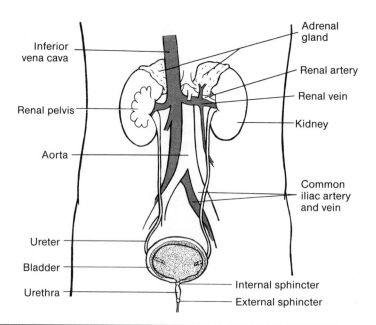

Figure 19-1

Organs of the urinary system, vasculature, and surrounding structures. The kidneys are located between the twelfth thoracic vertebra and third lumbar vertebra. The bladder is bisected to show placement of the ureter as it enters the bladder. Notice the renal vein is anterior to the renal artery.

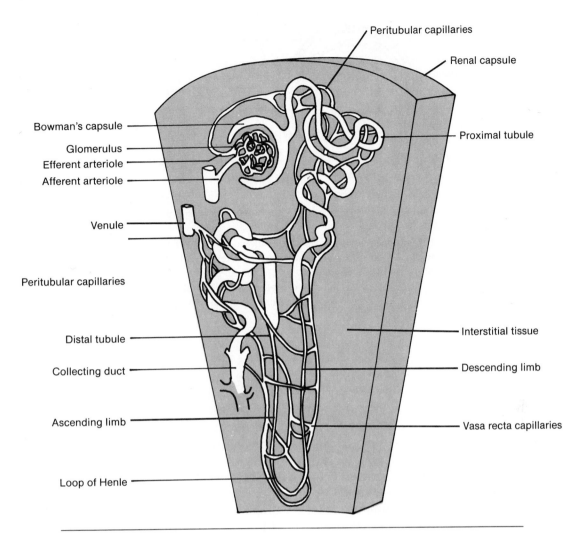

Figure 19-2

A nephron and its vasculature. The nephron is composed of Bowman's capsule, proximal tubule, loop of Henle (descending and ascending limbs), and distal tubule. Many distal tubules empty into a collecting duct. The renal capsule is the most exterior part of the kidney. Blood flows through the afferent arterioles to glomerular capillaries and the efferent arterioles divide into peritubular capillaries, which surround proximal and distal tubules, and the vasa recta capillaries, which surround loop of Henle and collecting duct. Both capillary systems return into a venule.

becomes the *distal convoluted tubule*. The distal tubule terminates in the collecting duct. Many *collecting ducts* join and form the renal calyces and subsequently the kidney pelvis. The *kidney pelvis* is small, holding 3 to 5 ml of urine. It is the last intrarenal structure before the ureter begins.

Blood flows to the kidney through the *renal artery*. This artery divides many times and eventually forms the *afferent arteriole* (Figure 19-2). The afferent arteriole divides into **glomerular capillaries** that unite to form the *efferent arteriole*. The efferent arteriole divides into two branches, the peritubular and vasa recta capillaries. The *peritu-*

bular capillaries surround the proximal and distal tubules, and the *vasa recta capillaries* surround the loop of Henle and collecting ducts. Both capillary systems drain into venules. The kidneys are very vascular and require a large blood supply for the high metabolic rate of the nephrons.

Function

The kidneys are organs of *regulation*. They regulate many substances such as water, electrolytes, nitrogenous wastes, acids, and bases; they also regulate bodily processes, such as blood pressure, through the production of urine and hormones.

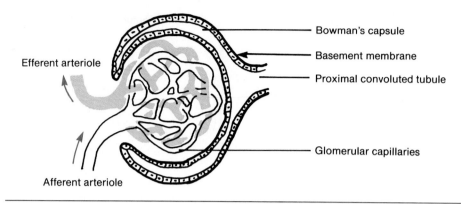

Figure 19-3

Enlarged view of Bowman's capsule and glomerular capillaries. Arrows depict direction of blood flow. Blood flows through the afferent arteriole into the glomerular capillaries where filtration occurs. The glomerular capillaries are surrounded by Bowman's capsule which becomes the proximal convoluted tubule. A continuous basement membrane supports the one-cell-thick wall of Bowman's capsule and proximal tubule.

Urine formation

There are two steps in urine formation, glomerular filtration and tubular processes.

Glomerular filtration. As blood flows through the **glomerular capillaries**, water and many substances filter from the blood, pass through the capillary wall and into Bowman's capsule (Figure 19-3). The main driving force for filtration is *hydrostatic pressure* in the glomerular capillaries. This pressure is due to systemic blood pressure that exerts a force against the glomerular capillary walls. For glomerular filtration to occur, systemic blood pressure must be maintained. If systemic blood pressure falls significantly, then glomerular filtration will decrease or even stop.

Another factor that influences glomerular filtration is the structural integrity of the glomerular capillaries and Bowman's capsule. Usually erythrocytes, leukocytes, platelets, and plasma proteins do not filter because they are too large to pass through the glomerular capillaries and Bowman's capsule. If these structures are diseased, blood cells and proteins may filter and be found abnormally in urine. *Proteinuria*, proteins in urine, is one sign of glomerular capillary disease.

The solution that is filtered through the glomerular capillaries into Bowman's capsule is termed the *glomerular filtrate*. It is composed mostly of water, electrolytes, creatinine, sugars, nitrogenous wastes, and bicarbonate. The volume of glomerular filtrate and the rate at which it is filtered is called the *glomerular filtration rate* and is approximately 125 ml/min. As glomerular filtrate

leaves Bowman's capsule and enters the proximal tubule, the second step of urine formation, tubular processes, begins.

Tubular processes. Throughout the length of the nephron, the tubular processes of reabsorption and secretion will selectively alter and reduce the glomerular filtrate to form urine. *Reabsorption* is the movement of substances from within the nephron to the surrounding capillaries (peritubular and/or vasa recta) and/or interstitial tissue, the cells between nephrons and blood vessels. *Secretion* is the movement of substances from within the capillaries and/or interstitium into the nephron. The following paragraphs briefly describe how tubular processes affect glomerular filtrate as it flows through the nephron.

In the proximal tubule approximately 60% to 70% of the glomerular filtrate is reabsorbed, and that includes water, most electrolytes, sugars, urea, and bicarbonate. Hydrogen ions and some drugs are secreted. In the descending loop of Henle, a small volume of water is reabsorbed and urea is secreted. In the ascending limb, chloride and sodium are reabsorbed.

In the distal tubule, the transport of many substances is regulated by extrarenal hormones. Aldosterone causes sodium reabsorption and potassium secretion. Chloride follows sodium. Parathyroid hormone increases calcium reabsorption and decreases phosphate reabsorption. Calcitonin decreases phosphate and calcium reabsorption. Hydrogen ions and ammonia are secreted.

The collecting duct determines the final volume and composition of urine. *Antidiuretic hormone (ADH)*, also called vasopressin, causes water reabsorption and forms a concentrated urine. Without ADH, water is not reabsorbed, and a dilute urine is excreted. **Urea** is reabsorbed and/or secreted depending on its concentration in the tissues surrounding the collecting duct.

Creatinine, an end product of muscle metabolism, is a unique substance because it is freely filtered through the glomerular capillaries but minimally affected by tubular processes. Therefore the amount of creatinine filtered is found in the urine. Because creatinine is only excreted by the kidneys, it is very useful in diagnosing and evaluating renal disorders.[18]

With acid-base imbalances, the kidneys correct changes in pH that blood buffers and lungs have started to correct. The kidneys regulate the bicarbonate level and neutralize and excrete acids. The urinary pH can vary from acidic to alkaline depending on the body's needs.

Renal hormones

The hormones that are released from the kidney and their actions are summarized in Table 19-1; renin is discussed further here. Angiotensinogen is synthesized and secreted by the liver. Renin converts angiotensinogen to angiotensin I. As angiotensin I circulates through the lung, an enzyme there converts it to angiotensin II. Angiotensin II stimulates thirst, causes peripheral vasoconstriction, decreases renin secretion, and stimulates aldosterone release. Aldosterone causes the plasma sodium level to rise by stimulating the reabsorption of sodium in the kidney, intestine, salivary glands, and sweat glands. The above system is frequently referred to as the *renin-angiotensin-aldosterone system*, and its overall goals are to maintain sodium, water, and blood pressure balances.[11,18]

NURSING ASSESSMENT

History and Physical Examination

This section highlights aspects of the history and physical examination distinctive to the urinary system. A discussion of a complete history and physical can be found in Malasanos and others.[13] Additional information on patient assessment for specific conditions is also presented in the section on Diseases and Disorders of the Urinary System. Several important nursing responsibilities associated with caring for a patient undergoing an assessment are to explain all procedures and tests and to make sure that the patient understands, to his/her satisfaction, the results of all procedures and tests.

Patient history—physical examination

Because the kidneys and ureters are located deep within the abdominal cavity, they are difficult to examine physically. It is even more difficult to obtain information about their function from a physical examination. The urinary system, however, is assessed during the abdominal part of a physical examination with the patient supine and nurse on the right side of the patient. Imagine the abdomen divided into four quadrants with the umbilicus as the center. Inspect the entire abdominal region, diaphragm to symphis pubis, from a standing position and then at eye level for raised masses. Usually these abnormalities are not present. Enlarged kidneys may be visible in the upper quadrants, and an enlarged bladder may be visible in the lower quadrants across the midline. Palpate and then percuss the abdomen. A distended bladder feels tense, smooth, round, and dull to percussion.[18]

Urinary tract pain

Pain associated with the urinary tract may be stimulated during a physical examination and can be felt from an area slightly below the ribs to the upper thighs. Typically, ureteral pain is felt in the groin or genital area, bladder pain is felt in the suprapubic to upper thigh area, and renal pain is felt at the *costovertebral angle* in the back. If the person feels tenderness or pain in any of these

Table 19-1

Renal Hormones	
Hormone	**Action**
Erythropoietin	Stimulates formation of red blood cells in the bone marrow
Kinins	Vasodilation
Prostaglandins	Renal vasodilation; some cause constriction
Renin	Converts angiotensinogen to angiotensin I
Vitamin D	Increases calcium and phosphate absorption from the intestine, bone, and kidney

areas, be as gentle as possible when touching the areas.

Unfortunately, extensive damage and even complete loss of a kidney can occur without the person feeling any pain because most of the kidney is without pain receptors. The renal capsule, however, is innervated with pain receptors, and if it is punctured, distended, or inflamed, a dull to sharp pain is felt. The rest of the urinary tract has many pain receptors and responds according to the pathologic condition. For example, a sudden obstruction, like a stone in the ureter, causes an abrupt onset of sharp pain.[17]

DIAGNOSTIC TESTS AND NURSING RESPONSIBILITIES

Urine

Collection of specimens

Methods. Urine can be collected by the clean-catch or voided-midstream method, bladder catheterization, or suprapubic aspiration of (the bladder) urine. All procedures should be thoroughly explained to the patient whether the patient, the nurse, or someone else does the collection. The clean-catch or voided-midstream method is explained first. After washing the hands, the external genitalia are washed thoroughly with soap and water. With a female the labia are separated; with an uncircumcised male the foreskin is retracted before voiding. The patient voids approximately 100 ml to wash out bacteria and leukocytes in the urethra, continues voiding, and then collects the urine in a sterile container. Only the outside of the container is touched, and it is covered as soon as the urine is voided into it.

Bladder catheterization and *suprapubic aspiration* are both invasive procedures that can cause urinary tract infections and are done when no alternative noninvasive method is available. These procedures are discussed under the section, Therapeutic Procedures. If the patient has a bladder catheter in place, a urine specimen can be collected using the aseptic technique. Newly excreted urine is taken from the drainage system, not old urine that has accumulated in the drainage bag. The exact method of urine collection can vary with the design of the drainage system, therefore read the manufacturer's instructions, but always use the aseptic technique.

Timing. If the urine cannot be taken to the laboratory immediately after it is collected, it is refrigerated. Substances in the urine change at room temperature, making the results of the urinalysis inaccurate. For example, red blood cells hemolyze, bacteria grow and consume glucose, and the pH changes. The frequency at which urine is collected depends on the requirements of the test and is explained in the next section.

Purposes. Although there are many reasons to analyze urine, this section will focus on urinalysis as it relates to structures, functions, and diseases of the urinary system. Additional information on urinalysis for specific conditions is presented in the section, Diseases and Disorders of the Urinary System.

A *routine or baseline* **urinalysis** assesses urine color, clarity, odor, specific gravity and/or osmolality, pH, glucose, ketones, proteins and related substance, sediment (which includes cells, crystals, casts, and bacteria or other microorganisms), and possibly enzymes and electrolytes. The first urine of the day is the most concentrated from an overnite fast; therefore it is the best specimen to use for a routine/baseline urinalysis especially to assess pH, osmolality, and sediment. Use the clean-catch method to collect urine. Although usually a minimum of 15 ml is required for routine urinalysis (check with the laboratory doing the test because some can do the urinalysis with less), it is helpful to send more urine so results can be double checked. If abnormalities are found, further testing can be done. Some patients with urinary tract disease may have less than 15 ml with any voiding; send what you have.

A *24-hour urine collection* can measure the total quantity of a substance or substances excreted in a day. This is helpful for substances excreted in varying concentrations throughout the day, such as hormones, creatinine, protein, urea, and glucose. A 24-hour urine collection can be started at any time using the following procedure.

1. Explain the entire procedure to the patient.
2. Prepare collection container per laboratory instructions; for example, refrigerate, add preservative, or both.
3. Designate time for collection to start. Patient voids at this time, and urine is discarded.
4. All subsequent voidings are saved. Using the clean-catch method, urine is voided into a receptacle and then poured into a collection container to prevent contamination with feces.
5. Collect the last urine specimen 24 hours from the starting time.

6. Send all urine in properly labeled containers to the laboratory immediately. If the collection is interrupted and some urine is omitted from the collection, the collection is stopped, urine discarded, and procedure restarted.

A *urine smear* and/or *culture and sensitivity* tests assess the urine for microorganisms and accompanying cells, and medications or drugs the organisms are most sensitive to. A few milliliters of urine collected by the clean-catch method and placed into a sterile container is required for these tests.

With a *serial urine collection* each voiding is saved in a separate container for a designated number of voidings, hours, days, or until some urinary characteristic is adequately assessed. For instance, after bladder surgery, hematuria (blood in the urine which appears reddish) can occur, and a serial urine collection is implemented. Each voiding is labeled, saved, and assessed for changes in **hematuria** (redness). Hopefully the redness diminishes with each voiding and the urine becomes yellow. If the hematuria persists, specific treatment is implemented. With a serial urine collection, the clean-catch method is adequate, and specimens can be assessed in a patient's room or a utility room, sent to a laboratory, or any combination of these.

Urinalysis

Urine is approximately 95% water and consists of excess water and excess substances that are end products from body metabolism. It is a valuable body fluid to assess because it tells us about renal function as well as other bodily processes.

Freshly voided urine has a slight *odor* caused by the breakdown of urea to ammonia. If urine stands for a period of time and/or has a large bacteria population, it will have a strong ammonia smell. The ingestion and excretion of certain foods, and/or medications, like asparagus, and vitamins, will also cause urine to smell differently.

The pale yellow to amber *color* of urine is due to the presence of urochrome pigments. Urine color can be changed by the presence of cells and by an increased urine concentration. The presence of red blood cells, **hematuria**, can cause urine color to range from yellow to bright red. White blood cells can make urine look whitish. Concentrated urine is usually dark yellow to orange.

Normally urine is *clear* and slightly acidic, although its *pH* range is 4.5 to 8. Urine will become cloudy and alkaline upon standing because of the breakdown of urea to ammonia, which increases the pH. Cloudiness can result from the presence of cells, bacteria, crystals, casts, or fat substances.

The kidneys are significant in regulating overall body fluid balance. They will excrete a concentrated urine when water needs to be conserved or a dilute urine when there is an excess of water. A measure of the kidneys' ability to concentrate or dilute urine is **urine osmolality** and ranges from 300 to 1200 mOsm/kg water. A very dilute urine is 300 mOsm/kg water, whereas a very concentrated urine is 1200 mOsm/kg water. It is helpful to measure urine osmolality and blood osmolality (approximately 290 mOsm/kg water) simultaneously to assess if the kidneys are accurately regulating body fluid balance. Urine *specific gravity* varies with the amount of solids in the urine such as cells, casts, and microorganisms, but urine osmolality is not affected by these substances; that is why urine osmolality is a more accurate measure of the kidneys' ability to concentrate or dilute urine. The range for specific gravity is 1.005 to 1.030 with the higher number indicating a more concentrated urine. Usually urine osmolality and/or specific gravity varies somewhat throughout the day and from day to day. If they become fixed or remain the same for consecutive voidings and days, this could indicate renal disease.[17]

Urea, an end product of *protein* metabolism, is found in urine and varies with protein intake and fluid balance. A small amount of proteinuria is insignificant, but quantities greater than 150 mg/24 hours should be investigated because that could indicate glomerular capillary disease. Proteinuria can cause urine to be foamy.

The kidneys regulate *electrolyte* balance. They excrete a variable amount of electrolytes per day as well as throughout the day. Urinary electrolyte excretion is influenced by many factors and accurately assessed with a 24-hour urine collection and analysis of blood electrolytes.

Glycosuria (glucose in the urine) is unusual except with hyperglycemia (elevated blood glucose) which can occur with diabetes mellitus or following an excessive ingestion of sugar. Rarely does glycosuria indicate renal disease.

A few epithelial cells, erythrocytes, leukocytes, and bacteria are normally found in urine. An excess of any of these *cells* could indicate a pathologic condition anywhere along the urinary tract. The site of the pathologic condition can usually be identified with further assessment. For instance, erythrocytes that originate in the kidney are usually broken and found with red blood cell casts, whereas erythrocytes from the lower urinary tract are not as broken and not found with red blood cell casts. Eosinophils (not usually found in urine) indicate a hypersensitivity reaction such as a rejection of a transplanted kidney.

Crystals and stones are not usually found in the urine, but either one can originate any place along the urinary tract. If found in the urine, their composition should be identified and the urinary tract assessed for more crystals and stones. They may not be the result of urinary tract disease but can cause it by obstructing the flow of urine.

Casts are formed within the nephron and are unique to renal disease. There are many types of casts, and each is associated with certain renal pathologic conditions. For example, white cell casts are composed of bits of leukocytes and are associated with renal inflammation, such as pyelonephritis.

Creatinine Tests
Plasma creatinine

Creatinine is an end product of muscle metabolism and is only excreted by the kidney. Plasma creatinine averages approximately 0.7 to 1.3 mg/dl and is relatively constant throughout the day and from day to day. Creatinine levels are slightly higher in men than in women because of men's larger muscle mass. When plasma creatinine rises, it indicates a decrease in renal function. A blood sample can be collected at any time to measure plasma creatinine.[17]

Creatinine clearance

Like plasma creatinine, *creatinine clearance* is a very specific test that assesses renal function, primarily glomerular filtration rate. Creatinine is filtered through the glomerular capillaries and passes through the rest of the nephron unaffected. Therefore the rate at which creatinine is excreted in the urine is similar to the glomerular filtration rate. Normal creatinine clearance is approximately 110 to 125 ml/min. To conduct the test, collect a 24-hour urine specimen and one blood specimen at the midpoint (twelfth hour) of the urine collection. When creatinine clearance decreases, it indicates a decrease in renal function.[17]

Blood Urea Nitrogen

Blood urea nitrogen (BUN) is an end product of protein metabolism primarily excreted by the kidney. BUN averages approximately 10 to 20 mg/ dl; it rises with a decrease in renal function or fluid volume and with an increase in catabolism and dietary protein intake. Because BUN is affected by multiple factors, it is correlated with changes in plasma creatinine to assess renal function. When renal function decreases, both plasma creatinine and BUN rise. With rapidly rising BUN and/or very elevated BUN, the nervous system can be affected and the patient can experience loss of memory, disorientation, confusion, and convulsions. Nursing interventions are focused on preventing injury by visiting and orienting the patient often, placing the call light within close reach for patient, and possibly putting the side rails up on the bed.

Kidneys, Ureters, and Bladder X-rays

A flat x-ray film is taken of the abdomen to visualize the kidneys, ureters, and bladder (KUB) and serves as a screening test before most other procedures.[15] A *KUB* visualizes the position, shape, size, and number of macroscopic or gross renal, ureteral, and bladder structures and surrounding bones. The only patient preparation required is an explanation of the procedure.

Pyelography
Excretory urography

Several methods using a radiopaque dye are employed for securing x-ray films of the urinary system. In an *excretory urography*, also called intravenous pyelography, dye is injected into a vein, circulates through the kidney and is excreted in the urine. A series of x-ray films are taken at short intervals while the dye is being excreted. This test determines the size, shape, and location of urinary tract structures and evaluates renal excretory function. Patient preparation includes an explanation of the procedure and posttest care, adequate fluid intake, clear empty gastrointestinal tract, an allergy history, and baseline information about renal function. The dye is **nephrotoxic** (poisonous to the kidney) and allergenic to some people.[9] A hydrated state helps the dye pass through the kidney and prevent renal damage.

Because the intravenous dye usually contains iodine, the patient should be questioned carefully concerning any allergies, especially to iodine or shellfish. A test dose is often given to determine the patient's sensitivity to the dye, but it is generally believed that such testing is not totally reliable. A negative reaction to a sensitivity test does not guarantee that the patient will not have a severe reaction to the injected dye. Therefore knowledgeable personnel are present during the test to observe for and treat an allergic response. Because fecal matter and gas in the intestinal tract will interfere with the visualization of the kidneys and the ureters on the x-ray film, a laxative or enema may be indicated before the test.

When the patient completes the test, he or she should drink plenty of fluids to help eliminate any dye left in the body. The patient is also observed for signs and symptoms of an allergic response and/or decreasing renal function.[18]

Retrograde urography

Retrograde urography is an invasive procedure that consists of passing a catheter or cystoscope into the bladder, passing small catheters into the ureters (*ureteral catheterization*), injecting a radiopaque dye, and taking x-rays. More x-rays can be taken as the catheters are removed and should be taken approximately 15 to 30 minutes after the initial x-rays to make sure all the dye is secreted. This test provides anatomical information about the urinary tract from the renal pelvis (Figure 19-1) through the urinary meatus and is often done when an obstruction is suspected. If necessary, urine specimens may be secured from each kidney before the dye is injected. Retrograde urography is often done in connection with cystoscopic examination. See the next section, Bladder Studies, for an explanation of the test and patient care.

After the test the patient needs to be observed for *urinary tract infection (UTI)*, hematuria, allergic response to the dye, and changes in urine output. Urinary tract infection can result from retrograde movement of organisms with catheter insertion and dye injection. Hematuria can be associated with UTI and/or result from injury to the urinary tract mucosa from the catheter or cystoscope. Ureteral edema can result from manipulation of the catheters and obstruct urine flow. Signs and symptoms of this are decreased urine output and possibly pain.

Although performing excretory and retrograde urographic tests provides very useful information about urinary tract structures and function, they can be hazardous to the patient's urinary tract. The nurse can try to minimize the hazards by properly assessing and preparing the patient and implementing posttest care that focuses on evaluating and preserving urinary tract function.[17]

Bladder Studies
Cystoscopic examination

The cystoscopic examination directly visualizes the inside of the urinary bladder, may be done with a retrograde urography, and is usually part of a complete urinary system assessment. A cystoscope is a long, metal, lighted instrument that is passed through the urethra into the bladder to observe the bladder and ureteral openings for abnormalities. The examination may be done while the patient is under a local or general anesthetic. Unless a general anesthetic is to be given, fluids are encouraged and the patient does not void before the examination. A sedative may be given shortly before the procedure to decrease anxiety. Be sure that the patient understands the procedure and his or her role in the procedure, especially if only a local anesthetic is used.

After the procedure the urine may be blood tinged or sometimes colored blue or red from the dye used to evaluate kidney function (retrograde urography). The patient should understand that the discoloration is expected and that it will clear. The patient may also have some discomfort, such as burning on urination or pain in the back. Analgesics, warm sitz baths, and external heat to the back and abdomen may relieve the discomfort. Severe pain warrants further investigation. Patients having a cystoscopic examination should always be observed for possible hemorrhage after the procedure.[14]

Cystography

A catheter is introduced into the bladder, urine is removed, a radiopaque substance is injected into the bladder, and x-rays are taken. The presence of stones, tumors, or any other pathologic condition is detected. Patient care is similar to cystoscopic examination and retrograde urography.[14]

Urodynamic studies

Various tests exist that evaluate bladder function and all phases of voiding; for example a cystometrography measures bladder pressure during bladder filling and voiding. Refer to McConnell and Zimmerman[14] for a thorough explanation of these tests and patient care.

Radioisotope Studies
Renography

A small amount of radioactive material is administered intravenously; it circulates through the kidney and is excreted in the urine. This test measures renal function. A graphic record (renogram) is made that traces the radioisotope through the kidney and assesses renal blood flow, glomerular filtration, and tubular secretion. Patient preparation includes an explanation of the test and an assessment of the patient's ability to sit or lie quietly for 30 to 60 minutes. There is no special posttest patient care.

Renoscan

The renoscan is a procedure that outlines the kidney by external scanning. After intravenous injection of a radioactive isotope, a scanning device, such as a scintillator, is passed over the patient's back directly above each kidney and counts the activity of the isotope. In the presence of tumors or nonfunctioning areas, the radioactive material will not be detected by the scan. Patient care is the same as for renography.

Ultrasonography

Ultrasound is a noninvasive procedure that provides almost immediate information. High-frequency sound waves are reflected over the desired body areas, transmitted to an oscilloscope, and recorded. There is no discomfort associated with ultrasound, but it is important to realize that the patient must be able to tolerate a prone position for approximately 30 minutes. Ultrasound may also be used for intrauterine detection of fetal genitourinary anomalies. This is especially significant when there is a history of genetic renal disorders. Fetal kidneys may be detected at a gestational age of as early as 12 weeks, and the bladder as early as 15 weeks.[19]

Computerized Tomography

Computerized tomography (CT) combines the basic principles of radiography with computer technology. Instead of broad x-ray beams passing through the patient to be captured on x-ray film, CT scanning uses a thin x-ray beam that is visualized on a computer screen. While the patient rests in a recumbent position, the thin x-ray beams are transmitted rapidly through the patient and assembled and integrated by digital computers. This information is developed into a cross-sectional image shown on the screen that gives a remarkable definition of body anatomy.[15]

Magnetic Resonance Imaging

Magnetic resonance imaging (MRI), formerly known as nuclear magnetic resonance (NMR), is a revolutionary imaging method that provides superior visual information about soft tissue. Short pulses of low-energy radio waves are introduced into the hydrogen nuclei of the tissue cells to create a magnetic field, and the resulting complex series of events is assembled as a tomogram that is far superior to the image provided by a CT scan.[15] It does not differentiate benign from malignant tumors. The patient must assume a recumbent position throughout the test.

Renal Biopsy

Tissue obtained from a renal biopsy is examined microscopically which helps to determine the nature and extent of renal disease. Biopsy of renal tissue may be accomplished by the open or closed method. Both are invasive procedures that require sterile technique. An *open renal biopsy* requires an operation with general anesthesia. An incision is made, the kidney is exposed, the biopsy needle is inserted into the kidney, a piece of tissue is extracted, and the area is closed and sutured.

The procedure for a *closed renal biopsy* (also called a percutaneous renal biopsy) is as follows. A local anesthetic is given, and the patient is placed in a prone position with a pillow under the abdomen. A patient who has undergone a kidney transplant is positioned to maximize access to the transplanted kidney, which is usually in the groin area. The patient is instructed to hold his or her breath while the biopsy needle is inserted through the skin and into the kidney. Confirmation that the needle is in the kidney is that it moves when the patient breathes, because the kidneys are in contact with the diaphragm and move with ventilation. A small fragment of tissue is obtained and the needle is withdrawn. After a specimen is obtained, pressure must be applied to the site along with a pressure dressing.

With either method of renal biopsy, hemorrhage is the most common complication. The patient must maintain bedrest for 24 hours in a supine position with a pressure dressing. The patient is assessed for pain and given analgesics as needed. Vital signs are evaluated frequently, as is the biopsy site and the dressing. The patient is encouraged to drink fluids to keep the urine diluted and prevent clot formation in the kidney, which could obstruct urine flow. Urine is evaluated for hematuria. The patient is also observed for signs and symptoms of urinary tract infection.[18] The patient may be fearful of the possible diagnosis, and waiting for the biopsy results may be stressful. Hence the nurse provides emotional support during this time.

THERAPEUTIC PROCEDURES AND NURSING IMPLICATIONS

Diuretics

Diuretics are substances and/or drugs that increase the urinary output. The excretion of large amounts of urine is **polyuria**; polyuria after the administration of a diuretic is called **diuresis**. Diuretics have different physiologic actions in the kidney and are classified by their actions, where the action occurs in the nephron, and/or if the diuretics are potassium-sparing or potassium-depleting. The more thoroughly renal physiology is understood, the easier it is to understand the action and side effects of diuretics and to take care of patients receiving them.

Table 19-2 lists some diuretics, and a few are explained briefly here. *Alcohol* and *caffeine* suppress the release of antidiuretic hormone (ADH) from the pituitary gland. When ADH is not present in the collecting duct, a copious dilute urine is secreted. *Spironolactone (Aldactone)* inhibits aldosterone from causing sodium reabsorption and potassium secretion in the distal tubule. Because sodium attracts water, excess water is excreted with the sodium. Potassium is reabsorbed and not excreted in excess in the urine. *Ethacrynic acid (Edecrin)* and *furosemide (Lasix)* inhibit the reabsorption of sodium primarily in the ascending loop of Henle and increase potassium excretion. An elevated concentration of electrolytes in the nephron attracts water, which increases the fluid volume and flow rate, and that decreases potassium reabsorption in the distal tubule.[9]

Major side effects of diuretics are an exaggeration of their physiologic actions. For instance, all diuretics cause **polyuria**, and with prolonged polyuria there is water loss that can result in a fluid volume deficit. Dehydration, therefore, is an important side effect that nurses and patients need to watch for. Signs and symptoms of fluid volume deficit are decrease in weight, concentrated urine, hard stool, sunken eyeballs, dry mouth, poor skin turgor, dizziness, orthostatic hypotension, increased hematocrit, and increased plasma osmolality. If a fluid volume deficit becomes severe enough, blood flow to the kidney can be so reduced that renal failure results.[12,18]

Table 19-2

Diuretics	
Generic name	**Trade name**
Acetazolamide	Diamox
Bumetanide	Bumex
Chlorothiazide	Diuril
Ethacrynic acid	Edecrin
Ethoxzolamide	Ethamide
Furosemide	Lasix
Hydrochlorothiazide	Esidrix
Indapamide	Lozol
Mannitol	Osmitrol
Meralluride	Mercuhydrin
Mercaptomerin sodium	Thiomerin
Metolazone	Diulo
Spironolactone	Aldactone
Triamterene	Dyrenium
Urea	Carbamide

The most reliable method for assessing body fluid changes is by weight. Weigh the patient daily and, if possible, record fluid intake and output. Weigh the patient at the *same* time each day with the *same* amount of clothing and on the *same* scale. Usually before breakfast, after the bladder has been emptied, is a beneficial time. Balance the scale before each weighing, and use a metric scale, if possible, because it is easier to calculate fluid changes on a metric scale. Compare daily weight changes with fluid intake and output changes; they should correlate. For example, if the weight change from one day to the next day is a loss of 1kg, then the fluid change should also be a loss of 1L (1kg = 1L = 2.2lbs). Teach patients how to weigh themselves and how to record fluid intake and output.

Instruct patients about the action, onset, and duration of diuretics so they will not be alarmed at the increased voiding and will know when to expect it and how long it will last. Diuretics are administered at certain times so that the patient's sleep is not disturbed.

Most diuretics cause potassium depletion by interfering with its reabsorption. Some diuretics directly affect the potassium reabsorbing mechanisms. Other diuretics, especially those that act proximal to the distal tubule, cause an increase in the volume of fluid in the nephron. An expanded fluid volume increases the fluid flow rate, and that sweeps potassium and other substances along so fast that they do not have time to be reabsorbed.

The nurse is alert to signs and symptoms of hypokalemia, such as undue fatigue, weakness, loss of appetite, loss of muscle tone, muscle cramping in the legs, arrhythmias, constipation, and abdominal distention. Blood levels of potassium are evaluated frequently. Dietary and/or drug potassium supplements are given as needed.[9,11,18]

Provision for Urinary Drainage

There are several types of urinary drainage procedures. The most common method is to allow the urine to flow by gravity. It is recommended that a closed drainage system be used for all patients needing urinary drainage. Closed systems have the drainage tube sealed to the container, whereas open systems are not sealed and allow air and microorganisms to enter the system freely.

Collection sets in widespread use contain sterile drainage tubing permanently connected to plastic containers. Most containers are flexible bags that have drains at the bottom of the bags to allow the urine to be emptied frequently. The end of the drain is protected by a cap, and the tube is fastened to the container when it is not being used. Most containers have valves at the top where the drainage tubing enters to prevent bacteria from invading the drainage tubing and traveling upward toward the urethra and bladder. Filter air vents are also located on the top of the containers and allow air to enter the system but prevent bacteria in the air from contaminating the urine. All collection containers have bed hangers, which keep the containers in an upright position and off the floor (Figure 19-4).

Catheter care

Most bladder catheters are made of rubber, whereas drainage tubing is clear plastic. Determination of urine clarity or color should be made by observing the urine in the tubing; the urine collected in the drainage bag does not give an accurate assessment. Specimens must only be taken from the port with a sterile syringe.

Patients whose condition necessitates the presence of indwelling catheters over extended periods are very susceptible to infection. This is especially true of chronically ill patients. Points to remember to help prevent infection are that the catheter should provide free flow of urinary drainage and should be comfortable for the patient. It should be secured to the inner upper thigh in females to eliminate tension on the bladder, and laterally to the thigh or lower abdomen in males

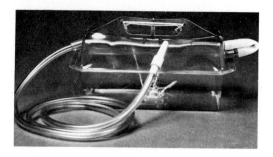

Figure 19-4

Urinary collection set. Drain-box container. (*Courtesy Abbott Laboratories, North Chicago, Ill.*)

to avoid pressure on the urethra at the penoscrotal junction, which can cause the formation of a fistula (see Figure 22-9). The drainage tubing may be placed over the thigh, downward between the legs, or under the patient's leg near the popliteal space. Excess tubing should be coiled on the bed and not allowed to loop below the collection container. Many collection sets provide an apparatus so that the tubing may be attached to the sheets in a proper manner. Care must be taken that the tubing does not become kinked or obstructed. If the urine flow is blocked, stasis occurs and provides a good media for bacteria to grow. The entire system should remain sterile and should not be disconnected. The collection set and tubing should not be lifted or elevated, since drainage may flow back into the bladder.

Using a catheter of the proper size is also important. If the catheter is too small, leakage may occur around it; if it is too large, it may be uncomfortable for the patient. Retention catheters are available in various sizes with balloons of 30- and 5-ml capacity. For most patients a size 16 or 18 French catheter with a 5-ml balloon is satisfactory and will be both comfortable and adequate for free drainage. Often, when a 30-ml balloon is used, the tip of the catheter may bend on the balloon and obstruct the flow of urine.

Free urinary drainage is facilitated when the patient receives adequate amounts of fluid. Adequate fluid intake helps prevent accumulation of mucus, minerals, and exudate, which may adhere to the catheter and cause obstructions. Adequate fluids also eliminate the necessity for irrigation. Crusts and secretions around the vulva or penis and around the catheter should be removed, and the general area should be cleansed as needed. There are differing opinions about cleansing

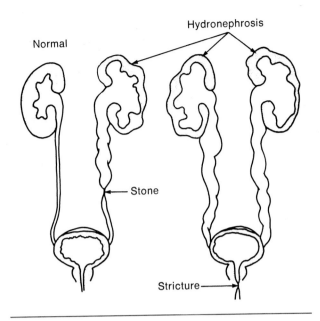

Figure 19-5
Hydronephrosis caused by obstruction of the urinary tract. Dilation occurs above point of obstruction.

methods, but washing the area with soap and water is now thought to be adequate.

When it is necessary for patients to have retention catheters indefinitely, the catheter and its tubing should be changed every 7 to 10 days, or more often if it becomes encrusted with organic deposits.

Pyelostomy, nephrostomy, ureteral, and cystostomy catheters. Several surgical procedures are performed on the urinary system in which the patient will return from the operating room with a catheter placed in the *kidney pelvis (pyelostomy)* or in the kidney **(nephrostomy)**. The nephrostomy catheter or tube is brought out through an incision in the flank and sutured to the skin. *Ureteral catheters* are passed through the urethra and bladder and to the ureters and the kidney pelvis. These catheters are attached to free drainage. Any catheter placed in the kidney pelvis is never clamped because obstructing the flow of urine causes increased pressure in the kidney pelvis, resulting in hydronephrosis and subsequent damage to the kidney (Figure 19-5). Care must be taken to prevent any displacement of these catheters, since reinsertion may not be possible. The nurse should observe the catheters frequently to be sure they are open and draining, and any evidence of failure to drain must be reported to the physician immediately. All drainage is measured and recorded. Sometimes a catheter is placed

in the bladder through an abdominal incision (**cystostomy** or *suprapubic tube*) and is attached to drainage at the bedside. All the equipment that is used for pyelostomy, nephrostomy, ureteral, and cystostomy drainage must be kept sterile (see pp. 508-509).

Catheter irrigation. A physician's order is needed for catheter irrigation. If the fluid intake is adequate and no blood clots occur, it should not be necessary to irrigate the urethral catheter unless the procedure is specifically ordered. Thirty milliliters of physiologic saline solution is usually sufficient to determine the patency of the catheter. After irrigation, the solution should return by gravity. If the irrigating fluid flows in well but does not return, a clot is usually present at the end of the catheter. The nurse should remember that catheter irrigation is done to keep the catheter open and draining, and not to irrigate the bladder.

If the patient has a bilateral pyelostomy and irrigations are ordered, separate equipment must be maintained for each catheter. The irrigating equipment and solution must be sterile; only 2 to 3 ml are used for the irrigation, depending on the physician's order. The solution must be injected with extreme care and gentleness, and its return by gravity should be observed. Failure of the solution to return must be reported, and additional solution should not be injected.

If a urethral catheter needs frequent irrigation, it may be practical to set up closed intermittent irrigation, using a Y connector (Figure 19-6). A bottle of sterile irrigating solution is elevated on a stand, and a sterile tubing leads from the irrigating solution to the Y connector, which is attached to the catheter. The third arm of the Y connector is attached to the drainage tubing. By releasing a clamp on the tubing to the irrigating solution, the nurse allows the desired amount of solution to flow into the patient's bladder. A clamp on the drainage tubing prevents the solution from immediately draining into the collection set. When the desired solution has entered the bladder, that clamp is turned off, and the clamp on the drainage tubing is released, allowing the solution to drain from the bladder under force of gravity. The drainage tubing is left unclamped until the next irrigation. The physician will order the kind of solution, the amount, and the interval for irrigation.

If continuous irrigation is necessary, the patient must have a triple lumen Foley catheter (or

Table 19-3

Urinary Drainage Systems

Catheter and origin	Irrigation	Clamp
Nursing intervention		
Indwelling bladder catheter	Only as needed to maintain patency; sterilize equipment with *each* irrigation; 30 ml of sterile normal saline gently instilled with gravity return	To obtain specimen or as ordered
Cystostomy catheter (suprapubic tube)	If necessary to disconnect system, close three-way stopcock before disconnecting to maintain column of urine in catheter and to maintain siphon action	On physician's order the suprapubic tube may be clamped 4 hours, then drained 30 minutes so bladder fills, and patient attempts to void through urethra while the tube is clamped
Ureteral catheters (through bladder and ureters to kidney pelvis)	Irrigate according to physician's order; irrigate with 2 or 3 ml of sterile solution	Never
Pyelostomy (kidney pelvis)	Only with physician's order; use 2 or 3 ml of sterile solution as ordered; irrigate gently with gravity return; separate sterile equipment for each catheter.	Never
Nephrostomy (kidney)	Only with physician's order and sterile equipment	Never

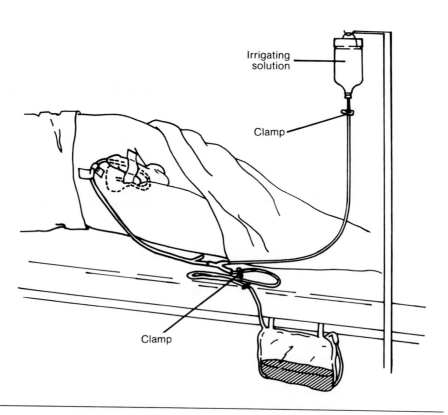

Figure 19-6
Retention catheter inserted for urinary drainage. Closed system with Y connector for intermittent irrigation. Continuous irrigation requires triple lumen catheter.

Measuring output	Drainage tubing	Care of site
Empty drainage bag every 8 hours or more often if filled to capacity	Place over thigh and tape to avoid trauma to urethra; maintain closed system with drainage bag attached to beds	Cleanse entire perineal area with soap and water as needed
Empty drainage bag every 8 hours or more often if filled; measure and record voided urine on separate record if catheter is clamped and patient voids	Secure to lower abdomen; attach catheter to closed drainage system	Apply sterile dry dressing to site; dressing may become saturated from leaking urine
Measure and record separately for each kidney; observe output hourly	Tape to thigh; maintain closed system and patency	Care as for bladder catheter if it enters meatus; apply sterile dry dressing if brought out on flank or abdomen
Measure drainage from each kidney and record separately	Maintain patency and closed system	Apply sterile dry dressing; change often to keep dry
Measure drainage and record separately	Maintain patency and closed system	Apply sterile dry dressing; change often to keep dry

a cystostomy tube and a urethral catheter) in the bladder to provide for continuous flow in and out of the bladder. The irrigation equipment is the same, except that a drip-o-meter is attached to the irrigating solution to regulate the rate of flow; the drainage tubing is left unclamped. In both intermittent and continuous closed bladder irrigation, it is important to keep an accurate record of the amount of irrigating solution used and to subtract this amount from the measurement of total drainage.

Patient care after catheter removal

Removal of the indwelling bladder catheter should be preceded by complete deflation of the balloon. The balloon should be deflated by aspirating the fluid that was instilled on its insertion rather than by cutting the catheter to allow the fluid to drain by gravity. The catheter should be inspected and the physician notified if it is not intact. After its removal the patient should be observed for retention or dribbling and checked often for residual urine. There may be a dribbling caused by dilation of the sphincter muscles. Frequently, the patient is unable to void normally, and sometimes catheterization and replacement

of the retention catheter may be necessary. If the patient voids only small amounts, the bladder may not be completely emptying. Occasionally, the capacity of the bladder may be temporarily decreased, and the patient will complain of discomfort soon after the removal of the catheter because the patient is unable to void. The patient should be instructed to assist in keeping a record of the time and the amount voided, and to observe the appearance of the urine. If blood appears in the urine, the physician should be notified. It is frequently necessary to maintain accurate output records for several days, especially if the patient has had urologic surgery.

Follow-up care

Many patients are dismissed from the hospital to their homes with indwelling catheters, draining wounds, and permanent appliances. There should be a planned program teaching the patient self-care insofar as he or she is competent. This includes three steps: (1) observation, (2) participation, and (3) practice under supervision. The patient will observe the nurse in the various procedures; at the same time the nurse explains, step by step, what is being done and the reason for it.

As the patient is able, he or she begins to assist the nurse or participate in the procedures, gradually assuming more and more of the care. Finally, the nurse allows the patient to give all the care, while observing to correct any mistakes and provide positive feedback.

When the patient leaves the hospital he or she should feel secure about knowing what to do and how to do it. There may be catheters or dressings posteriorly that the patient cannot reach, and a member of the family should be instructed in the care. In addition, hospitals should provide written instructions with a list of the home equipment needed for the patient or the family. In planning care for patients with urologic conditions, it has been found that each patient has her or his own special needs.

There should be a referral system between the hospital and the home health agency, and when it can be arranged, the home health nurse should visit the patient in the hospital before discharge. Information should be available to the home health nurse concerning the care needed and the instructions given the patient. The home health nurse will supervise or assist with the necessary care after discharge. The continuity of care between the hospital and the home provides a feeling of security for the patient and facilitates the process of rehabilitation.

DISEASES AND DISORDERS OF THE URINARY SYSTEM

Pathogenic organisms may gain entrance to the urinary tract by the bloodstream or from infections elsewhere in the body. The result may be an inflammatory process or an infection that may spread from the urethra upward to other parts of the system. Obstructions may occur along the tract from stones, strictures, tumors, or a kinked ureter. Tumors, either benign or malignant, may result in serious injury to the bladder, urethra, or kidneys. Injuries elsewhere in the body may also affect the kidney. Some diseases of the kidney may be the result of allergic factors, and others may be the result of degenerative changes.

Noninfectious Diseases

Glomerulonephritis is a term that encompasses several conditions affecting the glomerular capillaries of the kidney. Early classifications were based on the clinical picture of the disease. Since the advent of percutaneous renal biopsy and so-

phisticated techniques of electron microscopy, the newer classifications of the glomerulopathies are based on histologic and immunologic findings.

Acute poststreptococcal glomerulonephritis

Pathophysiology. Acute poststreptococcal glomerulonephritis (APSGN) is usually preceded by a recent infection of the pharynx or the skin (impetigo) caused by beta-hemolytic streptococcus. Antibodies develop and combine with an unknown antigen, possibly a protein (M) of the streptococcus, and form an *immune complex*. These immune complexes become trapped in the glomerular basement membrane (GBM) and cause inflammation. The inflammatory response in the glomeruli results in the passage of red blood cells and protein into the urine.

It is not yet known why some people develop the immune complex and APSGN after a streptococcal infection and others do not. The disease is most common in children, appears suddenly, and usually clears up with no residual damage. It may progress to a chronic form of the disease, however, when the patient is an adult.

Assessment. Urine output is reduced (**oliguria**) and will be rusty colored from the presence of red blood cells. Edema results from increased capillary permeability and is seen in the face, eyelids, and hands in the morning, and in the legs at night. A significant number of patients have circulatory congestion from fluid and sodium retention, resulting in dyspnea, cough, and pulmonary edema. Protein is found in urine, but blood levels of protein remain normal. The BUN and serum creatinine levels will be increased. Most patients will have mild to moderate hypertension at the onset that diminishes as the body eliminates the excess fluid.

Some cases will be more severe, resulting in **anuria** (absence of production of urine) and subsequent uremia. The prognosis is favorable if there is no preexisting renal disease or if proteinuria is not heavy or persistent. Patients may have some urinary abnormalities for several years after recovery. Follow-up studies are now revealing residual pathologic conditions, but evidence is not conclusive. Adults who develop the disease are more likely to develop chronic renal disease as a complication, resulting in end-stage renal failure.[6]

Intervention. Nursing diagnoses and interventions for APSGN are summarized in the box on page 511. Treatment of acute glomerulonephritis is symptomatic, aimed at relieving hypertension, circulatory congestion, and edema. The

NURSING CARE GUIDELINES
Acute Poststreptococcal Glomerulonephritis

Nursing diagnoses

- Activity intolerance related to fatigue and weakness secondary to renal dysfunction
- Anxiety related to unknown prognosis
- Potential impairment of physical mobility related to inactivity secondary to prolonged bedrest
- Fluid volume excess, edema, related to decreased renal excretion
- Knowledge deficit: signs and symptoms of fluid and electrolyte imbalance and side effects of corticosteroids and cytotoxic agents
- Potential for infection related to increased susceptibility secondary to corticosteroid therapy, immobility, invasive procedures
- Potential impaired skin integrity related to edema, bedrest
- Alteration in nutrition, less than body requirements, related to anorexia and restrictions of protein and sodium
- Potential for hyperkalemia related to decreased renal excretion of potassium.

Nursing interventions

- Maintain activity as tolerated
- Measure and record intake and output—report reduced output
- Measure urine output hourly if indwelling catheter present
- Observe urine for color and sediment and record
- Test urine for protein (albumin)

- Restrict fluids as ordered, based on urinary output and body weight
- Restrict protein intake as ordered, based on blood levels of nitrogenous wastes and urine output
- Give high-carbohydrate diet
- Check temperature, pulse, and respirations every 4 hours; report elevated temperature, galloping or irregular pulse, dyspnea, and coughing
- Check blood pressure every 4 hours—notify physician if systolic pressure is over 160 mm Hg or diastolic pressure is over 110 mm Hg
- Weigh patient daily
- Observe for edema and note location
- Measure abdomen daily to evaluate ascites
- Observe signs of hyperkalemia; administer ion resin exchanges for hyperkalemia
- Observe mental status at least once each shift and report changes, including confusion, headache, sleepiness, or tremors
- Institute seizure precautions if mental changes observed
- Teach patient about disease process and treatment

Expected outcomes

- Weight stable at level maintained before edema
- Blood pressure stable
- Urine negative for albumin and red blood cells
- Absence of edema
- Urine output appropriate for intake

patient will probably be allowed as much activity as can be tolerated. Bed rest is indicated in the acute stage until hematuria and proteinuria subside.

Fluids and sodium will be restricted if there is circulatory congestion or hypertension. Diuretics will be used, but vigorous diuresis and dehydration should be avoided. Antihypertensives are used to reduce the elevated blood pressure. Treatment of hypertension prevents additional damage to the renal microvasculature. Protein intake must be restricted if nitrogenous protein waste levels in the blood become increased (azotemia), but vigorous protein restriction is avoided.

Steroids and cytotoxic agents may help control the deposition of immune complexes.[18] Antibiotics do not help the patient but may be given to the family to prevent them from having the antibody reaction to the antigen associated with the preceding infection.

An increase in urine output and a corresponding weight loss signal improvement. The urine begins to clear itself of albumin and red blood cells, the blood pressure decreases, and the patient feels better. This usually begins about 3 weeks after the onset of the edema. When the weight and blood pressure are stable, edema and hematuria are gone, and the BUN level is decreased, dietary and activity restrictions may be lifted.

Nephrotic syndrome (nephrosis)

Assessment. The term nephrotic syndrome is used to describe the patient with massive proteinuria, hyperlipidemia, hypoalbuminemia, and edema. The edema accompanying the nephrotic syndrome causes a puffy face, distended eyelids, a bloated abdomen (ascites), and swelling in the lower extremities. The skin may have a waxy pallor because of the edema.

The syndrome has multiple causes and is characterized by increased glomerular permeability, which results in protein and fat found in the urine. The nephrotic syndrome is not a disease; rather, it is a group of symptoms found in many diseases affecting the glomeruli. It occurs with some infectious diseases, poisoning from chemical substances, toxemia of pregnancy, shock resulting from external burns, or coronary occlusion, and may follow a transfusion with incompatible blood. It is seen in membranous, proliferative glomerulonephritis and poststreptococcal glomerulonephritis. It is also found in diabetic glomerulosclerosis, systemic lupus erythematosus, renal vein thrombosis, syphilis, and some neoplastic conditions.[1,7]

Pathophysiology. The increased permeability of the glomeruli allows protein to leave the blood and enter the urine, producing proteinuria. The reduced serum protein level causes a decrease in plasma oncotic pressure. The inadequate plasma oncotic pressure reduces the natural force that draws fluid back into the capillary from the interstitial spaces. The excess fluid remaining in the interstitial space results in edema (Chapter 4). An unknown factor stimulates hepatic lipoprotein synthesis, which results in hyperlipidemia. Cholesterol and low-density lipoproteins are the first to elevate, followed by triglyceride levels. Fatty casts are found in the urine.

Intervention. Treatment usually consists of administration of diuretics to decrease the edema. Dietary restraints depend on the severity of the symptoms, but the diet should include high-protein foods and restrictions on sodium. Corticosteroids and cyclophosphamide (Cytoxan) are used in severe cases. Intravenous albumin is not usually administered because it is rapidly lost from the permeable glomeruli, but it may be used if edema is severe and generalized (*anasarca*). The individual is encouraged to continue normal activity unless the edema is severe.

Prevention and control of infection are important, since the patient is highly susceptible, and infection is one of the chief causes of death. Nursing care requires the monitoring of diuretic therapy; it includes weighing the patient daily, measuring the girth of the abdomen and extremities, the intake and output, and the protein and sodium intake. The patient may be anorectic, and small frequent feedings may be necessary to assure an adequate protein intake. The disorder may be acute or chronic, and the primary causative disease must be cured or controlled to relieve the condition.

Infectious Diseases
Cystitis

Pathophysiology. Cystitis is an inflammation of the lining of the bladder. It may be acute or chronic and is more common in females than males. The female urethra is shorter and straighter than the male urethra and therefore is more easily contaminated. In addition, the prostatic secretions in the male have antibacterial properties. Cystitis may be caused by bacteria that enter through the urinary meatus, or it may occur through catheterization, during which organisms in the urethra are carried into the bladder. Cystitis in women can occur after sexual intercourse, which promotes the introduction and ascent of pathogens. Infections may also be carried from the upper urinary tract, beginning with the kidney and involving the ureters and the bladder. In this instance the infectious organism gains entrance to the kidney by way of the bloodstream. Cystitis may result from nonbacterial factors such as injury to the lining of the bladder caused by instruments or a catheter.

Assessment. Symptoms are frequent urination, including nocturia, severe pain and burning in the urethra with urination, and a sensation of bearing down or pressure in the bladder and suprapubic area. Examination of the urine may show the presence of pus and may reveal blood. Frequently, specific pathogenic organisms are not found.[18]

Intervention. The first criterion of treatment is to establish the cause of the problem. Antispasmodic drugs, sulfonamide or antibiotic drugs, and preparations to acidify the urine may be ordered. The patient should be encouraged to drink water freely. Hot sitz baths and the application of heat to the abdomen may relieve pain. Phenazopyridine (Pyridium), a urinary antiseptic, may be given to relieve discomfort.

Cystitis during pregnancy creates special problems. The enlarged uterus causes some obstruction to the ureters, and glycosuria offers media for bacterial growth. Also, any therapy can place the fetus at risk.[1]

Nursing interventions should include teaching the patient to prevent recurrence of cystitis. The patient should be instructed to have regular follow-up examinations to rule out the presence of asymptomatic infections and to take medications as prescribed with a full glass of water. The patient should be advised to continue taking medication for the full time prescribed, even though symptoms may be relieved or disappear. Women who experience frequent urinary tract infections should be instructed to:

1. Cleanse the perineal area from front to back after each voiding and bowel movement.
2. Increase fluid intake and void every 2 to 3 hours during the day to empty the bladder and reduce growth of bacteria.
3. Void before and after sexual intercourse.
4. Wear absorbent cotton panties or those-lined with cotton in the crotch.

Pyelonephritis

Pyelonephritis is an acute pyogenic infection involving the parenchyma in one or both kidneys. Although *pyelitis* (infection of the kidney pelvis) may occur alone, it is considered rare.

Pathophysiology. Pyelonephritis is caused by bacteria: the *Proteus* group, *Escherichia coli,* and *Pseudomonas;* less common are the streptococcus and the staphylococcus bacteria. The infection may be brought to the kidney by the bloodstream or the lymphatic system from infection elsewhere in the body. It may also spread upward from the bladder. Factors that contribute to the disorder include obstructions that restrict urinary flow and examinations, such as cystoscopy and catheterization. Pyelonephritis may occur in persons with some neurologic diseases or with conditions that require long periods of immobilization during which urinary calculi may develop.

Assessment. The kidney becomes edematous and inflamed, and the blood vessels are congested. The urine may be cloudy and contain pus, mucus, and blood. Small abscesses may form in the kidney. The diagnosis is made by microscopic examination of the urine and urine cultures; an intravenous urography may be done. The symptoms may occur abruptly with fever, chills, an elevated leukocyte count, aching, pyuria and white blood cell cysts. There may or may not be pain in the back.[17]

Intervention. The treatment of the patient depends on locating and eliminating the cause. Sensitivity tests are done, and the appropriate antibiotic is administered. Bed rest is required during the acute period. Vital signs are recorded twice a day and weight daily. Fluid intake is encouraged, and all intake and output should be recorded. The patient should be observed for any difficulty in voiding, such as pain and burning. Urine should be observed for color. The patient should be kept warm, not exposed to drafts or chilling, and protected from respiratory tract infections.

Expected outcomes. With proper intervention the patient with pyelonephritis will have:

Normal temperature

Urinalysis without abnormalities

No back or flank pain

No fatigue

Obstructions of the Urinary System

Obstructions of the urinary system may result from many different causes and may be located anywhere from the kidney to the urinary meatus. Any prolonged obstruction will lead to serious pathologic conditions, since the glomerular filtration rate will be reduced, pressure within the kidney, ureter, or bladder may cause dilation, and excretion of creatinine, urea, and other substances will be reduced.

Renal calculi

Pathophysiology. A stone is called a **calculus,** the formation of stones is called **lithiasis,** and the presence of stones in the kidney is called *nephrolithiasis.* When stones occur in any other part of the urinary system, the location determines the term used, as in ureteral calculi. The exact cause of the formation of renal calculi is unknown, but some factors that contribute to their formation are known. Patients who are required to remain on a regimen of bed rest for long periods and paraplegic patients are likely to develop calculi because of stasis of urine and the release of increased amounts of calcium from bone. Some common organisms that cause infection of the bladder and kidney cause the urine to become alkaline. Calcium phosphate, a compound readily excreted by the kidneys, cannot dissolve in the alkaline urine and will form crystals around a shred of tissue or other substance in the kidney, resulting in stone formation. Patients requiring continuous urinary drainage often will develop kidney or bladder stones as a complication. Pathologic disorders such as senile osteoporosis, gout, infection, hyperparathyroidism, and disorders affecting the pH and concentration of the urine are believed to be contributing factors.

Assessment. Stones may be like tiny gravel, and the patient may be asymptomatic. Large stones with irregular branches may be present in the kidney pelvis; they are known as *staghorn* calculi and require surgical intervention. When stones occur in the kidney, pain may be present on the involved side and usually radiates from the flank to the crest of the ileum. Pus may be present in the urine, resulting from infection at the back of the stone. Hematuria, usually microscopic, results from injury to the mucous membrane from the rough, jagged edges of the stone.[7,18]

Ureteral colic is caused by a stone passing down or becoming lodged in the ureter. The pain is excruciating and radiates down the ureter and may extend to the thigh and the urethra. Nausea, vomiting, and sweating occur, and the patient feels weak and may faint.

Intervention. All urine from patients with renal calculi should be strained through gauze and carefully inspected. The patient is encouraged to drink at least 3000 ml of fluid in 24 hours, since increasing urinary output will facilitate passage of the stone. If infection is present, the appropriate antibiotic may be ordered. The patient is encouraged to remain active because stones are more likely to be passed if the patient is ambulatory.

Narcotics are required to relieve the pain, and an antispasmodic drug such as methantheline bromide (Banthine) or propantheline bromide (Pro-Banthine) may be ordered to relieve spasm.

Prevention is also important. Patients confined to bed should be turned regularly every 2 hours. Long periods of immobilization result in a loss of calcium from the bones and an increase of calcium in the bloodstream. High levels of calcium in the blood contribute to the formation of kidney stones. Adequate hydration will dilute the urine so that stones are less likely to form.[16] Isometric exercise and weight bearing exercise will reduce calcium lost from the bone. The use of the tilt table, the circle bed, rocking bed, and overhead trapeze provides exercise for the patient and helps in the prevention of stone formation.

Patients who require intervention for removal of large stones have several options. In addition to conventional open surgical techniques, percutaneous stone removal and extracorporeal shock-wave lithotripsy are being used successfully for stone removal or dissolution. Percutaneous stone removal is achieved through a nephroscope under fluoroscopy after the patient has received a local anesthetic. This method has the greatest success rate with renal pelvic and caliceal stones.[19] The nephrostomy tube is left in situ for several days. (See care of the patient with a nephrostomy tube on p. 507.)

Extracorporeal shock-wave lithotripsy consists of administering an epidural or general anesthetic to the patient and then placing the patient in a tank of water. The bottom of the tank is equipped with an electrode that exerts shock waves which fragment the renal stone.[19] The stone fragments may then be passed in the urine over the next several days. Since no incision is required, patients are hospitalized for only 1 or 2 days and can immediately return to work and other responsibilities. Some centers perform the procedure without anesthesia, thus further reducing the risk of complications. These patients report some discomfort when the shock wave is applied. Most patients develop localized bruising.

Hydronephrosis

Dilation of the kidney pelvis caused by obstruction of urinary flow is called **hydronephrosis.** Dilation of the ureter caused by obstructed flow is called *hydroureter.* Pressure develops as the urine is dammed up and may become high enough to cause damage to the kidney tissue. The obstruction may be caused by stones, tumors, kinking of a ureter, a congenital anomaly, or an enlarged prostate gland in a male (see Figure 19-5).

Intervention. The treatment is based on locating the obstruction, which may be done by a series of x-ray studies and tests. Depending on the cause, correction may be made and the condition cured. However, if the kidney has undergone considerable destruction, a **nephrectomy** may be necessary.

Traumatic Injuries

Injuries to the urinary system often occur in connection with injuries to other parts of the body. Injuries may be caused by gunshot wounds, penetrating wounds from sharp objects, and crushing injuries with fracture of the pelvis, which may cause rupture of the bladder or the urethra. Injuries resulting from external violence such as falls or blows may result in simple injury to the kidney or may completely shatter the kidney. All trauma victims should be observed for blood in the urine. The patient in shock will have a reduced blood supply to the kidney, and the urine output will be reduced. Initial interventions are aimed at stablizing vital signs and maintaining circulation and oxygenation of tissues. Assessment of the extent of injury determines the method of treatment, which may be conservative or may require surgical intervention.[6,18]

```
┌─────────────────────────────────────────┐
│   ┌───────────────────────────────────┐ │
│   │      NURSING CARE GUIDELINES      │ │
│   │          Renal Calculi            │ │
│   └───────────────────────────────────┘ │
```

Nursing diagnoses

- Anxiety related to fear of disease process, invasive medical procedure
- Comfort alteration (pain) related to passage of calculi, invasive procedure
- Knowledge deficit related to limited understanding of disease process, prescribed treatment
- Potential alteration in urinary elimination related to obstructing calculi

Nursing interventions

- Teach patient about disease process and treatments
- Encourage activity and ambulation
- Encourage patient to verbalize fears and concerns
- Explain all diagnostic tests, nursing measures, and physiology of ureteral colic and bladder spasm
- Give analgesics as frequently as ordered to relieve pain
- Encourage fluids to produce high urinary output of dilute urine—offer 200 ml every 2 hours (even) while awake and 400 ml during night
- Strain all urine and observe for sediment, crystals, and stones, and report findings; save any solids and send to laboratory for analysis; instruct patient on same
- Instruct patient and supervise dietary restrictions indicated by nature of stone as analyzed by laboratory

Expected outcomes

- Absence of pain
- Urine output of 1400 to 1600 ml every 8 hours
- Absence of calculi
- Can verbalize diet restrictions and be able to select appropriate foods for restricted diet

Tumors of the Urinary Tract

Kidney

Tumors of the kidneys are generally malignant and usually result from metastasis from the lung. The malignancy is often spread to the lungs and bones by the bloodstream. The primary symptom is blood in the urine; other symptoms are weight loss and fatique. The treatment is a nephrectomy and may be only palliative, since metastasis may have occurred. Wilms' tumor is one of the most common types of malignant tumors seen in children and a pediatric textbook should be consulted for further explanation.

Bladder

Tumors of the bladder may be benign or malignant. A complete urologic examination, including cystoscopy and a biopsy, is done to diagnose the problem. Cancer of the bladder is more common in men over age 50. Smoking, and exposure to dyes, chemicals, and ionizing radiation increase the risk of developing cancer of the bladder. The bladder is also a site of metastasis of cancer originating in the male prostate or female lower reproductive tract. The most common symptom is gross, painless hematuria. Urinary tract infection often develops as a complication of malignancy and produces symptoms of frequency, urgency, and dysuria. A distant metastasis may produce pelvic or back pain.

For malignancy, a partial or complete cystectomy may be performed. A complete cystectomy necessitates urinary diversion (p. 522). Radiation therapy or chemotherapy may be initiated. Chemotherapy may be given systemically or locally by instilling a solution into the bladder. Immunotherapy is in the experimental stage but offers hope for the future. Passive and adoptive methods have been tried.[8] BCG (Bacille Calmette Guérin) has been instilled into the bladder and allowed to remain a given time before withdrawal. This treatment offers the advantage of actual contact with the tumor; more investigation is needed, but preliminary cases suggest this and other immunotherapy methods should be studied.

Renal Failure

Renal failure is a broad term for kidneys that are unable to meet the demands of the body. It is described as acute or chronic, according to the time required for the development of the condition and whether it is short-lived or prolonged.

Acute renal failure

Acute renal failure may develop insidiously or suddenly, but the kidneys suddenly stop functioning. Acute renal failure proceeds through several well-defined stages.

Assessment. The first is the *onset stage*, that time from the precipitating event to the onset of oliguria or anuria, usually a short time. Next is the *oliguric-anuric stage*, in which output is less than 400 ml in 24 hours. This may last only for a day or two, or it may last for as long as 2 weeks. Then the kidney starts to recover and enters the *diuretic stage,* when urinary output increases and the BUN level stops rising and eventually falls to normal range. The *convalescent stage* begins when the BUN level is stable and ends when the patient returns to normal activity and urine output is normal. This may take several months, and some patients may develop chronic renal failure.

Pathophysiology. The causes of acute renal failure are numerous, but decreased renal blood flow and nephrotoxins are the most common causes. Postoperative shock produces hypotension that prevents the kidney from filtering the blood adequately. This decreased flow and lack of oxygen to the kidney may cause acute renal failure. Some other causes include burns, blood transfusion reactions, infections, antigen-antibody reactions (acute glomerulonephritis), and obstructions.

Changes that occur in the kidney include necrosis and a sloughing of the lining of the renal tubules. Areas of the nephron rupture, resulting in the formation of scar tissue. Blood chemistries show an increase in the BUN, plasma creatinine, and potassium and a decrease in pH (acidosis) and bicarbonate. Generalized edema, pruritus, headache, disturbance of vision, hypertension, and vomiting occur, and there is an odor of urine on the breath. The patient appears acutely ill.

Intervention. Treatment begins with determining the cause and correcting it if possible. Management focuses on fluid balance, electrolyte balance, nutrition, preventing infection, and educating the patient. The patient is kept alive while the kidney heals itself. The mortality rate is about 50% and the leading cause of death is infection.[17]

There is a tendency for nurses to become preoccupied with the patient's urine volume and blood chemistries and to forget that they are dealing with a very frightened human being. Nurses should be alert for and respond to the patient's behavior and provide the support and understanding needed in this difficult time.

Because daily weights and fluid output guide fluid replacement, careful recording is done. The diet is high in carbohydrates to prevent the breakdown of fats, which produces ketosis, and low in protein and potassium to reduce BUN and hyperkalemia. Fluids are restricted. Protein is increased as the nephron units begin functioning and BUN decreases. If the level of serum potassium continues to increase and becomes dangerously high, an exchange resin is administered to release the excess potassium. Medications should be evaluated to determine potential buildup. Conservative treatment is continued, and dialysis is indicated when the clinical condition or biochemical state is deteriorating. Peritoneal dialysis may be used unless very rapid dialysis is required or repeated dialysis is anticipated; then hemodialysis is used.[18] Dialysis is explained after the section Chronic renal failure.

The box at right summarizes nursing care of the patient with acute renal failure.

Chronic renal failure

Chronic changes in renal failure may be considered on a continuum that ranges from impairment to insufficiency to failure. *Renal impairment* is detected by changes in concentration and dilution of the urine. *Renal insufficiency* becomes apparent when the kidney cannot meet the demands of dietary or metabolic stress. *Renal failure* appears when the normal demands of the body cannot be met. As many as 80% of the nephrons may be lost before renal functional losses are detected. Hypertrophy and hyperplasia of the remaining nephrons permit an increase in their work load and in their ability to maintain function.[7] **Uremia** is a term that has been used for years to describe terminal renal failure and literally means urine in the blood. Although it is less popular now than formerly, the term is still used.

Pathophysiology. As renal function diminishes, the kidney loses its ability to adapt to varying intakes of foods and fluids. Polyuria and an inability to concentrate the urine are early signs of chronic renal failure. Later oliguria and anuria occur. An output of less than 400 ml of urine per day indicates failure.

The kidneys may be small and contracted or large and irregular in shape. The nature and extent of the underlying disease affect the rate of progression and the complicating factors. The most common causes are pyelonephritis, chronic glomerulonephritis, glomerulosclerosis, chronic urinary obstruction, severe hypertension, diabetes, gout, and polycystic kidney disease.[7,11]

Assessment. Patients with **chronic renal failure** have a characteristic dusky, yellow-tan, or gray color from retained urochrome pigments. The pallor of anemia is obvious. Pruritus and crawling or tickling sensations cause the patient to scratch the skin, producing excoriations that become infected. Abnormalities in clotting and capillary fragility permit large bruises and purpura to develop. The skin is dry and scaly because

---

NURSING CARE GUIDELINES
Acute Renal Failure

Nursing diagnoses

Anxiety related to prognosis

Decreased cardiac output related to dysrhythmias, drug intolerance, stress on heart function

Alteration in comfort related to infection, muscle cramps, acute pain

Ineffective individual coping related to anger, anxiety, denial, dependent behavior, depression

Alteration in family process related to complex therapies, hospitalization, illness of family member

Fear related to disease process, hospitalization, invasive medical procedure, powerlessness, real or imagined threat to well-being

Alteration in fluid volume (excess) related to decreased output

Grieving related to actual or perceived loss

Knowledge deficit related to limited understanding of disease process or prescribed treatment

Alteration in nutrition (less than body requirements) related to dietary restrictions, loss of appetite, nausea and vomiting

Powerlessness related to disease process, hospitalization

Ineffective breathing pattern (impaired gas exchange) related to fluid overload

Disturbance in self-concept related to body image, personal identity, role performance, self-esteem

Alteration in thought process related to impaired perception of reality

Alteration in urinary elimination related to decreased kidney function, decreased urine output

Nursing interventions

Teach patient about disease process and treatment

Measure and record urine output hourly; report if less than 30 ml per hour

Report any reduction in urine output

Restrict and regulate fluid intake as ordered and as permitted by output and weight gain

Weigh patient daily

Observe signs of fluid excess—dyspnea, tachycardia, pulmonary edema, distended neck veins, peripheral edema

Observe signs of elevated serum potassium (hyperkalemia) and administer ion exchange resins as ordered

Turn patient every 2 hours

Have patient cough and deep breath every 2 hours

Provide emotional support, anticipating needs

Limit dietary protein as necessary during oliguric phase

Restrict sodium intake as ordered

Anticipate treatment with dialysis

Expected outcomes

Blood chemistries to level before illness

Urine output greater than 30 ml per hour

Weight decreased to level maintained before illness

Absence of edema and respiratory distress

Lungs clear

No signs/symptoms of infection

Patient and family verbalize fears and concerns

---

of a decrease in oil gland activity and in subcutaneous tissue. Uremic frost may form as white or yellowish crystals on the skin. This is rarely seen unless dialysis is not implemented.

The patient will develop a nonbacterial stomatitis caused by the action of the urea-splitting flora of the oral cavity on the increased urea. This gives rise to a metallic taste in the patient's mouth. Anorexia, nausea, and vomiting are common. Metabolism of urea in the intestinal tract forms ammonia, which causes formation of ulcers that may then hemorrhage, causing melena. High levels of urea in the blood produce a general feeling of lethargy advancing to drowsiness, confusion, and eventual coma.

Elevation of the serum potassium level accompanies the loss of sodium and the elimination of hydrogen ions from the kidneys (the body's attempt to reduce acidosis). The high potassium level may cause dysrhythmias. For some reason calcium is not absorbed in the gastrointestinal tract, and low levels of calcium may produce muscle irritability followed by tetany or convulsions if not corrected. Acidosis progresses, depleting bicarbonates and stimulating the respiratory center to increase respirations. Thus a deep sighing form of breathing is a symptom of renal insufficiency, whereas in the late stages of uremia, hyperventilation is amplified to rid the body of carbonic acid along with water in the form of carbon dioxide.

The anemia that accompanies chronic renal failure causes air hunger and a mild dyspnea. Belching and hiccups are also common.

Hypertension will develop to compensate for the decreased oxygen-carrying capacity of the blood in anemia, and retinopathy may then occur.

Intervention. Ongoing teaching is the most

important nursing intervention implemented for the patient with renal failure. Chronic renal failure is treated by restriction of nutrients and fluids to levels that the kidneys are able to manage effectively, and by dialysis or renal transplantation. If dietary management is initiated early, the buildup of toxins can be prevented or minimized, and the impaired functional abilities of the kidneys can be more effective for a longer time. Transplant and dialysis are discussed later in this chapter.

Usually the diet is complex and managed by a renal dietitian. The diet contains enough protein to prevent tissue wasting but not so much as to contribute to the overload of its metabolic end products (urea). When even a minimum amount of protein cannot be handled by the kidneys, dialysis is required. The diet is high in calories from carbohydrates and fats, at least 2500 to 3000 calories daily. Without sufficient calories from carbohydrates and fats, the liver will form glycogen from amino acids (glyconeogenesis) and increase the metabolic end products of protein in the blood. Other dietary restrictions are related to the patient's degree of acidosis. Potassium is retained; therefore foods high in potassium could be restricted. Sodium is controlled at a level sufficient to replace sodium loss without causing fluid retention. Table salt is almost always eliminated, and commercially prepared low-salt foods are used. Boiling and processing fruits and vegetables removes potassium.

Fluid balance is of prime importance. The patient may have fluids equal to the amount excreted in the urine plus 300 to 500 ml to compensate for insensible fluid loss (fluids lost through the lungs, perspiration, and so on). Fluids in excess of the amount that can be eliminated are retained in the body, and the patient gains weight. Accurate records of all intake and output, as well as daily weights, are essential to the calculation of fluid replacement. Weighing the patient at the same time each day on the same scale with same amount of clothes is important.

The patient often complains of thirst, but the thirst associated with renal failure cannot be relieved by ordinary means. Factors that the nurse must consider in relation to the patient's thirst include the total amount of fluid allowed, condition of the patient's mouth, fluid output, diet, physical activity, and the patient's mental state. There are ways in which the nurse can space the fluid without giving more fluid than the amount permitted.

When fluids are restricted, the following methods of administering medications should be considered: (1) giving several medications at mealtime, (2) giving small pills and capsules rather than large ones that may require larger amounts of water to swallow, (3) using solid forms of medications rather than liquid forms, (4) using small glasses rather than large glasses (a small glass full of water has a better psychologic effect than a large glass with a small amount of water), and (5) realizing that a small amount of cold water will be more satisfying than warm water.

Dietary and fluid restrictions may be eased once the patient begins dialysis, but some treatment plans continue rigid control on the premise that this will prevent complications and improve the prognosis.

Thorough and frequent oral hygiene is necessary to relieve the effects of stomatitis and the metallic taste in the mouth. Vinegar (0.25% acetic acid) used as a mouthwash helps to neutralize ammonium. Hard candy, gum, and cold liquids help improve the taste in the mouth. The more critical the patient's condition, the more mouth care will be required, and in some cases it may have to be given hourly. Whatever method is used must meet the needs of the patient. The mouth may be dry because of dyspnea or because of the effects of receiving oxygen. Humidification of the air will provide moisture and relieve dryness.

Patients who are given a regimen of bed rest may develop decubiti or pulmonary complications and should be turned regularly and encouraged to breathe deeply. The use of an alternating air pressure pad may provide comfort for some patients. Skin care is extremely important in the care of patients with chronic renal failure. Mild soap such as Basis, a baking soda solution, or bath oil may be used to cleanse the skin. Lanolin or other ointments may be ordered to relieve itching. Nails should be kept short so the patient will not scratch and traumatize the skin.[10] Edematous areas should be supported with pillows and circulation stimulated through active or passive exercises. Edematous extremities should be elevated above the level of the heart.

If the patient's vision is failing, care should be taken to prevent injury. Padded side rails should be used for patients who are confused or disoriented. The nurse should be sure that an oral airway is kept at the bedside or nearby in case convulsions should occur.

Blood transfusions may be necessary, and

only washed donor cells may be used, especially if the patient is awaiting transplant. Antigens should not be introduced into the body unnecessarily because the formation of antigen-antibody complexes may limit the patient's ability to accept a donor kidney. Blood transfusions, together with hyperkalemia, fluid retention, and hypertension, may result in congestive heart failure. In treating congestive heart failure, it must be remembered that drugs normally excreted by the kidney, such as digoxin, will require reduced dosages and that diuretics that depend on glomerular filtration will not be effective.

Patients with chronic renal failure should be encouraged to participate in self-care activities and to remain active if their condition permits.

Dialysis

Hemodialysis. Hemodialysis is an extracorporeal mechanical method of removing waste products and establishing equilibrium of electrolytes and water when the kidneys are unable to perform their functions. Hemodialysis is accomplished by the use of the artificial kidney called a *dialyzer*, and may be used in (1) chronic renal failure, (2) acute renal failure, and (3) drug poisoning. Hemodialysis will not cure the damage caused by renal disease, but will remove waste products from the body and prevent damage to other organs until further treatment can be instituted and healing of the kidney takes place.

The process of hemodialysis is as follows: blood leaves the body and flows through sterile tubing, a sterile **dialyzer** (also called an artifical kidney), more sterile tubing, and back to the body. The dialyzer is composed of two compartments that are separated by a semipermeable membrane, which is similar to cellophane. In one compartment is the patient's blood and in the other compartment is the dialyzing solution that is chemically similar to blood. As the blood and the dialyzing solutions circulate on the two sides of the semipermeable membrane, waste products leave the bloodstream, cross the membrane, and enter the dialyzing solution, which is changed periodically. Therefore the dialysis process occurs across the semipermeable membrane inside the dialyzer. The dialyzer is attached to a hemodialysis machine that has different pumps and safety devices. Nurses with additional education conduct hemodialysis on patients, and the reader is referred to Lancaster[10] and Richard[18] for a thorough discussion of hemodialysis.

There are three basic circulatory accesses to remove and return the blood. The *external arteriovenous shunt* requires the insertion of cannulas in an artery and a vein, usually on the forearm (Figure 19-7). Each cannula is attached to the dialysis tubing during hemodialysis treatment, but otherwise they are attached to each other by a connector. This shunt is intended for short term use.

An alternative to the arteriovenous shunt is the insertion of a specially designed, double-lumen *catheter* through the subclavian or jugular vein. The catheter is designed so that blood is removed from a point proximal to the insertion site, routed through the dialyzer, and returned through a distal hole in the catheter. The Quinton catheter and Quinton-Mahurkar are examples (Figure 19-8). The subclavian or jugular site is easier to protect and maintain than the shunt site in the forearm. It can be used for a number of weeks. The site must be cleansed and redressed regularly, as for any long-term infusion catheter. The other method used to conduct dialysis involves an *arteriovenous fistula*, in which a vein is surgically anastomosed to an artery. The vein then becomes distended, and the vessel wall thickens and can be palpated easily so that needles can be inserted for dialysis hookup (Figure 19-7).

Patients can be maintained on dialysis therapy and their lives prolonged pending the possibility of a kidney transplant. When long-term dialysis is necessary for end stage renal disease, the patient may go to a dialysis center, usually two or three times weekly, and remain approximately 4 to 6 hours for the treatment. Some patients secure their treatment at night and go about their normal activities during the day. Smaller, portable units have been developed that allow the patient to be dialyzed anywhere. Many patients, with the help of an assistant, dialyze themselves at home.

Patients receiving dialysis therapy need a great deal of psychologic support and encouragement. Most patients realize the seriousness of their condition. They may become depressed and question why they are being kept alive. The patient's family members play a most important role.

Personnel who work with hemodialysis patients must be specially educated in anatomy, physiology, pathology of the kidney, and pharmacology. Usually each dialysis center has its own education program, lasting 6 to 12 weeks.

Peritoneal dialysis. Peritoneal dialysis was the original substitute for a nonfunctioning kidney. It can be performed in any hospital with min-

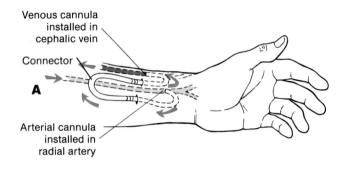

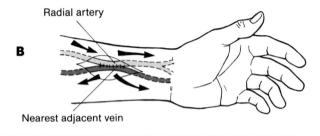

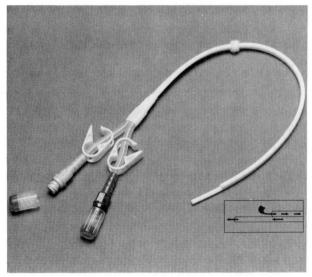

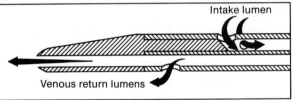

Figure 19-7

Hemodialysis circulatory accesses. **A,** External arteriovenous shunt. A cannula is inserted into a vein and another cannula is inserted into an artery. The two cannulas are joined by a connector. Arrows indicate the direction of blood flow. **B,** Arteriovenous fistula. An artery and vein are surgically anastomosed. Blood flows through the artery into the vein and arterilizes the vein. Arrows indicate the direction of blood flow.

Figure 19-8

A, This double lumen hemodialysis catheter is available for subclavian and femoral insertion. **B,** (Enlargement of small insert in Figure A). The distance between the venous return lumen and the return intake lumen assures minimal recirculation. *(Photos courtesy of Quintron Instrument Company, Seattle, Wash.)*

imum equipment, and new systems have been developed that can be used while the patient is ambulatory. In all types of peritoneal dialysis, a fluid is instilled into the peritoneal space by gravity, allowed to remain there long enough to collect waste products and excess electrolytes that have been left in the blood by the nonfunctioning kidney, then drained from the space and discarded. While in the peritoneal space, the fluid, called *dialysate,* bathes the peritoneal membrane. The waste products and electrolytes pass through the capillaries in the membrane, by the processes of osmosis and diffusion, into the dialysate. The chemical composition of the dialysate is designed to promote removal of products from the blood in the same way it functions in hemodialysis.

The catheter is inserted into the peritoneal cavity using a technique that is similar to abdominal paracentesis. A trocar, a large needle with a large bore, is inserted through a tiny incision made in the skin of the abdomen. During insertion, a stylet is in place in the bore of the trocar; after insertion, the stylet is removed, and a catheter with tiny holes running the length of all sides

is inserted through the trocar. The trocar is then withdrawn, and the catheter remains in the peritoneal cavity.

Next, 2000 ml of dialyzing solution is allowed to run into the peritoneal cavity and remain for 30 to 60 minutes. The solution is warmed before it is instilled to improve its effectiveness and to prevent chilling of the patient. The fluid is then drained by gravity. When 100 to 200 ml of solution remains in the cavity, another bottle of solution is connected and the process is repeated. Sterile technique is observed when inserting the catheter and caring for the site. All connections to the tubing and the addition of bottles of solution must be done in a manner that prevents contamination of the inside of the tubing, the site, and the solution.

During the procedure the patient should be observed for signs of abdominal or respiratory distress, change in vital signs, and bleeding. The amount of fluid instilled and drained should be carefully recorded. The patient should be weighed before and after the procedure. The catheter is removed when the process is completed. If the procedure is to be repeated in a day or two, the pathway to the peritoneal cavity may be kept open with a sterile plastic tube specially designed for this purpose. A sterile dressing is applied to the site; the incision is small and does not require repair with sutures.

Considering the time required for this procedure to remove the waste products, it is easy to see how hemodialysis, came to be the preferred method for the patient with chronic renal failure. It is not practical to spend 24 hours, every other day, confined to bed or a hospital unit, receiving a peritoneal dialysis treatment. Although hemodialysis does restrict the patient, it is at least less time consuming.

Continuous ambulatory peritoneal dialysis, or *CAPD* removes some of these restrictions from the patient with end-stage renal disease. It allows the patient to receive dialysis at home, during the night while asleep or while ambulatory at home, work, or play. A catheter is inserted surgically and is left in place and covered by a sterile dressing. The catheter is placed in the peritoneal space through an incision, and the distal end is tunneled through a 3- or 4-inch section of subcutaneous tissue on the abdomen, then brought out to the surface of the abdomen. This tunnel creates a barrier to prevent infection of the peritoneal cavity if the catheter site should become infected. The patient is taught to meticulously care for the catheter and site, using a sterile technique. Before and after connecting the dialysate tubing, the connection is disinfected with a povidone-iodine (Betadine) soak for about 20 minutes.

For nighttime dialysis, the dialysate instillation is regulated by a machine that automatically starts the flow of solution, times the period it remains in the cavity, and then allows the fluid to drain by gravity. Safety mechanisms are built into the machine to prevent fluid from being instilled if the previous instillation has not drained adequately. Multiple bottles of dialysate are hooked up to the machine, and it automatically instills each bottle in sequence. Used dialysate is likewise collected in multiple bottles that are weighed by the machine to verify complete elimination before the next bottle is instilled. An alarm sounds to waken the patient if any problem is sensed by the machine.

For daytime dialysis with continuous ambu-latory peritoneal dialysis, the patient attaches a small bag of dialysate to the catheter, instills it, then rolls it up and tucks it in an inconspicuous place while the dialysate is instilled. Later, the dialysate is drained into the same bag and discarded. The procedure is repeated as necessary to maintain the waste products in the blood at a safe level, usually four times each day. Research and development of new products and techniques continue to make life more *livable* for the patient dependent on dialysis.[18]

Renal transplantation

A renal transplantation is the procedure of placing a normal kidney from a donor into a person with nonfunctioning kidneys. The most successful transplants are those done with a sibling or family member with the same blood and tissue typing. By carefully matching the donor kidney with the recipient, kidneys from unrelated people and from cadavers are transplanted with fair success.

The patient may undergo a bilateral nephrectomy in preparation for the transplant if the kidneys are severely infected or if the patient has severe diastolic hypertension. This patient will experience a sense of loss, even though the absent kidneys were not functioning. The kidneys may both be left in place for transplant surgery, since the donor kidney is placed in the iliac fossa and receives its blood supply from the iliac arteries. Dialysis is necessary until the transplantation can be accomplished.

Postoperative care is centered around careful observation of hourly urine output and maintaining patency of the indwelling catheter along with the maintenance of intravenous fluid and electrolyte therapy. Massive diuresis or oliguria may be possible. Additional nursing measures are similar to those of any major surgical procedure. A central venous pressure line may be in place to monitor fluid needs. The patient is weighed daily to monitor fluid retention. The patient must be observed carefully for signs of *rejection* of the donor kidney, which include decreased urine output, increased blood pressure, fever, and swelling and tenderness at the site of the implanted kidney.

The major problem in transplantation is that of rejection. Before surgery the patient's immunologic responses are suppressed, and immunosuppressive therapy is continued long after discharge. Cyclosporin (Sandimmune), a drug obtained from soil fungus, has revolutionized the success of organ transplantation, including kidney transplants.[21] Cyclosporin may be used as a single immunosuppressant agent or in conjunction with steroids. Cyclosporin may be administered intravenously or orally. Because cyclosporin is prepared in an oil base, patients may find it unpalatable. Administering it with food or diluting it in chocolate milk may help the patient ingest the drug. Therapeutic levels of cyclosporin are carefully monitored with a radioimmunoassay since, ironically, elevated levels of cyclosporin are nephrotoxic.

Other drugs that may be used are azathioprine (Imuran), prednisone, and methylprednisolone (Solu-Medrol).

The patient will also be given furosemide (Lasix) to control fluid retention, aluminum phosphate gel (Phosphaljel) to protect the stomach during steroid therapy, hydralazine (Apresoline), and methyldopa (Aldomet) for the control of blood pressure, and sulfisoxazole (Gantrisin) and mystatin (Mycostatin) to prevent infections. The visible side effects of steroid therapy, namely moon face and weight gain, may be the greatest problem for the patient during recovery. As immunosuppressive therapy is withdrawn, the physical appearance returns to normal. The rejection may occur soon after surgery, or it may be delayed for months or even years after transplantation. The possibility of rejection is a very important factor to the patient. The patient must be encouraged and facilitated in expressing concerns about rejection and the long-term prognosis. The patient must be prepared for discharge and convalescence by being taught the importance of taking medications, keeping appointments with the physician or clinic, and keeping track of how he or she feels. Psychologically, the patient must adopt the new kidney.

OPERATIVE CONDITIONS OF THE URINARY SYSTEM

Many conditions affecting the urinary system require both medical and surgical treatment, and operative procedures are seldom done until a thorough urologic examination has been completed. The preoperative care of patients does not differ greatly from that of other surgical patients. When surgery involves the kidney, the patient's blood is typed and cross-matched in case transfusion should be necessary. The postoperative care differs from other kinds of surgery in that drains, tubes, or catheters are placed to remove urine.

Many patients after surgery on the urinary system will have draining wounds. Although patients may have understood this before surgery, when they are faced with the discomfort of wet dressings, the odor of urine, and the resulting skin irritation, they may become irritable and depressed and feel that adjustment is impossible. It may challenge the nurse to find ways to overcome these problems. Because dressings need to be changed frequently, Montgomery straps or laced dressings could be used to avoid irritation from adhesive tape. Small dressings changed frequently will keep the patient more comfortable than large bulky ones that become saturated, heavy, and foul smelling. A ureterostomy cup may be applied and attached to free drainage, or the disposable plastic urostomy bags may be used for some patients. Wound drainage bags are available that may be effective in some drainage problems. Any device used is only an adjunct to good nursing care, which includes cleansing the skin and protecting wounds from infection.

Cystectomy

A **cystectomy** is the surgical removal of the bladder and may be partial or complete. The surgery may be necessitated because of malignant tumors involving the bladder and adjacent structures. When the bladder is removed, the ureters are transplanted by one of the methods discussed in the following section to provide for urinary drainage. The nursing care is the same as that for patients having abdominal surgery. The prostate gland may have been removed through a perineal wound, and such wounds must be observed for evidence of hemorrhage. The patient will have a nasogastric tube connected to suction siphonage and will be given nothing by mouth for several days. During this time the patient should receive special mouth care at frequent intervals. If a partial resection of the bladder has been done, a catheter will be inserted into the remaining bladder, and precautions must be taken to prevent any pulling on the catheter. The tubing should be pinned to the sheet and sufficient slack allowed to permit the patient to turn.

Urinary Diversion: Ureteral Transplants

Several types of procedures are used to divert the flow of urine when required for treatment of bladder cancer, invasive cancer of the cervix, neuro-

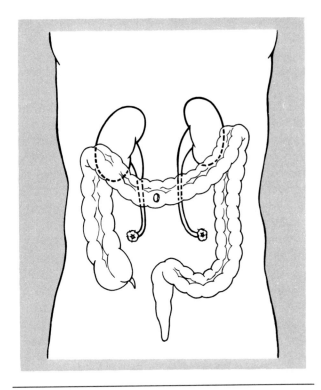

Figure 19-9

Cutaneous ureterostomy in which ureters are brought through skin onto abdomen.

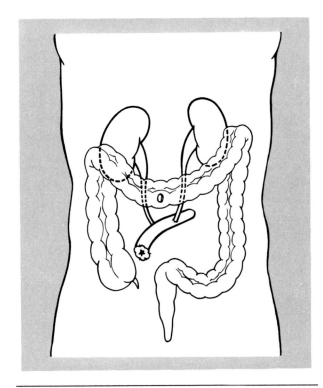

Figure 19-10

Ileal conduit.

genic bladder, and congenital anomalies. The *ureterosigmoidostomy* involves implanting the ureters into the large bowel, which is left intact so that both urine and feces are eliminated rectally. This technique is rarely used today because of the undesirable effects on the perianal skin resulting from chronically liquid stool. A variation of this procedure is the formation of an isolated rectal pouch into which the ureters are implanted, while the remainder of the bowel is diverted to form a sigmoid colostomy.

A second procedure, *cutaneous ureterostomy*, involves direct implantation of the terminal ends of the ureters onto the skin (Figure 19-9). The ureters may be joined so that there is only one stoma, or each ureter may be brought to the skin separately, forming two stomas. A third procedure, the *ileal conduit*, is a common method of urinary diversion at present (Figure 19-10). In this procedure a section of the ileum is resected from the small bowel, and its blood supply is preserved. The remaining small bowel is then anastomosed so that normal bowel function will be maintained. The resected segment of ileum is sutured closed at one end, forming a pouch, and the other end is sutured to the skin, forming a stoma. The ureters are transplanted into this segment of ileum, which forms a conduit that serves as a passageway for urine to flow from the body. It does not serve as a reservoir for urine.

A variation of the ileal conduit is the *continent urostomy (or Koch's pouch)*, in which the pouch is formed from the ileum. In this instance the reservoir can hold up to 800 ml of urine. A large segment of the ileum is structured into an internal pouch with two nipple valves. The ureters are implanted into the reservoir, and a portion of the ileal reservoir is brought out transcutaneously and fashioned into a stoma. Patients are taught to catheterize this pouch approximately four times a day, and they do not need to wear an external urinary appliance. A small bandage over the stoma is sufficient.[5]

Cutaneous ureterostomy

When the ureters have been transplanted to the abdominal wall skin, the patient may have soft rubber catheters in place for about 1 week if the ureters are small. It is important that the catheters drain adequately so that hydronephrosis does not develop.

If cutaneous ureterostomies heal properly, the patient can use ostomy bags instead of catheters for drainage. The bags may be applied to the skin with adhesive disks and may require changing only every 2 or 3 days. The technique for applying the bag is not difficult, but it does take practice. When the bag is first applied, the nurse must make sure that there is adequate drainage from the kidney. If the patient complains of any back pain, the appliance should be removed at once and reapplied. Sometimes obstruction to drainage is caused by angulation of the ureter or by temporary ureteral edema.

If the ureter is angulated or if there is stomal stenosis, the kidney will have to be drained permanently with a catheter. If the patient must wear ureteral catheters, he or she is taught to irrigate these each day. Patients must return to the physician every 2 to 4 weeks to have the catheters changed, or they are taught to change their own catheters. The catheters are anchored to the skin with adhesive tape, or a catheter disk with a belt is used. The catheters are attached by tubing to a drainage receptacle. This procedure is not commonly used, since infections occur frequently, causing a series of complications.

Ileal conduit (ileobladder)

The **ileal conduit** is a method of urinary diversion that results in fewer fluid and electrolyte problems and provides an added barrier to infection (the conduit). Preoperatively, the patient will have little or no special preparation of the bowel, since the ileum is considered sterile. Careful preoperative measurement and inspection of the abdomen for optimum placement of the stoma will facilitate movement and application of an appliance for urinary drainage postoperatively.

Postoperative complications related to abdominal surgery must be prevented. The abdomen should be observed for any changes that might indicate inflammation. Paralytic ileus can occur as a result of manipulation of the bowel. There is a possibility of urine leakage at the suture lines, which allows urine to enter the peritoneal cavity; the resultant inflammation causes pain, fever, nausea, and vomiting. The patient's abdomen will feel rigid and will be sensitive to the touch. A nasogastric tube is usually inserted to decompress the bowel until peristalsis returns. Oral intake is restricted or prohibited while the nasogastric tube is in place.

The patient will return from surgery with a catheter in place or with a temporary transparent appliance attached to the skin to collect urine. If the catheter is used, it is attached to a sterile gravity drainage system. The appliance is also attached to a drainage system to provide for the flow of urine, which will be continuous. Urinary flow must be maintained; if it is allowed to distend the conduit, it will cause back pressure on the kidneys, damaging them, or it will rupture the suture lines. The nurse must watch closely for low abdominal pain and decreased urinary output. Urine output may be measured hourly in the early postoperative period.

When the stoma has healed, a permanent (reusable) appliance is fitted to the patient. Disposable appliances are available (Figure 19-11) but are expensive; therefore patients may choose a reusable appliance. Proper application of the appliance will prevent leaking and irritation of the skin. The stoma is covered with gauze or a tampon to absorb urine while the area around the stoma is cleaned. A skin barrier such as Stomahesive may be applied directly to the skin before the appliance is applied, or the skin may be prepared in some other manner. It is essential to keep the skin dry before applying the appliance, or it will not adhere. Permanent appliances have a faceplate that is attached to the skin with cement or a double-faced adhesive. The collection pouch is attached to the faceplate. A permanent appliance can be worn for 3 to 7 days if applied properly. It is recommended that the patient purchase a second appliance so that one may be cleaned and aired while the other is worn.

The psychologic problems that result from urinary diversion are similar to those occurring from diversion of the intestinal tract. The necessity for the surgery has been a traumatic experience, and the patient must adapt to an altered body image. The patient must be supported and reassured when learning to care for the urostomy and encouraged to continue everyday activities once he or she has recuperated from surgery. It may be beneficial to consult an ostomy nurse specialist.

Postoperative intervention. The box on p. 526 lists the nursing diagnoses and nursing interventions following the patient's surgery to create a urinary diversion, including cutaneous ureterostomy and ileal conduit.

Cystotomy

A cystotomy is a surgical incision into the bladder and may be performed for various reasons, including the correction of prostatic hypertrophy in connection with suprapubic prostatectomy. It

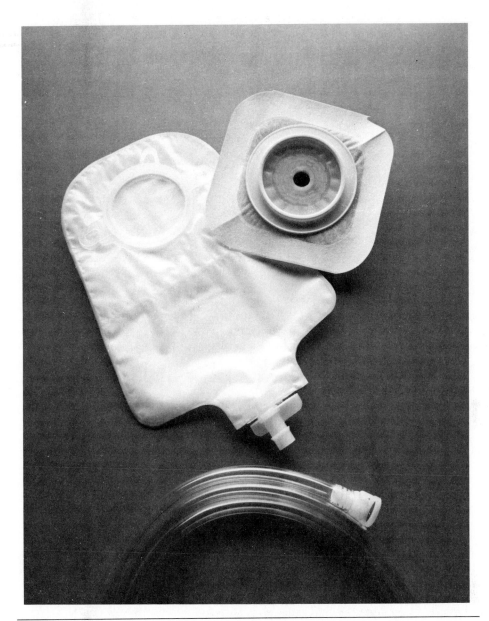

Figure 19-11
Disposable appliances for ileal conduit or other urinary diversion (urostomy). Faceplate attaches to skin as barrier and drainable bag attaches to flange on skin barrier. Drainage tube can be attached for nighttime use. *(Copyright 1983, Hollister Incorporated. All rights reserved).*

may be performed to remove tumors or stones from the bladder.

The preoperative care of the patient is the same as that for other abdominal surgery. When the patient returns from surgery, a drainage tube will have been inserted into the bladder, which may be connected to a drainage bag. The dressings will have to be changed frequently to keep the patient dry and comfortable. The skin must be kept clean, and a protective ointment may be used to prevent irritation. Blood pressure and pulse must be checked frequently during the immediate postoperative period, and the patient must be turned from side to side to prevent pulmonary complications.

Ureterotomy and Lithotomy

Surgery on the ureter is generally performed to remove a stone, to repair a severed ureter, or to do plastic repair of a stricture. If the stone is in

---

NURSING CARE GUIDELINES
Urinary Diversion, Postoperative Phase

Nursing diagnoses

- Activity intolerance related to anxiety, pain, weakness, fatigue
- Anxiety related to fear, prognosis
- Alteration in bowel elimination (constipation) related to decreased activity, painful defecation
- Alteration in comfort related to pain
- Ineffective individual coping related to anxiety, depression
- Fear related to disease process, hospitalization, powerlessness, real or imagined threat to well-being, surgical procedure
- Fluid volume deficit related to abnormal fluid loss, decreased fluid intake
- Impaired home maintenance management related to home environment obstacles, inadequate support system
- Knowledge deficit related to limited understanding of disease process, prescribed treatment
- Disturbance in self-concept related to body image, role performance, self-esteem
- Sexual dysfunction related to altered bladder control, body image, depression, impotence, physiologic limitations
- Alteration in urinary elimination pattern related to diversion

Nursing interventions

- Administer standard immediate postoperative care, for example, frequent vital signs
- Measure and record intake and output
- Report absence of urinary drainage immediately
- Maintain intravenous fluid and electrolyte infusions
- Provide mouth care every 4 hours while patient is awake
- Maintain patency of nasogastric tube, and cleanse and lubricate nostril through which tube passes
- Monitor return of peristalsis by observing for flatus, listening for bowel sounds once every 8 hours
- Administer nothing by mouth until ordered, based on return of bowel function
- Administer analgesics as ordered to relieve pain and facilitate movement
- Turn patient every 2 hours and encourage coughing, deep breathing, and leg exercises
- Ambulate as early as orders permit
- Maintain patency of drainage tubes
- Facilitate expression of feelings about altered body image
- Assess integrity and color of the stoma every shift
- Teach about disease process and treatment

Cutaneous ureterostomy

- Maintain patency of ureteral catheters
- Put ureterostomy cups or urostomy bags in place after catheters removed
- Dilate ureters with sterile catheters as ordered to assure patency and prevent ureteral stricture

Ileal conduit

- Maintain drainage bag over stoma or catheter in stoma to collect urine; attach catheter to gravity drainage
- Empty drainage bag every 2 hours; attach to gravity drainage bag at night
- Control odor of urine and in appliance by:
  Avoiding odor-producing foods
  Giving cranberry juice
  Adding commercial deodorizers to bag
  Washing permanent appliance with detergent and water and rinsing in vinegar water; air dry over night; patient uses two permanent appliances, alternating one each day or uses disposable appliances
- Change appliance and cleanse skin as follows:
  Remove appliance
  Bend over to drain conduit before cleansing skin
  Clean cement from skin with adhesive solvent
  Wash skin with soap and water
  Apply stomahesive skin barrier or powder for skin irritation
  Apply cement or liquid adhesive or double-faced adhesive disks and appliance
  Instruct patient and gradually involve the patient in care until self-care possible

Expected outcomes

- Adequate urinary drainage maintained
- Discomfort relieved
- No signs or symptoms of infection
- Actively participates in care
- Adequate nutritional and fluid states maintained
- Describes disease process, surgical intervention, and responsibility for care
- Relates less anxiety from fear of unknown, loss of control, or misinformation
- Shares feelings about control of elimination and bodily changes
- Patient and family verbalize fears and concerns
- Skin integrity maintained

the ureter, a *ureterolithotomy* is performed. Removal of the stone from the kidney is a *nephrolithotomy,* and removal of the stone from the kidney pelvis is a *pyelolithotomy.* Patients having a stone removed from the lower third of the ureter will have an abdominal incision, and care is similar to that for any patient with abdominal surgery. However, the incision will drain urine for several days after surgery, since the ureter cannot be closed with watertight sutures or strictures will form. Stones removed from the upper two thirds of the ureter and the kidney will necessitate a flank or kidney incision.

The postoperative care of the patient is directed toward the care of tubes and maintaining drainage. Occasionally, a catheter is inserted into the ureter, which serves as a splint while healing occurs. It is important that the catheter be kept in place at all times. When there is urinary drainage onto the skin, there must be frequent change of dressings and cleansing of the skin to prevent irritation and maceration. All urinary drainage should be measured and recorded.[18]

The box at right summarizes the nursing diagnoses and nursing interventions for the patient following lithotomy.

Nephrectomy and Nephrostomy

A **nephrectomy** is the surgical removal of the kidney and may be done because of tumors, chronic infection, or to provide a kidney for transplantation. No matter what the reason for the nephrectomy, the patient needs emotional support and an opportunity to express and discuss feelings about the loss of a body part.

A small drain may be placed in the wound for incisional drainage. When the patient has had a nephrectomy, there may be minimal amount of drainage from the wound for the first 24 to 48 hours, gradually diminishing.

Dressings should be checked frequently for evidence of fresh bleeding, since hemorrhage is always a possibility. Vital signs are watched, and any significant change in the pulse rate with restlessness should be reported to the physician. Gastrointestinal complications with nausea, vomiting, and abdominal distention may occur. Fluids by mouth may be restricted and a nasogastric tube inserted, which should be connected to suction drainage.

The most important postoperative concern is that good urinary drainage be established from the remaining kidney. The patient may have a retention catheter in place, which is connected to

---

> ### NURSING CARE GUIDELINES
> ### *Lithotomy, Postoperative Phase*
> ### *(ureterolithotomy, pyelolithotomy,*
> ### *nephrolithotomy)*
>
> **Nursing diagnoses**
> - Activity intolerance related to anxiety, pain, weakness, fatigue
> - Alteration in bowel elimination related to decreased activity, painful defecation
> - Alteration in comfort related to pain
> - Ineffective individual coping related to anxiety, depression
> - Fear related to disease process, hospitalization, powerlessness, real or imagined threat to well-being, surgical procedure
> - Fluid volume deficit related to abnormal fluid loss, decreased fluid intake
> - Knowledge deficit related to limited understanding of disease process, prescribed treatment
>
> **Nursing intervention**
> - Weigh daily
> - Use standard immediate postoperative care
> - Anticipate drainage from wound; secure dressing with Montgomery straps
> - Change sterile dressing as often as necessary to keep dry; use caution to prevent displacement of Penrose drain in wound
> - Maintain patency of bladder catheter
> - Measure and record intake and output
> - Observe color of urine
> - Relieve pain with analgesics as ordered
> - Splint incision during movement and coughing
> - Assist males to stand when voiding
> - Instruct on disease process and treatment
>
> **Expected outcomes**
> - Maintain adequate urinary drainage
> - Discomfort relieved
> - Actively participates in care
> - Relates less anxiety from fear of unknown or misinformation
> - Describes disease process, surgical intervention, and care
> - Adequate nutritional fluid status maintained
> - No signs or symptoms of infection

---

gravity drainage; if the patient does not void, catheterization may be ordered. All intake and output must be carefully measured and recorded.

The patient will find it difficult to breathe deeply because of the location of the incision. In some cases the thoracic cavity may have been opened, and the patient will have chest tubes connected to underwater drainage. Medication for pain should be given, after which the incision may be splinted and the patient encouraged to breathe deeply. The patient will be positioned according to the approach used for surgery. The patient is usually out of bed on the first postoperative day and ambulatory soon after. Most patients are able to tolerate a regular diet by the fourth postoperative day, with a fluid intake of approximately 3000 ml

When the patient leaves the hospital, he or she is advised to avoid heavy lifting and straining for 6 weeks, to maintain fluid intake, and to avoid alcohol. The patient should be advised to avoid respiratory tract infections and activities that might result in injury to the other kidney.

A *nephrostomy* is an incision into the kidney pelvis for the purpose of drainage. The postoperative care of the patient with a nephrostomy or pyelostomy is the same as that for nephrectomy except for the presence of catheters, which are attached to drainage (Figure 19-12). The nurse should watch carefully to be sure that the catheters do not become plugged with a blood clot. The physician's orders concerning turning the patient onto the affected side should be clearly understood. Drainage must be accurately measured and

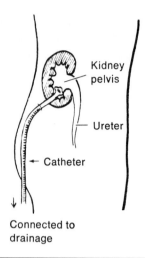

Figure 19-12
Nephrostomy with catheter in kidney pelvis. Catheter is brought out through skin incision and connected to tubing and gravity drainage.

recorded, and dressings about the tubes or wound may have to be changed frequently. The skin may be kept clean by washing with mild soap and water and dried to prevent irritation. If tubes have been placed in both kidneys, both tubes should be placed on one side of the bed. (For instructions on irrigating these tubes, see the discussion for catheter care on p. 507.)

NURSING CARE PLAN
Patient with Chronic Renal Failure

The patient is a 39-year-old female who comes into the outpatient dialysis unit for hemodialysis treatments three times per week because of chronic renal failure secondary to diabetic nephropathy. An internal arteriovenous fistula in her left arm is used as an access for dialysis. Physically, she has been tolerating the dialysis treatments well with only mild dizziness at the end of each session.

The dialysis nurses have noted, however, that Emily gets irritated about 1 hour into the treatment. She calls to the nurses to check the machine, solutions, or her blood pressure, all of which are normal.

Emily has been on dialysis treatments on a regular basis for 6 months. She is on the transplant list, awaiting a matched donor.

Past medical history
Diagnosed as having Juvenile Diabetes (insulin dependent) at age 8.

Good control until adolescence. Multiple hospitalizations from age 12 to 19. Periods of noncompliance, denial of the diabetes, and growth spurts.
Appendectomy at age 16.
First pregnancy at age 21. Baby a fetal demise at 39 weeks.
Second pregnancy at age 22. Complicated by preeclampsia. C-sectioned at 36 weeks, viable male infant weighing 10 lbs.
Third pregnancy at age 26. Mild toxemia, repeat C-section at 36 weeks, viable female infant weighing 9 lbs 15 oz.
Abdominal hysterectomy (uterus only) at age 29.
Hospitalized at ages 30 and 37 for severe episodes of vomiting leading to ketoacidosis.
Major illness at age 38, characterized by intractable vomiting, diarrhea, ketoacidosis, and coma. Diabetic nephropathy and retinopathy identified at that admission. Being followed closely by specialists for both conditions.

Immunizations up-to-date. Last tetanus booster 3 years ago.

No known food or drug allergies.

Has never smoked.

Family history

Incomplete as to biologic family. Adopted as an infant. Is in the process of petitioning the courts to obtain birth records to identify genetic relatives in the hopes of locating a matched donor.

Phychosocial data

Currently a housewife. Not employed outside of the home.

Has completed 2 years of junior college. Now attending a 4-year program, wants to obtain a degree as a counselor.

Divorced for 10 years. States she has a "friendly" relationship with her exhusband due to the children.

Has 2 children: 17-year-old Dan Jr., a high school sophmore, and 13-year-old Lisa, who is in the 8th grade.

Is living with her boyfriend David who is supportive and caring.

Current living situation for 6 years. Both children spend every other weekend with their father and stepmother.

Receives disability through Social Security, also on Medicaid (title 19).

Exhusband is a lawyer, contributes child support payments on a regular basis.

Owns own home—multi-level split style, but master bedroom on 1st floor.

Quality relationships with adoptive parents, siblings and ex-inlaws.

Religion: Lutheran, active in church, sings in the choir.

Hobbies: likes to read, garden, knit, and draw. Is an avid hockey fan, has season tickets to local professional team.

Because she does not feel well enough to drive after dialysis treatments, David brings her to the dialysis center during his lunch hour at noon, and returns to pick her up at 6 pm (treatment time is from 1-6 pm, Monday, Wednesday and Friday).

Assessment data

Height 5 ft 4 in Weight 118 lbs.

Oriented × 3 (time, place, and person).

Skin: Dry and scaly. Dusky color at times. Usually pale but has been noted to be gray. Signs of irritation from scratching evident on chest and arms. No signs of infection. Small areas of broken skin on right chest wall.

A-V fistula in left forearm (is right handed).

EENT: Full extraocular movements (EOMs). Wears glasses for nearsightedness. Last ocular visit 3 months ago.

Teeth in good repair. Visits dentist regularly.

Respiratory: Regular rate and rhythm (18-20). All lung fields clear to percussion and ascultation.

Breasts: Firm. No nipple discharge. No masses or tenderness on palpation (Practices breast self-examination monthly.)

Had mammogram 6 months ago, negative findings.

Abdominal: Soft, nontender, nondistended. Midline scar noted.

Cardiovascular: Apical rate 68. Best heard at apex. S1, S2 heard. All peripheral pulses felt.

Musculoskeletal: Full range of motion. Joints not inflamed or painful. Steady gait.

Lab data

Blood sugar (fasting) = 128. Does own blood sugar daily.

Hgb 9.4 Hct 27 WBC 8500 Platelets 300,000.

Electrolytes WNL now. Prior to dialysis, potassium was high.

Screened on a weekly basis.

BUN 38. Had been as high as 76.

Creatinine clearance varies depending on when tested in relation to dialysis. Felt to have some residual nephron function

Medications

NPH insulin 46 units daily.

Regular insulin 8 to 10 units on a sliding scale.

Colace 100 mg po prn.

Centrum vitamin tab 1 po daily.

NURSING DIAGNOSIS

Diversional activity deficit related to long hours of treatment and relative immobility during treatment, as evidenced by statements of boredom and frequent turning of the channel selector of the TV set.

Expected patient outcomes	Nursing interventions	Evaluation for expected outcomes
Patient will identify the personal meaning of her usual diversional hobbies and incorporate these into her treatment times.	Encourage patient to discuss drawing and sketching in detail. Ask her what parts of these activities are most meaningful.	Patient will feel free to discuss the prolonged immobility and her negative feelings toward it.

Expected patient outcomes	Nursing interventions	Evaluation for expected outcomes
Patient will choose a desired activity that she can engage in. Patient will satisfactorily engage in her chosen diversional activity during periods of immobility.	Initiate a discussion of past artwork and have her describe specific details that give her pleasure. Focus on what patient *can* do with one hand and her other senses while sitting for 5 hours, rather than on what she *cannot* do. Encourage patient to use her analysis of the meaningful aspects of gardening to find something related to these activities. If necessary, prompt patient with ideas related to her analysis such as listening to tapes on gardening, drawing plans for use of oils or colored pencils, writing stories about painting, or planning hockey moves. Let patient know that the environment can be adapted for her use (such as moving a larger table near by, allowing her time to set up before hooking up the dialysis machine). Have patient identify what she needs for her chosen daily activities and plan together how to obtain the materials. Observe for periods of frustration and assist. Let patient know that changes in her plans are possible (i.e., adding new activities).	Patient will identify those diversional activities that appeal to her while immobilized. Patient will select certain activities to engage her time and mind while immobilized. Patient will plan a range of diversional activities and feel comfortable in asking for assistance in setting them up.

NURSING DIAGNOSIS

Potential for fluid volume excess related to compromised regulatory mechanisms, as evidenced by changes in neurologic, cardiovascular, respiratory, and renal status.

Expected patient outcomes	Nursing interventions	Evaluation for expected outcomes
Patient will not experience fluid volume excess as evidenced by: stable weight, stable BP and pulse, absence of gallop rhythm, usual mental status, normal breath sounds, absence of dyspnea, peripheral edema, distended neck veins, and CVP within the normal range. Patient avoids any complications of excess fluid volume. Patient has normal skin turgor. Patient has electrolytes that are within the normal range. Patient states her ability to breathe comfortably.	Assess for and report signs and symptoms of fluid volume excess: significant weight gain, (greater than 0.5 kg/day) elevated BP and pulse, (BP may not be elevated if fluid has shifted out of vascular space), development of an S3 and/or S4 gallop rhythm, change in mental status, crackles and diminished or absent breath sounds, dyspnea, orthopnea, peripheral edema, distended neck veins, or elevated CVP. If respiratory difficulty, help patient into a semi-Fowler's position to facilitate breathing.	At home, or in the dialysis center, patient does not experience symptoms of fluid volume excess. Patient can cite the importance of self-monitoring and self-regulating of all necessary parameters (i.e., weight, fluid intake and output). Patient identifies what symptoms to report to her physician/the dialysis center. Patient states the importance of immediately reporting any changes to either her physician or the dialysis center.

Expected patient outcomes	Nursing interventions	Evaluation for expected outcomes
Patient keeps her fluid intake at 500 ml plus the amount of urine output daily. Baseline weight of 118 to 120 lbs is maintained. Urine specific gravity remains within 1.005 to 1.020.	Administer oxygen as needed. Remind patient of the necessity of restricting fluids to 500 ml plus urine out amount daily. Discuss the importance of weighing herself daily and comparing and contrasting findings. Remind her to phone the dialysis center if her weight gain is over 4 lbs. per day. Reinforce teachings regarding measuring specific gravity testings. Discuss her sodium and potassium restricted diet. List foods that are to be avoided. Refer her to a dietician to incorporate food restrictions into the ADA diet exchanges. Teach patient to test all stools for occult blood. Have her give a return demonstration. Provide a diet high in calories from carbohydrates and fats. Reinforce with patient the importance of monitoring I & O. Remind patient of the need for frequent oral hygiene. Discuss the use of hard sugarless candy, gum, and cold liquids to help improve the taste in her mouth.	She takes the responsibility of teaching her children/significant other these untoward changes.

NURSING DIAGNOSIS

Powerlessness related to chronic illness, as evidenced by statements of ambivalent feelings about dependence on others.

Expected patient outcomes	Nursing interventions	Evaluation for expected outcomes
Patient acknowledges her fears, feelings, and concerns about the current situation. Patient makes decisions regarding the course of treatment. Patient participates in self-care activities such as personal hygiene. Patient decreases her level of anxiety by citing stressors and identifying ways to change responses (control for her). Patient expresses feelings of regained control. Patient accepts and adapts to lifestyle changes.	Encourage patient to express her feelings. Set aside time for meaningful discussions regarding daily happenings. Accept her feelings of powerlessness as normal. Plan to be present (if possible) during situations where feelings of powerlessness are likely to be greatest, and offer therapeutic use of self. Identify and develop patient's coping strategies, strengths (sense of humor) and resources, (extended family) for support.	Patient verbalizes both positive and negative feelings about her current situation. Patient describes strategies for decreasing anxiety. Patient demonstrates increased control by participation in decision making related to health care. She actively participates in planning and carrying out some aspects of care and treatment. Patient communicates a renewed sense of power and control over the current situation.

Continued on next page.

Expected patient outcomes	Nursing interventions	Evaluation for expected outcomes
Patient projects ahead to when her kidney transplant will hopefully alter her need for dialysis treatments.	Discuss situations that provoke feelings of anger, anxiety and powerlessness to search for areas that she can control. Encourage participation in self-care. Provide positive reinforcement for her attempts. Make her feel like a member of the health team by asking her opinion. Provide opportunities for her to make decisions relating to care, treatment, positioning, and ambulation. Encourage her family and significant other to support her without taking control. Explain rules, policies, procedures, and schedules to decrease areas of potential conflict. Modify the environment when possible to promote a sense of control.	Patient projects and daydreams about the time when her kidney transplant will alter her illness and treatment needs.

NURSING DIAGNOSIS

Sexuality pattern alteration related to illness and medical treatment
as evidenced by statements of concern about sexuality.

Expected patient outcomes	Nursing interventions	Evaluation for expected outcomes
Patient acknowledges some type of a depressive episode and problems in sexual functioning. Patient voices her feelings about potential or actual changes in sexual activity/desire. She identifies ways to enhance pleasure and improve interpersonal communication with significant other. Patient regains a sexual desire after recovery from depression. Patient and significant other accept a referral for sexual counseling, if necessary.	Initiate a trusting therapeutic relationship with patient. Provide time for privacy. Encourage her to express her feelings openly in a nonthreatening nonjudgmental atmosphere. Discuss with patient and significant other expressions of affection to enhance their relationship, and past supportive roles, especially in times of crisis. Offer a referral to counselors or support persons/groups, (I can cope).	Patient describes crying episodes, the treatment plan, and all the effects on her sexual desire. She expresses her concerns to primary nurse and significant other. Patient identifies at least three activities to enhance pleasure and communication with significant other. Patient reports the return of sexual fantasies and desire for sexual activity. Patient indicates a willingness to follow through with a referral if the sexuality problem remains unresolved.

REFERENCES AND ADDITIONAL READINGS

1. Bereza DH: The kidney and pregnancy. In Richard CJ (editor): Comprehensive nephrology nursing, Boston, 1986, Little, Brown & Co, Inc.
2. Bowker C: Focus on urinalysis, part 2, Nurs Times Suppl 82:1, 1986.
3. Bowker C: Focus on urinalysis, part 3, Nurs Times Suppl 82:1, 1986.
4. Brenner BM and Lazarus JM: Acute renal failure, ed 2, New York, 1988, Churchill Livingstone Inc.
5. Brogna L and Lakaszawski M: Nursing management: the continent urostomy, J Enterstom Ther 13:139, 1986.
6. Brunner LS and Suddarth DS: Textbook of medical-surgical nursing, ed 6, Philadelphia, 1987, JB Lippincott Co.
7. Bullock BL and Rosendahl PP: Pathophysiology adaptations and alterations in function, ed 2, Boston, 1988, Scott, Foresman & Co.
8. Droller M: Immunotherapy and genitourinary neoplasia, part III, Infect Control Urol Care 6(4):12, 1982.
9. Govoni LE and Hayes JE: Drugs and nursing implications, ed 6, Connecticut, 1988, Appleton-Century-Crofts.
10. Irrgang SL: Classifications of urinary incontinence, J Enterstom Ther 13:62, 1986.
11. Lancaster LE, editor: Core curriculum for nephrology nursing, ed 2, Pitman, NJ 1990, AJ Jannetti Inc.
12. Lancaster LE: Renal response to shock, Crit Care Nurs Clin No Amer 2(2):221, 1990.
13. Malasanos L and others: Health assessment, ed 4, St Louis, 1989, The CV Mosby Co.
14. McConnell EA and Zimmerman MF: Care of patients with urologic problems, Philadelphia, 1983, JB Lippincott Co.
15. Palubinskas AJ: Imaging the urinary tract. In Smith DR, editor: General urology, Los Altos, Calif, 1984, Lange Medical Books.
16. Phipps WJ, Long BC, and Woods NF: Medical-surgical nursing concepts and clinical practice, ed 3, St Louis, 1987, The CV Mosby Co.
17. Richard CJ: Assessment of renal structure and function and causes of renal failure. In Lancaster LE (editor): Core curriculum for nephrology nursing, ed 2, Pitman, NJ, 1990, AJ Jannette Inc.
18. Richard CJ: Comprehensive nephrology nursing, Boston, 1986, Little, Brown & Co.
19. Sanders R: Intrauterine detection of genitourinary anomalies by ultrasound, Infect Control Urol Care 6(4):5, 1982.
20. Spirnak JP and Resnick MI: Urinary stones. In Smith DR, editor: General Urology, Los Altos, Calif, 1984, Lange Medical Books.
21. Trusler LA: OKT® 3: Nursing considerations for use in acute renal failure transplant rejection, ANNA J 17:4, 1990.
22. Williams RD: Urologic laboratory examination. In Smith DR (editor): General urology, Los Altos, Calif, 1984, Lange Medical Books.

CHAPTER

20

PROBLEMS AFFECTING
Sexuality

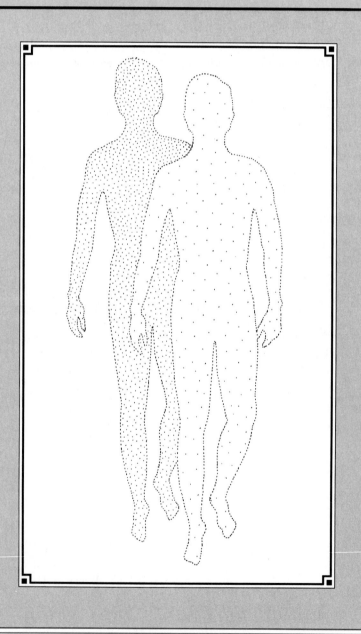

KEY WORDS

abortion
amenorrhea
benign prostatic hypertrophy
bilateral
climacteric
colposcopy
culdoscopy
curettage
dilation
dysmenorrhea
endometriosis
epididymitis
fimbriated
gynecology
hydrocele
hysterectomy
laparoscopy
mammography
mastectomy
mastitis
menarche
menopause
menorrhagia
metrorrhagia
ovulation
Papanicolaou smear test
pelvic exenteration
pessary
phimosis
prostatitis
puberty
vaginitis
varicocele
vulvovaginitis

OBJECTIVES

1. Discuss the physiology of menstruation and menopause.

2. Discuss the theories relating prostaglandins and progesterone to dysmenorrhea.

3. Identify those symptoms of menopause that are relieved by treatment with supplementary estrogen therapy.

4. Identify the purpose and nursing responsibilities for the following diagnostic tests: Papanicolaou smear, Schiller's test, breast examination, and Rubin's test.

5. Contrast the treatment of vaginitis caused by the Trichomonas organism with that caused by Candida albicans.

6. Identify the anatomical structures removed in simple vulvectomy.

7. Discuss medical indications for vulvectomy and its effects on female sexuality.

8. Discuss the effects of a hysterectomy on the woman's self-concept and sexuality.

9. Discuss the various classifications of abortion.

10. Discuss methods of breast reconstruction following a mastectomy.

11. Discuss the perioperative interventions for the following types of prostatectomy: transurethral, suprapubic, perineal, retropubic.

12. Describe the operative procedure and discuss the preoperative and postoperative intervention for the following methods of prostatectomy: transurethral, suprapubic, perineal, and retropubic.

13. Identify those procedures for prostatectomy that may result in incontinence, impotence, and sterility.

STRUCTURE AND FUNCTION
OF THE REPRODUCTIVE SYSTEM

The reproductive system includes the external genitalia of the male and female, as well as the internal organs associated with reproduction. The female and male breasts also play a role in sexual function and dysfunction. Sexual and reproductive development are influenced by the endocrine system, and the nervous system is involved in human sexual response.

The Female Reproductive System

The region encompassing the female external genitalia is usually referred to as the *vulva*. The vulva includes the mons pubis, a pad of fatty tissue that lies over the pubis; the labia majora and labia minora; the clitoris, located near the anterior folds of the labia minora; and the vaginal outlet, situated between the urinary meatus and the anus (Figure 20-1, *A*). The *perineum* is a muscular area lying between the anus and the vaginal outlet. The area of the perineum where the labia minora join posteriorly is called the *fourchette*. The clitoris enlarges during sexual stimulation and is a site of female orgasm. The vaginal outlet is the entrance to the vagina, located posterior to the bladder and anterior to the rectum and sigmoid bowel. The vagina functions as an organ of sexual pleasure, acts as an outlet for menstrual flow, and serves as a birth canal during delivery. The vagina is lubricated by secretions from two sets of glands, *Bartholin's glands* and *Skene's glands*. The cells of the vagina also provide some lubrication by producing secretions. During the childbearing period the epithelium that lines the vagina is arranged in transverse folds called *rugae*. After menopause the walls of the vagina become thin and smooth, resembling those of childhood. In the vagina and dividing the external genitalia from the internal organs is a thin fold of mucous membrane called the *hymen*. The hymen can become separated or torn during exercise, trauma, digital examination, or coitus.

The internal structures are located in the pelvic cavity and include the uterus, two fallopian tubes, and two ovaries (Figure 20-1, *B*). The *uterus* is a pear-shaped, hollow, muscular organ composed of three layers: the inner, **endometrial** layer, which is shed during menstruation; the middle layer, or *myometrium;* and outer layer, or *perimetrium*. The muscle layers are necessary during the labor of the birth process. The bulging,

upper part of the uterus is called the *fundus*. The lowest portion extends downward into the vagina and forms the cervix. The cervix has a narrow canal that has openings at the entrance and exit, called the *internal and external os*. The uterus is suspended in the pelvic cavity by the round, broad, and uterosacral ligaments. The two fallopian tubes are attached to and open into the upper part of the uterus. The distal end of the tubes has a **fimbriated** opening into the abdominal cavity; the ovaries are located near the distal end of each tube. The white, almond-shaped ovaries are attached to the uterus by a ligament. Each ovary consists of a cortex and a medulla; the ovarian follicles form within the cortex. From the time of menses the ovaries release an ovum each month, which is transported by a fallopian tube. The ovum is either fertilized in the tube and propelled to the uterus for implantation or shed with the endometrial lining of the uterus during menstruation (see Figure 20-1, *C*).

The female breast is composed of milk-producing glands called *acini;* the lactiferous ducts, which collect and deliver milk during lactation; and the nipple. The nipple is surrounded by a darkened area called the *areola*. The pigment of the areola deepens during pregnancy and with the use of oral contraceptives. The nipple is composed of erectile tissue and is capable of responding to sexual excitement. It is usually everted. *Montgomery's glands* are small elevations on the areola surrounding the nipple that secrete a lubricating and protective substance during lactation. The form of the breast is provided by subcutaneous and fatty tissue supported by the pectoralis major and pectoralis minor muscles. The female breast has a rich lymphatic system that drains from the breast to various nodes in the axilla.

The Male Reproductive System

The reproductive organs of the male include the penis, testes, vas deferens, seminal vesicles, and prostate gland. The penis is the primary organ of sexual pleasure in the male and also contains the urethra (Figure 20-1, *D*). The urethra is a long channel that runs from the floor of the bladder to the external opening, called the *urinary meatus*. The meatus is normally found at the end of the penis in the center of the glans penis, a bulging structure covered by a loose, retractable skin called the *prepuce,* or foreskin. The upper section of the urethra passes through the center of the

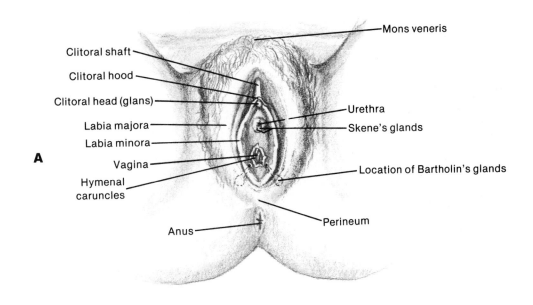

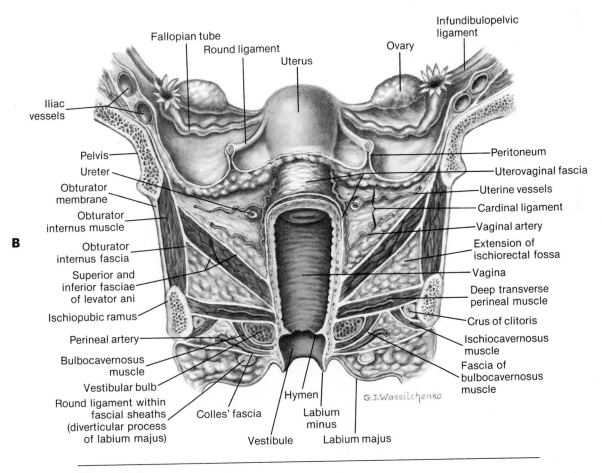

Figure 20-1

A, Female external genitalia. **B,** Posterior view of female internal reproductive organs.
(**A** *from Fogel CI and Woods NF: Health care of women: a nursing perspective, St Louis, 1981,*
The CV Mosby Co.; **B** *from Bobak I and Jensen MD: Essentials of maternity nursing, St Louis,*
1984, The CV Mosby Co.)

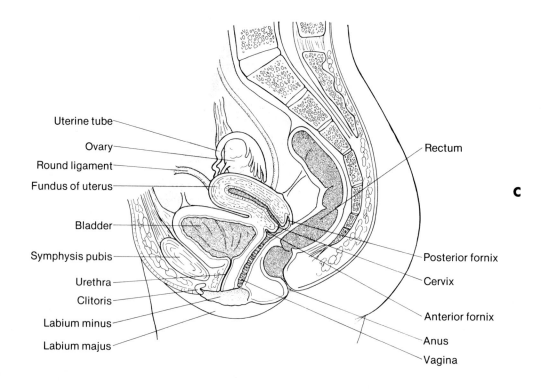

C

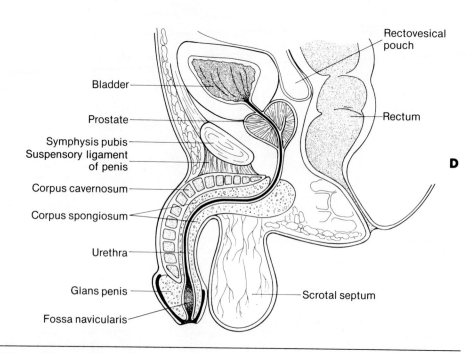

D

Figure 20-1 (continued)

C, Lateral view of female pelvis. **D,** Male reproductive organs.

prostate gland. The prostate secretes an alkaline fluid that is transported by ejaculatory ducts that pass through it. The testes are enclosed in and supported by the scrotum. Their location outside of the body allows them to maintain the sperm at a temperature lower than the rest of the body, which is essential for fertility. The **epididymis** is located along the upper side of the testes. The testes produce sperm and testosterone. As sperm are produced, they collect in the epididymis and are transported through the vas deferens to the ejaculatory ducts, where they are mixed with fluid from the seminal vesicles and the prostate gland. During coitus the seminal fluid and sperm are ejaculated into the upper urethra near the prostate and travel through the penis and into the vagina.

The breasts of the male do not contain the milkproducing glands or the subcutaneous and fatty tissue found in the female breast. The male breast, however, may enlarge in response to hormonal changes during puberty or in certain disease states. This abnormal enlargement is referred to as _gynecomastia_.

THE ROLE OF THE NURSE IN RELATION TO SEXUALITY

Nursing is concerned with total patient care. Illness or disease can adversely affect an individual's interest in sex or ability to function sexually. If a patient's condition or treatment raises sexual concerns or limits sexual ability, the nurse should provide an opportunity to discuss the situation with the patient. An attitude of nonjudgmental concern and caring on the part of the nurse will help provide an atmosphere conducive to discussion. It is also important to provide privacy when discussing sexual concerns so that the patient knows confidentiality will be maintained. When privacy is provided and there are no distractions, the patient will be better able to focus on sexual questions.

The nursing assessment of the patient with problems of the reproductive system is used to help the patient talk about sexual concerns and to help the nurse plan care, give information, or make referrals based on the patient's problems. The assessment can be done during the admission process while completing the history forms, or later, when a nurse-patient relationship has formed. The assessment does not have to be long and detailed. Its primary focus is to help the patient identify his or her sexual concerns.

The nurse should remember that words, tone of voice, and the phrasing of the question are important when assessing sexual function. It is important not to reveal your own sexual value system when you ask questions or make comments. Ask for clarification or additional information when an answer is unclear or incomplete. Be sure to use words that the patient understands. In some cases, this may mean using slang or "street words." The patient and the nurse should both be comfortable with word choices so that they both understand what the other is saying. Learning to talk about sexual concerns and feelings is often difficult for both the nurse and the patient. For the nurse, it is a skill that will develop with careful practice.

NURSING ASSESSMENT OF THE PATIENT WITH PROBLEMS OF THE REPRODUCTIVE SYSTEM

The nursing assessment should include information on the onset of menses and menopause in female patients, a record of all pregnancies and their outcomes, the type of birth control (if used), and the date of the last **Papanicolaou (Pap) smear test.** If the woman is still menstruating, the date of the beginning of her last menstrual period should be recorded, as well as the length in days and the frequency and character of flow of each period or any bleeding between periods. The nurse should also note if the woman is experiencing any of the symptoms related to premenstrual syndrome (PMS). These symptoms include weight gain, abdominal bloating, pelvic fullness and a variety of emotional responses. (PMS will be discussed in more detail later in this chapter.) The type and character of any pain or discomfort accompanying menstruation should also be reported. In the menopausal female, symptoms of hot flashes, headache, nervousness, palpitation, dizziness, insomnia, and irritability should be identified, if present. Urinary symptoms such as stress, incontinence, urgency, or frequency are indicative of gynecologic problems. When assessing male patients, the nurse should be aware that those who are experiencing (1) difficulty in voiding, (2) reduced urine stream pressure, or (3) difficulty in initiating the urine stream, may have enlargement of the prostate.

When assessing sexual functioning in the male and female, the nurse should know that chronic illnesses, such as hypertension, arthritis, and diabetes, and medication therapy can decrease sexual desire and sexual ability. Many individuals who take antihypertensives, such as propranolol (Inderal) and methyldopa (Aldomet) may find that they have a diminished libido. Men may have difficulty establishing an erection. Inform these individuals that their illness or medication may affect sexual desire and performance, and if problems occur, they should notify the physician. Many times a solution to the problem can be found, such as changing or lowering the dose of the medication

The nurse should ask about the presence of any unusual discharge from the vagina or penis and any itching or lesions on the genitalia. Changes in the breast of females and in the testes of males should be documented. Examine female breasts for symmetry and any soreness. The condition of the nipples should be described as everted or inverted, and the presence of cracks or fissures and discharge should be recorded.

Pain during intercourse or sexual dysfunction should also be investigated. Since this is a topic not easily approached without the establishment of rapport, a self-history may be used to facilitate the gathering of this and other information involving reproductive and sexual functioning. The indication of sexual problems in a self-history allows the patient to take the initiative and then gives the nurse the opportunity to verbalize and assess on these topics. Patients differ greatly in the degree of openness with which they will discuss symptoms related to reproductive and sexual function. This method gives the patient the opportunity to set the pace.

PHASES OF REPRODUCTIVE FUNCTION THROUGHOUT THE LIFE CYCLE

Puberty

Puberty is the period during which the body prepares for reproductive ability. It begins in males around age 12 and in females about age 10. Secondary sex characteristics begin to make their appearance. The size of the external reproductive organs increases, axillary and pubic hair grows in both the male and the female, the female breasts become larger, and the male voice deepens. In the female the first menstrual period (**menarche**) signifies the beginning of puberty. Some variation in age at onset of puberty and the menarche exists.

> ### Questions One Might Use In a Sexual Assessment
>
> You are starting to develop sexually. Has anyone talked to you about what that means?
>
> What things in your past have affected the way you feel about your sexuality today? Religion? Parents? Friends?
>
> Most of us have heard some sexual myths while growing up. Are there any that come to mind?
>
> Are there things in your present health status, lifestyle, or living situation that affect or influence your sexuality?
>
> How has your illness (or surgery) affected your sex life?
>
> What are your expectations for sex now that you are in menopause? Now that you have had a prostatectomy?

The first menstrual period usually occurs between age 12 and 16 years however, it may occur anytime from age 10 to 18 years.

If menses has not begun by age 15 or 16 years, a gynecologist should be consulted to rule out endocrine imbalance, an imperforate hymen, or congenital anomalies. The hymen normally has an opening that allows menstrual flow to occur, but if it is imperforate, there is no opening and the flow is held back.[30]

Along with the increase in size of the sexual organs in the male, the continuous production of sperm begins in the testes, stimulated by the *follicle-stimulating hormone (FSH)*. When the reproductive system begins to function, the male will experience nocturnal seminal emissions, usually around age 14. The muscles of the body become larger and give the male a more mature appearance.

All children need preparation for puberty through sex education. From the moment of birth the infant begins to respond to and reflect the attitudes of others who care for him. Parents are usually the most influential people during the developing years; consequently, they have a great impact on their children's attitudes regarding sexuality. Young children are curious and need direct and truthful answers to their questions. Although sex education in schools still arouses controversy, it is generally being accepted and incorporated into elementary and junior high schools. Often nurses are requested to teach basic sex education to small groups of children.

As the boy and girl approach maturity, they encounter many problems at a time when the physiologic organism is already required to make many adjustments, and they need guidance and wise counseling to help them establish patterns that will prepare them for adult life.

Menstruation

Menstruation is a cyclic process in females, occurring at fairly regular intervals between puberty and menopause and spanning a period of approximately 30 to 35 years. The onset of menstruation, **menarche**, is a normal physiologic process and does not indicate a state of illness or disability. Between menses there may be white vaginal discharge.[28]

A wide variation exists in the cycle and duration of the menstrual flow. A cycle of every 28 days may be normal for some persons, but for others it may be shorter or longer. **Ovulation** is the discharge of an ovum from a follicle in the ovaries. It occurs about 2 weeks before the onset of menstruation, regardless of the duration of the menstrual cycle. Ovulation begins some time after menarche, and a girl may be anovulatory for up to 2 years after her first period. Ovulation ceases at some time during menopause. For ovulation to occur, the anterior pituitary secretes FSH, which matures the ovarian follicle. With the release of a second pituitary hormone, *luteinizing hormone (LH)*, the mature follicle ruptures, discharging the ovum. The ovum is then drawn into the fimbriated end of the fallopian tube. After the ovum is released, the ruptured follicle is transformed into a small body filled with yellow fluid called the *corpus luteum*. If the ovum is fertilized by a spermatazoon in the fallopian tube, it implants itself in the endometrium of the uterus. If fertilization does not occur, the ovum leaves the body through the vagina. Whether or not the ovum is fertilized, the endometrium prepares for a possible pregnancy. The endometrium is a highly vascular glandular tissue that lines the uterus. The hormone estrogen, produced by the maturing ovarian follicle, begins the development of the endometrium. After the follicle ruptures and becomes the corpus luteum, it produces the hormone progesterone, which makes the endometrium richer and thicker. The production of FSH is now inhibited. If the ovum is not fertilized, the prepared endometrium degenerates and menstrual flow begins about 2 weeks after ovulation. After menstruation, the cycle begins again.[28] The flow usually lasts from 3 to 5 days, but for some women 6 or 7 days may be normal. The usual amount of blood loss is 30 to 180 ml. In the beginning an initial period may occur, then a skip of 2 or 3 months, followed by a normal period, after which the function proceeds in an orderly fashion. Brief periods with slight flow may occur and be perfectly normal, but if this pattern is continued over an extended time, medical consultation should be secured.

The nurse is often involved in counseling and teaching girls about menstruation. This process must always begin with an assessment of the individual's knowledge and feelings about menstruation. The nurse can then proceed to clarify any misconceptions and provide additional knowledge appropriate to the age and developmental level of the girl. Using terms such as "the curse" or "sick time" connotes a negative attitude and makes menstruation seem like an abnormal process. A more positive attitude about the normalcy of menstruation is fostered by the use of proper terminology, such as menstruating or "having my period." In addition to basic information regarding the process of menstruation, instruction should include hygiene measures and methods of sanitary protection. Either tampons or sanitary pads can be safely used by girls of any age. However, the possibility of toxic shock syndrome (TSS) related to tampon use has resulted in some specific guidelines regarding their use. (See information on TSS later in this chapter). Sanitary pads should be attached in the front and then the back and also removed from front to back to prevent contamination from the rectal area. A young girl may need to lubricate the tampon before it can be comfortably inserted. Even if not completely saturated, sanitary pads and tampons should be changed at least every three to four hours to prevent irritation and odor. Encourage proper handwashing before and after changing a tampon or pad to prevent infection. The nurse should stress proper menstrual hygiene.

Each female should be encouraged to lead a normal life at the time of menstruation. A program of personal hygiene, including sleep, rest, proper diet, exercise, and bathing should be continued. Exercise, with a few exceptions, is considered helpful in relieving minor discomfort. Although many taboos previously existed concerning bathing and washing the hair, there is no valid evidence of harm resulting from such procedures. A daily warm bath or shower is important, since there is often increased activity of the sweat glands during this time. Douches should not be used unless ordered by a physician. Coitus may be objectionable to women during their periods and they may choose to avoid it for aesthetic reasons.

Recent research has linked the discomfort associated with menstruation to the activity of prostaglandins, and treatment with antiprostaglandin drugs has been successful.[7] (See the section on dysmenorrhea for a more complete treatment of this topic.)

Hygiene

The nurse has numerous opportunities to instruct patients in personal hygiene measures. Cultural differences influence the habits and opinions of an individual; some cultures place great importance on cleanliness, others do not. The practice of douching was once considered by some to be essential to feminine hygiene. Routine douching is now discouraged because it is known to irritate the vaginal mucosa and upset the normal protective mechanisms of the vagina to resist infection. Genital odor rarely comes from the vagina but instead stems from the interaction of bacteria with oils secreted by the skin of the vulva. Old menstrual blood and seminal fluid remaining after coitus sometimes produce odor. A simple and effective douching solution can be prepared using 1 oz or 30 ml of white vinegar in a quart or liter of warm water. The solution is placed in a douche bag and instilled into the vagina under gentle pressure. Commerical preparations *are not* more effective and may contain perfumes that are irritating to the vaginal mucosa. Significant odor or drainage may indicate a retained tampon or other foreign body or some pathologic condition and should be further assessed. Soap and water cleansing of the perineal area is all that is normally necessary for feminine hygiene.

Sexual Role Behavior

In each stage of physical and emotional growth there are tasks related to development of behavior associated with the particular sexual role. Any condition or situation that interferes with the completion of these tasks may affect the development of sexual role behavior, but the process continues and evolves throughout the lifetime of an individual.

Sexual role or gender role is the public expression of behavior that implies masculinity or feminity. Gender identity is defined as the private or personal experience of one's maleness or femaleness. It is usually, but not always, congruent with the individual's gender or biologic sex. The development of gender identity and sexual role behavior is a complex process influenced by biologic, psychologic, and social factors.

Gender identity begins with the biologic event of conception, when the X or Y chromosome of the male combines with the X chromosome of the female. An XY pair influences the undifferentiated gonad of the embryo to become a testis at a gestational age of about 6 weeks; an XX pair differentiates the gonad as an ovary at about 12 weeks. If the fetus develops a testis, two hormonal secretions of the testis initiate the masculinization of the external genitalia. The development of the uterus, fallopian tubes, and upper vagina is suppressed by the müllerian-duct inhibiting factor. Testosterone promotes the growth of the wolffian ducts, from which develop the internal male reproductive structures and external genitalia.

The appearance of the external genitalia is the next factor in the development of sexual role behavior. The parents tailor childrearing practices in accordance with their perception of a daughter or a son. The child eventually becomes aware of his or her body, including the genitalia. The child's body and the responses of others to it influence juvenile gender identity.

At puberty the production of hormones affects sexual desire and further development of the genitals. These changes at puberty, combined with social influences, determine adult gender identity.

The Reproductive Years

All couples contemplating marriage should have complete physical examinations, including a serologic test for syphilis. Some states require testing for AIDS. At this time possible problems can be eliminated, and both people have the opportunity to discuss any questions concerning married life. Common questions concern birth control and family planning.

As a result of energy crises and a variety of other environmental problems, the world has been forced to realize that continued population expansion can only lead to a decrease in lifestyle standards. There has been much discussion about zero population growth as a means to ensure survival in the future. This, in addition to the desire to live a comfortable life without hardship and to provide the best for their children, has caused many couples to limit the size of their families.

Birth control (contraception)

Birth control or contraception is the voluntary prevention of pregnancy. The selected method of birth control depends on individual preference, religious beliefs, and cultural considerations. A complete history, physical examination, and laboratory tests may precede the prescription of some forms of contraception. Methods of birth control include: oral contraceptives, condoms, intrauterine devices (IUDs), diaphragms, foams, suppositories, jellies, and natural family planning.

Oral contraceptives (the pill) are combinations of estrogen and progesterone that act to inhibit ovulation. Taken as directed, oral contraceptives are almost 100% effective, but they can produce serious side effects and the benefits and risks must be evaluated on an individual basis.

Condoms are approximately 83% to 90% effective when used in combination with a spermicide. Care must be exercised in withdrawing the penis to prevent spillage of semen in or near the vagina.[6]

IUDs are plastic or metal devices that are placed in the uterus and act, it is believed, by preventing implantation of a fertilized ovum. Side effects and complications of these devices have decreased their popularity in recent years.

The diaphragm is a rubber device that fits under the symphysis pubis and covers the cervix. Used in combination with a spermicide, the diaphragm carries an effectiveness rate of approximately 83% to 90%.[6] The most important factor in using the diaphragm is that it fits well.

Foams, suppositories, and jellies are spermicide preparations that are readily available and convenient but less effective when used alone. Used in combination with mechanical devices, the effectiveness of each is enhanced. Newer forms of spermicide include the vaginal sponge and ring.

Natural family planning includes the basal body temperature, rhythm, and cervical mucus methods. They consist of abstaining from intercourse during carefully calculated times and require planning and dedication to be effective.

Newer contraceptives are currently being researched to increase the effectiveness rate and convenience. Tubal ligation for the female and vasectomy for the male are the current methods of permanent contraception.[6]

Menopause (Climacteric)

Menopause is defined as the cessation of menses associated with reduced ovarian function. It is diagnosed when a year has passed since the last menstrual period. The **climacteric** refers to the transition period during which reproductive function gradually diminishes and is eventually lost.

Menopause is often referred to as "the change of life"; however, for the well-adjusted person there should not be any appreciable change in the normal pattern of living. Menopause is a normal, physiologic process and simply means that the period of reproductivity has come to an end in the female. Marital relationships continue, people do not lose their minds, and the host of other conditions so often attributed to menopause may be unrelated to the physical process.

In the majority of women menopause occurs between 45 and 55 years of age, but it may occur earlier or later. Artificial menopause may be induced by the surgical removal of the ovaries or by deep internal radiation and radium placed in the vaginal canal. Although some women may stop menstruating abruptly, the usual pattern is a gradual tapering off. The flow may gradually decrease, with some irregularity of periods, and when the production of the ovarian hormone (estrogen) falls below the level necessary to stimulate the endometrium, menstruation ceases. The uterus, vagina, and vulva decrease in size. Several changes in the epithelial cells occur in the postmenopausal woman that affect the vagina, urinary tract, and oral cavity. These changes are believed to be caused by the loss of estrogen. A lack of estrogen also contributes to the development of osteoporosis.

With the cessation of menses most women do not experience any symptoms severe enough to require medical care. A few women may complain of hot flashes, which are warm feelings about the face and neck accompanied by sweating. Some women may also complain of headaches, nervousness, palpitation, dizziness, insomnia, and irritability. When the symptoms are severe enough to require medical care, some form of estrogen therapy may be advised. There is a great deal of discussion and some disagreement concerning the use of supplementary estrogens in menopausal and post-menopausal women. Some consider menopause a deficiency state that should always be treated with estrogen supplements. However, most physicians believe that treatment should be individualized.

Estrogen therapy is most effective in relieving hot flashes and night sweats. A patient with a history of uterine or breast cancer is not treated with estrogen, and patients receiving estrogen should have a regular examination for cancer of the uterus and breast.[30] If prescribed, estrogens may be administered orally, by injection, or transdermal patch. One form in common use is a naturally occurring estrogen (Premarin) derived from the urine of pregnant mares. When administered in combination with Provera, a progesterone preparation, the risk of uterine cancer is reduced. Mild sedatives, tranquilizers, or mood-elevating drugs may sometimes be prescribed to alleviate psychologic symptoms. The vaginal mucosa may atrophy and cause an irritating discharge. Vaginal creams with estrogen are effective in eliminating this discomfort. Emphasis should be placed on the normalcy of menopause, and women should be encouraged to pursue interests, hobbies, activities, and career.

Male climacteric

Climacteric occurs in males but is usually less pronounced, and many men will exhibit no symptoms. Some men may associate their approaching retirement with a loss of sexual power. Although sperm production may diminish, it does not stop completely. Some men do experience flushing and chills and may exhibit psychologic symptoms.

DISTURBANCES OF MENSTRUAL FUNCTION

Dysmenorrhea

Painful menstruation (**dysmenorrhea**) is the most common complaint associated with the menstrual process; at least one half of all women experience some degree of physical discomfort. The discomfort may occur with or without the presence of a pathologic condition. When pain and discomfort are severe enough to incapacitate the individual, a medical examination should be performed to rule out disease. Sometimes pain may result from fibroid tumors of the uterus, ovarian cysts, chronic inflammation of the fallopian tubes, displacement of the uterus, endometriosis, or narrowing of the cervical canal.

It has long been thought that dysmenorrhea may be related to immaturity, nonacceptance of the feminine role, an initial traumatic sexual ex-perience, fear of childbirth, or emotional problems. In many instances dysmenorrhea has been relieved after marriage and pregnancy; it is theorized that the hormonal changes of pregnancy may bring relief of symptoms. Those who believe that this disturbance is primarily emotionally based advise that the woman's self-satisfaction after childbirth results in reduction or elimination of symptoms. A more recent theory proposes that hypercontractility of the uterus resulting from higher than normal levels of prostaglandins may be the cause of dysmenorrhea. Prostaglandins stimulate smooth muscle contraction, and the uterus is comprised of smooth muscle. The evidence of prostaglandins in the menstrual flow of patients with dysmennorrhea supports this theory.[9] Whatever the cause, the symptoms and pain are real.

The discomfort of cramps, backache, and leg pain can often be relieved by rest, a heating pad or hot-water bottle applied to the abdomen, and a few simple exercises (Figure 20-2). If the flow is not profuse, a hot sitz bath may be taken. Heat is an especially effective treatment because it reduces muscle tone and increases circulation, thereby increasing oxygen to the muscle and relieving the ischemia.

Recent studies have shown that drugs inhibiting the production of prostaglandin (antiprostaglandins) have been effective in reducing or eliminating pain or other undesirable symptoms that sometimes accompany menstruation. Several over-the-counter (OTC) preparations are available for the treatment of dysmenorrhea. Aspirin, a drug frequently recommended to relieve dysmenorrhea, has been identified as having antiprostaglandin activity, which explains its effectiveness. Other drugs known to have antiprostaglandin action include mefenamic acid (Ponstel), ibuprofen (Motrin), naproxen (Anaprox), and indomethacin (Indocin). They are thought to be more effective than aspirin in reducing the production of prostaglandins.[9] These drugs were previously used primarily for their antiinflammatory action in diseases such as arthritis. In addition to reducing uterine cramping, the antiprostaglandin drugs are thought to reduce the gastointestinal symptoms of indigestion, nausea, vomiting, and diarrhea that accompany menstruation in some women. Prostaglandin activity is thought to increase contractility in the gastrointestinal tract as well, which also causes these symptoms.

It is recommended that these drugs be taken

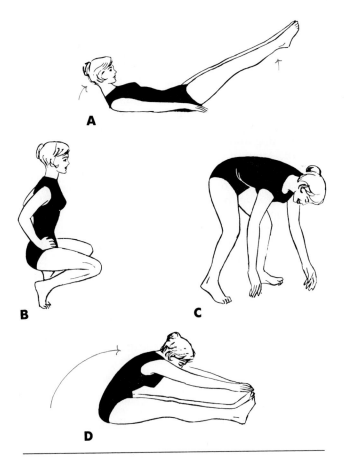

Figure 20-2
Sitting-up exercises for dysmenorrhea. **A,** Supine position with head and legs raised simultaneously; arms should be kept at side and legs straight. **B,** Deep knee bends; back should be kept straight. **C,** Monkey walk; keep hands flat on floor and walk about on hands and feet. **D,** Toe touching; keeping back straight and the legs straight, bend and touch toes with hands.

with the onset of menstruation and only for the 2, 3, or 4 days of the menstrual cycle in which the individual normally experiences discomfort. These drugs should only be taken to control symptoms. If taken in a limited dose, the chance of side effects is reduced.

There has been very little research in the area of dysmenorrhea despite its incidence to some degree in many women and its regularly incapacitating effect on many others.

Amenorrhea

Amenorrhea is the absence of menstruation, which is normal during prepuberty, after menopause, and during pregnancy and lactation. Amenorrhea may occur with some diseases, such as tuberculosis, nephritis, and certain distur-

bances. It may also occur as a result of change of climate or emotional factors. Nurses must be aware that nongynecologic surgery may cause amenorrhea for a period of time. Amenorrhea that exists before the beginning of menses is usually referred to as primary, whereas suppression of menstruation once it has occurred is called secondary amenorrhea. The treatment is based on the underlying cause and must be determined on an individual basis.

Menorrhagia

Menorrhagia refers to excessive menstrual flow, either in amount or duration. The condition is usually associated with some pelvic pathologic conditions such as uterine fibroids or with an endocrine disturbance or some other disease. Medical examination is always indicated, and if bleeding is severe, the individual should remain in bed with the foot of the bed elevated.

Metrorrhagia

Metrorrhagia is bleeding that occurs between regular menstrual periods and usually indicates the presence of some abnormal pathologic condition. It is often associated with a malignant condition of the reproductive system but may result from benign lesions of the cervix or the uterus.

Toxic Shock Syndrome

Although not related to menstrual function, *toxic shock syndrome (TSS)* usually affects healthy young women during their menstrual periods. This illness was first reported to the Centers for Disease Control in 1980. TSS also occurs in nonmenstruating women, and in men, but data suggests it is caused by continuous use of tampons during menstruation by women who have *Staphylococcus aureus* colonized in the vagina. TSS is characterized by the sudden onset of fever of 102°F (39°C) or higher, an erythematous macular rash (usually on the palms and soles) that desquamates in 7 to 24 days, systolic blood pressure below 90 mm Hg (in an adult), and involvement in three or more other organ systems. The systems most commonly involved are the gastrointestinal, muscular, mucous membrane, renal, hematologic, hepatic, central nervous, and cardiopulmonary. Nausea, vomiting, and diarrhea are common.

Danger signs of TSS may be accompanied by a sore throat, headache, decreased urine output, and confusion. Laboratory studies reveal elevated levels of blood urea nitrogen (BUN), serum cre-

---

Toxic Shock Syndrome (TSS) Danger Signs

1. Sudden onset of fever—102° F (39° C) or higher
2. Hypotension—Systolic pressure below 90 mm Hg
3. Rash—diffuse, erythematous macular rash

Guidelines for Tampon Use

Use tampons during time of moderate to heavy flow; change every 1 to 3 hours.

Avoid tampon use during times of light flow when vaginal walls are drier (usually at the beginning and end of the menstrual period).

Avoid tampon use at night. Use sanitary pads.

Avoid using superabsorbent tampons.

If high fever, vomiting, and diarrhea occur while using a tampon, see a health care professional at once.

If skin rash, sore throat, weakness, and flulike muscle aches occur while using a tampon, see a health care professional at once.

Stop using a tampon immediately if any of the above symptoms develop while wearing a tampon.

Avoid using tampons if you have a history of TSS, or stop using them for 3 to 4 months after the acute infection until cultures are negative for *S. aureus*.

---

atinine, creatine phosphokinase (CPK), serum glutamic-oxaloacetic transaminase (SGOT), bilirubin, and leukocytes in the blood (leukocytosis).

Treatment involves antibiotic therapy with betalactamase-resistant antistaphylococcal antibiotics such as nafcillin, oxacillin, cephalosporin, and fluid and electrolyte replacement. Careful monitoring of fluid intake, urinary output, and vital signs is necessary. Early detection and treatment will improve the prognosis. As many as 10% of all cases are fatal. Women who recover from TSS should be instructed to avoid tampon use for several menstrual cycles or until eradication of *S. aureus* in the vaginal flora can be documented. The risk of developing TSS in previously unaffected women can be reduced by wearing tampons during only part of the day or night and during only part of the menstrual cycle (see Guidelines for Tampon Use). All women should be warned about the danger of high-absorbency tampons.

Premenstrual Syndrome

The condition known as *premenstrual syndrome (PMS),* also called premenstrual tension, has been the subject of many current research studies. PMS is a set of both physical and emotional symptoms that begin approximately 7 to 10 days before the beginning of the menstrual period. Symptoms commonly associated with PMS include irritability, depression, insomnia, fatigue, weight gain, edema, abdominal distention, headache, and backache.[6] These symptoms usually disappear with the onset of the menstrual period.

The exact cause of this condition is not known and therefore, a great variety of methods are used to treat PMS. Information gained from a detailed history and a daily log of symptoms and mood changes covering several menstrual cycles can help determine a plan of treatment.[6] Medication may be prescribed for the relief of the more severe symptoms. A diuretic, such as chlorothiazide

(Diuril) may be prescribed to relieve the edema resulting from water and sodium retention. The nurse could suggest that the woman eat a diet low in sodium and high in complex carbohydrates 7 to 10 days before the beginning of the menstrual cycle. Improved nutrition has been suggested as a means to control symptoms. Joining a self-help group may be useful to women who have low self-esteem from lack of understanding of PMS.

NURSING RESPONSIBILITIES FOR DIAGNOSTIC PROCEDURES

Examination of the Female Patient

Female patients with problems of the reproductive system are seen in the gynecologist's office and are often treated on an outpatient basis. Since the reproductive system of the male patient is so intricately related to the urinary system, such patients are usually cared for by the urologist.

Physical examination

Examination of the patient begins with a complete history, which includes the menstrual history, history of any pregnancies, or past illness, and history of the present illness. The physical examination of the patient will include palpation of the breasts for evidence of cysts or tumors and examination of the pelvis. Nurses are employed in many physician's offices, and it is important for them to be familiar with the procedure for pelvic examination and their responsibilities in assisting the physician.

Pelvic examination

The nurse must understand that this examination may not be easy for the patient and may have long been delayed. The nurse should try to relieve the patient's anxiety, fears, and embarrassment by maintaining a caring attitude and explaining the procedure to her.

Often children have gynecologic problems and are brought to the physician by the parent. Young children are likely to have a profound sense of modesty and they may resist exposure for examination. Efforts should be made to secure the child's confidence and cooperation. The child should not be restrained, since this may cause traumatic results that can affect future behavior.

In preparation for the examination, the patient should be instructed to void and evacuate the bowel. Clothing below the waist should be removed to allow visualization of the genitalia and palpation of the abdomen. The breast examination is usually performed at the same time, and all clothing should be removed and the patient dressed in an examination gown.

Positioning the patient

The physician will determine the position in which the patient should be placed for the pelvic examination. It may be the lithotomy position, Sims' position, or the knee-chest position. (See a textbook on basic nursing for further information on these positions). The patient is usually placed in the lithotomy position with both legs elevated in stirrups and the lower third of the table pushed back and out of the way. The patient is then asked to slide her buttocks down so they extend just over the edge of the table. If an examination table is not available or if the patient cannot be moved to one, the examination can be performed in bed with the buttocks elevated on a firm surface, such as a wrapped bedpan. The patient should be carefully draped, and unnecessary exposure should be avoided. A sheet or bath blanket positioned diagonally will cover the chest, abdomen, and both legs; the lowest corner can be lifted to visualize the genitalia.

Examination procedure

The procedure begins with examination of the external genitalia. Then a bimanual examination of the uterus is performed. The physician inserts two fingers of a gloved hand into the vagina up to the cervix while using the other hand to place gentle pressure on the lower abdomen over the uterus. Pressure on the abdomen applies pressure to the fundus. This pressure will be felt by the patient from the fingers at the cervix if the uterus is in the proper position. Finally, a bimanual rectovaginal examination is performed by inserting the second finger into the vagina and the third finger into the rectum. The other hand is placed on the abdomen to palpate rectal and pelvic abnormalities. The nurse stays during the procedure to provide support to the patient, assist the examiner, focus the light, and provide instruments or equipment as needed. A Pap smear is often taken at this time. When the examination is complete, the patient should be cleansed of any lubricating jelly or secretions, and the legs should be removed from the stirrups simultaneously. The lower third of the table can be brought back into position before the legs. The patient can then be assisted to a sitting position on the side of the table and should be encouraged to stay sitting until she is sure she is not dizzy. The physician may wish to speak to the patient at this time or may return later after the patient has dressed to discuss further treatment.

Handling and cleaning of examination equipment should be performed with caution and while wearing latex gloves since many pelvic diseases are infectious.

Laboratory tests

The laboratory tests will include urinalysis; the *Papanicolaou cytologic test* for cancer; and smears and cultures from the vagina, cervix, and urethra, which may be examined for both infectious and noninfectious organisms. A complete blood count and a serologic test for syphilis are usually done. Examination of the male patient may include prostatic smears secured through massage of the prostate gland by the gloved finger placed in the rectum. A urine specimen is then secured for laboratory examination.

Papanicolaou smear. Pap smears are used to detect early cases of cervical cancer. For women of average risk, routine smears are recommended every 3 years after two negative tests 1 year apart.[2] The patient's or her family's history may reveal high risk and indicate more frequent testing. Many physicians recommend that their patients have a Pap smear and vaginal examination every year. A woman should begin routine testing at age 20 or before that time if sexually active. After age 40 or after a positive examination, yearly tests are recommended. The woman must understand the purpose of the test and the interpretation of results. Douching 24 hours before the test is contraindicated because cellular discharges to be examined may be washed away and negate the test. The patient should void, be placed in the dorsal lithotomy position, and then draped. The nurse may be asked to assemble the proper equipment for the physician, including a glass slide, vaginal speculum, wooden swab or spatula, a fixing solution of alcohol or formalin, and a cytology laboratory requisition. In some situations nurses obtain the sample for the smear, and frequently the nurse applies the sample to the glass slide after it is collected by the physician. Some laboratories interpret results using the categories below.[6]

Current laboratory practice uses a descriptive classification.

An infection can produce an abnormal Pap smear and reexamination is necessary following treatment of the infection.[6]

Schiller's test. Schiller's test is used for the early detection of cancer cells and to guide the physician in doing a biopsy. Usually the test involves the cervix, which is painted with an iodine solution. Glycogen, which is present in normal cells, will stain brown when the iodine solution is applied, but in the presence of cancer and some other conditions, the cells do not contain glycogen and will not stain when the iodine is applied. Thus the physician will be able to determine the exact areas from which a biopsy specimen should be taken.

Culdoscopy. A **culdoscope** is a long, metal, lighted instrument that can be inserted into the vagina and through Douglas' cul-de-sac, a pouch that lies between the uterus and the rectum. The test is usually performed in the operating room with the patient in the knee-chest position. An incision is made in the posterior fornix of the vagina, and the culdoscope is introduced through this incision to provide visualization of the pelvic organs. Preparation is routine for minor vaginal surgery, and postoperative care includes checking vital signs and observing for hemorrhage and infection. The incision usually heals rapidly, and douching and sexual activity are to be avoided for about 1 week or until permitted by the physician. Air embolism is a rare complication of this procedure.

Colposcopy. Colposcopy involves the examination of the cervix and vagina with an instrument containing a magnifying lens and light called a colposcope. The test is used after a positive Pap test or to further examine suggestive lesions seen during a vaginal examination. A biopsy may be performed, and photographs may be taken of suggestive lesions with the colposcope and its attachments. Patients whose mothers received DES (diethylstilbestrol) during pregnancy are monitored regularly using the colposcope. The patient is positioned in a lithotomy position, and the colposcope is introduced into the vagina. If a biopsy has been performed, the patient must be instructed to abstain from sexual intercourse and to avoid inserting anything in the vagina except a tampon until healing of the biopsy site is confirmed.

Cervical biopsy. A cervical biopsy is the surgical excision of tissue from the cervix for the purpose of histologic examination. Samples are taken from three or more sites around the cervix; the

---

Categories to Interpret Lab Results	
Class I	No abnormal cells are present
Class II	Atypical cells are identified; inflammation must be ruled out
Class III	Suggestive abnormal cells present
Class IV	Malignant cells present; carcinoma in situ
Class V	Malignant cells present; invasive cancer

Descriptive Terminology
Normal
Metaplasia
Inflammation
Minimal atypia—koilocytosis
Mild dysplasia
Moderate dysplasia
Severe dysplasia—carcinoma in situ
Invasive carcinoma

sites are determined by direct visualization with colposcopy or by iodine staining (Schiller's test). It is indicated in women with suggestive cervical lesions and should be performed when the cervix is least vascular, usually 1 week after menses. If findings indicate advanced dysplasia or carcinoma in situ, a cone biopsy may be performed in the operating room with the patient under general anesthesia to obtain a larger tissue specimen and allow a more accurate evaluation of the extent of dysplasia. Before this, a consent form must be signed, and the patient should void before the biopsy. The patient is instructed to avoid strenuous exercise for 8 to 24 hours after the biopsy. The outpatient should be allowed to rest briefly before going home. A tampon may be inserted by the physician after biopsy to help stop bleeding; the patient should be instructed to leave it in place for the time ordered by the physician, usually 8 to 24 hours. Some bleeding is expected, but bleeding heavier than menstrual flow should be reported to the physician. Tampons are not inserted by the patient until permitted by the physician. Douching and intercourse should be avoided for about 2 to 6 weeks as instructed. A foul-smelling, gray-green vaginal discharge will appear in a few days and remain for as long as 3 weeks. This discharge is caused by the healing of the cervical tissue, and the patient should be told to expect this.

Laparoscopy. A **laparoscope** is a small, fiberoptic instrument that is inserted through a small incision in the anterior abdominal wall. The procedure is used to detect abnormalities as well as to perform minor surgical procedures, such as lysis of adhesions, ovarian biopsy, tubal sterilization, removal of foreign bodies, and treatment of sites of endometriosis. Because laparoscopy is performed under anesthesia, the patient must fast for at least 8 hours before surgery. There is a danger of hemorrhage following the test and the possibility of peritonitis following the spilling of intestinal contents if a visceral organ is accidentally punctured. The patient will experience pain at the puncture site following the test. There will also be pain in the shoulder resulting from the air that was introduced into the peritoneal cavity to allow better visualization of the organs during the examination. Following the test, vital signs should be monitored per routine postoperative instructions, urinary output should be checked, and the patient should be ambulated. A normal diet may be resumed gradually and activity will be re-

stricted for 4 to 7 days as ordered by the physician. The pain in the abdomen and shoulder should disappear within 24 to 36 hours and will be relieved by aspirin or acetaminophen as ordered.

Hysterosalpingography. A hysterosalpingogram is an x-ray examination used to visualize the uterine cavity, the fallopian tubes, and the area around the tubes. To determine tubal and uterine abnormalities, fistulas, and adhesions, a radiopaque substance is injected in the uterus and up into the fallopian tubes as fluoroscopic x-ray films are taken. The structure and patency of the tubes may be examined. The presence of foreign bodies can also be detected; however, pelvic ultrasound is more commonly used for this purpose. Following the test, the patient may experience cramps and a vagal reaction resulting in a slow pulse rate, nausea, and dizziness. These symptoms should subside quickly. The patient must be watched for signs of infection, such as fever, pain, increased pulse rate, malaise, and muscle ache.

Pelvic ultrasonography. In this test high-frequency sound waves are passed into the area to be examined and are reflected to a transducer, which then converts the sound energy into electric energy and forms images on an oscilloscope screen that are similar to an x-ray film. Pelvic ultrasonography is used to detect foreign bodies; to distinguish between cysts and tumors; to measure organ size; to detect multiple pregnancies or fetal abnormalities; to evaluate the size, gestational age, growth rate, position, and viability of the fetus; and to determine the location of the placenta and the fetus during amniocentesis. The patient must have a full bladder during the examination to improve the image produced by the sound waves and to provide a landmark to define pelvic organs. The patient is asked to drink liquids, approximately 6 to 8 glasses of water, before the test and is instructed not to void. Immediately following the test, the patient should be allowed to empty her bladder. There is some question about the effects of ultrasound on the fetus. There has been no conclusive evidence of harm to the fetus or the mother during the 20 years it has been in use. However, a hypothetical risk exists that cannot be ignored. The patient must be fully informed regarding the benefits and potential risks of ultrasonography.[6]

Breast examination

The physician palpates the breasts during the examination. In recent years emphasis has been

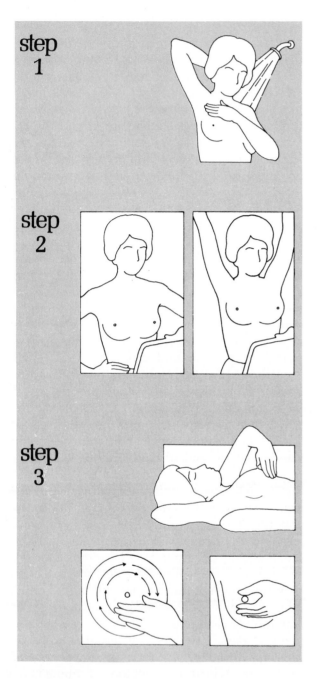

step
1

step
2

step
3

Figure 20-3
Breast self-examination. **1,** In the shower: Examine your breasts during bath or shower; hands glide easier over wet skin. With fingers flat, move them gently over every part of each breast. Use right hand to examine left breast, left hand for right breast. Check for any lump, hard knot, or thickening. **2,** Before a mirror: Inspect your breasts with arms at your sides. Next raise your arms high overhead. Look for any changes in contour of each breast—a swelling, dimpling of skin, or changes in nipple. Then rest palms on hips and press down firmly to flex your chest muscles. Left and right breast will not match exactly—few women's breasts do. Regular inspection shows what is normal for you and will give you confidence in your examination. **3,** Lying down: To examine your right breast, put pillow or folded towel under your right shoulder. Place your right hand behind your head—this distributes breast tissue more evenly on the chest. With left hand, fingers flat, press gently in small circular motions around an imaginary clock face. Begin at outermost top of your right breast for 12 o'clock, then move to 1 o'clock, and so on around the circle back to 12 o'clock. Ridge of firm tissue in lower curve of each breast is normal. Then move in an inch, toward nipple, keep circling to examine every part of your breast, including nipple. This requires at least three more circles. Now slowly repeat procedure on your left breast with pillow under your left shoulder and your left hand behind your head. Notice how your breast structure feels. Finally, squeeze nipple of each breast gently between your thumb and index finger. Any discharge, clear or bloody, should be reported to your physician immediately. *(Reprinted by permission of the American Cancer Society, Inc.)*

placed on teaching women to palpate their own breasts monthly. Early cancer of the breast is curable, and if every woman would take time to carefully examine her own breasts at regular intervals, many benign and malignant tumors would be discovered early. Nurses should become familiar with the procedure of breast self-examination (BSE) so that they may teach patients, friends, or members of their families (Figure 20-3).

Mammography

Mammography is a radiographic (x-ray) technique used to detect breast cysts or tumors, especially those not palpable on physical examination. The test uses relatively low radiation levels but is contraindicated during pregnancy. The patient stands and is asked to place one of her breasts on a table above an x-ray cassette. A compressor is placed on the breast, and the patient is instructed to hold her breath while a picture is taken from above. The machine is rotated, the patient is repositioned, and a lateral view is taken. The procedure is then repeated on the other breast. Abnormal tissues will be evident on the developed films. The current recommendation of the American Cancer Society is (1) a baseline mammogram for women 35 to 40 years of age, (2) women 40 to 49 years of age should have a mammogram at 1 to 2 year intervals, and (3) an annual mammogram for women 50 years of age and older. Women who have a family history of breast cancer, or have other risk factors, should have an annual mammogram.

Rubin's test (tubal insufflation)

Rubin's test is done to determine if the fallopain tubes are open when sterility is suspected. The test consists of injecting carbon dioxide gas into the uterine cavity under controlled pressure. If the tubes are open, the gas escapes through the tube into the peritoneal cavity, where it is absorbed. The test is usually done 2 to 6 days after the end of the menstrual period. The test is contraindicated if pregnancy is suspected, if any infection is present, or if the patient has recently had a dilation and curettage procedure. When the examination is completed and the patient sits up, she will experience discomfort in the right shoulder and neck. This pain is referred to the shoulder and neck from irritation of nerves under the diaphragm where the gas collects. The patient should be assured that the discomfort will last only a few minutes because the gas is absorbed quickly. An absence of pain or discomfort indicates that the tubes are not open.

Pregnancy tests

The most common laboratory tests for pregnancy are based on finding human *chorionic gonadotropin (HCG)* in serum or urine. The urine tests are widely available in kit form and are fairly accurate, simple, and inexpensive. The manufacturers of these kits claim that HCG can be detected in urine 42 days after the last menstrual period. Improper collection of the specimen, proteinuria, hormone-producing tumors, and other factors can produce false-positive or false-negative readings.[6]

Dilation and curettage (D and C)

Dilation and curettage is a procedure in which the cervical os is dilated and the inside of the uterus is scraped with a curette. There are three basic reasons for this procedure: (1) to secure tissue from the lining of the uterus (endometrium) for examination, (2) to control uterine bleeding, and (3) to clear the uterine cavity of any residue left after incomplete abortion. D and C is a surgical procedure requiring an anesthetic. Preoperative preparation of the patient is the same as that for most other surgical patients. Postoperative care includes observation of the patient for excessive vaginal bleeding and urinary retention. The patient may have packing in the vaginal canal, which is removed in 24 hours. The patient is usually ambulatory on the first day, and little or no analgesic is required. The patient is generally discharged from the hospital on the second day with instruction to report to her physician for follow-up care.

Examination of the Male Patient

Most men prefer to be examined by a male without a female present. Examination includes inspection and palpation of the external genitalia for abnormalities of structure, signs of infection such as discharge and swelling, and skin lesions. The penis is inspected for the presence and position of the urinary meatus. In the uncircumcised male the prepuce, or foreskin, must be retracted and the glans examined. If the foreskin does not retract easily, the patient may have **phimosis.** The scrotum should be examined for size, symmetry, and the presence and size of both testes; the left testis is often lower than the right. The scrotum contracts and becomes smaller when cold. It is easier to examine the testes when the scrotum is relaxed. For this reason, men are adviced to examine the testes monthly, while in a warm tub or shower. Routine examination provides for early detection of testicular cancer. The testes are also examined for masses, swelling, and movability. The prostate gland is examined through the rectum. A gloved and lubricated finger is inserted to palpate the prostate and determine size, shape, and consistency. Male breasts are examined for enlargement, lesions, discharge, and masses. The incidence of breast cancer in males is less than 1%, but men should be instructed to observe and report any changes in size, shape, and color and the presence of discharge or masses. If sterility is suspected, several examinations may be carried out, including examination of semen to determine the presence and characteristics of spermatozoa and examination to locate obstructions along the tubal route. A voided specimen may be collected after massage of the prostate gland for examination for cancer cells or tubercle bacilli. A biopsy of the prostate gland or the testes may also be done.

Semen analysis

This is a relatively simple and inexpensive test to evaluate fertility in the male. It is also used to detect semen in a rape victim, to identify the blood type of an alleged rapist, or to prove sterility in a paternity suit. Following a vasectomy, semen is analyzed to evaluate the effectiveness of the surgical procedure.

Semen may be collected after masturbation, after coitus, or by interrupting coitus. If the male prefers to collect the sample at home, the specimen must be kept from extremes in temperature and direct sunlight to avoid killing the sperm. When evaluating fertility, the physician may recommend refraining from intercourse from 2 to 5 days before collecting the specimen. The specimen must be brought in for examination within 3 hours after collection. The male is instructed to either masturbate and ejaculate in a clean container; to interrupt coitus just before ejaculating, withdraw the penis, and deposit the ejaculate in a container; or to collect during coitus by using a condom that has been washed with soapy water and dried to remove any spermicide. The entire specimen must be collected.

The specimen is analyzed for volume of seminal fluid, sperm count, and motility and shape *(morphology)* of the sperm through microscopic examination. When collecting semen from a female after rape or for evaluation of fertility, the physician employs a vaginal speculum and aspirates the specimen using a small syringe without a cannula or needle.

THE PATIENT WITH DISEASES AND DISORDERS OF THE REPRODUCTIVE SYSTEM

Venereal Disease

Venereal disease is discussed in Chapter 7.

Conditions Affecting the Female External Genitalia and Vagina
Vulvitis

Vulvitis may be either an acute or chronic inflammatory condition of the vulva. There are many causes, including an irritating vaginal discharge, infectious diseases, untreated diabetes, contraceptive pills, and trauma caused by scratching. There usually is severe itching and burning with redness and in some patients ulceration. Treatment consists of identifying and treating or removing the cause. Clothing that rubs or irritates the condition should be eliminated.

Vaginitis

Vaginitis is one of the most common disorders affecting the female. This condition affects females of any age group, from infants to the elderly.

Pathophysiology. Vaginitis is an inflammation of the vagina. Many factors are associated

with its occurrence. *Trichomonas vaginalis* is a flagellated protozoan and is a common cause of vaginitis. It is considered to be sexually transmitted in most cases. Vaginitis may also be caused by *Candida albicans,* a yeastlike fungus. This form can be commonly found in women with diabetes and during antibiotic or steroid therapy. Atrophic vaginitis occurs during preadolescence and after menopause and is caused by low levels of estrogen, resulting in a thinning of the vaginal lining. Bacterial vaginitis is caused by an interaction between the *Gardnerella* bacillus and another, unidentified bacterium. Simple vaginitis may be caused by faulty hygiene, tight clothing, or emotional stress.[6]

Assessment. The patient who has contracted vaginitis will complain of burning and itching of the vulva, vaginal discharge, and may report that she has pain on urination or intercourse. Examination of the vaginal walls will show a profuse foamy (bubbly) exudate if the cause of the vaginitis is *T. vaginalis.* If *C. albicans* is the causative agent, a thick cheeselike discharge results. Bacterial vaginitis produces a milklike discharge with a foul or fishy odor.

Intervention. Most persons with vaginitis caused by *Trichomonas* organisms are treated with metronidazole (Flagyl), either in a single dose of 2 g or 250 mg three times a day for 7 days. Both partners should be treated at the same time to avoid "Ping-Pong" reinfection.[6] Douches using 1 tablespoon of vinegar to 1 pint of warm water may be ordered to help remove excessive discharge and provide local comfort. Treatment for vaginitis caused by *C. albicans* is nystatin in the form of tablets for vaginal insertion (Mycostatin) or miconazole nitrate (Monistat 7) vaginal cream. Both are inserted with a specially designed applicator. Atrophic vaginitis in women past menopause is treated with estrogen vaginal creams. Pain during intercourse can be relieved with the use of vaginal lubricants. Bacterial vaginitis is treated with metronidazole (Flagyl) taken two or three times a day for 7 days. In all cases of vaginitis, patients should be instructed to maintain scrupulous cleanliness, especially after elimination, to ingest or apply medications as ordered, and to restrict sexual activity as recommended by the physician.[6]

Leukorrhea

Leukorrhea is an abnormal white or yellow discharge from the vagina. Under normal conditions there may be some increase in vaginal secretions at the beginning and end of the menstrual period, and this should not be confused with the increased discharge that occurs at other times. Leukorrhea is usually the result of some infection of the vagina or the cervix and may occur in uterine cancer. Medical examination and treatment should always be secured.

Vulvovaginitis (bartholinitis)

Vulvovaginitis is an inflammation of the vulva and vagina or of Bartholin's glands, which are located on either side of the vaginal opening. The condition may result from any of several pathogenic bacteria and is frequently seen in untreated gonorrhea. The ducts from the glands may become occluded by the inflammatory condition, and abscess formation occurs. The abscess may rupture spontaneously, or an incision and drainage may be necessary. Treatment includes administration of the appropriate antibiotic and hot sitz baths. The patient is usually treated in the physician's office or in an outpatient clinic.

Vesicovaginal and rectovaginal fistula

A vesicovaginal fistula is an abnormal opening from the bladder to the vagina. Rectovaginal fistula is an abnormal opening between the rectum and the vagina. A fistula can occur congenitally or can be caused by injury during childbirth, vaginal surgery, or as a result of tissue damage from Crohn's disease or invasive carcinoma. Surgical repair is indicated if the fistula does not heal. Healing is promoted by a dietary increase in vitamin C and protein, cleansing of the area with douches and enemas, rest, and oral antibiotics. A temporary colostomy may be necessary to keep the site clean. Soiling from leakage of urine or stool into the vagina is disturbing for the patient. Sitz baths, deodorizing douches, perineal pads, and protective pants will be necessary preoperatively. For those with an irreparable fistula, hygiene and comfort are ongoing concerns. If repaired surgically, a Foley catheter may be inserted postoperatively to prevent strain on the suture line caused by a full bladder.

Relaxation of the pelvic musculature: rectocele, cystocele, and uterine prolapse

Pathophysiology. The uterus is normally supported by pelvic muscles. These muscles can atrophy with age or weaken with childbearing, thus allowing the uterus to descend, impinge on other structures of the bladder and/or rectum, and protrude through the vaginal wall. A rectocele is the protrusion of the rectum through the vaginal wall; a cystocele is the protrusion of the bladder through the vaginal wall, and uterine prolapse is the collapse of the uterus into the vagina. In severe cases of uterine prolapse, the cervix may protrude through the external vaginal opening.

Assessment. These conditions cause a feeling of downward pressure in the patient, especially when she is standing or walking. Stress incontinence and urinary frequency and urgency accompany cystocele; rectal pressure, constipation, heaviness, and hemorrhoids are associated with rectocele; and uterine prolapse produces more severe urinary symptoms such as incontinence and retention. Constipation, backache, and vaginal discharge result from the increased pressure exerted by the prolapsed uterus. Some degree of prolapse occurs in many women, but treatment is not usually initiated unless symptoms are problematic.

Intervention. Uterine prolapse can be treated by inserting a pessary to support the uterus, by transvaginal surgical correction, or by removing the uterus (hysterectomy). Surgery is the preferred treatment, but the pessary will be used if the woman plans further pregnancies or is unable to withstand surgery. A **pessary** is a small appliance placed in the vagina to reposition the uterus. A sterile lubricant is applied for insertion, and the pessary is removed and cleaned about every 2 months by the physician to prevent infection. The pessary may cause vaginal irritation or erosion; therefore frequent and regular examinations by the physician are important. The patient must immediately report any unusual vaginal discharge or changes in voiding.[4,30]

Pelvic floor exercises are prescribed for younger women who experience prolapse after childbirth. The women alternately contracts and relaxes both the gluteal and perineal floor muscles to strengthen muscle tone (Kegel exercises).

Hysterectomy may be necessary in severe cases of uterine prolapse. Preoperative and postoperative care of the patient with vaginal or abdominal hysterectomy is covered later in this chapter.

Surgical repair of a cystocele involves shortening the muscles that support the bladder through a procedure called anterior colporrhaphy; repair of a rectocele is called posterior colporrhaphy. Both repairs may be done at the same time and are then referred to as an anteroposterocolporrhaphy or anteroposterior repair. Nursing diagnoses commonly seen in patients having colporrhaphy are identified in the boxed material.

NURSING CARE GUIDELINES
Colporrhaphy (Repair of Relaxed Perineal Muscles)

Nursing diagnoses

- Altered sexuality patterns related to postoperative restrictions on sexual intercourse for 6 weeks
- Alteration in comfort (pain) related to inflammation at site of surgical repair
- High risk for injury (strain on sutures at site of surgical repair) related to full bladder, straining during defecation
- High risk for infection related to contamination by fecal material and obstruction of vaginal drainage
- Knowledge deficit related to restrictions on physical activity and sexual intercourse
- Potential urinary retention related to inflammation in urinary meatus

Nursing interventions

- Check routine vital signs until stable
- Maintain patency of Foley catheter
- Have patient void every 4 hours after catheter is removed to prevent strain on sutures from full bladder
- Give and instruct patient on low-residue diet to promote soft stool
- Avoid cleansing enemas
- Instruct patient not to strain during defecation
- Apply ice pack to perineum first 24 hours postoperatively; heat lamp to perineum 20 minutes three times daily beginning second postoperative day
- Administer perineal care with sterile solution four times daily and after each voiding or defecation
- Apply anesthetic and antiseptic sprays to perineum as ordered
- Maintain low Fowler's position
- Instruct patient to avoid standing long periods and heavy lifting for several weeks after discharge and to avoid coitus until permitted by physician (about 6 weeks)

Expected outcomes

- After proper intervention following colporrhaphy, the patient will:
- Have urinary output of 30 to 60 ml per hour.
- Have stool formed but soft.
- Verbalize reasons to avoid straining during defecation and to empty bladder every 4 hours.
- Select foods from a menu that comply with restrictions of a low-residue diet and promote bowel function.
- Correctly perform perineal care and correctly identify prescribed solution and indications for care.
- State plans for restricting activity during recovery, including avoidance of straining when rising, standing long periods, doing heavy lifting, and engaging in coitus for 6 weeks or until permitted by physician.
- State plans for follow-up visits to physician.

Preoperative and postoperative intervention: colporrhaphy. Preoperative care for colporrhaphy is especially important in assuring as clean an operative area as possible. Patients may be admitted to the hospital before surgery and given a cathartic, followed by enemas to be sure the bowel is completely empty. A liquid diet for 24 hours before surgery will help to keep the bowel empty. The surgeon may order a cleansing vaginal douche on the evening before and the morning of surgery. The entire vaginal area is shaved, including the pubis and rectal area.

The postoperative care of the patient having colporrhaphy includes checking vital signs and observing frequently for hemorrhage. A retention catheter is usually inserted into the urinary bladder to keep it empty and prevent pressure on sutures. It is important to keep the fecal residue as soft as possible; some physicians order a liquid diet for several days, or they may order stool softeners to be given every night. An oil retention enema may be ordered, but cleansing enemas should not be given. A small, soft rubber tube should be used for the oil retention enema, and the patient must be instructed not to strain when defecating. External sutures may or may not be present, depending on whether perineal repair has been done. The nurse should understand the physician's orders concerning perineal care, since some physicians want the area to be kept completely dry. The heat lamp may be used two or three times a day for 20 to 30 minutes. If a solution rather than plain water is to be used in giving perineal care, the physician will order it; all equipment and supplies must be sterile to prevent infection.

The patient is usually kept in low Fowler's position to prevent pressure or strain on sutures.

When ambulation is allowed, the patient should be taught to roll out of bed. On discharge from the hospital, the patient should be advised against standing for long periods or lifting heavy objects for several weeks. Coitus must be avoided until healing is accomplished, about 6 weeks. The boxed material describes the nursing care of the patient following colporrhaphy.

Malignant lesions of the vulva

Malignant lesions of the vulva are relatively rare. They account for 3% to 4% of all gynecologic malignancies and occur most often in women after menopause. Although these lesions are easily visible, many women wait up to 3 years before seeking medical attention.[6] Cancer of the vulva is also being diagnosed in women between 20 to 40 years of age. There may be a correlation between onset of this disease and a history of infection with herpes simplex virus and papilloma viruses. These cancers grow slowly and metastasize late. Chronic vulvar dystrophies, such as leukoplakia, are considered premalignant. Malignant lesions can be of the in situ variety, involving just the tissues at the site of origin, or the invasive type. If lesions are invasive, extensive local spread occurs, particularly into the lymphatic channels.

Assessment. The most common complaint of patients with early vulvar cancer is pruritus (itching). The precancerous lesions of leukoplakia may be present and are seen as thickened white patches on the mucous membranes of the vulva.[6] The patient will frequently give a history of having used various salves, ointments, and lotions for symptoms of mild soreness before finally seeking medical care. Cardiovascular and degenerative diseases are often present because of the typical older age of these patients. Later symptoms include edema of the vulva and pelvic lymphadenopathy.

Intervention. Radiation therapy may be used if the disease has progressed beyond the operable stage. If the malignancy can be surgically removed, a vulvectomy is indicated.

A vulvectomy includes the removal of the external female genitals. It may be a partial procedure for biopsy purposes, a simple procedure for removal of a benign or an in situ type lesion, or a radical procedure for invasive malignant lesions. A simple vulvectomy is the removal of the vulva along with a margin of skin adjacent to the vulva. A radical vulvectomy includes the excision of skin from the symphysis pubis to the anus and may include removal of the inguinal lymph nodes in the groin on both sides. The excised areas are covered with a skin flap.

Preoperative care includes the same care as reviewed in Chapter 5. Wide areas of skin preparation should include the inguinal regions, vulva, and pubic and perineal area. The emotional preparation of the patient is important, and the nurse should listen to any apprehension or fears that the patient expresses. Fear of disfigurement and loss of a body part are common. Both before and after surgery the patient may show signs of a grief reaction such as depression, anger, denial, or withdrawal.

When the patient returns from surgery, a Foley catheter will be in the urinary bladder to prevent constriction of the urethra. Dressings may have to be changed frequently for several days because of the serous drainage from the wounds. A T binder may be used to hold dressings in place. The patient is placed in a low Fowler's position to prevent strain on the sutures. The patient should be turned every 2 hours, and when on her side a pillow should be placed lengthwise between her legs to support the upper leg and prevent strain. The wound is cleansed according to the physician's orders. Solutions often used for cleansing include hydrogen peroxide, and warm physiologic saline solution. The surgeon may prefer that wounds be exposed and that a heat lamp be used, since it stimulates circulation and promotes healing. Some physicians may order sitz baths, whereas others may believe that such baths increase the danger of wound infection. The patient is usually given a low-residue diet. Analgesics will be required for several days, and recovery is generally slow. The patient may be ambulatory by the third day, but the nurse should remember that ambulation must be gradual for the older person. Leg edema is common after surgery, and some patients may develop chronic leg edema. Elastic stockings, elevation of the legs, and avoidance of long periods of sitting or standing will help to provide better venous return. An important nursing function is the prevention of wound infection. Care should be taken to provide privacy when caring for the wound and to avoid any unnecessary exposure of the patient.[10,22]

Acceptance of and adjustment to her change in appearance may be difficult and the patient may need support in helping her husband accept the change in her appearance. The patient may experience difficulty in coitus because of loss of tissue in the supporting structures of the labia and vagina and possible constriction of the vaginal orifice. Constriction may require dilation or surgical revision.[4]

Expected outcomes. With proper intervention the patient with a vulvectomy will:

Have self-esteem intact as indicated by attention to personal hygiene and appearance.

Verbalize concerns about change in appearance of vulvar region and share concerns with husband or significant other.

Have wound approximated and healing with no signs of infection.

Void regularly in amounts greater than 150 ml.

State plans for restricting activity postoperatively that will strain operative area.

State plans for restriction of sexual activity until permitted by physician.

Verbalize understanding that constriction of vaginal orifice may occur postoperatively and require reconstructive surgery.

State plans for follow-up visit to physician.

Vaginal cancer

Cancer of the vagina, particularly in young women, is also rare, but the incidence is higher in women who have been exposed to the hormone DES prenatally.

Early detection makes it possible to completely remove the malignant area in the vagina. The vagina can then be reconstructed, using a split-thickness graft from the buttocks applied to a Silastic mold, which is sutured to the labia. The mold is removed a few days postoperatively after the graft shows evidence of taking. A lighter, more comfortable mold is created with a condom filled with tampons that is inserted until healing is complete.

DES syndrome

DES (diethylstilbestrol) is a synthetic form of estrogen that was prescribed for approximately 5 to 6 million women in the United States between 1941 and 1971. It was commonly used to treat women who were pregnant and who had: (1) one prior miscarriage, (2) diabetes, (3) toxemia, or (4) slight bleeding during pregnancy. A prescription audit showed that the drug was still being prescribed during pregnancy as late as 1974, despite the Food and Drug Administration (FDA) announcing in 1971 that the drug was contraindicated in pregnancy. This FDA restriction followed the discovery that several young women developed adenocarcinoma of the vagina and that each of them was the daughter of a women who had ingested DES during pregnancy. Studies were then conducted on other young women who had been exposed to DES in utero, and characteristic benign genital tract abnormalities were found in the majority. Follow-up studies continue to determine the risk of these women for developing malignancies. Daughters of women who took DES are encouraged to have a yearly gynecologic examination. There is some evidence that male offspring suffer congential abnormalities and infertility, but studies to date are inconclusive.

Conditions Affecting the Cervix and Uterus
Cervicitis

Cervicitis may be the result of an acute inflammatory condition of the vagina, or it may be a chronic condition resulting from lacerations occurring at the time of delivery, erosion, cysts, or a specific infection such as gonorrhea. The cause of erosion is not always known and is often believed to be congenital. It appears to be more common in women who are taking oral contraceptives. Cervicitis may occur in any woman, often producing no symptoms, and is detected only on a routine pelvic examination. Most physicians believe that untreated chronic cervicitis predisposes to cancer of the cervix; treatment includes examination and studies to exclude cervical cancer. If lacerations exist, they should be repaired surgically, and erosions may be cauterized. If the condition does not respond to conservative treatment, the patient may be admitted to the hospital and under general anesthesia have a cone-shaped portion of the cervix removed (conization).

Uterine displacement

Retroversion is a displacement of the uterus backward from its normal position. It frequently occurs as a congenital condition and may result from laceration at the time of delivery followed by lack of proper postpartum exercises. It may be caused by large tumors or cysts that tend to weaken the uterine supports or contribute to the formation of adhesions. The condition may present no symptoms, or it may be evidenced by backache, fatigue, a feeling of pelvic pressure, and leukorrhea. Treatment may be confined to exercises or to the placement of pessaries to hold the uterus in a normal position. Pessaries are inserted by the physician and should not cause the person any difficulty or discomfort. They may be worn for several months;

however, they must be removed at intervals by the physician, cleaned, and reinserted. The patient may be advised to use a douche several times a week, since there may be some vaginal irritation and discharge. For some persons abdominal surgery is needed to correct the condition.

Endometriosis

Endometriosis is the growth of endometrial tissue in abnormal sites, usually in the peritoneal cavity. The ovaries and the peritoneum are the most common sites. The uterus is an organ that sheds cells periodically. These are endometrial cells, and occasionally they become seeded throughout the pelvis and other organs. The exact cause is unknown, but possibly it is of congenital origin. Although these endometrial cells are not in the uterus, they are stimulated by the ovarian hormones and bleed into the nearby tissue, resulting in an inflammatory process. Adhesions, strictures, cysts, and infertility can result.[22]

The patient is usually asymptomatic until she is between 25 and 40 years of age. Symptoms that gradually begin to occur are pain during menstruation, which becomes progressively worse, fatigue, pressure in the pelvic organs, and general discomfort. Treatment with drugs that suppress ovulation for a time delays the stimulation of the cells and increases the chance of fertility when administration of the drug is stopped. When endometriosis is severe, removal of the uterus, fallopian tubes, and ovaries may be necessary.

Tumors

Fibroid. A fibroid, or myomatous tumor, is a benign growth of muscle tissue of the uterus. It occurs in 20% to 30% of all women and develops slowly between the ages of 25 and 40. Menorrhagia, abnormally long or heavy bleeding with menstrual periods, is the characteristic symptom. If the fibroid tumor becomes large enough to cause pressure on other structures, there may be backache, constipation, and urinary symptoms. Treatment is surgical removal. If the fibroid tumor is small, a myomectomy is performed to remove just the tumor. If the tumor is large or produces excessive bleeding, a hysterectomy is performed, preserving the ovaries if possible.

Malignant. Cervical cancer is the second most common form of malignancy affecting the female reproductive organs. Unfortunately, cancer of the cervix does not cause any symptoms during the early stages, and the condition is usu-ally far advanced before any signs appear. Although cervical cancer may occur in young adults, the incidence increases with age, with the greatest incidence in patients between 30 and 50 years of age. There is an increased incidence of cervical carcinoma in young women whose mothers took DES during pregnancy as treatment to prevent spontaneous abortion. The Pap smear test (p. 547) is being used widely and has had a primary effect on the decreasing mortality associated with cervical cancer. Carcinoma in situ is a preinvasive, asymptomatic carcinoma that can only be diagnosed by microscopic examination. Once it is diagnosed, it can be treated early without radical surgery and a cure results. Carcinoma in situ of the cervix is essentially 100% curable. All women over 20 years of age or who are sexually active should have a pelvic examination and Pap smear every 3 years after two negative examinations 1 year apart.[1] High-risk women should be examined more frequently, and many gynecologists prefer to see their patients yearly.

Uterine cancer occurs somewhat later in life, usually affecting postmenopausal women. The most common symptom is vaginal bleeding; there is no relationship between the amount of bleeding and the existence of cancer. Sometimes only a slight spotting occurs.

Treatment of cervical and uterine cancer varies with the extent of the cancer and age of the patient. For cancer in situ a conization or laser surgery may be performed, which removes a portion of the cervix. Other patients may have a simple hysterectomy. Radical surgery and radiation therapy are used for more advanced cancer (Chapter 9).

Conditions Affecting the Ovaries and Fallopian Tubes
Cysts and tumors

Many different kinds of ovarian tumors and cysts are benign; however, some may be malignant. Ovarian cysts may cause no symptoms, or they may result in a disturbance of menstruation, a feeling of heaviness, and slight bleeding. If a pedicle (a stemlike structure) is present, the cyst may become twisted on the pedicle, cutting off the blood supply. If this occurs, immediate surgery is required.

Cancer of the ovary has a 4% incidence rate among the cancers that occur in the female reproductive tract. The risk of ovarian cancer increases with age, with the highest rates being for women age 65 to 84.[2] It has been called the silent disease since early warning signs, prompting medical attention, rarely occur. As a result, ovarian cancer causes more deaths than cancer of the uterus. Vague lower abdominal discomfort and mild digestive complaints are early symptoms for some women.[6] Later symptoms include pelvic pain, anemia, and ascites.[22] It may be a primary site or can occur as a result of metastasis from the gastrointestinal tract, breast, pancreas, or kidneys. Treatment for cancer of the ovary depends on the severity of the malignancy. Surgical removal of the tumor is the preferred treatment. This may include radical excision of the uterus, ovaries, tubes, and omentum. Chemotherapy follows surgery.[6]

Salpingitis

Salpingitis is an inflammation of the fallopian tube caused by bacteria. The gonococcus is frequently the invading organism, but other bacteria such as the streptococcus or staphylococcus may be responsible for the infection. The causative organism usually enters the uterine cavity and from there finds its way to the tubes. The ovaries and the pelvic peritoneum may become involved, resulting in what is called *pelvic inflammatory disease.*

Pelvic inflammatory disease

Pelvic inflammatory disease (PID), also termed pelvic infection, is an inflammatory condition of the pelvic cavity that may involve the fallopian tubes (salpingitis), ovaries (oophoritis), pelvic peritoneum, or pelvic vascular system. The disease can be acute or chronic and can be caused by gram-negative bacteria, staphylococcus, streptococcus, or sexually transmitted organisms. It can be confined to one structure or be widespread in the pelvic cavity. The gonococcus is the most common causative organism (Chapter 7). Pathogens invade the pelvic organs during sexual intercourse, childbirth, the postpartum period, or abortion or may spill into the cavity following rupture of an infected organ such as the appendix. PID is more common in women using intrauterine devices for birth control.

Pathophysiology. Pathogenic organisms are usually introduced from the outside and enter the cervix from the vagina, move up through the uterus to the fallopian tubes, exit from the tubes, and enter the pelvic cavity. They may also enter the pelvis through thrombosed uterine veins or through the lymphatics of the uterus. When the

pathogens lodge in the fallopian tubes, the inflammatory process results in purulent material and subsequent adhesions, strictures, and obstruction. Infertility results when the tubes become occluded from this process. Partial tubal obstruction predisposes to ectopic pregnancy. Whereas the sperm may be small enough to pass through the stricture or obstructed area, the fertilized ovum is too large to make the return trip to the uterus and remains in the tube, where it begins to develop. Adhesions may produce symptoms severe enough to require removal of the uterus, fallopian tubes, and ovaries.

Assessment. Acute PID is characterized by severe abdominal pain, pelvic pain, malaise, nausea, vomiting, and fever with leukocytosis. A foul-smelling, purulent vaginal discharge may be present. The symptoms may be so mild that the woman ignores them. They may subside before the patient seeks medical care, and the disease then goes untreated. Lack of treatment or inadequately treated acute PID results in the chronic form. The patient will then complain of a chronic dull pain in the lower abdomen, backache, constipation, malaise, low-grade fever, and menstrual disturbances. Acute symptoms can also appear during periods of exacerbation. The patient's complaints are often vague and nonspecific. Examination reveals pain and tenderness in the lower abdomen, which increases with a vaginal examination. Masses will be felt if the fallopian tubes or ovaries are enlarged or if an abscess is present. Abscess formation is common in Douglas' cul-de-sac. If adhesions are present, the pelvic organs will be less movable. Smears and cultures will be taken from the vagina, cervix, or Douglas' cul-de-sac to identify the causative organism and determine the most effective antibiotic to be used. Laparoscopy may be performed to diagnose the disease by visualizing the reproductive organs and surrounding tissues.

Intervention. Hospitalization is usually required so the patient can receive intensive antibiotic therapy. Activity is restricted to bed rest, and the patient is placed in a mid-Fowler's position to prevent upward flow of drainage and the formation of abscesses high in the abdomen. Intravenous fluids may be necessary if the patient's condition requires restricted intake. The antibiotics will be given intravenously at first to ensure that blood levels of the drug are adequate to be effective against the causative organism. Heat to the abdomen or hot sitz baths may be ordered to improve circulation and provide comfort. Analgesics will be necessary for pain. Blood pressure, temperature, pulse, and respirations should be taken every 4 hours until the fever subsides. The patient should be observed for any increase or decrease in pain and any change in amount, color, odor, or consistency of vaginal drainage. Surgical removal of involved organs may be necessary.

Expected outcomes. After proper intervention the patient with PID will:

Be afebrile.

Have absence or reduction of pain and vaginal drainage.

Identify the point of entry and route of travel of organisms causing PID.

Identify signs and symptoms of recurrence.

List all medications to be taken after discharge, including time and frequency of each dose.

Indicate compliance with restrictions on activity, medication regimen, and recommendations for follow-up care.

Surgical Intervention for Conditions Affecting the Cervix, Uterus, Ovaries and Fallopian Tubes

Hysterectomy is the surgical removal of the uterus. A hysterectomy may be performed through an incision into the abdominal cavity (abdominal hysterectomy), or the uterus may be removed through the vagina (vaginal hysterectomy). In premenopausal women the ovaries are usually not removed unless some abnormal condition exists. Depending on the existing condition, the physician may consider it necessary to remove one or both ovaries or one or both fallopian tubes. Removal of both ovaries is called *bilateral oophorectomy*, and removal of both fallopian tubes is called *bilateral salpingectomy*. When the entire uterus, tubes, and ovaries are removed, the operation is called *panhysterosalpingo-oophorectomy*, or panhysterectomy. It may also be referred to as a total abdominal hysterectomy with bilateral *salpingo-oophorectomy* (TAH BSO). Removal of the body of the uterus, leaving the cervix in place, is termed a subtotal hysterectomy. In a total hysterectomy the entire uterus is removed, but the tubes and ovaries are left in place. The patient should understand that a hysterectomy does not necessarily mean that any organs will be removed other than the uterus. However, if there is evidence of disease affecting other organs, they will be removed at the same time as the uterus.

Surgery involving the female reproductive tract is upsetting to most women. Often the patient perceives the procedure as a threat to her femininity. If the patient is of childbearing age, she may be disappointed because she can no longer have children. Often patients will worry about the process of healing and the resumption of sexual activity. If cancer is suspected or found, fear of death may be present. The more thoroughly the patient is prepared for the surgery, the more satisfactorily she will recover, both physically and emotionally.

Abdominal hysterectomy

Preoperative intervention. Preoperative care is the same as that for patients having other kinds of abdominal surgery. The surgical preparation of the skin includes the abdomen, pubis, and perineum. The physician may order an antiseptic vaginal douche, and a Foley catheter may be inserted to keep the bladder from filling during surgery and causing strain postoperatively.

Postoperative intervention. Postoperative nursing care is concerned with the prevention of urinary retention, intestinal distention, and venous thrombosis. If a retention catheter was inserted, it should be kept patent and attached to closed drainage. If not, the patient must be checked frequently for bladder distention. The incidence of urinary retention is greater after a hysterectomy than after other types of surgery because some trauma to the bladder unavoidably occurs. Urinary retention leads to discomfort from distention and increases the danger of urinary tract infection. Before administering drugs for pain, the nurse should be sure that the discomfort is not from an overdistended bladder. Most patients are given intravenous fluids for 1 or 2 days, and the additional fluid may contribute to bladder distention. Every method should be used to assist the patient to void before catheterization; efforts should be instituted early, not delayed until the patient is miserable because of an overdistended bladder. If the patient does not have an indwelling catheter and is unable to void, catheterization every 8 hours may be necessary.

Intestinal distention is common following a hysterectomy. A nasogastric tube may be inserted. A small tap-water enema or a Harris flush may be ordered to help relieve distention. Early ambulation will help to return the bowel to normal function. As soon as bowel sounds have returned and flatus is being expelled, the patient is allowed

---

NURSING CARE GUIDELINES
Hysterectomy

Nursing diagnoses

- Alteration in comfort (abdominal pain) related to surgical incision and for gaseous distention.
- Altered sexuality patterns related to restrictions on sexual intercourse.
- Potential ineffective coping related to loss of reproductive function.
- Potential dysfunctional grieving related to loss of reproductive organ.
- Knowledge deficit related to restrictions on physical activity, lifting, sexual relations, and onset and management of menopause.
- High risk for infection related to interruption in integrity of skin and/or vaginal mucosa.
- Disturbance in self-concept (body image, selfesteem, and/or role performance) related to loss of reproductive organ and function.
- Potential urinary retention related to pelvic edema and discomfort.
- Potential alteration in peripheral tissue perfusion related to venous congestion in pelvis.

Nursing interventions

- Administer routine care immediately after anesthesia.
- Check abdominal or perineal dressing for hemorrhage; change as needed after primary dressing is removed by physician.
- Maintain intravenous infusion, as ordered.
- Administer nothing by mouth until peristalsis returns.
- Maintain patency of indwelling catheter or check for bladder distention every 8 hours; straight catheterize, as necessary.
- Catheterize for residual urine after voiding, if ordered.
- Check for bowel sounds and observe for abdominal distention every 8 hours.

- Apply heat to abdomen for gas pains, if ordered.
- Apply elastic stockings for patients at high risk; may be removed for bathing.
- Apply "pulsating" pneumatic stockings for clients at high risk for deep vein thrombosis, if ordered.
- Avoid sharp flexion of knees or thighs; do not place pillows under the knees.
- Dangle the patient the evening of surgery; encourage leg exercises until ambulating.
- Provide emotional support, allow patient to express fears and concerns related to loss of reproductive capacity.
- Teach patient to:
  Resume sexual intercourse in 4 to 6 weeks based on physician's order
  Resume normal activity gradually, but avoid heavy lifting and extreme exercise for 6 to 8 weeks
  Avoid driving for 3 to 4 weeks
  Return for postoperative medical examination as instructed by physician.

Expected outcomes

- Void regularly, with amounts greater than 150 ml and residual amounts less than 60 ml.
- Take regular diet without nausea or distention.
- Demonstrate negative Homan's sign.
- Demonstrate abdominal wound, if present, that is clean, dry, and approximated.
- Maintain self-esteem, evidenced by attention to personal hygiene and appearance.
- Freely express fears and concerns regarding loss of reproductive capacity and sexual identity.
- Discuss fears, concerns, and restrictions on sexual activity with sexual partner.
- State restrictions on heavy lifting for several weeks.
- State restrictions on coitus until physician permits.
- Identify date of follow-up visit to physician.

---

liquids by mouth with a gradual return to solid food. Nursing diagnoses commonly seen in patients after a hysterectomy are identified in the boxed material.

Patients undergoing pelvic surgery are more susceptible to venous stasis and phlebitis because of trauma to blood vessels. Patients who have varicose veins in the extremities must be carefully observed. The nurse should *not* raise the knee gatch, place pillows under the knees, or place the patient in a high Fowler's position. Active exercise

should be started as soon as the patient is fully conscious, and early ambulation helps to prevent venous stasis. Some surgeons order elastic antiembolism stockings to prevent stasis and to support venous flow.

Sedation such as meperidine (Demerol) may be ordered for relief of pain. Slight vaginal drainage may occur for a day or two, but any unusual bleeding should be reported to the physician. Checking vital signs and observing the abdominal dressing for evidence of bleeding should be routinely carried out. Most patients without complications are dismissed from the hospital in about 5 days. The box summarizes nursing diagnoses and intervention for the patient following abdominal hysterectomy.

Vaginal hysterectomy

Preoperative intervention. Skin preparation involves shaving the pubis and perineum. Some physicians will order prophylactic antibiotics and some an antiseptic vaginal douche. A primary source of postoperative infection is the vaginal vault. A Foley catheter will be inserted to drain the bladder during surgery, and an enema will be given.

Postoperative intervention. If a repair has been done along with the hysterectomy, the Foley catheter will remain in place for 4 or 5 days to prevent pressure on the sutures. Otherwise, it is removed postoperatively, and the patient must be observed for bladder distention and assisted to void. Other postoperative nursing care is essentially the same as that for repair of relaxed muscles.[20]

Discharge teaching: hysterectomy. Before the patient is discharged, she should know what changes to expect. She will no longer menstruate, and she should not have coitus until her physician permits, usually after the first checkup in 4 to 6 weeks. She may have worries concerning her ability to continue to share sexual pleasure. When a hysterectomy is done, the vaginal floor is reconstructed with ligaments, and most women should have the same capacity for sexual stimulation after surgery as before. Pain experienced during intercourse (dyspareunia) should be reported to the physician. Normal physical activity and light work may be done when the woman returns home; however, lifting heavy objects and more difficult activity must be avoided for a few weeks. Most women may return to work within 6 weeks.

Conditions Affecting the Breast
Acute mastitis

Mastitis is an inflammation of the mammary gland (breast) that often occurs during lactation but may occur any time. Although uncommon, mastitis may occur in both the male and the female as a complication of mumps. It is usually the result of the entrance of bacteria through a crack or fissure in the nipple. The infection may block one or more of the milk ducts, causing the milk to stagnate in the lobule. The infection may spread throughout the breast tissue and cause abscess formation. The infection usually causes an elevation of temperature, with pain and tenderness of the breast. The treatment consists of administration of antibiotic drugs, application of heat or cold, and support of the breast. Incision and drainage of an abscess may be necessary. Since the invading organism in mastitis is frequently the staphylococcus, isolation and care as outlined in Chapter 7 should be followed.

Mammary dysplasia (fibrocystic breast disease, chronic cystic mastitis)

Mammary dysplasia occurs in approximately one of three premenopausal women. It is characterized by the formation of a nodular type of benign cyst in the breast. The exact cause is unknown but may be related to some hormone imbalance. Many women go through life unaware of the condition or neglect diagnosis and treatment. The disease is not malignant and does not produce an inflammatory condition. Although it may involve both breasts, it is generally accentuated in one breast. The cysts may occur singly or may be numerous and vary in size and tenderness. Pain may be present and may become worse during the menstrual period. Treatment is usually conservative after cancer has been ruled out; however, the patient should examine her own breasts at monthly intervals and remain under medical supervision.

Tumors

Tumors of the breast can be benign or malignant. Benign tumors are not tender and are freely movable. An exact diagnosis can be made only by careful microscopic examination of the cells. Benign tumors should be surgically removed.

Breast cancer

Breast cancer is the most common cancer in women, but is now second to lung cancer in the number of deaths from cancer in women. It is estimated that 1 of 10 women in the United States will develop cancer of the breast.[1] One of every 100 cases is seen in males. The single woman is more likely to have breast cancer than the married woman, and married women who do not bear children are more likely to have breast cancer than married women who do have children. There also appears to be a lower incidence of breast cancer among women who breast-feed their infants for at least 3 months; however, some authorities ques-

---

Risk Factors for Breast Cancer
Family history: mother/sister
Nulliparous
First pregnancy after 35 years
Menarche before age 11
Menopause after age 50
History of cancer in one breast
Diet high in fat and protein
Obesity

tion this factor. Breast cancer is not hereditary, but some families have a greater incidence of breast cancer than others. Women over 35 years of age are at higher risk. The cause of breast cancer is poorly understood despite extensive research.[6]

Time is an important factor in the diagnosis and treatment of breast cancer; if discovered in the early stages, the possibility of cure is high. When the disease is localized in the breast, 85% will survive 5 years or longer. The 5-year survival rate is decreased to 53% when axillary nodes are involved.

Assessment. The American Cancer Society, Inc., has outlined a program for breast self-examination and through films and printed material has sought to encourage women to examine their breasts monthly to detect any abnormalities (Figure 20-3). Annual examination by a physician is recommended for women over age 50; those between age 20 and 40 should be examined every 3 years.[25]

The development of the disease is insidious, and pain is usually absent in the early stages. The only sign that may be present is a small, firm lump in the breast, not well defined or movable, which may be discovered only by careful examination. As the tumor increases in size, it attaches itself to the chest wall or to the skin above. A dimpling of the skin may be present, the nipple may be retracted or inverted, and a discharge from the nipple may be present. In some cases reddening of the skin may develop and if the tumor is large, a change in the contour of the breast may be present. Without treatment, the axillary lymph nodes become involved, ulceration may occur, and metastasis to the lungs, bones, liver, and brain may occur. A gradual state of ill health occurs, with weight loss and poor appetite.

Carcinoma of the breast usually arises in a single area in one breast. Almost half of these tumors occur in the upper outer quadrant and another fourth in the central or inner half of the breast. Tumors in the upper outer quadrant tend to metastasize first to the axillary lymph nodes, whereas those from the central portion metastasize to the internal mammary chain or lymph nodes (Figure 20-4).[8]

The diagnosis is based on mammography and incision of the tumor for laboratory microscopic examination.

Assessment should include exploration of the patient's feelings about and desire for reconstruction following a mastectomy. Reconstruction can be more successful when tissue is conserved at the time of surgery in planning for reconstruction. Methods of and indications for breast reconstruction are covered later in this chapter.

Intervention. If the malignancy is too far advanced to be removed surgically, the patient will be treated with chemotherapy and hormonal therapy. The goal is to improve the quality of the patient's life while increasing the duration of survival with the least number of untoward effects to the patient. The patient will not be cured, but if she responds to treatment, she will live a longer and less painful life than if not treated.

Operable carcinoma of the breast is treated by excision (lumpectomy, quadrectomy) or mastectomy. Chemotherapy or radiation or both may be used in addition to surgery.

Lumpectomy

When the malignancy is a single tumor of less than 4 cm or two small tumors lying closely together, it is becoming more common for the physician to offer an alternative to mastectomy. Informed patients who refused a mastectomy are seen as a major force in advancing research on conservative management of breast cancer. Several studies performed over the last 20 years have shown that rates of survival, distant metastasis and local recurrence are similar in patients treated with lumpectomy plus radiation and mastectomy plus radiation. If the likelihood of "cure" is considered equal, one can consider the cosmetic advantage of removing only the malignant tumor and a small amount (0.5 to 1 cm) of surrounding breast tissue. If malignant cells are found adjacent to the tumor, a mastectomy is recommended.

The surgeon removes a minimum amount of skin and the breast tissues are not approximated to preserve the appearance of the breast. The in-

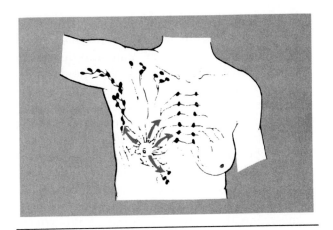

Figure 20-4

Mode of dissemination of breast cancer. *(From Bouchard R and Owens NF: Nursing care of the cancer patient, ed 4, St Louis, 1981, The CV Mosby Co.)*

cision is made to follow the contour of the breast. A separate incision is made in the axilla to dissect the axillary nodes for biopsy. At least five nodes lying lateral to (level I) and under (level II) the pectoralis minor muscles should be removed for review. If the nodes are removed from the lower two thirds of the axilla, the patient has better function and tolerance and less postoperative edema. If the nodes are negative, the axilla need not receive radiation therapy. Radiation treatments are given to the tumor site and internal mammary nodes up to five times weekly for 5 weeks. Tumor sites lying deep in breast tissue may be treated with an interstitial radiation implant. The patient must be hospitalized while the implants are in place.[21]

Mastectomy. The surgical removal of the breast for treatment of malignancy can be simple, radical, or modified radical. Some authorities believe that a subcutaneous mastectomy could be as effective as a simple mastectomy. *Subcutaneous mastectomy* involves an incision below the breast and the removal of the breast tissue below the skin. In a *simple mastectomy* the skin and tissue of the breast are removed, the edges of the remaining skin are sutured together, and the lymph nodes are left in place. Some surgeons think that preserving the lymph nodes is important in controlling the spread of malignant cells.

A *radical mastectomy* involves removal of the breast and the underlying tissues, including the muscles, axillary lymph nodes, vessels, and perhaps the entire mammary lymph node chain and supraclavicular nodes. The extent of surgery de-

pends on the spread of the neoplasm. However, a radical mastectomy is rarely performed today. When the malignant tumor is localized and examination of the lymph nodes is negative, most surgeons believe that a modified radical mastectomy should be done.

A *modified radical mastectomy* involves removal of all breast tissue, but with the pectoralis major and minor muscles left in place. Preserving these muscles prevents the formation of a hollow depression below the clavicle, thus reducing disfigurement. Hand and arm swelling are rare, and arm and shoulder motion are not affected. Scientific evidence of the effectiveness of the modified radical mastectomy has led to a shift in its general use. The cure rate for both the radical and the modified radical procedures seems to be the same. Irradiation may precede or follow a surgical procedure, but sufficient time must be allowed before or after surgery to avoid a delay in or interference with healing.

Often patients have delayed medical care and surgery so that the cancer has become invasive and therefore inoperable. In these cases radiation or chemotherapy or both may be used to retard the damaging effects of the malignant growth.

Preoperative intervention. The emotional preparation of the patient may be more important than the physical preparation. When a biopsy is positive, the patient and the physician together decide on the best course of action. The possibility of reconstructive surgery can be discussed at this time. Although this improves the patient's ability to accept the diagnosis and loss, it remains an enormous psychologic trauma. A female nurse has the advantage of providing woman-to-woman understanding and emotional support, which becomes even more important if the physician is male. Even the patient's husband may be unable to provide the understanding that the patient needs. He, too, should be given the opportunity to express his feelings and concerns. It is important to openly discuss the patient's fears, and this is best done by a nurse who has established a therapeutic relationship with the patient and family. It must begin on the day of admission by letting the patient know that the nurse is aware of her concerns and by helping the patient to express them. Identifying and labeling fears make them manageable. The nurse should respond to all questions in a way that keeps the patient talking. The "Reach to Recovery" program, sponsored by local chapters of the American Cancer Society,

Inc., will send volunteers who have had mastectomies to speak to individuals at the physician's request. Providing an opportunity to discuss the effects of a mastectomy with someone who has had one often gives needed reassurance to the patient facing or recuperating from such surgery. These services are not available in all communities and are not automatically requested by all physicians.

The physical preparation of the patient requires that a wide area of skin be shaved, including the axilla (Figure 20-5). Frequently, a radical mastectomy requires skin grafting, and the anterior surface of the thigh may be shaved, since the donor skin may be taken from this area. The physician will specify areas to be shaved. For some patients a blood transfusion or intravenous fluids may be administered preoperatively. If the patient's condition permits, a pint of blood will be taken from her preoperatively for administration at the time of surgery to avoid a chance of reaction. Other preparation is the same as that for other types of major surgery.

Postoperative intervention.   Postoperative nursing care should include checking vital signs and observation for symptoms of shock or hemorrhage, since many large blood vessels are involved in the procedure. Drains may be placed in the axilla to facilitate drainage, and some surgeons attach them to low suction. Other physicians use the Hemovac for drainage. Dressings are usually applied rather tightly and may tend to embarrass respiration and cause some pain and discomfort. When the vital signs are stable, the patient is placed in a 45-degree Fowler's position to promote drainage. The position should be changed frequently and deep breathing exercises encouraged. The patient may have considerable pain and should be given pain-relieving medication, but care must be exercised to prevent oversedation so that the patient will be able to breathe deeply to prevent atelectasis. Physicians differ in opinion concerning the best positioning of the affected arm. Some physicians include the arm in the dressing. If the arm is not included, it may be elevated on a pillow with the hand and wrist higher than the elbow and the elbow higher than the shoulder joint. This will facilitate the flow of fluids by the lymph and venous routes and prevent lymphedema. The arm should be observed for signs of circulatory disturbance such as coldness, lack of radial pulse, cyanosis, or blanching. The arm should be observed for edema, numbness, or inability to move the fingers, which should be reported immediately. The patient is allowed out of bed on the first or second postoperative day. The nurse must remember that balance may be poor and that the patient may need assistance to prevent falling. Fluids are permitted as soon as nausea ceases, and diet is usually or-

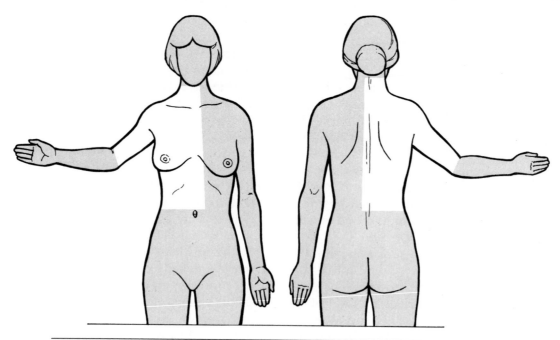

Figure 20-5

Area of skin to be prepared for mastectomy.

dered as tolerated. The patient may need help in cutting meat and in arranging food conveniently, since use of the arm on the affected side may be difficult. When drawing blood, administering intravenous fluids, or taking blood pressure, use the unaffected arm.

Rehabilitation. One of the primary aims of rehabilitation is to restore the use of the affected arm as soon as possible to prevent contracture. The physician will determine the time at which exercises may be started, depending on the presence of sutures and whether skin grafting has been done. If the donor site for skin used in grafting is the thigh, it must be carefully protected from infection. Often these areas are very sore and may cause the patient some pain and difficulty in walking. Some exercises that will help the patient regain use of the arm are shown in Figure 20-6. A small handbook entitled "Help Yourself to Recovery" is available from the American Cancer Society, Inc., for use by the nurse in teaching patients and for distribution to patients on the approval of their surgeon. If the "Reach to Recovery" visitor has been requested, she will bring a kit containing this manual along with a small pillow to aid in positioning, a length of rope and ball to use in exercising, and a temporary prosthesis made of washable cotton. The proper size for the prosthesis is determined at the time the visit is requested. The kit also contains information about permanent prostheses. The visitor will demonstrate and help the patient with the exercises if indicated by the physician. Conversation centers on clothes, prostheses, and returning to one's day-to-day routines.

When the patient is discharged, the home health nurse may visit the patient to encourage and reassure her and to supervise exercises.

Another important area for patient teaching is monthly self-examination of the remaining breast. If the patient had a simple or subcutaneous mastectomy, monthly breast examinations are still necessary because a rim of breast tissue is left and is a potential site of malignancy. Evaluation of the patient's ability to perform breast self-examination and her understanding of its importance is essential.

The box on p. 569 summarizes nursing diagnoses and intervention for the patient following mastectomy.

Choosing a prosthesis. The patient should not be fitted for a prosthesis for at least 6 weeks or as determined by her physician, and she should be encouraged to wait until she is psychologically ready to be fitted. A list of recommended fitters in the patient's geographic area will assist the patient in her selection. Information about types of prostheses available is also helpful. The "Reach to Recovery" visitor usually has this information. The public health nurse may be of help to the patient in following up suggestions made in the hospital concerning a prosthesis.

Breast prostheses are available in a variety of types, sizes, weights, and prices. They may be filled with rubber, air, fluid, or a gelatin-like substance. The surgeon should be consulted regarding the ideal weight of the prosthesis to provide proper balance and the width of the brassiere strap to prevent the tourniquet effect of a thin strap cutting into the shoulder. A proper fit of the prosthesis is essential to allow for normal posture and provide a natural appearance under clothing. A natural appearance is important because it can help the patient regain a positive self-image.

Breast reconstruction after mastectomy. Whereas a mastectomy is a curative treatment, the amputation of a breast is usually viewed as a tragic event, accompanied by loss of body image. Particularly in our society, where breasts are regarded by men and women alike as symbols of femininity, the loss can produce severe psychologic problems. Advances in the techniques of reconstructive mammoplasty hold the promise of restoring the contour and consistency of breast tissue to many mastectomy patients. Reconstruction is most feasible when less radical surgical procedures are performed. Early detection and treatment make the patient a good candidate for less extensive surgery. Most women experience some dissatisfaction with any type of external prosthesis, whether it be difficulty in wearing clothes or lack of normalcy in sexual relationships. It is becoming more common to replace the missing breast with an internal prosthesis whenever possible. Reconstruction may begin at the time of surgery. A temporary implant is inserted that is gradually expanded to stretch the remaining breast tissue. The permanent implant is put in place later. Consultation with a plastic surgeon before mastectomy provides the opportunity to explore the possibilities for reconstruction and perform the surgical procedure in a manner that is most likely to result in success (Figure 20-7).

Figure 20-6

Arm exercises after mastectomy. **A,** Pendulum swinging with arms relaxed and swinging free. **B,** Arm raising over head. **C,** Rope swinging with length of rope tied to doorknob and swinging with shoulder motion. **D,** Rope sliding by placing length of rope over pulley and sliding rope up and down. **E,** Wall climbing by standing with face to wall and climbing wall with hands, with fingers reaching as far as possible.

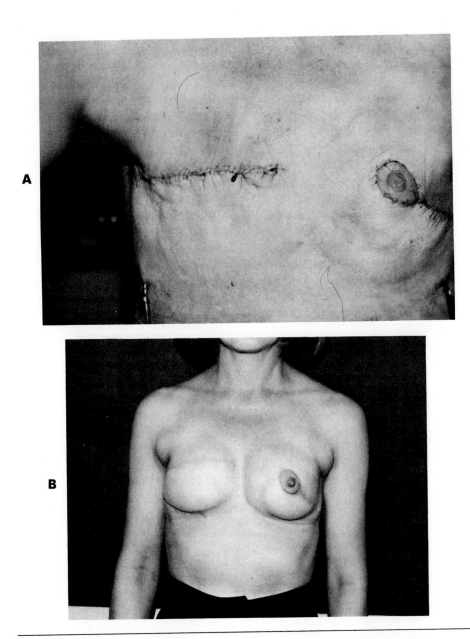

Figure 20-7

A, Immediate postoperative appearance after right simple mastectomy and left subcutaneous mastectomy. **B,** Appearance of patient shown in **A** after reconstruction of breast mounds.

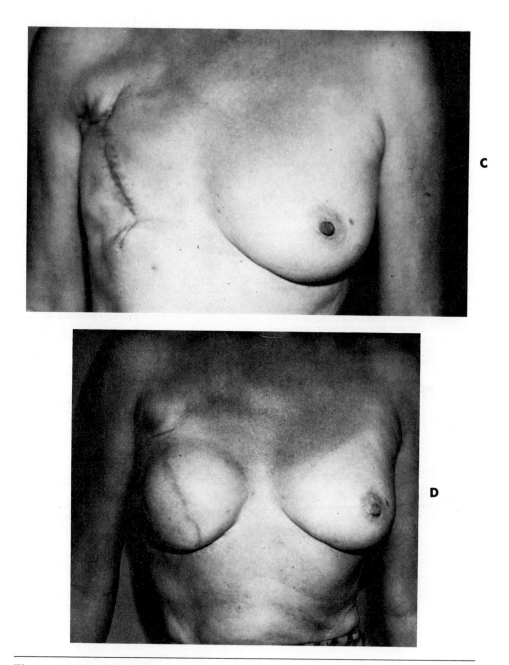

Figure 20-7 (continued)
C, Patient after modified radical mastectomy for carcinoma of breast. **D,** Appearance of patient shown in **C** several months after reconstruction of right breast.

NURSING CARE GUIDELINES
Mastectomy

Nursing diagnoses

- Anxiety related to uncertainty of prognosis or decisions about treatment
- Alteration in comfort (pain) related to incision in skin and muscles of chest wall
- Ineffective breathing pattern related to incision in chest wall
- Potential ineffective individual or family coping related to loss of breast and perceived loss of attractiveness
- High risk for injury to lymphatic system related to obstruction of lymph drainage
- Knowledge deficit related to prosthesis or reconstruction, activity restrictions, rehabilitation exercises, and support groups
- High risk for infection related to interrupted skin integrity and presence of drainage
- Disturbance in self-concept (body image and/or self-esteem) related to loss of breast

Nursing interventions

- Elevate affected arm with pillows above level of heart
- Check vital signs every 4 to 6 hours; use unaffected arm for blood pressures.
- Encourage early movement of affected arm
- Check dressings for signs of hemorrhage; reinforce as necessary
- Maintain patency and suction of Hemovac if present.
- Maintain intravenous fluids as ordered; do not infuse in arm on affected side
- Turn patient and encourage deep breathing and coughing every 2 hours
- Maintain bed in semi-Fowler's position to promote drainage
- Encourage active range of motion exercises of the legs

- Encourage exercise of the affected arm as soon as medically permitted
- Encourage expression of grief related to loss of breast and possible change in self-image
- Discuss the "Reach to Recovery" program and encourage participation
- Encourage early use of temporary breast forms and well-fitting brassiere as soon as permitted by physician
- Provide information on available community resources (Visiting Nurse, American Cancer Society, Prosthetic Suppliers)
- Teach patient to:
  - Continue prescribed arm exercises at home but stop at point of pain
  - Resume housekeeping activities gradually
  - Avoid deodorant on affected side until physician allows it
  - Report symptoms of infection (fever, redness, pain) to physician
  - Return for follow-up medical examination as prescribed
  - Conduct monthly breast self-examinations

Expected outcomes

- Verify absence of edema in arm of affected side.
- Perform exercises as ordered by physician.
- Verbalize fears, concerns, and feelings related to loss of breast and change in body image.
- Wound is dry, approximated, and healing.
- Donor site of graft (if present) is dry and healing, with granulation tissue present.
- State plans for use of appropriate temporary prosthesis and identify need to postpone fitting of permanent prosthesis until physician permits.
- Demonstrate procedure for breast self-examination and verbalize understanding of need to perform monthly on remaining breast or breast tissue.

CONDITIONS OF PREGNANCY

Abortion

The term **abortion** means the termination of pregnancy at any time before the fetus has attained the stage of viability, which is approximately 24 weeks. There are two main types of abortion: **spontaneous and induced.** The lay person uses the word "miscarriage" to denote a spontaneous abortion. It is estimated that 15% of all pregnancies end in spontaneous abortion. At least half of these are due to a defective fetoplacental unit, genetic defects, or implantation abnormalities.[14]

The exact causes of spontaneous abortions are unknown, but evidence indicates that some abortions are the result of defective germ plasm. Falls are not believed to be a significant cause of abortion.

It is customary to use the weight of the fetus as a criterion for defining abortion. Many author-

---

Classification of Abortion

1. Spontaneous abortion
   a. habitual
   b. threatened
   c. inevitable
   d. incomplete
   e. complete
   f. missed or retained
   g. septic
2. Induced abortion
   a. therapeutic
   b. legal
   c. criminal, or illegal

---

ities maintain that the fetus must weigh less than 500 g and have a crown-rump length of less than 16.5 cm.[14] In many states a birth certificate is prepared for any pregnancy terminating after the 20th week of gestation or when the fetus weighs 500 g or more.[28]

Habitual abortion is a term applied when three or more successive pregnancies are spontaneously interrupted. The situation frequently creates a severe emotional problem when a woman wants to have children.

Threatened abortion is indicated when vaginal bleeding or spotting occurs during the first 20 weeks of gestation. The cervix is not dilated, and with conservative treatment the pregnancy may continue uninterrupted. Treatment of threatened abortion includes limiting activity, and bed rest may be prescribed for 24 to 48 hours. If the bleeding stops, it usually does so within 48 hours.[14] The woman should be encouraged to avoid stress and fatigue and may be instructed to avoid intercourse until the pregnancy seems stable.

Inevitable abortion

In *inevitable abortion* the vaginal bleeding may be only spotting, or hemorrhage may occur with passing of clots. The cervix is dilated, and mild pelvic cramping occurs with gradual increase until all or part of the uterine contents are expelled. In inevitable abortion there is no chance of saving the pregnancy.

Incomplete abortion

In *incomplete abortion* only a portion of the products of conception has been expelled; bleeding continues and may cause severe hemorrhage. The part retained is usually fragments of the placenta. It is necessary to hospitalize the patient and prescribe a regimen of bed rest. Sedative drugs are administered and blood transfusions are given if the hemorrhage has been severe. Oxytocin may be administered to stimulate contractions of the uterus. If the residue is not expelled and bleeding continues, the patient is prepared for surgery, taken to the operating room, and given a light anesthetic; then a D and C is performed.

Complete abortion

In *complete abortion* the entire products of the conception are expelled. It is probable that many complete abortions occur without any major difficulty, and a physician does not see the patient.

Missed abortion

In *missed abortion* the fetus dies and is retained for 8 weeks or more before the 20th week of gestation. Weekly examinations of the fibrinogen level in the blood are done. No attempt is made to empty the uterus unless the level of fibrinogen begins to fall. Oxytocin may be administered to stimulate contractions and cause the fetus to be expelled.

Septic abortion

Evidence of *septic abortion* includes an elevation of temperature to 104° F (40° C) or more, with threatened or incomplete loss of the products of conception. The presence or absence of any other focus of infection is ruled out before establishing a diagnosis of septic abortion. The sepsis may be caused by any of several pathogenic organisms. If caused by *Clostridium perfringens*, a spore-forming organism, a powerful exotoxin is liberated. The patient is critically ill with the elevated temperature; the pulse is rapid; and headache, malaise, abdominal tenderness, and indications of pelvic peritonitis occur. The patient is isolated, and medical aseptic technique is carried out. Cultures from the cervix and the uterus are taken, and the appropriate antibiotics are administered. Intravenous fluids and blood transfusions may be given, and hydrocortisone and oxytocin (Pitocin) may be ordered. Septic abortion frequently results in serious complications, including acute renal failure, congestive heart failure, hemorrhage, and severe shock. The patient's condition will be considered in the physician's decision to do a D and C; however, opinions differ concerning the time when a D and C should be done. In some cases a hysterectomy may be performed.

Therapeutic abortion

Therapeutic abortion is the termination of pregnancy by a physician during the first trimester of pregnancy. Therapeutic abortion is usually indicated when the life or health of the mother must be protected. It is considered when there is hazard to the fetus such as rubella in the mother during the first trimester of pregnancy. Reputable physicians secure medical consultation or approval by an established committee before performing a therapeutic abortion.

Legal abortion

Legal abortion, the termination of a pregnancy at the request of the woman, is now available in all states, as the result of a Supreme Court ruling. On January 22, 1973, the U.S. Supreme Court ruled that all antiabortion laws were unconstitutional in the United States. In general, the court made the following ruling concerning abortion:

1. During the first 12 weeks, the state could not bar a woman from obtaining an abortion by a licensed physician.
2. Between 12 and 24 weeks the state could regulate the performance of an abortion in ways reasonable to the woman's health.
3. During the third trimester, the state could regulate and prohibit abortion except those deemed necessary to protect the woman's health or life.

In 1976 the U.S. Congress passed the Hyde amendment, which forbids the use of federal funds for abortions except for situations in which the woman's life is threatened. As a result, women with personal funds or private insurance are able to have abortions, whereas poor women who use federal funds for health care are denied the same opportunity.

Criminal or illegal abortion

Criminal or *illegal abortion* is abortion performed without legal approval. Many are self-induced, or they may be performed by nonprofessional persons known as "doctors," by midwives, or by lay persons. Since abortion has been legalized, the incidence of illegal abortion has decreased significantly. It should be noted that the number of illegal abortions cannot be estimated since they are not reported. Only if the woman encounters problems and is forced to consult a physician or clinic may the abortion be known. When serious complications develop, such as hemorrhage, renal failure, or sepsis, medical care will be sought. Maternal mortality is higher in illegal abortion than in spontaneous abortion.

Intervention

Interventions are planned according to the type of abortion, prognoses, and nursing diagnoses. All pregnant women should be taught to report any signs of vaginal bleeding or spotting to their health care provider. Women experiencing bleeding or spotting must be observed for hemorrhage. An exact pad count must be kept, and they may be weighed to determine the amount of blood loss. All clots and tissue must be saved for inspection and possible laboratory testing. The nurse must be aware of hospital policy concerning the disposal of the products of conception. The nurse should also understand and encourage the woman's religious beliefs and practices that might be appropriate at this time.

In preparing the woman for a D and C, the nurse uses the same procedures as those for the nonpregnant woman. Administration of medication, intravenous fluids, or blood transfusions is carried out according to physician's orders. An informed consent must be obtained.

Postoperatively, vital signs should be monitored routinely. The woman must be observed for vaginal bleeding and any signs of infection. She should be taught good hygiene practices and good nutrition. Since there has been blood loss, instruct her about foods high in iron, folic acid, vitamin C, and protein. Listen to her talk about the meaning of the loss of the pregnancy. The nurse should recognize that abortion may precipitate grief in the woman and that the grieving process takes time before it is resolved. The woman may need advice about birth control before discharge. A method of birth control may need to be prescribed by the physician, so the patient should be encouraged to consult with her physician before discharge.

Legalized abortions have brought about rapid changes in maternity nursing, which has always been focused on bringing new life into the world. Many nursing personnel have had difficulty accepting these changes, and many hospitals have used inservice education to help nurses to verbalize their feelings. Whatever the feelings of the individual nurse, the patient entering the hospital seeking an abortion should never face hostility or discrimination. The decision to seek an abortion may be a difficult one, and these patients have problems and worries similar to those of any other hospitalized patient. Nurses who believe that they cannot morally assist with an abortion should not work in an agency where they are performed.

Ectopic Pregnancy

Ectopic pregnancy is gestation anywhere outside the uterus. Rarely, but occasionally, it may be in the abdomen or the ovary; however, the most common site is the fallopian tube. When the ovum becomes implanted in the fallopian tube, it is referred to as *tubal pregnancy*. Infrequently, a tubal pregnancy may be palpated in the area near the uterus, but the first indication of tubal pregnancy occurs when the tube ruptures. Tubal pregnancy results from some condition within the tube that slows or prevents passage of the ovum through the tube to the endometrium of the uterus. Conditions such as inflammation from disease, narrowing of the tube, and an elongated or immature tube create a situation conducive to tubal pregnancy.

As the embryo increases in size, the tube stretches until it can no longer remain intact. The tube may rupture, releasing the entire products of conception into the abdominal cavity *(ectopic abortion)*, or the rupture may be small, and the embryo remains within the tube, but severe bleeding occurs from damage to the blood vessels. The length of time the tube remains intact with the developing embryo is variable and may be from 3 to 4 weeks or as long as 8 to 12 weeks.

Assessment

Frequently, the patient has missed one period and has noted slight spotting but may not know that she is pregnant. In the majority of patients rupture results in acute abdominal pain that occurs suddenly. The pain may extend to the shoulder and the rectal area. The patient becomes faint and pale and she may be in shock. Hemorrhage may be severe, and acute secondary anemia results.

Intervention

A ruptured tubal pregnancy is always an emergency and requires immediate surgery. There may be little time for preoperative preparation. The patient is treated immediately for shock by blood transfusions or intravenous infusion of lactated Ringer's solution. The nurse must anticipate the physician's needs and work quickly and efficiently.

NURSING CARE GUIDELINES
Abortion or Ectopic Pregnancy

Nursing diagnoses
- Fluid volume deficit related to blood loss
- High risk for infection related to retained products of conception
- Alteration in comfort; pain related to uterine cramping
- Potential spiritual distress related to loss and grief
- Ineffective individual coping related to death of fetus

Nursing interventions
- Check vital signs routinely
- Save all peripads, blood-soaked linens, clots, and tissue
- Monitor intravenous infusions
- Observe for bladder distention; catheterize as ordered
- Encourage verbalization of concerns and feelings related to loss
- Provide spiritual support and conduct religious practices if requested
- Instruct patient to:
    Take all medication as prescribed by physician
    - Return for medical examination as ordered by physician
    - Report signs and symptoms of infection or vaginal bleeding
    - Eat foods high in iron, folic acid, vitamin C, and protein
    - Refer patient to perinatal loss groups in community

Expected outcomes
- Vital signs stable and within usual limits
- Vaginal drainage reduced and free of unusual odor
- Voiding 30 to 60 ml/hr
- Verbalizes concerns and feelings
- Verbalizes discharge instructions and identifies referral source and date of medical examination

---

Postoperative care of the patient is the same as that for other abdominal surgery. Transfusions with whole blood may be necessary to combat the anemia. Uterine bleeding will occur for several days, and the patient must be observed for any unusual bleeding from the abdominal incision or from the vagina.

CONDITIONS AFFECTING THE MALE EXTERNAL GENITALIA

Congenital Malformation

Congenital malformations in the male involve the bladder, the urethra, and the penis. *Exstrophy of the bladder* is a major defect in which the abdominal wall has failed to close and the anterior bladder is open on the abdomen. A direct passage of urine to the outside occurs and it is difficult to keep the patient dry. *Epispadia* occurs when the male urethra is open somewhere along the upper surface (dorsal) of the penis, whereas in *hypospadias* the urethra is open at some point along the undersurface (ventral) of the penis. Most instances of hypospadias are minor and require no corrective surgery. Severe urethral defects require extensive urethroplasty. If surgery is required, no circumcision is done since the foreskin will be used in the procedure.[6] These defects require plastic surgery. When surgery for exstrophy of the bladder is done, a long hospitalization is usually necessary. The surgery is not always successful and is associated with some risk.

Conditions Affecting the Testes and Adjacent Structures
Epididymitis

The epididymis is a coiled tube approximately 20 feet long that lies on top of the testes in the scrotum and collects the spermatozoa. Any of several bacteria may cause an infection, including the streptococcus, staphylococcus, and colon bacillus. It may occur after prostatitis or infection of the urinary tract. It often occurs as a complication of gonorrhea. The patient may be ill with fever, chills, headache, nausea, and vomiting. Painful swelling of the scrotum, which may be unilateral or bilateral, occurs.

Treatment is to place the patient on a regimen of bed rest and support the scrotum. Heat or cold may be applied, and the appropriate antibiotic is administered. If abscess formation occurs, incision and drainage may be required.

Orchitis

Orchitis, an infection of the testicle, may result from injury or any one of the several infectious diseases such as influenza, pneumonia, or gonorrhea. It may also occur as a complication of mumps. Symptoms include fever, nausea, and painful swelling of the testicle. The treatment is the same as that for epididymitis.

Hydrocele and varicocele

A **hydrocele** is a collection of fluid between the testes and their outermost covering, the tunica vaginalis testis. The condition is often associated with some other disease or injury. Several methods of treatment are used, including aspiration of the fluid; injection of a sclerosing solution, which causes the walls of the sac containing the fluid to adhere; and surgical removal of the sac, which often is the best method of treatment to ensure cure. The scrotum should be supported with bandages or a commercial suspensory.

A **varicocele** is a form of varicosity that involves the veins of the spermatic cord. It is usually a painless and harmless condition, but if it causes pain the scrotum should be supported; if support fails to relieve the discomfort, ligation of the veins may be done.

Tumors

Tumors of the male reproductive tract are usually malignant. They commonly occur in the testes, the prostate, and on the penis. *Penile* tumors account for a small percentage of cancer in men. It is usually the result of poor hygiene practices and is rarely seen in men who were circumcised as infants. Treatment involves removal of the cancerous tumor, and partial or total removal of the penis may be necessary.

Testicular tumors are the second most common malignancy in men between the ages of 15 and 35 years of age, and account for 1% to 2% of all tumors in men. However, the disease also occurs in other age groups, so all men should be aware of the symptoms. Testicular carcinoma has a highly metastatic character.[3] Regular testicular self-examination (TSE) is currently recommended as an effective method for detecting cancer in its early stages (Figure 20-8). All males age 15 and older should perform TSE (see Guidelines, page 574).

Warning Signs of Testicular Cancer

A lump in either testicle
Any enlargement of a testicle
A feeling of heaviness in the scrotum
A dull ache in the lower abdomen or the groin
A sudden collection of fluid in the scrotum
Pain or discomfort in a testicle or in the scrotum
Enlargement or tenderness of the breasts[3]

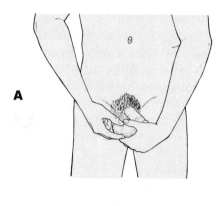

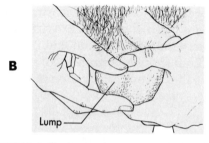

Figure 20-8

Testicular self-examination. **A,** Grasp testis with both hands; palpate gently between thumb and fingers. **B,** Abnormal lumps or irregularities are reported to physician. *(From Phipps, WJ, Long, BC, and Woods, NF: Medical-surgical nursing, concepts and clinical practice, ed 1, St Louis, 1987, The CV Mosby Co.)*

Treatment includes surgical removal of the testes and radiation. Chemotherapy is used in metastatic disease. A primary concern in caring for these patients is providing emotional support. These men may express fear and anxiety related to their sexual functioning as well as to the outcome of cancer treatment. Postoperative care includes: assessing the dressing over the scrotal wound, maintaining patency of the catheter if present, providing scrotal support, and maintaining a comfortable position. Men who have been treated for cancer in one testes have about a 1% chance of developing cancer in the other testicle. They should be checked yearly by their doctor and be encouraged to do testicular self-examination monthly.

Phimosis

Phimosis is a condition in which the orifice of the prepuce is too small to allow retraction over the glans penis. The condition is often congenital but may be acquired as a result of local inflammation or disease. The condition is rarely severe enough to obstruct the flow of urine but may contribute

---

to local infection because it does not permit adequate cleansing. A surgical procedure (circumcision) may be performed in which part of the foreskin is removed, leaving the glans penis uncovered. To prevent phimosis resulting from inflammation, circumcision is frequently performed on newborn infants before they leave the hospital. The procedure is also a rite performed in the Jewish religion.

Cryptorchidism (undescended testicle)

In embryonic life the testes are in the abdomen, and during the last 2 months before birth they descend into the scrotum. In some instances they remain in the abdomen or the inguinal canal. One or both testicles may be involved. They sometimes descend during the first few weeks of life. By 1 year of age the incidence of undescended testes in all boys is less than 25%. If the testes fail to descend, treatment with certain hormones is usually initiated. If results are not secured, surgery may be done; however, surgery is not always successful. Although the condition is fairly common in newborn infants, only a small number of adults are seen with an undescended testicle, indicating that the condition is generally self-correcting.

Ectopic testis

Ectopic testis means that undescended testes are outside the normal path for descent. Since their location may subject them more readily to injury, intervention to place them into the scrotum is done early. Hormone treatment has no effect on ectopic testis.

Torsion of the spermatic cord

A kinking and twisting of the spermatic cord and artery interrupts the blood supply to the testes. It can lead to ischemia and severe pain. The pain may be aggravated by scrotal elevation. The man will be prepared for surgery. The testes will be surgically fixed to the scrotal wall. If gangrene is present, the testes will be removed. The opposite testes is usually fixed prophylactically at the same time. Postoperative care includes application of ice to relieve swelling and discomfort. Care should be taken to place the ice cap under the scrotum, and the nurse should see that it is removed for short intervals every hour to prevent ice burn. The scrotum can also be elevated using a folded towel.[22]

Penile ulceration

Ulceration on the penis may result from many conditions, including syphilis, chancroid, and tuberculosis. Examination should be made as soon as possible so that proper diagnosis and treatment may be started immediately (see Chapter 7).

Conditions Affecting the Prostate Gland

The prostate is a firm, partially glandular, partially muscular body that surrounds the urethra at the bladder neck. It has five lobes. Conditions affecting the prostate include prostatitis, cancer, and benign prostatic hypertrophy.

Prostatitis

Prostatitis is an infection of the prostate gland by bacteria or virus. It can occur in an acute or a chronic form. Symptoms of acute prostatitis include fever, chills, lower back pain, perineal discomfort, dysuria, and urinary urgency and frequency. After confirming the diagnosis by culture of the urine and prostatic secretions, the patient is treated with antibiotics, rest, increased fluid intake, and analgesics.

Chronic prostatitis may affect as many as 80% of all men between the ages of 30 and 50. It may go undiagnosed for years until the patient seeks medical treatment at the onset of symptoms such as pain in the perineum, low back pain, or persistent urinary tract infections. Treatment includes antibiotic therapy and periodic digital massages of the prostate to increase the flow of infected prostatic secretions. The chronic inflammation may cause an increase in prostate size, resulting in obstruction of urinary flow and requiring surgical correction.

A third form of prostatitis does not involve bacterial infection. It is a chronic prostatitis also called *prostatosis*. It may be caused by excessive consumption of alcohol or caffeine and may also be a psychologic problem in a man with sexual dysfunction. There is congestion in the prostate gland, which is found on physical examination to be nontender and of normal consistency. The patient experiences mild urinary frequency and urgency, low back pain, and discomfort in the rectum, urethra, and perineal area. The patient may also experience a moderate loss of libido. The symptoms are usually self-limiting, and treatment involves removing the cause of the problem.

Cancer of the prostate gland

The prostate gland is the second most common site of cancer among men 55 to 74 years of age in the United States and is the third leading cause of death from cancer in men of that age group. Death rates from the disease have not changed significantly in the past 30 years. Early detection, radical surgery, and hormone therapeutic and chemotherapeutic drugs could improve the prognosis. Seventy percent of those with local disease and 35% of those with metastatic disease will survive 5 years or more.[20]

Early detection by routine rectal examination of nodules can lead to early treatment. For this reason, all men over age 40 should have annual routine rectal examinations done by a urologist. Detection of firm nodules on the posterior lobe indicates malignancy. The lesion may be the size of a marble before it can be palpated. Newer diagnostic techniques using ultrasound can detect lesions as small as 2 mm. Early symptoms are rarely present, but the patient may complain of dysuria and frequency of urination. Later the patient will experience a sciatic type of pain, urinary retention, and hematuria. The disease is usually far advanced by the time these symptoms appear.[8] Laboratory findings in the advanced stages include an elevated serum acid phosphatase.[20] Acid phosphatase is an enzyme that is normally present in large concentrations in the prostate gland. If metastatic carcinoma of the prostate gland ruptures the capsule surrounding the gland, the enzyme will be released into the bloodstream. An elevated alkaline phosphatase indicates bony metastases.

If the diagnosis is made while the malignancy is still a small nodule within the gland and no metastasis has occurred, a radical resection of the prostate gland is usually curative.[8] When cancer of the prostate gland is extensive, treatment may be only palliative. Treatment is designed to slow the rate of growth of malignant cells and to provide relief from pain. Several procedures may be used, including *cryosurgery* (freezing prostatic tissues) and radiation therapy. The surgical removal of the testes (*orchiectomy*) eliminates the male sex hormones that contribute to growth of cancer cells. The administration of estrogen (*stilbestrol*) in small doses also helps to slow the growth of malignant cells.[11] A combination of the hormone estradiol and the cytotoxic agent of nitrogen mustard, estramustine phosphate (Emcyt, Estracyt), has also been shown to be effective in halting the progression of the disease. It is thought that the hormone acts as a carrier of the nitrogen mustard to the hormonally receptive cancerous tissue. The drug is taken by mouth, produces few side effects, and in some patients rapidly relieves pain. It has proved effective in more than one third of patients who did not respond to hormone therapy alone.[18]

Benign prostatic hypertrophy

Simple enlargement of the prostate gland is a non-malignant disorder that affects men who are past 50 years of age. As the gland enlarges, it presses the urethra, causing urinary symptoms to develop. The urinary stream begins to slow and urination becomes frequent and painful, eventually progressing to complete urinary retention. Most men have some symptoms by age 55 years and many will eventually require surgery (prostatectomy) to prevent blockage of the urethra.

Prostatectomy

There are several methods by which the prostate gland may be removed. The method used is determined by the physician and will be the method best suited for the particular patient and his diagnosis. Nursing care will be determined by the type of surgery.

Each situation will present certain special problems of nursing care. Additional problems may occur, since most patients are men well past 50 years of age who may have other diseases from degenerative changes.

Preoperative intervention. The patient is usually admitted to the hospital before surgery. Because of the urinary frequency, the patient should be shown the location of the bathroom immediately on admission to the clinical unit. A series of laboratory tests are completed, including

---

> ### Four Methods of Prostatectomy
>
> 1. Suprapubic prostatectomy is accomplished by an incision through the abdomen; the bladder is opened, and the gland is removed with the finger from above.
> 2. Transurethral prostatectomy is done by approaching the gland through the penis and bladder using a resectoscope, a surgical instrument with an electric cutting wire for resection and cautery, to cut the lobes away from the capsule.
> 3. Perineal prostatectomy requires an incision through the perineum between the scrotum and the rectum.
> 4. Retropubic prostatectomy is the method in which an incision is made into the abdomen above the bladder, but the bladder is not opened. The gland is removed by making an incision into the capsule encasing the gland.

---

urine culture and urinalysis (one third of these patients have infected urine), BUN and serum creatinine to determine renal function, a hemoglobin and coagulation time to evaluate ability to withstand blood loss and control bleeding, and alkaline phosphatase to determine metastases if malignancy is suspected. An intravenous pyelogram is done to rule out renal mass or other abnormalities. An electrocardiogram, as well as a cystoscopic examination with biopsy, may precede a prostatectomy. Since blood loss may be extensive, blood typing and cross matching are usually ordered in case transfusion therapy is necessary. The nurse should be sure that the physician's orders for the various examinations are understood and that the request forms are properly completed and routed to the appropriate departments. Catheter drainage may or may not be ordered before surgery, but accurate records of urinary output must be maintained, including the interval and the amount of urine voided. Many patients may be instructed to help with maintaining the record. An enema will be given the night before to reduce the risk of straining during defecation, which could cause bleeding after surgery. Antiembolism stockings will be applied the morning of surgery. Nursing diagnoses and interventions commonly seen in patients after prostatectomy are identified in the boxed material on p. 577).

Postoperative intervention: transurethral prostatectomy. A transurethral prostatectomy

NURSING CARE GUIDELINES
Prostatectomy

Nursing diagnoses

- Potential sexual dysfunction: impotence related to or actual or perceived effects of prostatectomy on sexual functioning
- Sexual dysfunction: Retrograde ejaculation and altered fertility related to surgical intervention
- Anxiety related to uncertain outcome of surgery
- Alteration in comfort (bladder spasms) related to 30 ml catheter balloon or presence of clots
- Potential alteration in tissue perfusion related to hemorrhage
- High risk for injury related to straining during defecation
- Potential altered tissue perfusion in the lower extremities related to deep vein thrombosis
- High risk for infection related to indwelling urinary catheter
- Potential urinary retention related to edema in urethra after catheter removed
- Potential fluid volume excess related to excessive absorption of irrigating solution
- Potential disturbance in self-concept (body image) related to surgery involving reproductive organs
- Knowledge deficit related to activity restrictions after discharge

Nursing interventions

- Check temperature every 4 hours; blood pressure, pulse, and respiration every 2 hours
- Administer nothing by mouth until diet ordered; maintain intravenous fluids as ordered
- Measure and record intake and output
- Assess level of hydration and signs of fluid and/or electrolyte imbalance
- Maintain patency of indwelling catheter; instruct patient not to void around catheter; maintain gentle traction for 24 hours if ordered
- Administer continuous or intermittent catheter irrigation as ordered
- Observe drainage for color and consistency hourly

- If dressings are present, change frequently to keep dry
- Ambulate as ordered; avoid sitting
- Administer antispasmodics as ordered
- Instruct patient not to strain at stool for 6 weeks
- Inform patient he may resume sexual activity after 6 to 8 weeks
- Administer stool softeners and mild laxatives as ordered
- Apply antiembolism stockings while in bed
- Assess extremities for adequate tissue perfusion
- Avoid rectal temperatures and enemas
- After catheter is removed:
  Instruct patient to perform perineal exercises: press buttocks together, hold as long as possible, relax; repeat 10 to 20 times per hour
  Instruct patient to void whenever he feels urge
  Inform patient to expect dribbling of urine
  Continue to measure and record intake and output
  Observe for urinary retention or incontinence
- Maintain fluid intake of 2000 ml daily
- Administer low-residue diet after healing following perineal prostatectomy; administer regular diet 24 to 48 hours postoperatively after other procedures

Expected outcomes

- Absence of signs of infection
- Vital signs within normal limits
- Hematocrit and hemoglobin remain at preoperative levels
- Minimum urinary output of 60 ml/hr
- Urinary drainage reddish-pink to light pink 24 hours postoperatively with continuous irrigation; cherry red and clear with intermittent irrigation; urine clear in 7 to 10 days
- Patient remains free of bladder spasm
- Absence of pain and pallor in lower extremities
- Absence of symptoms of fluid and/or electrolyte imbalance

has the following advantages: the patient is ambulatory soon after the surgery, recovery is generally rapid, and a shorter period of hospitalization is required (see the boxed material). Postoperatively, the patient will have a Foley catheter connected to continuous closed bladder irrigation to reduce clot formation. Gentle traction is applied by taping the catheter against the thigh. This pulls the catheter balloon down against the bladder and

helps to control bleeding. The irrigation system should be assessed every hour to be sure patency is maintained and obstruction prevented. Closed drainage with intermittent irrigation of 20 to 30 ml normal saline is sometimes used; but clots are more likely to form and obstruct the catheter, and/or cause bladder spasms. The patient should be advised not to try to void around the catheter, since this will contribute to bladder spasm. The patient must be observed closely for hemorrhage, as it is always a possible complication. Most complications are likely to occur in the first 24 hours postoperatively. Blood pressure should be taken every 2 hours. Temperature should be taken every 4 hours; a temperature of over 101°F (38.3°C) by mouth indicates infection. A pulse rate below 60 should be reported; bradycardia can result if spinal anesthesia was used for a prolonged time. An elevation in pulse and drop in blood pressure indicates hemorrhage and shock. As a result of continuous closed bladder irrigation to cleanse the bladder, the drainage is expected to be reddish-pink to light pink within 24 hours after surgery. Without continuous irrigation the urine will be cherry red but clear. A deeper color indicates hemorrhage. Bright red drainage with numerous clots and viscous consistency, along with a falling blood pressure, indicates arterial bleeding and usually requires the patient to return to the operating room for further cautery. Venous bleeding is more common and is darker and less viscous. It can usually be controlled by applying traction to the catheter so that the ballooned end inside the bladder applies pressure to the prostatic fossa. This should be done by the physician but may be done by an experienced nurse who has been trained in the procedure. Traction is rarely maintained longer than 24 hours to avoid trauma to the external urinary sphincter.

If continuous irrigation is not ordered or maintained, a blocked catheter can result and can cause bladder distention and spasms. If drainage stops, the catheter is usually irrigated with a Toomey syringe and sterile normal saline. If gentle suction dislodges clots or tissue remnants, irrigation should be repeated after the initial saline instillation has drained. Irrigation should be repeated at least every 4 hours until the drainage is entirely free of clots. If the catheter will not clear, the urologist will have to remove it and insert another. As the urinary drainage clears, continuous irrigation is discontinued and straight drainage is maintained. The drainage may become deeper pink, since there is no irrigation solution to dilute the color. With increased fluid intake the color will lighten and eventually return to normal in 7 to 10 days. Stool softeners and mild laxatives will be ordered to prevent constipation. Straining must be avoided for 6 weeks after discharge to prevent pressure of the rectum against the prostatic fossa, which delays healing.

The patient is ambulated on the first postoperative day. He should avoid sitting, since it increases intraabdominal pressure and promotes bleeding. Ambulation should be increased to frequent short walks, and the patient should wear antiembolism stockings while in bed. He should be assisted to turn and deep breathe at frequent intervals.

When the catheter is removed, the patient will normally void small amounts, 15 to 30 ml. The amount of each voiding will remain small until the bladder is stretched to normal capacity. For 2 months the patient should void whenever he has the urge to prevent pressure of a full bladder on the surgical site before it is fully healed. The patient may experience dysuria, which may be helped by warm tub baths. Some patients have difficulty voiding, and others are incontinent after removal of the catheter. Incontinence is usually caused by bladder irritation and weakened sphincter muscles. Perineal exercises, performed by tightening and releasing the gluteal muscles, should improve control. Voiding problems usually disappear with time.

After discharge the patient is to void whenever he has the urge, avoid straining during defecation, and avoid constipation by taking prescribed stool softeners and laxatives and eating adequate fiber and fluids. Spicy foods should be avoided. Sexual activity can be resumed in 6 to 8 weeks. Erectile function should not be permanently affected but may be temporarily altered.

Suprapubic prostatetcomy

When a suprapubic prostatectomy has been done, the surgeon may place some agent such as gauze packing or a hemostatic bag into the depressed area where the gland was located to prevent hemorrhage. In addition, there will be some provision for urinary drainage through the abdominal incision. Drains or tubes such as a cystostomy tube may be used. Not all urologists use this method. If only small drains are used, a ureterostomy cup may be employed to collect urine and to keep the patient dry, whereas in other cases large abdominal dressings may be used. Abdominal dressings may have to be changed frequently to keep the patient dry, and enclosing them in some type of impervious material may help. In any procedure used, the patient must be watched closely for hemorrhage. The patient will need medication for pain, since bladder spasms may be severe and painful. The patient should be assisted and encouraged to turn frequently, and deep breathing exercises are especially important to prevent pulmonary complications. Ambulation for these patients is delayed. The catheter must be kept open and draining.

Retropubic prostatectomy

The patient having a retropubic prostatectomy has less discomfort than when other methods are employed. He will have a retention catheter and should be observed for hemorrhage. There are few or no bladder spasms, and there is no urinary drainage on the abdominal dressing. If urinary drainage is noted on the abdominal dressing, or if purulent drainage, fever, or increased pain with ambulation occurs, the physician should be notified. These symptoms may indicate deep wound infection or pelvic abscess.[22]

Perineal prostatectomy

Perineal prostatectomy may be performed because of benign prostatic hypertrophy, or a radical procedure through the perineum may be used for cancer of the prostate gland. When the surgery is for cancer, radical prostatectomy may be performed, removing the entire prostate gland, including the capsule, seminal vesicles, and the adjacent tissue. The remaining urethra is anastomosed to the bladder neck. Since the internal and external sphincters of the bladder lie close to the prostate, the patient is likely to experience some degree of urinary incontinence. He will also be impotent and sterile. Both the patient and his sexual partner must be made aware of the consequences of radical prostate surgery.[20]

A modified radical approach may also be performed for cancer of the prostate gland in which the nerves controlling erection are saved. Erectile function may be disturbed for 6 to 12 months, but most patients will eventually regain erection capabilities. This greatly improves the patient's outlook on the effects of the procedure. It is recommended only for well-localized prostatic lesions.

The preoperative preparation of the patient for perineal prostatectomy is essentially the same regardless of the purpose. The bowel is prepared by giving a laxative and enemas. Frequently, an antibiotic or sulfonamide drug may be administered preoperatively, and only clear liquids may be allowed on the day before surgery.

When the patient returns from surgery, he will have a retention catheter, which should be connected to sterile closed drainage. Extreme care should be taken to be sure that the catheter does not become obstructed or displaced. There is less possibility of hemorrhage and bladder spasms in the perineal approach to the prostate gland. Urinary drainage may occur on the perineal dressings, which will gradually decrease over a few hours. In a perineal prostatectomy temporary fecal incontinence may occur. The patient should be taught perineal exercises, and beginning them early will strengthen the rectal and urethral sphincter muscles. Patients having simple perineal prostatectomy for benign prostatic hypertrophy have no problem with urinary control.

The catheter is removed for some patients in about a week, whereas for others it may be several weeks. The patient should be instructed to perform perineal exercises and to void whenever he feels the urge. All patients should receive at least 3000 ml of fluid daily. After the first 24 to 48 hours most patients are allowed solid food, except for those having a perineal prostatectomy. During the immediate postoperative period the patient receives nothing by mouth, and liquids or a low-residue diet may be given until there has been time for healing.

Conditions Affecting Erectile Function

Any condition affecting erectile function causes the male a period of impotence. *Erectile dysfunction* is the failure to achieve penile erection in a sufficient manner for successful intercourse. This condition has many causes and the incidence tends to increase with age. *Hormonal disorders* that disturb the hypothalmic-pituitary-gonadal axis often cause erectile dysfunction.[18] *Vascular disorders* have a major effect on penile erection since it is a vascular event. Both arterial and venous disorders can be responsible for erectile dysfunction. *Neurological disorders* are caused by conditions that affect the brain, spinal cord, or peripheral nervous system.[1] Other causes include advanced syphilis, amyotrophic lateral sclerosis, and diabetes. *Surgical procedures* can compromise peripheral neural or vascular erectile tissue in the penis. Radical prostatectomy is an example of a surgical procedure that may cause impotence. *Trauma* to the lower urinary tract and pelvis can cause erectile dysfunction.

Treatment is based on the cause of the impotence and is planned after a complete history and physical are done. The nurse should remember that sexual dysfunction might be a result of physiologic, psychologic, and sociocultural factors. The female nurse must realize that the male patient may be embarassed and hesitant to speak to, or be examined by, a female nurse.

Prosthetic devices can be surgically implanted in the corporeal bodies on either side of the penis. They are easy to use but difficult to conceal in clothing.[4] The main complications with these devices are infection and erosion of the device through the skin. Postoperative care includes assessing the penile or scrotal incision for infection and noting amount and type of drainage during dressing changes.[4] Penile and scrotal swelling usually last 3 to 5 days. The patient should be instructed to avoid strenuous exercises for approximately 3 weeks. Sexual contact is also to be avoided for 3 weeks to promote healing. The male should also operate the device under direct supervision of his doctor to be sure he does it properly. The male should be instructed to promptly report any dysfunction in the device or any signs of infection.

Pelvic Exenteration

Pelvic exenteration is done for both sexes and for adults in all age ranges. Complete or total pelvic exenteration consists of the removal of the rectum, distal sigmoid colon, urinary bladder and distal ureters, interal iliac vessels and their lateral branches, all pelvic reproductive organs, and lymph nodes. In women, in addition, the entire pelvic floor and peritoneum, levator muscles, and perineum are excised. Urinary and fecal diversions are done. *Pelvic evisceration* and *pelvic sweep* are terms used interchangeably with pelvic exenteration.

The procedure is sometimes modified. An anterior pelvic exenteration removes the bladder and distal portion of the ureters, while the proximal portions are implanted in an ileal conduit. In women, the vagina, adnexa, pelvic lymph nodes, and pelvic peritoneum are removed as well. The normal bowel structure is preserved. In posterior pelvic exenteration the colon and rectum are removed and, in women, the uterus, vagina, and adnexa. Pelvic exenteration is indicated for carcinomas that are locally destructive and capable of growing to great size but that do not tend to metastasize and for tumors that are radioresistant or incurable by less radical surgery. The tumor must be confined to the pelvis without metastatic spread to distant sites and must be operable within the pelvis. The patient should be of an age and general physical and mental condition that make rehabilitation a reasonable goal. Exentera-

tion is an alternative to lethal disease, but the patient and spouse or supportive person must have a stronger than usual desire to live in order to cope with altered methods of fecal and urinary elimination and sexual intercourse. Their psychologic and sociologic status must be carefully evaluated preoperatively.

The patient will be admitted 5 or 6 days before surgery, and preoperative care must focus on the patient's psychologic needs, as well as physical preparation of the bowel with a low-residue diet, laxatives, a saline enema, and antibiotic therapy. A sulfonamide drug regimen for bowel cleansing may be used, but there is some controversy regarding the use of antibiotics for bowel cleansing. Antiembolism stockings will be applied, and a nasogastric tube may be inserted the morning of surgery. The women will douche daily with an antiseptic solution. Vitamin K therapy, to promote blood coagulability, may begin 2 to 3 days before surgery. The patient must be prepared to remain in bed for up to 1 week postoperatively as healing begins.

Postoperatively, the vital signs and blood pressure are taken hourly for approximately 48 hours. Then they are assessed every 4 hours for 7 days, or as long as necessary. Rectal temperatures are contraindicated. Intravenous therapy is maintained up to 4000 ml daily. All intake and output are measured. The operative site, the dressings, and all drainage tubes are also assessed hourly for the first 48 hours. Dressings should be reinforced and changed as ordered. Specific nursing care will be indicated by the extent of the procedure, the status of the wounds and/or ostomies that were created, and the patient's response to the surgery.

Self-worth

Exenterative surgery has a drastic effect on body image. Loss of the reproductive organs and the ability to have sexual intercourse may be a major handicap to the patient's rehabilitation. Society's emphasis on physical attractiveness will make it even more difficult for the patient to maintain a positive self-concept and strong male or female role identity after the loss of the ability to function in a reproductive capacity. Sexual readjustment may be a problem of great magnitude for the patient and his or her sexual partner. Vaginal reconstruction is possible, but it is usually done as a follow-up procedure. Segments of colon or ileum or skin grafts over a stent can be used. It is important for the nurse to facilitate the patient's expression of fears and concerns and to communicate the patient's needs to other members of the health team and community resources. Ostomy clubs can be of help to patients in their efforts to regain social mobility and maintain a realistic, yet hopeful, outlook on life.

NURSING CARE PLAN
Patient with a Repeat C-section

The patient is a 21-year-old female, Gravida 4, Para 4, who is 1 day postoperative from an elective repeat C-section. She has been receiving prenatal care at an inner-city clinic with good compliance to visits, and was estimated to be at 39 weeks gestation. Her L/S ratio was 2:1, therefore the C-section was planned. A viable male infant was delivered with Apgars of 9 at 1 minute and 9 at 5 minutes. Her previous pregnancies were all C-sections due to cephalopelvic disproportion (CPD).

Her general health is good with no known drug or food allergies. She took prenatal vitamins and iron during this pregnancy and denies the ingestion of any other meds. She does not smoke, but is subjected to "secondhand" smoke from the baby's father. She also underwent voluntary bilateral partial salpingectomy during this current surgery.

Past medical history

No major illnesses. All immunizations up to date. General health good.

Onset menses at age 12 years. Became sexually active at age 16.

First baby (boy, Alfredo Jr.) at age 17.

Second child (girl, Nina) at age 19.

Third child (girl, Carmen) at age 20. Plans to name new son Luis.

Negative history for diabetes, HTN, asthma, ETOH/ drug abuse.

Positive family history: Paternal grandmother with insulin-dependent diabetes mellitus (IDDM), Both maternal grandparents with hypertension, (HTN). All doing well under treatment.

Father of the baby (FOB), age 34. Has a positive ETOH abuse history in the past. Attended AA for 2 years, and currently not drinking. His health said to be excellent.

Psychosocial data

Unmarried. Has her own apartment where she lives with FOB and three other children. States that relationship with FOB is "good." He is also the father of the other 3 children.

Oldest of 6 children, all of whom still live at home with her parents.

Familial support is also provided by her extended family who live nearby (mother and 2 adolescent sisters), and frequently babysit and share cooking.

She left school in the ninth grade when she was pregnant with her first child. States she hopes to obtain her GED diploma after her first two children go to school.

Receives supplemental food and health care through Women, Infants, and Children, (WIC), and Title 19 (Medicaid).

Apartment has 3 bedrooms, adequate heat in the winter, but limited outdoor safe play areas for the children. She has her own laundry facilities, and they have a used car for transportation.

FOB works as a chef in a local restaurant. He is awaiting permanent status so as to receive medical insurance for himself and the children. States they will marry after that so the health insurance will benefit the entire family.

Assessment data
Known risks

Single parent, young maternal age.

Low economic status.

Many children close in age.

Lack of safe play areas for children.

Family history of diabetes, HTN.

Known strengths

Highly compliant to health care.

Positive coping strategies.

Increased trust in nursing/medical personnel.

Physical assessment WNL.

Support from FOB, and extended family.

Positive bonding with new son Luis.

Tolerating po fluids.

Immunizations up-to-date in other children.

Postpartal assessment

Breasts: Soft, no pain or edema. Nipples everted. Some colostrum expressed. No vein distention. Plans to bottlefeed.

Abdominal: Lower transverse incision following line of previous scar.
  Area clean and intact. No signs of redness or swelling.
  Dressing clean, no signs purulent material.

Continued on next page.

Abdomen soft with moderate distension. Positive passage of flatus, with bowel sounds heard in all four quadrants.

No bowel movement postop.

Fundus firm, at midline.

Lochia moderate rubra, patient changing pad every 4 hours with pad ½ full.

Respiratory: Lungs clear to percussion and ascultation.

No adventitious sounds. Chest with symmetrical movements

No dyspnea. RR 18, deep and regular.

Cardiovascular: Apical pulse strong and regular at 76. No murmurs.

S3 heard. Negative Homan's bilaterally

Vital signs stable.

Lab data

Hgb 10.3 Hct 30.0 Blood type A+. Patient and baby both rh +. All other lab values WNL.

Urinalysis WNL.

Medications

Prenatal vitamins tab 1 po daily.

Slow Fe tabs 2 po BID.

Colace 100 mg po BID

Mylicon 80 mg po TID.

Percocet tabs 1 to 2 po prn for pain.

IV fluids D5 with Lactated Ringer's 1000 ml every 12 hours. May D/C when po intake adequate.

NURSING DIAGNOSIS

Alteration in comfort (abdominal pain) related to surgical incision and gaseous distension, as evidenced by facial grimacing while turning, coughing, and deep breathing (TCDB), and by request for analgesia.

Expected patient outcomes	Nursing interventions	Evaluation for expected outcomes
Patient identifies characteristics of her pain. She articulates factors that intensify the pain, and modifies her behavior accordingly. Patient expresses a feeling of comfort and relief of pain.	Assess patient's pain symptoms. Teach her to identify the intensity on a scale of 1 to 10. As ordered, administer prescribed pain medications. (Percocet and Mylicon, the antiflatulent, as needed, and prior to ambulating or TCDB exercises). Ambulate patient for at least 10 to 15 minutes 2 times per shift. Teach patient to splint her incision with a pillow, during TCDB exercises, or when ambulating. Have her change position every 2 hours to avoid circulatory stasis. Provide back care rubs. Teach relaxation techniques. Instruct her as a nonbreast feeding mother, to wear a tight supportive bra or breast binder, and to apply ice packs as needed to reduce lactation. Assess for bladder distension. Implement measures to facilitate voiding, and provide appropriate patient teaching.	Patient states she is comfortable. She ambulates freely without excessive discomfort. Breasts are soft and nontender. Patient voids adequately without pressure or dysuria. Uterine afterbirth pains are minimal and relieved with prescribed medications.

NURSING DIAGNOSIS

Potential for infection related to interruption in integrity of skin as would be evidenced by signs of tissue inflammation, fever, increased WBC, and foul-smelling drainage.

Expected patient outcomes	Nursing interventions	Evaluation for expected outcomes
Patient regains skin integrity.	Assess for signs and symptoms of infection every shift.	Patient's oral temp remains below 100° F.

Expected patient outcomes	Nursing interventions	Evaluation for expected outcomes
Surgical wound heals without infection. Patient discusses care of the incision and need for asepsis.	Change the dressing every shift or as needed because of soiling. Teach patient the importance of good handwashing, especially as the wound heals and itchiness occurs. Monitor vital signs every 4 hours. Report any elevations. Obtain a blood culture if fever is over 102°. Monitor lab values to identify if WBC count is elevated. Teach patient the signs and symptoms of infection and instruct her to notify the clinic or her physician if any of these occur after discharge.	Postoperative vital signs and lab values are consistent with preoperative values. Patient's incision site remains free of erythema, edema, undue tenderness, warmth, induration, foul odor, purulent drainage, or other signs of infection. Wound edges are approximated and evidence of dehiscence is absent. Patient demonstrates skin inspection techniques. Patient discusses the signs and symptoms of infection and identifies when to phone in to the clinic or physician.

NURSING DIAGNOSIS

Potential for altered parenting related to economic problems and addition of new baby to family unit.

Expected patient outcomes	Nursing interventions	Evaluation for expected outcomes
Patient will exhibit positive parental attachment and behaviors of bonding (eye contact, physical touching, talking to new baby). Patient will communicate feelings and anxieties regarding the additional stresses that the new baby will bring to her household. Patient will express willingness to care for her son and demonstrate competent parenting skills. Both parents will demonstrate knowledge of neonate's developmental needs. Parents will support each other and discuss their available resources and willingness to use them. Siblings will visit and be introduced to their new brother.	Encourage patient to have the baby lie next to her in bed to faciliatate the "acqaintance process." Initiate discussion regarding the baby's looks and/or behaviors. Discuss the significance of the baby's name. Praise the baby in front of both parents. Discuss the need to be cautious about "isolation" with so many young children and the subsequent risks for dysfunctional parenting. Inquire into patient's ability to call on family members for assistance when needed. Remind both parents to take "time out" for themselves if possible. Encourage and praise patient for any baby care skills demonstrated. Include baby in all the teachings whenever possible. Encourage both parents to identify the "uniqueness" of this new son, and to discuss his developmental needs (i.e., trust). Provide parents with the telephone numbers of crisis hot lines, and/or community resources. Praise the siblings for visiting their new brother. Allow them to hear him cry and express himself.	Both parents initiate contact with their new son. Both parents voice their anxieties and fears about the potential for increased stressors within the family unit. Patient demostrates caring baby skills and gives evidence of attachment behaviors. Both parents identify the significance of their new son's name and feel prepared to relate a cultural and family connection to their choice. The parents give evidence of positive communication skills, and a supportive relationship. Siblings visit and give evidence of enjoyment of their new brother. The telephone numbers for community resources are placed in an accessible notebook by the parents.

Continued on next page.

NURSING DIAGNOSIS

Knowledge deficit related to restrictions on physical activity and
sexual relations, as evidenced by statements of inquiry.

Expected patient outcomes	Nursing interventions	Evaluation for expected outcomes
Patient will communicate a desire to learn to care for herself after a C-section. Patient will identify restrictions on her physical activity until incision heals. Patient will discuss her feelings related to changes in sexual identity since the elected tubal ligation.	Review with patient the process of involution to help her understand occurrences. Reinforce the importance of adequate nutrition and hydration to ensure proper healing and proper urinary and bowel elimination. Teach patient the importance of remaining on her prenatal vitamins. Discuss the importance of adequate rest and need to plan time for herself in the middle of the day when home. Encourage discussion of feelings related to sexuality. Provide privacy. Provide answers to specific questions. Help her to raise issues. Suggest the patient discuss her concerns with husband. Instruct patient to avoid coitus until physician permits (usually 4 to 6 weeks), but to expect same ability for sexual relations as before ligation surgery. Instruct patient to resume normal physical activity and light work, but to avoid heavy lifting for several weeks.	Patient grows in her ability to care for herself in an autonomous manner. Patient freely expresses her feelings and concerns regarding the loss of reproductive capacity and her new sexual identity. Patient outlines the plan for resuming activities of daily living upon return home. She includes plans for rest, nutrition, and hydration. Patient discusses the need to have "light" activities upon return home and to avoid heavy lifting.

REFERENCES AND ADDITIONAL READINGS

1. American Cancer Society, Inc.: Cancer facts and figures, New York, 1987, American Cancer Society, Inc.
2. Anthony CP and Thibodeau GA: Textbook of anatomy and physiology, ed 12, St Louis, 1987, The CV Mosby Co.
3. Beare P and Meyers P: Principles and practices of adult health nursing, St Louis, 1990, The CV Mosby Co.
4. Beyers M and Dudas S: The clinical practice of medical surgical nursing, ed 2, Boston, 1984, Little Brown & Co Inc.
5. Bobak IM and Jensen MD: Essentials of maternity nursing, ed 2, St Louis, 1987, The CV Mosby Co.
6. Bobak IM, Jensen MD, and Zolar MK: Maternity and gynecologic care: the nurse and the family, ed 4, St Louis, 1989, The CV Mosby CO.
7. Boston Women's Health Book Collective: The new our bodies, ourselves, New York, 1984, Simon & Schuster Inc.
8. Bouchard R and Owens NF: Nursing care of the cancer patient, ed 4, St Louis, 1981, The CV Mosby Co.
9. Brown MA and Woods NF: Correlates of dysmenorrhea: a challenge to past stereotypes, J Obstet Gynecol Neonatal Nurs 13(4):256-265, 1984.
10. Brunner LS and Suddarth DS: The Lippincott manual of nursing practice, ed 3, Philadelphia, 1982, JB Lippincott Co.
11. Brunner LS and Suddarth DS: Textbook of medical-surgical nursing, ed 5, Philadelphia, 1984, JB Lippincott Co.
12. Coyne CM, Woods NF, and Mitchell ES: Premenstrual tension syndrome, J Obstet Gynecol Neonatal Nurs 14(6):446-454, 1985.
13. Crooks C and Jones S: Educating women about the importance of breast screenings: the nurse's role, Cancer Nurs 12(3):161-164, 1989.
14. Dickason EJ, Schult MO, and Silverman BL: Maternal infant nursing care, St Louis, 1990, The CV Mosby Co.
15. Doyle J and Reilly N: Genitourinary problems. In RN nursing assesment, series 6, Oradell, NJ, 1985, Medical Economics Books.

16. Feather BL and others: Looking good after your mastectomy, Am J Nurs 87(8):1048-1049, 1987.
17. Frank EP: What are nurses doing to help PMS patients? Am J Nurs 86(2):136-140, 1986.
18. Gray ML and Broadwell DC: Genitourinary system. In Thompson JM and others: Mosby's manual of clinical nursing, ed 2, St Louis, 1989, The CV Mosby Co.
19. Griffith-Kenney J: Contemporary women's health: a nursing advocacy approach, Menlo Park, Calif, 1986, Addison-Wesley Publishing Co Inc.
20. Jones AG and Hoeft RT: Cancer of the prostate, Am J Nurs 82:826-828, 1982.
21. Lobo PA and Kahn FR: Conservative management of breast cancer by lumpectomy and radiation, Compr Ther 11(9):16-25, 1985.
22. Long B and Phipps WJ: Medical surgical nursing, ed 2, St Louis, 1989, The CV Mosby Co.
23. MacElveen- Hoehn P: Sexuality and cancer. In McCorkle R and Hongladarom G: Issues and topics in cancer nursing, Norwalk, Conn, 1986, Appleton-Century-Crofts.
24. Martin JP and others: Testicular cancer: from a medical model to a nursing model, Dimen Onc Nurs 2(2):5-11, 1988.
25. McConnell EA: Discovering a post T.U.R.P. complication, Nurs 89 19(9):96-98, 1989.
26. McKeon VA: Cruel myths and clinical facts about menopause, RN 52(6):52-59, 1989.
27. Patrick M and others: Medical-surgical nursing: pathophysiologic concepts, Philadelphia, 1986, JB Lippincott Co.
28. Reeder SR and others: Maternity nursing, ed 16, Philadelphia, 1987, JB Lippincott Co.
29. Richmond JB: Advisory on toxic shock syndrome, FDA Drug Bulletin, July 1980.
30. Scherer JC: Introductory medical-surgical nursing, ed 4, Philadelphia, 1986, JB Lippincott Co.
31. Thompson JJ and others: Clinical nursing, St Louis, 1986, The CV Mosby Co.
32. US Department of Health and Human Services: Breast cancer: understanding treatment options, Public Health Service Bethesda, Md, 1987, National Institutes of Health.
33. US Department of Health and Human Services: Mastectomy: a treatment for breast cancer, Public Health Service, Bethesda, Md, 1987, National Institutes of Health.
34. VanTyle JH and others: Premenstrual syndrome: diagnosis, etiologies, therapy, J Pract Nurs 38(4):19-27, 1988.

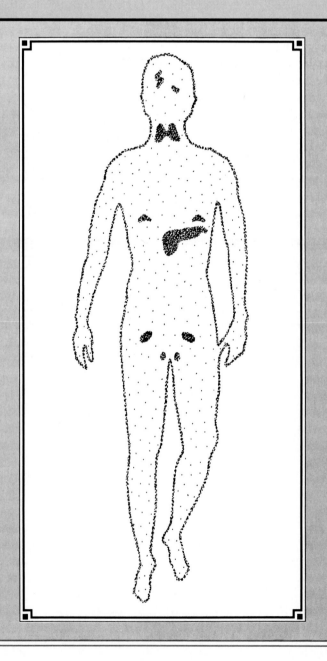

KEY WORDS

acetone
aldosterone
atrophy
calibrated
catecholamines
cretinism
diabetic
endogenous
exogenous
glucagon
glycohemoglobin
goiter
homeostasis
hormone
hyperglycemia
hyperglycemic hyperosmolar nonketotic
  coma
insulin reaction
ketoacidosis
ketonuria
ketosis
metabolism
renal threshold
tetany
type I diabetes
type II diabetes
ultrasonogram

OBJECTIVES

1. Discuss the nursing responsibilities to identify potential problems of the endocrine system.

2. Describe nursing interventions to manage patient responses to hypersecretion or hyposecretion of specific endocrine glands.

3. Describe the pathophysiology, course, prognosis, and treatment of diabetes mellitus.

4. Compare and contrast the risk factors, onset, and course of the acute complications of diabetes mellitus.

5. Outline the actions that patients and providers take to prevent, detect, and treat diabetic complications.

6. Discuss the palliative treatment goal of diabetes to reduce symptoms, control hyperglycemia, and prevent complications.

7. Describe some examples of patients' responses to diabetes mellitus that indicate the uniqueness of this disease.

8. Describe nursing interventions that foster self-care of diabetes activities of daily living.

ENDOCRINE GLANDS AND THEIR FUNCTION

The endocrine glands, or ductless glands, are sometimes called glands of internal secretion because they do not have ducts to carry their secretions to the outside, as do the exocrine glands. Instead, the secretions pass directly into the tissue fluid, from which they are picked up by the blood. The secretions of the endocrine glands are chemical substances called **hormones,** and they act as chemical messengers ultimately altering the activity of various body organs. Some of these hormones have been reproduced synthetically in the laboratory, whereas others are natural and are extracted from the glands of animals. The nurse who administers medications will be giving many of these commercially prepared hormone products, which are marketed under various trade names. Both the overproduction or under production of certain hormones may result in serious disease. In some cases, the very life of the individual may depend on an adequate supply of a particular hormone. When for some reason the gland fails to supply the normal requirement, a commercial preparation must be given to compensate for the deficiency. The most significant example of this situation is provided by diabetes mellitus.

The endocrine system is complete. Endocrine glands have many functions, and they are so interrelated and interdependent that to separate their activities and their importance would be extremely difficult. They regulate the metabolic processes that control energy production, fluid and electrolyte balance, growth, development, reproduction, and lactation. Hormones from endocrine glands help to maintain **homeostasis** and regulate blood pressure and neuromuscular contraction. They assist in maintaining fluid and electrolyte and acid-base balance. Secretions from some glands stimulate other glands to activity. A description of the endocrine glands (Figure 21-1) and their chief hormones follows.

The thyroid gland is the largest of the endocrine glands. It consists of two lobes and is located in the neck anterior to the trachea; one lobe is on each side of the trachea. The two lobes are connected with a strip of thyroid tissue called the *isthmus.* The thyroid gland stores iodine and secretes three hormones: thyroxine (T_4), triiodothyronine (T_3), and thyrocalcitonin (calcitonin). The primary function of the thyroid gland is regulation of metabolism, the rate at which nutrients are ox-

idized to provide energy for the body. Both T_4 and T_3 produce similar effects; T_4 however, acts more slowly and is longer lasting than T_3. Any disturbance in the secretion of T_4 may result in hyperthyroidism or hypothyroidism. A congenital absence of the thyroid gland causes **cretinism** in the infant, a deficiency of secretion may result in myxedema in the adult, and increased secretion may result in Graves' disease. Calcitonin is a hormone secreted by the thyroid gland that acts to decrease the level of calcium in the blood by increasing the movement of calcium from the blood into the bones.[42]

The parathyroids are usually four small glands, but there may be more or fewer. They are arranged in pairs and embedded in the posterior lateral lobe of the thyroid gland. The parathyroids secrete parathormone, which helps to maintain the homeostasis or relative consistency of the calcium levels in the blood and body fluids. The presence of this hormone tends to increase calcium in the blood and to increase the excretion of phosphates.[43]

The adrenal (suprarenal) glands are small bodies located above each kidney. Each gland is divided into two parts, the medulla and the cortex, and each part secretes different hormones. One hormone secreted by the medulla is epinephrine, prepared commercially as Adrenalin. Epinephrine has many uses, such as elevating the blood pressure, acting as a vasoconstrictor, and relaxing the bronchioles as in asthma. Since epinephrine is naturally released in stress situations and in anger, it is sometimes called the fight hormone. The other hormone secreted by the medulla is norepinephrine. The adrenal cortex secretes hydrocortisone (cortisol), corticosterone, aldosterone, and small amounts of sex hormones. Hydrocortisone and corticosterone have many functions in the body, but they primarily promote normal metabolism and resist stressful situations. **Aldosterone** regulates the level of sodium in the blood and body fluids. When a deficiency of these hormones occurs, Addison's disease results. Hypersecretion of aldosterone causes Cushing's syndrome.

The pituitary body (hypophysis) is often referred to as the master gland, since it is important in regulating many of the functions of the other glands. The pituitary gland is located in the sphenoid bone in the skull and secretes several hormones. It consists of two lobes, the anterior lobe and the posterior lobe.

The Anterior Lobe Secretes Seven Different Hormones:

growth hormone (somatotropin) Stimulates growth of bone and soft tissues

prolactin (lactogenic hormone) Initiates milk secretion.

thyrotropin Promotes and maintains the development of the thyroid gland.

adrenocorticotropic hormone (ACTH) Promotes and maintains the development of the adrenal cortex.

follicle-stimulating hormone (FSH) Stimulates the development of reproductive organs.

luteinizing hormone (LH) Stimulates the development of reproductive organs and secretion of progesterone and estrogens in the female and testosterone in the male.

melanocyte-stimulating hormone (MSH) Stimulates pigmentation of the skin.

The release of these seven hormones is controlled by the hypothalamus. The hypothalamus releases hormones that either stimulate or inhibit the release of hormones by the anterior lobe of the pituitary gland.

The posterior lobe of the pituitary gland secretes two hormones, vasopressin (antidiuretic hormone, or ADH) and oxytocin. ADH affects the amount of urine excreted because it causes a faster reabsorption of water from the kidney into the blood. When extremely large amounts of urine are excreted, this indicates an inadequate amount of ADH, a disorder known as diabetes insipidus. Oxytocin affects uterine contractions and lactation and is used in obstetrics to promote uterine contraction after delivery, thus preventing excessive bleeding.

In the female the gonads, or sex glands, include the ovaries which secrete estrogen, progesterone, and small amounts of androgens. Male sex glands are the testes, which secrete testosterone and androsterone. These hormones are important in the development of sex characteristics and in the reproductive process.

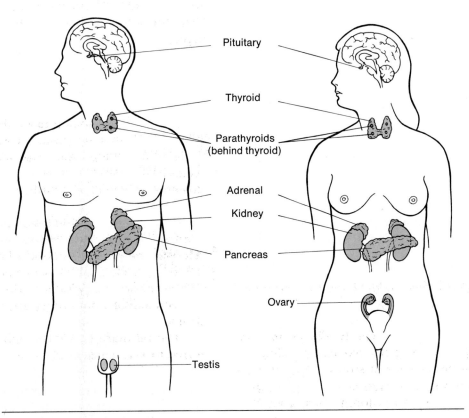

Figure 21-1
Location of endocrine glands.

The pancreas has both exocrine and endocrine functions. Pancreatic acinar cells have an exocrine function, whereas cells known as the islands of Langerhans have an endocrine function. There are two types of islet cells: *alpha cells*, which secrete **glucagon,** a hormone that elevates the blood sugar; and *beta cells*, which secrete insulin. Insulin is necessary for utilization of sugar by the body.

NURSING ASSESSMENT OF THE PATIENT WITH ENDOCRINE PROBLEMS

Endocrine problems are often difficult to assess because each of the hormones secreted by endocrine glands has different effects. Therefore the approach to assessment of the patient with an endocrine problem is to start with the medical history. It should be determined if the patient has any cardiovascular, pulmonary, renal, or neurologic problems. Hypertension should be noted, along with any previous endocrine disorders.

Signs and symptoms of endocrine disorders are varied as a result of the multiple systems that may be affected. Symptoms that should be assessed include changes in smell, taste, speech, skin, personality, and energy level. Potential problems such as visual disturbances, headaches, muscle weakness, excessive hunger, thirst, and urinary frequency should be assessed.

A history of medications taken by the patient is also important. Many medications have effects on the endocrine glands and could possibly contribute to the symptoms displayed by the patient.

Physical assessment of the endocrine system is difficult, since the thyroid gland is the only endocrine gland that is palpable. The primary assessment tool used for the endocrine system is inspection. Data should be collected on the individual's general appearance, apparent age, facial expression, and stature. Facial features and hair distribution should be assessed. The thyroid gland should be palpated to determine if it is enlarged or if any nodules are present.[8]

NURSING RESPONSIBILITIES FOR DIAGNOSTIC TESTS AND PROCEDURES

Many of the tests used to initially diagnose a possible endocrine disorder, to follow its course, and to evaluate the results of therapy are performed on blood and urine. The amount and kind of specific hormones can be estimated through chemical analysis of the blood and urine. When an excess or deficiency is suggested, further tests and procedures may be done to determine the effect on the body as a whole. Many of these tests require nursing interventions to ensure that specimens are collected properly. Some procedures require withholding food and fluids and collecting urine specimens. To ensure that the test results provide reliable information about endocrine status, procedures must be followed accurately.

Blood Chemistry

Analysis of endocrine gland functions is often done by hormone assay. Serum levels of hormones such as T_3 or T_4 will indicate if appropriate amounts of hormones are being secreted. However, not all hormone levels can be easily determined by blood level. Insulin secretion can best be estimated by measurement of blood glucose levels. High blood glucose levels indicate that insulin secretion is insufficient for the body's metabolic needs.[8]

Urinalysis

A 24-hour urine collection is necessary for hormone analysis. The collection may start at any hour. The nurse should secure a clean container sufficient to hold all urine voided for the 24-hour period. The procedure should be explained to the patient to avoid error, and the hour at which the collection was started should be carefully noted. Since the test measures substances *produced* within a 24-hour time frame, the bladder must be empty at the start of the test. The patient is asked to void, and the specimen is discarded, but all other urine voided from that hour is saved. The collection is completed at exactly the same hour the next day, at which time the patient voids and that urine becomes the last part of the specimen. It is the responsibility of the nurse to see that the patient voids the last specimen exactly 24-hours from the time the collection started.

Several precautions need to be taken in conducting urinalysis. First, the bottle should be clearly labeled with the patient's name, room number, and the date and time the collection began. Second, all urine must be collected and saved. Last, the container holding the urine must be maintained as specified for the diagnostic test. A preservative or refrigeration may be required. Patients should be taught to collect their urine and pour it into bottles containing preservatives and never to void directly into a bottle containing a chemical. If the preservative used is an acid, the patient should be instructed to notify the nurse when he or she voids and the nurse should pour the urine into the bottle to avoid burns.

Basal Metabolic Rate

The test for basal metabolic rate (BMR) measures the amount of oxygen consumed by an individual at rest who is in a fasting condition. A level considered normal for the individual is determined; a significant elevation above that rate usually indicates hyperthyroidism, and a rate significantly below normal indicates hypothyroidism. It is usually considered that plus or minus 15% is the average normal range of value for basal metabolism. However, many factors enter into the reliability of the test, and since there are more accurate measurements of thyroid activity, the BMR is used rarely. When it is used, it serves as a screening procedure and is followed with other tests.

Protein-Bound Iodine Test

The test for protein-bound iodine (PBI) is another indicator of thyroid function and is done on the serum from venous blood. It is not necessary to restrict food or fluids before the test; the blood specimen may be taken at any time. Before the test, however, iodine in any form must be restricted. This includes food (iodized salt), any of a large number of drugs that contain iodine, and all radiologic procedures that use a contrast medium. Because of the increased presence of iodine in the environment today, this test has become less reliable.

Radioactive Iodine Uptake

The test for radioactive iodine uptake measures the ability of the thyroid gland to concentrate ingested iodine. A small amount of radioactive iodine is administered orally to the patient, either in capsule form or in a colorless, odorless drink. The amount is called a *tracer dose*. After 24 hours the amount of radioactive iodine stored in the thyroid gland is measured by a Geiger counter—a type instrument called a *scintillator*, which is held near the thyroid gland. Persons with overactive glands will be found to store a high percentage of the iodine, whereas those with underactive glands will take up a small amount of the iodine. The normal thyroid gland will accumulate from 5% to 35% of the radioactive iodine within 24 hours.[28]

Another method of determining the radioactive iodine uptake is by measuring the amount of radioactive iodine excreted in the urine. All urine voided for 24 to 48 hours is saved and sent to the laboratory. The amount of iodine excreted is subtracted from the amount administered; the difference is the amount taken up by the gland. The same care should be exercised in collecting the urine as previously outlined.

Thyroid Ultrasonogram

The patient is brought to the x-ray area and a radiologic technique visualizes the tissue structure. Ultrasonic waves reflect the organ and a picture of the findings appears on an oscilloscope and paper printout.

Thyroid Scan

The patient is given radioactive iodine 131 (^{131}I) and the uptake is quantitatively measured by the external passing of the scintillator over the throat. The scintillator is connected to a recording device that provides a record of the activity. The scan is used in connection with other tests and is used to differentiate between a nonmalignant condition and a possible malignancy of the thyroid gland.

Triiodothyronine (T_3) Resin Uptake Test

In the T_3 resin uptake test a blood specimen is secured from the patient and ^{131}I is added to the blood in the laboratory. Normally, the red blood cells will take up 11% to 19% of the iodine. In hypofunction of the gland less will be taken up, whereas in hyperfunction more will be taken up by the red blood cells. The advantage of the test is that the patient does not have to be given the ^{131}I.

Nursing responsibilities

Several other thyroid function tests use ^{131}I. The nurse may not be directly concerned with the test but may have important functions related to the various tests. These responsibilities include reassuring the patient and encouraging him to cooperate. Patients should realize that they will not become radioactive as a result of the test. The collection of urine specimens must be absolutely correct, or the test results will not be valid. Care must be taken to be sure that the patient does not receive iodine before the test. Drugs that contain various iodine preparations, contrast mediums used in x-ray examinations, iodine used as a skin antiseptic, and iodized salt are all forms of iodine that should be avoided. The nurse should question the patient about any hypersensitivity to iodine before any testing using this drug is done.

Other diagnostic tests to detect or monitor the course of endocrine disturbances require some patient education. For the noninvasive test, computed tomography (CT scan), patients should be told that a picture of their gland will be taken by a machine that moves around them. *Magnetic resonance imaging* (MRI) is a new noninvasive test that uses a magnet, radiowaves, and computers to take an image of the entire body. It is a painless scanning and requires no special preparation. The presence of any metal within the patient's body such as pacemakers, heart valves, or clips, must be known before the test.

For invasive tests, such as arteriography, a contrast medium is injected into a vein and will go to the organ to be examined. X-ray pictures of the gland will be taken once it is visualized on the screen. Some people may feel a warm sensation, which is normal, when the medium is injected.

NURSING RESPONSIBILITIES FOR THERAPEUTIC PROCEDURES

The treatment for endocrine disorders varies greatly, depending on the type of disorder. There are, however, some nursing responsibilities that are the same regardless of the problem. First, and foremost is maintenance of the patient's airway. The airway should be patent, and the patient should be ventilating. Fluid and electrolyte balance should be monitored as necessary by recording fluid intake and urinary output and daily weights. Vital signs should be assessed, and neurologic status of the patient should be monitored when indicated.

Endocrine disorders are often traumatic, both physically and emotionally, and support should be given to the patient and his family. Many endocrine disorders, such as diabetes, require lifelong treatment that may be costly and inconvenient to the patient. Feelings of frustration are frequently experienced, and the nurse should help the patient and his family deal with these feelings by encouraging them to talk openly about the disorder and about the changes that will need to occur in their lifestyles.

Patient education is an essential component of the treatment of endocrine disorders and is the responsibility of both the nurse and the physician. Both patient and family must understand the dis-

order and be prepared to deal with the changes it may necessitate. Patients who understand the need for the diabetic diet will be more likely to comply with the diet than those who do not understand it. Medications to be taken by the patient should be explained. Patients and significant others should know the expected results, possible side effects, and methods to minimize side effects when possible. The nurse should also educate the patient regarding possible complications of the disorder. For example, patients with diabetes should know the difference between **ketoacidosis** and **insulin reaction** and the emergency treatment for both. Patient education is often the difference between compliance and noncompliance, and compliance is necessary for successful treatment of a disorder.[8]

THE PATIENT WITH DISEASES AND DISORDERS OF THE ENDOCRINE SYSTEM

Disorders of the Thyroid Gland
Simple (endemic) goiter

Any enlargement of the thyroid gland is called a **goiter.** *Endemic,* or *simple,* goiter results when dietary iodine is insufficient for synthesis of thyroxine. To compensate for the insufficiency, the pituitary secretes excessive amounts of thyroid-stimulating hormone (TSH), causing the gland to hypertrophy. Iodine deficiencies in food and water exist in certain areas of the United States, and it is in those areas that the occurrence of endemic goiter has been greatest. The marketing and use of iodized salt has reduced the incidence of this type of goiter.

Increased physiologic demands such as pregnancy, lactation, puberty, infections, and other body changes can also result in an inadequate iodine supply to meet the demands. For instance, endemic goiter is more common in girls and usually occurs just before puberty, after which it may completely disappear. Usually, these types of goiter produce no symptoms unless they grow large and exert pressure on adjacent structures such as the trachea. When this occurs, patients may experience mild neck discomfort, a chronic cough, difficulty in swallowing, and respiratory difficulty.[44]

The best treatment for goiters is prevention with adequate amounts of dietary iodine. However, once goiters have developed, treatment is aimed at decreasing the size of the gland with iodine and thyroid preparations. Large goiters may be surgically removed to relieve pressure or to improve appearance. Usually, a subtotal thyroidectomy is performed. Persons living in areas where there is a known deficiency of iodine in the water and soil should be encouraged to use iodized salt and eat foods rich in natural iodine, such as leafy vegetables and seafood.

Hyperthyroidism

Hyperthyroidism is caused by an overactive thyroid gland that produces an excess of thyroxine. The condition may be idiopathic, or it may result from hypertrophy, neoplasms, inflammatory processes, or autoimmune disorders. Often the condition follows infections or emotional stress. The disease is known by several names, including toxic goiter, thyrotoxicosis, exophthalmic goiter, and Graves' disease. The increase in hormone production increases all metabolic processes of the body and gives rise to a characteristic set of symptoms.

Assessment. The appetite is increased, but there is weight loss and the individual is thin. There is an increase in the systolic blood pressure, and the pulse rate is greatly increased, even while the individual is at rest. There may be enlargement of the thyroid gland. The skin is warm, and the patient perspires freely and is sensitive to heat. Palpitation, tachycardia, and atrial fibrillation may occur. When the fingers are extended, a fine tremor may be observed. Fatigue, weakness, a disturbance in menstruation, a disturbance in sleep, and constipation or diarrhea may exist. Profound personality changes may be present, with irritability, excitability, and crying episodes, which may occur spontaneously. Such personality changes are often difficult for friends and family members to understand. It is therefore important that nurses provide emotional support for the family, as well as for the patient, and to help them understand that a person's emotional state is related to hormonal changes and should subside as the hormone levels decrease.[37] There may be a bulging of the eyeballs, known as *exophthalmos*, which gives the patient a startled expression and may not be relieved even after treatment.

The diagnostic tests will show an increase above normal in the metabolic rate. A rapid and increased iodine uptake will be indicated in the radioactive iodine uptake test.

Intervention. The treatment of patients with hyperthyroidism is directed toward reducing the activity of the thyroid gland and the excessive production of thyroxine. The disease may be treated with antithyroid drugs, the surgical removal of the gland, or therapeutic doses of radioactive iodine.

Iodine preparations, Lugol's solution, and saturated solutions of potassium iodide (SSKI) may be given to reduce the symptoms of hyperthyroidism. They prevent the release of thyroxine but are effective only for temporary periods. Liquids are usually diluted with fruit juice, water, or milk and are administered through a straw to prevent staining of the teeth. Side effects include a metallic taste, epigastric discomfort, nausea, and vomiting. Iodine preparations are most useful before thyroid surgery or in emergency situations but are rarely used for long-term therapy.

Propranolol (Inderal) relieves many of the symptoms of hyperthyroidism, tachycardia, and hypertension. Because of its effectiveness, it is frequently used in conjunction with antithyroid drugs.

Radioactive iodine may also be given for hyperthyroidism. The drug acts the same as nonradioactive iodine, and after an oral dose it enters the bloodstream and becomes concentrated in the thyroid gland, where it destroys the cells. This treatment is inexpensive and is easily administered. Persons involved with patient care should wear gloves when giving radioactive iodine and when disposing of the patient's excreta. The major side effect is hypothyroidism.[26]

Each patient must be considered as an individual, and patience and tact may be required in meeting nursing needs. If exophthalmos is present, the eyes will need to be protected from irritation. The environment should provide rest and quiet and be free from annoying distractions. Since the patient is sensitive to warmth, the room should be private, well ventilated, and cool. Visitors should be limited to members of the family, and efforts should be made to interpret the patient's erratic behavior as a part of his disease. The patient needs emotional as well as physical quiet and should be protected from situations that increase emotional tension and anxiety. Psychotherapy is occasionally beneficial.

The diet should be high in calories and vitamins, with carbohydrate supplements. Extra servings should be available, and between-meal feedings may be given if sufficient calories are not taken with the regular meals. Patients should be permitted to choose food, especially if the appetite is poor, and a visit from the dietitian may be helpful in ascertaining the patient's likes and dislikes. If the patient is to be cared for at home, the public health nurse may visit the home and help the family plan the patient's care.

Thyroidectomy

The surgical removal of part or all of the thyroid gland may be done because of malignancy, exophthalmic goiter, or any other severe condition affecting the gland and adjacent structures. A thyroidectomy is not an emergency procedure, and the patient must have a normal thyroid functioning before surgery is done. This may require 2 to 3 months of drug therapy. Surgery is usually done only in cases of a carcinoma or large goiter. Nursing care after thyroid surgery requires more than routine postoperative care because of the location of the incision. Swelling around the incision can cause airway obstruction and a tracheotomy tray should be available for emergency intervention. The patient should be observed for **tetany** because of problems with calcium metabolism and also for voice changes due to injury of the vocal cords.

Thyroid crisis (storm) is a rare complication that can occur before surgery or during the initial postoperative period. It may also occur following severe physical or emotional stress. Increased amounts of thyroid hormones are released into the bloodstream, resulting in a sudden increase of metabolism. The heart rate, pulse rate, and temperature are elevated, and the patient is apprehensive, restless, and may finally become comatose and die. The patient is given oxygen, intravenous fluids, and sedatives and is placed on a hypothermia blanket to control temperature. The administration of cardiac drugs may be indicated if heart failure is imminent. This serious complication is the reason why the patient must be stabilized with antithyroid drugs preoperatively.

The boxed material summarizes nursing intervention for the patient with hyperthyroidism.

Hypothyroidism

Hypothyroidism is the result of an undersecretion of thyroxine by the thyroid gland or in some cases a complete lack of secretion. It may occur after surgical removal of the gland if too much thyroid tissue is removed. When the production of thyroid hormones is decreased, the symptoms are almost the reverse of those characterizing hyper-

---

NURSING CARE GUIDELINES
Hyperthyroidism

Nursing diagnoses
- Alterations in nutrition, less than body requirements related to increased metabolism
- Alteration in thought processes related to personality changes
- Sleep pattern disturbance related to increased metabolism
- Ineffective thermoregulation associated with increased metabolism
- Possible knowledge deficit
- Possible anxiety related to inability to control illness
- Possible ineffective individual and family coping related to personality changes

Nursing interventions
- Keep environment quiet and calm
- Limit visitors
- Monitor vital signs and temperature
- Promote diet high in protein, vitamins, calories, and fluids
- Discourage intake of caffeinated foods (coffee, cocoa, chocolate, cola, tea)
- Monitor for potential adverse effects of medications (rash, fever, conjunctivitis, generalized discomfort)
- Protect eyes from trauma, especially if exophthalmos (protrusion of eyes) exists
- Weigh patient daily
- Observe for respiratory problems, tetany or voice changes post-thyroidectomy
- Observe for signs of complications of hyperthyroidism (thyrotoxicosis, thyroid crisis or thyroid storm), including elevated temperature, rapid pulse and respirations, pain, dyspnea, confusion, restlessness, and alteration in level of consciousness
- Provide emotional support for patient and family
- Educate patient and family to watch for adverse effects of medications and for signs of thyroid crisis

Expected outcomes
- Verbalize the rationale for reducing environmental stimuli
- Follow a diet high in protein, vitamins, calories, and fluids
- Avoid intake of caffeine
- Describe the medication regimen and potential side effects of medications
- Discuss the need for protection of eyes from trauma
- Weigh self daily
- Recognize signs of complications of hyperthyroidism

thyroidism. Three conditions are recognized as resulting from hypothyroidism: myxedema, juvenile myxedema, and cretinism, all of which are actually forms of the same deficiency occurring at different ages.

Myxedema is the term applied to hypothyroidism in adults. The symptoms usually occur gradually and include sensitivity to cold, dryness of the skin and hair, weight gain despite a loss of appetite, and a gradually appearing dull facial expression, with thickening of the lips and puffiness about the lips and eyes. The individual becomes lethargic and may fall asleep at intervals; the speech is slurred, and the individual responds slowly. Impaired memory, personality changes, and depression may also occur. The pulse is slow, the basal metabolic rate is well below normal, and the PBI level is decreased.

The treatment is to replace the deficient hormone by administering synthetic triiodothyronine (T$_3$), levothyroxine, or desiccated thyroid. Replacement therapy is done gradually, and it may require 2 weeks or more for effects to be noticeable. A complete subsiding of symptoms may require up to 2 months or more of therapy, and once therapy is begun, it must be continued for life. Because thyroid hormone increases the metabolism, the patient's cardiovascular status must be monitored, especially during the initial weeks of therapy.[50]

Juvenile myxedema is similar to adult myxedema and varies in degree of severity. When the disease is moderately severe, both physical and mental growth is delayed. Puberty is also delayed, and the child tends to be lethargic. The treatment is administration of levothyroxine or desiccated thyroid, which is well tolerated by the child. The dose administered is sufficient to relieve the symptoms but not large enough to result in hyperthyroidism. The dosage will need to be readjusted periodically with increasing metabolic needs. Children are usually treated in an outpatient clinic or in a physician's office.

Emotional support is particularly important for these children; in addition to the normal changes of adolescence, they must also deal with the changes caused by hypothyroidism and its treatment. Adolescence is often associated with feelings of rebellion; therefore teaching the importance of management of hypothyroidism and compliance with therapy is essential.[50]

Cretinism is the result of a complete absence of thyroid secretion from birth, which may be caused by absence of the gland or its failure to secrete thyroxin. Intrauterine development is usually normal, but the characteristics of the condition may begin in the first few weeks after birth. The first symptoms are difficulty in nursing, failure to thrive, protrusion of the tongue, dry skin, constipation, and a hoarse cry. If the condition is not recognized early, irreversible damage may occur in physical and mental development. Because the effects of cretinism are easily prevented with an early diagnosis, many states have mandated testing of thyroxine (T$_4$) levels after birth.[38] The boxed material summarizes intervention for the patient with hypothyroidism (see p. 596).

Tumors of the thyroid gland

Tumors occurring in the thyroid gland may be benign or malignant and may be associated with hyperthyroidism. Enlargement of the thyroid from benign tumors is referred to as *nodular goiter*, and the tumors may be single or multiple. Some of the tumors secrete thyroxine, since they consist of the same kind of cells as those found in normal thyroid tissue. If they secrete appreciable amounts of the hormone, hyperthyroidism will develop, and the symptoms will be the same as those generally associated with hyperthyroidism. Surgical removal is generally indicated for the nodular type of tumors.

Carcinoma of the thyroid may be any of several types. Some types grow slowly and metastasize first to the lymph nodes, then to the lungs and bones. Other types progress rapidly, and some may be fatal within a few weeks. Surgery has proved to be the most satisfactory method of treatment, although radioactive iodine and x-ray therapy may be used in conjunction with surgery for some types. The nurse may care for patients for whom treatment is only palliative. The same physical care and emotional support are necessary as for all patients with terminal cancer.

Disorders of the Pancreas
Diabetes mellitus

Diabetes mellitus is the most common endocrine disorder in the United States. Approximately one in every twenty Americans is or will be affected by this metabolic problem. Diabetes mellitus is a chronic, currently incurable, health problem that results from defects in insulin action or secretion. It is a heterogeneous group of anatomic and chemical problems characterized by high blood glucose levels. In addition to the initially observed prob-

---

NURSING CARE GUIDELINES
Hypothyroidism

Nursing diagnoses

- Alteration in nutrition, more than body requirements related to decreased metabolism
- Alteration in thought processes related to personality changes
- Ineffective thermoregulation related to decreased metabolism
- Alteration in self-concept related to depression
- Possible knowledge deficit
- Possible ineffective individual and family coping related to personality changes

Nursing interventions

- Keep environment warm
- Promote care of skin with lotions
- Monitor effects of medications, especially those depressing central nervous system; drugs may be potentiated because of decreased metabolism
- Assess for signs of infection carefully, since resistance to infection may be decreased
- Prevent constipation by encouraging good bowel habits: exercise and eat diet high in fiber, fruits, and fluids
- Prevent hypoxia by encouraging deep breathing and moving
- Promote good nutritional status by decreasing caloric intake if necessary to promote weight loss
- Support patient and family emotionally during treatment, which usually leads to dramatic reversal of symptoms
- Educate patient and family to watch for side effects of therapy, such as tachycardia, sleeplessness, palpitations, and anxiety

Expected outcomes

- Verbalize principles of good skin care and demonstrate an ability to perform this care
- Describe the medication regimen and potential side effects of medications, (tachycardia, sleeplessness, palpitations, anxiety)
- Discuss signs of infection (redness, warmth, fever)
- Practice good bowel habits by exercising and eating a diet high in fruits, fiber, and fluids
- Follow a well-balanced diet and monitor weight
- Perform deep breathing and moving exercises every 1 to 2 hours

---

lem with carbohydrate metabolism, individuals who have diabetes mellitus also have a deficit in their conversion of proteins and fats.

Although the etiology of diabetes mellitus is currently unknown, there are probably diverse causes. Known risk factors for developing diabetes mellitus are heredity, environment, and lifestyle. Blood relatives of people who have diabetes, especially type II, are more likely to develop diabetes than are individuals not related to anyone with the disease. Overweight individuals and those who lead a sedentary lifestyle are more prone to develop type I diabetes mellitus. Certain viruses and autoimmune factors have been associated with the development of the disease and are thought to play a role in its etiology. Chickenpox-type viruses have been associated with the development of type I diabetes mellitus. The present thinking is that diabetes develops as a result of a combination of risk factors.

Diabetes is the leading cause of blindness, heart attack, stroke, and gangrene. Improvements in therapeutic techniques have increased the average life span of the individual who has diabetes, but more needs to be achieved in the prevention of complications of the disease.

Pathophysiology. The symptoms of diabetes mellitus result from insulin deficiency. Insulin is secreted by the beta cells in the islets of Langerhans in the pancreas. The deficiency may result because of diminished or absolute lack of insulin or as a result of resistance to insulin action at the cell level. Lack of enough usable insulin causes **hyperglycemia,** a high blood glucose level.

An adequate supply of insulin in the body is necessary for the body cells to combine oxygen and glucose to produce energy necessary for body functions. In the absence of insulin several metabolic changes occur. Glucose accumulates in the blood and is excreted in the urine. The body then is required to use proteins and fat for energy, which under certain conditions will lead to acidosis.

Diabetes mellitus is classified as either insulin dependent (IDDM), **type I;** or as noninsulin dependent (NIDDM), **type II.** Formerly IDDM individuals were classified as having juvenile-onset, or brittle, diabetes. NIDDM individuals previously were described as having stable, or adult-onset, diabetes. Clinically, many patients lie between the two extremes, and nursing interventions are directed toward individual responses to diabetes and its treatment, regardless of classification. But, because the pathogenesis, treatment, and possible complications of the types differ, the two classes will be discussed separately.

Assessment. The two classifications differ in respect to insulin dependency, onset and symptoms, and intensity of treatment. Type I diabetes frequently has a sudden onset marked by an excessive concentration of glucose in the blood and the presence of the three polys associated with diabetes: polyuria, polydipsia, and polyphagia accompanied by weight loss. Type II diabetes is characterized by a slow insidious onset and may go undetected for years.

Lack of insulin or a problem with its use at the cell level initiates a chain of events that accounts for the initial symptoms of type I diabetes. With an insulin deficiency, glucose cannot enter the cell and accumulates in the bloodstream. This is evidenced by a high blood sugar level, hyperglycemia. Because the body cannot use this glucose for food or energy, it keeps piling up until the kidneys excrete it. Glucose is dissolved in fluid in the bloodstream so when it is excreted by the kidneys (glycosuria), not only is it wasted, but so is the water in which it is dissolved. This accounts for the polyuria, or excessive urination. The increase in the amount of fluid lost makes the individual very thirsty (polydipsia) so he drinks extra liquids to maintain fluid balance. Instead of being absorbed into the cell, glucose is lost in urine. Since those calories were not used, the appetite mechanism is stimulated, the individual becomes very hungry, and eats an excessive amount of food, which is known as polyphagia. However, there is no weight gain because calories are wasted when the glucose is excreted into the urine.

Although diabetes is a complex phenomenon, the analogy of insulin helping to unlock the cell wall so that circulating glucose can enter into the cell has been used as a learning device for patients. The absorption of glucose into the cell, the resultant circulating glucose level, and its potential spill into urine are different, depending on the presence or absence of available insulin.

Individuals who develop type I diabetes are usually young, of normal weight or have recently experienced weight loss, and often present with polyuria, polydipsia, polyphagia, and **ketosis,** an accumulation of ketone bodies in the blood and tissues. When untreated, other symptoms that result include dry skin and mucous membranes, constipation, and signs of fluid and electrolyte losses. These undiagnosed individuals may develop **diabetic ketoacidosis** and die unless this process is stopped by **exogenous insulin,** insulin that is produced outside the body. People who have type I diabetes eventually require insulin to manage their diabetes.

Type II diabetes symptoms are usually so mild that the condition may exist undetected and untreated for a considerable period of time. Often individuals are middle-aged and overweight. They have some **endogenous** (produced within the body) insulin, but its secretion may be slow or subnormal. When this diabetes exists for a long time and is untreated, symptoms of varied severity may occur. These include skin infections such as boils and carbuncles and arteriosclerotic conditions, particularly of the eyes, kidneys, lower extremities, and coronary and cerebral blood vessels. Some people who have type II diabetes are able to keep the disease in check with diet alone, others require the addition of an oral hypoglycemic agent, and a third group require insulin.

Treatment goal. The therapeutic goal of diabetes management is to maintain as close to normal a blood glucose level as possible while allowing the patient to maintain a normal lifestyle. Diabetes cannot be cured but its symptoms can be controlled and its pathologic course may be kept in check. The therapeutic management of diabetes mellitus is palliative. The goals of symptom and hyperglycemia reduction, prevention of acute complications (insulin reaction, diabetic ketoacidosis, and **hyperglycemic hyperosmolar nonketotic coma**), and forestalling chronic complications (microvascular and macrovascular angiopathies) guide clinicians as they plan the diabetic regimen with and for the individual.

Priorities of nursing care are first concerned with immediate patient needs and then with long-range needs, since diabetes is a lifetime disease. Patients must assume a great deal of responsibility for their self-care management and become partners with the diabetes clinicians who provide the nursing, dietary, and medical supervision. Since individuals who have diabetes become managers of their chronic illness on a day-to-day basis, they are not always in a patient role. Therefore, instead of always labeling people who have diabetes as patients, consider referring to them as persons or individuals. The word **diabetic** should only be used as an adjective to describe a component of the regimen, such as diabetic diet. The label, diabetic, should never be used to refer to a person.

Diagnostic tests. The range of clinical symptoms of new-onset diabetes mellitus is from nothing to coma, depending on the type of diabetes and how long it had gone undetected. The sooner individuals who have diabetes mellitus are diagnosed and begin to control their disease, the more the anatomic problems associated with the disorder can be prevented. Since type II diabetes first appears with such mild symptoms, it may go undetected for years. Screening programs have been developed to increase the number of individuals with the disorder who are diagnosed. In contrast, individuals who have type I diabetes mellitus often have the recognizable classic symptoms of diabetes or progress to a state of acidosis that prompts medical attention. The initial diagnosis of diabetes mellitus is accomplished by analyzing the patient's blood or urine for the presence and amount of glucose or acetone.

Neither glucose nor acetone are normally present in urine. Their presence indicates the possibility of diabetes mellitus and the need for additional diagnostic tests. Glucose in urine means that the blood glucose level exceeded the **renal threshold,** that is, the blood glucose level for an individual that must be reached before circulating glucose is removed from the blood by the kidneys. **Acetone,** one of the ketone bodies produced in abnormally large amounts in uncontrolled diabetes mellitus, in the urine, means the body has rapidly broken down fats to use as energy and some of the breakdown product has been removed from the bloodstream and is present in urine. Dieting or ingestion of a highfat diet can also cause **ketonuria,** an excess of ketone bodies in the urine.

Glucose is always present in the blood. The amount varies according to a number of factors. Whether the blood sample is venous, capillary, or arterial and the type of blood specimen, such as whole, plasma, or serum, influence the value of the glucose detected. Fluctuations in amount of glucose occur secondarily to how recently and how much of what type foods the individual has eaten. Laboratory analyses can differ so that the upper and lower range of normal for a specific setting must be determined. All these factors have to be known before a decision can be made on the basis of blood glucose level as to the presence or absence of diabetes. The amount of glucose is reported in the number of milligrams (mg) present in 100 mililiters (100 ml) of fluid. One deciliter (1 dl) equals 100 ml and is the standard way the value

is reported. A value of 100 mg/dl means that 100 mg of glucose are present in 100 ml of plasma.

Consistency in the diagnosis of diabetes is being achieved by the use of criteria recommended by the National Diabetes Data Group of the National Institutes of Health.[31] The diagnosis of diabetes can be made for nonpregnant adults when one of the following signs is present: (1) classic symptoms of diabetes and hyperglycemia with a random plasma glucose level of over 200 mg/dl or greater, (2) a fasting venous plasma glucose level at least equal to 140 mg/dl on two occasions, or (3) an elevated venous plasma glucose level once after drinking glucose and before the 2-hour point *and* at the 2-hour point in an oral glucose tolerance test. A fasting plasma glucose level over 130 mg/dl should be an indication for further testing in children. Diabetic ketoacidosis can occur rapidly in young children, so early diagnosis and treatment is especially important.

An oral glucose tolerance test is done after an individual has eaten a well-balanced diet for 3 previous days. The person fasts from the evening before the test until the last specimen has been obtained. The day of the test an initial fasting blood sample is taken and sometimes a urine specimen is also obtained and sent to the laboratory. The patient is given a pure glucose drink. The very sweet tasting drink on an empty stomach may make the person feel a little nauseous. Since the test will be terminated if vomiting occurs, instruct the patient to assume a resting comfortable position during the test. Blood and urine samples are collected at various specified intervals until the test is complete. An elevated glucose level at the 2-hour point usually indicates some disorder of carbohydrate metabolism.

Another common test is a 2-hour postprandial blood sugar test that is drawn exactly 2 hours after the patient finishes the specified meal. Individuals who do not have diabetes mellitus would have a 2-hour postprandial blood glucose level that had returned to the normal fasting range.

Immediately after the diagnosis is made, healthcare providers monitor the status of the individual's diabetes and responses to treatment. Patients are taught to self-monitor their own condition as soon as possible. Patients learn the rationale for and techniques to correctly obtain the desired specimen and test it for the presence and amount of glucose or acetone.

Urine testing provides an approximation of the individual's blood glucose level. An individual's renal threshold determines when blood glucose spills over into urine. For adults with no renal problems this threshold is about 170 to 200 mg, which means the blood glucose level has to be minimally at the lower level of the range before any glucose could be wasted into the urine. Individuals determine their own renal threshold by recording their blood glucose values and comparing them with their urine glucose values. The lowest blood glucose value at which glucose spills into the urine is an estimate of the renal threshold.

When used, the timing of specimen collection is determined by whether or not the individual uses insulin. Urine specimens are collected approximately 30 minutes before mealtime and at bedtime for people who use insulin. Patients should be instructed to test a second voided specimen to avoid testing urine that has been allowed to pool in the bladder since a previous meal. Individuals who control their disease by only diet or with an oral hypoglycemic agent may test their urine after meals. Clinitest, Tes-Tape, or strips, may be used to test urine.

Some individuals prefer urine testing for monitoring diabetes. When their disease is stable enough to rely on urinary values to assess metabolic control, urine testing is an option. Although urine testing is becoming less frequently used, when done and interpreted accurately, it is an easy and inexpensive diagnostic test. Urine testing illustrates the wasting nature of diabetes mellitus. Each gram of glucose that is wasted in the urine means that 4 calories of energy or food are lost. If a patient with severely uncontrolled diabetes consistently spills 2% glucose (4 calories/ g × 0.02 = 0.08 calories/ml) and excretes 4 L (4000 ml) of urine in 24 hours, then 320 calories a day (0.08 × 4000 = 320) are lost.

The patient should be instructed to test urine for ketones if there is a large amount of glycosuria, the blood glucose level is over 240 mg/dl or there are symptoms of illness. When acetone is present in urine the body has metabolized fatty acids. This can occur during a usual overnight fast and a trace amount may be expected every morning. Conversely, larger amounts of ketone bodies can be a sign that the person requires more insulin.

Since it is desirable to keep the blood glucose in a range close to normal, a more accurate appraisal of blood glucose than can be achieved by urine testing may be necessary. Blood glucose determinations are often made on specimens collected in a fasting state. Insulin or oral agents should be withheld until after the specimen has been obtained. The patient should be told that breakfast will not be served until after the blood specimen has been taken.

Self-monitoring of blood glucose levels may be done with the use of commercial products such as visual strips and a meter. A finger stick is done and capillary blood is placed on the test strip. After waiting the correct amount of time, the reagent strip will turn a color depending on the amount of glucose in the blood. A color comparison of the strip to the chart indicates the amount of glucose present. Meters can automate the calculation and give a readout of the glucose level. Home measurement of blood glucose is recommended for individuals with type I diabetes and for those who require a strict control of their blood glucose levels.

The American Diabetes Association issued a policy statement strongly recommending that the following classes of patients self-monitor their blood glucose level.[2] Patients whose insulin doses require frequent adjustment on the basis of blood glucose levels are those who are (1) receiving intensive insulin therapy by insulin pump or multiple daily injections, (2) pregnant or plan to be, or (3) prone to hypoglycemia or may not experience warning signs of hypoglycemia.

Glycohemoglobin levels are another diagnostic test used in diabetes. Urine and blood glucose levels reflect the present, are easily influenced by recent events, and thus are used to determine insulin or dietary requirements. Glucose levels are not the equivalent of metabolic state. The glycohemoglobin level represents the degree of glucose control achieved during the previous several weeks and is a general indicator of long-term metabolic control. Glycohemoglobin production increases in the presence of hyperglycemia. An elevated glycohemoglobin level means that the patient's blood glucose levels were consistently high for 6 to 8 weeks previously. Since the palliative goal of diabetes therapy is to achieve good metabolic control without complications, glycohemoglobin levels are assessed periodically.

Providers and patients have to exercise some general cautions regarding the use and interpretations of diabetic diagnostic tests. The specific test and range of normal may differ from setting to setting. The important consideration is not to memorize lists of laboratory values, but to know what the normal ranges of values are in the setting where the specimen was analyzed.

Individuals who are taught to monitor their diabetes at home need to follow the same precautions that nurses in health care facilities take with similar diagnostic products. The most important caution is the most basic: read and carefully follow the manufacturer's directions! Wait the exact number of seconds required before examining the strip or solution for color change. Be sure to use the specific color chart or automatic device designed for the test. Observe the reagents and color strips to be sure they have not discolored or gone bad and would therefore be inaccurate. Test the calibration of instruments used to assure their accuracy and clean them regularly according to package directions. Store all testing materials in a place safe for both the product and the people who live in the same environment. There are many glucose meters on the market today. The patient should be instructed to investigate several before selecting one that meets their personal needs. Pharmacies that sell meters should be able to demonstrate the advantages and disadvantages of each meter.

Diet. Diet is the cornerstone of diabetes therapy. Several types of diabetic diets are calculated for the individual patient on the basis of caloric needs and nutritional requirements. Many patients with type II, mild diabetes are maintained on diet alone. One type controls calories only and is frequently prescribed for older obese patients who do not require insulin therapy. The metabolic picture of obese patients with type II diabetes will often improve after they reduce their weight.

For patients who have unstable type I diabetes, the diet is first calculated and then the amount of insulin necessary to metabolize it is established. A strict diet controls the amount of protein, fat, cholesterol, carbohydrate, fiber, and calories. Concentrated carbohydrate would be limited and the amount of food would be divided into specific amounts to be eaten at meals and for snacks at predetermined times.

Usually the food exchange lists prepared jointly by the American Diabetes Association, the American Dietetic Association, and the United States Public Health Service are used in planning the patient's therapeutic diet. Seven lists of exchangeable foods have been defined: (1) foods with a minimum caloric content that are allowed as desired, (2) vegetables, (3) fruits, (4) bread, (5) meat, (6) fats, and (7) milk. Each item on a specific list is equal in nutritional value and similar amounts are interchangeable with one another. A specified number of exchanges is allowed for each meal and snack, according to the caloric needs of the patient and the prescribed diet (Table 21-1).

The individual's usual lifestyle, preferences, and cultural differences are considered when the diet is planned. Since the discipline of dietary restrictions and the need to eat at prescribed time intervals are so demanding, it is critical that the diabetic diet be accommodated into the patient's routine as much as possible. Creativity of health care providers exercised within therapeutic guidelines can help minimize the tedium of following the same diet day after day. Individuals can be taught how to eat at fast food chains and to correctly "augment" their diet. For instance, a person who craves a large glass of orange juice in the morning but is allowed only 4 ounces can be taught to add 4 ounces of sugar-free orange tonic to their juice. Eight ounces of frosty, cold, orange juice—tasting liquid can be had for just one fruit exchange.

Diet therapy for people who have type I diabetes follows a strict time frame. When the action of insulin is at its peak, patients must have enough circulating glucose in their bloodstream to move into the cells. A specific amount of carbohydrate, protein, and fat in the form of food exchanges is calculated. The time frame for eating the exchanges is specified. Thus a package of peanut butter crackers eaten 3 hours after lunch, instead of being a casual snack, is an important component of an individual's diabetes therapy. A bedtime snack also prevents reactions during the night. Patients can be taught to exchange meals and snacks to accommodate special events in their life.

Insulin. Many individuals who have diabetes require insulin. In the United States, insulin is commercially derived from the pancreas of a pig or cow, or synthesized in the laboratory. The new synthetic human insulins (Humulin, Novolin) are the purest forms of insulin. Therefore, patients should not switch to synthetic insulin without close monitoring of dosage by the physician. The amount of insulin needed depends on the individual and will vary at different times for the same person. The type of insulin needed will also vary. The purpose of administering insulin is to replace the deficiency. Its action is to enable the body to metabolize food, absorb glucose into the cell, and thus to lower the blood glucose level. Many kinds of insulin are in current use. Each insulin has three expected time frames (1) *onset* is the time between

Table 21-1

1200 Calorie Diet Diabetic Patient Meal Plan					
Meal	Breakfast	Lunch	Afternoon snack	Dinner	Evening snack
Time	7 AM	12 PM		6 PM	
No. of choices					
Lowfat milk	½ cup	½ cup			½ cup
Vegetable		1		2	
Fruit	1	1		1	
Bread	1	1	1	1	1
Meat		1	1	2	
Fat	1	1		1	

Cholesterol 153g, Protein 61g, Fat 41g.

Table 21-2

Types of Insulin Available in the United States			
Type	**Action**	**Duration (hours)**	**Peak of action (hours)**
Regular (beef/pork or pure pork)	Fast acting	5-6	2-4
Novolin regular	Fast acting	5-8	2-5
Humulin regular	Fast acting	6-8	2-4
Velosulin	Fast acting	5-8	2-5
Lente (beef/pork or pure pork)	Intermediate acting	18-24	6-16
NPH (beef/pork or pure pork)	Intermediate acting	18-24	6-12
Novolin lente	Intermediate acting	18-24	7-15
Humulin NPH	Intermediate acting	14-24	6-12
Ultralente (beef/pork)	Long lasting	28-36	14-24
Humulin ultralente	Long lasting	24-28	8-20

Adapted from Sperling, M.A., Physicians' guide to insulin dependent (type I) diabetes. Alexandria: 1988, American Diabetes Association, Inc.

the injection of insulin and when it starts to be effective in the body, (2) *peak* is the time when the insulin action is at its highest, and (3) *duration* is the length of time the insulin effect is expected to last in the body. Insulins are classified according to their time frame of action and duration of effect as one of three types: (1) fast acting or short duration, (2) intermediate acting or medium duration, and (3) slow acting or long lasting (Table 21-2).

Product information circulars or current drug books provide precise data about the composition of specific insulins and their action. For patients, however, a range of possible times is not as helpful as learning when *their* insulin starts to work, peaks, and disappears. Diabetes clinicians examine patient records of blood and urine glucose and acetone levels and relate those values to food eaten, exercise, and symptoms of possible insulin reactions. They learn the approximate time after injection that insulin doses have their onset, peak,

and duration for that individual. Adjustments in dose are made until the best dose and type insulin is found to achieve the goal of as close to normal blood glucose levels as possible.

Since insulin is often stored in the refrigerator, it should stand at room temperature for several minutes before administration. Insulin used on a daily basis may be stored at room temperature for 1 month, as long as it is not exposed to direct sunlight or kept near a heat source. Once insulin bottles are opened they should be discarded after 3 months. Unopened insulin can be stored safely in the refrigerator until the expiration date on the bottle.

Insulin is administered in units that have been standardized so that no matter where it is purchased or from which pharmaceutical manufacturer it comes, it will be the same. Insulin is usually available in a concentration of 100 units/ml centimeter (U 100) and in a 10-ml vial in the United States. Insulin syringes are **calibrated** in

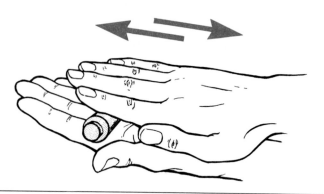

Figure 21-2

Method of mixing insulin. Vial is rolled between the palms.

units of 100 to correspond to that concentration of insulin (100 units/ml). Small (28 to 29) short (⅜- to ½-inch) needles are used. One-ml (100 unit) syringes are suitable for most patients. Low-dose syringes (that hold 50 units of U 100 concentrated insulin) are available for those who require minimum amounts of insulin. U-30 and U-25 insulin syringes are available now especially for use with pediatric patients. The most important consideration is that patients understand that each line on the U-100 syringe is two units while on all other syringes each line is one unit.

The skills required to inject insulin are less complex than the skills of drawing up insulin, and the patient may be fearful of the first self-injection. Therefore, if the patient is in a hospital setting and will be there for several days, the injection component of insulin administration can be learned as soon as patient condition allows.

Before teaching the mechanical skills for drawing up insulin, the patient should be assessed for ability to see the syringe markings and manual dexterity to handle the equipment. To draw up a single dose of insulin, the patient should be taught to check the label on the bottle to be sure it is the correct type. The insulin bottle should be gently rolled to ensure that all the sediment is mixed into the liquid (Figure 21-2). The insulin vial should be placed on a firm surface and its top cleaned with alcohol. The syringe should be handled carefully so as not to stress the small needle and sterile technique should be used. The patient should then remove the needle cover and draw in the amount of air equal to the amount of insulin to be removed from the vial. The air is injected into the vial and the vial is inverted in the patient's

hand so that the tip of the needle is covered by insulin and the bottle is not resting on the needle. The plunger is pulled halfway down the syringe and air bubbles are eliminated. Then the correct amount of insulin is withdrawn from the vial.

If the patient is receiving two insulins that can be mixed in the same syringe, some modifications are made in the previous procedure. To ensure patient consistency and avoid contamination the routine of drawing the shorter acting insulin first has been established at most diabetes centers. Both insulin vials are cleansed and placed on a firm surface. The amount of air to be injected into the longer acting insulin is drawn up and injected into the vial, and the needle is removed. Then the correct amount of air for the shorter acting insulin is injected into that bottle, the vial is inverted, the bubbles are removed, and the insulin is removed. Without letting any of the shorter acting insulin leave the syringe, the longer acting bottle is entered, the needle tip is covered, and the correct amount of insulin is withdrawn.

Patients are given precise instructions so that dose errors are avoided. If the patient's dose is 6 units of Regular insulin and 20 units of NPH insulin, the following instructions would be given so the patient would correctly draw up a total dose of 26 units. Draw up 20 units of air, inject it into the NPH vial, and remove the syringe. Draw up 6 units of air, inject it into the Regular vial, invert the bottle, cover the needle with insulin, fill the syringe halfway, remove the air bubbles, push-pull the plunger until there are exactly 6 units of insulin and no air in the syringe, and remove the syringe from the vial. Then, without losing any of the Regular insulin in the syringe, inject the

DOSE *10 Reg.*
      20 NPH

INSTRUCTIONS FOR MEASURING INSULIN

Mixed Dose

1. Turn cloudy bottle upside down and roll between hands.

2. Wipe off tops of bottles with cotton and alcohol.

3. Pull plunger to ..*20*. Put needle through top of cloudy bottle and push plunger down putting air into bottle. Take needle out empty.

4. Pull plunger to ..*10*... . Put needle through top of clear bottle and push plunger down. Leave needle in bottle.

5. Turn bottle upside down and pull plunger halfway down syringe. Push all insulin back in bottle;

6. Pull plunger halfway down syringe and check for bubbles.* If no bubbles present, push plunger to .*10*. units of regular insulin and take out needle.

    *If bubbles present, repeat step 5 before completing step 6.

7. Turn cloudy bottle upside down and stick needle through rubber top.

8. Pull plunger slowly to .*30*... units.
    (.*10*.. + *20*.). Take out needle.

9. Wipe skin with alcohol and cotton and pinch.

10. Pick up syringe like a pencil and push needle straight into skin. Push plunger down.

11. Release pinch, press alcohol next to needle and pull out.

Figure 21-3
Instructions for measuring insulin: mixed dose.

needle into the NPH vial, cover the tip of the needle with NPH insulin, and slowly pull the plunger back until it reaches 26 on the syringe. Then remove the needle from the NPH bottle and proceed with the injection. A total dose of 26 units (6 Regular and 20 NPH) were drawn into the same syringe. If too much insulin is pulled from the NPH bottle, it may not be pushed back into either bottle. The syringe is discarded and the patient must complete the process from step one. If mixing insulin is a problem for some patients, taking two separate injections may be a solution. Also, there are some premixed insulins on the market,

Mixtard 70/30 (pure pork) and Novolin 70/30 (human), that can meet the needs of certain patients whose dose is 30% Regular insulin and 70% NPH insulin (Table 21-2). Sample instructions for measuring insulin are found in Figure 21-3.

The method currently used for injecting insulin is to place the insulin in the space between the subcutaneous tissue and the muscle. Once the correct dose is prepared, the patient is taught to clean the skin and to pinch up a large fold of skin and fat. Holding the syringe like a pencil, the needle is injected into the skin at a 90-degree angle all the way to the hub. The insulin should be

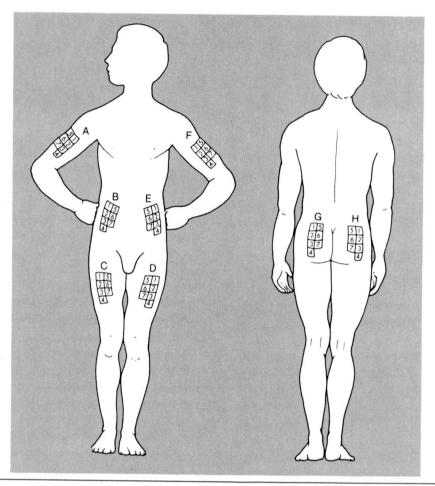

Figure 21-4

Injection sites for insulin. *(From Billings DM and Stokes LG: Medical-surgical nursing: common health problems of adults and children across the life span, ed 2, St Louis, 1986, The CV Mosby Co.)*

injected through the subcutaneous tissue into the loose space made by the pinch. Once all the insulin has been injected, the pinch of skin is released before the needle is withdrawn to avoid loss of insulin. The first time the patient self-injects insulin, the nurse should select a site that is easily reached from a comfortable position, such as the thigh when in a sitting position. The patient should be guided through the procedure and assisted as needed.

The sites for injection should be rotated with each injection to prevent lipodystrophy, which may interfere with absorption and may predispose to abscess formation. Possible injection sites should be chosen based on the condition of the skin, patient preferences, manual dexterity, and sensitivity of the individual to site changes. Pre-

ferred sites are the lateral surface of the upper arms, the abdominal tissue just below the rib cage, the anterolateral surfaces of the thigh, and the back (Figure 21-4). Any atrophied or hypertrophied area should be avoided, as should scar tissue, nevi, or moles. If insulin is given in the same site for a time, scar tissue forms, which leads to erratic absorption of the insulin. Exercising the arm or leg after injection may speed up insulin action and cause a reaction so injection sites need to be chosen carefully.

Once the prescribed dose of insulin has been injected, the patient should record the amount and site if a diabetes record is being kept. The used syringe and needle should be placed in a covered container (coffee can) before disposal. If the patient has been taught to reuse insulin equipment, the syringe should be stored for future use.

Another family member or available significant other should be taught the insulin administration technique in case the patient is ever in a situation where help is needed. For patients who have problems meeting acceptable skill levels in any components of the insulin administration process, problem solving should be done so that individuals are as independent as possible. For instance, if a patient cannot see well enough in the morning to accurately draw up insulin, but can manipulate injecting insulin, there are several alternatives. A visiting nurse can draw up a weeks' supply and leave them, a neighbor could be asked for daily assistance, or a magnifier or stop device could be used on the syringe. If the person can see better at the end of the day, which is not uncommon, then insulin for the next day can be drawn up the night before.

There are also several devices on the market to aid patients with injections. Some patients with unstable diabetes, after years of conventional therapy, may be candidates for intensive insulin therapy. There are two methods of intensive treatment. The first is with multiple injections of insulin and the second is the use of the insulin pump. Both of these treatments require motivation and special education, but do allow for greater flexibility in life style.

Oral agents. Several oral hypoglycemic drugs stimulate the islet cells of the pancreas to secrete more insulin. For these agents to be effective, the individual must have some endogenous insulin but requires additional insulin to maintain metabolic control. Therefore these oral hypoglycemic agents (OHAs) are suited for people who have type II diabetes, who cannot achieve control with diet therapy alone, and who do not require exogenous insulin to provide acceptable metabolic control. There are some possible complications from each of the drugs, the most common being hypoglycemia. Because sulfonylureas are detoxified in the liver, individuals who have liver problems must be monitored closely. The action of the drugs may be more intense in this group because the potential delay in their breakdown may cause an accumulation of the drug and increase the risk of hypoglycemia.

OHAs are not oral insulin. That is an important concept for the patient and family to understand. Currently, OHAs are sulfonylurea drugs. They are taken once or several times daily, depending on their duration of action. Like insulin,

OHAs are classified on the basis of how long they act. Tolbutamide (Orinase) is a short-acting (6 to 12 hours) OHA and is taken several times daily. Acetohexamide (Dymelor) and tolazamide (Tolinase) are intermediate acting (12 to 24 hours), so they are taken once or twice daily, depending on their duration of effect for specific individuals. Chlorpropamide (Diabinese) has a long duration (up to 60 hours), so it is taken daily. There are new oral agents on the market, glipizide (glucatrol) and glyburide (diabeta or micronase), that are known as second generation sulfonylurea drugs. These require much lower dosage to be effective so have lower incidence of side effects.

There has been some controversy regarding the use of OHAs. Since insulin therapy imposes such discipline on individuals' daily activities, OHAs are suited for certain people. If a patient has the type of diabetes that is uncontrolled by diet and more endogenous insulin stimulated by OHAs maintains their metabolic control, then one of those drugs is indicated.

Hygiene. People who have diabetes are believed to have a lowered resistance to infection, and abrasions or wounds heal more slowly than individuals who do not have diabetes. These observed phenomena may be secondary to an etiologic factor of immunologic suppression or may exist because of the effect of high blood glucose levels when diabetes is uncontrolled. The nursing implication from these observations is that hygiene for people who have diabetes must be a component of their therapeutic regimen. General skin care to prevent the accumulation of pathogenic organisms and prevent drying should be carried out daily.

Since many patients are at risk for foot problems because of potential complications from their diabetes, the most important aspects of hygiene is proper care of the feet. They should be washed daily with warm water (avoid hot water) and mild soap, and dried well. The area between the toes should be especially dry and no lotion or lanolin should be applied there. Nails should be filed slightly longer than the shape of the toe. Corns and calluses should be smoothed with a pumice stone or emery board. Patients should be told to avoid bathroom surgery and to consult a podiatrist for very tough toenails or corns that require cutting.

It is important that patients whose feet are "at risk" or their significant other examine the feet daily and report any problem to their physician.

Even a trivial injury should be reported early, since care for a minor problem can prevent its escalation into a major one. Other aspects of foot care include wearing properly fitting shoes, not going barefoot, and avoiding anything constricting (such as round garters or tightly fitting knee-high hose) that could decrease circulation to the feet. Shoes should be broken in gradually. Heating devices for the feet (e.g., hot water bottles) should never be used, and feet should never be soaked.

Exercise. One of the American pioneers in diabetes treatment, Dr. Elliot Joslin, viewed diet, exercise, and insulin as three frisky ponies that together control diabetes. After insulin became readily available as a therapy, the Joslin Clinic noted that patients who returned to farm work or other active jobs were in better metabolic control than their patients who had a more sedentary lifestyle. Exercise is believed to exert its physiologic benefit by changing the cell wall permeability so that movement of glucose into the cell is increased by directly lowering blood glucose levels, since glucose is used for energy, and by increasing the uptake of free fatty acids. Exercise also increases the level of high-density lipoproteins and lowers cholesterol and triglyceride levels. Individuals who have diabetes are at risk for cardiovascular diseases.

Just as diet and insulin therapies are individualized, so are exercise regimens. Diabetes clinicians are aware of potential complications from exercise and characteristics of those individuals for whom exercise would be considered dangerous. Therefore the specific exercise plan should be mutually decided by the patient (to fit into daily activities) and provider (to prescribe the proper amount and adjust the diet and insulin as necessary). Exercise may be contraindicated for some individuals. Others may need cardiovascular screening before an exercise prescription is given.

Weight control, lower insulin requirements, and a sense of well being are positive outcomes from an ongoing exercise program. Diabetes clinicians have to recognize that many individuals who do not have diabetes have a difficult time integrating regular exercise into their daily routine. For people who already integrate the activities required of diabetes management into their routine, the addition of exercise may be a difficult therapy to consistently achieve. This underscores the importance of patient and provider collaboration in developing diabetes activities of daily living that are acceptable to the individual who has the diabetes. An ideal plan that is too rigorous for the patient will not be followed. Realistic expectations that are easily assimilated into existing lifestyle patterns have a higher probability of being carried out by the patient.

Insulin reaction. The goal of diabetes therapy is to prevent or delay the onset of chronic complications without precipitating acute complications. Achieving a near-normal blood glucose level all the time is the ideal, but very hard to achieve in actuality. Shifts in blood glucose levels are inevitable, and these may result in one of the acute complications of diabetes. An insulin reaction, or hypoglycemic (low blood glucose) reaction, is the most common acute complication of diabetes, especially in patients who use insulin. Individuals who use insulin should be taught to expect to have insulin reactions, to learn when they are most likely to have a hypoglycemic event, and to recognize their own early warning signs. Patients and providers have to learn how to prevent, detect, and treat mild and severe reactions.

An insulin reaction results from either a drop in blood glucose level to a low amount not tolerated by the individual (usually under 60 ml/dl of blood) or a very rapid drop in blood glucose level. In the second case, a blood test would reveal a "normal" blood glucose level, but the individual would still experience and exhibit the symptoms of reaction. Once individuals recognize their reaction patterns, their opinion of whether or not they are in reaction is what determines if treatment is required. When in doubt, treat!

Hypoglycemic reactions are caused by too little circulating glucose, which is usually secondary to too much insulin or exercise and not enough food. An increased amount of insulin, not enough food at the time insulin is peaking, alcohol, or strenuous exercise without an insulin decrease or food increase may precipitate a reaction. Reactions come on very rapidly. They can be very mild or extremely severe. The most common symptoms are a trembling sensation, profuse perspiration, irritability, and dizziness. Additional signs may be generalized muscle weakness, headache, tingling sensations of the lips or tongue, blurred or double vision, an unsteady gait, palpitations, pallor, and hunger (Table 21-3). Without immediate treatment, the patient may become confused and comatose and have convulsions.

The immediate treatment is to raise the blood glucose level. Unless a patient is hospitalized and

Table 21-3

Characteristics of Diabetic Ketoacidosis and Insulin Reaction (Hypoglycemia)

	Diabetic acidosis	Insulin reaction
Cause	Dietary excesses Too little insulin Infection Decreased exercise with same dietary intake Another disease or condition that taxes available insulin Emotional stress	Dietary deficit Too much insulin Increased exercise without dietary supplement or insulin reduction
Symptoms	Early 　Gradual loss of appetite 　Increased thirst 　Nausea and vomiting 　Dry skin, flushed face 　Headache 　Weakness Later 　Kussmaul's respirations 　Sweet, fruity odor to breath 　Decreased blood pressure 　Increased pulse	Early 　Lassitude 　Lethargy 　Inability to concentrate 　Hunger Later 　Trembling sensation 　Profuse perspiration 　Irritability 　Generalized muscle weakness 　Blurred or double vision 　Headache 　Tingling sensation of lips or tongue
Blood glucose	Greater than 300 mg/dl	Less than 60 mg/dl
Urinary glucose	Positive	Negative
Progression	Gradual	Rapid
Intervention	Regular insulin Fluid and electrolyte replacement	Simple carbohydrate by mouth (orange juice, sugar) 20-50 ml of 50% glucose intravenously 1-2 mg of glucagon intravenously Mannitol if cerebral edema is present

hypoglycemia can be evaluated (blood tests are required before glucose is given) a quick-acting simple carbohydrate should be ingested. Some patients monitor their blood glucose level before treating so they can learn their blood glucose level and make an appraisal of how much carbohydrate to take. Doing this allows patients to gain a closer approximation of what symptoms they experience at various levels. Under no circumstances should treatment be delayed, since symptoms rapidly progress. If a suspected reaction is treated with 4 ounces of ginger ale and later on it is discovered that the patient was in error when the diagnosis was made, there is no harm done. Extra calories from the ginger ale are better than the risk of not treating or waiting too long.

Patients should be taught to carry a rapidly acting carbohydrate with them at all times so they can immediately treat suspected reactions and prevent serious ones. In a hospital setting, a conscious patient who experiences an insulin reaction is treated with fruit juice, regular tonic, honey, jelly, and the like. If a patient is unconscious, then nothing is given by mouth. One of two methods is used to quickly raise the blood glucose level. The length of time the patient has been unconscious and the setting where the patient was found determine which to use. If the patient is unconscious at home, or it is known that the patient just became unconscious, then glucagon would be the first treatment to use. **Endogenous glucagon** is a hormone secreted by the alpha cells of the islets of Langerhans. In the presence of low blood glucose levels glucagon is secreted, which stimulates the liver to break down glycogen, which in turn releases glucose into the bloodstream, and the blood glucose level is raised. An **exogenous glucagon** preparation would be given parenterally to stimulate a glucose release from stored glycogen.

Once conscious, the patient should ingest some easily absorbed carbohydrate and then some more complex food. Family members are taught to administer glucagon in the home setting by using one of the patient's insulin syringes and a glucagon kit. A side effect of glycogen is nausea so the patient and families should be told of this during the teaching session. After the initial treatment of an unconscious reaction, the patient and family should be instructed to investigate the cause. Repeated unconscious reactions should be avoided.

If the patient does not immediately respond to the glucagon, or if the patient has been unconscious for a while, intravenous glucose is required. A small amount of a very concentrated glucose solution (50%) is given, and patients usually respond rapidly. Additional complex carbohydrates, protein, and fat are provided as soon as the patient can tolerate them, since the intravenous glucose will rapidly pass from the bloodstream into the cells. Insulin reactions should not be overtreated. The day after a reaction, the patient will normally experience "rebound hyperglycemia." The ideal treatment for an insulin reaction is to give enough but not too much extra carbohydrate. One suggestion is to wait 10 minutes after giving carbohydrates; if the symptoms have not disappeared in that time, then repeat the carbohydrate.

When patients begin taking insulin, they may experience a reaction while their dose is being adjusted. This will help them know what a reaction feels like, which should dispel the fear of the unknown and give them confidence in how to treat future reactions. As individuals gain more experience with their illness, they should be able to detect initial warning signs, and learn their particular signs of impending reaction. One patient's growling stomach may indicate an insulin reaction is on its way, so it is particularly important for these individuals to be on the alert for feelings of "being low."

Patients need to be taught when to expect reactions and how to prevent them. Once people learn when their insulin peaks, they should be instructed to eat an appropriate snack a little in advance to prevent hypoglycemia. If strenuous weekend-only exercise is planned, then depending on body size and whether one wishes to gain or lose weight, either less insulin is used that day or more food is taken. Regularity in times of insulin administration, eating, and exercise is the best way to prevent insulin reactions. In case one experiences a reaction and becomes unconscious or demonstrates symptoms associated with intoxication, identification should be worn indicating to a stranger that the person has diabetes and that unusual symptoms mean a hypoglycemic reaction.

Diabetic acidosis (ketoacidosis). If the question, "Why treat diabetes?" is posed, the first response would be "to prevent diabetic acidosis." This serious acute complication of diabetes leads to death if untreated and is always considered an emergency. It may occur in an individual who had previously been undiagnosed and could even be the first indication of the disease. Ketoacidosis is more prevalent in individuals who have type I diabetes. Although it is unusual, it may occur in individuals who do not require insulin to manage their diabetes.

The immediate cause of diabetic ketoacidosis (DKA) is always lack of insulin and the subsequent accumulation of glucose and waste products from increased fat and protein metabolism. The onset is gradual and can be caused by any events that result in decreased available insulin or increased insulin requirements. Too little insulin, the flu, infection, or stress are some possible causes of DKA. Since the pathophysiology of DKA is similar to untreated uncontrolled type I diabetes, early DKA symptoms are similar to the classic signs of new-onset, type I diabetes. Initial symptoms are polyuria, polydipsia, and polyphagia, which may go unnoticed until some other symptoms such as nausea, vomiting, appetite loss, weakness, headache, dry skin, and flushed face occur (Table 20-2). Often patients think they have these symptoms because they have a virus. This is why all sick days are treated as if they might mean impending DKA.

Unchecked DKA can lead to complex metabolic processes that result in fluid and electrolyte loss, dehydration, starvation, and reduction in the acid-base buffering system. Late symptoms of DKA are related to these metabolic sequelae and include a sweet fruity breath odor, decreased blood pressure, increased pulse, and Kussmaul's respirations. Kussmaul's respirations, characteristic of late DKA, are a rhythmic cycle that includes a pattern of loud, deep, and rapid respirations followed by apnea. Body chemistries reflect this picture of metabolic acidosis. Patients exhibit high blood glucose levels, low pH and carbon dioxide, and altered electrolytes and have fatty acid breakdown products in (ketones) the urine. A blood glucose level may be well over 1000 mg/dl. This complication is the exact opposite of an insulin reaction. Usually the classic signs and symptoms of DKA allow the diagnosis to be made quickly. If symptoms are unusual and there may be doubt as to which acute complication has occurred, the patient should be treated for an insulin reaction. If the patient has DKA that is incorrectly diagnosed as an insulin reaction, and glucose is given, the only harm done is the waiting for a few minutes to see if the glucose is effective.

Patients with DKA look and feel seriously ill. They may become comatose if treatment is delayed. Emergency treatment is necessary to reverse the hyperglycemia, dehydration, acidosis, and electrolyte imbalance. Quick-acting insulin is given intravenously and is followed by subcutaneous or intravenous infusion of insulin. Rapid infusion of intravenous fluids are used to reverse the dehydration. Electrolytes are closely monitored and supplements are given as required. These seriously ill patients require intensive nursing care. The treatment goal for DKA is to reverse the metabolic imbalance without causing fluid overload or hypoglycemia.

Once the patient's condition has been stabilized, the cause of the DKA must be discovered. Alterations in diabetes management and education of the patient and significant other will be tailored to prevent future occurrences.

Hyperglycemic, hyperosmolar, nonketotic coma. A severe, but less frequently seen acute complication of diabetes is hyperglycemic, hyperosmolar, nonketotic coma (HHNC). Individuals who do not require insulin to manage their diabetes are susceptible to this problem. It is more common among elderly patients and may occasionally be the first indication that the individual has type II diabetes. The syndrome was named from its observed clinical signs and symptoms. There is no ketoacidosis, but the other defining characteristics of the problem, hyperglycemia and hyperosmolality, are very intense. Extreme dehydration is treated with massive amounts of fluid replacement, and very small amounts of insulin are used to reverse the hyperglycemia. These patients are critically ill and require intense monitoring as their metabolic problems are reversed.

Once the critical phase has passed, the cause of the HHNC must be discovered. Often it is secondary to an infection or another illness. This explains a general rule of thumb in diabetes management. No matter what other disease process may be present, metabolic control of diabetes has to be concurrent with other disease management.

Chronic complications. The second answer to the question "Why treat diabetes?" is to prevent, minimize, or delay the onset of chronic complications. Macrovascular and microvascular changes, functional disturbances in the nervous system, and infection are the major categories of impairment of long term or uncontrolled diabetes mellitus. A syndrome called diabetic triopathy results when severe pathologic changes have occurred in the peripheral nerves (neuropathy), eyes (retinopathy), and kidneys (nephropathy).

Individuals who have diabetes often develop macrovascular changes caused by atherosclerosis. These changes usually occur earlier and are more severe than in individuals without diabetes. Some diabetes clinicians estimate the anatomic changes of a patient's cardiovascular system to be consistent with that expected accoridng to their chronologic age plus the number of years they have had diabetes. These patients are in high-risk groups for problems with their peripheral vascular system, such as intermittent claudication or gangrene. Stroke and coronary artery disease also result from macrovascular changes.

Microvascular problems are caused by changes in the capillary basement membrane. High levels of circulating glucose in uncontrolled diabetes are believed to cause thickening and damage to these small vessels. Capillaries in the eye and kidney can be affected and cause retinal problems, leading to blindness and glomerulosclerosis that may cause renal failure. Other vision changes may occur from cataracts secondary to prolonged hyperglycemia.

High blood glucose levels probably account for the increased susceptibility that individuals with diabetes have for infections. Metabolic imbalances also contribute to problems that are evidenced in the central or peripheral nervous systems. Sensory and motor fibers can be affected and contribute to the "at-risk" foot. The ease with which individuals who have diabetes can acquire infections, poor circulation, which impedes, healing, and diminished sensation to lower extremities guide patient teaching regarding foot care. Patients are taught to observe their feet daily, since an abrasion or infection may be present but not felt.

Although the results of long-term randomized, controlled clinical trials to examine the relationship between glycemic control and vascular complications are not yet available, euglycemia (normal blood glucose level) is generally considered the best means to prevent the chronic complications of diabetes. The American Diabetes Association policy is that attempts at better control of diabetes should be standard therapy, within the limits of lifestyle alteration tolerated by each individual.

Other complications. Surgery, for whatever the reason, causes physiologic stress, regardless of whether one has diabetes or not. The individual who has mild type II diabetes that is under metabolic control by caloric dietary restrictions alone may require insulin for several days when hospitalized for major surgery. Patients who previously required insulin will have increased insulin requirements. One half of the anticipated insulin dose is usually given preoperatively and the remainder in the recovery room. An intravenous glucose solution runs during the perioperative period. Blood glucose levels are monitored closely, and supplemental insulin or glucose is administered as required.

Routine tests that require nothing by mouth can complicate the hospitalization of individuals who have diabetes. The length of the procedure and sensitivity of the patient to periods of fasting or withholding insulin determine what will be ordered for each individual. Some patients may tolerate half of their usual insulin dose (including rapidly acting insulin), whereas others may need to receive an intravenous glucose infusion.

In the home setting, unusual or sick days will require tailoring of the diabetic routine. Patients should learn how to adjust their diet when they go out to dinner and how to eat from a restaurant menu. Sick days should be treated as days of impending DKA or HHNC. More frequent diabetes monitoring should be done. Extra insulin may be needed even if only fluids such as regular ginger ale instead of a full diet are all that can be tolerated. Patients should be reminded that they must always take their insulin dose even if they are unable to eat due to nausea and vomiting.

Patient education. Because of its complexity, diabetes requires such an arduous treatment regimen that the American Association of Diabetes Educators has issued a position statement.[1] These educators believe that as a result of understanding the disease and its treatment, the person with diabetes can better participate in an individualized management plan. They recommend a careful adjustment of diet, exercise, and medications and suggest that individualized education be based on the person's intellect, motivation, physical ability, and social and personal resources.

One patient may be taught how to eat at a fast food restaurant chain by following a specific list of what to order. Another individual may have the ability to exchange foods quite accurately, and by following a few suggestions could eat within the diet at almost any restaurant. This same patient might be taught a sophisticated algorithm, whereby he could increase his usual insulin dose by 20% during a sick day. Conversely, the individual might be told, "Call your doctor to find out what to do whenever you feel you have the flu."

The most important feature of patient teaching is that its success depends on both the ability and willingness of individuals to incorporate their therapeutic plan into a daily routine. The experience of having diabetes is unique for each person. Therefore, in addition to achieving the goal of assuring that patients possess the requisite knowledge and skills to maintain metabolic control, the patient teaching plan must incorporate individual differences. Patient education for individuals who assume self-care management responsibilities usually held by providers of health care is a central feature of diabetes therapy.

Nursing interventions for people who have diabetes are directed toward the diagnosis and treatment of their actual and potential responses to both the disease diabetes and its treatment regimen. For individuals who are hospitalized and have diabetes, several routine nursing activities are incorporated into nursing care plans (see box on p. 612).

The steps of the nursing process are the organizing framework to summarize general nursing interventions for people with diabetes regardless of setting (see box below).

Expected outcome. The type of diabetes, general health status, personal ability, regimen complexity, and individual differences are some of the factors that determine expected outcomes for specific patients. Outcome criteria determine when patients are prepared to be the self-care manager of their disease, are ready for discharge from the hospital or diabetes teaching program, or require additional assistance or a change in their therapeutic plan.

Patients need to have adequate knowledge

about their diabetes, should have an understanding of the rationale that determines their individual care plan, and possess the requisite skills to manage their therapeutic regimen. An integration of patients' cognitive and behavioral skills should be demonstrated as they monitor, make decisions, and carry out their diabetes activities of daily living. Good metabolic control without acute complications is the expected therapeutic outcome.

Patients should understand the rationale for their treatment, based on the pathophysiologic condition that exists. This includes specific components of their therapy such as monitoring glucose level, giving medications, acting on the basis of blood and urine testing, and eating the correct foods. Blood and urine chemistry levels should be as close to normal range as possible. For example, a fasting venous plasma glucose level of 80 to 120 mg/dl, no sugar or acetone in preprandial urine specimens, a glycohemoglobin level less than 1.5 times normal (acceptable range for an individual with diabetes would be about 4.5% to 9%), and a 2-hour post prandial blood glucose level close to fasting range. Nurses are responsible for ensuring that patients demonstrate knowledge of the prevention, detection, and treatment of complications such as hypoglycemia and hyperglycemia. Specific expected outcomes for the hospitalized patient with diabetes mellitus are found in the boxed material.

Since there is no known cure or prevention for diabetes mellitus, early detection and careful treatment are the current therapeutic interventions. Individuals who develop diabetes become managers of their chronic illness and become partners with health providers who prescribe therapy. Nursing interventions must be guided to assist patients to successfully live with this disorder so that its catastrophic complications are prevented. Nursing creativity and ingenuity can make the difference between a regimen that is impossible for the patient to accept and one that accommodates individual differences.

Hypoglycemia

An abnormally low level of blood glucose may also occur in the absence of diabetes. It may be caused by disease of the liver or pancreas or disease of the pituitary or adrenal glands. The symptoms include hunger, weakness, anxiety, pallor, headache, sweating, and rapid pulse. One type known as functional hypoglycemia has an unknown cause. The symptoms are variable and frequently occur several hours after meals or exercise. The attacks may last from minutes to days. Treatment is based on relieving the immediate attack, followed by removing the cause when it is known. In mild attacks orange juice or hard candy may relieve the symptoms, whereas for patients with severe cases glucose may be administered intravenously. Patients may be given low-carbohydrate, high-protein diets with restriction of simple sugars; frequent small meals are usually prescribed. This type of diet should help prevent hypoglycemic episodes.

Disorders of the Parathyroid Glands
Hyperparathyroidism and hypoparathyroidism

Excessive secretion of parathormone may be caused by a benign tumor of one of the glands. The purpose of the hormone is to maintain a constant calcium balance in the blood. Too much parathyroid hormone causes a calcium imbalance by allowing the calcium in the bones to be removed and migrate into the bloodstream. The bones become weak, tender, and painful, and spontaneous fractures may occur. The appetite may become poor, constipation may be present, and there may be fatigue, depression, weight loss, and loss of muscle tone, making walking difficult for the patient. An increase in the blood calcium level occurs, and renal calculi composed chiefly of calcium salts may form in the kidney. Small tumors, which are detected by x-ray examination, may form in the bones. The treatment is surgical removal of the tumor or removal of the overactive gland. Following surgery, all symptoms should disappear and the bones will gradually strengthen.

When too little parathormone is secreted, the level of blood calcium decreases and phosphorus increases in the blood. The deficiency of the hormone may result from injury to the glands or the removal of too much parathyroid tissue during a thyroidectomy. The primary symptom is **tetany** resulting from the decreased level of blood calcium. There is muscular incoordination with tremor and muscular spasm. Laryngeal spasm and generalized convulsions may occur. The treatment is to elevate the blood calcium level by the administration of calcium salts, parathormone extract, and vitamin D. Depending on the severity of the condition, calcium gluconate in physiologic saline solution, parathormone solution, and vitamin D may be administered intravenously.

NURSING CARE GUIDELINES
Patient with Diabetes Mellitus

Nursing diagnoses

- Alteration in nutrition, less than body requirements related to insulin deficiency
- Anxiety related to inability to control illness
- Potential fluid volume deficit related to polyuria
- Disturbance in self-concept related to chronicity of illness
- Knowledge deficit related to complex management of illness
- Potential ineffective individual and family coping associated with chronicity of illness
- High risk for infection related to metabolic changes
- High risk for impaired tissue integrity related to metabolic change

Nursing interventions

- Monitor blood glucose levels (normal fasting level: 80 to 120 mg/dl)
- Promote nutritional status by planned diabetic diet
- Monitor vital signs
- Weigh patient daily
- Encourage moderate levels of activity, which lower blood sugar levels
- Test urine for ketones if blood glucose is over 240 mg/dl
- If patient is taking oral hypoglycemic agents, observe for adverse effects such as nausea, vomiting, rash, photosensitivity, and alcohol intolerance
- Monitor for signs of insulin reaction, such as diaphoresis (excessive perspiration), headache, tachycardia, and anxiety
- Observe for signs of diabetic ketoacidosis, such as nausea, vomiting, facial flushing, weight loss, polydipsia, and positive urine tests for sugar
- Provide emotional support for patient and family
- Educate patient and family regarding basic pathophysiology and management of diabetes
- Foster independence in self-care management
- Assess patient's health status, psychosocial functioning, and social support.
- Assess patient's and significant others' ability to comprehend and integrate their diabetes activities of daily living into their usual lifestyle pattern.

- Collaborate with patient, family, and diabetes clinicians to identify a therapeutic plan that provides the best metabolic control possible within the limitations of patient ability and acceptability.
- Decide how best to implement the plan so that patients become independent in self-management techniques as soon as possible without becoming overwhelmed.
- Incorporate the therapeutic plan of the patient care setting into the patient's individualized care plan. For example, use laboratory results of blood glucose values so patients can relate how they feel in relation to varying blood glucose levels, and those who take urine tests can learn their renal threshold.
- Promote patient confidence and independence in carrying out their diabetes activities of daily living. For example, under decreasing supervision, patients should draw up and inject their own insulin, SMBG, perform urine or blood test, and select foods for their meals and snacks.
- Evaluate the patient's skill level and coping ability so refinements can be made in the care plan.
- Collaboratively determine patient outcome expectations regarding the degree of metabolic control to be achieved, specific patient and significant other responsibilities in the home setting, and mechanisms to evaluate diabetes control, regimen ease/difficulty, and adherence to the therapeutic plan.

Expected outcomes

- Blood and urine chemistries close to normal range
- Basic pathology of diabetes explained
- Rationale for treatment regimen explained
- Prevent, detect, and treat hypoglycemia and hyperglycemia
- Foods exchanged properly
- Manages self-care on a sick day
- Nurse or physician called appropriately
- Complications prevented

Disorders of the Adrenal (Suprarenal) Glands

The body has two adrenal glands located immediately above the kidneys. Each adrenal gland consists of two parts, which function as separate glands. The outer part, the adrenal cortex, produces several different hormones that are essential to life. These include the glucocorticoids, the mineralocorticoids, and sex hormones. The glucocorticoids *cortisone* and *hydrocortisone* regulate much of the cell activity of the body and maintain an optimum internal environment for the body cells. They also regulate the body's ability to adapt to constant changes in the external environment. The mineralocorticoids help regulate electrolyte metabolism. **Aldosterone** is the most important mineralocorticoid, and its primary function is to maintain homeostasis of sodium concentration in the blood. Small amounts of the male hormone androgen and female hormone estrogen are also secreted by the adrenal cortex. The adrenal medulla secretes the **catecholamines** epinephrine and norepinephrine, two hormones that tend to increase and prolong the effects of the sympathetic nervous system. Epinephrine and norepinephrine primarily affect smooth muscle, cardiac muscle, and glandular activity and are responsible for the "fight or flight" response to stress situations.

Addison's disease

Hypofunction of the adrenal cortex resulting in insufficient secretion of hormones causes Addison's disease. The specific cause for the **atrophy,** or wasting away, of the gland is unknown, but it often is diagnosed after the patient has undergone stressful situations such as injury, infection or surgery. Recently, autoantibodies that react against adrenal tissues have been discovered in a significant number of patients. This finding suggests that Addison's disease may be an autoimmune process.

Symptoms result from inadequate amounts of adrenocortical hormones in the blood and body fluids. Common gastrointestinal symptoms are nausea, vomiting, anorexia, diarrhea, and abdominal pain. The patient may fatigue easily and show signs of hypoglycemia such as nervousness, increased perspiration (diaphoresis), headache, and trembling. These symptoms result from inadequate amounts of circulating cortisone and hydrocortisone. The normal fluid and electrolyte balance is interrupted, and the patient will have a deficiency of sodium and chloride and an excess of potassium because of insufficient aldosterone. Often the skin will develop a bronze color, and the patient will appear tanned.

Addison's disease is treated by reestablishing a state of normal hydration and then replacing hydrocortisone and fludrocortisone (Florinef). Both of these medications should be given after meals, since they may cause gastrointestinal upset. Once therapy is begun, it is essential that the patient understand that Addison's disease is a lifelong disorder and that medications should not be adjusted or stopped except under the guidance of the physician. Patients should avoid undue stress, both mental and physical, and should carry a Medic Alert tag or card identifying them as having Addison's disease and listing emergency measures to be taken.[43] An addisonian crisis is a serious exacerbation of the disease and may produce a severe drop in blood pressure, leading to shock, coma, and death. When this occurs, fluids are replaced with normal saline solution and hydrocortisone may be given intravenously.

Secondary hypoadrenalism

Steroid (hydrocortisone) therapy is commonly used in the treatment of asthma and ulcerative colitis. Long-term treatment with steroids leads to atrophy of the adrenal glands. If steroid therapy is withdrawn too suddenly, symptoms similar to those of Addison's disease occur. The patient feels lethargic and weak and may become hypotensive. The response to stress such as surgery may be severe depression; therefore it is important to know if a patient going into surgery has been receiving steroid therapy. Withdrawal from steroid therapy must be done very slowly under the supervision of a physician to allow the adrenal glands to recover.[43]

Cushing's syndrome

Hyperfunction of the adrenal cortex produces an excessive secretion of hormones from the gland and results in Cushing's syndrome. The cause is usually a tumor in the anterior pituitary gland or a tumor of the adrenal cortex.

Characteristic symptoms of Cushing's syndrome reflect exaggeration of the normal functions of adrenal hormones. These include weakness with muscle wasting; fat accumulation in the face, neck, and trunk; hemorrhagic tendencies; changes in secondary sex characteristics; hypertension; obesity; menstrual irregularities; hyperglycemia; irritability; and symptoms of fluid and electrolyte imbalance. The patient's appearance may be upsetting, especially to the woman affected by Cushing's syndrome, and the patient may withdraw from others.

Nursing care should convey acceptance and reassurance. Treatment usually involves surgical removal of the tumor, if possible. However, if the pituitary gland is involved, a hypophysectomy (removal of the gland) or irradiation of the pituitary gland may be performed.

A variety of chronic diseases are treated with adrenal steroids, although no adrenal disease is present. Examples of such diseases are rheumatoid arthritis, leukemia, emphysema, and ulcerative colitis. Drugs such as prednisone have potent antiinflammatory effects, which can be of great therapeutic value. However, most patients treated with adrenal steroids will develop Cushing's syndrome to a variable degree, and serious complications and side effects can occur. The nurse should be familiar with the untoward effects of the steroid preparations, and they should be reported if they are observed.

Some side effects of prednisone may be decreased if the desired therapeutic result can be obtained when the drug is given on alternate days. Other side effects may be minimized by patient education. For those individuals who are susceptible to weight gain, caloric control should be initiated at the beginning of steroid therapy. Females who develop a moon face should be instructed in makeup techniques and clothing to minimize the appearance of that side effect (e.g., avoid wearing turtle necks). Families should be instructed to expect mood swings in individuals who are taking steroids.

Pheochromocytoma

Pheochromocytoma is a catecholamine-producing tumor of the adrenal medulla. These tumors are generally small and benign, with only a tiny number being malignant. Pheochromocytoma is believed to be associated with neurofibromatosis and tumors of the thyroid gland and may be hereditary.[43]

Symptoms result from the hypersecretion of epinephrine and norepinephrine. The characteristic symptom is hypertension. However, the hypertension may be variable, being persistent and chronic or occurring in intermittent attacks. Because of the elevated blood pressure, pheochromocytoma is often confused with essential hypertension. Other symptoms may include severe headache, excessive sweating, nausea, vomiting, palpitation, and nervousness with acute anxiety. During an acute attack, tachycardia, hyperglycemia, and polyuria may occur.

The diagnosis of pheochromocytoma may be made by testing the urine for elevated levels of metanephrine (a by-product of epinephrine metabolism), using a 24-hour urine collection. When collecting the specimen, the urine should be kept on ice in a dark container and a preservative (hydrochloric acid) is necessary. Pheochromocytoma may also be diagnosed by urine levels of vanillylmandelic acid (also a metabolite of epinephrine), by intravenous pyelography, or by aortography. The treatment is removal of the tumor.

Adrenalectomy

Adrenalectomy is the surgical removal of the adrenal gland, usually because of a pathologic disorder such as a tumor. The preoperative preparation of the patient is the same as that for other abdominal surgery. The postoperative care may require the administration of hydrocortisone if the adrenal cortex has been removed. When surgery has been done because of pheochromocytoma, the patient's condition may be critical for the first 48 hours. Shock may occur because of the abrupt fall in the blood pressure. Blood pressure must be monitored continuously and the patient observed for hemorrhage, which may be external or internal. Central venous pressure is monitored, and the urinary output must be observed for signs of oliguria. Vasopressor drugs are administered intravenously. Caution should be used when administering narcotic drugs for pain, since some have a tendency to cause hypotension. After the critical period, the recovery progresses normally. If both adrenal glands are removed, the patient will need hormone replacement therapy for the rest of his or her life.

Disorders of the Pituitary Gland

The *hypophysis,* or pituitary gland, has been called the *master gland* because it exerts some control over the other endocrine glands. The anterior lobe secretes several hormones, including growth hormone, and the posterior lobe secretes two hormones, including the antidiuretic hormone (ADH).

A hypersecretion of the anterior lobe of the pituitary gland may result from a tumor affecting certain cells. The condition causes *acromegaly* in the adult and is characterized by the following; the features become coarse, the bones become large and heavy, the hands and feet become broad and massive, the chin protrudes, and the tongue enlarges. These effects are primarily caused by the effects of increased amounts of growth hormone circulating throughout the body. Surgical removal of the tumor is extremely difficult, and radiation therapy may be used in treatment of the condition. A congenital deficiency of the growth hormone results in *dwarfism* (midget), whereas a tumor affecting the growth hormone in childhood or adolescence causes the individual to grow extremely tall, resulting in *gigantism.*

Diabetes insipidus is a disease caused by failure of the posterior lobe of the pituitary gland to secrete sufficient amounts of ADH. ADH functions to increase the amount of water reabsorbed from the kidney tubules, and in its absence large amounts of water are excreted in the urine. Excessive fluid and electrolyte losses occur, producing symptoms such as dehydration, insatiable thirst, weakness, weight loss, and anorexia. Extracts of posterior pituitary lobes of animals or vasopressin (Pitressin) can be given parenterally for treatment of the condition. Lypressin (Diapid) is a synthetic medication identical to the ADH found in humans. It can be applied as a nasal spray several times a day.

Since the pituitary gland regulates many functions of the body and controls other functions through its influence on other glands, many disorders may result from an oversecretion or an undersecretion of its various hormones. Since many of these conditions occur only rarely, a discussion of them is not included in this book.

NURSING CARE PLAN
Patient with Hyperthyroidism

The patient is a 34-year-old female who is admitted to the medical unit for a diagnostic work-up after having palpitations, tachycardia, and an enlarged thyroid gland that was identified on a routine health visit to her private medical doctor (PMD).

Significant in her history is the fact that she has lost 20 lbs within the last 2 months without exercising or dieting. Her menstrual cycle has been erratic for the last 6 months with no menses for the last 3 months. She denies being pregnant. She states she is currently stressed over her husband's projected employment transfer to the West coast and away from her extended family. She complains of heat intolerance and frequent episodes of "sweating." She states she is easily fatigued and has had periods of insomnia and constipation. She describes herself as feeling irritable and having crying outbursts without warning.

Past medical history
T & A, age 10 years.

Appendectomy at 14 years old. No other surgeries.

Hospitalized × 3 for childbirth. All routine vaginal deliveries without complications.

Immunizations up to date.

No known food or drug allergies. Has recieved antiobiotics in past without problems.

Both parents alive and in good health. Both employed full time and supportive to their children.

Two brothers in good health. Both lawyers.

Identical twin sister recently diagnosed with Grave's disease.

Family history of HTN in maternal grandmother age 79.

Adult onset diabetes in paternal uncle, age 70. Good management.

Cancer of the breast in maternal aunt, deceased age 52.

Excellent health behaviors: yearly physical, Pap smear, mammogram.

Has never smoked. Denies use of alcohol and/or drugs. Some use of over the counter (OTC) cold remedies/analgesics (aspirin, tylenol).

Psychosocial data
Married 12 years. Quality relationship with husband. Dated 6 years while in college and after. Only stressor due to husband's frequent traveling with his work (Consultancy business and sales).

Own home. Has cleaning lady once per week.

Works part-time as librarian in media center at grammar school.

Has three children: Steve, age 9, Melissa, age 6, and Adam, age 5. All in excellent health.

Jewish faith. Children attend Hebrew school.

Has private health insurance.

Hobbies: avid reader, gardening, some traveling. Is a gourmet cook.

Assessment data
Thin, frail appearing woman with obvious exophthalmos. Height 5 ft. 8 in. Weight 118 lbs.

Skin: Warm with evidence of recent diaphoresis. No rashes, lesions, or bruises.

Musculoskeletal: Steady gait. Full range of motion all joints.

Fine tremors noted when fingers extended.

Neck: Diffuse swelling anterior portion neck. Isthmus of gland palpable. No specific nodules palpable.

Respiratory: Lungs clear to percussion and auscultation. RR 24-26. Regular rate and rhythm.

Cardiovascular: B.P. 146/84. (normal baseline = 118/72). Apical pulse 96-100. No bruits. All peripheral pulses symmetrical. Atrial flutter documented on ECG.

Abdominal: Bowel sounds heard all four quadrants. Slight distension.

Continued on next page.

Lab data

Hgb 12.1 Hct 37.8 WBC 8000 Platelets 320,000
BUN 16. Electrolytes WNL.
Thyroid ultrasonogram reveals marked diffuse swelling bilaterally.
Thyroid scan reveals a nonmalignancy condition
T3 triiodothyronine (T3) resin uptake test = 24% of iodine uptake.

Medications

SSKI 300 mg po every 4 hours. Dilute in 4 oz orange juice.
Inderol 20 mg po QID.
Colace 100 mg po daily.
Multivitamins tab 1 po daily.
Tylenol 300 mg po prn headache.

NURSING DIAGNOSIS

Alteration in nutrition, less than body requirements related to increased metabolism, as evidenced by rapid weight loss and chronic fatigue.

Expected patient outcomes	Nursing interventions	Evaluation for expected outcomes
Patient will show no futher evidence of weight loss and will take in at least 2000 calories daily. Patient communicates understanding of special dietary needs (high calorie, high carbohydrate). Patient develops a plan to monitor and maintain target weight at discharge.	Weigh patient daily (same time, same scale) and record results. Monitor fluid I & O (likes milkshakes as between-meal snacks). Provide high calorie, high carbohydrate diet. Assist her with menu choices and discuss rationale for choices. She likes pasta, some creamed soups, and fresh fruits. Patient hates broccoli. Refer to dietician for teachings related to incorporating special dietary needs into gourmet cooking. Monitor bowel sounds once per shift. Check for episodes of constipation. Hold colace if loose stools. Teach same to patient. Provide oral hygiene at least twice per day. Remind patient to try to eat at least 90% of each meal tray. Record results on calorie count sheet.	Patient remains at or above specified weight (125 lbs) and shows a steady increase of 2 lbs bimonthly. Patient consumes at least 90% of meals served and all of in-between snacks. Patient plans appropriate diet for discharge for 1 week post discharge. She can explain the rationale for her choices.

NURSING DIAGNOSIS

Body image disturbance related to exopthalmic appearance as evidenced by statements of anxiety and wearing dark glasses.

Expected patient outcomes	Nursing interventions	Evaluation for expected outcomes
Patient will acknowledge a change in her body image and will communicate her feelings related to that change. Patient will express positive feeling about herself. Patient will talk to someone who has also experienced the same problem. Patient demonstrates the ability to practice positive coping skills.	Assess patient's usual coping patterns. Encourage discussion of feelings by initiating comments related to self-esteem and self-worth. Cite behaviors of progress. Introduce patient to available personnel (by mutual consent) who have had similar condition (Not rare condition). Praise efforts to participate in self-care. Discuss hairstyle changes that might enhance self-image. Actively listen for expressions of anxiety.	Patient discusses the change in her body image. Patient takes an active role in planning hygiene and self-care. Patient expresses at least two positive feelings about herself daily. Patient identifies coping strategies that aid situations.

Expected patient outcomes	Nursing interventions	Evaluation for expected outcomes
	Guide thinking along postive channels. Protect eyes from trauma. Monitor for complete closure while asleep to prevent corneal drying.	

NURSING DIAGNOSIS

Sleep pattern disturbance related to increased metabolism.

Expected patient outcomes	Nursing interventions	Evaluation for expected outcomes
Patient will identify factors that prevent or facilitate sleep. Patient sleeps at least 6 hours nightly without interruption and expresses feelings of being well rested. Patient shows no physical signs indicative of sleep deprivation (dark circles under eyes, staring into space). Patient performs relaxation exercises at bedtime.	Ask patient what factors are conducive to sleep. Discourage intake of caffeinated foods such as coffee, cocoa, tea, chocolate, and cola drinks. Keep environment restful and calm. Plan to provide period for uninterrupted sleep. Provide patient with normal sleep aids such as back rubs, pillow, food, drinks, and personal hygiene measures. Ask patient to discuss sleep pattern from previous night. Teach patient relaxation techniques such as meditation, guided imagery, and muscle relaxation exercises. Plan medication schedule to allow for maximum rest. Limit visitors to those persons specified by patient. Reduce environmental stimuli at bedtime, (dim lights, soft music, closed doors).	Patient sleeps at least 6 hours without interruption, and expresses a feeling of being well rested. Patient does not exhibit signs and symptoms of sleep deprivation. Patient discusses lifestyle changes to induce sleep upon discharge to home. Patient performs relaxation techniques at bedtime.

NURSING DIAGNOSIS

Knowledge deficit related to physical status as evidenced by statements of "immediate recovery."

Expected patient outcomes	Nursing interventions	Evaluation for expected outcomes
Patient will communicate an understanding of physical changes brought about by overactive gland. Patient will set realistic learning goals. Patient expresses an interest in learning about condition. Patient practices new health related behaviors during hospitalization (selects appropriate diet, weighs self daily, and monitors food and fluid intake).	Ascertain what patient already knows about Grave's disease. Urge her to ask questions. Suggest she write down major concerns. Determine if she enjoys learning through media (is a librarian), such as videotapes, audiotapes, or books. Begin negotiating learning objectives with her. Plan mutual establishment of goals.	Patient discusses newly acquired knowledge. Patient develops realistic learning goals. Patient identifies specific changes in her lifestyle needed to promote optimal health. Patient discusses a reasonable time frame for condition to subside. Patient feels free to question the possibility of surgery if necessary.

Continued on next page.

Expected patient outcomes	Nursing interventions	Evaluation for expected outcomes
Patient develops a realistic plan to maintain health behaviors once home. Patient identifies the time frame needed before condition will subside.	Set times for discussion and include husband if needed. Discuss possible adverse side effects of medications. Answer any questions pertaining to the possiblity of surgery.	

REFERENCES AND ADDITIONAL READINGS

1. American Association of Diabetes Educators: Position statement: individualization of diabetes education and management, Diabetes Educator 8:48, 1982.
2. American Diabetes Association: Policy statement: self-monitoring of blood glucose, Diabetes Care 8(5):515+, 1985.
3. Anderson RM: Is the problem of noncompliance in our heads? Diabetes Educator 11:31-34, 1985.
4. Arky RA, Wylie-Rosett J, and El-Behri B: Examination of current dietary recommendations for individuals with diabetes mellitus, Diabetes Care 5:59-63, 1982.
5. Black RM: Diagnosis: pituitary tumor, Hosp Med 21(10):43-69, 1985.
6. Blonde L and Riddick FA: Hypothyroidism: clinical features, diagnosis, and therapy, Hosp Med 16(2):52-63, 1980.
7. Blonde L and Riddick FA: Hyperthyroidism: etiology, diagnosis, and therapy, Hosp Med 16(3):68-80, 1980.
8. Borg N and others: Core curriculum for critical care nursing, ed 2, Philadelphia, 1981, WB Saunders Co.
9. Cahill GF: Diabetes control and complications (editorial), Diabetes Care 6(3):310-311, 1983.
10. Cahill M (ed): Patient teaching, Springhouse Pa., 1987, Springhouse Corp.
11. Campbell K: 1990 Buyer's Guide Diabetes Forecast. 42(10):72-76, 1989.
12. Drury TF and Powell AL: Prevalence, impact, and demography of known diabetes in the United States. *Advance Data* (Feb. 12, 1986), US Department of Health and Human Services, Public Health Service, Pub. No. 114. Hyattsville, Md, 1986, National Center for Health Statistics.
13. Gotch PM: Teaching patients about corticosteroids, Am J Nurs 81(1):78-81, 1981.
14. Guthrie DW and Guthrie RA (eds): Nursing management of diabetes mellitus, ed 2, St Louis, 1982, The CV Mosby Co.
15. Hahn K: About insulin administration, Nurs 89 10(4):66-72, 1989.
16. Hamilton HK (ed): Diagnostics, Nursing 84 books, Springhouse Pa. 1984, Springhouse Corp.
17. Hoffmann JT and Newby TB: Hypercalcemia in primary hyperparathyroidism, Nurs Clin North Am 15:469-480, 1980.
18. Honigman RE: Thyroid function tests, Nurs 82 12(4):68-71, 1982.
19. Huzar J: Preventing acute complications, RN 52(8):34-39, 1989.
20. Huzar J and Cerrato P: The role of diet and drugs, RN 52(8):46-50, 1989.
21. Jenkins EH: Living with thyrotoxicosis, Am J Nurs 80:956-958, May 1980.
22. Kessler C: Protecting the adrenolectomy patient, Nurs 18(12):64, 1988.
23. Krall LP and Beaser RS: Joslin diabetes manual, ed 12, Philadelphia, 1989, Lea & Febiger.
24. Lockheart J and Griffin C: Action stat tetany, Nurs 18(8):33, 1988.
25. Lumley WA: Recognizing and reversing insulin shock, Nurs 89 19(9):34-41, 1989.
26. Martyn P: If you guessed cardiovascular disease, guess again, Am J Nurs 82:1239-1241, 1982.
27. Mecklenberg RS: Treating ketoacidosis, Practical Diabetology 9(2):13-17, 1990.
28. Mondahl BK: A change in size, Nurs Mirror 153(18):38-39, 1981.
29. Moriarty D and Stephens L: Factors that influence diabetes patient teaching performed by hospital staff nurses, Diabetes Educator, 16(1):13-35, 1990.
30. Murray P: Diabetes today. When hypoglycemia goes critical, RN 106:56-60, March 1983.
31. National Diabetes Data Group: diabetes in America: diabetes data compiled for 1984 NIH Pub. No. 85-1468, Washington, DC, 1985, US Government Printing Office.
32. Nemchick R: Diabetes today. A very different diet: a new generation of oral drugs, RN 97:41-45, 1982.
33. Nemchick R: Diabetes today. The news about insulin, RN 97:49-54, 1982.
34. Nemchick R: Diabetes today. Facing up to the long-term complications, RN 46(7):38-45, 1983.
35. Porter P: Patient education makes all the difference, RN 52(11):56-62, 1989.
36. Refkin H, (ed): Physicians guide to non-insulin dependent (type II) diabetes, ed 2, Alexandria, Va, 1988, American Diabetes Association, Inc.
37. Rockey P: Misbehavior of a thyroid, Emergency Med 13(5):203+, 1981.
38. Rogers MA and others: Improvement in glucose tolerance after one week of exercise in patients with mild NIDDM, Diabetes Care 11:613-618, 1988.
39. Rosenstock IM: Understanding and enhancing patient compliance with diabetic regimens, Diabetes Care 8:610-616, 1985.
40. Sanford S: Dysfunction of the adrenal gland: physiologic considerations and nursing problems, Nurs Clin North Am 15:481-497, 1980.
41. Sarsany S: Thyroid storm, RN 51(7):47-48, 1988.
42. Shaw K: The nature of the endocrine system. part 3. The thyroid gland, Nurs Mirror 144(22):26-28, 1977.

43. Shaw K: The nature of the endocrine system. part 6. The parathyroid glands and calcium metabolism, Nurs Mirror 144(25):28-30, 1977.

44. Solomon BL: The hypothalamus and the pituitary gland: an overview, Nurs Clin North Am 15:435-451, 1980.

45. Sperling MA, editor: Physicians guide to insulin dependent (type I) diabetes, Alexandria, Va, 1988, American Diabetes Association, Inc.

46. Thompson JM and others: Mosby's manual of clinical nursing, ed 2, St Louis, 1989, The CV Mosby Co.

47. Tomky D: Tapping the full power of insulin pumps, RN 52(6):46-48, 1989.

48. US Department of Health and Human Services: Third Annual Report of the National Diabetes Advisory Board—five years of progress, five years of promise, April 1980.

49. Wake MM and Bremsinger JF: The nurse's role in hypothyroidism, Nurs Clin North Am 15:453-467, 1980.

PROBLEMS AFFECTING
Neurologic Function

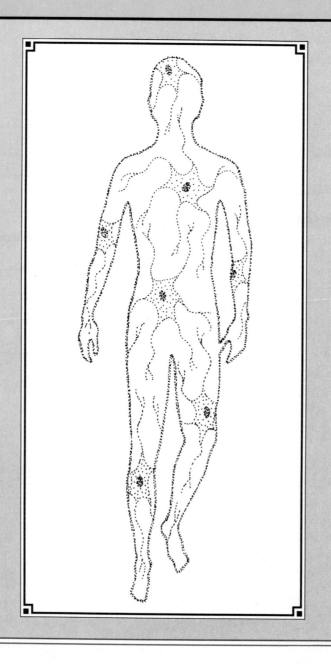

KEY WORDS

aphasia
ataxia
aura
canosognosia
cerebrospinal fluid
cholinergic crisis
coma
concussion
confusion
consciousness
convulsion
craniotomy
delirium
dysphagia
flaccid
hemianopia
hemiplegia
hyperreflexia
hyperthermia
intracranial pressure
laminectomy
muscle spasms
myasthenic crisis
opisthotonos
paraplegia
quadriplegia
reflex
rigidity
seizure
spinal shock
tremor

OBJECTIVES

1. Define the basic structure and function of the nervous system.

2. Discuss the purposes of the various neuro-diagnostic procedures.

3. Interpret the signs and symptoms of neurologic disturbances.

4. Recognize the significance of alterations in the patient's neurologic status.

5. List the characteristics of major neurologic conditions.

6. Identify the reasons underlying medical interventions for neurologic conditions.

7. Describe nursing interventions for patients with neurologic dysfunction.

STRUCTURE AND FUNCTION OF THE NERVOUS SYSTEM

The nervous system is the body's most highly organized and complex system. Its basic function is to transmit information throughout the body. The nervous system receives sensory information from the body's internal and external environment, interprets sensory input in the brain, and determines the body's responses to these sensory messages. In this way the nervous system controls and coordinates all the body's systems so they function as an integrated whole.

The nervous system is composed of two divisions: the central nervous system and the peripheral nervous system. The *central nervous system* is composed of the brain and the spinal cord. The *peripheral nervous system* is made up of 12 pairs of cranial nerves that emerge from the base of the brain, 31 pairs of spinal nerves that emerge from the spinal cord, and the autonomic system. Information to and from the brain and spinal cord is carried by the cranial and spinal nerves respectively.

The *autonomic nervous system,* a division of the peripheral nervous system, carries information to smooth muscle (heart, lungs, intestines, bladder) and glands (salivary, adrenal, pancreas). The autonomic system acts automatically; its functions are carried out without the individual's awareness. The autonomic system is divided further into the sympathetic and parasympathetic nervous system. The *sympathetic nervous system* produces generalized physiologic responses to prepare the individual for "flight or fight." Increased heart rate and blood pressure, an increased blood supply to the brain, skeletal muscles, and heart, and vasoconstriction of the blood vessels of the skin are examples. The *parasympathetic nervous system* produces more localized effects in particular organs, such as slowing the heart rate and increasing peristalsis. The parasympathetic nervous system balances the effects of the sympathetic nervous system, maintaining the body in a state of equilibrium.

The brain is divided into three major parts: the cerebrum, the brainstem, and the cerebellum (Figure 22-1). The *cerebrum* is divided further into the right and left hemispheres. The left hemisphere controls the right side of the body, and the right hemisphere, the left. Each hemisphere is made up of four lobes: the frontal, parietal, temporal, and occipital. The cerebrum receives, ana-

lyzes, and stores information for future use and controls conscious voluntary movements. The *cerebellum,* attached to the lower portion of the brain, assists in the coordination of voluntary movement and maintenance of muscle tone. The *brainstem* is the pathway for impulses between the brain and spinal cord. The vital centers for control of respiration, heart action, and vasoconstriction of blood vessels are located in the brainstem. All the sensory and motor pathways must pass through the brainstem on their way to the brain. Many of these pathways cross over in the brainstem, which explains why injury to one side of the brain may result in loss of function on the opposite side of the body.

The *spinal cord* is a slender cylinder of nerve tissue extending from the brainstem to the first lumbar vertebra, which is just below the waistline. The spinal nerves that innervate the legs extend beyond the end of the spinal cord to approximately the level of the hip. The function of the spinal cord is to transmit sensory information from the periphery to the brain and motor responses from the brain to nerves supplying muscles and glands. The spinal cord also serves as the connection for the reflex pathway (e.g., the knee-jerk reflex) that bypasses the brain.

The brain and spinal cord are protected from injury by a bony covering, by the meninges, and by **cerebrospinal fluid.** The bony covering of the brain is called the skull or *cranium;* the spinal cord

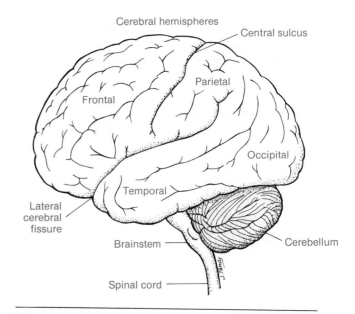

Figure 22-1

Major parts of the brain.

is encased within the *vertebral column*. The **meninges** are connective tissue coverings that completely enclose the brain and spinal cord. In addition to providing protection, the meninges contain blood vessels that carry blood to the brain and spinal cord. The brain and spinal cord are suspended in *cerebrospinal fluid,* a clear, watery liquid that fills the small spaces (ventricles) located within each hemisphere of the brain and that extends down into the spinal canal around the cord. It provides moisture and lubrication and cushions the brain and spinal cord from injury.

NURSING RESPONSIBILITIES FOR ASSESSMENT, AND DIAGNOSTIC TESTS AND PROCEDURES

The differential diagnosis of diseases of the nervous system includes a careful and thorough history and neurologic examination, as well as special tests and diagnostic procedures. A physician known as a neurologist usually performs the neurologic examination and determines the special tests and procedures to be performed. The nurse can provide additional information during this time through observation and recording of the patient's condition and behavior.

Basic Neurologic Examination

The purpose of the neurologic examination is to localize the site of a pathologic condition. A neurologic examination includes the systematic evaluation of the cranial nerves, including those of the senses (vision, hearing, taste, smell), the sensory system (touch, pain, temperature, position sense), and the motor system (gait, muscle strength and tone, coordination, muscle stretch reflexes such as the knee-jerk reflex). During the examination the patient is observed for mental and emotional state, as well as for his or her ability to speak and understand spoken words.

The neurologic examination includes assessments of function in five areas: cranial nerve function, **proprioception** and cerebellar function, musculoskeletal system, sensory fuction, and reflexes.[18] The cranial nerves and their functions are identified in Table 22-1. Proprioception and cerebellar function assessment provides information about the patient's balance and muscle coordination. Sensory function includes assessment of light touch, pain, temperature, and vibration. **Reflexes** are measured by stimulating a tendon (deep

Table 22-1

Cranial Nerves and Their Functions	
I Olfactory	Sense of smell
II Optic	Visual acuity
III Oculomotor	Movement of eye muscles
	Upper lid opening
	Pupillary reflexes
IV Trochlear	Movement: superior oblique eye muscles
V Trigeminal	Sensory of face
	Motor to muscles of chewing
VI Abducens	Movement of lateral rectus eye muscle
VII Facial	Motor to muscles of facial expression
	Sensory: taste, anterior two-thirds of tongue
VIII Acoustic	Auditory acuity
	Position in space: balance
IX Glossopharyngeal	Sensory position in space
	Motor to uvula
	Soft tissue of palate
	Sensory: taste in posterior one-third of tongue
X Vagus	Motor to muscles of pharynx and larynx
XI Hypoglossal	Motor to tongue
XII Spinal Accessory	Motor to sternocleidomastoid muscles and trapezius muscles

From Malasanos L, Barkauskas V, and Stoltenberg-Allen K: Health assessment, ed 4, St Louis, 1990, Mosby-Year Book Inc, p. 494.

tendon reflex) or the skin (superficial or cutaneous reflex) to produce a response. Certain reflexes (pathologic) are present only in disease or following injury to the central nervous system.

The nurse may be asked to assist with the examination. The equipment needed to perform a neurologic examination may be located on a special tray and should include a tongue blade, a pin with sharp and dull ends, a wisp of cotton, a tuning fork, a percussion hammer, a flashlight, and an ophthalmoscope. After the physical examination the neurologist may order special examinations, including x-rays, laboratory examinations and computerized tomography.

Examination of Cerebrospinal Fluid

Cerebrospinal fluid is a clear, colorless, odorless solution that bathes the brain and spinal cord. It

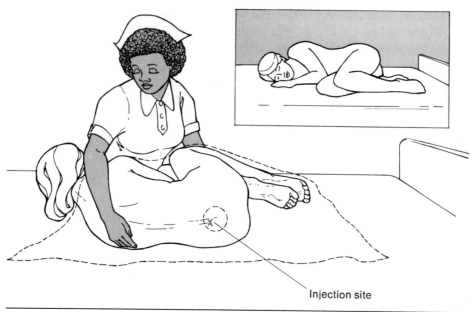

Injection site

Figure 22-2
Position of patient for lumbar puncture.

serves as a shock absorber and cushions the brain and spinal cord from injury during movement.

Lumbar puncture

A lumbar puncture consists of withdrawing a small amount of spinal fluid, usually 8 to 10 ml, for diagnostic purposes. The procedure usually is performed in the patient's room or in the outpatient clinic, with the patient being allowed to go home after its completion. Before the examination the nurse should explain the procedure to the patient, emphasizing the need to remain completely still. The patient should be reassured that a local anesthetic (procaine 1%) will be used but that some pressure or slight pain, which may extend down the legs, may be felt. The procedure usually takes only a few minutes to complete.

Before the procedure the nurse should assemble the equipment for the physician. Strict surgical asepsis must be maintained in any procedure in which direct penetration of the central nervous system is made. During the procedure the patient either is placed in the side-lying position near the edge of the bed with the knees pulled up, the back bowed, and the chin and knees close together, (Figure 22-2) or sitting up and bending forward. The procedure consists of inserting a small needle between the third and fourth lumbar vertebrae (level with top of hip bones), which is below the level where the spinal cord ends. The physician then measures cerebrospinal fluid pressure with a manometer. Several specimens of fluid are collected in test tubes, using care to ensure that specimens are labeled correctly and taken immediately to the laboratory for examination. Throughout the procedure the nurse should provide emotional support and encourage the patient to relax and lie quietly. The nurse should observe and record any significant reactions to the procedure, noting any changes in pulse, respiratory rate, or skin color.

After a lumbar puncture a common complaint is headache. Although its exact cause is unknown, the loss of cerebrospinal fluid may contribute to its development. Headache resulting from lumbar puncture is usually relieved by lying flat, applying an ice cap to the head, and administering mild analgesics.

Queckenstedt's test (lumbar puncture with dynamics)

Queckenstedt's test is performed in connection with the lumbar puncture when the physician suspects partial or complete blockage of cerebrospinal fluid circulation as a result of spinal tumor or dislocation or fracture of a vertebra. Performance of

Queckenstedt's test is contraindicated in the presence of suspected intracranial hemorrhage or increased intracranial pressure. A manometer is attached to the lumbar puncture needle, and the cerebrospinal fluid pressure is measured. Digital pressure is placed on the jugular veins of the neck. Normally, the cerebrospinal fluid pressure rises but then falls rapidly as the digital pressure is released. If a block is present in the canal, the cerebrospinal fluid pressure will scarcely be affected or will rise and fall slowly. To prevent possible anxiety and fright, the patient should be told in advance that pressure will be exerted on the neck for a few seconds.

Cisternal puncture

Cisternal puncture is another method of obtaining cerebrospinal fluid for examination. In this procedure the cerebrospinal fluid is obtained by inserting a short-beveled needle just below the occipital bone into the cisterna magna (Figure 22-3). The back of the patient's head may be shaved. The patient is placed in the lateral position with the head bent forward and held securely in place by the nurse. Cisternal puncture is frequently the procedure of choice on small children. Some physicians prefer it to lumbar puncture because headache is not as common.

Neuroradiologic Studies

Cerebral angiography, pneumoencephalography, ventriculography, and myelography are contrast studies that allow for detection of pathologic disorders of the brain and spinal cord. These procedures are done in either the x-ray department or the operating room. Most procedures require only a local anesthetic preceded by mild sedation, but in some cases a general anesthetic may be used. The nurse may not be concerned directly with the examination but will help to provide care of the patient before and after it is conducted.

Cerebral angiography (arteriography)

Cerebral angiography allows for visualization of the cerebral arterial system. A radiopaque substance is injected into an artery of the arm or neck and x-ray films of the head are taken. As the substance circulates in the arterial system, lesions such as cerebral aneurysms, tumors, or ruptured blood vessels can be seen.

Usually the femoral or brachial artery is used and pressure must be applied to the site after the procedure is finished. Following the procedure

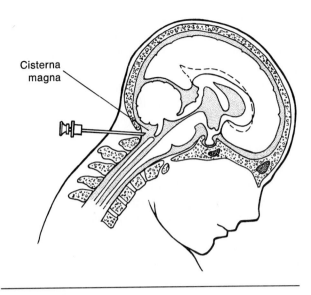

Figure 22-3
Cisternal puncture, showing location for insertion of needle.

the nurse should carefully inspect whichever site is used to ensure that bleeding has not occurred or that a hematoma has not developed. If the carotid artery is used, the nurse should observe for signs of respiratory distress after the procedure because edema around the site may compress the trachea. Patients with sensitivity to the contrast media may experience nausea and vomiting after the procedure.[10] Usually the patient tolerates the procedure well and can resume normal activities within a few hours. Occasionally, neurologic symptoms increase after the procedure or the patient has a delayed allergic reaction to the dye. An ice collar applied to the injection site helps prevent bleeding and local edema.

Pneumoencephalography (air encephalography)

Pneumoencephalography consists of the introduction of air or oxygen into the *subarachnoid space* after the removal of small amounts of cerebrospinal fluid through a lumbar or cisternal puncture. This procedure is performed to visualize accurately any abnormal shape or position of the ventricular and subarachnoid space. The procedure is technically difficult and uncomfortable for the patient, and severe headache, nausea, and vomiting are common after this examination. The headache caused by the air in the ventricular spaces usually subsides with 12 to 48 hours and may be relieved by administering analgesics, keeping the head of the bed flat, and applying an ice cap to the patient's head. Infrequently, severe reactions to pneumoencephalography occur, and the patient must be observed closely during and after the procedure for signs of seizures, shock, and increased intracranial pressure.[5] The procedure is contraindicated if increased intracranial pressure is present.

Ventriculography

Ventriculography is similar to pneumoencephalography except that air is introduced directly into the lateral ventricles (spaces within the brain) through small openings (burr holes) in the skull. The procedure usually is done in the operating room.

Myelography

Myelography is an x-ray examination of the spinal cord and vertebral canal following injection of air or contrast media (dye) through a lumbar puncture. The purpose of the procedure is to identify tumors of the spinal cord or ruptured intervertebral disks. Some dyes used in the procedure can cause serious irritation and must be removed on completion of the x-ray examination by drawing the dye back through the lumbar puncture needle. The patient should be observed closely for signs of an allergic reaction. Water-soluble contrast media are now available and cause fewer side effects because they are self-absorbing and nonirritative.

Computed tomography (CT scan)

The simplicity of this new noninvasive radiologic procedure, the low risk to patients, and the low exposure to x-rays have virtually revolutionized the diagnosis of neurologic disorders. Computed tomography (formerly known as computerized axial tomography, or CAT scan) is a diagnostic technique used to study the structure of the brain. Its three-dimensional views of the brain content allow for differentiation between intracranial tumors, cysts, edema, and hemorrhage. A narrow beam of x-rays is directed through the brain from one side of the head. A recording then is made of the amount of radiation not absorbed by the brain cavity. Through interpreting changes in density from that of normal brain tissue, a diagnosis can be made. The patient needs no special preparation for this procedure but should be told that his or her head will be immobilized in a snug-fitting rubber cone.

Two additional computerized techniques available at some of the larger health-care centers are magnetic resonance imaging (MRI) and posi-tron emission tomography (PET) scanning. The PET scan provides information about physiologic function rather than anatomy, which is the case with the CT and MRI scans.[3] The MRI scanner is useful for the diagnosis of demyelinating diseases and diseases resulting from neuronal degeneration.[8,19]

Electrodiagnostic Studies
Electroencephalography

Electroencephalography (EEG) is a graphic recording of the brain's electrical activity and can be performed on persons of any age. The EEG is not considered conclusive but may be helpful in locating the site of a lesion or determining the presence of epilepsy. The test is performed by placing small electrodes at specified locations on each side of the patient's scalp. The electrodes are connected by wires to a recording machine. The scalp should be clean, but no other preparation is necessary. The EEG is performed in a darkened room to avoid outside distractions and takes 1 to 2 hours to complete. Before the test the patient should not take stimulants or depressants of any kind (coffee, tea, colas, alcoholic beverages, or sedatives). No specific follow-up nursing care is required.

Electromyography

Electromyography (EMG) is a diagnostic test that measures and records the electrical activity of muscles. The EMG is useful in detecting dysfunction of the motor neuron, the neuromuscular junction, or muscle fibers. Either surface electrodes are applied to the skin's surface or needle electrodes are inserted into the muscle. Patients should be assured that they are in no danger of being electrocuted. Some discomfort may be felt, however, when the muscles are stimulated.

Other Tests
Echoencephalography

Echoencephalography is a diagnostic test that uses ultrasound to provide information about the position of the midline of the brain. It is useful in detecting cerebral masses that cause shifts in the brain from the midline. Ultrasonic pulses are beamed through the head in the temporoparietal region and a recording is made of the returning echoes.

Caloric test

The caloric test is done to evaluate equilibrium by testing the vestibular branch of the eighth cranial nerve. Lesions in the brainstem and the cerebellum can be differentiated using this test. Cold or hot water is allowed to drip into the ear and is stopped the moment the patient complains of dizziness or nausea or if the physician observes any symptoms such as nystagmus. If no signs or symptoms occur within 3 minutes, the irrigation is terminated. Each ear is irrigated separately; the entire procedure usually takes between 30 and 40 minutes to complete.

Brain scan

A solution of radioactive material is injected intravenously, and after 4 hours a Geiger counter or scintillator is used to determine the uptake of the material. If tumors are present in the brain, they tend to retain the radioactive material. Because minute amounts of radioactive material are used, the patient is not considered to be radioactive. When used with other tests and examinations, the isotope has been found to give good diagnostic data.

Nursing Intervention

The procedures just outlined are among the most common ones used. The specific nursing care before and after each depends on the patient, the particular hospital, and the physician. Most of these procedures require that signed permission be obtained from the patient. Patients having ventriculography and pneumoencephalography receive care similar to that given to any preoperative and postoperative patient (see Chapter 5). In addition, these patients should be observed closely for evidence of neurologic symptoms—for example, increased intracranial pressure, respiratory distress, and seizures.

The patient and family also will need accurate information and opportunities to ask questions and express concerns. Patients undergoing these procedures are likely to be stressed as a result of the factors that brought them to seek treatment and may be anxious about what the findings will mean to them and their families.

ALTERED STATES OF AWARENESS

Awareness or **consciousness** can be thought of as being on a continuum from a state of complete wakefulness to that of sleep or **coma**. A certain portion of the brainstem (reticular formation) is responsible for maintaining wakefulness. Another aspect of consciousness under the control of the cerebral cortex is the ability to perform complex mental activites. Thought, association, discrimination, judgment, and memory all are the responsibility of the cerebral cortex. Memory allows knowledge to be reproduced for use. These functions may be disrupted or disturbed temporarily after a head injury or in certain disease conditions. In addition, deterioration of brain cells and nerve tissue occurs with the normal aging process. Although the aged person may exhibit behaviors characteristic of patients with brain disorders, many are normal for the aging process.

The nurse who is in frequent contact with patients may be the first person to note changes in levels of awareness. Physicians rely on nurses to assess and record accurately any changes in the patient's neurologic status. Seemingly insignificant changes in behavior may be important in the diagnosis and treatment of the patient's condition. Therefore any changes should be documented carefully and reported at once.

Several descriptive terms have been used to explain the deviation from normal conscious behavior. The nurse should become familiar with the terms and be able to apply them correctly.

Consciousness-Unconsciousness

Because **consciousness** is a subjective state, various objective behaviors must be relied on to determine accurately the patient's level of consciousness. Such behaviors include the patient's responses to verbal and visual stimuli, responses to touch or painful stimuli, motor activity, reflex responses, and vital signs.

Coma

The comatose patient is in an abnormally deep sleep and cannot be aroused by external stimuli. **Coma** may result from brain disorders, metabolic disorders, trauma, and functional or psychiatric disorders. It is always to be considered a serious condition.

In an effort to standardize the reporting of consciousness level, an assessment tool has been developed that measures patient eye opening and verbal and motor response to verbal or painful stimuli. This scale, called the Glasgow Coma Scale (Table 22-2), is simple to use and allows rapid determination of the level of consciousness. The scale is divided into three sections, each of which measures a separate dimension of consciousness level. The first component assesses the patient's eye-opening response, the second his or her motor response, and the third his or her verbal

Table 22-2

Glasgow Coma Scale		
Test	**Response**	**Score**
Best eye opening	Opens spontaneously	4
	Opens to verbal command	3
	Opens to pain	2
	No response	1
Best motor response	Obeys verbal command	6
	Localizes to painful stimulus	5
	Withdrawal from painful stimulus	4
	Abnormal flexion to painful stimulus	3
	Abnormal extension to painful stimulus	2
	No response	1
Best verbal response	Oriented and converses	5
	Disoriented and converses	4
	Inappropriate words	3
	Incomprehensible sounds	2
	No response	1
	TOTAL	15

From Jennet B and Teasdale G: Lancet 1:878-881, 1977.

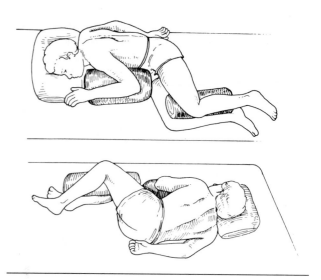

Figure 22-4

Positioning of comatose or unconscious patient.

response. Each of these segments is scored by the degree of responsiveness, as shown in Table 22-2.

Scores assigned to each of the sections are based on the patient's best response in that area. The individual subcategory scores are then totaled to determine the overall level of consciousness score, which can range from 3 to 15. The less responsive the patient, the lower the score; the more responsive the patient, the higher the score.

The tool has been used with some success in predicting morbidity and mortality following head injury.[1,14] Patients with Glasgow Coma Scale scores of 3 to 4 within the first 24 hours of coma have been found to have only a 7% chance of achieving independence, as compared with those who have scores of 11 or more, of whom 82% regain independence.

Intervention

Because unconsciousness may result from a number of conditions, medical treatment is directed toward identifying and treating the underlying cause. With loss of consciousness, the patient depends completely on the nurse for the basic needs of life and comfort. Nursing priorities should be to ensure adequate oxygenation of tissue and circulation of blood flow. The maintenance of a patent airway is vital. Frequent observation of the patient's vital signs and neurologic status is necessary. Prevention of the complications of immobility, such as pneumonia, contractures, and pressure areas, must always be a major concern of nursing (Figure 22-4). The general nursing interventions for the unconscious patient are summarized in the boxed material.

Confusion-Delirium

With damage to the cerebral cortex, changes in the patient's mental status occur. Patients may not recognize familiar persons (e.g., wife, son), be able to identify their home, or state the day, month, or year correctly.

Confusion (disorientation)

The elderly person, the posttrauma patient, or the patient with a severe illness who is apprehensive and anxious is often confused. **Confusion** is a state in which patients have poor memory, inability to think clearly, and impaired perception. They may make mistakes in identifying people or may misinterpret conversations. Disorientation to time and place may be an early indication of confusion. This state, which often worsens at night, may occur intermittently or go on for several days.

Delirium

Delirium is a symptom of a major distortion of cerebral function and may result from infections

---

NURSING CARE GUIDELINES
The Unconscious Patient

Nursing diagnoses

- Ineffective airway clearance
- Total incontinence
- Potential ineffective breathing patterns
- Potential impaired gas exchange
- Impaired swallowing
- High risk for injury
- Impaired physical mobility
- Potential alteration in nutrition, less than body requirements
- Potential alteration in oral mucous membranes
- Self-care deficit
- Potential impairment of skin integrity

Nursing interventions

- Ensure an open airway; insertion of an oral airway or tracheostomy may be necessary
- Position patient in lateral or semiprone position to facilitate drainage of oral secretions (Figure 22-4)
- Aspirate tracheal and oral secretions by suctioning patient as necessary
- Check vital signs, neurologic signs (pupillary reaction, reflexes) and levels of consciousness every 15 minutes for first several hours and then every hour for 24 hours
- Turn patient every 2 hours
- Maintain proper body alignment by positioning patient to prevent foot-drop, wrist-drop, and joint contracture

- Carry out passive range of motion exercises on all joints at least four times a day
- Use sheepskin pads, water mattresses, or alternating air flotation systems to prevent pressure sores
- Protect eyes from irritation and corneal ulceration—use eye shields, eye irrigations with physiologic saline, or eye lubricants and ointments as ordered by physician
- Monitor intravenous fluids or tube feedings closely; do not give unconscious patients oral fluids
- Carry out frequent oral hygiene
- Monitor patient's urinary output closely; if indwelling catheter is in place, tape to abdomen for male patient (Figure 22-9)
- Administer suppositories or enemas or both as necessary to maintain bowel elimination
- Provide emotional support and reassurance to family; allow family members to assist in care when feasible

Expected outcomes

- Maximum pulmonary function maintained
- Aspiration prevented
- Skin integrity maintained
- Adequate nutritional status maintained

---

causing high temperatures, toxic conditions, or brain disorders. Individuals who have used alcohol over a period of years may become delirious when they cannot obtain alcohol. This type of delirium is known as *delirium tremens* or *alcohol psychosis*.[17] Delirium is characterized by progressive disorientation to time, place, and, finally, persons. Delirious patients may become agitated and combative or withdraw and become secretive. They must be protected from injuring themselves or others. Delirium frequently involves misinterpretation of visual and auditory stimuli. For example, patients may claim they see snakes and worms crawling over the bed or hear voices that are not present. Talkativeness, overalertness, and insomnia occur. Lack of sleep frequently is cited as one of the important variables causing delir-

ium. Delirium may be seen in patients in intensive care units when they receive excessive sensory stimuli. Nursing care should be directed toward providing meaningful, reality-oriented information and protecting the patient from injury[17] (see the box on nursing interventions for the confused patient on p. 630).

Increased Intracranial Pressure

The cranial contents, brain tissue, vascular tissue, and cerebrospinal fluid all are contained within the body framework of the skull. Any increase in the amount of any of these contents will cause an increase in **intracranial pressure (ICP).** Some of the more common causes of this condition are cerebral edema, hemorrhage, tumor, or trauma. The symptoms of increased intracranial pressure

---

result from direct pressure to the cerebral contents. Prolonged increases in pressure will cause brain cells to die because of lack of oxygen. The nurse should report immediately any evidence of increased intracranial pressure so that treatment can be started at once. Increased intracranial pressure is considered to be an emergency situation. Observation of the patient should include the following[5]:

1. State of awareness—signs of increasing restlessness, confusion, delirium, or subtle changes in level of consciousness
2. Headache—constant and increasing in intensity
3. Vital signs—slowly falling pulse and respirations accompanied by a rise in blood pressure
4. Pupils—slow or sluggish reaction; unequal size of pupils or one pupil fixed and dilated

5. Motor response—muscle weakness or resistance to passive movement; evidence of *decorticate posturing* (adduction and abnormal flexion of arms with rigid extension and external rotation of legs) or *decerebrate posturing* (rigid abnormal extension of all extremities)

Early symptoms of rise in ICP include development or worsening of headache, confusion, drowsiness, and transient episodes of change in neurologic status.[20] Late signs include loss of consciousness, change in pupil size, widened pulse pressure, slowed pulse, and drecreased or irregular respiratory rate. By the time these late indicators appear, however, considerable damage to brain cells may have occurred. Close monitoring of early symptoms is essential to prevent serious injury as intracranial pressure rises. Any early indication of increased ICP should be reported immediately.

Intervention

Medical treatment for patients with increased intracranial pressure is directed toward removing the causative factor and reducing the cerebral edema and pressure. Drugs such as corticosteroids or mannitol may be given to promote diuresis. Nursing intervention is aimed primarily at early detection of signs of increased pressure and controlling any factors that may increase cerebral pressure further (see the box on p. 631).

Close monitoring of the ICP can be accomplished through the use of subarachnoid screws, epidural sensors, or intraventricular catheters. These devices allow for continuous measurement of ICP. The intraventricular catheter also facilitates the withdrawal or drainage of cerebrospinal fluid when the ICP rises above pathologic levels (>25 mm Hg). Care must be taken not to drain the ventricles too rapidly because subdural hematoma or subarachnoid hemorrhage can result.[22]

Seizure Disorders

The term **convulsion** frequently is used interchangeably with the term **seizure**. Convulsion refers only to the involuntary muscular contractions that occur during a seizure; seizure refers to the entire event. The term "fit" should be avoided because it is inappropriate. Seizures may occur at any age and are associated with a variety of diseases and disorders.

Seizures represent some disturbance of cerebral function in which a sudden, excessive, and

---

NURSING CARE GUIDELINES
Increased Intracranial Pressure

Nursing diagnoses
- Sensory perceptual alterations
- Self-care deficit
- Impaired physical mobility
- Potential ineffective airway clearance
- Potential ineffective breathing patterns
- Potential alteration in nutrition, less than body requirements
- High risk for injury
- Potential impaired swallowing
- Potential total incontinence
- Alteration in thought processes

Nursing interventions
- Elevate head approximately 30 degrees to improve cerebral drainage
- Check vital signs, blood pressure, neurologic signs, and level of consciousness every hour for first 24 hours
- Minimize situations that cause an increase in intracranial pressure—for example, vomiting, coughing, straining during bowel movements, or changing position
- Maintain an open airway and use oxygen therapy as ordered to prevent decreased oxygenation of brain tissue
- Monitor intravenous fluids closely; do not overhydrate by infusing intravenous solutions or blood transfusions rapidly
- Accurately measure intake and output
- Know the differences between symptoms of increased intracranial pressure and shock
- Check with physician about hyperventilating patient to keep P_aCO_2 at 25 to 30 mm Hg
- Report immediately to physician any changes in patient's condition

Expected outcomes
- Injuries prevented
- Maximum pulmonary function maintained
- Aspiration prevented
- Skin integrity maintained
- Adequate nutritional status and fluid intake maintained
- Participates in self care as appropriate
- Relates rationale for interventions

---

disorderly discharge of electric impulses from nerve cells occurs. Seizures occur with many illnesses, including some psychologic and neurologic conditions. They also may occur following a traumatic injury to the brain. Children are especially prone to seizures with temperature elevation. Seizures do not always follow any single pattern or form; their characteristics depend on the area of the brain from which they originate.

Seizure disorder is a term used to identify recurrent episodes of disturbances in cerebral functioning resulting in convulsive movements, loss of consciousness, and abnormal sensory or behavioral manifestations. Up to 4 million people in the United States have some form of this disorder. It has been one of the least understood conditions since ancient times, often being related to divine origin and clouded in superstition. Today the causes of seizures are better understood, and the condition usually can be controlled. In some cases, the cause may not be specifically identified (*idiopathic epilepsy*). An inherited tendency is thought to play a role in some. Other causes include metabolic disturbances, congenital malformations, trauma, and neurologic conditions of the cerebral cortex. Although several types of seizures exist, this discussion is limited to grand mal, focal, petit mal, and psychomotor seizures.

Grand mal (tonic-clonic) seizures

Grand mal seizures are the most common type, characterized by generalized convulsions and loss of consciousness. Patients often have some warning or sign of the approaching attack, which is called an aura, but almost immediately become unconscious, often falling. The attack may be immediately preceded by a cry, which occurs as the thoracic and abdominal muscles go into spasm, forcing air out of the lungs. The body becomes rigid, with legs extended straight, the jaws tightly clenched, and the hands gripped tightly (tonic phase). A temporary cessation of respiration with cyanosis may occur at this time. The eyes are wide open and pupils dilated. In a few seconds the convulsive stage begins, with all the muscles beginning to jerk and twitch violently (clonic phase). Bowel and bladder incontinence and profuse salivation occur. The convulsive state is of short duration, but the patient may remain unconscious or drowsy. The patient may then fall into a deep sleep that may last from several minutes to several hours. On awakening, the person will not remember having the seizure but may complain of headache, slight nausea, and general malaise. After the convulsive state some patients may become mentally confused and violent.

Occasionally, typical grand mal seizures are preceded by convulsive twitching in one part of the body, which spreads to other areas of the body. This type of seizure is called a *focal*, or *jacksonian*, seizure. Focal seizures may be limited to a specific part of the body, and a grand mal seizure may not occur.

Status epilepticus is a condition in which seizures recur without recovery between them. Respiration is disturbed, blood pressure is elevated, and sweating and elevation of temperature occur. The condition may continue for hours or days and is serious because brain damage is possible. Emergency treatment always is required.

Petit mal (absences) seizures

Petit mal seizures are a mild form of the disease in which an aura is not present, and only momentary loss of consciousness occurs. Tonic-clonic convulsions do not occur, and only a slight twitching of the face or nod of the head may be observed. A patient with petit mal seizures may have several attacks in a day. These seizures are common in children under 10 years of age, and often are outgrown at puberty. Because of the frequency of these attacks, children may have problems in school. Some patients experience both grand mal and petit mal convulsions.

Psychomotor (temporal lobe) attacks

Psychomotor attacks frequently are associated with brain damage, specifically of the temporal lobe. Patients do not lose consciousness but automatically perform normal actions although they are not aware of what is happening and cannot remember their actions afterward. Behavior may seem purposeless or inappropriate, and patients may have sensory disturbances. The individual may become drowsy, angry, or fearful or exhibit antisocial behavior. Attacks may last from 30 seconds to several minutes. This type of seizure disorder commonly is seen in children between ages 11 and 15.

Intervention

Treatment of seizure disorder is aimed at eliminating factors that precipitate seizures and control of seizures through regular administration of anticonvulsant medication. A program that includes regulation of rest, diet, activity, fluids, and med-

ication should be followed on a regular basis. Medication is prescribed for the purpose of preventing seizures, and any attempt on the part of the patient to skip, reduce, or otherwise alter the schedule of dosage may cause the return of serious seizures. Drugs in use for treatment of grand mal seizures and some psychomotor attacks include phenytoin (Dilantin), 0.2 to 0.6 g daily; phenobarbital, 0.06 to 0.02 g daily; primidone (Mysoline), 0.5 to 2 g daily; ethotoin (Peganone), 0.5 to 1 g daily; and carbamazepine (Tegretol), 1 to 1.2 g daily. The most effective drug in current use for petit mal seizures is ethosuximide (Zarontin), 0.5 to 2 g daily. Phensuximide (Milontin) and acetazolamide (Diamox) are of less value. Drugs may be used singly or in combination to enhance their action (synergistic effect) and decrease toxic side effects. All medication is administered in divided doses, and the patient should be observed for toxic effects such as skin rash, nervousness, drowsiness, fatigue, ataxia, and nystagmus. Because of the possible toxic effects from drugs, all patients should be under medical supervision. Periodic blood counts are performed because some drugs may cause depression of bone marrow. Surgery may be useful in treating a small number of persons with well-defined and localized seizures that do not respond to anticonvulsant medication.

The nurse should be aware of all patients with a history of seizures admitted to the hospital. Necessary precautions for the care of patients with seizures should be taken. In addition, the nurse should be aware and inform the physician of all anticonvulsant medications that the patient is taking because many of these drugs interact with other medications.

One of the most important responsibilities of the nurse in caring for patients with seizure disorders is patient education. Patients should understand the nature of their seizure activity, their medication programs, the potential side effects of drugs, and the danger of not taking medications exactly as prescribed. Also, the nurse should emphasize the importance of adequate rest, a well-balanced diet and avoidance of situations that may precipitate a seizure, such as extreme physical exertion, infection, and emotional stress. Patients should be advised not to participate in activities that may endanger their lives, such as working near dangerous machinery, climbing ladders, or swimming alone. Driving an automobile is permitted, providing seizures have been under complete control for an extended time.

People with epilepsy live in a world of insecurity and misunderstanding. They constantly anticipate and fear a seizure and its embarrassment. They often are rejected, avoided, and discriminated against and may become lonely individuals who need help. People with epilepsy should carry an identification card or wear a Medic Alert bracelet or tag.

The Epilepsy Foundation of America* can provide information and support to the patient and family.

Once a seizure has begun, the main responsibilities of the nurse are to protect the patient from injury and to accurately observe and record the patient's behavior before, during, and following the seizure (see box to the right). A careful and accurate recording from the initial onset of the seizure until its completion can assist the physician in locating the site of the cerebral lesion and in planning further care and treatment for the patient. Observation of the patient's seizure should include the following:

1. Exact time of onset, duration, and ending of the seizure
2. Presence or absence of preconvulsive signs (aura)—behaviors observed or anything patient says
3. Level of consciousness before, during, and after seizure (Table 21-1)
4. Progression and type of muscular activity—**rigidity** of muscles and joints (tonic phase) or jerking and twitching of muscles (clonic phase); parts of body involved; where convulsions began and how they progressed
5. Presence of cyanosis or respiratory difficulty
6. Presence or absence of urinary or fecal incontinence
7. Movements of tongue or eyeballs; note any pupillary changes
8. Postseizure behavior
9. Any injury that may have occurred during seizure

Depending on the patient's age and underlying disease condition, the physician may order diazepam (Valium), 5 to 10 mg, amobarbital (Amytal), 0.25 to 0.5 g, or phenytoin (Dilantin) 50 mg, intravenously. Dosages may be repeated if seizure

---

NURSING CARE GUIDELINES
The Patient with Seizures

Nursing diagnoses
- High risk for injury
- Ineffective airway clearance
- Ineffective breathing patterns
- Potential total incontinence
- Impaired swallowing
- Impaired physical mobility
- Self-care deficit
- Impaired verbal communication

Nursing interventions
- Do not leave patient unattended; do not attempt to move patient
- Insert plastic airway or padded tongue blade between patient's back teeth *only* if patient's jaw is relaxed; do not attempt to forcibly open patient's jaw if teeth are clenched
- Keep padded side rails up at all times; may be lowered during seizure
- Maintain patent airway and adequate ventilation; suctioning and oxygen may be necessary
- If patient is standing, lower carefully to floor and place pad under head
- Accompany patients with frequent seizures when ambulating
- Administer anticonvulsive medications as ordered; notify physician if patient is unable to take medication for any reason
- Accurately record all aspects of the seizure
- Respect dignity of patient—provide privacy if possible

Expected outcomes
- Injuries prevented
- Maximum pulmonary function maintained
- Aspiration prevented
- Participates in self-care as appropriate
- Relates rationale for interventions
- Demonstrates ability to understand and express self
- Demonstrates understanding of interventions

---

*Epilepsy Foundation of America, 4351 Garden City Drive, Landover, MD 20785

activity continues. In the presence of prolonged, continuous seizure activity, thiopental (Pentothal) or ether by inhalation may be used.

Abnormal Body Temperature Elevation (Hyperthermia, Hyperpyrexia)

Abnormally high temperature elevations—103°F (39.5°C) or above—may occur in patients with neurologic disease caused by malfunction of the temperature regulatory center in the hypothalamus. This condition, **hyperthermia,** may result from overwhelming infectious processes in the body or prolonged exposure of an individual to extremely high environmental temperatures (heatstroke or sunstroke). In heatstroke the body cannot dissipate heat as fast as it is being received from external sources. A notable absence of sweating, the usual protective mechanism that cools the overly heated body, occurs. Body temperature may be in excess of 106°F (41°C). During hyperthermia the increased body metabolism demands increased amounts of oxygen and glucose. In patients with cerebral disorders, hyperthermia may result in additional brain damage.

Patient care is focused on reducing the elevated body temperature. A number of methods may be used to lower the patient's temperature (see box to the right). Care should be taken that the patient's temperature is not lowered too rapidly. Heart irregularities or cardiac arrest or both may occur with sudden or excessive cooling.

THE PATIENT WITH DISEASES AND DISORDERS OF THE NERVOUS SYSTEM

Infectious Diseases
Meningitis

Meningitis is an inflammation of the meninges covering the brain and spinal cord. Common causes of the disease are meningococcal, pneumococcal, streptococcal, and *Haemophilus influenzae* infections. The causative organism may reach the meninges through the bloodstream after a systemic infection. Meningitis also may develop by direct extension from an adjacent infected area, such as in otitis media or mastoiditis. The disease often occurs in sporadic epidemics and is a threat where crowded conditions exist. Children are more frequently affected than adults because of their tendency to develop ear infections.

> ### NURSING CARE GUIDELINES
> *Abnormal Temperature Elevation*
>
> **Nursing diagnoses**
> - Ineffective thermoregulation
> - Hyperthermia
> - Self-care deficit
> - Potential fluid volume deficit
> - Potential alteration in thought processes
>
> **Nursing interventions**
> - Control room temperature with air conditioning or fans
> - Remove all excessive clothing and coverings from patient—only a light cover should be used
> - Ice bags may be applied to axillae, groin, and trunk areas—fill and reposition as necessary
> - Administer antipyretic drugs (aspirin or acetaminophen) as ordered
> - Monitor and record vital signs frequently—take rectal temperature at least every hour
> - Use electric cooling blanket as ordered—blanket should be placed under patient with protective covering between cooling blanket and skin surface
> - Observe patient's skin frequently for signs of ischemia, frostbite, edema, or discoloration
> - Cleanse and massage skin surfaces frequently
>
> **Expected outcomes**
> - Normal body temperature maintained
> - Participates in self-care as appropriate
> - Relates rationale for interventions
> - Demonstrates ability to understand and express self

The onset of symptoms varies according to the causative organism. Clinical symptoms usually develop within 48 hours, although meningococcal meningitis has a more rapid onset of 8 to 12 hours. The diagnosis is made through analysis of cerebrospinal fluid, including culture or smear examination to determine the causative organism. Symptoms of meningitis include headache, severely rigid and stiff neck (nuchal **rigidity**), markedly elevated temperature, lethargy, and confusion. As the disease progresses, nausea, vomiting, photophobia (intolerance to light), and convulsions frequently occur. **Opisthotonos** (arching of the back) may be seen.

Intervention. Treatment for meningitis includes prompt administration of antibiotic therapy. Aqueous penicillin or ampicillin is given intravenously in large doses. Tetracyclines, erythromycin, and sulfonamides may be used when the patient is sensitive to penicillin. Intravenous fluids usually are given during the acute phase and should be monitored carefully to prevent rapid infusion, which could result in cerebral edema. Analgesics and an ice bag may be used to relieve the headache. The patient should be placed in a quiet, slightly darkened room because of the photophobia and tendency for seizures. Isolation precautions are necessary for patients with meningococcal infections and may be required in some areas for all types of meningitis until the causative organism has been identified. Nose and throat secretions of patients should be handled with gloves, and extreme caution should be used to avoid transmission of the disease by contamination with respiratory secretions.

General supportive measures necessary for any acutely ill patient, including regular turning intervals, maintenance of good body alignment, and accurate monitoring and recording of fluid intake and urinary output, are required. Depending on the patient's condition, measures to control the elevated temperature and seizures may be necessary. The patient should have constant attendance and be observed for evidence of increased intracranial pressure. The outcome cannot always be predicted, and, if the patient recovers, residual damage such as blindness, deafness, mental retardation, or paralysis may occur.

Encephalitis

Encephalitis is an acute febrile illness with evidence of involvement of brain tissue. It may be caused by viruses, bacteria, fungi, chemical substances, toxins, or injury. It also may occur with or following one of the acute infectious diseases of childhood (measles, rubella) or may be a complication of measles, chickenpox, or rabies vaccination (postvaccinal encephalitis). Residual neurologic disorders may follow encephalitis, including a slowly developing parkinsonian syndrome. The disease occurs sporadically and in epidemics, with the greatest incidence during the late summer or fall months. On average, about 1400 cases occur each year in the United States, although during severe epidemics the total number of cases may be greater. Mortality is variable and ranges from a minimum of 5% to 70%.

Viral encephalitis is caused by several viruses, including the herpes simplex virus. Among the viral infections most commonly encountered are those caused by mosquitoes (arthropod-borne encephalitis). The virus is transmitted to humans by the bite of an infected mosquito. It cannot be transmitted from person to person. Evidence indicates the virus is harbored by several species of wild birds or horses. The mosquito becomes infected through biting these infected birds or animals. These forms of arthropod-borne encephalitis have been classified as St. Louis encephalitis, eastern equine encephalitis, western equine encephalitis, and Japanese B encephalitis. St. Louis encephalitis is the most common type, and several epidemics have occurred in recent years. Eastern encephalitis may have a mortality rate as high as 60% to 70%. Very young and elderly persons are most frequently affected, although persons of all ages may contract the disease. Each of the viral types is caused by a different virus, although they may be related.

The symptoms are fairly uniform for all types of encephalitis. The onset is sudden, with an elevation of temperature to 104° to 105°F (40° to 40.5°C), increased pulse rate, and severe headache unrelieved by analgesics. Symptoms include nausea, vomiting, tremor of the hands, tongue, and lips, stiffness of the neck, speech difficulty, and drowsiness. In severe cases convulsions, coma, and death may occur suddenly.

Intervention. For patients with viral encephalitis no specific treatment is indicated. Isolation is not required, since encephalitis is not transmitted from person to person. As a precautionary measure, however, some states require isolation up to 7 days, depending on the type of encephalitis. Nursing care requires careful observation of the patient, because progress of the disease may be rapid. The patient is critically ill, and nursing care is based on symptoms. Variations in level of consciousness and mental status should be considered in planning care for these patients. If respiratory difficulties occur, a tracheostomy and mechanical ventilation may be necessary. Seizures are not uncommon, and necessary precautions should be taken. Fluids may be given intravenously and a diet high in calories and proteins is given orally or by gavage. Hot, moist packs applied to muscles may relieve painful spasms. Meticulous oral hygiene and skin care are necessary because of profuse diaphoresis, incontinence, and a disagreeable mouth odor. Residual disabilities may result, requiring prolonged periods of rehabilitative therapy.

Poliomyelitis (infantile paralysis)

Poliomyelitis is an acute infectious disease caused by three different strains of viruses. The disease affects the motor cells of the spinal cord and brainstem. Poliomyelitis is a highly communicable disease transmitted through secretions from the nose and throat and through the feces of infected persons. The incubation period is 1 to 3 weeks.

One of the outstanding medical advances of this century has been the discovery and production of the Salk vaccine and Sabin oral vaccine for immunization against poliomyelitis. Through the efforts of physicians, health departments, and public education, the widespread use of these poliovirus vaccines has resulted in a sharp decline in incidence since 1955. During 1978 four cases, three of which were paralytic, were reported to the Centers for Disease Control. Currently, concern is being expressed about the public's laxity in obtaining immunizations, which could result in increased incidence of the disease. The nurse should encourage mothers to take infants and young children to their physicians or health departments for inoculations (see Chapter 7). Recently, a syndrome in survivors of poliomyelitis has been identified. This syndrome consists of chronic fatigue, muscle weakness in unaffected muscles, and respiratory impairment. The mechanism for the syndrome is unknown, although it is believed to be caused by slow disintegration of nerve axons, which carry impulses to the muscle from the nerve cell.[21]

Central nervous system syphilis

Lesions caused by the syphilis organism (*Treponema pallidum*) may develop in the central nervous system and cause a wide variety of complex neurologic conditions. The three forms of neurologic disorders most often encountered are meningovascular syphilis, tabes dorsalis, and general paresis.

Meningovascular syphilis. This pathologic condition consists of lesions in the meninges of the brain and inflammation of the arteries, which leads to narrowing and occlusion. The acute form resembles meningitis caused by other bacteria, with the significant difference being that both the blood and the spinal fluid are reactive for syphilis. Fever, headache, vomiting, and rigidity of the neck may be present; vision may be blurred and paralysis of facial muscles may occur. In the chronic form of syphilitic meningitis the fever is low grade and loss of weight occurs. The first overt signs of meningovascular syphilis usually develop about 6 to 7 years after the original infection.

Tabes dorsalis (locomotor ataxia). This type of central nervous system syphilis, which develops 15 to 20 years after onset of the infection, involves the spinal cord. Degeneration of the sensory nerve roots and nerve pathways in the posterior columns occurs. The sense of equilibrium is destroyed so that patients are unaware of the position of their feet and legs. Their gait becomes staggering and unsteady, and they walk with a slapping movement of the feet. Patients must keep their eyes on their feet to be able to walk and are unable to walk in the dark. Sharp, stabbing, lightning-like pains occur most frequently in the legs. In the neurologic examination patients are asked to close their eyes and stand with their feet together. When tabes dorsalis is present, patients sway and will fall. This is known as a *positive Romberg's sign*. The patient's vision also may be affected. They become undernourished and are incontinent and impotent. At intervals they have sudden acute attacks of pain involving the stomach accompanied by severe vomiting (gastric crisis).

General paresis. General paresis, a more common form of neurosyphilis, occurs 15 to 20 years after the initial infection. The lesions primarily involve the cerebrum, and a gradual deterioration and atrophy of the brain occurs. A condition in which general paresis and tabes dorsalis occur together is called *taboparesis*. Over time, a change in personality occurs. Outbursts of temper, extreme irritability, impaired judgment, and the development of delusions of persecution or of grandeur may occur. The patient may become paranoid and be dangerous. The condition grows progressively worse until the patient must be admitted for psychiatric intervention.

Neurosyphilis can be prevented by early and adequate treatment (see Chapter 7).

Degenerative Diseases

Degenerative diseases of the central nervous system refer to conditions in which premature degeneration of nerve cells and pathways with no identifiable cause occurs. Familial factors, toxic agents, metabolic defects, and viral and immunologic mechanisms all have been suspected as possible causes. These conditions may develop over a period of years and result in some degree of chronic disability. Nursing care is concerned primarily with the care given any patient with chronic disease. Other concerns are to provide encouragement and emotional support for the patient and family, and to help the patient be independent and self-sufficient as long as possible. The major degenerative conditions that will be reviewed here are multiple sclerosis, amyotrophic lateral sclerosis, Parkinson's disease, and Huntington's chorea. Myasthenia gravis, although not a degenerative disease, will be discussed because of similarities with the other conditions.

Multiple sclerosis (disseminated sclerosis)

Multiple sclerosis is a chronic disease of the nervous system characterized by remissions and exacerbations. The disease affects the myelin sheaths (segmented covering around nerve fibers) resulting in numerous areas of demyelinization of nerve fibers of the spinal cord and brain. Later, patches of sclerotic nerve fibers (plaques) develop at these sites. The symptoms and severity of the disease are quite variable, depending on the location and extent of the lesions. Remissions of symptoms occur when partial healing in the area of demyelinization occurs. The disease is chronically progressive because residual disability usually increases after each exacerbation.

Epidemiologic studies indicate that multiple sclerosis is related to some environmental factor or factors encountered in childhood and has a prolonged period of latency. In nearly two-thirds of cases, the first symptoms of the disease begin between 20 and 40 years of age, with the peak incidence occurring between 30 and 35 years.

An estimated 250,000 people in the United States currently have multiple sclerosis. Studies have shown a high incidence of the disease in cold, damp climates. The disease occurs in less than 1 per 100,000 persons in equatorial areas; 6 to 14 per 100,000 in southern United States and Europe; and 30 to 80 per 100,000 in Canada, northern United States, and Europe. The course of the disease is unpredictable, with the life span after onset varying from 13 years to greater than 25 years. Many individuals are able to maintain normal lifestyles before they succumb to complications of the disease.

Assessment. The onset of the disease may be acute or may develop slowly over months or years. Diagnosis of the disease in its early stages is difficult because of the variation of symptoms. Because no specific diagnostic test is available, patients frequently are misdiagnosed or thought to have emotional problems. Among the earliest symptoms are double vision (diplopia), spots before the eyes (scotoma), blindness, tremor, weakness or numbness of a part of the body, and fatigue. As the disease progresses, nystagmus, paralysis, disorders of speech, urinary frequency and urgency, and muscle incoordination occur. Severe spasticity of muscles resulting in contractures is a late manifestation.[9,15] Approximately one third of patients with multiple sclerosis develop mental changes. Symptoms and the severity of symptoms reflect the nerve fibers affected.

Intervention. No specific treatment for multiple sclerosis exists. During acute exacerbations the patient may be given corticosteroids and be placed on a regimen of bed rest. Continued use of corticosteroids and prolonged periods of bed rest should be avoided, however, because of their complications. After an exacerbation a concentrated program of physical and occupational therapy is indicated to regain function. The patient should be encouraged to remain as active as possible without becoming overly tired. Precipitating factors that cause exacerbations, including fatigue, cold, hot baths, and infections should be avoided. Because of sensory loss, muscle paralysis, and incoordination, special safety precautions are necessary. Heating pads should be avoided and patients should be instructed to check water temperature with uninvolved body parts. They should be cautioned about scatter rugs and polished floors, which may precipitate falls. They also should receive nutritional counseling because of their need for well-balanced diets high in vitamins.

An important responsibility of the nurse during hospitalization is patient and family education concerning all aspects of the disease process, methods of preventing complications of pressure ulcers and contractures, and ways to conserve energy to avoid fatigue. Work and social activities should be continued for as long as possible, although a change in occupation may be necessary to avoid fatigue. Self-help devices are available for patients with considerable disability. Patients and families should be taught about the disease and should be encouraged to avoid drugs or treatments that promise a cure.[9,15] They should be told about the National Multiple Sclerosis Society,* which provides printed material that may help the family in caring for the patient.

Amyotrophic lateral sclerosis

Amyotrophic lateral sclerosis (ALS) is a progressive degenerative disorder of the motor neurons of the spinal cord, brain stem, and motor cortex resulting in muscular weakness and atrophy. Approximately 8,000 to 10,000 persons in the United States are affected. The disease primarily affects men between the ages of 40 and 60 years. Its cause is unknown, but a familial susceptibility has been discovered.

Symptoms include progressive muscle weakness, with muscle twitchings being an early sign. As the disease progresses brain stem involvement causes difficulty in speech, chewing, and swallowing. No known treatment of the disease exists, and complete dependency and death usually occur within 2 to 6 years of onset. Death usually results from pneumonia or respiratory failure. Nursing care is aimed at supportive and symptomatic measures to improve the patient's well-being. The ALS Foundation can offer assistance to families of victims of the disease.[23]

Parkinson's disease (paralysis agitans, shaking palsy)

Parkinson's disease is a chronic progressive disease affecting the basal ganglia, a group of nerve cell bodies (nuclei) located deep within the cerebral hemispheres. Between 1 and 1.5 million persons have some degree of parkinsonism, with approximately 50,000 new cases being diagnosed each year. It is considered to be one of the most common neurologic disorders of the aged, with the first symptoms becoming apparent between ages 50 and 60. Parkinson's disease often leads to complete dependence.

Research has shown that patients with Parkinson's disease have a deficiency of the amine known as dopamine, a compound found normally in large amounts in the basal ganglia. Dopamine is necessary for the normal transmission of nerve impulses in the basal ganglia. Deficiencies of dopamine result in involuntary movements and disturbances of muscle tone and bodily posture. The exact cause of this disease is unknown, but a num-

ber of factors associated with deficiency of dopamine include encephalitis, arteriosclerosis, toxic substances (carbon monoxide and mercury), and certain tranquilizer drugs.

Assessment. The disease is characterized by **tremor**, imbalance (**ataxia**), **rigidity**, postural abnormalities, difficulty in starting movements (akinesia), and slowness in movement (bradykinesia). The tremor, frequently the first symptom reported, can best be described as a pill-rolling motion of the fingers. The tremor is rhythmic and rapid and may be limited to the fingers and hand or may involve the entire body. Typically, the tremor is more noticeable with the hand at rest and may even disappear with voluntary movement of the hand. It is aggravated by stress and anxiety and usually disappears with sleep. Rigidity of the muscles results in jerky, uncoordinated "cogwheel" movements. All complicated movements are slow and difficult to perform. The patient's gait typically is shuffling with very small steps. Some patients begin to take smaller and faster steps (propulsive gait), resulting in a danger of falling and associated movements such as arm swing may be lost. Postural disturbances also result from the rigidity. A stooped posture with the head and body flexed forward often results and the extremities remain flexed continuously. Other symptoms include a masklike facies, slow, monotonous speech, and drooling. Depression often results because these patients have difficulty talking, and they tend to withdraw from people because of their physical appearance. Parkinson's disease does not affect intelligence, and these patients may be starved for intellectual stimulation.

Intervention. No known cure for Parkinson's disease exists. Treatment is symptomatic, supportive, and palliative and includes psychotherapy, physical therapy, and drug therapy.

Levodopa (L-dopa), the immediate precursor of dopamine, is now considered the treatment of choice. L-Dopa (dihydroxyphenylalanine) has proved to be particularly effective in alleviating the symptoms of tremor and rigidity. The drug is converted to dopamine after passing the blood-brain barrier into the brain. The dosage of the drug is increased gradually until maximum benefit is gained with fewest side effects. Many patients are troubled by nausea and vomiting, postural hypotension, and cardiac dysrhythmias. Probably the most disturbing side effect to the patient is the abnormal involuntary movements of the tongue, jaw, and neck resulting in lip smacking

---

*National Multiple Sclerosis Society, 205 East 42nd St, New York, NY 10017.

and protrusion of the tongue. Agitation, delusions, and insomnia may occur. Carbidopalevodopa (Sinemet) is a preparation that enhances the therapeutic response to levodopa but reduces the side effects. Its effect is to decrease the peripheral metabolism of levodopa, making more levodopa available for use in the brain. Carbidopa reduces the amount of levodopa required by 75%. Giving small, divided dosages will also tend to reduce the side effects of levodopa. Ingestion of large amounts of protein and pyridoxine (vitamin B_6) reduces the therapeutic effect of L-dopa. Pyridoxine has no effect on carbidopa.[4,6]

Several other drugs have been used for their symptom-relieving effects, including the anticholinergics trihexyphenidyl (Artane), cycrimine (Pagitane), and benztropine (Cogentin). Other drugs found useful include antihistamines and amantadine (Symmetrel). These drugs may be given in combination with levodopa for their synergistic effect.[6]

In selected patients any of several surgical procedures may be performed. Stereotactic surgery (destruction of areas controlling specific functions) may be done in cases in which drug therapy has been unsuccessful. In this procedure destruction of a well-defined area of the basal ganglia is accomplished with alcohol or liquid nitrogen after burr holes have been made in the skull and a cannula inserted.

Nursing care of patients with Parkinson's disease is aimed at maintaining the patient's independence (see box to the right). The nurse can contribute significantly to the patient's successful adaptation in the home through a program of patient and family teaching emphasizing drug therapy, diet, elimination, and daily exercise. The patient with Parkinson's disease should be encouraged to work and participate in social functions as long as possible. Family members may need counseling to intelligently understand the disease condition and anticipate necessary adjustments in the home.

Huntington's chorea (hereditary chorea, adult chorea)

Huntington's chorea is a hereditary disorder of the basal ganglia and cerebral cortex. The onset of the disease typically occurs between ages 35 and 50. It is characterized by **choreiform** (rapid, jerky) movements and mental deterioration. No specific treatment for the disease exists. Tranquilizers and sedatives may be used to treat the

---

NURSING CARE GUIDELINES
Parkinson's Disease

Nursing diagnoses

- Impaired physical ability associated with uncoordinated movements
- Self-care deficit associated with altered movement patterns
- Anxiety related to inability to control illness
- High risk for injury related to altered movement patterns
- Alterations in bowel elimination, constipation related to altered movement pattern
- High risk for ineffective individual and family coping associated with chronicity of illness
- Potential hopelessness
- Potential knowledge deficit related to drug therapy regimen
- Self-concept disturbances related to change in body image

Nursing interventions

- Observe for L-dopa side effects—check pulse rate and rhythm four times a day; take blood pressure in lying and standing position
- Administer L-dopa with meals to decrease nausea
- Reduce stress- and anxiety-producing situations—allow patient plenty of time to perform such activities as eating and dressing
- Encourage patient to exercise and use all muscles and joints—range of motion exercises should be done several times a day
- Carry out regular daily exercise program to maintain function
  Practice writing and singing aloud
  Use march music and lines placed at intervals on the floor to encourage larger steps
  Encourage exercises to improve balance
- Use stool softeners and suppositories as necessary to prevent constipation
- Involve family and patient in all aspects of planning and giving care
- Provide emotional support to patient and family—be calm and reassuring

Expected outcomes

- Takes appropriate precautions to prevent injury
- Sets realistic goals
- Participates in self-care as appropriate
- Reports satisfaction with self-care despite limitations
- Relates rationale for interventions
- Describes own anxiety and coping patterns; uses coping mechanisms effectively
- Demonstrates ability to understand and express self
- Demonstrates initiative and autonomy in making decisions
- Describes methods to prevent constipation

symptoms but the disease pursues a steady progressive course, and death generally occurs about 15 years after onset.

Intervention. Nursing care is supportive and symptomatic and is aimed at maintaining independent functioning as long as possible. The psychologic effects of the disease can be tremendous. Because of the hereditary nature of the disease, genetic counseling is imperative. The fear of inheriting or transmitting the disease is always present in families of patients with Huntington's chorea.

Myasthenia gravis

Although myasthenia gravis is a fairly uncommon disease, an estimated 50,000 persons in the United States have been diagnosed with the disorder. The disease is neurologic only to the extent that a deficiency in neuromuscular transmission exists at the point where a motor nerve joins a skeletal muscle, causing a weakened contraction of the muscle.

Normally, nerve endings produce a substance called acetylcholine, which carries the nerve impulse from the nerve fiber to the muscle, causing it to contract. The muscle then produces an enzyme, cholinesterase, which inactivates the acetylcholine. The patient with myasthenia gravis produces either too little acetylcholine or too much cholinesterase; the result is insufficient muscle contraction, or weakness. The exact reason why the deficiency exists is essentially unknown, although recent investigations have indicated that it might be an autoimmune disease (see Chapters 2 and 26). The disease occurs most frequently in women between ages 15 and 40 and in men over age 50; women are affected more often than men. At present the disease can be fairly well controlled with drugs, although no known cure exists. Patients must learn to live with the disease for the rest of their lives. With understanding from physicians, nurses, and family, the patient may live a relatively normal life.

Assessment. The primary symptom is muscle weakness, which affects almost every muscle of the body, except those of the heart, intestines, and bladder. Muscle strength is characteristically stronger in the morning and progressively becomes weaker with continued use. The weakness may range from a slight reduction of strength after repeated use of a particular muscle to complete paralysis. Symptoms are aggravated by emotional upset, alcoholic intake, lack of rest, and respiratory tract infections. As a result of the muscle weakness, ptosis of the eyelid, and weakness of the muscles of swallowing, chewing, and speaking, are common occurrences. Shortness of breath may develop when walking.

The diagnosis of myasthenia gravis is made on the basis of history, physical examination, and electromyography. Administration of a test dose of neostigmine or edrophonium (Tensilon) produces dramatic improvement in muscle strength.

Intervention. Treatment of patients with myasthenia gravis depends on the severity of the disease. Maintenance doses of anticholinesterase drugs have been found effective in controlling symptoms. These include neostigmine (Prostigmin), pyridostigmine (Mestinon), and ambenonium (Mytelase). These drugs prevent the breakdown of acetylcholine by cholinesterase. The optimum dose for the patient is the smallest possible dose that will produce the greatest muscle strength. Overdosage can produce generalized weakness **(cholinergic crisis)**. Dysphagia and respiratory weakness during a cholinergic crisis may be so severe that mechanical ventilatory assistance is necessary. Corticosteroids may be used for patients who do not respond to these drugs. The purpose of the corticosteroids is to control the body's autoimmune response.

Because thymic tumors have been associated with myasthenia gravis, surgical excision of the thymus gland is performed in certain cases. The remission rate is approximately 40% to 50% if the procedure is done in the early stages. However, improvement after thymectomy may occur gradually over a period of years; therefore the immediate results of the surgery may not be known.

Nursing care of the patient with myasthenia gravis should emphasize careful monitoring and follow-up. The patient's status may change, requiring an adjustment in medication dosages. A **myasthenic crisis,** often difficult to distinguish from a cholinergic crisis, may occur. In an exacerbation of the disease a decreased response to anticholinesterase medication develops. Emergency measures usually are necessary at this time. The nurse must remember that drugs acting on the neuromuscular junction (morphine, barbiturates, tranquilizers, antibiotics such as streptomycin and neomycin) should not be administered to these patients. Careful observation is necessary when cardiac drugs such as quinidine sulfate or procainamide (Pronestyl) are given, since nerve conduction may be diminished.

Myasthenia gravis is a chronic disease that affects every aspect of the patient's life. It afflicts young people in the prime of life and can be a terrifying, life-threatening condition. Apprehension and fear may be great, with the patient never knowing when he may lose the ability to swallow, breathe, or move. Patients need the consistent reassuring care a nurse can give. Measures to conserve energy and muscle strength should be emphasized in preparing these patients for discharge. The patient should carry a Medic Alert identification card or wear a Medic Alert bracelet to ensure proper treatment during emergency situations. Helpful information can be obtained from the Myasthenia Gravis Foundation, Inc.*

Alzheimer's disease

Alzheimer's disease is a chronic degenerative disease with gradual, progressive loss of cognitive function. Women are affected more often than men and the disease usually involves people over 45 years of age. It is the major cause of dementia in the elderly. The cause of Alzheimer's disease is unknown, although arteriosclerosis, heredity, and autoimmune response are suggested as possible contributors.

Mental changes associated with the disease usually begin with forgetfulness and progress to inability to reason or recall information. In the terminal phase, cognitive function and emotional physiologic responses are lost. At present, no known treatment exists. Support for the patient and family is essential and community services may need to become involved.[2,15]

Cerebrovascular Accident (CVA, Stroke)

Cerebrovascular disease continues to be the third leading cause of death in the United States. At present, several factors tend to make statistical information unreliable; however, evidence indicates that the following trends may be anticipated. The frequency of cerebrovascular disease increases with age. As the number of persons age 65 and older rises, an increase in cerebrovascular disease can be expected to occur. Present mortality data show a greater frequency of CVA among men than among women, and the frequency is greater in the nonwhite than the white population. The incidence of hypertension and arteriosclerosis

bears a direct relationship to the incidence of cerebrovascular disease. Socioeconomic factors affecting the nonwhite population and the elderly may contribute to the lack of early and adequate medical care for hypertension, thus hastening the occurrence of a CVA.

Pathophysiology

Cerebral thrombosis, cerebral hemorrhage, and cerebral embolus are the three major causes of CVA. *Cerebral thrombosis*, the most common cause, results from occlusion of a blood vessel in the brain. A number of related medical conditions predispose to thrombus formation, but by far the most common cause is arteriosclerosis. In patients with arteriosclerosis, cerebral thrombosis is thought to follow clotting of the blood at a site where its flow is impeded by an arteriosclerotic plaque (Figure 22-5, *A*). Such arteriosclerotic changes are associated with increasing age, hypertension, and diabetes. The peak incidence for cerebral thrombosis is between 50 and 70 years of age.

Cerebral hemorrhage results from the rupture of a blood vessel in the brain (Figure 22-5, *C*). The rupture is usually in an arteriosclerotic vessel. The resulting blood clot destroys and replaces nearby brain tissue and interrupts transmission of nerve impulses through the affected area. Cerebrospinal fluid analysis shows a large amount of blood if the blood communicates with the ventricles or subarachnoid space. Related findings usually include a history of hypertension and cardiovascular disease. Cerebral hemorrhage usually is seen in patients between 40 and 70 years of age.

Cerebral embolus is the blockage of a cerebral blood vessel by a small blood clot, fat, air, or other substance that has been circulating in the bloodstream. Following blockage of the vessel, death of nerve tissue occurs in the area supplied by the occluded vessel. Cerebral embolism may occur in children with rheumatic heart disease or in middle-aged and elderly patients with coronary thrombosis and atrial fibrillation. CVAs also can be caused by arterial spasm, which reduces the blood flow to a specific area of the brain (Figure 22-5, *D*) or by compression of vessels by tumors, edema, large blood clots, or other disorders (Figure 22-5, *B*).

Assessment

Early symptoms and neurologic signs can vary considerably depending on the cause, location,

---

*Myasthenia Gravis Foundation, 53 West Jackson Blvd, Chicago, IL 60604.

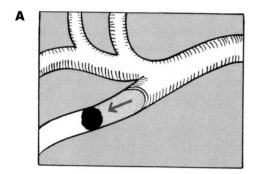

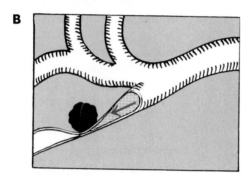

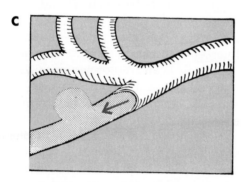

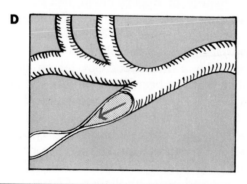

Figure 22-5

Causes of cerebrovascular accident. **A,** Formation of blood clot in blood vessel resulting in occlusion of vessel. **B,** Pressure on blood vessel resulting from blood clot, tumor, or anything compressing the vessel. **C,** Rupture of blood vessel in brain with hemorrhage into adjacent tissue. **D,** Closing of blood vessel resulting from spasm or contraction, causing blockage of blood flow.

and extent of the CVA. In approximately 75% of the cases resulting from thrombosis, warning signs consisting of mental confusion, dizziness, drowsiness, headache, or cerebral *transient ischemic attacks* (little strokes) precede the onset of a full CVA. These warning signs or transient ischemic attacks rarely precede CVAs caused by embolus or hemorrhage.

Cerebral transient ischemic attacks (TIAs) are brief (2 to 60 minutes), reversible, and caused by a temporary decrease or interruption of blood flow to an area of the brain. Symptoms of transient cerebral ischemic attacks may include visual or auditory disturbances, abnormal sensations in the extremities, dizziness, headache, slowing of thinking processes, or convulsions. Neurologic examinations performed between attacks are normal. Patients having transient ischemic attacks as a result of narrowing of an artery caused by arteriosclerotic plaque formation may benefit from surgical procedures such as carotid endarterectomy (see Chapter 16). Patients who are not candidates for surgery receive anticoagulant therapy to prevent future episodes and possible CVA. Low doses of aspirin have been found to be effective, particularly in males, as a type of anticoagulant therapy.

The general clinical picture is similar for CVAs of varying causes. Usually, the onset is sudden, without warning, with the patient falling to the ground. Headache, vomiting, convulsions, and coma may occur. Not infrequently, CVAs occur while individuals are asleep, awakening to find themselves paralyzed. Neurologic signs vary according to the location of the CVA in the brain. Generally, patients will have paralysis, sensory loss, confusion, disorientation, and memory loss. A patient with a CVA on the right side of the brain will have paralysis on the left side of the body (hemiplegia) because the motor nerve pathways cross from one side of the brain to the other in the brainstem (Figure 22-6). If the left side of the brain is involved in a CVA, the patient will have hemiplegia on the right side of the body. In addition, patients who have a CVA involving the left cerebral hemisphere may have difficulty speaking or understanding the spoken word **(aphasia).** Patients with damage to the right cerebral hemisphere (left **hemiplegia**) tend to have perceptual problems. They may not recognize their paralyzed side as being a part of themselves **(canosognosia)** and may ignore it altogether (visual neglect). In addition, they often are quite impulsive, believing

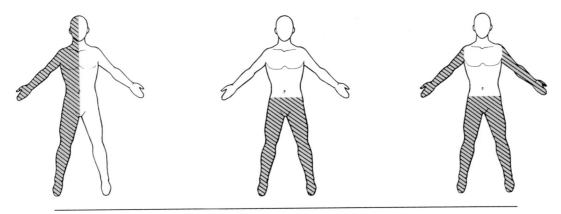

Figure 22-6
Damage to central nervous system may result in paralysis of some or all extremities.
A, Hemiplegia. **B,** Paraplegia. **C,** Quadriplegia.

they can perform acts that they are unable to.[7,13] Other problems associated with CVA include difficulty in swallowing **(dysphagia),** bladder and bowel incontinence, and loss of vision toward the paralyzed side **(hemianopsia).**

Intervention

Radical changes have taken place in recent years in the medical management and nursing care of patients with CVAs. If the patient survives the acute attack, the prognosis for life is good. With active rehabilitation many patients can become completely independent. The extent of the recovery depends on the location and the severity of the CVA. Not all patients will be restored to a useful life however; some will remain chronically incapacitated throughout life. Usually, if some evidence of recovery occurs within the first few weeks, the outlook is favorable. An intensive interdisciplinary health team approach will provide the patient with the best opportunity to regain lost function (see Chapter 12). The family and patient, when able, are an integral part of the therapy program and should be included in developing the plan of care.

Acute stage. During the acute stage, medical management and nursing care are directed toward saving the life of a critically ill patient. In essence, this is the care of the comatose or stuporous patient (see p. 629). Cerebral circulation must be maintained during this period to prevent ischemia of cerebral tissue. Any signs of circulatory collapse—decreased blood pressure with rapid pulse—should be reported promptly, and

correction of blood loss or initiation of antihypotensive drugs should be begun immediately. Anticoagulant therapy, heparin or warfarin, may be started to prevent further thrombosis. However, anticoagulant therapy is contraindicated if cerebral hemorrhage is suspected. In the first several days cerebral edema may threaten life. Dexamethasone in intravenous or intramuscular doses of 4 to 6 mg may be given every 6 hours. Any evidence of increased intracranial pressure should be reported and treated promptly. If the patient is conscious, frequent reassurance and explanations will help alleviate anxiety and fear. Careful monitoring of vital signs is necessary during this initial period to ensure adequate oxygenation of vital organs. The patient's blood pressure may be exceedingly high or low as a result of damage to the vasomotor centers in the brainstem. Neurologic assessment should be done at regular intervals to detect any neurologic complications or extension of the CVA. Seizure precautions should be implemented. Patients who have suffered a CVA are vulnerable to peripheral vascular disease such as thrombosis (see Chapter 16). Antiembolic elastic stockings may be applied to prevent stasis of blood and improve circulation in the lower extremities.

The environment should be quiet and well ventilated, and visitors should be restricted. The patient who suffers a mild CVA will usually not lose bladder control, but retention may occur, and the nurse should watch for bladder distention. Catheterization may be necessary.

The patient who is completely or partially paralyzed and who has limited ability to move about freely is subject to contracture formation, pressure ulcers, atrophy of muscles, thrombosis, and edema. Proper positioning and a regular turning schedule are imperative to prevent these complications. A written schedule for changing position may be useful. The following are important points in proper positioning:

1. Firm mattress or bed board to provide proper support
2. Frequent ankle pumping to prevent footdrop
3. Supine position—blanket or pillow between legs, trochanter roll or sandbags on outside of affected leg and thigh to prevent outward rotation, heels off mattress
4. Side-lying position—affected side for 30-minute intervals four times a day; unaffected side for 2-hour intervals; flex top leg and bring forward, support it with two or more pillows to maintain proper alignment of the hip; lower leg can be straight with the spine; top leg should never rest directly on bottom leg
5. Prone position—no pillow is used under head; a flat pillow is placed under abdomen to protect back; place elbows in flexion or extension; allow feet to extend over end of mattress; a small pillow may be placed under the ankles
6. Affected arm—90 degrees away from body with pillow between arm and body, arm supported on pillow with wrist higher than elbow and elbow higher than shoulder, hard roll or splint in hand to maintain functional position
7. Head—elevate 20 degrees with small pillow

The knee gatch should not be raised, and pillows should not be placed under the knees when the patient is in a supine position. This position contributes to contractures and thrombosis formation. Rubber rings and doughnuts under the coccyx and heels should never be used. Hyperextension of the head or flexion forward onto the chest may cause pressure on the veins of the neck.

Whenever the patient's position is changed, the patient's joints of both the involved and uninvolved side should be put through a gentle full range of motion (see Chapter 12). As soon as possible, the patient should be taught to use the nonparalyzed arm to exercise paralyzed extremities.

Aphasia. If the patient's CVA has affected the left hemisphere of the brain (right hemiplegia), damage to the speech centers may occur, resulting in aphasia. Aphasia is described as *receptive* or *expressive.* In receptive aphasia, patients have difficulty understanding what is said or reading what is written, whereas in expressive aphasia they have difficulty speaking and writing. Sometimes patients will be able to sing songs, count, or recite the alphabet and make statements such as "Good morning" or "How are you?" but be unable to communicate effectively. This is called *automatic* or *primitive* speech. Some patients will have minor word-finding problems or substitute similar or inappropriate words for the one desired. Several guidelines are useful when talking with the aphasic patient (see box on p. 645). Referral to a speech therapist is made when the patient's condition permits. Not being able to speak can be extremely frustrating to the patient, and encouragement and emotional support are essential during this period.

Dysphagia. Difficulty in chewing and swallowing (dysphagia) may occur as a result of damage to the cranial nerves controlling the gag and swallow reflex. Before oral food and fluids are given to the patient with a CVA, the swallow and gag reflex should be checked. If the condition persists for a time, a feeding tube may be necessary. Frequent oral hygiene, particularly after each meal, is necessary, since the patient will tend to accumulate food on the paralyzed side of the mouth (pocketing or squirreling). Measures to facilitate chewing and swallowing are necessary for these patients (see box).

Hemianopia. Hemianopia is the loss of one half of the patient's normal field of vision. The loss of vision occurs as a result of damage to the visual pathways as they travel from the eye to the visual center in the occipital lobe of the cortex. The visual loss occurs on the same side as the patient's paralysis. Frequently, the patient may seem unresponsive to stimuli when in actuality the lack of response is a result of visual loss.

Hemianopsia can be diagnosed by having the patient name or point to all objects seen without moving the head. The nurse should then compare what is named to its location around the patient. Modification of the patient's care plan can decrease anxiety and stress over the visual loss (see box on p. 645). The visual loss may disappear or lessen as the cerebral edema subsides.

Bladder and bowel incontinence. Damage to centers in the brain that control bladder and bowel function can result in a decreased awareness of bladder fullness and the need to defecate. The

NURSING CARE GUIDELINES
Problems Associated with Cerebrovascular Accident (CVA)

Nursing diagnoses
- Impaired verbal communication associated with aphasia and hemiplegia
- Impaired swallowing associated with hemiphagia and cranial nerve damage
- Sensory perceptual alterations associated with aphasia, hemianopsia, and cerebral hemisphere damage
- Impaired physical mobility related to hemiplegia
- Self-care deficit related to hemiplegia
- High risk for injury associated with visual and perceptual problems and hemiplegia
- Potential incontinence related to hemiplegia
- Potential ineffective airway clearance related to hemiplegia
- Potential alteration in nutrition, less than body requirements
- Potential alteration in oral mucous membranes
- Potential anxiety related to hemiplegia, aphasia, dysphagia, hemianopsia, and perceptual problems
- Self-concept disturbance related to body image change

Nursing interventions
Aphasia
- Talk slowly in normal tone of voice
- Use simple words, phrases, and short sentences
- Allow patient sufficient time to answer
- Eliminate distracting noises or stimuli
- State question that can be answered by "yes" or "no" or nod of head—determine reliability of patient's answers
- Listen carefully to patient's attempts to speak
- Do not force patient to talk if unable

Dysphagia
- Place patient in upright position with head slightly flexed
- Determine presence of gag and swallow reflex before attempting any oral fluids or foods
- Place food in mouth on nonparalyzed side
- Encourage patient to eat slowly and concentrate on coordinating chewing, breathing, and swallowing

- Ice tongue before feeding to increase muscle tone—may use popsicles or iced utensils
- Avoid giving patient milk and milk products, which cause thick, stringy secretions
- Give foods that are stimulating to taste and form a ball, for example, chilled pureed fruit

Hemianopsia
- Place patient so activity is toward nonparalyzed side
- Approach patient from nonparalyzed side
- Place personal objects within patient's vision
- As patient recovers, encourage to turn head toward paralyzed side to increase viewing area

Perceptual problems
- Provide sensory stimulation to affected side
- Have patient touch and handle affected extremities
- Use mirrors to improve sitting and standing balance
- Teach patient to check position of affected extremities visually
- Label clothes right, left, top, and bottom to reduce confusion in dressing

Expected outcomes
- Injuries prevented
- Maximum pulmonary function maintained
- Aspiration prevented
- Skin integrity maintained
- Adequate nutritional status maintained
- Demonstrates improved ability to express self
- Expresses decreased frustration with communication
- Participates in self care as appropriate
- Reports satisfaction in self-care despite limitations
- Demonstrates understanding of rationale for interventions
- Describes own anxiety and coping patterns; uses coping mechanisms effectively
- Demonstrates ability to understand and express self
- Achieves or maintains control of own body
- Shares feelings of changes in perception of self

problem can range from one of urgency and frequency to one of complete incontinence. When bladder and bowel incontinence persist, a program of retraining is necessary. The patient should be placed on a commode or taken to the toilet at prescribed intervals. Accurate records of amount and time of food and fluids and frequency

of voidings can be helpful in setting up a voiding schedule for each patient. Constipation may become a problem because of decreased mobility. Stool softeners or suppositories may be necessary. A consistent morning or evening bowel program will help to establish a routine evacuation pattern.

Perceptual problems. If the patient's CVA involves the parietal lobe of the right cerebral hemisphere (left hemiplegia), the patient's perceptual ability may be impaired. Some common disorders of perception include disturbances of body image, difficulty judging position, distance, or movement, and inability to recognize objects through the senses (vision, hearing, or touch). Measures to provide increased sensory input can help overcome some of these problems (see box p. 645).

Rehabilitation

Rehabilitation of the patient with a CVA begins on admission. Although it may be simpler and faster for the nurse to perform various tasks for the patient, the patient should be encouraged to perform activities that do not cause undue frustration. The patient should not be rushed during these activities. A sense of accomplishment is important and new learning experiences should be attempted only when the patient is well rested.

Independence in mobility, either walking or by using a wheelchair, will help to reduce the patient's feelings of helplessness. The nurse should teach the patient to transfer from bed to wheelchair and wheelchair to toilet by leading with the nonparalyzed side of the body. In assisting the patient to walk, the nurse should support the patient's weak side. A belt placed around the patient's waist and held by the nurse in back will help to maintain balance. A sling may be used to support the affected arm when the patient is walking to prevent separation of the shoulder joint (subluxation).

Patients who have suffered CVAs have experienced a sudden drastic change in body function that may be overwhelming. Although intellect usually remains intact, their bodies no longer react according to their wishes. They may not be able to speak intelligently, move at will, or control the most basic body functions. Their perceptions of themselves have been altered suddenly, and emotional reactions are to be expected. Many patients succumb to outbursts of anger, tears, or extreme withdrawal as a means of expressing their fear, anxiety, and frustration. Nursing personnel must understand the needs and feelings of patients and provide opportunities for patients to communicate in whatever way possible. Often nursing attitudes play an important part in what the patient accomplishes. The nurse who is calm and reassuring, recognizes small gains, and gives constant encouragement will stimulate the patient to continuous progress.

The nurse shares with other team members the responsibility for preparing patients for their return home. Both the patient and family should be involved in planning for care of the patient after discharge. The patient's home situation should be assessed and necessary physical changes made before discharge. The family should be encouraged to maintain as normal a home environment as possible, considering the patient's capabilities. Constant and consistent patient and family education is important to ensure adequate care with the least amount of stress on family members. If the family understands what may be anticipated, a smoother adjustment to the home situation will be made by both the patient and family.[7]

Cerebral Artery Aneurysm

A cerebral aneurysm is a round saccular distention of the arterial wall that develops because of a weakness in the wall.[5] It is the most frequent cause of subarachnoid hemorrhage, which is bleeding into the subarachnoid space of the brain. Although the cause of cerebral aneurysms is unknown, hypertension, polycystic disease, congenital defects in the wall lining, and trauma are probable contributors.

Cerebral aneurysms occur most often in people between the ages of 35 and 60 years. Symptoms are divided into those occurring before and those occurring after rupture or bleeding.[15] Before bleeding, most people are asymptomatic; some complain of headache, lethargy, and neck pain. After bleeding, the individual experiences violent headache, decreased consciousness, visual disturbances, and vomiting. Each of these symptoms is related to the increased intracranial pressure that results from the addition of blood into a contained space.

Patients with ruptured cerebral aneurysms are at risk for rebleeding, and with rebleeding the survival rate decreases. Rebleeding usually occurs around the seventh day following the initial bleed. *Cerebral vasospasm* (narrowing or constriction of the vessel) is another complication of cerebral aneurysm. It can result in ischemia to the brain and death if infarction of brain tissue is severe. Clinical signs vary depending on the location of the vasospasm but usually include decreased level of consciousness, motor weakness, visual defects, and respiratory pattern changes.

Surgery usually is indicated for treatment of cerebral aneurysm. The timing of the surgery is controversial, with some recommending early intervention and others recommending delay. For ruptured aneurysms, steroids (dexamethasone), antihypertensives (hydralazine), antipyretics (acetaminophen), stool softeners, anticonvulsants (phenytoin), and sedatives (phenobarbital) may be administered.

Nursing intervention is directed toward monitoring neurologic status and vital signs, preventing additional injury from ischemia or seizure activity, and providing support to the patient and family. A list of nursing diagnoses for patients with cerebral aneurysm, nursing interventions, and expected outcomes can be found in the box to the right.

Head Injuries

Trauma to the brain can result in death or permanent disability for people of all ages. Head injury is the major cause of death for persons between ages 1 and 44. Automobile and motorcycle accidents, physical assault, and industrial and military accidents account for the majority of head injuries. An estimated 70% of vehicular accidents result in injury to the head. Public education in the prevention of accidents and the use of safety measures such as safety belts and helmets is essential to lower the incidence of head trauma.

Head injuries are classified as *closed* if the skull covering the brain remains intact and *open* when injury penetrates the skull. Skull fractures may be linear (simple), in which the fracture resembles a line or single crack in the skull, depressed, in which fragments of bone press inward on cranial contents, or compound (perforated), in which a direct opening exists between the scalp laceration and the underlying brain tissue. A basal skull fracture involves the base of the skull and can be linear, comminuted or depressed.[15] Skull fractures include a simple break in the bony skull without any displacement of the bone; *depressed* fractures, when fragments of bone are pressing inward on the cranial contents; and *compound* fractures, when a direct opening exists between the scalp laceration and underlying brain tissue.

Assessment

Closed head injury can result in **concussion,** an immediate and momentary loss of brain function caused by a blow to the head. A momentary loss of consciousness occurs. The effect of such a blow to the head on the soft brain tissue encased in a closed cavity is one of sudden movement that comes to an abrupt halt. The degree of brain injury

---

NURSING CARE GUIDELINES
Cerebral Aneurysm

Nursing diagnoses

- Potential altered body temperature (hyperthermia)
- Altered bowel elimination (constipation)
- Altered comfort (acute pain)
- Impaired communication
- Fear (of surgery, of prognosis)
- High risk for injury related to ischemia or seizure activity
- Knowledge deficit related to aneurysm and care
- Impaired physical mobility
- Potential altered respiratory function
- Self-care deficit
- Self-concept disturbance
- Altered thought processes
- Altered tissue perfusion of brain cells

Nursing interventions

- Monitor neurologic and vital signs every 15 minutes initially and then every hour thereafter
- Notify the physician of any changes in vital signs or neurologic status
- Assess and document location and severity of headache
- Administer and evaluate effectiveness of prescribed medications
- Reposition patient at least every 2 hours
- Maintain seizure precautions
- Provide support to patient and family

Expected outcomes

- Injuries prevented
- Maximum pulmonary function maintained
- Aspiration prevented
- Adequate nutritional status maintained
- Skin integrity maintained
- Demonstrates improved ability to express self
- Normal body temperature maintained
- Participates in self-care as appropriate
- Demonstrates understanding of rationale for interventions
- Indicates increased comfort following pain relief measures
- Shares feelings of changes in perception of self

---

may be termed as minor if the patient rapidly regains consciousness and mental clearing. A **contusion** results when bruising or hemorrhage of the brain occurs. Loss of consciousness can sometimes occur, but loss of neurologic function (paralysis, confusion, speech and visual disturbances) persists. In any brain injury the potential for hemorrhage and hematoma formation always exists. A subdural hemorrhage results when bleeding into the subdural space between the dura and the arachnoid layers of the meninges occurs. An epidural or extradural hemorrhage occurs when blood hemorrhages into the space between the dura and the skull. Bleeding also may occur within the brain itself *(intracerebral hemorrhage or hematoma)*. It can occur from arteries or veins. Complications from bleeding (increased intracranial pressure and brain compression) develop more slowly from venous than arterial bleeding. Much of the damage to brain tissue occurs as a result of compression of cerebral contents from bleeding or edema rather than from the actual primary injury to vital centers of the brain itself. This compression results in decreased oxygen supply to nerve tissue and is referred to as *secondary injury*.

Intervention

After the immediate emergency care to maintain the patient's life (control of hemorrhage and maintenance of adequate ventilation), a number of diagnostic procedures (skull x-ray examination, angiogram, computed tomography) will be indicated, depending on the patient's condition. The patient should be examined carefully for additional injuries to the cervical spine, abdomen, chest, or extremities. The treatment of the head injury is primarily aimed at reducing and controlling cerebral edema and preventing compression of intracranial contents from depressed skull fractures, hemorrhage, or hematoma. Patients who have signs of cerebral edema will be given mannitol and dexamethasone (Decadron) intravenously to promote diuresis and reduce the cerebral edema. Surgical intervention is indicated for depressed skull fractures and intracranial hemorrhage as well as for subdural and epidural hematomas.

Care of the patient with head injury is focused on prompt recognition and treatment of respiratory insufficiency and increased intracranial pressure. The importance of maintaining a clear and patent airway to ensure effective respirations is discussed in the section on care of the unconscious patient, but needs to be reemphasized here. Impaired respiratory function can result in decreased oxygen supply to brain tissue and contribute to cerebral edema. The nurse should observe the patient closely for any changes of respiratory function, hyperventilation, hypoventilation, or irregular respiratory rates. Any signs of respiratory dysfunction should be reported immediately so treatment can be initiated.

A regular, frequent, and thorough check of the patient's neurologic status should be performed. The patient's level of consciousness is a major indicator of neurologic function; any changes should be reported immediately (Table 22-1). In addition, the patient should be closely observed for signs of increased ICP and seizures.

The nurse should carefully observe any patient with brain injury for serous or bloody drainage from the ears or nose. Drainage may indicate the meninges have been torn, resulting in leakage of cerebrospinal fluid. Such an opening may allow infection to be introduced into the cranial cavity from the nose or ears (meningitis). The ear or nose should not be cleaned because of the danger of introducing infection. Nasal suction should never be performed on these patients. The patient should be instructed to avoid coughing, sneezing, and blowing the nose. A soft, sterile cotton pad may be placed gently over the opening of the ear or nose, but the opening should not be plugged. The pad should be changed when moist, and the color, consistency, and amount of fluid present should be noted. The fluid should be checked for glucose, which is an indication of the presence of cerebrospinal fluid.

Fluid and electrolyte balance should be monitored closely. Intravenous fluids during the initial period may be restricted to 1500 to 2000 ml in a 24-hour period to control or eliminate cerebral edema. Increased urinary excretion of sodium or cerebral salt retention may occur following head injury. The care of the comatose patient and the patient with seizures is discussed on pp. 527-528 and 630-633.

One common complication following trauma to the brain is *stress ulceration* of the stomach and duodenum. These ulcers are thought to result from disturbances in the autonomic nervous system as a result of injury. Treatment is similar to that for any patient with an ulcer (Chapter 18).

The aftermath of brain injury will depend on the severity of damage to the brain tissue. The majority of patients with minor injuries will recover without any residual effects. Some patients will suffer from headache, dizziness, and mental changes for several months after injury. Seizures as a result of scar tissue may occur in some patients. Patients with moderate to severe injury will require long periods of rehabilitation. The patient and family will need understanding throughout the acute period and during convalescence to adjust to any residual disabilities.

Neuritis and Neuralgia

Neuritis and neuralgia are vague terms used by lay people to describe a variety of pains associated with peripheral nerves. Neuritis refers to nerve damage from tumors, infection, trauma, vascular and metabolic disorders, and toxic agents. Diffuse damage to multiple nerves is called polyneuritis.

Polyneuritis (multiple neuritis)

Polyneuritis results in degenerative changes in the peripheral sensory and motor nerve fibers. The degenerative changes result in both motor and sensory symptoms. The motor symptoms, which cause weakness and **flaccid** paralysis of the extremities, are often more significant than the sensory symptoms. Causes of polyneuritis include vitamin B deficiencies, malnutrition, alcoholism, ingestion of toxic substances, and prolonged gastrointestinal disease. Acute infectious polyneuritis is referred to as *Guillain-Barré syndrome*. Guillain-Barre syndrome is one of the most common diseases of the peripheral nervous system. Sensory symptoms may occur in the absence of any motor symptoms, but if motor involvement occurs sensory symptoms always will be evident. Motor symptoms may begin with weakness, disturbance of gait, and paralysis. The paralysis usually begins in the ankles and wrists and gradually extends up the extremity until complete paralysis results. Pain may occur early in some patients.

Guillain-Barré syndrome is divided into three stages: acute onset, which begins with development of symptoms and ends when no additional symptoms or deterioration are observed (usually around 1 to 3 weeks); plateau, which lasts for 1 to 3 weeks; and recovery, which may last for up to 2 years depending on the extent of involvement and loss of function. Permanent disability may be an outcome.[15]

Intervention. Treatment for patients with polyneuritis is directed toward controlling the underlying cause. Large doses of vitamin B complex are administered along with a well-balanced diet. The patient may be restricted to bed rest with a cradle to protect tender and painful feet and legs from the weight of bed covers. The application of moist heat to muscles may provide some relief from pain. Extreme caution should be taken to prevent burns to desensitized areas of the body. Gentle massage and passive exercises should be administered. Splints sometimes are used to prevent wrist-drop and foot-drop. Hot compresses may be employed to help maintain muscle tone and prevent atrophy of muscles.

Neuralgia

Neuralgia is a severe pain along the route of a nerve and may be the result of pressure at some point along the nerve pathway. Tumors, hypertrophic arthritis, and aneurysms are among some of the causes, but the disease also may occur when the cause is unknown. The more common types of neuralgia are intercostal neuralgia, sciatica, and trigeminal neuralgia.

Intercostal neuralgia. Intercostal neuralgia follows the course of the intercostal nerves, which extend from the thoracic cord to innervate the ribs. It may be from a tumor on the spinal cord or from arthritis. In herpes zoster, pain usually follows the intercostal nerves. Pain generally begins in the back and radiates toward the front; one or both sides may be affected. If the cause is known, it should be treated or removed. The neuralgic pain may be relieved with application of heat and mild analgesics.

Sciatic neuralgia (sciatica). Sciatica is an inflammation and pain along the course of the sciatic nerve. The pain, which may be mild or severe, may be felt in the back and the buttocks and extends down the back of the thigh and down the leg. In addition to pain, the nerve may be sensitive. Sciatica may occur without any known cause, but it frequently occurs from disorders of the sacroiliac joint or the lumbar spine. It may result from a ruptured intervertebral disk. The nerve also may be injured by carelessness in the administration of injections in the gluteal muscle. The cause should be located and treated. Patients will be more comfortable if they have a firm mattress with a board beneath. Moist heat and analgesic drugs will relieve much of the discomfort; however, the pain occasionally is acute enough to require narcotics. Traction also has been found helpful in relieving the disorder. Bed rest should be continued until the acute attack is over.

Trigeminal neuralgia (tic douloureaux). Trigeminal neuralgia is a facial neuralgia involving one of the branches of cranial nerve V (Figures 22-7 and 22-8). The condition occurs in persons of middle age and older, and with advancing years attacks increase in frequency. Although some the-

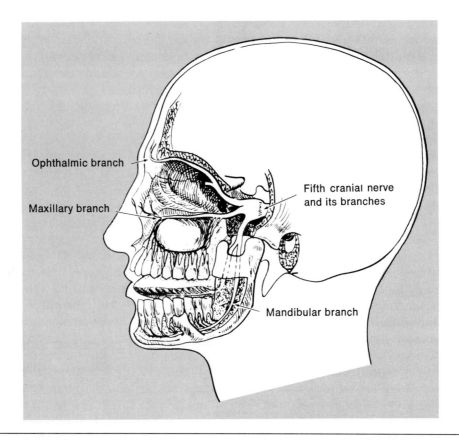

Figure 22-7
Cranial nerve V and its branches.

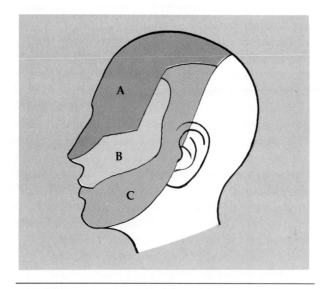

Figure 22-8
Areas supplied by three branches of cranial nerve V.
A, Opthalmic branch. **B,** Maxillary branch. **C,** Mandibular branch. Any of the branches may be involved in tic douloureux.

ories exist, in general, the specific cause is unknown. The pain comes in paroxysms lasting only a few seconds, but is extremely severe. The pain is felt only in the skin, and any activity that stimulates the area near the affected nerve will cause a paroxysm of pain. Certain locations on the face are called *trigger points,* and the slightest touch or stimulation of these areas may cause an attack. Many activities of daily living such as brushing the teeth, shaving, washing the face, combing the hair, or eating, as well as environmental factors such as change of temperature, cold air, a breeze or a draft, may precipitate an attack. The patient lives in a constant state of fear and anxiety, afraid to perform any activity that might cause an attack.

Several methods of treatment have been tried. Injections of alcohol or phenol often provide relief for several months. Vitamin B_{12}, analgesics for relief of pain, and sedatives for sleep and rest may be given. Antiepileptic drugs such as phenytoin (Dilantin), mephenesin (Tolserol), and carbamazepine (Tegretol) have been found to suppress or shorten the duration of attacks. The use of electric stimulation through implanted electrodes has been found helpful in blocking pain impulses. Administration of narcotics is contraindicated in these patients because of the possibility of addiction from prolonged use. Any of several surgical procedures that divide the nerve fibers and result in loss of sensation in the area may provide more permanent relief.

When caring for patients with trigeminal neuralgia, the nurse should remember that the patient may be completely exhausted from fighting attacks of pain. The patient may be malnourished from lack of food, because chewing may cause pain. The patient needs a nourishing diet with food of a consistency that does not require a great deal of chewing. Food should be served tepid rather than extremely hot or cold. The patient should be placed in a quiet environment away from breezes. Drafts and jarring of the bed should be avoided.

Surgical sectioning of the nerve results in loss of sensation, numbness, and stiffness along the pathway of the nerve. The nurse should be sure the patient is protected and instructed to prevent injury to the involved area. For example, if the ophthalmic branch is involved, protective eye care is necessary. If the maxillary or mandibular branch is severed, the patient must be instructed to avoid hot foods and fluids that could burn the mucous membranes and avoid biting the mucous membranes while chewing. Since sensation is lost to the mouth area, visual checks of the oral cavity should be made on the affected side.

Bell's Paralysis (Bell's Palsy)

Bell's paralysis, commonly called *Bell's palsy*, affects branches of cranial nerve VII. The condition may begin with slight pain and tenderness at the back of the ear and on the side of the neck, followed by paralysis of the muscles on one side of the face. The eye cannot close, the mouth is pulled to the opposite side of the face, and drooling occurs. An increase in lacrimation (tears) from the eyes occurs.

Intervention

Passive exercises, gentle massage, and moist cloths to the affected side of the face will help to improve muscle tone. Electric stimulation to the face often is used to stimulate return of function. Because the blinking reflex is lost in Bell's palsy,

special measures must be taken to protect the cornea of the eye from dust or dryness. Glasses and artificial tear solution are indicated. An eye patch may be worn at night. Occasionally, vasodilating drugs may be given to increase circulation to the area, and steroids may be given to reduce edema.

More than 80% of the patients recover without residual effects after a few weeks. When the paralysis appears to be permanent (after 1 year), surgical anastomosis of the facial nerve to the spinal accessory or hypoglossal nerve may be performed.

Spinal Cord Injuries

Spinal cord injury (SCI) resulting in loss of sensory and motor function is an increasing cause of serious disability. The Paraplegia Foundation has estimated that between 125,000 and 200,000 persons in the United States have sustained SCI. This number is increased by 12,000 new cases annually. Although spinal cord damage may result from tumors, infections, congenital defects, and degenerative diseases, by far the most common causes are vehicle and diving accidents, falls, and gunshot and knife wounds. The injury may result in complete transection of the spinal cord, resulting in complete paralysis and loss of sensation below the level of injury. When the spinal cord is partially transected, the effects are less severe and disabling. An injury in the cervical or high thoracic region may result in **quadriplegia,** whereas an injury in the thoracic or lumbar region results in **paraplegia** (Figure 22-6).

Emergency intervention

Any person with a suspected spinal cord injury should be handled with extreme caution to prevent further damage to the cord. Spinal cord injury should be suspected in any person who cannot move the arms or legs, complains of tingling or lack of feeling in any extremity, or complains of back pain. Any unconscious individual who has sustained a head injury should be handled as if a back injury has been sustained until proved otherwise. The person should not be moved until properly trained emergency personnel are available. If the patient must be moved, at least four or five persons should be available to lift the patient carefully onto a firm, hard board with one person holding the patient's head. Extreme care must be taken to keep the head, neck, and back in straight alignment. Pillows should not be placed under the head, but a small roll may be placed under the neck if a cervical neck injury is suspected. If the injury appears to be in the lower thoracic spine or lumbar region, a small roll under the lumbar spine may be more comfortable. The head should be supported on either side and should not be turned or allowed to tilt forward or extend backward.

Early intervention

The early intervention for patients with spinal cord injury is aimed at reducing the effects of the injury, maintaining alignment of the spine, and stabilizing it to prevent further damage. Research has shown that additional damage to the cord can occur as a result of edema, hemorrhage, and vasoconstriction of nearby blood vessels resulting from norepinephrine excretion at the site of the injury. Specialized treatment at a spinal cord trauma center is preferable. During this initial period the patient should be monitored closely for signs of shock and circulatory collapse. In persons with cervical cord injury, the muscles of respiration may be affected, and mechanical ventilation may be necessary.

Restoration of alignment and stability of the spine usually is accomplished with traction and braces. If the spinal cord is being compressed by bony fragments or a herniated disc, a laminectomy may be performed. In cervical injuries, halo traction may be used to reduce the fracture and maintain proper alignment of the neck. The halo hoop is initially connected to weights at the top of a turning frame or bed. Once the patient's respiratory status is stable, the hoop is disconnected from the weights and is attached to a body vest or cast. The CircOlectric bed should not be used during the early stages because of the increased pressure placed on the vertebral column when the patient is in the upright position.

Spinal shock

Immediately after a spinal cord injury, a period of complete inactivity of the nervous system occurs below the level of injury. This period of **spinal shock** may last from 1 week to several months and is characterized by flaccid paralysis, loss of all sensation, reflex activity and autonomic function below the level of the injury, and bowel and bladder dysfunction. Because of the loss of muscle tone, these patients are extremely susceptible to many of the complications of immobility, particularly pressure ulcers, thrombophlebitis, and renal calculi. Conscientious and expert nursing care

during this acute period can help prevent many of these complications.

Daily care

Immediately after the injury, a disturbance of the heat-regulating mechanism occurs so the patient does not perspire below the level of injury. This may result in an elevation of temperature. The loss of temperature regulation results in a phenomenon referred to as *poikylothermia*—the tendency of the body to take on the temperature of the surrounding environment. If the environment is hot, the patient's temperature will rise; if the environment is cold, the patient's temperature will fall. The patient should be instructed to avoid extremes in temperature to prevent the undesirable effects of hyperthermia or hypothermia. In addition, the skin must receive meticulous care. The use of powder is to be discouraged, since it holds moisture and contributes to maceration of the skin. Wrinkles in sheets and clothing must be removed to ensure that pressure areas do not develop.

The patient with quadriplegia cannot use a traditional push-button bell signal to summon help. Special devices, such as a bladder-type call bell, should be obtained to allow the patient the maximum amount of independence possible.

Relief of pain. The administration of pain-relieving drugs depends on the location and extent of pain. To avoid respiratory impairment, narcotic drugs are not given to patients with cervical cord injuries. The use of narcotics should be avoided whenever possible because of the potential for addiction. Medications should be given orally when possible, and injections should not be given below the level of the injury because desensitized tissue does not have normal circulation.

Edema. As a result of the loss of muscle tone and sympathetic activity, the hands, feet, and ankles of SCI patients often become edematous. Elastic support hose and abdominal binders can help control the pooling of blood in the abdomen and lower extremities, which can result in low blood pressure. Elevation of the legs also will help control this problem.

Positioning. Keeping the body in functional position is essential to prevent contractures. The use of soft foot supports, trochanter rolls, and hand splints or rolls can help maintain normal functional position of joints. Passive range of motion exercises to all joints (Chapter 12), if performed religiously, can prevent contracture formation even in the presence of spastic muscles. A regular turning schedule with massage of bony prominences is necessary to prevent pressure ulcers.

Elimination. In patients with severe spinal cord injuries, urinary retention often occurs. An indwelling catheter usually is inserted in the emergency room. For female quadriplegic patients, an indwelling catheter may be necessary if they are unable to manage self-catheterization. For male quadriplegic patients and for male and female paraplegic patients, intermittent catheterization is the method of choice and should be begun as soon as possible after admission.

Intermittent catheterization is less likely to result in chronic urinary tract infections and penoscrotal fistula formation in males. When an indwelling catheter is in place, it should be taped to the abdomen of males (Figure 22-9) and to the inner thigh of females. This will help prevent complications associated with prolonged tension and pressure from the catheter.

Patients are catheterized intermittently to maintain urine volumes of 500 to 600 ml at each voiding. Consistent volumes greater than this amount can result in overstretching of the bladder and can increase the potential for formation of urinary crystals. In addition, autonomic hyperreflexia can occur when the bladder is overdistended. Frequent urine cultures should be collected, and symptomatic urinary tract infections should be treated with appropriate antibiotics.

Since bowel function is affected, fecal impaction should be guarded against. Stool softeners such as dioctyl sodium sulfosuccinate (Colace, Peri-Colace, Doxinate) should be used on a routine basis. With the additional use of bisacodyl (Dulcolax) or glycerin suppositories, constipation and fecal impaction should be prevented. The suppository should be administered early in the morning, because this is the time when the gastrocolic reflex is the strongest. Digital stimulation may be required—particularly during the early stages of the bowel program. Enemas should be avoided, to be used only when other methods fail. The instillation of liquid into the bowel can result in an autonomic hyperreflexic response.

Diet. A high-protein, high-calorie diet is essential during the acute stage. Fluid intake should be at least 3,000 ml to help prevent urinary tract infections and calculi formation. Citrus juices, which cause an alkaline urine, should be avoided.

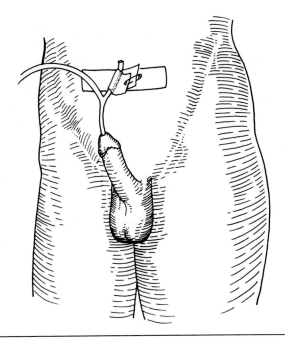

Figure 22-9
Catheter taped to abdomen of male patient.

Patients may be given ascorbic acid tablets to maintain an acidic urine. Initially the patient with quadriplegia must be fed, but many patients can eventually feed themselves using the various assistive devices available.

Muscle spasms. After the resolution of spinal shock, **muscle spasms** may occur. These generally are not treated unless they become severe and often will resolve over several weeks. Spasms can be aggravated by bladder stones, pressure ulcers, physical contact, systemic infection, and anxiety. Any precipitating factor should be identified and removed, when possible. Diazepam (Valium), dantrolene (Dantrium), or baclofen (Lioresal) are prescribed if the spasms are severe enough to interfere with rehabilitation efforts or are distressing to the patient.

The presence of muscle spasm does not indicate a return of normal function. Patients and families frequently misinterpret the significance of the spasms, hoping that the movement of an extremity reflects a positive sign. They will need accurate information and considerable support as they move through the adaptation process associated with spinal cord injury.

Autonomic hyperreflexia (dysreflexia). Autonomic **hyperreflexia** is an emergency condition occurring in patients with cervical or high thoracic injuries. It occurs as a result of an exaggerated and uncontrolled response of the sympathetic nervous system to external stimulation. Some of the common causes are bladder or bowel distention, enemas, digital rectal stimulation, bladder irrigations, infection, or skin ulcers. The condition is characterized by pounding headache, markedly elevated blood pressure, which may be as high as 300 mm Hg, flushed face, "goose flesh," and a slow pulse. Once the cause of the attack has been identified and corrected, the symptoms usually subside without further treatment. When the symptoms of hyperreflexia occur, the nurse should immediately check for bladder distention, plugged catheter, or other causes so the problem can be corrected. If the bladder is distended, the patient should be catheterized immediately. In cases of fecal impaction, a local anesthetic ointment should be inserted into the rectum before any attempt is made to remove the impaction. The preceding emergency nursing measures should be attempted immediately. The physician should be notified that the patient has had an episode of autonomic hyperreflexia or if these measures are ineffective. If the above interventions fail, rapid-acting antihypertensive medications such as methyldopa hydrochloride (Aldomet), will be required. The patient and family should have a complete understanding of this problem and how to correct it before the patient's discharge.

Rehabilitation

Rehabilitation begins immediately, and the primary objective of care is to assist the patient in achieving an optimum level of physical and mental function within the limits of the disability. The extent of functional return for patients with spinal cord injury will depend on the remaining muscle power available. The higher the level of injury, the more muscles involved—and the greater will be the disability. With long-term physical and occupational therapy, patients can learn to use remaining functional muscles and adaptive devices to achieve independence in daily activities. Ambulation with or without bracing may be attempted in selected patients with lumbar or sacral injuries. The nurse plays an important role during this period in teaching the patient and family aspects of self-care so that many of the potential complications of chronic disability can be prevented.

Bladder and bowel reconditioning are considered major goals during rehabilitation. If the par-

alyzed person can regain continence of bladder and bowel function, the patient's self-confidence and potential for successful rehabilitation will improve. Once the spinal shock phase has passed, bladder and bowel reconditioning should be initiated. A rigid program of regulated fluid intake and attempts to void is begun. Many patients will be able to empty their bladders through stimulation of the voiding reflex by tapping over the bladder area, stroking the inner thighs, or pulling pubic hairs. Catheterization for residual urine is done routinely to prevent distention and to determine the effectiveness of bladder emptying. The goal of bowel reconditioning is to achieve a regularly scheduled emptying of the bowel by methods previously cited. The time selected should be convenient for the patient after discharge. As soon as patients can maintain an upright position, they should be assisted to the toilet to facilitate evacuation.

Sexual counseling has been an area frequently neglected in the past. Many SCI patients will have concerns regarding their potential for normal sexual activity. The nurse should be aware that some patients may be embarrassed or reluctant to ask questions related to sexual functioning. If the nurse does not feel comfortable with or capable of answering the patient's questions, a referral to the appropriate resource person in the hospital should be made.

Adjustments to paralysis are difficult, with extreme changes in body image being required.[24] The grief process, including such behaviors as anger, depression, denial, and withdrawal can be anticipated. Often these patients do well when interacting with others having similar problems.

Rupture of the Intervertebral Disk

Between adjacent vertebrae is a flattened disk of cartilage (intervertebral disk) that is slightly compressible and allows for limited flexibility of the spine. Intervertebral disks also act as shock absorbers to protect the vertebrae from jars and jolts. Sometimes these disks rupture, and the soft, gelatinous substance in the center (nucleus pulposus) escapes. This mass then may compress the spinal cord or exert pressure on nerves—causing neurologic symptoms. The disks in the lumbar region are the ones most commonly affected, although cervical disk disorders are not infrequent.

Low back pain is generally the initial symptom, with acute attacks occurring as the result of some slight movement. The pain eventually radiates over the buttock down the leg to the ankle along the course of the sciatic nerve. The patient may experience tingling or numbness in the foot and spasms in the leg; depending on the amount of pressure on the nerve, gait may be affected.

Heavy lifting or twisting of the back usually precipitates the onset of pain. In cases of herniation of cervical disks, hyperextension of the neck (whiplash) may be the precipitating factor. Rupture of the intervertebral disk is now considered to be one of the major causes of severe, recurrent low back pain.

Intervention

Conservative methods of treating ruptured intervertebral disks are tried initially unless symptoms of cord compression are present. Complete bed rest on a firm mattress with a bed board underneath is essential. Strong analgesic medication (Empirin with codeine) may be necessary to relieve the discomfort. Muscle relaxants such as diazepam (Valium), carisoprodol (Soma), or methocarbamol (Robaxin) often are helpful. If an inflammatory process is involved, indomethacin (Indocin) or ibuprofen (Motrin) may be given. The use of pelvic traction for lumbar disks is controversial. However, cervical traction with a halter has been found helpful for patients with cervical disks. Lying on the side with knees and hips flexed helps relieve the tension on the lumbar and sacral nerves. Another position of comfort for the patient with low back pain is on the back with the head of the bed elevated and the knee gatch up. This helps to lengthen the muscles of the back and legs to prevent muscle spasms. A small pillow placed under the lumbar region of the back also will help relieve the tension. Physical therapy, applying moist heat to the lumbar area, light massage, or the use of infrared heat with muscle exercises often is ordered.

When the patient is allowed out of bed, a back brace or corset can be worn to provide additional support to the back. With ruptured cervical disks, a cervical collar usually is worn to keep the neck in a neutral or slightly flexed position. After the pain subsides, the patient usually is started on a series of corrective exercises to strengthen the abdominal and back muscles. If conservative treatment is ineffective or neurologic symptoms increase, a laminectomy is performed.

The nurse can be helpful in teaching the patient correct body mechanics when bending, lifting, or turning in bed. The patient should be ad-

vised not to twist or strain the back during movement. General care of the patient is similar to that of any patient who must be immobilized for a period of time. Attention should be given to maintaining adequate fluid intake and elimination. Mild laxatives may be necessary.

An experimental procedure called *chemonucleolysis* is being performed in some areas as a final step in the conservative treatment of herniated lumbar disks. In this procedure an enzyme is injected into the disk, and the damaged tissues are dissolved. Conservative treatment of cervical disk herniation consists of bed rest, immobilization of the neck with a stabilizing collar, and intermittent cervical traction.

Laminectomy

A **laminectomy** is a surgical procedure to remove bone, cartilage, projecting intervertebral disk, or spinal cord tumor. The posterior arch of the vertebra is removed so the spinal cord is exposed and the disk or tumor can be removed. A spinal fusion also may be done during the operation. Spinal fusion consists of the removal of a piece of bone from another area of the body (iliac crest or rib) and grafting it onto the vertebrae. This provides a firm, bony union in a weakened area of the vertebral column. Metal wires or rods also may be attached to the vertebrae to provide additional support to the area. A laminectomy may involve the cervical, thoracic, or lumbar vertebrae; however, the thoracic vertebrae are less often involved. A partial or hemilaminectomy can be performed to remove a herniated disk. A spinal fusion is not necessary, since the defect resulting is negligible.[1]

Preoperative intervention. Preoperative care of the patient is essentially the same as that for most surgical patients (Chapter 5). If a spinal fusion is to be done, the bone grafts may be taken from the leg or the crest of the ilium, and this area also is prepared. The patient may be apprehensive and needs reassurance. An explanation of what to expect postoperatively will help to relieve anxiety.

Postoperative intervention. General postoperative care is similar to that for other types of surgical procedures (Chapter 5). After a laminectomy, the patient's spine must be kept in a position of correct alignment. Turning and activity orders vary according to the surgeon. Some patients are allowed out of bed on the operative day, whereas others are kept on a regimen of bed rest from 10 to 14 days. When the patient is allowed out of bed, a back brace or corset may be required, and low-heeled shoes are preferred to bedroom slippers. General principles of nursing care for patients after a laminectomy are summarized in the box to the right.

When spinal fusion is performed with laminectomy, recovery is slower and an extra wound must heal. If bone has been taken from the leg, the extremity should be handled carefully. Ambulation of patients who have had spinal fusion should be gradual. Patients should be taught to bend from the hips, keeping the back straight. They will be more comfortable if they use a straight chair when sitting.

Tumors of the Brain and Spinal Cord

All tumors of the brain, whether benign or malignant, are potentially fatal unless treated. Death from untreated tumors results from the compressive effects of a space-occupying lesion or from progressively increasing intracranial pressure. Tumors can originate within the brain tissue (gliomas) or outside of the brain tissue in the meninges (meningiomas). Brain tumors tend to occur in young adult life or middle age.

Symptoms of intracranial tumors are caused by localized destruction or compression of brain tissue and vary according to the location and size of the lesion. Initially, tumors may exist with very few noticeable symptoms. Often a slight slowing of mental functioning or change in personality is the only abnormal behavior. Occasionally, seizure activity, particularly when onset occurs in middle age, is a dramatic early sign. Malignant tumors may result from metastasis from lesions elsewhere in the body, but primary tumors of the brain do not metastasize outside the brain.

The specific symptoms presented may provide clues to the location of the tumor. The nurse can help localize the site of the tumor by observing and recording focal symptoms such as muscular weakness, hearing and visual disturbances, dizziness, and speech or sensory deficits.

The generalized classic symptoms of brain tumors are those of gradually increasing intracranial pressure. Headache tends to occur at night or on awakening in the morning. The location and nature of the headache varies considerably but increases in intensity as the tumor grows. Coughing, straining, or stooping often aggravates the headache. Nausea and vomiting appear in about one third of the patients and may accompany the headache. Nausea and vomiting appear in about

---

NURSING CARE GUIDELINES
Postoperative Care: Laminectomy Patient

Nursing diagnoses
- Alteration in comfort: pain
- Potential impaired physical mobility
- Self-care deficit
- Potential ineffective breathing patterns
- Potential sensory perception alteration
- High risk for infection
- Potential alterations in patterns of urinary elimination

Nursing interventions
- Check postoperative orders carefully
- Place patient on firm mattress
- Keep head of bed flat until ordered otherwise
- Check patient's vital signs and monitor motor and sensory function in all extremities—report any muscle weakness and numbness or tingling to the surgeon
- Observe dressing for signs of hemorrhage or cerebrospinal fluid leakage
- If cervical laminectomy was performed, closely observe quality and rate of respirations
- Maintain correct body alignment at all times
- Turn patient in logroll fashion with a turning sheet every 2 hours; caution patient not to attempt to turn self
- Check for urinary retention; catheterize patient as necessary
- Assist patient to ambulate when ordered; encourage patient to walk erect and not to bend forward
- Avoid having patient sit in chair for long periods—use only straight chair

Expected outcomes
- Maximum pulmonary function maintained
- Aspiration prevented
- Infections prevented
- Participates in self-care as appropriate
- Demonstrates understanding of rationale for interventions
- Reports increased comfort following pain relief measures
- Maintains continency, voiding voluntarily

---

one third of the patients and may accompany the headache. Some patients may vomit unexpectedly and forcibly, without any preceding nausea (projectile vomiting). Other symptoms include papilledema, dizziness, and changes in level of consciousness.

Before considering surgery, the exact location of the tumor must be determined. In addition to a complete history and neurologic examination, various diagnostic procedures referred to earlier in this chapter are performed. These could include skull x-ray examinations, electroencephalography, angiography, and computed tomography or magnetic resonance imaging.

When possible, brain tumors are treated by surgical removal of the tumor. Many tumors are malignant and infiltrate the brain tissue, making complete excision impossible. If complete removal of the tumor is not possible, surgery is followed by radiation therapy or chemotherapy (Chapter 9). Radiation therapy is the treatment of choice for inoperable tumors. Many chemotherapeutic agents are not effective for brain tumors, since they do not pass the blood-brain barrier.

Spinal tumors

Spinal cord tumors occur less frequently than those involving the brain, and the majority are benign. They tend to occur in young or middle-aged adults and most often involve the thoracic region. Spinal tumors may originate from spinal cord tissue (intramedullary) or from surrounding tissue (extramedullary). Metastasis to the vertebral column from various primary sites can cause pressure on the cord or may involve the cord itself.

Symptoms of spinal cord tumors vary depending on the level and location of the tumor. Neurologic symptoms develop below the level of the tumor and cause both sensory and motor changes. A disturbance in gait may occur, and spastic paraplegia may develop. When the tumor affects the cervical spinal cord, quadriplegia results. One of the early symptoms may be numbness, tingling, and pain in parts of the body supplied by the nerves from the affected area. The diagnosis may be made by lumbar puncture, CT or MRI, or myelography. Treatment is surgical removal of the tumor by laminectomy or radiation therapy or both. Surgical removal should occur before the tumor exerts pressure on the spinal cord and deprives the cord of an adequate blood supply. If the cord is not permanently damaged, the symptoms of neurologic deficit may be reversible.

Craniotomy

A **craniotomy** is a surgical opening through the cranium for the purpose of removing a tumor, evacuating hematomas, or relieving intracranial pressure. The patient is admitted to the hospital for a complete neurologic workup when the surgery is elective.

Preoperative intervention. Preoperative preparation of the patient and family includes a thorough explanation of the intended procedure and possible outcomes. The nurse can be most helpful in providing emotional support and accurate information during this stressful period. Routine preoperative procedures are carried out and may include hypothermia in preparation for surgery (Chapter 5). The head is shaved in the operating room or the evening before in the patient's room. The scalp is shampooed and any lesions or abrasions reported. A clean towel then is pinned around the patient's head. The patient and family should understand that the hair is to be cut, and long hair is saved and given to the patient. Today the use of commercial wigs and hairpieces helps in the adjustment to having the head shaved. The patient usually is not given an enema, and the usual preoperative drugs often are omitted, although codeine is sometimes given. Corticosteroids may be administered preoperatively to control cerebral edema. A retention catheter usually is placed into the urinary bladder.

Postoperative intervention. Usually after craniotomies, patients are placed in the intensive care unit under close observation until their conditions stabilize. The care of these patients is complex and requires highly skilled nursing care. In some hospitals continuous monitoring of the patient's temperature, pulse, respirations, intracranial pressure, and electrocardiogram is done. The nurse should be prepared to handle emergencies such as cardiac or respiratory arrest. Many of these patients will be unconscious for a time after surgery, and care appropriate to the unconscious patient should be followed. Principles of care are similar for all patients with intracranial surgery (see box on p. 658).

During convalescence the patient may continue to have neurologic deficits that existed before surgery and that have not been completely relieved. The physical therapist can help with ambulation and muscle-strengthening exercises. When the patient is discharged from the hospital, a visit from a public health nurse may be desirable. Patients need constant encouragement and reassurance and should be urged to do everything for themselves within the limits of their abilities.

NURSING CARE GUIDELINES
Postoperative Care: Craniotomy Patient

Nursing diagnoses
- Alteration in comfort: pain
- Potential impaired physical mobility
- Self-care deficit
- Potential ineffective breathing patterns
- Potential alteration in sensory perception
- Potential impaired verbal communication
- High risk for infection
- Potential alteration in nutrition, less than body requirements

Nursing interventions
- Position patient according to site of surgery—do not place on operative side if large tumor or bone was removed; elevate head of bed
- Check vital and neurologic signs at frequent intervals
- Observe patient for signs of increased intracranial pressure and seizure activity
- Observe dressings for signs of bleeding and leakage of cerebrospinal fluid
- Maintain asepsis in handling all dressings
- Observe for signs of neurologic deficits (paralysis, sensory loss, difficulty in swallowing or speaking)
- Maintain activity or position restrictions as ordered
- Do not place patient in Trendelenburg's position without physician's order
- Do not suction patient through nose
- Ice bags may be used to relieve headache and facial edema; analgesics may be necessary
- Prevent straining by patient; avoid use of restraints, enemas; avoid coughing or vomiting
- Provide calm, quiet environment

Expected outcomes
- Maximum pulmonary function maintained
- Aspiration prevented
- Infections prevented
- Adequate nutritonal status maintained
- Communicates effectively
- Participates in self-care as appropriate
- Demonstrates understanding of rationale for interventions
- Reports increased comfort following pain relief measures

NURSING CARE PLAN
Patient Who is Confused

The patient is a 19-year-old male who was brought into the trauma center by the police after having been found wandering aimlessly along a dirt road by a passing motorist. Details of the patient's accident are still not complete, but the police found an overturned smashed motorcycle about 500 feet from where the patient was discovered. Upon arrival, it was noted that the patient was not wearing a helmet and had a strong odor of alcohol on his breath. A blood alcohol level was drawn as well as other drug toxicology studies, but the results are being kept confidential on the advice of his lawyer. Identification was made via a wallet found near the cycle. His vital signs have been stable, although difficult to obtain, as he has been combative since his arrival. Physical examination has also been hard to accomplish due to his altering states of cooperation.

He has a large facial laceration extending from just above the right eyebrow to the center midhair line (approximately 8 cm). Frontal swelling is noted along his forehead. Skull x-rays are negative for a fracture, and he has had a cranial CAT scan. The laceration was sutured with 6-0 nylon sutures and xylocaine.

He is moving all extremities without evidence of pain or tenderness. Abdominal trauma is being questioned as he has guarding and wincing on palpation of the left upper quadrant. Serial hematocrits have been stable, ruling out a ruptured spleen. Vital signs are stable and his pupils are equal and reactive to light. He has been uncooperative in testing his hand grasp. His condition is felt to be stable, but he is being admitted for observation due to the ingestion of unknown substance(s) and possible loss of consciousness at the scene of the accident. His score on the Glasgow coma scale is 12, with orientation only to self.

Past medical history

Provided by anxious parents who were notified once identification had been established.

Generally good health. Recently passed Army physical exam and was awaiting orders to attend basic training. Had plans to join the Reserves to obtain their college assistance program.

Immunizations up-to-date. Last tetanus booster 2 years ago due to a foot laceration with sutures.

No known food or drug allergies.

No history of hospitalizations/surgeries.

Psychosocial data

Lives with parents and 3 younger brothers.

Second year of college; business major.

Reported to be in scholastic jeopardy due to low grades.

Active in sports, likes basketball best.

Has part-time job at local McDonald's.

Has had driver's license since age 16.

One conviction of driving while intoxicated (DWI), age 18.

Has attended mandatory DWI classes. License just renewed

Covered by parents health insurance.

Protestant religion. No active church involvement.

Said to have many girlfriends, recently depressed over loss of special girlfriend.

Assessment data

Well-developed, well-nourished male who is oriented to self only. Cannot state orientation to time, place, or persons

Does not appear to recognize parents.

Vital signs stable: T 99 R, P 84, R 22, B.P. 126/78.

Skin: Color good. Multiple abrasions on right forehead. Sutures dry and intact. No evidence infection.

Abrasions also on right chest wall. No drainage.

No rashes, no edema.

Head: Patent nares. No discharge.

Cut on upper lip. Central upper incisor loose.

EENT: Full extra ocular movements (EOMs). Pupils round, equal, and react to light accommodation. Visual acuity intact.

No complaints of dizziness or diplopia.

Respiratory: Regular rate and rhythm. No use of accessory muscles.

Chest movements symmetrical. Clear to percussion and ascultation. No rales, rhonchi, or rubs.

Abdominal: Soft. Slight tenderness in upper left quadrant, with some guarding on palpation. Nondistended. Bowel sounds present all quadrants.

Musculoskeletal: Moving all extremities well. Full range of motion.

Equal grasps and sensations. DTR's intact, 2+ and symmetrical.

Babinski sign negative. Unable to test for Romberg's sign.

Is right handed.

Neuro: Follows commands inconsistently. Speech rambling. Some echolalia.

No memory of events prior to accident.

Cannot name president of United States, or identify basic colors.

Will count to 10 only. No ability to add or subtract.

Periods of increased agitation and crying.

Unable to test all cranial nerves, due to lack of cooperation.

Will shrug shoulders, blink, raise eyebrows, smile, frown, and yawn.

Cardiovascular: Apical pulse 82 and regular. No diaphoresis.

Lab data

Hct stable at 34-36. Checked every 3 hours for first 24 hours.

Hgb 12.2 Oxygen saturations stable at 96-98.

Platelets, electrolytes, liver function tests (LFTs), BUN, FBS, all within normal limits.

Urinalysis WNL. No gross or microscopic hematuria.

Chest x-ray and flat plate of abdomen all negative.

Medications

No medications.

IV 1000 ml D5W in Ringers Lactate at 80 ml per hour.

IV removed by patient. Decision to restart pending tolerance of po fluids.

Clear liquid diet. Advance as tolerated. Nursing judgment.

NURSING DIAGNOSIS

Sensory perceptual alterations related to head trauma, and question of drug ingestion as evidenced by confusion, anxiety, and apprehension.

Expected patient outcomes	Nursing interventions	Evaluation for expected outcomes
Patient will obtain orientation to persons, place, and time (in addition to self). Patient will not show signs of cerebral tissue perfusion related to an interruption of cerebral blood flow. Patient will show an interest in his external environment. Patient will show a decrease in anxiety and agitation levels. Patient will demonstrate an increased ability to react to reality.	Assess patient for signs and symptoms of decreased cerebral tissue perfusion: dizziness, syncope, blurred or dimmed vision, diplopia, or any change in his visual field. Monitor for a decreased level of consciousness, seizures, paresthesis, motor weakness, paralysis and unequal pupils, (late sign) or an absent pupillary reaction to light.	Patient does not show signs of altered tissue perfusion related to an interruption in cerebral blood flow. Patient's level of consciousness does not deteriorate. Patient communicates in a lucid manner. Patient reestablishes a sleep-wake cycle.

Continued on next page.

Expected patient outcomes	Nursing interventions	Evaluation for expected outcomes
	Monitor his vital signs every 2 hours until stable. Report any deviations from the baseline. Orient patient to reality: call him by name. Tell him your name and why you are with him. Give background information (time, place, and date) frequently throughout the day. Orient him to his environment, including sights and sounds. (Example: "This is a hospital. I am a nurse caring for you. You are hearing the food cart go down the hall.") Have his parents bring in photos and personal articles from home. Talk to patient while providing care. Encourage the family to discuss past and present events with him. Arrange to be with him at predetermined times to avoid feelings of isolation. Turn on the TV and radio for short periods of time, based on his interests to help him orient to reality. Hold his hand while talking to soothe him. Monitor his response. Continually monitor neurologic signs and report changes immediately. Always approach in a calm gentle manner to avoid startling him. Encourage regular sleep patterns and routines. Encourage the family to visit frequently. Provide reassurances and explanations to aid their understanding of his condition. Suggest that friends send cards rather than visit or call during the acute stage.	Upon discharge, patient will be oriented to self, person, place, and time. Patient's periods of agitation, anxiety, and confusion will be diminished or absent.

NURSING DIAGNOSIS

Potential for injury related to the question of drug ingestion and cerebral trauma.

Expected patient outcomes	Nursing interventions	Evaluation for expected outcomes
Patient is protected from injury while in an agitated and/or confused state. Patient identifies factors that could increase potential for injury.	While orienting patient to the environment, state his boundaries. Assess his ability to use the call bell.	Patient will remain safe and free of injury while in a confused state. Patient cooperates in keeping himself free from harm. Parents incorporate safety teachings into discharge plans.

Expected patient outcomes	Nursing interventions	Evaluation for expected outcomes
Patient cooperates in applying safety measures to prevent injury. Family develops strategies to maintain safety upon discharge to home. Patient optimizes ADLs within sensiomotor limitations.	Keep the side rails up at all times, with the bed in the low position, with the wheels locked. Keep a light on at night to prevent any falls. Conduct a close watch on him, especially when agitated. Teach the family about the need for safe illumination, especially if he has distorted images. Monitor his gait when ambulating. Have two people if he is unsteady. Have a system in place to call for assistance if he is extremely agitated. Assist patient when eating. Monitor for safe use of utensils. Have him do as much self-care as possible (i.e., brushing teeth). Praise him for any attempts. Discuss the need for nonskid slippers or sneakers when ambulating. Assess his visual acuity prior to ambulation. Discuss safety upon return home with his parents. Inquire into their ability to remain home with him until he feels safe. Discuss the impact of patient's confusion on his younger siblings.	

NURSING DIAGNOSIS

Impaired verbal communication related to the questionable history of drug ingestion, and the cerebral trauma, as evidenced by periods of crying, echolalia, and garbled speech.

Expected patient outcomes	Nursing interventions	Evaluation for expected outcomes
Patient's needs are met by staff and his family. Patient grows in his ability to answer direct questions correctly. Patient communicates his needs and desires without undue frustration. Patient uses an alternate method of communication (temporarily).	Speak slowly and distinctly when addressing patient. Stand where he can see and hear you. Reorient him to reality. Use a large calendar and reality orientation boards. Use short simple phrases and yes and no questions, especially when his frustration level is high. Be prepared to repeat the words or directions. Monitor for signs of understanding. (nodding his head, frowning). Encourage his attempts at communication. Listen carefully for identifiable words. Provide reinforcement when he is lucid.	Patient's needs are met consistently. Patient and his family communicate at a satisfactory level. Patient correctly answers two direct questions. By the time of discharge, patient's echolalia is gone and his speech is no longer garbled. Patient communicates his basic needs (i.e., use of the urinal, need for privacy) to staff and his family via gestures and sign language prior to his regaining oral ability.

Continued on next page.

Expected patient outcomes	Nursing interventions	Evaluation for expected outcomes
	Allow ample time for a response. Do not answer questions for him. Teach his family the same. Do not pretend to understand if you do not. This will only add to his confusion. Remove distractions from environment during his attempts to communicate (i.e., lowering the sound on the TV). Adjust his care plan as progress develops.	

NURSING DIAGNOSIS

Pain—headache related to cerebral trauma, as evidenced by crying and wincing with head movement and swelling in the frontal area of his head.

Expected patient outcomes	Nursing interventions	Evaluation for expected outcomes
Patient will obtain relief from his headache as evidenced by verbalization of headache relief, relaxed facial expression, and body posturing. Patient will show increased participation in activities.	Determine how patient usually responds to pain. Assess for nonverbal signs of headache, (wrinkled brow, clenched fists, squinting, rubbing head, avoidance of bright lights and noises). Assess for any verbal attempts at communication of pain. Assess for factors that seem to aggravate his head pain. Implement measures to relieve the pain (quiet environment, dim lights, avoidance of any sudden movements). Provide nonpharmacological measures for headache relief (e.g., cool cloth to forehead, back rub, distraction). Involve family to assist in soothing his pain by gentle touch. Administer nonnarcotic analgesics if ordered. Monitor results. Consult physician if above action fails to relieve his headache.	Patient will experience relief from his headache. By his body language, patient will indicate that aggravating factors have been decreased or eliminated. Patient will cooperate more fully in his neurologic assessments and participate in nursing care activities.

REFERENCES AND ADDITIONAL READINGS

1. Bates D: Predicting recovery from coma, Br J Hosp Med 29:276-282, 1983.

2. Beck C and Heacock P: Nursing interventions for patients with Alzheimer's disease, Nurs Clin North Am 23:95-124, 1988.

3. Budinger TF: Noninvasive image analysis in critical care medicine: major innovations described, Crit Care Monitor 2(5):1, 1985.

4. Burns EM and Buckwalter KC: Pathophysiology and etiology of Alzheimer's disease, Nurs Clin North Am 23:11-29, 1988.

5. Conway-Rutkowski BL: Carini and Owens' neurological and neurosurgical nursing, ed 8, St Louis, 1982, The CV Mosby Co.

6. Delgado JM and Billo JM: Care of the patient with Parkinson's disease: surgical and nursing interventions, J Neuro Nurs 20:142-158, 1988.

7. Doolittle ND: Stroke recovery: review of the literature and suggestions for future research, J Neuro Nurs 20:169-173, 1987.

8. Engler MB and Engler MM: Magnetic resonance imaging: an overview and safety considerations, J Emerg Nurs 12:360-364, 1987.

9. Ferguson JM: Helping an MS patient live a better life, RN 50(12):22-27, 1987.

10. Fisher J: What you need to know about neurological testing, RN 50(1):47-55, 1987.

11. Friedman-Campbell M and Hart CA: Theoretical strategies and nursing interventions to promote psychosocial adaptation to spinal cord injuries and disability, J Neurosurg Nurs 16:335-342, 1984.

12. Grove TP and others: A man alone . . . and afraid: caring for a patient with Guillain-Barre syndrome, Nurs 87 17(12):44-48, 1987.

13. Hahn K: Left vs right: what a difference the side makes in stroke, Nurs 87 17(9):44-47, 1987.

14. Hall K, Cope DN, and Rappaport M: Glasgow outcome scale and disability rating scale: comparative usefulness in following recovery in traumatic head injury, Arch Phys Med Rehabil 66:35-37, 1985.

15. Hickey JV: The clinical practice of neurological and neurosurgical nursing, ed 2, Philadelphia, 1986, JB Lippincott Co.

16. Jennett B and Teasdale G: Aspects of coma after severe head injury, Lancet 1:878-881, 1977.

17. Kirk E and Bradford LT: Effects of alcohol on the central nervous system: implications for the neuroscience nurse, J Neuro Nurs 19:326-335 1987.

18. Malasanos L, Barkauskas V, and Stoltenberg-Allen K: Health assessment, ed 4, St Louis, 1990, the CV Mosby Co.

19. Newman F, Ogburn-Russell L, and Rutledge JN: Magnetic resonance imaging: the latest in diagnostic technology, Nurs 87 17(1):44-47, 1987.

20. Pallett PJ and O'Brien MT: Textbook of neurological nursing, Boston, 1985, Little, Brown & Co.

21. Purtilo DT and Purtilo RB: A survey of human diseases, ed 2, Boston, 1989, Little, Brown & Co.

22. Robinet K: Increased intracranial pressure: management with an intraventricular catheter, J Neurosurg Nurs 17:95-104, 1985.

23. Stone N: Amyotrophic lateral sclerosis: a challenge for constant adaptation, J Neuro Nurs 19:166-173, 1987.

24. Whitney FW: Relationship of laterality of stroke to emotional and functional outcome, J Neuro Nurs 19:158-165, 1987.

PROBLEMS AFFECTING
Vision and Hearing

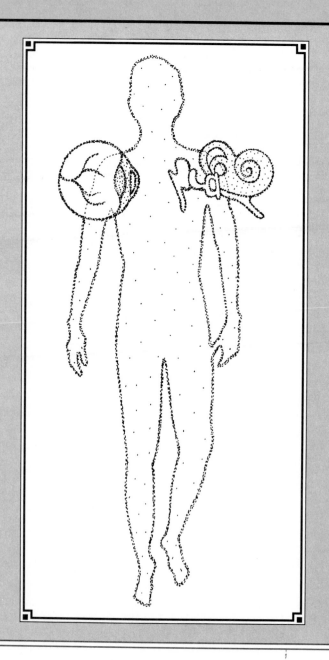

KEY WORDS

astigmatism
audiologist
cataract
cerumen
conjunctivitis
cryosurgery
diplopia
eustachian tube
glaucoma
hyperopia
iridectomy
keratitis
keratoplasty
labyrinthitis
mastoiditis
Meniere's syndrome
miotic
mydriatic
myopia
ophthalmologist
otitis media
otologist
otosclerosis
pinna
refraction
stapedectomy
strabismus
tonometry
trabeculoplasty
uveitis

OBJECTIVES

1. Associate the anatomic parts of the eye and ear to the functions of sight and hearing.

2. Identify the purpose and procedure for common diagnostic tests involving the eye and ear.

3. Describe the use of the tonometer in measuring intraocular pressure.

4. Explain the importance of detecting and removing contact lenses from injured or unconscious patients.

5. Differentiate between the signs and symptoms of hordeola, conjunctivitis, trachoma, blepharitis, keratitis, uveitis, and iritis.

6. Discuss the relationship between injury to the cornea and corneal ulcers.

7. Describe the postoperative nursing interventions for a patient receiving a corneal transplant.

8. Discuss the assessment of, prevention of, and interventions for glaucoma and its role in causing blindness.

9. Describe the symptoms of cataracts and the nursing interventions following cataract extraction.

10. Identify the signs and symptoms of retinal detachment.

11. Discuss the emergency care of the patient with an eye injury.

12. Identify observations that would indicate hearing impairment in an infant or child.

13. List the guidelines for talking to a hearing-impaired person.

14. Describe the signs and symptoms of otitis media.

15. Define otosclerosis and describe the surgical procedure (stapedectomy) used to correct the condition.

16. Discuss the postoperative nursing interventions for the patient having a stapedectomy.

17. Identify the activity restrictions for the patient following tympanoplasty.

18. Identify the symptoms of Meniere's syndrome.

STRUCTURE AND FUNCTION OF THE EYE AND EAR

The Eye

The eye is a highly specialized sense organ, a large portion of which lies protected within a bony cavity, with only the anterior portion exposed (Figure 23-1). The eye has three coats. The external, or fibrous, coat comprises the white, opaque **sclera,** covering four-fifths of the eye, and the **cornea,** a transparent, avascular, curved layer covering the anterior one fifth of the eye. The cornea bends light rays entering the eye and focuses the resulting images slightly behind the retina. The sclera, the protective layer of the eye, is penetrated around the optic nerve by blood vessels and the nerves that lead to the interior of the eye.

The middle, or vascular, coat is also known as the **uveal tract** and consists of the choroid, iris, and ciliary body. The **choroid** lies between the sclera and retina and is firmly attached on its inner surface to the retina. The blood supply of the choroid nourishes the retina, and the choroid's dark pigmentation prevents internal reflection of light. The **iris** is the colored part of the eye that can be seen through the cornea. It is composed of muscle fibers that regulate the amount of light entering the eye by changing the size of the **pupil,** the circular opening in its center. Behind the iris lies the crystalline **lens,** a biconvex, transparent structure enclosed in a capsule of transparent elastic membrane that can change its shape to focus light rays precisely on the retina. The shape of the lens is controlled by the ciliary muscle contained in the external aspect of the **ciliary body.** The internal surfaces of the ciliary body secrete **aqueous humor,** the watery fluid that fills the anterior and posterior chambers of the eye—the spaces in front of and behind the iris. The fluid passes from the posterior chamber, through the pupil, to the anterior chamber, and then is drained off through spaces at the angle formed by the iris and cornea into a circular venous channel called **Schlemm's canal.** The ciliary body connects the choroid with the periphery of the iris.

The third and inner coat is the **retina,** a delicate membrane in which the fibers of the optic nerve are spread out in a complicated network of nerve cells, rods, and cones lined with pigment epithelium. The posterior portion of the retina is called the **optic fundus.** Near its center lies a circular, depressed, white to pink area where the optic nerve enters the eyeball called the **optic disc.**

It contains no photoreceptor cells; thus it is insensitive to light and is known as the blind spot. Just lateral to the optic disc is a small, oval, yellowish area called the **macula lutea** or macula. At the center of the macula is a depressed part known as the **fovea centralis,** the area of most acute vision. Blood is supplied to the retina by its central artery, which enters the eyeball with the optic nerve. Drainage is accomplished through a corresponding system of retinal veins that join to form the central vein of the retina, which exits along the path of the optic nerve. The space between the lens and the retina is the **vitreous chamber,** which contains a colorless, transparent gel called the **vitreous body,** or **vitreous humor.**

Vitreous humor maintains the shape of the eye and supports the retina. If the vitreous were to be lost, such as by a penetrating injury, the eye would collapse.

The eye rests on a cushion of fat within its bony orbit. Six voluntary **(extrinsic)** muscles attached to the outside of the sclera control the movements of the eyes. The action of these muscles is coordinated to allow binocular vision, the concerted use of both eyes working together. Branches of several cranial nerves control these muscles. Involuntary **(intrinsic)** muscles within the eye control the shape of the lens and the size of the pupil.

The accessory organs of the eye include the eyebrows, eyelids and their muscles, eyelashes, conjunctiva, lacrimal glands and their ducts, and sebaceous glands.

Vision is the result of light rays entering the eye; as they pass through various structures of the eye, they must produce a clear image on the retina. When the image is produced on the retina, visual receptors in the eye are stimulated, thus causing a nerve impulse to be transmitted to the visual center in the brain.

The Ear

The ear consists of three parts: external, middle, and inner (Figure 23-2). The external portion is composed of the visible **auricle,** or **pinna,** and the **external auditory canal.** The auricle acts as a collecting trumpet for sound waves and directs them toward the auditory canal (external acoustic meatus), where they are further directed toward the tympanic membrane. Modified sweat glands in the auditory canal, called **ceruminous glands,** secrete **cerumen** (earwax).

The **tympanic membrane** (eardrum) separates

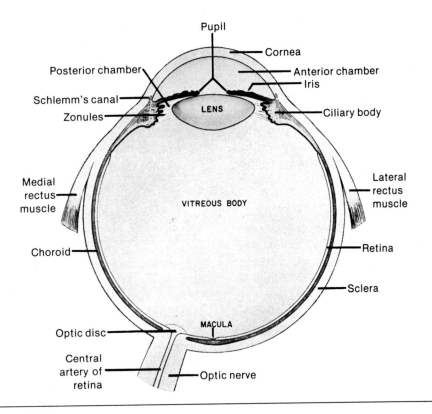

Figure 23-1
Cross section of eye. *(From Saunders WH and others: Nursing care in eye, ear, nose, and throat disorders, ed 4, St Louis, 1979, The CV Mosby Co.)*

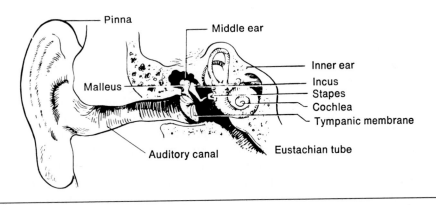

Figure 23-2
Diagram of ear.

the external from the middle ear. The skin of the auricle, containing hairs and glands, is continued into the auditory canal and covers the external surface of the tympanic membrane, where it becomes very thin and hairless. The internal surface of the tympanic membrane is covered with mucous membrane. The normal membrane appears pearly gray and shiny. The external surface of the tympanic membrane is supplied by the auriculotemporal nerve, and some innervation is supplied by a small auricular branch of the **vagus nerve** (cranial nerve X). This nerve may also contain some glossopharyngeal and facial nerve fibers.

The middle ear, or **tympanic cavity,** is an air-filled space located within the junction of the petrous and mastoid parts of the temporal bone. It is separated from the external ear by the tympanic membrane. The tympanic cavity is lined with a continuous mucous membrane that also lines the posterior auditory tube (eustachian tube), the mastoid air cells, and the mastoid antrum. The **eustachian tube** connects the middle ear with the nasopharynx; its function is to equalize pressure in the middle ear with atmospheric pressure, thereby allowing free movement of the tympanic membrane. Air can enter or leave the tympanic cavity through the eustachian tube to balance pressure on both sides of the membrane. The middle ear contains three small bones called the auditory ossicles, each of which is named to describe its shape: the **malleus** (hammer), **incus** (anvil), and **stapes** (stirrup). The malleus is attached to the tympanic membrane, the incus is attached to the malleus, and the stapes is attached to the incus. The other end of the stapes fits into the **oval window** (fenestra ovalis), which leads to the inner ear. These bones receive sound vibrations from the tympanic membrane and transmit them to the inner ear. Another opening to the inner ear is covered with a membrane and is called the **round window** (fenestra rotunda).

The inner ear (labyrinth) consists of the bony (or osseous) labyrinth, which contains the vestibule, cochlea, and semicircular canals. A membranous labyrinth within the bony labyrinth contains two small sacs, the **utricle** and **saccule,** in which a fluid called **endolymph** is found. **Perilymph** surrounds the utricle and saccule, which are suspended within the vestibule. The cochlea is a snail-shaped tube containing the cochlear duct with the receptors for the cochlear branch of the vestibulocochlear nerve—cranial nerve VIII— and the sense of hearing. The semicircular canals and the utricle contain the receptors for the vestibular branch of cranial nerve VIII concerned with maintaining a sense of equilibrium. Several other structures and supporting parts are contained within the inner ear, and students who wish a more detailed review should consult a textbook of anatomy.

The auditory center for hearing is located in the temporal lobe of the cerebrum, and stimulation of this center results in hearing. Sound waves enter the ear through the auditory canal and cause the tympanic membrane to vibrate. The vibrations are transmitted from the tympanic membrane through the bones of the middle ear. One of the three small bones, the stapes, moves against the oval window, causing vibrations that are trans-mitted through the fluid of the cochlea and end up at the round window, where they are dissipated. The passing of the pressure wave from the oval to the round window stimulates the hair cells of the **organ of Corti** to move and send the stimulus to the membrane of Corti. These impulses are received by the cochlear branch of the auditory nerve and are transmitted to the brain, where they are perceived as sound.

NURSING ASSESSMENT OF THE PATIENT WITH EYE PROBLEMS

The assessment begins with a thorough nursing history, including information about the patient's medical condition, past surgery, and current symptoms. The chief complaint, such as change in vision, redness, itching, floating spots, discharge, or halos should be investigated and documented. The nurse should assist the patient in identifying how long the problem has been present, when it is most intense, and if anything helps to relieve it. The nurse can also assess the person's vision, the response of the pupils to light, the ability of the eyes to look in the same direction, and follow a light. The placement of the eyes within its bony orbit is assessed and whether it is sunken or protruding should be noted.

Diagnostic Tests and Procedures
Physical examination: eye

A complete physical examination is important in the treatment of diseases of the eye. When the underlying cause is diabetes, syphilis, or arteriosclerosis, treatment of the cause must accompany any treatment of the eye. The physician may order x-ray examinations, examination of the blood, or neurologic examination. A thorough eye examination often leads to the discovery of serious diseases in other parts of the body.

Eye examination

Several eye tests are used to detect eye diseases and disorders of vision.

Snellen's chart. Acuity refers to the clearness of vision, or the person's ability to see. The most common method for determining acuity of vision is testing with a Snellen eye chart, a method used in schools, industry, and physicians' offices as a screening examination. The chart consists of rows of letters arranged in various sizes that a person should be able to see at various distances from the chart. If individuals are able to read the letters marked 20 at a distance of 20 feet, they are considered to have 20/20 vision, which is normal vision. However, if only the rows of larger letters marked 30, 40, or even 200 are read correctly, the person is said to have 20/30, 20/40, or 20/200 vision, indicating a loss of visual acuity. Sometimes the vision in one eye may be 20/20, and the test will indicate a loss of vision in the other eye. When the individual is wearing glasses, the test is usually performed both with and without the glasses. One form of the chart consists of the letter "E" arranged in various positions. Young children, illiterate adults, or those with language problems may be tested with this chart by having them point in the direction faced by the open end of the E, or match a handheld E to the one on the chart. Questions have been raised as to whether very young children are capable of using the E chart, and, as a result, various other kinds of charts using pictures or simple geometric forms, for example, are being developed and tested.

Amsler's grid test. A grid composed of horizontal and vertical lines that form 5-mm squares is used to detect scotomas or blind spots in the central 20 degrees of visual field and to evaluate the presence, stability, or progression of macular disease. Covering one eye and wearing any corrective lenses usually worn, the patient is instructed to stare at a dot centrally located on the grid. The patient should be able to see the dot, and the lines on the grid should appear straight. All four sides of the grid should be visible. The patient is asked to describe and outline any area where the grid is distorted or absent. A pathologic condition of the macula is suggested if the patient describes a gray area or an area where lines are missing or distorted **(metamorphopsia).** This test is for initial screening only and must be followed by ophthalmoscopy, visual field testing, and fluorescein angiography to further evaluate the presence of disease.[52]

Perimetry. This test is used to examine the central and peripheral visual fields. It is useful to follow the progression of **glaucoma,** which affects peripheral vision and can result in blindness. The three common methods used are the **tangent screen, goldmann perimeter,** and **computerized perimeter.** The tangent screen examination is performed to determine loss of vision in the central visual field. The patient fixes his or her eye on a target on a screen. Test objects are then brought from the periphery into the visual field, and the

patient is asked to signal when the object is seen. This is repeated at 30-degree intervals on the screen, and the examiner marks the point at which the object is noted. Each eye is tested separately. The normal blind spot caused by the projection of the optic nerve into the visual field is located. The test is normal if the blind spot appears in the appropriate location and the visual field forms a circle extending 25 degrees in all directions. The ability to see only half of the visual field is called **hemianopsia.** It often occurs following a cerebrovascular accident, and plotting the visual field can help determine the location of the lesion in the brain.[52] The Goldmann perimetry test is a more accurate test of visual field defects. A hollow, white spheric bowl is placed in front of the patient. Lights of variable size and intensity are brought in from the periphery. Boundary lines of perception are formed which are plotted on a sheet to make a visual field plot. **Computerized, automated perimetry** test, the most sophisticated and sensitive test, uses this same method but eliminates variables introduced by the examiner.[52]

Color vision tests. Color vision tests assess the ability to recognize differences in color. The most commonly used is the **Ishihara test** (polychromatic plates). The cones of the retina contain three pigments that are sensitive to color—specifically, red, green, and blue, the primary colors of light. Mixtures of these pigments allow perception of other colors. A color vision deficiency may be inherited as a sex-linked recessive trait; it affects approximately 8% of males and less than 1% of females. It may also be acquired as a result of retinal disease.[52] The test is performed to screen for disease of the retina or to screen applicants for employment in which accurate color perception is vital. The driver's eye examination also tests for the ability to differentiate color to determine whether the driver has the ability to see and interpret stoplights. Colored dots are arranged on a background of randomly mixed colors. A person with normal color vision will be able to identify all patterns or symbols on the test field. A patient with a deficiency will be unable to identify patterns or symbols in the color he is unable to see. True color blindness—**achromatopia,** or the inability to see any color—is rare; the patient sees all colors as shades of gray. Other visual impairments usually accompany true color blindness. Inherited color deficiencies affect both eyes; acquired deficiencies may affect only one eye or part of the visual field.[52]

Refraction. Refraction enables images to be focused on the retina and directly affects visual acuity. It is the bending of light rays by the cornea, aqueous humor, lens, and vitreous humor in the eye. The ability of the eyes to bend light rays and form images on the retina is measured in a routine eye examination or whenever a patient complains of a change in vision. The ophthalmologist can perform a refraction by using a retinoscope or by questioning the patient while placing trial lenses before his or her eyes. Lenses can then be prescribed to correct the error in refraction and thus improve vision. Common eye problems involving errors in refraction include **myopia,** or nearsightedness (light rays focus in front of the retina because the eyeball is too long); **hyperopia,** or farsightedness (light rays focus behind the retina because the eyeball is too short); **presbyopia** (the inability of the lens to change its shape or to accommodate and focus on close objects as a result of aging); and **astigmatism** (lack of uniform refraction of light rays resulting in a blurring of vision). Astigmatism is usually caused by unequal curvature of the cornea. Refraction may be done with or without the use of cycloplegics, drugs used to inhibit accommodation by the lens. The drops are more commonly used in children than adults. Before the drops are instilled, the patient's history should be checked for hypersensitivity to dilating eye drops **(mydriatics** and **cycloplegics)** and for the presence of narrow-angle glaucoma. Patients with narrow-angle glaucoma use constricting eye drops **(miotics)** to open the angle of the eye and increase the flow of aqueous humor. Mydriatics and cycloplegics will close this angle, restricting flow and increasing pressure in the eye. Blindness may occur from damage to the optic nerve caused by increase in pressure.

Exophthalmometry. This test uses an instrument called an exophthalmometer to measure the forward protrusion of the eye and to evaluate an increase or decrease in the condition known as exopthalmos, the abnormal forward protrusion of the eye seen in thyroid diseases and other conditions that displace the eye in the orbit.

Slit-lamp examination. The slit lamp is an instrument equipped with a special lighting system and a binocular microscope. It is used to examine in detail the anterior segment of the eye, which includes the eyelids, eyelashes, conjunctiva, sclera, cornea, tear film, anterior chamber, iris, crystalline lens, and vitreous face. If abnormalities are detected, special devices can be attached to allow more detailed examination. Mydriatic drops are not used unless the disease condition requires dilation for comfort and adequate illumination. If a corneal ulcer or abrasion is detected, a fluorescein stain may be applied to provide better visualization.[8]

Schirmer's tearing test. The function of the major lacrimal glands responsible for tearing can be tested by inserting a strip of filter paper into the lower conjunctival sac. The amount of moisture absorbed by the paper is measured and compared to the normal level. The accessory lacrimal glands of Krause and Wolfring, responsible for maintenance of adequate corneal moisture, can be tested by instilling a topical anesthetic before inserting the paper. The anesthetic inhibits reflex tearing by the major lacrimal glands caused by the filter paper so that only the basic tear film produced by the accessory glands is measured.

Tonometry. Tonometry is used to measure intraocular pressure (IOP), which normally ranges between 12 to 21 mm Hg. This range is maintained by the balance between the production and outflow of aqueous. In certain diseases such as glaucoma, there is an obstruction of the flow of aqueous and, as a consequence, pressure will increase. **Applanation tonometry** (Figure 23-3) is the most accurate and frequently used method to measure IOP. Anesthetic drops (0.5% proparacaine) and fluorescein dye are placed in the eye; the tonometer, which is attached to a slit lamp, is placed onto the cornea. **Schiotz tonometry,** although an older technique, has the advantage of being a portable hand-held method and is useful in clinics or at the bedside. In this method only one drop of anesthetic is required before the tonometer is placed on the eye (Figure 23-4).

Ophthalmoscopy. The ophthalmoscope is an instrument that permits visualization of the vascular and nerve tissue in the fundus of the eye, including the optic disc, retinal vessels, macula, and retina. Mydriatic eye drops are instilled to dilate the pupil, if necesssary for good visualization. Drops may not be necessary if the lighting in the room can be reduced and there is sufficient light in the ophthalmoscope. The test is performed to identify changes in the blood vessels in the eye and to detect tumors and other diseases of the eye (Figure 23-5).

Fluorescein angiography. This test allows the examination of the microvascular structures of the retina. Sodium fluorescein is injected intravenously, and multiple photographs of the fundus

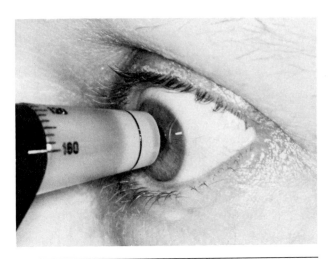

Figure 23-3

Applanation tonometer. Provides a more precise measurement of intraocular pressure. *(From Saunders WH and others: Nursing care in eye, ear, nose, and throat disorders, ed 4, St Louis, 1979, The CV Mosby Co.)*

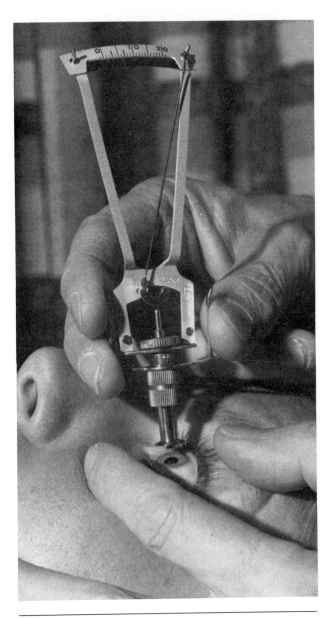

Figure 23-4

Schiotz tonometer used to measure intraocular pressure. *(From Saunders WH and others: Nursing care in eye, ear, nose, and throat disorders, ed 4, St Louis, 1979, The CV Mosby Co.)*

are taken using a special camera. The patient is prepared for the test by dilating the pupils with mydriatic drops. Food and fluids are allowed, but the patient may be instructed to eat lightly before the test. Photographs may be taken just before the dye is injected, and then more are taken in rapid sequence just after the dye is injected. Delayed photographs may be taken 20 minutes after injection of the dye. The blood vessels of the retina normally fill with the dye within 12 to 15 seconds after injection. The rate at which the blood vessels fill and the presence of obstruction and abnormalities can be detected in the photographs by a specialist.[8]

Ocular ultrasonography. Ocular ultrasonography involves the transmission of high-frequency sound waves through the eye and the measurement of their reflection from ocular structures. It is especially helpful if the view of the fundus is clouded by an opaque medium such as a cataract or a vitreous hemorrhage. It may also be used to measure the length of the eye and the curvature of the cornea in preparation for surgery. Lesions within the eye and in the orbit may be located as well.

Loss of Sight

In the United States approximately 0.2% of the population is blind. Blindness is legally defined as a visual acuity with correction of 20/200 or less in the better eye or a visual field of no greater than 20 degrees. Loss of vision may be congenital or acquired and may occur suddenly or gradually. Several pathologic conditions may result in varying degrees of blindness, including diabetes, hypertension, inflammation of the choroid and retina, retinal detachment, infectious diseases such as syphilis, certain poisons such as grain alcohol, and injuries. A gradual loss of vision may be caused by cataracts and glaucoma. Cerebral disorders can affect the optic nerve, as can malignant

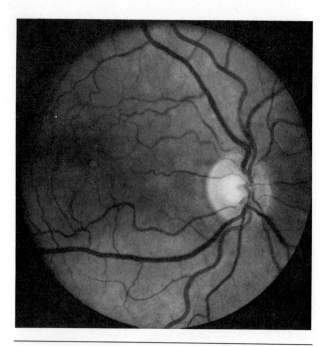

Figure 23-5

Optic nerve and retinal blood vessels as seen with ophthalmoscope. *(From Saunders WH and others: Nursing care in eye, ear, nose, and throat disorders, ed 4, St Louis, 1979, The CV Mosby Co.)*

lesions that occur in children, such as retinoblastoma. Many children were permanently blinded between 1930 and 1950 because of the excessive use of oxygen in the premature newborn nursery, which caused retinopathy of prematurity. Rubella occurring in the pregnant woman is implicated as a cause of cataracts and glaucoma in the infant.

Refractive Errors of the Eye

When light rays enter the eye, they must focus directly on the retina. To reach the retina, the rays pass through several structures in the eye, and in doing so are bent so that they will fall directly on the receptors in the retina. Sometimes an abnormal condition exists in some of the structures so that bending of the light rays—refraction—may not permit the image to focus directly on the retina (Figure 23-6). These defects are called **errors of refraction.** The patient may complain of eyestrain, headache, and sometimes of nausea. To overcome the error, the person must have an eye examination and glasses fitted to correct the refractive error. This examination is also called refraction.

Guidelines for Interacting with Blind People

1. Always introduce yourself each time you come into contact with a blind person, unless you are well known to him or her.
2. If the blind person is a patient in hospital, knock on the door before entering the room.
3. Never touch the person before you speak. They may not have heard you approaching and you may startle them.
4. Explain what you will be doing before you start.
5. Let the person know when you are leaving the room. It is embarrassing for the person to discover they are talking and no one is there.

Tips to Facilitate Independence in Blind People

1. When helping a blind person walk, let him or her take your arm.
2. Keep furniture and other commonly used objects in specific places.
3. Encourage family and friends not to move objects in the blind person's usual environment without permission.
4. Put food, cooking utensils, and supplies in specific locations in the refrigerator or cupboard.
5. Place clothing in specific locations in closets and drawers or label with an identifying mark.
6. Use the hours on the face of the clock to identify placement of objects; for example, the potatoes on the plate are at 6 o'clock.

Myopia (nearsightedness)

Persons with myopia have a defect that may be in the eyeball or in the bending of the light rays. The rays are brought to focus too soon, or in front of the retina. As a result, distant visions will be blurred rather than clear. Myopia may become progressively worse in some young persons, and it is important for the individual to remain under the care of the ophthalmologist. A surgical technique called **radial keratotomy** has been developed that corrects the defect by changing the curvature of the eye.

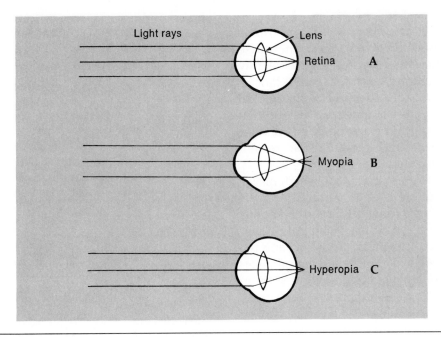

Figure 23-6
Refractive errors of eye. A, Light rays entering eye are brought to focus directly on retina, resulting in normal vision. B, Light rays focus in front of retina, resulting in myopia. C, Light rays focus at back of retina, resulting in hyperopia.

Hyperopia (farsightedness)

In persons with hyperopia the light rays do not bend sharply enough or soon enough to focus the object on the retina, and the point of focus is behind the retina. The individual will see distant objects clearly, but near vision will be blurred. Examinations such as those with the Snellen eye chart may not show this condition. A small eye chart may be held 15 inches from the patient's eyes to test for a defect in near vision.

Presbyopia

The ability to focus on near objects (**accommodation**) diminishes with age. This inability, called **presbyopia,** is caused by loss of elasticity of the lens. As a consequence, most people over 40 will require glasses for reading and close up work.

Astigmatism

Astigmatism is a defect in the curvature of the eyeball surface, usually of the cornea but sometimes of the lens. Exact regularity of the curvature probably does not exist in many persons, but defects may be too slight to cause any trouble. However, when the irregularity is severe, all light rays do not bend equally, and the individual will suffer from eyestrain and blurred vision. When the ophthalmologist fits glasses for astigmatism, the glasses should be worn constantly.

Strabismus

Strabismus is a condition that occurs when the eyes are not perfectly aligned. The deviation can be in any direction; inward (eso), outward (exo), upward (hyper), downward (hypo), or in a rotary direction. If the deviation is present under binocular viewing conditions it is called a **tropia.** For example, **esotropia,** the most common type of strabismus, would be a turning in of the eye toward the nose. If the deviation is present only after binocular vision is interrupted by covering one eye, it is called a **phoria.** Strabismus can also be classified as paretic or nonparetic. **Paretic strabismus** results from paralysis of one or more extraocular muscles. **Nonparetic strabismus** is caused by problems in fusion, accommodation, or errors of refraction that result in problems of muscle balance. Strabismus is present in 2% of all children. Many people think that strabismus can be outgrown. This almost never occurs and if the child is to have binocular vision and good visual acuity, treatment must begin as early as possible.

Contact Lenses

As more people wear contact lenses, the nurse may be regularly asked about them. The nurse should know that these lenses are constantly being improved and are worn for many kinds of visual defects and disorders. The individual should have the eyes examined by an ophthalmologist to be sure that no serious eye disease exists, and contact lenses should be recommended by the ophthalmologist.

A contact lens is a small, thin, polished, plastic disk that is ground on its outer surface to correct vision deformities; its inner surface corresponds to the shape of the eye. It may be lightly tinted and is held in place by capillary attraction and the upper eyelid. The lens is moistened before insertion, and the conjunctival secretions provide lubrication and prevent irritation of the cornea. There are many advantages to wearing contact lenses, but the wearer must take precautions to avoid abrasions of the cornea. Causes for abrasions include prolonged wearing of improperly fitted lenses, tilting of the lens when removing or inserting it so that the edge of the lens scratches the cornea, or scratching the cornea with the fingernail. Abrasions are also caused by an inadequate flow of tears under the lenses.

It is important for the nurse to realize that an injured person may be wearing contact lenses, and unless they are removed, serious damage to the cornea may result (Figures 23-7 and 23-8). A light flashed into the eye from the side will cast a shadow on the iris, which will enable the nurse to detect the lens as the patient blinks his eyes.

A variety of contact lenses are worn today. The hard contact lens was the original type and is still prescribed today although less frequently. Soft and gas-permeable lenses are most common. Soft lenses offer little correction for corneal astigmatism and require greater care than the gas-permeable and hard lenses. Several types of very thin soft lenses have made longer wearing time possible.

The presence of the contact lens increases the metabolic rate of the cornea. The cornea normally receives its oxygen supply through the exchange of gases in the atmosphere and tears. When the eyes are closed, the cornea experiences a reduction in oxygen supply, but the reduced metabolism that occurs with sleep reduces the need for oxygen. The presence of a contact lens, however, increases the need for oxygen while the closed eyes interfere with its availability. If the contact

1. **DETERMINE IF PATIENT IS WEARING CONTACT LENSES:**
   a. Ask
   b. Check I.D. Card
   c. Check Medic Alert Medallion
   d. Look for contact lenses

2. **IF YOU SUSPECT THE LENSES ARE STILL ON THE EYE:**
   a. Apply adhesive tape strip to patient's forehead or adjacent area and label "Contact Lenses"
   b. Consult emergency aid file when time permits

3. **IF THE LENSES ARE FOUND:**
   a. Place in a case or bottle and label with patient's name (Mark "right" or "left," if known)
   b. Record on emergency tag

*Provided as a public service
by the
AMERICAN OPTOMETRIC ASSOCIATION*

Figure 23-7

Suggested emergency care for patients wearing contact lenses. *(Reprinted with permission of the American Optometric Association, St Louis.)*

lens is not removed, the damage to the cornea is directly related to the time the lens has been in place. Should corneal damage occur it will most likely affect the epithelium of the cornea, which is the outermost layer. Damage therefore is seldom permanent. Care must be taken to avoid damaging the cornea while removing the contact lens. Instructions for removing the different types of lenses are given in Figure 23-8. To determine which type of lens the patient is wearing, the size of the lens is examined in relationship to the cornea. The hard lens is always smaller than the cornea. The soft lens extends 1 to 2 mm beyond the corneal scleral junction. It is important to remove contact lenses from an injured person regardless of the type of lens. If the nurse is unable to remove the lenses, an ophthalmologist or optometrist should be called to remove them. Contact lenses removed from an injured or dying person should be placed in bottles labeled "right" and "left" with the patient's name and protected from loss or damage. Soft and gas-permeable lenses should be stored in saline solution.

Color Blindness

The inability to distinguish colors may be congenital or acquired, and it may be partial or complete. Acquired color blindness may be the result of injury or disease of the nervous mechanisms concerned with vision. Partial color blindness is

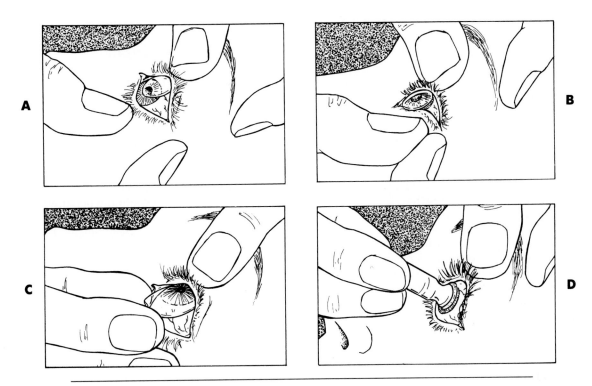

Figure 23-8

A, To remove hard lens, place thumb or finger directly on margin of lid at base of eyelashes and raise lid. Use same procedure with other hand to lower bottom lid. Recenter lens before removing. **B,** Slowly bring lids together, trapping contact lens between lid margins. Eyelid will break tear layer adhesion of contact lens, which will be ejected as lid forces it outward. **C,** Soft lens will move as lids are manipulated. If it does not seem slippery, it must be moistened with saline solution before attempting to remove it to avoid peeling epithelial tissues from corneal surface. To remove soft lens, raise upper lid with one hand and pinch lens with fingers of other hand. It will be removed easily if it is moist and may be removed even it it is off center in eye. **D,** Kits that contain contact lens suction cup are available in many emergency rooms. Suction cup is effective for removing hard and scleral lenses, but it cannot be used with soft lenses.

more common in men than in women, is rare in blacks, and is generally a congenital condition inherited as a sex-linked characteristic. The most common type of color blindness is **red-green blindness,** a condition in which persons do not see red or green as such but see them as yellow or blue in different intensities of saturation. A person may be color blind in one eye only, and will distinguish colors normally.

Some states require a person applying for a driver's license to be tested for color blindness. When an individual is found to be color blind in both eyes, he is taught to distinguish traffic lights by their location. Awareness of the defect often makes the person with color blindness a more cautious driver than the individual with normal color vision.

THE PATIENT WITH DISEASES AND DISORDERS OF THE EYE

Several nursing procedures are often necessary in caring for patients with diseases and disorders of the eye. These include the instillation of eye drops and ointments (see box on p. 676), the administration of eye irrigations (see box on p. 676), and the application of warm or cold compresses. Absolute cleanliness is essential, and the hands should be washed before beginning any procedure and should be washed after nursing each patient. All equipment must be clean, and in some situations sterile supplies and equipment may be required. The nurse should review these procedures and understand the precautions necessary in each procedure.

Instillation of Eye Drops

1. Wash your hands before doing any procedure on the eye.
2. With one hand put a finger on the patient's cheek just below the eye on the bony socket. Gently pull down until a small pocket is formed between the eyeball and lower lid.
3. Have the patient tilt his or her head back and look up. Place a drop into the pocket that you have formed (conjunctival sac).
4. Have the patient gently close both eyes for a minute to let the drop absorb.
5. If another drop is to be instilled, wait 3 to 5 minutes before the next one is put in.
6. The same procedure is followed for putting in ointments. The ointment is squeezed into the conjunctival sac from the inner to outer side of the eye. If putting in drops and ointment at the same time, the ointment goes in last.
7. Avoid touching any part of the eye with the medication container.

Eye Irrigation

1. Prepare the solution. Normal saline or lactated Ringer's solution is frequently used.
2. Position the patient comfortably with the head turned to one side.
3. Use a kidney basin or other appropriate means to catch the irrigating solution.
4. Direct the irrigating solution over the eye from the nasal to the temporal side of the eye. Avoid letting solution flow into the nonaffected eye.
5. Hold the eye open if necessary so that it is thoroughly cleansed. Do not instill the irrigating solution too forcefully.

Eye Irrigations

The equipment and procedures for an eye irrigation will vary depending on the purpose of the irrigation. If the purpose is to cleanse the eye postoperatively, sterile cotton balls moistened with solution can be used. The upper lid, lower lid, and lashes are gently cleansed using a new cotton ball for each. If the purpose is to remove secretions, a plastic squeeze bottle filled with solution may be all that is needed. On the other hand large amount of fluids will be needed for removing chemical irritants. Bags of solutions, such as an IV bag with tubing attached are useful. The tubing allows the fluid to be directed more easily onto the eye.

Inflammatory and Infectious Eye Disorders
Styes (external hordeola)

It is commonly but inaccurately believed that styes are a sign of weak eyes; they are from infections of Zeis' or Moll's glands in the eyelid. An internal hordeolum is an infection of a meibomian gland.[52] Styes are characterized by a small inflamed swelling at the edge of the eyelid. Staphylococcus is frequently the causative organism. As the swelling increases, the stye may rupture spontaneously and drain pus, after which healing occurs. Occasionally the condition becomes chronic, with the occurrence of repeated infections.

The application of warm, moist compresses will help to relieve pain and facilitate suppuration. Medical care is seldom required, but in some cases incision and drainage and administration of the appropriate antibiotic may be necessary. Precautions should be taken to avoid squeezing or picking of the stye to prevent spread of the infection.

Chalazion

A chalazion is a sterile granulomatous inflammation of a meibomian gland. It frequently begins with inflammation and tenderness but does not have the acute signs of inflammation seen in a hordeolum. The common symptom is a painless bump that develops over several weeks. If the chalazion gets large enough it may press on the cornea and cause astigmatism. In the early stages, warm moist compresses may help the inflammation subside. Antibiotic or sulfonamide drugs may also be prescribed. Chalazions frequently need to be removed surgically by the ophthalmologist. They can recur and malignancy needs to be ruled out in these instances.

Conjunctivitis

Conjunctivitis is an inflammation of the conjunctiva of the eye, and there are several forms of the disease. Conjunctivitis may be the result of an allergy and will usually clear when the offending allergen is removed. It may also result from bacteria or injury.

Acute catarrhal conjunctivitis

This most common type of conjunctivitis is often referred to as **pinkeye.** In temporate climates it is commonly caused by the pneumococcus organism. In tropical climates the Koch-Weeks bacillus, *Haemophilus aegyptius,* is the most frequent cause.[52] Conjunctivitis is frequently encountered as an epidemic among schoolchildren, spread through droplet infection. The conjunctiva becomes red, with burning and a mucopurulent secretion.

The eyelids are usually stuck together in the morning, and warm, moist compresses may be applied to soak the crusted lids. Eye irrigations using physiologic saline solution may be ordered. The specific organism should be identified, and the disease may be treated with a sulfonamide or antibiotic. Steroid therapy is contraindicated when infections are present, although it may be of value when the cause is an allergy. Drops are usually instilled during the day, and an ointment is used at night. Discharge from the eye should always be removed before medication is applied. Persons with the infection should have their own towels and washcloths and should not use public swimming pools. Children with the disease should not attend school until the infection has cleared, which will be in about 1 week.

Purulent conjunctivitis

Purulent conjunctivitis is marked by profuse purulent discharge. It is usually caused by *Neisseria meningitidis* and *Neisseria gonorrhoeae.* This form is not self-limiting and can lead to corneal perforation and vision loss if not treated.

The disease may be treated with penicillin, which is administered intramuscularly and instilled into the eye. The sulfonamide drugs may also be used. Other treatment may consist of placing warm compresses on the eye and cleansing the purulent exudate from the lids. The patient may be isolated and medical asepsis must be carried out. A gown is worn by the nurse, and precautions should be taken to protect the eyes from contamination. Disposable gloves should be worn when carrying out treatments to the eye.

Ophthalmia neonatorum refers to any purulent conjunctivitis of the newborn acquired from an infected birth canal. State laws require that erythromycin (0.5%) or tetracycline (1%) ophthalmic ointment or drops be instilled in the eyes of all newborn infants to prevent the disease. Although ophthalmia neonatorum occurs as a result of maternal gonorrhea, it is now most commonly caused by chlamydia. Erythromycin and tetracycline are effective in preventing chlamydial eye infections and are the drugs of choice in preventing ophthalmia neonatorum. Prophylactic agents should be given shortly after birth, but a delay of up to 1 hour is acceptable and may facilitate initial parent-infant bonding by not interfering with the infant's vision.

Trachoma

Trachoma is a communicable disease caused by chlamydia that frequently affects all the members of a family. It is transmitted by the common fly and by direct contact with infected eyes or through the use of common towels, washbasins, and washcloths. The incidence is greatest where overcrowding and poor hygiene conditions exist. It is almost nonexistent in the United States but is prevalent in Asia, Africa, and parts of South America. It is the major cause of blindness in the world today.[35]

The disease begins with inflammation of the conjunctiva, which becomes chronic and is accompanied by formation of granules on the lids; the conjunctiva has a characteristic reddish blue appearance. The disease progresses slowly, with changes in the conjunctival tissue and a tendency to form corneal ulcers. The disease will ultimately lead to blindness. Patients with longstanding cases may develop **entropion,** which is a turning in of the eyelid that requires surgical correction.

Treatment is with sulfonamide, tetracycline, or erythromycin administered orally for 3 to 5 weeks. Close supervision is necessary because all members of the family must be treated if they are infected, and personal hygiene practices must be improved or reinfection may occur.

Marginal blepharitis

Marginal blepharitis is a chronic inflammatory process involving the margin of both eyelids and may be caused by bacteria, allergy, and degenerative diseases. The most common type is **seborrheic.** The patient frequently has a history of a seborrheic condition of the scalp, commonly known as dandruff. The skin and scalp are often found to be excessively oily. Itching and burning of the eyelids may be the first symptoms. The lids are red and inflamed, and fine, crustlike scales form at the base of the eyelashes. Ulcerations may develop.

Treatment consists of the application of warm, moist compresses to soften the crusts, which are then removed with a cotton swab dipped in baby shampoo to clean the lid margins.[52] Application of such drugs as sulfacetamide ophthalmic ointment may be prescribed at bedtime in patients prone to the disease. Cleanliness of the hair, skin, and scalp is especially important in controlling the disease. If a seborrheic condition of the scalp is present, it must be treated to control the blepharitis.

Keratitis

Keratitis, an inflammation of the cornea, appears in several different forms; its cause may not always be known. Interstitial keratitis frequently accompanies congenital syphilis. Allergies, viral infections, and diseases such as smallpox, herpes simplex, or nerve disorders can be causative factors. Keratitis causes pain, sensitivity to light, lacrimation, eyelid spasms, and redness with inflam-

mation. The disease is always serious because it may result in scars on the cornea, and if the scars occur near the pupil, vision will be affected.

Treatment consists of identifying and removing the cause when possible. Antibiotics or antiviral medications may be given to treat infection. Warm, moist compresses may be employed, along with the application of ointments and the use of dark glasses. If patients are in such distress that they are unable to open their eyes, activity is restricted for safety reasons, and the eyes may be covered to avoid eye movements (Table 23-1 and Table 23-2).

Corneal ulcers. Ulcers on the cornea may result from trachoma, injury, or extension of infection from the conjunctiva and may be present with keratitis. Infection can occur even after a minor injury to the cornea, so a physician should always be consulted for treatment. Permanent damage

Table 23-1

Antiinfectives

Drug (generic and trade name)	Preparation	Action	Nursing considerations
Antibiotics			
Bacitracin 500 U/g ointment	half inch 2-4 times daily in conjunctival sac	Broad spectrum. Treatment of ocular infections	Warn patient that ointment will blur vision. Keep tube closed to avoid contamination.
Erythromycin 1%	half inch 1-2 times daily	As above	
Neomycin sulfate	As above	As above	
Polymyxin B, 10,000U, bacitracin 400U, hydrocortisone 10 mg (1%), neomycin sulfate 3.5 mg, in combination (Cortisporin)	As above	As above	
Sulfonamides			
Sulfisoxazole (Gantrisin)	1-2 drops; frequency depends upon severity of infection	Active against gramnegative and grampositive organisms	Watch for hypersensitivity to sulfonamides
Sulfacetamide sodium (Sulamyd)			
Antiviral agents			
Idoxyuridine (IDU) solution	1 drop hourly; 2 drops hourly at night	Used against keratitis caused by herpes simplex.	Administer with caution in pregnant women. Stress importance of taking as prescribed. Frequency of administration decreases with healing.
0.1% ointment (Stoxil)	half inch strip every 4 hours		
Trifluridine 1% (Viroptic)	1-2 drops every 2-3 hours		

and loss of vision can be prevented by prompt treatment. The seriousness of the condition depends on the extent of the ulcer and its location. Superficial ulcers usually heal without complication, but if the ulcer is severe and deep, the possibility of perforation is always present, which might be injurious to sight. After healing, a scar will remain, which will interfere with sight if it is in the line of vision.

Symptoms generally are pain, sensitivity to light, increased lacrimation, and twitching or spasm of certain eye muscles.

Treatment depends on the seriousness of the ulcer. The extent of the ulcer is determined by placing a drop of fluorescein in the conjunctival sac, which will stain the affected area green. The slit lamp is then used to examine the eye and locate the ulcer. Treatment may consist of instillation of atropine to place the eye at rest, warm compresses to relieve pain, cauterization with silver nitrate or heat, and antibiotic and steroid drugs.

A large, thick contact lens called a **bandage contact** may be used to protect the eye and promote healing. Dressings are not used when infected lesions are present, since they favor bacterial growth and limit the flow of discharge from the eye. Corneal ulcers may result in corneal scarring or perforation, which can produce partial or permanent blindness.

Corneal transplant (keratoplasty). Corneal transplant surgery may be done on certain persons to restore sight. The conditions for which a corneal transplant may be done include scarring as the result of injuries or infection, corneal ulcer, and degeneration of the cornea.

There are two types of corneal transplants. A **penetrating keratoplasty** involves full-thickness replacement. Young donors are preferred because their endothelial cells are healthier. Donor eyes should be removed as soon as possible after death and transplanted within 48 hours. A **lamellar keratoplasty** is a partial-thickness procedure. After removal from the donor, corneas for this procedure may be frozen, dehydrated, or refrigerated for several weeks. The current shortage of available corneas could be reduced if more people would donate their eyes at death to an eye bank.

Postoperative care of the patient is designed to prevent any disruption of the wound, infection, or rejection of the cornea. Patients are usually kept in bed and helped to the bathroom until the effects of the anesthetic have worn off and are discharged on the first to third day postoperatively. A patch and shield are usually kept on for the first day, and the shield is worn at night or when resting

Table 23-2

Steroids			
Drug (generic and trade name)	Preparation	Action	Nursing considerations
Prednisolone acetate 0.125% (Econopred mild, Pred-mild) 1% suspension (Econopred Plus, Pred Forte)	1-2 drops every 4-6 hours	Reduces the inflammatory process	Watch for complaints of decreased vision and pain in the eye. Teach patients the side effects of long-term usage: increased IOP, interference with wound healing, cataract formation
Dexamethasone alcohol (Maxidex) 0.1% suspension, 0.5% ointment	1-2 drops every 4-6 hours. May be given hourly in severe infections		
Sulfacetamide 10%, prednisolone acetate 0.5% (Metimyd)	1-2 drops every 4-6 hours		
Fluromethalone 0.1% (FML)	1-2 drops every 4-6 hours		
Combination drug: Dexamethasone alcohol 0.1%, neomycin 3.5 mg, polymyxin 6000 u suspension/ointment (Maxitrol)	1-2 drops every 4-6 hours		

NURSING CARE GUIDELINES
Eye Surgery

Nursing diagnoses
- Anxiety related to fear of loss of sight
- Potential ineffective breathing pattern related to effects of anesthesia and restrictions on coughing
- Deficit in diversionary activity related to postoperative restrictions
- Knowledge deficit related to administration of medications and activity restrictions after discharge
- Alteration in sensory perception (visual) related to eye dressings

Nursing interventions
Preoperative care

- Orient patient to his or her surroundings
- Facilitate patient's expression of fears regarding decreased vision
- Instruct patient to wear dark glasses if dilating drops have been instilled
- Maintain a hazard-free environment for the patient
- Prepare the affected eye by washing the skin of that side of the face with pHisoHex or surgical scrub solution the night before and the morning of surgery
- Instruct patient regarding postoperative restrictions specific to surgery
- Inform patient that a patch and shield will be worn on the operated eye after surgery
- Instruct patient in postoperative deep-breathing exercises
- Provide early light breakfast if surgery is to be done under local anesthesia or administer nothing by mouth to the patient if a general anesthetic will be used
- Administer antibiotics and other eye drops or ointments as ordered by the physician

Postoperative care

- Position patient on back or turn to unoperated side if turning is permitted
- Restrict activities as ordered by the physician
- Announce your presence when entering the patient's room because one or both eyes may be patched
- Raise side rails to protect patient from injury and to provide a sense of security
- Place call bell or signal within easy reach of the patient
- Keep the eye patch or shield or both in place as applied by the physician
- Assist patient when he or she is initially ambulating postoperatively
- Report severe eye pain immediately

---

to protect the eye. Regular eyeglasses can be worn during the day. Combination steroid-antibiotic eyedrops and short-acting cycloplegics are usually prescribed and the patient should continue taking these after being discharged. The patient needs to be taught how to administer the drops and check the eye daily for signs of rejection. Sudden decrease in vision, increase in redness or presence of pain that lasts longer than 24 hours should be reported to the doctor.

Corneal grafts heal slowly because of the lack of blood supply to the area. The incision to remove the damaged cornea is made at the point where the cornea meets the sclera. Healing is improved when the new avascular cornea is attached to the vascular sclera. Infection may occur easily, and strict asepsis must be maintained. The graft will take 3 weeks or more to heal firmly. The amount of activity that is permitted will depend on the procedure and the individual physician. All orders should be clearly written, and the nurse should be sure that they are understood.

(The box above summarizes general nursing diagnoses and interventions for the patient having eye surgery.)

Uveitis

The uveal tract is the middle layer of the eye and includes the ciliary body, iris, and choroid. **Anterior uveitis** is the preferred term for infection involving the iris (iritis) and the ciliary body (iridocyclitis). **Posterior uveitis** refers to involvement of the choroid in choroiditis and chorioretinitis.

Frequently, the cornea may be affected; this condition is considered serious and may cause blindness. The inflammation may be from unknown cause, or it may result from diseases such as tuberculosis or syphilis. It may also be caused by viruses or by a protozoal parasite such as *Toxoplasma*. Pain in the eye is a primary symptom,

Table 23-3

Mydriatics/Cycloplegics			
Drug	**Preparation**	**Action**	**Nursing considerations**
Phenylephrine hydrochloride (Neosynephrine, Mydfrin)	1-2 drops in each eye. Repeat after 5-10 minutes as necessary	Mydriatic—dilates pupil; sympathomimetic	Should not be used in patients with narrow-angle glaucoma
Atropine .25-2% solution, 0.5-1% ointment	1 drop twice a day	Cycloplegic—dilates pupil, paralyzes accommodation; long acting	Effect can last 2 weeks. Use with caution in infants and young children
Homatropine 25% solution	1 drop two to three times daily	Same as atropine; not as long acting	As above
Cyclopentolate hydrochloride (cyclogyl)	1-2 drops in each eye. Repeat as necessary	Dilates pupil; paralyzes accommodation	Burns on instillation
Tropicamide 0.5, 1% solution (mydriacyl)	As above	As above	All cycloplegics have photophobia and inability to do close-up work; advise patient to wear dark glasses.

accompanied by sensitivity to light, tearing, disturbance of vision, and contraction of the pupil.

Treatment includes keeping the pupil dilated with 1% atropine sulfate or cyclopentolate 1% (cyclogyl) to prevent formation of anterior or posterior synechiae (adhesions) between the iris and cornea or lens. Corticosteroids may be administered, and if a causative organism can be identified, the appropriate therapy is given. Warm, moist compresses relieve pain and inflammation, and analgesics may be required for pain. Dark glasses are worn during convalescence to protect against sensitivity to light.

The nurse should remember that children are more sensitive to atropine than adults and that poisoning may occur unless care is taken. The nurse should be careful in applying warm compresses to the eye, since the eyelids are particularly sensitive to heat and may be easily burned (Table 23-3).

Sympathetic ophthalmia

Sympathetic ophthalmia is a bilateral uveitis that occurs after a penetrating wound to the eye in the area of the ciliary body. It can develop as early as 10 days and as late as several years following the injury. It has also occurred after intraocular sur-

gery for cataract or glaucoma. The occurrence is rare. The cause is unknown but is probably related to hypersensitivity to some element of the pigment-bearing cells in the uvea.

The patient complains of **photophobia** (sensitivity to light), and blurred vision and inflammation will occur first in the injured eye and then in the sympathizing eye. Treatment consists of local and systemic corticosteroids. An injured eye may be removed to prevent the development of sympathetic ophthalmia. This is a radical approach, and the patient must be fully informed of the risks involved. If the disease occurs and is not treated, bilateral blindness will slowly develop.

Noninfectious Eye Disorders
Retinopathy of prematurity

Retinopathy of prematurity (retrolental fibroplasia) is a disease found in 25% to 30% of infants whose birth weight is less than 1700 grams or those who are premature. Besides low birth weight, risk factors are length of time on oxygen and the concentration of oxygen given to the infant.[8] The disease results in partial or total blindness and is seen only in premature infants. Its incidence decreased in the 1960s with improved control of oxygen therapy, but is increasing now as the number of surviving premature infants increases, especially those weighing less than 1000 grams.

Contrary to previous belief, there is no "magic number" that indicates a safe level of oxygen for a premature infants. It was once thought that anything under 40% oxygen concentration was safe, but it is now known that any level is dangerous if it raises the infant's oxygen level too high. Tests on the blood to determine oxygen level are performed frequently on premature infants receiving oxygen therapy, but the best indicators of adequate oxygen are the symptoms displayed by the infant. The nurse must observe the infant carefully and frequently so that high levels of oxygen are not administered unnecessarily.

Glaucoma

Each year about 4000 Americans are blinded by glaucoma. One out of every seven blind persons has lost the sense of sight because of glaucoma. The most disturbing aspect of these facts is that blindness from glaucoma can be prevented by early detection and treatment. It is estimated that two out of every 100 Americans over age 40 have glaucoma and are in danger of losing their sight as a result. Because this loss of sight can occur before the patient is aware of any symptoms, glaucoma is called the "sneak thief" of sight. Since the most common form of the disease (90% have open, or wide-angle, glaucoma) is painless and involves loss of peripheral vision, progressing slowly over a period of years, the patient may be experiencing severe vision loss without being aware of it.

Glaucoma may be detected early with a simple test using a tonometer to measure intraocular pressure (Figures 23-3 and 23-4). Glaucoma may occur at any age, but, since it is most common in persons age 40 or older, persons in this age group should be tested every 2 to 3 years. If there is a family history of glaucoma, people over 40 should be tested yearly. The local Society for the Prevention of Blindness can be consulted for information regarding free glaucoma testing in each community.

Pathophysiology. Glaucoma may occur as a primary condition without any known cause, or it may be secondary to other disorders such as injuries or infection. In primary glaucoma an inherited predisposition is believed to be a factor.

Glaucoma causes an increase in the intraocular pressure within the eye. Continued pressure may cause damage to the optic nerve. Under normal conditions aqueous humor is formed by the ciliary body and secreted into the posterior chamber, from which is flows between the iris and the lens through the pupil into the anterior chamber. After reaching the anterior chamber, it drains out over a fine meshwork called the trabecula into Schlemm's canal, located near the angle of the anterior chamber, from which it finally drains into the general circulation. The rate of production of aqueous humor and the outward flow remain constant, and thus normal intraocular pressure is maintained. However, when pathologic changes occur at the angle of the anterior chamber that prevent a normal outflow, the intraocular pressure increases because the balance between production and outflow has been disrupted. There are two types of primary glaucoma: **narrow-angle glaucoma** and **wide-angle glaucoma.** Narrow-angle, or closed-angle, glaucoma results from a narrowing of the angle that leads to the drainage canal. In wide-angle glaucoma the angle is unaffected, but the aqueous cannot penetrate the trabeculae to enter Schlemm's canal. At least 90% of primary glaucoma is the wide-angle type. There is no cure for glaucoma, but early diagnosis and treatment will prevent blindness and help to control intraocular pressure. Chronic glaucoma may appear initially in one eye, but both eyes will become involved.

Assessment. Acute narrow-angle glaucoma occurs with a sudden onset of blurred vision, followed by excruciating pain localized in and around the eye. The patient sees a rainbow-colored halo around lights. Nausea and vomiting are often present. Pupils will be fixed and moderately dilated. Without immediate treatment, blindness may occur. Chronic wide-angle glaucoma develops slowly, and the patient may be unaware of any early symptoms. One of the earliest signs is an impairment of peripheral vision. Patients complain of halos around lights, blurred vision, disturbance of color vision, and eye fatigue. They also may find that they require frequent change of glasses. The progress of the disease is followed by assessment of the visual fields and the optic disc. The optic disc will become cupped as the pressure remains high and the visual fields will become restricted as peripheral vision loss increases.

Intervention. Acute narrow-angle or closed-angle glaucoma is a medical emergency. The closed chamber angle must be opened to permit outflow of the aqueous humour. Medical treatment will be attempted first, but surgery is often necessary.

The initial treatment includes the instillation of miotic drugs into the eye. Miotic drugs help to improve the drainage of aqueous humour by constricting the pupil and pulling the iris out of the chamber angle, thus opening the out-flow path for the aqueous humour. Osmotic agents such as mannitol may be given intravenously, or glycerol may be given orally in iced lemon juice. Carbonic anhydrase inhibitors (e.g., Diamox) may be given orally or intramuscularly to help decrease the production of aqueous. Nausea and the accompanying pain will also be treated with medication. This treatment should reduce ocular pressure within 4 to 6 hours, and if surgery is necessary, it is usually postponed for a day or so until the eye is less inflamed. In the absence of treatment, the high pressure will cause death of the nerve fibers and loss of vision. Once the acute episode has been relieved, the surgical procedure of choice for acute narrow-angle glaucoma is iridectomy.

In **iridectomy** a small hole is made in the iris to provide drainage of the aqueous humour. The surgical opening also allows the iris to fall back and thus deepens the anterior chamber. The iridectomy is usually performed in the upper segment of the iris. Because the upper eyelid normally covers the upper segment of the cornea, it covers the iridectomy, which improves the cosmetic effect and also covers this newly made accessory pupil. Because glaucoma is a bilateral disorder, an iridectomy is usually performed prophylactically on the other eye within a short time after the initial procedure. Postoperatively, the patient can be ambulated immediately, and no dressings are worn. Medications will be used to mobilize the pupil, often by alternating drugs that dilate and those that constrict. Laser iridectomy with the argon or Nd:YAG laser is now commonly used in narrow-angle glaucoma. It is a safer procedure than surgical iridectomy and has a high success rate. It is used to prevent as well as cure this type of glaucoma and can be performed in the physician's office.

Chronic open-angle glaucoma is usually treated medically. Traditional treatment involves the use of miotic eye drops and beta-adrenergic blocking agents, which improve drainage of aqueous humor and control intraocular pressure, although they do not cure the condition. Miotics commonly used include pilocarpine in a 1% to 4%

solution, and carbachol, 0.75%, both cholinergic medications. Anticholinesterase medications such as demecarium bromide, 0.06% to 0.25%, and echothiophate iodide, 0.03% to 0.25%, are the longest acting miotics available but have high rates of complications. A pilocarpine gel (Piloplex) can be used once or twice daily rather than every 6 hours, as required with drops.

For the elderly patient who may have difficulty remembering to use the eye drops daily, the "Occusert" method of eye drop administration may be used. A polymer membrane, medicated with pilocarpine, is placed into the conjunctival sac. The medication is released slowly by osmosis and lasts for 1 week, at which time it must be replaced. Timolol (timoptic), a beta-adrenergic blocking agent, is the drug of choice and has several advantages over pilocarpine. Less of the drug is needed to maintain intraocular pressure without fluctuation, so the drug can be administered less frequently (twice a day) and many of the undesirable effects of miotics are reduced, such as loss of accommodation, miosis, and cataractogenesis. Another beta-blocker, betaxolol (Betoptic) is also used and has fewer systemic side effects, such as bronchoconstriction. Epinephrine eye drops, which are sympathomimetic, are believed to decrease aqueous humor production and increase the outflow of aqueous humor.[52] Drugs known as carbonic anhydrase inhibitors are given systemically, because they indirectly affect the production of aqueous humor. These drugs include acetazolamide (Diamox) and methazolamide (Neptazane), which are administered orally. The nurse in the physician's office or in the hospital should be alert for toxic reactions to drugs used to treat glaucoma. Side effects or toxic reactions may include tingling of the hands, loss of appetite, skin rash, drowsiness, weakness, blood dyscrasias, and central nervous system disturbances. When patients are hospitalized, individually marked bottles of eye drops should be used. Extreme care must be taken to be sure that the right medication is given to the right patient.

When medical treatment fails to control the intraocular pressure, surgery must be done. The objective of surgery is to provide for the escape of aqueous humor and the reduction of intraocular pressure. **Laser trabeculoplasty** and **surgical trabeculectomy** are two common procedures. Laser trabeculoplasty reduces intraocular pressure by applying 100 or more laser burns around the trabecular meshwork. The patient needs to be monitored closely for a few hours following trabeculoplasty as a rise in intraocular pressure may occur for 1 to 4 hours following the procedure. In some people the trabecular meshwork continues to deteriorate despite the treatment; they may require filtration surgery **(trabeculectomy).** However, control for glaucoma for more than 10 years has been noted. In a trabeculectomy, a new channel for drainage of aqueous is created by removing a section of the sclera, which usually includes Schlemm's canal and the trabecular meshwork (Figure 23-9). Nursing care following trabeculectomy includes routine postanaesthesia care, protection of the eye with a patch and shield, and maintaining comfort in the eye upon which surgery has been performed. Medications such as cycloplegics, combination steroid-antibiotics, and antiglaucoma agents may be ordered. It is important to remember that antiglaucoma medication is also required in the eye that was not operated on.

Cyclodiathermy and cyclocryopexy are also procedures used in the surgical treatment of glaucoma. They are usually done as last resorts for cases of uncontrollable glaucoma. These procedures directly reduce the amount of aqueous formation by damaging the ciliary body through either diathermy or **cryosurgery.**

The patient with glaucoma must remain under medical care, and treatment is continued for life; most patients will be cared for in the ophthalmologist's office. All treatment is planned for the individual patient. Persons with glaucoma should wear a Medic Alert tag or carry a card to indicate that they have glaucoma.

Cataracts

Pathophysiology. A cataract is a slowly progressive disorder in which there is an opacity of the lens of the eye. Because light must pass through the lens to reach the retina, any opacity will result in impairment of vision. The disorder may occur at any age and may be caused by several conditions. Cataracts are classified as developmental, such as those present at birth (congenital), and degenerative, such as those resulting from aging, injury, allergy, or systemic diseases such as diabetes. Cataracts caused by the degenerative changes of aging (senile cataracts) develop slowly with advancing years, and patients may be 70 years or older before sight is sufficiently impaired to require surgery. A change in the normal metabolism of lens tissue appears to exist. Congenital cataracts may be caused by rubella in the mother during the first trimester of pregnancy.

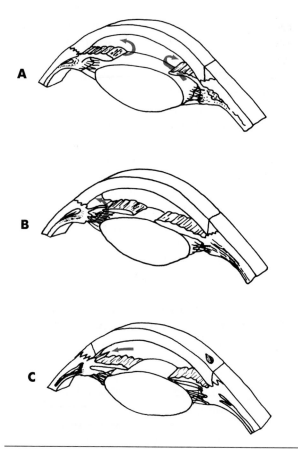

Figure 23-9

In the normal eye; **A,** Aqueous produced by ciliary body flows through Schlemm's canal to return to general circulation. In acute congestive, or narrow-angle, glaucoma; **B,** Angle of anterior chamber is too narrow and aqueous cannot enter canal. Treatment (center) includes use of miotics to constrict pupil and widen angle and laser trabeculoplasty and peripheral iridectomy to provide supplementary channel. In chronic wide-angle glaucoma; **C,** The problem is that aqueous cannot penetrate trabeculae to enter canal. When drug treatment is no longer effective, trabeculectomy, or laser trabeculoplasty may be performed to improve aqueous outflow by enlarging canal. *(Adapted from Kornzweig AL: Visual loss in the elderly, Hosp Prac 12(7) and from Reichel W (editor): The geriatric patient, New York, 1978, HP Publishing Co Inc. Reproduced with permission.)*

Symptoms caused by cataracts may include gradual impairment of vision in varying degrees, blurring, and sensitivity to glare. Some patients may experience double vision and distortions of sight. There is no pain associated with cataracts.

Cataract extraction. The only cure for a cataract is surgery, and surgical procedures for the eye have evolved to a high state of perfection. It is no longer necessary to wait for a cataract to mature before its removal. This is determined on an individual basis, depending on the patient's need for improved vision. If the cataract is present in only one eye and the other eye is normal, surgery may be delayed indefinitely. Generally, senile cataracts are removed when the sight in the better eye is failing and is interfering with the patient's daily routine.

Preoperative intervention. Most cataract extractions are now performed with the patient under local anesthesia. Most patients are admitted the day of surgery and are discharged later that day unless complications occur. Some patients may require longer hospitalization. Most patients admitted for surgical removal of cataracts are elderly persons whose vision is impaired in one or both eyes because of the disorder. Patient's who have minimum vision may have fears about the success of the surgery and the danger of losing the vision that they have. The nurse caring for these patients should realize that they have poor vision and need to be oriented to their room and hospital procedures. When patients feel comfortable and secure in their room and know what to expect, their fear and apprehension will be decreased. Since a metal shield and patch will be worn on the eye after surgery, this should be explained to the patient. The physician may order the lashes of the affected eye to be clipped. Rubbing the scissors with petroleum jelly (Vaseline) will catch the hair that should be trimmed to about 3 mm from the lid margin. The physician will order antibiotic eye drops and antibiotic ointment the day before surgery to prevent bacterial growth. Mydriatic drops may be ordered to dilate the pupils before some surgical procedures. In addition, the physician may order the face washed with a surgical scrub such as chlorhexidine the evening before and the morning after surgery. If the procedure is to be performed with the patient under a local anesthetic, the patient may be allowed to have a light breakfast. The surgery is sometimes performed with the patient under a general anesthetic, which requires that the patient take nothing by mouth after midnight.

Surgical intervention. There are two surgical procedures for the extraction of cataracts: **intracapsular extraction** and **extracapsular extraction.** In intracapsular extraction the lens and the anterior and posterior capsule in which it lies are all removed (Figure 23-10, *A*). After the zonules that attach the lens to the ciliary body are dissolved, a cryoprobe cooled to $-60°$ F is inserted into the lens. The lens then reacts and adheres to the probe and is easily removed (Figure 23-10, *B*).

In extracapsular extraction the capsule is opened, the lens and anterior capsule are removed, and the posterior capsule is left in place. Extracapsular extraction is now the most common procedure because the intact posterior capsule allows insertion of a posterior chamber intraocular lens. This procedure has a lower incidence of complications than the anterior chamber lens implant. Implantation of a lens eliminates the need to wear cataract glasses or contact lenses following surgery, and 90% of all cataract removals now include lens implant. **Phacoemulsification,** another technique for cataract extraction, uses ultrasonic frequencies to emulsify the lens; the lens material can then be aspirated through a needle inserted into a small incision. In this instance the posterior capsule is left in place.

Postoperative intervention. It was once necessary for the patient to remain in bed for 2 weeks following cataract extraction, with the head immobilized with sandbags. Improved surgical equipment and techniques eliminate the need for severe restrictions, and the procedure can be performed on an outpatient basis with the patient going home to rest within 1 to 2 hours after the surgery is completed. If the patient is hospitalized discharge will be within 1 or 2 days, depending on the patient's general health status and coexisting medical conditions. The patient returns from surgery with the eye patched and covered with a metal or plastic shield. This patch and shield are left in place until the physician changes the patch and inserts eye drops the day after surgery.

The eye shield is always worn during sleep to protect the eye from accidental injury. The patient's own glasses can be worn while awake. Dark glasses may be helpful as the eyes are frequently sensitive to light. Pressure on the eyeball during removal of the shield is avoided by first releasing the tape above the eye and then pulling the shield down off of the cheek. When inserting drops, the patient is instructed to rest the hand on the bony orbit below the eye. Activity restrictions are aimed at preventing an increase in intraocular pressure, which would place strain on the suture lines. The patient should not lie on the operative side or stomach, and the head should be slightly elevated. Stooping, bending over, sneezing, and heavy lifting should be avoided; straining at stool caused by constipation should be prevented; and heavy work should be avoided for 4 to 6 weeks. The patient can resume a normal diet as tolerated. After the anesthetic wears off, the patient may experience aching and a scratch-

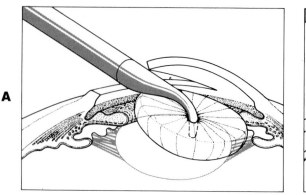 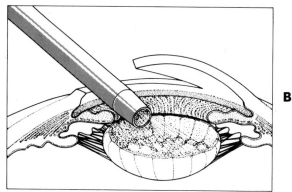

Figure 23-10

Cataract extraction. **A,** Intracapsular, when lens and capsule are removed. **B,** Extracapsular, when lens and only the anterior part of the capsule are removed. *(From Beare PG and Meyers JK: Principles and practice of adult health nursing, ed 1, St Louis, 1990, The CV Mosby Co.)*

iness about the eye, which is often described as feeling like the patch is rubbing against the eyeball. These discomforts can be relieved with aspirin or acetaminophen. If the patient experiences severe pain across the side of the head, nausea, or vomiting, the physician should be notified. This could indicate an increase in intraocular pressure, and the physician may order medication to reduce it. The patient is instructed on the use of any medications ordered. Frequently, steroid drops are given four times a day for 2 to 3 weeks and then gradually decreased over the next 4 to 5 weeks. Miotic drops may be used for the first day or so postoperatively. If there are any indications of iritis then mydriatic drops are started. Some ophthalmologists order mydriatic drops routinely. Occasionally there is a rise in intraocular pressure and the person may be put on timoptic drops until the pressure is controlled. After lens extraction the eye is considered aphakic, which means there is an absence of the lens. The aphakic eye has no power of accommodation and has lost much of its refractive ability. Aphakia must be corrected by glasses, contact lenses, or an intraocular lens implant to attain clear, functional vision. The eyes are periodically checked for refraction, and when the measurement is the same on two consecutive examinations, usually 2 to 3 months after surgery, permanent lenses are prescribed. If the patient will be wearing contact lenses, they will be fitted at this time.

Cataract glasses require a thick lens—lighter now because it can be made of plastic but still readily noticeable. Cataract glasses magnify ob-

jects about 25%, making them seem closer and interfering with eye-hand coordination. Doorways appear curved, and peripheral vision is restricted. If the other eye has not had a lens extraction, the lens for that eye must blur out vision so the patient will see with only the operated eye. The vision of the two eyes cannot be equally corrected. If both eyes have had cataract extractions, binocular vision is possible. The patient will need time to become accustomed to the visual distortions caused by the cataract glasses. Walking and climbing stairs with assistance must be practiced. Contact lenses do not create the overmagnification and distortion seen with cataract glasses, but many patients lack the dexterity required to insert and remove them properly.

Implantation of the intraocular lens eliminates the need for wearing cataract glasses or contact lenses postoperatively. For the patient who would have difficulty adjusting to either of these and who does not suffer from any of the diseases that contraindicate lens implantation, it is an option. Existing myopia or hyperopia can be corrected with the properly implanted lens power. There is little magnification of images, resulting in improved depth perception, full visual field, and binocular vision. The implant is present 24 hours a day, eliminating the hazards of operating without the aid of glasses or contact lenses. The lens cannot be detected in the eye unless one looks very closely. Although the lens is usually implanted at the time of surgical removal of the original lens, it is possible to implant a lens years later. The eye with the false lens is termed "pseudo-

---

NURSING CARE GUIDELINES
Cataract Surgery

Nursing diagnoses

- Anxiety related to surgery and uncertain outcome
- Knowledge deficit related to restrictions on bending, stooping, lifting, coughing, and sneezing
- Potential injury related to sensory deficit, lack of awareness of surroundings
- Altered visual sensory perception related to cataract, eye patch, or aphakia
- Alteration in comfort: pain related to inflammation, increased intraocular pressure

Nursing interventions
Preoperative care

- Orient the patient to surroundings
- Explain what the patient will see and hear during the surgery
- Administer antibiotic or mydriatic eye drops or both as prescribed
- Teach deep-breathing exercises
- Instruct the patient not to stoop, bend, cough, or sneeze after surgery; explain to the patient that a metal shield and patch will be worn when returning from surgery
- Instruct the patient on instillation of eye drops, eye care, and signs and symptoms of infection.

Postoperative care

- Advise the patient to move slowly in bed
- Turn patient to unoperated side
- Announce yourself when entering the room, since the patient's eye is shielded
- Remind the patient not to bend or stoop
- Assist patient in deep breathing
- Follow the activity orders of the physician
- Administer antiemetic drugs as prescribed for nausea and vomiting
- Report sudden pain in the eye

Expected outcomes

- Be able to administer eye medications and apply shield safely and without pressure on eyeball (may be performed by family member)
- Verbalize restrictions in activities of daily living
- Identify date of follow-up visit to physician
- Ambulate safely with temporary glasses, contact lenses, or intraocular implant
- Have absence of severe pain, nausea, and vomiting
- Perform eye care satisfactorily

---

phakic." The box above summarizes commonly related nursing diagnoses and nursing care of the patient having cataract surgery.

Diabetic retinopathy

Diabetic retinopathy is a complication of diabetes mellitus that involves noninflammatory vascular changes in the retina (Chapter 21). It causes 12% of new cases of blindness each year and the prevalence increases with the duration of diabetes. It is divided into two forms: background and proliferative retinopathy. In the early, nonproliferating stage, retinal blood vessels swell and microaneurysms occur and rupture, producing hemorrhages. In the proliferating stage, new blood vessels grow from the existing retinal vessels in a process called *neovascularization*. Formation and contraction of scar tissue can result in retinal detachment. There has been no treatment for this condition, but the progress of this complication can now be delayed with the use of argon laser panretinal photocoagulation. Treatment consists of a series of three or four applications, with a total of several thousand laser spots applied to each retina, sparing the optic disc, macula, and vessel arcades. Treatment must begin when the patient shows neovascular changes. Photocoagulation is used to destroy the peripheral area of the retina, resulting in a diminished metabolic demand. The new vessels that have formed then tend to disappear. There may be some loss of vision or acuity, but total blindness is delayed.

Macular degeneration

Macular degeneration is also referred to as senile macular degeneration because it is the most common cause of blindness in the elderly. The macula is the central portion of the retina. The cause is believed to be an abnormality in the pigment epithelium of the retina. Environmental and artificial lighting can damage the photoreceptor cells of the retina and cause this degeneration. There is an inherited tendency and myopia is considered a predisposing factor.

Early in the disease small, round, yellow spots, called drusen, will appear around the major blood vessels in the retinal epithelium. The drusen cause changes in structure in the cones of the retina and result in scar formation. Where scars form, vision is decreased. The scarring continues until the entire macula is destroyed. One eye may be affected, but it is usually bilateral.

Assessment. The patient will first complain of a sudden onset of blurred central vision. Some will describe a blind spot (scotoma) in the center of the field of vision. Other symptoms may include distortions, such as seeing a bend in a straight line, change in size of objects, or change in color. Peripheral vision is retained but the patient is unable to read, drive, watch television, or distinguish faces. Progression of the disease is detected with the Amsler's grid test (p. 669). There is no cure available. The structural changes that cause bleeding and scar formation can be slowed down with the use of laser photocoagulation. The patient will need rehabilitation services to cope with the loss of vision.

Retinal detachment

Pathophysiology. The retina is the innermost coat of the eye, and a retinal detachment means that the layers of the retina have become separated. The term detachment is not really accurate as the whole retina is not usually involved. The detachment is normally between the retinal sensory and pigment layers. Injuries, disease, or degeneration may cause small holes or tears to occur in the retina. When this happens, it allows vitreous humor from the large chamber in the back of the eye to seep in between these two layers, causing them to separate. This condition is known as primary, or rhegmatogenous, detachment. In secondary, or nonrhegmatogenous, detachment, the retina separates without a break as a result of a disease process such as tumor, inflammation, or vitreous traction that produces subretinal fluid. In either type, the blood supply to the retina is reduced, and the vision is blurred or lost in that area. When the macula lutea is involved, vision is more likely to be permanently affected. The macula is the point of clearest vision on the retina. Unless the retinal detachment is treated immediately, it will continue to enlarge and become total resulting in blindness in the involved eye.

Assessment. Symptoms depend on the location and size of the separation. The condition may occur spontaneously with sudden loss of vision, or the person may see flashes of light and have blurring of vision. Often the patient will complain of floaters, which are black spots or lines in the path of vision. This is not to be confused with the constant presence of one or more black "floaters" that many people have before their eyes. Instead, the person with a detached retina sees a sudden shower of floating opacities. Flashing lights appear later, and then a dark blot appears in a portion of the visual field of the affected eye. This usually appears in side vision rather than central vision. The dark blot is not always immediately recognized by the patient if there is good vision in the opposite eye. Diagnosis and determination of the exact location and extent of the separation is easily made by the ophthalmologist with an ophthalmoscope. Ultrasound and tomography are also valuable when opacities in the media obstruct the view of the fundus.

Nursing diagnoses for retinal detachment are identified in the box on p. 689.

Intervention. Treatment is always surgical for primary retinal detachment. Treatment of secondary detachment is control of the causative disease or reduction of inflammation with corticosteroid therapy. If discovered early, a retinal break may be repaired by cryotherapy or laser photocoagulation, and separation of the retina will be prevented. After primary detachment, scleral buckling is the preferred surgery. The operation consists of two steps: reattaching the retina by cryotherapy, laser photocoagulation, or diathermy, then securing the reattached area in place with a tiny silicone plate and in some cases a silicone cinch around the eyeball. This is known as a *scleral buckle.* In cryotherapy a cryoprobe is touched to the sclera, producing a cold burn of the choroid with no damage to the sclera. In the procedure involving photocoagulation with a laser beam, strong beams of light are focused under direct vision through the cornea and lens of the eye onto a small area of flat retina, causing an aseptic choroiditis. This allows the retina to adhere firmly to the underlying choroid. Silicone rubber sponges and silicone bands can then be buckled to the surface of the sclera with Dacron suture. A silicone band may be applied to crimp the sclera and choroid to the retina, and the lesion created in the choroid will reattach itself to the retina.

When the subretinal fluid is too great in volume to allow the retina to sink to the area of choroiditis created by therapy, it will have to be released through an incision in the sclera. There is

NURSING CARE GUIDELINES
Detached Retina

Nursing diagnoses

- Anxiety related to concern for loss of sight and uncertain outcome
- Impaired mobility related to positioning to maintain detached area in dependent position
- High risk for injury related to sensory deficit
- Knowledge deficit related to activity restrictions and possible surgical repair
- Altered visual sensory perception related to decreased vision or eye patching
- High risk for infection related to surgical repair
- Alteration in comfort related to sensitivity to light and lid swelling from surgical trauma

Nursing interventions

- Maintain activity restrictions
- Position the patient as ordered by the physician to maintain the detached area in a dependent position
- Administer medications as ordered by the physician for comfort
- Explain surgical treatment and postoperative restrictions
- Visit frequently—provide radio or television for orientation
- Administer cold compresses or ice packs four times a day
- Dim room lights, keep curtain closed, encourage the wearing of dark glasses
- Institute safety precautions as appropriate; assistance to bathroom, side rails

Expected outcomes

- Vision clear
- Patient expresses fears and concerns
- Absence of infection at surgical site
- Verbalize and comply with restrictions for positioning and activity
- Ambulate safely and avoid sudden movements
- Demonstrate proper and safe administration of eye medications
- Verbalize and demonstrate proper cleansing of the eye
- Identify date of next visit to physician and indicate compliance with follow-up care

Vitrectomy. A vitrectomy is the removal of all or part of the diseased vitreous body. It is often performed in conjunction with surgery for retinal detachment to remove the detached retina floating in the vitreous. The membranes are gradually cut and aspirated, and the fluid is replaced with sterile fluid to maintain intraocular pressure. The instruments for this procedure include a fiberoptic light source, a cutting instrument, and aspirating instrument, which are inserted through three openings.

Preoperative intervention. The box at right summarizes nursing care of the patient undergoing retinal detachment surgery and a vitrectomy. The patient is usually admitted to the hospital the same day as the diagnosis is made to limit activity and prevent further damage. The restrictions in activity will vary depending on the site of the detachment and whether the macula is involved. People who have small peripheral detachments, for example may have few restrictions and the eye may or may not be patched. In contrast, people who have a detachment that threatens the macula may be placed on strict bed rest with bilateral patching. Nursing care needs to be adapted to the restrictions and constraints placed on the patient. Abrupt change of events and the fear of blindness can produce a great deal of anxiety in the patient. The patient should be helped to verbalize these fears and should receive answers to all questions about the condition, the treatment, and the prognosis. The nurse can assist the patient in bringing queries to the physician.

Preoperative teaching should include activity restrictions. The patient should be instructed that the eyelashes may be trimmed before surgery to prevent infection or irritation. The patient should also be informed that the area around the eye will be black and blue after surgery; this discoloration will disappear. The pupil is dilated with both mydriatic and cycloplegic eye drops to permit examination of the retina and prevent iritis. If the patient will be given a general anesthetic, food and fluids are not allowed after midnight. The nurse should plan to spend some time with the patient at frequent intervals to provide opportunity for verbalizing fears and providing support.

Postoperative intervention. The patient will return from surgery with one or both eyes bandaged. Position should be maintained according to the physician's orders, usually so that the area of detachment is in a downward position. If an air, fluid, or gas bubble has been injected into the

danger of infection following this procedure, as well as incarceration of the retina in the scleral incision.[16] In more complex cases of detachment the retina may need to be pushed into place through injection into the vitreous of gas, oil, or some form of mechanical tamponade.[33]

eye during surgery, the patient is positioned so the bubble will press against the retinal area that needs to be flattened. Usually, the bubble is posterior in the vitreous, so the patient lies prone with the head down and turned slightly on a small pillow. The surgeon will indicate the position in the orders. Vital signs are taken frequently until stable and then as required. The patient is encouraged to deep breathe but not to cough to avoid pressure on the eye. Vomiting increases intraocular pressure and should be prevented if possible. Specific activity orders should be obtained from the physician. Pupil dilation is maintained with mydriatic and cycloplegic drops. Antibiotic and corticosteroid drops may be used to reduce inflammation and prevent infection. Discharge teaching should begin as soon as the patient is ready. The patient may be discharged anywhere from 1 to 3 days postoperatively but may stay as long as a week. Light activity and watching television is permitted. Reading may or may not be. If the patient has had gas instilled into the vitreous they may be restricted from flying for several weeks or longer. There will be edema and discoloration about the affected eye and the patient should be advised to clean the eye using warm water and cotton balls two to three times a day to soften and remove secretions and crusts that form about the eyelashes. The patient is instructed to keep appointments with the ophthalmologist following discharge. The first appointment is usually made prior to discharge. Not all retinal detachments will be corrected by the surgery; surgery may have to be repeated for some patients and others may develop new areas of detachment.

Injuries to the Eye

Injuries to the eye may be the result of foreign bodies, thermal or chemical burns, abrasions, and lacerations or penetrating wounds. Neither the nurse nor the patient can assess the damage resulting from an injury to the eye; therefore all injuries should be seen by the ophthalmologist. If the injury is slight, nothing has been lost, but if it is serious, immediate medical care may mean saving vision or even the eye.

Corneal drying

The cornea must be lubricated to remain healthy. Inadequate tears and lack of protection by the lids are common causes of corneal discomfort and damage. Tear deficiency may be caused by lacrimal gland disease or may occur spontaneously with age. Faulty lid closure may accompany facial paralysis and sagging facial muscles, and prominent eyes occur with thyroid disease (exophthalmos). The unconscious patient is in great danger of corneal damage because the lids do not close properly. Within hours the patient can suffer surface necrosis and permanent scarring. It is an important responsibility of the nurse to prevent this damage by closing the lids and protecting the cornea with a lubricant as necessary. Prolonged wearing of contact lenses can also cause drying.

Foreign bodies

Irritation by foreign bodies is one of the most common types of injury and may be from dust particles, loose eyelashes, or cinders, which may lodge in the conjunctiva or become embedded in the cornea. Foreign bodies under the upper lid may cause irritation of the cornea from the movement of the lid and result in considerable discomfort to the patient. Foreign bodies should not be removed from the cornea because of the high risk of abrasion. Usually the foreign body will move to the sclera, and it can then be removed with a clean handkerchief or a cotton swab dipped in physiologic saline or by irrigating the eye with physiologic saline. The patient should be instructed to look up, and the lower lid may be pulled down and the conjunctival sac examined. If the foreign body is under the upper lid, the lid should be everted over a match or applicator. The patient is instructed to look down, and the examiner grasps the lashes and pulls the lid downward. Placing the applicator across the lid, the lid is drawn up over the applicator and everted. The lid must be held onto to keep it everted. Any person with a foreign body in the eye that cannot be easily removed or that has been in the eye for some time should be examined by an ophthalmologist.

Burns

Burns may be caused by acids, alkalies, hot metal, flashes from acetylene blowtorches, or exposure to the ultraviolet rays of the sun. Whatever the cause, the burn must be considered an emergency. If chemicals are accidentally splashed into the eye, prolonged washing of the eye with plain tap water should be initiated immediately. This first-aid measure will prevent formation of permanent scar tissue more effectively than any other treatment. The eyelids should be separated and cool water poured gently over the eyeball for 15 to 20 minutes. Medical care should then be sought. Persons suffering burns caused by heat such as flash burns, burns from overexposure to the sun, and burns from fireworks should be taken immediately to an ophthalmologist. No home or first-aid treatment should be attempted in this situation.

Abrasions and lacerations

Superficial abrasions have numerous causes; although painful at the time, they usually do no serious harm. If the abrasion is deep, scarring may result. Antibiotics are generally used to prevent infection, and the eye may be covered with a pad. Lacerations of the eyelids are not serious and are treated like lacerations elsewhere. However, laceration of the eyeball may be extremely serious because it may affect vision and sometimes results in loss of the eye.

Penetrating wounds

Penetrating wounds are especially serious because they invariably introduce infection into the eye and may destroy eye structures. Total blindness in the eye can result. All penetrating injuries of the eye should be treated immediately by an ophthalmologist. Both eyes should be covered with shields while transporting the patient to the physician to reduce injury from movement involved in vision. A shield can be improvised in the home using the bottom of a paper cup taped securely to the face. Usually, it is easy to recognize that an eye has been perforated, although not always. The iris of the eye often will move to plug the wound, resulting in an irregular pupil. Tiny wounds such as caused by a needle or thorn often are self-sealing and cannot be seen. The foreign body may have pierced the eye and entered the intraocular space, threatening the retina itself. The possibility of infection is high, and occasionally the infection can spread out of the eye and even have fatal consequences. Some wounds can be repaired surgically if the area is clean and relatively free of contamination. If the wound is extensive, enucleation is indicated.

Eye Enucleation

Eye enucleation, the surgical removal of the eyeball, may be necessitated because of a severe injury, the need to relieve pain when the patient is blind, the presence of malignant tumors, or for cosmetic purposes when the patient has been blinded from injury or disease. The surgery may include the removal of the entire eyeball, only the contents of the eyeball, or the eyeball and all the related structures.

Preoperative intervention

The preoperative care of the patient includes discussing the way the patient feels about the surgery. When a malignancy is present, the nurse may expect the patient to be depressed and worried. A sympathetic, understanding approach to the patient is essential. Although the patient may be assured that a prosthesis may be used, an overly optimistic attitude should be avoided. However, when surgery is done to relieve pain, the patient may look forward to its relief, and the emotional reaction will be one of optimism.

Postoperative intervention

When the patient returns from surgery a pressure dressing will be placed over the eye and will be left in place for 24 hours. The patient should be observed for any evidence of hemorrhage, pain on the affected side, and headache, which should be reported immediately. During surgery, a plastic ball implant covered by the muscles and conjunctiva maintains the shape of the eye, and a plastic conformer placed over the conjunctiva maintains the eyelid's integrity while the eye heals. When the eye socket has healed, usually after 2 to 6 weeks, the patient may begin wearing a prosthesis. The patient should be instructed in the use and care of the prosthesis, care of the socket, and instillation of medications. A referral should be made to the oculist for the making and fitting of the prosthesis.

Today prostheses are generally made of plastic throughout, including paint, iris, veins, and sclera. Plastic is preferred to glass because it is tougher and does not break easily. In addition, the plastic eye can be built up or cut down as the shape of the person's socket changes. Plastic also has a much longer life span and an adult can expect to get several years of comfortable wear.

At one time people were encouraged to remove their prosthesis on a regular basis for cleaning. However, it has been learned that removal on a regular basis can cause mild irritation of the socket. Consequently, many people now find it only necessary to have the artifical eye cleaned at their annual visits to the oculist. The salt and protein deposits that build up on the prosthesis are removed by polishing. If the eye must be left out of the socket, it should be stored in water or contact lens solution. Occasionally, people with artificial eyes will complain of dry eye caused by lack of lubrication. Artificial tears or an oily lubricant is often helpful. Points to reinforce with patients include: (1) If there is a need to wipe the eye, the person should rub the eye toward the nose with the eyes closed. Wiping the eye away from the nose may cause it to fall out. (2) The eye should not be exposed to alcohol, ether, chloroform, or any solvent because these solutions can damage the eye. (3) The person should wear a protective patch or swimming goggles, or remove the eye and store it when participating in water sports. (4) The person should be encouraged to protect the remaining eye through the proper use of safety devices such as safety glasses.

NURSING ASSESSMENT OF PATIENTS WITH EAR PROBLEMS

Hearing assessment of the patient begins with his or her past and present medical condition, noting especially past surgeries and current symptoms. Several observations and symptoms are important in a proper assessment.

Diagnostic Tests and Procedures
Ear examination

Several methods exist for determining hearing loss; the tests vary in accuracy and purpose.

Otoscopy. Otoscopy is the direct visualization of the external auditory canal and the tympanic membrane through an instrument called an otoscope. It is performed before any other auditory or vestibular tests.

Voice tests. Voice tests may be done by whispering or speaking in a lower tone of voice. The individual is placed at a distance of 20 feet and turned sideways so that the ear to be tested is toward the examiner; the other ear is covered. The person is asked to repeat the whispered or spoken words. The method is of value only as a screening test to locate individuals who need to be more thoroughly examined.

Audiometry. A more accurate examination is done with the audiometer, which produces tones of varying pitch and intensity. The patient wears earphones that are attached to the audiometer. The individual listens to various tones and indicates when the sound is heard. The audiometer test provides information concerning quantitative and qualitative measurement of hearing and provides the otologist with information that can help to determine the kind of treatment needed.

Tuning forks. Hearing tests may also be done by using tuning forks that are made to vibrate and are placed at various locations near the ear. The Weber and Rinne tests are useful in distinguishing

---

> ### Symptoms of Ear Problems
>
> 1. Pain or discomfort in one or both ears.
> 2. Sudden or gradual hearing loss.
> 3. Progressive or sudden unilateral hearing loss.
> 4. Complaints of tinnitus or chronic dizziness.
> 5. Air-bone conduction gap assessed by special tests.
> 6. Visible signs of blockage in the ear canal from wax or foreign objects.
> 7. Congenital or traumatic deformities of the ear.

between sensorineural and conductive hearing loss. The Weber test, which detects nerve loss (sensorineural), uses bone conduction to test lateralization of sounds. A tuning fork is vibrated and placed in contact with the skin at a point on the midline of the skull, preferably halfway between the front and back of the head or on the top of the forehead. The sound will not be perceived in the ear with the deficit or will be less audible; instead it will carry laterally to the good ear. In the Rinne test the base of a vibrating tuning fork is placed on the mastoid process of the temporal bone until the person can no longer hear it. The tuning fork is then placed in front of the ear, where under normal circumstances it can still be heard, indicating that air conduction lasts longer than bone conduction.

Testing hearing in young children. Infants as young as a few days and very young children may be tested for hearing loss. These tests depend on observation of reflex action of the child when exposed to sound stimuli. To administer the tests, a person must be especially trained in the technique. However, the nurse working in the nursery or in pediatrics may contribute to the identification of infants or young children who may have hearing loss by making a few careful observations, such as the following, which should be reported to the physician:

1. Child cannot be awakened unless touched
2. Comfort measures fail unless infant is held
3. Child fails to respond to sounds or loud noises
4. Child shows lack of interest in noisemaking toys unless they are in the child's hands
5. Child fails to respond to own name

Vestibular tests
Falling and past-pointing tests. Dysfunction in the vestibule of the ear and the cerebellum of

the brain may result in dizziness, loss of equilibrium, or **nystagmus** (involuntary rhythmic movement of the eyeball). Patients can be tested for vestibular and cerebellar dysfunction with the falling and past-pointing tests. In the falling test the patient is observed while standing with feet together, standing on one foot, standing heel to toe, and walking forward and backward heel to toe—each time with eyes open and then with the eyes closed. Marked swaying or falling indicates dysfunction. In the past-pointing test the patient is instructed to reach out and touch the examiner's index finger, which is held at shoulder level, then to lower his or her arm and touch the finger again with the eyes closed. The test is repeated using the finger of the examiner's opposite hand. The degree and direction of past-pointing is observed.

Electronystagmography. In this test eye movements in response to specific stimuli are recorded. Nystagmus following a head turn is normal, but prolonged nystagmus is abnormal. The test is used to determine the presence and location of a lesion in the vestibule of the ear; to help identify the cause of dizzines, vertigo, or tinnitus; and help diagnose unilateral hearing loss of unknown origin. It employs a battery of tests using multiple stimuli, including hot and cold water, to elicit nystagmus.

Hearing Impairment

Hearing loss may be congenital, or it may occur later in life as a result of disease or injury. Persons are considered hard of hearing when their hearing is defective but they can function with a hearing aid or some other device that amplifies sound. Hard-of-hearing persons may sometimes recover their hearing through surgery. The deaf person cannot be helped by medical treatment and must depend on lipreading and sign language for communication. About one of ever 500 adults in the United States is deaf. Deaf persons will have difficulty in speaking if they have been without hearing since birth. Those who have lost their hearing after they have learned to speak are able to speak quite normally. Even persons born deaf who have some residual hearing can learn to speak intelligibly and be understood by relatives and friends. The inability to speak with normal rhythm and tone is not a sign of poor intellectual capacities. The terms "deaf mute" and "deaf and dumb" are resented by deaf persons and should not be used. The deaf person must have training in lipreading and speech training.

Types

Hearing loss may be conductive, affecting only the external or middle ear, or it may be sensorineural (nerve deafness), in which the inner ear is involved. Conductive deafness may be caused by an obstruction of the auditory canal that prevents sound waves from reaching the inner ear. The problem may be an accumulation of cerumen in the auditory canal, or it may be caused by otosclerosis in the middle ear that prevents transmission of sound vibrations from reaching the inner ear. For these persons surgery may restore hearing. In some cases there may be a congenital absence of the auditory canal or the tympanic membrane. In conductive deafness only the intensity of sound is affected.

In sensorineural deafness the auditory canal and the middle ear may receive the vibrations normally, but they go no further. This is because of degeneration of the nerve fibers of the auditory nerve or the hearing center in the brain. Damage may result from tumors, head injuries, or other causes such as congenital syphilis that affect cranial nerve VIII. Nerve deafness may occur in babies born to mothers who had rubella during the first trimester of pregnancy. A type of nerve deafness that usually involves high-frequency sounds may occur as part of the aging process. Persons with nerve deafness talk loudly, and there is confusion and distortion of sounds with poor speech discrimination. When nerve deafness is congenital or acquired during infancy and early childhood, speech is generally affected. Such children usually need training in lipreading and special education. Sensorineural or nerve deafness is permanent and irreversible, but research brings hope for finding a treatment in the future. An electronic cochlea has been devised that is implanted in the inner ear and conducts impulses to the higher centers in the brain. However, for the present most people with nerve deafness must be helped to live without the ability to hear.

Hearing Aids

Advertisements for hearing aids appearing in many magazines, newspapers, and television may confuse the hard-of-hearing person. The nurse can be helpful by advising the individual to consult an otologist. After careful examination, if the otologist considers the hearing loss to be irreversible, the patient will be referred to the nearest speech and hearing clinic. Technicians in these clinics evaluate the type of hearing loss and recommend the hearing aid best suited to the indi-

Signs of Hearing Loss

1. *Fatigue*—Straining to hear conversations is tiresome and often leads to irritability.
2. *Speech deterioration*—"Flat voice", incorrect pronunciation, or omitting words because sounds are produced incorrectly.
3. *Indifference*—Lack of hearing can cause disinterest and depression.
4. *Social withdrawal*—Withdrawing from social gatherings occurs when the person is unable to communicate.
5. *Insecurity*—Improper hearing may cause the person to say or respond in the wrong manner leading to feelings of embarrassment and insecurity.
6. *Indecision/procrastination*—Hearing problems lead to loss of self-confidence, which in turn makes decision making more difficult.
7. *Suspiciousness*—As only parts of conversations are heard, hearing-impaired people suspect that they are being talked about.
8. *False pride*—Pretending to hear normally often causes others to believe that the person has normal hearing.
9. *Loneliness and unhappiness*—Enforced silence can lead to many frightening experiences, giving the person a sense of not belonging.
10. *Dominating conversations*—By dominating conversations the person has control of the group, thereby eliminating embarrassment.

vidual. The hearing aid is of little value to the individual with total nerve deafness; these persons must be trained in lipreading. The hearing aid is only designed to amplify sound; in persons with conduction deafness, in which the problem is one of intensity of sound, a hearing aid may help. The hearing aid amplifies all sound, including background noise. This can cause confusion and actually make it more difficult to hear conversation. For this reason, patients sometimes reject the hearing aid, saying that they can hear better without it. Patients should be taught to use the hearing aid only at times and places where it improves hearing. The hearing aid consists of three parts: a microphone that picks up sound and converts it into electric signals, an amplifier that intensifies the signal, and a receiver that converts the signal back into an intensified sound. The hearing aid may be used along with auditory training and lipreading. There are various types of hearing aids, including those that may be used about the head. They may be built into the glasses, worn behind the ear, or worn in the auditory canal. Other types may be worn on the torso.

The successful use of a hearing aid depends on the individual's feelings about the disability and the use of a hearing aid. Not all persons will be able to adjust to the device, and elderly persons may find it more difficult. Deafness, whether progressive or sudden in onset, produces anxiety and fear in the patient. The possibility of becoming cut off from familiar surroundings, losing friends, losing a job, and becoming isolated often leads to the patient's withdrawal from society. Many patients will deny the defect and refuse assistance. Hearing aids can play an important part in improving residual hearing, thus lessening the emotional impact of approaching deafness. Proper care of the hearing aid can eliminate several problems and increase the person's confidence in using this device. Whistling noises can indicate a loose or improperly worn mold. Poor amplification can result from dead batteries, wax buildup, or incorrect volume control. Pain while wearing the mold may not only show improper fitting but also signs of an infection in the ear or surrounding area.

Speaking to the Hearing Impaired

You should face the patient so that your lips are visible. Do not raise your voice to any great extent, but do speak more slowly and distinctly than usual. Avoid the use of the high tones, since they are more difficult to hear for the deaf person. If the patient does not understand what you have said, rephrase your statement using different words to say the same thing and pointing to the object you are talking about, whenever possible. Some letters and sounds are more difficult to distinguish than others. If the patient cannot hear you at all and cannot read your lips, then write out your message. It is important to communicate in some way with the deaf person to prevent feelings of loneliness.[13] Sign language is a useful tool and the nurse who works often with the hearing impaired should learn to sign.

THE PATIENT WITH DISEASES AND DISORDERS OF THE EAR

External Ear

Certain disorders of the external ear may affect hearing and cause pain and discomfot. Common disorders include infection, obstruction, injury, and perforation of the eardrum (Figure 23-2).

Infections

Boils are a common type of infection and may be extremely painful. Large boils may obstruct the auditory canal and cause impairment of hearing. They have a tendency to recur unless properly treated. The infectious agents are usually staphylococcal bacteria, which gain entrance to the subcutaneous tissue through a scratch or injury that may occur in removing wax or a foreign body. Relief may be obtained by the application of nonsterile warm compresses, a hot-water bottle, or an electric heating pad. Treatment may include instillation of drops containing antibiotics or cortisone. Also, a solution of aluminum acetate, known as Burow's solution, may be instilled into the auditory canal. If the infection extends to the regional lymph nodes, oral or intramuscular administration of antibiotics may be required. Drugs such as aspirin or codeine may be needed to relieve pain for patients with severe infection.

Other types of infections include those caused by fungi, which are rather uncommon. Various forms of dermatitis may ocur, particularly in persons with diabetes. Other generalized infections such as erysipelas or eczema may involve the external ear.

Obstructions

Children frequently put foreign bodies into their ears that obstruct the auditory canal. Parents and nurses should not attempt to remove foreign bodies because of the danger of pushing them farther into the canal. When the foreign body consists of vegetable matter such as corn, peas, or beans, which children are likely to put into the ear, irrigation should not be done because the fluid will cause the object to enlarge. A common cause of obstruction is the accumulation of cerumen, which may plug the canal. Sometimes it pushes against the eardrum and hardens, causing irritation of the drum and pain. Cerumen can be softened by placing warmed oil or glycerin in the ear for 2 or 3 days; it is then removed by gentle irrigation with a syringe or a Water Pik on *low* power. Irrigation of the ear is done less frequently than in the past and should be done under the direction of a physician. Warm water between 105° and 110°F (40.6 and 43.3°C) should be used because water that is too hot or too cold will cause pain or dizziness. Placing the tip of the syringe at the meatus and aiming towards the roof of the ear canal will give the best results. If injury to the tympanic membrane is suspected, irrigation should not be performed.

Insects such as cockroaches can enter the ear canal, causing discomfort and hearing loss. This problem is commonly seen where roaches are prevalent. An insect in the auditory canal can generally be killed by instilling a few drops of warm oil and then irrigating the canal with warm water. If the insect is alive, the physician may gently spray lidocaine in the ear to cause the insect to exit.

Injury

Injury to the external ear may result from many causes and consists of contusions, abrasions, or lacerations. Occasionally, there is loss of the pinna without interference with hearing. However, the congenital absence of the pinna may include absence of the canal and eardrum, resulting in total deafness in the ear.

Perforation

Perforation of the eardrum may ocur as a result of a fracture of the skull or a severe blow to the ear. It may result from otitis media (infection in the middle ear) in which there is a spontaneous rupture of the drum, with accompanying deafness, dizziness, nausea, and vomiting. Medical care should be secured to avoid or prevent spread of the infection.

Middle Ear

The middle ear is connected with the posterior part of the nose by the eustachian tube. Equalization of air pressure on both sides of the eardrum is maintained by air entering the middle ear through this tube. Infection from the nose and throat may reach the middle ear through the eustachian tube. Sometimes the tube may become inflamed or plugged with mucus, resulting in diminished hearing. The middle ear contains the organs for transmitting sound to the inner ear, and if they become diseased, deafness may result (Table 23-4).

Otitis media

Infection may enter the middle ear through the eustachian tube as the result of acute upper respiratory tract infections or infectious diseases such as measles or scarlet fever. Children are more susceptible to otitis media, because during the early years of life, the eustachian tube is more horizontal than in later years. This favors the conduction of infection from the respiratory passageways into the middle ear. It is most common in infants because the eustachian tube is shorter, wider, and

Table 23-4

Ear Medications

Drug	Preparation	Action	Nursing considerations
Hydrogen peroxide	Solution 1.5%, 3%	destroys bacteria by chemical action. Fill ear canal, wait until bubbling stops, drain out of ear canal.	Administer: to ear canal to facilitate removal of ear wax; can be diluted 1:1 with water or saline solution. Evaluate: for irritation rash, skin breaks, dryness, scales.
Acetic acid (Vosol, Domeboro, Otic)	Solution 2%, pH 2.8; 1-2 drops daily for 3 days.	provides antibacterial action to decrease ear infection; used for swimmer's ear to normalize pH and for infections of external ear canal.	Administer: solution should be warmed to body temperature after ear wax has been removed by irrigation. Evaluate: pain reduction: increased redness and swelling may indicate an underlying infection; instillations may cause temporary dizziness.
Isopropyl alcohol	Solution 70%-85%	used to dry ear canal	used in dermatitis and eczema to keep skin dry in ear canal; toxic reactions are rare
Aminoglycoside (Neomycin Sulfate, Neobiotic)	Topical; instill 1-3 drops 3-4 times daily for 7-10 days; reassess	antibiotic used to break down protein synthesis causing bacterial death.	Administer: warm to body temperature; doses should be evenly spaced to maintain blood levels.
Bacitracin and Polymyxin B	Topical Adult/child instill 1-3 drops 2-3 times daily for 7-10 days.	Bacteriostatic, bactericidal; effective for gram-negative bacteria.	Administer and store at room temperature; hypersensitivity reaction rare in local application but can occur if given along with systemic form of the drug; usually given in combination with other products.
Cortisporin (Sofracort, Synlar)	Topical; 2-3 drops 3-4 times daily for 7-10 days; reassess	decreases swelling; antibacterial agent	Administer and store at room temperature; can cause hypersensitivity reaction; preparation is usually in combination with other products.
Burow's Solution Acetic acid 2% in aluminium acetate	Topical solution 2.5%-10%	astringent, antiseptic	Administer: remove debris from ear canal prior to use; avoid eyes; can be used alone or in combination with other solutions or ointments.
Boracic Acid (boric acid)	Topical ointment, powder	very weak germicide; nonirritating	Administer: toxic reactions to topical use are rare; very toxic if taken internally.

straighter. In addition, the infant lies flat in bed most of the time and infected materials move easily from the respiratory tract to the middle ear. Children and adults should be taught to blow their nose with the mouth open to reduce the probablility of infection being forced from the respiratory tract up to the middle ear. The infection may cause an abscess, and the condition is then called **purulent otitis media.** The eardrum becomes red and swollen, and there is severe pain in the ear, with fever and impairment of hearing. The parent may often suspect the disease in an infant or young child when crying is accompanied by pulling at the ear and rolling the head from side to side.

Because the mucous membrane lining the middle ear is continuous with parts of the mastoid process, the added danger of extension of the infection into the mastoid cells is always present.

Intervention. The patient with acute purulent otitis media is usually restricted to bed rest and given amoxicillin for a week. The eardrum may rupture from the pressure in the middle ear, or the physician may incise the drum, which is called **paracentesis,** or **myringotomy.** A light general anesthetic or local anesthetic using an ionesthetizer is usually necessary when a myringotomy is done. The ionesthetizer anesthetizes the eardrum through ion transfer with the use of a local anesthetic solution and an electrode in the ear canal.

Ear Instillations
1. Turn the patient's head to the side with the affected ear upright.
2. In adult patients, the auricle should be pulled upward and backward.
3. In children, the auricle should be pulled downward.
4. Instill the prescribed number of drops (usually 3 or 4) into the ear opening without touching the meatus.
5. Pump the tragus once or twice to remove the air locks and drive the solution forward.
6. To improve contact with the inner ear, have the patient lie on the side for 5 to 10 minutes before the medication is instilled.

This method is ideal for outpatient procedures. Drainage from the ear is generally bloody at first but becomes purulent. Small tissues should be used to remove the drainage, or cotton should be placed loosely at the external opening of the auditory canal so as not to obstruct the flow of drainage. The area about the external ear should be kept clean, since the drainage will cause severe irritation if allowed to remain on the skin. After a myringotomy the temperature drops and the pain is usually relieved. However, if medication for pain is needed, aspirin is generally given. Purulent otitis media is often caused by the streptococcus or staphylococcus organism, and the appropriate antibiotic is administered. Unless proper treatment is given, the condition may become chronic, and the individual may have a draining ear for months or even years. The patient should be protected from chilling and observed for an increase in pain or temperature, which may indicate need for an additional incision or may be a sign of extension of the infection.

The box on p. 698 summarizes nursing care of the patient with otitis media.

Mastoiditis

Mastoiditis is a complication of acute purulent otitis media. Sometimes the infection may extend to the brain, with the formation of brain abscess or the development of meningitis. The infection from the mastoid cells may drain away through the auditory canal. However, if this does not occur, the cells will be destroyed. Symptoms associated with acute mastoiditis are elevation of temperature, increased pain, and tenderness over the mastoid area. There may be swelling, which tends to push the ear forward.

Mastoidectomy

Usually a myringotomy and large doses of antibiotics will cure mastoiditis. If bone destruction has occurred, a simple mastoidectomy may be necessary. Before the development of antibiotics, acute purulent otitis media and acute mastoiditis were common occurrences. However, because of antibiotic drugs, these diseases occur less often today.

Preoperative intervention. The preoperative care of the patient undergoing a mastoidectomy is the same as that for other surgical patients. A careful explanation should be given to all patients concerning removal of hair, and only the necessary amount of hair should be removed. An area of approximately 1½ to 2 inches around the ear is shaved.

Postoperative intervention. When the patient returns from surgery, the ear will be covered with a large pressure dressing secured with bandages about the head. When the patient has recovered from anesthesia, he may be placed in a semi-Fowler's position. As soon as nausea subsides, oral fluids and diet as tolerated by the patient may be given. Fluids may be administered by the intravenous route if nausea is persistent. Medication is given to relieve pain as necessary. Temperature, pulse, and respiration rates are measured every 4 hours and recorded. Some drainage may occur through the dressing; if necessary, the nurse may reinforce the dressing, but the dressing is changed only by the physician. Antibiotics are usually ordered as indicated.

The patient should be observed for evidence of hemorrhage, which might appear as bright red blood on the dressing. Stiffness of the neck may occur from positioning during surgery, but if stiffness is accompanied by headache, visual disturbances, or signs of facial paralysis, it should be reported to the physician.

Tympanoplasty

Tympanoplasty is the name given to a group of surgical procedures designed to restore hearing loss caused by perforation of the tympanic membrane or necrosis of one of the ossicles of the middle ear, usually following chronic otitis media. The simplest form is a myringoplasty, in which the perforation in the eardrum is closed and reinforced with a tissue graft. Other types do more

---

NURSING CARE GUIDELINES
Otitis Media

Nursing diagnoses
- Alteration in comfort (pain) related to pressure and inflammation in the ear
- High risk for injury related to vertigo and diminished hearing
- Alteration in auditory sensory perception related to disruption in conduction of sound
- Sleep pattern disturbance related to ear discomfort
- Potential impairment of skin integrity of the ear because of drainage

Nursing interventions
- Check vital signs every 4 hours
- Observe location, duration, intensity, and characteristics of pain
- Administer antibiotics as ordered; report symptoms of headache, slow pulse, vomiting, and vertigo
- If the ear is draining, place cotton loosely in the external ear outside the ear canal and cleanse the ear frequently to keep free of irritating drainage

Expected outcomes
- Inflammation and pain reduced
- Outer ear clean and dry
- Hearing maintained

---

than close the defect and may involve the bones of the middle ear.

Postoperative intervention. The patient should lie on his unaffected side with the affected ear upward for about 12 hours after surgery. The inner dressing in the ear canal is not disturbed, but the outer dressing is changed if it becomes saturated. The patient is likely to experience vertigo and nausea after surgery. Care should be taken during ambulation, and antiemetics should be administered as ordered. The patient must keep the ear dry, and avoid sneezing or blowing the nose, but if this is necessary, the mouth should be kept open to avoid build up of pressure. The patient may not swim or travel by air until healing is complete; however, once the healing is complete, patients will have few restrictions. Antibiotics will be administered for about 5 days postoperatively.

Otosclerosis

The middle ear contains three little bones that function in transmitting sound to the inner ear. Normally, the stapes vibrates against the oval window through which sound reaches the inner ear. In otosclerosis a new growth of bone forms, causing the footplate of the stapes to become fixed in the oval window, preventing it from transmitting sound. Otosclerosis is the most common cause of conductive deafness. The cause of otosclerosis is unknown, but it is believed that there is a hereditary predisposition to the disorder. The loss of hearing may first be detected during the adolescent years and may be discovered through audiometer testing. Usually, the loss affects both ears, although one may be more severely involved than the other. The hearing impairment continues to increase slowly until the person reaches 40 years of age or older, by which time the loss may be great. Presently, there is no medical treatment that will cure the disorder or impede its progress. A surgical procedure called a **stapedectomy** will restore hearing in approximately 90% of patients.

Stapedectomy

A stapedectomy represents one of the most significant advances in ear surgery. Surgical procedures preceding the stapedectomy included stapes mobilization and fenestration, but both provided only temporary restoration of hearing. Today the stapedectomy is considered the treatment of choice for otosclerosis. In this procedure the stapes is removed and replaced by a small piece of wire or a plastic piston. This is attached to a graft of fat, vein, or Gelfoam, which covers the oval window. Occasionally, the footplate of the stapes will be left in place and the prosthesis placed through it. Sound travels from the incus to the wire or plastic piece, which vibrates the tissues of the oval window. Liquids of the inner ear then pick up the vibrations, and nerve impulses are initiated.

Preoperative intervention. Preoperative preparation of the patient is essentially the same as that for other surgery. A local anesthetic is generally given to avoid the postoperative effects of general anesthesia. The patient should be advised to wash the hair before entering the hospital to avoid the danger of getting water into the ear after surgery. The patient should be given an explanation of the surgery and know what to expect postoperatively.

Postoperative intervention. Postoperatively, the patient is kept flat in bed for the first 24 hours, and he should not blow his nose; in addition, all head movements should be kept at a minimum. After 24 hours the patient may be allowed up but should not get up alone. He should rise slowly, keeping the head level, and should walk slowly with the head and torso in line. There will be a dressing and packing in the auditory canal. Slight drainage may appear on the dressing, but any bright red blood should be reported. The patient should be carefully observed for signs that might indicate complications such as meningitis or facial paralysis. Facial nerve paralysis may occur immediately postoperatively because of injection of anesthetic near the nerve. Function should return in about 4 hours. Dryness of the mouth or decreased taste sensation may occur from injury to the chorda tympani nerve during surgery. These symptoms will eventually pass but may last for several months. Vertigo may occur from trauma, loss of perilymph, or labyrinthitis. Care must be taken in ambulating the patient with vertigo. A sensation of sloshing of the ear may indicate a collection of serous fluid in the middle ear. Otitis media can occur as a complication of the surgery. Because eating may be painful, administration of an analgesic before meals will increase comfort. A liquid diet is given postoperatively with a gradual increase to soft foods as tolerated. If nausea and vomiting occur, antiemetics may be ordered. The patient may be discharged from the hospital in 3 or 4 days and should be aware that hearing is not instantly restored with the surgery but that instead it will return gradually over several weeks. The patient should be instructed to keep the dressing dry, to avoid getting water in the ear, (thus hair washing and swimming are not allowed) and is taught to maintain a sterile technique while changing the dressing.[17] Situations should be avoided in which there are air pressure changes, such as traveling on airplanes with poorly pressurized cabins.

Inner Ear
Labyrinthitis

The labyrinth is a system of cavities within the inner ear that communicate with one another. Labyrinthitis is an inflammation of these structures, usually resulting from an extension of infection from the middle ear. The characteristic symptom is severe dizziness, causing a disturbance of equilibrium. In patients with severe cases nausea and vomiting may occur, and there is generally some impairment of hearing.

Intervention. The condition is usually treated with antibiotic drugs. The patient is restricted to a regimen of bed rest, and side rails should be placed on the bed. The patient should be instructed not to get up without assistance because of the danger of falling. If nausea and vomiting are severe, intravenous fluids and antiemetic drugs to control vomiting may be administered.

Meniere's syndrome

The symptoms of Meniere's syndrome result from an increase in the endolymph, which causes an increased pressure in the inner ear. An imbalance of the autonomic nervous system results in a spasm of the internal auditory artery, causing the increased pressure. However, the cause is unknown, and there is no specific treatment.

The major symptom is severe vertigo, which is the sensation of seeing and feeling motion that is not present. There may be nausea and vomiting, ringing in the ears, and ultimately loss of hearing.

Intervention. The nursing care of the patient should provide for safety by placing side rails on the bed. The symptoms cause the patient anxiety, apprehension, and distress, and any movement may increase the severity of his symptoms. The nurse should explain all procedures to the patient and allow him to move in a way that causes him the least discomfort. Because the appetite is poor, the patient may need encouragement to eat. In severe prolonged attacks, intravenous fluids may be administered.

Although some patients may respond to medical treatment, others do not. The patient is usually advised to avoid smoking and may be prescribed a low-sodium diet to help control edema. Vitamins have provided relief for some older patients, and meclizine (Bonine) and nicotinic acid have been effective in relieving symptoms in others.

Surgery may be performed to relieve severe vertigo. If there is considerable hearing loss in the affected ear, and if hearing in one ear is not affected, the destruction of the membranous labyrinth may be done. This type of surgery results in permanent deafness in the ear. When the loss of hearing is minimal, ultrasonic surgery may relieve symptoms and preserve hearing. Bell's palsy may complicate ultrasonic surgery but will clear in several weeks.

NURSING CARE PLAN
Patient with Detached Retina

The patient is a 26-year-old male who was brought to the emergency department by one of his caretakers after complaining of "blurred vision," and "seeing out of only one half of his right eye."

The patient is a moderately retarded young man who requires assistance in his activities of daily living (ADLs). He can feed and dress himself and be responsible for toileting and hygiene, but needs assistance with time management and decision making. He is considered "trainable" and can function semi-independently in many self-care skills.

Opthalmic exam revealed that the patient has a right detached retina and he was admitted for surgery on the following day. His overall health status is good. He has known allergies to ragweed (hay fever every summer) codeine, xylocaine, and strawberries.

Past medical history

Some information from old records.
Premature birth at 32 weeks. Unknown cause.
Required oxygen for first 3 weeks of life.
Periods of apnea and bradycardia during first month of life.
Bilateral inguinal hernia repair at 3 months.
Grand mal seizures started at age 6 years. Currently under control with Tegretol. Last seizure 1 year ago.
Mild cerebral palsy—wears short leg braces.
Moderate level mental retardation.
Has never smoked/negative alcohol use.
Has chronic constipation.

Family history

Mother age 52. Alcoholism × 30 years.
Father age 60. No available data.
Brother age 20 years, history of mental illness, and autism.

Psychosocial data

Lived with biologic family until 7 years old.
Seizures plus social conditions within family prompted Children's Protective Services to intervene.
History of foster families. Unknown period of time.
Resided in residential state school from age 14 to 19.
Special education classes until age 21.
  Can write own name, count to 30, and read on a primary level. Has very short attention span.
Has lived in current group home for 7 years.

Considers other residents his "family." Particularly attached to "Joe," his primary caretaker.
Biologic family no longer in area. Minimal visits or contacts.
Has Medicaid and Title 19.
Social Security disability income.
Works in local grocery store as "bagger."
Excellent work record and attendance.
Occasional "temper tantrums" at home, usually over TV or household chores. Information provided by Joe who will remain in continual attendance daily while hospitalized.

Assessment data

Height 5 ft 6 in, weight 146 lbs.
Pleasant young man with dull facies.
Oriented ×3 (time, place, and person). Dependent on caretaker to respond to some questions. Otherwise cooperative.
Skin: intact—no signs rashes or bruises.
Respiratory: Regular rate and rhythm (16-18). No use accessory muscles. Lungs clear to percussion and ascultation.
Cardiovascular: Slight pectus excavatum. Apical rate heard best to right of midclavicular line. Regular rate and rhythm (68-70). No bruits, all pulses intact.
Abdominal: Slight distention—bowel sounds heard in all four quadrants.
Musculoskeletal: Full range of motion for all joints. Said to have "unsteady gait" without braces.

Lab data

ECG, chest x-ray normal.
Hgb 14.1 Hct 42 WBC 9,000 Platelets 325,000
BUN 14 Electrolytes WNL.
Urinalysis: No abnormalities.

Medications

Tegretrol 200 mg BID.
Colace 100 mg BID.
Cyclogyl eye drops 1 in right eye every 4 hours.
Predulose opthalmic eye drops 2 OD every 6 hours.
Sodium Sulamyd 30% opth sol. 2 drops QID and hs.
Compazine 10 mg I.M. prn nausea.
Valium 5 mg po QID.
Seconal 100 mg po hs.

NURSING DIAGNOSIS

Anxiety related to visual disturbance and being in unfamiliar environment as evidenced by shaky voice and hesitant responses.

Expected patient outcomes	Nursing interventions	Evaluation for expected outcomes
The patient describes his perception of the visual problem. Patient experiences reduced anxiety by identifying persons familiar to him. The patient copes with current medical situation without having severe anxiety. Patient uses support systems to assist him with coping.	Determine patient's level of knowledge. Orient him to his surroundings. Encourage him to "touch" all equipment (BP cuff, stethescope). Use simple terms in explaining what is expected of him. Encourage any questions. Speak gently when entering room (both eyes patched). Tell him when you are leaving. Remind him that his caretaker is always present. Have patient introduce his attendent caretaker from the group home. Reorient patient as often as necessary as to where he is and why the bed is different from his at home. Provide ample time for patient to respond to care measures. Prepare patient for any changes (eye drops), give short simple explanations geared to his level of understanding. At the first signs of anxiety, hold his hand and reassure him.	Patient will demonstrate reduced preoccupation with fears and will give evidence of a level of trust in his caretakers and nurses. Patient will state (in basic terms) what his visual condition is and that the eye patches are temporary. Patient will cooperate with his treatment regimen.

NURSING DIAGNOSIS

Potential for injury or infection related to eyes patched and sensation of "itchiness" with healing.

Expected patient outcomes	Nursing interventions	Evaluation for expected outcomes
Patient's eyes remain free from all signs and symptoms of infection. Vital signs, temperature, and lab values remain within the normal range. Patient remains in designated position (usually prone) as determined by his surgeon. Patient cooperates with the need to maintain bedrest and allows his caretakers to assist him with voiding and eating.	Keep bed at lowest level to floor. Orient patient to the use of and the need for side rails. Frequently remind patient to remain on bed rest. Assess his ability to use the call bell. Keep it near at all times. Immediately postoperative, take vital signs every 15 minutes until stable and then once per shift for 24 hours. Give tranquilizer medication as ordered to promote cooperation. Keep radio or TV on softly to his favorite stations or programs. Encourage his attendant caretaker to read to him when awake. Encourage deep breathing exercises when ascultating lungs. Remind patient not to cough. Monitor for signs of nausea and medicate with Compazine to prevent vomiting.	Patient's eye incision site remains free of erythema, edema, purulent drainage, and other signs and symptoms of infection. Patient's vital signs and lab values remain within his baseline data. Patient discusses the need for safety measures such as side rails. Patient remains in the designated postoperative position and does not attempt to get out of bed. Patient cooperates in some self-care activities within the sensori-motor limitations posted by his eye patches and enforced bed rest.

Continued on next page.

Expected patient outcomes	Nursing interventions	Evaluation for expected outcomes
	Performing active and passive range of motion exercises and antiembolism exercises every shift. Advance diet slowly as tolerated (clear liquids first). Teach patient the importance of not rubbing eyes or bandages. Have patient perform hand washings four times a day, especially at bedtime or after using the bedpan or urinal. Perform basic infection prevention teachings with attendant caretaker every shift.	

NURSING DIAGNOSIS

Knowledge deficit related to activity restrictions.

Expected patient outcomes	Nursing interventions	Evaluation for expected outcomes
Patient states an understanding of what he has been taught. He can recite back all the instructions by his date of discharge. Significant others (caretakers) express willingness to help patient maintain maximum independence.	Advise patient of need to move slowly in bed. Maintain bed rest with both eyes patched for 48 hours postsurgery. Position patient in the prone position with his head downward and turned slightly (may use small pillow). Instruct patient not to forcefully cough. Remind him of the need to deep breathe every 2 hours when awake. Discuss importance of quiet activities upon discharge. Avoid crowds or any situation where he might have rapid or jolting movements. Teach patient of need to eat lightly to avoid vomiting. Have him cite his favorite foods (cereals, fruits, and pizza). Provide written discharge instructions to his caretakers outlining the specific activity restrictions. Question if other residents pose a physical threat to patient. Have patient list his favorite "quiet" activities. Praise his efforts at cooperation.	Patient (and his caretakers) discuss the effects of visual loss on his lifestyle. Patient can list what he is to avoid and how he is allowed to ambulate (slowly and steadily with no rapid movements). Patient does not lose any of his self-care skills previously attained due to his hospitalization and/or surgery. Caretakers cite ways to assist patient to attain his maximum level of functioning.

REFERENCES AND ADDITIONAL READINGS

1. Affel EL: Ophthalmic ultrasonography: a scan, J Ophthal Nurs Technol 9:52-56, 1990.
2. Allen MN: Adjusting to a visual impairment, J Ophthal Nurs Technol 9:47-51, 1990.
3. American Foundation for the Blind: Directory of services for the blind and visually impaired in the US, ed 23, New York, 1988, The Foundation.
4. Arentsen JJ: The dry eye, J Ophthal Nurs Technol 6:134-137, 1987.
5. Barker-Stotts K: Action STAT! Hyphema, Nursing 18(12):33, 1988.
6. Bentz LN: Caring for and communicating with blind and visually impaired persons, J Visual Impair Blindness 81:472-481, 1987.
7. Bishop VE: Visually handicapped people and the law, J Visual Impair Blindness 81:53-58, 1987.
8. Boyd-Monk H and Steinmetz CG: Nursing care of the eye, Norwalk, Ct, 1987, Appleton & Lange.
9. Boyd-Monk H: Examining the external eye, Nursing 10(5):58-63, 1980.
10. Brunner LS and Suddarth DS: Textbook of medical surgical nursing, ed 6, Philadelphia, 1988, JB Lippincott Co.
11. Bull TR: A color atlas of ENT diagnosis, ed 2, London, 1987, Wolfe Medical Books.
12. Capino DG and Leibowitz HM: Age-related macular degeneration, Hosp Pract 23(3):23, 1988.
13. Carbary L: Deafness: the silent world, Nurs Care 9:13-16, 1976.
14. Carver JA: Cataract care made plain, AJN 87:626-630, 1987.
15. Centers for Disease Control: Recommendation for prevention of HIV transmission in health care settings, MMWR 36(25), 1987.
16. Clemens G: Nursing role in fluorescein angiography, J Ophthal Nurs Technol 4(4):32-35, 1985.
17. Conover J and Cober J: Caring for the hearing impaired, Nurs Clin North Am 5:497, 1970.
18. DeBase R and others: Postintraocular lens implants, Geriatr Nurs 9(6):342-343, 1988.
19. Dungca DU and others: Temporal arteritis and sudden irreversible vision loss, Ophthal Nurs Forum 2(1):2-4, 1986.
20. Edmonds SE: Resources for the visually impaired, J Ophthal Nurs Technol 9(11):14-15, 1990.
21. Folley FM and others: Alkaline injury to the eye, Ophthal Nurs Forum 5(1):1-4, 6-8, 1989.
22. Fong ACO: Acquired immune deficiency syndrome and ophthalmology, J Ophthal Nurs Technol 8(5):189-192, 1989.
23. Frank A and Werfel N: ECCE with phacoemulsification, J Ophthal Nurs Technol 7:62-67, 1988.
24. Glover SF: Update on scleral buckling: a fight for sight (pictorial), Today's OR Nurse 8:8-12, Jan. 1986.
25. Goldstein J: Ocular side effects of systemic drugs, J Ophthal Nurs Technol 5:103-105, 1986.
26. Goldstein J: Pharmacology of ophthalmic drugs, anesthetics, mydriatics, cycloplegics and ocular hypotensives, J Ophthal Nurs Technol 6(1):146-150, 1987.
27. Goldstein J: Pharmacology of ophthalmic drugs: antiinflammatory and antiinfective agents, J Ophthal Nurs Technol 6(2):193-197, 1987.
28. Halpern BL: Sexually transmitted diseases and the eye, Contact Lens Forum, 31-40, Oct 1989.
29. Hamrick S and others: Therapeutic ultrasound, AORNJ 47:950-960, 1988.
30. Hankewich M: Nursing grand rounds: hyphema, J Ophthal Nurs Technol 5(5):169-173, 1986.
31. Hearing loss: basic anatomy of the ear (pictorial), Hosp Med 22(7):160, 1986.
32. Holt JE: Eye disease: changes with aging—natural or a sign of disease? Consultant 26(7):69-72, 1986.
33. Hosein AM: The use of silicone oil in vitreoretinal surgery, J Ophthal Nurs Technol 7:126-129, 1988.
34. Lawlor MC: Common ocular injuries and disorders, J Emerg Nurs 15(1):36-43, 1989.
35. Luckman J and Sorensen KC: Medical-surgical nursing: a psychophysiologic approach, ed 3, Philadelphia, 1987, WB Saunders Co.
36. MacInnis B: Lasers and the eye, Med N Am 33:6045-47, 1989.
37. Maise AR, Silberman R, and Trief E: Aging and visual impairment, J Visual Impair Blindness 81:323-325, 1987.
38. Micucci J: Automated versus Goldmann perimetry, J Ophthal Nurs Technol 5(3):94-99, 1986.
39. OTC eye drops and blindness, Nurses Drug Alert 12(7):56, 1988.
40. Pappas JJ and others: Hearing loss: new techniques to correct defects and enhance sounds, Consultant 26(9):129-132, 1986.
41. Pashby T: Eye injuries in sports, J Ophthal Nurs Technol 8:99-101, 1989.
42. Ponchillia SV and LaGrow S: Independent glucose monitoring by functionally blind diabetics, J Visual Impair Blindness 82:50-53, 1988.
43. Roach VG: Endophthalamites: an ocular emergency, J Ophthal Nurs Technol 8:203-205, 1989.
44. Roach VG: What you should know about diabetic retinopathy, J Ophthal Nurs Technol 7:166-169, 1988.
45. Shakin EP and Lucier AC: Retinitis pigmentosa, J Ophthal Nurs Technol 9:6-9, 1990.
46. Smith S: Diabetic retinopathy, Insight XIV(4):22-26, 1989.
47. Smith S: Day care cataract surgery: the patient's perspective, J Ophthal Nurs Technol 6:50-55, 1987.
48. Smith SJ and Drance SM: Difficulties patients have at home after cataract surgery, Can J Ophthalmol 19(1):6-9, 1984.
49. Smith SJ: Sensory deprivation and the ophthalmic patient, J Ophthal Nurs Technol 8:148-154, 1989.
50. Spencer RE: Transitions: being blind in a sighted world, J Ophthal Nurs Technol 7:220-222, 1988.
51. Vader L: End stage glaucoma and enucleation: an ophthalmic nursing challenge, Ophthal Nurs Forum 3(4):1-8, 1987.
52. Vaughan D and Asbury T: General ophthalmology, Los Altos, Calif, 1987, Lange Medical Publishers.
53. Vickers R: A psychological approach to attitudes toward blind persons, J Visual Impair Blindness 81:326-327, 1987.
54. Whitton S: Managing detachment with retinal tacks, J Ophthal Nurs Technol 5(3):91-93, 1986.
55. Yanuzzi LA, Gitter K, and Judson PH: Lasers in ophthalmology, J Ophthal Nurs Technol 7(6):199-203, 1988.

CHAPTER

24

PROBLEMS AFFECTING
Skin Integrity

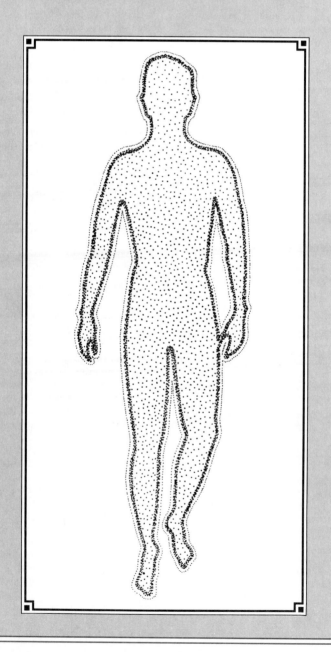

KEY WORDS

atrophy
autograft
bleb
bulla
comedones
crust
debridement
decubitus ulcer
dermatologist
dermis
epidermis
eschar
excoriation
fissure
gumma
heterograft
homograft
macule
nodule
papule
pruritus
pustule
sebaceous
seborrhea
sebum
shearing force
tinea
ulcer
urticaria
vesicle
wheal

OBJECTIVES

1. Identify the functions of the skin.

2. Describe the correct methods for applying open and closed wet dressings and administering a soak or therapeutic bath.

3. Identify measures to prevent and treat decubitus ulcers (pressure necrosis).

4. Differentiate between the signs and symptoms of folliculitis, furuncles, and carbuncles, and identify the usual causative organism of each.

5. Describe the lesions and transmission of impetigo.

6. Differentiate signs, symptoms, and intervention for the various forms of ringworm (tinea).

7. Differentiate between the causes of: chafing, prickly heat, plant poisoning, exfoliative dermatitis, and drug dermatitis.

8. Describe lesions and interventions for psoriasis and eczema.

9. Discuss the facts essential to teaching the patient to control systemic lupus erythematosus.

10. Differentiate between herpes simplex types I and II and herpes zoster.

11. Describe nursing measures to provide relief for the patient with pruritis.

12. Differentiate skin tumors.

13. Describe methods for the prevention and treatment of pediculosis.

14. Describe the prevention of airway obstruction, shock, and infection in the burn patient.

15. Describe the following methods of treatment for burns: exposure, hydrotherapy, wet dressings, occlusive dressings, mafenide acetate, silver nitrate, silver sulfadiazine, and povidone-iodine.

16. Discuss the rehabilitation phase and discharge planning and teaching for the burn patient.

17. Discuss the role of the nurse in caring for the patient with a skin graft.

STRUCTURE AND FUNCTION OF THE SKIN

The skin is the largest organ of the body and is often referred to as the *integumentary system*. It is considered an organ because of its physiologic structure and its many functions (Table 24-1). The skin is usually thought of as having two distinct layers: the **epidermis** and the **dermis** (Figure 24-1); however, a third layer of tissue, the subcutaneous tissue, may be included because of its function in helping to protect other body tissues. The epidermis is the outermost layer, and it actually has four layers or regions, sometimes called *strata* (stratum basale, stratum spinosum, stratum granulosum, stratum corneum). The three outermost regions consist of dead cells that are constantly being pushed to the surface and shed, while new cells are being developed in the innermost region. The principal substance of the outside layer of the epidermis is *keratin*, which provides a waterproof covering that prevents the skin from drying and has a slightly acid reaction, producing the acidity of the skin, which acts as a barrier to invading

Table 24-1

Functions of the Skin

Function	Epidermis	Dermis	Subcutaneous
Protection from dehydration	Keratin renders skin impervious to water, preventing undue water loss	Sebaceous glands render skin impervious to water, preventing undue water loss	
Protection from mechanical injury	Mechanical strength protects underlying structures; layer is thicker where subject to more friction (palms, soles of feet)	Mechanical strength from collagen fibers, elastic fibers, ground substance	Mechanical shock absorber
Protection from infection	Dry external surface inhibits growth of microorganisms Cells reproduce rapidly if skin damaged or torn to repair surface, provided dermis intact	Lymphatic and vascular tissues capable of inflammatory and immune response; first line of defense against microorganisms	
Protection from ultraviolet light	Melanin absorbs UV light and protects subepidermal layers		
Temperature regulation	Sweat glands secrete sweat, taking energy from the skin to reduce skin temperature and to evaporate sweat, thus reducing core body temperature	Dilation or constriction of blood vessels will promote or inhibit heat conduction, convection, radiation, and evaporation	
Vitamin synthesis	When exposed to sunlight, synthesizes Vitamin D from dehydrocholesterol in malpighian cells; supplements Vitamin D taken with food		
Sensory organ	Transmits sensations through neuroreceptor system	Relays sensations to brain	Contains large pressure receptors
Communication	Blushing and facial expressions communicate wide range of emotions		
Preservation of self image	Epidermal diseases such as psoriasis, can alter body image and self esteem	Dermal diseases such as scleroderma, can alter body image and self esteem	

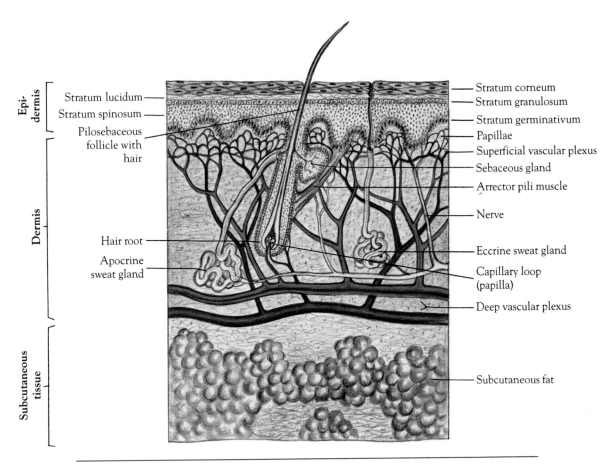

Figure 24-1

Structures of the skin. *(From Thompson JM et al: Mosby's Manual of clinical nursing, ed 2, St Louis, 1989, The CV Mosby Co.)*

pathogens. Hair and nails are a specialized form of keratin that has become dry and firm. The epidermis also contains the pigment *melanin*, which provides the coloring of the skin and helps prevent cancer from developing in the skin by shielding the skin from excessive exposure to sunlight. There is an increased synthesis of melanin on exposure to ultraviolet lights—the process involved in suntanning. Black-skinned people have larger melanin pigment granules than light-skinned people. There are no blood vessels in the epidermis, thus it receives its nourishment and fluids through seepage of lymph from blood vessels below.

The dermis, or true skin, is closely attached to the epidermis and consists of two layers. The uppermost layer (superficial layer) contains small elevations that project upward into the epidermis. The reticular or deeper layer contains numerous capillary blood vessels and nerve fibers. (This is why bleeding and pain occur when a person pricks a finger.) Some of the nerve fibers have receptors for hot and cold, others for touch and pressure, and some are concerned with vasodilation and vasoconstriction. The dermis also contains the sudoriferous (sweat) and sebaceous (oil) glands. All the structures are held together by fibrous and elastic connective tissue. The elasticity of this tissue decreases with the aging process, causing the skin to take on a wrinkled appearance.

Beneath the dermis is a layer of subcutaneous tissue, also called *superficial fascia*. The subcutaneous tissue, closely adherent to the dermis, provides support and through small arteries and lymphatics maintains a blood supply to the dermis. Subcutaneous tissue contains large amounts of fat and some sweat glands. The thickness of the skin and the amount of subcutaneous tissue vary on different parts of the body.

The nails, hair, and sebaceous and sudoriferous glands and their ducts are appendages of the skin.

The sebaceous glands secrete an oily substance called **sebum**, which keeps the hair from becoming brittle. The gland may open into a hair follicle or may open onto the skin. The oil on the skin forms a protective covering that prevents the rapid evaporation of water from the skin surface. The vernix caseosa on the newborn infant is an accumulation of sebum from the sebaceous glands.

The sweat glands originate as blind coiled tubes with ducts that ultimately open on the surface of the skin as pores. These glands are distributed over the entire body but are more numerous on the forehead, palms of the hands, and soles of the feet. The sweat glands are important because they function in regulating body heat through evaporation of water from the skin surface.

The hair and nails are subordinate to the skin. The appearance of the nails will change during illness, and they may become brittle and easily broken, whereas in old age they may be rough and thickened.

The skin functions as a sense organ, provides a protective covering, serves as an organ of excretion, helps to regulate body temperature, provides information about the environment, plays a significant role in communicating with others, and is involved in vitamin synthesis.

Because of the numerous nerve endings in the skin, its function as a sense organ is of primary importance. Through the sense of touch the nurse is able to take the patient's pulse, touch the patient's skin and know if it is hot or cold, determine the presence of a draft in the patient's environment, or determine if the room is too warm and in need of improved ventilation.

The unbroken skin is the first line of defense against pathogenic organisms. The skin protects deeper tissues from injury and loss of body fluids. The excretory function of the skin is limited, but one of its most important functions is to help regulate body temperature. This is accomplished in two ways: (1) evaporation of sweat from the body and (2) dissipation of excess heat into the air when blood vessels dilate, bringing more blood, and thus increased heat, to the skin surface.

NURSING ASSESSMENT OF THE SKIN

In health or disease the normal skin tells many things about an individual, and in many situations it may provide valuable diagnostic clues to disease. Nursing personnel should routinely observe the color of the skin, its texture, presence of rashes or lesions, and characteristics of the hair and nails. Cyanosis, pallor, profuse sweating, and skin rashes are some of the conditions observed that may help to identify disease. In a state of health most persons take their skin for granted and pay too little attention to it, but when disease affects the skin, they become greatly disturbed. Skin that is well cared for and free from disease is a psychologic, social, and economic asset. It contributes to a feeling of well-being, to social acceptance, and to educational and employment opportunities.

ASSESSMENT AND DESCRIPTION OF SKIN LESIONS

Certain types of skin lesions are peculiar to specific disorders and help the **dermatologist** identify the disease. Some diseases are characterized by an orderly sequence of skin lesions. With chickenpox, red macules surmounted by vesicles first appear (dew drop on a rose petal), then umbilication, and finally crusting (Figure 24-2). Several different types of lesions may be present in an individual at the same time. Below are some of the typical types of skin lesions.

atrophy A wasting or thinning of body tissue, typically occurring with the aging process and with some neurologic diseases.

bleb An irregular elevation of the epidermis filled with serous or seropurulent fluid. It may be large in size and is seen in certain forms of severe dermatitis.

bulla A vesicle greater than 1 cm in diameter.

crust A dry exudate, commonly called a *scab*, occurring in impetigo, smallpox, chickenpox, and eczema.

excoriation An abraded or denuded area of skin. Unless expert care is given, it may occur where there is drainage, as with a colostomy.

fissure A groove, crack, or slit in the skin.

gumma A tumorlike lesion similar in appearance to an abscess. It is characteristic of late syphilis.

macule A discolored spot on the skin that may be of various colors and shapes. It is neither raised nor depressed.

nodule A raised solid lesion that is deeper in the skin than a papule.

papule A small, solid elevation varying from the

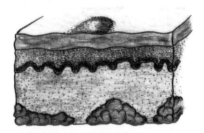

Macule: flat, nonpalpable, change in skin color, smaller than 1 cm (e.g., freckle, petechia).

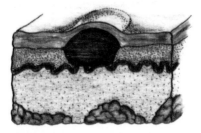

Papule: palpable, circumscribed, solid elevation in skin, smaller than 0.5 cm (e.g., elevated nevus).

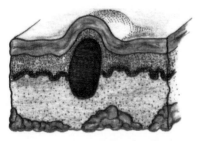

Nodule: elevated solid mass, deeper and firmer than papule, 0.5-0.2 cm (e.g., wart).

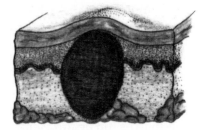

Tumor: solid mass that may extend deep through subcutaneous tissue, larger than 1-2 cm (e.g., epithelioma).

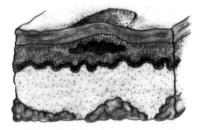

Wheal: irregularly shaped, elevated area or superficial localized edema; varies in size (e.g., hives, mosquito bite).

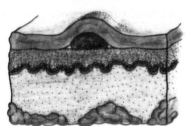

Vesicle: circumscribed elevation of skin filled with serous fluid, smaller than 0.5 cm (e.g., herpes simplex, chickenpox).

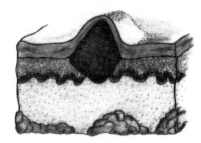

Pustule: circumscribed elevation of skin similar to vesicle but filled with pus, varies in size (e.g., acne, staphylococcal infection).

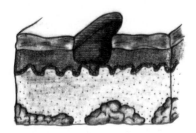

Ulcer: deep loss of skin surface that may extend to dermis and frequently bleeds and scars, varies in size (e.g., venous stasis ulcer).

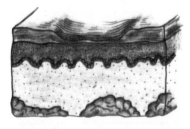

Atrophy: thinning of skin with loss of normal skin furrow and skin appearing shiny and translucent, varies in size (e.g., arterial insufficiency).

Figure 24-2

Types of skin lesions. *(From Perry AG and Potter PA: Clinical nursing skills and techniques, ed 2, St Louis, 1989, The CV Mosby Co.)*

size of a pinhead to a pea. It may be observed in eczema, measles, smallpox, and syphilis.

pustule A small elevation filled with pus. It is characteristic of impetigo and acne vulgaris.

scale A small, thin flake of dry epidermis seen in eczema and psoriasis.

scar The mark left on the skin after repair of deep tissue loss.

ulcer An open lesion on the skin with loss of deep tissue (epidermis and part of dermis) often healing with a scar. The classic example is the decubitus ulcer.

vesicle A blisterlike elevation on the skin containing serous fluid. It occurs in herpes simplex, chickenpox, and impetigo.

wheal Elevation of varying size and irregular

shape. If extensive, wheals may run together. They are characteristic of various allergic reactions and are often referred to as hives.

NURSING RESPONSIBILITIES FOR DIAGNOSTIC TESTS AND PROCEDURES

Most skin disorders can be diagnosed using a carefully taken history, the patient's complaints, and observation of the lesion. A personal history should include allergies, sleep habits, occupation, medications, recent travel, contact with others, and anxiety. It is also important to find out when and where the lesion first appeared and the direction of its spread; whether it is constant or comes and goes; if it is wet or dry; and if itching is present. Four important observations must be made, including identification, distribution, shape, and arrangement of the lesion. Careful observation and recording of this information can be of great value to the physician in making the correct diagnosis. Sometimes the dermatologist may wish to make a bacteriologic study, in which case scraping or swabbing of the lesion is necessary. Various kinds of fungi can be identified by this method. At other times a biopsy may be done for pathologic examination.

NURSING RESPONSIBILITIES FOR THERAPEUTIC PROCEDURES

Nursing care of the patient with skin disorders may involve several nursing procedures, including therapeutic baths, wet dressings, soaks, and the application of various topical medications.

Therapeutic Baths

Therapeutic baths are used for several purposes, including disinfecting and deodorizing, relieving pruritis, achieving a soothing effect, and softening and lubricating the skin. Soap, oils, medications, or a variety of substances such as oatmeal, starch, baking soda, or a combination of these may be used. Ordinary laundry starch or cornstarch may be used and is prepared in the same way as for laundry purposes. Several kinds of laundry starch contain bluing and are lightly scented, and these should not be used for therapeutic baths. The starch may be cooked, using 1 cup of starch moistened with cold water and 2 quarts of boiling water. A combination of uncooked starch and baking soda in the proportion of 1 part soda to 4 parts starch may be prepared as a paste and added to the water. For a bath, oatmeal may be prepared by placing 2 cups of oatmeal and 1 quart of boiling water in a double boiler and cooking for approximately 45 minutes. The oatmeal mixture is then put in a gauze bag and placed in the tub of water, and the bag is swished in the water. The oatmeal mass may be expressed from the bag and applied gently over the patient's body, but it is washed off before he leaves the bath. Bran is prepared in the same way as oatmeal, using 4 cups of bran. Commerical oatmeal preparations, such as Aveeno, are available and ready to add to the bath water. To prevent lumping, the commercial mixture should be dissolved under running water and then dispersed throughout the bath water.

The temperature of the water for therapeutic baths, should be 95° to 100° F (35° to 37.8° C), and the tub should be three-fourths full or sufficiently full to cover the involved area. The bath may be given for 20 to 30 minutes several times a day. Warm water should be added to maintain a constant temperature, but the temperature should not exceed 100° F (37.8° C). Very hot water is not good for the skin (due to the drying and vasodilation effects) and particularly not for persons with skin diseases.

Since some preparations may cause the tub to be slippery, extreme care should be taken to prevent the patient's slipping in the tub. When the patient is removed from the tub, the skin should be patted dry to avoid irritation or damage, and medication, if order, is applied. The patient should be prevented from chilling.

Wet Dressings

Wet dressings are used for many types of skin diseases. Dressings may be open or closed, and warm or cold, depending on the therapeutic effect desired. Evaporation of the solution in an open dressing initiates vasoconstriction, which provides a cooling effect and relieves the **pruritus** (itching) that accompanies some diseases. The moisture will soften crusts and stimulate drainage. Some solutions, such as Dakin's solution, will retard the growth of bacteria on the skin and prevent infection. Open wet dressings should not be covered with impermeable materials. Because of rapid evaporation, frequent changing or wetting is necessary. Pieces of soft old muslin, fluffs, or abdominal gauze are preferred to cotton, which has a tendency to pack down. Dressings must be clean but not necessarily sterile unless indicated by the overall condition of the patient (e.g., immunocompromised).

Wet dressings under occlusion (closed wet dressings) are used to help hydrate the epidermis to allow more effective absorption of topical medications. The dressings may be used on an isolated area or as a total body treatment (mummy wrap) for patients with extensive or generalized involvement. If the area being treated is limited, wet the dressing in the prescribed medicated solution and apply it directly to the area. The surrounding skin should be protected from moisture and the medicated solution by applying petroleum jelly or other suitable protective substances. Wet dressings should be thoroughly saturated but should not drip. Dry towels are wrapped around the closed wet dressing.

A warm, moist dressing is wrapped in thin plastic material and secured with a gauze bandage. A constant temperature heating pad may be used to keep the dressing warm; in this case, the dressing should *not* be wrapped in plastic because of the danger of burning the patient. Wet the dressing with an Asepto syringe; however, if drainage is present, it is preferable to remove the entire dressing and reapply. Solutions frequently used for wet dressings include physiologic saline solution, magnesium sulfate solution, 0.5% aluminum acetate (Burow's) solution, diluted sodium hypochlorite (Dakin's) solution, and 1:4000 potassium permanganate solution. Boric acid should *not* be used for widespread, raw areas because of its toxic effects, but it is safe and soothing for small irritated areas. This limited use is a major disadvantage. Even continuous wet dressings should be removed periodically to allow the skin to dry and to observe the status of the affected area. Cold dressings should be removed every 6 hours for at least 30 minutes. The same dressings can be soaked and reapplied if not contaminated with drainage. The bed and pillow should be protected when wet dressings are used. Due to the risk of maceration and decreased frequency of wound observation, continuous wet dressings should be used cautiously and on a limited basis.

When topical medicines such as medicated creams need to be applied, wet the dressing material with warm tap water and apply it over the medicine. Dry towels (for limited area) or bath blankets (for mummy wrap) are then placed on top of the dressing. This not only keeps the moisture in, but provides warmth for the patient as the dressings begin to cool. Generally these dressings are left in place for 20 to 30 minutes and a lubricating agent is applied over the affected areas to provide occlusion until the next wet dressing is applied. A mummy wrap is the dressing of choice when treating patients with generalized skin disorders that are erythematous, eczematous, or exfoliating (psoriasis, eczema, mycosis fungoides).

Soaks

Soaks may be ordered to loosen necrotic tissue, promote suppuration, or hydrate the skin to increase the absorption of topical medications. When an extremity is involved, a basin or tub large enough to submerge the part should be secured. If open lesions are present, the container should be sterilized. The solution, temperature, and frequency and duration of the treatment is prescribed by the physician. Burned patients may be placed in physiologic saline soaks for the purpose of debridement. The tub is thoroughly scrubbed and disinfected before the soak. Sometimes whirlpool baths are used for the same purpose.

Paste Boots

Boots are frequently used for patients with certain kinds of dermatitis and ulcers on the lower extremities. Several commercial preparations containing water, gelatin, glycerin, and zinc oxide are available. One preparation, Dome-paste bandage, is impregnated with the materials, which simplifies its application. The extremity is elevated about 30 minutes before applying the boot. An ointment may be applied to the skin lesions and covered with a thin gauze dressing. The paste bandage is then applied from the ankle to the knee, with greater pressure on the ankle and reduced pressure near the knee. This increases venous return and is particularly beneficial in patients with venous stasis ulcers. Two layers of stockinette are applied as an outer dressing. The boot is changed every 5 to 8 days.

Emotional Support

Patients with skin disorders may have a long road to travel before recovery is complete. Serious skin problems often become chronic, and the patient must learn to live with this disability. When lesions are on the face and exposed parts of the body, the fear of disfigurement is ever present. The patient believes what society thinks is extremely important. He often believes that others are afraid he has an infectious disease and that he is shunned and rejected for real or imagined reasons. As a result, he may isolate himself and withdraw into a world of his own. In children and adolescents the impact on personality may be serious. Although few patients with skin disorders may be admitted to the hospital, they are everywhere. Probably few persons escape some type of skin disorder during their lifetimes.

The nurse may be a source of encouragement to patients whether they are in or out of the hospital. First, nurses should know that skin disease is rarely fatal and that few diseases are contagious. Next, nurses should analyze their own feelings toward the patient. If they find the patient repulsive, they will be unable to give him support when he needs it. The nurse must care for the patient with warmth and understanding and convey a feeling of acceptance. Gentleness in removing and applying dressings, keeping wet dressings wet, and carrying out treatments on time will help make the patient feel secure. The nurse should avoid a "hurry-up" attitude and should be able to spend more time with the patient to reassure him of interest and acceptance and encourage verbalization of his feelings about the disease.

Decubitus (Pressure) Ulcers

Necrotic ulcers commonly are a cause of considerable discomfort for the patient and require costly nursing time and dressings. An ulcer is defined as an area of skin in which the entire epidermis has been destroyed. **Decubitus ulcers**, or pressure ulcers, are the result of localized trauma causing lack of blood supply to tissue. These ulcers can appear anywhere on the body but the greatest incidence is over bony prominences (Figure 24-3). Pressure over these areas of bony prominences cuts off the blood supply, deprives the cells of nutrition, and prevents elimination of waste from the cells. Anything that hinders this process interferes with cell function and eventually leads to cellular death (necrosis). This results in a pressure sore or decubitus ulcer. Tissue destruction can occur rapidly, and when the skin is broken, there is a rapid destruction of the underlying tissues. The ulcer frequently becomes infected with *Escherichia coli*.

There are many factors that put a patient in danger of developing decubitus ulcers. The most common are predisposing disease states (diabetes mellitus, cardiovascular disease, anemias, neuropathies, renal disease, and pulmonary disease), apparent age versus chronologic age, weight, medications, allergies, abnormal laboratory values (albumin, total protein, hemoglobin, hematocrit, total lymphocyte count), dietary restrictions, general status of skin integrity, mental status, decreased mobility/activity, decreased sensory perception, nutritional status, and aggravating factors (moisture, friction, shear).

The actual cause is sustained pressure. Both the amount and duration of pressure are important. Skin may experience high pressure for a short time without breaking down, whereas low to moderate pressure sustained for an extended period will often result in skin breakdown. The surgical patient may develop pressure sores after a prolonged period on the operating table.

Prevention of aggravating factors of moisture, friction, and shear become solely the nurses' responsibility. Sustained moisture (incontinence, diaphoresis), over-hydrates the skin and results in maceration. Maceration impairs the protective function of the skin which will allow for further breakdown and/or infection.

Friction occurs when a patient is pulled over a surface. This action can strip the epidermis causing an open erosion. Lifting patients to move them rather than pulling will greatly decrease this risk factor.

The fragile skin of elderly patients is particularly susceptible to friction tears that may lead to infection and further tissue breakdown. **Shearing force** is another factor related to development of pressure sores. Shearing occurs when two or more tissue layers slide on each other, causing subcutaneous blood vessels to become kinked or stretched. This obstructs blood flow to and from the area supplied by those vessels, resulting in necrosis. Every patient in a hospital bed experiences shearing force when the head of the bed is elevated 30 degrees or more. As the head is raised, the patient slides toward the foot of the bed. Those tissues attached to bony structures move with the patient, but because of the friction between the linen and the skin, the outer skin layers tend to stay in a fixed position. This exerts "shearing force" and diminishes blood flow to the sacral area, causing tissue necrosis.

Prevention

The cost of caring for one patient with a decubitus ulcer has been estimated to be $2000 to $10,000.

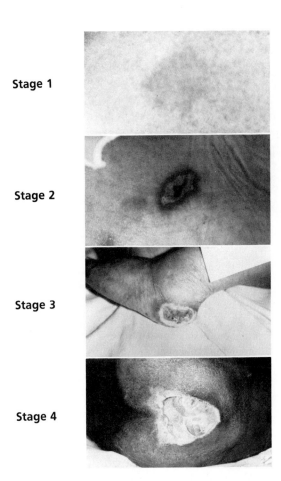

Stage 1   Region of pallor, mottling, followed by erythema.
Early lesion: erythema blanches, lesion may be painful.
Late lesion: erythema does not blanch, may be soft or indurated; edge is usually irregular.

Stage 2   Superficial epithelial damage, may range from a heel blister to as much as a 4 mm tissue loss over the buttocks. Surrounding area is red and scaley with irregular borders.

Stage 3   Destruction of tissue has involved the subcutaneous layers. Surface of ulcer will likely be smaller than internal diameters.

Stage 4   Tissue destruction extends through subcutaneous layers into muscle and bone. Ulcer edge appears to "roll over" into the defect and is a tough fibrinous ring.

Figure 24-3

Pressure ulcer stages. *(From Perry AG and Potter PA: Clinical nursing skills and techniques, ed 2, St Louis, 1989, The CV Mosby Co.)*

Despite preventive measures, they continue to occur, and curative measures have left much to be desired. Researchers have worked diligently to discover a safe way to prevent this painful and costly complication. Prevention basically depends on the amount of nursing care necessary to protect areas susceptible to breakdown. There is no substitute for conscientious nursing care. Nursing procedures include (1) a dry, unwrinkled surface, (2) freedom from irritating substances such as crumbs in the bed, (3) frequent change of position, and (4) frequent massage of threatened areas. A reddened or erythematous area is the first sign of pressure. In the light-skinned patient a red color change is seen; in the black-skinned patient the erythematous area may be detected by an increase in skin temperature or a darkening or lightening of that patient's normal skin color. The nurse should also inspect the black-skinned person for edema at the suspected pressure site. Edematous skin will feel slick and tight when touched with the back of the finger. Erythema should disappear within a short time after pressure is eliminated and will often respond to gentle massage. If edema occurs and redness remains for 15 minutes after pressure is relieved, pressure sore development should be suspected.[8]

Vigorous massage should be avoided because it may hasten ulceration. Massaging the skin around existing ulcers should be avoided because it may cause unnecessary trauma and spread infection. The use of soap should be limited, since the alkali in soap will produce cracking and chapping of dry skin.[48] The old method of using doughnuts and rubber rings is discouraged because these devices create rings of pressure that further restrict circulation. Preventing decubitus ulcers in long-term and elderly patients requires intensive nursing care and is not an easy task. Ulcers may occur quickly from only slight pressure; this is especially true with elderly persons.

The health and nutritional status of the patient will contribute to development of pressure sores. Protein, Vitamin C, and Vitamin B are essential for normal cell growth and healing.[8] A person who is ill requires additional protein to replace that lost through tissue breakdown. At the same time, protein and vitamin intake are frequently diminished because of anorexia or inability to eat, leading to deficiencies of these nutrients.

Adequate hydration is necessary to maintain skin turgor and prevent infection. Inadequate Vitamin C contributes to capillary fragility, making tissues more susceptible to trauma and interrupted blood flow.

The free circulation of air stimulates the peripheral circulation of blood, and the bedding may be elevated over a bed cradle to allow free flow of air. The judicious and proper use of various devices as adjuncts to nursing care is helpful in preventing decubitus ulcers but should never be used to replace good nursing care.

Devices that augment nursing care

Increased concern of this devastating problem has resulted in development of products for both the prevention and care of decubitus ulcers. To avoid confusion, the products should be looked at in a generic way with classifications that may simplify choices for intervention.

Equipment for pressure reduction/relief varies considerably both in effectiveness and cost. The nurse must be able to make a cost effective choice to deliver the highest quality of care to the patient.

Mattress overlays

The first level of intervention would be classified as mattress overlays. These may be convoluted foam or air products. Convoluted foam products must be at least 4 to 6 inches thick to provide pressure reduction (Figure 24-4). Anything less than 4 inches provides comfort but no significant

Figure 24-4

Convoluted foam mattress. *(From Perry GA and Potter PA: Clinical nursing skills and techniques, ed 2, St Louis, 1989, The CV Mosby Co.)*

pressure reduction. These foam products are indicated for the ambulatory patient or the patient with limited mobility who is at risk for skin breakdown or, has a stage I, II, or III (see Table 24-2) decubitus ulcer and is at risk for further breakdown but is not draining excessively. If the patient has documented stage I or II and presents with a need to reduce excessive moisture (incontinence, perspiration) an air mattress overlay is indicated (Figure 24-5). Good nursing care along with a turning schedule must be included when using these products.

Patients with stage III or IV, or multiple stage II's involving more than one surface can benefit from a low-air-loss mattress. If the patient has all of the above parameters and is in end-stage cancer, has pulmonary complications, sepsis or needs pain management, an oscillating low-air-loss bed would be more appropriate.

Specialty beds

A low-air-loss with pulsation, or air-fluidized (high-air-loss) bed is indicated for the patient with fresh skin graft, skin flap, or burn. These beds are contraindicated for patients with unstable spinal cord injuries. Low-air-loss speciality beds help reduce moisture and manage pain. Turning sched-

Table 24-2

Stages of Decubitus Ulcers

Stage	Color concept
Stage I	
Redness not resolving within 30 minutes of pressure relief; reversible with intervention	Redness, no wound
Stage II	
Loss of epidermis possibly to dermis; blistering may be present; free of necrotic tissue	Red wound, clean, healing wound
Stage III	
Loss of epidermis and dermis; involves subcutaneous tissue; shallow crater or covered with eschar; may have necrotic tissue, sinus tract formation, exudate, and/or infection	Yellow wound, some exudate; infection may be present
Stage IV	
Deep tissue destruction extending through subcutaneous tissue and fascia; may involve muscle and/or bone. Deep crater; may have necrotic tissue, sinus tract formation, exudate, and/or infection	Black wound, necrotic tissue

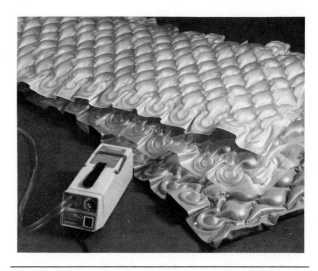

Figure 24-5

Inflated air mattress. *(Courtesy Gaymer Industries, Inc., Orchard Park, NY. From Perry GA and Potter PA: Clinical nursing skills and techniques, ed 2, St Louis, 1989, The CV Mosby Co.)*

ules are recommended. An oscillating low-air-loss speciality bed provides programmable turning of patients from side to side to promote drainage of lung secretions, enhance venous return from lower extremities, and facilitate urine flow. They are indicated for use for the hemodynamically unstable patient who cannot tolerate sudden position change or requires pain management.

Air-fluidized therapy provides pressure relief on a high-air-loss surface. This speciality bed is indicated for patients who require minimal movement to avoid skin damage by shearing forces (posterior grafts, or flaps). Turning schedules are recommended, though not mandatory. This bed is also contraindicated for patients with unstable spinal cord injury.

The last types of speciality beds are oscillating support and special function. Oscillating support beds provide continuous turning of the patient from side to side to prevent and treat the complications of immobility. This bed may be used with spinal cord injury. The special function bed includes a pressure-relieving surface that provides continuous pulsating air suspension. It has the same indications as the low-air-loss bed with the addition of pulsation. It is indicated for the patient who needs pain management even though there is no evidence to support the therapeutic effect of pulsation.

Treatment of decubitus ulcers

In addition to equipment developed to relieve or reduce pressure, many products treat decubitus ulcers. There are agents for cleansing and debridement, topical medications (antimicrobials, antiseptics, antibiotics), exudate absorbers (beads, pastes), and dressing materials.

Cleansing agents

Cleansing agents include normal saline, hydrogen peroxide, povidine-iodine, sodium hypochlorite (Dakin's solution), acetic acid, and prepared wound cleansers. The ideal method for a wound to heal would be to allow the body's own healing mechanisms to occur—supplementing only with soap and water or normal saline—promoting optimum healing. Effective wound healing can be inhibited by the indiscriminate use of antiseptics.[12] Normal saline is appropriate and safe for all wounds. Hydrogen peroxide is a mechanical cleansing agent that acts by effervescent action to promote the removal of wound debris and bacteria. This mechanical action has been shown to destroy fibroblasts; therefore it should be used judiciously. Povidine-iodine is effective against bacteria, viruses, and fungi. However, if improperly diluted, it will destroy macrophages and fibroblasts. Sodium hypochlorite (Dakin's solution) controls odor and is appropriate for *Staphylococcal* and *Streptococcal* infections. It helps liquify necrotic tissue but also destroys fibroblasts if improperly diluted. Acetic acid is used in wounds infected with *Pseudomonas*, but destroys fibroblasts even when diluted.[12]

There are several prepared wound cleansers available on the market. Most contain a wetting agent and a blend of moisturizers that help soften eschar for debridement and removal of debris. Use each product according to the recommendations of the manufacturer.

Debridement

Debridement can be accomplished surgically, chemically, or mechanically. Surgical debridement is aggressive, fast, and selective. It may be performed at the bedside or in the operating room. Chemical debridement is accomplished with commercially available enzymatic debriding agents (Elase, Santyl, Travase). Enzymatic debridement is aggressive, less selective, and slower than surgical debridement. The least aggressive form of debridement is mechanical. This can be accomplished with gauze, a soft brush, or a sponge. It is nonselective, painful, and may be destructive to surrounding tissue. Wet-to-dry dressings are an excellent way to mechanically debride a wound but are often removed inappropriately and may cause bleeding and pain.[53]

Stage II, III and IV ulcers with a large amount of necrotic tissue may be debrided by surgical or chemical methods. Stage III and IV ulcers with moderate amounts of necrotic tissue and wound exudate may be debrided effectively with mechanical methods.

Topical medications

Antimicrobials, antiseptics, and antibiotics can be in the form of cream, ointment, solution, or spray. Topical agents should be chosen for their antibacterial effectiveness and for their ability to enhance, not inhibit, healing. For instance, an occlusive ointment may cause maceration or encourage the growth of resistant organisms. Some topical agents interfere with neutrophils, fibroblasts, and endothelial cells in the healing process.

Exudate absorbers

Exudate absorbers (absorption dressings) include, but are not limited to, moist gauze, copolymer starches, and dextranomers. They act by absorbing excess exudate, obliterating dead space, and keeping the wound surface moist. Dead space impairs the wound healing process and predisposes to abscess formation. When packing the wound with any of these dressings do not pack too tightly. This will impair circulation and damage healthy tissue.[12] A new exudate absorber on the market is the calcium alginate dressing. Calcium alginates are derived from brown seaweed. They are easily applied and absorb a large amount of wound exudate.[15]

Dressing materials

Dressing materials are numerous and varied. For simplification they will be classified as transparent film dressings, hydrocolloids, foam dressings, hydrogels, and protective barriers. Transparent film dressings are semipermeable adhesive dressings that allow exchange of oxygen and moisture vapor but do not allow the passage of fluid or bacteria. They are indicated for use in superficial (stage I or II) dermal ulcers, skin grafts, donor sites, and minor abrasions. Hydrocolloids are adhesive dressings that absorb small to moderate amounts of exudate while interacting with the wound to form a liquid gelatinous substance that maintains a moist healing environment. They may be used on superficial, minimally exudating pressure ulcers and skin tears. Hydrocolloids are occlusive and not permeable to gases. Therefore, they are contraindicated for infected wounds, deep wounds with tunnel tracts, or undermining.

Foam dressings are nonadherent hydrophilic polyurethane that absorbs heavy amounts of exudate while maintaining a moist healing environment. This type of dressing is indicated in highly exudative stage III and IV pressure ulcers and is often used for leg ulcers. Hydrogels are water polymer gels that act to provide a moist wound healing environment while absorbing excess exudate. Hydrogels also clean and debride the wound. This type of dressing is appropriate for all stages of wound healing but often indicated in stage III and IV pressure sores and leg ulcers. Hydrogels may be used in necrotic wounds.

Protective barriers (skin sealants) provide a protective coating, usually in alcohol solution, that is applied to the skin. This coating forms a second skin and protects the injured area while it heals. This is particularly successful for stage I wounds or on any open area where tape or adhesive products may be applied.

Nursing intervention

A thorough assessment of the patient must be undertaken before any interventions are begun. Depending on the specific needs and condition of the patient, an individualized plan can be formulated. Several objective factors must be considered when assessing the patient for risk. These include general state of skin, general state of health, mental status, degree of mobility and activity, level of sensory perception, nutritional status, and aggravating factors such as moisture, friction, and shear. Contributing factors must also be taken into consideration when developing interventions. These include predisposing disease states (diabetes mellitus, cardiovascular disease, anemias, neuropathies, renal disease, pulmonary disease), apparent age versus chronologic age, weight, medications, allergies, serial laboratory values (albumin, total protein, hemoglobin, hematocrit, total lymphocyte count), and dietary restrictions.

If a patient is found to be at risk and has no skin breakdown, interventions should be aimed at prevention. Interventions should include placing the patient on a pressure reducing/relieving device (mattress overlay), inspecting the skin regularly for redness or evidence of breakdown (at least every 8 hours), institute measures to reduce shearing forces and friction (keep head of bed flat or below a 30-degree angle), use a draw sheet to turn, apply powder on surfaces contacting the skin, avoid direct contact with plastic or vinyl surfaces (such as chux), and encourage and assist ambulation. If the patient is incontinent or diaphoretic, measures must be implemented to prevent breakdown secondary to moisture. Breathable absorptive pads, fecal incontinence collectors, and/or external urinary catheters may be used. Incontinence care kits are invaluable for cleaning and protecting the skin. Adult diapers are available, but should be used judiciously and assessed at least every 2 hours for changing. Poor nutrition and hydration must be addressed if present. Intake and output records should be initiated, fluid intake should be encouraged if not contraindicated, and a dietary consult should be requested for nutritional assessment.

When a decubitus ulcer is already present, the above interventions and an individualized plan for treatment of the ulcer must be instituted to enhance healing. Before any plan of care can be initiated, the ulcer must be staged (Table 24-2). In addition to staging, a new classification of wounds has been introduced. It is the red-yellow-black system of wound classification.[4] It allows the nurse or physician to look at a wound and quickly assess the interventions needed. Red wounds may be acute or chronic. Acute red wounds may be caused by traumatic or surgical injury with frank bleeding or evidence of recent hemostasis. Chronic red wounds have clean pink to bright or dark red granulation tissue (seen after necrotic tissue is removed). The goal with a red wound is protection. This is accomplished with an atraumatic, gentle cleansing or irrigation with appropriate cleanser, and then covering the wound with appropriate dressing material (gauze, hydrogel, hydrocolloidal) and/or appropriate topical medication.

Yellow wounds have soft necrotic tissue, "slough," or thick tenacious exudate ranging in color from creamy ivory to yellow-green. The goal with a yellow wound is cleansing. This may be accomplished by aggressive wound cleansing with soap and water followed by a thorough rinsing. Mechanical debridement, occlusive dressings (transparent film, hydrocolloidal, hydrogel), and topical medication is indicated.

The black wound is a wound covered by thick necrotic tissue (**eschar**). The primary goal with this wound is debridement, which may be accomplished surgically or chemically. There are some occlusive dressings that may be employed to promote softening of eschar via autolysis. These include hydrogel sheets, hydrophilic beads, powder, or paste, or continuous moist saline gauze dressings (change every 8 hours). A black wound cannot be staged until the eschar is removed.[4]

Wounds should be continuously assessed during treatment in order to adjust treatment as wound progresses. For example a yellow wound will become a red wound when exudate is no longer present and the wound exhibits a red, granulating base. The treatment should be adjusted to that of a red wound. A wound may possess the characteristics of two different classifications. In this case interventions are based on the worst classification (see page 718).

NURSING CARE GUIDELINES
Decubitus Ulcer

Nursing diagnoses
- Impaired skin integrity related to ulcerated area over coccyx
- High risk for injury, infection, related to impaired skin integrity

Nursing interventions
- Assess nutritional status
- Turn every 2 hours
- Apply 4- to 6-inch foam or air mattress overlay to standard bed or suggest specialty bed suited to patient's condition.
- Keep skin dry
- Use draw sheet to lift and turn patient
- Maintain head of bed below 30-degree angle
- Dressings, cleansing, and medication as ordered by the physician

Expected outcomes
- Ulcer decreased in size
- Ulcer free of infection
- Pink healthy tissue apparent/continues to increase

THE PATIENT WITH DISEASES AND DISORDERS OF THE SKIN

Although most diseases and disorders of the skin are treated by the dermatologist as medical or dermatologic conditions, some require surgical treatment. Both the medical and surgical aspects in relation to the disease are considered in this chapter.

Bacterial Diseases
Folliculitis, furuncles, carbuncles, and felons
Folliculitis is the infection of a hair follicle. It is usually caused by staphylococci and most commonly occurs on the scalp, the extremities, or the bearded areas of the face. Chronic folliculitis of the beard is called *sycosis barbae*.

A *furuncle* (boil) is an acute infection of one hair follicle or sebaceous gland, usually caused by the staphylococcus bacterium. A *carbuncle* is similar to a boil, except that the infection infiltrates into the surrounding tissue and results in several boils. Carbuncles are also caused by the staphy-

lococcus bacterium. A *felon* is an infection of the end of a finger. It may result from a puncture wound such as a pinprick, or it may occur without a known cause. The streptococcus bacterium is a common cause of felons.

Assessment. The lesion of folliculitis consists of a pustule surrounded by an area of erythema and appears as a raised dome around the follicle. The pustule weeps, forming a crust, and the hair seems to be growing from the center of the crust. Pain will occur if the infection spreads to the dermis surrounding the follicle. A furuncle begins as a small, red, edematous, painful area on the skin of the face, neck, axilla, forearm, buttocks, groin, or legs. It may appear as only a tiny pimple and abate spontaneously, or it may continue to increase in size and in a few days give evidence of pus formation. Carbuncles are most commonly found on the back of the neck and upper back. As the infection gradually comes to the surface from the deeper tissue, there will be several openings discharging pus. The site of a felon on a finger is red and edematous, and there is severe, throbbing pain. Both carbuncles and furuncles occur most frequently in poorly nourished and debilitated individuals and may be a sign of uncontrolled diabetes mellitus.

Intervention. Early treatment of these localized infections will prevent complications and systemic spread. If hair follicles are permanently damaged, hair will not grow from them. The skin of the area is cleansed with an antibacterial soap to remove excess moisture, oil, and grease. The skin surrounding the lesion should be cleansed carefully to prevent spread of the infection. Warm, moist compresses are used to promote suppuration. If the lesion does not rupture and drain spontaneously, surgical incision and drainage will be necessary. The patient will also be given antibiotic therapy. In the larger lesions, such as the carbuncle, incision may be necessary to remove cellular debris after suppuration begins.

Most patients with furuncles and carbuncles are cared for in the physician's office. If the patient is hospitalized, wound isolation procedures should be initiated until drainage subsides. The patient must be taught to prevent contamination of others in the hospital and at home by careful handwashing after contact with any drainage and by careful disposal of dressings or other materials that may be contaminated. Clothing and linens used by the patient should not be shared by other household members. Prevention requires the maintenance of adequate nutrition and hygiene measures.

Impetigo contagiosa

Impetigo is a superficial contagious skin disease caused by *staphylococcus* and *streptococcus* bacteria. The disease occurs primarily on the face and hands, but may be transmitted to other exposed parts of the body (Figure 24-6). It may occur at any age but is most commonly seen in children. The disease is spread by direct and indirect contact. It is common for an insect bite to become infected by the *staphylococcus* or *streptococcus* organism which results in impetigo. Poor health and nutrition, a warm, humid environment, and antecedent pruritic skin eruptions may also predispose a patient to impetigo.[19]

Assessment. The disease begins as a vesicopustule on the skin, which ruptures, leaving a red, oozing erosion. The erosion becomes covered by a characteristic yellow (honey-colored) crust. The infection may spread from an existing lesion to other areas on the body so that several lesions may be present at the same time.

Intervention. The treatment consists of removing the crust by soaking with warm physiologic saline solution or hydrogen peroxide. After removal of the crust, any of several topical ointments may be applied. Polymyxin (Aerosporin), bacitracin (Baciguent) or mupirocin 2% (Bactroban) are the most commonly used agents. Sometimes an antibiotic is administered orally. Individuals with the disease should be provided with individual towels and washcloths.

Most state laws do not require isolation or exclusion from school. However, the local school system may not permit school attendance of children with impetigo. More adequate treatment can be given if the child is kept at home for a few days.

Fungal Infections
Tinea (ringworm)

Ringworm can affect any part of the body. Each form of the disease is given a name beginning with the word tinea and ending with a word that describes the part of the body being affected. Tinea capitis is ringworm of the scalp, tinea barbae affects the beard and mustache, tinea corporis is ringworm of the body, tinea cruris is ringworm of the groin, tinea manuum is ringworm of the hand, and tinea pedis is ringworm of the foot, also called athlete's foot.

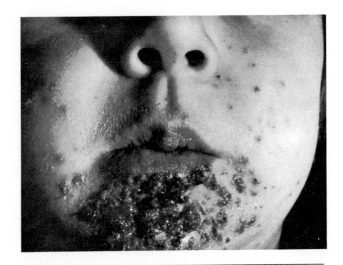

Figure 24-6

Impetigo contagiosa. *(From Phipps WJ et al: Medical-surgical nursing: concepts and clinical practice, ed 4, St Louis, 1991, The CV Mosby Co.)*

Tinea capitis. Tinea capitis, better known as ringworm of the scalp, occurs primarily in preadolescent children. The lesion is easily recognized and appears as a scaly bald spot with hairs breaking off at the surface (Figure 24-7). Occasionally, the patient will develop an inflammatory reaction to the fungus and will develop boggy areas with pus called *kerion*. Treatment of ringworm is usually successful with oral griseofulvin. If kerion are present, they should be treated topically with compresses and hydrogen peroxide along with oral steroids. Patients receiving cortisone should not be given griseofulvin at the same time. When the infection is severe, there may be patches of baldness on the scalp. This loss of hair is usually temporary, and the hair will return when the infection subsides. This infection is contagious; therefore all members of the family should be examined. The patient's personal toilet articles such as comb and brush should not be used by other members of the family. The individual is usually treated in the physician's office or in a clinic; however, the patient may have been admitted to the hospital for another condition. If tinea capitis is discovered in a hospital patient, it should be called to the physician's attention, and the nurse should take protective precautions.

Tinea corporis. Tinea corporis is a form of ringworm that occurs on the body. It is characterized by congested patches that are slightly elevated and may present a scaly appearance (Figure 24-7). The lesion increases in size gradually,

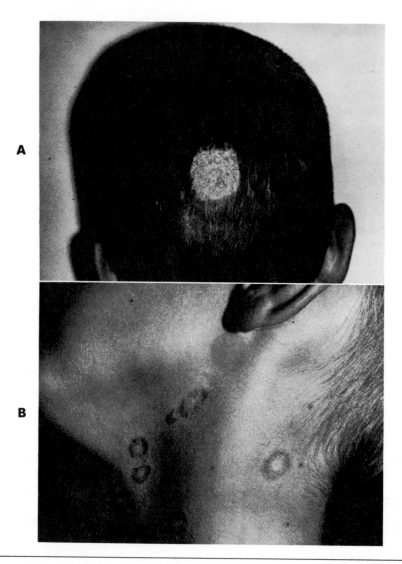

Figure 24-7

A, Tinea capitis. **B,** Tinea corporis. *(From Phipps WJ et al: Medical-surgical nursing: concepts and clinical practice, ed 4, St Louis, 1991, The CV Mosby Co.)*

with the center clearing. Treatment with a topical fungicide is satisfactory if only a few lesions are present. For more extensive cases, griseofulvin is used.

Tinea barbae. Tinea barbae occurs in the beard and is characterized by a soft nodular type of lesion with edema of the face. The nodules may break down and become suppurative. The hairs of the beard become loose and slip out, leaving bald areas. Several preparations have been used in the treatment of the condition, including ammoniated mercury ointment, griseofulvin, and copper undecylenate.

Tinea cruris. Tinea cruris is commonly called jock itch. It is more common during hot weather and is aggravated by friction caused by tight-fitting clothing. The lesion usually affects both sides of the groin equally and may extend to cover the entire groin, giving a butterfly appearance. Itching is prevalent, and the folds of the skin in the groin frequently become macerated. Treatment involves keeping the area cool and dry, wearing loose, absorptive clothing, and applying an antifungal preparation as prescribed.

Tinea pedis. Tinea pedis, or athlete's foot, is a common disorder affecting the feet, although it may be spread to other parts of the body, particularly the hands, where it is called tinea manuum. The causative fungal organism is often *Epidermophyton flocosum*, but the tinea may be caused by other organisms. It is generally believed that the infection is contracted in showers, around swimming pools, and in similar moist places; however, absolute proof of this method of transmission is lacking. The fungus is widespread in the environment, and there is evidence that some individuals are more sensitive than other persons. If these hypersensitive persons come in contact with the fungus, they may contract the disease.

Assessment. The infection usually begins between the fourth and fifth toe and first appears as small fissures with peeling at the borders. The infection spreads to the other toes, where the epidermis may become macerated. When the dead skin is removed, the new epidermis soon becomes infected. During the acute stage, vesicles may form containing serous fluid, later becoming purulent and eventually drying. If untreated, the infection may become chronic, spreading to the sole, heel, and arch and extending to the top of the foot. In both the acute and chronic stages there is usually severe itching. Allergic reaction to shoes will frequently cause lesions that mimic athlete's foot; these can be differentiated when the lesions are found covering the dorsal and ventral surfaces of the foot, whereas the skin between the toes remains clear.

Intervention. Several agents may be used in the treatment of tinea pedis, including zinc undecylenate (Desenex) and tolnaftate. Oral griseofulvin may be given for weeks or months if the condition is severe. Emphasis should be placed on keeping the feet dry and careful drying, especially between the toes; the use of a medicated foot powder with clean cotton socks is recommended. When caused by yeast organisms, amphotericin B is used. The tetracyclines are prescribed when the diphtheroid bacterium is the cause.

Dermatitis

Dermatitis is an inflammatory condition of the skin resulting from a wide variety of causes and characterized by varying types of skin manifestations. In most cases it results in redness, itching, and various kinds of skin lesions.

Erythema intertrigo (chafing)

Chafing occurs when two skin surfaces rub together. It results in redness and may cause maceration of the skin. Frequent sites are the areas between the thighs, in the axillae, and under the breasts. In infants chafing may occur in the folds of the skin, particularly about the neck. Obese persons are more likely to be affected. Treatment includes cleansing with mild soap and water, patting the area dry, and powdering with cornstarch. Good personal hygiene and avoidance of strong or irritating soaps are important. In extreme cases the application of hydrocortisone cream (Hytone) may be required. Before applying a hydrocortisone cream the area should have a KOH prep done to rule out fungal infection.

Miliaria (prickly heat)

Miliaria is a condition in which the flow of sweat from the eccrine sweat glands, found on all skin surfaces, is hindered. The cause of miliaria includes both environmental and physiologic factors. Persons exposed to extremes of temperature and humidity for long periods, those overprotected by clothing, those with high body temperature, and obese persons are most likely to suffer from attacks of prickly heat. Infants swathed in excessive clothing and blankets are especially susceptible. The condition occurs more frequently during hot weather.

Assessment. Tiny red papules appear on the skin, usually on the trunk, but may cover the entire body. The lesions are accompanied by burning, prickling, and itching. An infant with prickly heat will be restless and fretful.

Intervention. Treatment consists of cooling or soothing baths and thorough drying by patting. Emollient baths such as the starch bath may provide relief for persons with severe cases. The application of calamine lotion is generally effective, and cornstarch or other nonirritating powders may be used. The condition is usually of short duration and can be prevented by avoiding extremes of heat and humidity and by wearing absorbent and porous clothing.

Dermatitis venenata (plant poisoning)

Allergic dermatitis occurring as the result of contact with certain plants is frequently referred to as ivy poisoning, sumac poisoning, or poisoning by other specific kinds of plants. Individual susceptibility is an important factor in this type of dermatitis. Although many different plants and shrubs may cause the condition, some of the more common ones are poison ivy, poison sumac, poison oak, and poison elder.

Assessment. Symptoms will vary from a mild redness to severe systemic reactions and gangrene. The primary lesions are most frequently found on the parts of the body contacted by the irritant, usually the hands, arms, face, and legs. The skin may become erythematous, which may be followed by the formulation of papules, vesicles, and pustules in a characteristic linear distribution. Facial edema can be seen in patients exposed to airborne allergens (i.e., when the plant is burned). The tissue may be edematous, and severe itching and burning may occur.

Intervention. When the individual is aware of contact with a poisonous plant, the exposed parts should be washed immediately with strong soap and water. Washing will not be effective unless it is done soon after contact. After lesions have appeared, soap and water should not be used. Cool, open, wet dressings, using 1:20 solution of aluminum acetate (Burow's solution) or physiologic saline solution, may be applied three times a day for 30 minutes to cool and relieve pruritus. The dressings should not be wrapped in plastic. After the administration of the wet dressings, corticosteroid ointment or cream may be applied. The steroid ointments are available under trade names such as Kenalog and Aristocort. Oral antihistamines such as chlorpheniramine maleate (Chlor-Trimeton) may also be ordered to relieve pruritus.

Exfoliative dermatitis

Exfoliative dermatitis, also known as exfoliative erythroderma, is a serious and sometimes fatal condition. It may be secondary to several conditions such as preexisting skin disease (psoriasis, eczema), drug hypersensitivity (particularly antibiotics, anticonvulsants, and antiinflammatory agents), or underlying malignancies (leukemias, lymphomas, visceral malignancy). Patients who are receiving gold salts should be carefully observed, since a form of exfoliative dermatitis may develop. Mercury can also cause the condition.

One commonly used source of mercury is merbromin (Mercurochrome). When merbromin is applied to the skin, it is absorbed systemically. It has been found to be a weak antibacterial agent and carries great risk of causing harm to the patient. One study reported the death of an infant resulting from mercury poisoning after application of merbromin to an omphalocele (herniation of organs into the umbilical cord at birth). Use of merbromin should be questioned, especially when it involves a relatively large open area capable of absorbing the mercury in large amounts.

This severe form of dermatitis is seen less often today because the use of chemotherapeutic agents has replaced the heavy metals formerly used to treat some diseases.

Assessment. The disease begins as rapidly progressing generalized erythroderma, followed by fine scales or thick sheets of desquamation. Pruritus may be severe; widespread lymphadenopathy (enlarged lymph nodes), hepatosplenomegaly (enlarged liver and spleen), and low grade fever are common. Generalized vasodilation and hypothermia may cause severe chills. Patients are at risk for cardiac failure due to increased amounts of blood being shunted to the skin surface. There is a high degree of iron loss with the desquamation, and electrolyte imbalance results from the impaired integument. Hospitalization is required to deliver intensive topical treatment and to monitor for complications.[19]

Interventions. Pruritus may be relieved with colloidal baths followed by topical steroids under occlusion (mummy wraps). High doses of antihistamines are administered and in very severe cases systemic steroids may be used. Because of the patient's inability to control body temperature, the environment needs to be carefully controlled to ensure warmth. Special mouth, eye, and lip care and prevention of pressure necrosis are important nursing functions. The patient should be observed for any awkward reaction to topical or systemic medicines. The nurse must convey acceptance and understanding and allow the patient to express fears and concerns.

Dermatitis medicamentosa (drug dermatitis)

The term *dermatitis medicamentosa* is applied to skin eruptions caused by drugs, regardless of the method of administration. Almost any drug may cause a reaction in certain individuals, and with the development of many new drugs and their increased use, the incidence of such reactions will increase.

Assessment. The characteristics of drug reactions range from mild erythema to severe conditions that may be fatal. Every type of skin lesion reviewed in this chapter may be seen in various reactions to drugs. It is more important than ever that the nurse be aware of the possibility and observe patients for evidence of any skin lesion. It is also important to question patients concerning any undersirable side effects of a drug that they have experienced previously; the same drug given to the same patient again will produce a similar or more severe reaction.

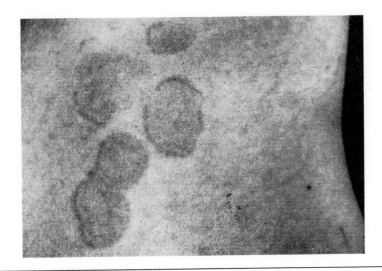

Figure 24-8
Urticaria. *(From Billings DM and Stokes LG: Medical-surgical nursing: common health problems of adults and children across the life span, ed 2, St Louis, 1987, The CV Mosby Co.)*

Intervention. Immediate detection of a drug reaction is essential in preventing severe consequences. When the patient is hospitalized, a thorough drug history should be taken, including over-the-counter medications. All drugs that the patient is currently taking should be held and the physician consulted immediately.

Dermatitis caused by drugs will usually subside upon withdrawal of the medication. However, resolution may take up to 2 weeks. Treatment should be instituted to relieve the distressing symptoms from the skin lesions. Intervention is based on the patient's symptoms and may include antihistaminic drugs. In some cases corticosteroid agents in the form of lotions may be applied topically. In severe cases the corticosteroid agents may be given orally for their systemic effect.

Urticaria

Urticaria is the presence of hives or wheals (Figure 24-8). The condition may be associated with a number of systemic diseases such as hepatitis, Hodgkin's disease, lupus erythematosus, leukemia, rheumatic fever, dental and sinus infections, and infestations. It may be seen as a cholinergic response to heat, cold, or ultraviolet light, or a reaction to certain foods. Genetic predisposition and psychogenic factors have also been seen as causative agents. Often the cause is not readily apparent, which is disturbing to patients and health care workers alike. Urticaria may be acute, lasting less than 12 hours, or chronic, lasting more

than 6 weeks. Respiratory distress, hoarseness, abdominal pain, vomiting, diarrhea, arthralgia, headaches, and central nervous system dysfunction may accompany select cases of urticaria. Angioedema (swelling of the face) is the most severe complication seen with urticaria. This is a medical emergency and the patient should seek treatment immediately. When urticaria appears suddenly, check whether the patient is taking any new drugs. If so, they should be stopped immediately and the physician notified.[19]

Contact dermatitis

Contact dermatitis is usually found on the face, neck, and backs of the hands, the forearms, the male genitalia, and the lower legs. The borders of the reaction are frequently well defined, which aids in determining the cause. The lesions appear abruptly and always itch. The lesions may be red, oozing, or scaly. A careful history is essential in determining the cause of contact dermatitis.

Cool compresses applied for 1 hour, three times daily, will relieve itching. Topical steroids will relieve skin inflammation, and in serious cases systemic steroids such as prednisone may be prescribed. Systemic antihistamines and topical antihistamines are not used because the condition is not related to histamine release.

Erythema multiforme

Erythema multiforme is a reactive skin disorder in which the individual lesions have a characteristic target (iris or bull's-eye) configuration (Figure

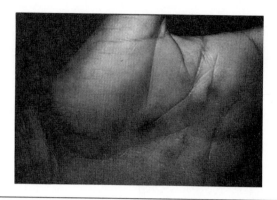

Figure 24-9

Erythema multiforme. *(From Thompson JM et al: Mosby's manual of clinical nursing, ed 2, St Louis, 1989, The CV Mosby Co.)*

24-9). The lesions can be caused by drugs, or by viruses such as herpes simplex and vaccinia. They can also be caused by systemic infections such as pneumonia, meningitis, or measles; in some cases the cause cannot be identified. The lesions may last long enough to cause erosion of the lips, eyelids, and genitalia. Large areas of skin may eventually slough off, and the disease can be fatal. Stevens-Johnson syndrome, the most serious form of erythema multiforme, has a mortality rate of 15% to 20%.

Assessment. The lesions are called iris or bull's-eye lesions because they are depressed in the center and have raised, reddened borders. They are found on the skin and the mucous membranes. Fever, chest pain, and joint pain may precede the eruption.

Intervention. The underlying cause must be discovered and eliminated, if possible. If the patient is taking any drugs, all except those essential to life should be discontinued. Large dosages of steroids are given, and the lesions will disappear within 2 weeks if a drug is responsible. Baths, soaks, and dressings will be used to reduce the discomfort of the lesions. Adequate fluids and nutrition will promote healing. Special mouth care will be needed if lesions appear in the mouth.

Psoriasis

Psoriasis is a genetically determined chronic disease of epidermal proliferation. The exact incidence of the disorder is probably unknown, and estimates vary widely. It has been estimated that approximately 2% to 3% of the U.S. population has had psoriasis at some time. The disease usually begins between the ages of 10 and 35 years but may be seen at any age. The exact cause is unknown, but the disease is not contagious.

Pathophysiology. Epidermal metabolism is accelerated resulting in the migration of immature cells to the skin surface. The immature cells form a thick adherent silvery scale on well-demarcated, erythematous elevated plaques. Psoriasis may appear in areas of trauma (Koebner's phenomenon) such as surgical incision, sunburn, cuts, abrasions and other chemical or mechanical injury. In about 5% to 10% of the cases, psoriatic arthritis may develop and may be acute or chronic. The arthritic condition resembles rheumatoid arthritis; however, opinions vary as to whether it is a form of rheumatoid arthritis or a separate disease. The arthritis may accompany the skin disease, or the skin eruption may exist for several years before the arthritis makes its appearance.

There is no cure for psoriasis, but the disease may undergo extensive clearing or even long remissions. The disease tends to improve in the summer months when the lesions are exposed to ultraviolet rays of the sun. Emotional stress, systemic infections, obesity, excessive alcohol ingestion, injury to the skin, and pregnancy exacerbate the disorder.

Assessment. The disease is characterized by well-demarcated, erythematous, scaly lesions presenting bilaterally and symmetrically with a predisposition for elbows, knees, scalp, genitalia, and gluteal cleft but may be generalized (Figure 24-10). There may be a single lesion or multiple lesions. Small lesions may coalesce to form large irregular patches called *plaques*. The adherent scales may be removed with resultant pinpoint bleeding which is called the Auspitz sign of psoriasis. Research reports indicate that 92% of patients with psoriasis complain of itching, but there appears to be no relationship between the degree of itching and the severity of the disease.

There are four basic types of psoriasis: plaque, guttate, psoriatic erythroderma, and pustular. The plaque type is the most common and appears as well-defined areas, often with raised borders, and ranging in size from several millimeters to extensive areas. Guttate (droplike) psoriasis often occurs following an infection, usually streptococcal, and is commonly seen in school-aged children; thus it is often initially misdiagnosed as one of the childhood diseases. The more severe forms include psoriatic erythroderma, in which plaque or guttate psoriasis may become confluent and form large areas of erythematous psoriatic patches

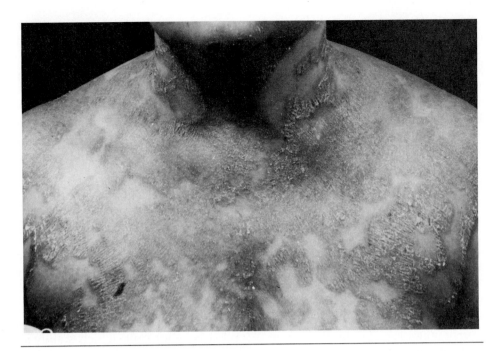

Figure 24-10

Generalized psoriasis. *(From Phipps WJ et al: Medical-surgical nursing: concepts and clinical practice, ed 4, St Louis, 1991, The CV Mosby Co.)*

that may involve the entire body surface. This form of psoriasis is often recalcitrant to treatment and may last for long periods. The more common forms of psoriasis may evolve into pustular psoriasis when the plaques become covered with small pustules, usually involving the palms and soles.

Intervention. There are a number of different methods of treatment. Several topical drugs have been used and frequently bring about a remission. These drugs include 1% to 10% crude coal tar in petroleum jelly (Vaseline), coal tar and sulfur ointment, coal tar shampoo, 0.25% anthralin (Dithranol), and cortisone. In many cases ultraviolet light B (shortwave spectrum of light) accompanies the topical tar treatment (Goeckerman therapy). Systemic therapy with antimetabolites, such as methotrexate, used in the treatment of leukemia, may be used in severe cases of psoriasis. Since this drug is potentially toxic to the liver, an initial liver biopsy is recommended. This is followed by regular blood work to evaluate liver and renal function, white blood cell count, hemoglobin, and hematocrit. One of the newest forms of treatment involves the systemic oral administration of methoxsalen (Psoralen) followed by long-wave ultraviolet light treatments. This treatment is called PUVA (Psoralen and ultraviolet light administra-

tion) and has been very effective. The patient is given Psoralen, then exposed to ultraviolet light A (long-wave spectrum of light) 2 hours after ingestion of the drug. Side effects include itching, sunburn, nausea, headache, and photosensitivity (especially in the retina). Patients should be advised to avoid exposure to the sun while taking Psoralen.

Continued research has produced a new oral medication that is a synthetic form of vitamin A or an aromatic retinoid. It is effective in the treatment of psoriasis, but side effects limit its usage. It is recommended for adults and is used with extreme caution in women of child-bearing age. Retinoids and vitamin A are not the same compounds, and people should be cautioned not to take large doses of vitamin A in the hope of duplicating this synthetic drug.

Systemic steroids are not used because of the dangerous side effects of long-term therapy. Short-term use will produce remission but is frequently followed by a flare-up in which the disease is worse than it was before treatment. The arthritic condition is treated in the same manner as rheumatoid arthritis. Psoriatic arthritis tends to remit when psoriasis remits and becomes worse when psoriasis exacerbates.

Although most psoriasis patients can be

treated on an outpatient basis, occasionally the severity or extent of involvement warrants confinement for supervised care. Usually this involves the use of Goeckerman's method, which employs the combined therapy of crude oil tar medications and ultraviolet light. In various areas of the United States this intense form of treatment is now available in a psoriasis day-care program that allows the patient to return home at night.

Treatment for each patient must be individualized, and the patient should know that treatment is only palliative. Unless the patient knows, understands, and accepts the disease, he or she may be led to quacks who continuously advertise cures. The patient needs a great deal of emotional support because the psychologic effects of the disease may be severe. The nurse must convey with words and actions the feeling of acceptance of both the patient and the disease. The patient must know that the nurse is not repelled by his or her appearance, and touching can do a great deal for self-image. The patient must be taught to care for the disease and to realize the importance of continuing treatment after discharge.

Eczema

Eczema is a term applied to a group of diseases characterized by many types of lesions. The disease may be related to allergic conditions (Chapter 26), hereditary and emotional factors, drugs, and various other contactants, which can be occupational, recreational, or everyday household exposures. Eczema frequently occurs among industrial employees whose work brings them into contact with dyes, tars, and other toxic agents. Various kinds of cosmetic agents and metallic fibers in clothing may also irritate eczematous conditions, or cause contact eczema (contact dermatitis).

Assessment. Whatever the cause, there is always itching, and scratching may cause secondary infection. Lesions may be vesicular in type and tend to rupture, leaving a moist surface (weeping), and they may form crusts. In some types of eczema the skin becomes dry and scaly and has a leathery appearance.

Interventions. If possible, the cause of the disorder should be found and removed. Treatment is based primarily on relief of itching, and every effort should be made to keep the patient as comfortable as possible. It is also necessary to combat secondary infections. There are many preparations used for these purposes, and every

patient must be treated on an individual basis, based on the cause and characteristics of the condition. In most cases of eczema the use of soap is contraindicated because of its drying effect on the skin. The topical application of corticosteroid creams and ointments has replaced most other forms of treatment. Because of the extreme discomfort and anxiety suffered by many patients with eczema, tranquilizing drugs are frequently given.

The nurse should be familiar with the methods of applying various topical preparations and should observe each patient carefully for undesirable effects, which should be reported promptly to the physician. The patient also needs understanding and reassurance from the nurses.

Acne vulgaris

Acne vulgaris is an inflammatory disease of the pilosebaceous unit, which mainly affects the face, chest, back, and shoulders. Adolescents are most widely affected by the disease, and severe cases may require medical intervention. The disease usually declines in the early twenties, but it can continue into the forties and fifties. It is not uncommon for the first presentation to occur in the patient's forties, fifties, or even sixties.[13] Both men and women may be affected, with the higher incidence occurring in males.

The acne begins with the appearance of **comedones** (blackheads) that plug the ducts of the sebaceous glands and are the result of increased secretion of sebum from the glands. The inflammatory process within the duct soon leads to the formation of papules and pustules on the skin.

Assessment. The papules, pustules, and comedones that characterize acne are found on the face and back. In addition to assessing the location and severity of the lesions, the nurse must assess the patient's reaction to the disorder and understanding of the causes. The psychologic effects are often more serious than the disease. Acne vulgaris occurs at a time when adolescents are concerned with personal appearance, and the unsightly skin condition may seriously interfere with personality development. It is also important to evaluate the patient's understanding of the treatment prescribed.

Intervention. Treatment for the condition is nonspecific and is directed toward reducing inflammation and infection, reducing blackhead formation, and developing a program of good personal hygiene. The skin should be kept scrupulously clean by washing with soap and water several times a day. A preparation containing hexachlorophene will help to reduce the staphylococcus population on the skin. Keratinous agents that cause drying, such as salicylic acid and resorcinol, may be used to produce a peeling of the skin and the removal of keratinous plugs to prevent the development of comedones and cysts. Cleansing agents are used to remove excess sebum from the skin and thus prevent the development of comedones. Tetracycline, minocycline, or erythromycin may be prescribed by the physician to prevent infection and thus reduce the probability of scarring. Existing comedones can be removed by the physician with an extractor and pustules opened with a blade every week or two. Small doses of estrogens administered to girls just before the menstrual period have helped to relieve the oily condition of the skin and retarded the formation of sebum. The patient should be advised against squeezing the lesions, which may worsen the condition and lead to scarring. Stress should be placed on developing a program of adequate diet, sleep, and wholesome physical activity. The restriction of certain foods in the diet, such as chocolate or fried foods, does not seem to have any effect on the prevention or treatment of acne. Iodized salt will make acne worse in sensitive people.

The most severe cases of acne, cystic acne, are being treated with isotretinoin (Accutane), a derivative of vitamin A, called a retinoid. This oral medication has potentially serious side effects and must be used with caution. A female who becomes pregnant while taking the drug has a high risk of birth defects in the infant. Other possible side effects include dry skin, hair loss, eye irritation, nosebleeds, and muscle and joint pain. Increased blood levels of cholesterol and triglycerides occur in 25% of patients and increase the risk of heart disease. The cost is about $150 per month for the medication alone. After a few months of treatment the condition can be cured.

When scarring is severe, the physician may recommend removal of the scars by chemical face peeling or dermabrasion. Chemical face peeling is also performed in the treatment of fine wrinkles, and both procedures are used to remove abnormal pigmentation, freckles, or scars from trauma or other skin diseases as well as acne. Chemical face peeling involves the application of a phenol-base chemical to the entire face followed by a mask of waterproof adhesive. The medication causes a burning sensation, and the patient will require medication to control apprehension and relieve pain. After 6 or 8 hours the face becomes edematous. The patient is not allowed to move about except to go to the bathroom for 48 hours. The dressings are removed after 48 hours, and the appearance of the skin will be similar to that of a second-degree burn. During the next 24 hours a bacteriostatic medication, thymol iodide powder, will be applied with a cotton applicator to the entire surface three or four times. Following this series of treatments, a lubricating ointment such as A and D ointment is applied to facilitate the separation of the crust that will form on the skin. After an additional 24 hours the face may be washed with plain water. Facial redness will persist for several weeks, and the patient will not feel comfortable being seen by others for as long as 3 or 4 weeks. Cosmetics may be applied at the end of 3 weeks, but exposure to the sun is not permitted for 3 to 6 months because the natural protective mechanism against the sun, melanin, is diminished.

An alternative to chemical face peeling is dermabrasion, or surgical planing. This procedure involves scraping, sandpapering, and brushing the skin to remove the epidermis and some superficial dermis. The remaining dermis will produce new cells and form a new epethelial layer in the dermabraded areas. The procedure can be performed by hand with coarse, abrasive paper or mechanically by using a rapidly rotating wire brush. The patient must be fully informed about the procedure and the appearance of the skin after its completion. After the procedure, pressure dressings may or may not be used, depending on the physician's preference. If dressings are used, they are removed after 48 hours, and the skin will have the appearance of a recent sunburn. A crust will begin to form, and vaseline or cocoa butter may be used to relieve tightness. The crust will separate in about 14 days; the skin will appear red. The patient must avoid direct sunlight for 3 to 4 months and use a sunscreen to protect the skin from exposure to the sun. It should be emphasized to the patient that even with repeat treatment deep scarring may not be completely eliminated, only improved. All patients who are candidates for dermabrasion should be questioned as to their expectations of the outcome of treatment. Some patients set their expectations too high and this needs to be addressed before the procedure is undertaken.

Certain acne scars can be treated with a new method involving the injection of collagen implants (Zyderm Collagen Implant). This brand is a highly purified form of collagen, the natural protein that provides the structure of skin and many other tissues in humans and animals. The collagen fibers form a latticework that lend structural support for the growth and development of surrounding cells and blood vessels. The Zyderm Collagen Implant is prepared from bovine skin that has been purified to remove materials that are unacceptable to the body. The material is implanted through a fine needle into the scar or depression, filling the depression and raising the skin to the level of the surrounding tissue. A series of treatments may be necessary. There will be mild soreness and redness at the site immediately after implantation, and soft lumps may be felt for several weeks. When the implant is incorporated by the body, it cannot be distinguished from normal tissue. A test dose is injected into the forearm to determine possible allergy before treatment is initiated.

Lupus Erythematosus

Lupus erythematosus is not strictly a disease of the skin and could be appropriately placed in a number of chapters in this text. It is a chronic inflammatory disease involving the connective tissues of the body. Since these tissues are found in almost all regions and areas of the body, almost any part or organ may be affected. The disease may be confined to the skin, as in discoid lupus erythematosus (DLE), or may become generalized, as seen in systemic lupus erythematosus (SLE).

DLE is a skin ailment characterized by disklike lesions with raised, reddish edges and sunken centers. They are most likely to appear on the arm, neck, face, scalp and may leave scars when they subside. DLE is rarely fatal, but it is irritating and painful. Few patients with the discoid form go on to develop the systemic form.

Systemic lupus erythematosus (SLE)

The cause of this disease is unknown, but theories include autoimmunity, predisposition, and drugs. The autoimmune theory proposes that SLE is an abnormal reaction of the body against its own tissues. The predisposition theory identifies such factors as physical or mental stress, streptococcal or viral infection, exposure to sunlight or ultraviolet light, vaccines, and x-ray treatments as pre-

disposing certain persons to this disease. It has been observed in successive generations of some families, so genetics may also be a predisposing factor. The drugs suspected of triggering SLE include sulfa forms, penicillin and other antibiotics, certain birth control pills, and individual drugs such as hydralazine and procainamide. Women are 10 times more likely to have SLE than men, and most of these women are of childbearing age. These patients are more susceptible to having miscarriages, premature births, and stillbirths. The fetus who reaches full-term is not usually affected by the mother's disease. The disease is also more common in blacks than whites, and it is rare in Asia. The incidence has been estimated at somewhere between two and five people per 100,000 population.

Pathophysiology. SLE can affect the skin, kidneys, central nervous system, heart, lungs, blood vessels, serous membranes, joints, and muscles, either singly or in combination. The inflammation occurs in connective tissue common to all organs, so involvement usually becomes more widespread with time. Because it can affect so many organs, it is difficult to describe a classic group of symptoms and to distinguish it from other diseases. The Diagnostic and Therapeutic Criteria Committee of the American Rheumatism Association has issued a list of 14 preliminary criteria. The presence of four or more of the 14 either serially or simultaneously during any interval of observation constitutes a diagnosis of SLE (see the box at right).

Pregnant women who demonstrate signs of preeclampsia should be tested for SLE, since this may be the early signs of the disease. About 75% of all patients with SLE live 5 years or longer after diagnosis, and this disease is most likely to prove fatal in the patient with kidney or neurologic involvement. Early diagnosis and treatment improve the prognosis, and developments in hemodialysis and renal transplant techniques are improving the outcome for those who experience renal failure. The life expectancy following diagnosis has almost doubled in the last 10 years.

Assessment. Symptoms vary from patient to patient, since the same organs may not be involved. The patient must understand this or may become confused and lose confidence in the physician when discussing treatment with other patients with the disease. The earliest symptoms often include fatigue, chills, occasional fever, and stiff aching joints on arising, usually followed sev-

---

Systemic Lupus Erythematosus is Indicated by the Presence of Four or More of the Following:

1. Facial erythema (butterfly rash)—diffuse flat or raised rash over the bridge of the nose; may be present on only one side of the face
2. Discoid lupus erythematosus—patches of redness or thickened red, raised, coin-shaped patches covered with scales and involving plugged follicles; may be present anywhere on the body, including the face.
3. Raynaud's phenomenon—intermittent attacks in which the hands or some of the fingers of each hand become cold, pale, painful, and then deeply cyanotic; symptoms are relieved by warming the hands
4. Alopecia—rapid loss of large amounts of scalp hair
5. Photosensitivity—an unusual skin reaction from exposure to sunlight
6. Ulcers in the mouth or nose
7. Arthritis without deformity but involving pain on motion, tenderness, swelling in the joints of the feet, ankles, knees, hips, shoulders, elbows, wrists, hands
8. LE cells—an unusual cell can be identified in the blood of patients with systemic lupus erythematosus; if one of these cells is seen in two or more specimens, or two in one specimen, the test is considered positive
9. Chronic false-positive serologic test for syphilis
10. Profuse proteinuria—over 3.5 g of protein excreted in the urine per day
11. Cellular casts—examination of the urine reveals casts that may be red blood cells, hemoglobin, granular, tubular, or mixed in type. When casts are found in the urine, they indicate a pathologic condition in the kidney. They are named to reflect their composition and shape; for example, red blood cell casts are composed of red blood cells, indicating a leakage of red blood cells into the urine. Many contain albumin because albumin often pours out into the urine in diseases involving the kidney; since systemic lupus erythematosus sometimes causes a type of glomerulonephritis, the presence of casts in the urine can be considered one of the criteria for diagnosis
12. Pleuritis or pericarditis or both—patient experiences pleuritic pain, a pleural rub is heard by the physician, or x-ray examination reveals thickening and fluid in the lungs; pericarditis is detected by electrocardiogram or can be heard by the physician as a rub
13. Psychosis or convulsions or both—uremia and drugs must be ruled out as a cause
14. One or more of the following—hemolytic anemia, leukopenia (white blood count less than 4000/mm^3 on two or more occasions), thrombocytopenia (platelet count less than 100,000/mm^3)

---

eral months later by a rash on the face and scalp and loss of hair in patches (alopecia). About 70% of patients develop skin eruptions, and about 40% develop a characteristic butterfly rash over the bridge of the nose and the cheek. The rash and hair loss become worse on exposure to the sun. The rash sometimes spreads to the arms, trunk, or legs, causing a flushed sunburned look or a scarred, patchy coinlike look. Chest, stomach, and muscle pain may occur, or fluid may accumulate in the feet, ankles, or chest. Pericarditis is the most frequent cardiac involvement. Women may experience irregular menstrual periods and may have difficulty in conceiving a child during an exacerbation of the disease. Pregnancy is less safe when there are kidney or neurologic abnormalities; thus the pregnant patient with SLE must be watched closely. The blood presure may become highly elevated. Protein, casts, and red blood cells in the urine indicate renal involvement, usually in the glomeruli, which become inflamed as a result of the deposit of immune complexes in the glomerular basement membrane. Convulsion, cranial nerve involvement, and psychoses may occur with central nervous system involvement. Symptoms tend to come and go, and most can be relieved and even reversed with proper treatment.

Because of the widespread effect of the disease, a number of laboratory tests are performed to aid in diagnosis. In addition to routine blood work, chest x-ray examinations, electrocardiograms, and urinalysis, the urine is examined for creatinine clearance to evaluate kidney function. More specific tests include blood tests for the LE cells, as well as the ANA (antinuclear antibody) and the anti-DNA test, which are positive.

Intervention. Treatment is aimed at reducing

the inflammatory process. High doses of aspirin are prescribed, often in combination with magnesium-aluminum hydroxide (Ascriptin) to reduce stomach distress. Indomethacin (Indocin) is also antiinflammatory and should be taken at bedtime with a snack to prevent stomach distress and provide maximum relief from early morning joint stiffness and pain. Corticosteroids such as prednisone are used for more severe symptoms. The topical steroid flurandrenolide 0.05% is prescribed in ointment form (Cordran ointment) for the facial lesions and as a lotion (Cordran lotion) for the scalp. If sun sensitive, the patient must use a sunscreen containing paraminobenzoic acid (PABA), which is available from many manufacturers without a prescription. Hydroxychloroquine (Plaquenil), an antimalarial whose action in the treatment of SLE is unknown, is prescribed only for severe skin lesions and may cause macular degeneration resulting in permanent blindness. Frequent eye examinations must be made to detect the early signs of this side effect. Immunosuppressive therapy is being used experimentally with patients who do not respond to conservative treatment. Patients must consult their physician before receiving any immunizations or before taking birth control pills and over-the-counter drugs such as vitamins. If receiving steroids, the patient should be instructed to wear a Medic Alert bracelet. Hot baths or shower are used to relieve joint pain and stiffness, and an exercise program is prescribed to maintain mobility, strength, and endurance.

In addition to providing measures to relieve pain and supervising prescribed exercises, nursing care is concerned with patient education. The patient must understand the disease, its symptoms, and the treatment prescribed in order to control the disease. Return of symptoms or the onset of new symptoms must be reported immediately. The response to drug therapy must be carefully observed and reported to the physician. The patient must make alterations in lifestyle to obtain more rest and avoid exposure to the sun. It may be necessary for the patient to wear clothing that completely covers the body and head, to use a sunscreen on those small areas of exposed skin, and to avoid the sun at midday while it is strongest. Fluorescent lighting is another source of ultraviolet light that may need to be avoided. The patient's self-concept may be affected by the disease, as well as by the restrictions imposed with treatment. It is important to make the patient

feel comfortable and free to express concerns and ask questions. The patient's family must also understand the disease and its treatment to be able to provide the support necessary for the patient to live with the disease. It is important to inform the patient of community groups available for supplying information and support. The Lupus Foundation of America* and the Arthritis Foundation† are two national sources. There may be a "lupus club" in your area, and if so, the patient should be advised of its availability but not pressured to join. With early diagnosis and control of the disease, aided by discoveries resulting from research into its causes and treatment, the patient will be able to make the most of the years ahead.

Viral Infections
Herpes simplex

Herpes simplex is a viral disease caused by herpesvirus hominus. This virus has two types, with type I being the most common and the one usually found in gingivostomatitis (cold sore). Type II, or genital herpes, is the one usually found in lesions of the penis or cervix and in disseminated herpes of the newborn. (See Chapter 19.)

Assessment. Herpes simplex type I is characterized by the appearance of a group of small vesicles on an erythematous base. It was originally thought that HSV I could only be found on the skin and mucous membranes of the lip or nose (Figure 24-11). This has since been proven incorrect. HSV I has been cultured from lesions on the genitalia. The disease often occurs when other acute infections are present but may occur in the absence of any other condition. It was once thought that canker sores on the mucous membrane of the mouth may have been caused by this same virus, but it has now been demonstrated that they are not herpetic lesions. Herpes simplex is usually of short duration, but it is a recurring condition. The virus has the ability to persist in a latent state in certain tissues and to cause repeated infection despite the presence of circulating neutralizing antibodies. The appearance of the lesion, often called a cold sore, is often associated with certain stimuli such as sunlight, menstruation, fatigue, and emotional stress, which are thought to trigger viral replication and result in disease.

Herpes simplex type II is found in about 20% of the adult population and is more prevalent in

---

*First National Bank, 100 Federal, Boston, Mass. 02241.
†3400 Peachtree Rd. NE, Atlanta, Ga. 30326.

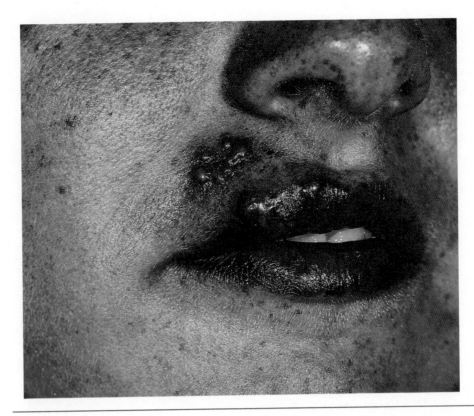

Figure 24-11
Herpes simplex type I. *(From McCance KL and Huether SE: Pathophysiology: adults and children, St Louis, 1989, The CV Mosby Co.)*

lower socioeconomic groups and in sexually active persons. The virus produces genital herpes and results in ulcerative or necrotizing lesions of the uterine cervix or the vulvar area in women. In men it produces ulcerations on the penis. The ulcerations are painful and tend to recur. It must be remembered that females may have asymptomatic lesions of the cervix that continually shed the virus. It is extremely important to evaluate pregnant women to decide if vaginal delivery is safe.

The herpes virus can also produce acute encephalitis and is the most common cause of sporadic acute encephalitis in the United States.

Intervention. Although little can be done to prevent recurrence of herpes type I or type II, once infected, the patient can be educated in methods of preventing the spread of the disease. Direct contact with lesions should be avoided. Hot compresses may provide relief from the discomfort of the lesions, and topical application of alcohol or spirits of camphor may be helpful. Repeated vaccination with smallpox vaccine was once recommended to try to prevent herpes labialis; the value

has not been proved, however, and it is contraindicated because of the risks of the complications of smallpox vaccine. There is presently no cure for the diseases caused by the herpesvirus type I or type II, but a drug has been introduced that shortens episodes of the disease. Acyclovir is an antiviral drug active against herpes simplex types I and II, herpes zoster varicellosus, Epstein-Barr virus, and cytomegalovirus. Intravenous, oral, and topical (Zovirax ointment 5%) forms of the drug are available.

Herpes zoster (shingles)

Herpes zoster is often classified as a neurologic disorder because the lesion is located in one or more of the spinal ganglia with involvement of the skin area supplied by the nerve fibers. The disease is caused by the herpes zoster virus (herpesvirus varicellosus), which is also the cause of chickenpox (varicella). The virus can lie dormant in exposed individuals, including those who have developed chickenpox after exposure. Herpes zoster occurs when the dormant virus is activated. Individuals who have not had varicella

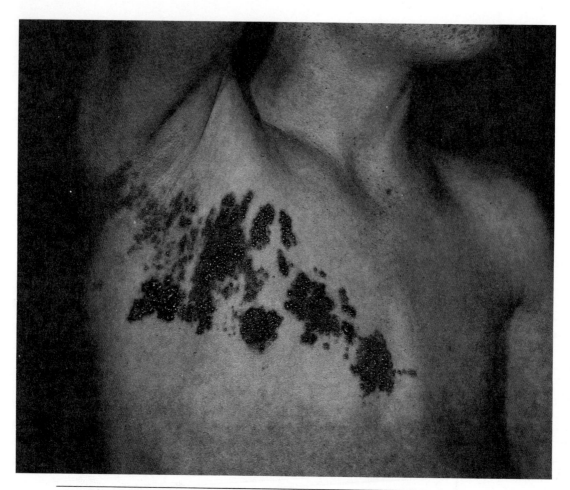

Figure 24-12

Herpes zoster. *(From McCance KL and Huether SE: Pathophysiology: adults and children, St Louis, 1989, The CV Mosby Co.)*

may develop it after exposure to the vesicular lesions of persons with herpes zoster. Herpes zoster can be a serious condition in any adult and may even lead to death from exhaustion in the elderly and the debilitated. It often occurs in persons with Hodgkin's disease and other cancers because of reduced cell-mediated immunity.

The virus can lie dormant in exposed individuals, including those who have developed chickenpox after exposure. Herpes zoster occurs when the dormant virus is activated.

Assessment. The skin lesions usually follow the dermatomes: the segments of the skin surface that are divided according to the nerves that innervate them (Figure 24-12). Since the lesions follow these nerve pathways, they rarely cross the midline of the body and may appear only on one side. If lesions cross the midline, internal malignancy may be suspected. The patient may have a slight temperature, malaise, and loss of appetite,

with severe pain in the skin area before development of the rash. After 1 or 2 days, an inflamed, edematous area appears where papules turning to vesicles are arranged in groups following the sensory nerves from the posterior to the anterior. The most common location of the lesions is the thoracic region. But the disease may occur on the thighs, lower abdomen, or forehead. About one third of the patients have involvement of cranial nerve V (trigeminal nerve) with lesions on the face, eyes, and scalp. If the rash occurs along the branches of cranial nerve V, the patient should be observed for facial paralysis and eye or ear disturbances. A neurologic pain occurs in paroxysms and is worse on movement and at night. The pain may persist long after the skin manifestation has subsided; it is then called *postherpetic neuralgia*.

Intervention. The disease is self-limiting, and acyclovir and vidarabine are used in severe cases and in immunocompromised patients. Analgesics are given for pain and narcotics may be required for severe pain. The injection of a local anesthetic agent into the nerve has been attempted to control pain by blocking its transmission. If begun early enough, this method also seems to provide protection against the development of postherpetic neuralgia. Lotions may be used to relieve the discomfort from the skin rash. Methscopolamine bromide (Protamide) a colloidal solution of a proteolytic enzyme, has proved valuable in relieving pain and reducing the rash. It has been reported that patients treated with methscopolamine bromide have not experienced the postherpetic pain. Some patients may be treated with corticosteroids such as methylprednisolone (Medrol) to reduce inflammation and to shorten the period of acute pain, but these agents have no effect on the healing of the skin lesions. If secondary infection occurs, antibiotics are administered.

Patients with herpes zoster may be hospitalized, and emotional depression frequently accompanies the disease. The nurse may find the patient irritable and uncooperative. Patience and understanding will be needed in caring for these patients.

Disorders of Pigmentation
Lentigo (freckles)

Freckles are collections of skin pigment that result from quantitative changes in melanin. They may occur in certain persons on exposure to the sun in summer and tend to disappear in winter. Persons with severe cases may have the freckles removed by dermal abrasion, but assurance cannot be given that they will not return.

Chloasma (liver spots)

Patches of pigmentation that may be yellowish brown, brown, or black occur on various parts of the body. They are more common in women and are often seen during pregnancy or at the time of menopause. The condition is not the result of disease of the liver.

No treatment is necessary, unless the lesions occur on the face and the person is sensitive about them for cosmetic reasons. They may be removed with various bleaching preparations, but the procedure is not recommended.

Disorders of Glands
Seborrhea (oily skin)

Some persons have an excessive secretion of oil from the sebaceous glands that is accentuated on the face, neck, and scalp, where the oil glands are most abundant. It is often associated with other conditions such as acne vulgaris, seborrheic dermatitis, eczema, and seborrheic warts. Although the condition is normal for some persons, particularly women, it not only detracts from personal appearance but also predisposes to other more serious skin conditions.

Treatment consists of washing frequently and thoroughly with soap and water and avoiding the use of greasy creams. Preparations containing salicylic acid or sulfur or both may be rubbed into the affected areas several times a day. If the hair and scalp are affected, Sebucare lotion may be applied to wet hair once or twice daily and thoroughly massaged into the scalp.

Sebaceous cyst (wen)

A sebaceous cyst, commonly called a *wen*, is often seen on the scalp and may become large. It is the result of obstruction of the sebaceous duct in the presence of continued secretions from the gland. These tumors contain an accumulation of sebum, which develops an offensive odor. The treatment is surgical incision, with measures to prevent infection.

Hyperhidrosis (excessive sweating)

Excessive sweating occurs in relation to several conditions, including diseases such as tuberculosis and hyperthyroidism, conditions in which severe pain is present as in renal colic, and certain acute heart attacks. It may also occur in some shock states and toxic conditions or after the administration of antipyretic drugs. Under normal conditions excessive sweating usually occurs when a person is exposed to extremes of heat or severe physical exercise. Excessive sweating may predispose the individual to skin disease or irritation.

Treatment is directed toward removing the cause, and nursing care should concern keeping the bed and clothing dry, sponging and drying the skin, and protecting the patient from exposure.

Axillary hyperhidrosis may be controlled by topical application of most of the commercial agents on the market. These preparations act by closing the pores and may occasionally cause a mild irritation. Excessive hyperhidrosis of the feet can be relieved by washing several times daily, drying thoroughly, and dusting with a medicated foot powder.

Anhidrosis (absence of sweating)

Anhidrosis is a normal result of the aging process accompanied by decreased activity of the sebaceous glands, which causes dryness of the skin. It can also be a very serious condition seen in younger individuals in which the temperature regulating mechanism (sweating) is disturbed. If temperature regulation is severely affected, the chance of heat prostration increases. This disorder is characteristic of diabetes mellitus, nephritis, hypothyroidism, and several skin diseases and may follow the administration of drugs such as atropine.

There is no specific treatment for the condition as such, except the use of superfatted soaps and the application of creams or oils. Treatment of the causative factor may provide relief.

Pruritus (Itching)

Pruritus is a symptom that accompanies many disorders, including a variety of skin diseases, systemic diseases, allergic reactions, and anhidrosis in the elderly person. The response of the individual is to scratch, and it is generally useless to tell him not to scratch, since his reply will probably be, "I can't help it." In fact, scratching is almost an automatic, unconscious act.

Whenever possible, treatment is based on removing or treating the cause. In treating small children, splinting of the arms or the use of mitts may be necessary to prevent scratching. Cold wet dressings, emollient baths, and emollient lotion containing phenol or menthol may be used, or the physician may prescribe a lotion containing a steroid drug. Some patients may benefit from antihistaminic drugs.

The nurse should do everything possible to provide comfort for the patient and to relieve the emotional tension often associated with pruritic conditions. Maintaining a cool, even room temperature and providing a quiet environment and some diversional activity will help to relieve itching.

Tumors of the Skin

Tumors of the skin are among the most common of all tumors and generally affect exposed parts of the body such as the face and back of the hands. Persons whose occupations expose them to wind, sun, and frost are often affected. Most patients with skin tumors are in the older age group. Skin tumors may be benign or malignant, and most malignant tumors can be easily diagnosed and cured. Benign tumors include the keloid, angioma, nevus, wart, and keratoses.

Keloid

The keloid is an overgrowth of fibrous tissue occurring at a scar site. The shape may be irregular and small, or it may increase to the size of the hand. The tumor may develop after inflammation or ulceration from burns or traumatic injuries. It is not known why the condition occurs. It is more common in blacks.

There is no uniform opinion concerning treatment. The lesion may be erythematous, irritated, and painful. Pain may be relieved by injection of a glucocorticoid (Aristocort, Kenacort) diluted 1:5 with lidocaine (Xylocaine). Surgical removal followed by x-ray therapy will be effective in about half the cases.

Angioma

Angioma is a benign skin tumor that consists of dilated blood vessels. There are several types of angiomas—one is congenital, called a *birthmark* by many people. The skin may have an area of purplish color known as *port-wine stain*. The stain is not elevated and may be large. Port-wine stains frequently are found on the face and may cover an entire side of the face. Treatment may consist of electrolysis, or x-ray therapy, which usually is for cosmetic purposes only.

The *spider angioma* is an acquired condition often accompanying disease of the liver, which consists of a network of venous capillaries that radiate outward in a spiderlike fashion. It generally fades and disappears as the primary condition improves.

Nevus (mole)

The mole is a nonvascular tumor, many of which are pigmented and may be present at birth. There are many different types of nevi, almost all of which are harmless. However, the raised black mole, although benign, may become malignant if it is located where it is subjected to constant irritation. It is generally advisable for these moles to be excised as a precautionary measure.

Verruca (wart)

Warts are common and may occur at any age; however, the largest number are found in persons between 10 and 30 years of age. There are several different types; some occur as single lesions, others are multiple. They are caused by a virus, and it is believed that they are contagious, but the exact mode of transmission is unknown. A common type of wart is found on the hands and arms, including areas around the nails. They occur on the feet, legs, face, and neck and vary in size and color. Another type that appears on the face and neck tends to be elongated. The plantar wart develops on the weight-bearing part of the foot and may be painful. Warts are flat, and removal of the horny epidermis leaves a slightly bleeding surface. Some warts are moist and may occur in persons with gonorrhea; others that occur in infectious syphilis are called *condylomata*. Warts occurring in gonorrhea and syphilis are frequently located about the genital area. Condylomata tend to coalesce and form large, cauliflower-like lesions.

Treatment of warts depends on the type of wart, the location, and the number. Plantar warts may be especially difficult to treat; they may be treated with preparations containing salicylic acid. In a large number of cases warts disappear spontaneously. Dietary supplements of vitamin A have been found to be effective in treating and preventing warts in some individuals.

Keratoses

Keratoses are generally considered precancerous lesions, of which there are many types. Some occur in elderly persons as senile keratoses and are most likely to become malignant. Surgical removal is generally indicated. Some forms of keratoses, such as solar or actinic, appear in persons who have been exposed to the sun and whose skin has been damaged by it. Others are found in persons past middle age as seborrheic dermatoses. These are less likely to become malignant but should be kept under observation.

Malignant tumors

Skin cancer can be prevented, and if diagnosed early, can be cured. The thousands of skin cancer deaths each year can be partially attributed to public ignorance about prevention and laxity among professionals in assessing skin lesions. Skin cancer may be caused by frequent contact with carcinogenic chemicals, such as those found in coal tar, pitch, and pesticides; overexposure or chronic exposure to the sun's ultraviolet rays; repeated scar-producing injuries, especially burns; and radiation treatment. Fair-skinned people are more susceptible to cancer from sun exposure because they have less melanin, which keep the sun's ul-

traviolet rays from penetrating the skin. The ultraviolet rays are believed to set off a genetic reaction that results in skin cancer. There are three types of skin cancer: basal cell, squamous cell, and malignant melanoma. The first two types are the most common and are easily cured if detected and treated early. Malignant melanoma is rarer but is the most dangerous to the patient.

Assessment. Assessment begins with a determination of the patient's risk for developing skin cancer. An investigation of his lifestyle, occupation, geographic location, and hobbies will reveal factors that predispose to skin cancer. Careful assessment of the skin of the entire body is important, including hidden areas between the toes and fingers and in the folds of the skin.

Basal cell carcinoma is seen most often in fair-skinned people who have had overexposure to the sun. It is usually found on the nose, eyelids, cheeks, rim of the ear, or trunk. There are two forms: nodular and superficial. The nodular form is elevated and firm to palpation and has an ulcerated center, raised margins, and a waxy or pearly border. The superficial type is flat and has a crusted or red center and a raised or pearly border.

Squamous cell carcinoma usually develops on areas exposed to radiation, mainly the head (especially on the lips) and hands. It can be an elevated, nodular mass or a large, fungus-like mass. It spreads more rapidly than basal cell carcinoma.

Malignant melanoma may appear without warning, beginning in or near a mole or other dark spot in the skin. The important warning signs are the ABCDs of melanoma. **A**symmetry: one side does not match the other. **B**order irregularity: the edges are notched, ragged, or blurred. **C**olor: the pigmentation is not uniform; shades of tan, brown, or black appear; dashes of red, white, or blue may be seen in the lesions. **D**iameter: generally greater than 6 ml (about the size of a pencil eraser). The patient should see a physician if any of the following conditions are observed in a mole: the ABCDs, scaling, oozing, bleeding, spread of pigmentation, or change in sensation.

There is an inherited tendency to develop malignant melanoma, and melanoma-prone families can be identified by the presence of numerous B-K type nevi on the skin. Recently identified as *dysplastic nevus syndrome (DNS)*, this condition often leads to the development of malignant melanoma and is characterized by many large and unusual moles. The moles often number more than 100 and are usually larger than 5 mm. Their pigmentation is unusual, combining brown, black, red, and pink in a single mole. They are found on the back and chest and may even be found in the scalp and on the breast. Patients with DNS or multiple nevi should be seen regularly by a physician to detect changes warning of malignancy. The patient must also be instructed to regularly and systematically observe the moles so that early detection of change is possible. Any change in size or color of a mole, flaking, ulceration, bleeding, or sudden elevation of a once-flat mole should be reported immediately to the physician. Patients with fewer or no moles must likewise be alert for changes in warts, moles, scars, and birthmarks. Any unusual finding should be documented completely, including location, size, color, surface characteristics, and appearance of surrounding area. Documentation should also include the patient's observations of the lesion, including time of appearance, recent changes, irritation from clothing, and past treatment.

Intervention. Skin cancer is treated with a number of methods, including surgical excision, radiation, cryosurgery, and electrodessication and curettage. More resistant and larger lesions are treated more effectively with a method called *Mohs' surgery,* named after Frederich Mohs, who developed the technique more than 30 years ago. The technique originally involved the application of a chemical fixative to the visible part of the skin cancer to eliminate blood flow during excision. Modern laboratory procedures and improved surgical techniques have eliminated the need for chemical fixation, and the technique is now performed on fresh tissue. The tissue is examined microscopically as it is removed, until all malignant tissue is excised. The wound can be immediately reconstructed, which was not possible when the chemical fixative was used. It is relatively painless and can be performed on an outpatient basis. The procedure is now known as microscopically controlled excision or Mohs' surgery—fresh-tissue technique.

After surgery, instruction in wound care is necessary. If the wound is left open to heal by secondary intention, it will be dressed postoperatively with the application of a topical antibiotic and a nonadherent dressing (most surgery units have their own protocols). The dressing is generally changed twice a day, and the wound is cleansed every time. This may be done with diluted hydrogen peroxide, but caution should be taken since the action of hydrogen peroxide may disturb the granulating tissue. The antibiotic ointment is reapplied at each dressing change. The ointment keeps the wound moist to prevent formation of eschar. Patients should understand the need to care for the wound as prescribed, using careful handwashing to prevent secondary bacterial infection.[39]

Disorders of the Appendages
Alopecia (loss of hair)

Loss of hair may result from several causes, including the normal thinning of the hair as a condition of the aging process. Hair is sometimes lost after long and debilitating diseases such as fevers. A characteristic alopecia occurs in early syphilis and is marked by loss of hair in round patches; it may progress until the scalp presents a moth-eaten appearance. *Alopecia areata* results in patches of baldness that may appear suddenly and tend to spread from the edges. After several round patches of baldness occur, regrowth of hair begins but may not be permanent. Finally, however, the hair is replaced, and spontaneous recovery takes place after several months.

Hypertrichosis and hypotrichosis

The excessive growth of hair may be congenital or acquired or may result from a hereditary tendency. In congenital hypertrichosis, hair may cover moles or the skin over a spina bifida. Acquired hypertrichosis may be the result of endocrine disturbance and is frequently seen as a growth of hair on the upper lip and on the chin of women. It may also be the result of a hereditary predisposition. The most satisfactory method of removing superfluous hair is by electrolysis.

Hypotrichosis is an absence of hair or a deficiency of hair. The condition may be the result of skin disease or endocrine factors. When the cause is endocrine disturbance, correction should be made if possible.

Hair transplants. The problem of baldness is more common in men than in women. As an alternative to wearing hairpieces, it is now possible to elect to have a hair transplant for cosmetic purposes. The majority of balding males retain healthy hair on the back and sides of the head. These hair follicles can be relocated by a transplant procedure. Dozens of small plugs of hair are removed and relocated in the areas where hair is thin or absent. Patterns of grafts are removed from the balding area and replaced by the healthy growing hair grafts from the donor area. Treatment is usually performed in two or three sessions, and each session lasts 1 or 2 hours. Sessions are spaced at a minimum of 2 weeks to allow adequate healing and to establish circulation through the transplant area. New hair should begin to appear about 12 weeks after the transplant.[16]

Nail disorders

Disorders of the nails may be associated with diseases elsewhere in the body or may be caused by congenital defects or infection. The nails may be soft or brittle. Changes in the shape and contour may occur, and nails may grow into the soft tissues at the side (ingrown nails). *Paronychia* (runaround) is an infection that begins on the side of the nail, often from a hangnail or injury, and finally encircles it. The infection loosens the nail from the matrix and may become painful. Frequently, surgical removal of the affected part of the nail is necessary. Wet dressings, using 1:2000 to 1:10,000 potassium permanganate and the application of neomycin ointment may relieve the condition. Fungal infections of the nails respond poorly to ordinary methods or treatment and may take months for cure.

Infestations
Pediculi (lice)

Three types of *Pediculus* infest human beings: P. *humanus* var. *capitis*, P. *humanus* var. *corporis*, and P. *pubis*.

P. *capitis* is the head louse, which lives on the scalp and attaches its eggs (nits) to the hair. The nits are attached to the hair by an adhesive substance that makes them difficult to remove. The louse bites the scalp to seek nutrition by sucking blood, causing severe itching and scratching. Severe infestations may result in secondary infection, which includes enlargement of lymph glands in the neck. The present recommended treatment is the use of Kwell (1% gamma benzene hexachloride) shampoo, which is applied to the hair and scalp and lathered for 4 to 5 minutes, after which the hair is rinsed and combed to remove the nits. The treatment may be repeated in 24 hours. A newer preparation, RID, is sold without a prescription and tests have shown it to be as effective as Kwell, while causing fewer adverse reactions.

P. *corporis* is a body louse that may be found in the seams of underclothing. Scratch marks may appear on the skin in the area of clothing seams. Treatment consists of boiling the underwear, which kills the louse and the nits. However, all bedding and clothing must be washed and boiled and pillows and blankets treated. It is believed that clothing that cannot be washed and boiled will be safe for wearing if stored and not worn for one month, since the lice cannot live without a human organism as a source of nutrients. Kwell, cream or lotion, or RID is applied to the affected areas after bathing thoroughly.

P. *pubis* (*Phthirus pubis*) is found primarily in the genital area; however, it may infect the axilla, eyebrows, beard, and eyelashes. The lice may be contracted from toilet seats, bedclothes, clothing, and sexual intercourse. Treatment involves a warm bath and applying Kwell cream. The cream should be applied over the entire body and left on for 24 hours. If necessary, the treatment may be repeated. If RID is used, it is applied to the entire pubic region, left on for 10 minutes, and then washed off. This application is repeated daily for 3 consecutive days.

Scabies (itch)

Scabies, an infectious skin disease, is caused by the itch mite, a parasite that burrows under the skin. A warm, protected environment fosters the growth of the parasite, and it is spread easily by direct contact with another person who is infested. Even handholding or simply shaking hands can transmit scabies from one individual to another. Contact with infected clothing or linens can spread scabies, but the mite does not jump from one person to the other and does not survive very long in clothing or linens. Outbreaks of scabies were common until World War II and then began a decline only to make a vigorous comeback in recent years. It is not uncommon to find scabies on patients in nursing homes and hospitals. Scabies may occur in epidemics or endemics. An individual can develop immunity to the disease, but the mechanism of this immunity is not clearly understood.[1]

Assessment. The nurse can prevent the spread of the disease to other patients and also prevent contracting the disease by being alert to the symptoms. A person is more likely to contract scabies from someone whose disease is not diagnosed than from one who has been identified and treated. The disease is recognized by the presence of itching and multiform lesions, or lesions "of many shapes." Papules and vesicles are common, and characteristic S-shaped burrows are often, but not always, present. Secondary bacterial infection and scratching may result in pustules and edema. Delay in treatment may lead to secondary skin lesions or the development of an eczematous condition.

The characteristic location of the lesion varies with age. Children will have involvement of the palms, soles, head, and neck. Adults will rarely have lesions in these areas but will have them on the flexor surfaces of the wrist and elbows, on the waist, buttocks, male genitalia, and female breast. Burrows can be found between fingers and around the umbilicus. The characteristic itching intensifies at night. A definite diagnosis may require examination of scrapings taken from lesions on the skin.

Burns

Burns are injuries to body tissue and may be caused by heat (dry or moist), electricity, chemicals, or radiant energy. There are about 2 million burn cases each year, and about 7% to 8% of these patients require hospitalization. About one fourth of those hospitalized will have major burns or significant associated injuries requiring treatment in a specialized burn unit or burn center.

Classification by severity

The American Burn Association classifies a burn as minor, moderate, or major, based on the following criteria:

Minor burn. Deep partial-thickness burns involving less than 15% TBSA (total body surface area) in adults or less than 10% TBSA in children, or a full-thickness burn of less than 2% TBSA that does not involve special care areas (i.e., face, eyes, ears, hands, feet, or perineum).

Moderate burn. Deep partial-thickness burns of 15% to 25% TBSA in adults or 10% to 20% in children, or full-thickness burn less than 10% TBSA not involving special care areas.

Major burn. Deep partial-thickness burns totaling more than 25% TBSA in adults or 20% in children. All full-thickness burns of 10% TBSA or more. Other factors such as inhalation or electrical injuries and the age and health status of the individual are considered in classifying a burn as major.[14]

Determination of Burn Depth

Burns are classified as partial-thickness or full-thickness, depending on which layers of the skin have been damaged (Figure 24-13). Partial-thickness burns destroy and damage tissue into the dermis. A superficial or shallow partial-thickness burn will be reddened, warm, and painful and will blanch and refill after applying fingertip pressure. The epidermis is damaged, but this keratinized layer is rapidly replaced by underlining cells. A deep partial-thickness burn is characterized by blisters, which usually increase immediately in size, and involves the dermis. Enough epithelial cells remain around the hair follicles and sweat glands to produce new skin, provided the cells are not destroyed during treatment. Shallow and deep partial-thickness burns are comparable to the burns previously classified as first and second degree.

Full-thickness burns (previously classified as third degree burns) destroy all of the layers of the skin, extending into the subcutaneous tissue, and may involve muscle and bone. If the burned area is reddened but does not blanch and refill with fingertip pressure, it is considered full thickness. Full-thickness burns appear leathery and may be white, brown, red, or black. Small, thin-walled vesicles may be present. There is no sensation of pain at first because sensory nerve fibers in the dermis have been destroyed; sensation and pain return as the tissues recover. Since burns are usually a mixture of full- and partial-thickness injuries, some pain is usually present. Full-thickness burns must be grafted to heal—there are no cells remaining and regeneration is therefore impossible. These burns were previously classified as third and fourth degree.

Determination of Burn Extent

There are two methods used to estimate total area of burn injury: the rule of nines and the Lund and Browder Chart. For both methods you color a chart as found in Figure 24-14, using red for areas of full-thickness or third degree burns and blue for deep partial-thickness or second degree burns. With the rule of nines, you add the percentages listed for each burned area. For example, burns on the right arm and anterior trunk would total 27%. When children are burned, these percentages must be adjusted. The percentage of an infant's head is twice that of an adult's, whereas a 10-year-old's head is about one and one half that of an adult. The trunk is considered about two thirds that of an adult. The Lund and Browder Chart is considered more accurate because it divides the body into more sections and also makes

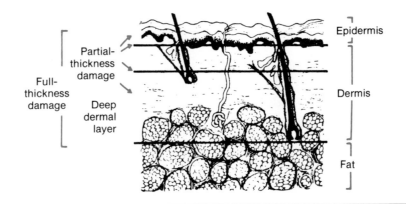

Figure 24-13

Diagram of skin showing depth of burn. *(Courtesy Dr. H. Harrison. From Jacoby FG: Nursing care of the patient with burns, ed 2, St Louis, 1976, The CV Mosby Co.)*

adjustments for age-related changes in body size. To use the Lund and Browder Chart, note the red and blue colored areas, find the column that reflects the patient's age, and then add the percentages for each area of the body burned. A two-year-old child with burns on the right arm (R.U. arm., R.L. arm., R. hand) and anterior trunk would have burns on 26.5% of the body, while the percentage for an adult with burns in the same areas would be estimated at 22.5%.

Phases of hospitalization

The hospital care of the seriously burned patient has been classified into three phases: the emergent period, the acute period, and rehabilitation. The emergent period begins with the burn injury and includes the first stage and initial care as determined by the severity of the injury; this period ends when the patient is stable and begins to diurese and no longer requires fluid therapy. The acute period is centered around care of the wounds to prevent infection and promote healing. Rehabilitation involves all that is required to help that patient return to his previous or optimum level of functioning. Many aspects of rehabilitation, however, must be initiated from the time of admission and early care. The following sections on burn care deal with total patient needs throughout these periods.

First aid

The first priority is to prevent further injury by extinguishing any flames still present or by removing the victim from the electric contact in the event of an electricity burn. Flames should be smothered by wrapping the patient in a blanket or rolling him on the ground. In the case of a chemical burn, all contaminated clothing should be removed and the skin rinsed generously with water to remove the chemical. The extent of any burn can be limited by the application of cool water. This reduces the temperature of the skin, lessens tissue destruction, and may prevent a full-thickness burn from occurring. If the burns are extensive, application of ice or ice water to a large area of the skin could produce total body hypothermia, followed by fatal cardiac arrhythmias. Therefore ice or ice water should be applied either for brief periods or to limited areas of the skin. No attempt should be made to apply ointments or give medications. The victim should be wrapped in a clean sheet or blanket and taken immediately to the hospital for emergency treatment.

Once the cause of the burn has been eliminated, the next priority is to maintain or provide a patent airway. Any bleeding that is present should be stopped. Shock may be present and should be treated. The burn victim is usually conscious and in pain. The rescuer should reassure the victim and explain what is being done during this time.

Assessment and intervention. During the emergent period shock is a major problem for the burn patient; it can be managed with proper nursing intervention. Suctioning may be necessary to remove aspirated secretions in maintaining a patent airway. Humidified oxygen should be administered, since carbon monoxide inhaled in a smoke-filled space is displaced from hemoglobin more rapidly if the patient is breathing 100% oxygen rather than room air.[36] Smoke inhalation, par-

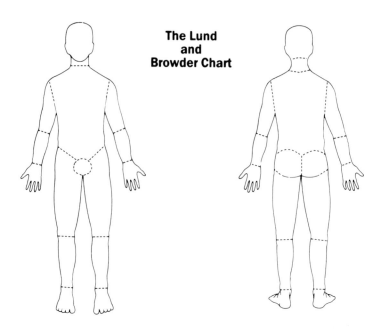

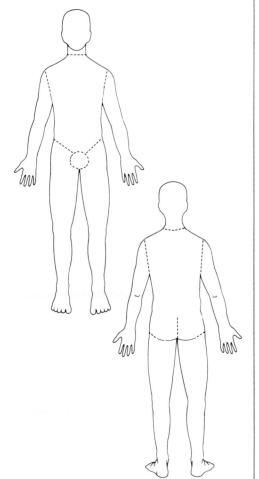

The Rule of Nines

Head and neck	**9%**
Right arm	**9**
Left arm	**9**
Posterior trunk	**18**
Anterior trunk	**18**
Right leg	**18**
Left leg	**18**
Perineum	**1**
	100%

The Lund and Browder Chart

AREA	AGE-YEARS					% 2°	% 3°	% TOTAL
	0-1	1-4	5-9	10-15	ADULT			
Head	19	17	13	10	7			
Neck	2	2	2	2	2			
Ant. Trunk	13	17	13	13	13			
Post. Trunk	13	13	13	13	13			
R. Buttock	2½	2½	2½	2½	2½			
L. Buttock	2½	2½	2½	2½	2½			
Genitalia	1	1	1	1	1			
R.U. Arm	4	4	4	4	4			
L.U. Arm	4	4	4	4	4			
R.L. Arm	3	3	3	3	3			
L.L. Arm	3	3	3	3	3			
R. Hand	2½	2½	2½	2½	2½			
L. Hand	2½	2½	2½	2½	2½			
R. Thigh	5½	6½	8½	8½	9½			
L. Thigh	5½	6½	8½	8½	9½			
R. Leg	5	5	5½	6	7			
R. Foot	3½	3½	3½	3½	3½			
L. Foot	3½	3½	3½	3½	3½			
					Total			

Figure 24-14

Estimating burn size. *(Adapted from Lund C and Browder N: The estimation of areas of burns, Surg Gynecol Obstet 1944.)*

ticularly in the combustion of synthetic materials and inhalation of toxic chemical by-products by the victim, may also result in damage to the respiratory tract and produce laryngeal edema. Early laryngeal edema can be detected by wheez-ing on inspiration, the use of accessory muscles for respiration, and increased hoarseness. The patient with inhalation injuries is at great risk for developing bronchial pneumonia.

Damage to the capillary system occurs in the

burn area, along with damage to the body cells; both injuries cause water and electrolytes to shift from the plasma to the interstitial fluid. This fluid accumulation causes edema and in partial-thickness burns is evidenced by blisters. In full-thickness burns the same process occurs, but the destroyed layers of the skin, or eschar, may trap the edema fluids beneath them. If the wounds are circumferential, covering all sides of an extremity, a tourniquet effect is created. Circumferential wounds on the torso can affect respiration, whereas those involved in the neck may obstruct the airway. Pulses distal to the wound, respirations, and airway patency must be checked hourly. If edema causes complications in any of these areas, an escharotomy—cutting through the burned skin layers—is performed to relieve the constriction.

It can be expected that an adult with 15% or a child with 10% of the body burned will be suffering from some degree of shock. The accumulation of edema fluids in the burned area and the loss of fluids from injured tissues result in a decrease in the amount of circulating blood plasma. When the volume of the bloodstream falls, blood pressure drops, circulation decreases, and less oxygen is available to all body tissues. This process leads to shock; if treatment is not instituted, acute renal failure and damage to the kidneys and other organs will occur. Metabolic acidosis may result. This shift of fluids, electrolytes, and albumin from the capillaries to the burned tissues occurs in the first 24 to 48 hours following the injury. Shock is the usual cause when a patient dies in the first 72 hours following a burn.

The nurse caring for a newly burned patient must be constantly alert for symptoms of burn shock. Restlessness is a common sign of hypoxia and may indicate onset of shock. The pulse will increase before the blood pressure falls, and respirations will also increase. Urine flow is scant or absent. (See the boxed material.) To prevent burn shock, administration of intravenous fluids is usually the first emergency treatment given to the severely burned patient. Many combinations of fluids may be used, depending on the physician's preference; Ringer's solution plus albumin may be given to combat protein loss. Fluids may be administered rapidly until urine flow is established, then regulated to maintain a urine output of 30 to 50 ml per hour. An indwelling catheter is inserted, and it is the nurse's responsibility to measure the output, urinary pH, and specific

gravity each hour. The specific gravity and hematocrit value may be elevated because of the shift of fluid from the circulating blood in the vascular spaces to the burn tissue. Almost every burn patient is extremely thirsty, but must not be allowed to drink water, since this tends to dilute body electrolytes. The patient is given nothing by mouth; intravenous fluids are administered instead. In patients with major burns a nasogastric tube will be inserted to prevent gastric dilation, since peristalsis will slow or stop altogether as a normal body response to stress.

With time, the capillary walls return to normal and the fluids accumulated in the tissues reenter the bloodstream. The electrolytes return with the fluid. This process is detected by a marked increase in urinary output or diuresis. If the kidneys are damaged or diseased, the patient is at great risk for kidney failure. This shift of fluid and electrolytes back into the vascular system also puts an extra volume load on the heart and lungs. Patients with a prior history of heart or lung problems should be monitored very closely for signs of congestive heart failure or pulmonary edema. Since electrolytes are also returning to the bloodstream, it would be dangerous to administer additional electrolytes to the patient in the intravenous fluids. The fluids, however, are still needed, so dextrose and water are administered. The onset of diuresis signals the end of the emergent period of care. The nurse, continually observing the patient, notes this change in status and reports to the physician so the treatment plan can be modified. Formulas such as Parkland's and Brooke's have been developed to help determine the volume of fluid replacement. The use of these formulas depends on precise monitoring by the nurse. Determining the fluid needs of the burn patient requires accurate checking of intake and output and vital signs every hour, as well as frequent monitoring of weight and hematocrit levels.

Initial treatment of the wound involves cleansing with a diluted solution of povidone-iodine (Betadine) or pHisoHex (one part povidone-iodine or pHisoHex to three or four parts water). The wound should then be rinsed thoroughly and covered with moist saline dressings. If the wounds cover a great deal of the body, the saline should be warm and the patient should be kept covered with a sheet to prevent excessive heat loss. After all the wounds are cleansed, the saline dressings may be covered with dry dressings or may be replaced with dry sterile dressings. If the wound

NURSING CARE GUIDELINES
The Patient with Burn Injuries

Nursing diagnoses

- Fluid volume excess/deficit related to fluid shifts/loss of skin integrity
- Fear related to pain, hospitalization, unknown outcomes of burn injury
- Pain, acute related to tissue injury, wound care
- Potential impaired gas exchange related to inhalation injury
- High risk for infection related to burn wound, respiratory or urinary stasis
- Altered nutrition: less than body requirements related to increased metabolic needs, impaired gastrointestinal function, loss of body fluid
- Body image disturbance related to burn injury potential long-term dependency and therapy

Nursing interventions

- Assess and record vital signs. I and O, lung sounds and weight, evidence of edema or respiratory distress
- Assess and document wound or other drainage Encourage/restrict fluids to maintain predetermined I and O
- Review electrolyte levels and other lab tests-report abnormalities to physician
- Monitor urine output, specific gravity, daily weight
- Assess and document level of orientation and weakness
- Institute safety precautions and rest periods PRN
- Spend time with patient; listen to fears and concerns
- Identify patient support systems and use in planning care
- Explain hospital resources such as counseling, social services, and pastoral care and initiate referrals as requested
- Assess and document patient pain levels on a scale of 0 to 10 every 2 to 3 hours
- Use a variety of comfort measures such as positioning and massage to increase patient comfort
- Teach patient relaxation, distraction, and guided imagery techniques
- Consult with the physician, O.T., and others to assist in pain management
- Assess lung sounds, respiratory rate and depth, skin color, and sputum production every 4 to 8 hours or more often as needed
- Monitor lab values and report changes. Administer oxygen as needed
- Reduce oxygen need by using pain and anxiety reduction techniques and pacing activity as needed
- Monitor for signs and symptoms of infection and document findings:

elevated temp and pulse
appearance of wound
urine output and appearance

- Use special protective techniques to reduce risks of contamination for patient and to prevent transfer of infection present to self and other patients
- Instruct patient and family on signs and symptoms of infection and factors that reduce risk
- Daily weight, monitor I and O, calorie count, lab values
- Assess bowel sounds and gastrointestinal function and document
- Encourage fluids, high-protein, and high-calorie foods, if permitted
- Arrange consultation with dietician and reinforce instructions
- Encourage family to bring in preferred foods, if allowed, and modify environment as possible to provide pleasant mealtime experience
- Encourage patient and family to verbalize feelings, concerns, and grief
- Assist patient and family to identify personal strengths and coping strategies
- Identify in- and out-patient resources and help pt to contact as needed
- Provide care that maintains privacy and personal dignity

Expected outcomes

- No evidence of fluid deficit:
    Vital signs within normal limits (Specify for individual)
    Balanced I and O
    Serum electrolytes, hemoglobin, hematocrit within normal limits (specify) mucous membranes moist, denies thirst, tissue turgor elastic
- No evidence of fluid excess:
    No evidence of edema
    Weight constant (specify range)
    Lung sounds clear
    Vital signs within normal limits (specify)
- Able to verbalize fears and concerns
- Identifies strategies to reduce fear
- Able to rest, sleep and participate in care and decision making
- States pain 0 to 3 on scale of 10 and reports relief of pain after medication
- Able to rest, sleep 6-8 hours every night and participate in ADLs without significant increase in pain levels
- Demonstrates ability to use noninvasive techniques such as relaxation, distraction, and guided imagery for pain relief

- Lungs clear, no congestion or hoarseness
- Skin pink, no cyanosis
- ABGs within normal limits for pt
- Demonstrates ability to DB and use supportive oxygen equipment
- Afebrile
  WBCs within normal limits
- Urine clear—no sx of UTI
- No purulent drainage or odor from burned areas
- Patient and family verbalize signs and symptoms of infection and risk factors

- Daily intake of _____ calories (3000 to 5000 usual range
- Serum albumin, nitrogen levels within normal limits I and O equal
- Can describe prescribed diet and indicates willingness to follow it
- Acknowledges actual change in appearance and function
- Maintains relationships with significant others/staff
- States willingness to use identified resources after discharge

is a result of a chemical injury, it is washed with copious amounts of warm water before cleansing and covering with a dry dressing.[46] Strict asepsis is essential to avoid wound contamination and subsequent infection.

Morphine sulfate or diazepam (Valium) or both may be given to reduce pain and apprehension. Medications are not given intramuscularly because tissue absorption is poor in the burn patient as a result of the reduced blood supply to the tissues. Reduced dosages given intravenously have been found effective. Antibiotics and tetanus prophylaxis are usually given.

The initial treatment of the patient will take place in the hospital emergency room. If a burn treatment center is available, the patient with major burns will be transferred there as soon as his initial needs are met. The patient's clothing should be placed in a bag and sent with the patient to the burn center, where the staff may need to examine its composition. If admitted to the general hospital, the patient will be placed in an intensive care unit or a regular medical or surgical unit. The patient should be placed in reverse isolation in a private room in a clean area of the hospital. Nursing diagnoses commonly seen in the patient with burns are identified in the box at left and above.

Expected outcomes: emergent period. The following should be observed in the burn patient after proper intervention during this period:
Causes of further injury removed
Arterial blood gases within normal limits
Peripheral pulses palpable
Urinary output greater than 30 ml per hour
Blood pressure above 100/70
Expresses feelings of safety and comfort
Bowel sounds present, with passing of flatus
Lungs clear, respiration within normal limits

The Acute Phase

During the acute, or initial hospitalization phase, the major burn victim is usually cared for in a special burn unit. The burn care team consists of the physician, nurse, social worker, and the many therapists who must coordinate activities to plan for the successful treatment of the patient.

Objectives of Treatment

Each patient must be considered individually because the cause, depth, and extent of the burn, the patient's age, preexisting disease, and the patient's emotional reaction to the injury will determine the methods of treatment selected by the physician. Although different methods are employed, the basic objectives are always the same:
1. Prevention and treatment of shock
2. Relief of pain
3. Prevention of infection
4. Healing of open wounds
5. Restoration of normal function and appearance
6. Preservation of emotional equilibrium
7. Return to the social and work environment

Methods of Wound Treatment—Medical Management

Initially, the burn wounds are cleansed and debrided. Hair is clipped or shaved to reduce infection potential. If a burn wound is to heal without surgical intervention, various therapies are needed to keep the area free from dead tissue and bacteria. Wound healing is slow, with the dangers of infection, scarring, and contracture formation ever present. This form of burn treatment generally includes the use of hydrotherapy, topical antimicrobials, and occlusive dressings.

Hydrotherapy

Hydrotherapy, or tubbing the burn victim, is usually used in combination with some other method. Once a day, for not more than 30 minutes, the patient is immersed in a solution of either normal saline, plain water, or a balanced electrolyte solution. Nonirritating cleansing agents may also be used. Dressings are removed before the patient is placed in a tub unless they are adhered to the wound. Immersion in the solution facilitates removal of dressings that have adhered and loosens slough, eschar, exudate, and topical medications. The tub also provides an excellent place for the patient to be bathed and exercise his extremities. A whirlpool provides the ideal form of hydrotherapy.

The tub must be cleaned thoroughly between each use, and the use of plastic liners for the tub can save time and prevent cross-contamination. The patient is placed on a narrow frame called a plinth, and plastic covers are available. Long plastic gloves are worn by the person working with the patient in the tank, and plastic aprons, masks, and caps must be worn if the patient's wounds are exposed. The patient must be observed for chilling. Patients with newly grafted areas are not usually given full body baths until the graft is healed, which takes 3 to 7 days. If there is a fine-mesh inner gauze over a fairly fresh grafted area, it should be left in place while the patient is in the tub. The gauze over a donor area is also not disturbed unless it loosens.

Topical antimicrobials

Mafenide acetate (Sulfamylon Acetate). Organisms most often involved in infection of burn patients include *Staphylococus aureus*, hemolytic streptococci, and *Pseudomonas aeruginosa*. Mafenide has been found to be a safe, effective adjunct in preventing infection, and some believe that it is more effective than silver nitrate.

Silver nitrate method. The use of silver nitrate for treating burns is based on its bacteriostatic and infection-preventing properties. After thorough cleansing of the wounds, the burns are wrapped with dressings saturated with a solution of distilled water containing 0.5% silver nitrate. The dressings must be thoroughly soaked and thick enough to hold large amounts of solution. The entire dressing is then covered with two layers of prebleached stockinette. The dressings must be rewet every 2 to 4 hours so that the solution is in direct contact with the skin at all times.

Povidone-iodine ointment. Povidone-iodine ointment 10% and solution (Betadine) are now being used in the care of burn wounds because of their broad spectrum of microbicidal action. Betadine ointment can be used alone or in conjunction with Betadine solution and may be used with or without dressings.

Silver sulfadiazine 1%. Silver sulfadiazine 1% (Silvadene) was approved for general use in the United States in 1974. It is a water-soluble cream that can be applied directly to the burn area using a sterile gloved hand. The wounds may be left exposed, and the cream is reapplied, as necessary, when it is rubbed off. A layer of cream 2 to 4 mm thick should be applied so that the wound is not visible through the cream. A single-layer gauze dressing can be impregnated with Silvadene and applied to the wound and secured with stretch gauze or tube dressings. If the wounds are draining heavily or are infected, the dressings may be changed as often as three times a day. Silvadene cream can be bactericidal for up to 48 hours. The area covered with the cream must be cleansed thoroughly to prevent buildup.

Sulfonamide therapy is known to increase the possibility of brain damage caused by elevated bilirubin levels (kernicterus). For this reason, Silvadene should not be used for a pregnant woman who is near term, on premature infants, or on infants during their first month of life.

Surgical Management

Surgical care of burn wounds may involve only periodic debridement (removal of dead tissue) of an area that is being treated by the medical methods above. If the burn wound is severe and no dermis remains to allow tissue regeneration, skin grafting will be necessary. This involves removal of dead tissue and possibly the underlying fatty tissue and the application of a skin graft or an artificial covering. Closing a burn wound quickly will decrease the potential for infection and scarring. It also results in decreased pain and fluid loss. The only permanent graft is an **autograft,** skin that is removed from a donor site on the burn victim. Any other form of wound cover is temporary and will eventually be rejected by the burn victim's immune system. Since the burn victim is initially medically unstable and unable to withstand autografting procedures, temporary grafts play a major role in early therapy. These include:

1. **Homograft (allograft).** The skin from another person. This may be from a living

relative or, more commonly, from a cadaver or skin grown in a culture. These may remain in place 3 to 5 weeks before rejection occurs.

2. **Xenograft (heterograft).** Skin from another animal species. Pig skin is the most common with the major disadvantage being early breakdown and potential for infection.

3. **Synthetic skin substitutes.** One example is collagen dressings (Biobrane). They have a long storage life and can provide wound cover for 2 months or longer until autograft is possible.[14]

In addition to classification by material, grafts are also categorized by depth (Figure 24-15). A full-thickness graft includes the epidermis and all of the dermis and is generally used for reconstruction. When a full-thickness graft is taken, the donor site will also need grafting. A split-thickness graft leaves some dermis at the donor site, which allows that site to heal. The split-thickness graft may be applied as is to the burn wound as a sheet graft for the best cosmetic result. It may also be altered after removal from the donor site by a mechanical device that creates a mesh pattern of small slits. This mesh graft can be expanded to cover a larger surface area and allows drainage from the wound site.

The patient receives a general anesthetic for the grafting procedure, and on return from the operating room will have two surgical sites that require care: the donor site and the grafted area. There are various types of dressings used for the grafted area, including fine-mesh petroleum gauze held in place by cotton pads and bandages. Some physicians prefer that the area be left open to the air. Most physicians apply a light pressure dressing to ensure that the graft will remain in close contact with the burn site. Care must be taken by the nursing staff during the first 48 hours not to move the patient in any manner that would disrupt this surface contact. If dressings are used, the nurse never removes them unless told to do so by the physician. In other cases dressings are applied and a daily inspection may be done for evidence of infection. Since many methods are used, the nurse will have to become familiar with the particular procedure desired by the physician. The care of the donor site will also vary. It may be covered with gauze and pressure bandages, or it may have a layer of fine-mesh gauze and be left open to the air. Analgesics may be needed for pain, and the ambulatory patient often finds that

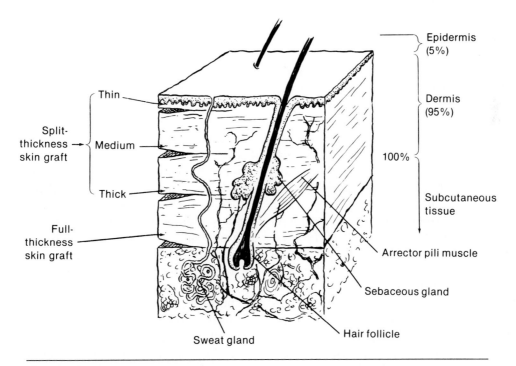

Figure 24-15
Layers of skin involved in various types of skin grafts. Thickness of epidermis and dermis pictured here is typical of that found on lateral thigh of adult.

he has more discomfort from the donor site than from the grafted area. When the donor site is the thigh, walking may be difficult. Not all grafted skin may grow, and repeat grafts may be required.

Nursing Management During the Acute Phase
Monitoring weight and intake and output
Careful measurement in recording fluid intake and urinary output is important to determine proper fluid replacement and to prevent complications. Obtain and record a preburn weight for the patient, since it will assist the physician in determining the patient's fluid needs.

Positioning. Proper positioning of the patient is important to prevent contractures, decubitus ulcers, foot drop, and pulmonary complications. Care of the patient may be facilitated by using a specialty bed that alternates pressure on body surfaces. Flotation therapy has been used successfully for severely burned patients. Flotation prevents pressure areas and allows blood flow to all areas of the body. This enhances nourishment of the cells, promotes healing, and helps to prevent decubitus ulcers. The sensation of floating is soothing and relaxing and lessens pain and tension, and the patient is able to move about more freely. The physical therapist may assist with both passive and active range of motion exercises, and the patient should be encouraged to assist with his own exercises. The patient should not be placed in Fowler's position, and the knee gatch of the bed should not be elevated, since both will contribute to contractures. When the patient is in the supine position, hyperextension of the head will help to prevent contractures when the neck is burned. Splinting and exercise programs may be instituted to prevent deformities. A major objective of care is to encourage the patient to participate actively in his own care when his condition has stabilized. Depending on the patient's condition, early ambulation is encouraged.

Prevention of infection. Some hospitals maintain rooms in which dressings are changed under aseptic conditions, or sometimes patients are taken to the operating room for dressing changes, and light anesthetics are administered. Medical centers and large hospitals are developing self-contained burn units. Regardless of the method of treatment used, all personnel caring for the patient should observe the practice of thorough handwashing before providing any care. When dressings are changed and while providing any care when the exposure method is used, a gown, mask, and sterile gloves must be worn, and

the patient should wear a mask to protect himself from organisms present in his own respiratory tract. If visitors are allowed in the room, they should be required to follow the same procedure. Antibiotics are usually administered to the patient to aid in preventing infection. Treatment will depend partly on the conditions surrounding the injury. Persons with respiratory tract infections should not be allowed near the patient. When there are burns about the perineal area, care must be taken to prevent infection from fecal contamination. This may be especially important, and difficult, in children.

Relief of pain. When burns are severe, the patient will need medication for pain. When severe edema is present, medication to relieve pain should be given intravenously. Morphine or meperidine hydrochloride (Demerol) may be given intravenously as a continuous infusion or via a patient-controlled analgesia (PCA) pump. Medication should be given prior to any treatment or procedure that will be painful to the patient.

Diet. Nothing is given by mouth for the first 24 to 48 hours. Many burn patients have nausea and vomiting, and a nasogastric tube is usually inserted to prevent abdominal distention and paralytic ileus. After 24 hours if there is no vomiting, oral fluids may be started. When the physician has ordered a clear-liquid diet, the nurse should offer 30 to 60 ml an hour and increase the amount as tolerated. If the patient can tolerate it, a high-calorie, high-protein diet will be started in 7 to 10 days. Caloric requirements may exceed 5000 daily. Until the patient is able to consume a diet that can provide the required calories, parenteral hyperalimentation may be necessary. If the gastrointestinal tract is capable of absorbing nutrients, enteral hyperalimentation may be used. The oral fluids taken by the patient in the early days of treatment will not provide the required nutrients and calories, and enteral hyperalimentation will improve the patient's nutritional status and therefore the prognosis. Even the patient consuming a full, general diet may lack the appetite to eat the amount and variety of foods needed to deliver the total calorie requirement. Small, frequent feedings should be given. The use of between-meal high-protein drinks will aid in meeting caloric requirements.

Supportive care. After admission of the patient, the bed may not be changed before the second or third day, and a sufficient number of persons should be available to assist. Medication for pain should be administered 30 to 45 minutes before beginning the procedure. Thereafter the bed is changed only as necessary. The patient needs special mouth care, and lemon juice and glycerin may be used. If the lips are not burned, cold cream or a water-soluble jelly should be applied. A retention catheter is usually inserted, and care should be taken to prevent urinary tract infection by maintaining a sterile closed system of drainage.

If the feet have not been burned, ambulation is generally ordered as soon as possible for the patient. This helps to improve appetite and elimination and to raise the patient's spirits. Soaks or tub baths may be ordered to remove dressings and to prevent damage to the tissues or to remove eschar before skin grafting. The bathtub should be thoroughly scrubbed with soap and water and disinfected, and the temperature of the water should be 100° F (37.8° C).

Emotional care. The burn patient has many emotional problems, especially fear of disfigurement. If the burn is the result of carelessness, there are bound to be feelings of guilt. Most patients realize that long weeks of recovery lie ahead, and the worry over loss of income and expenses may cause endless anxiety. The patient's family may have emotional problems and guilt feelings. Both the patient and the family need opportunities to talk about their problems, and these opportunities may be provided by the nurse, the hospital social worker, or the religious counselor. Plans to assist a family financially may relieve worry. Diversional activities should be provided for the patient to help fill unused time and may be helpful in preventing contractures.

Expected outcomes: acute period

The following results should be seen in the burn patient during the acute period of hospitalization after proper intervention:

Formation of infection-free granulation tissue on burn sites

Graft sites and donor sites free of infection

No pressure sores

Consumption of full diet without nausea or distention

Normal temperature, pulse, and respirations

Full range of motion

Self-esteem intact

Verbalized concerns regarding changes in body image

The rehabilitation period

The patient with major burns usually leaves the hospital with the prospect of a long period of re-

habilitation. In addition to further pain, grafting, and reconstruction in the years ahead, the burn victim must deal with the social and emotional trauma of a profoundly altered body image, as well as the changes in social relationships that may result. Many burn victims are young children and are particularly affected by the social stigma of being "different" from their peers. Long-term physical, social, and psychologic therapy, as well as the financial burdens that these impose, require careful coordination and planning by the burn unit staff before discharge.

At the time of discharge a number of factors must be considered to smooth the transition from patient to citizen. These are not solely nursing responsibilities, but the nurse may need to coordinate home care activities. Discharge planning should include consideration of the following areas:

1. *Emotional adjustment.* The patient and family may experience problems during the rehabilitative period. The hospital social worker may intervene, or the nurse should arrange for psychologic follow-up.

2. *Dressing procedures.* Instructions and supplies should be provided if the family is to continue changing dressings at home. What seems simple in the hospital setting may be problematic in the patient's kitchen or bathroom, so home care follow-up and supervision should be provided.

3. *Exercise, splinting, and activities of daily living.* The nurse should observe the patient doing these activities prior to discharge. The physical therapist and/or occupational therapist may make follow-up visits to help with these programs.

4. *Medications.* All medications, dosage, effects, and possible contraindications should be fully explained to the patient and family and their level of understanding evaluated.

5. *Return visits and phone numbers for problems.* The patient should be given written instructions for scheduling follow-up care. Arrangements for transportation should be made prior to discharge. Phone numbers of burn unit personnel should be given to the patient for use in case of questions or problems.

6. *Home care or community agency follow-up.* If the hospital does not have a follow-up procedure, arrangements should be made with a community home care agency to provide these services.[14]

NURSING CARE PLAN
Patient with Systemic Lupus Erythematosus

The patient is a 46-year-old female who comes to the emergency department via ambulance with complaints of fever, fatigue, left arm swelling, cellulitis of the left hand, generalized skin pain, weight loss, and overall malaise. She is currently 3 weeks post-surgery for thyroid adenoma and has been maintained on broad spectrum antibiotics. She exhibits the signs and symptoms of systemic lupus erythematosus. In addition to the above symptoms, she has chest pain, alopecia, and photosensitivity. She is allergic to tape, compazine, tylenol, betadine, demerol, codeine, epinephrine, and perfumes.

Past medical history

Hypoglycemia. Lactose intolerance.
Cholecystectomy 1984 (7 years ago).
Hysterectomy, oophrectomy 1988 (3 years ago).
Has cluster headaches (takes 2 Fiorinol tablets 7 times per day).
Wolff-Parkinson White (WPW) syndrome (accelerated conduction syndrome).
Thyroid adenoma surgery 3 weeks ago.

Family history

Father age 72 years—Coronary bypass surgery 2 years ago. Overall health good at current time.
Mother age 68 years—History of mitral valve prolapse.
Sister age 44 years—Also with history of mitral valve prolapse.

Psychosocial data

Unmarried. Lives alone and states she has many close supportive friends.
Employed by large medical center as a pastoral counselor.
Is a registered nurse. Formerly a nursing instructor.
Religion: Roman Catholic—States strong source of comfort.
Has never smoked. Denies use of alcohol and drugs.

Assessment data

Skin: Face has rashlike appearance. More noticeable on left side.
Oral mucosa shows healing of lesions on tongue. Small indentations on right and left sides of tongue.

Both arms affected with skin rashes. Right upper arm has three 1-cm slightly reddened areas that are sensitive to touch.
Entire right arm with edema. On palpation, feels warm.
Radial pulse present.
Left arm appears red and blanched. Is warm and tender to touch.
Diminished radial pulse.
Musculoskeletal: Limited range of motion in both arms due to pain.
Able to bear own weight on legs.
All joints appear swollen.
Respiratory: Lungs clear to auscultation. Regular rate and rhythm (range of 16-20). No signs retractions.
Cardiovascular: Apical pulse 72. Best heard at apex. Normal S1 and S2.
Abdominal: Slightly distended. Bowel sounds heard in all four quadrants. Liver not palpable. Several red, swollen, rashlike areas on abdomen (approximately 1 to 2 cm each). Sensitive and warm to touch.
Lower extremities: Scaly patches present anterior thigh right leg. Bilateral pedal edema.

Lab data

WBC 7,800 Hgb 7.9 Hct 22.8 BUN 19 Electrolytes WNL
Creatinine 0.5 Platelets 82,000.

Vital signs

Currently within normal limits. Fever resolved.
Difficulty in obtaining blood pressure due to bilateral arm skin irritation and edema.

Medications

(Patient taking Fiorinal tablets, 14 per day at home. Agrees to wean off while in hospital.)
Fiorinal tablets, 1 five times per day.
Nystatin oral suspension po QID.
Micro K 10 mg daily.
Clotrimazole troche 10 mg po QID.
Premarin 0.3 mg po daily.
Kenalog in orabase po TID and HS.
Multivitamin with mineral tab 1 po daily.
Solu-medrol 60 mg IV piggy back every 8 hours.
Normal saline flush 2 ml to hep lock BID.

NURSING DIAGNOSIS
Potential for infection related to interruption in skin integrity as evidenced by rash, lesions, and mouth ulcers.

Expected patient outcomes	Nursing interventions	Evaluation for expected outcomes
On a daily basis, patient shows no further evidence of skin breakdown. Patient demonstrates skin inspection techniques prior to discharge. Patient performs routine skin care while in hospital in preparation for discharge.	Inspect skin every shift. Describe and document skin condition. Report changes. Perform prescribed treatment regimen for skin. Avoid all soaps and perfume products. Monitor lab values. Check vital signs for increasing infection. Maintain infection control standards. Teach to patient. Provide mouth care at least every shift. Inspect for new oral lesions. Provide supportive measures. Assist with general hygiene and comfort measures. Administer pain medication and monitor effectiveness. Use egg crate mattress. Change position at least every 2 hours when awake. Encourage patient to express her feelings related to skin condition.	Patient's skin lesions remain infection free and show signs of healing as evidenced by presence of granulated tissue and decrease in the size and depth of lesions. Patient's mouth lesions improve leading to increased nutritional intake. Patient demonstrates skin inspection techniques and performs routine skin care. Patient is maintained in proper body alignment and has a degree of comfort while resting.

NURSING DIAGNOSIS

Mobility impairment related to decreased range of motion and muscle weakness.

Expected patient outcomes	Nursing interventions	Evaluation for expected outcomes
Patient demonstrates increased mobility. Patient shows no evidence of contractures, venous stasis, thrombus formation, or skin breakdown. Patient attains the highest degree of mobility possible within the confines of her disease. Patient states her feelings about limitations.	Encourage patient to verbalize pain or discomfort. Observe nonverbal cues of pain, including favoring a body part and grimacing. Observe patient's ability for mobilization daily. Report any changes or progress. Provide supportive measures—padding to skin areas that are prone to breakdown (heels, elbows). Encourage patient's active movement by assisting devices such as trapeze bar, walker, or cane. Implement range of motion exercises every shift, especially after administration of pain medications. Progress from passive to active ROM, as tolerated. Reposition patient every 2 hours and provide meticulous skin care. (Use patient's own hypoallergenic products). Reinforce teachings regarding need for increased mobilization.	Patient demonstrates increased mobility. Patient shows no evidence of contractures, skin breakdown, venous stasis, thrombus formation, hypostatic pneumonia, or other complications. Patient attains highest mobility level possible. Patient discusses limitations imposed by mobility problems and states adaptations needed in ADLs.

Continued on next page.

Expected patient outcomes	Nursing interventions	Evaluation for expected outcomes
	Teach relaxation exercises. Discuss use of distraction methods. Plan care with rest periods between. Promote progressive mobilization to maximum patient tolerance. Encourage patient to discuss feelings related to altered mobility.	

NURSING DIAGNOSIS

Alteration in nutrition related to nausea, vomiting, decreased appetite, and mouth lesions as evidenced by weight loss, dehydration on admission, and muscle weakness.

Expected patient outcomes	Nursing interventions	Evaluation for expected outcomes
Patient shows no further evidence of weight loss. Patient consumes a minimum of 2000 calories per day. Patient develops a plan to monitor and maintain target weight at discharge. Patient's mouth lesions show improvement on a daily basis.	Obtain and record patient's weight daily. Monitor fluid intake and output. Force fluids up to 800 ml per shift. Offer ginger ale and fruit juices that are favorites. Discuss food preferences identifying cultural and dietary selections. Patient prefers a vegetarian diet with rice at all meals. Assess and record bowel sounds every shift. Monitor for distention and constipation. Provide small portions per feeding with between-meal snacks. Discuss high calorie foods and advantages to using them. Provide mouth care prior to and after meals while lesions are most painful. Teach relaxation techniques at first signs of nausea. Refer to dietary consult to explain Kilocalorie body needs. Maintain daily calorie count and identify progress to patient.	Patient shows no further evidence of weight loss. Patient tolerates prescribed diet and can state foods especially high in nutritive value. Patient does not exhibit signs of nausea, vomiting, constipation, diarrhea, or hypoglycemia. Patient consumes the specified amount of calories daily and identifes her plan to maintain caloric intake once discharged.

NURSING DIAGNOSIS

Impaired coping related to the threat to her self-image as evidenced by projection of blame and expressed need for control.

Expected patient outcomes	Nursing interventions	Evaluation for expected outcomes
Patient will verbally describe herself and state a sense of control. Patient will participate in self-care and engage in decisions regarding treatment. Patient will accept responsibility for her own behavior and will interact with her family and others in a socially acceptable manner.	Encourage patient to write a list of positive and negative traits of herself. Provide a structured daily routine. Help patient to make treatment related decisions and encourage autonomy.	Patient uses two positive terms to describe herself. Patient initiates and completes at least three self-care activities daily. Patient makes decisions related to ADLs, self-care and/or treatments. Patient socializes with others.

Expected patient outcomes	Nursing interventions	Evaluation for expected outcomes
	Actively listen to patient when discouraged. Provide positive feedback when patient assumes responsibility for own behavior and care. Allow time for patient to discuss the impact that chronic illness has had on her life. Encourage increased use of family or friend (resources). Help family support patient's level of independence. Inform patient and her family of community resources and support groups available (VNA, Meals on Wheels, and Friendly Visitors). Discuss use of wig to promote self-image.	Patient describes her past methods of coping and identifies positive strategies to assist in this chronic illness.

REFERENCE AND ADDITIONAL READINGS

1. Baerm RL: Current views on the management of pediculosis and scabies. Introduction, Cutis cutaneous medicine for the practitioner: The management of scabies and pediculosis, Proceedings of a Symposium (Suppl):5-6, 1981.
2. Bullock BL and Rosendahl PP (editors): Pathophysiology: adaptations and alterations in function, Boston, 1988, Scott, Foresman & Co.
3. Cooke WM et al: Wound care, New York, 1986, Churchill Livingstone Inc.
4. Cuzzell J: Wound care forum: the new RYB color code, AJN 88(10):1342-1346, 1988.
5. Dagher FJ (editor): Cutaneous wounds, New York, 1985, Futura Publishing Co Inc.
6. Dyer C: Burn wound management: an update, Plastic Surg Nurs 8(1):6-12, 1988.
7. Feller I and Jones CA: Basic burn care, Ann Arbor, Mich., 1975, National Institute for Burn Medicine.
8. Feustel DE: Pressure sore prevention: aye, there's the rub, Nursing 82 12(4):78-83, 1982.
9. Hanson B and Hemmingway B: The great imitator, understanding lupus erythematosus, J Pract Nurs 31(6):13-16, 1981.
10. Hill MJ: The skin: anatomy and physiology, Dermatol Nurs 2(1):13-17, 1990.
11. Kinzie V and Lace C: What to do for the severely burned, RN 43:47-51, 1989.
12. Krasner D (editor): Chronic wound care: a clinical source book for healthcare professionals, King of Prussia, Penn, 1990, Health Management Publications.
13. Laudano JB, Leach EE and Armstrong RB: Acne: therapeutic perspectives with an emphasis on the role of isotretinon, Dermatol Nurs 2(6):328-336, 1990.
14. Martin LM: Nursing implications of today's burn care techniques, RN 43(5):26-32, 1989.
15. Motta GJ: Calcium alginate topical wound dressings: a new dimension in the cost-effective treatment of exudating dermal wounds and pressure sores, Ostomy/Wound Management 25:52-56, 1989.
16. The plain truth about hair transplants, Brecksville, Ohio, Cleveland Hair Clinics.
17. Rasmussen E: The diagnosis and management of scabies in adults. Cutis cutaneous medicine for the practitioner: The management of scabies and pediculosis, Proceedings of a Symposium (Suppl):7-9, 1981.
18. Robinson JK: Moh's surgery for skin cancer, Am J Nurs 82:282-283, 1982.
19. Rosen T, Lanning M, and Hill M: The nurse's atlas of dermatology, Boston, 1983, Little, Brown and Co Inc.
20. Willey T: High-tech beds and mattress overlays: a decision guide, AJN 89(9):1105-1252, 1989.
21. Yotter M: Contact dermatitis: nursing intervention, Dermatol Nurs 2(5):267-269, 1990.

PROBLEMS AFFECTING
Mobility

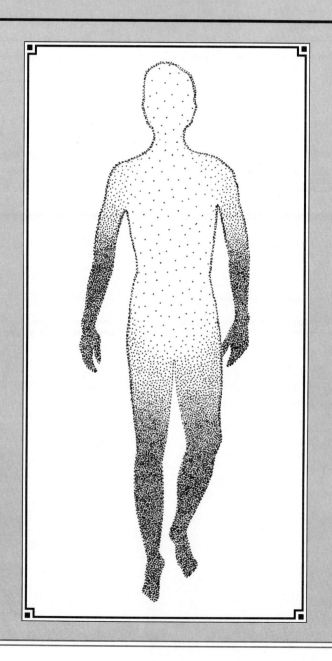

OBJECTIVES

1. Describe the structure and function of the musculoskeletal system.

2. Discuss the physiology of fracture healing, including the role of hematomas, granulation tissue, and callus formation.

3. Compare the pathophysiology, findings, and nursing interventions for patients with rheumatoid arthritis and osteoarthritis.

4. Discuss the drugs and dietary restrictions used in the treatment of gout.

5. Define and describe the assessment of bursitis.

6. Differentiate between osteomyelitis and tuberculosis of bone.

7. Discuss the nurse's role in the diagnosis of and intervention for torticollis and congenital dislocation of the hip.

8. Compare and contrast the interventions for sprains, dislocations, and fractures.

9. Discuss the nursing care of the patient in a Thomas splint with a Pearson attachment.

10. Identify the various types of fractures.

11. Discuss the advantages of treating hip fractures by internal fixation.

12. Identify nursing measures that promote drying, and preserve shape and integrity of a newly applied cast.

13. Describe methods for assessing circulation, nerve damage, and infection in a body part enclosed in a cast or splint.

14. Discuss the advantages and disadvantages associated with each type of turning frame.

15. Discuss the nursing measures for preparing the patient who has had an amputation and is being fitted with a prosthesis.

16. Differentiate between the assessment of muscular dystrophy and cerebral palsy.

17. Identify nursing measures that help prevent complications associated with immobility.

18. Discuss the psychosocial needs of immobilized patients and their families.

STRUCTURE AND FUNCTION OF THE MUSCULOSKELETAL SYSTEM

Structure

The musculoskeletal system consists of bones, joints, and muscles. Within this system, muscles are attached to bones by fibrous cords called *tendons.* Bones are held together at the joints by bands of tough tissue called *ligaments. Cartilage* is a somewhat flexible tissue connecting bones and acting as a shock absorber; for example, cartilage is found between the vertebrae of the spinal column.

Bones are composed of living cells surrounded by an intercellular matrix. This intercellular substance around bone cells is infiltrated with calcium salts, making bones hard and providing strength and rigidity. This *calcified intercellular substance* is permeated by a system of tiny canals filled with tissue fluid, through which bone cells are nourished and waste is removed.

Bones are of various shapes. *Long bones* are found in the extremities, *short bones* in the hands and feet. Flat bones protect vital structures such as the brain and organs located in the thorax. Irregular bones include the vertebrae and other small bones found throughout the body.

Each long bone consists of six major parts. The *diaphysis* is the long shaft of the bone, and the two *epiphyses* are the ends. The *medullary cavity* is the space filled with bone marrow. In the adult, the medullary cavity is filled with fatty yellow marrow and the ends of the long bones contain blood forming red marrow. This cavity is lined with the *endosteum,* which consists of cells that form new bone as needed. The *periosteum* is the fibrous membrane that covers the outside of the bone, except at the joints, and contains blood vessels, lymphatic vessels, and nerves. The inner layer of the periosteum also contains bone-forming cells. Finally, each end of the long bone is covered with *articular cartilage,* which cushions blows to the joint.

Bones in children are more flexible than those in adults. As bones grow, more calcium is deposited and they become rigid and inflexible. With advanced age, however, calcium may be lost from bones, causing them to become porous and brittle.

To effectively put the patient's joints through a full range of motion, the nurse should have an understanding of joints. Some joints are freely movable, such as the hinge joints in the elbows and knees. The motions of these joints are called flexion and extension. Shoulder and hip joints are ball-and-socket joints and have a rotating motion. Other joints are slightly movable. For example, the joints between the vertebral bodies provide limited motion of the spine. Some joints are immovable and are found in places such as the cranium. Only those joints that are freely movable can be put through a full range of motion.

Although movement of the body depends largely on contraction of the muscles, mobility is actually a cooperative function of bones, muscles, and joints.

Function

The musculoskeletal system has other functions beside locomotion. The bony framework supports the body in an upright position and protects vital organs. Blood cells are formed in the marrow of bones, and bones deposit calcium, which may be used to supply a deficiency in the body fluids. Injury and disease may affect any part of the system and result in deformity or impairment of functions. Some disorders involve both nerves and muscles and are called *neuromuscular disorders.*

POSITION, EXERCISE, AND BODY MECHANICS

Proper positioning of the patient confined to a regimen of bed rest is essential. This is a nursing intervention, and medical orders are not necessary except in certain surgical procedures in which physician's preferences vary. Orthopedic patients may be required to remain in plaster casts, traction, or other stabilization devices for prolonged periods. Nursing care must emphasize positioning to prevent **contractures,** deformities, or other complications of immobility.

Active and passive exercise of muscles of both the affected and the unaffected extremities is essential for maintaining muscle tone, preventing complications, and preparing for ambulation. Frequently, an exercise program tailored to the individual will be initiated soon after immobilization. Active and passive movement of joints through their full range of motion should be incorporated into the daily activities of physical care and ambulation. Patients may fear that moving a casted extremity or doing prescribed exercises will cause further injury—many are afraid to wiggle their fingers and toes. Specific exercises that prevent thrombophlebitis and help maintain muscle tone include *antithromboembolic* exercises of the calf muscle, along with *quad-setting* and *gluteal-setting* isometric exercises. These are to be performed in the supine position. To encourage circulation and prevent thrombus and embolus development in the calf muscle, patients fully extend their legs and push the back of their knees down on the bed while dorsiflexing their foot. For quad-setting, patients tighten their quadriceps muscles; for gluteal-setting, they tighten and pinch their buttocks together. With each of these exercises, patients may be advised to hold the position to the count of 10. They also may be advised to repeat these exercises 10 times every hour while awake. Exercises designed to strengthen muscles in preparation for ambulation include prescribed weight lifting and *bridging* exercises. To perform the bridging exercise, patients flex their unaffected leg at the knee. They push down on the bed with the sole of their feet, while lifting their back and buttocks off the bed, using the trapeze. They hold themselves in the lifted position with their backs straight for as long as possible. They also may be advised to do this 10 times an hour while awake.

Emphasis also has been placed on the importance of turning patients to prevent pulmonary complications. Too often a comfortable patient objects to being disturbed, and the moving of an obese or comatose patient or a patient in a body cast or traction presents a special challenge for the nurse. However, research has confirmed that turning the patient as little as 12 degrees is sufficient to prevent pulmonary complications, stimulate circulation, and prevent decubitus ulcers. Therefore, all immobilized patients should be turned at least every 2 hours.

The tilt table is a device for helping the patient adjust to an upright position before ambulation. Patients confined to bed rest for long periods may develop hypotension when they sit or stand. Gradual elevation using a tilt table, helps prevent the problem. The tilt table is used to prepare the patient for crutch walking and ambulation and to reduce osteoporosis that develops from immobilization. It also may prevent urinary tract infection by decreasing the pooling of urine in the bladder that results when the patient remains in a supine position.

After injuries to the musculoskeletal system, many patients will need to be taught the proper methods of standing, sitting, walking, stooping, and lifting. Nurses who use their bodies skillfully will be in a much better position to help teach their patients about body mechanics. Consideration of body mechanics will conserve energy, prevent injuries to muscles, avoid fatigue, and promote work efficiency.

NEUROVASCULAR INTEGRITY

Neurovascular impairment is a threat in patients with orthopedic conditions and must be relieved promptly. Impairment of circulation or nerve function can result in tissue necrosis or loss of the use of an extremity. Damage to nerves and blood vessels may result from trauma, surgery, or tight bandages, splints, and casts. Assessment and intervention for arterial vascular compromise is discussed later in this chapter in relation to the serious complication of compartment syndrome. Temporary impairment of the venous circulation in the extremities is more common and should be suspected when edema, coolness, pallor or cyanosis, pain, and numbness or tingling are observed in the fingers or toes. These symptoms may be accompanied by sluggish capillary refill in the nail beds along with absence of radial, pedal, or tibial pulses.

Assessment

To perform an accurate neurovascular assessment, the nurse should always compare the findings in the affected extremity with those in the unaffected extremity. Extremities should be positioned correctly, with the affected arm or leg elevated. An accurate description of sensations should be elicited from the patient. Using the same hand (rather than two hands) to access both extremities may provide a more accurate assessment. To determine true coolness in the affected extremity, both feet must be felt because many people have cool feet under normal circumstances. The foot of the affected extremity may be warmer than the other because of the normal inflammation associated with trauma and surgery. Edema accompanied by warmth and a light, rosy, flesh color usually does not indicate harmful circulatory impairment, particularly if other signs are absent or if it occurs within 48 to 72 hours after trauma or surgery. This warmth and edema will gradually subside. Edema with pallor, cyanosis, and coldness is a sign of circulatory impairment. If swelling is difficult to determine, a comparison of the wrinkles on the toes or fingers of both feet or hands may show stretching of the tissue on the digits in question, indicating slight edema (see box at right).

The *blanching sign* is a test of the rate of capillary refill, which signals the adequacy of circulation. When the nail of each toe or finger is compressed and immediately released, the nail bed should rapidly change from white to pink. Slow or sluggish capillary refill indicates decreased circulation. Each digit should be checked for sensation and motion because all are not innervated by the same nerve. Localized numbness and the inability to flex and extend the digits indicate nerve compression. Increased pain may accompany circulatory impairment. A clear description of the pain with regard to its precise location (along a nerve, over a bony prominence), intensity, and response to movement should be obtained from the patient before pain medication is given.

Palpating the pedal, tibial, or radial pulse may be difficult or impossible when a cast or bandage renders these areas inaccessible. At times, the nurse may be able to reach under a bandage to locate the pulse. Caution must be used, however, if an incision or open wound is underneath and sterile gloves may be required to protect from inadvertent contamination. The presence and strength of the pulse in the affected extremity should be identified and compared to that in the unaffected extremity.

Immediately following surgery or the application of a cast, a neurovascular assessment should be performed every 30 minutes thereafter. Frequently, patients will describe transient tingling and numbness in an extremity, resulting from general immobility. Flexing fingers and toes will relieve this, and the patient should be encouraged to flex whenever these symptoms occur. Neurovascular assessments should be completely and accurately recorded. The previous status of the patient's circulation should be reviewed before each subsequent neurovascular assessment. Such a review provides a baseline for evaluating progress or deterioration of circulatory integrity. When circulatory impairment is suspected, the physician should be notified. Repositioning and elevating the extremity may alleviate the symptoms. Treatment may involve loosening or removing a cast or bandage. Modification of a cast is discussed later in the section on the patient with a cast.

NURSING CARE GUIDELINES
Neurovascular Integrity

Nursing diagnoses

- Alteration in peripheral tissue perfusion related to injury/treatment
- High risk for injury related to neurovascular impairment

Nursing interventions

- Position extremities in alignment; elevate affected extremity
- Compare affected extremity with unaffected extremity, using same hand for palpation
- Test capillary refill
- Check *each* digit for sensation and motion
- Document location and characteristics of pain
- Palpate pedal, tibial, or radial pulses and compare to unaffected extremity
- Look for edema with pallor, cyanosis, and coldness
- Elicit description of sensations from patient

Pain

Specific types of musculoskeletal injuries or disorders produce specific types of pain therefore the nurse must know the nature of the pain to effectively assess and alleviate it. One must differentiate between pain as an expected outcome and pain as a diagnostic sign. Types of pain and how to assess pain are discussed in Chapter 6.

Patients who sustain fractures frequently describe acute, deep, severe pain at the time of injury, which persists until the fracture is reduced and medication is given. This is an expected outcome of traumatic fractures. The pain accompanying a fractured hip can be severe because of muscle spasms and trauma to surrounding nerves. Once a fracture is reduced, the pain becomes more localized and gradually subsides as healing takes place. A recurrence of severe pain after a fracture is reduced and healing begins signals that something is wrong.

A constant aching pain may be the first sign that neurovascular integrity is being compromised. This pain may be increased with passive movement of the extremity and will be accompanied by other signs of neurovascular impairment, such as numbness, paralysis, coolness, and paleness. These findings are diagnostic of a circulatory problem that must be corrected promptly.

Pain associated with spinal column disorders frequently accompanies a long-standing back problem and ranges from sudden and sharp to constant or intermittent aching pain. The pain may extend down one or both extremities and often is influenced by voluntary movement or positioning of the patient. Ongoing precise assessment of the frequency, location, and influencing activity of the pain is necessary for determining progress in both conservative and surgical treatment of spinal disorders.

Because pain associated with musculoskeletal disorders may be severe and persistent, the nurse can anticipate that pain medications may be needed regularly until the pain subsides. Pain medication should be given once the pain has been assessed thoroughly. Additional measures to alleviate the pain by repositioning the affected body region also should be initiated.

The Patient with a Cast

Casts are applied to fractured extremities or other parts of the body for the purpose of maintaining correct alignment of bones during healing. Casts are most frequently applied to fractures that are reduced by closed manipulation. They may also be applied following realignment involving open reduction with internal fixation, as well as following other surgical repairs (see intervention for fractures later in this chapter). Usually, the cast is applied to extend beyond the joints above and below the fracture site.

The application of a plaster cast may be anticipated by the patient, but more often accompanies an unexpected fracture. Once the cast is applied, the patient is faced with a frustrating limitation of movement and an interruption of fulfilling roles and responsibilities. His emotional adjustment may be difficult. The nurse should recognize the patient's need to have many questions answered and to be supported in his adjustment to a changed level of function.

Care of cast

A newly applied cast will set quickly but will take up to 48 hours to dry completely. During this drying time the cast must be handled with the palms of the hands rather than with the fingers to prevent indentations that could create pressure. Casts are positioned and elevated on pillows to prevent pressure from the firm mattress and reduce swelling. Positioning with pillows is shown in Figures 25-1 to 25-3. Cast drying is accompanied by considerable heat, which should be explained to the patient. Ice bags are placed along the side of a cast for 48 hours to combat this heat and to help reduce swelling of the extremity. Once the cast has dried, it should be examined for rough edges, which may need to be trimmed slightly or covered with adhesive *petals*. Petals are rectangular or oval pieces of adhesive with rounded corners, approximately 1 inch by 3 inches in size, which are slipped under the edge of the cast, brought over the edge, and adhered to the top of the cast. Cotton wadding or a stockinette will have been applied under the cast to provide smooth edges. Further care of a plastic cast includes maintaining cleanliness and preventing moisture, which may soften the plaster and cause the cast to crack. Protecting a cast around the genital area from urine and stool can be accomplished by tucking plastic inside the cast and taping it to the outside. If this is done, the skin beneath the plastic must be checked regularly for evidence of irritation or maceration. Use of powder under the cast should be avoided because moisture from the patient's body may cause the powder to clump, resulting in pressure against the skin.

Cleaning a plaster cast is difficult, but small stains on the outside of the cast can be removed by gently rubbing with scouring powder on a dampened dry cloth. Rubbing baby powder on a cast will whiten it and lend a pleasant smell. Spraying the cast with a plastic coating or painting it with white shoe polish is generally not recommended because this prevents the cast from "breathing." Bathing with a cast is possible if the cast is covered with a leakproof plastic bag, and the cast is not submerged.

Performing regular neurovascular assessments on all patients with casts is a critical nursing function. During the neurovascular assessment, the nurse should also feel the entire cast for excessive local warmth and should sniff it for any putrid odor. These signs, along with the patient's description of a localized burning sensation, signal the presence of tissue necrosis from localized cast pressure. When a cast is applied, bony prominences and areas with nerves close to the skin are usually well padded. However, these sites are particularly susceptible to cast pressure, local necrosis, or neurovascular impairment. In the arm, sites are located at the condyles and olecranon processes of the elbow and at the radial and ulnar

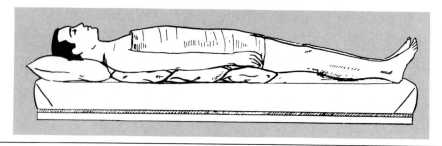

Figure 25-1
Placement of pillows to receive patient in wet body cast.

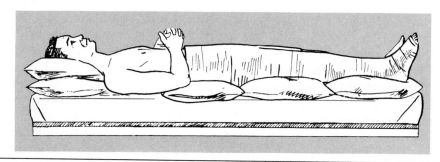

Figure 25-2
Placement of pillows to receive patient in wet hip spica cast.

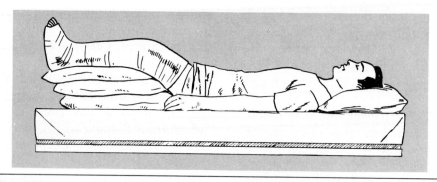

Figure 25-3
Placement of pillows to support extremity in long-leg cast.

styloids; in the leg, at the popliteal space, head of the fibula, lateral aspect of the knee, lateral and medial malleoli, and the heel. Specific measures to relieve circulatory impairment and localized pressure include lengthwise splitting of a cast or cutting a window over the area of pressure. An oscillating saw (cast cutter) is used by the physician to accomplish this; the patient should be assured that the cast will not cut into the skin.

A cast should also be observed for external bloody drainage. This may be expected with certain types of open reduction procedures. The area of drainage should be circled, dated, and timed on the cast; its progression should be monitored, recorded, and reported. Drainage may occur in the direction of gravity, therefore careful examination of the underside of the cast is essential, although the site of an incision may be on the anterior surface of the extremity. Because evidence of bleeding on the cast and development of odor from necrotic tissue may not occur until after considerable blood or tissue has been lost, the nurse should monitor the extremity carefully for other indicators of blood loss and tissue damage.

Skin care of areas close to the cast and of the entire body is important because casts can be heavy and patients may have difficulty moving in bed. Regular inspection of areas usually resting on the bed is vital. Patients need assistance in regular turning and should be positioned in good body alignment with firm supportive pillows. Itching under the cast as the wound heals is usually inevitable and is probably the greatest annoyance to the patient. Little can be done to alleviate this, unless a gauze running the length of the cast was inserted at the time of application, which the patient can pull back and forth. Patients should be cautioned against using knitting needles, wire hangers, or foreign objects to scratch under the cast.

Currently lightweight alternative materials are available for casting. Generally, they consist of fiberglass or fabric tape impregnated with a resin, plastic, or polyurethane hardening agent. These casts dry faster and are lighter, stronger, more porous, less itchy, and easier to move around with than plaster casts. They also are more expensive and are used for casts that do not require frequent changing.

Cast removal

When a cast is removed, the extremity should be moved carefully and supported at the joints. If the patient has been in a cast for a long time, some decalcification has occurred and a spontaneous fracture is always a possibility. In addition, the patient may experience some discomfort once the external support is removed. The skin should be cleansed gently. Exercises to restore strength and mobility are begun. Weight bearing may be restricted until total bone healing takes place.

The box on p. 760 summarizes nursing care of the patient with a cast.

Hip spica and body casts

Hip spica and body casts are large, cumbersome casts. They are worn for long periods (5 months or longer) and require special techniques for turning and general care of the patient. These casts surround the entire trunk and may make the pa-

tient claustrophobic. The hip spica cast extends from below the axilla to the entire length of one or both legs. It is applied to immobilize hip fusions, congenital hip dislocations, or fractures of the hip and femur. The body cast extends from the neck or upper chest to the groin or thigh. It is applied to immobilize spinal fractures, to protect spinal surgery, and to treat scoliosis. Confinement in these casts can be very frightening, with the patient needing to make adjustments to being confined within the cast. The patient may have to eat smaller or more frequent portions of food to be comfortable. A cast that is too tight can cause respiratory complications if the lungs cannot expand fully. The most serious complications from a tight cast is the development of "cast syndrome," which occurs when the superior mesenteric artery presses on or obstructs part of the duodenum. Symptoms of nausea, vomiting, abdominal pain, or intestinal obstruction require that the cast be removed to alleviate the condition. Generally, body casts have a window placed over the diaphragm to allow for expansion of the lungs and to prevent the development of cast syndrome.

The Patient with an Orthopedic Device
Traction

Traction may be applied to any of the extremities, the cervical area, or the pelvic region. *Cervical traction* may be caused when there is severe injury to the cervical vertebrae or spinal cord. *Pelvic traction* may be indicated to relieve pain from injury of the lower back, frequently in the lumbar region. The purpose of traction may be to relieve muscle spasm, which often occurs because of disease or injury. For patients with certain kinds of fractures, traction may be necessary to keep bones in place while healing of bones and soft tissue occurs. It may be used to reduce dislocations or to correct or relieve contractures.

Traction means "pulling." When traction is applied to a lower extremity because of a broken bone, the two ends of the bone are pulled into place. The force of the traction must be stronger than the force of the contraction of surrounding muscles to relax or "stretch" those muscles and allow the bone fragments to be brought into correct alignment. The physician decides on what type of traction and its placement, as well as the weight applied to achieve the desired results. When applied correctly, traction must be equal to countertraction. **Countertraction** is applied either by the patient's own body weight, as in Buck's

NURSING CARE GUIDELINES
The Patient with a Cast

Nursing diagnoses

- Alteration in comfort (pain) related to bone displacement and muscle spasm
- Potential alteration in bowel elimination (constipation) related to inactivity and altered position for elimination
- Deficit in diversional activity related to restrictions imposed by cast
- Impaired management of home maintenance related to restrictions on activity
- High risk for injury related to falls, neurovascular impairment
- Knowledge deficit related to diet to promote bone healing and correct use of ambulatory assistive devices
- Impaired physical mobility related to cast
- Alteration in nutrition (potential for more than body requirements) related to reduced activity
- Self-care deficit in feeding, bathing/hygiene, and dressing/grooming related to cast
- Actual or potential impairment of skin integrity related to trauma, cast irritation, or immobility
- Alteration in tissue perfusion related to edema and cast constriction
- Potential altered respiratory function related to imposed immobility or restricted respiratory movement secondary to cast (body)[1]

Nursing interventions
While cast dries

- Place patient on firm mattress
- Handle cast with palms of hands
- Explain to patient that he or she will feel heat as cast is drying
- Do not cover cast until it is completely dry
- Do not speed drying with heat or lamps; cast may dry on outside but remain weak inside and crack
- Elevate extremity on plastic-covered pillows or support curves of body cast with small pillows
- Avoid weight bearing on walking leg cast for 48 hours

When cast is dry

- Attend to all complaints—they may be a warning of impending complications; do not medicate for pain until cause of pain is clearly identified

- Observe for signs of pressure—pain, burning, and odor
- Check circulation—observe for pain, numbness, tingling, edema, color, blanching and capillary refill, skin temperature, inability to move fingers or toes, and presence and rate of pulse; compare to other extremity
- Protect cast in perineal area from soiling with plastic sheeting
- Cleanse cast with almost dry cloth and abrasive soap or cleanser; whiten and freshen by rubbing in baby powder
- Pull stockinette up and over edge of cast
- Cover edge of cast with adhesive tape petals
- Inspect skin under and at edge of cast for irritation
- Instruct patient not to insert wire hangers, knitting needles, or other sharp instruments to scratch skin under cast
- Assist patient with isometric exercise of affected extremities
- Actively exercise unaffected joints in addition to isometric exercise

When cast is removed

Explain to patient that cast cutter vibrates and cannot cut or injure

After cast is removed, support part with pillows in same position as when part was in cast

Move extremity gently

Wash skin with soap and water, followed by gentle massage with lanolin or baby oil

Assist patient in performing prescribed muscle-strengthening exercises

- If lower extremity is involved:

  Instruct patient to elevate foot when sitting to prevent edema

  Apply elastic bandage or elastic stocking as ordered to provide support

  Reinforce physician's instructions about weight bearing; usually limited after removal of leg cast

Expected outcomes

- Knows rationale for cast application
- Cast integrity is maintained
- Neurocirculatory status is normal
- Cares for cast, observing condition of skin and extremities

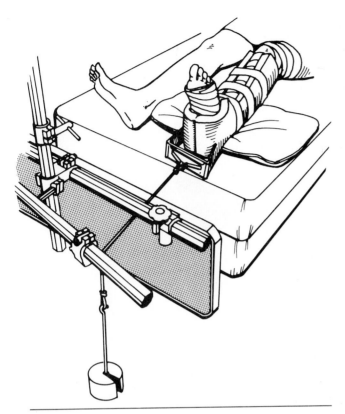

Figure 25-4
Buck's extension. Heel is supported off bed to prevent pressure on heel. Weight hangs free of the bed. Foot is well away from footboard of bed. The limb should lie parallel to the bed unless prevented, as in this case, by a slight knee flexion contracture. *(From Phipps WJ, Long BC, and Woods NF: Medical-surgical nursing: concepts and clinical practice, ed 1, St Louis, 1987, The CV Mosby Co.)*

expansion, or by other weights or devices. Traction may be applied as *skin traction,* in which some material with an adhesive surface is applied directly onto the clean dry skin, or as skeletal traction, in which various devices such as pins or wire are placed through a bone. For cervical traction, tongs or pins, as in the halo ring, are placed against the outer table of the skull. Occasionally, patients are placed in balanced suspension with a splint. This type of traction is generally used to maintain an extremity in a specific position after surgery and may not involve skin or skeletal traction. In all types of traction, ropes, pulleys, weights, and countertraction will be used.

Among the commonly used types of traction is *Buck's extension,* a form of running skin traction applied to the lower extremities (Figure 25-4). Adhesive material is attached to the skin the length of the limb to a point 1 inch above the

malleolus. The adhesive material is then attached to a footplate, which is attached to a rope. The rope is placed over a pulley at the foot of the bed, and the desired weight is attached at the end. This is a simple type of traction that can be adapted for home use. It cannot be used if there is an open wound in the area to be covered by adhesive or if the patient is allergic to the adhesive material.

Regardless of the materials and method used to apply Buck's extension, the nursing care of the patient's extremity is the same. Impaired circulation resulting from compression of the dorsalis pedis artery must be prevented. Decreased circulation to this area can result in ischemia, which causes paralysis. The bony prominences of the foot and ankle must be observed for evidence of strap pressure and felt or cotton should be used to protect the Achilles tendon from irritation.

The upper aspect of the calf also should be examined closely. The peroneal nerve lies close to the surface in this area and compression against the bone can result in paralysis and plantar flexion and inversion of the foot. The area should be well padded before the tape is applied, and the foot should be observed daily for the tendency to turn inward toward the midline of the body. Any complaints of burning or pain under the tape should be reported immediately.

An innovation in the application of Buck's extension has been developed by the DePuy Company. The usual adhesive straps wrapped with Ace bandages are replaced with a foam rubber boot, which is secured with a velcro strap. The boot has a footplate at the bottom and comes in sizes to fit children and adults. The foam boot is applied directly to the skin, and weights are attached to the spreader bar. When applied correctly, the edges of the boot come together or overlap completely. If the patient does not require continuous traction, the boot can be removed easily for bathing and ambulation (Figure 25-5).

Bryant's traction is used for children weighing under 35 pounds with a fracture of the shaft of the femur. Buck's extension is applied to both legs, which are then flexed at the hips to about 90 degrees. The ropes are attached to each footplate and are strung over two pulleys on an overhead bar at the level of the child's pelvis, maintaining the legs in suspension at right angles to the body. A second set of pulleys is placed overhead near the foot of the bed to allow free suspension of the weights. When the weights are applied, the child's hips should be elevated just

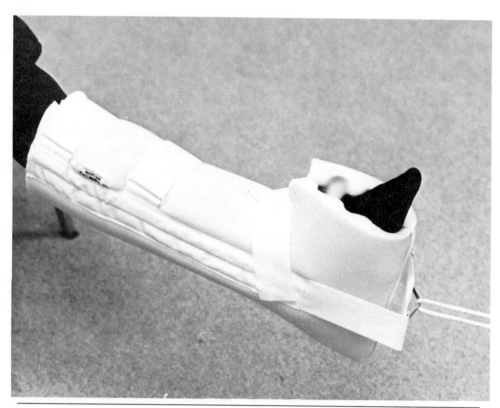

Figure 25-5
Foam boot splint used to apply skin traction to lower extremities. Black stocking provides contrast for photography only; boot is applied directly to skin. *(Courtesy DePuy, Warsaw, Inc.)*

off the bed. This position is maintained for 2 to 4 weeks until an adequate callus is formed at the fracture site. Some type of restraint often is necessary to keep a young child in the proper position. The position of the bandages should be checked to prevent pressure over the dorsum of the foot or around the heel cord. The child's limbs must be checked frequently for discoloration, pallor, loss of motion, or loss of sensation. Treatment with Bryant's traction usually is followed with the application of a hip spica cast.

Russell's traction consists of skin traction, often Buck's extension, in addition to a sling under the knee that is attached to ropes and pulleys to provide suspension (Figure 25-6). The rope is brought overhead to a pulley and then down to a pulley at the foot of the bed. The same rope is brought back to a pulley on the footplate of Buck's extension and then back over the foot of the bed to a fourth pulley before dropping down to the attached weight. This creates running traction plus a balanced traction or countertraction. It may be used in fractures of the femur or hip and coun-

tertraction is provided by elevating the foot of the bed.

Firm pillows should support the entire thigh and calf, maintaining a 20-degree angle between the bed and the hip and leaving the heel free of the bed. The popliteal space under the sling should be examined frequently for irritation. A piece of felt placed in the sling may prevent wrinkling and reduce pressure areas. Because the affected limb is suspended rather than resting on the bed, movement will not alter the position of the traction. The suspension apparatus takes up any slack in the traction caused by movement, and the line of the traction remains unchanged. This provides greater freedom of movement for the patient and greater ease for the nurse providing care.

A *Thomas splint*, either half ring or full ring, frequently is used in another type of suspension traction (Figure 25-7). When the half-ring splint is used, the half ring is positioned over the anterior aspect of the thigh. Proper weights and adequate countertraction prevent the half ring from

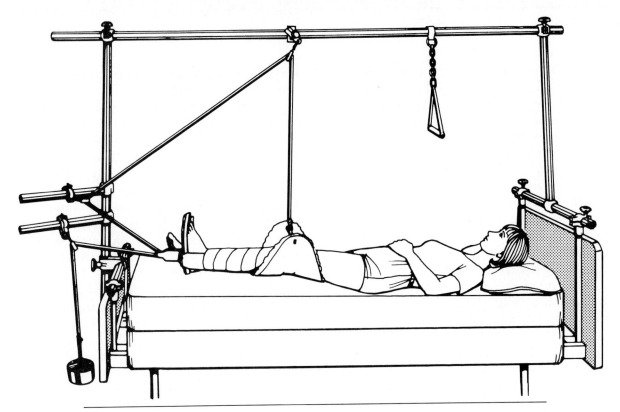

Figure 25-6

Russell traction. Hip is slightly flexed. Pillows may be used under lower leg to provide support and keep the heel free of the bed. *(From Phipps WJ, Long BC, and Woods NF: Medical-surgical nursing: concepts and clinical practice, ed 1, St Louis, 1987, The CV Mosby Co.)*

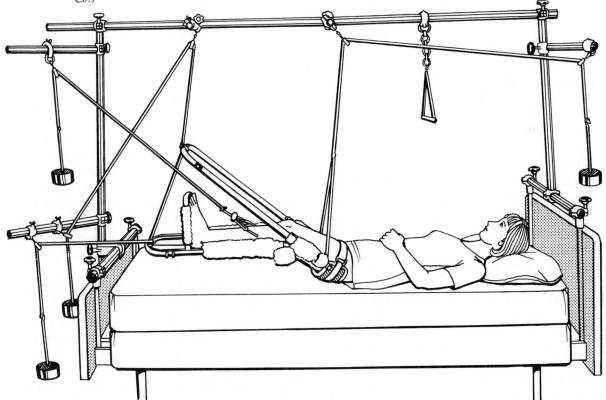

Figure 25-7

Balanced suspension with Thomas splint and Pearson attachment. This apparatus can be used alone, or, as in this case, with skeletal traction. *(From Phipps WJ, Long BC, and Woods NF: Medical-surgical nursing: concepts and clinical practice, ed 1, St Louis, 1987, The CV Mosby Co.)*

causing pressure in the groin and on the anterior aspect of the thigh. The full ring of a Thomas sling is covered with smooth, moisture-resistant leather. Pressure from the ring on the adductor and ischial area must be avoided at all times. A Pearson attachment can be fastened to a Thomas splint to support the leg from the knee down. The *Pearson attachment* usually is horizontal to and just high enough to swing clear of the bed. The patient's knee should correspond with the point where the Pearson attachment is fastened to the splint. The limb is usually held in a neutral position or in slight **internal rotation** and **abduction**. The patient must be positioned straight in bed; when lying diagonally, abduction is lost. The patient in suspension traction may turn toward the limb in traction.

Skeletal traction. Traction can be applied directly to the bone by surgically inserting a pin or wire into the bone. The *Steinmann steel pin* and *Kirschner wire* are most commonly used. Weights are attached to the pin or wire while the patient is placed in suspension traction.

Cervical traction. Cervical traction is a form of skeletal traction used to immobilize the cervical and upper thoracic spine. Tongs or a halo ring containing metal pins are placed against the patient's skull and traction is applied. When tongs are used, the points of the tongs either rest against the skull or pierce it slightly; with the halo ring, the pins are placed approximately 0.05 mm into the skull. Insertion of pins is generally performed under local anesthesia.

The advantage of halo traction is that it can be attached to a rigid vest, allowing for the patient to sit upright and to ambulate. Caution must be used when the patient is upright because peripheral vision is restricted and the patient's balance is affected by the weight of the halo vest, which is approximately 7 pounds.[16]

Whenever skeletal traction is used, care of the pin or wire insertion site is required. Aseptic technique must be used to prevent infection, which can be severe if bacteria enters the wound and infects the underlying bone. Pin care consists of cleaning the area around the pin or wire with sterile solution (usually normal saline) and drying thoroughly. Evidence of redness, inflammation, or drainage from the pin site should be reported to the physician.

Pelvic traction. Pelvic traction is applied by using a canvas girdle that fits snugly over the crests of the ilia and the pelvis. On either side are webbing straps joined to form one strap on each side at about midthigh. These are attached to ropes and weights. Light weights are applied at first and gradually increased. The iliac crests must be examined frequently for pressure, and padding may be necessary for thin patients.

Nursing intervention. The nurse usually is not responsible for constructing traction. Many hospitals have personnel who are trained and responsible for setting up the type of traction ordered by the physician. If such persons are not available, the physician assumes the responsibility for constructing the traction.

In many instances the patient will be required to lie flat in bed and may not be permitted to sit up or turn fully on either side. The nurse caring for patients in traction must be familiar with the amount of movement the physician allows.

The skin around the edge of the adhesive tape must be observed for irritation or abrasion. If the tape seems to be pulling or loosening, it must be reinforced or replaced. Extremities should be checked several times a day for color, numbness, cyanosis, pallor, pain, and edema. The skin over the ankles and the heel must be watched for pressure areas and irritation. The patient's position and body alignment in bed are extremely important, as is avoiding **internal** or **external rotation** of extremities.

The patient should be positioned in good alignment at all times. The traction, height of backrest, knee elevator, and elevating blocks should not be changed unless ordered by the physician. Although the patient usually is turned toward the affected side, specific turning instructions should be obtained from the physician before a regular turning schedule is begun. The skin beneath and around the traction splint (Figure 25-6) or sling should be observed frequently for signs of pressure. In addition, the traction weights should hang free of the frame or bed and should never rest on the floor.

When giving care, several persons may be needed to lift the patient so the back may be washed and massaged. Inspection of the sacral area for pressure points should not be overlooked. Massage of the area should be done several times a day and may be accomplished by running the hand under the back without lifting the patient. The bottom of the bed is changed from the unaffected side, or top to bottom, and small blankets, sheets, or split linen may be used to cover the patient when large ones interfere with place-

---

NURSING CARE GUIDELINES
The Patient in Traction

Nursing diagnoses

- Alteration in comfort (pain) related to bone displacement, muscle spasm, and tissue trauma
- Potential alteration in bowel elimination (constipation) related to inactivity and altered position for elimination
- Deficit in diversional activity related to restrictions imposed by traction
- Impaired management of bone maintenance related to hospitalization
- High risk for injury related to accidental disturbance of line of pull and weight of traction
- Knowledge deficit related to diet to promote healing and prevent urolithiasis and to exercises to promote circulation and bone healing
- Impaired physical mobility related to traction
- Alteration in nutrition (potential for more than body requirements) related to decreased activity
- Self-care deficit in feeding, bathing/hygiene, dressing/grooming, and toiletting related to traction
- Actual or potential impairment of skin integrity related to trauma, skin or skeletal traction, or immobility
- Alteration in tissue perfusion related to edema

Nursing interventions

- Keep patient in good alignment
- Never change heights of backrest, knee elevators, or elevating blocks unless ordered by physician
- Never remove traction unless ordered by physician

- Place patient on firm mattress; hinged bedboard often is used for additional support
- Ensure ropes and pulleys are in straight alignment with fracture site
- Check equipment frequently to be sure ropes are not frayed, are unobstructed and move freely in pulley grooves, knots are tied securely, and weights hang freely
- Weight applied in skin traction should not exceed tolerance of skin; condition of skin must be inspected frequently
- Frequently check pin or wire insertion site when skeletal traction is used; be alert for odors, signs of local inflammation, or other evidence of osteomyelitis
- Check skin frequently for evidence of pressure or friction over bony prominences
- Encourage active motion and exercise of unaffected joints
- Check for circulatory impairment—numbness, cyanosis, edema, color, and pain
- Encourage self-help and independence within limitations of traction
- Obtain specific orders on how patient can move—turning is not allowed with running traction; slight turning, usually to affected side, is allowed with balanced suspension

Expected outcomes

- Knows rationale for traction and observes condition of skin and extremities
- Traction alignment is maintained
- Neurocirculatory status is normal

---

ment of ropes or mechanical devices. An orthopedic bedpan and female urinal may be desirable for bowel and bladder elimination. When a large pan is needed as in the case of an enema, a plastic-covered pillow should be placed lengthwise along the back when the patient is lifted onto the pan. In many cases an overhead trapeze is provided, and patients can assist by lifting their hips.

Good oral care and a diet high in calcium, protein, iron, and vitamins are important. Foods high in roughage may help to prevent constipation. Active and isometric exercises help to prevent osteoporosis in the immobilized patient. Osteoporosis occurs because calcium leaves the bone of the immobilized patient. As it leaves the bone, it enters the serum, causing elevated levels of se-

rum calcium. These high serum levels produce an alkaline urine, which can lead to the formation of urinary calculi. Fluids should be forced to help prevent this complication. The patient also should be encouraged to cough, deep breathe, and actively exercise the unaffected extremities; the affected extremity should not be exercised unless specifically ordered by the physician.

The box above identifies nursing diagnoses and summarizes nursing care of the patient in traction.

Frames

Several types of frames may be used for orthopedic, neuromuscular, or burned patients. The *Balkan frame* consists of a wooden or steel framework that attaches to the regular hospital bed. The frame has adjustable pulleys and a trapeze attached to an overhead bar. The Balkan frame is used for patients in traction and should be placed on the bed before traction is instituted.

The *Bradford frame* is a rectangular steel frame with two pieces of canvas stretched tightly and laced to the frame. A space is left between the pieces of canvas at the level of the buttocks to place the bedpan. The frame comes in several sizes and may be suspended to the bed with hooks, or it may be suspended in the bed on blocks or boxes. The canvas is usually covered with a sheet, or frame covers with tapes sewed to the sides for attachment to the frame may be used. If sheets are used, they must be tightened several times a day to avoid wrinkling under the patient. Because the frame is narrow and suspended, patients must be protected from falling. When children and unconscious or disoriented adults are placed on a Bradford frame, some type of restraint is required.

The *Stryker Wedge Turning frame* and *Foster frame* allow for changing the patient's position from supine to prone without interfering with body alignment (Figure 25-8). They are similar to the Bradford frame but fit into a pivoting device at the head and foot of the frame, where they are held firmly by pins. Two frames are used, a posterior and an anterior. The posterior frame has an opening in the canvas to allow for the use of a bedpan. Both frames have canvas covers over which a sponge rubber mattress is placed and then covered with a specially fitted sheet.

Nursing care of the patient on a Stryker Wedge Turning frame or Foster frame is simplified because the patient is turned easily, allowing for skin care and frequent change of position. When giving morning care, the anterior part of the body is bathed. A pillow is placed lengthwise across the legs. The patient is covered with a sheet, and if a thin foam rubber mattress is used, it is placed over the sheet. The anterior frame is then placed on top of the patient. The frame is fastened at the top and bottom ends to the pivoting device, and straps are secured around both frames and the patient. Two persons should be present during turning, one at the head and one at the foot of the frame. The pivot pins are removed, and the frame is turned so the patient is in the prone position. A steady, uninterrupted turn will help prevent the patient's fear of falling while being turned. The pivot pins are replaced to hold the frame firmly in place, the straps are removed, and the posterior frame and bedding are removed. The posterior part of the body may then be washed

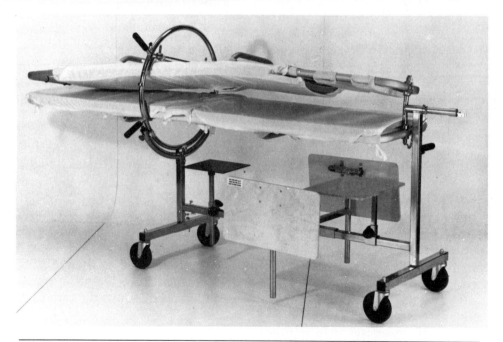

Figure 25-8

Stryker Wedge Turning frame provides ease in turning for skin care and change of position for patient who might otherwise be immobile. *(Courtesy Stryker Corp, Kalamazoo, Mich.)*

and the back massaged and observed for any pressure areas.

The frame is equipped with armrests, a footboard, and an attachment for the head. When the patient is in the prone position, pillows should be placed on the armboards for the arms, and the toes should extend over the edge of the canvas. When in the supine position, the patient's heels should be elevated off the frame to prevent pressure areas from developing; also, the bedpan may be placed under the patient below the frame and between the canvas space. Patients on Stryker or Foster frames can do many things for themselves, including oral care, feeding, reading, or other diversional activities.

The nursing care is similar to that for any patient who is immobilized. Reassurance and an explanation of what the patient can expect during the turning procedure should be provided in advance, since most patients are apprehensive about falling when first placed on these frames.

The *CircOlectric bed* is a vertical turning bed that may be operated electrically by one person. It has an anterior frame, which is attached when the patient is to be turned to the prone position. As the patient is turned, the head rises and the feet are lowered. The bed may be placed in a variety of positions, including the sitting and standing positions and may be used with traction (Figure 25-9).

Figure 25-9

CircOlectric bed simplifies turning of patient and facilitates early ambulation. Bed may be operated by patient and may be tilted to standing position. *(Courtesy Stryker Corp, Kalamazoo, Mich.)*

Several new beds have been designed for the management of immobilized patients. Among these are mattresses filled with water, air, or air forced through silicone beads. These beds help the patient move, yet minimize the potential for constant pressure against skin and bone prominences. *Kinetic beds* also are available. They provide constant side-to-side movement of the patient while maintaining proper alignment of fractures in the thorax, pelvis, spine, or extremities.

Each of the beds has distinct advantages and certain limitations associated with its use. Because they all are expensive to use, their potential benefit to the patient should be evaluated carefully. A social worker should be contacted to assist in determining whether the patient's medical insurance will cover the cost of the bed's use. When possible, the patient and family should participate in the final decision about the use of the bed.

Splints

Splints are used to support or immobilize an area of the body in a specific position. They are made of a variety of materials such as plywood, lightweight aluminum, plastic, or casting materials. Plywood splints generally are used for first aid only. In treating a fractured finger or an injury in which immobilization of the finger is desired, a tongue blade is used. Aluminum splints are made for right or left extremities and provide for support of the foot or thumb. They may be short for the lower leg or long enough to reach the hip. The splint is held in place by elastic bandages or gauze and has the advantage of allowing for the application of wet dressings for the care of ulcers or other superficial injuries. Occasionally, casts are bivalved (cut in two along both sides) and made into removable shells. This allows access to the affected area, while maintaining mobilization.

Other types of splints are used for patients with specific orthopedic conditions. Some kinds of splints, such as the *Thomas splint,* are used in combination with traction (Figure 25-7). When splints of any kind are used, the nurse must observe the skin for pressure areas and use care when handling the extremity involved.

Other orthopedic devices

Crutches and braces and their care were discussed in Chapter 12. Plastic or rubber heels may be incorporated into the cast to allow the patient to walk on the extremity. Sometimes an iron called a *walking iron,* extending up into the cast is used.

Only certain kinds of fractures lend themselves to walking casts, and the orthopedic surgeon will decide if such a cast can be used safely. The patient must always be cautioned about the outward rotation of the foot when walking.

Various types of *collars* or *neck supports* are designed to immobilize the head and to take the weight of the head off the spine. These generally are used temporarily while healing occurs and may not be required at night.

Corsets and *back braces* are used to immobilize the spine and to prevent the patient from engaging in activities that would cause further harm to the spine. Braces may have steel supports in the back, and corsets usually lace in front. Patients are measured for the supports, which are then made specifically for their needs. A cotton T-shirt is worn under the brace to prevent skin irritation and to absorb perspiration. The brace or corset should be put on with patients in recumbent positions before they arise in the morning.

Intervention

The treatment of patients with orthopedic conditions is considered a surgical specialty, since many require minor or major surgical procedures. Most patients will be cared for in an orthopedic or surgical service. Certain basic aspects of nursing care apply to most orthopedic patients, and many of these procedures have been referred to in this and other chapters.

All patients with fractures should have bedboards, a firm mattress, and an overhead trapeze. Cast care is the same for all patients, regardless of the extent of the cast. Extreme care must be taken to protect devices such as traction equipment, splints, or tongs so that the corrective procedure is not jeopardized. Skin care is a must for orthopedic patients, and because many patients are hospitalized for several weeks, the nurse should remember that good personal hygiene includes care of the nails and hair. The immobilized patient may have problems with elimination, therefore a diet high in roughage or the use of mild laxatives or enemas may be necessary. Adequate fluid intake must be ensured to promote bowel function and to prevent urinary tract infection and the formation of urinary calculi (Chapter 19). Isometric exercises will retard osteoporosis that accompanies immobility. Prescribed exercises should be carried out with the assistance of the physical therapist and members of the nursing staff. Maintaining flexibility of unaffected joints, muscle tone, and function is important for preventing contractures and fostering rehabilitation. Open surgery may be performed on bones, tendons or muscles, and the immediate postoperative care is essentially the same as that for any surgical patient. All wounds must be protected from contamination.

One of the most important interventions for patients with musculoskeletal conditions involves the recognition and support of their psychosocial needs.[3] Individuals who suddenly are hospitalized because of injuries sustained during an accident or who are receiving medical care for chronic musculoskeletal disorders are certain to have questions and concerns about how injuries or illnesses will affect them and their families. In addition, patients who are elderly or who are hospitalized for long periods may show signs of confusion and disorientation. Consistent attention by the nurse to the patient's socialization and adaptation needs will help to prevent or alleviate these concerns.

THE PATIENT WITH DISEASES AND DISORDERS OF THE MUSCULOSKELETAL SYSTEM

Congenital Deformities

Many congenital deformities affect bones, joints, and muscles. Some are recognized at birth, whereas others may not be observed for months or even years. Common congenital deformities may include clubbed feet or fingers, dislocated hips, webbing of fingers or toes, and spina bifida. Part or all of the extremities may be missing, multiple fingers or toes may be present, and multiple deformities may be noted in the same child. When the pediatrician makes a thorough examination of the newborn infant soon after birth, defects are more likely to be discovered. The nurse assigned to work in obstetrics or in the nursery should watch for any unusual fold of tissue in the buttocks, failure to move extremities normally, or limitation of movement of a joint. The nurse should be suspicious if any of these signs is observed and should notify the physician promptly.

For children with orthopedic conditions, assistance is available through the Department of Health and Human Services. The program of services to crippled children is administered through local health departments, and parents should be advised to contact the public health nurse or the hospital's department of social services for additional information.

Clubfoot

Congenital clubfoot may affect one or both feet and may be mild or severe. The condition involves an **adduction** and inward rotation of the foot. The foot resists being placed in normal position when manipulated, and when released the foot will return to its former state. If the condition is mild, it may be overlooked. A hereditary tendency toward clubfoot has been noted and when present, the infant should be examined carefully, since other malformations may be present.[10] Early detection and treatment of clubfoot results in complete correction. The longer treatment is delayed, the longer the period of treatment and the less certain the outcome.

For patients who have mild cases, exercise may be all that is required. Most patients, however, are treated by application of plaster casts and by manipulation. Casts may be changed at frequent intervals in the beginning, and the intervals will be extended later. The parents should know that correction will take several months, and the appointments for medical care should be kept faithfully. When the deformity has been corrected, the child will be fitted with special orthopedic shoes.

The care of the infant with casts on the feet requires frequent checking of circulation. The casts should not be allowed to become wet or damp. Because the infant will be treated in the outpatient clinic or the physician's office, parents should be taught how to watch for pressure or circulatory disturbance, how to protect the top of the cast against moisture, and how to care for chafing of the skin. Young infants may outgrow the cast quickly, and chafing and irritation may result. Parents should be cautioned to observe the skin and cast closely and to report any unusual condition to the physician. When clubfoot fails to respond to treatment by manipulation and casts, surgery may be necessary.

Nurses who are employed in public health departments may help parents understand the importance of early treatment and continued medical supervision for several years after satisfactory correction has been achieved. The possibility exists that the deformity will recur, and if neglected, may require radical treatment.[10]

Torticollis (wryneck)

Torticollis, or congenital wryneck, may be observed during the first few weeks after birth. Although no general agreement has been reached about its cause, it is commonly believed to be the result of injury during birth. During birth the sternocleidomastoid muscle is torn, and hemorrhage resulting in a hematoma occurs. The result is a fibrotic mass of scar tissue in the muscle, which produces loss of elasticity and contraction of the muscle fibers. The ear on the affected side is pulled down toward the shoulder, and the chin points toward the opposite unaffected shoulder. If the defect is not recognized and treated early, deformity of the jaw and face on the affected side occurs.

When the defect is discovered during the first few weeks of life, correction may be achieved by the use of heat, massage, and gentle stretching. The mother can perform the stretching exercises by turning the head gently to the unaffected side and back about 25 times, repeating the process three times a day. Without treatment, the defect is considered permanent by the time the infant is 8 months old, and surgery is required.[10] After surgery a cast may or may not be applied, depending on the extent of the procedure and the technique of the particular surgeon. If a cast is applied, it may cover the chest, neck, and head. After about 6 weeks, it is replaced by an orthopedic collar that is worn for several more weeks. When a cast is applied, it must be protected. Care should be taken not to let crumbs drop inside the cast and irritate the skin.

Dislocation of the hip

Congenital dislocation of the hip is a developmental error that usually is the result of poor development of the hip socket (acetabulum) into which the femur fits. Although the actual defect may be present at birth, often dislocation does not occur until the child begins to stand or walk. Early detection is important if good results are to be obtained from corrective measures.

Signs of the disorder vary according to age. It may be detected in the infant by abducting the hips or by placing the child's legs in a froglike position while lying on his back. Resistance or limited abduction is a meaningful sign. When the leg is abducted, a click is sometimes heard, and one knee may be lower than the other. As the child grows older, walking may be delayed, one leg may appear shorter, an extra gluteal fold may be observed, and a waddle or limp may be present.

When the condition is mild, treatment may consist of using extra diapers or a pillow to keep the legs in a position of abduction. The child may be given an anesthetic and the legs manipulated to place the head of the femur into the acetabulum, after which a cast is applied with the legs in the position of extreme abduction. After removal of the cast an adjustable abduction splint may be used. X-ray films are taken at frequent intervals to monitor the development of the joint. When walking is permitted, it should be undertaken gradually.

The nursing care of the child depends largely on the corrective method used and the age of the child. Most children will be treated through the outpatient clinic or the physician's office. When a cast is applied, the child is hospitalized for about 48 hours to permit drying. Routine cast care is needed. Perineal care for the child is important to prevent soiling and damage to the cast. During this time the nurse has the opportunity to teach parents how to care for the cast and the child and how to protect the cast from becoming wet. In some situations, before open or closed reduction, the physician may wish to have traction applied to bring the femoral head into a more satisfactory position for reduction and to avoid excessive manipulation.[10]

Arthritis

Arthritis belongs to a group of diseases commonly called *rheumatic disorders*, which involve inflammation of a joint. Exactly how many persons in the United States have some form of arthritis is unknown, although it is the number one crippling disease in the United States. Estimates vary widely, but at least 50 million Americans are affected and at least 4 million of these are dependent and unable to work, attend school, or participate in social functions.[12] Not all persons with arthritis are completely incapacitated. Many go about their daily activities, at home and at work, with only varying degrees of discomfort.

Many types of arthritis exist, but the most common are rheumatoid arthritis, rheumatoid spondylitis, and osteoarthritis (degenerative joint disease). Forms of arthritis often accompany other diseases such as psoriasis (see chapter 24), rheumatic fever, infectious diseases such as gonorrhea, and gout, which is a metabolic disease.

In providing care and services for the arthritic

patient, goals should be established that include medical and nursing care during the acute stages and long-range plans to maintain the patient in the best possible condition. Emphasis should be placed on prevention of infectious diseases that may be associated with arthritis, prevention and correction of deformities, teaching activities of daily living, and providing a psychosocial environment in which the patient and family can accept and live comfortably with a chronic disability. To accomplish these goals, the physician, psychiatrist, psychologist, nurse, physical therapist, occupational therapist, religious counselor, social worker, vocational counselor, and public health nurse may need to be involved.

Rheumatoid arthritis and rheumatoid spondylitis

Rheumatoid arthritis is the most serious form of the disease and leads to severe crippling. The disease may occur at any age, but most frequently affects persons between 20 and 45 years of age. Rheumatoid arthritis in infants and children is a chronic systemic disease affecting many organs and tissues, including joints. Children between 2 and 4 years of age are most commonly affected.

Pathophysiology. Research has failed to find a specific cause of the disease, but rheumatoid arthritis is now considered to be an autoimmune disease. Most people with rheumatoid arthritis have an unusual antibody in their bloodstream, and it appears that they make antibodies against their own antibodies. The individual is believed to damage his own antibodies while defending against infection. These damaged antibodies are then interpreted by the body's defense system as foreign, and are attacked, causing the inflammatory response.[15] This theory would explain why patients with rheumatoid arthritis frequently have a history of a recent infection of some type. The disease may develop rather insidiously, or it may have an acute onset. Remissions occur and symptoms subside, but subsequent attacks follow, and a chronic state slowly develops. The disease affects the joints, first causing an inflammation of the joint membrane. As the disease progresses, granulation tissue fills the joint and the normal joint cartilage is destroyed. The joint cavities fill with scar tissue and adhesions, causing stiffness, pain, and complete immobility. Swan-neck deformities of the hands and fingers are shown in Figure 25-10.

The early symptoms of rheumatoid arthritis are loss of weight, loss of appetite, muscle aching, malaise, fever, and swollen painful joints. Complaints of joint stiffness, especially on rising in the morning, are common. During the early course of the disease considerable muscle spasm occurs, and any effort to move the affected joints is painful. The diagnosis is established by a variety of

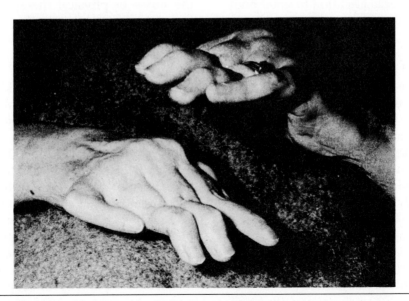

Figure 25-10

Swan-neck deformities of fingers in rheumatoid arthritis. *(From Phipps WJ, Long BC, and Woods NF: Medical-surgical nursing: concepts and clinical practice, ed 1, St Louis, 1987, The CV Mosby Co.)*

findings. The rheumatoid factor (RF) titer is elevated, indicating that an abnormal serum protein concentration is present. The erythrocyte sedimentation rate is elevated, and x-ray films show progressive damage to the joints.

Intervention. The care of the patient is directed toward maintaining function, relieving pain, preventing deformities. Minimizing stress is important because stress has been found to be associated with increased symptom severity and difficulty adjusting to the disease.[7] One of the most distressing factors in the treatment of rheumatoid arthritis is that some patients obtain unprofessional advice in hopes of relieving their symptoms. As a result, they may wear copper bracelets, drink potions of vinegar and honey, wear beans or potatoes around their necks, or sit in uranium mines. Patients hear about these "cures" through well-meaning friends and relatives who may be acquainted with someone whose symptoms seemingly disappeared with similar therapy. The disease is characterized by alternating periods of exacerbation and remission, thus the patient who adopts quackery as treatment may experience a normal remission and attribute the improvement to the "cure." As a result, the supposed cure is believed to be valuable, despite medical advice to the contrary. Patients should seek medical attention early so that pain and joint deformity can be minimized.

During acute attacks rest is important, and the nurse should give special attention to good body alignment. Boards should be placed under the mattress to provide a firm bed. The extremities should be straight without pillows under the knees, and the knee gatch on the bed should not be raised. A bed cradle should be used to keep bedclothing off painful joints. Sandbags or trochanter rolls should be used to prevent outward rotation of the extremities. The patient should be positioned so that the back is straight, and a small pillow is placed under the head. Hip and knee flexion is to be avoided.

Aspirin generally is considered to be the drug of choice to decrease both pain and inflammation. It may be given in fairly large doses and should be taken with food to avoid gastric upset. The drug indomethacin (Indocin) also is antiinflammatory and analgesic, although it is no more effective than aspirin. Phenylbutazone (Butazolidin) has similar effects on the rheumatoid arthritic patient; however, its effectiveness appears to be limited and serious side effects can occur. Gold compounds are selected for some patients, usually those who are not responding to other forms of treatment. These medications are slow acting, and the patient must be watched carefully for side effects while receiving the drug. Adrenocorticosteroids (cortisone, prednisone, hydrocortisone) are given if more conservative treatment fails. These drugs may produce dramatic relief of symptoms, although they do not cure the disease. Rather severe side effects can result, however, and once the medication is discontinued, the patient may have a full return of original symptoms. Usually the patient is maintained on the lowest dose of corticosteroids that will produce an improvement in the condition. Hydrocortisone acetate injected into joints results in immediate relief of pain and a temporary halt of the destructive process, usually lasting for several weeks.

The use of heat is helpful in relieving pain and may include hot moist packs, hot tub baths, electric blankets, heat cradles, paraffin baths, and whirlpool baths. Some of the joint deformities that are the most severe are caused by patients assuming a comfortably flexed position. Once the acute stage is passed, a program of physical therapy must be established. A planned program of rest and activity is important. Active exercise should be a part of the therapeutic plan so that normal functioning of the joints may be maintained. Exercises should be simple and may be taught by the nurse or physical therapist. No special diet is required for the arthritic patient, but a well-balanced diet and adequate fluid intake should be encouraged.

After recovery from acute attacks the patient may return to work and should be encouraged to remain active. Many patients with rheumatoid arthritis remain independent and self-sufficient for 20 or 30 years.

Rheumatoid (ankylosing) spondylitis is an inflammation of the vertebrae and sacroiliac joints and may affect part or all of the spine, resulting in complete rigidity. The rheumatoid process may cause a bowing outward of the thoracic spine (kyphosis). Treatment of the condition is similar to that for rheumatoid arthritis, except that the program of exercise is designed to prevent kyphosis. Exercises are planned to keep the spine straight and to maintain range of motion in the cervical spine. The patient should be positioned on a firm bed with bedboards and should not use a pillow.

Osteoarthritis (degenerative joint disease)

Osteoarthritis is the result of the normal wear and tear placed on joints over the years. The process may be hastened by joint trauma or obesity. It is the most common form of arthritis and begins to make its appearance in persons past middle life. Most people have some degree of osteoarthritis by the time they reach 60 years of age. The disease damages the cartilage in the joints, and although pain and stiffness result, they usually do not cause crippling. Several factors contribute to development of the disease. Engaging in occupations in which prolonged strain is placed on joints, obesity, poor posture, and injury to a joint favor early development of osteoarthritis. The joints most often affected are the spine, knees, fingers, and hips. Osteoarthritis of the hand, with characteristic Heberden's nodes, is shown in Figure 25-11.

Treatment for the disease should include a reduction in weight if obesity is present and a regular program of exercise to maintain range of joint motion. Analgesics such as aspirin, 10 to 15 grains three or four times daily after meals, may be given to relieve pain. Also, phenylbutazone (Butazolidin), 100 mg two or three times daily, indomethacin (Indocin), or ibuprofen (Motrin), 400 mg four times a day, may be ordered by the physician. In patients with severe joint pain, hydrocortisone acetate may be injected into the synovial cavity and usually provides pain relief for several weeks. The patient should have a program of rest, and joints should be protected from continuing wear and strain. The application of moist heat with baths, soaks, packs, or paraffin baths may afford temporary relief.

Surgical intervention for arthritis

A variety of surgical procedures are available to prevent progressive deformities, relieve pain, improve function, and correct deformities resulting from rheumatoid or osteoarthritis. Tendon transplants can be done to prevent the progressive deformity caused by muscle spasm. The excision of the synovial membrane of a joint, a **synovectomy,** is helpful in rheumatoid arthritis to maintain joint function. An **osteotomy,** a cutting of bone to correct bone or joint deformities, may be performed to improve function or relieve pain. Severe joint destruction may be treated with an **arthrodesis,** which is a surgical fusion of the joint in a functional position. An **arthroplasty** involves plastic surgery on a diseased joint such as the elbow, hip,

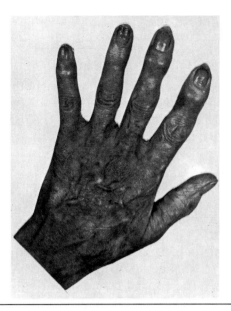

Figure 25-11

Osteoarthritis of hand. Note enlargement of distal joints of index, middle, and little finger (Heberden's nodes). *(From Phipps WJ, Long BC, and Woods NF: Medical-surgical nursing: concepts and clinical practice, ed 1, St Louis, 1987, The CV Mosby Co.)*

knee, or shoulder to increase mobility. Sometimes an arthroplasty involves the removal of a portion of the joint and replacement with a **prosthesis** made of metal or synthetic material. *Arthrotomy* is a broad term that refers to the surgical opening of a joint. *Arthroscopy* involves the introduction of an instrument or scope into a joint to examine it. Some surgical procedures can be performed through the arthroscope.

A hip arthroplasty is a common procedure when arthritis involves the head of the femur and acetabulum. In this type of surgery a Vitallium cup is cemented into the arthritic acetabulum to receive the head of the femur. The most recent development in hip reconstruction is total hip replacement. A white plastic cup is cemented in place to replace the damaged acetabulum. A stainless steel or Vitallium ball on a stem replaces the head of the femur, which is surgically removed. The stem is cemented into the femoral canal, and the new head fits precisely into the plastic acetabulum, providing friction-free movement in the joint. The cement used is a soft, surgical bone cement that hardens quickly and stabilizes the prosthesis to prevent future erosion of the surrounding bone. If the patient experiences an adverse reaction to the cement, a remote possibility, the prosthesis would have to be surgically removed. The procedure is performed for damage resulting from trauma or congenital deformities, as well as for arthritis.

Preoperatively, the patient is taught to use the overhead trapeze and to elevate the buttocks. The affected hip and groin are scrubbed twice daily with a surgical scrub to minimize the risk of postoperative infection. In addition to coughing and deep breathing, the patient is taught to perform isometric exercises of the quadriceps and gluteal muscles, to keep the toes pointed up, to flex the ankles frequently, and to flex and extend the knee of the unaffected extremity. These exercises are continued postoperatively to improve circulation, prevent emboli, and reduce joint stiffness and muscle weakness. Thigh-high antiembolism stockings are applied before or during surgery.

A Hemovac usually is placed in the wound during surgery to provide closed wound suction. The patient is moved from the operating table to the bed to reduce the chance of dislocation during transfer at a later time. If traction is used, it is applied at this time.

Postoperatively, the affected leg must be maintained in abduction; some surgeons apply traction, and others order only the use of an abduction pillow between the legs. The *abduction pillow* is a large, hard triangular pillow with Velcro straps on each side to attach to each leg. The straps must be fastened firmly while turning the patient to maintain the extremity in abduction. The patient may not be turned unless ordered by the physician. If turning is allowed, it is to the unaffected side with additional pillows to support the affected extremity in abduction. The patient must be observed for any adverse reaction to the cement, phlebitis, urinary retention, and infection, as well as for circulation and sensation in the affected leg. Some elevation in temperature is expected, but a fever persisting after the fifth to eighth day indicates infection. A plan of weight bearing and physical therapy will be ordered by the physician, with some patients getting out of bed very soon after surgery. Patients experience an immediate relief of joint pain after surgery and have relatively normal range of motion in the hip. They also report the quality of their lives to be significantly improved after total hip replacement.[17]

The patient is not to sleep on the operative side for 2 months and should maintain the limb in extension and abduction when getting out of bed. Sitting is not allowed in the early postoperative period, and extreme flexion of the hip, such as sitting in a low chair or stooping, must be avoided for several weeks to reduce the chance of dislocation. Exercises are performed while the patient is supine or standing.[16] Because prosthetic devices for hip replacement are continually being developed and improved, the therapy prescribed and restrictions imposed will vary. Some new devices do not require cement, and the patient is allowed to sit in a chair on the second postoperative day and progress to full weight bearing in 10 to 12 days.

Total knee replacements are now being done for arthritic conditions involving the knee, and procedures also have been developed to replace shoulder, elbow, and finger joints.[8] Following knee replacement, the extremity may be placed in a motorized splint that continually flexes and extends the knee to an angle predetermined by controls on the machine.

Gout (gouty arthritis)

Gout is a metabolic disease resulting from an accumulation of uric acid in the blood. The disease may be primary, caused by a hereditary metabolic error, or it may be secondary to some other disease process and to certain drugs. The disease usually appears in middle life. It does not occur before puberty in the male or before menopause in the female. The disease almost exclusively attacks men.[2] It takes about 20 years for sufficient urates to accumulate in the body before causing symptoms when the disease is primary. When gout is the result of a negative response to drugs, its symptoms may develop rapidly over several days.

Gouty arthritis can affect any joint in the body, but 20% of first attacks occur in a joint of the great toe. Although first attacks may occur in other joints, the great toe is involved in 80% of persons with the disease (Figure 25-12). Typically, the onset occurs at night with excruciating pain, swelling, and inflammation in the affected joint. The pain may be of short duration, returning at intervals, or it may be severe and continuous for 5 to 10 days. The patient may never have more than one attack throughout his entire life, or attacks may continue at intervals of months, gradually coming closer together.

The diagnosis is based on the finding of a high blood level of uric acid. Several drugs are used in the treatment of the disease. For acute attacks colchicine is administered orally or may be given intravenously. When administered orally, 0.5 mg

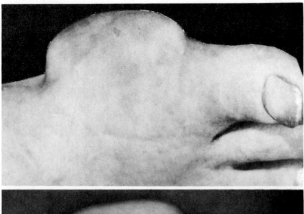
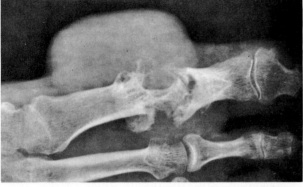

Figure 25-12

Gout of long duration. Tophaceous mass at base of great toe, as well as destructive bone and joint changes shown in x-ray, are associated with extensive urate deposits. *(From Phipps WJ, Long BC, and Woods NF: Medical-surgical nursing: concepts and clinical practice, ed 1, St Louis, 1987, The CV Mosby Co.)*

may be given hourly until 12 doses have been given. The drug is discontinued if gastrointestinal symptoms develop, and if the patient has not had relief from the pain, phenylbutazone (Butazolidin) will be ordered. Indomethacin (Indocin) is a potent antiinflammatory drug useful for controlling gout in patients who suffer frequent attacks despite prophylactic dosages of colchicine. The high doses required tend to cause headache, dizziness, and epigastric pain, so dosages should be reduced quickly and discontinued as soon as possible. In some cases daily doses will prevent acute attacks.[2]

A factor in the treatment of gout is the prevention of tophi and gouty arthritis. **Tophi** are deposits of uric acid that may form in various parts of the body, including the kidneys. Uric acid stones may develop here and destroy kidney tissue. Drugs may be given to prevent these disorders from occurring or to relieve them when present. Drugs in use include allopurinol (Zyloprim),

probenecid (Benemid), and sulfinpyrazone (Anturane).[2] Allopurinol decreases the production of uric acid in the body and must be taken regularly to prevent acute attacks and tophi formation. Probenecid increases excretion of uric acid by the kidney, thus reducing the amount in the body. It must be taken daily to be effective. Each patient is treated on an individual basis, and the period during which these drugs are to be administered depends on the stage of the disease and the practices of the individual physician. The patient may need to continue receiving drugs over several years. No special diet has been found to be effective, although foods high in purine, such as liver, kidney anchovies, sardines, and sweetbreads should be avoided. The diet should be well balanced, with a high water intake. During an acute attack the patient should be prescribed a regimen of bed rest, and painful joints should be protected from bedcovers by a bed cradle.

Bursitis

The bursae are small sacs located in the shoulder, elbow, knee, hip, and foot. They contain a small amount of fluid that lubricates areas in which movement may cause friction. The bursae may become inflamed, causing an acute bursitis, or inflammation extending over a long period may result in chronic bursitis and the formation of calcium salt deposits. Bursitis generally is the result of injury, strain, or prolonged use of the bursae, as in active exercise. It also may occur secondary to infection elsewhere in the body.

The subdeltoid region is the most frequent location of inflammation. Subdeltoid bursitis is characterized by severe pain that may radiate down the arm into the fingers. Treatment consists of supporting the arm in a sling and administering an analgesic for pain. Hydrocortisone may be injected into the bursae. Several other methods of treatment may be used, including administering a local anesthetic, inserting needles, and washing out the calcium deposits. Range of motion exercises should be started as soon as possible. In chronic bursitis pain occurs during use of the affected part; treatment includes analgesics to relieve pain and physical therapy. Surgical removal of hardened calcium deposits may be necessary.

Infectious Diseases and Disorders
Osteomyelitis

Osteo- is the prefix meaning bone; therefore, osteomyelitis is inflammation of the bone. The most common cause of the disease is the introduction of pathogenic bacteria into the bone in penetrating injuries such as gunshot wounds or in compound fractures with bones protruding. Acute osteomyelitis may result from infections elsewhere in the body, and then the pathogenic bacteria are carried to the bone by the bloodstream. Because many infections are now treated with chemotherapeutic drugs, fewer cases of osteomyelitis result from bloodstream infection.

Chronic osteomyelitis may recur throughout life. Complete elimination of the disease depends on the thoroughness of the removal of dead bone and prolonged use of antibiotics. No uniform method of treating patients with osteomyelitis exists. For some patients surgery may be performed to remove necrotic bone. Antibiotics generally are given, and immobilization may be helpful. Much depends on the age and the condition of the patient.[16]

The wounds caused by the disease are painful, and the nurse should exercise gentleness when moving the affected part. Wounds often are irrigated with hydrogen peroxide or other antiseptic or antibiotic solution, and strict asepsis must be maintained. Contractures may occur unless care is taken to see that the patient is positioned properly. New foci of infection may develop, and the patient should be observed for any sudden elevation of temperature, which should be reported at once. The diet should be high in calories, protein, and vitamins. Because osteomyelitis patients often are children, some diversional activity should be planned.

Tuberculosis of the bone

Tuberculosis caused by the tubercle bacillus may affect any bone or joint. The infection usually is acquired from contact with patients who have infectious tuberculosis. Bone and joint tuberculosis is not infectious unless draining lesions are present or unless it is accompanied by infectious pulmonary tuberculosis. Tuberculosis of bones and joints occurs primarily in children between 2 and 12 years of age. Often it results from the child associating with older persons who have pulmonary tuberculosis. Tuberculosis of the spine (Pott's disease) is the most common form and accounts for greater than 50% of bone and joint tuberculosis. Tuberculosis of the hip is next in frequency.

Pott's disease (tuberculosis of the spine)

The symptoms of tuberculosis of the spine usually begin with muscle spasm and stiffness. The patient tends to avoid any activity that involves bending the back. The small child may be irritable and fretful and may cry out at intervals, particularly at night. The lower dorsal or the upper lumbar portion of the spine is most frequently involved. As the disease progresses with the softening and destruction of bones, deformity occurs, giving a humped appearance known as gibus, or kyphosis. Abscesses without inflammation may occur at various sites on the body, along the spine, in the hips, or in the groin.

An important factor in treatment is absolute immobilization of the spine. The child may be placed on a Bradford frame in hyperextension, or casts and braces may be used. The administration of streptomycin, para-aminosalicylic acid (PAS), and isoniazid (INH) in addition to proper nutrition, sunshine, and fresh air is considered important in the plan of therapy. No shortcut to cure is available, and treatment must extend from months to years.

Tuberculosis of the hip

Tuberculosis of the hip may be observed in the very young child who limps and walks on the toes of the affected side. Stiffness of the joint and pain, which is often referred to the knee, may be present. In treating young children, the hip is placed at rest, whereas the treatment of older children may include surgery followed by immobilization.[16]

Nursing care is the same as for any patient in a cast, on a frame, or in traction. Good nutrition, immobilization, and rest are basic factors in the treatment of bone or joint tuberculosis. Patients usually are hospitalized initially and then discharged. Parents must have specific instructions about care of the child, and demonstrations are helpful. If the disease is diagnosed early, antituberculous drugs such as para-aminosalicylic acid, isoniazid, and streptomycin sulfate are effective in treating the disease. However, the disease is characterized by relapses and complicating factors.

Traumatic Injuries

Traumatic injuries to the musculoskeletal system are responsible for a large number of hospital admissions among all age groups. Many less severe injuries, including contusions, sprains, and strains, are cared for in outpatient clinics or in the physician's office.

Contusions

Contusions are the most common and the simplest type of injury to the musculoskeletal system. Contusion is synonymous with bruise and is the result of an external injury to the soft tissues. A sharp blow to the eye, arm, or thigh are examples of injuries that cause a simple contusion. The injury causes a rupture of small blood vessels and subsequent bleeding into tissues, resulting in an *ecchymosis*, the familiar discoloration often called a "black-and-blue spot." When the contusion is severe, a large amount of blood may collect in the tissue, resulting in a hematoma.

Treatment generally includes elevation of the part and application of cold, which may be in the form of cold compresses or an ice cap. After 24 hours, if there is no further bleeding, heat may be applied to relieve muscle soreness.

Sprains

A sprain involves ligaments, tendons, and muscles and occurs as the result of twisting or wrenching a joint beyond its normal range of motion. When this occurs, ligaments are torn, and tendons may be pulled from the bone. Blood vessels are ruptured, causing contusions with ecchymosis; pressure on nerve endings results in pain. As the result of a disturbance of circulation and lymph drainage, muscle spasm occurs, with a tendency to edema. Sprains of the ankle or wrist joint are common examples.

Immediately after the injury, weight bearing or other pressure on the joint should be avoided. Any walking on a sprained ankle, for instance, will cause further bleeding into soft tissues. The involved extremity should be elevated to promote drainage away from the injury; an ice cap should be applied for the first 24 hours to constrict blood vessels and ensure control of further bleeding. After this, mild heat may be applied to encourage circulation and healing and to relieve soreness in the area. Treatment should include x-ray examination to rule out the possibility of a fracture. The joint is then immobilized by a splint and Ace bandage or a cast if the sprain is severe. Occasionally, taping the foot will achieve enough immobilization for healing to occur. The support is removed in 2 to 3 weeks. If the ankle joint is in-

volved, minimum weight bearing is permitted at first and is increased gradually as the discomfort subsides. If the ankle has been casted, active exercises should be performed after cast removal and before full weight bearing begins.

Dislocations

A dislocation may be congenital, as in the case of a congenitally dislocated hip, discussed earlier in this chapter; it may be caused by a disease process in the joint; or it may be caused by trauma. A dislocation results in the temporary displacement of a bone from its normal position within a joint. It is accompanied by stretching and tearing of ligaments and tendons, a fracture may sometimes occur at the same time. A dislocation results in severe pain, deformity, and loss of function.

The treatment of patients with dislocations is usually done with the patient under a general anesthetic; the displaced parts are manipulated manually into normal position. Sometimes the fluoroscope may be used to assist the surgeon. The affected part is then immobilized in splints, bandages, or a cast until the injured tissues have healed. When a fracture accompanies a dislocation, achieving an effective outcome may be more difficult than with dislocation alone.

Nursing care of the patient includes observation for signs of impaired circulation, such as loss of sensation, pain, or tingling and numbness. The care of casts is reviewed earlier in this chapter.

Fractures

A fracture is the same as a break and results from some force (blow, crushing, twisting) that places more stress on the bone than it can absorb. Decalcification and brittleness of bones—osteoporosis—occur in the aging process and make bones increasingly unable to withstand external stresses. In elderly persons, this process may result in fractures occurring with very little stress to bones and joints. Metastatic cancer and tumors of bone weaken bones also and may result in fractures with little or no stress; these are called *pathologic fractures*. Fractures may occur directly at the point stress is applied, or the fracture may be some distance away from this point. Various kinds of fractures exist, and the method of treatment varies with the location and type. Whenever a fracture takes place, some injury to the soft tissues and some bleeding occurs, since the bones have their own blood supply.

Fractures are classified in four broad ways. First, they are described as either *open (compound)* or *closed (simple)*, meaning that the fracture either does or does not protrude through a break in the skin (Figure 25-13). Open fractures generally are more serious because they are accompanied by considerable soft tissue damage, require surgical treatment to repair, and involve a break in the body's first line of defense against infection—the skin. In other words, the fracture has been compounded by the injury to the skin and by the possibility of infection. Because closed fractures do not involve a break in the skin, bones may be realigned by external manipulation only. The use of the term "simple" is avoided because it is misleading, since no fracture is simple in its treatment and the potential for problems exists.

Fractures are also described according to their appearance. Greenstick, complete, comminuted, impacted, transverse, oblique, and spiral fractures are examples (Figure 25-14).

greenstick fracture Incomplete fracture common in children because their bones are softer and more flexible than adult bones. The bone is broken and bent but still secured on one side.

complete fracture The bone is completely broken through and severed on all sides.

comminuted fracture The bone is splintered into three or more fragments at the site of the break.

impacted fracture One broken end of a bone is driven or wedged into the opposite end of the fractured bone by external force. In long bones, this creates a shortening of the extremity.

transverse fracture The break runs directly across the bone.

oblique fracture The break runs along a slant to the length of the bone.

spiral fracture The break coils around the bone.

Third, fractures are described according to their location on the bone, namely, proximal, midshaft, or distal (Figure 25-15).

Fourth, fractures are described according to their displacement. Figure 25-16 shows that fragments may be displaced sideways, may override the opposite fractured surface, may angulate or create a bend in the bone, and may rotate away from the fracture site. Any displacement of bone fragments will result in soft tissue damage, and the patient is likely to experience severe pain, swelling, and muscle spasms in the early stages of healing.

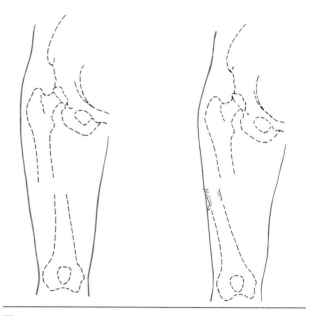

Figure 25-13
A, Closed fracture. **B,** Open fracture with bone protruding through skin.

Assessment

Signs and symptoms of a fracture will vary with its type and location and may include pain and swelling (particularly at the time of injury), tenderness and muscle spasms, deformity, and loss of function. Sometimes symptoms may not be present at the time of injury. Often injury to other body parts occurs simultaneously, and the patient may be admitted unconscious and in severe shock. The treatment of any general systemic condition takes precedence over treatment of the fracture.

An accurate diagnosis of the fracture is made by x-ray or fluoroscopic examination. The physician also will want to know exactly how the accident happened, since this has a bearing on the type of fracture and the method of treatment.

Intervention

To treat a fracture, the bone segments must be realigned. The realignment of a fracture is termed *reduction.* Fractures are reduced by closed or open methods. In *closed reduction* the bones are externally manipulated into position and immobilized with external devices such as casts, splints, or traction. In *open reduction* the bones are exposed and aligned through a surgical incision and may be fixed in position with wires, nails, plates,

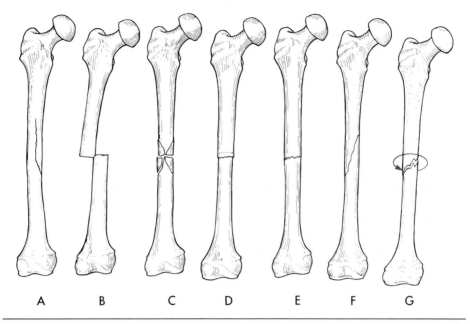

Figure 25-14
Description of fracture by appearance: **A,** greenstick; **B,** complete; **C,** comminuted; **D,** impacted; **E,** transverse; **F,** oblique; and **G,** spiral.

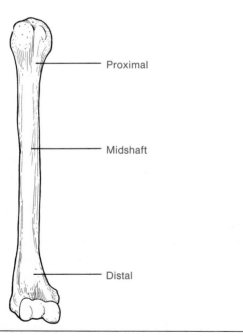

Figure 25-15
Location of fractures.

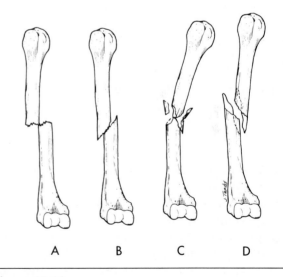

Figure 25-16
Displacement of fragments: **A,** sideways; **B,** override; **C,** angulate; and **D,** rotate.

screws, bolts, or any combination of these. The use of these devices is called *internal fixation* (see page 780). As with closed reduction, external devices may also be used for immobilization of the extremity.

Fracture healing

Whereas other parts of the body heal by the formation of scar tissue, bones heal by the formation of new bone. When a fracture occurs, the bone is broken, soft tissues are damaged, and the periosteum is torn. The bleeding that occurs results in the formation of a hematoma surrounding the area within 24 hours. The coagulation of this blood forms a loose fibrin mesh, which acts as a framework for the early stages of growth of the new bone. An inflammatory reaction follows, causing the fibrin mesh to be replaced by granulation tissue. Within 6 to 10 days the granulation tissue contains calcium, cartilage, and osteoblasts and is termed **callus.** Callus unites the bone so the cast can be removed, but the bone cannot withstand unprotected stress. The bone is immature and is gradually replaced by mature bone in the process of ossification. Remodeling of the bone is the process in which bone tissue consolidates and compacts the bone in relation to its function. This final step in fracture healing requires the stresses of muscle action and weight bearing. After remodeling, the bone is considered to be in union and may be used unprotected.

The time required for healing of fractures varies and is influenced by the type of fracture, the bone involved, and the age and condition of the patient and his bones. For example, displaced fractures take longer to heal than those with no displacement of fragments. Bones of the arms heal in 3 months, as contrasted with 6 months for a long bone of the leg. Solid callus may be present in the fracture of a child within 3 weeks but may take 6 to 8 weeks in a young adult. That same fracture may not develop good callus formation for 3 to 4 months in an elderly person.

The complete union of fractured bones may be prevented or delayed by infection, poor circulation, inadequate nutrition, necrosis, and improper immobilization or fixation. When a fracture does not form a bony union within the usual amount of time, *delayed union* occurs, requiring extended immobilization. *Nonunion* results when healing fails to occur, requiring revision or bone grafting to stimulate callus formation. Faulty reduction or improper immobilization may cause *malunion* of a fracture, resulting in deformity and disability and requiring surgery for repair. *Aseptic* or *avascular necrosis* is literally a clean death of the bone resulting from loss of blood supply to the fracture site.

Over the past 10 years, the use of *electrical bone stimulators* to treat persistent nonunion of fractures has gained popularity. With this technique, the normal negative electrical potentials occurring along fracture sites are stimulated by use of a small generator. New bone forms as a result of the increased electronegativity.[9]

The system contains a generator and electrodes that are implanted percutaneously or through direct surgical incision. The stimulator (generator) may be either embedded internally between nearby muscles or may remain externally attached by lead wires. The decision about which technique to use depends on the patient, the location of the fracture, and the preference of the surgeon involved. External immobilization of the fracture with a cast or splint is required. The electrodes are removed after 3 months, and if the fracture is completely healed, gradual movement and weight bearing of the extremity are begun.

No discomfort should be felt by the patient while the electrodes are in place. Pain at the site of the cathode may indicate localized infection or displacement of the electrode wire and should be reported immediately. Nursing intervention includes preoperative and postoperative teaching and assessment for local infection at the insertion site.

Fractures of the hip

Because more people are living longer now, the incidence of hip fractures among older persons is increasing. Because of the brittleness of bones, older people need only a slight fall to sustain a fracture of the hip or arm. Hip fractures occur spontaneously in older people, which means that the patient falls as a result of the fracture rather than suffering the fracture as a result of the fall. Regardless of the cause, the patient with a fractured hip will experience pain in the fracture site, the affected extremity will shorten, and the foot will turn outward (external rotation). Healing of a bone as large as the hip takes a long time in the elderly, predisposing them to numerous complications. They are at risk for atelectasis and pneumonia, deep vein thrombosis, decubitus ulcers, urinary retention, constipation, and mental confusion or depression.

Newer methods of treatment allow for greater mobility earlier than was previously possible after hip fracture. Different kinds of fractures occur, so methods of treatment vary. Basing the decision on x-ray examination, the surgeon determines the method to be used. The care of patients in casts and traction is reviewed earlier in this chapter; a discussion of internal fixation by nailing is presented here.

Nailing means that a nail or rod made of stainless steel and Vitallium is inserted through the marrow cavity of one bone fragment and driven across the site of the fracture into the marrow cavity of another bone, thus holding the fractured bones in correct anatomic position. Not all fractures can be nailed, but when this procedure is possible, it allows many patients to be out of the hospital in a few weeks, walking on crutches. In some kinds of fractures a prosthetic device may be used. These usually are inserted when the neck of the femur has been fractured and the blood supply necessary for healing has been disrupted. The head and neck of the femur are surgically removed and replaced with a ball and stem (Austin-Moore or Bateman prosthesis), which fits into the shaft of the femur. This enables the patient to bear weight directly on the leg in a short time. These techniques offer the advantage of early ambulation and help to prevent complications commonly associated with immobility.

Intervention. The patient with internal fixation is given a general anesthetic for the procedure, after which vital signs are checked frequently until stabilized. After internal fixation, turning and moving the patient can begin. The patient's position should be changed from side to side, every 2 hours. When the patient is turned on the unaffected side, the fractured extremity should be supported with pillows and remain in the same line as the rest of the body. When the patient is in the supine position, the knee may be slightly flexed, and the extremity should be supported from the hip to the ankle with sandbags or a trochanter roll to prevent outward rotation. Pillows may be used to support the legs and keep the heels off the bed. Because physicians vary in what activity they permit, the nurse should understand exactly what the physician wishes done.

An orthopedic or pediatric bedpan may be more comfortable for the patient. The elderly patient should be observed for fecal impaction, and mild laxatives or small enemas may be ordered. Intake and output records should be maintained.

With the physician's permission the patient may be taught muscle-setting exercises such as quadriceps-setting, tightening gluteal and abdominal muscles, plantar flexion, and dorsiflexion of the feet. All joints should be exercised, except the affected leg, and the patient may be encouraged to use the trapeze to move and exercise the arms. Exercise of the affected leg must be ordered by the surgeon.

In most instances the patient is out of bed in a chair on the day after surgery. Elderly patients may tire easily and should not be left sitting for long periods; usually 1 hour two or three times a day is sufficient. Because the appetite may be poor, allowing the patient to be up at mealtimes may improve intake. Depending on the patient's age and progress, the use of crutches may be permitted in 3 to 6 months; weight bearing is allowed when healing is complete.

When a prosthesis such as the Austin-Moore or Bateman is inserted into the femur, the limb is kept in a neutral position, with slight abduction to prevent dislocation. The patient may be placed in traction to maintain this position and is not turned unless ordered by the physician. In this case the patient is lifted off the bed for back care. If turning is permitted, the patient is placed on his unaffected side, and abduction is maintained by placing pillows between his legs. Muscle exercises are encouraged. Partial weight-bearing may be allowed in 10 to 14 days and full weight-bearing in about 4 weeks. Specific exercises, activity, and weight-bearing restriction must be ordered by the physician.

Colles fracture

Colles fracture is a classic fracture of the wrist in which the distal end of the radius is broken off and displaced backward so that the wrist drops down. It is termed the "silver fork" deformity because the curve of the lower arm, wrist, and fingers resemble the contour of a silver fork or table fork. The fracture usually is caused by breaking a fall with the outstretched hand. Treatment involves reduction with application of a cast or splint. Skeletal traction may be necessary.

Complications. Serious complications of fractures include pulmonary embolism, fat embolism, gas gangrene, tetanus, and compartment syndrome. Because of prolonged immobility, patients with fractures of the lower extremities are particularly susceptible to pulmonary embolism, which may be secondary to thrombophlebitis or which may occur spontaneously. Measures to prevent pulmonary embolism include prophylactic anticoagulation, early ambulation, exercises, and the use of elastic stockings. Sudden respiratory distress with acute substernal pain and signs of shock should alert the nurse to suspect pulmonary embolism. Treatment includes oxygen administration to support respiration, anticoagulant therapy, and general emergency measures. Fat embolism develops most commonly in young adults who sustain multiple, crushing-type fractures, such as those occurring from motorcycle accidents or industrial injuries. Although rare, fat embolism is life threatening because the released fat droplets can effectively occlude capillaries of the pulmonary circulation, causing brain hypoxia and tissue death. Measures to prevent fat embolism include cautious and minimum manipulation of bone fragments with immediate immobilization. Mental disturbance, respiratory distress, and signs of shock occurring within 72 hours after injury are signs of fat embolism. The classic appearance of petechiae on the upper chest and axillae and blood-tinged sputum may accompany these early signs. Treatment includes the administration of high concentrations of oxygen, control of shock, and all symptomatic measures to sustain life.[13]

Gas gangrene and *tetanus* occur rarely but must always be considered as possible complications when a compound fracture has been sustained through a small or puncture-type wound. Both are caused by anaerobic bacteria, which produce rapid and life-threatening results. Gas gangrene is a rapid destruction of tissue, signaled by an acute, fulminating infection with fever, wound pain, gas bubbles, and edema. Untreated, the condition progresses to systemic toxemia and death. In tetanus the bacteria affect the nerves, causing muscle twitching, severe spasms, and inability to open the mouth (lockjaw), and progressing to severe seizures that can be stimulated by the slightest movement or noise. Treatment for both conditions includes wound debridement, hyperbaric oxygen, and antibiotic therapy; anticonvulsive drugs are given for seizures. Amputation of the affected limb may be necessary.

Compartment syndrome. Compartment syndrome is the progressive development of arterial vessel compression and circulatory compromise, which can rapidly result in a permanent contracture deformity of the hand or foot, called *Volkmann's contracture* (Figure 25-17). Fractures of the forearm or tibia usually precede the onset of muscle swelling within the inelastic fascia, which forms compartments for the muscles of the forearm and lower leg. Entry and exit openings to each compartment are only large enough to allow passage of major arteries, nerves, and tendons. When the muscle within a compartment swells as

Figure 25-17

Well-established Volkman's contracture with clawhand and flexion of wrist and fingers. Note atrophy of forearm. *(From Larson CB and Gould M: Orthopedic nursing, ed 9, St Louis, 1978, The CV Mosby Co.)*

a result of severe trauma or compression of a cast, blood vessels within the muscle are compressed and muscle ischemia results. A vicious cycle is set in motion in which histamine is released, capillaries dilate, additional swelling occurs, blood flow is decreased further, more ischemia results, and so on.

Within 6 hours the condition can progress to irreversible muscle ischemia, with compression of the arteries, nerves, and tendons entering the compartment. Paralysis and sensory loss follow, and the contracture and permanent disability of the extremity may be complete within 24 to 48 hours. Careful assessment by the nurse of the neurovascular integrity of fractured extremities can interrupt the development of compartment syndrome. Sharp pain is the first symptom, which increases with passive movement of the hand or foot. This is accompanied by an inability to flex the fingers or toes, numbness, coldness, and lack of pulse.

Frequent assessment of the affected extremity is essential and should include observation of skin color and tension. Palpation will detect changes in temperature, pulse rate, and capillary refilling time. A decreased pulse rate and slowed capillary refilling time do not occur until late in the course of clinical events, however.[4]

Muscle strength should be tested, and increased pain associated with muscle stretching should be reported. Tissue pressure measurements can be taken to determine the extent of tissue compression within the fascial compartment. Normally, pressure is recorded at 0 mm Hg. When pressure rises to 10 to 30 mm Hg less than the patient's diastolic blood pressure, tissue ischemia begins.[4]

Continued elevated pressures in the presence of decreased sensory and motor function necessitate surgical intervention. A *fasciotomy* (incision into the fascia) is performed to relieve pressure within the compartment and allow return of normal blood flow to the area. Postoperatively, the patient is observed for signs and symptoms of infection. The extremity is elevated above the level of the heart and range of motion exercise is begun.

General nursing intervention. The patient with a fracture needs a well-balanced diet, and opinions differ on the value of vitamin and mineral supplements in hastening bone repair. Fluids should be provided. Exercise of the unaffected joints, muscle-setting exercises, skin care, and elimination are important considerations in patient care. Internal fixation has simplified nursing care for many patients with fractures and shortened the period of hospitalization, but many patients will require hospitalization for several weeks. For these patients some form of occupational therapy should be available. If activity is restricted, the complications that result from immobility must be anticipated and prevented.

Whiplash injuries

Whiplash injury to the musculoskeletal system is the result of a combination of severe flexion and extension of the neck. The injury may cause a compression fracture of the cervical vertebrae or result in tearing of muscles and ligaments. Although the injury may be severe enough to cause paralysis and loss of consciousness, most whiplash injuries do not produce immediate symptoms. Symptoms often do not appear until 4 or 5 days after the injury. At that time headache, spasm of neck muscles with loss of motion, and a drawing sensation in the back of the neck may be noticed. Pain may be referred from one side of the head to the base of the skull, and vision may be disturbed. If the injury has been severe enough to injure a nerve root, neurologic symptoms may occur.

Treatment should be secured immediately after injury because without treatment the condition may become chronic. Methods of treatment vary; however, the patient may be admitted to the hospital for several days and a regimen of bed rest prescribed. Cervical traction employing a head halter may be used, as well as the application of heat and massage. The patient may be fitted with a neck support to be worn when he is up. After approximately 4 weeks, physical therapy and exercise are begun to strengthen neck muscles.

Rickets

Rickets is a disease affecting the bones, causing retardation of growth and bone development. The disease occurs in infants and young children and is the result of vitamin D deficiency, which is associated with calcium-phosphorus balance in the body. The condition is more likely to develop in the presence of substandard hygienic conditions, inadequate nutrition, and lack of sunshine. Rickets sometimes results in severe orthopedic deformity.

Education and emphasis on infant care have done much to prevent the occurrence of rickets in the United States, but it remains prevalent in many parts of the world in which poor nutrition standards exist. Addition of Vitamin D to milk sold in the United States has also reduced the incidence of this disease.

Many symptoms are characteristic of the rachitic child. Curvature of long bones, which are soft because of the lack of mineral deposits, occurs; bowleg is an example of this bending. The head has a square appearance and may flatten in back or on the side if the infant lies too long in one position. The closure of the anterior fontanel and development of the definition are delayed. Pigeon breast, knockknee, and enlargement of the wrist and ankles may occur.

The treatment is administration of vitamin D, exposure to sunlight, and improvement in general nutrition.

Bone Tumors

Tumors of the bone may be primary or secondary and may be benign or malignant. Several types of benign tumors exist, and their cause is not always known. Benign tumors do not metastasize to other parts of the body and usually produce few symptoms, with pain being the most common. Benign tumors are diagnosed by x-ray examination and biopsy. Most are removed surgically.

Several different kinds of malignant bone tumors exist. One type of primary malignant tumor, *osteogenic sarcoma*, occurs in younger persons and metastasizes to the lungs, from which the malignant cells are carried throughout the body by the bloodstream. The long bones are usually affected, and amputation generally is required.[3] Other types of malignant tumors affect the flat bones, often involving other types of tissues. Carcinoma of the prostate, lung, breast, thyroid, and kidney may metastasize to the bones, where destruction of the bone and spontaneous fractures result. In most cases of bone tumor, both benign and malignant, pain and declining health are the primary symptoms. In some forms, anemia, elevation of temperature, swelling, and platelet disturbance occur. Treatment depends on the type of tumor, extent of involvement, location, and presence of malignant lesions in other parts of the body.

Amputation

The amputation of an extremity or a portion of it may be necessary because of malignant bone tumor, injury, diabetic gangrene, or any condition that threatens the patient's life unless the procedure is performed. Occasionally, amputation may be an emergency procedure performed when a severe accident has nearly severed the extremity. Generally, it is an elective procedure, and the final decision rests with the patient. The exchange of a leg for a life, particularly when life expectancy may not be too long, is not an easy decision to make. Patients need all the emotional support and understanding possible. They should know preoperatively about prostheses; often a visit from a person using a prosthesis is helpful.

Advances in microsurgery techniques have made reattaching severed limbs possible. The equipment and skills for accomplishing this procedure are not available in many communities, and patients may need to be transferred to another hospital where these services are available.

Preoperative intervention

The patient's general condition will be evaluated carefully, and routine laboratory examinations will be performed. If the patient is diabetic, an evaluation of his diabetic status will be determined. Other examinations such as electrocardiograms and chest x-rays may be ordered by the physician. Intravenous fluids may be given to combat dehydration, and a blood transfusion may be ordered if anemia is present. The skin will be prepared according to the hospital procedure (Figure 25-18). Surgery may be performed under *regional hypothermia*, in which case the extremity is packed in ice for several hours preoperatively.

Postoperative intervention

Today the months of stump wrapping and conditioning before being fitted with a prosthesis have been eliminated. Patients are fitted with a rigid temporary prosthesis either immediately after surgery or when the stump is healed and sutures removed. Every amputee should receive a temporary prosthesis as soon as possible after surgery. The patient benefits psychologically, and complications are prevented.

Upon return from surgery, the patient should be watched for signs of shock, and vital signs should be checked at frequent intervals until stabilized. The dressings or compression cast should be observed for evidence of bright red blood. In case of severe bleeding, the nurse should apply manual pressure to the site and contact the physician immediately. If oozing from the stump occurs, the nurse may reinforce the dressing but should never attempt to change it without a physician's order. Because many amputations are performed on persons between 60 and 70 years of age, the patient must be observed carefully for shock, pulmonary complications, or cardiovascular collapse. Suction equipment and oxygen should be at the bedside, and intravenous fluids and emergency drugs should be available for immediate use. Patients may be cared for in an intensive care unit where drugs and equipment are readily available. Elderly patients may have problems with urinary incontinence, and the dressing may have to be protected to prevent contamination of the wound.

The postoperative care of the patient with an amputation is directed toward preparing the stump for a prosthesis, preventing contractures of the hip or nearest joint, maximizing wound healing, and facilitating adaptation to an altered lifestyle. Providing support to the patient who has undergone amputation is an important component of nursing care. Loss of a limb results in grieving and fear about how the individual will function and interact with others. When psychologic response to the loss is severe, it can result in ineffective rehabilitation.[14]

If a temporary prosthesis has not been applied, the stump is wrapped with elastic compression bandages to shrink and shape the stump.

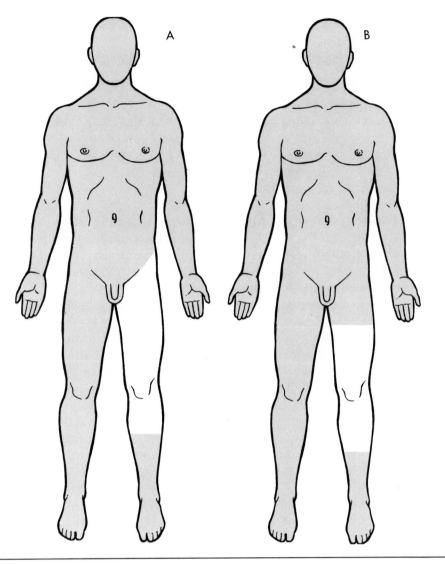

Figure 25-18
Area of skin to be prepared for amputation. **A,** Midthigh amputation. **B,** Below-the-knee amputation.

Before healing occurs, every effort must be made to prevent infection of the wound. The stump may be elevated by raising the foot of the bed for the first 24 hours. When the patient is in the supine position, the stump should rest flat on the bed. The patient should be encouraged to spend some time each day in the prone position with a pillow tucked under the lower trunk and the stump for support (Figure 25-19). The stump should not be flexed over the unaffected leg. When in the prone position, the patient may begin pushup exercises to strengthen arm and shoulder muscles. When in the supine position, the patient may begin exercises of the leg unless this causes strain on the suture line.

With immediate postsurgical prosthesis fitting, a sterile stump sock is pulled over the stump when surgery is complete. Pressure areas are protected with felt pads. The stump is wrapped with elastic plaster-of-Paris bandages to form a rigidly firm dressing, which prevents swelling and protects the stump from injury. As soon as the dressing is dry, a prosthetic device with a foot is applied. The nurse must be alert for edema that may prevent weight bearing, and if the dressing is damaged or comes off, the physician must be notified immediately. Compression bandages should be applied until the physician arrives.[3] Brief ambulation with limited weight bearing is possible within 24 hours. Gradually, ambulation

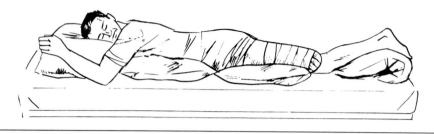

Figure 25-19

Patient in prone position following amputation. Note position of pillows.

is increased, although weight bearing is limited until healing is complete.[12]

This method minimizes stump edema, reduces the risk of embolism, and prevents contractures that preclude subsequent use of a prosthesis. With the application of a compression cast to the stump, the wound cannot be inspected and the risk of necrosis at pressure points exists.

If no complications occur and the wound has healed, the sutures are removed and a temporary prosthesis made of plastic or plaster of Paris is provided 2 to 3 weeks after surgery. At this time, the patient is allowed partial weight bearing. Unless complications develop, the patient may bear full weight on the prosthesis within 6 weeks, and a permanent prosthesis is supplied within 3 months.

Patients may need to be taught balance and crutch walking before leaving the hospital; they often are referred to the physical therapy department. The patient should be instructed to wash and dry the stump thoroughly once a day when healing is complete. If any abrasion occurs, the physician should be consulted immediately.

Phantom limb pain

Patients may have little pain from the surgical procedure or may complain of pain in the amputated limb. This pain, referred to as phantom limb pain, frequently occurs during the first few weeks after surgery and is most intense during the initial 6 months after the amputation.[11] The exact mechanism of phantom limb pain is not completely understood, although a combination of physiologic and psychologic factors may be involved. Investigators have found that preoperative limb pain is associated with phantom pain in the immediate postoperative period.[11]

Until recently, measures used to treat phantom limb pain have been ineffective. Consequently, a number of individuals have been unable to be fully rehabilitated because of the extreme discomfort associated with the application of the prosthesis and their inability to participate in programs of muscle strengthening and ambulation training.

Encouraging results have been seen over the past few years with the use of *transcutaneous electrical nerve stimulation* (TENS) for the relief of phantom pain.[5] Patients experiencing limb pain after amputation are being instructed to attach a TENS unit to the nonamputated limb at a site comparable to where the pain is felt in the amputated limb. The relief from pain is believed to be the result of the inability of the cerebral cortex to distinguish the origin of the impulse. The impulses generated by the TENS unit "override" the pain impulses, breaking the cycle of pain and relieving the discomfort.[5]

The child amputee

Congenital absence of limbs can occur and children of all ages may have amputations because of disease or injury. The meaning of the event to children depends on their age. For the adolescent, the experience may be profoundly traumatic. Small children who are treated by parents as invalids may become completely dependent, rather than self-sufficient.

The child amputee faces some special problems that must be recognized. When a prosthesis is fitted, regular medical supervision and changes must be made coincident with the growth process. The child with a prosthesis is likely to suffer from fatigue more readily than other children. Active children frequently sustain trauma to the stump, and edema may result from excessive pressure within the socket of the prosthesis. The socket must fit properly because abrasions and irritations of the stump will occur if it does not. In some parts of the United States child amputee clinics are available to assist children and their families.

NEUROMUSCULAR CONDITIONS

A number of neurologic conditions affect the musculoskeletal system. Low back pain may be caused by a ruptured intervertebral disk or may result from muscle strain caused by poor alignment of the vertebral column or excessive activity. *Carpal tunnel syndrome* and *thoracic outlet syndrome* both involve tingling and numbness of the upper extremities and impair function. These conditions are discussed in Chapter 22.

Muscular Dystrophy

Progressive muscular dystrophy is the term applied to a number of neuromuscular disorders of genetic origin in which a slow degeneration of muscle fibers occur. Muscular dystrophy is caused by an inherited genetic defect.[18] Carriers of the gene can now be identified, and the disease can be detected before symptoms arise by determining blood levels of the enzyme creatine phosphokinase. Because physicians are not required to report the disease, the number of actual cases is not known. Several types of the disease occur, the most common appearing at age 2 or 3 years (Duchenne's muscular dystrophy). The onset of other types generally occurs in the teens and during the second and third decades of life. The most common type occurs classically in men who have received the defective gene from their mother.

Muscular dystrophy affects voluntary muscles, which become weak, atrophy, and waste away. The mother of a young child with the disease may first become concerned when she notices that the child stumbles and falls more than others and has difficulty running. The child tends to walk on the toes with a waddling gait and has difficulty rising from the floor *(Gowers' sign)* because the muscles of the pelvic girdle are weak. The calf muscles become enlarged, and the heel cords contract. A hollow develops in the back, and the abdomen protrudes. The fibers of the enlarged calf muscles are replaced by fat and fibrous tissue. The muscles of the thighs, hips, and shoulders atrophy as the child grows older. In later stages extensive wasting of muscles and deformity of limbs and spine occurs. The heart muscle may become involved, which ultimately leads to death. These patients are susceptible to respiratory tract infections, which contribute to the early death of many. Antibiotics have helped prolong life and a great deal of research has been done, but no cure exists and the prognosis is poor.

Intervention

The aim of treatment is to help the child live a normal life. Regular school should be attended as long as the physical condition permits, after which the child should attend a school for the handicapped. The child must be encouraged and helped to continue active use of muscles to help maintain strength and independence. Long-term bed rest may hasten atrophy. Prevention of contractures is important.

The family will need instruction and guidance in caring for the child, as well as rehabilitation aids for lifting and transporting. Assistance can be obtained through the local chapter of the Muscular Dystrophy Association of America, founded in 1950. The association provides school facilities, physical therapy, braces, wheelchairs, and other items needed by patients and their families.

Cerebral Palsy

Cerebral palsy is a broad term applied to a variety of conditions characterized by impaired functional muscle control resulting from an abnormality in the cerebral areas that affect these functions. The cause may be any condition that produces cerebral anoxia and hemorrhage or trauma. It may occur during the prenatal period, during or after delivery, or later in life. If the injury produces irreversible damage to any cerebral areas affecting neuromuscular function, cerebral palsy results.

Many types of cerebral palsy exist and the disease is classified on the basis of symptoms and the extent of involvement. The disease results in motor disability and is characterized by spasticity and involuntary movements related to walking, talking, or any activity requiring muscular coordination. The disorder may be recognized soon after birth or during the first few months of life. Much can be done to help the child, but no treatment to correct the cerebral defect is available.

The person with cerebral palsy may have multiple disabilities in addition to motor function. Many have impairments of vision, hearing, and speech, convulsive disorders, and mental retardation. In addition, psychologic, emotional, and social problems occur. The care and treatment of the child with cerebral palsy requires the help of every person on the health care team. Teaching is basic to the program. The child may need speech therapy and may have to be taught all of the activities of daily living. Work with parents is vitally important.[19]

NURSING CARE PLAN
Patient with Below the Knee Amputation

The patient is an 88-year-old female with a history of noninsulin dependent diabetes mellitus (NIDDM type II). She enters the hospital for a left, below the knee amputation due to gangrene and poor circulation in the left leg. She states that she has enjoyed good health until this "circulation" problem. Additional medical data reveals that she has a history of hypertension. She has never smoked nor used alcohol.

Past medical history

Appendectomy at age 17.
Total hysterectomy at age 46 due to fibroid tumors.
Fractured left femur at age 55 after a fall from bicycle. Healed without sequelae.
Denies any COPD, hypertension, or cardiac disease.
Diabetes discovered on routine physical at age 62. Takes Diabinese 0.2 gr daily in morning. Follows ADA exchange diet with good control.
No known food or drug allergies. Has received antibiotics in the past without problems.

Psychosocial data

Currently resides in an extended care facility due to increasing problems in performing activities of daily living (ADLs), and lack of available family resources. She has been a widow for 9 years and has no children. She is a retired elementary school teacher who engaged in physical sports until age 70.

Assessment data

Patient alert and oriented × 3 (time, place, and person).
Blood pressure stable at 130/70. Afebrile.
Respiratory: Lungs clear. Able to demonstrate effective cough.
   Rate 18-20, regular depth and rhythm.
Abdominal: Soft, nontender, nondistended. Bowel sounds heard in all four quadrants.
Skin: Clear with the exception of a reddened area 2 by 3 cm on coccyx with a small open area (1 cm) on left buttock.
   No rashes or evidence of bruising.
Cardiovascular: Pulse 68-72 apical rate. Regular without murmurs or thrills.
   Pulses on right leg paplable (femoral, popliteal, and pedal).
   Pulses on left leg thready and feeble (femerol and popliteal.
Wound assessment: Stump dressing dry and intact. In good alignment.

Lab data

Hgb 13.1 Hct 40. Electrolytes WNL.
Serum glucose 238.
Urinalysis WNL. Chest x-ray WNL. ECG WNL. All other lab data WLN.

NURSING DIAGNOSIS

Alteration in self-concept related to disturbance in body image from left below the knee amputation as evidenced by statements of depression and periods of crying.

Expected patient outcomes	Nursing interventions	Evaluation for expected outcomes
Patient will achieve a positive self-concept prior to discharge as evidenced by stated feelings of optimism, decreased periods of crying, and verbalization of will to live. Patient will talk with someone who has experienced the same loss.	Inform patient that feelings of depression are expected after a loss of a body part. Provide time to listen. Discuss fears. Encourage feelings. Explore resources among friends. Arrange for patient to interact with others who have similar problems.	Patient acknowledges a change in body image. Patient takes an active role in planning aspects of daily care. Patient expresses her emotions associated with the change in body image. Patient expresses at least one positive feeling about herself daily. Patient participates in discussion with person with a similar change in body image.

NURSING DIAGNOSIS

Aleration in comfort: phantom sensations related to nerve stimulation secondary to amputation as evidenced by soreness in left leg when moving, sensation of "feeling" blanket on missing foot.

Expected patient outcomes	Nursing interventions	Evaluation for expected outcomes
Patient will identify pain characteristics. Patient will articulate factors that intensify pain and modify behavior accordingly. Patient will discuss phantom pain and express a feeling of comfort and relief from pain.	Explain the sensation of "phantom limb." Assess patient's physical pain. Have the patient describe the pain on a scale of 1 to 10. Administer pain medications.	Patient identifies pain characteristics. Patient discusses phantom pain. Patient expresses a feeling of comfort and pain relief.

NURSING DIAGNOSIS

Impaired physical mobility related to left, below the knee amputation as evidenced by need of assistance when moving and inability to perform own ADLs.

Expected patient outcomes	Nursing interventions	Evaluation for expected outcomes
Patient will perform self-care activities to tolerance level. Patient will carry out isometric exercises. Patient will avoid risk factors that will lead to activity intolerance. Blood pressure, pulse, and respiratory rate will remain within prescribed range during periods of activity.	Maintain patient in proper body alignment. Turn and position the patient at least every 2 hours. Establish turning schedule while dependent. Increase mobility by having patient move into chair, commode, and geriatric chair. Teach patient to move self in bed. Monitor deep breathing and coughing exercises. Encourage the use of the unaffected leg to change positions in bed. Accompany patient to physical therapy department if possible. Perform range of motion exercise every 2 to 4 hours when awake. Encourage and praise behaviors of independence. Encourage active movement by using trapeze or other assistive devices. Assess patient's physiologic response to increased activity (blood pressure, respirations, heart rate, and rhythm).	Patient demonstrates isometric exercises. Patient explains rationale for maintaining activity level and states at least five risk factors for activity intolerance. Patient performs self-care activities in preparation for discharge. Patient does not exhibit evidence of cardiovascular or respiratory complications during or after activity.

Continued on next page.

NURSING DIAGNOSIS

Impaired skin integrity related to decreased mobility and bedrest as evidenced by reddened and open skin on coccyx.

Expected patient outcomes	Nursing interventions	Evaluation for expected outcomes
Patient experiences no further skin breakdown.	Change patient's position at least every 2 hours.	Patient's skin has no further skin breakdown.
Patient maintains adequate skin circulation. Patient communicates understanding of preventive skin care measures. Patient sustains adequate food and fluid intake.	Keep skin clean and dry. Avoid use of irritating soap; rinse skin well. Use preventive skin care devices as needed, such as an alternating pressure mattress, sheepskin, pillows, and/or padding. Protect bony prominences and massage gently to increase circulation. Keep linen clean, dry, and free of wrinkles or crumbs. Monitor nutritional intake; encourage adequate hydration. Leave reddened area exposed to air; turn patient off area. Teach patient and friends the importance of remaining off reddened areas.	Reddened areas show signs of improved circulation. Patient's mucous membranes remain intact. Patient eats at least 80% of each meal and takes extra fluids every 2 hours when awake. Patient remains clean and dry at all times. Her position is changed at least every 2 hours. Patient's weight remains within her established limits. Patient lists preventive skin care measures.

REFERENCES AND ADDITIONAL READINGS

1. Adams RD and Victor M: Principles of neurology, ed 4, New York, 1989, McGraw-Hill Inc.

2. Andreoli TE and others: Cecil's essentials of medicine, ed 2, Philadelphia, 1990, WB Saunders Co.

3. Brunner LS and Suddarth DS: Textbook of medical-surgical nursing, ed 6, Philadelphia, 1988, JB Lippincott Co.

4. Burg ME: Compartment syndrome, Crit Care Q 6(1):27-32, 1983.

5. Carabelli RA and Kellerman WC: Phantom limb pain: relief by application of TENS to contralateral extremity, Arch Phys Med Rehabil 66:466-467, 1985.

6. Carpenito LJ: Handbook of nursing diagnosis 1989-90, Philadelphia, 1989, JB Lippincott Co.

7. Crosby LJ: Stress factors, emotional stress and rheumatoid arthritis disease activity, J Adv Nurs 13:452-461, 1988.

8. Follman DA: Nursing care concerns in total shoulder replacement, Orthop Nurs 7(3):29-31, 1988.

9. Geier KA and Hesser K: Electrical bone stimulation for treatment of nonunion, Orthop Nurs 4(2):41-50, 1985.

10. Hilt NE and Cogburn SB: Manual of orthopedics, St Louis, 1980, The CV Mosby Co.

11. Jensen TS and others: Immediate and long-term phantom pain in amputees: incidence, clinical characteristics and relationship to preamputation limb pain. Pain 21:267-278, 1985.

12. Luckman J and Sorensen KC: Medical-surgical nursing, ed 3, Philadelphia, 1987, WB Saunders Co.

13. Mims BD: Fat embolism syndrome: a variant of ARDS, Orthop Nurs 8(3):22-27, 1989.

14. Pinzer MS, Graham G, and Osterman H: Psychologic testing in amputation rehabilitation, Clin Orthop 229:236-240, 1988.

15. Reckling JB and Neuberger GB: Understanding immune system dysfunction, Nurs 87 17(9):34-41, 1987.

16. Schoen DC: The nursing process in orthopedics, Norwalk, Conn, 1986, Appleton & Lange.

17. Selman SW: Impact of total hip replacement on quality of life, Orthop Nurs 8(5):43-49, 1989.

18. Stewart NJ: Perceptual and behavioral effects of immobility and social isolation in hospitalized orthopedic patients, Nursing Papers 18(3):59-74, 1986.

19. Whaley LF and Wong DL: Essentials of pediatric nursing, ed 3, 1989, St Louis, The CV Mosby Co. 1989.

PROBLEMS AFFECTING
Immune Response

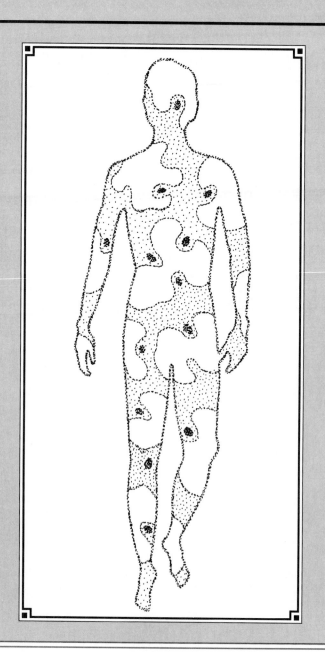

KEY WORDS

AIDS
allergen
allergist
anaphylaxis
antigen
antihistamine
atopic
autoimmune disease
cell-mediated immunity
desensitization
eosinophils
epinephrine
genetic
humoral immunity
hypersensitivity
immunodeficiency virus
immunotherapy
lacrimation
opportunistic infection
reaginic IgG antibody
rhinitis
sensitized
universal precautions
urticaria

OBJECTIVES

1. Define hypersensitivity.

2. Differentiate between immediate and delayed hypersensitivity.

3. Explain the action of histamine in allergic reactions.

4. Identify the major manifestations associated with allergic conditions.

5. List the major assessment techniques used for allergic conditions.

6. Identify the primary therapeutic techniques in the treatment of hypersensitivity.

7. Identify diseases attributed to autoimmunity.

8. Discuss the nursing responsibility in the intervention for a patient in anaphylactic shock.

9. Define primary and secondary immune system deficits.

10. List the common medical interventions in the treatment of primary immune deficiencies.

11. Discuss the nursing care of a patient with a primary immune system deficiency.

12. Identify the nursing interventions for a patient with AIDS.

13. List the major medical interventions in the treatment of patients with AIDS.

EXCESSIVE, IMMUNE RESPONSES

Allergy

The condition now known as **allergy** or **hypersensitivity** was first observed in 1832. However, it was not until 1890 that serious study was undertaken. Robert Koch was the first to observe and describe the allergic reaction after he administered the tuberculosis test for diagnosis of tuberculosis. The term "allergy" was not used until 1906, when von Pirquet used it to describe changes associated with repeated contact with various antigenic substances. Since that time, the word allergy has been accepted to designate hypersensitivity in certain individuals. The terms "allergy" and "hypersensitivity" are used interchangeably.

Although many factors associated with immunity and hypersensitivity remain unknown, research has accomplished a great deal in a short time. The diagnosis and treatment of allergic disorders is a medical specialty and the physician treating these disorders is called an **allergist.**

An allergy is an inappropriate and excessive response of the immune system to certain substances that are not harmful to most persons (see Chapter 2). When an individual contacts the offending substance **(antigen),** his body is immediately stimulated to produce either antibodies or sensitized white blood cells, called **T lymphocytes,** to defend itself against the offending antigen. When the same antigen is contacted again, the antibodies or sensitized cells that have been produced react with the antigen and destroy or neutralize the antigen. This results in a group of symptoms that we refer to as manifestations of allergy.

The **genetic** transmission of the predisposition to allergy occurs in some families. If a parent has an allergic disorder, the offspring may develop an allergic condition at some period during their lifetime; however, it does not necessarily mean that the allergy will be the same type as the parent's allergy. The homeostasis of the body plays an important role when the individual has an inherited predisposition to allergy. Any episode that disturbs the homeostatic balance, such as severe infection, pregnancy, or endocrine dysfunction, may cause or exacerbate an allergy.

An allergen may be transmitted directly from the mother to the fetus in utero by the placental blood supply. When the infant has been sensitized in utero to a specific allergen, contact with the allergen after birth may cause an allergic reaction.

Allergens can be classified as inhalants, ingestants, injectants, contactants, or infectants. The most common inhalants are pollens from grasses, weeds, trees, grains, and dust. Allergy caused by inhaling these pollens is usually seasonal and occurs when flowering and pollination occur. The most common type of allergy caused by pollens is hay fever. Ingestants are usually foods to which the individual may be hypersensitive. The most common offenders include the proteins of cow's milk, egg white, chocolate, strawberries, shellfish, and nuts. Among the injectants are drugs such as penicillin or other antibiotics. Horse serum that may be used in making antitoxins may cause severe reactions. The venom from a snake bite or stings from some insects may cause a reaction in a hypersensitive person. Some individuals may be sensitive to contactants such as laundry powders, cosmetic preparations, nickel compound used in costume jewelry, rubber compounds used in elastic, and the sap from plants such as poison ivy or poison oak (Figure 26-1). Factors related to infectants have been demonstrated in tuberculosis, typhoid fever, and anthrax.

Pathophysiology

Most allergies are caused by an antigen-antibody reaction that results in damage to some of the body's tissues. This type of response is called an **immediate** reaction. The tissues of the body commonly involved are called target organs and are those tissues that come in frequent contact with the external environment, such as the skin, mucous membranes, respiratory tract, and gastrointestinal tract. A summary of hypersensitivity reactions is found in Table 26-1. Types I, II, and III reactions are related to **humoral immunity** and are the immediate result of interactions involving circulating antibodies. Type IV reactions are delayed, are related to **cell-mediated immunity,** and are the direct result of interactions involving **sensitized** lymphocytes.

Immediate hypersensitivity. Individuals with Type I immediate hypersensitivity reaction must first come into contact with an allergen. The body may respond by forming specific antibodies that will react with the allergen. Although this is essentially a normal mechanism, the hypersensitive individual produces an altered form of antibody called the **reaginic IgE antibody** (Chapter 2). The nonallergic person would produce the IgG antibody. Subsequent contact with the allergen will initiate an antigen-antibody reaction that will

Table 26-1

Summary of Hypersensitivity Reactions[2,11,21]

Type		Etiology	Examples
I	Immediate	IgE bound to mast cells, which degranulate and release histamine and other chemical mediators	Atopic (inherited) Hay fever Urticaria Insect-sting reactions Anaphylaxis
II	Cytotoxic	Antigen-antibody complex and complement cause cell lysis. IgG and/or IgM mediated	Transfusion reactions Drug reactions
III	Immune complex	Antigen-antibody complexes deposit in blood vessels and tissues, causing acute inflammation	Systemic lupus Erythematosus Serum sickness Glomerulonephritis
IV	Cell-mediated	Sensitized T lymphocytes and macrophages cause tissue destruction	Tuberculosis reaction (delayed skin response) Contact dermititis Transplant rejection

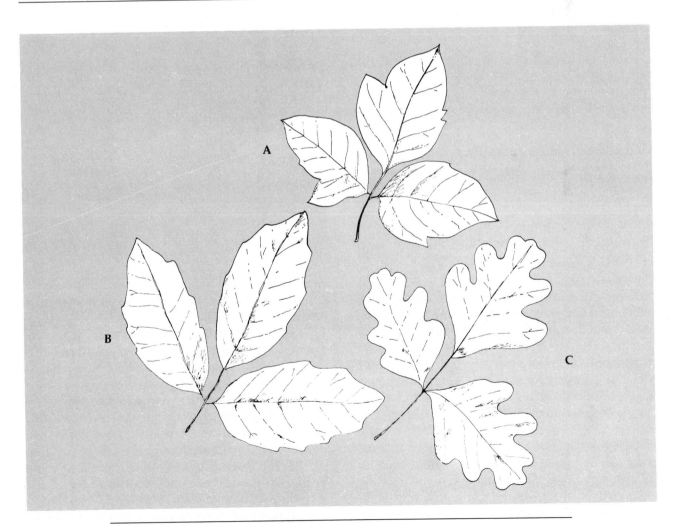

Figure 26-1

Plants and shrubs that frequently cause severe skin reactions. **A,** Poison ivy. **B** and **C,** Types of poison oak.

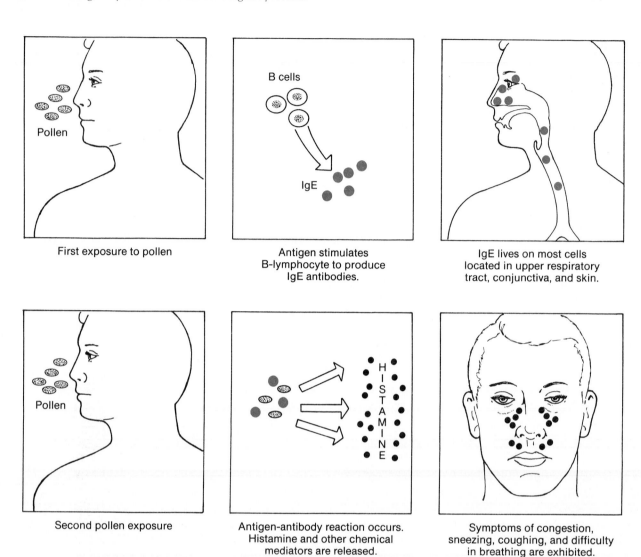

First exposure to pollen

Antigen stimulates
B-lymphocyte to produce
IgE antibodies.

IgE lives on most cells
located in upper respiratory
tract, conjunctiva, and skin.

Second pollen exposure

Antigen-antibody reaction occurs.
Histamine and other chemical
mediators are released.

Symptoms of congestion,
sneezing, coughing, and difficulty
in breathing are exhibited.

Figure 26-2
Allergic response to ragweed pollen.

damage tissues. Enzymes such as histamine and histamine-like substances are released from mast cells in the target organ to which the reaginic antibody and antigen have become attached. This process causes increased vascular permeability, constriction of smooth muscle, and an increased secretion from mucous glands; a local inflammatory response is initiated.

The symptoms of this type of allergy are caused by the effects of these chemicals and the lactation of the tissue in which the antigen-antibody reaction is occurring. If a sensitized person inhales ragweed pollen, the antigen-antibody reaction will take place in the respiratory tract. Histamine causes vasodilation, and vessels become more permeable, allowing fluids to escape into the body tissues and causing edema. Constriction of smooth muscle lining the airway plus increased mucous secretion may all lead to symptoms of congestion, sneezing, coughing, and difficulty breathing (Figure 26-2).

Inhalants usually cause congestion of the nasal mucosa, sneezing, a thin watery nasal discharge, red itching conjunctivae, and increased lacrimation. Allergens entering through the digestive tract may produce nausea, vomiting, and diarrhea. Various contact substances cause urticaria and dermatitis. Typical skin reactions such as hives or wheals are localized areas of swelling that are red, hot, and itchy. Hives can also develop in the gastrointestinal tract, on the lining of the respiratory passageways, and along blood vessels. When histamine causes spasm and constriction of the bronchioles, bronchial asthma may occur. Many local Type I reactions are atopic or inherited. Usually the symptoms of atopic allergy

Table 26-2

Emergency Care of Individuals in Anaphylactic Shock

Signs and symptoms	Nursing interventions	Expected patient outcomes
Rapid, shallow breathing; bronchospasms; dyspnea; cyanosis; restlessness; "sense of doom"; irritability; laryngeal edema	Prepare for oropharyngeal intubation or surgical insertion of tracheotomy; oxygen therapy per order; Prepare for administration of antihistamines such as benadryl 50-100 mg IM, aminophylline IV drip; administer corticosteroids to decrease inflammation, as ordered.	Maintain patent airway Demonstrates effective breathing pattern
Hypotension Rapid, thready pulse	Administer 0.1 ml to 0.5 ml 1:1000 epinephrine solution SC or IM into upper arm and massage site to hasten absorption; prepare to administer vasopressor drugs such as levarterenol bitartrate (Levophed) and high-dose dopamine (Intropin); monitor pulse and blood pressure q 3-5 minutes until stable	Maintain hemodynamic stability, as evidenced by blood pressure and pulse in normal range
Edema and itching at site of injection or insect bite	Place a tourniquet above the site of the antigen. Remove tourniquet q 10-15 minutes or until reaction is under control; apply ice	Reduce systemic absorption of the antigen

are localized to the site of the antigen-antibody reaction. However, if large amounts of chemicals are released, they may enter the circulation, causing systemic effects. Drug allergies, for example, may cause a variety of reactions, from fever and skin rash to **urticaria,** anaphylactic shock, and death.

Allergic reactions from insects

The bites or stings of various insects may cause local or systemic reactions. The local reaction that occurs at the site of the bite or sting is not considered to be an allergic reaction. However, when systemic reactions occur, the symptoms are consistent with allergy. Stings by bees, wasps, hornets, and yellow jackets may produce systemic reactions that vary from mild urticaria and itching to respiratory embarrassment, shock, loss of consciousness, and death. The antigen-antibody reaction may be to all insects or to only one specific insect. The same process of antibody formation occurs as with other antigens. The first sting may cause no trouble, but if the individual should be stung again, a reaction may occur. The speed with which the reaction develops is in direct proportion to its severity. If a large number of stings occur at the same time, the reaction may be immediate and can be fatal because of the large amount of toxin injected. When the stinger is left in the skin, it should be scraped off; squeezing should be

avoided. See Table 26-2 for immediate intervention.

The best treatment is prevention. Patients with a known allergy to insect stings should carry an emergency medical information card or dog tag that explains the problem. See box on page 798 for prevention of severe insect sting reactions.

Anaphylactic Shock

Anaphylactic shock, is a systemic response to a type I, hypersensitivity reaction. It is potentially fatal and can appear within minutes in people who have been previously sensitized to the allergen. It is a sudden, severe, systemic reaction that is a true medical emergency. It follows exposure to a substance to which the individual is extremely sensitive. Although it is relatively rare, it occurs after the injection of vaccines, drugs, foreign sera, or allergenic extracts that are used in desensitization. Penicillin, bee or wasp venom, and substances containing iodine, which are frequently used as a contrast medium for x-ray examinations, are common causes of anaphylaxis. Foods containing iodine are often implicated.

Assessment

Initial symptoms of anaphylaxis are edema and itching in the eyes and ears and/or at the site of injection, sneezing, and apprehension. In seconds or minutes edema of the face, hands, and other parts of the body can occur. Respiratory distress from bronchospasm, sneezing and coughing, wheezing, dyspnea, and cyanosis follows. Edema of the larynx and laryngospasm may lead to death. Gastrointestinal symptoms such as nausea and vomiting, abdominal pain, and diarrhea may be present. Cardiovascular signs such as dysrhythmias, tachycardia, or bradycardia may be followed by circulatory collapse, which is indicated by a falling blood pressure, pallor, and loss of consciousness. In extreme cases death may occur in 5 to 10 minutes after onset of the reaction. See Table 26-2 for the immediate nursing interventions for an individual suffering from anaphylactic shock.

Cytotoxic

A type II (cytotoxic) hypersensitivity reaction occurs when an incompatible blood product is given to a patient. The antigen responsible for the antigen-antibody reaction is the donor red blood cell. This cell reacts with the recipient's antibody and complement to cause cell lysis. See Chapter 17 for more information on this and other types of transfusion reactions. Some drug reactions are also cytotoxic reactions.

Immune Complex

A type III hypersensitivity reaction results in the formation of immune complexes. This product of the antigen-antibody reaction is deposited in the tissues. Inflammation results and causes damage in the affected organ system. One example is the response to the beta hemolytic streptococcus that results in acute poststreptococcal glomerulonephritis, causing the nephrons of the kidney to become damaged (Chapter 19).

Cell-Mediated

Delayed reactions, type IV hypersensitivity, may be local or systemic and may be delayed from hours to days. This type of hypersensitivity is a result of an alteration in the cell-mediated immune response where entire lymphoctyes (T cells) become sensitized to the antigen (Table 26-1). Antibodies are not produced, but instead the whole cell attacks the antigen and destroys it. The most common example of a delayed reaction is the tuberculin skin test. Individuals who have been previously sensitized to the antigen will respond to an intradermal injection of old tuberculin with erythema and induration after 24 to 48 hours. Allergic contact dermatitis is the most common immunologic disorder treated by dermatologists. The most common sensitizing antigens are poison ivy, rubber compounds used in elastic, and nickel used in costume jewelry and buttons. These combine with skin proteins creating a non-self antigen. A localized irritation of the skin (eczema) will result, characterized by redness, edema, and scaling. Organ transplant rejection is also believed to be a type of delayed sensitivity. The individual's history as it relates to tension-producing situations, infection, endocrine disturbance, and work-related activities may be significant. Geographic movement may be important because of change of climate or exposure to new kinds of allergens (Figure 26-3). Include all the relevant assessments clearly in the patient's chart and in the nursing care plan. See the boxed material at right for appropriate nursing diagnoses for patients with allergies.

A thorough physical examination is done, which involves a complete blood count and differential count. **Eosinophils** are white blood cells that normally comprise 1% to 3% of all leukocytes. During an allergic reaction, the number of circulating eosinophils frequently increases greatly, and they collect at sites of antigen-antibody re-

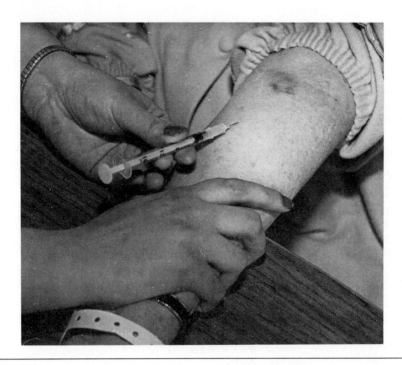

Figure 26-3
Interdermal skin testing for allergic response. *(Courtesy Copley Memorial Hospital, Aurora, Ill.)*

Nursing Diagnoses for Patients with Allergic Conditions

- Potential for injury related to allergic conditions
- Ineffective airway clearance related to nasal congestion and bronchospasms
- Pain related to hives or contact dermatitis
- Knowledge deficit related to allergens, diagnostic tests, and treatment regimens
- Impaired skin integrity related to contact dermatitis
- Altered family processes related to change of environment
- Alteration in cardiac output related to anaphylactic shock
- Alteration in nutrition related to nausea and vomiting
- Sleep pattern disturbance related to side effects of medications
- Ineffective individual coping related to variable nature of allergic reactions and necessity of altering lifestyle

actions, such as in the nasal secretions. Another diagnostic blood study is the radioallergosorbent technique (RAST) test, which uses a sample of the patient's blood to test for the presence of reaginic (IgE) antibodies.

Assessment of People with Atopic Allergies

About 40 million Americans have some type of allergy.[17] Because these hypersensitivity reactions occur so frequently, nurses in all fields must learn to appropriately assess the allergy patient. A careful and thorough allergy history is essential in identifying possible allergens. See Figure 26-4 for an example of a complete allergy assessment. Genetic and congenital factors are extremely important in helping to establish a diagnosis. Patients should be asked about any family history of allergies and any previous allergic experiences that they may have had. Any past allergic reactions must be recorded and described in the assessment.

Skin tests

There are several methods of doing skin tests, including the scratch test, intradermal test, and patch test. Testing is often started using the

ALLERGY SURVEY SHEET

Name _John Richards_   Age _36_   Sex _M_   Date _Sept. 3, 1989_

I. **Chief complaint:** _Stuffy nose + watery eyes_
II. **Present illness:** _Wheezing, clear nasal discharge, itchy eyes for 5wks._
III. **Collateral allergic symptoms:** _Same symptoms last fall._

Eyes:	Pruritus ✓	Burning —	Lacrimation ✓	
	Swelling ✓	Infection —	Discharge —	
Ears:	Pruritus —	Fullness —	Popping —	
	Frequent infections —			
Nose:	Sneezing ✓	Rhinorrhea ✓	Obstruction —	
	Pruritus ✓	Mouth breathing —		
	Purulent discharge —			
Throat:	Soreness —	Post-nasal discharge ✓		
	Palatal pruritus ✓	Mucus in the morning —		
Chest:	Cough —	Pain —	Wheezing ✓	
	Sputum —	Dyspnea —		
	Color —	Rest —		
	Amount —	Exertion —		
Skin:	Dermatitis —	Eczema —	Urticaria —	

IV. **Family allergies:** _Father had eczemas. Mother none._
V. **Previous allergic treatment or testing:** _no_
   Prior skin testing: _none_

Drugs:	Antihistamines	Improved _yes_	Unimproved
	Bronchodilators	Improved _yes_	Unimproved
	Nose drops	Improved _yes_	Unimproved
	Hyposensitization	Improved _not done_	Unimproved —
	Duration —		
	Antigens —		
	Reactions —		
	Antibiotics } _not used_	Improved —	Unimproved
	Steroids	Improved —	Unimproved

VI. **Physical agents and habits:**

Bothered by:

Tobacco for — years	Alcohol —	Air cond. —
Cigarettes — packs/day	Heat —	Muggy weath. —
Cigars — per day	Cold —	Weath. chngs. —
Pipe — per day	Perfumes —	Chemicals —
Never smoked ✓	Paints —	Hair spray —
Bothered by smoke _yes_	Insecticides —	Newspapers —
	Cosmetics —	

Figure 26-4

Allergy survey sheet *(From Patterson R: Allergic diseases, ed 3, Philadelphia, 1985, JB Lippincott Co.)*

scratch test method. A small scratch is made through the skin with a blunt instrument, but not deep enough to cause bleeding. The allergen may be a powder, liquid, or paste. When the test is done on the forearm, a control is placed on the other arm. After application of the allergen, an area of redness and a wheal will appear in 15 to 30 minutes if the individual is sensitive to the antigen, whereas the control will not show any reaction.

The intradermal test may be used without prior use of the scratch test, or it may be used only for the antigens that failed to react to the scratch test. A minute amount (0.01 to 0.02 ml) of the antigen is injected into but not through the skin with a tuberculin syringe and a No. 26-gauge

VII. When symptoms occur:

Time and circumstances of 1st episode: *Aug./Sept. 1988*
Prior health: *good*
Course of illness over decades: progressing ____✓____ regressing _____
Time of year:
  Perennial ___✓___   Exact dates *Aug./Sept. 1988*
  Seasonal ___✓___   *Aug. 1- present 1989*
  Seasonally exacerbated ___✓___
Monthly variations (menses, occupation): *none*
Time of week (weekend vs weekdays): *no*
Time of day or night: *no*
After insect stings: *no*

VIII. Where symptoms occur:

Living where at onset: *Kansas City, Kansas*
Living where since onset: *Kansas City, Kansas*
Effect of vacation or major geographic change: *until June 1988 lived in N.W. Pennsylvania*
Symptoms better indoors or outdoors: *indoors*
Effect of school or work: *better at work inside*
Effect of staying elsewhere nearby: *none*
Effect of hospitalization: —
Effect of specific environments: *went to a park with increased severity of symptoms*
Do symptoms occur around:
old leaves ___✓___ hay ___✓___ lakeside ___—___ barns ___—___
summer homes ___—___ damp basement ___—___ dry attic ___—___
lawnmowing ___✓___ animals ___—___ other ___—___
Do symptoms occur after eating: *no*
cheese ___—___ mushrooms ___—___ beer ___—___ melons ___—___
bananas ___—___ fish ___—___ nuts ___—___ citrus fruits ___—___
other foods (list) *none* _____
Home: city ___—___ rural ___✓___
  house ___✓___ age *10 yrs.*
  apartment ___—___ basement ___✓___ damp _____ dry ___✓___
  heating system ___✓___ *Forced*
  pets (how long) *none* dog ___—___ cat ___—___ other ___—___

Bedroom:	Type	Age	Living Room:	Type	Age
Pillow	*foam*	*3 yrs.*	Rug	*nylon*	*1 yr.*
Mattress	*foam*	*5 yrs.*	Matting	*nylon*	*1 yr.*
Blankets	*thermal*	*5 yrs.*	Furniture	*wood & nylon fabric*	*1 yr.*
Quilts	*none*	—			
Furniture	*wood*	*5 yrs*			

Anywhere in home symptoms are worse: *no* _____

IX. What does patient think makes him worse: *outside Aug./Sept.*

X. Under what circumstances is he free of symptoms: *in air conditioning*

XI. Summary and additional comments:

Figure 26-4 cont'd

needle (Figure 26-4). The test is read in about 10 minutes, and the sensitivity reaction is similar to that of the scratch test.

Patch tests may be used for suspected allergy to specific substances for which commercial allergens are not available. The allergen is applied to the skin, covered, and then secured with adhesive tape. The patch is removed in 2 to 3 days and the skin examined. Appearance of erythema or a wheal indicates sensitivity to the allergen. The nurse must be alert for any reaction that might indicate that the patient is developing a generalized allergic reaction. Sudden difficulty in breathing, a change in vital signs, pallor, or dizziness should be reported to the physician at once. A syringe of 1:1000 epinephrine (Adrenalin) should be available for immediate use. All patients undergoing testing should be kept under surveillance for at least 20 minutes following the testing procedures. In the event that the patient has a reaction, follow the procedure outlined in Table 26-2.

Mucous membrane sensitivity tests

Tests may also be made by placing the allergen into the conjunctival sac of the eye. Nothing is placed in the opposite eye, which serves as a control. If the test is positive, itching of the conjunctiva and increased **lacrimation** will occur. The eyes are then flushed with physiologic saline solution to remove the allergen, and 1 or 2 drops of a 1:1000 aqueous solution of epinephrine is placed in the conjunctival sac. The nasal cavity may also be used for testing; the allergen is sprayed or sniffed into one nostril. The opposite nostril serves as a control. A positive reaction will cause sneezing, nasal congestion, and a thin, watery discharge. Because of the discomfort caused to the patient, mucous membrane testing is not widely used.

Elimination testing

When food is believed to be the cause of allergy, the patient may be given an elimination diet to determine the specific food causing the trouble. Either of two methods may be used. The patient may be asked to keep a record of all food eaten for a given period. Then one food, such as milk, chocolate, or wheat products, is eliminated from the diet. By gradually eliminating specific foods from the diet, the food causing the allergy may be identified. The other method is to give the patient a diet consisting of foods that usually do not cause allergy. The diet is followed for a week, and if allergic symptoms continue, changes are made in the diet. If symptoms continue, it is generally considered that food is not the cause of the allergic reaction. However, if symptoms disappear, other foods are added to the diet until the patient develops allergic symptoms. That food is then considered to be the probable cause, and it is eliminated from the diet. This type of testing may be used to identify the cause of urticaria (see Chapter 24). Elimination testing is also used for patients with contact dermatitis. Offending agents such as cosmetics, hair spray, and certain types of clothing are eliminated until the dermatitis disappears. These agents gradually are reintroduced to identify the causative agent.

Nursing Interventions for People with Allergies

Nursing interventions for people with allergies includes education on avoidance therapy, administering drug therapy, and assisting with immunotherapy (**desensitization**). Patients should be educated on the importance of maintaining optimal health and getting enough rest and controlling stress. The emotional status of the patient will influence the severity of the allergy symptoms and the effectiveness of the allergy treatment.

Allergen avoidance

The best treatmet for an allergy is to prevent the person from coming in contact with the allergen. The specific allergen must be identified and necessary adaptations made. This may completely change a person's way of life. It may mean moving to another environment, a change in employment, or a change in the type of clothing worn. When animal dander is a factor, it may be necessary to remove household pets or to avoid contact with farm animals. Picnicking or hiking into the woods may have to be eliminated. Installing air-conditioning, damp mopping and dusting, and keeping windows closed may help to prevent some allergic attacks when caused by household dust or other allergens in the air. Rainy, damp, humid weather is often associated with asthma. The use of a dehumidifier to remove moisture from the air may be beneficial in preventing attacks of asthma. Individuals with allergies are advised to avoid exposure to infections. A common cold may precipitate an allergic reaction. It may be necessary for the individual to make many changes in his environment and personal way of life. Adaptations made by the person with an allergy may also affect members of the patient's family.

Drug Therapy

Drugs commonly used to treat allergies are antihistamines, epinephrine, topical decongestants, and corticosteroids. As a result of the antigen-antibody reaction, histamine is released from the cells and is primarily responsible for allergic symptoms. Drug therapy is designed to counteract the effects of the histamine. Antihistamines are most useful in allergic conditions affecting the nasal mucosa (such as hay fever), **rhinitis,** itching, and acute urticaria. They are also used for motion sickness, nausea and vomiting, vertigo, and sleeplessness.

Antihistamines block the action of histamine on the bronchioles and blood vessels; the major side effect from these drugs is drowsiness. Persons who are taking any of this group of drugs are advised not to drive motor vehicles. Other side effects include dizziness, dryness of mucous membranes, and weakness. There are many antihistaminic preparations on the market. Some of the newer, nonsedating antihistamines, such as terfenadine (Seldane), may be better tolerated although they are more expensive and not necessarily more effective.[17]

Antihistamines may be administered orally, and some are available for parenteral injection or administration rectally. The most commonly used antihistamines are outlined in Table 26-3.

Epinephrine (adrenalin) has several uses. In allergy it is used for serious hypersensitivity such as anaphylactic shock. A 1:1000 aqueous solution is used for parenteral injection. Epinephrine counteracts the actions of histamine and helps reverse the pathology that has occurred. It increases the strength and force of the heartbeat, increases blood pressure, and relaxes the smooth muscles of the respiratory tract.

Topical decongestants exhibit an antiallergy effect causing shrinkage of congested nasal mucous membranes. Phenylephrine (neosynephrine) is one of the most widely prescribed topical nasal decongestants. The drug should be used at intervals of at least 4 hours to prevent rebound congestion. This can occur after prolonged and repeated vasoconstrictor stimulation initiates a compensatory vasodilation and subsequent increased secretions. When this occurs the drug treatment should be discontinued.[33]

Corticosteroids are not generally used in allergic disorders because of their serious side effects. However, steroid preparations are marketed as ointments, creams, and lotions for topical application. They are used in allergic dermatosis and applied two or three times a day. Corticosteroids may be given to a patient with life-theatening asthma, but usually only after other forms of medication have failed. Corticosteroids are also administered in some immediate allergic reactions, including anaphylactic shock or an allergic reaction to penicillin and other severe drug reactions. Corticosteroids help reduce the inflammatory reaction and aid in recovery. Hydrocortisone succinate (Solu-Cortef) is often used.

Immunotherapy

Immunotherapy or desensitization, as it is sometimes called, is a form of immunization, the purpose of which is to stimulate the production of a

Table 26-3

Major Antihistamines Currently in Use

Drug	Dosage	Action	Nursing considerations
Diphenhydramine (Benadryl)	25-50 mg PO tid or qid or 10-50 mg IM or IV	Blocks the effects of histamine, thereby blocking the constriction of bronchial, GI, and vascular smooth muscle, and skin nerve endings. (same for all 4 drugs)	Advise patient that drowsiness may occur; administer drug at bedtime to decrease symptoms. Sleepiness may decrease after 2-3 days. Advise patient not to drive or engage in activities that require alertness. Advise patient to avoid alcohol or other CNS depressants, which increase sedative effect. Instruct patient to increase fluids or suck on sugarless candy if dry mouth occurs. Consult with physician to discontinue antihistamines 4 days before allergy skin testing to avoid masking results. When administered parenterally, use deep IM and Z-tract method to prevent SC irritation.
Tripelennamine (Pyribenzamine)	25-50 mg PO q4-6 hours not to exceed 600 mg/day; 100 mg PO, bid or tid if sustained release tablets		
Chlorpheniramine (Chlor-trimeton, Teldrin)	4 mg PO in regular tablets q4-6 hours, not to exceed 24 mg/day; 8-12 mg PO bid of sustained release tablets; 5-20 mg IV		
Terfenadine (Seldane)	60 mg PO bid		

more common form of antibody, the IgG antibody, rather than the reaginic IgE antibody. When small amounts of the extract of the antigen are administered by injection at varying intervals for an extended time, IgG antibodies are produced that have a greater affinity for the allergen than the IgE antibody. This causes the serum titer of the IgE antibody to decrease, and therefore the reactions typical of atopic allergy are prevented. The antigen-antibody reaction that occurs with the IgG antibody does not stimulate histamine release from mast cells.[23,25]

The extract is usually given weekly and the amount is gradually increased with each injection until the largest dose that causes no reaction is given. This is considered to be the maintenance dose. Desensitization has been most effective in hay fever. Persons who have a seasonal allergy are advised to begin injections early, before allergic symptoms appear. This is not a lifetime regimen; most allergists consider a routine course to last for 3 to 4 years.[17]

Autoimmune Disease

As a result of genetic differences, the human body rejects anything that is not of itself. This is the reason that human organ transplants are usually rejected by the recipient. It is also why skin for grafting is taken from a site on the recipient's own body and transferred to the site for grafting. The individual becomes both the donor and the recipient. Recently, considerable attention has been given to what is called **autoimmune disease.** Under usual conditions the body will suppress the production of antibodies that would injure its own body. For reasons not clearly understood, the body loses self-identity and produces antigenic substances that stimulate antibody or sensitized lymphocyte formation that will react against itself. Diseases and disorders that result from this reaction are called autoimmune diseases or autohypersensitivity, and they may affect the eyes, skin, joints, thyroid gland, kidneys, brain, and vascular system. Some diseases currently believed to be autoimmune are found in the box above right. Intensive study and research are continuing to produce a better understanding of autoimmunity.[29]

Autoimmune diseases are usually treated with drug therapy aimed at interfering with the immune response. Immunosuppressants, such as azathioprine (Imuran), and corticosteroids, such as prednisone (Deltasone), may be administered.

Diseases Considered to be Autoimmune in Nature
Rheumatoid arthritis
Systemic lupus erythematosus
Idiopathic thrombocytopenic purpura
Myasthenia gravis
Pernicious anemia
Hashimoto's thyroiditis
Glomerulonephritis
Multiple sclerosis
Ulcerative colitis
Juvenile insulin dependent diabetes

Antiinflammatory drugs, such as salicylates (aspirin) and ibuprofen (Motrin) may be given for symptomatic relief.[33]

DEFICIENT IMMUNE RESPONSES

Immunodeficiencies or deficient immune responses affect one or more of the major components of immunity: T cells, B cells, complement, and leukocytes (see Chapter 2). Immune deficiencies are classified according to etiology as either **congenital** or **acquired.** Congenital, or inherited, deficiencies are categorized as primary disorders, whereas acquired deficits are designated as secondary deficits. Regardless of the classification, these deficient responses produce similar effects. Persons with an immune system deficit are susceptible to life-threatening infections and often have limited prognoses for survival. Some specific disorders are associated with other severe health problems that contribute to the dismal prognosis. See Table 26-4 for more information on primary immunodeficiencies and the appropriate nursing care of these patients.

Primary Immunodeficiencies

Parents and families of infants and children diagnosed with DiGeorge's syndrome, **severe combined immunodeficiency disease** (SCID), or Wiskott-Aldrich syndrome need tremendous support both financially and emotionally. If the disorder is genetic, the parents need counseling regarding the risk for having another child with the same deficiency. Parents need help dealing with the prognosis of an early death of their child as do

Table 26-4

Primary Immunodeficiencies

Disease and etiology	Nursing diagnoses	Nursing interventions
Hypogammaglobulinemia: B cell deficiency in male infants.	Potential for infections related to inadequate immune system	Educate parents and patients to recognize and avoid infections and to seek prompt treatment when infection occurs. See box on page 807, High risk for infection.
IgA deficiency: IgA deficiency with normal IgG levels; allergies and autoimmunity occur frequently.	Potential for infection related to inadequate immune system; potential ineffective airway clearance related to anaphylaxis; pain related to autoimmunity	Educate parents and patients to recognize and avoid infections and to seek prompt treatment when infection occurs.* See box on page 807, High risk for infection. Identify allergens through allergy assessment. Monitor blood transfusions carefully for reaction. Assess pain level and plan care to minimize discomfort.
DiGeorge's syndrome: Partial or complete absence of thyroid gland	Potential for infection related to inadequate immune system; knowledge deficit regarding signs of tetany; potential dysfunctional grieving related to anticipated loss	Educate parents and patients to recognize and avoid infections and to seek prompt treatment when infection occurs.* See box on page 807, High risk for infection. Monitor levels Educate family on signs of tetany Provide support to integrate the anticipated loss of the child and find meaning in the time the child is living.
Wiscott-Aldrich syndrome: Low IgM levels and decreased T-cell immunity; thrombocytopenia and eczema are common manifestations.	Potential for infection related to inadequate immune system; potential for injury related to increased susceptibility to bleeding; pain related to eczema	Educate parents and patients to recognize and avoid infections and to seek prompt treatment when infection occurs.* See box on page 807, High risk for infection. Assess and report signs of bleeding. Apply hydrocortisone cream to affected skin as ordered.
Severe Combined Immunodeficiency Disease (SCID): Both B cell and T cell immunity is absent; bone marrow transplant effective if done quickly.	Potential for infection related to inadequate immune system; potential alteration in oral mucous membranes related to infection; potential decreased nutrition related to diarrhea; potential alteration in skin integrity related to bone marrow rejection	Educate parents and patients to recognize and avoid infections and to seek prompt treatment when infection occurs.* See box on page 807. Assess for and maintain adequate hydration. Assess oral mucous membranes q4 hours. Plan meals to minimize discomfort. Do not administer live vaccines. Avoid invasive procedures. Assess for bone marrow rejection as evidenced by rash and sloughing of skin.

*See box on p. 807.

the siblings. Referrals at the appropriate time to hospice groups, visiting nurses associations, and community agencies for financial support are important facets of nursing care for these families. School nurses and teachers should also be contacted when appropriate. A national support group started by parents of children with immune deficit disorders has many state chapters.*

Secondary Immunodeficiencies

Secondary deficient immune responses are acquired and are attributed to various, often multiple etiologies. Age is a factor that affects the immune response of the very young and the very old. Babies who have lost their natural immunity and have not yet developed a mature immune system are very susceptible to infections. The elderly exhibit both thymus gland and T-cell function deterioration. These cellular changes combined with physiologic changes (Table 26-5) make the elderly more susceptible to infections.[37] Malnutrition, cancer and cancer treatments such as cytotoxic chemotherapy and radiation therapy, surgery and anesthesia, therapeutic induction of immunosuppression as used in transplantation procedures, and chronic use of corticosteroids have all been implicated as factors causing acquired immune deficits. Malignant diseases of the immune system like multiple myeloma and chronic lymphocytic leukemia are associated with humoral immune deficits; malignancies of the cell-mediated immune system such as Hodgkin's disease impair T-cell function. Other factors such as prolonged distress and bereavement have been correlated with immunosuppression. A recent and tragic example of an acquired, or secondary, immune deficiency is the acquired immune deficiency syndrome (AIDS).

Pathophysiology

Secondary, or acquired, immune system deficits vary in the degree to which the immune system is depressed. Generalized immune deficits occur more often in acquired than in primary states, thus presenting difficulty in isolating and correlating each etiologic factor with a specific disorder.

When the humoral immune system is predominantly affected, the individual is subject to similar recurrent bacterial infections as occur in

*The Immune Deficiency Foundation P.O. Box 586, Columbia, MD 21045.

Table 26-5

Physiologic Changes in the Elderly

Change	Consequences
Gastrointestinal tract	
Decreased HCl secretion	Decreased destruction of organisms
Decreased motility	Ineffective removal of organisms
Genitourinary system	
Decreased bladder elimination	Greater opportunity for microbe growth
Decrease in mucosal barrier	Increased entry of organisms
Respiratory system	
Decreased effectiveness of cilia	Poor removal of inhaled organisms
Decrease in elastic recoil	Decreased alveolar ventilation
Decreased tidal volume when lying flat	Collapse of alveoli (atelectasis)
	Decreased macrophage function
	Impaired gas exchange
	Lower blood oxygen levels
Reduced muscle strength	Labored breathing
Impaired cough/gag reflexes	Decreased ability to remove particles and organisms
	Increased risk of aspiration
Cardiovascular system	
Decrease in cardiac output	Decrease in oxygen delivery to tissues
Increased peripheral resistance	Increased risk of ischemic injury
Fragile capillaries	Increased risk of damage
	Decreased oxygen/nutrient supply to tissues
Skin	
Decreased elasticity	More easily torn or traumatized, permitting organisms to enter body

From Beare PG and Myers J: Principles and practice of adult health nursing, St Louis, 1990, Mosby-Year Book, Inc.

primary hypogammaglobulinemia. Invasion by gram-positive and gram-negative bacilli is facilitated: in some patients these are the organisms that coexist with the body as part of the normal flora. In the hospitalized patient, virulent organisms that reside in the environment colonize the skin and oropharynx, thereby increasing vulnerability to life-threatening bacterial infections.

T-cell or cell-mediated responses suppressed by the factors described earlier limit the individual's ability to resist infections too, but in this instance the causative organisms are viruses, fungi, and protozoa. These intracellular organisms, so called because of their ability to escape phagocytosis and opsonization by penetrating cell membranes, are usually effectively neutralized by the T lymphoctyes. Some of these organisms are part of the normal flora of the skin, the mucous membranes of the small intestine, and the oral cavity. When these organisms proliferate, as they do in the immunosuppressed patient, they result in systemic and local infections. These infections are termed **opportunistic** as are those caused by endogenous bacteria.

NURSING CARE OF PEOPLE WITH IMMUNODEFICIENCIES

Because infection is the major sign of immunodeficiency, the nurse must focus assessment and intervention on preventing and treating infec-

tions. Performing a complete nursing assessment will help to identify patients who at risk for immunodeficiencies. Reviewing lab studies and conducting a physical exam can identify an actual infection. See below for the appropriate nursing interventions for patients at high risk for infections.

Acquired Immunodeficiency Syndrome

As the name implies, AIDS is an acquired, or secondary, immune system disorder. Presently an incurable and fatal disease, AIDS is caused by the human immunodeficiency virus (HIV). This virus is transmitted in three ways: through sexual contact, by exposure to infected blood, and perinatally from mother to neonate. It may take from 6 to 12 weeks for a person to manufacture enough antibodies to test positive to HIV (HIV+). The HIV+ diagnosis is made when a series of blood tests, starting with enzyme-linked immunoabsorbent assay (ELISA), followed by the Western blot, a more specific test is repeatedly reactive.[24] The presence of HIV antibodies does not necessarily mean that a person has AIDS. It is only after the development of severe symptoms of immunodeficiency, AIDS dementia, opportunistic infections, or malignancies that the AIDS diagnosis is

---

High Risk for Infection: Nursing Interventions

1. Careful handwashing before, during, and after care.
2. Monitor temperature every 4 hours and report elevations to physician.
3. Monitor pulse rate every 4 hours and report elevations to physician.
4. Monitor lab values, especially CBC.
5. Assess mouth for lesions, color changes, or discomfort every 4 hours.
6. Assess rectum for tenderness, irritation, or redness.
7. Check bowel daily.
8. Auscultate lungs every 8 hours and report adventitious sounds.
9. Note, report, and document any changes in sputum—color, odor, amount, or consistency.
10. Assist patient to turn, cough, and deep breathe every 2 hours.
11. Ambulate patient if tolerated; if not, reposition every 2 hours.
12. Range of motion exercises should be performed every 4 hours if mobility is limited.
13. Monitor skin turgor every 8 hours.
14. Assess skin for redness, lesions, or swelling every 8 hours.
15. Keep skin clean, dry, and well lubricated with daily bathing.
16. Assess for pain or burning on urination and for color of urine.
17. Inspect all IV line sites for redness, swelling, or pain.
18. Maintain strict asepsis with dressing changes, IV dressing site changes, and suctioning.
19. Invasive procedures—injections, enemas, or rectal temperatures—should not be performed.
21. Fresh flowers, fresh vegetables, or water-filled vases are not permitted in the room.
22. Screen visitors and staff for colds, nausea, vomiting, and fever.
23. Maintain patient in a private room or protective isolation if required.
24. Instruct patient and family on signs and symptoms of infection.
25. Instruct patient and family on how to perform personal hygiene.

made. See the box at right for the Centers for Disease Control's classification system for HIV infections.[4]

AIDS occurs primarily in homosexual men (60%) and intravenous drug users who share needles (20%). Infants born to or nursed by an HIV+ mother, recipients of blood transfusions performed before 1985, and the heterosexual partners of HIV+ persons are also at risk for becoming infected. HIV does not spread by casual contact; so far there have been no cases of other members of an AIDS patient's family contacting the disease.

Present estimates by public health officials indicate that 1 to 1½ million Americans are infected with the AIDS virus (HIV), known also as the human T cell lymphotropic virus III (HTLV III). Prediction by these officials is that 25% to 30% of infected individuals will develop AIDS within the next few years. Because AIDS is a relatively new phenomenon, no one can predict with absolute accuracy whether these estimates will hold true; also the time interval from infection to disease manifestation is not fully known. Some experts predict that the incidence rate will be closer to 50% of those infected. In either case, the United States health care system and all individuals affected by the disease will be severely strained economically and emotionally. Over 120,000 people have been diagnosed with AIDS using the definition proposed by the Centers for Disease Control; approximately 70,000 of these have already died.

Clinical manifestations

It takes between 6 and 12 weeks for antibodies to develop to the HIV after the initial infection takes place and may take up to 1 year. During that time the patient may or may not have symptoms that indicate infection. Some individuals experience flulike symptoms similar to those seen in mononucleosis. During the variable incubation period between infection and AIDS (1 to 10 years), most patients have persistent and generalized lymphadenopathy. This may be accompanied by night sweats, fever, diarrhea, fatigue, weight loss, and unusual infections like oral candidiasis. These symptoms are somtimes called **AIDS-related complex (ARC)**. In a few infected persons the virus directly attacks the central nervous system, producing headaches, forgetfulness, and inability to concentrate. Recent studies suggest that dementia sometimes occurs before AIDS is diagnosed.[10] Some of these infected individuals even-

---

> ### Centers for Disease Control Classification System for HIV Infection
>
> **Group**   **Description**
>
> I   Acute HIV infection; documented seroconversion
>
> II   Asymptomatic seropositives; no present or previous signs or symptoms of infection
>
> III   Persistent, generalized lymphadenopathy, defined as ≥1 cm nodes at ≥2 extrainguinal sites
>
> IV   Severe AIDS-related diseases
>
> A   Constitutional disease: unexplained fever, diarrhea, weight loss
>
> B   Neurologic disease: unexplained dementia, neuropathy, or myelopathy
>
> C-1   Opportunistic infections
>
> C-2   Other infections: oral hairy leukoplakia, multidermatomal herpes zoster, recurrent *Salmonella* bacteremia, nocardiosis, tuberculosis, oral candidiasis
>
> D   Opportunistic malignancies: Kaposi's sarcoma, non-Hodgkin's lymphoma, primary CNS lymphoma
>
> E   Other conditions

---

tually will develop AIDS within the next 10 years (see the box on page 809). For most persons there is a long interval between acquiring the initial infection and developing fullblown AIDS; living with this phenomenon stimulates many concerns about the quality of life.

Because of their severely impaired cellular immunity, AIDS patients are susceptible to multiple opportunistic infections and unusual malignancies. Infections are difficult to control and can recur despite what appears to be good responses to treatment. For 60% of HIV+ patients, *Pneumocystis carinii* pneumonia (PCP) is the progression to AIDS. This slow-developing, parasitic lung infection occurs only in immunosuppressed patients. PCP is treated with trimethoprim-sulfame thoxazole (Bactrim, Septra) or Pentamidine (Pentam 300 or aerosol). Antiinfective therapy can be successful for this disease. Kaposi's sarcoma manifests as multiple red to purple, oblong, non-

---

NURSING CARE GUIDELINES
AIDS[20,31]

Nursing diagnoses

- High risk for infection related to inadequate immune system
- Social isolation related to stigma attached to AIDS diagnosis
- Alteration in nutrition: decreased related to loss of appetite, oral discomfort, or high metabolic needs.
- Activity intolerance related to weakness, fatigue, and malnutrition.

Nursing interventions

- Reduce stigma of isolation by respecting patient's dignity.
- Encourage patient to express feelings of isolation; provide support and feedback.
- Assure patient and significant others that AIDS does not spread by ordinary physical contact and encourage casual interactions.
- Confer with other experts to establish a plan to decrease social isolation. Specify plan.
- Assess and chart behaviors indicative of social isolation.
- Explain rationale for protective isolation to patient and family.
- Encourage telephone contact with significant others.
- Make local and national support groups or hot lines available to patient (AIDS information number 1-800-342-AIDS).
- Assess and document signs of malnutrition (weight, weakness, serum albumin, stomatitis, etc).
- Monitor and document food intake.
- Confer with physician about need for supplements, tube feedings, and total parenteral nutrition.

- Develop meal plan with patient: meal schedules, eating environment, likes/dislikes, food temperature.
- Assess oral mucous membranes every 8 hours and provide appropriate interventions to decrease pain.
- Encourage high protein and high carbohydrate foods.
- Weigh patient qod.
- Assess and document level of tolerance to activities.
- Provide for periods of rest by scheduling treatments, minimizing room noise, and limiting visitors.
- Assist patient with hygiene as needed.
- To improve activity tolerance, instruct patient on energy-saving techniques and improve nutritional status.
- Encourage progressive activity as tolerated. Assess pulse, respiration, blood pressure, presence of dyspnea, cyanosis, and pain as indicators of overactivity.

Expected outcomes

- Verbalizes signs and symptoms of infection
- Verbalizes factors that may increase risk of infection
- Verbalizes a decrease in loneliness and sense of isolation
- Maintains relationships with significant others.
- Maintains weight at ___ lbs
- Tolerates prescribed diet
- Exhibits healthy gums and oral mucous membranes
- Demonstrates ability to alternate activity with appropriate rest periods.
- Verbalizes increased comfort while performing activities

---

tender, slow-growing skin tumors that may involve lymph nodes, lung, and the GI tract (Figure 26-5). Kaposi's sarcoma is treated with chemotherapy, radiation therapy, and interferon, although none of these approaches are curative. Cytomegalovirus (CMV), a viral infection, has an overwhelming incidence in AIDS patients. Ganaclovir (DHPG) slows the progress of retinitis caused by CMV. This drug has a strong suppressive effect on the immune system, which often forces it to be discontinued. At present there is no effective treatment for CMV. Candidiasis and

other fungal infections may be treated with amphotericin B, an antifungal agent with renal function toxicity. Herpes simplex virus 1 and 2 are treated with acyclovir (Zovirax).[21]

Pathophysiology

AIDS is a sexually transmitted and blood-borne disease; the HIV virus is transmitted through semen and blood. The disease is not transmitted through casual contact. Sexual intercourse, whether anal or vaginal, between infected partners spreads the virus. All men and women who

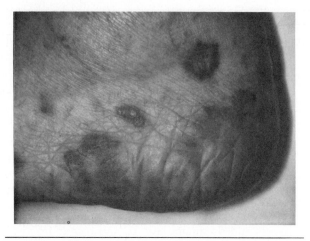

Figure 26-5
Violaceous plaques, purplish in color, of Kaposi's sarcoma on the heel and lateral foot.

have multiple sex partners are at risk. The virus invades the body during intercourse through breaks in the vaginal or rectal mucosal membrane, penis, or skin. Sharing of needles and syringes among intravenous drug abusers is another route of transmission; infected blood may have contaminated the needles or syringes and is a source for AIDS transmission among this group. Transfusions of infected blood or blood products before 1985 accounts for the incidence in non–high-risk groups. Maternal transmission of the virus before or during birth and possibly via breast milk are the routes of transmission in infants of high-risk mothers.

The virus affects the immune system by attaching itself to the T4 or helper T-cell subpopulation of T lymphocytes. It invades the T4 cell and directs the cell to manufacture viral genetic products and proteins. This results in a decrease in helper T-cell number and function. Because the helper T-cell plays a role in both humoral (B-cell) and cellular (T-cell) immunity, this virus causes an impairment in antibody production and T-cell immunity, therefore AIDS virtually cripples the normal protective immune response of the body.

Intervention

Treatment of AIDS remains largely supportive. There is no cure for AIDS and mortality is high. Zidovudine (Retrovir) is the first drug to receive FDA approval for treating AIDS and ARC. Zidovudine, once known as AZT, is still the only drug known to slow the progress of this disease. Although it is not curative, it decreases incidences

of opportunistic infections, improves appetite, and allows patients to live longer. Some patients also experience better neurologic functioning. Zidovudine, an antiviral drug, inhibits the replication of HIV. It does not clear HIV from cells that are already infected, so patients must keep taking it to prevent the disease from advancing. They also must continue to practice safe sex and take other precautions against transmitting the disease to others. Unfortunately zidovudine is not without serious hematologic side effects. Significant anemia and agranulocytopenia can appear within several weeks of therapy. These effects make the drug useless to about 50% of AIDS patients. The cost of the drug, which is about $600 a month, adds to the financial concerns of the AIDS patient.[19,33]

The AIDS diagnosis may affect every system of the body and every facet of a person's life. The nurse has a large role in assessing the many needs of these patients and designing appropriate plans for care. For a sample nursing care plan that may be developed for the AIDS patient, see page 812. The role of the nurse is supportive and is focused on minimizing the distress from the numerous manifestations of the disease. Providing psychologic support is essential, since the essence of nursing care is to assist the patient and family through an enormous assault to the human spirit (Figure 26-6). Body image changes are frightening as the wasting and mental status changes associated with progressing disease take hold. Fear of having transmitted the disease to loved ones and the experience of ostracism can be overwhelming. Physical symptoms such as the drenching sweats that occur daily are managed with frequent linen changes and bathing and special skin care. Prevention of decubiti includes the use of protective devices on the bed. Assisting the patient to maintain independence while conserving energy by balancing activity with frequent rest periods is important. Encouraging the patient to perform consistent frequent oral care will relieve the discomfort of a *Candida* infection. Sitz baths to relieve impaired perirectal mucosal integrity are offered three or four times a day. Maintaining safety is very important for the confused, demented patient and involves keeping bedside rails up, assisting with ambulation, ensuring a safe environment, and frequent reality orientation.

Education of the patient and family in the management of AIDS is extremely important. Informing the patient and the family about the

Figure 26-6
Compassionate support. *(Courtesy VNA Hospice Home Care Program.)*

modes of transmission of the virus is essential to halting the spread of the disease. Patients should be informed that the virus is spread through semen and blood and that sexual intercourse should be avoided if the person is infected. Condoms have been recommended as a means to prevent spread but it is not known if the virus can be blocked by the thin membrane of most commercially available condoms. Abstaining from oral-genital sex is also recommended. Infected persons should not share toothbrushes or razors and women partners of infected persons or high-risk women should prevent pregnancy, since the virus can be transmitted to the fetus. Persons who have a positive antibody test should inform health care personnel before receiving treatment. They should also notify partners and never donate blood, organs, tissue, plasma, or sperm or share needles or syringes if they abuse drugs.

In the hospital, the nurse prevents the spread of the AIDS virus by following infection control recommendations. When the patient is capable of performing self-care activities, only gloves need be worn to handle blood and other specimen collections. The CDC guidelines for universal precautions to prevent transmission of HIV are listed at right.[5] Other isolation procedures should be initiated if the patient has a communicable opportunistic infection. The major risk for health care workers has been associated with handling sharp objects. From a single needlestick with a needle that has been in contact with infected blood, the infection rate is estimated to be about 0.5% or 1 in 200.[24] Precautions to prevent needlestick injury by the nurse must be adhered to strictly.

The nurse should be well informed about this dreaded disease that is epidemic among high-risk groups and in many areas of the world. It is essential that the nurse avoid the hysteria associated with AIDS and maintain a professional demeanor. This involves correcting misinformation, providing accurate information, and above all, protecting the patient's basic human right to privacy. The diagnosis should be kept confidential and patient records guarded against invasion by others who may engage in unethical practices. Quality of care can only be achieved when that care is ethically based.

PRECAUTIONS TO PREVENT TRANSMISSION OF HIV

Universal Precautions

Since medical history and examination cannot reliably identify all patients infected with HIV or other blood-borne pathogens, blood and body-fluid precautions should be consistently used for *all* patients. This approach, previously recommended by CDC and referred to as "universal blood and body-fluid precautions" or "universal precautions," should be used in the care of all patients, especially including those in emergency care settings in which the risk of blood exposure is increased and the infection status of the patient is usually unknown.

1. All health care workers should routinely use appropriate barrier precautions to prevent skin and mucous-membrane exposure when contact with blood or other body fluids of any patient is anticipated. Gloves should be worn for touching blood and body fluids, mucous membranes, or nonintact skin of all patients, for handling items or surfaces soiled with blood or body fluids, and for performing venipuncture and other vascular access procedures. Gloves should be changed after contact

with each patient. Masks and protective eyewear or face shields should be worn during procedures that are likely to generate droplets of blood or other body fluids to prevent exposure of mucous membranes of the mouth, nose, and eyes. Gowns or aprons should be worn during procedures that are likely to generate splashes of blood or other body fluids.

2. Hands and other skin surfaces should be washed immediately and thoroughly if contaminated with blood or other body fluids. Hands should be washed immediately after gloves are removed.

3. All health care workers should take precautions to prevent injuries caused by needles, scalpels, and other sharp instruments or devices during procedures; when cleaning used instruments; during disposal of used needles; and when handling sharp instruments after procedures. To prevent needlestick injuries, needles should not be recapped, purposely bent or broken by hand, removed from disposable syringes, or otherwise manipulated by hand. After they are used, disposable syringes and needles, scalpel blades, and other sharp items should be placed in puncture-resistant containers for disposal; the puncture-resistant containers should be located as close as

practical to the use area. Large-bore reusable needles should be placed in a puncture-resistant container for transport to the reprocessing area.

4. Although saliva has not been implicated in HIV transmission, to minimize the need for emergency mouth-to-mouth resuscitation, mouthpieces, resuscitation bags, or other ventilation devices should be available for use in areas in which the need for resuscitation is predictable.

5. Health care workers who have exudative lesions or weeping dermatitis should refrain from all direct patient care and from handling patient-care equipment until the condition resolves.

6. Pregnant health care workers are not known to be at greater risk of contracting HIV infection than health care workers who are not pregnant; however, if a health care worker develops HIV infection during pregnancy, the infant is at risk of infection resulting from perinatal transmission. Because of this risk, pregnant health care workers should be especially familiar with and strictly adhere to precautions to minimize the risk of HIV transmission.*

---

*Courtesy Centers for Disease Control, 1987.

NURSING CARE PLAN
Patient with Acquired Immunodeficiency Syndrome (AIDS)

The patient is a 37-year-old male who reenters the medical unit after having been discharged 3 months ago. He is HIV+, and has been receiving outpatient therapy for chronic symptoms such as fever, night sweats, diarrhea, fatigue, and weight loss. He currently is experiencing dyspnea, shortness of breath (SOB), and cough, which began 2 days ago. The SOB has intensified, causing him to become anxious and at times confused. Pneumocystis carinii is confirmed by assessments, x-rays, and cultures. He is admitted for further evaluation, nursing care, and treatment.

He has no known food or drug allergies.

Does not smoke or tolerate "second-hand" smoke. Denies use of alcohol or drugs.

Past medical history

Generally healthy until 1 year ago when he developed generalized lymphadenopathy. Sought medical advice immediately. Blood test confirmed presence of HIV antibodies. Started on azidothymidine (AZT) and Bactrim DS on an outpatient basis. Progress monitored by private medical doctor. History of 50 lbs weight loss in 6 months.

Depression for 3 months. Is receiving psychotherapy on a weekly basis. Risk behavior of homosexual activity since age of 18 years old.

Psychosocial data

Has significant other (SO) partner Jeff, with whom he has had a 6 year relationship. (Jeff unwilling to be tested for AIDS at this time).

Supportive relationship with lover. Family lives out-of-state. Both parents are well, and in their early 60s. Planning to retire soon from professional careers. Said to be adjusting to Thomas's homosexual disclosure and illness. Have been to visit two times.

One brother age 35, and a sister age 30. Both well.
No family history of HTN, diabetes, or renal disease.
Cancer history in both sets of grandparents, (now deceased).
Self employed as a dentist. Has been unable to maintain practice.
In process of selling practice and applying for disability benefits under Social Security.
Issue of "confidentiality" requested by Thomas as "giving up" license to practice denotes surrendering to illness.
Owns own home. Easy entrance access.
Has private medical insurance through group practice. Anxious over continuing coverage once illness progresses.
Religion: Protestant—attends services only on holidays. Has discussed illness with Minister.
Hobbies: Likes listening to classical music.
Follows sports on TV. Interested in antique cars.

Assessment data

Frail, thin male who appears much older than his stated age.
Flat affect with very little verbal exchange—Responds to questions but offers no extra information. Some eye contact.
Height 5 ft 10 in. Weight 130 lbs
Oriented × 3 (time, place, and person). Color pale.
Vital signs: T 100.6, p 92, R 38. B.P. 140/70.
Skin: Warm, dry, and intact. No signs rashes, bruises, or decubiti.
EENT: Mucous membranes moist. No mouth lesions
Extra ocular motions (EOM's) intact.
Both nares patent.
Prominent cheek bones from apparent weight loss.
Generalized lymphadenopathy—cervical, postauricular, and axillary nodes bilaterally.

Respiratory: Rate 36-40 range, labored with increased use of accessory muscles. Dyspnea on exertion (DOE). Bilateral wheezes heard both lower lobes, greater on expiration than inspiration.
Adventitious sounds heard all lung fields.
"Guarding" chest while coughing. Nonproductive cough.
No sputum.
Abdominal: Wasted appearance. Decreased tone. Hypotonic bowel sounds heard all four quadrants.
Musculoskeletal: Range of motion all joints with some obvious degree of discomfort. Unsteady gait. Positive peripheral pulses.
No edema in ankles or feet.

Lab data

RBC 3.09 Hgb 8.1 Hct 29 WBC 18,000 Cholesterol 105.
Platelets 300,000 Electrolytes: Na. 145 Pot. 4.2.
Chloride 108 CO2 24.
Blood gases: ph. 7.36, Pco2 47, HCO3 28, Po2 78, 02 sat. 82%.
ECG: WNL.
Chest x-ray shows infiltration both lungs.
Urinalysis: WNL.
Stool culture: positive for Giardia Lamblia.

Medications

Retrovir 200 mg po every 4 hours.
Flagyl 400 mg IVPB every 6 hours (Infuse over 1 hour).
Bactrim DS tabs 2 po every 8 hours.
Valium 5 mg po every 4 to 6 hours prn anxiety.
1000 ml D5W with 10 meq KCL every 8 hours.
Oxygen at 6 L via nasal cannula.
Universal precautions maintained.

NURSING DIAGNOSIS

Altered protection related to immunosuppression as evidenced by infections, cough, weakness, and dyspnea.

Expected patient outcomes	Nursing interventions	Evaluation for expected outcomes
Patient demonstrates use of protective measures including conservative use of energy, maintenance of balanced diet, and obtainment of adequate rest.	Monitor vital signs every 4 hours (more frequently if abnormal).	Patient's vital signs and lab values remain within normal range.
Patient shows no evidence of skin breakdown. Pathogens in cultures show a decrease. WBC and diff. count stay within normal range. Respiratory secretions are clear and colorless.	Teach protective measures including the need to rest, conserve energy, and eat a balanced diet.	Cultures do not exhibit pathogen growth.
IV sites show no signs of inflammation.	Offer small, frequent feedings. Have the dietician visit to calculate kilocalories needed for maintenance.	Patient demonstrates appropriate personal and oral hygiene.
	Patient likes breads, sweets, sherberts, and ginger ale.	Respiratory secretions remain clear and colorless.
	Monitor I & O.	Urine remains clear, yellow, odorless, and free of sediment.
	Encourage him to eat at least 90% of his meals and all of the snacks.	IV sites do not show signs of inflammation.
		Patient's fluid intake remains at specified level.

Continued on next page.

Expected patient outcomes	Nursing interventions	Evaluation for expected outcomes
	Provide relief for symptoms (fever, chills, malaise). Teach stress management and relaxation techniques. Monitor WBC count daily. Report deviations from baseline. Culture urine, respiratory secretions any wound drainage according to hospital policy/physician orders. Help patient wash hands before and after each meal and after using the bathroom, bedpan, or urinal. Assist patient to ensure that perineal area is clean after elimination to decrease the risk of hemorrhoids or perineal abcess. Offer oral hygiene every 4 hours when awake. Use strict aseptic technique when suctioning airway, inserting IV lines, or providing any wound care. Change IV tubing and give site care according to hospital protocol (usually 24 to 48 hours). Rotate IV sites every 48 to 72 hours if possible. Provide tissues and disposal bag for expectorated sputum. Help turn patient every 2 hours when awake. Provide skin care, especially over bony prominences. Use sterile water for humidification/nebulization of oxygen. Encourage fluid intake of at least 2000 ml daily to help mucous secretions. Offer high protein supplements. Patient will drink strawberry Ensure, 90 ml (if chilled) as snack. Keep on reverse isolation. Check visitors or staff for any minor infections.	Patient consumes specific amount of protein and nutritional intake daily. Patient demonstrates a normal pattern of rest, activity, and sleep.

NURSING DIAGNOSIS

Anticipatory grieving related to advancement of illness, as evidenced by behavioral manifestations.

Expected patient outcomes	Nursing interventions	Evaluation for expected outcomes
Patient identifies the perceived potential of his illness and expresses his feelings related to it. Patient exercises control by making decisions related to his dental practice and care while hospitalized.	Help patient to discuss his fears by establishing a trusting relationship. Plan time with each shift to sit with and actively listen to him. Give private time with friend and his family.	Patient expresses his feelings about his illness. Patient communicates understanding of the stages of grief. Patient accepts feelings and behavior brought on by the potential loss.

Expected patient outcomes	Nursing interventions	Evaluation for expected outcomes
Patient uses healthful coping mechanisms to deal with potential loss. Patient seeks a support group. Patient discusses plans to include family and his friend to provide emotional support.	Help patient to understand the grieving process and to accept his feelings as normal. Emphasize patient's identified strengths. Provide positive reinforcement for effective coping behaviors. Inform him of existing support groups in the facility/community. Offer to contact clergy of his choice. Accept his negative feelings as his way of responding to the illness. Provide privacy, dignified care, and acceptance on a daily basis.	Patient uses healthful coping mechanisms. Patient contacts a support group within 2 weeks of hospitalization. Patient shares his feelings with his family, friend, and/or his clergy.

NURSING DIAGNOSIS

Decisional conflict related to surrender of dental practice and license, as evidenced by delayed decision-making and vacillation between alternative choices.

Expected patient outcomes	Nursing interventions	Evaluation for expected outcomes
Patient states his feelings about the current situation. Patient discusses his concern about potential conflict of disclosure (friend is also a partner in the groups practice of three). Patient identifies positive and negative consequences of his decisions. Patient makes minor decisions related to daily activities. Patient accepts assistance from peers, family, and clergy. Patient reports feeling comfortable about his ability to make appropriate rational choices.	Acknowledge patient's feelings. Be supportive and use a nonjudgmental approach. Help him to identify available options and their possible consequences. Help patient make decisions about daily activities. Keep him oriented to reality. Encourage visits with family, friend, clergy, and peers. Demonstrate respect for his right to choose decisions based on values and beliefs.	Patient openly expresses feelings about necessary decisions that he faces. Patient describes conflicts related to illness, disclosure, and treatment. Patient identifies consequences of potential choices. Patient makes at least two care-related decisions daily. He expresses increased comfort in dealing with conflicts.

NURSING DIAGNOSIS

Powerlessness related to chronic illness, as evidenced by sadness, crying, and passivity.

Expected patient outcomes	Nursing interventions	Evaluation for expected outcomes
Patient acknowledges fears and feelings about current situation. His level of anxiety decreases by changing responses to stressors. Patient expresses feelings of regained control. Patient accepts and adapts to his lifestyle changes.	Encourage patient to express his feelings. Set aside time for discussion. Allow silence. Listen for clues of expression. Accept his feelings of powerlessness as normal. Try to be present during situations when feelings of powerlessness are likely to be greatest to help him cope in a positive way.	Patient verbalizes both positive and negative feelings about current situation. Patient describes strategies for reducing anxiety. Patient demonstrates control by participation in decision making related to care. Patient actively plans and executes aspects of decision making regarding future of dental practice.

Continued on next page.

Expected patient outcomes	Nursing interventions	Evaluation for expected outcomes
	Identify and develop patient's coping mechanisms, strengths, and resources. Discuss situations that provoke feelings of anger anxiety or powerlessness. Encourage participation in self-care as much as possible. Provide as many opportunities as possible for him to make decisions regarding care (positioning, rest, choosing an IV site, visiting, fluid and food choices). Modify the environment when available to meet his self-care needs (commode, lounge chair). Encourage family and friend to support patient without taking control. Reinforce patient's rights as stated in "Patient Bill of Rights." Identify and arrange to accommodate his spiritual needs.	Patient includes friend in a discussion of his feelings and/or needs. Patient identifes the potential for appointing a "power of attorney" as his illness progresses. Being a part of that decision leads to his increased feelings of dignity.

REFERENCES AND ADDITIONAL READINGS

1. Barrick B: Caring for AIDS patients: a challenge you can meet. Nurs 88:50, 1988.
2. Beare P and Myers J: Principles and practice of adult health nursing, St Louis, 1990, Mosby–Year Book, Inc.
3. Buisseret PS: Allergy, Sci Am 247:86-95, 1982.
4. Centers for Disease Control: Classification system for human T-lymphotropic virus type III/lympthadenopathy virus type III infections, MMWR 35:334, 1986.
5. Centers for Disease Control: Recommendations for prevention of HIV transmission in health-care settings, MMWR 36(2S):1987.
6. Centers for Disease Control Update: Acquired immunodeficiency syndrome and human immunodeficiency virus infection among health care workers, MMWR 37:229, 1988.
7. Cohen F: Immunologic impairment, infection and AIDS in the aging patient, Crit Care Nurs Q 12(1):38, 1989.
8. Cummings D: Caring for the HIV-infected adult, Nurse Pract 13(11):28, 1988.
9. Ganong W: Review of medical physiology, ed 13, Norwalk, Conn, 1987, Appleton & Lange.
10. Grabbe L: Identifying neurologic complications of AIDS, Nurs 89:66, 1989.
11. Griffin J: Hematology and immunology: concepts for nursing, Norwalk, Conn, 1986, Appleton & Lange.
12. Gurewich I: AIDS in critical care, Heart Lung 18(2):107, 1989.
13. Gurka A: The immune system: implications for critical care nursing, Crit Care Nurse 9(7):24, 1989.
14. Harmon AL and others: Anaphylaxis: sudden death anytime, Nursing 10(10):40-43, 1980.
15. Jackson M and Lynch P: The epidemiology of HIV infection: AIDS and health care worker risk issues, Fam Comm Health 12(2):34, 1989.
16. Jacobs K and Piano M: The clinical picture of AIDS: underlying pathological processes. In Durham J and Cohen F (editors): The person with AIDS: nursing perspectives New York, 1987, Springer Publishing Co.
17. Jacobs RL, Meltzer ED, and Selner JC: Rhinitis: not just hay fever, Patient Care 23(6):168, 1989.
18. Kinney M, Packa D, and Dunbar S: AACN'S clinical reference for critical care nursing, ed 2, New York, 1988, McGraw-Hill Co.
19. LaChariete C and Meisenhelder J: Zidovudine: flawed champion against AIDS, RN 52:35, 1989.
20. Lederer J and others: Care planning pocket guide: a nursing diagnosis approach, ed 3, Redwood City, Calif., 1990. Addison-Wesley Publishing Co Inc.
21. Luckmann J and Sorenson K: Medical-surgical nursing: a psychophysiologic approach, ed 3, Philadelphia, 1987, WB Saunders Co.
22. Marcus R and the CDC Cooperative Needlestick Surveillance Group: Surveillance of health care workers exposed to blood from patients infected with the human immunodeficiency virus, N Eng J Med 319:1118, 1988.
23. Middleton E, Reed CE, and Ellis EF: Allergy: principles and practice, St Louis, 1978, The CV Mosby Co.
24. National Institute for Occupational Safety and Health in collaboration with Center for Infectious Diseases, Centers for Disease Control: Guidelines for prevention of transmission of HIV and hepatitis B virus to health care and public safety workers, Atlanta, 1989.
25. Patterson R: Allergic diseases, ed 3, Philadelphia, 1985, JB Lippincott Co.
26. Reckling J and Neuberger G: Understanding immune system dysfunction, Nurs 87:34, 1987.
27. Robertson S: Drugs that keep AIDS patients alive, RN 52:35, 1989.

28. Roitt I: Essential immunology, ed 5, London, 1984, Blackwell Scientific Publications Inc.
29. Smith AL: Microbiology and pathology, ed 12, St Louis, 1980, The CV Mosby Co.
30. Stites DP and others: Basic and clinical immunology, ed 5, Los Altos, Calif, 1984, Lange Medical Publications.
31. Ulrich S, Canale S, and Wendell S: Nursing care planning guides, Philadelphia, 1986, WB Saunders Co.
32. Ungvarski P: Coping with infections that AIDS patients develop, RN 51:53, 1988.
33. Williams B and Baer C: Essentials of clinical pharmacology in nursing, Springhouse, Penn, 1990 Springhouse Co.

Appendix A

Normal Reference Laboratory Values

Blood, Plasma, or Serum Values		

| Determination | Reference range | |
	Conventional values	SI units
Acetoacetate plus acetone	0.30-2.0 mg/dl	3-20 mg/L
Acetone	Negative	Negative
Acid phosphatase	Adults: 0.10-0.63 U/ml (Bessey-Lowry)	28-175 nmol/s/L
	0.5-2.0 U/ml (Bodansky	
	1.0-4.0 U/ml (King-Armstrong)	
	Children: 6.4-15.2 U/L	
Activated partial thromboplastin time (APTT)	30-40 sec	30-40 sec
Adrenocorticotropic hormone (ACTH)	6 AM 15-100 pg/ml	10-80 ng/L
	6 PM <50 g/ml	<50 ng/L
Alanine aminotransferase (ALT)	5-35 IU/L	5-35 U/L
Albumin	3.2-4.5 g/dl	33-55 g/L
Alcohol	Negative	Negative
Aldolase	Adults: 3.0-8.2 Sibley-Lehninger units/dl	22-59 mU/L at 37° C
	Children: approximately 2 × adult values	
	Newborns: approximately 4 × adult values	
Aldosterone	Peripheral blood:	
	Supine: 7.4 ± 4.2 ng/dl	0.08-0.3 nmol/L
	Upright: 1-21 ng/dl	0.14-0.8 nmol/L
	Adrenal vein: 200-800 ng/dl	
Alkaline phosphatase	Adults: 30-85 ImU/ml	
	Children and adolescents:	
	<2 years: 85-235 ImU/ml	
	2-8 years: 65-210 ImU/ml	
	9-15 years: 60-300 ImU/ml	
	(active bone growth)	
	16-21 years: 30-200 ImU/ml	
Alpha-aminonitrogen	3-6 mg/dl	2.1-3.9 mmol/L
Alpha-1-antitrypsin	>250 mg/dl	
Alpha fetoprotein (AFP)	<25 ng/ml	

Blood, Plasma, or Serum Values—cont'd

Determination	Reference range	
	Conventional values	SI units
Ammonia	Adults: 15-110 μg/dl	47-65 μmol/L
	Children: 40-80 μg/dl	
	Newborns: 90-150 μg/dl	
Amylase	56-190 IU/L	25-125 U/L
	80-150 Somogyi units/ml	
Angiotensin-converting enzyme (ACE)	23-57 U/ml	
Antinuclear antibodies (ANA)	Negative	
Antistreptolysin O (ASO)	Adults: ≤ 160 Todd units/ml	
	Children:	
	Newborns: similar to mother's value	
	6 months-2 years: ≤50 Todd units/ml	
	2-4 years: ≤160 Todd units/ml	
	5-12 years: ≤200 Todd units/ml	
Antithyroid microsomal antibody	Titer <1:100	
Antithyroglobulin antibody	Titer <1:100	
Ascorbic acid (vitamin C)	0.6-1.6 mg/dl	23-57 μmol/L
Aspartate aminotransferase (AST, SGOT)	12-36 U/ml	0.10-0.30 μmol/s/L
	5-40 IU/L	5-40 U/L
Australian antigen (hepatitis-associated antigen, HAA)	Negative	Negative
Barbiturates	Negative	Negative
Base excess	Men: −3.3 to +1.2	0 ± 2 mmol/L
	Women: −2.4 to +2.3	0 ± 2 mmol/L
Bicarbonate (HCO_3)	22-26 mEq/L	22-26 mmol/L
Bilirubin		
Direct (conjugated)	0.1-0.3 mg/dl	1.7-5.1 μmol/L
Indirect (unconjugated)	0.2-0.8 mg/dl	3.4-12.0 μmol/L
Total	Adults and children: 0.1-1.0 mg/dl	5.1-17.0 μmol/L
	Newborns: 1-12 mg/dl	
Bleeding time (Ivy method)	1-9 min	
Blood count (see complete blood count)		
Blood gases (arterial)		
pH	7.35-7.45	
P_{CO_2}	33-45 mm Hg	4.7-6.0 kPa
HCO_3^-	22-26 mEq/L	21-28 nmol/L
P_{O_2}	80-100 mm Hg	11-13 kPa
O_2 saturation	95%-100%	
Blood urea nitrogen (BUN)	5-20 mg/dl	3.6-7.1 mmol/L
Bromide	Up to 5 mg/dl	0-63 mmol/L
Bromosulfophthalein (BSP)	<5% retention after 45 min	
CA 15-3	<22 U/ml	
CA-125	0-35 U/ml	
CA 19-9	<37 U/ml	
C-reactive protein (CRP)	<6 μg/ml	
Calcitonin	<50 pg/ml	<50 pmol/L
Calcium (Ca)	9.0-10.5 mg/dl (total)	2.25-2.75 mmol/L
	3.9-4.6 mg/dl (ionized)	1.05-1.30 mmol/L
Carbon dixoide (CO_2) content	23-30 mEq/L	21-30 mmol/L
Carboxyhemoglobin (COHb)	3% of total hemoglobin	
Carcinoembryonic antigen (CEA)	<2 ng/ml	0-2.5 μg/L
Carotene	50-200 μg/dl	0.74-3.72 μmol/L
Chloride (ClI)	90-110 mEq/L	98-106 mmol/L
Cholesterol	150-250 mg/dl	3.90-6.50 mmol/L

Continued on next page.

Blood, Plasma, or Serum Values—cont'd

Determination	Reference range	
	Conventional values	SI units
Clot retraction	50%-100% clot retraction in 1-2 hours, complete retraction within 24 hours	
Complement	C_3: 70-176 mg/dl	0.55-1.20 g/L
	C_4: 16-45 mg/dl	0.20-0.50 g/L
Complete blood count (CBC)		
Red blood cell (RBC) count	Men: 4.7-6.1 million/mm³	
	Women: 4.2-5.4 million/mm³	
	Infants and children: 3.8-5.5 million/mm³	
	Newborns: 4.8-7.1 million/mm³	
Hemoglobin (Hgb)	Men: 14-18 g/dl	8.7-11.2 mmol/L
	Women: 12-16 g/dl (pregnancy: >11 g/dl)	7.4-9.9 mmol/L
	Children: 11-16 g/dl	1.74-2.56 mmol/L
	Infants: 10-15 g/dl	
	Newborns: 14-24 g/dl	2.56-3.02 mmol/L
Hematocrit (Hct)	Men: 42%-52%	
	Women: 37%-47% (pregnancy: >33%)	
	Children: 31%-43%	
	Infants: 30%-40%	
	Newborns: 44%-64%	
Mean corpuscular volume (MCV)	Adults and children: 80-95 μ^3	80-95 fl
	Newborns: 96-108 μ^3	
Mean corpuscular hemoglobin (MCH)	Adults and children: 27-31 pg	0.42-0.48 fmol
	Newborns: 32-34 pg	
Mean corpuscular hemoglobin concentration (MCHC)	Adults and children: 32-36 g/dl	0.32-0.36
	Newborns: 32-33 g/dl	
White blood cell count (WBC)	Adults and children >2 years: 5000-10,000/cm³	
	Children ≤2 years: 6200-17,000/mm³	
	Newborns: 9000-30,000/mm³	
Differential count		
Neutrophils	55%-70%	
Lymphocytes	20%-40%	
Monocytes	2%-8%	
Eosinophils	1%-4%	
Basophils	0.5%-1%	
Platelet count	150,000-400,000/mm³	
Coombs' test		
Direct	Negative	Negative
Indirect	Negative	Negative
Copper (Cu)	70-140 μg/dl	11.0-24.3 μmol/L
Cortisol	6-28 μg/dl (AM)	170-635 nmol/L
	2-12 μg/dl (PM)	82-413 nmol/L
CPK isoenzyme (MB)	<5% total	
Creatinine	0.7-1.5 mg/dl	<133 μmol/L
Creatinine clearance	Men: 95-104 ml/min	<133 μmol/L
	Women: 95-125 ml/min	
Creatinine phosphokinase (CPK)	5-75 mU/ml	12-80 units/L
Cryoglobulin	Negative	Negative
Differential (WBC) count		
Neutrophils	55%-70%	
Lymphocytes	20%-40%	
Monocytes	2%-8%	
Eosinophils	1%-4%	
Basophils	0.5%-1%	

Blood, Plasma, or Serum Values—cont'd

Determination	Reference range Conventional values	SI units
White blood cell count (WBC)	Adults and children >2 years: 5000-10,000/cm³	
	Children ≤2 years: 6200-17,000/mm³	
	Newborns: 9000-30,000/mm³	
Differential count		
Neutrophils	55%-70%	
Lymphocytes	20%-40%	
Monocytes	2%-8%	
Eosinophils	1%-4%	
Basophils	0.5%-1%	
Platelet count	150,000-400,000/mm³	
Coombs' test		
Direct	Negative	Negative
Indirect	Negative	Negative
Copper (Cu)	70-140 μg/dl	11.0-24.3 μmol/L
Cortisol	6-28 μg/dl (AM)	170-635 nmol/L
	2-12 μg/dl (PM)	82-413 nmol/L
CPK isoenzyme (MB)	<5% total	
Creatinine	0.7-1.5 mg/dl	<133 μmol/L
Creatinine clearance	Men: 95-104 ml/min	<133 μmol/L
	Women: 95-125 ml/min	
Digoxin	Therapeutic level: 0.5-2.0 ng/ml	40-79 μmol/L
	Toxic level: >2.4 ng/ml	>119 μmol/L
Erythrocyte sedimentation rate (ESR)	Men: up to 15 mm/hour	
	Women: up to 20 mm/hour	
	Children: up to 10 mm/hour	
Ethanol	80-200 mg/dl (mild to moderate intoxication)	17-43 mmol/L
	250-400 mg/dl (marked intoxication)	54-87 mmol/L
	>400 mg/dl (severe intoxication)	>87 mmol/L
Euglobulin lysis test	90 min-6 hours	
Fats	Up to 200 mg/dl	
Ferritin	15-200 ng/ml	15-200 μg/L
Fibrin degradation products (FDP)	<10 μg/ml	
Fibrinogen (factor I)	200-400 mg/dl	5.9-11.7 μmol/L
Fibrinolysis/euglobulin lysis test	90 min-6 hours	
Fluorescent treponemal antibody (FTA)	Negative	Negative
Fluoride	<0.05 mg/dl	<0.027 mmol/L
Folic acid (Folate)	5-20 μg/ml	14-34 mmol/L
Follicle-stimulating hormone (FSH)	Men: 0.1-15.0 ImU/ml	
	Women: 6-30 ImU/ml	
	Children: 0.1-12.0 ImU/ml	
	Castrate and postmenopausal: 30-200 ImU/ml	
Free thyroxine index (FTI)	0.9-2.3 ng/dl	
Galactose-1-phosphate uridyl transferase	18.5-28.5 U/g hemoglobin	
Gammaglobulin	0.5-1.6 g/dl	
Gamma-glutamyl transpeptidase (GGTP)	Men: 8-38 U/L	5-40 U/L 37° C
	Women: <45 years: 5-27 U/L	
Gastrin	40-150 pg/ml	40-150 ng/L
Glucagon	50-200 pg/ml	14-56 pmol/L

Continued on next page.

Blood, Plasma, or Serum Values—cont'd

Determination	Reference range	
	Conventional values	SI units
Glucose, fasting (FBS)	Adults: 70-115 mg/dl	3.89-6.38 mmol/L
	Children: 60-100 mg/dl	
	Newborns: 30-80 mg/dl	
Glucose, 2 hour postprandial (2-hour PPG)	<140 mg/dl	
Glucose-6-phosphate dehydrogenase (G-6-PD)	8.6-18.6 IU/g of hemoglobin	
Glucose tolerance test (GTT)	Fasting: 70-115 mg/dl	
	30 min: <200 mg/dl	
	1 hour: <200 mg/dl	
	2 hours: <140 mg/dl	
	3 hours: 70-115 mg/dl	
	4 hours: 70-115 mg/dl	
Glycosylated hemoglobin	Adults: 2.2%-4.8%	
	Children: 1.8%-4.0%	
	Good diabetic control: 2.5%-6%	
	Fair diabetic control: 6.1%-8%	
	Poor diabetic control: >8%	
Growth hormone	<10 ng/ml	<10 µg/L
Haptoglobin	100-150 mg/dl	16-31 µmol/L
Hematocrit (Hct)	Men: 42%-52%	
	Women: 37%-47% (pregnancy: >33%)	
	Children: 31%-43%	
	Infants: 30%-40%	
	Newborns: 44%-64%	
Hemoglobin (Hgb)	Men: 14-18 g/dl	8.7-11.2 mmol/L
	Women: 12-16 g/dl (pregnancy: >11 g/dl)	7.4-9.9 mmol/L
	Children: 11-16 g/dl	
	Infants: 10-15 g/dl	
	Newborns: 14-24 g/dl	
Hemoglobin electrophoresis	Hbg A$_1$: 95%-98%	
	Hgb A$_2$: 2%-3%	
	Hgb: F: 0.8%-2%	
	Hgb S: 0	
	Hgb C: 0	
Hepatitis B surface antigen (HB$_s$AG)	Nonreactive	Nonreactive
Heterophil antibody	Negative	Negative
HLA-B27	None	None
Human chorionic gonadotropin (HCG)	Negative	Negative
Human placental lactogen (HPL)	Rise during pregnancy	
5-Hydroxyindoleacetic acid (5-HIAA)	2.8-8.0 mg/24 hours	
Immunoglobulin quantification	IgG: 550-1900 mg/dl	5.5-19.0 g/L
	IgA: 60-333 mg/dl	0.6-3.3 g/L
	IgM: 45-145 mg/dl	0.45-1.5 g/L
Insulin	4-20 µU/ml	36-179 pmol/L
Iron (Fe)	60-190 µg/dl	13-31 µmol/L
Iron-binding capacity, total (TIBC)	250-420 µg/dl	45-73 µmol/L
Iron (transferrin) saturation	30%-40%	
Ketone bodies	Negative	Negative
Lactic acid	0.6-1.8 mEq/L	
Lactic dehydrogenase (LDH)	90-200 ImU/ml	0.4-1.7 µmol/s/L

Blood, Plasma, or Serum Values

Determination	Reference range	
	Conventional values	SI units
LDH isoenzymes	LDH-1: 17%-27%	
	LDH-2: 28%-38%	
	LDH-3: 19%-27%	
	LDH-4: 5%-16%	
	LDH-5: 6%-16%	
Lead	120 μg/dl or less	<1.0 μmol/L
Leucine aminopeptidase (LAP)	Men: 80-200 U/ml	
	Women: 75-185 U/ml	
Leukocyte count (see complete blood count)		
Lipase	Up to 1.5 units/ml	0-417 U/L
Lipids		
Total	400-1000 mg/dl	4-8 g/L
Cholesterol	150-250 mg/dl	3.9-6.5 mmol/L
Triglycerides	40-150 mg/dl	0.4-1.5 g/L
Phospholipids	150-380 mg/dl	1.9-3.9 mmol/L
Lithium (see Table 14-2)		
Long-acting thyroid stimulating hormone (LATS)	Negative	Negative
Magnesium (Mg)	1.6-3.0 mEq/L	0.8-1.3 mm/L
Methanol	Negative	Negative
Mononucleosis spot test	Negative	Negative
Nitrogen, nonprotein	15-35 mg/dl	10.7-25.0 mmol/L
Nuclear antibody (ANA)	Negative	Negative
5'-Nucleotidase	Up to 1.6 units	27-233 nmol/s/L
Osmolality	275-300 mOsm/kg	
Oxygen saturation (arterial)	95%-100%	0.95-1.00 of capacity
Parathormone (PTH)	<2000 pg/ml	
Partial thromboplastin time, activated (APTT)	30-40 sec	
P_{CO_2}	35-45 mm Hg	
pH	7.35-7.45	7.35-7.45
Phenylalanine	Up to 2 mg/dl	<0.18 mmol/L
Phenylketonuria (PKU)	Negative	Negative
Phenytoin (Dilantin)	Therapeutic level: 10-20 μg/ml	
Phosphatase (acid)	0.10-0.63 U/ml (Bessey-Lowry)	0.11-0.60 U/L
	0.5-2.0 U/ml (Bodansky)	
	1.0-4.0 U/ml (King-Armstrong)	
Phosphatase (alkaline)	Adults: 30-85 ImU/ml	20-90 units/L
	Children and adolescents:	
	<2 years: 85-235 ImU/ml	
	2-8 years: 65-210 ImU/ml	
	9-15 years: 60-300 ImU/ml (active bone growth)	
	16-21 years: 30-200 ImU/ml	
Phospholipids (see Lipids)		
Phosphorus (P, PO_4)	Adults: 2.5-4.5 mg/dl	0.78-1.52 mmol/L
	Children: 3.5-5.8 mg/dl	1.29-2.26 mmol/L
Platelet count	150,000-400,000/mm³	
P_{O_2}	80-100 mm Hg	
Potassium (K)	3.5-5.0 mEq/L	3.5-5.0 mmol/L
Progesterone	Men, prepubertal girls, and postmenopausal women: <2 ng/ml	6 nmol/L
	Women, luteal: peak >5 ng/ml	>16 nmol/L

Continued on next page.

Blood, Plasma, or Serum Values—cont'd

Determination	Reference range	
	Conventional values	SI units
Prolactin	2-15 ng/ml	2-15 μg/L
Protein (total	6-8 g/dl	55-80 g/l
Albumin	3.2-4.5 g/dl	35-55 g/L
Globulin	2.3-3.4 g/dl	20-35 g/L
Prothrombin time (PT)	11.0-12.5 sec	11.0-12.5 sec
Pyruvate	0.3-0.9 mg/dl	34-103 μmol/L
Red blood cell count (see Complete blood count)		
Red blood cell indexes (see Complete blood count)		
Renin		
Reticulocyte count	Adults and children: 0.5%-2% of total erythrocytes	
	Infants: 0.5%-3.1% of total erythrocytes	
	Newborns: 2.5%-6.5% of total erythrocytes	
Rheumatoid factor	Negative	Negative
Rubella antiboyd test		
Salicylates	Negative	
	Therapeutic: 20-25 mg/dl (to age 10: 25-30 mg/dl)	1.4-1.8 mmol/L
	Toxic: >30 mg/dl (after age 60: >20 mg/dl)	>2.2 mmol/L
Schilling test (vitamin B_{12} absorption)	8%-40% excretion/24 hours	
Serologic test for syphilis (STS)	Negative (nonreactive)	
Serum glutamic oxaloacetic transaminase (SGOT, AST)	12-36 U/ml 5-40 IU/L	0.10-0.30 μmol/s/L
Serum glutamic-pyruvic transaminase (SGPT, ALT)	5-35 IU/L	0.05-0.43 μmol/s/L
Sickle cell	Negative	
Sodium (Na^+)	136-145 mEq/L	136-145 mmol/L
Sugar (see glucose)		
Syphilis (see Serologic test for, fluorescent treponemal antibody, veneral disease research laboratory)		
Testosterone	Men: 300-1200 ng/dl	10-42 nmol/L
	Women: 30-95 ng/dl	1.1-3.3 nmol/L
	Prepubertal boys and girls: 5-20 ng/dl	0.165-0.70 nmol/L
Thymol flocculation	Up to 5 units	
Thyroglobulin antibody (see Antithyroglobulin antibody)		
Thyroid-stimulating hormone (TSH)	1-4 μU/ml	5 m U/L
	Neonates: <25 μIU/ml by 3 days	
Thyroxine (T_4)	Murphy-Patee:	50-154 nmol/L
	neonates: 10.1-20.1 μg/dl	
	1-6 years: 5.6-12.6 μg/dl	
	6-10 years: 4.9-11.7 μg/dl	
	>10 years: 4-11 μg/dl	
	Radioimmunoassay: 5-10 μg/dl	
Thyroxine-binding globulin (TBG)	12-28 μg/ml	129-335 nmol/L
Toxoplasmosis antibody titer		

Blood, Plasma, or Serum Values—cont'd

Determination	Reference range	
	Conventional values	**SI units**
Transaminase (see Serum glutamic-oxaloacetic transaminase, serum glutamic pyruvic transaminase)		
Triglycerides	40-150 mg/dl	0.4-1.5 g/L
Triiodothyronine (T$_3$)	110-230 ng/dl	1.2-1.5 nmol/L
Triiodothyronine (T$_3$) resin uptake	25%-35%	
Tubular phosphate reabsorption (TPR)	80%-90%	
Urea nitrogen (see Blood urea nitrogen)		
Uric acid	Men: 2.1-8.5 mg/dl	0.15-0.48 mmol/L
	Women: 2.0-6.6 mg/dl	0.09-0.36 mmol/L
	Children: 2.5-5.5 mg/dl	
Venereal Disease Research Laboratory (VDRL)	Negative	Negative
Vitamin A	20-100 g/dl	0.7-3.5 μmol/L
Vitamin B$_{12}$	200-600 pg/ml	148-443 pmol/L
Vitamin C	0.6-1.6 mg/dl	23-57 μmol/L
Whole blood clot retraction (see Clot retraction)		
Zinc	50-150 μg/dl	

From Pagana KD and Pagana TJ: Diagnostic testing and nursing implications: a case study approach, ed 3, 1990, Mosby–Year Book Inc.

Appendix B

Vaccines Available in the United States, by Type and Recommended Routes of Administration		
Vaccine	**Type**	**Route**
BCG (bacillus of calmette and guerin)	Live bacteria	Intradermal or subcutaneous
Cholera	Inactivated bacteria	Subcutaneous or intradermal*

DTP
  (D = diphtheria)
  (T = tetanus)
  (P = pertussis)
	Toxoids and inactivated bacteria	Intramuscular

HB (Hepatitis B)	Inactive viral antigen	Intramuscular
Haemophilus influenzae b		
—polysaccharide (HbPV)	Bacterial polysaccharide	Subcutaneous or intramuscular†
—or conjugate (HbCV)	or polysaccharide conjugated to protein	Intramuscular
Influenza	Inactivated virus or viral components	Intramuscular
IPV (inactivated poliovirus vaccine)	Inactivated viruses of all 3 serotypes	Subcutaneous
Measles	Live virus	Subcutaneous
Meningococcal	Bacterial polysaccharides of serotypes A/C/Y/W-135	Subcutaneous

MMR
  (M = measles)
  (M = mumps)
  (R = rubella)
	Live viruses	Subcutaneous

Mumps	Live virus	Subcutaneous
OPV (oral poliovirus vaccine)	Live viruses of all 3 serotypes	Oral
Plague	Inactivated bacteria	Intramuscular
Pneumococcal	Bacterial polysaccharides of 23 pneumococcal types	Intramuscular or subcutaneous
Rabies	Inactivated virus	Subcutaneous or intradermal‡
Rubella	Live virus	Subcutaneous
Tetanus	Inactive toxin (toxoid)	Intramuscular§

Td or DT‖
  (T = Tetanus)
  (D or d = diphtheria)
	Inactivated toxins (toxoids)	Intramuscular§

Typhoid	Inactivated bacteria	Subcutaneous¶
Yellow fever	Live virus	Subcutaneous

*The intradermal dose is lower.
†Route depends on the manufacturer; consult package insert for recommendation for specific product used.
‡Intradermal dose is lower and used only for preexposure vaccination.
§Preparations with adjuvants should be given intramuscularly.
‖DT = tetanus and diphtheria toxoids for use in children aged <7 years. Td = tetanus and diphtheria toxoids for use in persons aged ≥7 years. Td contains the same amount of tetanus toxoid as DTP or DT but a reduced dose of diphtheria toxoid.
¶Boosters may be given intradermally unless acetone-killed and dried vaccine is used.
(From Morbidity and Mortality Weekly Report, Vol 38/No 13, March 8, 1991, Centers for Disease Control, Atlanta, Ga, US Department of Health and Human Services.)

Appendix C

Recommended Immunization Schedule for Persons ≥7 Years of Age Not Immunized at the Recommended Time in Early Infancy		
Timing	**Vaccine(s)**	**Comments**
First visit	Td#1*, OPV#1†, and MMR‡	OPV not routinely recommended for persons aged >18 yrs
2 mos after Td#1, OPV#1	Td#2, OPV#2	OPV may be given as soon as 6 wks after OPV#1
6-12 mos after Td#2, OPV#2	Td#3, OPV#3	OPV#3 may be given as soon as 6 wks after OPV#2
10 yrs after Td#3	Td	Repeat every 10 yrs throughout life

*Td—Tetanus and diphtheria toxoids, adsorbed (for adult use) (for use after the seventh birthday). The DTP doses given to children <7 years who remain incompletely immunized at age >7 years should be counted as prior exposure to tetanus and diphtheria toxoids (e.g., a child who previously received 2 doses of DTP needs only 1 dose of Td to complete a primary series for tetanus and diphtheria).

†OPV—Poliovirus vaccine live oral, trivalent: contains poliovirus types 1, 2, and 3. When polio vaccine is to be given to persons >18 years, poliovirus vaccine inactivated (IPV) is preferred. See ACIP statement on polio vaccine for immunization schedule for IPV (2).

‡MMR—Measles, mumps, and rubella virus vaccine, live. Persons born before 1957 can generally be considered immune to measles and mumps and need not be immunized. Since medical personnel are at higher risk for acquiring measles than the general population, medical facilities may wish to consider requiring proof of measles immunity for employees born before 1957. Rubella vaccine can be given to persons of any age, particularly to nonpregnant women of childbearing age. MMR can be used since administration of vaccine to persons already immune is not deleterious (see text for discussion of single vaccines versus combination).

(From Morbidity and Mortality Weekly Report, Vol. 38/No. 13, March 8, 1991, Centers for Disease Control, Atlanta, Ga, U.S. Department of Health and Human Services.)

Glossary

AIDS Acquired immune deficiency syndrome.

ARDS Adult respiratory distress syndrome.

abduction Movement of the extremity away from the midline of the body.

abortion The termination of pregnancy before the fetus is viable.

abscess A localized infection with an accumulation of pus.

abuse To use wrongly or excessively.

acetone A by-product of fat metabolism.

acceptance Approval or the willingness to accept.

acidosis Increase in hydrogen ion concentration resulting from accumulation of acid products or depletion of bicarbonate reserves.

acromegaly A chronic disease caused by an oversecretion of the growth hormone of the pituitary gland. In the adult it may be caused by a tumor.

active immunity Immunity acquired during a person's lifetime as a result of exposure to infectious organisms.

acute care Those services that treat the acute phase of illness or disability, the purpose of which is the restoration of normal life processes and functions.

acute pain Discomfort of relatively short duration; useful in that it provides information relating to injury or pathology.

acute renal failure Temporary loss of renal function usually with a sudden onset.

adaptation Modification to meet a new or changed situation.

addiction Psychologic dependence on a drug; a behavioral pattern of compulsive drug use characterized by overwhelming involvement with getting and using the drug. Withdrawal symptoms specific to the drug occur after cessation of intake.

addictive disorders Physiologic dependence on a chemical or organic substance resulting in withdrawal symptoms on cessation of intake.

adduction Movement of the extremity toward the midline of the body.

adhesion Joining of two parts by an abnormal fibrous band.

adjustment disorders An inability of the individual to adapt to new situations or changes in life or an inability to modify behavior, which overwhelms the person's coping skills and defense mechanisms.

ADL Activities of daily living.

aerobic Describes a pathogen that requires free oxygen to live.

affective disorders One of a group of disorders that has a primary disturbance of emotions or mood as a major feature. It can be chronic or episodic.

agent A factor, such as a microorganism, where presence or relative absence is essential for the occurrence of a disease.

aging A nonpathologic process that gradually results in loss of cells and physiologic reserves.

airway A metal, plastic, or rubber device used to keep the tongue from obstructing the trachea.

aldosterone A steroid hormone produced by the adrenal cortex to regulate sodium and potassium in the blood.

alkalosis A condition in which the alkalinity of the body is increased.

alkylating agent A drug used as nitrogen mustard and related compounds used in the treatment of cancer.

allergen Any substance to which some individuals react abnormally.

allergist A physician trained in the diagnosis and treatment of allergic diseases and disorders.

Alzheimer's disease A chronic brain disorder that involves a progressive destruction of brain tissue. This can begin when a patient is in their forties, and results in slurred speech, growing lapses of memory, involuntary muscle movements, and gradual intellectual deterioration.

ambulation Not confined to bed; walking.

ambulatory care All health services provided on an outpatient basis to those who visit a hospital or other health care facility and depart after treatment on the same day.

amenorrhea Absence of menses; normal before puberty and during pregnancy.

amputee A person who has lost one or more of the extremities.

anabolism A constructive process by which food is converted into living cells.

anaerobic Describes a pathogen that will not live in the presence of oxygen.

analgesic A drug that will relieve pain.

analysis Second step in the nursing process, sometimes combined with or implied as part of the first step, assessment. Involves the evaluation of data for the purpose of determining the patient's needs and problems and developing a nursing diagnosis.

anaphylaxis An immediate reaction from sensitivity to a foreign protein.

anastomosis Surgical connection between two normally distinct structures or segments of a structure (arteriovenous anastomosis); connection of an artery to a vein (intestinal anastomosis); connection of two previously distant portions of the intestine. Can occur pathologically as well.

anemia A blood disorder caused by a reduction of erythrocytes and hemoglobin.

anesthesia Administration of a substance that causes loss of bodily sensations.

aneurysm Dilation of blood vessels into a saclike bulge.

anger An expression of anxiety resulting from real or perceived threats.

angina pectoris Paroxysms of pain caused by decreased blood supply to the myocardium.

angioplasty Percutaneous transfusional coronary angioplasty dilates the coronary vessel wall through mechanical compression.

anhidrosis Lack of sweating.

anion A negatively charged ion.

ankylosis Stiffening of a joint caused by infection or irritation, and the development of fibrous tissue in the joint.

anorexia Loss of appetite.

antibody An immune substance produced within the body in response to a specific antigen.

anticipatory grief Expectation of loss of someone or something highly valued.

anticoagulant A drug that lengthens the prothrombin time and helps to prevent thrombosis and embolism.

antigen A substance that stimulates the immune process.

antihistamine A drug used in the treatment of allergic disorders and motion sickness.

antimetabolite An agent that is used primarily in treating leukemia in children.

antiseptic Any agent that retards the growth of bacteria.

antispasmodic A drug used to relieve spasms of smooth muscles.

antitoxin A serum that is used to combat the toxin produced by a microorganism.

anuria Failure of the kidneys to secrete urine.

anxiety Feeling of uneasiness or apprehension in which the source is often unknown.

anxiety disorders Disorders that have anxiety as the most outstanding symptom. These disorders include posttraumatic stress disorder, phobic disorder, panic disorder, and obsessive-compulsive disorder.

aphasia Loss of the ability to speak.

apnea A temporary absence of breathing.

apoplexy Cerebrovascular accident.

appendicitis Acute inflammation of the appendix.

arrhythmia Any deviation from the normal rhythm of the heartbeat.

arteriosclerosis Hardening of the arteries caused by the formation of fibrous plaques and loss of elasticity.

arthrodesis Surgical fusion of a joint in a functional position.

arthroplasty Plastic surgery on a diseased joint to increase mobility.

articulation Point at which two bones are joined together as in a joint.

ascites Accumulation of fluid in the peritoneal cavity.

asepsis A condition of freedom from pathogenic organisms.

asphyxia Suffocation caused by a decrease of oxygen and an increase of carbon dioxide.

assessment The first step in the nursing process. It demands the collection and recording of data related to the patient and the family for the purpose of identifying patient problems.

It includes the physical and emotional signs and symptoms presented by the patient as well as information obtained from other sources such as the patient's chart, laboratory report, and family visitors.

asthma A chronic bronchial disease caused by spasm of the bronchial tubes accompanied by edema.

astigmatism A defect in the curvature of the cornea or the lens of the eye.

ataxia A lack of coordination of motor movements.

atelectasis Collapse of the lung; may be total or partial.

atherosclerosis A degenerative process of the blood vessels characterized by fatlike deposits along the walls of the vessels.

atopic Pertaining to a state of hypersensitivity that is influenced by heredity.

atrial fibrillation An arrhythmia of the atria consisting of rapid, irregular, and ineffective contractions.

atrophic Wasting away of an organ or part of the body.

atrophy To waste away or decrease in size.

atropine An alkaloid of belladonna; may be administered with a narcotic as preoperative medication.

audiologist A person trained in the detection of hearing problems and the administration of hearing tests; advised persons in the use of hearing aids.

aura A visual sensation experienced by the epileptic person before having a seizure.

auricular fibrillation An arrhythmia of the atria characterized by rapid irregular rate of contraction.

autoclave An apparatus using steam and pressure to sterilize.

autogenous Made from within the body. A vaccine made from organisms taken from a person is an autogenous vaccine.

autograft Tissue taken from the same donor as the recipient.

autoimmunity A condition in which antibodies are produced by one's own body, causing immunization against the body's own proteins.

autonomy The ability or tendency to function independently.

bacteremia Presence of bacteria in the bloodstream.

bacterial endocarditis Infection affecting the valves and the lining of the heart.

bactericidal Describes an agent that kills bacteria.

bacteriophage A virus that attacks bacteria.

bacteriostatic Describes an agent that prevents multiplication of bacteria.

bargaining A mutual agreement.

barium A silver-white chemical agent used as a contrast medium in x-ray examination of the gastrointestinal tract.

bends Abdominal cramps caused by a rapid change from increased atmospheric pressure to normal pressure.

benign Describes a nonmalignant growth or tumor.

benign prostatic hypertrophy Enlargement of the prostate gland.

bereavement Deprivation, such as in loss by death.

bilateral On both sides.

biliary Relating to the gallbladder, liver, and their ducts.

biliary colic Acute pain caused by obstruction of the cystic duct, usually because of a stone.

biopsychosocial The interrelationship of physical, emotional, and social factors.

bleb An irregular elevation of the epidermis filled with serous fluid.

blood dyscrasias Diseases of the blood and the blood-forming organs.

blood urea nitrogen (BUN) An end product of protein metabolism found in the blood.

body image Way in which a person views own body; may mean acceptance in care of a deformity.

boil Cutaneous superficial infection of short duration.

bone marrow transplantation Placement of bone marrow from one person to another.

braces Mechanical device used for support, usually of an extremity.

bradycardia A cardiac arrhythmia marked by an unusually slow heartbeat.

brain stem Subdivision of the brain located above the spinal cord containing the midbrain, pons, and medulla.

bronchiectasis A chronic disease of the lungs in which there is a dilation of the bronchi; may affect both lungs or only a portion of one lung.

bronchitis An inflammatory condition of the bronchial tubes.

bronchography X-ray examination of the bronchi using a radiopaque substance.

bronchoscopy Examination of the bronchi and a portion of the lungs with a lighted instrument.

bulla A vesicle greater than 1 cm in diameter.

bursitis Acute or chronic inflammation of a bursa caused by injury, disease, or unknown factor.

calculus Many stones.

calibrated Marked or graduated to provide for accurate measurement.

callus (1) Thickening of skin from continuous irritation; (2) fibrous tissue formed at the site of a fracture.

cannulation Procedure of placing a cannula into the body, as into a vein.

capsule Mucilaginous envelope surrounding some forms of bacteria.

carbuncle A boil with infiltration into adjacent tissues finally opening in several places on the skin.

carcinogenic Anything capable of producing cancer.

carcinoma A malignant growth with a tendency to infiltrate or metastasize to other tissues.

cardiac output The volume of blood expelled by the ventricles of the heart.

cardiogenic shock Interference with pumping action of the heart causing insufficient vascular circulation.

cardiogram A tracing of the electric activity of the heart.

cardiospasm A spasm of the cardiac valve between the esophagus and the stomach; generally, a functional disorder.

carrier One who harbors germs of a disease and transmits the disease to others while having no symptoms of the disease oneself.

case management Coordination and supervision of all aspects of health care for an individual patient, including delivery of care and evaluation of effectiveness.

catabolism Destructive process by which complex substances are broken down into simpler ones; opposite of anabolism.

cataract An opacity of the lens or the capsule of the eye.

catecholamines Hormones that tend to increase and prolong the effects of the sympathetic nervous system.

cation A positively charged ion.

cell-mediated immunity Acquired immunity characterized by the dominant role of small T-cell lymphocytes.

cellular immunity Acquired immunity that results in sensitization of whole lymphocytes to the invading agent.

central venous pressure A measurement to determine the ability of the right side of the heart to receive and pump blood.

cerebellum Part of the hind brain functioning to coordinate movements.

cerebral edema Increased fluid accumulation in the interstitial areas of the cerebrum.

cerebral palsy A chronic neuromuscular disorder affecting motor coordination.

cerebrospinal fluid Fluid surrounding the brain and spinal cord.

cerebrum Main portion of the brain in the upper half of the cranium forming the largest part of the central nervous system.

cerumen Earwax; a yellowish or brownish waxy secretion in the external ear canal.

chancre Lesion of primary syphilis occurring at the point of inoculation.

chemotherapy Treatment of disease with chemical drugs.

Cheyne-Stokes respiration Respiration in which the rhythm and depth vary with periods of apnea.

cholangiography X-ray examination of the biliary tree after injection of a radiopaque dye.

cholecystectomy Surgical removal of the gallbladder.

cholecystitis Inflammation of the gallbladder.

cholecystography X-ray examination of the gallbladder by use of a radiopaque dye to determine the shape and position of the organ.

cholelithiasis A condition in which calculi are present in the gallbladder or one of its ducts.

cholesterol A substance present in all body tissues and fluids. It may be increased or is thought to be a factor in the development of atherosclerosis.

cholinergic Nerve fibers that liberate acetylcholine when an impulse passes through the nerve; a drug that resembles the action of acetylcholine.

choreiform Resembling chorea.

chronic acute pain Acute pain lasting longer than 6 months; may be continuous or intermittent.

chronic benign pain Pain that persists for 6 months or longer in which the pathologic cause is not progressive or life-threatening. The pain serves no useful purpose and should be treated as a disease.

chronic disease A disease involving structure or function or both and that may be expected to continue over an extended period.

chronic malignant pain Pain associated with cancer or other progressive disorders.

chronic renal failure Loss of renal function usually with a prolonged onset.

cilia Hairlike projections in nasal cavities, trachea, and bronchi.

CircOlectric bed A type of electrically operated bed that permits easy turning and moving of the patient.

circumvent To go around or to prevent.

cirrhosis Disease characterized by death of liver cells and their replacement by scar tissue.

climacteric Synonymous with menopause.

coalesce To run together as in measles.

coccidioidomycosis A disease of the lungs caused by inhaling spores of fungi from the soil.

colectomy Surgical removal of part or all of the colon.

collagenase (ABC) ointment Ointment found to be effective in the treatment of decubitus ulcers.

colonization Presence of an infective agent in the body. Similar to infection.

colostomy A surgical procedure for the purpose of providing an artifical passageway for fecal material from the colon to the outside.

colposcopy Examination of the cervix and vagina by means of a lighted instrument with a magnifying lens called a colposcope that is inserted into the vagina.

coma A deep sleep from which the person cannot be aroused.

comedomes Blackheads.

compartment syndrome The progressive development of arterial blood vessel compression and circulatory compromise (reduced blood supply). Can rapidly result in permanent contracture deformity of the hand or foot called Volkmann's contracture; can occur with injury to forearm and lower leg, with or without fracture.

computerized tomography A computer-aided x-ray examination that visualizes soft tissues better than conventional x-rays.

concurrent disinfection Daily handling and disposal of contaminated material or equipment.

concussion A violent jarring of the brain against the skull.

confusion Altered orientation to time, person, or place.

congenital Existing at birth.

conization A surgical procedure in which a cone-shaped piece of tissue is removed from the cervix.

conjunctivitis Inflammation of the conjunctiva of the eye.

conscious The part of the mind that is one's awareness.

contamination Soiling with any infectious material.

continuity Uninterrupted connection, succession, or union.

contracture A shortening or tension of a muscle that affects extension.

control Restricting the spread of infectious processes.

contusion Bruise; black and blue spot caused by rupture of small blood vessels.

convulsion Involuntary contraction of voluntary muscles.

corpuscle Blood cell; any small mass in the body.

coryza An acute upper respiratory infection; a common cold.

countertraction An opposing force or pulling in the opposite direction.

craniotomy A surgical opening of the cranium for exploration or removal of a tumor or blood clot.

creatinine Nonprotein substance in the blood, synthesized from three amino acids. Normally excreted by the kidney.

creatinism A condition resulting from complete absence of the thyroid gland or its secretion at birth.

crossinfection Transmission of an infection from one patient to another who is already ill with another disease.

crust A dry exudate, commonly called a scab.

cryoprecipitate A fraction of fresh blood plasma; used to control bleeding in hemophilia.

cryosurgery Surgical techniques using an intrument that applies extreme cold to destroy tissue. Used in cataract surgery.

cryptorchidism A condition of an undescended testicle.

culdoscopy A diagnostic procecure; an incision through the posterior cul-de-sac and inserting of a culdoscope to visualize the pelvic organs.

curettage A surgical procedure in which a cavity is scraped with an instrument called a curet.

cutdown Incision through the skin for the purpose of placing a needle or catheter into a vein.

cyanosis A bluish color of the skin caused by inadequate oxygenation of the blood.

cyst Saclike, nonmalignant tumor; may contain fluid or cheeselike material.

cystectomy Removal of the urinary bladder.

cystitis Inflammation of the urinary bladder.

cystocele Protrusion of the bladder into the vagina.

cystography X-ray examination of the urinary bladder after injection of a radiopaque substance.

cystoscope Lighted instrument for examination of the inside of the urinary bladder.

cystostomy A surgical opening of the urinary bladder through an abdominal incision and drainage by a catheter through the abdominal wound.

debridement Removal of infection or necrotic tissue from a wound.

decomposition Dissolution into simpler chemical forms.

decompression Reduction of pressure.

decubitus ulcer Necrotic ulcer caused by pressure over bones where there is little fat and subcutaneous tissue.

defense mechanisms (1) Unconscious processes used to alleviate anxiety; (2) physical structures or processes that protect against stresses from the environment.

defibrillation Application of a current countershock to the chest wall to stop ventricular fibrillation.

degeneration Gradual deterioration of the normal cells and body functions.

dehiscence Separation of a surgical incision.

delirium A global cognitive impairment of memory and organization of thought.

delirium tremens A form of alcoholic psychosis.

delusion False belief that contradicts the individual's knowledge or experience.

dementia A global cognitive dysfunction with impairment in short-term and long-term memory, orientation, abstract thinking, judgment, and personality changes. Also referred to as organic brain syndrome.

demineralization A decrease of mineral or inorganic salts that occurs in some diseases.

denial Refusal to accept a situation.

depolarization The reduction of a membrane potential to a less negative value.

depression Feeling of inadequacy or sadness.

dermatologist A physician trained in the diagnosis and treatment of skin diseases and disorders.

dermatomycosis Superficial mycotic infections of the skin, hair, and nails.

dermis True skin just below the epidermis.

desensitization Injection of extracts of antigenic substances causing immunization against specific antigens.

desquamation A scaling or flaking of the skin after certain infectious diseases or in psoriasis.

diabetic A person with diabetes caused by a deficiency of insulin being secreted by the islands of Langerhans.

dialyzer A machine used to separate or remove certain substances from the blood when the kidneys fail to perform their normal function.

diffusion Movement of molecules from an area of higher concentration to an area of lower concentration.

digitalization Administration of digitalis in doses sufficient to achieve the maximum physiologic effect without toxic symptoms.

dignity Feeling of worth.

diplopia A condition of the eye in which a person sees double.

direct contact Touching of two individuals or organisms done in association with a carrier in an infective state.

disease Any condition in which either the physiologic or psychologic functions of the body deviate from what is considered to be normal.

disinfectant A chemical that when applied to inanimate objects will destroy microorganisms.

dislocation Separation of a bone in a joint from its normal position.

disseminated intravascular coagulation (DIC) An acute bleeding disorder resulting in a hypercoagulable state.

dissociative disorders Disorders that involve the mental defense of splitting off some part of consciousness, identity, or particular behavior on a temporary basis.

distraction techniques Procedures that prevent or lessen the perception of pain sensations by focusing attention on sensations unrelated to pain.

distributive care The pattern of health care that concerns itself with environment, heredity, living conditions, lifestyle, and early detection, usually directed toward continuous care of persons not confined to health care institutions.

diuresis Increase in urinary output.

diuretic A drug used to increase urinary output.

documentation The act of recording patient assessments and nursing interventions in the patient's chart. The chart is a permanent record that is considered a legal document and is also audited to evaluate charges and quality of care.

donor A person who gives or furnishes blood, skin, or body organs for use by another person.

dorsiflexion A bending backward from a neutral position.

DRG (diagnosis related group) A designation in a system that classifies patients by age, sex, diagnosis, treatment procedure, and discharge status, predicting use of hospital resources and length of stay. Currently utilized as basis for system of prospective payment under Medicare.

drug dependency Addiction to a drug.

dwarfism Abnormal smallness of body caused by undersecretion of the growth hormone from the anterior pituitary gland.

dyscrasias Diseases of the blood.

dysmenorrhea Painful menstruation.

dysphagia Difficulty in swallowing.

dyspnea Shortness of breath or difficult, labored breathing.

dysrhythmia Any disturbance or abnormality in a normal rhythmic pattern, specifically, irregularity in the brain waves or cadence of speech.

ecchymosis Large amount of bleeding into the tissues.

eclampsia A condition occurring during pregnancy characterized by convulsions, hypertension, and edema.

ego In Freudian theory, the part of the personality structure containing the instinctive drives and urges.

electrocardiogram Graphic recording of the electric potential resulting from the electric activity of the heart.

electroencephalograph Graphic recording of brain waves within the deep structures of the skull.

electrolytes Salts of various minerals that are in solution in the body.

embolectomy Surgical removal of a blood clot from a vein.

embolism Foreign substance in the bloodstream; may be fragment from a blood clot or an air bubble.

embryonic Pertaining to the embryo.

emphysema Overinflation and other destructive changes in alveolar walls, resulting in loss of lung elasticity and decreased gas exchange.

empyema Presence of pus in the pleural cavity.

endemic Describes the presence of a few cases of a disease in a community continuously.

endogenous From within.

endogenous depression A depression that has no recognizable loss, stressor, or other identifiable cause, and is seen as arising from intrapsychic sources.

endometriosis A disease caused by groups of cells growing in the pelvic cavity. The cells are similar to those of the uterine mucous membrane.

endorphins Substances produced by the brain that mimic the effects of opiates such as morphine.

endotoxin A toxin that is released when the cell disintegrates.

enteritis Inflammation of the intestines.

enucleation Surgical removal of the eyeball.

enuresis Involuntary voiding of urine; bed-wetting.

environment All factors that influence the life and survival of a person.

eosinophils Granular leukocytes. Number is increased during an allergic reaction.

epidemic Occurrence of a large number of cases of a disease in a specific area at a given time.

epidemiology Study of factors related to epidemics of disease, their control, and their methods of spread.

epidermis The superficial layers of the skin, made up of an outer, dead portion and a deeper living, cellular portion.

epididymitis Inflammation of the epididymis.

epidural analgesia The process of achieving regional anesthesia of the pelvic, abdominal, genital, or other area by the injection of a local anesthetic into the epidural space of the spinal column.

epinephrine A hormone secreted by the adrenal medulla; prepared commercially as Adrenalin.

episodic care Care provided by the nurse to the medical or surgical patient who is hospitalized in an acute care or extended care facility with a goal of cure or improvement in a specific illness or crisis.

epistaxis Nosebleed.

erythema A redness of the skin.

erythroblastosis A congenital blood disease of the newborn in which there is a reaction of the Rh-negative antibodies of the mother with the Rh-positive antibodies of the infant.

erythrocytes Red blood cells.

erythropoiesis Production of erythrocytes.

erythropoietin A glycoprotein hormone synthesized mainly in the kidneys and released into the bloodstream in response to anoxia.

eschar Slough of tissue resulting from a burn.

Escherichia coli A species of organism found in the intestinal tract of humans and animals.

esophagoscopy Examination of the esophagus by the use of the endoscope.

estrogen A hormone excreted by the ovaries.

ethical dilemmas Situation requiring a choice between two equally desirable or undesirable alternatives.

ethylene oxide A gas used in sterilization of surgical supplies and equipment.

etiologic Describes the cause of diseases or disorders.

eustachian tube Tube connecting the middle ear with the pharynx.

euthanasia The intentional death of a person suffering from an incurable disease; mercy death.

evaluation The final stage of the nursing process. Patient progess is compared to previously identified expected outcomes of each nursing action prescribed for a problem. This requires the continued assessment of the patient.

evisceration Opening of a surgical incision permitting the viscera to protrude to the outside.

excoriation An abrasion or denuded area of the skin.

exfoliative cytology Microscopic study of the cell used for diagnostic purposes.

exogenous From outside the body.

exotoxin A toxin or poison secreted by an organism.

expertise Skill and knowledge of a person by reason of special training.

extended-care facility Institution devoted to providing medical, nursing, or custodial care for an individual over a prolonged period of time. Includes intermediate and skilled-care facilities.

external rotation Turning away of a limb from the midline of the body.

extracorporeal Outside the body; used to describe a method of bypassing a patient's heart and lungs by using the heart-lung machine; used in open heart surgery.

extrasystole A form of cardiac arrhythmia in which heartbeats occur sooner than expected.

exudate Pus containing dead cells, phagocytes, bacteria, and tissue fluids.

factitious disorders Symptoms or disorders voluntarily produced by a patient for unconscious reasons.

family Two or more persons who are related by blood, marriage, or adoption and who live together over a period of time.

fibrillation Tremor or rapid contraction of the heart.

filter A device for separating one substance from another.

filtration Movement of fluid and electrolytes by the pressure or force that is exerted as a result of the weight of the solution.

fimbriated Demonstrating fingerlike projections at the end of the fallopian tubes.

fissure A crack or slit in the skin.

flaccid Limp; cannot be controlled.

flagella Hairlike projections extending from some bacterial cells making them capable of movement.

flotation therapy Semiweightlessness produced by various types of equipment; used in prevention and treatment of decubitus ulcers.

fomite Any object or material that may hold or transmit pathogenic organisms.

frostbite Freezing caused by exposure to extreme cold; seen as white patches on skin that do not redden on pressure or as deeper lesions involving subcutaneous tissue.

functional assessment Admission examination of patient's functional abilities.

functional nursing An approach to nursing service that uses auxiliary health workers trained in a variety of skills. Each person is assigned specific duties or functions that are carried out for all patients on a given unit. Assignments are made in relationship to the skill levels of the worker. This follows the "assembly line" approach.

functional psychosis Major emotional disorder characterized by derangement of the personality and loss of the ability to function in reality; not directly related to physical processes.

fungi Microbes from the plant kingdom, of which there are many different kinds. Some are harmless and some cause disease.

gangrene Necrosis of tissue caused by cutting off the blood supply.

gastrectomy Partial or complete surgical removal of the stomach.

gastritis Inflammation of the stomach generally caused by ingestion of contaminated food.

gastroscopy A direct visualization of the stomach with a gastroscope.

gate control theory Proposes that pain impulses transmitted from nerve receptors through the spinal cord to the brain can be altered or blocked in the spinal cord or brain.

genetic Pertaining to origin or inherited.

geriatrics A medical specialty dealing with problems of aging and the aged.

germicide An agent that destroys bacteria.

gerontology The scientific study of the process of aging and of the problems of the aged. The science of gerontology is interdisciplinary and includes the social, biologic, and psychologic aspects of aging.

glaucoma An eye disease caused by increased intraocular pressure; may cause blindness if not treated.

glomerular capillaries Cluster of blood vessels surrounded by Bowman's capsule.

glomerulonephritis A type of nephritis in which the glomerulus of the kidney is involved.

glucagon A hormone, produced by the alpha cells in the islets of Langerhans, that stimulates the conversion of glycogen to glucose in the liver.

glycohemoglobin A type of hemoglobin that has a sugar attached (glycosated) that is increased in poorly controlled diabetes. It is an indicator of glucose levels over several weeks.

glycosuria Presence of sugar in the urine.

goiter Any abnormal enlargement of the thyroid gland.

gonads Sex glands; testes in the male and ovaries in the female.

gram negative Term used in identifying bacteria after staining with a dye. Color can be removed with a solvent.

granulocytes Leukocytes identified by shape of the nuclei and coloring of their cytoplasm.

grief A severe emotional reaction to loss.

gumma A tumorlike lesion that is similar in appearance to an abscess.

gynecology A medical specialty concerned with diseases and disorders of the female reproductive system.

habitat Natural environment where a plant or animal, including humans, resides.

hallucination A mental aberration based on seeing or hearing things that do not exist in reality.

hallucinogenic Describes an agent that causes changes in personality or causes hallucinations.

hashish A resinous mixture contained in the flowering tops of *Cannabis sativa* plant.

health Defined by the World Health Organization as "a state of complete physical, mental, and social well-being and not merely the absence of disease."

Health Maintenance Organization (HMO) Created by the Social Security Amendments of 1972 to provide comprehensive services to enrollees on the basis of a predetermined fixed cost or rate, without regard to the extent or frequency of services. These services may be given directly by the HMO or through arrangements with others and include the services of primary care and specialty physicians and institutional services.

heat stroke Disturbance in body heat—regulating mechanism resulting in elevated body temperature and hot dry skin; may be damaging to brain cells.

hematemesis Vomiting of blood.

hematocrit A measure of the volume of red blood cells and the plasma.

hematogenic shock A shock state caused by loss of blood or plasma internal or external.

hematuria Blood in the urine.

hemianopia Defective vision or blindness in half the visual field.

hemiplegia Paralysis affecting one side of the body.

hemodialysis Artificial method of removing urea and nitrogenous wastes from the blood when the kidneys fail to function normally.

hemoglobin electrophoresis A test used to identify various abnormal hemoglobins in the blood; may indicate genetic disorders such as sickle cell anemia.

hemophilia A group of hereditary bleeding disorders.

hemoptysis Hemorrhage that may be from the lungs, trachea, or larynx.

hemorrhage Escape of blood from a broken vessel.

hemorrhoids Varicosities of the anal canal; may be internal or external.

hepatic coma Comatose condition caused by liver failure; believed to result from accumulation of nitrogenous substances in the blood, especially ammonia.

hepatitis Inflammation of the cells of the liver; two types—hepatitis A and hepatitis B.

herniorrhaphy Surgical repair of a hernia.

herpes simplex Cold sore or fever blister.

herpes zoster Shingles; caused by a virus that affects the nerve roots of the posterior ganglia; same virus that causes chickenpox.

heterograft Tissue taken from an animal or a species other than a human donor.

hiatus hernia Protrusion of a structure through the diaphragm about the esophageal opening.

high risk Applied to groups of persons considered to be more susceptible to infections or diseases than other individuals.

histoplasmosis A benign disease of the lungs caused by a fungus.

Hodgkin's disease A malignant disease affecting the lymph nodes; once considered highly fatal but is now being cured.

holistic care Care of the total or whole person including physiologic, psychologic, and sociologic needs.

home health care Health services provided in the client's place of residence for the purpose of promoting, maintaining, or restoring health or minimizing the effects of illness and disability.

Homemaker service A service to provide assistance in the home for elderly or sick persons; federal program under the Older Americans Act.

homeostasis A relative constancy in the internal environment of the body that is naturally maintained by adaptive responses that promote health survival.

homograft A graft taken from a person other than the recipient.

hormone A chemical substance secreted by an endocrine gland; some prepared commercially.

hospice An approach to providing support for the terminally ill patient and significant others, addressing physical, emotional, and spiritual needs.

host An organism, which may be a human, from which another obtains its nourishment.

human needs Those needs basic to every individual and identified by Maslow as physiologic, safety and comfort, love and belonging, and esteem and self-actualization.

humoral immunity Acquired immunity that results in lymphocytes forming antibodies that are specific to the invading agent.

Huntington's chorea A rare abnormal hereditary condition characterized by chronic, progressive chorea and mental deterioration that terminates in dementia.

hydrocele A collection of fluid in the testicle.

hydrolysis Splitting of a compound into parts by adding water. In digestion, enzymes reduce large molecules into small particles so that they may be absorbed.

hydronephrosis Distention of the kidney pelvis with urine caused by an obstruction along the urinary route.

hypaxial Beneath the axis of the vertebral column.

hyperalimentation A method of providing complete nutritional requirements by the intravenous route.

hypercalcemia Excess of calcium in the extracellular fluid.

hypercapnea Excess of carbon dioxide in the blood.

hyperchloremia Excess of chloride in the blood.

hyperglycemia Excess of glucose in the blood.

hyperglycemic, hyperosmolar nonketotic coma A diabetic coma in which the level of ketone bodies is normal, caused by hyperosmolarity of extracellular fluid.

hyperkalemia Excess of potassium in the extracellular fluid.

hypernatremia Excess of sodium in the extracellular fluid.

hyperopia Farsightedness.

hyperplasia Increased number of cells causing a part to be enlarged.

hyperreflexia Exaggeration of reflexes.

hypersensitivity An abnormal sensitivity to certain substances.

hypertension A consistent elevation of blood pressure above normal.

hyperthermia Highly increased temperature.

hypertonic A solution having an osmotic pressure higher than the one with which it is being compared.

hypertrophy Enlargement of an organ that may or may not be caused by disease; increase in the size of the cells comprising an organ.

hypervolemia Increase in the amount of extracellular fluid.

hypocalcemia Deficit of calcium in the extracellular fluid.

hypochloremia A decrease in the chloride level in the blood serum.

hypochromia Below normal color, as in a low index of the color of hemoglobin.

hyponatremia Deficit of sodium in the extracellular fluid.

hypospadias Congenital malformation of the male urethra.

hypostatic pneumonia Pneumonia caused by a person's remaining in the same position for long periods.

hypothermia An adjunct to anesthesia produced by lowering the body temperature below normal. It may be local or general.

hypotonic A solution having an osmotic pressure lower than the one with which it is being compared.

hypovolemia Decrease in the amount of extracellular fluid.

hypoxia Deficiency of oxygen in the tissues.

hysterectomy Surgical removal of the uterus; may be abdominal or vaginal, total or partial.

iatrogenic A disorder produced inadvertently by a physician as a result of treatment for another disorder.

icterus index A test to measure the amount of yellowness in the blood serum.

id In Freudian theory, the part of the personality structure that contains the instinctive drives and urges.

ileal conduit Method of urinary diversion. Ureters are implanted into a section of dissected illeum, which is then sewed to an opening in the abdomen.

ileostomy A surgical procedure in which an artificial passage from the ileum to the outside of the abdomen is constructed.

ileus Failure of peristalsis leading to intestinal obstruction.

immunity Resistance to a specific disease.

immunization Process of becoming immune to certain diseases; usually refers to injections to develop active acquired immunity.

immunoglobulins (Ig) Serum proteins that include several groups of globulins; formerly called gamma globulins.

immunologist A person trained in the science of immunity.

immunotherapy A special treatment of allergic responses; administers increasingly large doses of the offending allergens to gradually develop immunity.

impetigo Contagious skin disease.

implementation Category of nursing behavior. One of five steps in the nursing process in which the actions necessary for accomplishing the health-care plan are initiated and completed. Includes performance of or assisting in performance of activities of daily living, counseling and teaching, giving care, supervising and evaluating staff members, and recording and exchanging information relevant to the client's continued health care.

incontinence Inability to retain urine in the bladder.

incubation period Time between exposure to a disease and the appearance of the first symptoms.

independence Capable of performing activities of daily living without assistance.

indirect contact Touching of an object contaminated with an infective organism.

infection Entry and multiplication of an infective agent in the body of man or animal. May or may not cause infective disease.

infectious disease A disease that may be transmitted from person to person either by direct or indirect contact.

infiltration Passing of fluid through, as when intravenous fluid passes into the tissues; usually caused by needle being displaced from the vein.

inner child Refers to the child ego state described by the Redecision Theory, which is found in any person, regardless of chronologic age.

insulin reaction Syndrome caused by too much circulating insulin.

intermediate-care facility A facility that provides care for chronically ill or disabled individuals in which room and board are provided but skilled nursing care is not.

internal rotation Turning of the limb toward the midline of the body.

intervention One step in the nursing process. The actual implementation of the most suitable actions chosen for a given situation, which may include direct patient care, health teaching, or other activities for the benefit of the patient or the supervision of such activities.

intracranial pressure Pressure within the cranium.

intrathecal analgesia Injection into the subarachnoid space of the spinal chord; a lumbar puncture must be performed.

intravenous therapy Administration of fluids or drugs or both into the general circulation through a venipuncture.

intussusception Telescoping of the intestine; may involve any part of the small or large intestine.

iodophor An antiseptic or disinfectant agent that combines iodine with another agent, usually a detergent.

ion An atom or group of atoms carrying an electric charge.

ionizing radiation Rays of energy that break atoms into smaller, electrically charged particles called ions.

iridectomy Surgical procedure in which a small hole is made in the iris to provide drainage of aqueous humour when acute, narrow-angle glaucoma has caused the angle to narrow and obstruct drainage.

ischemia A temporary interruption of the blood supply to any area.

ischemic heart disease Pathology of the heart resulting from lack of oxygen.

isoenzyme An enzyme that may appear in multiple forms, with slightly different chemical or other characteristics, and be produced in different organs, although each enzyme performs essentially the same function.

isometric exercise Exercise done by a patient in which he contracts and relaxes a muscle.

isotonic Solution that is compatible with the normal tissue by having the same osmotic pressure.

isotope A chemical element that has been made radioactive.

jaundice A condition in which a yellow color affects the skin and the sclera of the eyes caused by an accumulation of bile pigments in the blood.

keloid A benign overgrowth of fibrous tissue.

keratitis Inflammation of the cornea of the eye with formation of ulcers.

keratoplasty Corneal transplant.

ketoacidosis Acidosis resulting from the body's inability to neutralize keto acids from abnormal fat metabolism.

ketonuria Presence in the urine of excessive amounts of ketone bodies.

ketosis The abnormal accumulation of ketones in the body as a result of a deficiency or inadequate use of carbohydrates.

Klebsiella A species of bacteria that lives in the intestinal tract and may cause serious infections.

Koplik's spots White spots on a reddened base found in the throat in measles.

labyrinthitis Inflammation of the labyrinth of the inner ear.

lacrimal fluid Tears secreted by the lacrimal glands.

lacrimation Increased secretion from the lacrimal glands.

laminectomy Surgical procedure for ruptured intervertebral disk or for fusion.

laparoscopy Examination of the interior of the abdomen with a laparoscope.

laparotomy Any surgical procedure for which the abdomen is opened.

laryngectomy Surgical procedure for the removal of the larynx.

leukapheresis Selective removal of leukocytes from blood that has been withdrawn from the patient and then reinfused.

leukemia Serious and usually fatal disease of the blood.

leukocyte White blood cell.

leukocytopenia A reduction in the number of leukocytes.

leukocytosis Great increase in leukocytes occurring in many kinds of infections.

leukopenia An abnormal decrease in the number of white blood cells to fewer than 5000 cells per cubic millimeter.

leukoplakia White spots formed on the mucous membrane of the mouth that may become malignant.

leukorrhea White or yellow vaginal discharge.

life-island A plastic bubble enclosing a bed that is used to provide a germ-free environment.

life span The longest period of time a typical individual can be expected to live.

ligature Suture used in surgery to tie or ligate a blood vessel.

lithiasis Formation of stones of calculi.

living will A written agreement between a patient and the physician to withhold heroic measures if his condition is irreversible.

lobectomy Surgical removal of a lobe of a lung.

long-term care Those services designed to provide symptomatic treatment, maintenance, and rehabilitative services for patients of all age-groups in a variety of health care settings.

lumen Passageway within a tube such as the lumen of blood vessels.

lymph nodes Small structures of lymphatic tissue containing lymphocytes, the function of which is filtration and phagocytosis.

lymphangitis Inflammation of one or more lymph vessels.

lymphocytes A lymph cell or white blood cell: develops in the bone marrow.

lymphoma A malignant type of tumor.

lysergic acid diethylamide (LSD) A hallucinogenic agent causing changes in mood and personality.

lysis A gradual decrease of symptoms of a disease, also a laboratory procedure to indicate decomposing of an agent by another agent.

macrophage Large phagocyte cell that wanders about.

macule A discolored spot on the skin that may be of various colors and shapes. It is neither raised nor depressed.

magnetic resonance imaging An imaging method that provides superior visualization of soft tissue. Utilizes harmless low energy radio waves to create a magnetic field. When introduced into the hydrogen nuclei of soft tissues, a complex series of events occurs and is assembled as a tomogram.

malaria A disease caused by a protozoan and transmitted by the *Anopheles* mosquito.

malignant Describes a disease that is a threat to life, usually applied to cancer.

mammary gland Synonymous with the female breast.

mammography X-ray examination of the breast.

marijuana *(Cannabis sativa)* Same plant as hashish but contains less resin and is less psychoactive.

mastectomy Surgical removal of the breast; may be simple or radical.

mastitis Inflammation of the breast.

mastoiditis Inflammation of the cells of the mastoid process.

Meals on Wheels Program designed to prepare food and take hot meals to elderly or physically handicapped persons.

mediastinum Space between the lungs that contains the heart.

Medicaid Federal- and state-supported program to provide hospital and medical care for certain eligible persons.

medical-surgical nursing The nursing care of patients whose conditions or disorders are treated pharmacologically or surgically.

Medicare Federal program to provide hospital and medical care for persons 65 years of age or older.

menarche First menstruation occurring at the time of puberty.

Meniere's syndrome A condition involving an increase in pressure following an increase in the endolymph in the inner ear, producing the symptoms of vertigo, nausea and vomiting, and ringing in the ears.

meninges Membrane enclosing the brain and spinal cord.

meningitis Infection and inflammation of the meninges.

menopause Climacteric or the cessation of menses representing the end of the reproductive period.

menorrhagia Excessive menstrual flow either in quantity or duration.

mental health A state of being in which a person has a reasonably satisfactory balance of personality structure.

mental illness Any psychiatric illness that has been identified by various recognized authorities. A condition in which the person experiences enough psychic pain to cause interference with successful life functioning.

mental status The degree of competence shown by a person in intellectual, emotional, psychologic, and personality functioning as measured by psychologic testing with reference to a statistic norm.

mental retardation A condition in which there is an absence of normal mental growth and development.

mescaline Derivation of peyote cactus and classified as a hallucinogenic agent.

metabolism Sum of all processes that go on within the body, including the breaking-down and wearing-out processes and the regeneration and building-up processes.

metastasis Spreading of cancer cells by the bloodstream or lymph from one part to another part of the body.

methadone Synthetic narcotic analgesic agent used to replace heroin; considered addictive.

metrorrhagia Bleeding between regular menstrual periods.

miotic A drug that causes contraction of the pupil of the eye.

molecule Smallest particle of an element or compound.

monocyte A large mononuclear leukocyte.

mononucleosis An infectious disease characterized by swelling of the lymph nodes, especially the cervical nodes.

motivation Providing an incentive to cause a person to move or to act in a particular way

multisystem A corporation that manages a group

of hospitals. Hospitals may or may not be owned by the managing system.

muscle spasm A severe muscular contraction.

myasthenic crisis Acute episode of muscular weakness.

mycotic Pertaining to a disease caused by a fungus.

mydriatic A drug that dilates the pupils of the eyes.

myelin Fatlike substance forming a sheath around certain nerve fibers.

myelography X-ray examination of the spinal column after injection of a radiopaque substance.

myelosuppression Inhibition of the function of the bone marrow.

myocardial infarction Disorder caused by obstruction or thrombus of a coronary artery or its branches, depriving the myocardium of its blood supply and causing death of the tissue affected.

myopia Nearsightedness.

myxedema Hypothyroidism in adults causing changes in the physical appearance and mental apathy.

narcotic A drug that may be an opium derivative or synthetic narcotic-like agent used to relieve pain and produce sleep. All narcotic drugs are habit forming and under government control.

natural immunity Immunity acquired by an infant as a result of maternal antibodies crossing the placental barrier and entering fetal circulation.

nebulization A method of spraying a drug into the respiratory passages; may be used with or without oxygen to carry the drug to the lungs.

necrosis Death of tissue.

necrotic tissue Dead tissue or small groups of cells.

neobladder Urinary diversion by transplanting the ureters into a constructed segment of the sigmoid colon.

neoplasm Abnormal tumor growth; may be benign or malignant.

nephrectomy Surgical removal of a kidney.

nephritis Inflammation of the kidney; may be acute or chronic.

nephron Nephron and its component parts comprise the structural and functional unit of the kidney.

nephrosclerosis Sclerosis of the blood vessels of the kidney, usually associated with hypertension.

nephrosis (nephrotic syndrome) Degeneration of renal tissue with inflammation; may occur with glomerulonephritis

nephrostomy Surgical wound on the flank and placement of a catheter into the kidney pelvis for the purpose of drainage.

nephrotoxin A substance that is destructive to the kidney.

neurogenic shock Shock resulting from peripheral vascular dilation as a result of neurologic injury.

neurotransmitters The chemicals responsible for message transmission across the synapse. Examples include dopamine, substance P, endorphins, and enkephalins.

nodule Small solid node that can be detected by touch.

normal flora Microscopic cells normally present on skin and mucosal surfaces that may include *Staphylococcus*, *Streptococcus*, and other bacteria.

normovolemic shock Shock resulting from a disproportion between the normal volume of blood and the size of the vascular bed.

nosocomial Hospital-acquired infection.

nursing care plan The proposed plan of care for each patient, preferably written, that is intended to communicate, to prevent complications, to assure continuity of care, to identify and ensure patient teaching, and to provide for discharge planning. It must include statements that identify the patient's problems and proposed nursing intervention as well as measurable expected outcome.

nursing diagnosis A concise statment describing a combination of signs and symptoms that indicate an acute or potential health problem that nurses are licensed to treat and are capable of treating.

nursing history The documented findings of a thorough patient assessment including the physical and emotional signs and symptoms presented by the patient as well as information obtained from other sources.

nursing home A long-term or extended care facility that provides nursing, medical, and rehabilative care as well as furnishing residential and personal services.

nursing process A dynamic interpersonal problem-solving process that facilitates a person's potential for health. The steps in the process include assessment, planning, intervention, and evaluation.

nystagmus A continuous movement of the eyeball; may be associated with labyrinthitis.

occlusion Blockage of a passageway.

occult blood A minute or hidden quantity of blood that can be detected only by means of a chemical test or by microscopic or spectroscopic examination. Often present in stools of patients with gastrointestinal lesions.

oncology Branch of medicine dealing with tumors.

onconogenes Certain genes in the cell that can somehow be activated and cause cells to become malignant.

oophorectomy Surgical removal of an ovary.

opacity Omitting light or opaque to light rays.

ophthalmia neonatorum Infection of the eyes of the newborn with the gonococcus organism.

ophthalmologist A physician trained in the diagnosis and treatment of eye diseases and the correction of vision defects with lenses.

opiate Drug derived from opium.

opisthotonos Arching of the body caused by rigidity of the spine.

opportunistic pathogen A microbe that produces illness only in the compromised host.

orchitis Inflammatory condition of the testes caused by infection, injury, or malignancy.

organic psychosis Major emotional disorder characterized by derangement of the personality and loss of the ability to function in reality; caused by an underlying physical process resulting in damage to the brain.

orthopedic Describes disorders of the musculoskeletal system.

orthopnea Ability to breathe only in the upright position.

oscilloscope An instrument that records a visual wave on a screen.

osmolarity The osmotic pressure of a solution expressed in osmols or milliosmols per kilogram of the solution.

osmosis Diffusion of water through a semipermeable membrane.

osmotic pressure Pressure of a fluid that determines its ability to pass through a semipermeable membrane.

osseous Pertaining to bone.

osteoarthritis A degenerative type of arthritis affecting the joints; characteristic of the aging process.

osteomyelitis Infection and inflammation of a bone.

osteotomy Cutting of bone to correct joint or bone deformities.

otitis media Abscess of the middle ear.

otologist A physician trained in the diagnosis and treatment of diseases and disorders of the ear.

otosclerosis A disease of the middle ear in which changes in the stapes occur that prevent transmission of sound to the inner ear.

ovulation Discharge of a mature ovum from the ovarian follicle.

oxygenation The process of combining or treating with oxygen.

pacemaker A mechanical device used to provide electric stimulation in heart block; may be temporary or permanent.

pain Whatever the patient experiencing it says it is, existing whenever he says it exists.

palliative Giving temporary relief but not cure.

pancreatitis Inflammation of the pancreas.

pandemic A disease that is widespread in a geographic area or throughout the world.

panhysterectomy Surgical removal of the uterus and the cervix.

Papanicolaou smear test A cytologic test for the detection of cancer cells.

papule A small solid elevation on the skin varying in size from a pinhead to a pea.

paralytic ileus A decrease or absence of intestinal peristalsis.

paraplegia Paralysis of the lower part of the body below a point of injury to the spinal cord.

paroxysm Spasmodic attacks that recur at periodic intervals.

paroxysmal atrial tachycardia Very rapid heart beat beginning suddenly and ending abruptly.

passive immunity Immunity acquired by injecting a serum into the body that produces an immediate but temporary immune response.

patient-controlled analgesia Self-administration of pain medications by means of a mechanical device.

pathogen An organism capable of causing disease.

pathophysiology Changes in the physiologic function caused by pathologic disease.

patient The individual who initiates, plans, and actively participates in his or her health care.

pelvic exenteration Removal of all reproductive organs and adjacent tissues.

penicillinase An enzymelike substance produced by some bacteria that affects the antimicrobial properties of penicillin.

peptic ulcer An ulcer occurring in the wall of the stomach or the duodenum.

perfusion Procedure of introducing a chemical drug to an isolated part of the body by way of the bloodstream.

periosteum Specialized connective tissue covering all bones.

peristalsis Involuntary wavelike contraction of muscles of the gastrointestinal tract.

peritoneal dialysis A method of removal of waste products from the blood by way of the peritoneal membrane.

personality The unique combination of behavior patterns, attitudes, and traits of an individual.

personality disorders A group of mental disorders in which there are maladaptive patterns of behavior, often identifiable by adolescence or earlier.

pertussis Whooping cough.

pessary A device used to support the uterus in a normal position.

petechiae Small pinpoint hemorrhagic spots on the skin.

Peyer's patches Areas of lymphoid tissue on the mucous membrane of the small intestine that become elevated and inflamed in typhoid fever; may become ulcerated and rupture, causing hemorrhage.

phagocyte Cell that engulfs and ingests bacteria or other material.

phagocytosis Ingestion and digestion of bacteria at the scene of an infection.

phenylketonuria Hereditary disease in which there is a faulty utilization of the amino acid phenylalanine.

phimosis A narrowing of the prepuce opening so that the foreskin of the penis cannot be retracted.

phlebotomy Incision of a vein for the purpose of removing blood.

phobia Abnormal fear.

physical dependence The altered state produced by the repeated administration of a drug. When the drug is stopped, withdrawal symptoms occur.

pica A craving to eat substances that are not foods, such as dirt, clay, chalk, glue, or hair.

pinna Auricle of the ear, or the cartilaginous external ear.

pinworm Small parasitic worm that matures in the large intestine and crawls to outside of rectum to deposit its eggs.

placebo An inactive substance or procedure that is used with a patient under the guise of an effective treatment. It is used to satisfy a patient's symbolic need for drug therapy or as a means of control in research studies.

planning That stage of the nursing process that involves the development of an orderly mental or written design of action based on needs and the real or potential problems that have been identified in the patient. It is this stage in which nursing actions or interventions are proposed and goals or expected outcomes are identified.

plaques Atherosclerotic fatty deposits found in the intima of blood vessels; often the coronary arteries are affected.

plasmapheresis Process of separating the plasma and the red blood cells.

Platyhelminthes Flatworms.

pleurisy Inflammation of the pleura.

pneumonectomy Surgical removal of a lung.

pneumonia An acute inflammation of the lungs, often caused by inhaled pneumococci.

pneumothorax A collection of air or gas in the pleural space causing the lung to collapse.

pollinosis An allergic condition, same as hay fever.

polycythemia An abnormal increase in the number of erythrocytes in the blood.

polyp A small tumorlike growth projecting from a mucous membrane.

polyuria Increased urinary output.

populations Aggregation of individuals, often with specific characteristics in common.

porcine graft Temporary biologic heterograft taken from the skin of a pig.

posttraumatic stress syndrome An anxiety disorder that originates with a traumatic event and is characterized by nightmares, flashbacks, physiologic symptoms, and acute anxiety attacks. This disorder can occur soon after the traumatic event, or can occur years later.

preferred provider organization (PPO) An organization of physicians, hospitals, and pharmacists whose members discount their healthcare services to subscriber patients.

primary care The first contact in a given episode of illness that leads to a decision of what must be done to help resolve the problem. It is provided by the individual who is responsible for the continuum of care, such as maintenance of health, evaluation and management of symptoms, and appropriate referral. This is usually provided by a physician; however, some primary care functions are now handled by nurses with advanced education and experience.

primary nursing An approach to nursing service that closely resembles the original case method. The primary nurse assumes complete responsibility for the total care of the patient from admission to discharge. When off duty, the primary nurse is assisted by other nurses who follow the directives of the plan of care established. Each primary nurse is assigned a group of patients, preferably no more than five.

primary prevention Involves activities promoting general well-being as well as specific protection for selected diseases, such as immunizations for diphtheria, measles, and tetanus.

priority Order of importance.

problem-oriented medical record (POMR) A system of record-keeping that involves the identification and numbering of patient problems. All progress notes and orders are directly related to patient problems, and each entry must consist of four parts designated by the acronym SOAP—subjective data, objective data, assessment, and plan.

problem-oriented record (POR) See problem-oriented medical record.

proctoscopy Examination of the rectum with an endoscope passed through the anus (proctoscope).

proctosigmoidoscopy Visualization of the sigmoid colon and rectum.

prognosis Expected outcome of a disease.

proprietary Operated for profit.

prospective payment Third party reimbursement based on predetermined cost rather than actual costs incurred.

prostatitis Inflammation of the prostate gland.

prosthesis Any artificial device used to replace a missing part of the body.

prosthetist A person skilled in making and fitting prostheses.

Proteus morgani A species of bacteria that may cause infectious diarrhea in infants.

Proteus vulgaris A species of bacteria found in feces, water, and soil; a frequent cause of urinary tract infection.

Protozoa A phylum of unicellular organisms.

pruritus Itching of the skin.

Pseudomonas Microorganism found on the skin or in the intestinal tract of humans; may be the cause of hospital-acquired infections. It is resistant to most antibiotics.

psilocybin Active agent of the *Psilocybe mexicana* mushroom; classified as a hallucinogenic agent.

psoriasis A chronic skin disease characterized by scaly patches and desquamation.

psychoneurosis An emotional maladaptation whose chief characteristic is anxiety.

psychophysiologic reactions Physical disorders resulting from an inward bodily channeling of anxiety and stress.

psychoses A major organic or emotional disorder resulting in an inability to function effectively in life; there may be loss of contact with reality.

psychosomatic Refers to disorders for which no pathologic condition can be found.

ptosis A dropping from the normal position, such as ptosis of the eyelid in facial paralysis.

puberty Period at which the ability to reproduce begins.

pulmonary edema A condition in which left ventricular heart failure occurs, causing a slowing of the systemic circulation and backup of returning blood; a serious condition.

pulmonary embolism A condition that is usually caused by a blood clot that breaks away from its place of origin and travels by the bloodstream to the lungs, where it lodges in a small vessel.

pulmonary emphysema A chronic obstructive disease of the lungs in which there is an overdistention of the alveoli.

pulse deficit Difference between the radial pulse rate and apical pulse rate.

Purkinje's fibers Continuation of the bundle of His that extends into the muscle walls of the ventricles.

purpura Bleeding into the skin.

purulent Describes a discharge containing pus.

pustule An elevated skin lesion containing pus.

pyelitis Inflammatory condition of the kidney pelvis.

pyelography X-ray examination of the kidney pelvis and may include the ureters after injection of a radiopaque medium.

pyelonephritis An inflammatory condition that involves the kidney pelvis and extends into kidney tissue.

pyloric spasm Severe and painful spasm of the pyloric valve.

pyuria Pus in the urine.

quadriplegia Paralysis of all four extremities.

quarantine Isolation for a given time that prohibits person-to-person contact; used in infectious diseases.

Queckenstedt's test A test used in the diagnosis of obstruction of the spinal cord.

radioactive substance Any substance capable of giving off rays resulting from disintegration such as radium.

radiation therapy Treatment of neoplastic disease by use of gamma rays or x-rays.

radioisotope A chemical element that has been made radioactive and emits rays of energy.

radiopaque A substance that cannot be penetrated by any form of radiation; used in x-ray examination of internal structures.

reaginic antibody IgE immunoglobulin that is elevated in hypersensitive individuals.

reality orientation A small group activity in which the group leader emphasizes time, day, month, weather, and so on.

referred pain Pain felt at a site other than its origin.

reflex An involuntary act.

refraction Bending of light rays entering the eye; also used in correction of abnormal bending of light rays by the ophthalmologist.

regression Going backward.

regurgitation Usually applied to the return of food or fluids from the stomach.

rehabilitation Process of assisting an individual after a disabling event has occurred.

reimbursement Repayment for an expense or loan.

relaxation techniques Procedures that help the patient achieve freedom from mental and physical tension or stress.

reminiscing Recalling past events or experiences.

remission Relief from symptoms or temporary improvement; opposite from exacerbation.

remotivation The use of special techniques that stimulate patients to become motivated to learn and interact.

renal threshold The maximum amount of a substance that can be reabsorbed by the renal tubules at which point the excess is excreted into the urine.

residual Refers to the part remaining, such as urine remaining in the bladder after catheterization.

respite Period of relief from responsibilities for the care of a patient.

reticuloendothelial system Main bodily defense to protect humans from harmful agents; responsible for phagocytosis and elimination of cellular debris in inflammatory conditions.

retinopathy Noninflammatory condition resulting in small vessel changes in the eyes.

retirement Period in one's life when one leaves a job and enters another phase of life.

retrospective payment Reimbursement payment to agencies after service has been provided.

rhinitis Inflammation of the nasal mucosa.

rhizotomy A neurosurgical procedure in which a pain pathway in the brain stem is severed.

rickettsiae Small bodies that occupy an intermediate position between bacteria and viruses.

rigidity Inflexibility.

ringworm A skin disorder caused by a fungus.

risk factors A factor that causes a person or a group of people to be particularly vulnerable to an unwanted, unpleasant, or unhealthful event.

roentgen Unit for measuring radiation, such as in x-rays.

rose spots Small rose-colored spots on the abdomen occurring in typhoid fever.

sarcoma A type of malignant tumor.

scale A small thin flake of dry epidermis.

scar A mark left on the skin after repair of tissue.

Schick's test A subcutaneous skin test to determine immunity to diphtheria.

schizophrenia Psychotic behavior in which there are a variety of subgroups; consists of alterations in association, affect, ambivalence, autism, and attention.

scintillator A device used to measure the amount of radioactive material in a part of the body.

scolex Segment of the tapeworm that forms the head with hooks or suckers.

sebaceous glands Oil glands that secrete sebum.

seborrhea An increased secretion of sebum from the sebaceous glands.

sebum Secretion from the sebaceous glands.

secondary prevention The level of prevention of illness that focuses on early diagnosis and implementing measures to stop the progression of disease processes or handicapping disability.

sedimentation rate Rate at which red blood cells settle when blood is placed in a test tube.

seizure A sudden loss of consciousness, such as in epilepsy.

self-actualization The fundamental tendency toward the maximum realization and fulfillment of one's human potential. Highest need in Maslow's hierarchy of human needs.

senescence Process of becoming old, or old age.

sensitized Describes tissues that have been made susceptible to antigenic substances.

septicemia A bloodstream infection resulting from invasion of the blood by bacteria or their toxins.

sexuality A person's need for comfort, touch, companionship, and love that may or may not be expressed through sexual activity.

shearing force Causing two contacting parts to slide upon one another.

shearlings Sheepskins used on the bed to help prevent decubitus ulcers.

sickle cell disease Congenital disease marked by sickle-shaped red blood cells; occurs most commonly in blacks.

sigmoidoscopy Examination of the sigmoid colon with a sigmoidoscope.

sinoatrial node Cells located in the right atrial wall that contract to set the rate the heart will beat; initiated electric conduction system of the heart; called the pacemaker.

sinus bradycardia A slowing of the heart action to 60 beats per minute or less.

sinus tachycardia Rapid beating of the heart in excess of 100 beats per minute.

situational depression A depression that occurs as a result of a specific, identifiable event or events in which feelings of sadness and loss do not resolve within a normal period of time.

skilled nursing facility (SNF) A nursing home that provides 24-hour nursing services, regular medical supervision, and rehabilitation therapy.

SOAP The acronym that designates the four parts of each entry in a problem-oriented record—subjective data, objective data, assessment, and plan.

socioeconomic Interaction of social and economic factors.

sordes A foul accumulation of secretions and crusts about the teeth and gums caused by lack of oral care.

spastic Describes involuntary muscular contractions resulting in rigidity.

specificity theory Proposes that pain messages are carried from pain receptors along pain (nerve) pathways to pain centers in the brain.

sphincter Muscles that are circular in shape and that constrict an anatomic opening, such as the anal sphincter.

spinal shock Syndrome directly following acute spinal cord injury.

spirometer Mechanical device to measure vital capacity.

splenectomy Surgical removal of the spleen.

splenomegaly Enlargement of the spleen.

spores Bacilli that are capable of changing into resistive forms that can exist at high temperatures and in the presence of ordinary disinfectants.

standards An evaluation that serves as a basis for comparison when evaluating similar phenomena or substances, or as a standard for the practice of a profession.

stapedectomy Surgical procedure to correct otosclerosis, a disorder that prevents sound from reaching the inner ear.

Staphylococcus Species of bacteria often responsible for hospital-acquired infections.

stasis Slowing or stopping the normal flow.

stenosis Narrowing or constriction of a passageway, such as in the valves of the heart—mitral stenosis.

sterilization Process of destroying all pathogenic microorganisms.

stigma A mark of disgrace.

stimulus Any action or agent that causes changes or action in an organ or part.

stoma An opening onto the skin created by an artificial passageway; may also apply to the normal opening of a pore.

stomatitis Inflammation of the mucous membranes of the mouth.

strabismus Crossed eyes.

strawberry tongue Strawberry-like appearance of the tongue in scarlet fever.

streptococcus Species of bacteria that probably causes the most illness in man.

stump Distal portion of an extremity after amputation.

stuporous Describes deep sleep with diminished sense of feeling and responsiveness.

subconscious Partial responsiveness of the mind to impressions made by the senses.

subculture An ethnic, regional, economic, or social group with characteristic patterns of behavior that distinguish it from the larger culture or society.

substance P A chemical secreted by pain nerves; a neurotransmitter.

suicide Self-destruction.

sunstroke Disorder caused by overexposure to the sun.

superego In Freudian theory, that part of the personality structure that contains society's mores. It often may be self-critical.

surveillance Supervising or watching a person or a condition.

synovectomy Excision of the synovial membrane of a joint.

tachycardia A cardiac arrhythmia that results in a very rapid beating of the heart.

team A decentralized system in which the care of a patient is distributed among the members of a team of various professionals and/or family and friends.

team nursing A nursing service approach that employs the skills of a variety of nursing personnel in providing comprehensive care for the patient. The leader, a registered nurse, is assisted in the care of a group of patients by other nurses, LVN/LPNs, nursing assistants, and orderlies. The leader assigns and directs patient care based on input from team members.

tenacious Describes secretions that are sticky and stringy and tend to hold together.

terminal disinfection Cleaning of equipment and airing of room after the release of a person who has had an infectious disease.

tertiary prevention The level of prevention of illness that deals with rehabilitation of a disabled patient to return the person to a level of maximum usefulness.

tetany A paroxysmal type of spasm involving the extremities.

thanatology Study of death and dying.

therapist A person skilled in various therapeutic techniques.

thermography Technique of determining surface temperature of the body through photography.

thoracotomy A surgical opening into the thoracic cavity.

thrombocytopenia Decreased number of platelets in the circulating blood.

thrombophlebitis Inflammation of a vein caused by a thrombus.

thrombosis Presence of a blood clot.

thrush An infection of the mouth and throat caused by a fungus; usually occurs in infants.

tinea Ringworm; disease is further differentiated by the area of body affected. Tinea capitis—scalp; tinea barbae—beard and mustache; tinea corporis—body; tinea cruris—groin (jock itch); tinea manum—hand; tinea pedis—foot (athlete's foot).

tissue macrophage Any phagocytic cell of the reticuloendothelial system including cells in the liver, spleen, and connective tissue.

tolerance State in which increasingly larger doses of a drug are needed to provide the same effect as was produced by the original dose.

tonic Refers to tension of contraction.

tonometry Measurement of intraocular pressure.

tonsillectomy Surgical removal of tonsils.

tophi A deposit of urates in tissues around joints; seen in gout.

toxemia Presence of toxins or poisons in the blood.

toxicity State of being poisonous.

trabeculae Portion of the eye in front of the canal of Schlemm and within the angle created by the iris and the cornea.

trabeculectomy Surgical removal of a section of corneoscleral tissue, usually including the canal of Schlemm and the trabecular meshwork. Increases outflow of aqueous humor in patients with chronic side-angle glaucoma.

trabeculoplasty Use of the laser to apply burns in the trabecular meshwork to improve aqueous humour outflow in chronic, wide-angle glaucoma.

tracheostomy Permanent opening into trachea after tracheotomy.

tracheotomy An incision is made into the trachea through the neck below the larynx to gain access to the airway below the blockage of a foreign body, tumor, or edema of the glottis.

traction Exerting a force that pulls or draws on a muscle or organ.

transcutaneous electrical neural stimulation (TENS) Alteration of pain sensations by stimulating peripheral nerves by the application of electric current to the skin.

transected Cut across or severed.

transplantation Surgical transfer of an organ from a donor to a recipient.

tremor Involuntary trembling of body or extremities.

triage System of assigning priorities in treating patients in a disaster or emergency situation.

trichinosis Infection with trichina, a worm found in pork.

trichomoniasis Infection with the *Trichomonas* parasite.

type I diabetes Insulin-dependent diabetes mellitus.

type II diabetes Noninsulin-dependent diabetes mellitus.

ulcer An open lesion on the skin with loss of deep tissue.

ultrasonogram An instrument that measures and records the reflection of pulsed or continuous high-frequency sound waves to detect abnormalities.

unconscious The part of the mind that is only rarely in one's awareness. It contains experiences or data that may be too painful to recall.

unfinished business Concerns of the dying patient requiring resolution before death can be accepted, ranging from financial factors to interpersonal relationships.

universal precautions CDC-recommended "universal blood and body fluid precautions." (Prevent injury from needles and sharp objects; wear protective devices during resuscitation; avoid patient and equipment contact if draining lesion exists in health-care worker.)

urea Chief end-product of protein metabolism, excreted by the kidney.

uremia Accumulation of urinary constituents in the blood causing a general toxic condition.

ureterotomy Incision into a ureter.

urinalysis Analysis of components of urine.

urine osmolality Measurement of the concentration of urine.

urticaria Hives; an allergic reaction characterized by the appearance of wheals on the skin.

uveitis Inflammation of the uveal tract, which lies between the coats of the eye and includes the ciliary body, iris, and cornea.

vaccine A pathogen whose virulence has been reduced and which is used as prophylaxis against a disease.

vaginitis Inflammation of the vagina.

varicocele A varicosity or dilation of veins in the spermatic cord.

varicosities Dilated veins.

vasogenic shock Shock resulting from peripheral vascular dilation caused by factors (toxins) that directly affect blood vessels.

vector An insect, rodent, or arthropod that carries disease and transmits it to humans.

vegetative bacteria Bacteria that do not form spores.

vehicle Mode of transmission of an infective agent from its source to a susceptible host.

venous access device An intravenous pump which patients use to give themselves limited doses of fast-acting analgesics at onset of pain.

ventilation The movement of air in and out of the lungs.

ventricles Small cavities such as in the heart or brain.

ventricular fibrillation Disorganization of the heartbeat that may cause cardiac arrest without prompt treatment.

ventricular tachycardia Rapid contraction of the ventricle with reduced cardiac output.

ventriculogram A diagnostic procedure in which air is injected into the cerebral ventricles and x-ray films are taken.

vertigo A sensation characterized by the movement of objects or of self-movement; an extreme form of dizziness.

vesicle A blisterlike elevation on the skin containing serous fluid.

vesiculation Formation of vesicles.

virology Study of viruses.

virulence Strength of an organism to produce disease.

viruses Infective agents that cause several diseases.

viscosity Thickness of a fluid that causes it to resist flow.

visual analog scale A rating scale using a line to represent a continuum with the ends marked for the two extremes of pain.

vital capacity Amount of air that can be retained in the lungs after a full inspiration.

vulvovaginitis Inflammation of the vagina, the vulva, and usually the vulvovaginal glands.

Wangensteen suction A suction-siphonage method to remove secretions from the stomach.

wen A cyst that often occurs on the back of the scalp.

wheal An elevated type of rash on the skin, such as in urticaria.

withdrawal syndrome A syndrome of serious symptoms when the use of a drug is discontinued.

wound healing Repair of a break in the skin.

wound infection Invasion of a wound by pathogenic microorganisms that reproduce and multiply causing injury.

Index

t indicates table
f indicates figure

A

Abdomenal distention, 448
  after surgery, 125
Abdominal resection, 447
Abdominal surgery, 447-449
Abduction, 265
Abduction pillow, 774
Abortion, 569-572
  classification of, 570
  nursing personnel and, 571, 572
Abscess(es)
  causes of, 28
  manifestations of, 38
Absorption of nutrients, process of, 436, 437
Acceptance as emotional stage of dying, 222, 223
Acetaminophen, 136*t*
Acetic acid, 716
  ear infection and, 697*t*
Acetohexamide, 605
Acetone, 598
Acetylsalicylic acid (aspirin), 136*t*
  ulcers and, 469
Achromatopia, 669
Achromycin; *see* Tetracycline
Acid, 87
Acid-base imbalance, 87-91
Acid fast bacilli (AFB) isolation, 183
Acidosis, 87
  diabetic, 607*t*, 608, 609
  metabolic, 88, 89*t*
  respiratory, 90, 91*t*
Acne vulgaris, 726-728
Acquired immunodeficiency syndrome (AIDS), 145, 153, 164, 166, 167, 812-816
  intervention for, 810-811
  nursing care guidelines for, 809
  nursing care plan for patient with, 812-816
  pathophysiology of, 809, 810
  prevention and control of, 167
  pulmonary infections and, 340
ACTH; *see* Adrenocorticotropic hormone
Activities of daily living (ADLs), 258, 285
Acuity of vision, 668

Acupuncture, 115, 116
Acute care, 7
Acute poststreptococcal glomerulonephritis, 510, 511
Adaptation, 26
Addiction, 137, 138
Addictive disorders, 57, 58
Addison's disease, 613
Adduction, 265
Adenoids, enlarged, 342
Adenovirus, 29
ADH; *see* Antidiurectic hormone
Adjuvant therapy, 202
ADLs; *see* Activities of daily living
Admission of patient, 102
Adrenal glands, 588
  disorders of, 612-614
Adrenalectomy, 614
Adrenalin; *see also* Epinephrine
  allergy therapy and, 803
Adrenocorticotropic hormone (ACTH), 589
Adult respiratory distress syndrome (ARDS), 334, 335
Adventitious sounds, 314
Advil; *see* Ibuprofen
Aerobacter aerogenes, wound infection from, 126
Aerobic bacteria, 26
Aerosol therapy, 320, 321
Affective disorders, 55
Afferent arteriole, 497
African sleeping sickness, 30
Age, falls and confusion and, 287, 288
Aging
  causes of, 235
  factors affecting, 233-237
  intelligence and, 236
  memory and, 236, 237
  physiology of, 237-246
  retirement and, 234, 235
  sensory system and, 239, 240
Agnosia, 294
Agranulocytes, 405, 406
  normal values for, 410*t*
A-hydrocort; *see* Hydrocortisone sodium succinate
AIDS; *see* Acquired immunodeficiency syndrome
AIDS-related complex (ARC), 167, 808

Air embolism
  blood transfusion and, 414
  intravenous therapy and, 93
Air swallowing, 476
Airborne transmission, 173
Airway
  artificial, 117*f*
  obstruction of, 395-397
  postoperative care and, 116, 117
Albumin
  calcium and abnormal levels of, 82
  serum, 407
Alcohol
  abuse of or addiction to, 57
  as antiseptic, 181
  delirium and, 629
  pregnancy and, 34
  ulcers and, 469
  urinary system and, 505
Alcohol psychosis, 629
Aldactone; *see* Spironolactone
Aldehydes, disinfection and, 181, 182
Aldosterone, 72, 612, 613
  function of in body, 588
Alimentary tract, 436; *see also* Gastrointestinal system
Alkaline phosphatase, normal values of, 442
Alkalosis, 87
  metabolic, 88, 89*t*
  respiratory, 88-90
Alkylating agents, cancer treatment and, 208-209
Allergen avoidance, 802
Allergens, 794
Allergic conditions, nursing diagnosis for patients with, 799
Allergic reaction
  from insects, 797
  to penicillin, 42
Allergy, 794-803; *see also* Hypersensitivity
  atopic, assessment of, 799-802
  drug treatment for, 802, 803
  nursing interventions for, 802-804
Allergy survey sheet, 800*f*, 801*f*
Allogeneic transplantation, 212
Allograft, 744, 745
Alopecia, 736
Alpha receptors, 355
Alprazolam, 63*t*

ALS; *see* Amyotrophic lateral sclerosis
Aluminum hydroxide, 468, 469
Alveolar ducts, 310, 311*f*
Alveoli, 310, 311*f*
Alzheimer's disease, 57, 243, 641
Ambulation, 252
    after surgery, 122, 123
Ambulatory care, 9
Amcill; *see* Ampicillin
Amenorrhea, 545
American Cancer Society, 192
    guidelines for cancer-related check-
        ups, 197*t*
    mammography, recommendation of,
        550
American Diabetes Association, self-
        monitoring guidelines of, 599
American Heart Association, life sup-
        port standards and, 393-395
American Nurses' Association (ANA),
        definition of nursing of, 11
American Red Cross
    blood collection and, 408
    cardiac life support standards and,
        393-395
Aminoglycoside(s)
    administration, dose, and side effects
        of, 44*t*
    ear infection and, 697*t*
Amitriptyline hydrochloride, 63*t*
Ammonium compounds (quats), disin-
        fection and, 181
Amphojel, 468, 469
Ampicillin, 44*t*
Amputation, 784-786
    nursing care plan for patient with,
        788-790
    prosthesis and, 784-786
Amputee, 276, 277
    child, 786
Amsler's grid test, 669
Amyotrophic lateral sclerosis (ALS),
        638
Anaerobic bacteria, 26
Anal sphincter spasm, 475
Analgesia
    patient-controlled, 138
    spinal, 138
Anaphylactic shock, 94, 797, 798
Anaprox; *see* Naproxen
Anastomosis, 465
Android obesity, 31
Anectine; *see* Succinylcholine
Anemia, 415-422
    causes of, 31
    nursing care guidelines for, 423
Anesthesia, 110-116
    alternative forms of, 115, 116
    epidural, 114, 115
    equipment used for, 111*f*
    infiltration, 115
    malignant hyperthermia and, 116
    spinal, 114
    topical, 115
    types of, 113-116
Anesthesiologist, 112

Anesthetic(s); *see also* Regional anes-
        thetics
    characteristics and nursing considera-
        tions of, 112*t*
Anesthetist, 112
Aneurysm, 385, 386
    cerebral, 646, 647
Anger as emotional stage of dying, 222
Angina pectoris, 376, 377
Anginal syndrome, 376, 377
Angiogram, 370
Angiography, 370
    cerebral, 625
    fluorescein, 670, 671
    pulmonary, 316
Angioma, 734
Angioplasty, 391
Angiotensin, 499
Anhidrosis, 734
Anion(s), 70
Anion gap, 88
Anoxia, signs and symptoms of, 117
Antacid, peptic ulcers and, 468, 469
Anthrax, 28
Antibiotic(s), 42-44*t*
    administration, dose, and side effects
        of, 43*t*, 44*t*
    cancer treatment and, 208-209
    eyes and, 679*t*
Antibodies, 40
Anticholinergics, 469
    action and nursing considerations of,
        108*t*
Anticoagulant drugs, administration of,
        379
Antidepressant(s), 62
    action and side effects of, 63*t*, 64*t*
    elderly and, 250
Antidiuretic hormone (ADH), 72, 499,
        589
Antigen(s), 39, 794
Antihistamines, allergy therapy and,
        802, 803
Antiinfectives for eyes, 679*t*
Antimetabolites, cancer treatment and,
        208-209
Antimicrobials, topical, for burns, 744
Antisepsis, 180-182
Antiseptic, 180-182
Antitoxins, immunity and, 147, 148
Antiviral agents, eyes and, 679*t*
Antrectomy, 470
Anuria, 510
Anxiety, 51-53
Anxiety disorders, 53, 54*t*
Aphasia, 294, 644
Aplastic anemia, 420, 421
    nursing care plan for patient with,
        429-433
Apnea, 312
Appendages, disorders of, 736, 737
Appendectomy, 447
Appendicitis, 457-459
Appliances for urinary diversions, 524,
        525*f*
Apraxia, 294

APSGN; *see* Acute poststreptococcal
        glomerulonephritis
Aquathermia pack, 38
Aqueous humor, 666
ARC; *see* AIDS-related complex
ARDS; *see* Adult respiratory distress
        syndrome
Argyle Double Seal unit, 325
Aristocort; *see* Triamcinolone
Arterial occlusive disease, 386
Arterial pulse, assessment of, 358
Arteriography, 625
Arteriole, afferent, 497
Arteriosclerosis, 237, 371
Artery(ies)
    coronary, disease of, 376-378
    heart disease and disorders and, 385-
        389
    renal, 497
Arthritis, 770-774
    surgical intervention for, 773, 774
Arthrodesis, 773
Arthroplasty, 773
Arthroscopy, 773
Arthrotomy, 773
Artificial eye, 277
Ascariasis, 162, 163
Asepsis, 109
Asphyxia, 312
Aspiration of bone marrow, 411, 412,
        413*f*
Aspirin, 135, 136*t*
    inflammation and, 43
    menstruation and, 544, 545
    ulcers and, 469
Assessment; *see also* Nursing assess-
        ment
    in nursing process, 13, 14
    of pain, 132-135
Asthma, 331, 332
Astigmatism, 670, 673
Atarax; *see* Hydroxyzine hydrochloride
Atelectasis, 333, 334
Atherosclerosis, 237, 368, 371
Athlete's foot, 30, 720, 721
Ativan; *see* Lorazepam
Atmospheric pressure, illness related
        to, 32
Atopic allergies, assessment of, 799-802
Atrial fibrillation, 362, 363
Atrioventricular (AV) junctional tissue,
        354
Atrium, 352
    dysrhythmia and, 361-363
Atrophic urethritis, 270, 271
Atrophy, 708
Atropine sulfate, 108*t*
Audiometry, 692
Aureomycin; *see* Chlortetracycline hy-
        drochloride
Auricle, 666
Auscultation
    cardiac, 357
    in respiratory problem assessment,
        314
Austin-Moore prosthesis, 781

Autism, 55*t*
Autoclaving, 109
Autoimmune disease, 804
Autologous blood, 408, 409
Autologous transplantation, 212
Autonomic nervous system, 622
Autonomy, 284
Aventyl; *see* Nortriptyline hydrochloride
Awareness, altered states of, 627-634
Azo Gantanol; *see* Sulfamethoxazole

B
Baby boomers, 5
Bacille Calmette Guerin (BCG), 152
Bacilli, 28
Bacitracin, ear infection and, 697*t*
Bacteremia
    manifestations of, 38
    nosocomial, 177, 178
Bacteria, 26-29
    respiratory tract infection and, 336
Bacterial disease, 148-155
Bactericidal chemotherapeutic drugs, 41
Bactericide, 180-182
Bacteriostatic chemotherapeutic drugs, 41
Badge for radiation exposure, 207
Bag(s)
    ice, 39
    ileostomy, 451
Balance and gait, 287
Balkan frame, 765, 766
Barbiturate(s); *see also* Short-acting barbiturates
    action and side effects of, 63*t*
    elderly and, 250
Bargaining as emotional stage of dying, 222
Barium enema, 200, 441, 442
Barnard, Christiaan, 218
Barnes-Redo prosthesis, 463
Baroreceptors, 355
Barriers, protective, for skin, 717
Bartholinitis, 553
Basal cell carcinoma, 735
Basal metabolic rate (BMR), 591
Base bicarbonate deficit and excess, 89*t*
Base excess, normal values of, 315*t*
Bases, 87
Basic food groups, 248
Basophils, 35, 405
    normal values for, 410*t*
Bateman prosthesis, 781
Bath(s), 38
    therapeutic, 710
BCG; *see* Bacille Calmette Guerin
Bed(s)
    CircOlectric, 767, 768
    Gatch, 319, 320
    specialty, 714, 715
Bedsore, 269
Beijerinck, Martinus, 29
Bell's palsy, 651
Bell's paralysis, 651
Benadryl; *see* Diphenhydramine
Bends, 32

Benign tumors, 193-195
Benzathine penicillin G, 43*t*
Benzocaine (Solarcaine), 114*t*
Benzodiazepines, action and side effects of, 63*t*
Bereavement, 223, 224
Beriberi, causes of, 31
Bernstein test, 440
Beta receptors, 355
Betadine, burns and, 744
Bicarbonate, 90, 91
Bicillin; *see* Benzathine penicillin G
Bicyclic, 64*t*
Bile, 484
    digestion and, 437
Biliary system
    diagnostic tests for disorders of, 442-444
    diseases and disorders of, 484-488
    terminology for, 485
Bilirubin, 477
Bilirubin test, 442
Biological response modifiers (BRMs), 212, 213
Biopsy, 198
    cervical, 548, 549
    liver, 443
    renal, 504, 505
Bipolar disorder, 55
Birth control, 543
Bladder, 496
    studies of, 503
    tumors of, 515
Bladder training, 270-273, 290
Blanching sign, 756
Bleb, 708
Bleeding, gastrointestinal, 481
Bleeding time, 409
Blepharitis, marginal, 677, 678
Blind people, interacting with, 672
Blindness, 672
    color, 675
Block, heart, 365, 366
Blood, 353, 402-433
    analysis of, 201
    autologous, 408, 409
    collection of, 408, 409
    components of, 353, 411*f*
    cross-matching of, 412, 413
    diagnostic tests on, 409-413
    diseases or disorders of, 415-428
    donation of, 408
    examination of, 314, 315
    function of, 404
    normal reference laboratory values for, 819-825
    precautions in contact with, 183, 187
    Rh factor of, 412, 413
    structure of, 404-406
    testing of, 408
    typing of, 412, 413
    universal precautions and, 184-188
    volume of, 353
Blood cells, 35
Blood chemistry, 412, 590

Blood count, 367, 409
    differential, 406
    normal values for, 410*t*
Blood cultures, 367
Blood dyscrasias, 415-428
Blood flow through heart, 352*f*
Blood fractions, 406-408
Blood gas(es), 368
    analysis of, 411
    arterial, 315
    interpretation of values of, 90
Blood loss, 405
Blood pressure, 368, 369
    in assessment of cardiovascular system, 357-359
    elderly and, 237, 251
    hypertension and, 371-374
    mean arterial, 373
    postoperative, 117
Blood transfusion
    nursing responsibilities for, 413, 414
    reactions to, 414*t*
    elderly patient and, 252
    infection and, 36
Blood type, 412, 413
Blood urea nitrogen (BUN), 502
Blood vessels, 353
BMR; *see* Basal metabolic rate
Body cast, 759
Body fluid(s)
    nature of, 70, 71
    precautions in contact with, 183, 187
    universal precautions and, 184-188
Body image, surgery and, 100
Body mechanics, musculoskeletal system and, 754
Body substance isolation, 188
Body temperature, 31
    abnormal elevation of, 634
    heart rate and, 355
Boil(s); *see also* Furuncle(s)
    causes of, 28
    of external ear, 695
Bone(s), 754
    tuberculosis of, 776
    tumors of, 783, 784
Bone marrow
    aplastic anemia and, 420, 421
    aspiration of, 411, 412, 413*f*
    transplantation of, 212, 421
Boot, paste, 711
Boracic Acid, ear infection and, 697*t*
Boric acid, 182
    ear infection and, 697*t*
Borrelia burgdorferi as cause of Lyme disease, 153
Bowel function after surgery, 120
Bowel sounds, 448
Bowel training, 273, 274
Bowman's capsule, 496-498*f*
Braces, 277, 278
Brachytherapy, 203
Bradford frame, 766
Brain, 622
    tumors of, 656, 657

Brain scan, 627
Brainstem, 622
Breast(s), 536
    cancer of, 561, 562
    conditions affecting, 561-569
    examination of, 549, 550
    prostheses and, 565
    reconstruction of, 565-568
    tumors of, 561
Breast self-examination (BSE), 196, 550
Breath sounds
    location of, 311f
    in respiratory problem assessment,
        314
Breathing
    postoperative care and, 116, 117, 119,
        120
    respiratory problems and, 318, 318
Brevital; see Methohexital
BRMs; see Biological response modifiers
Bronchi, 310, 311f
Bronchiectasis, 341
Bronchioles, 310, 311f
Bronchitis, 29
    chronic, 330, 331
    intervention in, 337
Bronchoscopy, 199
    in diagnosis of respiratory problems,
        316, 317
Bryant's traction, 761, 762
BSE; see Breast self-examination
Buerger's disease, 387
Bulla, 708
BUN; see Blood urea nitrogen
Bundle of His, 354
Burn(s), 738-747
    assessment of and intervention for,
        739-743
    classification of, 738
    depth and extent of, 738, 739
    estimating size of, 740f
    of eye, 691
    first aid for, 739
    methods of treatment for, 743-746
    nursing care guidelines for patient
        with, 742, 743
    nursing management of, 746-748
    objective of treatment for, 743
    rehabilitation and, 747
    shock and, 741
    surgical management of, 744-746
Burow's solution, ear infection and,
        697t
Bursitis, 775
Butyrophenones, action and side effects
        of, 63t
Bypass, coronary artery, 389

C

C-section, nursing care plan for patient
        with repeat, 581-584
Caffeine
    pregnancy and, 34
    ulcers and, 469
    urinary system and, 505
CAL; see Chronic airflow limitation

Calcitonin, 588
Calcium, 81-84
    physiologic functions of, 31
Calcium carbonate, peptic ulcers and,
        468, 469
Calcium gluconate, magnesium and, 86
Calculi; see Renal calculi
Calculus, 513
Callus, 780
Calor, 35
Caloric test, 626, 627
Camalox, 469
Cancer, 190-215
    biological response modifiers and,
        212, 213
    bone marrow transplantation and,
        212
    of breast, 561, 562
    causes of, 195, 196
    cervical, 557
    chemotherapy and, 208-212
    colorectal, 465, 466
    diagnostic tests and procedures for,
        198-201
    drugs used in treatment of, 208, 209
    emotional care and, 213, 214
    esophageal, 463
    laryngeal, 342-344
    of lung, 344
    of mouth, 462, 463
    of ovary, 557, 558
    overview of, 192-195
    pathophysiology of, 193-195
    prevention and control of, 196-198
    of prostate gland, 575, 576
    protective steps against, 196
    radiation therapy for, 202-208
    rehabilitation and, 214, 215
    risk factors of, 196
    self-help groups and, 215
    of skin, 735, 736
    of small intestine, 465
    of stomach, 464, 465
    surgery and treatment for, 202
    testicular, 573
    of thyroid, 595
    treatment of, 201-213
    uterine, 557
    vaginal, 556
    warning signals of, 197
Candida albicans, 30
    thrush (candidiasis) and, 453
    vaginitis caused by, 552
Candidiasis, 453
Cannula, infection and, 177
Capsule, 27
Carbenicillin, 44t
Carbidopalevodopa, 639
Carbolic acid, disinfection and, 181
Carbon dioxide, partial pressure or ten-
        sion of, 315
Carbonic acid, 90, 91
Carbuncle(s), 718, 719
    causes of, 28
    manifestations of, 38
Carcinogen(s), 195, 196

Carcinoma, 195
    skin and, 735
Carcinoma in situ, 557
Cardiac catheterization, 370, 371
Cardiac cycle, 353, 354
Cardiac dysrhythmias, 361
Cardiac output, 362
Cardiac surgery, 389-392
    nursing care guidelines for, 392
Cardiogenic shock, 93, 380
Cardiopulmonary resuscitation, 393-395
Cardiospasm, 475
Cardiovascular problems
    arteries, veins, and lymphatics and,
        385-389
    cholesterol and, 368
    drugs used in patients with, 378t
    nursing assessment of, 355-359
    rehabilitation and, 392, 393
    risk factors and, 355, 356t
Cardiovascular system
    aging and, 237-239
    diseases and disorders of, 371-385
    structure and function of, 352-355
    surgery of, 389-392
Cardioversion, 363
Carina, 310
Carrier, 145
Cartilage, 754
Cast(s), 757-759
    body, 759
    nursing guidelines for patient with,
        760
Cataract(s), 684-687
Cataract surgery, 685-687
Category specific isolation, 182-187
Catheter(s), 174; see also Indwelling
        catheter(s)
    follow up care and, 509, 510
    irrigation of urethral, 507-509
    for urinary drainage, 506-510
    whistle-tip, 318, 319
Catheterization
    bladder dysfunction and, 273
    cardiac, 370, 371
Cations, 70
CCRC's; see Continuing care retirement
        communities
CCU; see Coronary care unit
Cecum, 436
Cefazolin, 44t
Cefotoxin, 44t
Celbenin; see Methicillin sodium
Cell(s)
    abnormalities of, 32-34
    cancer and, 193-195
    immunity and, 40, 41
Cell-mediated immune response, 798,
        799
Cellular immunity, 40, 41
Cellulitis, manifestations of, 38
Centers for Disease Control, classifica-
        tion system for HIV infection of,
        808
Central nervous system, 622
    degenerative diseases of, 636-641

Central venous lines, 93
Central venous pressure (CVP), 368
Centrioles, 34
Cephalexin, 44*t*
Cephaloridine, 44*t*
Cephalosporins, 42
    administration, dose, and side effects
        of, 44*t*
Cephalothin sodium, 44*t*
Cerebellum, 622
Cerebral angiography, 625
Cerebral embolus, 641
Cerebral hemorrhage, 641
Cerebral palsy, 787
Cerebral thrombosis, 641
Cerebrospinal fluid, 623-626
Cerebrovascular accident (CVA), 237,
        238, 641-646
    assessment of, 641-643
    intervention for, 643-646
    nursing care guidelines for, 645
    rehabilitation and, 646
Cerebrum, 622
Cerumen, 666
    ear obstruction and, 695
Ceruminous glands, 666
Cervical biopsy, 548, 549
Cervical cancer, 557
Cervical traction, 764
Cervix, conditions affecting, 556, 557
Cesium-137, 204
Cestoda, 161, 162
Chafing, 721
Chalazion, 676, 677
Chambers of heart, 352
Checkups, cancer-related, guidelines
        for, 197*t*
Chemical(s), health problems and, 32
Chemical dependence, 32
Chemipen; *see* Phenethicillin potassium
Chemistry, blood, 412
Chemonucleolysis, 655
Chemoreceptors, 355
Chemotherapy, 40-45
    in cancer treatment, 208-212
    education for patient and, 210
    mouth and throat problems and,
        210
    side effects and suggested nursing
        actions of, 211*t*
    for tuberculosis, 152
Chest
    drainage of, 324-326
    surgery of, 344-346
    wounds of, 346
Cheyne-Stokes respiration, 312
Chickenpox, 156, 157
Child amputee, 786
Children
    hearing tests for, 693
    laryngitis and, 335, 336
    tetracyclines and, 42
Chloasma, 733
Chloramphenicols, administration,
        dose, and side effects of, 44*t*
Chlordiazepoxide hydrochloride, 63*t*

Chloride (Cl), 86, 87
    physiologic functions of, 31
Chlorine, disinfection and, 181
Chloromycentin; *see* Chloramphenicol
Chlorpheniramine, 803*t*
Chlorpromazine hydrochloride, 63*t*
Chlorpropamide, 605
Chlortetracycline hydrochloride, 44*t*
Chlor-trimeton; *see* Chlorpheniramine
Cholangiography, 443, 485
Cholangitis, 485
Chole, 485
Cholecystectomy, 447, 485, 486-488
    postoperative nursing care guidelines
        for, 489
Cholecystitis, 484, 485
Cholecystography, 443, 485
Cholecystostomy, 488
    postoperative nursing care guidelines
        for, 489
Choledocho, 485
Choledocholithiasis, 485
Choledochostomy, 488
    postoperative nursing care guidelines
        for, 489
Cholelith, 485
Cholelithiasis, 485-488
Cholera, 28, 29
Cholesterol, 368
Chordotomy, 140
Chorea, 639, 640
Choroid, 666
Christmas disease, 425
Chronic airflow limitation (CAL), 328-
        332
Chronic obstructive pulmonary disease
        (COPD), 328-332
    nursing care guidelines for, 329
Chvostek's sign, 83
Chyme, 437
Cigarette smoking; *see* Smoking
Cilia, 34, 310
Cimetidine (Tagamet), 108*t*
    ulcers and, 469
CircOlectric bed, 767, 768
Circulating nurse, 110
Circulation, 350-401
    lymphatic, 353
    portal, 482*f*
    postoperative care and, 116, 117
    pulmonary and systemic, 353
Circulation overload, 414
Cirrhosis, 478-483
    nursing care guidelines for, 480
    nursing care plan for patient with,
        490-493
    surgical intervention in, 481-483
Cisternal puncture, 625
Cl; *see* Chloride
Cleansing agents, 715, 716
Climacteric, 543, 544
Clonidine, 58
Clostridium, 154
Clostridium perfringens, septic abortion
        caused by, 570
Cloxacillin monohydrate sodium, 44*t*

Clubfoot, 769
CMV; *see* Cytomegalovirus
Coagulation, 368
    normal values for tests of, 410*t*
    tests for, 409, 410
Coagulation factors, 408
Coccidioidomycosis, 30
Codeine, 136*t*
Cold; *see also* Common cold
    healing process and, 38, 39
Cold sore, 29
Colic, ureteral, 514
Colitis, 456-458
Collagen, 36
Collar, ice, 39
Colles fracture, 781, 782
Colon, 436, 437
Colonoscopy, 199, 441
Color blindness, 675
Color classification of decubitus ulcer
        stages, 715*t*, 717
Color vision tests, 669
Colorectal cancer, 465, 466
Colostomy
    nursing care and, 449-453
    nursing care guidelines for, 454
Colporrhaphy, 554, 555
Colposcopy, 548
Coma, 627, 628
    diabetic, 609
    hepatic, 483, 484
Comminuted fracture, 778
Common cold, 29, 335
Communicable disease(s)
    bacterial, 148-155
    control of, 145-148
    infectious process and, 144, 145
    nursing's role in prevention of, 148
    public education about, 148
Communication, 60-62, 96
Community acquired infections, 140-
        169
Compartment syndrome, 782, 783
Compazine; *see* Prochlorperazine
Compensation
    blood gasses and, 90, 91
    as defense mechanism, 52*t*
Complete fracture, 778
Compress, 38
Computed tomography (CT), 200, 201
    in diagnosis of respiratory problems,
        316
    of gastrointestinal system, 443
    for neurologic disorders, 626
    of urinary system, 504
Computer, 5
Concussion, 647
Condoms, 543
Conduction system, cardiac, 354, 355*f*
Confusion, 294, 295, 628
    nursing care plan for, 630, 658-662
Congenital deformities, 769, 770
Congenital malformation in males, 573
Congestive heart failure, 381-385
    nursing care guidelines for, 383
    nursing care plan for, 397-400

Conjunctivitis, 677
Consciousness, 627, 628
Conscious mind, 48
Constipation, 244, 291, 292, 475
Contact dermatitis, 723
Contact isolation, 183, 185
Contact lenses, 674, 675
Contact transmission, 173
Continent urostomy, 523
Continuing care retirement communities (CCRCs), 8
Continuity in patient care, 276
Contraception, 543
Contraction(s)
    of heart muscle, 359
    premature atrial, 361, 362
    premature ventricular, 363, 364
Contrast medium, 201
Contrast x-ray, 199
Control, 180
Contusion(s), 647, 777
Convalescence, 252
Conversion as defense mechanism, 52t
Convulsion(s), 630
COPD; *see* Chronic obstructive pulmonary disease
Cord, spermatic, torsion of, 575
Cornea, 666
    ulcers on, 678
Corneal drying, 690
Corneal transplant, 678, 679
Coronary artery, disease of, 376-378
Coronary care unit (CCU), 366, 367
Corporatization of health care, 5
Corpus luteum, 541
Cortef; *see* Hydrocortisone
Cortef acetate; *see* Hydrocortisone acetate
Corti, organ of, 668
Corticosteroids, 43, 45t
    allergy therapy and, 803
    depression and, 58
Corticosterone, 588
Cortisol; *see* Hydrocortisone
Cortisone, 43
Cortisone acetate, 45t
Cortisporin, 697t
Cortogen acetate; *see* Cortisone acetate
Cortone, 45t
Cortril acetate; *see* Hydrocortisone acetate
Coryza, acute, (common cold), 335
Cost of health care, 5-7
Coughing
    postoperative care and, 119, 120
    respiratory problems and, 318, 318
Count, blood; *see* Blood count
CPR; *see* Cardiopulmonary resuscitation
Crackles (rales), 314
Cranial nerves, 623
Craniotomy, 657
Creatinine, 499
Creatinine tests, 502
Crede maneuver, 291
Creosol, disinfection and, 181
Cretinism, 595

Criminal abortion, 571
Crohn's disease, 455, 456
Cross-matching of blood, 412, 413
Croup, 335, 336
Crust, 708
Crutches, 278-281
Cryoprecipitate, 408
Cryosurgery, 32
    cancer and, 202
Cryptorchidism, 574
Crystals in urine, 502
Crysticillin; *see* Procaine penicillin G
CT; *see* Computed tomography
Culdoscopy, 548
Culture, 27
    blood, 367
Curare, 114
Cushing's syndrome, 613, 614
Cutaneous ureterostomy, 523, 524
Cutdown, 91
CVA; *see* Cerebrovascular accident
CVP; *see* Central venous pressure
Cyanosis, 312
Cycle, cardiac, 353, 354
Cycloplegics, 670, 681t
Cyclosporin, organ transplantation and, 521, 522
Cyclothymic disorder, 55
Cyst(s)
    of female reproductive system, 557, 558
    sebaceous, 733
Cystectomy, 522
Cystic fibrosis, 328
Cystitis, 512, 513
Cystocele, 553-555
Cystography, 503
Cystoscopic examination, 503
Cystotomy, 524, 525
Cytology, exfoliative, 198
Cytomegalovirus (CMV), 167, 809
Cytoplasm, 32
Cytotoxic hypersensitivity reaction, 798

D

D and C, 551
Dakin's solution, 716
Datril; *see* Acetaminophen
Day hospital, 253
Deafness, 693, 694
Death, 216-231
    causes of among elderly, 233
    definition of, 218
    fear of, 219, 222
    following traumatic injury, 225
    procedures following, 227
Debridement, 716
Declomycin; *see* Demeclocycline
Decompression; *see* Gastrointestinal decompression; Intestinal decompression
Decubitus ulcer(s), 269, 292, 293, 712-718
    color classification of wounds and, 715t, 717
    nursing intervention for, 717, 718

Decubitus ulcer(s)—cont'd
    prevention of, 712-714
    stages of, 715t
    treatment of, 715-717
Defense mechanisms
    for controlling anxiety, 51-53
    physiologic, 34-39
Deformities, congenital, 769, 770
Degenerative joint disease, 773
Dehiscence, 126, 127f
Dehydration, 73
Delirium, 242, 294, 628, 629
Delirium tremens, 629
Delivery systems, nursing, 17
Delta-Cortef; *see* Prednisolone
Deltasone; *see* Prednisone
Delusions, 55t
Demeclocycline, 44t
Dementia, 56, 57, 242, 294
Demerol; *see* Meperidine HCl
Demulcents, 318
Denial
    as defense mechanism, 52t
    as emotional stage of dying, 222
Departments of health, 9
Dependence
    chemical, 32
    drug, 137, 138
Depolarization, 359
Depression, 55, 58, 59, 294
    assessment of, 58, 59, 287
    as emotional stage of dying, 222
Dermatitis, 721-728
Dermatitis medicamentosa, 722, 723
Dermatitis venenata, 721, 722
Dermatomycosis, 30
Dermis, 707
DES; *see* Diethylstilbestrol
DES syndrome, 556
Desipramine hydrochloride, 63t
Desquamation, 204
Detached retina, 688, 689
    nursing care plan for patient with, 700-703
Deviated septum, 341, 342
Dexamethasone suppression test, 56
Diabetes, 605
Diabetes insipidus, 614, 615
Diabetes mellitus, 595-611
    care plan for hospitalized patient with, 612
    chronic complications of, 609-611
    diagnostic tests for, 598, 599
    insulin and, 600-605
    pathophysiology of, 596, 597
    patient education and, 610
    retinopathy and, 687, 688
    treatment goals management of, 597
Diabetic, 31, 597
Diabetic retinopathy, 687, 688
Diabinese; *see* Chlorpropamide
Diagnosis, nursing, 14, 15
Diagnosis related groups (DRGs), 6
Diagnostic procedures, nursing responsibilities for, 444
Dialysis, 519-521

Diaphragm, 543
Diastole phase of cardiac cycle, 353
Diazepam (Valium), 63*t*, 108*t*
   depression and, 58
   elderly and, 250
Dicarbosil; *see* Calcium carbonate
Dicloxacillin, 44*t*
Diet
   burn management and, 746
   cardiac problems and, 384
   colostomy and, 450
   in diabetes therapy, 600, 601*t*
   elderly and, 244, 248
   ileostomy and, 451
   peptic ulcer and, 468
   postoperative, 120
   renal failure and, 518
   sodium restricted, 373
   surgery and, 104, 105
Diethylstilbestrol (DES), 556
   cancer and, 195
Diffusion, fluids and electrolytes and, 71, 72
DiGeorge's syndrome, 805-807
Digestion
   accessory organs of, 476-493
   process of, 436, 437
Digestive system, 436; *see also* Gastrointestinal system
   aging and, 243, 244
   diseases and disorders of, 437, 438
Digitalis, 363, 384
Digoxin, 378*t*
Dihydroxyphenylalanine, 638, 639
Dilation and curettage (D and C), 551
Dilaudid; *see* Hydromorphone hydrochloride
Dilemma(s), ethical, 284
Diphenhydramine, 803*t*
Diphenylmethanes, action and side effects of, 63*t*
Diphtheria, 28
Diplococci, 27, 28
Disability, emotional response to, 263, 264
Discharge, manifestations of, 38
Discharge planning, 126, 127
Disease
   causes of, 26
   chemical and physical agents of, 31, 32
Disease specific isolation, 183, 184
Disinfection, 180-182
Disk, intervertebral, rupture of, 654, 655
Dislocation, 777
   of hip, 770
Displacement as defense mechanism, 52*t*
Disseminated intravascular coagulation, 94
Disseminated sclerosis, 637, 638
Dissolution therapy, oral, for gallstones, 486
Distention of abdomen, detecting, 448

Distraction in pain management, 139, 140
Diuresis, 505
Diuretic(s), 383, 384, 505, 506
   potassium and, 78
Diverticula, 459
Diverticulitis, 459, 460
Documentation, nursing, 16
Dolophine; *see* Methadone hydrochloride
Dolor, 35
Domeboro; *see* Acetic acid
Dopamine, deficiency of, 638
Douching, 542
Doxycycline, 44*t*
Drain(s), 121, 122*f*
Drainage
   chest, 324-326
   postoperative care and, 117, 118*f*
   systems for, 122*f*
   in therapy for respiratory problems, 319, 320
   urinary, 506-510
Drainage precautions, 183, 187
Dressing(s)
   materials for, 716
   postoperative care and, 117, 120, 121
   wet, 710, 711
DRGs; *see* Diagnosis related groups
Droperidol, 112*t*
Drug(s)
   abuse of or addiction to, 57
   addiction and, 137, 138
   for allergy treatment, 802, 803
   anesthesia and, 110-115
   antibiotic, 43*t*, 44*t*
   anticoagulant, 379
   for cardiac disorders, 378*t*
   chemotherapeutic, 41-45, 208, 209
   for congestive heart failure, 383, 384
   geriatrics and, 250, 251
   health problems and, 32
   hypoglycemic, oral, 605
   noninotropic, 95
   in organ transplantation, 521, 522
   for pain, 135-137
   for peptic ulcers, 468, 469
   psychotropic, 62-64*t*
   for seizures, 632
   for symptoms accompanying menstruation, 544-545
   for tuberculosis, 152
   vasoactive, 95
   vasopressor, administration of, 379
Drug dermatitis, 722, 723
Dry desquamation, 204
Drying, corneal, 690
Ducts, alveolar, 310, 311*f*
Dullness in percussion of chest, 314
Duodenum, 436
Duracillin; *see* Procaine penicillin G
Dying, 216-231
   emotional stages experienced in, 222, 223
   fear of, 219, 222
   hospice movement and, 225, 226

Dying—cont'd
   nursing care and, 224-229
   nursing interventions and, 226, 227
Dying patient, nursing care of, 224-225
Dymelor; *see* Acetohexamide
Dynapen; *see* Dicloxacillin
Dyscrasias, blood, 415-428
Dysentery, 30
   causes of, 28
Dysmenorrhea, 544, 545
Dyspareunia, 561
Dysphagia, 463, 644
Dysplasia, mammary, 561
Dysplastic nevus syndrome (DNS), 735, 736
Dyspnea, 312
Dysreflexia, 653, 654
Dysrhythmia, 361

E

Ear(s); *see also* External ear; Inner ear; Middle ear
   diseases and disorders of, 695-700
   instillations of, 696
   medications for, 697*t*
   structure and function of, 666-668
Ear problems
   assessment of, 692-695
   diagnostic tests and procedures for, 692, 693
   symptoms of, 692
Eardrum, 666, 667
   perforation of, 695, 696
Earwax, 666
Ecchymoses, 427
Ecchymosis, 777
Echocardiogram, 370
Echoencephalography, 626
Ectopic pregnancy, 572
Ectopic testis, 574
Eczema, 726
Edecrin; *see* Ethacrynic acid
Edema, 74
   in assessment of cardiovascular system, 359
   pitting, 359
   pulmonary, acute, 333, 380, 381
Education, nursing, 11, 12
EGD; *see* Esophagogastroduodenoscopy
Ego, 48
Elavil; *see* Amitriptyline hydrochloride
Elbow, range of motion of, 265
Elderly; *see also* Aging; Geriatrics
   demographics of, 232, 233
   factors affecting dietary patterns of, 244
   group work with, 253, 254
   hospitalized, 251, 252
   nursing of, 246-252
   nutritional needs of, 248
   personal hygiene and, 248, 249
   physiologic changes in, 238*t*, 806*t*
   preventing injury to, 246, 247
   providing comfort for, 247, 248
Electrical bone stimulators, 780

Electrical cardiac conduction, normal, 354, 355f
Electrocardiogram (ECG), 359
   interpretation of, 360, 361
Electrocardiography, 359-361
Electrodiagnostic studies for neurologic disorders, 626
Electroencephalography (EEG), 626
   in determination of death, 218
Electrolyte(s), 68-97
   in body fluid, 71t
   imbalances of, 72-91
   heart rate and, 355
Electromyography (EMG), 626
Electronic cardiac pacemaker, 366
Electronystagmography, 693
Electrophoresis, hemoglobin, 409
Elimination
   bowel, problems affecting, 434-493
   spinal cord injuries and, 653
   surgery and, 105
Elimination testing, 802
Embolectomy, 391, 392
Embolism
   postoperative, 126
   pulmonary, 332, 333
Emotional disorders, 53
Emotional problems, development of, 53
Emotional response to disability, 263, 264
Empathy, 60
Emphysema, 328-330
Empyema, 340, 341
   in diagnosis of respiratory problems, 317
Encephalitis, 155, 635, 636
Encephalography air, 625, 626
Endocarditis, bacterial, 375
Endocardium, 352, 375
Endocrine function, problems affecting, 588-619
Endocrine glands, 588-590
Endocrine problems
   diagnostic tests and procedures for, 590-592
   nursing assessment of patient with, 590
   nursing responsibilities and, 592
Endocrine system, diseases and disorders of, 592-617
Endogenous infections, 173
Endolymph, 668
Endometriosis, 557
Endoplasmic reticulum, 34
Endorphins, 131, 132
Endoscopy of gastrointestinal tract, 440
Endotoxins, 37
Endotracheal intubation in therapy for respiratory problems, 321
Enema
   barium, 441, 442
   preoperative, reasons for, 105
Enflurane (Ethrane), 112t
Enteric precautions, 183, 186

Enteritis, 455, 456
Enterococcus faecalis, nosocomial infections and, 173, 174
Enucleation, 691, 692
Environment, infectious process and, 144
Enzyme(s)
   digestion and, 437
   serum, 367
Eosinophils, 35, 405
   normal values for, 410t
Epicardium, 352
Epidermis, 706, 707
Epidermophyton floccosum, tinea pedis caused by, 720, 721
Epididymis, 539
Epidural anesthesia, 114, 115
Epinephrine, 588
   allergy therapy and, 803
Epistaxis, 328
Epstein Barr virus, mononucleosis and, 157
Equanil; *see* Meprobamate
Erectile function, conditions affecting, 579, 580
Erection, penile, 579, 580
Erikson, Erik, personality development theories of, 49, 50
Erythema intertrigo, 721
Erythema multiforme, 723, 724
Erythematosus; *see* Lupus erythematosus; Systemic Lupus erythematosus
Erythropoietin, 499t
Erythrocin; *see* Erythromycin
Erythrocytes, 404, 405; *see also* Red blood cells
   disorders of, 415-422
Erythromycin, 42, 44t
Erythromycin estolate, 44t
Erythropoietin, 404
Escherichia coli
   decubitus ulcers and, 712
   nosocomial infections and, 173, 174
   penicillinases and, 42
   ulcerative colitis and, 458
   wound infection from, 126
Eskalith; *see* Lithium carbonate
Esophagogastroduodenoscopy (EGD), 440, 441
Esophagoscopy, 199
Esophagus, 436
   cancer of, 463
Esotropia, 674
Estrogen, 543, 544
Ethacrynic acid, 505
Ethics, long term care and, 284
Ethrane; *see* Enflurane
Ethylene oxide, 109, 110
Eustachian tube, 668
Evaluation, nursing process and, 16
Evisceration, 126, 127f
Exchange, fluid and electrolyte, 71, 72
Excoriation, 708
Excretory urography, 502, 503
Exenteration, pelvic, 580, 581

Exercise(s)
   arm, after mastectomy, 566f
   diabetes and, 606
   for dysmenorrhea, 545f
   musculoskeletal system and, 754
   postoperative, 121, 122
   for range of motion, 265-267
Exercise tolerance test (ETT), 369, 370
Exfoliative cytology, 198
Exfoliative dermatitis, 722
Exogenous infections, 173
Exophthalmic goiter, 593
Exophthalmometry, 670
Exotoxins, 37
Expectorants, 318
Extended care facilities, 8
External ear, diseases and disorders of, 695, 696
Extracellular fluid
   composition imbalances of, 76-91
   diagnosis of deficit or excess of, 74t, 75t
   volume imbalances of, 72-76
Extracorporeal shockwave lithotripsy, 486
Exudate, 36
   manifestations of, 38
Exudate absorbers, 716
Eye(s)
   antiinfectives for, 679t
   artificial, 277
   diseases and disorders of, 676-692
   foreign bodies in, 690, 691
   injuries to, 690, 691
   irrigations of, 676
   prostheses for, 692
   refractive errors of, 672-674
   structure and function of, 666, 667f
Eye disorders
   inflammatory and infectious, 676-681
   noninfectious, 681-690
Eye enucleation, 691, 692
Eye examination, 668-672
Eye problems
   diagnostic tests and procedures for, 668-672
   nursing assessment of patient with, 668-676
Eye surgery, nursing care guidelines for, 680

F

Fallopian tubes, conditions affecting, 557-559
Falls, 287-289
Family of patient, 264
Famotidine (Pepcid), 108t
Farsightedness, 673
Fat(s), saturated, foods high in, 368
Fear of death and dying, 219, 222
Federal Drug Administration, blood donation and, 408
Felons, 718, 719
Fenestra ovalis, 668
Fenestra rotunda, 668
Fentanyl, 112t

Fever
definition of, 31
postoperative, 125
scarlet, 150
Fiber optic tubes, 199
Fibrillation, 362, 363
ventricular, 365
Fibrinogen, 407
Fibrocystic breast disease, 561
Fibroid tumor, 557
Fibrosis, cystic, 328
Filtration
fluids and electrolytes and, 71, 72
glomerular, 498
Fissure(s), 708
anal, 473
Fistula
anal, 473
rectovaginal and vesicovaginal, 553
Flagella, 27
Fleming, Alexander, 42
Flora, normal, 26
Fluid(s), 68-97; *see also* Body fluid(s);
Cerebrospinal fluid
imbalances of, 72-91
intake and output of, 251, 252
in intravenous therapy, 72, 73*t*
oral, 39
pathophysiology of shifts of, 74-76
Fluid and electrolyte exchange, 71, 72
Fluorescein angiography, 670, 671
Fluoroscopic x-ray in diagnosis of respi-
ratory problems, 316
Fluoroscopy, 199, 370
Fluothane; *see* Halothane
Fluoxetine hydrochloride, 64*t*
Fluphenazine dihydrochloride, 63*t*
Flutter, atrial, 362, 363*f*
Foam dressings, 716
Follicle-stimulating hormone (FSH),
540, 589
Folliculitis, 718, 719
Folstein Mini-Mental State Exam, 286
Fomites, 145
Food(s)
cholesterol and, 368
iron and, 418
potassium rich, 384
saturated fat and, 368
Food exchanges, 600
Food groups, basic, 248
Food poisoning
salmonella and, 153, 154
staphylococcal, 149, 150
Foot problems, diabetes and, 605,
606
Forane; *see* Isoflurane
Foreign bodies
in ear, 695
in eye, 690, 691
respiratory system and, 342
Foster home, 253
Fourchette, 536
Fovea centralis, 666
Fractionation, 203
Fractions; *see* Blood fractions

Fracture, 777-783
healing of, 780
of hip, 780, 781
intervention for, 778, 779
nursing intervention for, 783
reduction of, 778, 779
of wrist, 781, 782
Frames, 765-768
Freckles, 733
Freud, Sigmund, 48
Functional assessment, 285, 286
Functional nursing, 17
Fungi, 30
Furosemide, 505
Furuncle(s), 718, 719
causes of, 28
manifestations of, 38

G

Gait
and balance, 287
crutch walking and, 279-281
Galactose tolerance test, 442
Gallbladder, 436
diseases and disorders of, 484-488
Gallstones, 485-488
therapy for, 486
Gamma globulin, 407
Gangrene
causes of, 28
gas, 154, 155
manifestations of, 38
Gantanol; *see* Sulfamethoxazole
Garamycin; *see* Gentamicin sulfate
Gas(es), blood; *see* Blood gas(es)
Gas gangrene, 154, 155, 782
Gastrectomy, 447, 470-472
Gastric analysis, test for, 438-440
Gastric gavage, 444
Gastric lavage, 444
Gastric perforation, 470
Gastric resection, 470-472
Gastritis, 454, 455
Gastroenteritis, 455
Gastrointestinal decompression, 445,
446
nursing care guidelines for, 439
Gastrointestinal series (GI), 200, 441,
442
Gastrointestinal system
accessory organ disease and disor-
ders and, 476-493
diagnostic tests for disorders of, 438-
442
diseases and disorders of, 437, 438,
453-476
functional disorders of, 474-476
inflammatory diseases of, 453-461
structure and function of, 436
therapeutic techniques for, 444-447
Gastrointestinal tract, benign tumors
of, 466
Gastroscopy, 199
Gastrostomy, 447
care of patient with, 463, 464
Gatch bed, 319, 320

Gate control theory of pain, 131
Gavage, gastric, 444
Gelusil, 468, 469
Gender
determination of, 542
falls and confusion and, 287, 288
Genitalia
female, conditions affecting, 552-556
male, conditions affecting, 573-581
Gentamicin sulfate, 44*t*
Geopen; *see* Carbenicillin
Geriatric Depression Scale, 287
Geriatric patient; *see* Geriatrics
Geriatric suicide, 236
Geriatrics, 230-255; *see also* Aging; Elderly
aging and, 233-237
alternatives to institutional care and,
252, 253
cardiovascular system and, 237-239
causes of death and, 233
definition of, 232
digestive system and, 243, 244
drug use and, 250, 251
hospitalized elderly and, 251, 252
integumentary system and, 240, 241
mental health and, 235, 236
musculoskeletal system and, 241, 242
neurological system, 242, 243
nursing and, 246-252
nursing homes and, 252, 253
physiology of aging and, 237-246
progress and research in, 233
reproductive system and, 246
respiratory system and, 245, 246
sensory system and, 239, 240
sexuality and, 249
urinary system and, 244, 245
German measles; *see* Rubella
Germicide, 180-182
Gerontology, definition of, 232
GI; *see* Gastrointestinal series
Gland(s)
adrenal; *see* Adrenal glands
endocrine; *see* Endocrine glands
Montgomery's, 536
parathyroid, disorders of, 611
pituitary, *see* Pituitary gland
prostate; *see* Prostate gland
sebaceous, 708
skin disorders and, 733, 734
sweat, 708
thymus, aging and, 235
thyroid, 588
Glasgow Coma Scale, 627, 628
Glaucoma, 682-684
Glipizide, 605
Globulin, gamma, 407
Glomerular capillaries, 496-498*f*
Glomerular filtration, 498
Glomerulonephritis, 510, 511
Gloves, infective materials and, 184
Glucagon, 590, 607, 608
Glucatrol; *see* Glipizide
Glucose
in blood, 598

Glucose—cont'd
    self monitoring of, 599, 600
Glutaraldehyde, disinfection and, 181,
        182
Glyburide, 605
Glycohemoglobin, diabetes and, 599
Glycopyrrolate (Robinul), 108*t*
Glycosuria, 501
Goiter, 592, 593
    nodular, 595
Gold-198, 204
Golgi complex, 34
Gonococcus, 28
Gonorrhea, 166
    causes of, 28
Gout, 774, 775
Gowns, infective materials and, 184
Graft, skin, 744-746
Gram negative organism, 27
Gram positive organism, 27
Grand mal seizures, 631, 632
Granulation, manifestations of, 38
Granulation tissue, 36
Granulocytapheresis, 408
Granulocytes, 35, 405
    normal values for, 410*t*
Granulocytopenia, 405
Graves' disease, 593
Greenstick fracture, 778
Grief, 223, 224
Groups, self-help, 215
Growth hormone, 589
Guillain-Barre syndrome, 649
Gumma, 708
Gynoid obesity, 31

H

H₂ receptor antagonists, action and
        nursing considerations of, 108*t*
Haemophilus aegyptius, 677
Hair, loss of, 736
Hair transplants, 736, 737
Haldol; *see* Haloperidol
Hallucinations, 55*t*
Haloperidol, 63*t*
Halothane (Fluothane), 112*t*
Handicapped, tools and procedures to
        assist, 281
Handwashing, 180
Haptens, 40
HCFA; *see* Health Care Financing
        Agency
Head injuries, 647-649
Healing, 36
    of fractures, 780
    wound, after surgery, 122
Health
    defined, 4
    mental, 50
Health Care Financing Agency (HCFA),
        6
Health care
    cost and reimbursement and, 5-7
    delivery of, 7
    home, 296-305
    other facilities for, 9, 10

Health care—cont'd
    phases of, rehabilitation in, 259, 260
    trends affecting, 4, 5
Health care team, 10
Health care workers, universal precau-
        tions and, 184-188
Health maintenance organization
        (HMO), 8, 9
Hearing, 668
    aging and, 239, 240
    in infants and young children, 693
    problems affecting, 664-703
Hearing aids, 694
Hearing loss, 693-695
    signs of, 694
    speaking to patient with, 695
Heart
    anatomy of, 352, 353
    monitoring of, 359-361
    neurohumoral controls of, 354, 355
Heart block, 365, 366
Heart disease
    coronary artery and, 376-378
    hypertensive, 371-374
    pregnancy and, 385
    rheumatic, 374, 375
Heart failure; *see* Congestive heart fail-
        ure
Heart rate, 360
    disorders of, 361-366
Heart rhythm, 360, 361
    disorders of, 361-366
Heart sounds, 353, 354
    characteristics of, 358*t*
Heartburn, 475, 476
Heat
    external, shock and, 95, 96
    healing process and, 38, 39
Heat lamps, 39
Heating pads, elderly patients and, 247
Heimlich chest drainage, 325, 326
Heimlich maneuver, 342, 395, 396
Helminthic infestations, 161-163
Hematocrit, 409
    normal values for, 410*t*
Hematuria, 501
Hemianopia, 644
Hemianopsia, 669
Hemodialysis, 519, 520*f*
Hemo-Drain, 121
Hemoglobin, 405, 409
Hemoglobin electrophoresis, 409
Hemophilia, 425-427
Hemoptysis, 125, 318
Hemorrhage, 415, 416
    postoperative, 125
Hemorrhagic anemia, 415, 416
Hemorrhagic disorders, 425-429
Hemorrhoidectomy, 474
Hemorrhoids (piles), 473, 474
Henderson, Virginia, 10, 11
Hepatic coma, 483, 484
Hepatitis, 159; *see also* Viral hepatitis
Hernia, 472, 473
    hiatus (hiatal), 473
Hernioplasty, 472

Herniorrhaphy, 447, 472
Herpes simplex, 29, 730, 731
Herpes simplex virus (HSV), 167, 168
Herpes varicella-zoster (V-Z) virus, 156,
        157
Herpes zoster (shingles), 29, 157, 731-
        733
Herpesvirus, 29
Heterograft, 745
Hexachlorophene, disinfection and, 181
Hiatus (hiatal) hernia, 473
Hierarchy of relative prepotency, 18
Hip
    dislocation of, 770
    fracture of, 780, 781
    range of motion of, 265
    tuberculosis of, 776
Hip spica, 759
His-Purkinje system, 354
Histamine test, 438-440
Histoplasmosis, 30
History, patient, 103
HIV; *see* Human immunodeficiency vi-
        rus
Hodgkin's disease, 195, 422-424
Holistic care, 4
Home care, 253
Home health agencies, 9
Home health care, 296-305
    long term care and, 304
    nursing in, 301-305
    reimbursement for, 303, 304
    services for, 299, 300
    team for, 300, 301
Home health services, 299, 300
Homeostasis, 4, 18, 26
Homograft, 744, 745
Hookworms, 163
Hordeola, 676
Hormone(s), 588, 589
    antidiuretic, 499
    cancer treatment and, 208-209
    electrolyte and fluid balance and, 72
    follicle-stimulating, 540
    heart rate and, 355
    luteinizing, 541
    renal, 499
Hospice care, 9, 225, 226
Hospital(s), 7, 8
    day, 253
    infection acquired in, 178-189
Host, 144, 145
Hot water bottle(s), 38, 39
    elderly patients and, 247
Housing, elderly and, 234
HSV; *see* Herpes simplex virus
Human chorionic gonadotropin (HCG),
        551
Human immunodeficiency virus (HIV),
        145, 166, 167, 807-811
    clinical manifestation of, 808, 809
    precautions to prevent transmission
        of, 811, 812
    tuberculosis and, 153
    universal precautions and, 184-188
Human needs, 18-21, 48

Humidification, 320, 321
Humidifier(s), 175, 321
Humoral immunity, 40
Huntington's chorea, 57, 639, 640
Hydrocele in males, 573
Hydrocolloids, 716
Hydrocortisone, 45*t*
  function of in body, 588
Hydrocortisone acetate, 45*t*
Hydrocortisone sodium succinate, 45*t*
Hydrocortone; *see* Hydrocortisone
Hydrogels, 716
Hydrogen peroxide, 182, 716
  ear infection and, 697*t*
Hydromorphone hydrochloride, 136*t*
Hydronephrosis, 514
Hydrotherapy for burns, 744
Hydroureter, 514
Hydroxyzine hydrochloride, 63*t*
Hydroxyzine pamoate, 63*t*
Hygiene
  diabetes and, 605, 606
  sexuality and, 542
Hymen, 536
Hyperacidity, 475, 476
Hyperalimentation, 447
Hyperbaric oxygen, 323
Hypercalcemia, 83, 84
Hypercapnia, 312
Hypercarbia, 312
Hyperchloremia, 87
Hyperglycemia, 596
Hyperhidrosis, 733
Hyperkalemia, 79-81, 82*t*
Hypermagnesemia, 86
Hypernatremia, 77, 78*t*
Hyperopia, 670, 673
Hyperparathyroidism, 611
Hyperphosphatemia, 87
Hyperpyrexia, 634
Hyperreflexia, 653, 654
Hypersensitivity, 794-803; *see also* Allergy
  immediate, 794-797
Hypertension, 371-374
  elderly and, 237
  intervention for, 373, 374
  stepped-care treatment of, 374
Hyperthermia, 31, 32, 634
Hyperthyroidism, 593, 594
  nursing care plan for patient with, 615-618
  nursing guidelines for, 594
Hypertonic fluid, 73
Hypertrichosis, 736, 737
Hypertrophy, benign prostatic, 576
Hyperventilation, 312
Hypervolemia, 73, 74, 75*t*
Hypnosis, 115, 116
Hypnotic, elderly and, 250
Hypoadrenalism, secondary, 613
Hypocalcemia, 83, 85*t*
Hypochloremia, 86, 87
Hypochromia, 417
Hypochromic anemia, 416-418
Hypogammaglobulinemia, 805*t*, 806

Hypoglycemia, 611
Hypoglycemic drugs, oral, 605
Hypoglycemic reaction, 606-608
Hypokalemia, 78, 79, 80*t*
Hypomagnesemia, 84-86
Hyponatremia, 76, 77
Hypoparathyroidism, 611
Hypophysis, 614
Hypothalamus, 589
Hypothermia, 31, 32
Hypothermia as anesthesia, 115
Hypothyroidism, 594, 595
  nursing care guidelines for, 596
Hypotrichosis, 736, 737
Hypoventilation, 312
Hypovolemia, 72, 73
Hypovolemic shock, 93, 415, 416
Hypoxia, 312
Hysterectomy, 447, 559-561
  nursing care guidelines for, 560
Hysterosalpingography, 549

I

^{131}I, 591, 592
I can cope, 215
Ibuprofen, 136*t*
  menstruation and, 544, 545
Ice, healing process and, 39
Ice bag, 39
Ice collar, 39
ICF; *see* Intermediate care facility
ICP; *see* Intracranial pressure
ICU; *see* Intensive care unit
Id, 48
Identification as defense mechanism, 52*t*
Ig; *see* Immunoglobulins
Iga deficiency, 805*t*
Ileal conduit, 523, 524
Ileobladder, 523, 524
Ileocecal valve, 436
Ileostomy
  continent or pouch, 453
  nursing care and, 449-453
  nursing care guidelines for, 454
Ileum, 436
  paralytic, 449
Illegal abortion, 571
Illness
  defined, 4
  division between mental and physical, 48
Ilosone; *see* Erythromycin estolate
Ilotycin; *see* Erythromycin
Imaging, 198-201
  magnetic resonance, 201
Imipramine hydrochloride, 63*t*
Immune complex, hypersensitivity and, 798
Immune response
  deficient, 804-807
  excessive, 794-804
  problems affecting, 793-817
Immunity, 39-41
  active, 146, 147
  cellular, 40, 41

Immunity—cont'd
  humoral, 40
  natural, 145, 146
  passive, 147, 148
Immunization, 145-148
  contraindications for, 147
  for influenza, 337
Immunization schedule, 146*t*, 827
Immunocompetent, 39
Immunodeficiencies, 804-807
  nursing care of people with, 807-811
  primary, 804-806
  secondary, 806, 807
Immunoglobulin (Ig), 40, 146-148
Immunology, 39
Immunotherapy, 803, 804
Impacted fracture, 778
Impairment, hearing; *see* Hearing loss
Impetigo, 28
Impetigo contagiosa, 719
Implant, collagen, 728
Incontinence; *see also* Urinary incontinence
  bladder and bowel, 644, 645
Incus, 668
Inderal; *see* Propanolol
Indigestion, 475
Indocin; *see* Indomethacin
Indomethacin, menstruation and, 544, 545
Indwelling catheter(s), 73
Infant(s)
  hearing tests for, 693
  retinopathy and, 681, 682
  sulfonamide therapy and, 744
Infantile paralysis, 636
Infarct, 378
Infarction; *see also* Myocardial infarction
  pulmonary, 332, 333
Infection(s), 26, 36-38; *see also* Communicable disease(s); Nosocomial infections
  burn management and, 746
  classification of, 37
  community-acquired, 140-169
  endogenous and exogenous, 173
  fungal (mycotic), 30
  helminth, 161
  manifestations of, 38
  nursing intervention in high risk for, 807
  respiratory, health and social aspects of, 346, 347
  salmonella, 153, 154
  staphylococcal, 148-150
  streptococcal, 150
  superficial or systemic, 30
  surgery and, 100
  of surgical wounds, 126
  urinary tract, 174
  viral, 29
Infection control in hospitals, recommendations for, 178
Infection control committee, 178
Infection control practitioner, 178

Infectious disease; *see* Communicable disease(s)
Infestations, 737, 738
Infiltration, intravenous therapy and, 91, 92
Inflammation, 35, 36
Inflammatory process, 35, 36
Influenza, 158
    intervention in, 336, 337
Informed consent, 102
Inhalant agents, characteristics and nursing considerations of, 112t
Inhalation anesthesia, 113
Injury
    elderly patient and, 246, 247
    to external ear, 695
    eye, 690, 692
    head, 647-649
    physical agents of, 31, 32
    spinal cord, 651-654
Inner ear, 668, 699, 700
Innover; *see* Droperidol
Insects, allergic reaction from, 797, 798
Inspection in respiratory problem assessment, 313
Instillations, ear, 696
Institutional care, alternatives to, 253, 254
Instruction, preoperative, for patient, 103, 104
Insulin, 590, 600-605
    instructions for measuring, 603f
Insulin reaction, 606-608
Integumentary system; *see also* Skin
    aging and, 240, 241
Intelligence, aging and, 236
Intensive care unit (ICU), 118, 119
Intermediate care facility (ICF), 8
International Association of Laryngectomees, 215
Intervention, infection and inflammation and, 38, 39
Intervertebral disk, rupture of, 654, 655
Interviewing techniques, 13, 14
Intestinal decompression, 445, 446
Intestinal obstruction, 461, 462
Intestine(s) *see also;* Large intestine; Small intestine
    inflammation of, 455, 456
Intoxication, water, 74
Intracranial pressure (ICP), 629, 630
Intraoperative care, 108-116
Intrauterine devices (IUDs), 543
Intravenous agents, characteristics and nursing considerations of, 112t
Intravenous drugs, 113, 114
Intravenous therapy, 91-96
    bacteremia and, 177, 178
    elderly patient and 252
    postoperative care and, 117, 118
Intradermal test, 800, 801
Intubation in therapy for respiratory problems, 321
Iodine
    as antiseptic and disinfectant, 181
    radioactive, 208, 209, 591, 592

Iodine-125, 204
Iodine preparations, 593
Iodophors as antiseptic and disinfectant, 181
Ionizing radiation, 202
Ions, 70, 71t
Iridectomy, 683
Iris, 666
Iron
    administration of, 416, 417t
    average normal daily requirements for, 416t
    foods high in, 418
Iron-deficiency anemia, 416-418
Irrigation
    colostomy and, 450
    of eye, 676
    throat, 320, 321
    of urethral catheter, 507-509
Ishihara test, 669
Islands of Langerhans, 436
Isocarboxazid, 64t
Isoenzymes, cardiac, 367
Isoflurane (Forane), 112t
Isolation, 182-187
    body substance, 188
    disease specific, 183, 184
    emotional support and, 188, 189
    instruction cards for, 183-187
    pneumonia and, 339
Isolation perfusion, 211, 212
Isoniazid (INH), 152
Isopropyl alcohol, ear infection and, 697t
Isordil; *see* Isosorbide dinitrate
Isosorbide dinitrate, 377
Isotope, radioactive, 204, 205
Itch, 737, 738
Itching, 734

J

Jackson-Pratt suction apparatus, 121
Jejunum, 436
Jock itch, 720
Joint(s), 754
    range of motion and, 265-267
Joslin, Elliot, Dr., 606
Jugular venous pressure, 359

K

Kanamycin sulfate, 44t
Kantrex; *see* Kanamycin sulfate
Kaposi's sarcoma, 808, 809
    AIDS and, 167
Keflex; *see* Cephalexin
Keflin; *see* Cephalothin sodium
Keloid, 734
Kenacort; *see* Triamcinolone
Kenalog; *see* Triamcinolone acetonide
Keratin, 706, 707
Keratitis, 678, 679
Keratoplasty, 678, 679
Keratoses, 735
Keratotomy, 673
Ketaject; *see* Ketamine
Ketalar; *see* Ketamine

Ketamine, characteristics and nursing considerations of, 112t
Ketoacidosis, diabetic, 607t, 608, 609
Ketonuria, 598
Kidney, 496
    tumors of, 515
Kinins, action of, 499t
Knee, range of motion of, 265
Koch, Robert, 108, 150
Koch's pouch, 523, 453
Koplik's spots, 155
Korotkoff sounds, 258
Kussmaul respirations, 88, 608
Kwashiorkor, 31
Kwell shampoo, 737
Kynex; *see* Sulfamethoxypyridazine
Kyphosis, 241

L

Laboratory examinations, cardiovascular disease and, 367, 368
Laboratory studies in diagnosis of cancer, 201
Laboratory values, normal reference, 819-827
Lactogenic hormone, 589
Laetrile, 213
Laminectomy, 655, 656
Lamp, heat, 39
Langerhans, islands of, 436
Lanoxin; *see* Digoxin
Laparoscopy, 549
Laparotomy, 447
Large intestine, 436
    digestion and, 437
Laryngectomy, 343, 344
Laryngitis, 335, 336
Larynx, 310, 311f
    cancer of, 342-344
Laser cholecystectomy and, 486
Lasix; *see* Furosemide
Lavage, gastric, 444
Laxatives, 475
Legal abortion, 571
Legionella pneumophila, 155
Legionnaires' disease, 155, 338
Lens(es), 666
    contact, 674, 675
Lentigo, 733
Lesions, skin; *see* Skin lesions
Leukapheresis, 408
Leukemia(s), 195, 424, 425
    nursing care guidelines for, 426
Leukocytes, 35, 405, 408; *see also* White blood cells
Leukocytosis, 39, 405, 422
Leukopenia, 405, 422
    chemotherapy and, 210
Leukorrhea, 552, 553
LeVeen shunt, 481-483
Levo Dromoran; *see* Levorphanol tartrate
Levodopa (L-dopa), 638, 639
Levorphanol tartrate, 136t
Librium; *see* Chlordiazepoxide hydrochloride

Lice, 737
Licensed practical nurse (LPN), 11, 12
Licensed vocational nurse (LVN), 11, 12
Lidocaine (Xylocaine), 114t
Life, prolongation of, 218, 219
Life cycle, reproductive function and, 540-544
Life expectancy, 5, 232
Life support, 218, 219
    cardiac, 393-395
Lifestyle, hypertension and, 372
Ligaments, 754
Ligation, vein, 388
Lister, Joseph, 108
Lithane; *see* Lithium carbonate
Lithiasis, 513
Lithium carbonate, action and side effects of, 63t
Lithonate; *see* Lithium carbonate
Lithotomy, 525-527
Lithotripsy, 486
    extracorporeal shock-wave, 514
Liver, 436
    diagnostic tests for disorders of, 442-444
    digestion and absorption and, 437
    diseases and disorders of, 476-484
Liver biopsy, 443
Liver function test, 442
Liver scanning, 443
Liver spots, 733
Living will, 219, 220f, 221f
Living with cancer, 215
Lobectomy, 344, 345f
Local anesthetics; *see also* Regional anesthetics
Lockjaw, 782
Locomotor ataxia, 636
Long-term care, 7, 282-295
    assessment guidelines in, 285-287
    ethical dilemmas in, 284
    home health care and, 304
    risk and specific care issues in, 287-295
Loop of Henle, 496, 497
Lorazepam, 63t
Loridine; *see* Cephaloridine
Loss; *see also* Blood loss; Hearing loss
    of hair, 736
    of sight, 672
Lumbar puncture, 624, 625
Luminal; *see* Phenobarbital
Lumpectomy, 562, 563
Lung(s), 310, 311f
    cancer of, 344
    coccidioidomycosis and, 30
    foreign bodies in, 342
    histoplasmosis and, 30
Lupus erythematosus, 728-730; *see also* Systemic lupus erythematosus
Lupus Foundation of America, 730
Luteinizing hormone (LH), 541, 589
Lyme disease, 153
    causes of, 28, 29
Lymph, 353

Lymph node(s), 34, 35, 353
    in assessment of cardiovascular system, 359
Lymphangitis, 389
Lymphatic circulation, 353
Lymphatic fluid, 353
Lymphatics, heart disease and disorders and, 385-389
Lymphocytes, 35, 40, 794
    normal values for, 410t
Lymphoma, 195
Lysol, disinfection and, 181
Lysosomes, 34
Lysozyme, 34

M
Maalox, 468, 469
Macrolides, 42
    administration, dose, and side effects of, 44t
Macrominerals, 31
Macrophages, 36
Macula, 666
Macular degeneration, 688-690
Macule, 708
Mafenide, 41t
Mafenide acetate, burns and, 744
Magnesium, 84-86, 468, 469
    physiologic functions of, 31
Magnesium sulfate, 86
Magnesium trisilicate, 468, 469
Magnetic resonance imaging (MRI), 201
    for neurologic disorders, 626
    of urinary system, 504
Make Today Count, 215
Makeup, surgery and, 106, 107
Malaria, 30, 160, 161
Malformation, congenital, in males, 573
Malignant melanoma, 735, 736
Malignant neoplasms, sites of, 193f
Malignant tumors, 193-195
Malleus, 668
Malnutrition, 30, 31
    elderly and, 248
Mammary dysplasia, 561
Mammography, 200, 550
Manic-depressive illness, 55
Mantoux test, 151
MAO inhibitors; *see* Monoamine oxidase inhibitors
MAP; *see* Mean arterial blood pressure, 373
Marasmus, 31
Marplan; *see* Isocarboxazid
Mask(s)
    infective materials and, 184
    oxygen by, 323
Maslow, Abraham
    human needs theories of, 18-21, 48
    criteria for normal personality of, 51
Mastectomy, 563-569
    nursing care guidelines for, 569
    reconstruction of breast after, 565-568
Mastication, 436
Mastitis, 561
Mastoidectomy, 697, 698

Mastoiditis, 696, 697
Matching, cross, of blood, 412, 413
Materials, dressing, 716
Mattress overlays, 714
McGill-Melzack Pain Questionnaire, 133
Mean arterial blood pressure (MAP), 373
Measles, 146, 147, 155, 156
Mediastinum, 310
Medicaid, 6
    home health care and, 305, 306
Medical patient, 12
Medical surgical nursing, 12
Medicare, 6, 233
    home health care and, 305, 306
Medication(s)
    addiction and, 137, 138
    for ear, 697t
    long term care and, 287
    oral versus parenteral administration of, 137
    pain, 135-137
    preoperative, 107, 108
    topical, 716
Mefenamic acid, menstruation and, 544, 545
Mefoxin; *see* Cefotoxin
Melanin, 707
Melanocyte-stimulating hormone (MSH), 589
Melanoma, malignant, 735, 736
Mellaril; *see* Thioridazine hydrochloride
Membrane(s)
    cell, 32
    mucous, 34
Memory, aging and, 236, 237
Menarche, 540, 541
Meniere's syndrome, 699, 700
Meninges, 623
Meningitis, 634, 635
    causes of, 28
    meningococcal, 155
Meningococcus, 28
Menopause, 543, 544
Menorrhagia, 545
Menstrual function, disturbances of, 544-546
Menstruation, 541, 542
Mental health, 50
    aging and, 235, 236
Mental illness, organic brain changes and, 56, 57
Mental status, assessment of, 286, 287
Meperidine, 112t
Meperidine HCl (Demerol), 108t
Meperidine hydrochloride, 136t
Meprobamate, 63t
Metamorphopsia, 669
Metastasis, 194
Metazoa, 161-163
Methadone hydrochloride, 136t
Methicillin sodium, 44t
Methohexital (Brevital), 112t
Methyldopa, depression and, 58
Meticorten; *see* Prednisone
Metrorrhagia, 545

Microbes, 26-30
Microbiology, 26
Micronase, 605
Microorganisms, 26-30
Microscopy, fluorescent, 29
Midazolam HCl (Versed), 108t
Middle ear, 667, 668, 696-699
Midicel; see Sulfamethoxypyridazine
Miliaria, 721
Miltown; see Meprobamate
Minerals; see Macrominerals; Trace minerals
Minocin; see Minocycline
Minocycline, 44t
Miotics, 670
Miscarriage, 569
Mitochondria, 34
Mobility, problems affecting, 752-791
Mobitz type heart block, 365
Mole(s), 734
    skin cancer and, 735, 736
Monitoring
    in burn management, 746
    of heart, 359-361
    self, for diabetes, 599, 600
Monoamine oxidase inhibitors, action and side effects of, 64t
Monocytes, 35, 405, 406
    normal values for, 410t
Mononucleosis, 422
    infectious, 157, 158
Mono-vacc test, 151
Montgomery straps, 121
Montgomery's glands, 536
Morphine, 112t
    dying patient and, 226
Morphine sulfate, 108t, 136t
Motivation in rehabilitation, 274, 275
Motrin; see Ibuprofen
Mouth
    cancer of, 462, 463
    inflammation of, 453, 454
Movement, joint, 265-267
MRI; see Magnetic resonance imaging
Mucous membrane sensitivity test, 802
Mucous patches, 165
Multiple sclerosis, 637, 638
Multisystems in health care, 5
Mumps (parotitis), 157
    vaccine for, 147
Muscle(s)
    heart, 352, 353
    pelvic, relaxation of, 553-555
    sphincter; see Sphincter muscle
Muscle relaxants, 114
Muscle spasms, 653
Muscle strength, 287
Muscular dystrophy, 787
Musculoskeletal conditions, intervention for, 768, 769
Musculoskeletal system
    aging and, 241, 242
    diseases and disorders of, 769-786
    infectious diseases and disorders of, 775, 776
    neuromuscular conditions and, 787

Musculoskeletal system—cont'd
    structure and function of, 754
    traumatic injury to, 776-783
Myasthenia gravis, 640, 641
Mycifradin; see Neomycin sulfate
Myciguent; see Neomycin sulfate
Mycobacterium tuberculosis, 150, 151, 153
    as cause of tuberculosis, 339
Mycotic infections, 30
Mydriatics, 670, 681t
Myelocytes, 405
Myelography, 626
Myeloma, 195
Myelosuppression, chemotherapy and, 210
Myocardial infarction, 378-385
    complications of, 380-385
    intervention for, 379, 380
    nursing care guidelines for, 380
Myocardium, 352
Myomatous tumor, 557
Myopia, 670, 673
Myringotomy, 696
Myxedema, 595

N

Nafcillin sodium, 44t
Nail disorders, 737
Nailing, bone, 781
Naproxen, menstruation and, 544, 545
Narcotic(s), action and nursing considerations of, 108t
Narcotic analgesics, 112t
Nardil; see Phenelzine dihydrogen sulfate
Nasal cavities, 310, 311f
Nasal polyps, 341, 342
National Cancer Act, 192
National Cancer Institute information line, 198
National Multiple Sclerosis Society, 638
National Nosocomial Infections Study (NNIS), 173
Nausea, postoperative, 124
Nearsightedness, 673
Nebulizer(s), 175, 321
Neck, range of motion of, 265
Necrosis, manifestations of, 38
Needs; see Human needs
Neisseria gonorrhoeae, 166, 677
Neisseria meningitidis, 155, 677
Nematoda (roundworms), 162, 163
Nembutal; see Pentobarbital Sodium
Neobiotic; see Aminoglycoside
Neomycin sulfate, 44t
Neoplasms, 193-195; see also Malignant neoplasms
Nephrectomy, 527, 528
Nephrolithiasis, 513
Nephrolithotomy, 527
Nephron, 496, 497
Nephrostomy, 527, 528
Nephrotic syndrome, 511, 512
Nerve, cranial, 623
Nerve block, peripheral, 115

Nervous system
    autonomic; see Autonomic nervous system
    central; see Central nervous system
    diagnostic tests and procedures for, 623-627
    diseases and disorders of, 634-658
    infectious diseases of, 634-636
    parasympathetic; see Parasympathetic nervous system
    peripheral, 622
    structure and function of, 622, 623
    sympathetic; see Sympathetic nervous system
Neuralgia, 649-651
Neurectomy, 140
Neuritis, 649-651
Neurogenic shock, 93, 94
Neurologic examination, 623
Neurologic function, problems affecting, 620-663
Neurological system, aging and, 242, 243
Neuromuscular conditions, 787
Neuroradiologic studies, 625, 626
Neurovascular integrity, 755-769
    nursing care guidelines for, 756
Neutrophils, 35, 405
    normal values for, 410t
Nevus, 734
Newborn, purulent conjunctivitis and, 677
Nifedipine, preparation, action, and nursing considerations of, 378t
Nightingale, Florence, 10, 11
Nipple, 536
Nitro-Bid; see Nitroglycerine
Nitroglycerin, administration of, 377
Nitroglycerine, 378t
Nitrostat; see Nitroglycerine
Nitrous oxide, 112t
NNIS; see National Nosocomial Infections Study
Node(s); see Lymph node(s)
Nodule, 708
Non-Hodgkin's lymphoma, 195
Noncontrast x-ray, 199
Noninotropic drugs, 95
Nonnarcotic analgesics, 112t
Nonsteroidal antiinflammatory drugs, 43, 135
Normal reference laboratory values, 819-827
Normovolemic shock, 93
Norpramin; see Desipramine hydrochloride
North American Nursing Diagnosis Association (NANDA), 14
Nortriptyline hydrochloride, 63t
Nosebleed, 328
Nosocomial bacteremia, 177, 178
Nosocomial infections, 37, 170-189
    control and prevention of, 178-189
    emotional support and, 188, 189
    incidence of, 172, 173
    methods of transmission of, 173

Nosocomial infections—cont'd
    policies and procedures for control
        of, 182-189
    preventive policies and procedures
        for, 180-182
    surveillance and, 178-180
Novocain; *see* Procaine
Nucleus, 34
Nuprin; *see* Ibuprofen
Nurse(s)
    circulating, 110
    and health care team, 10
    rehabilitation and, 260, 261
    scrub, 110
Nursing
    abortion and, 571, 572
    in coronary care unit, 366, 367
    definition of, 10, 11
    delivery systems and, 17
    education and scope of practice and,
        11, 12
    medical surgical, 12
    rehabilitation, 258-264
    standards of practice in, 12, 13
    surgical, 101
    theory in practice of, 17, 18
    therapeutic relationship in, 59-62
Nursing assessment
    of depression, 58, 59
    in long-term care, 285-287
    surgery and, 102, 105
Nursing care plan, 15
Nursing diagnosis, 14, 15
    respiratory problems and, 348, 349
Nursing history, 13
Nursing homes, 252, 253
Nursing process, 13-16
Nutrient, 30, 31
Nutrition, 30, 31; *see also* Diet
    elderly and, 248
    problems affecting, 434-493
    total parenteral, 446, 447
Nutritional imbalance, 30, 31
Nystagmus, 693

O

O₂ saturation, normal values of, 315*t*
Obesity, 31
Oblique fracture, 778
Obstruction(s); *see also* Intestinal ob-
        struction
    airway, 395-397
    of ears, 695
    of respiratory system, 341, 342
    of urinary system, 513, 514
Occupational Heath and Safety Admin-
        istration (OSHA), health
        care workers and, 188
Occupational therapist (OT), rehabilita-
        tion and, 261, 262
Ocular ultrasonography, 671, 672
Oily skin, 733
Older Americans Act, 233
    home health care and, 304
Oliguria, nursing care plan for, 397-400
Omnipen; *see* Ampicillin

Oncogenes, 196
Oophorectomy, 447
Open heart surgery, 389
Operative day, care on, 105-108
Operative team, 110
Ophthalmia, 681
Ophthalmia neonatorum, 677
Ophthalmoscopy, 670
Optic fundus, 666
Oral contraceptives, 543
    depression and, 58
Oral dissolution therapy, 486
Oral fluids, 39
Oral hypoglycemic agents (OHAs), 605
Orchiectomy, 576
Orders, preoperative, 104, 105, 107,
        108
Orem, Dorothy, 11
Organ(s)
    accessory, of digestion, 476-493
    preferred provider, 9
    reproductive, male, 538*f*
Organ of Corti, 668
Organelles, 32-34
Organic brain syndrome, 56, 57
    medications and, 251
Orinase; *see* Tolbutamide
Orthodiagraphy, 370
Orthopedic conditions, 768, 769
Orthopedic devices, 759-769
Orthopneic patient, 312
OSHA; *see* Occupational Health and
        Safety Administration
Osmolality of urine, 501
Osmosis, fluids and electrolytes and,
        71, 72
Osteoarthritis, 773
Osteogenic sarcoma, 784
Osteomyelitis, 775, 776
    causes of, 28
Osteoporosis, 241, 242
Osteotomy, 773
Otic; *see* Acetic acid
Otitis media, 696
    nursing care guidelines for, 698
Otosclerosis, 698
Otoscopy, 692
Outpatient surgery, 101
Ovaries, 536
    cancer of, 557, 558
    conditions affecting, 557-559
Overlays, mattress, 714
Overload, circulation, 414
Ovulation, 541
Oxacillin sodium, 44*t*
Oxygen
    hyperbaric, 323
    by mask, 323
    by nasal cannula, 322, 323
    partial pressure or tension of, 315
    precautions in use of, 323
    premature infants and, 682
Oxygen saturation, 315
Oxygen therapy, 322, 323
Oxytetracycline, 44*t*
Oxytocin, 589

P

P wave, 360, 361
PAC; *see* Premature atrial contraction
Pacemaker, electronic, 366
Pack, aquathermia, 38
Paco₂, 315
Pain, 128-141
    assessment of, 132-135
    burn management and, 746
    chest, 376
    definition of, 130
    drugs for, 136*t*, 137*t*
    dying patient and, 226
    function of, 130
    management of, 135-140
    musculoskeletal injuries and, 756,
        757
    nature of, 130-135
    neurosurgical procedures for blocking
        of, 140
    noninvasive interventions for, 139,
        140
    nursing care guidelines for, 140
    phantom limb, 786
    postoperative, 118, 123, 124
    responses to, 132*f*
    theories of, 130, 131
    types of, 132
    urinary tract, 499, 500
Palliative surgery, 202
Palpation
    in assessment of cardiovascular sys-
        tem, 356
    in respiratory problem assessment,
        313
Palsy
    Bell's, 651
    cerebral, 787
Pancreas, 436
    diseases and disorders of, 488-490,
        595-611
    function of, 590
Pancreatectomy, 489, 490
Pancreatitis, 488, 489
Pancuronium (Pavulon), 114
Pancytopenia, 420
Panmycin; *see* Tetracycline
Pao₂, 315
Pap smear, 198, 547-549
Papanicolaou (pap) smear, 198, 547-549
Papilloma, 29
Papovavirus, 29
Papule, 708, 709
Paracentesis, 696
Paralysis, Bell's, 651
Paralysis agitans, 638, 639
Paralytic ileus, 449
Paranoia, 56
Parasites, 161-163
Parasympathetic nervous system, 355,
        622
Parathormone, 72
Parathyroid glands, disorders of, 611
Parathyroids, 588
Parenteral fluids, 177
Paresis, 636

Parkinson's disease, 638, 639
  nursing care guidelines for, 639
Paronychia, 737
Parotitis, 157
Partial pressure of carbon dioxide and oxygen, 315
Partial thromboplastin time, 409, 410
Paste boots, 711
Patch test, 801, 802
Patches, mucous, 165
Pathocil; *see* Dicloxacillin
Pathogen(s), 36-38, 144
Pathogenicity, factors influencing, 37
Patient(s)
  admission of, 102
  defined, 4
  dying, 216-231
  geriatric, 230-255
  rehabilitation and, 260
  rights of, 20, 21
Patient care
  physiologic aspects of, 24-45
  psychologic aspects of, 46-65
  total, concept of, 4
Patient history, 103
Patient's Bill of Rights, 20
Pavulon; *see* Pancuronium
Payment systems, 5-7
PCA pump, 124
Pco₂, normal values of, 315*t*
Pearson attachment, 764
Pediculi, 737
Pediculus capitis, 737
Pediculus corporis, 737
Pediculus humanus, 737
Pellagra, 31
Pelvic examination, 547
Pelvic exenteration, 580, 581
Pelvic inflammatory disease (PID), 558, 559
Pelvic muscles, relaxation of, 553-555
Pelvic traction, 764
Pelvis, female, 538*f*
Pen-Vee-K; *see* Penicillin V potassium
Penicillin, 42, 43*t*, 165, 166
  administration, dose, and side effects of, 43*t*
Penicillin G potassium, 43*t*
Penicillin V potassium, 43*t*
Penicillinases, 42
Penile ulceration, 575
Penrose drain, 121
Pentazocine, 136*t*
Pentids; *see* Penicillin G potassium
Pentobarbital Sodium (Nembutal), 108*t*
Pentothal; *see* Thiopental sodium
Pepcid; *see* Famotidine
Peptic ulcer(s), 466-472
  complications and, 469, 470
  drug therapy for, 468, 469
  nursing care guidelines for, 468
Perceptual problems, 465, 646
Percussion
  in assessment of cardiovascular system, 356, 357

Percussion—cont'd
  in respiratory problem assessment, 313, 314
  in therapy for respiratory problems, 319
Percutaneous transluminal coronary angioplasty (PTCA), 391
Perforation
  of eardrum, 695, 696
  gastric, 470
Pericarditis, 352, 353
Pericardium, 352
Perilymph, 668
Perimetry, 669
Perineum, 536
Peripherally inserted central catheter (PICC), 93
Peristalsis, 436, 437
Peritoneal dialysis, 519-521
Peritonitis, 460, 461
Permitil; *see* Fluphenazine dihydrochloride
Pernicious anemia, 418, 419
Personal care, 8
Personal hygiene, elderly patient and, 248, 249
Personality
  development of, 49, 50
  disorders of, 56
  normal, criteria for, 51
  structure of, 48, 49
Perspiration, 34
Pertofrane; *see* Desipramine hydrochloride
Pertussis, 28
PES format in nursing diagnosis, 14
Pessary, 553
Petechiae, 427
Petit mal seizures, 632
pH, 87
  of blood, 315
Phacoemulsification, 685
Phagocytosis, 35, 405
Phantom limb pain, 786
Pharyngitis, 29
  acute, 335
Pharynx, 310, 311*f*
Phenelzine dihydrogen sulfate, 64*t*
Phenergan; *see* Promethazine
Phenethicillin potassium, 43*t*
Phenobarbital, 63*t*
Phenol, disinfection and, 181
Phenothiazines, action and side effects of, 63*t*
Pheochromocytoma, 614
Pheresis, 407
Phimosis, 574
Phonocardiogram, 370
Phoria, 674
Phosphate, 87
Phosphorus, physiologic functions of, 31
Phthalylsulfathiazole, 41*t*
Phthirus pubis, 737
Physical agents of injury to body, 31, 32

Physical restraint of patient, 288, 289
Physical therapist, 261
Physician, rehabilitation and, 261
Physiologic aspects of patient care, 24-45
Picornavirus, 29
Pigmentation, disorders of, 733
Piles, 473, 474
Pillow, abduction, 774
Pinkeye, 677
Pinna, 666
Pinworms, 163
Pitting edema, 359
Pituitary gland, 588
  disorders of, 614, 615
Placebos, 138
Plan, nursing care, 15
Planning, nursing process and, 15
Plant alkaloids, cancer treatment and, 208-209
Plant poisoning, 721, 722
Plaque, 371
  in blood vessels, 237
Plasma, 353, 404, 406
  normal reference laboratory values for, 819-825
Plasmodium falciparum, 160, 161
Platelet(s), 406, 407; *see also* Thrombocytes
  normal values for, 410*t*
Platyhelminthes (flatworms), 161, 162
Pleura, 310, 311*f*
Pleural friction rubs, 314
Pleural space, 310, 311*f*
Pleurevac, 325, 326*f*
Pleurisy, 340, 341
PMS; *see* Premenstrual syndrome
Pneumocystis carinii
  AIDS and, 167
  pneumonia caused by, 340
Pneumocystis carinii pneumonia, AIDS and, 808
Pneumoencephalography, 625, 626
Pneumonectomy, 344, 345*f*
Pneumonia, 337-339
  caused by staphylococcus bacteria, 339
  causes of, 28
  nosocomial, 174, 175
  nursing care guidelines for, 340
Pneumonitis, 29
Pneumothorax, 333*f*, 334
  tension, chest drainage and, 324, 325
Po₂, normal values of, 315*t*
Poikylothermia, 652
Poisoning; *see* Food poisoning
Polarization, 359
Poliomyelitis, 29, 636
Pollen, ragweed, allergic response to, 796*f*
Polycillin; *see* Ampicillin
Polycythemia, 421, 422
Polydipsia, 597
Polymyxin B, ear infection and, 697*t*
Polyneuritis, 649
Polyp, nasal, 341, 342

Polyphagia, 597
Polys, 405
Polyuria, 505
Ponstel; *see* Mefenamic acid
Pontocaine; *see* Tetracaine
Portal circulation, 482*f*
Positioning, 267-269
   burn management and, 746
   musculoskeletal system and, 754
Positron emission tomography for neurologic disorders, 626
Postoperative care, 123-127
   comfort and safety measures in, 119
   complaints and complications and, 123-125
   coughing and deep breathing and, 119, 120
   discharge planning and, 126, 127
   nursing guidelines for, 123
Postoperative complaints, 123-125
Postoperative complications, 125, 126
Postoperative preparation for return from surgery, 345, 346
Postural drainage, 319-320
Potassium, 77-81
   deficit of, 78, 79, 80*t*
   excess of, 79-81
   foods rich in, 384
   heart rate and, 355
   physiologic functions of, 31
   sources of, 80
Pouch
   colostomy and, 450
   Koch's, 453, 523
Povidine-iodine, 716
Poxvirus, 29
PPS; *see* Prospective payment system
PR interval, 360, 361
Practice, nursing
   scope of, 11, 12
   standards of, 12, 13
   theory in, 17, 18
Precautions
   universal, 811, 812
   in use of oxygen, 323
Prednisolone, 45*t*
Prednisone, 45*t*
Preeclampsia, 728
Preferred provider organization (PPO), 9
Pregnancy, 34
   blood volume and, 353
   conditions of, 569-572
   cystitis and, 512
   ectopic, 572
   heart disease and, 385
   herpes simplex virus and, 168
   rubella during, 156
   SLE and, 728
   sulfonamide therapy and, 744
   tests for, 551
   tetracyclines and, 42
Preload, 368
Premature atrial contraction (PAC), 361, 362

Premature ventricular contraction (PVC), 363, 364
Prematurity, retinopathy of, 681, 682
Premenstrual syndrome (PMS), 539, 546
Preoperative care, 98-108
   interventions and planning in, 103-108
   preparation and, 102-108
Preoperative orders, 104, 105, 107, 108
Preoperative preparation for chest surgery, 344, 345
Presbyopia, 670, 673
Pressure; *see also* Blood pressure
   atmospheric, 32
   central venous, 368
   pulmonary artery, 368, 369
   skin breakdown and, 269, 270
   wedge, pulmonary artery, 368, 369
Pressure sores, 292, 293
Pressure ulcers; *see* Decubitus ulcers
Prevention
   definition of, 180
   of illness, levels of, 4
Prickly heat, 721
Primary care, 7
Primary health care, 259
Primary nursing, 17
Problem oriented record (POR), 16
Procaine (Novocain), 114*t*
Procaine penicillin G, 43*t*
Procardia; *see* Nifedipine
Prochlorperazine, 63*t*
Proctocolectomy, 451
Proctoscopy, 441
Proctosigmoidoscopy, 199
Projection as defense mechanism, 52*t*
Prolactin, 589
Prolixin; *see* Fluphenazine dihydrochloride
Promethazine (Phenergan), 108*t*
Propanedols, action and side effects of, 63*t*
Propranolol, 593
   administration of, 377
   depression and, 58
   preparation, action, and nursing considerations of, 378*t*
Prospective payment systems (PPSs), 6
Prospective reimbursement, 6
Prostaglandins, 499*t*
Prostaphlin; *see* Oxacillin sodium
Prostate gland, 539
   cancer of, 575, 576
   conditions affecting, 575-579
Prostatectomy, 576-579
Prostatic hypertrophy, 576
Prostatitis, 575
Prostatosis, 575
Prostheses, 276, 277
   amputation and, 784-786
   breast, 565
   for eye, 692
   surgery and, 106
Protective barriers for skin, 717
Protein-bound iodine test, 591

Proteinuria, 498
Proteus vulgaris, 126
Prothrombin time, 409
Protoplasm, 32
Protozoa, 30
Protozoal disease, 160-163
Providone-iodine ointment, 744
Proximal convoluted tubule, 496, 497
Prozac; *see* Fluoxetine hydrochloride
Pruritus, 734
Pseudomonas, 716
Pseudomonas aeruginosa, 173
   wound infection from, 126
   burns and, 744
Psoriasis, 724-726
Psychoanalysis, 48
Psychologic aspects of patient care, 46-65
Psychologic care, respiratory problems and, 318, 318
Psychomotor attacks, 632-634
Psychopharmacology, 62
Psychoses, 53-56
Psychosocial support, 96
Psychosomatic disorders, 57
Psychotropic drugs, 62-64*t*
Ptyalin, 437
Puberty, 540, 541
Pulmonary angiography in diagnosis of respiratory problems, 316
Pulmonary circulation, 353
Pulmonary edema, 333, 380, 381
Pulmonary embolism, 332, 333
Pulmonary function tests, 315, 316
Pulmonary infarction, 332, 333
Pulse
   arterial, 358
   in assessment of heart function, 361
   elderly and, 251
   postoperative, 117
   venous, inspection of, 359
Pulse pressure, 95
Pump(s)
   for patient-controlled analgesia, 138
   PCA, 124
Pupil, 666
Purkinje fibers, 354
Purpura, 427
Purulent discharge, 38
Pustule, 709
Pyelitis, 513
Pyelography, 502, 503
Pyelolithotomy, 527
Pyelonephritis, 513
Pyloroplasty, 470, 471
Pylorospasm, 475
Pyopen; *see* Carbenicillin
Pyribenzamine; *see* Tripelennamine
Pyrimal; *see* Sulfadiazine

Q

Q wave, 360, 361
QRS complex, 360, 361
Quaternary ammonium compounds, disinfection and, 181
Quats, disinfection and, 181

R

Queckenstedt's test, 624, 625
Quinaglute; *see* Quinidine gluconate
Quinidine, 363
Quinidine gluconate, 378*t*

R factor, 88
Rabies, 29
Radiation, ionizing, 202, 203
Radiation therapy, 202-208
    external, 203, 204
    nursing intervention and, 203-207
    sealed internal, 204-207
    self-protection and, 207
    unsealed, 207, 208
Radioactive iodine, 208, 209, 591-593
Radioactive iodine uptake, 591
Radiography in diagnosis of respiratory
        problems, 316
Radioisotope, 201
Radioisotope studies, 503, 504
Radiotherapy; *see* Radiation therapy
Radium, 204
Radon, 204
Ragweed pollen, allergic response to,
        796*f*
Ranitidine (Zantac), 108*t*
    ulcers and, 469
Rash(es)
    chickenpox and, 156
    measles and, 155
Rate
    basal metabolic, 591
    sedimentation, 367, 410, 411
Rationalization as defense mechanism,
        52*t*
Rauwolfia alkaloids, 63*t*
Raynaud's disease, 386, 387
Reabsorption, 498
Reach to Recovery, 215
Reaction(s)
    allergic, from insects, 797, 798
    cytotoxic hypersensitivity, 798
    hypersensitivity, 795*t*
    insulin and hypoglycemic, 606-608
Reaction-formation as defense mecha-
        nism, 52*t*
Reality orientation, 254
Receptors, 355
Record(s), 16
Recovery room, 116-119
Rectocele, 553-555
Rectovaginal fistula, 553
Rectum, 436
Red blood cells, 353, 404, 405; *see also*
        Erythrocytes
    normal values for, 410*t*
    packed, 408
Redecision theory of personality struc-
        ture, 49
Reduction of fractures, 778, 779
Referred pain, 132, 133*f*
Refraction, 670
    errors of, 672-674
Refractive errors, 672-674
Regional anesthetics, 114, 115

Registered nurse (RN), 11, 12
Regression, 55*t*
    as defense mechanism, 52*t*
Rehabilitation, 256-281
    bladder and bowel training and, 270-
        273
    burn management and, 747
    cardiac, 392, 393
    focus of, 259
    after mastectomy, 565
    motivation in, 274, 275
    nursing approaches to, 264-281
    for patient with cerebrovascular acci-
        dent, 646
    programs for, 262, 263
    in spinal cord injuries, 654
    teaching in, 275, 276
    team for, 260, 262
    techniques in, 265-269
Rehabilitation nursing, 258-264
Rehabilitation team, 260-262
Reimbursement
    for health care services, 5-7
    for home health services, 303, 304
Rejection in renal transplantation, 521,
        522
Relaxants, muscle, 114
Relaxation
    in pain management, 140
    of pelvic musculature, 553-555
Reminiscing, 254
Renal artery, 497
Renal calculi, 513, 514
    nursing care guidelines for, 515
Renal failure, 515-522
    chronic, nursing plan for patient
        with, 528-532
Renin, 373, 499
Renin-angiotensin system, 373, 374
Renography, 503, 504
Renoscan, 504
Reovirus, 29
Repolarization, 359
Repression as defense mechanism, 52*t*
Reproductive function, life cycle and,
        540-544
Reproductive problems
    examination of female patient with,
        546-551
    examination of male patient with,
        551, 552
    laboratory tests for, 547-549
    nursing assessment of patient with,
        539, 540
Reproductive system
    aging and, 246
    diseases and disorders of, 552-569
    female, 536, 537
    function and structure of, 536-539
    male, 536-539
Reproductive years, 542, 543
Resection
    gastric, 470-472
    submucous, 341
Reserpine, 63*t*
    depression and, 58

Residential care, 8
Resonance in percussion of chest, 314
Respiration, 308-349
    Cheyne-Stokes, 312
    control of, 310
    deviations from normal, 312
    external and internal, 310
Respiratory assistance, cardiac surgery
        and, 390, 391
Respiratory disorders, postoperative,
        126
Respiratory isolation, 183, 184
Respiratory problem(s)
    altered status of respiration and, 312
    diagnostic procedures for, 314-317
    diseases and disorders and, 328-342
    health and social aspects of, 346, 347
    infectious conditions and, 335-341
    noninfectious conditions of, 328-335
    nursing assessment of patient with,
        313, 314
    nursing diagnoses and, 348, 349
    nursing responsibilities in
        diagnosis of, 314-317
        therapy for, 317-327
    obstructions and, 341, 342
    rehabilitation and, 346, 347
    therapeutic techniques in, 317-327
    tumors and, 342, 344
    upper respiratory tract infections
        and, 336, 341
Respiratory system, 310, 311*f; see also*
        Respiratory problem(s)
    aging and, 245, 246
    diseases and disorders of, 328-342
    infectious conditions of, 335-341
    noninfectious conditions and, 328-335
    obstructions of, 341, 342
    tumors of, 342, 344
Respiratory tract
    inspection of, 313
    intervention in infections of, 336, 341
Response, therapeutic, 60, 61
Restraint, physical, of patient, 288, 289
Retina, 666
    detached, 688, 689
Retinopathy
    diabetic, 687, 688
    of prematurity, 681, 682
Retirement, aging and, 234, 235
Retrograde urography, 503
Retrospective reimbursement, 6
Retroversion, 556, 557
Rh factor, 412, 413
Rheumatic disorders, 770-775
Rheumatic fever, 374, 375
    causes of, 28
Rheumatic heart disease, 374, 375
Rheumatoid arthritis, 771, 772
Rheumatoid spondylitis, 772
Rhizotomy, 140
Rhonchi, 314
Rhythm; *see* Heart rhythm
Ribosomes, 34
Rickets, 783
Rickettsae, 29

Rickettsia, 159
Rickettsial disease, 159, 160
RID, 737
Right(s) of patient, 20, 21
Ringworm, 30, 719-721
Rinne test, 692, 693
Risk
    for infection, nursing interventions
        and, 807
    for injury from falls, assessment of
        factors in, 288*t*
Risk factors
    for breast cancer, 562
    cardiac, 355, 356*t*
Robinul; *see* Glycopyrrolate
Rocky Mountain spotted fever, 29, 159,
    160
Rogers, Carl, 59
Romberg's sign, 636
Roundworms, 162, 163
Rubella (German measles), 29, 156
    immunization and, 147
Rubeola, *see* Measles
Rubin's test, 551
Rubor, 35
Russell's traction, 762, 763*f*

S

S sounds, 353, 354; *see also* Heart
        sounds
S wave, 360, 361
Saccule, 668
Salmonella, infections from 153, 154
Salpingectomy, 447
Salpingitis, 558
Sandimmune; *see* Cyclosporin
Sanguineous discharge of, 38
Sao₂, 315
Sarcoma, 195
    osteogenic, 784
Saturated fat, foods high in, 368
Scabies, 737, 738
Scale, 709
Scar, 709
Scar tissue, 36
Scarlet fever, 150
    causes of, 28
Schedule, immunization, 146*t*, 827
Schiller's test, 548
Schilling test, 411
Schirmer's tearing test, 670
Schizophrenia, 54, 55*t*
Schlemm's canal, 666
Sciatica, 649
Sclera, 666
Sclerosis of nervous system, 637, 638
Scratch test, 800
Scrub nurse, 110
Scurvy, 31
Seatworms, 163
Sebaceous cyst, 733
Sebaceous glands, 708
Seborrhea, 733
Sebum, 708
Secobarbital Sodium (Seconal), 108*t*
Seconal; *see* Secobarbital Sodium

Secondary health care, 259, 260
Secretin, 437
Secretion, 498
Secretion precautions, 183, 187
Sedation
    of elderly patients, 251
    prior to surgery, 105
Sedative(s)
    action and nursing considerations of,
        108*t*
    coughing and, 318
    elderly and, 250
Sedimentation rate, 367, 410, 411
Seizure(s), 630-634
    nursing care guidelines for, 633
Seldane; *see* Terfenadine
Self-actualization, 19
Self-care, 12
Self-examination
    breast (BSE), 196, 550
    testicular (TSE), 573, 574*f*
Self-help groups, 215
Self-monitoring for diabetes, 599, 600
Semen analysis, 551, 552
Sengstaken-Blakemore tube, 481
SENIC; *see* Study of Efficacy of Nosoco-
        mial Infection Control
Senility, 56, 57
Sensitivity tests, 27
Sensory changes, long-term care and,
    287
Sensory system, aging and, 239, 240
Septic shock, 94
Septicemia
    causes of, 28
    manifestations of, 38
Septum, deviated, 341, 342
Serous discharge, 38
Serpasil; *see* Reserpine
Serum
    immunization and, 146-148
    normal reference laboratory values
        for, 819-825
Serum albumin, 407
Serum enzyme tests, 367
Services, home health, 299, 300
Severe combined immunodeficiency
        disease, 805-807
Sexuality, 274
    conditions affecting male genitalia
        and, 573-581
    diagnostic procedures and, 546-552
    elderly and, 249
    problems affecting, 534-585
    reproductive years and, 542, 543
    role behavior and, 542
    role of nurse in relation to, 539, 540
Sexually transmitted diseases, 163-168
    characteristics of, 164*t*
SGOT, normal values of, 442
SGPT, normal values of, 442
Shaking palsy, 638, 639
Shaving, 176
    of patient, 105, 106*f*
Shearing force, 712
Shigella, 154

Shigellosis, 154
Shingles, 29, 731-733; *see also* Herpes
        zoster
Shock, 93-96
    anaphylactic, 797, 798
    assessment of, 95
    body response to, 94
    burns and, 741
    hypovolemic, 415, 416
    intervention for, 95, 96
    postoperative, 125
    spinal, 652
Shock therapy, 64
Short Portable Mental State Question-
        naire, 286
Short-acting barbiturates, 112*t*
Shoulder, range of motion of, 265
Shunt(s)
    LeVeen, 481-483
    peritoneovenous, 481-483
    portacaval, 481
    splenorenal, 481
Sickle cell anemia, 419, 420
Sight, loss of, 672
Sigmoidoscopy, 441
Silvadene; *see* Silver sulfadiazine 1%
Silver nitrate, 182
    burns and, 744
Silver sulfadiazine, 41*t*
Silver sulfadiazine 1%, burns and, 744
Simulation in radiation therapy, 203
Sinemet; *see* Carbidopalevodopa
Sinus dysrhythmia, 361, 362*f*
Sinus node, 354
Sinusitis, 336
Skeletal traction, 764
Skilled nursing facility (SNF), 8
Skin
    bacterial diseases of, 718, 719
    breakdown of, 269, 270
    cancer of, 735, 736
    diagnostic tests and procedures for,
        710
    diseases and disorders of, 718-751
    disorders of pigmentation of, 733
    emotional support and disorders of,
        711, 712
    fungal infections of, 719-721
    gland disorders of, 733, 734
    nursing assessment of, 708
    preparation of for surgery, 105
    pressure sore formation and, 293
    problems affecting, 704-751
    structure and function of, 706-708
    therapeutic procedures for, 710-718
    tumors of, 734-736
    viral infections of, 730-733
Skin graft, 744-746
Skin lesions, 708-710
Skin tests, 799-802
Skull fracture, 647
SLE; *see* Systemic lupus erythematosus
Slit-lamp examination, 670
Small intestine, 436
    cancer of, 465
Smallpox, 29

Smell, aging and, 240
Smoking
    health problems and, 32
    pregnancy and, 34
    ulcers and, 469
Snellen's chart, 668, 669
SNF; *see* Skilled nursing facility
Soaks, 38, 711
SOAP system of record keeping, 16
Sodium, 76, 77, 78*t*
    diagnosis of deficit of, 77*t*
    diagnosis of excess of, 78*t*
    diet and, 384
    hypertension and, 372, 373
    physiologic functions of, 31
Sodium hypochlorite, 716
Sofracort; *see* Cortisporin
Solarcaine; *see* Benzocaine
Solu-Cortef; *see* Hydrocortisone sodium
    succinate
Solutes, 70
Solutions, intravenous, 72, 73*t*, 91
Somatic disorders, 57
Somatotropin, 589
Sore throat, 150
Sores, *see* Decubitus ulcers; Pressure sores
Sound(s); *see also* Heart sounds
    bowel, 448
    Korotkoff, 358
Space; *see* Pleural space
Speaking to hearing impaired, 695
Speech, laryngectomy and, 344
Spermatic cord, torsion of, 575
Sphincter muscle(s), 436, 437
    spasms of, 475
Spinal analgesia, 138
Spinal anesthesia, 114
Spinal cord, 131*f*, 622
    injury to, 651-654
    tumors of, 656, 657
Spinal shock, 652
Spiral fracture, 778
Spirilla, 28, 29
Spirochetes, 28, 29
Spirometer, 316
Spironolactone, 505
Spleen, 35, 427, 428
Splenectomy, 428, 447
Splenomegaly, 427, 428
Splint(s), 768
    Thomas, 762-764
Spondylitis, 772
Spore, 27
Spots, liver, 733
Sprain(s), 777
Sputum, examination of, 315
Squamous cell carcinoma, 735
ST segment, 360, 361
Staining, bacteria and, 27
Standards of nursing practice, 12, 13
Stapedectomy, 699
Stapes, 668
Staphcillin; *see* Methicillin sodium
Staphylococci, 27, 28

Staphylococcus aureus, 28, 148, 149
    burns and, 744
    as cause of toxic shock syndrome,
        545
    nosocomial infections and, 173
    penicillinases and, 42
    surgical wounds and, 176
    wound infection from, 126
Staphylococcus epidermidis, 28
Starling's law, 75
Status epilepticus, 632
STDs; *see* Sexually transmitted diseases
Stelazine; *see* Trifluoperazine
Stenosis, 375
Stepped-care treatment of hypertension, 374
Sterilization, 109, 110
Steroid(s), 43, 45*t*
    eye inflammation and, 680*t*
Steroid therapy, 613, 614
Sting reaction, prevention of, 798
Stomach, 436
    cancer of, 464, 465
    inflammation of, 454, 455
Stomatitis, 204, 453, 454
Stone(s)
    removal of, 525-527
    in urinary system, 513, 514
    in urine, 502
Stool, examination of, 442
Strabismus, 673, 674
Strawberry tongue, 150
Streptococci, 27, 28, 719
Streptococcus pneumoniae, 28
Streptococcus pyogenes, 150
Streptococcus viridans, 375
Streptomycin, 152
Streptomycin sulfate, 44*t*
Stress, surgery and, 100
Stress ulcers, 467
Stressor, 4
Strict isolation, 183
Stripping, vein, 388
Stroke, 237, 238; *see also* Cerebrovascular accident
Stryker Wedge Turning frame, 766, 767
Study of the Efficacy of Nosocomial Infection Control, 173
Styes, 676
Subconscious mind, 48
Subcutaneous tissue, 707
Sublimation as defense mechanism, 52*t*
Submucous resection, 341
Succinylcholine (Anectine), 114
Suctioning, 318, 319
Suffocation, 312
Suicide
    assessing patient's risk for, 59
    geriatric, 236
Sulamyd; *see* Sulfacetamide
Sulfacetamide, 41*t*
Sulfadiazine, 41*t*
Sulfamethoxazole, 41*t*
Sulfamethoxypyridazine, 41*t*
Sulfamylon; *see* Mafenide
Sulfamylon Acetate, 744

Sulfathalidine; *see* Phthalylsulfathiazole
Sulfonamide(s), 41, 744
    eyes and, 679*t*
Superego, 48, 49
Surfactant, 310
Surgery
    abdominal, 447-449
    cardiac, 389-392
    cataract, 685-687
    chest, 344-346
    in cirrhosis intervention, 481-483
    eye, nursing care guidelines for, 680
    on female reproductive tract, 559-561
    gallbladder, 486-488
    for hernia repair, 472
    for intestinal obstruction, 461, 462
    intraoperative care and, 108-116
    palliative, 202
    in peptic ulcer treatment, 470-472
    preoperative and postoperative care
        and, 98-127
    in treatment of cancer, 202
    urinary system, 522-528
    on veins, 388
Surgical asepsis, 109
Surgical nursing
    objectives of, 101
    preoperative preparation and, 107
Surgical patient, 12
Surgical wound infection, 175-177
Surital; *see* Thiamylal
Surveillance for hospital associated infections, 178-180
Swallowing, air, 476
Sweat glands, 708
Sweating
    absence of, 734
    excessive, 733
Sympathetic nervous system, 355, 622
    hypertension and, 372, 373
Sympathetic ophthalmia, 681
Syngeneic transplantation, 212
Synlar; *see* Cortisporin
Synovectomy, 773
Synthetic skin substitutes, 745
Syphilis, 164-166
    causes of, 28, 29
    central nervous system, 636
Systemic circulation, 353
Systemic infections, 30
Systemic lupus erythematosus (SLE),
        728-730
    nursing care plan for, 748-751
Systole phase of cardiac cycle, 353

T

T lymphocytes, 794
T tube, 487, 488
T wave, 360, 361
Tabes dorsalis, 636
Taboparesis, 636
Tachycardia, 364, 365
Tagamet; *see* Cimetidine
Talwin; *see* Pentazocine
Tampon(s), 545, 546
Tapeworms (cestoda), 161, 162

Taste, aging and, 240
Team
    health care, 10
    home health care, 300, 301
    rehabilitation, 260-262
Team nursing, 17
Technology, health care and, 4, 5
Tegopen; *see* Cloxacillin monohydrate sodium
Teldrin; *see* Chlorpheniramine
Telematics, 5
Teletherapy, 203
Temperature, body; *see* Body temperature
Tendons, 754
TENS; *see* Transcutaneous electrical nerve stimulation
Tension, blood gas, 315
Terfenadine, 803*t*
Terminally ill patients, nursing care and, 224-229
Terramycin; *see* Oxytetracycline
Tertiary health care, 260
Tertiary intention, 36
Test(s)
    Amsler's grid, 669
    Bernstein, 440
    bilirubin, 442
    blood, 409-413
    blood donation, 408
    caloric, 626, 627
    for cancer, 198-201
    for cardiovascular disease, 367-370
    coagulation, 409, 410
    color vision, 669
    creatinine, 502
    dexamethasone suppression, 56
    for diabetes mellitus, 598-600
    exercise tolerance, 369, 370
    galactose tolerance, 442
    for gastric disorders, 438-442
    Ishihara, 669
    liver function, 442
    Mantoux, 151
    Mono-vacc, 151
    mucous membrane sensitivity, 802
    nursing responsibilities for, 444
    pap smear, 198
    for pregnancy, 551
    protein-bound iodine, 591
    pulmonary function, 315, 316
    Queckenstedt's, 624, 625
    for reproductive problems, 547-549
    rinne, 692, 693
    Rubin's, 551
    Schilling, 411
    Schirmer's tearing, 670
    Sciller's, 548
    sensitivity, 27
    skin, 799-802
    tine, 151
    triiodothyronine (T3) resin uptake, 591
    tuberculin, 151
    for tuberculosis, 151, 152
    tuning fork, 692, 693

Test(s)—cont'd
    vestibular, 693
    voice, 692
    Weber, 692, 693
Testes
    conditions affecting, 573-575
    surgical removal of, 576
Testicle, undescended, 574
Testicular cancer, 573
Testicular self examination (TSE), 573, 574*f*
Testing, elimination, 802
Testis, ectopic, 574
Tetanus, 782
    causes of, 28
Tetracaine (Pontocaine), 114*t*
Tetracin; *see* Tetracycline(s)
Tetracycline(s), 42, 44*t*
Theory in nursing practice, 17, 18
Therapeutic relationship in nursing, 59-62
Thiamylal (Surital), 112*t*
Thiopental (Pentothal) sodium, 112*t*
Thioridazine hydrochloride, 63*t*
Third spacing, 73
Thomas splint, 762-764
Thoracentesis in diagnosis of respiratory problems, 317
Thoracic cage, 310
Thoracotomy, 323-326
Thorazine; *see* Chlorpromazine hydrochloride
Threadworms, 163
Throat, foreign bodies in, 342
Throat irrigations, 320, 321
Thrombocytes, 406; *see also* Platelets
Thrombocytopenia, 204, 210, 211
Thrombophlebitis, 387, 388
    intravenous therapy and, 92
Thromboplastin time, partial, 409, 410
Thrombosis, postoperative, 126
Thrombus, 126
Thrush, 453
Thymus gland, aging and, 235
Thyroid gland, 588
    carcinoma of, 595
    disorders of, 592-595
Thyroid ultrasonogram, 591
Thyroidectomy, 594
Thyrotoxicosis, 593
Thyrotropin, 589
Tic douloureaux, 649-651
Ticar; *see* Ticarcillin disodium
Ticarcillin disodium, 44*t*
Tick(s), 29, 153
    Rocky Mountain spotted fever and, 159, 160
Tine test, 151
Tinea (ringworm), 719-721
Tinea barbae, 720
Tinea capitis, 719
Tinea corporis, 719, 720
Tinea pedis, 720, 721
Tissue; *see also* Granulation tissue; Scar tissue
    subcutaneous, 707

Tissue sampling, 198
Tofranil; *see* Imipramine hydrochloride
Tolazamide, 605
Tolbutamide, 605
Tolerance, drug, 137
Tolinase; *see* Tolazamide
Tomography; *see* Computed tomography
Tongue, strawberry, 150
Tonometry, 670, 671*f*
Tonsillectomy, 342
Tonsillitis, 336
    causes of, 28
Tonsils, enlarged, 342
Tophi, 775
Topical antimicrobials for burns, 744
Topical decongestants, allergy therapy and, 803
Topical medications, 716
Torsion of spermatic cord, 575
Torticollis, 770
Total parenteral nutrition (TPN), 446, 447
Total patient care, concept of, 4
Touch, aging and, 240
Tourniquets, rotating, 381, 382*f*
Toxic goiter, 593
Toxic shock syndrome (TSS), 149, 545, 546
Toxin, 37
Toxoids, 146
TPN; *see* Total parenteral nutrition
Trabeculectomy, 683, 684
Trabeculoplasty, 683, 684
Trace minerals, 31
Trachea, 310, 311*f*
    foreign bodies in, 342
Tracheostomy, 326, 327
Tracheotomy, 326, 327
Trachoma, 677
Traction, 759-765
    nursing care guidelines for patient in, 765
Tranquilizer(s), 62, 63*t*
    action and nursing considerations of, 108*t*
    elderly and, 250
Transcutaneous electrical nerve stimulation (TENS), 138, 139, 786
Transfer of patient, 270
Transfusion; *see* Blood transfusion
Transient ischemic attacks, 642
Transmission of infectious diseases, 145
Transplant(s)
    corneal, 678, 679
    hair, 736, 737
    ureteral, 522-524
Transplantation
    bone marrow, 212, 421
    renal, 521, 522
Transport of patient, 108
Transverse fracture, 778
Trench mouth, 453
Treponema pallidum, 165, 636
Triamcinolone, 45*t*
Triamcinolone acetonide, 45*t*

Trichinella, 163
Trichinellosis (trichinosis), 163
Trichinosis, 163
Trichomonas vaginalis, vaginitis caused
  by, 552
Trichomoniasis, 30
Trifluoperazine, 63*t*
Triflupromazine hydrochloride, 63*t*
Triiodothyronine (T3) resin uptake test,
  591
Tripelennamine, 803*t*
Tropia, 674
Trousseau's sign, 83
TSS; *see* Toxic shock syndrome
Tubal insufflation, 551
Tube(s); *see also* Fallopian tubes
  decompression, 445, 446
  eustachian, 668
  fiber optic, 199
  gastrostomy, 463
  laryngectomy, 343
  postoperative care and, 120
  Sengstaken-Blakemore, 481
  T, 487, 488
  tracheostomy, 321*f*, 326, 327
Tuberculin test, 151
Tuberculosis, 339
  of bone, 776
  causes of, 28
  of hip, 776
  nursing intervention for, 152
  pulmonary, 150-153
Tubular process, 498
Tumor(s), 193-195
  of adrenal medulla, 614
  of bone, 783, 784
  of brain and spinal cord, 656, 657
  of breast, 561
  causes of, 33
  of female reproductive system, 557,
    558
  of gastrointestinal system, 462-466
  of male reproductive system, 573, 574
  of organs, accessory, of digestion,
    490
  of respiratory system, 342, 344
  of skin, 734-736
  of thyroid gland, 595
  of urinary tract, 515
Tums; *see* Calcium carbonate
Tuning fork tests, 692, 693
Tylenol; *see* Acetaminophen
Tympanic membrane, 666, 667
Tympanoplasty, 698
Typhoid fever, 28
Typhus, 29
Typhus fever, 29
Typing of blood, 412, 413
Typmpanic sound in percussion of
  chest, 314

U

UI; *see* Urinary incontinence
Ulcer(s); *see also* Decubitus ulcer(s);
    Peptic ulcer(s)
  on cornea, 678

Ulcer(s)—cont'd
  duodenal and gastric, comparison of,
    469*t*
  on skin, 709
  stress, 467
Ulceration of penis, 575
Ulcerative colitis, 456, 457
  nursing care guidelines for, 458
Ultrasonogram, thyroid, 591
Ultrasonography
  of gastrointestinal system, 443
  ocular, 671, 672
  pelvic, 549
  of urinary system, 504
Ultrasound, 201
Unconscious mind, 48
Unconsciousness, 627, 628
  corneal damage and, 690
  nursing care plan for, 629
Undescended testicle, 574
Undoing as defense mechanism, 52*t*
Unipen; *see* Nafcillin sodium
United Ostomy Association, 215
Universal precautions, 184-188, 811, 812
Urea in urine, 501
Uremia, 516
Ureteral colic, 514
Ureteral transplants, 522-524
Ureterolithotomy, 527
Ureterosigmoidostomy, 523
Ureterostomy, cutaneous, 523, 524
Ureterotomy, 525-527
Ureters, 496
Urethra, 496, 536
Urethritis, 270, 271
Urinalysis, 500-502, 590, 591
Urinary diversion , 522-524
  appliances for, 524, 525*f*
  nursing care guidelines for postoper-
    ative stage of, 526
Urinary drainage, 506-510
Urinary incontinence (UI), 270-273, 289-
    291
  elderly and, 249
Urinary system, 494-533
  aging and, 244, 245
  anatomy of, 496-497
  diagnostic tests of, 500-505
  diseases and disorders of, 510-522
  function of, 497-499
  infectious diseases of, 512, 513
  noninfectious diseases of, 510-512
  nursing assessment of, 499, 500
  obstructions of, 513, 514
  operative conditions of, 522-528
  patient history and physical examina-
    tion and, 499
  structure of, 496, 497
  traumatic injuries to, 514
Urinary tract, tumors of, 515
Urinary tract infection, 174
Urine
  analysis of, 500-502
  collection of, 500, 501
  formation of, 498, 499
  retention of, after surgery, 124

Urine testing, 598, 599
Urodynamic studies, 503
Urography, 502, 503
Urostomy, continent, 523
Urticaria, 723
Uterine cancer, 557
Uterine prolapse, 553-555
Uterus, conditions affecting, 556, 557
Utricle, 668
Uveal tract, 666
Uveitis, 679, 681

V

Vaccination for influenza, 158
Vaccine(s)
  BCG (bacille Calmette Guerin), 152
  immunization and, 146-148
  for influenza, 337
  measles, 156
  mumps, 157
  rubella, 156
  types of and routes of administration
    for, 826
Vagina, 536
  cancer of, 556
  conditions affecting, 552-556
Vaginal irrigations, 34
Vaginitis, 552
Vagotomy, 470, 471
Vagus nerve, resection of, 470, 471
Valium; *see* Diazepam
Values, normal reference laboratory,
  819-827
Valve(s)
  ileocecal, 436
  of heart, 353
Varicocele in males, 573
Varicose veins, 388
Vascular system, 353
Vasoactive drugs, 95
Vasogenic shock, 93, 94
Vasopressor drugs, 379
Vasospasm, cerebral, 646
Vectorborne transmission, 173
Vectorcardiogram, 370
Vehicle transmission, 173
Vehicles for transmission of infections,
  145
Vein(s)
  heart disease and disorders and, 385-
    389
  varicose, 388
Vein ligation, 388
Vein stripping, 388
Venous access devices, 138
Ventilation, 310
  mechanical, 321, 322
Ventilation systems, 176
Ventricle(s), 352
  dysrhythmias and, 363-365
Ventricular fibrillation, 365
Ventriculography, 626
Verruca, 734, 735
Versed; *see* Midazolam HCl
Vesicle, 709

Vesicovaginal fistula, 553
Vesprin; *see* Triflupromazine hydrochloride
Vessels, blood, 353
Vestibular tests, 693
Vibramycin; *see* Doxycycline
Viral disease(s), 155-159
Viral hepatitis, 476-478
  comparison of types of, 479t
  nursing care guidelines for, 477
  prevention of, 478
Viral infection, 29
Virology, 29
Virulence, 37
Virus(es), 29, 30; *see also* Human immunodeficiency virus
  cancer and, 195
  herpes, 167, 168
  herpes varicella-zoster (V-Z)
Vision
  aging and, 239
  problems affecting, 664-703
Vistaril; *see* Hydroxyzine pamoate
Visual analog scale for assessment of pain, 133
Vital signs, elderly and, 251
Vitamin B_{12}; *see also* Pernicious anemia
  Schilling test for, 411
Vitamin D, 499t
Vitamin deficiency, 31
Vitrectomy, 689, 690
Vitreous chamber, 666
Vitreous humor, 666
Vocational Rehabilitation Act, 262, 263
Vocational therapist, 262

Voice tests, 692
Voiding
  postoperative, 118, 120
  record of, 290
Volkmann's contracture, 782, 783
Vomiting
  postoperative, 124
  psychic, 476
Von Willebrand's disease, 409, 425
Vosol; *see* Acetic acid
Vulva, 536
  malignant lesions of, 555, 556
Vulvectomy, 555, 556
Vulvitis, 552
Vulvovaginitis, 553

W

Walking with crutches, 278-281
Warning signals of cancer, 197
Warning signs of testicular cancer, 573
Wart(s), 29, 734, 735
Water intoxication, 74
Waveform(s), 359
Weber test, 692, 693
Wedge pressure, pulmonary artery, 368, 369
Wens, 733
Wenckeback block, 365
Wheal, 709, 710
Wheelchair, pressure relief for patient in, 270
Wheezes, 314
Whiplash, 783
White blood cells, 353, 405; *see also* Leukocytes
  disorders of, 422-425

White blood cells—cont'd
  normal values for, 410t
  radiation and, 204
Will; *see* Living will
Wiscott-Aldrich syndrome, 805-807
Withdrawal, 55t
Workers, health care, precautions for, 184-188
World Health Organization, definition of health of, 4
Wound(s)
  burn, 744-746
  chest, 346
  healing of, 36, 122
  penetrating, of eye, 691
  surgical, infection of, 126, 175-177
Wrist, fracture of, 781, 782
Wryneck, 770

X

X-ray(s), 199-201, 370
  in diagnosis of respiratory problems, 316
  therapy and, 202-208
  of urinary system, 502, 503
Xanax; *see* Alprazolam
Xenograft, 745
Xylocaine; *see* Lidocaine hydrochloride

Z

Zantac; *see* Ranitidine
Zollinger-Ellison syndrome, 466
Zyderm Collagen Implant, 728

Nursing Diagnosis Profiles

Calcium Deficit: Hypocalcemia, 84

Calcium Excess: Hypercalcemia, 85

Extracellular Fluid Deficit, 74

Extracellular Fluid Excess, 75

Magnesium Deficit: Hypomagnesemia, 85

Magnesium Excess: Hypermagnesemia, 86

Metabolic Acidosis: Base Bicarbonate Deficit or Metabolic Acid Excess, 89

Metabolic Alkalosis: Base Bicarbonate Excess, 89

Potassium Deficit: Hypokalemia, 80

Potassium Excess: Hyperkalemia, 82

Respiratory Acidosis: Carbonic Acid Excess, 91

Respiratory Alkalosis: Carbonic Acid Deficit, 90

Sodium Deficit: Hyponatremia, 77

Sodium Excess: Hypernatremia, 78

Spiritual Distress, 228

Nursing Care Plans

Patient Who is Confused, 658

Patient with AIDS, 812

Patient with Aplastic Anemia, 429

Patient with Below the Knee Amputation, 788

Patient with Chronic Renal Failure, 528

Patient with Cirrhosis, 490

Patient with Congestive Heart Failure and Oliguria, 397

Patient with Detached Retina, 700

Patient with Hyperthyroidism, 615

Patient with Pneumonia, 347

Patient with a Repeat C-section, 581

Patient with Systemic Lupus Erythematosus, 748